Travel Disc

This coupon entitles you to special discounts
when you book your trip through the

TRAVEL NETWORK®
RESERVATION SERVICE

Hotels ♦ Airlines ♦ Car Rentals ♦ Cruises
All Your Travel Needs

Here's what you get: *

♦ A discount of $50 USD on a booking of $1,000** or more for two or more people!

♦ A discount of $25 USD on a booking of $500** or more for one person!

♦ Free membership for three years, and 1,000 free miles on enrollment in the unique Travel Network Miles-to-Go® frequent-traveler program. Earn one mile for every dollar spent through the program. Redeem miles for free hotel stays starting at 5,000 miles. Earn free roundtrip airline tickets starting at 25,000 miles.

♦ Personal help in planning your own, customized trip.

♦ Fast, confirmed reservations at any property recommended in this guide, subject to availability.***

♦ Special discounts on bookings in the U.S. and around the world.

♦ Low-cost visa and passport service.

♦ Reduced-rate cruise packages and special car rental programs worldwide.

Visit our website at http://www.travelnetwork.com/Frommer or call us globally at 201-567-8500, ext. 55. In the U.S., call toll-free at 1-888-940-5000, or fax 201-567-1838. In Canada, call at 1-905-707-7222, or fax 905-707-8108. In Asia, call 60-3-7191044, or fax 60-3-7185415.

* To qualify for these travel discounts, at least a portion of your trip must include destinations covered in this guide. No more than one coupon discount may be used in any 12-month period, for destinations covered in this guide. Cannot be combined with any other discount or promotion.
**These are U.S. dollars spent on commissionable bookings.
***A $10 USD fee, plus fax and/or phone charges, will be added to the cost of bookings at each hotel not linked to the reservation service. Customers must approve these fees in advance. If only hotels of this kind are booked, the traveler(s) must also purchase roundtrip air tickets from Travel Network for the trip.

Valid until December 31, 1999. Terms and conditions of the Miles-to-Go® program are available on request by calling 201-567-8500, ext 55.

GRD123

"Amazingly easy to use. Very portable, very complete."

—Booklist

♦

"The only mainstream guide to list specific prices. The Walter Cronkite of guidebooks—with all that implies."

—Travel & Leisure

♦

"Complete, concise, and filled with useful information."

—New York Daily News

♦

"Hotel information is close to encyclopedic."

—Des Moines Sunday Register

Frommer's®
7th Edition

GREECE
FROM $50 A DAY

The Ultimate Guide to Comfortable Low-Cost Travel

by John Bozman & Kyle McCarthy

Macmillan • USA

ABOUT THE AUTHORS

Kyle McCarthy began travel writing with a series of articles for the *China Daily* newspaper, and she has since written about budget and adventure travel for *Cosmopolitan, Backpacker, Connections,* and several airline magazines. Kyle was one of the original authors of *Frommer's Thailand* and is now the editor-in-chief of *Family Travel Forum.*

John Bozman writes novels, plays, and screenplays; his most recent effort is *Maria & Ari,* a drama about Maria Callas and Aristotle Onassis. He has traveled extensively in Europe, Latin America, and Southeast Asia, and is the current author of *Frommer's Thailand.* He also contributes chapters on Greece to *Frommer's Europe from $50 a Day* and *Frommer's Europe.*

MACMILLAN TRAVEL

A Simon & Schuster Macmillan Company
1633 Broadway
New York, NY 10019

Find us online at **www.frommers.com**
or on America Online at Keyword: **Frommers**.

ISBN 0-02-861572-7
ISSN 1042-8410

Editors: Charlotte Allstrom, Art Vandalay
Production Editor: Michael Thomas
Design by Michele Laseau
Digital Cartography by Ortelius Design and Peter Bogaty.

SPECIAL SALES

Bulk purchases (10+ copies) of Frommer's and selected Macmillan travel guides are available to corporations, organizations, mail-order catalogs, institutions, and charities at special discounts, and can be customized to suit individual needs. For more information write to Special Sales, Macmillan General Reference, 1633 Broadway, New York, NY 10019.

Manufactured in the United States of America

Contents

List of Maps

INVITATION TO THE READER

In researching this book, we discovered many wonderful places—hotels, restaurants, shops, and more. We're sure you'll find others. Please tell us about them, so we can share the information with your fellow travelers in upcoming editions. If you were disappointed with a recommendation, we'd love to know that, too. Please write to:

Frommer's Greece from $50 a Day
Macmillan Travel
1633 Broadway
New York, NY 10019

AN ADDITIONAL NOTE

Please be advised that travel information is subject to change at any time—and this is especially true of prices. We therefore suggest that you write or call ahead for confirmation when making your travel plans. The authors, editors, and publisher cannot be held responsible for the experiences of readers while traveling. Your safety is important to us, however, so we encourage you to stay alert and be aware of your surroundings. Keep a close eye on cameras, purses, and wallets, all favorite targets of thieves and pickpockets.

WHAT THE SYMBOL MEANS

✪ Frommer's Favorites

Our favorite places and experiences—outstanding for quality, value, or both.

The following abbreviations are used for credit and charge cards:

AE	American Express	EURO	Eurocard
CB	Carte Blanche	MC	MasterCard
DC	Diners Club	V	Visa
DISC	Discover		

A NOTE ON ACCENT MARKS

To aid the reader in the pronunciation of Greek words, we have added an accent mark to indicate where you should put the stress. Getting the right pronunciation *can* be important, especially if you are asking for directions or are buying, say, a train or bus ticket. Thus, for example, in Leofóros Vassiléos Konstandínou (King Constantine Avenue, in Athens), the accents tell you that the words should be pronounced Leh-oh-*FOH*-rohs Vah-see-*LEH*-ohs Kohn-stahn-*DEE*-noo.

ACKNOWLEDGMENTS

This is the seventh edition of our guide to Greece, revised and, we hope, made even more user-friendly. We are especially grateful to the Greek National Tourist Organization, in New York and throughout Greece, and Tassoula Christofidis.

Once again we are deeply indebted to our helpful and informative friends in Greece: Peter and Dimitri Cocconi, Kostas Zissis, John Polychronides, Kim Sjogren, Eleni and Dimitris Sarlas, Tony and Nick Droseros, Sotiris and Marianne Nikolis, Yanna and Dimitris Skalidis, Soula and Dimitris Ghikas, Stavros and Julia Paterakis, Loucas and Yuli Ziras, Aris Ziras, the Diareme family, Rena Valyraki, Susan Spiliopoulou, Despina Kitini, Emily Stassinopoulou, Kathy Gavalas, Capt. Manolis Grillis, Michalis Valaris, Alexis Zikas, Vassilis Vassilatos, Ares Talares, Lefteris Trakos, Theo Spordilis, Sakis Papias, and last but certainly not least, the ever-gracious Thanos and his excellent staff.

Special thanks to all our readers who take the time to contribute to our guide with their comments and suggestions.

Many thanks also to our friend and resourceful researcher M. J. ("Lily") Nolan Kelly for her invaluable contributions. And our continuing gratitude to the staff at Macmillan Travel who put everything together.

FIND FROMMER'S ONLINE

Arthur Frommer's Outspoken Encyclopedia of Travel (www.frommers.com) offers more than 6,000 pages of up-to-the-minute travel information—including the latest bargains and candid, personal articles updated daily by Arthur Frommer himself. No other Web site offers such comprehensive and timely coverage of the world of travel.

The Best of Greece from $50 a Day

Some arrive on cruise ships; others come with a backpack looking for a good time. But these travelers and everyone in between want to see the best of Greece—the art treasures and grand structures from its ancient, storied past; its haunting archaeological sites; the places where myth and history come to life; its unrivaled museums; and its unspoiled, traditional villages. That's not to mention the elemental appeal of sun and sand, as well as its open-air markets, bouzouki clubs, and tavernas. These elements from the past and the present combine to create something magical, and we've written this guide for travelers who may need to watch their expenses but who want to touch a little of this magic all the same.

1 The Best Ancient Sites

Ever since the amazing discovery of the tomb of King Philip of Macedonia at Vergina in the late 1970s, there has been a rekindled interest in Greek archaeology. The spectacular traveling museum show "The Search for Alexander" in the 1980s, and the highly acclaimed restoration of the Parthenon taking place in the 1990s have received tremendous publicity around the world. New excavations and older digs (those going on for more than 100 years) are attracting the greatest interest in decades. A complete description of Greece's innumerable sites goes far beyond the scope of this book. We recommend any of the fine books written by such qualified Greek archaeologists as Manólis Andrónicos, Spíros Marinátos, or J. A. Papapostólou (all published by Ekdotikí and sold at bookstores and museums) as a companion guide as you explore the ruins.

- **The Acropolis** (Athens): Athens is dominated by the Parthenon, one of the Seven Wonders of the Ancient World. This masterpiece of classical architecture and engineering remains an enduring testimony to Greece's Golden Age. See chapter 5.
- **Epidaurus** (Peloponnese): You'll find the remains of the most renowned *asklépio* (center of healing arts) in the Hellenic world, a fine museum, and a well-preserved amphitheater where world-class performances of Aeschylus, Sophocles, Euripides, and Aristophanes are presented each summer. See chapter 7.
- **Mycenae** (Peloponnese): You can walk through its famous Lion Gate and imagine King Agamemnon leading the Greeks to

conquer Troy. The site of the greatest of all Mycenaean fortress palaces is still very impressive. See chapter 7.

• **Olympía** (Peloponnese): The Olympics were begun here in 776 B.C., and you can still run in the original Stadium, wander among the impressive ruins of the Sacred Precinct, and enjoy the treasures (including the Hermes of Praxiteles) housed in its fine museum. See chapter 7.

• **Knossós** (Iráklio, Crete): Despite its controversial reconstruction, this evocative site is where King Minos ruled the powerful Minoan capital. It was his daughter Ariadne who helped Theseus kill the Minotaur and escape the celebrated Labyrinth. See chapter 8.

• **Akrotíri** (Santoríni): The best preserved of all Minoan cities, thought to be the legendary lost Atlantis. Visit with a tour guide to better appreciate its historical and cultural importance. See chapter 9.

• **Délos** (Cyclades): This island birthplace of Apollo and Artemis was once considered the holiest of sanctuaries. Now you can hop over on a day trip from Mýkonos to visit the remains of one of the Mediterranean's most important trade centers. See chapter 9.

• **Delphi** (Central Greece): Delphi was the "navel of the earth" to the ancients, home of the greatest oracle, site of the Pythian Games, and one of the richest repositories of ancient treasures. Don't miss its excellent museum. See chapter 11.

2 The Best Beaches

• **Loutrá Kyllíni** (Elía, western Peloponnese): South of the ferry-spoiled port beach at Kyllíni, west of the picturesque fortress town of Kástro and accessed by the drive leading to a plush, gated resort are several kilometers of empty, broad, gold-sand beach. Sunbathers and families with small children travel from afar to enjoy its calm waters. See chapter 7.

• **Elía Beach** (Mýkonos): The longest beach on one of the world's premier fun-in-the-sun islands, Elía is sheltered, broad, and sandy, offering some shady spots for protection from the golden rays. Although it's one of the farthest beaches from town, everyone comes (with or without clothes). High season brings high style; low season brings some privacy. See chapter 9.

• **Milopótas Beach** (Íos): One of Greece's longest sandy beaches is lined with small inns, and filled with young partiers. Fortunately, it's maintained by resourceful locals who keep the ambience, sand, and water clean. A younger and less-well-to-do crowd than on Mýkonos makes this place fun. See chapter 9.

• **Lálaria Beach** (Skiáthos): Not nearly as crowded as more accessible Koukounariés, Lálaria is framed by white limestone cliffs with natural arches cut by the elements. The gleaming limestone and marble pebble beach creates a highly reflective seabed where the Aegean literally sparkles. See chapter 12.

• **Pórto Katsíki** (Lefkáda): Well known even though it's off the beaten path, this beach is most beautiful when seen from the road's end at the top of a jagged cliff. Before you hike down, study the white, pebbled, half-moon cove and pick your spot. See chapter 14.

• **Mýrtos** (Kefalonía): On an island where tourism is of secondary importance, go for the locals' favorite. Mýrtos is a broad, flat beach whose pearl-colored pebbles extend into a gently whispering surf. Great for swimmers and toddlers. See chapter 14.

- **Emborió** (Híos): It takes work and time to get here, but you'll find a long, shimmering black-pebble beach tucked into an ebony cove formed by volcanic activity. It is lovely and mysterious in its isolation. Don't forget your sandals. See chapter 16.

3 The Most Scenic Villages & Ports

- **Hýdra** (Hýdra): A national monument with a horseshoe-shaped harbor surrounded by grand slate-gray Italianate architecture. Since cars are banned from the entire island, strolling the meandering cobblestone lanes is a very special pleasure. See chapter 6.
- **Haniá** (Crete): Handsome Venetian ruins line Crete's most beautiful and impressive harbor. Wander the narrow lanes leading back to a proud past, or relish the heady mix of colorful local culture, excellent food, swinging nightlife, and interesting shopping. See chapter 8.
- **Mýkonos town** (Mýkonos): Sure it's too famous for its own good, and it's been overexposed on a million postcards. It's overpriced and overrun by tourists in the summer. But somehow it manages to hold on to its rugged good looks. This wonderful town has ample charm and more than a vestige of self-respect. It's still a thrill. See chapter 9.
- **Ía** (Santoríni): The most beautiful village along the spectacular Caldera, it survived a devastating earthquake in 1956 and profited from some tasteful reconstruction. A famous spot on a world-famous island, it's crowded during the day—but a quieter, more sophisticated atmosphere prevails after dark. See chapter 9.
- **Hóra** (Folégandros): This is the most beautiful and unspoiled town in the Cyclades, high atop a spectacular cliff and mercifully free of traffic. There's a picture-perfect old *kástro* (castle), the handsome all-white Panayía Church on the hillside above it, and surprisingly good accommodations. See chapter 9.
- **Sými:** Around the little harbor rise symmetrical tiers of pastel-yellow neoclassical homes. An archaeological decree has succeeded in preserving this ghost town, which was abandoned by earthquake refugees in the 1950s. Although it's somewhat touristy now, developers haven't yet managed to spoil this photographer's haven. See chapter 10.
- **Skópelos:** This amazingly preserved, whitewashed port town is adorned everywhere with pots of flowering plants. Beneath its traditional Greek facade is a sophisticated local community. See chapter 12.
- **Métsovo** (Epirus): Superbly situated in the mountains east of Ioánnina, Métsovo is serene and full of rustic Greek charm. This hill town is refreshing in summer and invigorating in the winter ski season, with a number of fine small chalets and restaurants serving hearty local cuisine. See chapter 13.
- **Fiskárdo** (Kefaloniá): This north-coast fishing village is the only one on the island that survived the earthquake of 1953. Its picture-postcard traditional homes have largely been renovated into quaint guest houses, and the port offers timeless views of the Ionian Sea. See chapter 14.
- **Pyryí and Mestá** (Híos): These are the two most interesting villages in the mastic-growing region. Pyryí is the only village in Greece painted with white-and-gray geometric patterns, which give the buildings a surreal op art quality. Nearby Mestá is a 14th-century medieval fortress. Its yard-thick walls form a labyrinth of interconnected streets with hidden, traditional hotels. See chapter 16.

4 The Most Intriguing Religious Sites

- **Dafní Monastery:** This is the largest and best preserved of Greece's many Byzantine monasteries, with handsome architecture and impressive mosaics. It's easily reached from Athens. See chapter 5.
- **Eleusis:** The most sacred of ancient Mysteries, it was destroyed by Alaric the Goth in A.D. 396. It's a sorry sight now, yet still there's an eerie and deeply mysterious atmosphere lingering. You'll see the original Ploutonion Cave into which Hades abducted Persephone, and the well where her mother Demeter's grief and neglect created the seasons on earth. See chapter 5.
- **Church of Panayía Evangelístria** (Tínos): The most revered Eastern Orthodox shrine in Greece is a neoclassical gem, crammed with treasures. This cathedral is set above the pleasant port of Tínos, on one of the most hospitable islands of Greece. See chapter 9.
- **Pátmos:** The island is dominated by the fortress monastery honoring the cave home of the exiled Disciple John the Younger. Here he had his vision of the Apocalypse and wrote the Revelations. The whole island has a rare spiritual quality; you'll seldom find people who love, respect, and revere their home more. See chapter 10.
- **The Monasteries of Metéora** (Kalabáka, Thessalía): These small Byzantine monasteries were somehow constructed atop rocky spines. Though only four remain active, those you can visit are incredibly spiritual, mysterious, and otherworldly. See chapter 11.
- **Mt. Áthos** (Macedonia): The impressive "Holy Mount" on the easternmost of Halkidikí's fingerlike peninsulas—from which women have been excluded since 1060—is an independent religious state comprising 20 monasteries. They can be entered only with special permission, but are worth looking at from a distance via one of the cruise ships that sail from Thessaloníki. See chapter 15.
- **Néa Moní** (Híos): This is an important site and one of Greece's oldest monasteries (despite the name "New Monastery"), though today it barely functions. The skulls of those slaughtered in a Turkish massacre are matter-of-factly displayed. The mosaics illuminating the monastery's ruined chapel are eerily moving. See chapter 16.

5 The Best Museums

- **National Archaeological Museum** (Athens): It's simply the best in the country, hands down. Highlights include the golden "Treasure of Agamemnon" discovered by Heinrich Schliemann, an unmatched collection of ceramic vessels, a handsome bronze *Poseidon* preserved 2,000 years by the sea, and two incredible *Aphrodites* that embody our very concept of beauty. See chapter 5.
- **Museum of Cycladic and Ancient Greek Art** (Athens): A superb display of astonishing Cycladic and ancient Greek treasures. See 5,000-year-old objects that resemble the work of Joan Miró and other modernists. The exhibits are so well labeled you won't even need a museum guide. See chapter 5.
- **Archaeological Museum of Olympía:** Besides the much celebrated *Hermes* by Praxiteles, there are pediments and metopes from the Temple of Zeus, remarkable for their preservation and attention to anatomical detail and expression, as well as a number of objects related to the Games. See chapter 7.

- **Archaeology Museum** (Iráklio, Crete): This fine museum contains Neolithic, Hellenic, and Roman finds from throughout Crete, but its Minoan collection is especially important. It includes surprisingly vivid frescoes from Knossós, elegant bronze and stone figurines, and exquisite gold jewelry. See chapter 8.
- **Goulandrís Museum of Modern Art** and **Museum of Sculpture** (Ándros): These heavily endowed, recently built sister museums contain the personal art collection of the Goulandrís family, who made their fortunes from shipping. World-class 20th-century paintings and sculpture are immaculately displayed. Call before you go; both are open limited hours in summer. See chapter 9.
- **Delphi Museum** (Delfí): Besides its famous life-size bronze charioteer with his sparkling eyes, there are two magnificent Archaic *koúri*, a room of silver and gold treasures, and an excellent collection of classical sculpture. See chapter 11.
- **Archaeological Museum of Thessaloníki:** Some may think that gazing on the skeleton of Alexander the Great's father and his funerary treasures is a bit macabre. But what a collection! See it and make up your own mind. See chapter 15.

6 The Best Natural Wonders

- **Samariá Gorge** (Crete): The "Grand Canyon of Greece" is 11 miles long (making it the longest gorge in Europe) with vertical walls reaching up to 1,625 feet. Pleasant and not strenuous for hikers (if you take your time), in spring it's awash with an incredible array of wildflowers. See chapter 8.
- **The Caldera of Thíra** (Santoríni): One of the world's most striking geological sights is this crater, averaging 5 miles in diameter. It was created by the explosion of a colossal volcano between 1647 and 1628 B.C. See chapter 9.
- **Metéora** (Kalabáka, Thessalía): Awesome gray pinnacles of rock were left when the sea retreated from the plain of Thessaly 30 million years ago. You may recall the daredevil rock-climbing of James Bond in *For Your Eyes Only,* a film that featured this strange and beautiful landscape dotted with monasteries. See chapter 11.

7 The Best Destinations for Romance

- **Piraeus:** 6:30am: Leave your main suitcase at your Athens hotel and take along only your essentials. 7am: Stroll along the waterfront and inspect the vessels sailing this morning. Get on the first ship that appeals to you, order a *nesfrappe* to bring out on deck, then ask where your ship is going. 8am: Sail to anywhere. So long as it's not a famous destination, you'll be able to find a room-to-let at the port when you disembark. See chapter 5.
- **Monemvassía** (Peloponnese): Rent a room off-season at the Hotel Malvasia, hidden on the island castle known as the Gibraltar of Greece. Tucked inside stylishly comfortable quarters, you can light a fire and imagine being imprisoned within this rocky fortress, or dress for a wind-blown stroll along the rocky promontory while the Aegean seethes at your feet. See chapter 7.
- **Tínos** (Cyclades): When the tourist hordes seem to be everywhere, we return to one of the most Greek of the Greek islands, Tínos. If you can get an old brass bed at the Hotel Tinion, leave the French doors open so the port breeze blows in during your siesta. Sleep late, wander the lanes filled with religious paraphernalia, take local buses anywhere and explore; be sure to dine after 10pm near the port. Voilà! You're back in the Greece you dreamed of discovering. See chapter 9.

- **Ía** (Santoríni): Get married in a town that's used to celebrating in a big way. Musicians lead the lucky couple along a marble pedestrian main street through the charming village. After a civil or religious ceremony, everyone enjoys a special feast in a local restaurant. Send the family away, then honeymoon in one of the excellent nearby caldera-view accommodations—at half the cost and with half the hassle of a wedding at home. See chapter 9.
- **Mt. Pelion** (Central Greece): Explore the heavily wooded hills around Mt. Pelion, looking for the tree nymphs and centaurs that once roamed the region. Smell the evergreens, pick wildflowers, and wander unannounced into timeless village squares for a glass of *krassí*, some pita bread, and a wedge of homemade cheese. You'll need only a room at a traditional welcoming *arhondikó*, hiking boots to stray off the beaten path, and each other. See chapter 11.
- **Delphi:** Visit the archaeological site after sunset, refresh yourself at the Castalian Spring, pose your question to the most famous oracle of ancient times, then wait and listen. . . . See chapter 11.

8 The Best Festivals Worth Planning For

- **Admiral Andreas Miaoulis Festival** (Hýdra): This week-long celebration lures every type of vessel to one of the prettiest harbors in Greece. Warships and gunboats moored offshore fire salutes periodically, and sailors of all stripes roam the port. Held during Navy Week in May.
- **Summer Theater Festivals:** In July and August you'll be able to see classical Greek dramas, performed in Greek, at Athens, Epidaurus, Thassos, Dion, and Dodona, among other places. Our three favorites: the gorgeous odeon at Epidaurus with its superb acoustics; the time-worn, intimate amphitheater at the archaeological site of Dion, near Mt. Olympus; and the site of the Oracle of Zeus Dodona in Epirus, where the atmosphere is mystical.
- **Pre-Lenten Carnival** (Pátra): Though its celebrations aren't on a scale with Mardi Gras festivities in New Orleans, you'll still be delighted to see this huge, modern port come alive with parades and parties in February.
- **Greek Orthodox Easter:** In any small Greek town, arrange to stay put for Good Friday, join worshipers at Holy Saturday's Midnight Mass, and share in Easter Sunday's Pascal Lamb feast. We love the coziness of the village of Aráhova (Central Greece) and the traditional ethnic purity of festivities on Kárpathos (Dodecanese), but this is Greece's favorite holiday and is celebrated everywhere in April.

9 The Best Affordable Hotels

- **Marble House Pension** (Koukáki, Athens; ☎ 01/923-4058): This pension is situated on a quiet cul-de-sac in an authentic Greek neighborhood south of the Acropolis. It's not the most convenient or the fanciest, but it's our choice because of the incredible bargain prices and exceptionally friendly, helpful, and caring staff. This is a comforting base from which to explore the big city. See chapter 4.
- **Hotel Byron** (Nafplio; ☎ 0752/22-351): You can find a less expensive choice if you're really intent on watching your wallet, but you can't find a prettier or more romantic lodging than this elegantly restored, 18th-century mansion perched on a hillside high above the touristy port. It's worth the extra price. Details such as marble-topped tables, lace curtains, Oriental rugs, and private terraces soothe the weary traveler. See chapter 7.

- **Chrissi Avgi Hotel** (Kástro, Peloponnese; ☎ 0623/95-224): This choice offers quality service, fine food, and castle views from its location in a tiny, very charming town. The two magnificent, centuries-old olive trees and the gracious owners make this contemporary residence a classically Greek experience. See chapter 7.
- **Doma Hotel** (Haniá, Crete; ☎ 0821/51-772): A former neoclassical mansion on the waterfront east of downtown has been converted into a comfortable and charming hotel by its gracious owner. The guest rooms are furnished with her family heirlooms, and the top-floor dining room offers a unique Cretan dining experience. See chapter 8.
- **Hotel Poseidon** (Iráklio, Crete; ☎ 081/245-360): This longtime favorite budget choice has an unusually well-informed staff who can make your travels around this huge island much easier. It's pleasantly modern, in a cool hillside location well above the hot, noisy city and close to the new port. See chapter 8.
- **Chateau Zevgoli** (Náxos; ☎ 0285/22-993): This restored Venetian mansion is in the charming, labyrinthine old quarter of town. The lobby/dining area is decorated like a local living room with antiques and family treasures. The cozy rooms are distinctively furnished in traditional style, and modern bathrooms and central heat assure total comfort. See chapter 9.
- **Santoríni Tennis Club Apartments** (Santoríni; ☎ 0286/22-122): Nestled in the sleepy village of Kartarados is a complex of white-stucco, early 19th-century Cycladic homes. Traditionally furnished, vaulted-ceiling rooms (some are former stables) offer kitchens, colorful weavings, and lofts that sleep two to five. Each is unique and very Greek in style. The pool and tennis courts make it an excellent choice for families. See chapter 9.
- **Hotel Australis** (Pátmos; ☎ 0247/31-576): When the Michalis family returned from Australia, they brought back with them plans for a clean, contemporary, port-view pension. Fortunately, their very Greek love of the land overpowered them and their inn has become hidden behind bougainvillea, geraniums, carnations, and other greenery. See chapter 10.
- **Hotel La Luna** (Rhodes; ☎ 0241/25-856): It's true that the seven wallpapered, eclectically decorated rooms don't have private baths. However, common showers have been built in a 300-year old Turkish *hamam,* a domed steam room that still evokes the wealth of the immigrant family that once owned this home. See chapter 10.
- **Arhondikó Hotel** (Corfu; ☎ 0661/36-850): If you request a room on the first two floors of this 1903 mansion–turned–guest house, you'll still enjoy cathedral ceilings and murals. The upper-floor rooms are simpler but perfectly spacious for families traveling together. Fresh flowers from the garden breakfast area fill antique urns on each landing. See chapter 14.
- **Kýma Hotel** (Híos; ☎ 0271/44-500): Built as a private villa in 1917, the Kýma was later converted into a very special hotel with a friendly, capable, and hospitable staff. The original architectural details have been preserved in the dining room, where an especially good breakfast is served. See chapter 16.

10 The Best Affordable Restaurants

- **Taverna Strófi** (Athens; ☎ 01/921-4130): After 14 years of regular visits to Greece, we always choose this place for our first meal in Athens. Nothing thrills us more than the excellent *mezédes,* attentive service, and perfect Acropolis view from the spacious roof terrace. See chapter 4.

- **Thanasis** (Athens; ☎ **01/324-4705**): This ever-busy souvláki stand just off Monasteráki Square has the best french fries in town, as well as tasty skewers of meat in pita. You won't mind the brusque service when you check out these no-nonsense prices. The line of cabbies offers assurance that you've reached the birthplace of authentic gyros. See chapter 4.
- **Taverna Klimatería** (Methóni, Peloponnese; ☎ **0723/31-544**): Not on the water, not glamorous, it's just a pleasant garden setting. But wait until you taste the delicious creations of chefs who are dedicated to the tradition of fine Greek cooking (usually an oxymoron). They grow their own produce in season and pride themselves on the quality of every morsel they serve. See chapter 7.
- **To Liotrívi** (Artemóna, Sífnos; ☎ **0284/32-051**): This is our favorite taverna on an island famous for its excellent cooks. Outdoors on the roof, on the square, or in their enlarged dining rooms, you can enjoy such delectable local specialties as *povithokeftédes* (croquettes of ground chickpeas) or a mouth-watering beef fillet with potatoes baked in foil. See chapter 9.
- **The Old Inn** (Hóra, Náxos; ☎ **0285/26-093**): Excellent food is served in a relaxing, tree-shaded courtyard, surrounded by the old inn's original parlors. You'll appreciate the enormously varied continental menu as well as the unique-in-Greece children's menu. Kids can await their meals in Mickey's Garden, a sandbox and play area filled with an array of toys. See chapter 9.
- **Yiánnis Taverna** (Old Town Rhodes; ☎ **0241/36-535**): Here you'll find generous portions of hearty moussaká, stuffed vegetables, and meat dishes, friendly service, and exceptionally good prices for this pricey area. See chapter 10.
- **Gregory's Taverna** (Vathý harbor, Ithaca; ☎ **0674/32-573**): Once you've taken the chartered boat or the half-hour walk to reach Gregory's, you may wonder why you made the effort. But you'll understand once your food arrives. After we update each edition of this book, our meal at Gregory's is the one we long remember. Order the grilled octopus, a snapper that swam by that afternoon, the superbly dry house wine, or a meaty lobster fresh from its trap. See chapter 14.
- **Ta Nicía** (Thessaloníki; ☎ **031/285-991**): This intimate little place 1 block off the harbor specializes in the freshest local seafood cooked in an original nouvelle Greek manner. Delicious mussels, crab, and cuttlefish are served with simple elegance. See chapter 15.

Getting to Know Greece 2

Most of you probably already have mental images of Greece that have been shaped by photographs and postcards, memories of the *Iliad* and *Odyssey* that stretch back to childhood, the music and dance of *Zorba the Greek,* reproductions of the *Venus de Milo* and the *Winged Victory of Samothrace,* vague recollections of myths of centaurs, muses, and Olympian gods. And of course, most travelers are in search of the sun, the deep blue of the Aegean Sea, and the dazzling white of cube-shaped houses. We hope you'll seek out your own combination of the sensual and intellectual pleasures that can be found in Greece.

This chapter is designed to help you understand what you'll see—and most people do need a refresher course, since it may have been a while since you last read anything about the ancient Greeks. The history section below, by no means exhaustive, serves to put into context the events, cultural details, speculative tidbits, and mythological tales discussed later in our book, as we consider the country region by region.

But don't become overwhelmed by antiquity's many silent and majestic monuments. Enjoy the Greece of today: the European sophistication of its cities, with their cosmopolitan nightlife; and the myriad islands offering sun and fun, water sports and hiking, inexpensive accommodations, and healthy dining. It's a country whose spirit is as bright and lively and colorful as its landscape. The Greek people continue the tradition, alive since Homer's time, of welcoming guests with *philoxenía*—or open arms.

1 The Regions in Brief

Greece is the southern part of the Balkan peninsula in the northeastern Mediterranean Sea. It has nearly 6,000 islands—though fewer than 200 of them are inhabited—strewn all around and far to the south. Though the Balkans have been perennially troubled, caught in the crucible of several thousand years of turbulent history, Greece itself remains somehow relatively constant.

The mainland is bordered on the north by Albania, the former Yugoslavia, Bulgaria, and Turkey, its former overlord and archenemy.

The islands are divided mostly along geographical lines into seven major groups: the **Saronic Gulf islands** near Athens and east of the

Greece

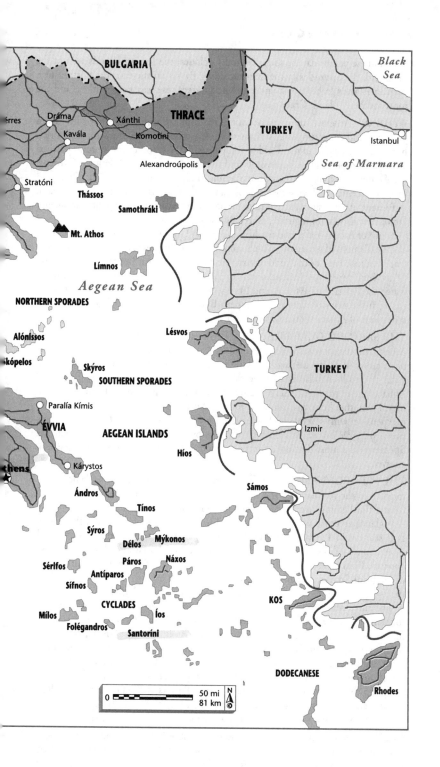

Peloponnese peninsula; the south-central **Cyclades;** the **Ionian islands** west of the mainland; the **Sporades** (sometimes including Évvia) on the east; the northeastern **Aegean islands** father north and east; the **Dodecanese** east near Turkey; and the most southerly island, **Crete.**

ATHENS   Athens (Athína) is, of course, the capital of Greece. It may suffer from pollution and congestion, but still, there are few cities in the world with such a rich history and few sights in the world to compare with the silent, evocative ruins perched atop the Acropolis. Here, too, you'll find the ancient Agorá, the National Gardens, the Temple of Olympian Zeus, the Stadium (built for the first modern Olympiad in 1896), scenic Mt. Hymettus (Imittós), and the refreshing Monastery of Kessariani.

  Piraeus, its port since ancient times, is one of the busiest in the Mediterranean and famous for its vibrant nightlife, especially its *rebétika* clubs.

  South of Athens you'll find wealthy and stylish Glyfáda, the Apollo Coast, and the austere Temple of Poseidon, which commands the impressive hilltop overlooking Cape Soúnio. Fans of the goddess Artemis may want to visit her temple at Brauron (Vravróna). Marathon (Marathónas), to the northeast, is where the Athenians defeated the Persians in 490 B.C. and from which Diomedon ran the 26 miles to Athens with the news of victory. The superb Byzantine Monastery of Dafní is only 6 miles west of Athens on the way to Corinth.

THE SARONIC GULF ISLANDS   The Saronic Gulf islands are the closest to Athens and the most easily accessible—but that very accessibility means that they're often crowded on the weekends and in the summer. **Aegina** (Éyina) is worth at least a day trip to its handsome and pleasant port of Aegina and the lovely Temple of Aphaia, one of the best preserved and most beautifully situated of all Archaic buildings. In another hour you can reach touristy **Póros,** which is pleasant and relatively inexpensive, with several good beaches. The whole island of **Hydra** (Ídra) is a national preserve on which vehicles are not allowed, a real gift, if a tad expensive. **Spétses** is the most distant, a pretty and sophisticated island, on which traffic is allowed.

THE PELOPONNESE   The Peloponnese (Pelopónnisos) is a peninsula now separated from the mainland by the Corinth Canal, which was begun by Nero in A.D. 67 and finished just over a century ago by a French construction company.

  A glance at a map will reveal at least a dozen places of major interest: the important seaport of **Pátra; Olympia,** famous for its games; **Mycenae,** from which Agamemnon led the Greeks against Troy; **Argos,** home of Jason and most of the Argonauts; **Epidaurus,** with its perfect amphitheater and Asclepion; the beautiful port of **Náfplio; Sparta,** which won the Peloponnesian War with its famous discipline; the Byzantine ghost city of **Mystrá; Kalamáta;** and "sandy" **Pylos.**

  The three remote southern fingers of the Peloponnese are largely unspoiled by tourism. The Venetian fortress at **Monemvassiá,** the "Gibraltar of Greece," is peaceful and otherworldly except in the summer and on holidays when Greeks reclaim and overrun it. **The Máni** is remote and wild, its people known for their independent spirit, with the cool underworld of the caves of Pirgou. The highway along the coast from Areópoli to Kalamáta is especially varied and spectacular. Below Pylos and past Navaríno (Navarone in Italian), where the Great Powers of Britain, France, and Russia accidentally defeated the Turkish fleet and ended the War of Independence, are **"the Eyes of Venice"**—the lovely castles at Methóni and Koróni—and good beaches.

CRETE   Crete (Kríti) is the largest and most southerly of the islands, something of a land unto itself, with great diversity and its own special character. It offers spectacular scenery, impressive Minoan ruins, and beautiful Venetian remains. Noteworthy attractions include the bustling capital of **Iráklio,** with its excellent archaeological museum; nearby **Knossós;** handsome and pleasant **Réthymnon;** lovely **Haniá,** which offers Venetian fortifications and makes a good base for excursions to **Samariá gorge;** and excellent beaches.

THE CYCLADES The Cyclades probably need little introduction, since they're among the most popular and accessible of the islands.

Spectacular **Santoríni** and swinging **Mýkonos** are world famous, sophisticated, and expensive, especially in the high season. **Páros** is the transporation hub of the Cyclades. Away from its port of Parikía, it's not too crowded or expensive; it's an excellent place for water sports, especially windsurfing. **Sýros** has the capital, largest city, and administrative center of the Cyclades, **Ermoúpolis** ("Hermes City"); it's not well known among tourists and thus is a good place to find an authentic taste of Greece without sacrificing the amenities. **Náxos** is large, mountainous, and largely self-sufficient because of its agriculture—a pleasant place to eat, shop, and escape the hordes. Or you could join them for a beer bust on **Íos. Tínos** is a religious retreat, where little English is spoken and foreign tourists are noticed only if they seem lost (then they're given genuine attention). Shy **Sífnos** offers a more enjoyable escape, and **Folégandros** is even more remote and detached.

THE DODECANESE The Dodecanese ("Twelve Islands" in Greek) are farther south than the Cyclades. They're generally well developed and easily accessible—perhaps too well.

Rhodes is the best known of the Dodecanese; decades of unflagging popularity with foreign visitors have not ruined the island, but it's not an easy visit. A trip there is certainly expensive and may not be a good value unless you're careful.

Little **Sými** owes its popularity to overflowing Rhodes (from which it's easily visited), its relative serenity, and its pretty yellow neoclassical architecture. Lovely **Kos** was in ancient times famous as a "cure" resort; now it's much too popular with budget tour groups, though with a little effort you can still find it well worth visiting. Sponges gave **Kálymnos** its livelihood until recently, but now it's accommodating the overflow tourists from adjacent islands, especially along its attractive west coast. **Léros,** with several mental institutions, served as a place of exile during the junta; whether it will be a refuge or a sentence for you will depend on how carefully you arrange your stay. Holy **Pátmos** is a very special island, which probably needs little introduction if you know your New Testament history; it's a refuge for the spirit and a joy to the senses.

CENTRAL GREECE Then there's what we conveniently call Central Greece (Stereá Elládos). This includes **Attica** (Athens County, you might say) and sometimes the big island of **Évvia.**

The high point is the stellar **Mt. Parnassus** (Parnassós), often covered with snow and shrouded with clouds—the Muses may still linger here.

Delphi (Delfí), in the shadow of Mt. Parnassus, is one of the most beautiful and deeply impressive places in Greece. The town itself is very pleasant, the remains of the Oracle of Apollo and the surrounding Sanctuary are endlessly fascinating, and the museum alone would be worth the trip. Also in the vicinity you'll find the handsome Byzantine monastery of **Ossios Loukás;** several lovely mountain villages, including **Aráhova,** which is a ski resort in the winter; **Itéa,** on the Gulf of Corinth, for those who require a dip in the sea; lovely **Galaxídi;** and historic **Dióstomo** or Lepanto (*Lefpákto*), where the European fleets defeated the Turkish.

THE SPORÁDES The Sporádes, off the east coast of mainland Greece, are verdant and surrounded with particularly clear water, but they're not quite as picturesque

The Gods & Goddesses of Mt. Olympus

Here's a brief summary of the major gods and goddesses (and their areas of influence) that appear in the literature, mythology, and folklore of classical Greece:

Aphrodite: Goddess of love and beauty; mother of Eros, messenger of love.

Apollo: God of light, music, learning, and prophecy.

Ares: God of war.

Artemis: Goddess of the hunt and of the moon; twin sister of Apollo.

Asclepius: God of medicine and healing.

Athena: Goddess of wisdom and patron of the arts and crafts; daughter of Zeus and protectress of Athens.

Cronus: The most powerful god during the Saturnian Age; father of Zeus, Hera, Poseidon, Hades, Demeter, and Hestia. Zeus took his place as leader on Mt. Olympus.

Demeter: Goddess of agriculture, mother of Persephone.

Dionysus: God of wine. The performance rituals honoring him were the basis for all Greek drama.

Hades: God of the Underworld.

Hephaestus: God of fire and metalwork. He made the armor that protected Achilles throughout the Trojan War.

Hera: The beautiful but jealous and exacting wife of Zeus.

Hermes: Messenger of the gods. He led the dead to the Underworld.

Hestia: Goddess of the hearth and family life. She was honored throughout Greece in homes and public buildings with a flaming altar.

Poseidon: God of the sea and fresh waters. He wielded a trident and caused earthquakes.

Zeus: Supreme diety; father of Apollo, Artemis, Athena, Ares, Hephaestus, numerous demigods, and all men. His weapon was the thunderbolt and his symbol was the eagle.

as the Ionians. They're accessible from Athens, via bus to Ayios Konstandínos then by hydrofoil or ferry, or from the port of Vólos.

Skiáthos, which can also be reached by air, is the most sophisticated, most expensive, and best developed—perhaps too developed—because of its many beautiful fine-sand beaches. **Skópelos** is more rugged, with fewer good beaches, but it's being developed more slowly and thoughtfully, and Skópelos town is one of the most beautiful ports in Greece. **Alónissos** is more remote and less touristy, but it has its share of attractions, and its people are friendlier. **Skýros** is also quite isolated (it's reached by ferry from Kými on Évvia), so it has maintained its own character and traditions (wild ponies still run free).

WESTERN GREECE & THE IONIAN ISLANDS   West of Thessaly is the mountainous region of **Epirus** (Ípiros), with its lovely mountain villages, such as Métsovo, and the wild and nearly deserted Zagóri, now being avidly explored by trekkers. South of the busy capital, Ióannina, and its tranquil lake are the remains of the famous Oracle of Zeus at Dodona (Dodóni). Unlike most of Greece, Epirus is densely forested in the north and rather overlooked by tourists—possibly partly because its people are not especially outgoing—but nature lovers and hikers will love it.

The **Ionian islands** are among the greenest and most beautiful of Greek islands, though they sometimes seem more Italian than Greek, and their inhabitants are not known for friendliness and hospitality. These islands are quite far from Athens, though fairly convenient for people coming from Italy. **Corfu,** the best-known Ionian island, is remarkably beautiful, sophisticated, and expensive. **Lefkáda,** which is accessible by car (no need for a ferry), is not especially attractive at first sight, but the interior is very pleasant and the south coast has some lovely beaches. **Ithaca** (Itháki) is more famous as the home of wily Odysseus than as a tourist destination, but it has a beautiful harbor at Vathý, a handsome interior with rugged hills and evergreen valleys, plus a few pretty if rocky beaches. Unspoiled **Kefalonía** is a large island with sensational scenery and several excellent beaches. **Zákynthos,** the southernmost Ionian island and convenient to the Peloponnese, has much to offer in the spring and fall, though its handsome Venetian architecture was significantly damaged by an earthquake in 1953.

NORTHERN GREECE—MACEDONIA, THRACE & THESSALY The unhappy and much-contested story of the northern region we call **Macedonia** (Makedonía) is a tangled one. Most of the region is part of Greece, but part of it was a republic in the former nation of Yugoslavia.

The name **Thessaloníki** celebrates the Macedonian victory over the Greeks at the battle of Chaeronea in Thessaly in 338 B.C by Philip II, Alexander's father. It's a thriving cosmopolitan capital, the second-largest city and port in Greece, with Roman ruins, marvelous Byzantine churches, a superb archaeological museum, an important yearly international trade fair, and a busy but pleasant atmosphere.

Alexander the Great country itself is mostly to the west and south at Pélla, Véryina, and Dión. To the south stretches the three-fingered peninsula of **Halkidikí** and holy **Mt. Áthos,** which can be visited only by men, and only with permission. **Kavála,** the pretty port where the Apostle Paul first stepped ashore in Europe, and nearby **Philippi,** where he also preached and where the armies of Anthony and Octavian (later Emperor Augustus) defeated those of Brutus and Cassius, are east.

East of Macedonia is the region that in ancient times was known for its wild redhaired people, **Thrace** (Thráki), which now has a large Muslim population. From its capital, **Alexandroúpoli** (City of Alexander), you can catch a ferry to Samothráki or continue on by bus or train to Istanbul (Konstantinópoli) or Bulgaria.

South of Macedonia and mighty Mt. Olympus lies **Thessaly** (Thessalía), famous since antiquity for its pastoral life, which continues there today (along with agriculture) on the central plains around the big easygoing capital of **Lárissa. Vólos,** the place from which Jason and the Argonauts set sail, is today a major seaport, where you can catch a ferry to the Sporádes. The wild slopes of **Mt. Pelion** (Pílio) are now covered with orchards (centaurs are no longer seen), and Thessaly has a number of charming traditional villages, beautiful beaches, and gracious people. In western Thessaly the monasteries of **Metéora** perch atop their towering rocks, spectacular and serene.

THE NORTHEASTERN AEGEAN ISLANDS These are the most remote and least visited of the major islands—which in itself should pique some interest. **Sámos** is only a few miles from Turkey, with regular ferry service to Kuçadasi and Ephesus, lots of good tourist facilities, good beaches, and several interesting sights. **Híos** is known for its wealthy shipowners, mastic (from which chewing gum is made), its handsome medieval villages, and the warm hospitality of its people. **Lésvos** is

probably best known as the birthplace of Sappho, the greatest of all lyric poets. It's a prosperous island and not dependent on tourism, though it has important resort havens in the north at beautiful Mólivos and in the south at Plomári. **Límnos** is a fertile volcanic island, strategically located at the mouth of the Black Sea, and perhaps best known today for its luxurious Akti Mirina resort complex. Lonely **Samothráki** has its Sanctuary of the Great Gods, where important fertility mysteries were celebrated in ancient times, but there are few tourist facilities on the island. Far-northern **Thássos** has lots of development because it's quite close to the mainland—maybe a little too close.

2 Greece Today

In the few years since the 1992 unification of Europe, Greece (then barely considered part of the Common Market) has changed more than it did in the preceding five decades! It's as if the cradle of civilization had finally reached adulthood.

One of the most important changes we've seen is that Greece is no longer an "exotic" country. It's as European as you'd expect Italy or Spain to be, with few donkeys to be seen on the shoulders of the new superhighways.

We remember when the only people who wore black were homebound widows, and Greeks were puzzled by fashionable visitors who wore black. We recall when unmarried daughters were supervised during the day and kept home in the evening—after dark, only men were seen in a *kafenion* (coffee house), where wizened old Greek men sat for hours nursing mud-black coffee while playing *távli* (backgammon).

But with the economy fizzling for so long, Greeks continued to flee to the cities and abroad. Political, economic, and social changes accelerated. Now, widows and 40-something Greek women go to work wearing the latest casual outfits from Paris and Milan. Greek girls in miniskirts and Doc Martins can be seen in clubs, at the newest wine bars, and on the beaches of Mýkonos and Santoríni. In the 1990s, it's their turn to flirt with young foreign visitors and to openly date Greek men. And those wizened old men have shaved off their handlebar mustaches and relocated to fashionable espresso bars (where they still play *távli*).

As we began our research for this edition, we worried about finding anything uniquely Greek left for readers heading to the most popular destinations. But "Greekness," however, remains tenacious—if not in the sense we used to mean: flocks of sheep everywhere, tavernas lined with dusty old wine casks, fishermen mending their nets in port. Now you'll find beef cattle in the fields, good bottled wine from the best vineyards, and fishermen chartering their caïques to far-off beaches.

As for the economy, much of the country is now too arid for cultivation after many decades of overdevelopment and 4,000 years of deforestation (for shipbuilding, fuel, and unsuccessful attempts to replace the native trees with the more lucrative but shallow-rooted olive tree). Tanker ships and desalination plants must supply water for many of the inhabited islands. Only about a fourth of the population is still engaged in farming, contributing less than 15% of the gross national product; the main products are grains, fruits, vegetables, olives, cotton, tobacco, livestock (goats for milk and sheep for meat), and increasingly fish farming. In 1991 the European Community (now the European Union) placed two popular Greek exports, feta cheese and the anise-flavored liqueur called *oúzo,* on its protected-products list. Tourism is now the country's biggest industry, followed by shipping.

In this EU-backed economy Greeks can finally afford to go to Greek resorts. Although accommodations and restaurants have become more expensive for foreigners, chic islands and out-of-the-way villages now lure Greek visitors in equal measure.

And, luckily, some things will never change. The Greeks' enduring love of sea and sky, their need to sit under the stars all night and argue politics, that fierce pride in their chaotic homeland, and the philosophy of *philoxenía,* or welcoming of strangers, still remain.

So, although your trip to Greece may not be what it would have been 5 years ago, it's sure to include much more contact with the locals. And that remains one of the best reasons to go!

3 History 101

According to archaeological finds, Greece had a long prehistory that extended back into the Neolithic Age (at least 6000 B.C.). Its earliest recorded history, beginning some 3,000 years later, can be divided into four main periods: the Minoan, the Mycenaean (or Helladic), the Archaic, and the Classical.

The years 2600 to 1500 B.C. were dominated by the Minoan culture, which flourished on Crete and, archaeologists speculate, on Santoríni, near settlements of the lesser-known Cycladic civilization.

The Mycenaean civilization, which lasted from about 1900 to 1100 B.C., was centered in the Peloponnese. In the 12th century B.C. the Mycenaeans were overrun by the Dorians, who invaded from the north, ushering in a 400-year period, 1200 to 800, that is referred to as the "Dark Ages."

The Classical era, so called because the arts, culture, and democracy of the Greeks reached their peak at this time, extends from 600 B.C. to the death of Alexander the Great in 323 B.C.

ANCIENT CIVILIZATIONS

EARLIEST SETTLERS   Pottery dating from as early as 6000 B.C., found in Macedonia, Thessaly, and the Cyclades, confirms the existence of settlements that later developed into a primitive Neolithic culture. About 2600 B.C. a wave of emigrants from what we now know as the Middle East brought copper to Greece. Archaeologists have found traces of another race at Phaistós, on Crete, from about 2300 B.C.; several sites abandoned about 2000 B.C. suggest that northern invaders overran Greek settlements about this time.

After this transitional period, Minoan culture became predominant during the middle Bronze Age (2000–1580 B.C.).

MINOAN CIVILIZATION   Around 1900 Sir Arthur Evans, a British archaeologist who had been conducting excavations on a Cretan hillside near Iráklio, came upon the remains of what appeared to be an enormous structure. The discovery of the royal

Dateline

- 3000–1400 B.C. Minoan culture flourishes on Knossós (Crete); Theseus slays the Minotaur in his Labyrinth.
- 1400–1150 B.C. Jason and the Argonauts; Agamemnon, Achilles, and the battle of Troy.
- 1200–1100 B.C. The Dark Ages.
- 800–600 B.C. Athens unites with towns of Attica; Homer composes the *Iliad* and the *Odyssey;* Draco proclaims severe laws; Solon reforms constitution.
- 520–430 B.C. Persian Wars; Themistocles fortifies Piraeus.
- 492 B.C. Diomedon runs 26 miles from Marathon to Athens to announce Athenian victory.
- 480 B.C. Aeschylus wins Athens drama festival.
- 480–430 B.C. The Classical Age: the Parthenon is built; Pericles is in power; Aeschylus, Sophocles, and Euripides are at work.
- 430–400 B.C. Peloponnesian War; naval battle of Syracuse; Erechtheum on Acropolis completed; Aristophanes writes comedies; Pericles dies; Socrates drinks hemlock; Sparta triumphs over Athens.
- 360–300 B.C. Macedonian Age: Alexander the Great conquers; Aristotle founds school.
- 200 B.C.–A.D. 300 Roman Period: Rome sacks Corinth.

continues

- 31 B.C. Octavian crowned first emperor of Rome.
- A.D. 300–1200 Constantine builds Constantinople; Crusaders build forts.
- 1204–1797 Venice rules duchies in the Ionian Isles, the Peloponnese, and other isles.
- 1453 Fall of Constantinople.
- 1453–1821 Period of Turkish rule.
- 1821–1829 Greek War of Independence.
- 1833 Prince Otto of Bavaria appointed first king of Greece.
- 1863–1913 Prince William of Denmark rules as George I; a liberal constitution is adopted; Greece regains much of its territory from the Turks; economy flourishes.
- 1917 Greece joins Allies during World War I.
- 1923 League of Nations organizes massive resettlement of Muslim and Greek Orthodox citizens.
- 1940–1941 Italians and Germans invade Greece; George II flees; resistance forms.
- 1944 British and Greek forces liberate the country.
- 1946 Greece joins United Nations; plebiscite returns George to throne.
- 1946–1949 Civil war between Communist and right-wing forces.
- 1947 George II dies; his brother Paul becomes king.
- 1951 Greece joins NATO.
- 1952 Women achieve the right to vote.
- 1964 King Paul dies; he is succeeded by his son Constantine.
- 1967 Military junta takes over; Constantine II flees country.
- 1973 Monarchy abolished.

continues

palace at Knossós, Crete's ancient capital, caused a sensation. The complex of multistoried buildings, many of them now partly restored, proved the existence of a civilization more advanced than hitherto supposed.

Indeed, not only in architecture but also in physical works, commerce, and the arts, the peaceful Minoans achieved a rare degree of sophistication. They were gifted artisans, producing beautiful frescoes for their unfortified palaces and probably for homes in their colony at Akrotíri, on the southwestern coast of Santoríni. (The best preserved of these frescoes are on display in the archaeological museums of Iráklio and Athens.)

By the 16th century B.C. the Minoans had founded colonies at Miletus, on the coast of Asia Minor near Sámos, and on Kálymnos, Rhodes, and Kýthira. Goods from as far away as Egypt and Syria have been excavated at Minoan sites, and the eggshell-thin, multicolored Kamáres ware they produced has been found throughout the Mediterranean. The most fascinating find may be a collection of tablets, thought to be royal records, written in syllable symbols and numerals that have not yet been fully deciphered, referred to as Linear A.

Almost as intriguing as the culture of the Minoans is the mystery surrounding the disappearance of their civilization. The late Greek archaeologist Spyrídon Marinátos, who headed the excavation of Akrotíri, and other archaeologists have postulated that a colossal volcanic eruption on Santoríni in about 1640 B.C. caused a tidal wave that wiped out Knossós and Crete's northern shore. (This explosion may have been responsible for the disappearance of the mythical Atlantis). Evidence suggests that some of the Minoan cities, including Knossós, recovered but were overrun about a century later by the Mycenaeans.

MYCENAEAN CIVILIZATION   As early as 2600 B.C. Asian tribes, later called Pelasgians, were settling in the Peloponnese. Their pottery and sculpture, found in Asia Minor, Egypt, the Cyclades, and on Crete, indicate that the Minoans had direct contact with their eventual successors.

It took the hard work and imagination of Heinrich Schliemann, the 19th-century German amateur archaeologist, to forge the link. In 1870, in a quest to prove the veracity of Homer's *Iliad,* Schliemann began excavating at Hissarlik, on the northwestern coast of modern Turkey. After 6 years of exploring the multilevel ruins of ancient Troy, he continued to the eastern coast of the Peloponnese, searching for evidence of Homer's Greek heroes. The royal shaft graves he uncovered at Mycenae, filled with gold masks, jewelry, and pottery, convinced him, albeit wrongly, that he'd found King Agamemnon's tomb.

This civilization that developed on the Peloponnese peninsula was centered in Mycenae, where a warrior king ruled from his fortified palace, with important citadels at Pýlos and Tíryns. These people achieved new heights in architecture and bronze work. By the 14th century B.C. shaft graves had evolved into *thóli,* beehive-shaped burial vaults cut into the mountainside, a significant engineering feat for that time.

Nestor's palace at Pýlos displays another Mycenaean invention. Unlike other palaces, it was built around a *mégaron,* a reception hall with a central hearth and columned portico at one end, the forerunner of the classic Greek temple. Linear B tablets found at Pýlos prove that their syllabic script was an early form of ancient Greek.

- 1974 Turkey invades Cyprus and junta collapses; Constantine Caramanlís becomes prime minister.
- 1981 Greece joins European Economic Community; liberal PASOK (Panhellenic Socialist Movement) party, under Andréas Papandréou, wins election.
- 1989 Charges of corruption bring down Papandréou government.
- 1990 Conservative New Democracy elects Caramanlís president.
- 1991 Athens celebrates 2,500 years of democracy.
- 1993 New elections called; PASOK reelected.
- 1996 Prime Minister Papandréou resigns and is succeeded by Kostas Simítis.

A militaristic mood prevailed in the Mycenaean centers. Cyclopean wall fortifications (so called because the ancients thought that only huge monsters could stack the tremendous boulders seen today) began appearing about 1300 B.C., the same time that smaller villages were falling to outside invaders. Mycenaean trading ships ran pirate raids against other Mediterranean sailing ships.

Historians think this was the period of the Trojan War, which Homer chronicled in his *Iliad* nearly 500 years later. At about this time the first Greek colonies were established in Asia Minor, and the Phoenicians dominated commerce in the Aegean.

Archaeologists think that the Dorians (from the Balkans) eventually overran and destroyed the Mycenaean civilization. Although the Dorians were Greek-speaking, they were not culturally advanced, and the region plummeted into the Dark Ages. There is little archaeological evidence from this period. What was found in the Keramikós Cemetery in Athens (dating from 1100 to 750 B.C.) comes from old-fashioned cist graves, not seen for a millennium. Both ceramics and iron jewelry indicate that culture retrogressed. Some scholars think that bronze-working may have lapsed because trade restrictions made it difficult to obtain tin, a component. Others associate the use of iron for metalwork with Anatolian and Middle Eastern tribes and believe that these peoples were related to the Dorians.

Art historians call this the Protogeometric Period because the pottery found from Athens was decorated with concentric circles or painted geometric forms. Trade with other, more sophisticated cultures seems to have resumed after 900 B.C. Skillfully crafted geometric period vases have been excavated in Phoenicia and Egypt, indicating that a new, broader range of trading partners helped pull Greece from the Dark Ages.

CLASSICAL CIVILIZATION

The Classical period, from about 600 to 300 B.C., is considered Greece's Golden Age. In three centuries the Greeks left an unrivaled cultural legacy: the democratic government of Solon and Pericles; the natural science of Pythagoras and Hippocrates; the historical writings of Herodotus and Thucydides; the dramas of Aeschylus, Sophocles, and Euripides; the comedies of Aristophanes; the philosophy of Socrates, Plato, and Aristotle; the art of Phidias, Praxiteles, and countless others.

GROWTH OF THE CITY-STATE   The mountainous, inhospitable Greek terrain made the city-state *(pólis)* a practical social unit. By 800 B.C. the barbaric tribes that had overrun mainland Greece and destroyed the centralized authority and economy of the Mycenaeans were settling into agricultural communities. Inhabited settlements, isolated from their neighbors by mountain barriers, clustered in fertile valleys. Homes were built upon any plateau *(acrópolis)* that could more easily be defended against invaders. As trade increased, agriculture became more specialized.

The city-state of Athens, for example, turned its farmland into vineyards and olive groves, not only for their export value but because of the crops' suitability to the arid terrain. The once-fertile inland was being eroded because of deforestation (to build ships and unsuccessful attempts to replace native trees with olive trees) and overgrazing. In the 4th century B.C. Plato wrote of the region: "What now remains, just as on small islands, compared with what used to be, is like the body of a sick man, with all the rich and fertile earth fallen away." The lack of arable land to satisfy an increasing population led the city-states to found colonies abroad.

Greece was now entering what archaeologists call the Archaic Age. About 750 B.C. the colony of Cumae (north of Naples) was founded by Greeks from Kými, Halkís, and Erétria on Évvia. Soon after, Syracuse in Sicily, Messalía (Marseilles), and Byzántion (Istanbul) were settled by Greeks. By 600 B.C. there were 1,500 overseas colonies linked to mainland Greece by language, custom, and religion. All others in the ancient world were considered *bárbari.*

The largest growing city-states were Corinth and Megara on the Peloponnese, Aegina and Athens in Attica, and the islands of Rhodes and Sámos. In order to maintain their colonies, these city-states felt they needed to expand commercially and industrially. The wealth amassed by the lower classes through such pursuits as trade, commerce, and craftsmanship led to the establishment of some economic equality among the social classes. The army, once the exclusive province of the landed gentry, now recruited *hoplites*—common soldiers who could pay for their own armor. Usurers began to prey on small farmers, who were hard hit by the growing specialization in food for trade. Social upheaval in every class generated changes in government.

FIRST DEMOCRACY   At the dawn of the Classical period some city-states attempted democratic governments, in which popular assemblies ruled; and some established oligarchies, giving power to aristocratic councils. All governments had similar precepts: a magistracy (which evolved from the old tribal kings) led by a religious, military, or judicial figure; a council or senate made up of elder advisers, often the aristocracy; and an assembly of the people, who could act on the council's recommendations.

In 594 B.C. Solon established a code of laws and a democratic framework for Athens. He canceled farmers' debts and attempted to restore an egalitarian social order. He also established public-works programs, festivals, and athletic events. Later, under Pericles, civil servants would collect salaries, so that all would be able to participate in the democratic process. Revenue was raised from taxes on voteless foreign residents as well as citizens, customs, and allied city-state "protection." The rich in Athens were "supertaxed"—they were required to pay for equipping a trireme, staging a play, or a chorus rehearsal.

The next important government reform in Athens was instigated by the tyrant Cleithenes (in 510 B.C.) when he acceded to revolutionary demands made by the aristocratic council (Areopagus). Every citizen was a member of a *démos,* or civil parish, of which there were 168 in Athens. These were arranged in groups of 10 and then mixed in order to achieve a geographic and ethnic blend of tribal members. A Supreme Court of nine representatives from the council was voted on annually, and the people's assembly was increased to 500 members. A president was elected by the assembly on a rotational basis from among tribal leaders.

Athenian leaders dispensed with their critics through the process of *ostrakismós,* in which members wrote the undesired person's name on a discarded pottery fragment *(óstrako).* The top scorer would be banished for 10 years, but without loss of property or status.

Aristotle summed up democracy this way: "You can't have a state of 10 citizens. But when you have 100,000, it is no longer a *polis.* [It should be small enough for] the citizens to know each other's characters. Where this is not the case, both elections and decisions at law are bound to suffer." The Greeks were very proud of their political democracy; in fact, it was to defend their political system in the Ionian colonies that Greece faced its first great challenge, the Persian Wars.

THE PERSIAN WARS   The mighty Persian Empire had long kept a covetous eye on Greece, targeting it as a potential conquest. Emperor Cyrus consolidated the Greek colonies in Asia Minor under Persian rule in 546 B.C., and in 499 B.C. these Ionian cities, now under Darius, revolted. Aristagoras, the tyrant of Miletus, went first to Sparta, then to Athens to plead for help against Darius. The following year 20 ships from Athens and 5 from Erétria sailed for Ephesus. After 4 years of battle the Persians prevailed, but Darius was determined to punish Athens for its aid. In 492 B.C. his first naval expedition was shipwrecked by a storm off Mt. Áthos on the easternmost tip of Halkidikí, but he soon sent another, this time to the Bay of Marathon, northeast of Athens. The badly outnumbered Athenian troops, together with their Plataean allies, camped at Marathon to await requested Spartan reinforcements. The messenger Pheidíppides ran 150 miles to Sparta in less than 2 days, but found the Spartans unwilling to march before the end of a lunar holiday. Miltíades, one of the Athenian generals, decided to attack, concentrating on the vulnerable Persian wings, which quickly collapsed. Darius's troops fled back to their ships and sailed immediately for Cape Soúnio, hoping to catch Athens unguarded. According to Herodotus, a young soldier, Diomedon, ran the 26 miles (42 kilometers) to Athens still in his armor, cried "We won!" then fell dead. (The long-distance marathon was added to the modern Olympic games to commemorate his run.) Miltíades and his men rushed after him to defend but lose their city.

The Persians did not accept their defeat at Marathon well; therefore, under Darius's son, Xerxes, two pontoon bridges were constructed across the Hellespont (Dardanelles), and a canal was dug through Halkidikí to prevent the possibility of another storm foiling revenge. In May of 480 B.C., Xerxes set off with about 180,000 troops, including foreigners (Indian, Ethiopian, Egyptian, and Phoenician infantry and Arabs on camelback). The Greeks had their naval defense at Cape Artemision, north of Évvia, and a land defense at the Thermopylae Pass. After several days of intense battle at sea, the Greek naval forces fled south and found refuge in the Bay of Eleusis, near the island of Salamís. The Spartan general Leonídas and 7,000 men were guarding Thermopylae, a natural land barrier preventing the Persians from reaching southern Greece. After 3 days of fighting, a traitor, Ephíaltes, led the Persians over another nearby pass. Aware of the hopeless situation, Leonídas ordered the majority of his troops to retreat and 300 Spartan and Boeotian soldiers stayed behind to guard their retreat. They fought bravely to the last man, and their immortal epitaph can still be seen at Thermopylae: "Stranger, tell the Spartans that here we lie in obedience to their word."

At Salamís the Athenian leader, Themistocles, heeding the Delphic oracle's prophecy that "wooden walls" would save Athens, ordered all the city's warships manned. He then sent a Greek slave to act as a traitor and to encourage Xerxes to attack immediately. The Persians were lured into the narrow bay, where the smaller and more maneuverable Greek triremes easily defeated them while Xerxes watched from the headland above. Xerxes withdrew to the Hellespont. During the following spring, the Persian general Mardonius recaptured Attica, inflicting heavy damage. Then the Spartan leader Pausánias rallied his troops to battle the Persians at Plataea, near Thebes; the Persians were defeated, and soon after the remaining Persian fleet was burned off Cape Mykále, on the coast of Asia Minor.

The Persian invasions should have made it clear to the Greeks that they needed a common defense, but Athens and Sparta soon became involved in an open rivalry. Sparta had already surrounded itself with the Peloponnesian League, and in 478 B.C. Athens countered by founding the Delian League, so called because its administrative center was on the sacred island of Delos. Some 200 city-states in the Aegean, in Thrace, and along the Asia Minor coast joined the league, contributing ships and funds in order to assure protection from Athens. In turn, Athens used the league to augment its own power in the region. As military strength became the city's primary concern, Athenians elected a brilliant general *(strategós)*, Pericles, to lead them.

ATHENS UNDER PERICLES   During the rule of Pericles (461–429 B.C.), Athens prospered and achieved cultural preeminence in the Greek world. Its democracy was strengthened. The state now began to pay those who served it, allowing a greater number of citizens to enter public service. Magistrates had to be elected, and government operations were centralized in the *thólos*, next to the council in the Agorá. All business was screened by the council before it went to the people's assembly, but any citizen could bring a grievance before the assembly.

Because there were 250 council seats and members could hold only two nonconsecutive terms in a lifetime, many Athenians became involved in the political process. Wealthy landowners and the military had traditionally controlled local politics; now a new breed of orators (demagogues) rose to represent the naval and civilian working class. Slaves were still common but many were skilled, had the right to vote, and ran their own businesses, paying their owners a royalty on earnings.

Pericles himself came from an aristocratic background but was a staunch supporter of democratic government. Contemporary writers describe him as an intelligent, skillful orator and a brilliant military strategist. Lesser politicians conceded that he was uncorrupted by his almost total power over the city, yet they used his highly publicized affair with a courtesan against him in his declining years.

In 447 B.C., as part of a major public-works program, Pericles ordered construction to begin on the Parthenon. For the project, he used funds from the Delian League's coffers, dismissing objections by other members. In 437 B.C. the Propylaea and a new odeum, or covered theater, were added to the Acropolis. Pericles also commissioned several temples—of Poseidon at Cape Soúnio, Nemesis at Rhamnous, and Hephaestus in Athens, overlooking the Agorá—as well as the Hall of Mysteries at Eleusis.

Pericles was an avid supporter of the arts, and his politically astute social programs served to promote the performing and visual arts. In 460 B.C. he commissioned his friend Phidias to sculpt a huge chryselephantine (gold-and-ivory) statue of Zeus for the sanctuary at Olympia. Phidias was already known to Athenians for his *Athena Promachus,* a huge bronze statue of the goddess constructed on the Acropolis to celebrate Athens's victory over the Persians. When the architects Ictinus and Callicrates began designing the Parthenon, Phidias was put in charge of all its sculptural ornamentation.

During Pericles' time the theater flourished. The first dramatic diversion from the solemnity of religious rituals came in 520 B.C., when Thespis introduced a *hypokrítes,* or play actor, reciting narratives. In 477 B.C. Aeschylus, Greece's first major tragic poet, added a second actor and further dialog, in his play *The Persians,* to create a more complex plot. After him the young Sophocles, who won the Athens drama competition in 468 B.C., introduced a third actor, as well as painted scenery. Best known for his *Antigone* and *Oedipus Rex,* Sophocles wrote more than 100 popular dramas. They were presented three at a time, followed by a farce, or so-called satyr play, as was the custom. The third great tragedian, Euripides (b. 480 B.C.), wrote realistic, psychologically penetrating, and often politically controversial plays, for example, *Medea, The Trojan Women,* and *The Bacchae.* He made use of the *deus ex machina,* a device to lower a god onto the stage to intervene in a hopeless situation.

Comedy, too, was very popular. The leading comic poet was Aristophanes, whose witty social and political commentaries enjoyed great success. Despite the frequent burlesque nature of his plays, they contained many fine lyrical choral passages. In *The Knights, The Wasps, Lysistrata,* and a handful of other surviving comedies, Aristophanes satirizes politicians, Athenian courts, modern music, Athens's imperial policies, even the battle between the sexes. In *The Clouds* he mocks the great philosopher Socrates, for running "a logic factory for the extraclever." At the factory, says one of the characters, "they teach you (if you pay enough) to win your arguments whether you're right or wrong." Some historians believe that Aristophanes' play led the Athenians to condemn Socrates, the perennial gadfly, to death in 399 B.C.

Athens's unique Golden Age under Pericles was short-lived. In 430 B.C. the first of two devastating plagues struck the city, killing nearly a third of its population. Many felt that the gods were indicating their displeasure with Pericles, whose aggressive attempts at land expansion were opposed by some of the other city-states, especially Sparta, Athens's chief rival. When Athens was at its weakest, its unbridled urge for conquest brought about the first major inter-Greek conflict, the Peloponnesian War.

SPARTA   Today the word "spartan," which means "warlike, hardy, disciplined," derives from the inhabitants of ancient Sparta (see chapter 7, "The Peloponnese"). Originally Sparta was merely a collection of villages without any natural means of defense, and thus it was dependent on the skill and ferocity of its soldiers. In the 9th century B.C. the legendary Lykurgus formed a more cohesive city-state with laws that provided for universal military training, rigid discipline, and the supression of liberty and luxury.

According to Plutarch, a committee of elders evaluated the physical condition of babies at birth; the weaklings were left on the slopes of Mt. Taygetus to die. Hardier infants were bathed in wine (an assurance of their good health) and raised to be unafraid of the dark, tolerant of all foods, and uncomplaining. At the age of 7 all boys were taken by the state for athletic training and basic education. They were underfed so that they might resort to stealing, which was believed to foster cunning and resourcefulness, two qualities especially prized in battle; if caught, they would be punished *for being caught.* They had to participate in violent team games and long, solo wilderness missions to develop their endurance. At age 20 young men attempted to win election to a *syssition*, a military unit in which they would spend their adulthood. Women lived at home but were given rigorous physical training as well to ensure that they would bear strong children. Wives could meet their husbands only secretly at night; if their husbands were sterile, the women would be lent to other men so that they could bear children.

The government of Sparta was run by two kings, who kept a check on each other. There was no political unrest among the citizenry because Spartiates (landowning, full-blooded descendants of Spartan parents) had no class distinctions; work was performed by their *helots* (state-owned slaves). In architecture, as in the other arts, the strict Spartan lifestyle discouraged creative expression. Nevertheless, the Spartans were extremely patriotic, brave, and proud of their city's achievements, and their political stability was the envy of many of their contemporaries.

THE PELOPONNESIAN WAR   Sparta had consolidated the Peloponnesian League into a powerful military alliance with the best land forces in Greece, but its naval forces were no match for those of Athens's Delian League. Pericles' initial forays outside of Attica had angered Sparta and its allies, but it was not until Athens began meddling in Corinth's affairs in the Ionian Sea (431 B.C.) that war was declared. Pericles directed Athens's offense at sea and was usually victorious. Spartan land raids into Attica were ineffective; Athens defended itself by retreating safely behind its fortifications and the "Long Walls" that connected the city with Piraeus and Phalerum. Protracted warfare proved devastating to both sides; in the captured colonies, men were killed and their wives and children sold into slavery. Plague broke out again in besieged Athens in 429 B.C. and killed a sixth of the population, including Pericles. The disorganized Athenian leadership chose a bolder offensive. Political greed motivated most of the Athenians' forays, and the resentment of many Delian League allies only accelerated Athens's downfall. After inconclusive fighting, a truce was declared in 421 B.C., but it was to last only 3 years.

Athens then turned a covetous eye on the prosperous colony of Sicily. A huge fleet was sent to capture the island but failed; the Sicilian expedition marked the second phase of the war. Thucydides, the great historian, blames Athenian arrogance for the humiliating naval defeat; only a few sailors escaped after the last great battle at Syracuse harbor, in 413 B.C. Alcibiades, the nephew of Pericles, first betrayed Athens in the Sicilian fiasco by turning to Sparta, then betrayed Sparta by joining the Athenian fleet off Sámos for the last phase (412–404 B.C.) of the war. By this time Sparta had traded its Ionian colonies for Persian support. After years of battling in the Ionian and Aegean seas, the Athenian fleet was defeated. Xenophon, another historian of the war, writes that Athens's Long Walls were immediately torn down "to the music of flute-girls and with great enthusiasm" and the victors demanded the surrender of all but 12 ships. Perhaps the greatest tragedy of this outcome was that Athens, fit to rule and at its prime culturally, was denied the only chance it had ever had to unite all of Greece under its aegis.

DECLINE OF THE CITY-STATES   Nearly 30 years of conflict devastated every city-state that had been involved in the Peloponnesian War. There was rampant inflation, widespread unemployment, and constant food shortages. There was no work for slaves, the poor sought jobs as mercenary soldiers, and the rich were subsidizing farmers. In 399 B.C. war broke out again. This time the Persians were asking Sparta to support them against the Asian Greek colonies. Within 4 years the Boeotian League, a confederation of central Greek city-states—Athens, Thebes, and several Peloponnesian League members that had been betrayed by Sparta—was formed to resist Sparta and Persia. The Persian king, Artaxerxes, fearing a protracted and costly war, demanded that Sparta make peace with the other Greek city-states.

From 378 to 371 B.C. Thebes, under the leadership of the brilliant King Epaminóndas, was the major power on the Greek mainland. After the Theban victory at the Battle of Leuctra, in which the Spartans were crushed, Epaminóndas led his troops on a conquest of the Peloponnese, liberating Messenia and founding the model city of Megalópolis. Athens was so alarmed by Thebes's growing power that it sided with Sparta. The struggle came to a climax at Mantínea in 362 B.C. where Epaminóndas fell in battle; his death so disheartened the Boeotians, who were winning, that they retreated. The Greek city-states were in hopeless disarray.

PHILIP OF MACEDONIA   Meanwhile the power of several northern kingdoms was growing. Athens regained some political stability under the leadership of Demosthenes, its greatest orator, and it undertook, along with Thebes, a series of preemptive incursions into Thessaly and Macedonia itself. During a Theban-led raid, Macedonia's young Prince Philip was taken hostage; he was later released and assumed the throne in 359 B.C.

Demosthenes warned the Athenians that they should strengthen their fleet to protect Athens's interests in northeastern Greece as a first step toward meeting the challenge of Philip, whose ambition was sure to lead him to attack Athens sooner or later. In yet another shift of alliances, Persia joined Athens, Thebes, and other Greek cities to form a united front against Philip. In 338 B.C., at the Battle of Chaeronea, Philip defeated the combined Greek forces and emerged as the undisputed leader of Greece.

The two greatest influential thinkers in the 4th century B.C. were Plato and Aristotle. Plato's philosophy was based on truth as a way of life—the belief that physical objects are impermanent representations of eternal ideas, and that these ideas alone give true knowledge. His thinking was idealistic; he had nothing but disdain for the imperfections of democratic politics, which he mocked in his *Republic*. He wrote the definitive treatise on Socrates' ideas, but never formalized his own ideas in writing. Nevertheless, the Academy he founded attracted the top Greek minds until A.D. 529, when Emperor Justinian put an end to all pagan institutions.

Plato's "best pupil," Aristotle, was born in Halkidikí, but came to Athens as a young man and studied with Plato for nearly 20 years. Philip brought him to Macedonia to tutor young Alexander, who surely benefited from his teacher's vast knowledge of the natural world, logic, and rhetoric. When, in 335 B.C., Aristotle left Alexander's court, he founded a school in Athens, near the Temple of the Apollo Lykeios. His Lyceum offered courses in rhetoric, logic, ethics, politics, and biology. His thinking was more practical and better formulated than Plato's, and his ideas dominated Western thought for nearly 1,000 years after his death. Alexander's breadth of interest and his commitment to unifying all the known races of the world in one kingdom was greatly influenced by the teachings of Plato and Aristotle.

ENTER ALEXANDER THE GREAT   When Philip was assassinated in 336 B.C., he was succeeded by his son, Alexander, who also assumed Philip's position as general of the League of Corinth. Alexander had been remarkably precocious in developing military and political skills; at age 18 he served as a general in the Battle of Chaeronea, and would soon use his talent to full effect in his brief but illustrious career.

In 334 B.C. Alexander began his conquest of Persia, ostensibly to avenge past invasions of Greece, but more likely to replenish Macedonian coffers. Reportedly he carried a copy of the *Iliad* with him throughout his Asian campaign, and he

❷ Did You Know?

- In 1997 Thessaloníki was recognized as the Cultural Capital of Europe.
- In 1991 Greece celebrated 25 centuries of democracy. The official ceremony, attended by prominent world figures, was held in Athens, at the *bema* (forum) atop Pnyx Hill where, in the 6th century B.C., the statesman Cleisthenes exhorted the Athenian assembly to accept his democratic reforms.
- In 500 B.C. Athens opened the first municipally run garbage dump, decreeing that all waste had to be disposed of 1 mile outside the city walls.
- Among the engineering feats of ancient Greece was a tunnel built on the island of Sámos by Eupalinos, a Megarian architect, in the 6th century B.C. to bring water from nearby mountain springs to the island's capital, Pythagório. The tunnel was dug some 1,000 yards through the mountain by workers who started at both ends and met in the middle, only about 1 inch off their marks.
- The gleaming marble Panathenaic stadium in the middle of Athens was built in 1896 for the first of the modern Olympic Games, which took place in Greece. It occupies the site of a 4th-century B.C. stadium where the quadrennial Panathenaic Games were held. Like the original, of which it is a faithful copy, the stadium is 1 stade (about 606 feet) long, the standard measure of the Olympic foot race.
- According to *Science News,* geochemists studying glacial ice cores in Greenland have found copper and lead emissions dating back 2,500–4,000 years. They believe smelting in ancient Greece caused some of the earliest air pollution.
- There are 7.5 million Greeks living abroad, sending home more than $1 billion annually.
- Greece is the third-largest wine producer in Europe. More than 25% of its wine is produced from grapes grown in the Peloponnese.
- Flokáti, the shaggy woolen rug made in Greece, is actually hand-woven from wool imported from New Zealand. Greece's many sheep are bred for their meat rather than their wool.
- The 20-station extension of the Athens Metro, due to open in late 1998—but probably delayed due to unexpected archaeological finds and added excavation— is budgeted at $2.8 billion. The city government projects it will transport 450,000 commuters daily and reduce automobile emissions by 35%.
- Each day in Athens, 500,000 *souvlakia* and 1,000,000 cups of coffee are sold.

demonstrated his political acumen by stopping at Troy to make sacrifices to Athena, following in the footsteps of every young Greek man's hero, Achilles. During the first 2 years of his campaign he captured Miletus, Tyre, Phoenicia, Palestine, and Egypt after difficult fighting, personal injuries, and great hardship for his troops. Alexander spent the winter of 332–331 B.C. in Egypt, founding the city of Alexandria, the first and greatest of the 16 Alexandrias he would found along his route of conquest. Later in 331 B.C. he routed Darius at Gaugamela, but refused Darius's offer of a settlement. He continued east to Babylon, Sousa, and Persepolis, where he burned down the old palace of Xerxes in revenge for the slaughter at Thermopylae. Darius, now left with only a handful of troops that were difficult to control, was killed at Ecbatana by Bessos, the murderous satrap of Bactria, who hoped to impress Alexander by the deed. Alexander, however, gave Darius a royal funeral and had Bessos executed. Alexander continued east until all opposition in the rugged, inhospitable eastern mountains had been crushed. In 327 B.C. he decided to invade India.

About this time Alexander began emulating Persian ways, including requiring his many new Persian advisers to prostrate themselves on the ground before him. His Greek troops, who would bow only before the gods, were offended by this behavior. Most wanted to return to their homeland and felt that they'd accomplished all they had set out to do, but they continued to follow Alexander because of personal loyalty and respect. Within the year Alexander and his army crossed the river Indus (in modern Pakistan), but the seasonal monsoon vanquished his troops' morale. They refused to continue across the Hyphasis River. After fruitless pleading, Alexander agreed to turn back. But nearly a year of arduous trekking, hunger, thirst, and natural disasters passed before Alexander arrived back at Sousa. There, he celebrated by marrying a Bactrian princess and presiding at a ceremony in which some 10,000 of his men married Asian women. He retired thousands of Macedonian soldiers and tried to replace them with Persian recruits, angering many loyal troops, who felt betrayed.

Alexander was planning to conquer Arabia when he fell ill (some say from malaria, others suggest poisoning, alcoholism, or venereal disease) and died in Babylon in June of 323 B.C. This brilliant military tactician and charismatic ruler contributed much to the knowledge of natural sciences and spread Greek culture to much of the known world. Unfortunately no one else was capable of governing his unwieldly empire, and so it was split into four parts, all of which grew again under the influence of Hellenistic civilization.

GREECE AFTER ALEXANDER

THE HELLENISTIC ERA   From Alexander's death (323 B.C.) to the crowning of Octavian as the first Roman emperor (31 B.C.), Greek culture dominated, remarkably, a world where Greeks had little political control. A common form of the Greek language, *koiné,* spread throughout the Mediterranean (the New Testament was later written in it) as individual city-states and colonies were absorbed by and influenced large kingdoms. The increase in worldwide trade and travel also led to the integration of Greeks with other races. By the Roman era a very cosmopolitan and sophisticated whole had evolved from the mixture of new cultures and traditions.

After Alexander's death Greece itself united into the Hellenic League in order to secure its freedom from Antipater, the Macedonian leader. After the Hellenic League's defeat at Lamía, Antipater's navy soundly defeated the Athenian navy in the Dardanelles. Athens surrendered and never regained her former status.

For 20 years the rest of Alexander's empire was at war. Antipater's son, Cassander, ruled Macedonia and installed Demetrius to rule over Athens. Alexander's former bodyguard, Ptolemy, headed the Hellenistic Empire from Alexandria, Egypt. He worked to preserve Alexander's ideals, and even smuggled Alexander's body into Alexandria so that a tomb could be built for him. Ptolemy's empire flourished until 31 B.C., when Cleopatra and Mark Anthony were defeated. The leader of Alexander's footguards, Seleucus, consolidated his Asian holdings along the lines of the old Persian Empire and established his capital at Antiochus (named after his son) in Syria. The Seleucid Empire was the most visible remnant of Alexander's former glory, but it, too, slowly dwindled in strength since no effort was made to unite its diverse people.

GREECE UNDER THE ROMAN EMPIRE   Greece and Carthage allied themselves against the Romans for the first Macedonian War in 215 B.C. Troops under Philip V resisted the Romans through another war, but in 205 B.C. Greece fell. Not until the Romans defeated the combined forces of the Achaean League (146 B.C.), however, was Greece made a province, subjected to Roman laws and forced to pay tribute. In 146 B.C. Corinth was leveled, and in 86 B.C. rebelling Athenians were massacred by Sulla. Ruthlessly putting down the rebellion of the poorer classes, the Romans rewarded some property holders with positions as local magistrates. Roman civil wars fought on Greek soil also caused much damage to Greece and its economy.

After the 2nd century A.D., when little of value remained in Greece, the Romans became more lenient with their Greek subjects. They began building public works, restored some cities, and brought Greeks into local government. Hadrian revived old religious festivals and founded a new Panhellenic League. The Romans enthusiastically adopted the Hellenistic culture and its artisans. In this period of "antiquarianism," early masterpieces were reproduced, old dramas were restaged, and classical philosophies and old dialects were revived. The writer Plutarch (A.D. 46–120) stirred Roman interest by praising Greek heroes, ethics, religion, and philosophy in his series of biographies, *The Lives*. In the mid–2nd century Pausanius wrote a scholarly account of Greece's archaeological history that not only helped sustain Roman interest in Greek culture but also contributed to educating the Western world about Greece's past.

THE BYZANTINE ERA   In Greece the 3rd century A.D. was marked by invasions of European barbarians that caused great destruction. Although the declining Roman Empire couldn't afford to repair the damage, the emperor Claudius II did guarantee the Greeks' physical safety. Christianity had now grown into a powerful force within the Roman Empire. At the end of the 3rd century Diocletian divided Greece into several dioceses, with Constantinople as the capital. Greek art and goods were shipped to the Asian city, increasing trade and bolstering local Greek communities. In 394 the emperor Theodosius I abolished the Olympic Games and all "pagan" rituals, but many Greeks continued to follow their old beliefs.

Under the Isaurian dynasty (8th century) the country was divided into *themes,* many of which prospered as the wealth of the Byzantines grew. The themes became feudal principalities after Constantinople fell to the Crusaders in 1204. New Latin conquerors and old Byzantine rulers—notably the Venetians, French, Aragonese, Sicilians, and Catalans—fought over and traded the principalities. A Frank, Geoffroy de Villehardouin, administered the principality of Morea, one of the most prosperous of its day. The Palaeologi, Byzantine rulers, retook Morea in 1262, renamed it the Peloponnese, and made Mystrá their capital (see chapter 7).

From 1204 to 1797 Venice held many Greek duchies, leaving an architectural legacy that is still admired today. The Ionian Islands; Methóni, Koróni, Argos, Monemvassiá, and Náfplio on the Peloponnese; and Crete, Évvia, Náxos, and other islands still bear evidence of this heritage. Overall, the ecclesiastical rule of the Byzantine era provided a period of self-confident growth for Greece from its state of neglect at the end of the Roman period to the nationalistic spirit and strength it would need to defend itself against its next conqueror.

TOURKOKRATÍA   The word *tourkokratía,* for the period of history when Greece was under the rule of the Ottoman Empire (1453–1821), is still spoken with resentment. Much of the Greek mainland had already been taken when Constantinople (now Istanbul) fell to Sultan Mohammad II in 1453. Although some individual islands resisted annexation to the empire for years, many Greek cities found Ottoman rule preferable to that of the Franks or Venetians. In theory the Greek Orthodox religion was tolerated so long as it permitted political loyalty to the Ottomans. Under Suleiman the Magnificent the Greeks also enjoyed freedom of trade and language;

strong Ottoman forces protected the mainland from attack by its former feudal over-lords and extended a small amount of autonomy to local governments.

For the Greeks, of course, life without freedom was intolerable. They were obli-gated to pay a per-capita tax for the "privilege" of living under Ottoman rule, real estate and commerce were taxed, and, worst of all, about 20% of the male children were sent to Istanbul for training as *janissaries* (servants to the sultan). The janissary system was abolished in the 1600s, but until then some Greeks actually took advan-tage of its educational opportunities to rise within the ranks of Turkish government. (When the revolution came, the "Turkish" Greeks did not forget their homeland.) In the 18th century Catherine the Great, empress of Russia, encouraged rebellion among her Orthodox brethren. The first uprising, centered in the Peloponnese in 1770, was forcibly put down without the promised Russian intervention. When Catherine tried to stir up trouble in 1786, most Greeks ignored her, although in Epirus there was an unsuccessful revolt against the local sultan, Ali Pasha.

During the next few decades oppressed Greeks were inspired by many world events: They witnessed the French Revolution, the American Revolution, other na-tionalist rebellions, and the fall of Napoleon. Ali Pasha had eroded Ottoman rule in the north by annexing all the neighboring territories. In response, Greek aristocratic and intellectual classes contemplated revolt, while Greeks in Europe sought support for their cause. When Ali Pasha decided to split from the empire in 1820, it provided a perfect opportunity for Greeks to demand their freedom. The War of Independence (1821–29) eventually won liberation for Greece, but the fledgling nation suffered from fragmented forces, conflicting allegiances, and disparate goals.

During the 2 years between the decisive Battle of Navarino, in which a combined British, French, and Russian naval force accidentally defeated a much larger Turk-ish fleet (following which Greece was granted independence under the Treaty of Lon-don), and Russia's war on Turkey (settled by the Treaty of Adrianople), Greece extended its boundaries north and south of the originally negotiated borders. Ioánnis Capodístrias, a noted leader in foreign affairs, took office as president on January 18, 1828. Wealthy Greeks thought Capodístrias's democratic reforms were excessive, while liberals felt he was autocratic and too willing to accept a king. Capodístrias was assassinated by an aristocratic dissident in Náfplio in 1831, leaving the government in chaos. The European powers attempted to support the weakened democracy by sending in French troops to keep order while hastily convening the Conference of London, which proclaimed Greece an independent kingdom.

THE MODERN ERA

One hallmark of Greece's modern history was Europe's imposition of a monarchy on the country; another was its territorial disputes. At the Conference of London, Greece was granted the Peloponnese, the mainland north to the Árta-Vólos line, and some of the Aegean Islands (but not Crete or Sámos), all to be guarded by Britain, France, and Russia. Greece's first monarch, Prince Otto (Othon) of Bavaria, arrived in 1833. Two issues caused considerable resentment: Greece had not yet expanded to its previous boundaries, and all positions in Othon's government were held by Bavarians. In 1843 Greek wartime leaders and rebel forces stormed the royal palace, demanding the removal of foreign advisers and a new constitution. Othon complied and drafted a new constitution providing for a National Assembly. His increasingly autocratic rule, however, caused popular discontent. In 1862 minor mutinies led to a full-scale revolt in Athens and Othon was deposed. Britain led the push to impose a new king and ceded the Ionian Islands to Greece to sweeten the deal. In 1863 young Prince William of Denmark accepted the Greek throne under the name

George I, king of the Hellenes—which indicated the intention of territorial expansion and helped fuel the "Great Idea," the dream of a new Greek empire.

During his long reign (1863–1913), Greece enjoyed relative prosperity and some technological advancement. Thessaly, Macedonia, Epirus, and most of the Aegean islands were reunited. In 1896 a major uprising occurred on Crete, leading to a war between Turkey and Greece. A peace treaty was arranged by the European powers in 1897 and in 1898 the Turks left Crete. The Europeans, instead of allowing Crete's union with Greece, installed Prince George of England as high commissioner under the sultan's suzerainty. The compromise was actively opposed by Elefthérios Venizélos, a prominent Cretan who led the struggle for union. As a result of his effective leadership, the European powers withdrew their troops in 1908.

THE BALKAN WARS   In 1909, Venizélos was summoned to Athens by the military (who wanted political reform) and made prime minister. He revised the constitution and effected social and financial reforms. At the same time he pressed for the independence of the rest of Greece. In 1912 Greece joined the Balkan League in a war against Turkey, winning back Epirus, Macedonia, Sámos, and Crete. Greece's fragile peace was, however, shaken by the assassination of King George; he was succeeded by his son Constantine, who had been a hero during the war.

The Treaty of London abolished the Turkish Empire and returned the occupied lands to the Balkan League. Disputes arising over their disposition led to the Second Balkan War, in which Serbia and Greece were allied against Bulgaria. The Truce of Bucharest, signed in 1913, left Bulgaria a small part of Macedonia and access to the Aegean, and created Albania from part of Epirus. However, the Turks and Italians refused to give up their occupation of the Aegean and Dodecanese islands. World War I put an end to this shell game.

WORLD WAR I   The war provoked a division in Greece. King Constantine insisted on neutrality, but his wife was the kaiser's sister and many felt that he really sided with Germany. Prime Minister Venizélos sided with Britain and France. Venizélos was dismissed, and Constantine maintained Greece's neutrality until June 1917, when the Allies demanded Greek participation in the war. Constantine left the country in protest, and Venizélos returned as prime minister. Military successes in Macedonia strengthened Venizélos's bargaining position with the Allied powers at the Versailles peace conference in 1919.

In 1919 the Allies encouraged Greece to retake Smýrna (now Izmir) but failed to provide military support, and the Greco-Turkish War that ensued was disastrous for Greece. In 1923 the League of Nations insisted on the resettlement of Muslim and Greek Orthodox citizens; more than a million Greeks in Turkey were forced to emigrate to Greece. Because of the Greeks' Asia Minor fiasco, Constantine was relieved of his throne. His successor, George II, reigned for only a year.

In 1924 Admiral Pávlos Koundouriótis was proclaimed first president of the new Republic of Greece, which lasted only 11 turbulent years. Venizélos, as leader of the antiroyalist Liberal Party, reappeared several times in an effort to take control. The royalist Popular Party, which stepped in after one of Venizélos's failed coups, restored the monarchy of George II in 1935.

The Communists won a narrow victory in the general election of 1936, but King George permitted a military takeover by Gen. Ioánnis Metaxás. Metaxas, citing a Communist threat, imposed a quasi-fascist dictatorship that lasted until World War II.

WORLD WAR II & CIVIL WAR   Greece entered World War II in October 1940. Until then it had been neutral, but when Italy demanded that Italian troops be allowed to cross into Greece from neighboring Albania, Metaxás is said to have responded with a firm *"Óchi!"* (no). (*Ochi* Day, October 28, is now a national holiday.) The Italians invaded but were forced back into Albania. In 1941 the German army struck through Yugoslavia, promised British support failed to materialize, Metaxás conveniently died, the king fled, and Greece quickly capitulated. The Nazi occupation, which lasted until 1944, was typically savage; half a million Greeks starved to death, thousands of others were slaughtered, and most of the Jewish population was deported and exterminated.

During the war a heroic resistance movement sprang up throughout the country made up of communist and socialist forces (EAM-ELAS) as well as rightest rebel forces (EDES). The two fought each other as well as the Germans. By the summer of 1944 the Communists, having consolidated their power, formed a provisional government in the north. Despite popular objection, the British insisted on the return of King George, and British troops fired on EAM-ELAS demonstrators in Athens, sparking a vicious civil war. It lasted 5 years, ending with the defeat of the Communists. During that time the United States, under the Truman Doctrine (1947), provided extensive military and economic aid to the rightest government, which was especially ruthless in its suppression of any opposition. Both sides were guilty of atrocities. The psychological damage made a greater impact on Greek politics than any other conflict since the Peloponnesian War.

POSTWAR GREECE   In 1946 a rigged plebiscite returned George II to the throne. He died a year later, however, and was succeeded by his brother, Paul. In 1952, after a series of unstable coalition governments, Field Marshal Alexander Papágos formed a government headed by his Greek Rally Party. In the intervening period Greece regained the Dodecanese islands (1948) and joined the North Atlantic Treaty Organization (1951).

Under a newly adopted constitution, Greek women were given the right to vote in 1952. A program of national reconstruction was instituted by Papágos and continued by his successor (1955), Constantine Caramanlís. The country allied itself firmly with the West and tried to settle some of its differences with its neighbor and NATO ally, Turkey. In 1959 the issue of Cyprus's sovereignty was resolved by the Zurich Accord among Greece, Turkey, and Britain (which ruled the island); it granted Cyprus independence and provided for the sharing of power between the island's Greek and Turkish communities.

Caramanlís remained in power until 1963, when a left-of-center coalition led by George Papandréou narrowly defeated the ruling Conservative Party. In 1964, after new elections in which the left increased its hold on Parliament, King Paul died and was succeeded by his son, Constantine II. A battle of wills between the elderly Papandréou, a veteran Venizélist, and the young monarch soon led to Papandréou's resignation and a protracted period of political instability as one government succeeded another. Finally, in April 1967 a group of colonels, headed by George Papadópoulos, seized power, dissolved Parliament, and banned political activity. The king and his family went into exile.

In 1973 the military junta abolished the monarchy, and Papadópoulos proclaimed himself president of the new republic. He promised to restore civil liberties and to schedule national elections the following year, but he was soon ousted by hard-line officers. With U.S. backing, the junta consolidated its grip, imposed rigid censorship, and imprisoned and tortured those who opposed it. In July 1974, in the wake of an Athens-inspired coup in Cyprus that led to a Turkish invasion of the island, the military junta yielded power to civilian leaders. Caramanlís, who had gone into exile in France after his 1963 defeat, returned as head of an interim government.

In late 1974 a plebiscite rejected the return of the monarchy, and the following year Parliament ratified a new constitution providing for a republican form of government. Caramanlís and his New Democracy Party won a majority in national elections; they returned to office in 1977. In 1980 Caramanlís stepped down as prime minister to become president of the republic; in that role, he presided over Greece's entry into the European Community (now European Union) as a full-fledged member in 1981. That same year Greek voters elected the country's first Socialist government, headed by Andréas Papandréou, the Harvard-educated son of George Papandréou. In 1985 strains between the Conservative Caramanlís and the leftist Papandréou led to the election of a new president, Chrístos Sartzetákis.

In 1989 charges of corruption brought down the Panhellenic Socialist Movement (PASOK). The new prime minister, Constantine Mitsotákis, and his New Democracy majority in Parliament elected Caramanlís to a new 5-year term as president in 1990.

The Conservative government set about to reverse many of the Socialists' free-spending policies, which had led to high inflation and a crippling national debt. An austerity program was mandated by the European Union as a condition for further EU aid to Greece. Outlays for social services were reduced, public-employee raises were limited, and public-utility rates were increased—measures that, as expected, touched off a series of labor strikes.

The government lost popularity because of its economic policies and eventually lost its parliamentary majority over a foreign-policy issue that had aroused nationalist passions—the dispute with the neighboring former Yugoslav Republic of Macedonia over that state's adopted name, "Macedonia," and national symbols (among them the star of Vergina, identified with Alexander the Great), which Greece regards as inherently Greek. Foreign Minister Antónis Samarás, accusing Mitsotakis of being too eager to settle the issue "against Greece's interests," resigned, bolted from New Democracy, and formed his own rightist group, Political Spring. Others defected from the governing party also, and in 1993 new elections were called.

The Socialists, under Papandréou, returned triumphantly to power. They moderated their socialist program, although they renationalized public transportation and slowed down the previous government's privatization program. They also exacerbated the "Macedonia" issue by imposing an economic embargo on the new nation of Macedonia (still referred to as FYROM or Skopye in the Greek press), which depends heavily on trade through the port city of Thessaloníki. Meanwhile, New Democracy chose a new leader, Miltíades Evert, the former mayor of Athens.

In early 1996 Papandréou resigned because of failing health and was succeeded by Kostas Simítis, a more moderate technocrat known for his even temper, methodical manner, and pro–European Union attitudes. Though frictions with Turkey have heated up again, the elections of September 1996 were quieter than usual and Simítis led the Socialists to a solid victory—162 of 300 parliamentary seats. He calmly warned the nation to tighten its belt because of spending for military preparation for conflict with Turkey, and also to be able to meet EU standards for inclusion in the European Common Currency by the end of the century. He must curb inflation and drastically reduce government spending.

Impressions

We are all Greeks.

—Shelley, *Preface to Hellas,* 1821

4 A Legacy of Art & Architecture

Ancient Greek art and architecture had a profound influence on the Western world's aesthetic sensibilities. From the "Grecian bend," coined to describe the forward-leaning gait so fashionable in 19th-century England, to the timeless images of Isadora Duncan's graceful dancing on the steps of the Parthenon, to the bold "Greek profile" universally praised as beautiful, we have absorbed certain principles of classic Greek style into our common culture.

Art historians have traced classical Greek art directly from the Mycenaean empire. The large amount of pottery found (much of it made in Athens) had simple geometric patterns applied in black paint to a terra-cotta ground, thus giving the era (1100–700 B.C.) the names "protogeometric" and "geometric."

The **Lion Gate at Mycenae,** the best known example of stone construction from the Bronze Age, dates from 1250 B.C. The huge, irregular, hand-hewn building stones (the gate's lintel is carved from one 10- by 12-foot block, sculpted with bas-relief lions) were typical of those stacked into cyclopean walls widely seen in Peloponnesian architecture from this era.

After the 8th century B.C., potters began to incorporate friezes of sticklike figures, chariots, and animals into their designs. Soon, Greek sailors introduced metalware and ivory to Cyprus and Asia Minor. Artisans began carving more voluptuous humans and animals, hammering bronzes, and doing filigree and granulation work in gold. Vase painting soon reflected these new undulating forms from the East. Trade with Egypt sparked an interest in monumental sculpture and architecture, and by the 6th century B.C. the residents of many Greek outposts in Italy and along the Mediterranean shore were constructing huge stone temples.

Corinth's Temple of Apollo (mid–6th century B.C.) is the oldest extant Doric temple in Greece. The baseless fluted columns end in simple round "cushion" capitals similar to but more graceful than the cigar-shaped Doric columns of the Temple of Hera in Paestum, Italy (which also dates from this period). Doric columns typically supported a frieze that was divided into triglyphs (vertical bands), separated by metopes (often sculpted areas) in a style derived from both Mycenae and Egypt. The basic temple hall was the cella, surrounded by a colonnaded stoa.

The eastern Greek settlements and Aegean islands were influenced by the Near Eastern and Oriental cultures with whom they traded, and they adapted the more graceful Ionic column as the basic element in building. The **Temple of Artemis at Ephesus,** Turkey, with its multitiered and sculpted bases, slender fluted columns, and double volute capitals, is one of the earliest examples.

During this period, bold stone male (*koúros*) and, less often, female (*kóre*) statues, their feet firmly planted in a frontal stance, were created as attendants to the gods or memorials over graves. The **National Archaeological Museum** in Athens has an excellent collection of these monumental figures and examples of the more naturalistic sculpture that developed. By the time construction began on Athens's **Acropolis** in the 5th century B.C., Phidias and his team of extraordinary sculptors were working on the lush, naturalistic figures that decorated the Parthenon frieze. The Acropolis's decorative sculptural elements are widely believed to be among the finest classical-era art ever produced.

The monuments of the Acropolis are among the greatest architectural achievements of all time. The Doric Temple of Athena Parthenos (Virgin)—the **Parthenon**—designed by Mnesicles, was built between 447 and 433 B.C. with plans by Ictinus and Callicrates. Ictinus's other great work, the **Temple of Vassae in the Peloponnese,** introduced the Corinthian capital (a crown of acanthus leaves under two Ionic volutes). The **Erechtheum** (421–405 B.C.) is the Acropolis's most unusual structure, with its Porch of Maidens and ornate Ionic columns. After the Acropolis, construction flourished throughout Attica: public buildings, courts, and markets were designed in what would be known as the "classical" style.

As classical artists honed their skills and their work became more sophisticated, many were given free rein to create for beauty's sake rather than for functional or religious purposes. **Bronzes,** now made by the lost-wax casting process, began to rival marble sculpture in detail and the figure's ease of movement. Intricately sculpted folds of cloth revealed the muscles and flesh of male statuary as well as sensuous female anatomy. In the 5th century B.C. **Myron** contributed his famous *Discus Thrower* and **Polyclitus,** his much copied and imitated *Spear Bearer.* The 4th century B.C. brought us the bronze *Marathon Boy;* the **Praxiteles** marble *Hermes with Dionysos* (for Olympia) and his *Aphrodite of Cnidos;* and the graceful circular *thólos* temple at Delphi. **Lysippus,** the favored sculptor of Alexander the Great and another star in the art world, is known primarily from later Roman copies of his work.

Although the huge tomb of Mausolus (mausoleum) at **Halicarnassus** (now Bodrum, in Turkey) dates from the late 4th century B.C., within Greece itself monumental architecture was still limited to public buildings, particularly theaters. They were typically designed with a large *orchestra* for the actors and chorus, surrounded by tiers of marble seats built into a hillside. The **theaters at Delphi, Delos, Megalopolis, and Epidaurus** are typical examples.

As Alexander the Great (ruled 336–323 B.C.) carved out his empire, he brought the Greek arts and culture to the people of Asia, as far east as the Indus River in Pakistan, north to southern Russia, and south to Egypt. The eastern and Asian influences that Greeks were exposed to in their turn, and the gifts of tribute and royal patronage that flowed back to Greece, catapulted the classical period of art and architecture right into the Hellenistic. The blossoming of Greco-Buddhist art in Gandhara (now the Swat Valley of Pakistan) is one of the most beautiful offspring of this cultural marriage.

The overornate works from the Hellenistic era, such as the Acropolis at Pergamum, Turkey; the stoa of Attalos, in Athens; the Temple of Didyma in Miletus, Turkey; the *Winged Victory of Samothrace* and the *Venus de Milo* (both in the Louvre); and the Colossus of Rhodes all reflect a new interest in overscale figures, intense movement and emotion, softly blurred details, and mannered, dramatic expressions. Simultaneously, techniques of glassblowing were refined and portrait painting on murals and vases became more common. Though some earlier works had been polychrome, we have very few examples of paintings. The art of mosaic with tesserae (cubes of glass or stone) flourished; some particularly beautiful examples can be seen at Alexander's capital at Pella in northern Greece.

After the Romans sacked Corinth in 156 B.C., pure Greek art and architecture almost disappeared. Since the Romans were great admirers, however, they commissioned Greek artists to copy the well-known classics and create new works. We begin to see a nostalgia for the classical period appearing together with the more ornate style preferred by the Romans. As their conquest of the East continued, the Romans spread Greek ideals of esthetic beauty throughout the Western world, establishing for us this artistic and cultural legacy.

5 The Birth of Bouzouki

The familiar melody to which Zorba danced in *Zorba the Greek* is typical of *bouzouki* music, a traditional folk music still heard at social gatherings or sung by old-timers.

New Wave

Yanni has joined the pantheon of one-name celebrities with worldwide fame, but few people realize that his music is indigenously Greek. New Wave (Néo Kýma) developed in the *boîtes* of Athens, intimate nightclubs where students gathered in the early 1960s to discuss politics and improvise music. As in the case of English-language folk music of the time, this music was heavily politicized and influenced by liberal ideas—specifically, the *rebétika* that protested social and economic injustice and openly espoused communism. The Junta closed these alternative-music venues during its reactionary grip (1967–74), but it failed to suppress the music itself.

Today New Wave has grown to encompass the international near-symphonic style popular with everyone from New Agers to senior citizens searching for something more accessible and relaxing than rap, grunge, and techno-pop. Some dismiss it as mere Muzak, but they fail to recognize that the movement also sparked such a musical phenomenon as Yórgos Daláras, an immensely popular musician often called the "Greek Springsteen," who has a growing international reputation and wide range of expression.

The bouzouki "sound" (or *rebétika,* as the Greeks know it) actually began in the 1920s, mainly in the backstreets of Piraeus. The port of Athens was filled with *rebetes*—petty criminals, down-and-out prostitutes, and druggies—along with a huge wave of impoverished immigrants from Asia Minor, who brought with them a Turkish musical heritage. They began playing soulful folk music on their acoustic bouzoukis (which bear some resemblance to mandolins) in the smoky dives and hash dens along the harbor.

The late Mános Hadjidákis, one of the greats of modern Greek music and composer of the film score for *Never on Sunday,* captured the spirit of rebétika: "[I was] dazed by the grandeur and depth of the melodic phrases. . . . I believed suddenly that the song I was listening to was my own—utterly my own story."

The style of music developed in much the same way that the blues developed in America, and by the 1950s these tunes had caught the fancy of well-to-do Greeks, who empathized with their lyrics of lost love, unemployment, death, family squabbles, sunken ships, and other crises. Popular musicians added a rhythm section, amplification, and often piano accompaniment to create the lively, spirited sound we now associate with Greek films and modern bouzouki clubs. Whereas in the film *Zorba the Greek* Anthony Quinn was carried away and danced a *zeibékiko* (an intensely personal expression of feeling) to Mikis Theodorakis's haunting music, visitors now leap up en masse to join hands in the *syrtáki,* one of the simpler folk dances taught by light-footed waiters. So the next time you see a Greek transported in dance or caught up in the frenzy, look for the tears behind the smiles and the laughter.

6 Dining with the Greeks

Greece is definitely a three-meals-a-day country. The emphasis is on a big midday lunch (about 2pm), followed by a siesta, a reviving coffee or snack at 6pm, and then a lighter but usually longer dinner around 9 to 11pm.

Most people are familiar with souvlaki, moussaka, Greek salads, and baklava pastry, but in Greece a wide variety of other foods (usually prepared with vegetables, meats, fish, and olive oil) will keep you trying something new for weeks.

Retsína: Not Your Average Taste of the Grape

Pine resin gives this wine its special flavor, and newcomers have been known to gasp and mutter "turpentine!" The flavor originally came from untreated pine barrels where the wine was stored—though the theory that pine was used because other wood was unavailable or too expensive is probably incorrect. Occasionally you'll hear someone explain that Greek wines are so good that wine-makers have had to spoil them intentionally to keep the Italians from taking them all away. Pine resin does extend the shelf life of wine, and Greeks have learned to savor it—and with a little patience, so can you. Today the EU has set the acceptable content of resin at 1%, and so you probably won't find any retsína that's breathtakingly pungent. If you haven't tried this wine, you really should; a taste for it is surely more easily acquired than for scotch.

The morning meal you typically receive in most guest houses is one of our pet peeves. It's generally quite meager despite the term "brekfest complet." However, now that hoteliers have realized that they can charge you $5 for something more substantial, many of our favorite small inns have added eggs, cheese, yogurt with honey, biscuits, and cake to their buffet tables. In small towns your best bet may be a bakery or the local *kafenío* (unfortunately, they're becoming more difficult to find), where you can order fresh-brewed Greek coffee, bread, and sometimes eggs, yogurt, or cheese pie.

Lunch presents lots of options, from retsína and fish to gyros or "tost," at those uniquely Greek sandwich shops where your choice of fillings is pressed onto a roll or hero with a waffle iron.

Dinner is the time to sample everything, drink some wine, and then take an evening stroll. In the Appendix you'll find a list of typical Greek menu items; in addition, familiar items such as pizza, pasta, and steaks are available almost everywhere. Many tavernas welcome you right into the kitchen to take a look around, enjoy the aromas, and point out what you want. The only rule of thumb about Greek restaurants is that you'll probably have to help the proprietor pay for decor and location—especially if the restaurant is along the harbor.

Although tap water on the mainland and on most islands is potable (on some islands the water comes from desalination plants and tastes terrible), most locals and visitors prefer bottled water; it's widely available, both in restaurants and at news kiosks and markets. Major international-brand sodas and Greek-produced juices can also be bought in most places.

Beer and wine (the latter produced throughout the country) are readily available and inexpensive. Amstel and Heineken are the most popular beers; other imported beers, such as Henniger, Kaiser, and Tuborg, tend to be more expensive.

Some of the favorite bottled wines include Nykteri from Santoríni, Samiana from Sámos, Robola and Yentilini from Kefaloní, Liyeri from Páros, and Ayio Ritiko from the Mt. Áthos region of northern Greece. Dependable labels include Achaïa-Clauss, Boutari, Calliga, Kambas, Lac des Roches, and Porto Carras. In certain wine-producing regions ask for *krassí,* the locally aged house wine.

Among the less expensive but more potent drinks are *retsína,* a wine flavored with pine resin (and often home-brewed), and *oúzo,* an anisette liquor that's usually mixed with water before drinking.

7 Recommended Reading

Greece has produced or inspired some of the greatest literary works ever created. The following is a sampling of books that we've enjoyed during our travels and that would make worthy companions on any journey through Hellas.

Over the years, Mary Renault's books have inspired countless readers. Renault, who died in 1983, wrote more than a dozen books, mostly historical novels, that breathe life into the ancient Greek past. Among her best known are *The King Must Die, The Mask of Apollo,* and *Fire from Heaven.*

If you haven't already read Homer's *Odyssey* and *Iliad,* the blind poet's mythological and historical epics, we would certainly encourage you to do so. Prose translations, such as those by W. H. D. Rouse, are easier to read and are actually more faithful to the original; however, among the verse translations, those by Robert Fitzgerald capture more of the original spirit than do those by Edith Hamilton. On the other hand, Hamilton's *Mythology* is a good reference book and makes for lively reading. Robert Graves's *The Greek Myths* is more demanding but more rewarding.

One of our favorite books on Greece is *From Alpha to Omega (The Life and Times of the Greek Alphabet),* by Alexander and Nicholas Humez, a volume that uses the Greek alphabet to describe some of the more remarkable aspects of ancient Greek life, while winding you around the authors' etymological finger.

If you want an overview of Greek art and architecture, we think the best is *The Greeks, an Introduction to Their Culture,* by Robin Sowerby. You might even pack a copy of John Boardman's classic *Greek Art* (Oxford University Press), then look around in Athens bookstores for the excellent Ekdotikí collection of museum and archaeology guides.

As for fiction, Henry Miller's *The Colossus of Maroussi* and the novels and travel books of Lawrence Durrell *(The Alexandria Quartet* and *Prospero's Cell)* are fine works by modern writers. *The Magus,* which takes place on Spetses, is one of John Fowles's best and a perfect book to read while lying on the beach.

No list of suggested books about Greece would be complete without some by the country's national writer, Níkos Kazantzákis: *Zorba the Greek* and *A Modern Sequel to the Odyssey* (which is 33,333 lines long) both capture the essence of the Greek soul. C. P. Caváfy (translated by Rae Davin), Greece's most important modern poet, is to verse what Kazantzákis is to prose. Byron is one of the most famous European poets to glorify Greece; Elizabeth Langford's *Byron's Greece* retraces his journeys and includes artwork illustrating his love affair with the country.

Literary buffs should get Richard Stoneman's *Literary Companion to Travelling in Greece,* and the accidental tourist can read Helen Miller's *Greece Through the Ages.* The armchair traveler will relish Patrick Fermor's personal journeys in *Mani: Travels in the Southern Peloponnese* or his *Roumeli: Travels in Northern Greece.* Romantics have long been wooed by Lawrence Durrell's guide, *The Greek Islands.*

3

Planning an Affordable Trip to Greece

It's completely possible to have a rich and rewarding travel experience without spending a fortune—and that doesn't have to mean that you sacrifice fun or comfort. That goal has been foremost in our minds ever since we began researching this guide years ago.

In this chapter, we'll tell you what you need to know in advance, and show you exactly how to set up your trip to find the best bargains.

1 How This Book Can Save You Money: The $50-a-Day Premise

With this guide, you can see the best of Greece without spending a fortune. In the pages ahead, we'll show how to save money on lodgings and food, as well as how to cut costs on transportation, sightseeing, shopping, and nightlife.

Since we steer clear of tourist traps and expensive diversions, you'll come closer to experiencing the real Greece and enjoy a truer slice of life. There's great joy in not only discovering a bargain, but meeting people and learning a lot while you travel.

This guide knows what inexpensive travel is all about, but differs from some of its competitors. For example, we believe in paying a little more from time to time in order to secure accommodations that are reasonable in price, but also clean, decent, and welcoming. Likewise, we don't believe in confining ourselves to a diet of cheap fast food. We've picked places to dine that are simple but good, serving authentic, hearty Greek fare. We also know that you'll feel like splurging sometimes, so we've offered slightly more expensive choices for those occasions—places that are memorable and still offer great value.

Budget travel isn't just about cutting expenses on the road. It's about bringing you into contact with the locals—the folks who run the local guest houses and tavernas. We've tried to put you in touch with genuine, warm, and sincere people who, in addition to earning a living in the tourist trade, take delight in welcoming visitors to their country.

Arthur Frommer, the pioneering publisher of this series, writes that over the years Frommer's readers have discovered a major principle of travel: "That the less you spend, the more you enjoy; that the less you spend, the better you encounter the realities of the countries you visit, and thus receive the most lasting rewards of the travel experience."

The daily budget of $50 a day promised in the title of this book is meant to cover your basic living costs while on the road: three meals a day, and half the price of a simple double room. The $50-a-day budget roughly breaks down like this: about $25 for a hotel room (probably a Class C or D hotel or a first-class pension, with private toilet/bath facilities plus continental breakfast) and about $25 a day for three meals (dining in the Greek style: a big meal at midday, a snack about 6pm, and a light supper). You won't live like a jet-setter on this amount, but you can enjoy comfortable accommodations and varied meals. Needless to say, if you insist on doing things American style, it will cost you more.

The $50-a-day figure does *not* include your transportation, admission to museums or historic sites, shopping purchases, or evening entertainment. However, we have listed the best budget choices for transportation, sightseeing, shopping, and nightlife, so that even in these areas you can be sure of the best value for your money.

There are a few caveats regarding the $50-a-day figure. If you're traveling alone, you may have to spend a little more (perhaps $55 to $60 a day) for the same accommodations and dining recommended here for couples or larger groups traveling together. If you plan to visit some of the more upscale islands (for example, Corfu, Mýkonos, Santoríni, Rhodes, or Crete), prices are likely to be higher; in this case, you may need to count on spending $60 or $70 a day per person. If you really want to save money on your trip to Greece, it's best to go during the spring or fall; you can save even more by going in winter—which is totally off-season.

And what about the word "from" in this book's title? We've phrased it that way for a reason. We want to be able to include establishments that are slightly more expensive than the $50-a-day budget, but are still terrific buys. We want to offer you places that have unique historical, cultural, or architectural features and let you decide when you're ready to splurge. No place has been included in this book that doesn't offer value, even if it's slightly higher than the figures listed above. (Conversely, we'll tell you about many bargains that could allow you to manage for even less than $50 a day). We've assumed that you demand more comfort than you did in your student days, so we haven't sent you to any marginal properties. We promise to bring you comfortable lodgings, great food, and loads of fun for a reasonable price!

2 Visitor Information & Entry Requirements

VISITOR INFORMATION

Before leaving home, you can obtain travel information as well as a basic profile about Greece and its highlights from the **Greek National Tourist Organization (GNTO).** The GNTO has offices in the following major cities:

IN THE UNITED STATES   **New York:** 645 Fifth Ave., 5th Floor, New York, NY 10022 (☎ **212/421-5777;** fax 212/826-6940). **Chicago:** 168 N. Michigan Ave., 4th Floor, Chicago, IL 60601 (☎ **312/782-1084;** fax 312/782-1091). **Los Angeles:** 611 W. 6th St., Suite 2198, Los Angeles, CA 90017 (☎ **213/626-6696;** fax 213/489-9744).

IN CANADA   **Toronto:** 2 Bloor St. W., Cumberland Terrace, Toronto, ON M4W 3E2 (☎ **416/968-2220;** fax 416/968-6533). **Montréal:** 1233 rue de la Montagne, Suite 101, Montréal, QC H3G 1Z2 (☎ **514/871-1535;** fax 514/871-1498).

IN THE UNITED KINGDOM London: 4 Conduit St., London WIR DOJ (☎ **0171/734-5997;** fax 0171/287-1369).

IN AUSTRALIA Sydney: 51–57 Pitt St., Sydney, NSW 2000 (☎ **2/241-1663;** fax 2/235-2174).

ENTRY REQUIREMENTS

Citizens of the United States, Australia, Canada, and New Zealand, and most other countries (except members of the European Union) are required to have a valid passport, which is stamped upon entry and exit, for stays of up to 90 days. All U.S. citizens, even infants, must have a valid passport, but Canadian children under 16 may travel without a passport if accompanied by either parent.

Longer stays must be arranged with the **Bureau of Aliens,** Leofóros Alexándras 173, Athens (☎ **01/770-5711**).

Citizens of the United Kingdom and other members of the European Union are required to have only a valid passport for entry into Greece, and it's no longer stamped upon entry. Children under 16 may travel without a passport if accompanied by either parent.

CUSTOMS

Greece permits you to bring in most personal effects duty free; some water-sports equipment, such as windsurfers, can be brought in only if a Greek citizen residing in Greece guarantees that they will be re-exported. Divers may also experience difficulty bringing in scuba equipment.

There's no restriction on the number or value of traveler's checks on either entry or exit, though amounts over US$1,000 must be declared. No more than 10,000 drachmas per traveler may be imported or exported.

Be careful about antiques that you buy in Greece; the laws protecting Greek antiquities are very strict, and no genuine antiquities may be taken out of the country without prior special permission from the **Archaeological Service,** at Odós Polygnótou 3 (3 Polygnotus St.), in Athens.

3 Money

The unit of currency in Greece is the **drachma** *(drachmí* in Greek), abbreviated **Dr.** It takes the form of both coins and bills. (The drachma was also used in ancient Athens; see the coin exhibits in the city's Numismatic Museum.)

As of this writing, US$1 = 240 Drs. Because of constant fluctuations in the exchange rate, however, and also because of possible increases in prices since the European Union inaugurated a single market, you should *use the figures in these pages only as a general guide.*

Coins come in denominations of 5, 10, 20, 50, and 100 Drs. Bills come in denominations of 50 Drs (blue), 100 Drs (red), 500 Drs (green), 1,000 Drs (brown), 5,000 Drs (blue), and 10,000 Drs (green and brown). There always seems to be a shortage of (or a reluctance to make) change in many places. If you know that you're

Impressions

Marvelous things happen to one in Greece—marvelous good things which can happen to one nowhere else on earth.

—Henry Miller, *The Colossus of Maroussi,* 1942

The Greek Drachma

For U.S. Readers   At this writing, $1 = 240 Drs (or 1 Dr = 0.4¢). This was the rate of exchange used to calculate the dollar values given in the table below and throughout this edition.

For U.K. Readers   At this writing, £1 = 370 Drs (or 1 Dr = 0.2p). This was the rate of exchange used to calculate the pound values in the table below.

Note: International exchange rates fluctuate from time to time and may not be the same when you travel to Greece. Therefore, this table should be used as a guide for approximate values only.

Drs	U.S.$	UK£
25	0.10	0.07
50	0.21	0.14
100	0.42	0.27
250	1.04	0.68
500	2.08	1.35
1,000	4.17	2.70
1,500	6.25	4.05
2,000	8.33	5.41
2,500	10.42	6.76
3,000	12.50	8.11
4,000	16.67	10.81
5,000	20.83	13.51
7,500	31.25	20.27
10,000	41.67	27.03
12,500	52.10	33.78
15,000	62.50	40.54
17,500	72.92	47.30
20,000	83.33	54.05
22,500	93.75	60.81
25,000	104.17	67.57

going to be buying some inexpensive items or paying small sums, ask for 1,000-Dr bills when you exchange currency.

Some coins may seem to be worth peanuts, but you'll need them for tipping, telephones, and trolleys.

Note: In the following pages, the dollar equivalents have been rounded off to the nearest dollar for the sake of simplicity.

TRAVELER'S CHECKS   Traveler's checks are the safest way to carry cash in Greece. Purchase them before leaving home, and always carry the checks and your receipts separately.

The most popular issuers of traveler's checks are: **American Express** (☎ **800/ 221-7282** in the U.S. and Canada); **Citicorp** (☎ **800/645-6556** in the U.S. and Canada, or 813/623-1709, collect, from anywhere else); **Thomas Cook**

What Things Cost in Athens	U.S.$
Taxi from airport to the city center	10.00
Local telephone call	.08
Double room at a B-class hotel	105.65
Bathless double room in a pension	32.15
Lunch for one at a tavérna	8.80
Dinner for one, with wine, at a restaurant	14.50
Bottle of beer	2.20
Soda	1.30
Cup of Greek coffee	1.30
Roll of ASA 100 Kodacolor film, 36 exposures	9.10
Admission to National Archaeological Museum	10.00

(☎ **800/223-7373** in the U.S. and Canada, or 609/987-7300, collect, from anywhere else); and **Interpayment Services** (☎ **800/221-2426** in the U.S. and Canada, or 800/453-4284 from most anywhere else).

Most British banks can issue their account holders a **Eurocheque** card and chequebook, which can be used at most cash machines and at Greek banks for an annual fee plus a 2% charge.

CREDIT/CHARGE CARDS & ATMS   You'll find that carrying credit and charge cards may be useful for hotels, major purchases, and larger restaurant bills—and they're all but required for renting a car. **Visa** is the most readily accepted, though **MasterCard, American Express, EuroCard,** and **Diners Club** are widely recognized.

ATMS are becoming increasingly common in Greece. Ask your bank or credit-card company if your card will be accepted in Greece, remember to double-check your cash-advance limits, and ask if your PIN (personal identification number) will need to be reprogrammed for use abroad.

Many smaller hotels will accept your credit/charge card *only* if you agree to pay their commission (usually 6%); therefore, you can save money by finding the nearest ATM.

CURRENCY EXCHANGE   There's no need to worry about arriving in Greece without Greek currency; at the Athens airport there are branches of the major banks where you can probably get a better exchange rate than at most banks in your home country.

Post offices are usually the best places to change money because the transaction fee is generally lower (about 300 Drs); in smaller towns the post office hours are longer and the wait is usually shorter.

In some cases it may be cheaper and easier (or even necessary) to pay with a check drawn on a Greek bank. This can be arranged by a large commercial bank or by a specialist such as **Ruesch International,** 825 14th St. NW, Washington, DC 20005 (☎ **800/424-2923** or 202/408-1200), or in the U.K. at 18 Saville Row, London W1X 2AD (☎ **0171/734-2300**); it performs a wide variety of conversion-related tasks, usually for only $2 per transaction.

Mutual of Omaha/Travelex, 1225 Franklin Ave., Garden City, NY 11530 (☎ **800/377-0051** in the U.S.), provides foreign currency exchange at more than 30 U.S. airport locations or through the mail. If you exchange $500 or more, they

What Things Cost on Corfu	U.S.$
Taxi from airport to the city center	5.50
Local telephone call	.08
Double room at a B-class hotel	108.35
Bathless double room in a pension	41.30
Lunch for one at a taverna	10.10
Dinner for one, with wine, at a restaurant	28.60
Bottle of beer	2.10
Soda	1.25
Cup of Greek coffee	1.25
Roll of ASA 100 Kodacolor film, 36 exposures	11.20
Admission to archaeological museum	2.10

What Things Cost on Póros	U.S.$
Local telephone call	.08
Double room at a B-class hotel	65.40
Bathless double room in a pension	28.10
Lunch for one at a taverna	6.95
Dinner for one, with wine, at a restaurant	23.45
Bottle of beer	1.25
Soda	1.05
Cup of Greek coffee	.85
Roll of ASA 100 Kodacolor film, 36 exposures	10.50

promise to buy back from you up to 30% of your remaining foreign currency within 30 days at the same rate without a service charge. Annual or short-term flight insurance policies are also available.

4 35 Money-Saving Tips
SAVING ON AIRFARES

A good travel agent with the latest software can help you find the best fare available for the period when you want to go.

Make your plans as early as possible, since advance-purchase tickets can be a big factor in saving money—but if you're a gambler, the opposite strategy can pay off, too. Last-minute bookings can sometimes be a bargain, if you're flexible and willing to take a chance. (Virgin Atlantic offers great deals on last-minute bookings.)

Never accept the first airfare you're quoted. Keep calling, keep questioning, until all reasonable options have been exhausted and you've priced all the airlines that fly to your destination. Airfares change constantly, so don't assume the first fare you're offered is the end of the story.

1. Try to fly midweek, when rates are usually lower than during weekends. .
2. Fares drop dramatically in the off-season (and you'll miss those summer crowds). You may not want to go in winter, since it's not beach weather, but spring and fall are lovely times to travel. You can find great round-trip fares and package deals.
3. **Virgin Atlantic Airways** (☎ 800/862-8621) offers consistently well-priced fares. Call them first in your search for the best deal.
4. Scour the weekend travel section of your local newspaper, plus the Sunday edition of the *New York Times* or the *Los Angeles Times* for ads for discount fares and charter operators. London's *Time Out* also advertises many discount vendors or bucket shops.
5. Call several consolidators (discount air-ticket sellers who profit by buying unused seats in bulk from various airlines) and be prepared to leave on short notice. Recommended consolidators include **Council Charter** (☎ 800/223-7402), **Travac** (☎ 800/872-8800), **Travel Avenue** (☎ 800/333-3335), and **Unitravel** (☎ 800/ 325-2222).
   You might also try calling ☎ 1-800-FLY-4-LESS, a ticketing service that specializes in finding the lowest airfares.
6. If you want to stop elsewhere in Europe, then reach Greece by train, bus, or ferry, try calling **Icelandair** (☎ 800/233-5500), which offers great bargains on flights from New York to Luxembourg.

SAVING ON ACCOMMODATIONS

7. From early May to the first of July you can save 20% to 45% off the high-season room rates (if you're not shy about bargaining), and at least 20% to 30% off the high-season rates from the first of September until the autumn closing.

SAVING ON DINING

Food is relatively more expensive in Greece than it is in North America, Australia, or New Zealand, and you'll need to spend a larger share of your budget on food here than you would when traveling in your own country. We've listed hundreds of options throughout this book where you can find the best bargains; the strategies outlined below will help you save money, too.

8. Buy groceries at the local market or at the minimarkets that are becoming increasingly common. (Bottled drinking water can cost three times as much in a restaurant as at a grocery store.)
9. The simple stand-up places where working-class Greeks themselves eat offer the best values. Many visitors on a budget choose such typically Greek food as *souvlákia, yíros* (gyros) in *píta* bread, *tirópites* (cheese pies), *tost* (toasted sandwiches), and pizza.
10. Seafood is the most expensive item on any menu. Fish and shellfish are often sold by the kilogram and can cost you up to 16,000 Drs ($67) per pound. We're never confident about the touted freshness of the day's catch, except on some of the smaller islands.
11. Some restaurants offer fixed-price menus, which can be a fairly good value if you have room for very large portions.
12. We often order just a variety of *mezédes* (appetizers) plus vegetables. They're usually freshly made and dependably tasty.
13. In most places you can find a bakery with fresh, tasty, substantial bread and rolls at very reasonable prices.
14. When choosing Greek fast food, such as *souvlákia* and *yíros,* follow the advice of our friend Markos: If the spindle of meat is "skinny" in the morning, it may not be fresh (go elsewhere or choose something else).

15. When ordering beverages, consider *oúzo, retsína,* or the *krassí* (house wine); they all tend to be cheaper than beer or soda.

16. If you must drink beer, stick with the domestic Amstel and Henniger. Heineken is a bit more costly. Imports, such as Kaiser and Kronenberg, are more expensive. Cans are more expensive than bottles, which are returnable.

17. Many hotels either include breakfast in the room rates or else charge about 1,200 Drs ($5) for bread, butter, jam, and coffee or tea. You'll seldom find a cheaper breakfast at outside restaurants; an American breakfast with eggs might cost 2,200 Drs ($9.15).

18. *Kouloúria* (pretzel-like rolls with sesame seeds), which many Greeks grab from street vendors for breakfast, are quite cheap—usually 50 Drs (20¢)—and tasty; they make a quick and easy addition to a skimpy breakfast.

19. In most places, simple *estiatória,* where a few dishes are precooked and displayed in a steam case or selected from the kitchen, are less expensive than at a *tavérna,* where your food will be cooked to order.

20. Greek desserts at restaurants are rarely very interesting. Save your money and broaden your experience by buying a dessert after your meal at a *zaharoplastío* (pâtisserie or sweet shop), where you'll have a larger and more intriguing selection.

SAVING ON SIGHTSEEING

Many of Greece's most interesting sights are free. You can stroll around Athens for days, enjoying an endless succession of experiences, without paying a single entrance fee. There's no charge to see a harbor, the market, the quiet lanes in an old part of town. Greeks will frequently include you in their celebrations, and you couldn't pay even if you wanted to.

21. If you're a senior citizen or a student, you may be eligible for discounts on admission fees. Don't forget to bring along proper ID.

SAVING ON NIGHTLIFE

22. One of the best parts of Greek nightlife is the evening *vólta* ("turn"), and you can join the sociable stroll for absolutely nothing. In many tavernas supper is followed by music and dancing.

23. Outdoor cinemas, though less common than they once were, are generally inexpensive and fun—except for those who must have quiet during a movie. Music bars, discos, and *rebétika* clubs are more expensive, but admission usually includes the first drink. (Budget travelers surely know how to nurse a drink!)

MONEY MATTERS

24. Generally, traveler's checks are the safest and most dependable means of carrying funds. Don't forget that some banks, credit-card companies, and organizations, such as the AAA and credit unions, offer lower commission fees to members or waive them altogether.

25. Don't worry about arriving in Greece without currency. Branches of the major Greek banks are located at the Athens airport, and they'll offer you a better rate than you'd get at home.

26. When changing money on the road, note that banks and post offices offer the best exchange rates.

27. Credit/charge cards are accepted in most places, though some hotels and businesses will tack on a surcharge, and some restaurants will refuse them except to pay larger bills.

28. ATMs are becoming increasingly common, but check in advance whether a given card will be accepted in Greece, what fees will be imposed, and what withdrawal

amounts make sense (clearly you wouldn't want to have to pay a $2.50 fee for a $20 withdrawal).

SAVING ON TRANSPORTATION

29. Greece has a good, efficient, inexpensive intercity bus system. You'll pay more for direct air-conditioned service, but local buses can be awfully slow and smoky, and you may have to hold a fellow passenger's chicken.

30. Bikes are easily and cheaply rented in most resort areas. Mountain bikes are increasingly common, but costlier. Mopeds are more expensive and, because of the terrain, poor surfaces, and sometimes nonexistent shoulders, less safe. Motorbikes are even more expensive and more dangerous. Greece is no place to try out your *Easy Rider* fantasies.

31. You can usually save money by reserving a car before you leave home—though this will give you less flexibility. If you decide to rent one in Greece, shop around; it's a good idea to carry along and display brochures from competitors to show that you're shopping. Local car-rental companies are often much less expensive than the big international companies—though there's less assurance of quality and service. Never try to save money by skimping on insurance.

32. If you must take a taxi or *caïque* (water taxi), look around for other visitors to share the cost. When supply outstrips demand, talk to several drivers and try to bargain discreetly.

33. Hydrofoils are generally twice as fast and twice as expensive as regular ferries. Ferries are more relaxing and fun, as well as more conducive to meeting people; on the other hand, they're more likely to cause seasickness—though less likely to be delayed or canceled because of bad weather.

SHOPPING

34. Generally speaking, the closer you are to where an item is produced, the less expensive it will be. If you buy a handmade article from the craftsman, family, or friends, you'll make sure that they're rewarded for fast-disappearing skills, and the article will become at least a bit more special. Since most souvenir items are now made in Athens, you'll probably find that they're less expensive there than on the more popular islands, such as Mýkonos, Santoríni, Rhodes, and Corfu.

35. Bargain, bargain, bargain. Except in department stores and posh shops, prices are usually negotiable. What's the harm in trying?

Figure out what a fair price would be, aim just below it—not at the half price accepted as a starting point by many bargaining cultures—and negotiate patiently. Keep a sense of humor and perspective. Bargaining is a learned skill and something of a game—surely more important to the seller than to you. Try not to take a negative approach—it isn't nearly as effective in Greece as it may be elsewhere. Many a Greek would rather lose a sale than sustain a blow to pride. But play it cool. If you show too much obvious interest, it's likely to drive up the price. Let your interest move on to something else. Drift away. If there are two of you, one can take the role of the neutral party.

5 When to Go

Although costs in Greece are much lower if you travel between September and June, you need to be aware that on most of the islands, nearly all of the hotels and restaurants are closed from late September/mid-October to late April/early May.

From early May to the first of July you can save 20% to 45% off the high-season room rates (if you're not shy about bargaining), and at least 20% to 30% off those rates from the first of September until the autumn closing.

In the spring and fall, Greece has fewer visitors (the busiest months are July and especially August); the country is much more beautiful; the weather is cooler, more temperate, and somewhat more stable; and the strong northern *meltémi* winds are not blowing.

Each year, as more and more visitors learn about the variations in climate, they seem to be going to their favorite islands earlier in the season. At the most popular resorts (Mýkonos, Santoríni, Rhodes, Corfu, Crete) hoteliers have begun to develop a "shoulder," or middle, season, when they feel that they can charge a little more for their rooms because of the increased demand. Nevertheless, spring is still a great time to visit.

CLIMATE   Greece has a generally mild climate: cool winters (that hover around 55° to 60°F in Athens and the south and 45° to 50°F in Thessaloníki and the north) and *meltémi* breeze-cooled summers (about 85° to 95°F throughout the country). The Greek National Tourist Organization claims that Greece enjoys 3,000 hours of sunshine each year! The best seasons to visit are spring (late April to June) and fall (mid-September to November) when the sun is less intensely blinding, the wildflowers are out, and there are fewer visitors. However, with fewer tourists, many facilities close, especially from mid-October to mid-April on the islands.

HOLIDAYS   The following are legal national holidays in Greece: **New Year's Day** (January 1), **Epiphany** (January 6), **Shrove Monday** (41 days before Easter), **Independence Day** (March 25), **Good Friday through Easter Monday** (remember: the Greek Orthodox Easter often falls on a different Sunday than Easter in non-Orthodox countries), **May Day** (May 1, Labor Day), **Whitmonday** (50 days after Easter), **Assumption of the Virgin** (August 15), *Óhi* **Day** (October 28), and **Christmas** (December 25–26).

On these days, government offices, banks, post offices, and most stores are closed. Certain museums and attractions, however, may remain open to the public. Many restaurants are also open. For further information, inquire at your hotel or check such English-language publications as *The Athenian* (a monthly) available in Athens and elsewhere.

GREECE CALENDAR OF EVENTS

Hundreds of special events—folkloric, religious, festive, and cultural—take place throughout the year all over Greece. For a complete list, contact the Greek National Tourist Organization.

January
- **Feast of St. Basil.** A national holiday, celebrated with traditional New Year's cake, or *píta*, and an exchange of gifts. January 1.
- **Epiphany.** The Blessing of the Waters, a religious ceremony celebrating Christ's Baptism, is held throughout Greece, although the most spectacular spot to visit is Piraeus. January 6.

February
- **Carnival.** Carnival is celebrated throughout Greece for 3 weeks during February or March every year (ending the night before the beginning of Orthodox Lent). Pátra has one of the largest and most colorful celebrations, with a chariot parade, traditional Greek theater, and wild Saturnalia (private and public parties with drinking, dancing, and general lack of inhibition). Masked revels are also held in

Macedonia. On the island of Skýros the pagan "Goat Dance" is performed before Lent. In Athens people drink even more than usual and bop each other on the head with plastic hammers.

April

- **Nightly sound-and-light performances,** Athens and Rhodes. These continue through October.
- **Easter.** There are celebrations all over Greece. The island of Hýdra, in particular, has colorful Good Friday ceremonies.

  On Pátmos you can witness the **Niptíras,** a reenactment of the Last Supper that's performed only on Pátmos (in the square outside the Monastery of St. John) and in Jerusalem. The festivities and holy days extend from the Monday before Easter to the following Tuesday, when there's great feasting and dancing in Xanthos Square.
- **Anniversaries dedicated to St. Spyrídon,** patron saint of Corfu. Mid-April.

May

- **Flower Festival.** May 1.
- **Anniversary of the Ionian Islands' union with Greece** in 1864. Celebrated mostly on Corfu. May 21.
- **Navy Week Festival.** Celebrated throughout Greece. In Vólos there's a reenactment of the departure of the Argonauts' expedition; on Hydra the event is turned into a celebration of Admiral Andréas Miaoúlis (1769–1835), a hero of the War of Independence. End of May.

June

- **Wine festivals.** These are held at Dafní, about 6 miles outside Athens, on Rhodes, and in other locations. Free wine-tasting, as well as dancing at outdoor tavernas. Mid-June.
- ✪ **Athens Festival.** Featuring music, drama, and dance. Begins at the Herod Atticus Theater, at the foot of the Acropolis, and on Lykavittós (Lycabettus) Hill. Performances continue until the end of September.

  Performances are often sold out well in advance. Contact the Greek Tourist Organization (EOT) for the current schedule or call the Athens Festival at ☎ **01/ 323-2771** or 01/322-3111 for information. Tickets go on sale 2 weeks prior to the performance at the Athens Festival Box Office, Odós Stadíou 4 (in a pedestrian shopping mall off Voukourestíou Street near Sýntagma Square); the box office is open daily from 8:30am to 2pm and 5 to 7pm. Tickets for the Epidaurus Theater Festival can also be purchased here. Athens Festival tickets cost 900 to 11,500 Drs ($3.75 to $47.90); any remaining seats can be purchased from the Herod Atticus box office between 6:30 and 9pm on the day of the performance. Check with the EOT or the *Athens News* or *Athenscope* (at newsstands) for festival information.
- **Miaoúlis Festival,** Hýdra. This event celebrates a famous naval victory during the War of Independence, in which the Hydriot Admiral Andréas Vókos, known as Miaoúlis (1769–1835), defeated the superior Ottoman fleet. The battle is re-created each year, complete with the burning of a fireship, exploding cannons, and fireworks. Reserve a room well ahead of time. End of June.

July

- **Lykavittós Festival,** Athens. An open-air festival held each summer at the theater on top of Lykavittós (Lycabettus) Hill. A funicular running from the top of Ploutárchou Street in Kolonáki will sweep you up to a restaurant, from which it's just a short walk to the panoramically situated modern bowl, where contemporary dance, music, and theatrical performances are given several evenings each week. For a schedule and ticket information, contact the **EOT** (☎ **01/322-3111**) or the **Lykavittós Theater** (☎ **01/322-1459**). Tickets can be bought at the Athens Festival box office or at the gate (ask about free transportation for ticket holders).

- **Pátra International Festival.** Complete with concerts, art shows, and the usual hoopla. Young Greek directors such as Victor Arditti have presented experimental plays; major name musicians have appeared here. Call ☎ **061/278-730** for schedule information. July and August.
- **Wine Festival,** Alexandroúpolis. Begins in mid-July and runs for 4 weeks.
- **Epidaurus Festival.** Classical Greek dramas are staged in the ancient amphitheater. Performances continue through early September.
- **Northern Greece National Theater performances.** Ancient Greek dramas staged in the open-air theaters at Philippi and on the island of Thássos. Performances continue through August.
- **"Dionysia" Wine Festival,** on the island of Náxos. Mid-July.
- **Wine Festival,** Réthymno, Crete. Throughout July.

August
- **Art exhibition,** Skýros island. First week of August.
- **Ancient Greek dramas,** performed in the open-air theater at Dión, near Mt. Olympus, and at the ancient theater at Dodóna. Mid-August.
- **Hippokrateia Festival,** on the island of Kos. Ancient drama, musical performances, and a reenactment of the Hippocratic Oath. Mid-August.

September
- **Thessaloníki International Trade Fair.** Mid-September.
- **Thessaloníki Film Festival and Festival of Popular Song.** End of September.

October
- **Demetrius Festival,** Thessaloníki. Featuring music, opera, ballet.
- **Athens Open International Marathon.** This race commemorates the run of Diomedon to announce the Athenian victory over the Persians at the Battle of Marathon (490 B.C.). The race begins outside the village of Marathon and continues along Diomedon's course for exactly 42.195 kilometers (26.2 miles) to the Panathenaic Stadium built for the first modern Olympic Games (1896) in Athens. There is no qualifying time to enter the race. Applicants should contact **SEGAS,** Leofóros Syngroú 137, 17121 Athens (☎ **01/932-0636;** fax 01/934-2980), for information.

November
- **St. Andrew's Day,** celebrating the patron saint of Pátra. November 30.

6 Planning an Active Vacation

ADVENTURE TRAVEL   For those seeking unusual travel experiences, several tour operators and academic groups offer adventure trips to Greece and the islands. One of our favorite expedition groups, **Mountain Travel–Sobek, Inc.,** 6420 Fairmount Ave., El Cerrito, CA 94530 (☎ **800/227-2384** or 510/527-8100), sometimes offers summer treks through the Píndos Mountains and the Zagóri in northern Greece. Another fine expedition group is **Exodus Expeditions,** 9 Weir Rd., London SW12 OLT (☎ **0181/675-5550;** fax 0181/673-0779).

We would also like to recommend **Trekking Hellas,** Odós Filellínon 7, 105 57 Athens (☎ **01/323-4548;** telex 226040 HIM; fax 01/325-1474). This excellent group arranges sea-kayaking journeys, hikes across the Víkos Gorge in the Víkos-Aóos National Park, ascents of Mt. Olympus, mountain hiking in northern Greece, and Zodiac inflatable boat trips around Crete. They also rent out most of the equipment you might need for an adventure trip, including sleeping bags and tents.

HIKING & ROCK CLIMBING   Independent hikers and rock climbers will appreciate **Armoutis,** at Odós Ifestou 20, near the Monastiráki Flea Market, in Athens (☎ **01/331-0434**). It sells boots and outdoor fashion, waist packs, climbing ropes, harnesses, maps, and other essentials for the active life. Kyle had a great time hanging out there and longed for enough leisure time to translate their Greek-only guide *Climbing in Athens.*

In the United States, hikers might want to contact the **Appalachian Mountain Club,** 5 Joy St., Boston, MA 02108 (☎ **617/523-0636**), regarding organized hiking and sailing trips to Greece.

Serious rock jocks with time to explore the country might want to order *Exotic Rock: Travel Guide for Rock Climbers* (1996, $24.95) before leaving home; its section on Greece could be helpful in planning an itinerary. Call the GORP Catalogue at ☎ **1-888/994-GORP** for information.

NATURE TRIPS   Bird-watchers and general nature buffs should contact **World Nature Tours, Inc.,** P.O. Box 693, Silver Spring, MD 20918 (☎ **301/593-2522**), which offers annual trips to northern and northeastern Greece, in conjunction with the University of Thessaloníki.

SKIING   Most visitors don't associate Greece with winter pleasures, but actually, many Greeks enjoy skiing down the (relatively gentle) slopes at Mt. Parnassos, about a 2^1/$_2$-hour drive north of Athens.

At Fterolaka and Kellaria, the Greek Tourist Organization has opened the full-service **Parnassos Ski Centre** to manage 20 ski slopes, chair lifts, tow bars, a ski school, snack cafes and restaurants, equipment-rental service, child-care center, and first-aid department. Contact the Greek Tourist Office (EOT) or the Parnassos Ski Centre, 320 04 Arachova Viotias (☎ **0234/22-689** or 02343/22-493; fax 0234/22-695), for more information.

WINDSURFING   This is one of Greece's most popular water sports and can be enjoyed on most islands. On the most popular islands, even the less-frequented beaches have gear for rent and experienced young men waiting to teach you. The rates vary, but lessons run about 1,500 to 2,500 Drs ($6.25 to $10.40) per hour. Páros in the Cyclades, the Dodecanese island of Kos, and the Ionian island of Lefkáda have windsurfing schools with week-long packages organized by European tour operators. For more information, see chapters 9, 10, and 14, respectively, or contact the **Greek Windsurfing Association,** Odós Filellínon 7, 105 57 Athens (☎ **01/323-0330** or 01/323-0068).

YACHTING   Is there anything more romantic or glamorous than chartering a yacht to sail the Greek islands? Information and a listing of yacht brokers can be obtained from any office of the Greek National Tourist Organization. For information on special rules and regulations governing yachting and the chartering of these boats in Greece, contact the **Greek Yacht Brokers and Consultants Association,** Leofóros Possidónos 11, 174 55 Alimos (☎ **01/985-0122;** fax 01/985-0130).

Our budget suggestion for sampling the high life: contact the **Greek Islands Cruise Center,** 4321 Lakemoor Dr., Wilmington, NC 28405 (☎ **800/341-3030;** fax 910/791-9400) or in Athens (☎ **01/898-0879;** fax 01/894-0952), to find out about its low-cost cruise packages through the islands.

7 Health & Insurance

STAYING HEALTHY You'll probably experience few health problems while traveling in Greece. The tap water is safe to drink, the milk is pasteurized, and health services are good. Occasionally the change in diet may cause some minor diarrhea, so you may want to take some antidiarrhea medicine along.

Bring along in your carry-on luggage a large enough supply of any prescription medication you need. Just to be on the safe side, ask your doctor to write you new prescriptions using the generic name—not the brand name.

If you need a doctor, your hotel can recommend one or you can contact the American embassy or consulate. Before you leave, you can obtain a list of English-speaking doctors from the **International Association for Medical Assistance to Travelers (IAMAT),** in the United States at 417 Center St., Lewiston, NY 14092 (☎ **716/ 754-4883**); or in Canada at 40 Regal Rd., Guelph, ON N1K 1B5 (☎ **519/ 836-0102**).

Those with a chronic illness should discuss their travel plans with their physician. For such conditions as epilepsy, diabetes, or significant cardiovascular disease, wear a Medic Alert identification tag, which will immediately alert any doctor to your condition and provide the number of Medic Alert's 24-hour hot line from which your medical records can be obtained. Contact the **Medic Alert Foundation,** P.O. Box 1009, Turlock, CA 95381 (☎ **800/344-3226**).

INSURANCE Before purchasing any additional insurance, check your homeowner's, automobile, and medical insurance policies as well as the insurance provided by credit/charge-card companies and auto and travel clubs. You may have enough off-premises theft coverage or your credit/charge-card company may even provide cancellation coverage if you purchase your ticket with a its card.

Remember: Medicare covers U.S. citizens traveling only in Mexico and Canada.

To submit any claim you must always have complete documentation, including all receipts, police reports, medical records, and so forth.

Here are a few companies that can provide further information:

Travel Guard International, 1145 Clark St., Stevens Point, WI 54481 (☎ **800/ 782-5151**), offers comprehensive travel packs that cover just about everything, including emergency assistance, accidental death, trip cancellation or interruption, medical coverage abroad, and lost or stolen luggage, based on the cost of the trip. Be sure that you understand the restrictions, however.

Travel Insurance Pak, Travel Insured International, Travelers Insurance Co., P.O. Box 285568, East Hartford, CT 06128 (☎ **800/243-3174** or 860/528-7663), offers health and accident, lost or damaged luggage, and trip-cancellation insurance.

Mutual of Omaha (Tele-Trip), 3201 Farnam St., Omaha, NE 68131 (☎ **800/ 228-9792** or 402/342-7600), provides foreign medical coverage, with a 24-hour hot line and worldwide assistance. It also offers trip-cancellation, lost or stolen luggage, and standard accident insurance, as well as other coverage.

Wallach & Co., HealthCare Abroad, 107 W. Federal St. (P.O. Box 480), Middleburg, VA 22117 (☎ **800/237-6615** or 540/687-3166; fax 540/687-3172), offers health and accident coverage, including medical evacuation and accidental death and dismemberment compensation. Trip-cancellation insurance is also available.

8 Tips for Travelers with Special Needs

FOR TRAVELERS WITH DISABILITIES Before you go, there are many agencies that can help you with advance-planning information.

For example, contact the **Travel Information Service** (☎ **215/456-9603**). It charges $5 per package, which provides the names and addresses of accessible hotels, restaurants, and attractions, often based on firsthand reports of travelers who have been there.

You may also want to subscribe to *The Itinerary,* P.O. Box 2012, Bayonne, NJ 07002 (☎ **201/858-3400**), for $12 a year. This bimonthly travel magazine is filled with news about travel aids for the handicapped, special tours, information on accessibility, and other matters.

The free booklet *Air Transportation of Handicapped Persons* can be obtained by writing to Free Advisory Circular No. AC12032, Distribution Unit, U.S. Department of Transportation, Publications Division, M-4332, Washington, DC 20590.

You may also want to consider joining a tour for disabled visitors. You can obtain the names and addresses of tour operators offering such tours by contacting the **Society for the Advancement of Travel for the Handicapped,** 347 Fifth Ave., Suite 610, New York, NY 10016 (☎ **212/447-7284;** fax 212/725-8253). Annual membership dues are $45 ($25 for senior citizens and students).

For the blind or visually impaired, the best source of information is the **American Foundation for the Blind,** 11 Penn Plaza, Suite 300, New York, NY 10001 (☎ **800/232-5463** or 212/502-7600).

FOR GAY & LESBIAN TRAVELERS   The **International Gay Travel Association,** P.O. Box 4974, Key West, FL 33041 (☎ **800/448-8550**), can advise you about travel opportunities, agents, and tour operators.

You might want to subscribe to *Our World,* a gay and lesbian travel magazine, at 1104 N. Nova Rd., Suite 251, Daytona Beach, FL 32117 (☎ **904/441-5367**). A monthly newsletter, *Out and About,* which also contains information about gay travel, can be ordered by calling ☎ **800/929-2268.**

In Athens, the gay organization **Akoe Amphi** can be found at Odós Zalóngou 6 (P.O. Box 26022), 100 22 Athens (☎ **01/771-9221**). The **Autonomous Group of Gay Women** can be contacted through The Women's House, Odós Románou Melódou 4, Likavitós (☎ **01/281-4823**).

The *Greek Gay Guide,* published by Kraximo Press, P.O. Box 4228, 102 10 Athens (☎ **01/362-5249**), is available at some kiosks.

FOR SENIORS   Some senior discounts may require that you belong to a recognized association for seniors; otherwise, your passport is an adequate proof of age. For plane travel in Greece, passengers 60 years of age and older are entitled to a 20% discount.

Before you go, obtain a copy of *Travel Tips for Senior Citizens* (publication no. 8970), available for $1 from the Superintendent of Documents, U.S. Government Printing Office, Washington, DC 20402 (☎ **202/783-5238**). Another publication, *101 Tips for the Mature Traveler,* is available free from Grand Circle Travel, 347 Congress St., Boston, MA 02210 (☎ **800/248-3737** or 617/350-7500).

Saga International Holidays, 222 Berkeley St., Boston, MA 02116 (☎ **800/343-0273**), offers all-inclusive tours for seniors (50 years of age or older). Insurance, except for cancellation coverage, is included in the price of the tours. There's a yearly membership fee.

The **American Association of Retired Persons (AARP),** 601 E St. NW, Washington, DC 20049 (☎ **800/424-3410** or 202/434-AARP), offers members information about discounts on airfares, car rentals, and hotels.

The **National Council of Senior Citizens,** 1331 F St. NW, Washington, DC 20004 (☎ **202/347-8800**), publishes a monthly newsletter that includes travel tips.

The annual membership fee is $12 ($16 per couple), which entitles members to discounts on lodging, car rental, and supplemental medical insurance.

Elderhostel, 75 Federal St., Boston, MA 02110 (☎ **800/733-9752** or 617/426-7788), offers study programs for people over 60 at more than 1,800 educational and cultural institutions throughout the world.

FOR STUDENTS   In the United States the largest travel service for students is **Council Travel** (a subsidiary of the Council on International Educational Exchange), 205 E. 42nd St., New York, NY 10017 (☎ **212/822-2600**), with branches in Boston (☎ **617/266-1926**), Los Angeles (☎ **310/208-3551**), Miami (☎ **305/670-9261**), and many other college towns. **CIEE** provides details about budget travel, study abroad, work permits, and insurance, and it sells **International Student Identity Cards** and **International Youth Cards** ($15) to bona fide students, as well as a number of helpful publications, including the *Student Travel Catalogue* ($1 by mail, free in person).

In Athens, the **International Student and Youth Travel Service,** Odós Níkis 11 (☎ **01/323-3767**), issues student cards to students with appropriate ID.

A **Hostelling International** membership can save students money in more than 5,000 hostels in 70 countries, where sex-segregated dormitory-style accommodations cost about $8 to $20 a night. For information, contact **Hostelling International / American Youth Hostels,** 733 15th St. NW., Washington, DC 20005 (☎ **202/783-6161**). Annual membership costs $10 for those under 18, $25 for those 18 to 54, $15 for those 55 and over, and $35 for families. The *AYH Guide to Budget Accommodations,* vol. 1, which lists European hostels, costs about $15, including postage.

For a complete listing of youth hostels in Greece, contact the Greek Tourist Organization (EOT) or, for further information, the **Greek Youth Hostel Federation,** Odós Dragatsaníou 4, 105 59 Athens (☎ **01/323-4107** or 01/323-7590).

9 Getting There

Two popular ways of traveling to Greece are by ferry (from Italy) and by air; most people fly. Considering the many price breaks, promotions, and charters available, you can certainly find a bargain airfare.

Although inexpensive express trains and buses connect the major European cities with Athens and Thessaloníki, your EurailPass is valid only on ferry service from Italy and travel within Greece.

BY PLANE

Olympic Airways (☎ **800/223-1226**), the national carrier of Greece, schedules daily nonstop flights to Athens from New York, twice-weekly flights from Boston, and weekly flights from Montréal and Toronto.

Within Greece, Olympic Airways is the major carrier. You can purchase tickets for Olympic flights within Greece in conjunction with your international ticket. To obtain a copy of Olympic's *Summer Timetable,* contact the airline's offices at 647 Fifth Ave., New York, NY 10022, or in Athens at Odós Óthonos 6, near Sýntagma Square (☎ **01/926-7251**). See "Getting Around," below, for sample airfares.

TWA (☎ **800/892-4141**) provides service to Athens from throughout the United States, with connections through New York; and **Delta** (☎ **800/241-4141**) serves Athens from a number of U.S. cities.

British Airways (☎ **800/247-9297**) schedules flights to Athens from a number of major cities, all stopping in London. **Virgin Atlantic** (☎ **800/862-8621**) provides daily service from Los Angeles and New York (or Newark), several times weekly from other cities, stopping in London; it often has substantially lower promotional fares.

KLM (☎ **800/882-4452**) flies from 10 major U.S. cities to Athens, all stopping en route in Amsterdam. **Sabena** (☎ **800/955-2000**) offers flights to Athens from Atlanta, Boston, Chicago, and New York, all stopping in Brussels. **Lufthansa** (☎ **800/645-3880**) has extensive service to Athens, Thessaloníki, and Crete from 10 U.S. cities, Canada, and points in Europe via its Frankfurt hub—a convenient stopover for those en route to or from Greece.

CHARTERS   Every year various companies offer charter flights to Athens. Generally, you must book a seat a month or so in advance for flights in June, July, or August; the price depends on the length of your stay, what day of the week you're departing, and at what time of year you plan to go.

Homeric Tours (☎ **800/223-5570** or 212/753-1100) is one of the oldest-established charter companies, and we have often enjoyed their friendly, efficient service. In 1996 they charged as little as $549 for round-trip flights departing from New York in the spring and $599 to $699 for round-trip flights during the high season. **Tourlite International** (☎ **800/272-7600** or 212/599-3355) charges somewhat higher rates for its flights from New York to Athens on scheduled airlines. Both companies offer low-cost tour, car-rental, cruise, and hotel packages. Inexpensive but restrictive charter packages are offered by several British and German tour operators from points in Europe direct to many islands.

Warning: Greek regulations prohibit visitors on charter flights from leaving and then reentering the country; the idea is to prevent visitors who plan to spend their time and money in Turkey from taking advantage of subsidized landing fees in Greece.

FLIGHTS FROM ELSEWHERE IN EUROPE   Many people may want to visit other parts of Europe, then travel to Greece by train, bus, or ferry. **Icelandair** (☎ **800/223-5500**) has long been a budget favorite. In 1997 during the low season the airline charged between $369 and $843 (during the high season between $616 and $1,121) for a round-trip ticket from New York to Luxembourg. There are no restrictions on stays within Europe for up to 1 year; you're also entitled to a stopover in Iceland! Icelandair schedules daily flights to Europe from New York, with additional departures from Baltimore/Washington, D.C., and Orlando, Florida.

BY TRAIN

A EurailPass offers unlimited first- or second-class train travel throughout Europe. It also enables you to ride the ferryboat—the Hellenic Mediterranean Lines (the Eurail correspondent company) that links Bríndisi, Italy, and the island of Corfu (Kérkyra) as well as the cities of Igoumenítsa and Pátra on the Ionian coast. (*Note:* You must declare your intention to stop on Corfu or Igoumenítsa—and we don't recommend the latter unless you plan to travel in northern Greece.)

Once in Greece, EurailPass holders can use the country's network of trains and buses that make up part of the Railway Organization of Greece (**Organismós Sidirodrómon Elládos,** or **OSE**).

Contact the **Council Travel Service,** a subsidiary of the Council on International Educational Exchange, at its main office, 205 E. 42nd St., New York, NY 10017 (☎ **212/822-2600**), or a travel agent familiar with rail travel, for information on obtaining a EurailPass, which must be purchased in the United States. A special 1-month Eurail Youth Pass (second class only) is available for $598 for those under

26 from **Rail Europe** (☎ 800/438-7245; fax 800/432-1329). European residents under 26 can obtain an InterrailPass for unlimited travel throughout Greece.

There's train service from Istanbul in the east, and from Bucharest and Sophia, though it's slow and not included in any of the passes mentioned. Contact the OSE's main office, at Odós Károlou 1, Athens (☎ 01/821-3882), for information. (During our last visit, service to Belgrade had supposedly been resumed, but it was still at best irregular because of the ongoing fighting in the former Republic of Yugoslavia.)

BY BUS

Magic Bus International, the company that once operated those indomitable overlanders, no longer runs its own bus service; however, it still has an office in Athens, at Odós Filellínon 20, near Sýntagma Square (☎ 01/323-7471; fax 01/322-0219), and can book seats for a twice-weekly London–Athens express bus (and other nondomestic points) for about $150 one-way; it also offers low airfares.

If you're heading north, check bus fares also at **ISYTS Ltd.,** Odós Níkis 11, 2d Floor, Sýntagma Square (☎ 01/322-1267).

BY SHIP

Several cruise ships ply the scenic waters between Italy's Adriatic coast and Greece's Ionian coast. The trip from Pátra to Bríndisi (the most common crossing) takes about 20 hours. They provide a lounge, snack bar, dining room, deck with sun chaises—what more do you need? For information about schedules (at least one ship leaves from either Pátra or Igoumenítsa for Brindisi or Ancona daily in the summertime), contact **Hellenic Mediterranean Lines** (the EurailPass people) in Brindisi, at Corso Garibaldi 8 (☎ 0831/528-531), or call its office in Pátra, Odós Pende Pigadion & Polythechniou (☎ 061/652-521; fax 061/652-775). **Anek Lines,** Leofóros Amalías 54, Athens (☎ 01/323-3481; fax 01/323-4137), and **Strintzis/Minoan Lines,** Leofóros Vassiléos Konstandínou (King Constantine Avenue) 2, Athens (☎ 01/751-2356; fax 01/752-0540), offer similar service, and the latter ferries cars to and from Venice.

During the low season, one-way fares run from 12,000 Drs ($50) for a deck chair (tourist class) to 36,000 Drs ($150) for a two- or three-bed outer cabin with a view. Many companies offer 20% to 25% off for those with student ID cards. See chapter 7 for more information about leaving Greece via ferry.

You can also cruise between Greece and Limassol, Cyprus, or Haifa, Israel; contact the **Poseidon Lines** office at Leofóros Alkyonidon 32, Voúla (☎ 01/965-8300; fax 01/965-8310), or **Salamis Lines,** Odós Filellínon 9 (☎ 01/429-4325).

Note: For information about sailings to Turkey from the various Greek Aegean islands, check the individual island listings in chapter 10, "The Dodecanese" (see Rhodes or Kos), and chapter 16, "The Northeastern Aegean Islands" (see Sámos, Híos, Lésvos).

PACKAGE TOURS

If you're interested in a guided tour of Greece, either with a group or with your own private party, we recommend the travel experts who have helped Frommer's readers for years: **Viking Star Tours,** Odós Artemídos 1, 166 74 Glyfáda (☎ 01/898-0829; fax 01/894-0952). Peter Cocconi and his knowledgeable staff will help you plan a trip tailored to your interests; they specialize in yacht cruises and offer discounts of up to 25% to Frommer's readers on last-minute bookings on their 7-day cruise to the Cyclades. They also discount coach land tours and other cruise packages.

Peter's brother, Dimitri Cocconi, runs **Educational Tours and Cruises** at the same address (☎ 01/898-1741; fax 01/895-5419) or in the United States at 14 (R)

Wyman St., Medford, MA 02155 (☎ **800/275-4109** or 617/396-3188; fax 617/396-3096). This organization specializes in a wide variety of cultural and educational land and sea tours, and also books standard 1- to 4-day Chat Tours and Key Tours.

Another brother, Mike Cocconi, can be reached at the **Greek Island Cruise Center,** 4321 Lakemoor Dr., Wilmington, NC 28405 (☎ **800/341-3030** or 910/350-0100; fax 910/791-9400).

10 Getting Around

Even if you don't speak Greek, you'll discover that getting around the country is relatively easy since many Greeks speak some English, and most young people speak it rather well. You'll also find transportation inexpensive, efficient, and pleasant.

BY PLANE

Flying makes it possible to travel quickly from one island directly to another (for example, Crete to Santoríni or Rhodes to Mýkonos) or via Athens. However, during the high season plane travel can be something of an ordeal; bumped passengers, delayed flights, and incorrectly written tickets are common. Make your reservations as far in advance as possible, then confirm your reservations within 24 hours of your flight. Be sure to get to the airport at least an hour before departure time.

Greece's major domestic airline is **Olympic Airways;** its Athens office can be reached by calling ☎ **01/926-7251.** If you fly to Greece on Olympic, you can purchase tickets for flights within Greece when you get your international ticket; this could save you money if the exchange rate increases during your visit.

Another airline that connects Athens with Thessaloníki, Rhodes, and Iráklio (Crete) is **Air Greece;** you can contact their Athens office at ☎ **01/325-5011.**

Note: If you decide to change or cancel your reservation on a domestic flight, you may have to pay a penalty—as much as 30% if you change or cancel within 24 hours of your scheduled departure time; as much as 50% if you do so within 12 hours of your departure time.

Passengers 60 years of age and older are entitled to a 20% discount.

The following are sample one-way airfares from Athens to the islands:

One-Way Airfares from Athens

Destination	Fare
Corfu (Kérkyra)	19,300 Drs ($75)
Crete (Iráklio)	20,880 Drs ($87)
Híos	13,800 Drs ($57.50)
Kos	20,000 Drs ($83.35)
Lésvos (Mytilíni)	15,250 Drs ($63.50)
Mýkonos	17,000 Drs ($70.85)
Páros	16,800 Drs ($70)
Rhodes	24,000 Drs ($100)
Santoríni (Thíra)	20,500 Drs ($85.50)
Skíathos	14,650 Drs ($61)

BY TRAIN

The slow but pleasant and reliable railroad system in Greece is run by the Railway Organization of Greece (OSE). The OSE maintains railroad and bus stations side by side in Athens. The main stations for domestic travel are the Lárissa Station (Stathmós

Laríssis) for northern Greece and the Peloponnese Station (Stathmós Peloponnísou) for southern Greece.

For most domestic train travel, you can purchase your ticket half an hour before departure time from the ticket window at the train station (open daily from 6am to 11pm).

For international train travel or for information, contact the OSE office at Odós Siná 6, off Akadimías Street (☎ 01/362-4402), or Odós Károlou 1 (☎ 01/522-2491), both near Omónia Square; or at Odós Filellínon 17 (☎ 01/323-6747), near Sýntagma Square. Tickets can be purchased for all international buses and domestic or international rail trips. All offices are open Monday to Saturday from 8:30am to 6pm.

BY BUS

Public buses are a cheap and easy way to travel around Greece. In Athens and other cities, kiosk news vendors sell tickets and are a good source of local bus information. When you hop on, have your ticket ready to be canceled.

Long-distance buses usually leave from one of the convenient central stations; check with the Greek National Tourist Organization for current schedules. (*Note:* Inside Greece itself, the Greek National Tourist Organization is known simply as the Greek Tourist Organization, Ellinikós Organismós Tourismoú, abbreviated EOT.) EurailPass holders are entitled to use the OSE train network free of charge; however, sometimes it's worth the money to take a bus belonging to KTEL (the privately run bus network) because of its more direct and convenient service.

Make sure you know the correct pronunciation of your destination (a friend of ours who wanted to buy a ticket to Mycenae, but pronounced it *Maïsíne* instead of *Mikínes*, was given a ticket to the town of Messíni, at the southern end of the Peloponnese). After you board the bus, try to sit near the driver, so that he can tell you when to get off. Tickets can be purchased at the station or from the conductor on board. Express buses from major centers (Athens, Pátra, Thessaloníki) usually sell reserved seat tickets for long trips; before paying for a regular or reserved seat, try to figure out how comfortable your seat and the bus will be (for example, is it air-conditioned?). Buses can be noisy, hot, crowded, and smoky, but they're usually fun.

BY CAR

For **emergency road service,** call ☎ 104; for **tourist information,** call ☎ 171.

RENTALS   Renting a car in Greece is an expensive proposition, but one that makes sightseeing much easier and more pleasurable. Try to include other travelers so that you can share expenses. Driving can be adventurous, since Greece has the highest auto accident rate in Europe. So drive cautiously and make sure you've purchased the maximum insurance available. Most car-rental companies require drivers to have a valid driver's license, be at least 21 years old (24 years old for some models), and use a major credit or charge card (or leave a cash deposit).

The major rental companies in Athens are: **AutoEurope** (☎ 01/960-0935; fax 01/960-0937); **Avis** (☎ 01/322-4951; fax 01/322-0216); **Budget** (☎ 01/921-4771; fax 01/922-4444); **HellasCars** (☎ 01/923-5353; fax 01/923-5397); **Hertz** (☎ 01/994-2850; fax 01/933-3970); and **Interrent-Europcar** (☎ 01/924-8810; fax 01/922-1440). All have several offices throughout the mainland and the islands and will book cars in advance. (You can save a a lot of money by booking and paying for your car before leaving home, but you'll have less flexibility.)

The smaller, Greek-owned companies tend to offer lower rates. **Viking Star Tours** (☎ 01/898-0879) and many hotels can also arrange car rentals at discount rates. Daily rates start at about $50, plus 30¢ per kilometer, and weekly rates start at about

$500, with unlimited mileage for the smallest Suzuki. Remember that gasoline (*venzína,* sold by the liter) costs almost $3 per gallon.

LICENSES All valid U.S., Canadian, European, and Australian licenses will be accepted for 1 year after your arrival in Greece. To obtain an international driver's license in the United States, apply at the nearest **American Automobile Association (AAA)** office (☎ **800/AAA-HELP**); you must provide two 2-by-2-inch photographs, a photocopy of your state driver's license, and a $10 fee. Canadians can get the address of the nearest branch of the **Canadian Automobile Club** by calling its national office (☎ **800/336-HELP**).

The Greek Automobile and Touring Club, **ELPA,** can extend your license. It will also supply you with maps and information.

BY TAXI

Our least favorite means of transportation is the taxi. In Athens, taxis can be very difficult to find. Either they have an odd number on a day when only even numbers are allowed to enter certain areas, or they're already carrying an Athenian who's not going in your direction (group rides are allowed because of the taxi shortage; each passenger pays the difference between the final meter reading and the reading when he or she entered); or, if the taxi is empty, the driver may refuse to pick you up when he realizes you're a visitor—usually because of potential communication problems. Outside Athens, it's easier to get a taxi.

Beware of the following typical taxi tricks:

• Some taxi drivers will pick up a group of tourists and insist (illegally) that every passenger pay the full metered fare.
• A few taxi meters include a decimal point for the obsolete *leptó* ($^1/_{100}$ of a drachma), and drivers often don't speak up when unwitting tourists pay 12,000 Drs instead of 1,200 Drs for their ride.
• Late at night, taxis at airports, ferry piers, and train and bus stations may refuse to use their meters and demand a flat rate, usually 100% to 300% higher than normal.
• Taxis at airports often overcharge tourists for the nominal additional fees (see "Getting Around" in chapter 4, "Athens," for more information).
• Drivers often adjust their meter so that it runs at twice the speed, even though your destination is not outside the city limits, where this practice is authorized. Check the small window to the right of the drachma display on the face of the meter for "1"; it should read "2" only after midnight or outside the city limits.
• A driver may want to take you to another hotel (where he can get a commission). Politely refuse.

We warn you about these scams so that you'll be well informed; however, we don't want you to become paranoid. Taxi fares are quite reasonable, and most Greek cabbies are honest and competent. If possible, try to learn from a local what the approximate fare should be before you enter a taxi; then you'll have some basis for judgment.

For taxis with meters, the initial charge is 200 Drs, plus 60 Drs per kilometer from 5am to midnight; after midnight the rate is doubled. There's an additional charge of 300 Drs for airport service, 160 Drs to take you to or from the train or bus station, plus 60 Drs for each piece of luggage. You'll have to negotiate with unmetered taxis, but drivers are usually honest and even helpful.

BY FERRY

Most visitors will probably sample the ferryboats, either the large ships leaving from Piraeus and other ports or the smaller, interisland boats. Ferries are usually the most relaxing way to travel, and they offer a great opportunity to meet other travelers. They can sail through higher winds and rougher seas than smaller craft, but in such weather their slow roll can lead to seasickness.

The best way to plan your island itinerary is to get a map from the National Tourist Organization (EOT) that shows—by dotted lines—most of the routes between islands, plus the weekly schedule of departures from Piraeus (the major port) and Rafína (a nearby Attica port that services the Cyclades more quickly and more cheaply than Piraeus). Remember that these ferries run less often from mid-September to mid-May, so you'll need to plan your vacation time accordingly. Also, certain travel agents sell tickets for specified lines. Shop around for prices and ask to see a photo of your interisland vessel; a larger ship can be much more comfortable if the seas are rough.

Arrive at least an hour before departure time (interisland boats often depart before their scheduled time) to buy your ticket from a dockside agent. In Athens you can purchase ferryboat tickets and book cabins (great fun!) on night ferries in advance at the **Galaxy Travel Bureau,** Odós Voulís 35 (at Apóllonos), Sýntagma Square (☎ **01/322-9761;** fax 01/322-9538); open daily except Sunday.

HellasTours, a Thomas Cook representative, at Odós Karayóryi tís Servías 4, Sýntagma Square (☎ **01/322-0005;** fax 01/323-3487), is a full-service agency that changes money without commission for its clients. The nearby **Summertime Tours,** in the arcade at Odós Karayóryi tís Servías 10 (☎ **01/323-4176**), offers discounts on its services.

In each chapter on an island group, we've tried to indicate the frequency and variety of ferry sailings and have suggested that you speak to the local tourist office or port authority or to a travel agent for schedule information. *Note:* Those taking ferries from the Dodecanese Islands to Turkey will have to submit their passport and payment to a travel agent 1 day in advance of departure.

Here are sample tourist-class fares from Piraeus to some Aegean destinations. The embarkation tax and value-added tax (VAT) will add a few hundred drachmas for all classes. Fares should be about 10% less during the low season.

Tourist-Class Boat Fares from Piraeus

Destination	Fare
Íos	4,900 Drs ($20.50)
Iráklio (Crete)	5,750 Drs ($24)
Kos	6,950 Drs ($29)
Lésvos (Mytilíni)	5,775 Drs ($24)
Monemvassiá (Peloponnese)	3,950 Drs ($16.50)
Mýkonos	3,950 Drs ($16.50)
Náxos	4,000 Drs ($16.65)
Pátmos	5,900 Drs ($24.60)
Rhodes	7,650 Drs ($31.90)
Sámos	5,300 Drs ($22.10)
Santoríni	4,900 Drs ($20.40)

From Vólos, in central Greece, to the nearby Aegean island of Skíathos, the fare is 2,650 Drs ($11).

Along the Ionian coast, some sample fares are: from Igoumenítsa to Corfu, 950 Drs ($3.95); from Pátra to Kefalonía, 3,140 Drs ($13).

Hydrofoils and sea jets (high-speed catamarans) are about twice as fast as the ferries, and are less likely to cause seasickness. But they cost about twice as much and offer less freedom of movement and provide a more limited view. They currently service Crete, the Cyclades, the Dodecanese, some of the Ionian islands, some of the Northeast Aegean islands, the Saronic Gulf islands, and some coastal cities in the Peloponnese (see the relevant chapters for more information).

A Note on Seasickness

This unpleasant subject is very much a part of island hopping for many people, particularly in May and August when the seas can be rough. If you're susceptible, purchase some meclizine (Bonine), cyclizine (Marezine), or dimenhydrinate (Dramamine)—all readily available without prescription—and take it the night before your ferry trip. They cause drowsiness, but you shouldn't mind that while you're sleeping, and the benefits last for up to 24 hours. Kyle and her family loved the new elasticized bracelets that utilize the principles of acupressure.

Don't eat within 2 hours of your boat's departure, and make sure that your last meal is light.

Here are some suggestions in case you're reading this while bobbing around on a ferryboat: Don't put your head down, and don't stay inside (unless there's a threat of being washed overboard!). Get some fresh air, breathe deeply and evenly, and focus on the horizon (or some other fixed point in the distance) to help your brain get in sync with your inner ear. If, despite everything, your lunch rebounds on you, eat dry soda crackers and don't drink fluids.

BY MOPED

Mopeds are probably the most common form of private tourist transportation. They're a fun, practical, and cheap way (about $15 to $30 per day) to sightsee in the islands. Before renting one, though, make sure you feel comfortable about riding along steep, sand- or gravel-strewn roads with poor or nonexistent shoulders, where cars know no speed limits. Since visitors are reluctant to accept a helmet from one of the few vendors who have them (we hope you'll decide to wear one), choose a slower, easier-to-balance moped rather than a small 125cc motorcycle. Organize your belongings so that the luggage straps are secure.

And *take a close look at your moped* before driving off. Check especially for faulty brakes. Also, since many visitors experience accidents but don't report them to the rental shop, the next renters end up with bent frames that make steering and balancing the bikes difficult and unpredictable.

A NOTE ON STREET NAMES

As you try to get around in Greek cities and towns, there are a few things you should know about street names.

The Greek word for "street" is *Odós.* The word for "avenue" is *Leofóros,* abbreviated *Leof.* In this guide, the Greek words are used in full addresses.

Street names appear in the genitive case. Thus, *Leofóros Vassilíssis Sofías,* in Athens, should be read "Avenue of Queen Sophia." The words for Queen (*Vassílissa,* gen. *Vassilíssis*) and King (*Vassiléfs,* gen. *Vassiléos*) appear in the city's major thoroughfares abbreviated in both cases " *Vass.*" (You will not be tested on grammar.)

Searching for the Real Greece

We've become increasingly frustrated with the blight of group-oriented tour companies on the Greek landscape. Some places that were once genuinely Greek destinations have become international-style apartment towns in the name of catering to these groups (this has happened to many beach towns in particular—they've lost their Greek character as they've become peppered with bars, discos, and motorcycle-rental shops). Greek traditions and customs have largely disappeared in these areas, which are unfortunately the very sites that most tourists are eager to visit.

In many lesser-known destinations, however, you can still find much that's genuinely Greek.

You might begin your tour in **Rafína,** the port east of Athens; it's a far more congenial place than Piraeus and more convenient to the famous Cyclades. Instead of glamorous, sophisticated, thoroughly European, and expensive islands like Mýkonos, Páros, and Santoríni, we suggest touring the less developed and lesser-known islands of Tínos, Náxos, Sífnos, and Folégandros.

Crete, an island that has undergone some of the heaviest development in recent years, is still worth a visit, especially if you concentrate on the town of Iráklio (to see the archaeological museum and nearby Knossós), the mountain village of Spíli, and the old Venetian cities of Réthymno and Haniá in the west.

For most people, a trip through the Dodecanese must include a visit to Rhodes and perhaps Kos, and might end on the northeast Aegean island of Sámos, with a quick side trip to Ephesus in Turkey. A better route, if you care about authenticity, is visiting Sými and Pátmos, and if you can make it, Kárpathos. On Sámos, visit the old town in Vathí and the village of Manolátes, then head for Híos or northern Lésvos—you can cross to Turkey from these islands, too.

In the Sporades, we like northern Skópelos (around Glóssa), Alónissos, and especially the island of Skýros; in other words, consider passing up trendy Skíathos.

The northern part of mainland Greece is the least explored and most ethnically interesting region. Among our favorite areas are the monasteries on Mt. Áthos (unfortunately, only men are allowed to visit), Kastoriá, and north to the Albanian border; the lovely rural mountain villages of Epirus, especially Métsovo; the Zagória region; the outcrop-topped monasteries of Metéora and across the mainland to Mt. Pílio.

No trip to Greece would be complete without a visit to Delphi and the Peloponnese peninsula; however, after visiting the archaeological sites, why not head west to Kástro (with its nearby beaches), to the mountain village of Andrítsena, or south to the Máni (the most remote part of the southern Peloponnese)?

If you have the time to explore the Ionian islands, instead of—or at least in addition to—beautiful, but overdeveloped and increasingly expensive Corfu, consider a minicruise from Kefalonía to Ithaca and Páxos (including a beach stop on Antipáxos).

We're confident that if you explore some of these more out-of-the-way areas you'll be amply rewarded with exciting, authentically Greek experiences.

The names of squares are kept in the nominative case in this guide. Thus, instead of *Platía Syntágmatos* (Square of the Constitution), the main square in Athens, we say simply Sýntagma Square. If you were to ask for directions to Sýntagma, you would be readily understood.

SUGGESTED ITINERARIES

If You Have 1 Week

Since most travelers begin their trip in Athens, explore the fascinating capital first. The main attractions are the Acropolis, National Archaeological Museum, the Museum of Cycladic and Ancient Greek Art, and Pláka, the city's lively, characteristic quarter.

Try to fit in a day trip to the Temple of Poseidon at Soúnio, at the southern tip of Attica.

On your fourth day, head west to the Peloponnese to ancient Corinth, the theater at Epidaurus (especially during the summer, when the theater offers a full schedule of classical Greek plays), the extensive excavations at Mycenae, south to beautiful Náfplio, then west to the elegant museum and site at Olympia.

If you still have the energy and time, head north to Greece's premier destination, Delphi. You could arrange to see some of these places by joining a group tour.

If You Have 2 Weeks

Follow our suggested itinerary for the first week (above). The second week should be spent island hopping. In order to make the best use of your time (and avoid transportation problems) it would be better to focus on one particular island group. The two most varied and easily accessible island groups are the Cyclades and the Sporades.

Consider the Cyclades: maybe Mýkonos (and by all means Délos), Páros, and Santoríni, with an excellent combination of archaeological sites, fine beaches, a sophisticated resort and shopping scene, and classic island architecture—with rests on the more peaceful and traditional Náxos, Tínos, or Sífnos.

The best of the Sporades include Skíathos, Skópelos, and Skýros, all of which are slightly less crowded and less expensive, but offer sensational beaches and a more traditional Greek lifestyle (especially on Skýros).

If You're Interested in Archaeology

The following destinations highlight archaeological excavations, museums, and medieval cities. This cross-country trip will take between 3 weeks and a month.

Start at Athens, where you'll want to take in the Acropolis, the National Archaeological Museum, the Museum of Cycladic and Ancient Greek Art, Soúnio, Dafní, and Aégina.

Then head east to the Cyclades, stopping on Mýkonos (Délos and the Maritime Museum), Ándros (the Museum of Modern Art and the Archaeological Museum of Ándros), and Santoríni (Akrotíri).

Next it's south to Crete—in particular, the town of Iráklio, where you'll take in Knossós and the archaeology museum. East of Crete, in the Dodecanese, lie Rhodes (Líndos), Kos (Asklepion), and Pátmos (Hóra).

Now head north to the northeast Aegean islands of Sámos (where you'll see the Efpalinion Tunnel, the Heraion, and the archaeology museum) and Lésvos (which boasts the Theóphilos Museum).

Now back on the northern mainland, you can take in the highlights of Thessaloníki (the archaeology museum, a walking tour of the major churches, Philippi, Vérgina) and Metéora.

South to the Peloponnese is Olympia (with an optional trip to Vássae and Mystrá if you're driving), Mycenae, Epidaurus, and ancient Corinth. And heading back north to central Greece, you won't want to miss Delphi (and Óssios Loukás).

If You Just Want Beautiful Beaches

Instead of presenting an itinerary here, we'll mention some of our favorite beaches and party spots, not in any particular order.

We love the many beaches on **Mýkonos,** Milópotas Beach on **Íos,** Mátala on **Crete,** the sandy strips of southeastern **Kos,** Embório on **Híos,** several beaches on **Skíathos,** the island of **Antipáxos,** Mýrtos on **Kefalonía,** and the newly accessible beaches on **Lefkáda.**

There are many other smaller beaches in more remote locations, but the ones we've mentioned here are all worthy of a special visit if you're longing for a place in the sun.

If you want to escape the hordes of summer visitors, there are certain out-of-the-way locations where you're bound to find the empty beach you've dreamed about or the perfect Greek fishing village that has all but disappeared. Try the Cyclades (especially the western Cyclades, including **Sífnos** and **Folégandros**) and the Sporades (northern **Skópelos, Alónissos,** and **Skýros**). We particularly enjoy the Dodecanese and the Ionian islands. In the Dodecanese you can find not only a large resort island such as Rhodes or Kos, with its ancient ruins, but also such smaller gems as **Sými** and **Pátmos.** The Ionians offer sophisticated **Corfu,** but more intrepid island hoppers enjoy stopping on **Ithaca, Páxos, Antipáxos,** and **Kefalonía.**

11 What You Need to Know About Accommodations Before You Go

In Greece, particularly during the high season (mid-June to mid-September), those traveling alone often have to pay for a double room, even though the "official" price for a single is 80% of the posted rate for a double. Therefore, our $50-a-day formula works best for two, three, or more people traveling together. *Note:* The prices given in this book are always high-season rates, unless otherwise noted.

On the islands there has been a trend among builders to bypass Greek government regulations (and restrictions on new hotel construction) by putting up small "apartment" buildings along the coast. These usually consist of simple studio and one-bedroom apartments, with fully stocked minikitchens, linens, and periodic maid service. They have become popular with Europeans, who frequently travel with their families and prefer to stay on one island for their 2- or 3-week vacation. As vacation rental units and older family hostels are being modernized, their Greek owners prefer to create apartments, thereby eliminating the need for a reception area (with a telephone switchboard) and the expectation that breakfast will be served. In some cases we've mentioned several of the better-value apartments; most of them, however, are booked by local travel agents and you cannot make a reservation by writing or calling.

Since our reviews generally focus on the small hotels and pensions that we prefer, we want to emphasize a few points. First of all, Greece is not a "fancy" country; in fact, its elegant style is based on simplicity and sparseness of design. The government ratings (deluxe and Class A, B, C, D, and E hotels or first-, second-, and third-class pensions) and loose maximum price controls are based on such factors as the facilities, size of rooms, and number of bureaus rather than on whether there are carpets, chandeliers, and VCRs in each room. Rental rooms and guest houses, though sometimes licensed, are not rated.

We have tended to focus on the Class C (simple "motel") and D (basic "hostel") hotels as well as first-class pensions (which generally run $40 to $70 for a double, often with continental breakfast, during the high season), but occasionally we've included a Class A or B hotel (which comes with the amenities of a typical American hotel) when we felt that you might want to treat yourself like royalty.

Most newer hotels are quite plain (Class C); you can generally expect to find an elevator, private bathrooms, air-conditioning (occasionally) for an extra fee, telephones, a lobby, a TV lounge/bar, and a breakfast room. From our perspective, the best pensions are the harder-to-find, older converted mansions, villas, or restored portside hotels with frescoed ceilings, winding staircases, wrought-iron balconies, and marble floors. (Staying with a Greek family is becoming a thing of the past, except in the less-visited inland villages.)

In our hotel listings we pay most attention to such factors as cleanliness, character of the hotel, and whether the staff is friendly and helpful. Of lesser concern is the size of the room and whether it has a television set and private bathroom (less expensive rooms have only a sink; there's usually a toilet/shower directly across the hall).

If you plan to travel to any of the popular island resorts during the high season, you'll need to make reservations as far in advance as possible. You can call or write directly to any of the hotels we recommend, or you can write to the **Hellenic Chamber of Hotels,** Odós Stadíou 24, 105 64 Athens, Greece (☎ **01/323-7193;** fax 01/322-5449). The chamber will expedite your reservation (for a 10% commission); it can also suggest alternative accommodations in a similar category if your first choice is not available. If you arrive without reservations, the local tourist office, portside hawkers, travel agents, or tourist police can help you find a hotel or private room.

FAST FACTS: Greece

Banks   Banks are open to the public Monday to Thursday from 8am to 2pm and Friday from 8am to 1:30pm. Some banks are open additional hours for foreign currency exchange.

Business Hours   Greek business hours take some getting used to. The typical 6-day work week is as follows: Monday and Wednesday from 8:30am to 3pm; Tuesday, Thursday, and Friday from 8:30am to 2:30pm, then they reopen from 5 to 8:30pm; and Saturday from 8:30am to 3:30pm. The afternoon siesta typically lasts from 3 to 5pm. However, many businesses that cater primarily to tourists forgo the afternoon siesta and offer expanded hours, from 9am to 11pm daily. Most government offices are open Monday to Friday from 8am to 3pm, and are closed Saturday and Sunday. Call ahead to check the hours of any business you'll be dealing with.

Drugstores   Drugstores *(farmakía,* singular *farmakío),* your first source of medical help, can be found all over Greece; they rotate their schedules so that there's almost always one drugstore open in each neighborhood. Check with your hotel for the one nearest you.

Electricity   Electric current in Greece is 220 volts AC, 50 cycles; two-post plugs are required. Some of the larger, deluxe hotels have 110-volt outlets in the bathrooms for electric shavers.

Embassies and Consulates   See "Fast Facts: Athens" in chapter 4.

Emergencies   See "Police," below.

Language   Modern Greek retains much of the vocabulary of ancient Greek but differs from it in grammar and pronunciation. To confuse matters a bit further, the founding fathers of the modern Greek nation tried to introduce *katharévousa,* a more formal "purified" form of the language, which is still used for government decrees and by newspapers, but the original, less formal *dimotíki* (demotic) is used in everyday conversation and has been adopted by most important writers. Modern Greek has absorbed many foreign words—Turkish, Italian, Slavic, and now English.

Although Greek has a different alphabet, it's not difficult to pronounce (see the Appendix at the end of this book).

You may want to learn a little Greek before your trip. There are several excellent phrase books, such as Berlitz's *Greek for Travellers,* which comes with an audiocassette. Don't be shy, once you get to Greece, about using the expressions you've learned; your effort alone, however faltering, will draw an appreciative response.

Mail As in most countries, you can receive mail addressed to you, c/o Poste Restante, General Post Office, City (or Town), Island (or Province), Greece. You'll need a passport to claim your mail. American Express card holders can receive mail for a nominal fee at any American Express office or agent throughout Greece.

Measurements Greece uses the metric system. It also, however, has an additional unit of weight—the oke *(oká),* which is equal to about 2.8 pounds.

Photographic Needs Cameras, accessories, and film are readily available, though more expensive, in Greece. One-hour photo shops are increasingly common. A 36-exposure roll of Kodacolor Gold (100 ASA) costs about 2,400 Drs ($10).

Police Wherever you are in Greece, first contact the local tourist police (local phone numbers are noted in each chapter) for assistance with tourist information, crime reports, or medical emergencies. There will usually be an English-speaking officer available. If not, contact the local police.

Rest Rooms Let's start with Greek toilets. For the most part, they're clean and they work, even in public parks and museums. Carry tissues with you, and pay attention to the signs you'll see everywhere: Don't try to flush the tissues down the toilet—use the receptacles provided. Even if there's no sign, don't put any paper products in the toilets (the old system can't cope!). It's much easier to find a trash bin than to explain in Greek that the toilet has just flooded.

With a little patience you'll soon learn to use and appreciate a "Danish" shower. (Believe those signs that say GREECE IS GOING DRY. Pátmos must have its water shipped in from Sámos; on Santoríni it's trucked from the springs at Kamáres; and in even the most fortunate places it's scarce and expensive.) Grasp the nozzle in one hand and turn the water on long enough for it to get warm and to soak yourself, then turn it off while you lather up; turn it back on to rinse. Standing or sitting with your back to the corner and directing the spray carefully will minimize the water in the rest of the bathroom when there's no curtain. (Yes, we know it doesn't sound like a lot of fun, but you can find luxury elsewhere, and you'll be conserving a precious resource.)

Safety Crime is not a serious problem in Greece. Pickpocketing, purse snatching, and beach theft, however, do occur in tourist areas. Be aware and alert at all times, even in the most heavily touristed areas.

Taxes and Service Charges Unless otherwise noted, all hotel prices include a service charge, usually 12%, and tax; the latter consists of a 6% value-added tax (VAT) and a 4.5% community tax. In most restaurants, a 13% service charge is added, along with an 8% VAT (in Athens, there's also a 5% city food tax). A VAT of 18% is added to rental-car rates.

Telephones To call a number in Greece from abroad, dial the international access code (011 in the United States and Canada), then 30 (the international country code for Greece), plus the area or city code (minus the first zero), then the local number.

In Greece, **pay telephones** require a 20-Dr coin. After depositing the coin, you'll hear an irregular beeping sound; that's your dial tone. A regular beeping sound indicates that the line is busy.

Telephones using the *telekárta* card-phone system can be found nearly everywhere; cards—starting at 100 units for 1,300 Drs—can be purchased at OTE (see below) and news kiosks. (Kiosks usually still let you use their telephone for 20 Drs, and in remote areas may even let you make a long-distance call.)

You can make **long-distance calls,** whether within Greece or internationally, from almost any hotel, but you'll find that the surcharges add between 50% and 100% to your telephone bill. The alternative is to make your calls from any of the conveniently located centers of the national telephone system, OTE (Organismós Tilepikinonión Elládos, or Telecommunications Organization of Greece). At OTE centers you can dial long-distance calls directly and pay for them in cash; you can also make collect calls, but they may require up to an hour's wait, as may credit-card calls.

Be warned: The cost of a long-distance call can be high, even at OTE. On our last visit, a call to the United States cost 750 Drs ($3.15) per minute. But there is an alternative: If you have a telephone credit card from AT&T, MCI, Sprint, or Excel, you can access that company's international network and have your calls billed directly to your card. For AT&T service dial ☎ 00800-1311; for MCI service dial ☎ 00800-1211; for Sprint dial ☎ 00800-1411. When you use your credit card, you can reduce the cost of calling home by more than 50%; a service charge, however, will be added by the telephone company to each call. You can make credit-card calls from any OTE center for a small fee or from your hotel for no fee. The larger OTE centers usually have a fairly recent collection of international telephone books.

In making long-distance calls, you must use the appropriate **area codes.** Within Greece, area codes always begin with a zero (but if you're calling Greece from abroad, omit the initial zero). For example, to call a number in Athens from outside the city, use the area code 01. (If you're calling locally, within an area code, dial just the local number.) To make a call to North America, first dial the Greek international access code 00 (double zero), then 1 (the country code for the United States and Canada), then the area code and the local number itself.

Time Greece is 2 hours ahead of Greenwich mean time. With reference to North American time zones, it's 7 hours ahead of eastern standard time, 8 hours ahead of central standard time, 9 hours ahead of mountain standard time, and 10 hours ahead of Pacific standard time.

In Greece, the European system of a 24-hour clock is used officially, so that, for example, noon is 1200, 4pm is 1600, and 11pm is 2300. Popularly, however, expressions such as "2 in the afternoon" and "8 at night" are used.

Tipping A 10% to 15% service charge is included in most restaurant bills and is reflected in the two columns of prices next to menu items. Nevertheless, it's customary to leave an additional 5% to 10% for the waiter. Often, on small bills, people leave change up to the nearest 100 Drs. This rule applies to taxi fares as well. (Greeks, by the way, don't usually tip taxi drivers; however, visitors are expected to do so.) Small tips to chambermaids and porters (200 to 500 Drs) are always appreciated.

Settling into Athens 4

Athens is unique among the great capitals of Europe. The golden marble columns of the Parthenon, crowning the rocky slope of the Acropolis, have brought travelers to this capital of the ancient world for more than 2,000 years.

Yet Athens's renown as the birthplace of democracy and its rich store of antiquity's finest art and architecture represent just two aspects of this fascinating city. (If you follow news accounts of the current subway construction, you'll see how rich the city's ancient past still is.) Today's visitors find intriguing evidence of Athens's Byzantine heritage in its tiny, old churches and its Turkish heritage in its bustling Eastern-style markets.

Put all this in the midst of a sprawling city of 4 million people embracing a new European lifestyle and you'll have some idea of the vibrancy and excitement that infuse contemporary Athens.

Many big-city problems have arrived. Congestion is one, aggravated by a recent influx of Eastern European refugees, some homeless, wandering the city's streets in search of work. Traffic and noise are another—the city has more than a million cars. A third problem (which stubbornly persists despite efforts by one government after another, including vexing traffic restrictions) is pollution. The city's noxious smog, called *néfos* by the Athenians, clouds the air on many days, especially during the summer.

Serious as these problems are, they haven't dampened the city's energy and vibrancy. Greeks are at their liveliest when most other people are fast asleep—late at night and into the early morning. The shops and markets and vegetable stalls, particularly those in Monastiráki and around Omónia Square, open almost at the crack of dawn. By 8am traffic is already heavy, with the sound of car horns impatiently signaling the start of another day. The cafes downtown are abuzz with activity as bleary-eyed office workers jostle each other for a quick cup of coffee while scanning their favorite newspaper for the latest political gossip.

At 2 or 3pm most businesses shut their doors for the officially sanctioned siesta, a period of rest and fortification at the height of the midday heat. The whole city, it seems, heads home for lunch (the biggest meal of the day) and an hour or two of sleep.

Beginning around 8 or 9pm, the city gets its second wind. Crowds pour into Athens's streets, tavernas, restaurants, and bars, filling them until well past midnight. Sometime around 2am Athenians wander home for a few hours of shut-eye before they begin anew.

1 Orientation

If you haven't been to Greece before, you may be surprised at the size of Athens. It's a sprawling metropolis; as a result, most transportation terminals lie outside the heart of the city.

ARRIVING & DEPARTING
By Plane

There are three terminals at **Ellinikón International Airport,** located in the eastern suburb of Glyfáda. (A new airport is presently under construction at Spáta, near Marathon, northeast of Athens.) The East Terminal (Anatolikó) handles the international flights of all scheduled airlines except Olympic Airways. The West Terminal (Dytikó) handles only Olympic flights, both domestic and international. Many charter flights now use the "Charter Terminal," the former U.S. military facility, to the south. A shuttle service operates between the two main terminals every hour from 8:30am to 8:30pm.

Arriving travelers will find the same services at the two main terminals, but fewer services at the Charter Terminal. Foreign-currency exchange booths offer the same rates as downtown banks; luggage carts are available for 200 Drs (85¢; make sure you have enough Greek currency before collecting your baggage); the national telephone system (OTE) offers international telephone and fax service; there are tourist information centers (inside the departure area of the East Terminal and across the street at the West Terminal), cafes, and restaurants. The airport's only luggage-storage facility is located outside the East Terminal.

TRANSPORTATION FROM THE AIRPORT INTO ATHENS To reach downtown Athens from Ellinikón International Airport, you have several alternatives that vary in cost and speed, in the usual inverse relationship. (Parts of central Athens are closed to traffic, to curb air pollution, and you may have to walk a few blocks.)

A **taxi** (available at both the East and West terminals) ride from the airport to Sýntagma Square should cost 2,000 to 2,500 Drs ($8.30 to $10.40). With little traffic the trip should take 20 to 30 minutes, but during rush hour it might take 1 to 1½ hours.

But there are important caveats about taking a taxi:

• Make sure that the meter is on. Some drivers will try to offer a "special" off-meter price. Don't accept it under any circumstances; stop the cab and call for a policeman before you leave the airport.

• If you've won that battle, check the meter as the cab drives away; drivers must keep it on the single-fare counter, indicated by a "1" in a small window on the meter. A "2," indicating double fare, is acceptable only for out-of-town or midnight-to-5am trips. Be bold—question any discrepancy immediately.

• Drivers may add an airport charge of 300 Drs ($1.25), plus 100 Drs (40¢) for every piece of luggage over 22 pounds. It's customary to give the driver a small tip—10% to 15%.

From the West Terminal only, the **Olympic Airways bus** leaves every half hour between 6:30am and 8:30pm from outside its international terminal (adjacent to its domestic terminal), taking Olympic's passengers to the airline's office at Leofóros Syngroú 96 (in Koukáki) or to Sýntagma Square, where buses are normally available to other parts of the city. The fare is 200 Drs (85¢), and you must have exact change.

Burial Mound at
  Marathon ❷
Dafní Monastery ❹
Ferries to the
  islands at the
  port of Piraeus
  (Pireás) ❺
Kessarianí Monastery ❻

Sanctuary of Artemis
  at Vravróna ❼
Sanctuary of Eleusis
  at Eléfsina ❸
Sanctuary of Nemesis
  at Rhamnous ❶
Sanctuary of Poseidon
  at Soúnion ❽

Airport ✈ Mountain ▲▲ Cruise Ship Terminal 🚢

You can catch an airport-bound bus at the Syngroú Avenue Olympic office. (We hope this information remains current during your visit, but because of the subway construction and funding problems, service can be erratic.)

Starting at the West Terminal and stopping at the East Terminal, an **express bus**—the blue double-decker **no. 91** or single-decker **no. 90**—runs every half hour from 5am to midnight, and then every hour from 1 to 5am, taking passengers to Sýntagma Square or Omónia Square. (Because of subway construction the bus now stops first at Omónia.) The fare is 200 Drs (85¢), but from midnight to 6am it goes up to 250 Drs ($1.05). This bus leaves from the northwest corner of Sýntagma Square (in front of the Bank of Macedonia-Thrace) as well as from Stadíou Street at Omónia Square for the return trip.

If you really want to save money, and if you have the time, you can take public **bus no. 133,** which plies the coastal route and stops at Posidónos Street outside the airport grounds. For 80 Drs (35¢) it, too, will take you to Sýntagma Square. However, you must buy a ticket from the bus kiosk or a newsstand before boarding and then have the ticket stamped after boarding.

TRANSPORTATION TO/FROM PIRAEUS   If you're skipping Athens and heading straight for the island boats, take a taxi to Piraeus; the fare for the half-hour trip is 1,500 to 2,000 Drs ($6.25 to $8.35). To keep those costs down, you can take public **bus no. 19** from either terminal to Karaïskáki Square in Piraeus for 300 Drs ($1.25).

To those travelers who think they can return from the islands on an overnight boat and then connect with an early-morning homeward flight, we can only say "Good luck!" Of course, some may succeed, but a great many people have been foiled by delayed boat arrivals and Athens's early-morning gridlock. We advise you to allow an extra day. You'll also face a conspiracy of taxi drivers, who meet the boats and offer one fare—4,000 Drs ($16.65)—to go anywhere. Pass them by and walk to the nearest major street, where you'll probably find an honest taxi driver. Or catch bus no. 19 at Karaïskáki Square.

BY TRAIN

If you're arriving from northern Europe or the north of Greece, your OSE train will pull into the main station, **Lárissa Station** (Stathmós Laríssis), near Karaïskáki and Omónia squares.

Trains coming from the Peloponnese arrive and depart from the ornate **Peloponnese Station** (Stathmós Peloponnísou) next door or in Piraeus. (See chapter 5 for information about the Piraeus Peloponnese Station.) The beaux-arts Peloponnese Station has smoked-glass panes, crystal-and-gilt chandeliers, and a marvelously carved wooden ticket booth with graceful wrought-iron dividers (a treat for the train buff).

Note: The Lárissa Station has a bank booth (open Monday to Saturday from 7:30am to 10pm and Sunday from 11am to 10pm) and an OTE center for local and long-distance telephone calls. Across the street is a police station.

Taxis are available at all hours from the parking area outside the train stations and should cost less than 900 Drs ($3.75) to Sýntagma Square. Trolley no. 1 (which you can catch in front of Lárissa Station) goes to Sýntagma Square and Koukáki, passing through Omónia Square. (You can pick it up on the southwest corner of at Sýntagma Square.) The fare is 80 Drs (35¢). You must purchase a ticket before boarding the trolley, either from a transit kiosk near the bus stop or from a newsstand.

BUYING TICKETS WHEN YOU'RE READY TO DEPART   You can buy OSE train tickets through a travel agent or at the Omónia Square **ticket office,** at Odós

Károlou 1 (☎ **01/524-0647**) or at Odós Filellínon 17 (☎ **01/323-6747**), which is more convenient to Sýntagma. Your seat and car number (smoking or nonsmoking) will be specified when you get your ticket.

BY BUS

KTEL BUSES   There are two principal stations for the national bus company (KTEL) in Athens. **Terminal A,** at Odós Kifíssiou 100, is where you'll find buses to Pátra, the Peloponnese, the Ionian islands, and all points south and west. Public bus no. 51 will take you from this terminal to the corner of Zínonos and Menándrou streets, near Omónia Square; from there you can catch a bus or trolley to Sýntagma (board at Sýntagma for the return trip).

At **Terminal B,** Odós Liossíon 260, you'll find buses heading northward to Delphi, Thebes, Évvia, Metéora, and other points north and east. Bus no. 24 will take you to and from Amalías Avenue, in front of the entrance to the National Garden, a couple of blocks south of Sýntagma Square. Check with the tourist police (☎ **171**) or the Greek Tourist Organization (EOT) office (☎ **01/323-4130**) for current schedules and fares.

OSE BUSES   The domestic railroad company, OSE, also offers some long-distance bus service. Its international buses to/from Italy, Germany, Belgium, and Great Britain, as well as to/from Bulgaria and Turkey, depart from the Peloponnese Station in Athens. Tickets can be bought at its ticket offices.

BY CAR

Arriving in Athens by car can be more than confusing, but most drivers will want to follow the signs to Sýntagma Square, the center of the city. Most car-rental agencies, incidentally, are based nearby on Amalías and Syngroú.

BY BOAT

The most enjoyable way to reach Athens from the port of **Piraeus** is to take the metro (subway). (If you're coming from abroad, however, you may find that your pier is far from the metro station; also, if you have heavy bags, you may want to take a bus or cab instead.) This old-fashioned subway is the fastest way through Athens's traffic congestion, but it makes only a few stops in the city center. The two closest stops to Sýntagma Square, the heart of Athens, are Monastiráki (about a 10-minute walk west of Sýntagma, noted for its flea markets) and Omónia Square (a major transportation hub).

Tickets, which cost 75 Drs (30¢) to any stop on the line, should be purchased either at the ticket machines or at the manned booths. The metro runs every 10 minutes from 5am to 12:10am.

There's also bus service to and from Piraeus. Green bus no. 40 runs every 15 minutes between 5am and 1am and hourly between 1am and 5am from Akti Xaveriou

---

Impressions

Athens, the eye of Greece, mother of arts and eloquence.
—Milton, *Paradise Regained,* 1671

In Athens I saw . . . a spirit . . . which a thousand years of misery had not squelched.
—Henry Miller, *The Air-Conditioned Nightmare,* 1945

Athens leaves me cool.

—Henry Adams, 1898

Athens at a Glance

American Express
  Office **9**
First Aid Station **4**
EOT (Greek Tourist
  Organization) **8**
National Archaeological
  Museum **3**
Olympic Airways Office **11**
OTE (Telecommunications)
  Office at Omónia
  Square **5**
OTE (Telecommunications)
  Office at Sýntagma
  Square **7**
The Parthenon **2**
Post Office (Main)
  at Omónia Square **6**
Post Office at
  Sýntagma Square **10**
Theseum Station **1**

Church ✝
Information *i*
Post Office ✉

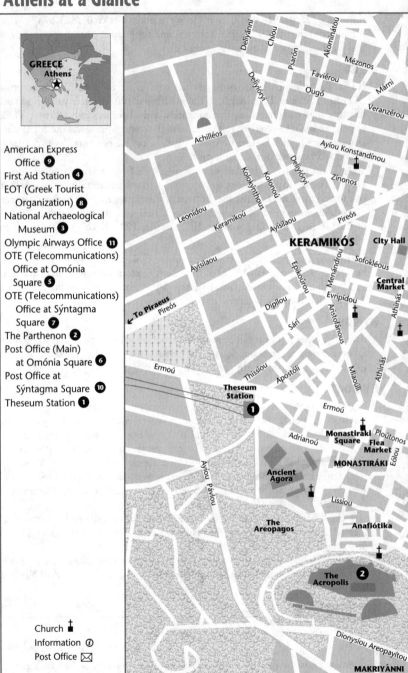

3-0512

72

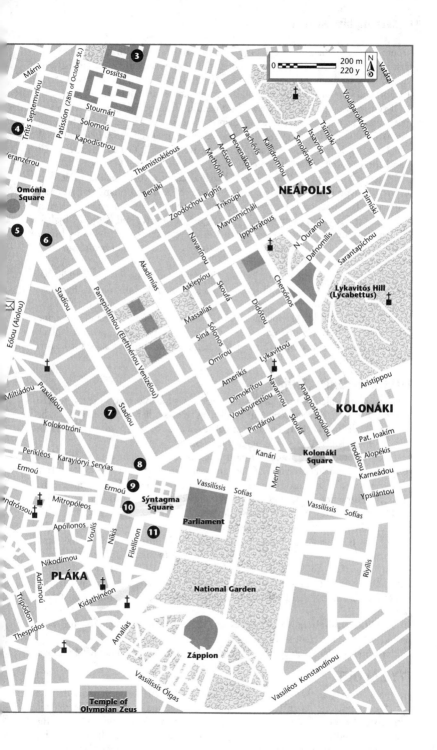

(south side of the harbor, several long blocks from most piers) to Filellínon Street, just off Sýntagma Square. (The metro stop is more convenient to most ferries.) Bus no. 49 runs between the more convenient Platía Karaïskáki (northeast side of the harbor) and Omónia, but the trip can sometimes take nearly an hour.

If you must take a taxi, be prepared for banditry from the taxi drivers who meet the boats. The normal fare on the meter from Piraeus to Sýntagma should be about 1,800 to 2,000 Drs ($7.50 to $8.30), but some drivers try to charge as much as 5,000 Drs ($20.85). Pay it if you're desperate, but better yet, walk to a nearby street, hail another taxi, and insist on the meter.

If you've landed by hydrofoil at **Zéa Marina** (about a 10-minute taxi ride west of Piraeus), you'll find the taxi choices slim and the rates exorbitant. To avoid an outrageous fare, walk up to the main street and take bus no. 905, which goes between Zéa and the Piraeus subway station. (Catch the bus up the hill from the hydrofoil marina, on the side street next to the subway station.) You must buy a ticket at the small ticket stand near the bus stop or at a newsstand before boarding the bus.

If you've landed at the port of **Rafína** (about an hour's bus ride east of Athens), you'll see a sloping bus stop with several buses in line up the hill from the ferryboat pier. Inquire about the bus to Athens; it runs often and will take you to the Áreos Park Terminal, at Odós Mavrommatéon 29, near the junction of Alexándras Avenue and Patissíon Street (about 25 minutes by trolley from Sýntagma Square or 1 block from the Victoria Square metro stop). From the terminal, buses leave for Rafína every half hour.

VISITOR INFORMATION

The most convenient source for a wide range of visitor information is the **tourist police;** they offer 24-hour service in English, as well as other languages, and can be reached by dialing ☎ **171.** The tourist police are also the people to contact in case you have travel-related problems or emergencies.

In Greece, the **Greek Tourist Organization** is known simply as **EOT** (Ellinikós Organismós Tourismoú). The EOT has an information desk (☎ **01/969-9500**) in the arrivals area of the East Terminal of Ellinikón International Airport, open daily. Tourist information at the West Terminal is provided by the tourist police.

The most convenient EOT office in Athens itself (☎ **01/322-2545** or 01/323-4130) is right on Sýntagma Square (the government and tourist center) at Odós Karayóryi tís Servías 2 (2 Karageorge of Serbia St.), outside the National Bank of Greece. It's open Monday to Thursday from 8am to 2pm and 3:30 to 6:30pm, Friday from 8am to 1:30pm and 3 to 8:30pm, Saturday from 9am to 2pm, and Sunday and holidays from 9am to 1pm. The EOT has a wide range of free brochures; bus, ferry, and train schedules; hotel listings; and good maps of Athens and Greece.

The **EOT administrative offices** (☎ 01/322-3111) are a few blocks northwest, at Odós Amerikís 2 (2 America St.).

There's also an EOT office at Zéa Marina; ask at the hydrofoil office for directions.

CITY LAYOUT

It's hard to imagine that only about 150 years ago Athens was little more than an obscure outpost with fewer than 10,000 inhabitants. Period engravings show shabby, single-story wooden homes flanking the Acropolis and Agorá. Beyond them the barren hills and plains of the Attica peninsula spread far into the distance. Today metropolitan Athens radiates out from the center city; Sýntagma Square is at the hub, and the surrounding suburbs include Kifissiá to the north, Kaisarianí to the east, Piraeus to the southwest, and Glyfáda (adjacent to the airport) and Vouliagméni to the south.

Athens's approximately 4 million residents live within a 150-square-mile area that's rapidly bumping up against the mountains and the sea. The city is such a magnet that roughly 40% of the entire population of Greece lives within its borders!

THE NEIGHBORHOODS IN BRIEF

Most of the attractions and services of interest to visitors are in the city center, within a triangle defined by Sýntagma Square to the east, the Acropolis to the southwest, and Omónia Square to the north. The neighborhood of Monastiráki, with its flea market and ancient ruins, is near the center of the triangle. (Subway construction will likely cause some inconvenience in this area for the next few years.)

Sýntagma Square   Draw a straight line between the Acropolis and Lykavittós, Athens's two major hills, and the midpoint is Sýntagma Square—the tourist, government, and business center. The old royal palace, which stands guard over the landscaped square on the east side, is now home to the Greek Parliament (Voulí) and the Tomb of the Unknown Soldier, where you can see the theatrical changing-of-the-guard ceremony performed by white-skirted, pompom-shoed *évzones*. Behind and beside the Parliament building are the verdant acres of the National Garden, an oasis of quiet greenness in the bustling city. The exclusive neighborhood of Kolonáki lies northeast from here, Omónia Square northwest, Monastiráki west, and Pláka and the Acropolis southwest.

In Sýntagma Square you'll find the queen of Athens hotels, the Grande Bretagne, which is a useful landmark. Walking counterclockwise around the square, which is presently dominated by metro construction, you'll come to two banks that offer foreign-exchange services (each one also has an EOT window and an American Express office), as well as familiar fast-food outlets. On the south side of the square, as well as on nearby side streets, you'll find airline offices, travel agents, foreign-exchange offices, bookstores, and numerous tourist-oriented shops.

The airport and other public buses leave from various stops around the square, as well as along Amalías Avenue to the south. Check with the bus-ticket booth near the General Bank of Greece office for the current location of the stops.

Mets   A residential area south of Sýntagma Square, between the Temple of Zeus and the First Cemetery and next to Ardítos Hill, Mets is noted for its many fine old garden houses, which give the area a villagelike aspect reminiscent of Old Athens. Named after a popular cafe, Metz, which once flourished here, it has become a favorite of the city's literati. Mets has several stylish boutiques and art stores as well as bars and a famous taverna along Moussoúri Street. The nightlife reflects the conservative tastes of its residents, many of whom are young professionals.

Kolonáki   The chic shopping district at the base of Lykavittós Hill, Kolonáki is a 10-minute walk northeast of Sýntagma Square. Although this section has lost some of its glamour to the nouveau suburbs, Kolonáki remains Athens's best in-town address. Lykavittós Hill offers a stunning view (when the smog clears) of the entire metropolitan area, and it has a contemporary outdoor theater with a diverse program of music and theater. There's a funicular railway that runs up the hill from the upper streets of Kolonáki.

Pláka   A favorite with visitors, Pláka is located just a few blocks to the southwest of Sýntagma and extends to the base of the Acropolis and around to the Agorá. A residential quarter in ancient times, it was settled again in the 19th and early 20th centuries by wealthy merchants, who built luxurious multistory wood-and-marble mansions with finely crafted interiors. Today some of those mansions remain as homes, but most have been transformed into bars, bouzouki clubs, restaurants, shops, and offices. Despite the rows of T-shirt and souvenir shops, the back lanes of this old neighborhood retain a charm that leads us to recommend a number of hotels and restaurants in this area.

Makriyánni/Koukáki   Makriyánni is the area just south of the Acropolis, a fairly fashionable neighborhood with a few affordable hotels, some good retaurants, and a growing number of shops. South and west is the quiet middle-class neighborhood of Koukáki, one of Athens's best-kept secrets, where we've found several small, well-priced hotels and pensions. The streets are a mix of early 20th-century and modern town houses, the restaurants are seldom patronized by visitors, and there's nary a souvenir shop to be found. Buses and trolleys run frequently along Koukáki's main streets, stopping at Sýntagma (only a short walk away) and elsewhere. Syngroú, the wide boulevard that goes to Piraeus, Glyfáda, and the two terminals of Ellinikón International Airport, runs along the edge of the neighborhood; in this area you'll find most of the car-rental agencies, the public bus to Piraeus, and Olympic Airways' main office (the airport bus arrives and departs from here after it leaves Sýntagma).

Monastiráki   This small neighborhood is west of Sýntagma Square north of the Acropolis, and next to the Agorá. Its name, "Little Monastery," derives from the fact that a monastery once stood here. At the convenient metro stop here, you can catch the subway south to Piraeus or north to Omónia Square and continue all the way up to suburban Kifissiá; close by are a couple of Athens's best budget hotels. The area is an extensive labyrinth of shops as well as home to a world-famous weekend flea market. Just to its north is the city's busy Central Market.

Omónia Square   If you look at a map of Athens, you'll come to the conclusion that all roads lead to Omónia Square, a handy metro stop (now almost overwhelmed by construction work). Two parallel streets connect Omónia with Sýntagma Square: Panepistimíou, where you'll find the university, the National Library, and the Academy; and Stadíou, with Kolokotróni Square and the main OTE (public telephone) office.

For many years Omónia (Harmony) Square was the commercial and tourist center of Athens. Today, however, since many businesses have moved away, a large number of homeless refugees from Eastern Europe have moved in, and many of the local hotels have gone downhill, the area resembles New York's Times Square of the 1980s (before its current redevelopment). We no longer recommend hotels here. Nevertheless, although this is not the safest or most attractive part of town, it's still one of the most interesting spots. There are meat and vegetable markets and huge department stores; the National Archaeological Museum is just a few steps away.

Exárchia   Exárchia, the neighborhood around Exárchia Square, is about a 15-minute walk north from Omónia Square. For many years it existed in the shadow of its famous neighbor, the National Archaeological Museum. But now it has become a lively hangout for urban professionals, students, visiting intellectuals, and local families. Athenians who flock to the cafes and tavernas around its mimosa-filled square wonder a bit about rumors of drug-dealing nearby, but you'd never guess that there was a problem while enjoying a cup of Greek coffee at one of the cafes.

The Suburbs   One of the ritziest suburbs is **Kifissiá,** well to the north of downtown Athens, where the houses are big and modern. A stroll down one of Kifissiá's nicer streets will remind you of an American suburban neighborhood. Farther north is pine-covered **Drossiá,** a suburb that's especially noted for two things: first, it's always 10° cooler here than in Athens itself, and second, it serves the best *penirlí* (boat-shaped cheese bread) in Greece. **Glyfáda,** south of Athens, is a residential area for many diplomats and—perhaps convenient for them—home of the airport. The residents and shops here are cosmopolitan and chic. Farther south on the coast is **Vouliagméni,** noted for its beach and one of Greater Athens's best hotels—the Astir Palace.

2 Getting Around

The area covered by most visitors is small enough to negotiate just by walking. Sometimes you have no choice, since parts of the central city are closed to traffic in order to reduce air pollution. (We suggest navigating the smaller streets parallel to the big avenues to further avoid the congestion, noise, and stifling emissions.)

If you plan to cover a larger area, we suggest taking a taxi since they're so cheap—usually less than the 500-Dr ($2.10) minimum—if you can get one.

BY SUBWAY

One of Athens's surprises is its clean, quiet, and efficient subway system. Though consisting of only one line, with a second line under construction, the metro (as the Greeks call it) is a great way to get from Sýntagma Square (using the nearby Monastiráki stop) or Omónia Square to Piraeus or the National Archaeological Museum.

Other stops include Néo Fáliro, which is convenient for diners heading to Mikrolímano; Victoria Square, near the Green Park bus or railroad station; Monastiráki, for sightseeing in Pláka or the Agorá or for shopping in the flea market; and Kifissiá (a prosperous outer suburb).

Subway tickets can be purchased from ticket machines or at booths in the station; for most destinations, a one-way fare is 75 Drs (30¢), and for longer distances, 100 Drs (40¢). Trains run approximately every 10 minutes between 5am and midnight. *Remember to validate your ticket;* the penalty for traveling without a validated ticket is 1,500 Drs ($6.25).

BY BUS & TROLLEY

Trolleys and local buses are among the most convenient ways to get around the city. Trolleys no. 1 and 5 go almost everywhere of interest to the visitor: Sýntagma Square, the National Archaeological Museum, Omónia Square, Lárissa Station, and the Koukáki region behind the Acropolis. At every stop (indicated by a yellow triangle), the trolleys' numbers and final destinations are posted.

You must buy your ticket before boarding, either at one of the small ticket booths near some stops or at most news kiosks. The fare is 75 Drs (30¢). Once on board, you must use one of the small machines to validate your ticket; failure to do so can result in a 1,500-Dr ($6.25) fine.

Always check your route with with your hotel reception desk or with local passengers waiting at the stop since route numbers change frequently. If you're not certain about the route, call the tourist police.

Many trolley lines run from 5am to midnight. Athens bus routes often coincide with trolley routes or partially overlap them and then extend outward in different directions. Main routes are noted on the free EOT map.

BY TAXI

Traveling by taxi in Athens is an adventure and not always a pleasant one. We've noted the problem with taxis at the airport (see "Orientation," earlier in this chapter); similar problems face you in the city.

Although there are taxi stands scattered throughout the city, you may have to hail a taxi. Since taxis are required to pick up as many additional passengers as possible who are going in the same direction, don't give up if the rooftop light is turned off. Keep waving—a taxi may stop for you! If the taxi picks up additional passengers, each one is supposed to pay the difference between the fare shown on the meter when he got in and when he got out of the taxi. Although you should be required to pay only your fair share, visitors often end up paying more.

The surest way to get a taxi (and your only strategy after midnight) is to call one yourself or, if possible, have the desk clerk at your hotel or a waiter at the restaurant call one. A radio surcharge of 500 Drs ($2.10) will be added to the meter, but it's worth it.

Surcharges are allowed for pickups from the airport (300 Drs/$1.25) and from the train or bus station (200 Drs/85¢), plus a baggage charge of 80 Drs (35¢). Taxi waiting time is charged at 1,400 Drs ($5.85) per hour. If you're suspicious of any charges, ask to see the official rate sheet that all taxis are required to carry. If you've been gouged, get the taxi number and report the driver to the tourist police.

BY CAR

We don't recommend that you try to drive around Athens. The streets are confusing and it's very difficult to find parking space. If you want to hire a car and driver, check with the desk at your hotel or a travel agent. For car-rental information, see "Getting Around" in chapter 3.

FAST FACTS: Athens

Airline Offices   Many international carriers have ticket offices in or near Sýntagma Square. **British Airways** is at Odós Óthonos 10 (☎ 01/325-0601); **Delta** is at Odós Óthonos 4 (☎ 01/331-1668); **Lufthansa Airlines** is at Leofóros Vassilíssis Sofías 11 (☎ 01/369-2111); **TWA** is at Odós Xenofóndos 8 (☎ 01/322-6451).

For information on **Olympic Airways'** schedules and fares, call or visit its main office, at Leofóros Syngroú 96 (☎ 01/926-7251). For reservations, call ☎ 01/966-6666.

For general and flight information at the East Terminal (non-Olympic flights), call ☎ 01/969-9466. For Olympic flights at the West Terminal, call ☎ 01/936-3363.

American Express   The main office is on Sýntagma Square, at the corner of Ermoú Street (☎ 01/324-4975; fax 01/322-7893). If you plan to receive mail there, the mailing address is Odós Ermoú 2, Sýntagma Square, 102 25 Athens, Greece. American Express will cash and sell traveler's checks, accept claims for lost and stolen charge cards and traveler's checks, store luggage for 300 Drs ($1.25) per day, make travel arrangements or book tours, accept mail for card members (others pay 500 Drs/$2.10 per collection), and wrap and send parcels. Office hours are Monday to Friday from 8:30am to 4pm and Saturday from 8:30am to 1:30pm. The office closes an hour earlier in winter, and mail service ends at 4:30pm weekdays. When transacting business at AmEx, don't forget to bring along your passport.

During off-hours, if you need to report lost or stolen charge cards or checks, call collect to the American Express office in London (☎ 44-0171/930-4411).

Area Code   The country code for Greece is **30.** The area code for Athens is **01.**

Banks   The **National Bank of Greece** on Sýntagma Square (☎ 01/322-2255) is open Monday to Thursday from 8am to 2pm and 3:30 to 6:30pm, Friday from 8am to 1:30pm and 3 to 8:30pm, Saturday from 9am to 3pm, Sunday and holidays from

9am to 1pm. The extended evening and weekend hours are for foreign exchange only and are shorter from October to April. (This branch offers the added bonus of an EOT office inside for visitor information.) Official banking hours throughout Greece are Monday to Thursday from 8am to 2pm and Friday from 8am to 1:30pm.

International banks with local offices include **Citibank,** Odós Othonos 8 (☎ **01/322-7471**); **Bank of America,** Odós Panepistimíou 39 (☎ **01/324-4975**); and **Barclays Bank,** Odós Voukourestíou 15 (☎ **01/364-4311**).

Automatic teller machines (**ATMs**) are becoming increasingly common in commercial areas. Ask your bank or credit card company whether your card can be used in Greece; if so, request a directory of locations and ask if your PIN needs to be reprogrammed.

Bookstores   The biggest of the foreign-language bookstores in Athens is **Eleftheroudákis,** at Odós Panepistimíou 17 (☎ **01/331-4180**). Its new eight-floor megastore has an enormous selection of travel, language, international literature, even children's books and toys, plus a music shop and cafe. There's also a large branch at Odós Níkis 4 (☎ **01/322-2255**), just behind Sýntagma Square. Also good is **Pandelídes,** at Odós Amerikís 11 (☎ **01/362-3673**), which accepts secondhand books for credit. Another personal favorite (with a much more eclectic, student bent) is **Compendium,** at Odós Níkis 28 (☎ **01/322-1248**); it also buys used books in return for store credit. For a look at the many fine guides and art books, as well as the photography-filled books about Greece, go to the retail store of **Ekdotiki** (Ekdotike), at Odós Omírou 11 (☎ **01/360-8911**). For stationery supplies, head straight to the best: **A. Pallis,** at Odós Ermoú 8, on the corner of Voulís, near Sýntagma Square (☎ **01/323-1128**).

Currency Exchange   In Greece, banks, post offices, and even travel agencies are authorized to change money at government-posted rates of exchange. Hotels will often change traveler's checks for guests, but at rates lower than those offered by banks. The maximum commission is 4%.

Several travel agents near the National Bank of Greece on Sýntagma Square offer foreign exchange late into the evening; their rates, however, may not be competitive. Because of bank holidays and periodic labor strikes, you may suddenly find banks in Greece closed for a day or several days; therefore, we recommend that you always have extra drachmas on hand.

Dentists and Doctors   Most embassies or consulates can provide a list of recommended dentists and doctors. Call the Citizens Services section during business hours. In an emergency, call the main number anytime.

Drugstores   Most drugstores *(farmakía)* around Sýntagma Square have personnel who speak English. Every pharmacy posts a notice on its door indicating where the nearest all-night pharmacy is located. The *Athens News* also lists pharmacies open after normal hours.

Embassies and Consulates   The embassy of the **United States** is at Leofóros Vassilíssis Sofías 91 (☎ **01/721-2951**). Hours for its Citizens Services section are 8:30am to 5pm Monday to Friday. The embassy of **Canada** is at Odós I. Yenadíou 4 (☎ **01/725-4011**). The embassy of the **United Kingdom** is at Odós Ploutárchou 1 (☎ **01/723-6211**). **Australia** has a consulate at Odós D. Soútsou 37 (☎ **01/644-7303**).

Emergencies   In an emergency call the **tourist police** at ☎ **171;** an English-speaking police officer is on duty 24 hours a day. If that line is busy, dial ☎ **166** for an **ambulance** or ☎ **199** for the **fire** department. The general **police**

emergency number is ☎ **100** (at that number, however, you may not reach an English-speaking officer). Check with your embassy for advice on medical assistance.

For **lost-and-found information,** call the traffic police (☎ **01/523-0111**). For **lost passports,** contact the alien police (☎ **01/362-8301**).

Any theft should be reported immediately to the tourist police, since all insurance policies require a police report for reimbursement. A police report is also required when you're replacing a lost passport or airline ticket. You'll need an English translation, as well, if the report is in Greek.

Hospitals   There are many hospitals in the Greater Athens area, but the only one that can be fully recommended is the **Hygeia** (pronounced Iyía) **Diagnostic and Therapeutical Center,** Odós Erythroú 4 at Kifissiás Street, north of Sýntagma Square, toward the Olympic Stadium, near the suburb of Filothéï (☎ **01/682-7940**). It's a private hospital and will require proof of payment before admission (credit and charge cards are accepted).

In an **emergency,** dial ☎ **171** or ☎ **166** for information on the nearest hospital. You'll probably be sent to a government hospital, but may not want to stay. Even at a government hospital you'll be expected to pay for any treatment (Blue Cross or other American insurance policies are not accepted). Citizens of the European Union, however, will not have to pay.

Luggage Storage/Lockers   Many hotels (and, surprisingly, hostels as well) will store your excess luggage for you while you cavort in the islands or wherever. Some will accept it for free; others charge 300 to 500 Drs ($1.25 to $2.10) per day per piece. The **Pacific Ltd. Travel** office, Odós Níkis 26, off Sýntagma Square (☎ **01/324-1007**), has a formal luggage-storage system. Each piece costs 400 Drs ($1.65) per day, 700 Drs ($2.90) per week, 2,000 Drs ($8.35) per month. It's open Monday to Saturday from 7am to 8pm and Sunday and holidays from 7am to 2pm.

In Piraeus there's luggage storage inside the subway terminal, but it's costly. Both railway stations (Lárissa Station and Peloponnese Station) provide luggage-storage facilities.

Maps   The Athens map provided free by the Greek Tourist Organization is very good. The best commercial map, called *Athens, Piraeus, Salonica,* is published by John Glavas; it's available at newsstands in these three cities.

Newspapers/Magazines   The *Athens News,* a daily newspaper, is published locally in English; it's available at kiosks everywhere for 150 Drs (65¢). The *International Herald Tribune* hits the newsstands after 7pm each day. *Athenscope,* a weekly magazine, is full of information, restaurant reviews, and cultural and recreational listings, as well as articles of interest to English-speaking visitors; it's available at most news kiosks for 300 Drs ($1.25).

Police   See "Emergencies," above.

Post Office   The general post office (GPO) is a half block from Omónia Square at Odós Eólou 100, open Monday to Friday from 7:30am to 8pm, Saturday from 8am to 3pm, Sunday from 8am to 2pm. There's also a branch at Mitropóleos Street, just off the square, with the same hours. *Poste restante* mail can be directed either to Omónia Square (where anything marked "GPO" will go) or to Sýntagma Square. (Bring your passport when picking up *poste restante* mail.)

The post office for sending parcels (surface mail is painfully slow and not much cheaper than air mail) is at Odós Stadíou 4. Leave any internationally bound parcels unwrapped until they've been inspected there.

Post offices also offer outbound fax service; some offer foreign-currency exchange.

A first-class letter or postcard costs 120 Drs (50¢), while express mail service costs 4,000 Drs ($16.65) for 500 grams (approximately 1 pound).

Safety   Athens ranks among the safest capitals in Europe. There are few reports of violent crimes. Pickpocketing, however, is not uncommon, especially in Pláka and the Omónia Square area, on the metro and buses, and in Piraeus. We advise travelers to avoid Omónia and the backstreets of Piraeus at night. As always, leave your passport and valuables in a security box at your hotel. Carry a photocopy of your passport, not the original.

Telephones/Telefaxes/Telegrams   The main office of the Telecommunications Organization of Greece (OTE) is Odós Stadíou 15 (2 blocks from Sýntagma Square). This and the Omónia Square branch are open daily from 8am to 10pm. The OTE office at Odós Patissíon 85 (near Victoria Square) is open 24 hours. There are other, smaller OTE exchanges in Athens, usually with more limited hours of operation.

Telegrams, telexes, and telefaxes can also be sent through the OTE offices. Some post offices offer fax service.

Transit Information   For bus routes, ferry schedules, and other transit information, call the Tourist Police at ☎ **171.**

---

3 Accommodations You Can Afford

Since most visitors want to see the Acropolis and the nearby sights, we've made a concerted effort to find reasonably priced accommodations in this central area. Many visitors have complained that it's difficult to find a room that's quiet enough to get a good night's sleep, and so we've done our best to avoid hotels on major streets (unless they offer air-conditioning and/or double-paned windows) and next to bouzouki clubs.

For pure convenience, the hotels of Monastiráki, touristy Pláka, and central Sýntagma can't be beaten. We especially recommend Koukáki for its quiet residential backstreets and the feeling it conveys of a real Greek neighborhood; although it's not conveniently situated, it's only a short walk from the Acropolis and buses are available to go elsewhere.

Note: We strongly advise that you reserve well ahead of time, since the best-value lodgings are often full.

AROUND SÝNTAGMA SQUARE

Because Sýntagma Square is such an important central location, there are only a few budget hotels in this area.

Hotel Achilléas. Odós Lekká 21, 105 62 Athens. ☎ **01/323-3197.** Fax 01/324-1092. 32 rms, all with bath. A/C TEL. 14,500–15,700 Drs ($60.40–$65.40) single; 19,000–20,400 Drs ($79.15–$85) double; 25,300 Drs ($105.40) triple. Rates include breakfast. AE, DC, EURO, MC, V.

The Achilléas, on a quiet side street near Sýntagma Square, was fully renovated in 1995. Its pleasant yellow rooms are spacious, most have plenty of light, and several provide balconies. Breakfast is served in the first-floor garden dining room. Don't be discouraged by the dim off-street entrance—good value awaits you inside.

Hotel Hermes. Odós Apóllonos 19, 105 57 Athens. ☎ **01/323-5514.** Fax 01/323-2073. 45 rms, all with bath (tub or shower). A/C TEL. 16,000 Drs ($66.65) single; 20,500 Drs ($85.40) double; 25,650 Drs ($106.90) triple. Rates include breakfast. AE, DC, EURO, MC, V.

Conveniently located near Pláka—just a couple of blocks from the cathedral (*mitrópolis*)—yet reasonably quiet, this hotel is pleasant, comfortable, and ably

Athens Accommodations

Annabel's Youth Hostel **4**
Athenian Inn **10**
Athens International
  Youth Hostel **3**
Attalos Hotel **5**
Dioskouros Guest House **17**
Hostel Aphrodite **2**
Hotel Achilleas **11**
Hotel Acropolis House **16**
Hotel Adonis **15**
Hotel Exarchion **8**
Hotel Hermes **13**
Hotel Nana **1**
Hotel Nefeli **14**
Hotel Plaka **12**
Hotel Tempi **6**
Museum Hotel **7**
YMCA (XEN) **9**

Church ✝
Information ⓘ
Post Office ✉

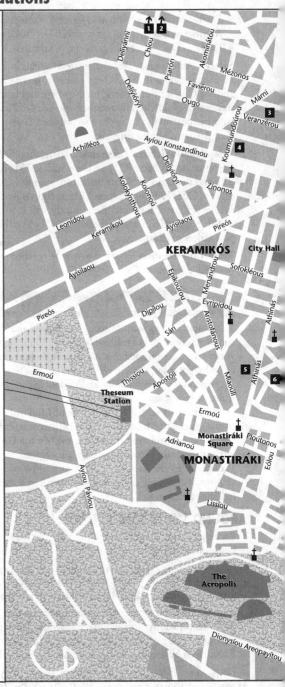

3-0513

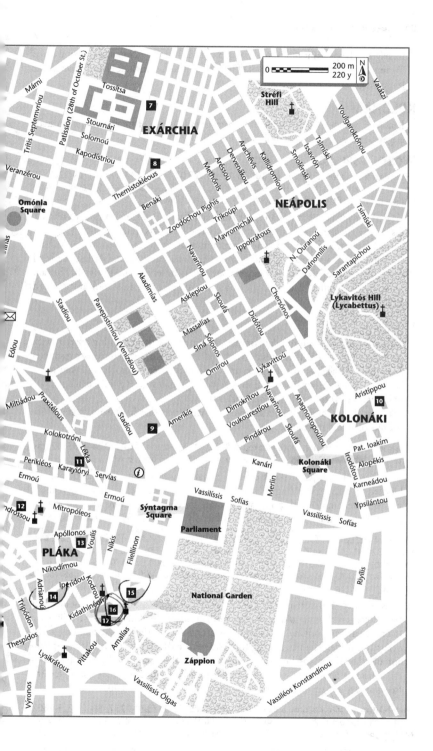

managed. The pleasant roof garden, with a fine view of the Acropolis, is a good place for lunch, dinner, or a sunset drink. The buffet breakfast includes ham, cheese, and boiled egg.

KOLONÁKI

Kolonáki, which rises up a slope of Lykavittós Hill, is one of the most sophisticated, elegant, and expensive neighborhoods in Athens.

WORTH A SPLURGE

Athenian Inn. Odós (C)háritos 22, 106 75 Athens. ☎ **01/723-8097.** Fax 01/724-2268. 28 rms, all with bath. A/C TV TEL. 18,900 Drs ($78.75) single; 28,200 Drs ($117.50) double. Rates include breakfast. Rates about 20% lower off-season. AE, EURO, DC, V.

One of the few hotels in this area, the Athenian is a charming hideaway that attracts discerning travelers. The international clientele prizes its quiet location (3 blocks east of Kolonáki Square), spacious accommodations (renovated in 1996), and friendly, informative staff. (A quote from the hotel guest book: "At last the ideal Athens hotel, good and modest in scale but perfect in service and goodwill. Hurrah. Lawrence Durrell.") Many of the rooms have balconies that look out toward Lykavittós Hill.

PLÁKA

This is the top choice for budget travelers because it's such a charming quarter, with enticing shopping, excellent restaurants, and lively nightlife. Vehicles are excluded from most of Pláka, so roaring trucks and motorcycles aren't a problem. If your room isn't too close to a nightspot with music, you'll probably get a good night's sleep—unless you're up enjoying the nocturnal activity.

Many of our choices in this section are small hotels that have been created from the old villas and mansions.

Dioskouros Guest House. Odós Pittakoú 6, Pláka, 105 58 Athens. ☎ **01/324-8165.** 12 rms, none with bath. 7,400 Drs ($30.85) single; 9,250 Drs ($38.55) double. MC, V.

The Dioskouros is just 1 block off busy Amalías Avenue, but most of the noise is blocked by a larger building. It's an old home with a big, winding staircase and a simple hostel ambience that appeals to young travelers. The rooms are a bit shabby but bright and clean. The management is friendly and offers 10% discounts on tours.

✪ **Hotel Acropolis House.** Odós Kodroú 6–8, Pláka, 105 58 Athens. ☎ **01/322-2344.** Fax 01/324-4143. 25 rms, 11 with bath (shower); 4 suites. TEL. 9,500 Drs ($39.60) single without bath; 15,000 Drs ($62.50) double without bath, 16,800 Drs ($70) double with bath; 19,550 Drs ($81.45) suite. Rates include continental breakfast. Add 4,000 Drs ($16.65) for air-conditioning. V (on request).

This restored 150-year-old villa at the south end of Voulís Street is one of our top choices, with more old-world charm than most. The Choudalákis family have maintained many original classical architectural details, such as the molding and a decorative frieze. The newer wing (only 60 years old) isn't as special, but it's pleasant and the toilets (one for each room, but across the hall) are fully tiled and modern. There's a book-swap spot and a washing machine you can use for a small fee (it's free after a 4-day stay). The best views are from rooms 401 and 402.

Hotel Adonis. Odós Koudroú 3, Pláka, 105 58 Athens. ☎ **01/324-9737.** Fax 01/323-1602. 25 rms, all with bath (shower); 1 suite. TEL. 9,800 Drs ($40.85) single; 13,800 Drs ($57.50) double; 16,450 Drs ($68.55) suite. Rates include breakfast. No credit cards.

This quiet hotel near the southern end of Voulís Street has central heating, an elevator, and a pleasant roof garden (where breakfast is served) with a great view of the

Accommodations & Dining South of the Acropolis

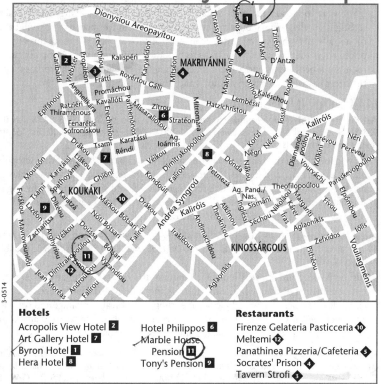

Hotels

Acropolis View Hotel **2**
Art Gallery Hotel **7**
Byron Hotel **1**
Hera Hotel **8**

Hotel Philippos **6**
Marble House
Pension **11**
Tony's Pension **9**

Restaurants

Firenze Gelateria Pasticceria **10**
Meltemi **12**
Panathinea Pizzeria/Cafeteria **5**
Socrates' Prison **4**
Tavern Strofi **3**

3-0514

Acropolis. The rooms are plain but the floors and furnishings are new. Ask for a room with a balcony; they're large enough for sunbathing.

Hotel Byron. Odós Výronos 19, Pláka, 105 58 Athens. ☎ **01/325-3554.** Fax 01/323-0327. 20 rms, all with bath (shower). MINIBAR TEL. 15,000 Drs ($62.50) single; 20,600 Drs ($86) double. Rates include breakfast. No credit cards.

The rooms here are neat and cheerful. The six front ones are a tad noisy, but they offer balconies and a view of the Acropolis. The rooms in the back are quieter and overlook nearby rooftops and gardens.

Hotel Nefeli. Odós Iperídou 16, Pláka 105 58, Athens. ☎ **01/322-8044.** 18 rms, 17 with bath (12 with shower, 5 with tub). TEL. 13,800 Drs ($57.50) single with bath, 8,980 Drs ($37.40) single without bath; 17,250 Drs ($71.90) double with bath. Rates include breakfast. AE, V.

This small, charming hotel, near the southern end of Voulís Street, is the perfect place for getting away from the bustle and noise of the city. Its rooms are spotless, though small, and its marble-floored hallways are lined with botanical prints. We like it for its central location, the quiet street, and the old-fashioned ceiling fans in some of the rooms (12 rooms have air-conditioning).

WORTH A SPLURGE

Hotel Plaka. Odós Kapnikaréas 7 (at Mitropóleos St.), Pláka, 105 56 Athens. ☎ **01/322-2096.** Fax 01/322-2412. 67 rms, all with bath (38 with shower, 29 with tub). A/C TV TEL. 19,600 Drs ($81.65) single; 25,800 Drs ($107.50) double. Air-conditioning 2,000 Drs ($8.35) extra. Rates include breakfast. AE, DC, EURO, MC, V.

If you want to spend a few extra drachmas for a step up in hotel living, try the Pláka. Its bright, spotless white lobby sets the tone. The fresh and attractive rooms and bathrooms, as well as the hallways, are decorated in shades of blue. We think this higher-priced alternative is a good value in a great location. Request a rear, Acropolis-facing room for a better view and a more peaceful night's rest, although the rooms facing the street have double-glazed windows and private balconies.

MAKRIYÁNNI/KOUKÁKI

Art Gallery Hotel. Odós Erechthíou 5, Koukáki, 117 42 Athens. ☎ **01/923-8376.** Fax 01/923-3025. 22 rms, all with bath (shower). TEL. 11,100 Drs ($46.25) single; 13,400 Drs ($55.85) double. No credit cards.

As you might expect from its name, this small hotel 3 blocks south of the Acropolis has an artistic bent, and the newly renovated reception area is very attractive. Polished hardwood floors, ceiling fans, and a tiny cage elevator add a warm, homey feeling to this half-century-old house that's been home to several artists, whose paintings are now on display. The rooms are plain but comfortable.

Hotel Hera. Odós Falírou 9, Makriyánni, 117 42 Athens. ☎ **01/923-6682.** Fax 01/924-7334. 49 rms, all with bath (shower). A/C TEL. 13,200 Drs ($55) single; 18,800 Drs ($78.35) double. No credit cards.

Just off Makriyánni Street, 1 long block south of the Acropolis, this attractive, modern hotel has large, arcaded picture windows and a slate-tiled rooftop bar. The spacious, double-height lobby includes a coffee shop and a breakfast lounge and bar with a view of the back garden. The rooms are simply furnished but carpeted and comfortable, with piped-in music. The top-floor rooms offer balconies.

✪ Marble House Pension. Odós Zinní 35A, Koukáki, 117 41 Athens. ☎ **01/923-4058** or 01/922-6461. 17 rms, 9 with bath (shower). TEL. 6,960 Drs ($29) single without bath, 5,600 Drs ($34) single with bath; 10,680 Drs ($44.50) double without bath, 11,800 Drs ($49.15) double with bath. Oct–May, rooms can be rented by the month for 70,000 Drs ($292). No credit cards.

Among the more intimate hostels, this is the friendliest place and offers the best value. There's a giant fuchsia bougainvillea climbing its marble facade at the end of a quiet cul-de-sac—a perfect place for kids to play. Although quite close to a major thoroughfare, the neat, efficient rooms are remarkably quiet, and they all have ceiling fans. Several of the front-facing rooms have balconies. Although the accommodations are basic, the personal service and convivial company are outstanding. The affable Thanos and his staff treat all guests like royalty. It's our favorite homey base for sightseeing; it's also a great place to stay if you have an early flight—they'll store your luggage for free. The Marble House is just 2 blocks from the Olympic Airways office on Syngroú Avenue (where you can also catch the bus to Piraeus) and a block from the trolleys that will whisk you to Pláka and Sýntagma.

Tony's Pension. Odós Zacharítsa 26 (off Propiléon St., 6 blocks from the Acropolis), 117 41, Athens. ☎ **01/923-0561.** 26 rms, all with bath (shower); 11 apts. TV TEL. 9,200 Drs ($38.35) single; 10,900 Drs ($45.40) double; 16,500 Drs ($68.75) apt. Monthly rentals available at 20% off the day rate. V.

Tony's Pension is a tastefully modern update of the wildly popular hostel the owner has been running since 1972. Each floor has a common kitchen and a TV lounge. Students, fashion models, and singles dominate the ever-lively scene at Tony's; if it's impossible for you to get a room here, good-natured Tony or his multilingual wife, Charo, will contact one of his pension-owner colleagues to try to arrange another accommodation for you. Eleven studio apartments offer kitchenettes, air-conditioning, and minibars.

WORTH A SPLURGE

Hotel Acropolis View. Odós Webster 10, Philopáppou, 117 42 Athens. ☎ **01/921-7303.** Fax 01/923-0705. 32 rms, all with bath. A/C TEL. 17,150 Drs ($71.45) single; 22,800 Drs ($95) double. Rates include breakfast. AE, EURO, MC, V.

This pretty little hotel on the slope of Philopáppou Hill just west of Makriyánni may suit the urge to splurge in some of our readers. It's on a quiet, winding lane between Propiléon and Rovértou Gálli streets, and some of its rooms and the rooftop bar live up to the name with a spectacular view of the Acropolis. The small rooms are equipped with most modern amenities and private bathrooms; many of the rooms have recently been renovated.

Hotel Phillipos. Odós Mitséon 3, Makriyánni, 117 42 Athens. ☎ **01/922-3611.** Fax 01/922-3615. 48 rms, all with bath. A/C TV TEL. 19,300 Drs ($80.40) single; 26,500 Drs ($110.40) double. Rates include breakfast. AE, DC, EURO, MC, V.

This is another hotel above our budget, but we're so pleased with it that we think it's worth a splurge. Completely renovated in 1994 in keeping with its sleek art deco design, it's amazingly quiet for its busy location, 3 blocks south of the Acropolis. The rooms are small but pretty in pink, and there's a laundry service.

NEAR MONASTIRÁKI

There are a few hotels near Monastiráki and the central market area, which bustles during the day but quiets down considerably at night. They're conveniently located near the metro stop, Pláka, and Sýntagma Square.

✪ **Attalos Hotel.** Odós Athinás 29, 105 54 Athens. ☎ **01/321-2801.** Fax 01/324-3124. 80 rms, all with bath. TEL. 9,200 Drs ($38.35) single; 11,500 Drs ($47.90) double; 16,900 Drs ($70.45) triple. Air-conditioning 2,000 Drs ($8.35) extra. AE, V.

This excellent-value lodging, 2 blocks north of the Monastiráki metro stop, has been popular with readers of this book and has been rising in our esteem. The entrance is nearly hidden by nearby businesses and the lobby is modest, but the rooms are exceptionally quiet and comfortable. (Those staying in the lower front rooms will probably want to spring for air-conditioning.) The staff is particularly capable, friendly, and helpful. The beautifully landscaped rooftop bar provides a superb view of the Acropolis and is a great place for a drink. The Attalos also offers free luggage storage and a discount for our readers.

Hotel Tempi. Odós Eólou 29, 105 51 Athens. ☎ **01/321-3175.** Fax 01/325-4179. 24 rms, 6 with shower only. 5,200 Drs ($21.65) single without bath; 8,625 Drs ($35.95) double without bath, 9,775 Drs ($40.75) double with shower only. AE, MC, V.

This cheap alternative for the student crowd is located on a pedestrian-only shopping street 3 blocks northeast of the Monastiráki metro stop. Pleasantly situated across from placid, car-free St. Irene Square, this well-managed, freshly painted lodging is a friendly place, if a bit worn. The homey touches include hallway murals of Greece, a laundry room with ironing facilities, free luggage storage, and a paperback-lending library. Six of the rooms have showers, but all toilets are shared.

AROUND EXÁRCHIA SQUARE

There are a couple of decent hotels near Exárchia and the National Archaeological Museum—good places to stay if you're especially interested in this extraordinary collection of ancient art.

Hotel Exarchion. Odós Themistokléous 55, 106 83 Athens. ☎ **01/360-1256.** Fax 01/360-3296. 49 rms, all with bath. TEL. 8,000 Drs ($33.35) single; 9,250 Drs ($38.55) double. No credit cards.

The modern Hotel Exarchion offers comfortable rooms, most of which have balconies. The lobby is decorated with handsome photographs of classical sites, and there's a large rooftop where you can eat or drink while you watch students debate in the square below.

Museum Hotel. Odós Bouboulínas 16, 106 82 Athens. ☎ **01/360-5611.** Fax 01/380-0057. 58 rms, all with bath (shower). TEL. 6,300 Drs ($26.25) single; 9,200 Drs ($38.35) double. Rates include breakfast. AE, DC, V.

This bright, pleasant hotel is so close to the National Archaeological Museum that all its balconies overlook the museum's tree-filled park. It's a good value in a good location—far from the madding crowd.

NEAR THE RAILROAD STATION

The only reason to stay in this area is for a convenient overnight between trains, saving time and taxi fare.

Hotel Nana. Odós Metaxá 27, 104 39 Athens. ☎ **01/884-2211.** Fax 01/882-3220. 50 rms, all with bath (shower). A/C TEL. 12,000 Drs ($50) single; 14,550 Drs ($60.65) double. No credit cards.

Just south of the park across from the Lárissa Station, the Nana provides clean, well-maintained rooms with some amenities, including air-conditioning. Request a rear-facing room to assure enough quiet for sleeping. There's 24-hour room service from the downstairs Nana Café, a popular local hangout.

SHOESTRING CHOICES

Several lodgings in Greece belong to the Greek Youth Hostel Federation (GYHF). For a complete listing, contact the Greek Tourist Organization (EOT) or, for further information, the **Greek Youth Hostel Federation,** Odós Dragatsaníou 4, 105 59 Athens (☎ **01/323-4107** or 01/323-7590).

Annabel's Youth Hostel. Odós Koumoundoúrou 28, 104 37 Athens. ☎ **01/524-5834.** 17 rooms (3 with bath), 36 beds. 4,500 Drs ($18.80) double without bath, 5,750 Drs ($23.95) double with bath; 2,000 Drs ($8.35) dorm bed. V.

This old hostel seems to be perpetually undergoing a change of management, but during our last visit we found it spruced up a bit and cleaner than ever. Even the neighborhood—3 blocks west of Omónia Square—showed signs of improvement.

Athens International Youth Hostel. Odós Victor Hugo 16, 104 37 Athens. ☎ **01/523-4170.** Fax 01/523-4015. 138 beds. 2,500 Drs ($10.40) dorm bed. Rates include breakfast. No credit cards.

This is by far the best hostel in Athens—a clear sign that the neighborhood west of Omónia Square is improving. The completely renovated rooms sleep two to four people in good, firm beds and provide private showers and lockers. To stay here, you must either join the IYHF—3,000 Drs ($12.50)—or pay an additional 500 Drs ($2.10) daily. There's a shared kitchen for use by members, a laundry facility, and no curfew.

Impressions

We are lovers of the beautiful yet simple in our tastes, and we cultivate the mind without loss of manliness.
                                   —Pericles, in Thucydides' *The Peloponnesian War,* ca. 430 B.C.

Hostel Aphrodite. Odós Einárdou 12 (at Michaíl Vodá, near Lárissa Station), 104 40 Athens. ☎ **01/226-6686.** Fax 01/822-0732. 28 rooms (8 with shower). 5,000 Drs ($20.85) single without bath; 6,000 Drs ($25.00) double without bath, 7,250 Drs ($30.20) double with bath; 7,250 Drs ($30.20) triple without bath; 9,200 Drs ($38.35) quad with bath. No credit cards.

This clean, well-maintained hostel offers some of the best budget accommodations in Athens, though its location—northeast of the railway stations, 5 blocks northwest of Victoria Square—is inconvenient. The hostel offers hot showers, a safe for valuables, an information desk, a sun roof, and free luggage storage. The basement breakfast room also serves as a gathering place for travelers who want to exchange information.

YWCA. Odós Amerikís 11, 105 62 Athens. ☎ **01/362-4291.** 30 rooms, 80 beds. 4,600 Drs ($19.15) single without bath, 6,325 Drs ($26.35) single with bath; 7,200 Drs ($30) double without bath, 9,000 Drs ($37.50) double with bath; 9,200 Drs ($38.35) triple without bath. No credit cards. Closed Dec–Jan 15.

Women will find spotless lodging at bargain prices at the YWCA (XEN in Greek), which is located a block off Panepistimíou Street. A few rooms are available for married couples. Call or write ahead, since this is a convenient and popular place.

4 Great Deals on Dining

The following is a quick rundown of our favorite restaurants by specialty.

Of the **tavernas,** the best (although a splurge choice) is **Myrtia,** near the Olympic Stadium. The best combination of food and view of the Acropolis is **Taverna Strófi,** in Koukáki. For music and a good casual Greek place, try **Taverna Xinos** in Pláka. The latter two are open evenings (closed Sunday). Good, moderately priced food, and a young and lively crowd can be found at **Socrates' Prison** in Makriyánni.

For **continental cuisine,** the best European old-world ambience with homemade light snacks and desserts is found at **To Tristrato** in Pláka.

A good **vegetarian** restaurant is hard to find, but most tavernas serve a variety of vegetable dishes. One of our reader's recommendations is the **Eden Vegetarian Restaurant.**

Ouzerís, casual bars, are a superb Greek invention, a place to nurse an *oúzo* (a strong, anise-flavored liquor) and munch on varied appetizers *(mezédes).* Our favorite Athens ouzerí is **Yiali Kafines** in Kolonáki, but it's closed in the summer. **Kouklis Ouzerí** is a good backup.

For a midday break, midafternoon lift, or late-night treat of **dessert and coffee,** try **Dionysos-Zonar's** near Sýntagma Square, a typical ice-cream and confection parlor. The best array of ice cream is at the **Firenze Gelateria Pasticceria,** in Koukáki. For stand-up coffee and sweets, we like the murals and 1930s brass decor and great java blends of the **Brazilian** off Sýntagma Square.

SÝNTAGMA SQUARE

The center of Athens offers plenty of eating choices, from fast food to fine Chinese cuisine.

Apotso's. Odós Panepistimíou 10. ☎ **01/363-7046.** Reservations not required. Most items 350–2,000 Drs ($1.45–$8.35). No credit cards. Mon–Fri 11am–5pm, Sat 11am–4pm. GREEK.

This classic, high-ceilinged taverna, decorated with old tin signs, wine and oúzo bottles, and tiny marble-top tables, is tucked away at the end of a cul-de-sac between some of Sýntagma Square's best shops. Apotso's provides good, moderately priced food in an authentically Athenian environment that attracts lots of shoppers and

Athens Dining

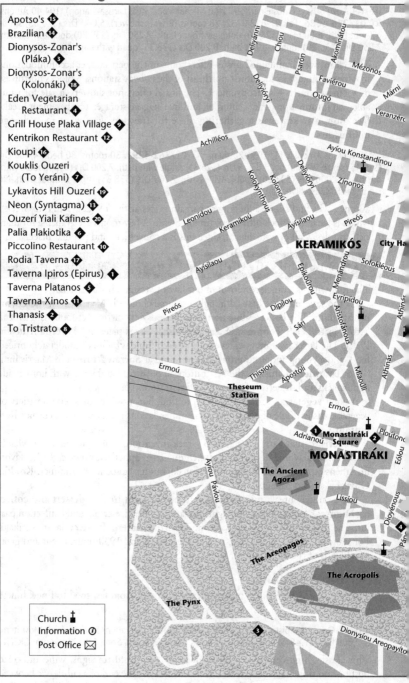

Church ✝
Information ⑦
Post Office ✉

9612

90

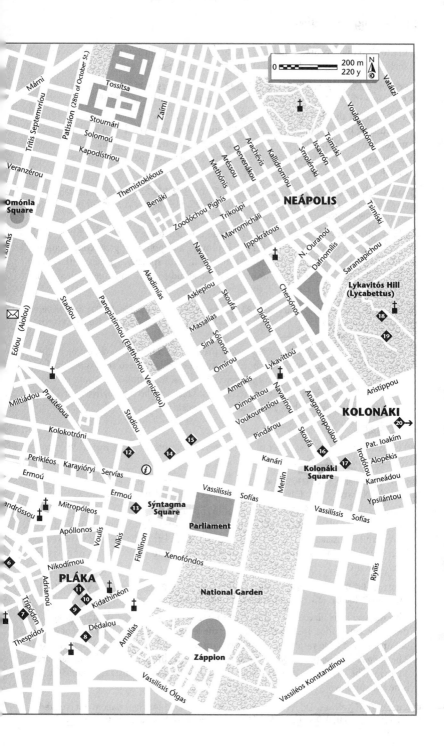

midtown businesspeople at lunch. *Mezédes* (appetizers), delicious plates of fresh salad, small fried fish, *keftédes* (meatballs), and regional cheeses are served.

Brazilian. Odós Voukourestíou 1. ☎ **01/323-5463.** Coffee/snacks 360–1,100 Drs ($1.50–$4.60). Mon–Fri 7am–8:30pm, Sat 7am–4pm (until 9pm in winter). COFFEE BAR.

Turn right at the Wendy's on Sýntagma Square, walk half a block, and you'll find the bustling Brazilian on the left—a 1930s-style coffeehouse filled with working Athenians, newspaper-reading travelers, or shoppers deep in conversation. Inside is our favorite spot to stand and drink a quick espresso or grab a pastry or sandwich. You can also sit outside.

✪ Kentrikon Restaurant. Odós Kolokotróni 3. ☎ **01/323-2482.** Reservations not required. Main courses 1,500–4,200 Drs ($6.25–$17.50). AE, DC, EURO, MC, V. Mon–Fri noon–6pm. GREEK/INTERNATIONAL.

Many discerning travelers try to put aside a lunch hour for this spacious, air-conditioned upscale restaurant. Service is prompt and polite—a great combination when you're waiting for a delectable lamb ragoût with spinach, chicken with okra, or the Kentrikón's special macaroni. Don't be afraid to walk into the kitchen and peek into the pots; it is, after all, the Greek way.

Neon. Odós Mitropóleos 3. ☎ **01/322-8155.** Snacks 200–650 Drs (85¢–$2.70); sandwiches 450–900 Drs ($1.90–$3.75); main courses 1,000–2,500 Drs ($4.15–$10.40). No credit cards. Daily 8am–2am. INTERNATIONAL.

This new addition to the Neon chain is convenient, if not quite as charming as the original restored kafeníon on Omónia Square. The sleek art deco style is perfect for the no-nonsense food and cafeteria service. You're sure to find something to your taste—maybe a Mexican omelet, a Green Forest salad, spaghetti bolognese, salad bar, or sweets ranging from Black Forest cake to tiramisù.

KOLONÁKI

This is an upscale area, so most of Kolonáki's restaurants are more expensive; some are also smoky and more than a bit snobby.

Kioupi. 4 Kolonáki Sq. ☎ **01/361-4033.** Reservations not required. Meals 1,200–2,300 Drs ($5–$9.60). No credit cards. Daily 11am–11pm. Closed evenings in summer. GREEK.

The only decent budget place we know of in this expensive area is just northwest off the square on Odós Skoufá. You'll find the usual Greek dishes, such as stuffed tomatoes and moussaká, and occasionally even fish. Turn left at the bottom of the steps, point out what appeals to you, and it will be brought to your table by one of the friendly waiters.

Lykavittos Hill Ouzerí. Lykavittós Hill (above Kolonáki Sq.). Reservations not required. Main courses 750–2,400 Drs ($3.15–$10). No credit cards. Daily 11am–midnight. GREEK.

This magical little place is one of our favorite spots in Athens. It's about halfway up the hill by car or foot. It's a popular bar for the leisurely enjoyment of a glass of oúzo or wine, with a wide variety of well-priced and reasonably tasty *mezédes* (appetizers). The *tirópita* (cheese pie), *saganáki* (fried cheese), and chicken and lamb souvláki are all good. The view from here, over the city to Piraeus and the distant Saronic Gulf, is best at sundown.

✪ Ouzerí Yiali Kafines. Odós Ploutárchou 18. ☎ **01/722-5846.** Reservations not required. Menu items 600–3,000 Drs ($2.50–$12.50). No credit cards. Mon–Sat 12:30–5pm and 8pm–2am. GREEK.

⑪ Affordable Family-Friendly Restaurants

Neon *(see page 92)*   For its varied and tasty choices, quick service, and reasonable prices, this cafeteria is a great place to relax after a full morning of shopping or sightseeing.

Dionysos-Zonar's *(see page 96)*   A must stop at Lykavittós Hill, if only for the spectacular view of Athens. Take the funicular or walk up the hill (good exercise for the whole family) and splurge on a snack. Try the Dionysos-Zónar's off Sýntagma Square for some good desserts at a more convenient location.

Floka   Athens's oldest and best chain of pâtisseries has beautiful desserts that taste as good as they look. There are convenient branches near Sýntagma, in the arcade at the corner of Panepistimíou and Voukourestíou, and south of the Acropolis at Makriyánni and Dimitrakopoúlou.

The owners of Yiali Kafines (the name is Turkish but everything else is Greek) head for the islands in the summer, so many readers will miss this great little treat. If you get lucky and find it open, try the *seftaliés* (Cypriot meatballs), codfish croquettes with skordaliá, and tabbouleh salad. Sit outside on the quiet side street and knock down a few ouzos; you'll go away happy.

Rodia Taverna. Odós Aristípou 44. ☎ **01/722-9883.** Reservations not required. Main courses 600–2,500 Drs ($2.50–$10.40). No credit cards. Mon–Sat 8pm–2am. GREEK.

This is a romantic, old-fashioned taverna below street level in one of Kolonáki's oldest homes, at the foot of Lykavittós Hill. In the winter meals are served in Rodiá's dark interior, where patterned tile floors, lace curtains, and kegs of the house *krassí* (wine) serve as decoration. At other times small tables are placed out in the vine-shaded back garden. Specials include octopus in mustard sauce; oregano or lemon beef; fluffy, divine *bourékkis;* and, for dessert, fresh halvá.

WORTH A SPLURGE

Dionysos-Zonar's. Atop Lykavittós Hill. ☎ **01/722-6374.** Reservations recommended. Main courses 2,500–7,200 Drs ($10.40–$30). AE, DC, MC, V. Daily noon–11pm. Closed Jan 31–Feb 28. CONTINENTAL.

This Dionysos can be reached by the funicular that begins at the head of Ploutárchou Street above Kolonáki Square. The funicular deposits you at the top of Athens's highest peak, just perfect for an overview of the glittering city, especially at sunset. This branch of Dionysos also features an international menu, and at lunch offers salads and sandwiches for 1,000 to 3,400 Drs ($4.15 to $14.15).

PLÁKA

Pláka is the most popular neighborhood for dining, so you'll find plenty of choices. We don't like restaurants that have staff members drag us in off the street; unless a restaurant really appeals to you, resist any efforts to get you inside the door. (Remember: If the food is really good, a restaurant won't need to resort to such tactics.)

Grill House Plaka Village. Odós Kydathinéon 28. ☎ **01/324-6229.** Most items 720–3,000 Drs ($3–$12.50). No credit cards. Daily 11am–1pm. GREEK.

If you're not in the mood to sit down and make a big production of a meal, this simple, clean, family-run gyro joint in the heart of Pláka is a good choice. For 1,500

Drs ($6.25) you get a savory plate with a skewer of pork or chicken souvláki, pita bread, salad, fries, and some tzatzíki.

Kouklis Ouzeri (To Yeráni). Odós Tripodón 14. ☎ **01/324-7605.** Reservations not required. Most items 400–800 Drs ($1.65–$3.35). No credit cards. Daily 11am–2am. GREEK.

Continue up Kydathinéon to Théspidos and climb toward the Acropolis to find this popular old favorite with a small terrace. Diners are presented with a large tray containing about a dozen plates of *mezédes:* appetizer portions of fried fish, beans, grilled eggplant, taramosalata, cucumber-and-tomato salad, olives, fried cheese, sausages, and other seasonal specialties; choose those that appeal to you. With hearty bread and a liter of the house *krassí* (wine) (850 Drs/$3.55), you can have a substantial meal on a budget.

Palia Plakiotika. Odós Lissíou 26. ☎ **01/322-8722.** Reservations required on weekends. Main courses 1,600–4,000 Drs ($6.65–$16.65); fixed-price dinner 4,500 Drs ($18.75). No credit cards. Daily 7pm–2am. GREEK.

As the name implies in Greek, this is one of the oldest tavernas in Pláka. This beautiful split-level garden, with vines tumbling down its trellised walls, provides a refreshing sanctuary on a hot summer's night. The typical taverna fare is a bit more expensive than that offered by some of the competition, but we think it's worth the extra cost since there's Greek music and the lively local crowd frequently joins in.

Piccolino Restaurant. Odós Sotíros 26 (at Kydathinéon). ☎ **01/324-6692.** Reservations not required. Main courses 1,200–4,500 Drs ($5–$18.75). AE, DC, MC, V. Daily 11am–2am. GREEK/ITALIAN.

We had ignored this excellent place just west of the Metamorphosi Church (probably because of the many tourist traps around it) until several readers raved about its food and friendly service. We found the moussaká delicious, with a sweet-spicy aroma, and the chicken souvláki moist and tender, both served in ample portions by an attentive staff.

We took our friends Monika and Stavros back for their review, and they were also enthusiastic.

Taverna Platanos. Odós Dioyénous 4. ☎ **01/322-0666.** Reservations not required. Main courses 1,500–2,400 Drs ($6.25–$10). No credit cards. Mon–Sat noon–4:30pm and 8pm–midnight. GREEK.

This is one of the last of a vanishing species—a taverna in Pláka that's still truly Greek. The food is traditional and free of the shortcuts usually taken to rip off tourists (such as frozen vegetables and microwave moussaká). Tables are scattered around a shaded bend in this quiet back lane near the Agorá, and time seems to stand still with the rhythmic sounds of cicadas under the noonday sun. We like Platanos for the hearty fare and timeless atmosphere.

✪ Taverna Xinos. Odós Angélou Yéronda 4. ☎ **01/322-1065.** Reservations recommended. Main courses 2,000–2,800 Drs ($8.35–$11.65). No credit cards. Mon–Fri 8pm–12:30am. Closed July. GREEK.

This place is a classic. Tucked in back of a narrow, pebble-paved lane near Iperídou Street, its walls graced with Dionysian folk-art murals, Xinos offers superb food to the accompaniment of live music. Its informal atmosphere draws guests in aloha shirts as well as the suit-and-tie crowd. It's highly recommended by Greeks, who consider it one of the finest restaurants in Athens. (Some of our readers, however, have complained about the service. We recommend that you make reservations for after 9pm.) Try the excellent lemony stuffed grape leaves, the tasty moussaká with fresh ground spices, the lamb fricassee in an egg-lemon and dill sauce, or the veal stew with tomatoes and potatoes.

✪ **To Tristrato.** Odós Dédalou 34. ☎ **01/324-4472.** Reservations not required. Light meals 960–2,280 Drs ($4–$9.50). No credit cards. Mon–Fri 2pm–midnight, Sat–Sun 11am–midnight. Closed Aug. SNACKS/DESSERTS.

This is one of our favorite light-meal and dessert places—a small 1920s-style tearoom adjoining a triangular rose garden near Ayíou Yéronda Square. Run by a group of lovely women, this New Age cafe has it all: fresh fruits and yogurt, omelets, fresh-squeezed juices, divine cakes—everything healthy and homemade. To Tristrato isn't cheap, but it's the perfect spot for a leisurely weekend brunch, afternoon tea, light supper, or late-night dessert.

MAKRIYÁNNI/KOUKÁKI

The neighborhoods south of the Acropolis—a short walk from Pláka—have several fine restaurants, and they're rarely jammed with tourists.

✪ **Firenze Gelateria Pasticceria.** Odós Dimitrakopoúlou 42. ☎ **01/922-7156.** Pastries and ice cream 900–1,800 Drs ($3.75–$7.50). No credit cards. Daily 10am–2am. DESSERTS.

As you explore Athens, you'll pass an endless stream of cafes serving coffee and desserts (most of which, we think, are made in the same subterranean kitchen and beamed all over the city). Pass them all by for this comfortable and hip spot at the corner of shady Drákou Street. Ice cream lovers from all over the city embrace the superb *gelati* and *graniti* (sorbets), with such fruit flavors as strawberry, melon, banana, kiwi, and more, as pure and fresh as can be. The pastries—tarts, cheesecakes, rich cream cakes—are superior, with cappuccino and espresso that are the best in town. Outdoors under the trees or in the marbled modern indoor space, you'll find it well worth the walk.

Meltemi. Odós Zinní 26. ☎ **01/902-8230.** Reservations not required. Menu items 600–2,150 Drs ($2.50–$8.95). No credit cards. Mon–Sat noon–1:30am. GREEK.

If you're arriving at or leaving from the Olympic Airways office on Syngroú Avenue at Zinní, this nearby ouzerí is a superb stopover for a light meal and drink. Trees and big white umbrellas shade the distinctive blue chairs and tables. Choose from the fresh shrimp, eggplant with grilled cheese, homemade sausages, various salads, daily specials—sophisticated Greek cuisine at its best.

Panathinea Pizzeria/Cafeteria. Odós Makriyánni 27–29. ☎ **01/923-3721.** Reservations not required. Main courses 850–2,600 ($3.55–$10.85). V. Daily 8:30am–1am. GREEK/INTERNATIONAL.

Our friend Suzanna recommended this unpretentious place, across from the Center for Acropolis Studies, for its ample "English" breakfast. It soon became John's favorite budget stop, and he can personally recommend the Greek plate, country salad, moussaká, chicken souvláki, rigatoni with four cheeses, and almost any pizza.

Readers Recommend

Eden Vegetarian Restaurant, Odós Lissíou 12 (at Mnesikléous), Pláka (☎ **01/324-8858**). "Not to be missed, even if you're not a vegetarian. I've sampled nearly the entire menu and never had a disappointment. Don't miss the tzatziki if you're a garlic fan. For dessert try their yogurt with honey and walnuts."

—Kathryn A. Price, Woodland Hills, Calif.

Socrates' Prison. Odós Mitséon 20. ☎ **01/922-3434.** Reservations not required. Main courses 1,250–2,700 Drs ($5.20–$11.25). V. Mon–Sat 7pm–1am. Closed Aug. GREEK/CONTINENTAL.

This favorite of discerning travelers and hip young locals is only a block south of the Acropolis. You dine at long, family-style tables or outdoors in summer. The meat dishes are well prepared and come in large portions, the salads are fresh, and the retsína is flavorful. New additions on the menu include such continental dishes as pork roll stuffed with vegetables and salade niçoise.

✪ **Taverna Strófi.** Odós Rovértou Gálli 25. ☎ **01/921-4130.** Reservations recommended in summer. Main courses 1,200–3,000 Drs ($5–$12.50). AE, DC, MC, V. Mon–Sat 7pm–2am. GREEK.

The stunning Acropolis vista from the rooftop garden, the excellent food, and the sophisticated ambience draw Athens's arts patrons and performers from the Odeum of Herod Atticus across the road. Vassilis and Damiano Manologlou offer a varied cuisine, marked by interesting cheeses, fine olive oils, and the freshest of ingredients. We especially like the superb *mezédes* (appetizers) and the excellent lamb and veal courses. In the winter the Manóloglous add a Saturday brunch with 20 *mezédes* and oúzo. Make your summer reservations for 10pm and you can avoid the tourist crush and sometimes hurried service.

WORTH A SPLURGE

Dionysos-Zonar's. Dionysíou Aeropayítou Ave. (southwest of the Acropolis). ☎ **01/923-1936.** Reservations recommended. Main courses 2,500–7,200 Drs ($10.40–$30). AE, DC, MC, V. Daily noon–11pm. CONTINENTAL.

On the side of Philopáppou Hill, commanding a magnificent view of the Acropolis, is one of the branches of Dionysos. The decor is modern and not very interesting, and the international menu is high-priced (there's an undistinguished coffee shop on the lower level). But nothing can detract from the view of the Parthenon, especially after 9:30pm, during the sound-and-light show.

MONASTIRÁKI

Taverna Ipiros (Epirus). 15 Ayíou Philíppou Sq. ☎ **01/324-5572.** Main courses 1,200–2,000 Drs ($5–$8.35). No credit cards. Daily noon–midnight. GREEK.

This good budget place, a couple of blocks west of the Monastiráki metro stop on a crowded little square in the heart of the flea market, serves good regulation Greek food in generous portions at fair prices. (Be sure to take a table that belongs to this unpretentious little place, rather than one belonging to a competitor.)

Thanasis. Odós Mitropóleos 69. ☎ **01/324-4705.** Reservations not required. Main courses 350–2,200 Drs ($1.45–$9.15). No credit cards. Daily 9am–2am. GREEK.

Thanasis is the hottest souvláki stand in town, conveniently located near the Monastiráki metro station. Locals flock here for the takeouts, and taxi drivers stopping for a quick snack sometimes block the street during the day. The grill is smoking as flea market vendors and tourists chow down on the delicious souvláki and excellent french fries. The atmosphere is informal and the price is right. A great budget choice.

Exploring Athens 5

After several days, most visitors to Athens, especially first-timers, seem to have had enough of the congested capital. The smog, the heat (in July and August), and the noise can become rather oppressive. So, before you, too, begin to falter, go straight to the heart of the city—the ancient Acropolis, high above the frenetic modern metropolis. There, amid the silent ruins, you'll find tranquillity, cool breezes, and the inspiration of 2,500 years of history.

The magnificent achievements of the 5th century B.C., concentrated on this 512-foot-tall limestone mound, still dominate the cityscape. No matter how far the boundaries of Athens extend, the Acropolis remains the storehouse of the city's soul. And for good reason. The Athens of Pericles was a historical epiphany: The idea of political democracy; the outpouring of revolutionary forms of drama, poetry, philosophy, and science; and the creation of extraordinary works of art and architecture set off an explosion that, within a century and a half, would shake the world.

A visit to the Acropolis, the Odeum of Herod Atticus at the foot of the hill, and the nearby Agorá (the ancient marketplace, or *archéa agorá* in Greek) will move you with the power and nobility of the ancient buildings that still stand there, albeit in various states of ruin. For amid their walls and columns, in this city that Pericles called the "school of Hellas," there once flourished some of the greatest poets and thinkers of Western civilization: the philosophers Socrates, Plato, and Aristotle; the dramatists Aeschylus, Sophocles, and Euripides; the comic poet Aristophanes; the historians Herodotus, Thucydides, and Xenophon; the orators Lysias, Isocrates, and Demosthenes. Their tragedies and comedies are still performed today; their philosophical and historical works are still studied and debated; their speeches—on liberty and freedom of thought and the importance of each citizen taking part in the affairs of his state—are still a source of inspiration.

SUGGESTED ITINERARIES

If You Have 1 Day

If you have only 1 day in Athens, head first for the Acropolis and then visit the National Archaeological Museum. In the evening, go listen to some bouzouki or *rebétika*.

If You Have 2 Days

Spend your first day as outlined above. On day 2, stroll through Pláka, look at other archaeological sites, and visit the Goulandris Museum of Cycladic and Ancient Greek Art.

If You Have 3 Days

A visit of 3 days will enable you to be more leisurely. In addition to the suggestions given above, try the cafes in Mitrópoleos Square or the National Gardens for people-watching. Sample different kinds of Greek food and wine, and shop for trinkets in the flea market or better souvenirs in Pláka.

1 The Acropolis

Many of the ancient city-states in Greece were built around a high promontory of land called an *acropolis*. This "high city" was fortified for better defense, and the population would withdraw there for refuge from marauding forces. Since it was higher (and therefore closer to the gods), the acropolis was also a place of worship. The Acropolis of Athens was considered a sacred spot even in Neolithic times. Archaeological evidence suggests that mystical cult worship was practiced there as long as 5,000 years ago.

Beginning in the 7th century B.C., monumental temples and sacred buildings were constructed. In 480 B.C. the Persians invaded Athens and burned the city and the Acropolis structures. After the Greek naval victory at Salamís and land battle at Plataea, the returning Athenians swore that they would leave the temples in ruins as an eternal reminder of the barbarity of the invaders. (Excavations between 1885 and 1891 led to the discovery of the "Persian V Deposit," pits filled with sculptural and architectural fragments that had been carefully buried after this destruction.) The Athenians soon reconsidered their pledge, and under Pericles, the wealthy, newly democratic, and invigorated city-state began an intensive rebuilding program.

One of the best guides to the site is *The Acropolis* (Ekdotiki), written by the late Greek archaeologist Manolis Andronikos. It includes illustrations that attempt to re-create the Acropolis as it once was.

Only four major buildings remain, but even in ruins they still convey the grace, style, and technical achievement of the Golden Age.

ADMISSION & OPEN HOURS   Admission to the entire site and the museum is 2,000 Drs ($8.35) for adults, 1,500 Drs ($6.25) for senior citizens, and 1,000 Drs ($4.15) for students. It's free on Sunday and public holidays.

The site is open Monday to Friday from 8am to 6:30pm, and on Saturday, Sunday, and holidays from 8:30am to 2:30pm. The museum doesn't open until 11am on Monday, and in the winter (November to March) the site and museum close at 5pm.

The entrance to the Acropolis is on the west end, and it can be approached from the north by bearing south from Monastiráki past the Roman Forum or from the south via Dionysíou Areopayítou Street from just west of the Odeum of Herodes Atticus.

THE PROPYLAEA

This grand entryway, begun in 437 B.C., led worshippers from the temporal world into the spiritual atmosphere of the sanctuary. The architect Mnesicles' graceful structure introduced a revolutionary design concept: the mixture of Doric and Ionic principles. The Propylaea has an outer and an inner facade of six Doric columns, which

The Athens Festival

Since 1955 the Athens Festival, held in one of the world's most beautiful ancient theaters, the Odeum of Herod Atticus (built in A.D. 161 and reconstructed after World War II) has attracted international audiences with theater, ballet, and musical performances by well-known traditional and modern artists. Martha Graham's and Maurice Béjart's companies have performed in a revival of the Dionysia performances begun by Peisistratus, ruler of Athens during the 6th century B.C. The Bolshoi and Kirov ballets, the London Philharmonic, the Deutsche Staatsoper Berlin, and many other internationally acclaimed groups have also been featured. The celebrated National Theater of Greece stages classical Greek dramas in modern Greek. In recent years we've caught performances as diverse as Gounod's *Faust* and the rhythm sensation *Stomp!* Some performances are given in the open-air theater on Lykavittós Hill, as well as at the ancient theater at Epidaurus, in the Peloponnese.

Performances are often sold out well in advance. Contact the Greek Tourist Organization (EOT) for the current schedule or call the Athens Festival (☎ **01/323-2771** or 01/322-3111) for information. Tickets go on sale 2 weeks prior to the performance at the **Athens Festival Box Office,** Odós Stadíou 4 (in a pedestrian shopping mall off Voukourestíou Street near Sýntagma Square); the box office is open daily from 8:30am to 2pm and 5 to 7pm. Tickets for the Epidaurus Theater Festival (see chapter 7, "The Peloponnese") can also be purchased here. Athens Festival tickets cost 900 to 11,500 Drs ($3.75 to $47.90); any remaining seats can be purchased from the Herod Atticus box office between 6:30 and 9pm on the day of the performance. Check with the EOT or the *Athens News* or *Athenscope* (at newsstands) for festival information.

created five entryways on both sides of the building. To support the massive roof, columns in the lighter, more graceful Ionic style were installed inside as well.

THE TEMPLE OF ATHENA NIKE

The Temple of Athena Nike is situated to the right of the Propylaea and is dramatically visible from the upper staircase to the Acropolis plateau. This elegant, white-marble monument was built over the site of an earlier altar dedicated to the goddess of Victory for the Panathenaic Festival almost 150 years before.

Pericles commissioned the architect Callicrates to build a new temple at a time when Athens was about to embark on the Peloponnesian War. In 425 B.C. an additional protective parapet, decorated with a sculptural frieze expressing the Athenians' hope for final victory, was added to the temple. Fragments of this frieze, including the lovely 5th-century B.C. *Nike Unlacing Her Sandals,* can now be seen in the Acropolis Museum (behind the Parthenon; see below).

THE ERECHTHEUM

As you pass through the Propylaea, you'll see the Erechtheum on your left, on a site where the Ancient Temple, dedicated to Poseidon, god of the spring that bubbled up life-giving water to previous generations of Acropolis inhabitants, and to Athena, goddess of the sustaining olive tree, once stood. Pericles ordered this new temple built to replace the one burned by the Persians. Work on the temple was halted by the Peloponnesian War and by Pericles' sudden death (from a plague), but it resumed in 421 B.C.

Athens Attractions

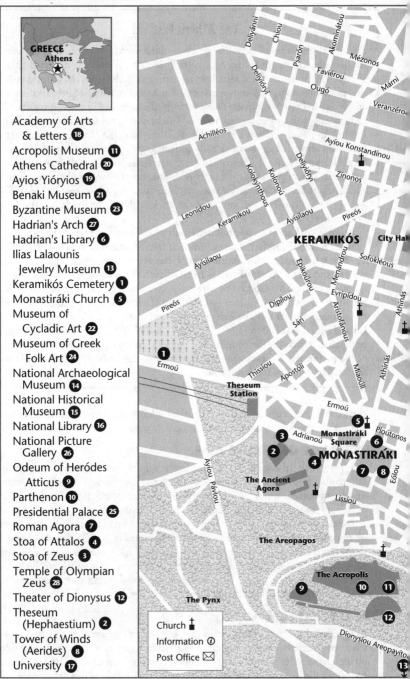

Academy of Arts
& Letters **18**

Acropolis Museum **11**

Athens Cathedral **20**

Ayios Yióryios **19**

Benaki Museum **21**

Byzantine Museum **23**

Hadrian's Arch **27**

Hadrian's Library **6**

Ilias Lalaounis
Jewelry Museum **13**

Keramikós Cemetery **1**

Monastiráki Church **5**

Museum of
Cycladic Art **22**

Museum of Greek
Folk Art **24**

National Archaeological
Museum **14**

National Historical
Museum **15**

National Library **16**

National Picture
Gallery **26**

Odeum of Heródes
Atticus **9**

Parthenon **10**

Presidential Palace **25**

Roman Agora **7**

Stoa of Attalos **4**

Stoa of Zeus **3**

Temple of Olympian
Zeus **28**

Theater of Dionysus **12**

Theseum
(Hephaestium) **2**

Tower of Winds
(Aerides) **8**

University **17**

3-0516

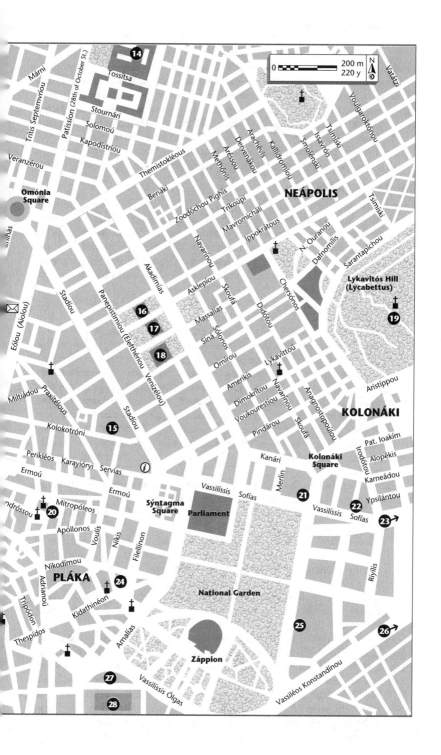

The Erechtheum has three basic parts: the main temple, the northern extension, and the famous Porch of the Maidens. The main temple is divided in order to accommodate the two deities to whom it is dedicated—Athena (the eastern half) and Poseidon (the western half). The covered porch, used in rituals, had graceful stone maidens, called Caryatides, instead of columns. The original five maidens have parted ways: One sailed with Lord Elgin to London in the early 19th century and is now in the British Museum; more recently her four sisters have also been removed, because of Athens's corrosive pollution, to the Acropolis Museum. The concrete copies that now appear in their place lack the grace of the originals.

THE PARTHENON

The most magnificent of structures, the ✪ **Parthenon,** is sadly suffering from the effects of Athens's *néfos,* the cloud of sulfur dioxide that often hangs over the city; the *néfos* combines with rain and dew to create an acid rain that dissolves the marble first into plaster and then into dust. Fortunately, the Greek government, with the assistance of the United Nations, has already been able to undertake much preservation work with special funds and the talents of an international advisory committee of architects and scientists.

The Parthenon is the largest Doric temple ever completed in Greece, and it's the only one made entirely of Pentelic marble, from Mt. Pentelicus, northeast of Athens. Most of it was built in 9 years (447–438 B.C.) at an extravagant cost.

Pericles commissioned the architects Ictinus and Callicrates to design a temple that would give Athenians "eternal honor." The sculptor Phidias insisted that it be wide enough and tall enough to house his planned 40-foot-high statue of Athena Parthenos (Virgin), to be made of gold and ivory. The design followed much of the floor plan of the original temple but was expanded to include 8 columns on its shorter sides and 17 on its longer sides, thereby meeting the classical requirement that the long sides must be twice as long, plus 1 column more to add grace. Every stone in the structure is trapezoidal in shape and was cut to fit its own unique position. Iron support beams, where needed, were sheathed in flexible lead to allow for expansion and to prevent corrosion.

Phidias is credited as the master of the Parthenon because of the extensive sculptural work he and his students created for the facade. Fragments of Athena's fight against the Giants (*Gigantomachy*), from the building's eastern side, can be seen in the Acropolis Museum.

The famous Parthenon frieze (most of which comprises the Elgin Marbles now in the British Museum in London) depicted the Panathenaic Procession, the annual event that drew hundreds of thousands of worshippers to the Acropolis, wending their way up the hillside, bearing gifts, children, and the aged in hand. The individuality and expressiveness of these Athenians is impressive; even the worn and pollution-eroded frieze left in place on the western side of the Parthenon evokes their former beauty.

In the early Christian era the Parthenon was turned into a church by the Byzantine emperor Theodosius II. Later the Franks had its wall crenelated and constructed a tower in the Propylaea. In the 15th century it became a mosque for Turkish conquerors, who kept a harem in the Erechtheum. Turned into a powder store, it was hit in 1687 by a Venetian bombardment, which caused 28 columns to fall, along with most of the interior cella; much of Phidias's frieze was also destroyed. The Turks masked the disfigurement with the trappings of a mosque, replete with minaret. Earlier, the Propylaea, also filled with gunpowder, was nearly destroyed when it was

Above the low roofs of Athens the Acropolis rises on its pedestal of rock: astonishing, dramatic, divine, with at the same time the look of a phantom.
—Edmund Wilson, *Europe Without Baedeker,* 1947

Since 146 B.C. Greece has been selling foreigners the Age of Pericles, and this is what meets the traveler on arrival.
—Kevin Andrews, *Athens,* 1967

struck by lightning. Indignities never cease—in 1981 the Parthenon was jolted more than an inch off its base by an earthquake.

After the Turks left (in 1834), efforts were undertaken to try to restore some of the ruins. Much was missing. Several years earlier Thomas Bruce, earl of Elgin and ambassador to the sultan, had obtained permission from the Turks to diagram, analyze, and finally take away, for "safekeeping," the carved stones and masonry that remained on the Acropolis—and they're still in the British Museum. The Greeks deeply resent the fact that some of their finest artifacts from antiquity are housed in a foreign land, and they've been trying to repatriate them. (You might recall the efforts of a former minister of culture, Melina Mercouri.)

ACROPOLIS MUSEUM

A discreet white building just behind the Parthenon houses a small collection of items from the Acropolis; there's some superb sculpture, including the Gigantomachy pediment from the Ancient Temple to Athena that had previously stood on the site of the Erechtheum. There are a few extraordinary Classical-era sculptures attributed to Phidias, which do justice to his reputation. The large collection of *korae* (statues of the young women who attended Athena) are particularly beautiful. In their strong faces, bright eyes, and robust figures we can trace the lineage of many of the Greeks we see today. Some coloration is still preserved on their pure marble surface. (We might be repulsed if we could see the Acropolis and its sculpture painted in their original, vivid colors!)

OTHER MONUMENTS AT THE ACROPOLIS

A major thoroughfare, Dionysíou Aeropayítou, runs below and parallel to the south side of the Acropolis rock. At its eastern end, at the edge of the Pláka, are the rocky remains of the 5th-century B.C. **Theater of Dionysos,** the birthplace of drama, where as many as 13,000 eager Athenians came to watch works by Aeschylus, Sophocles, Euripides, and Aristophanes. Next to it was the site of the Asclepium, built when Socrates brought that cult worship to Athens.

The long, arcaded **Stoa of Eumenes,** built by the king of Pergamum in the 2nd century B.C., runs west to the **Odeum of Herodes Atticus.** Herod (Herodes), an important patron of the arts, used his enormous wealth to create many monuments in Athens. This 5,000-seat roofed theater was built between A.D. 161 and 174 for his wife, Regilla. The theater impressed audiences of the day with its mosaic floor, white-marble seats, and huge cedar roof. The odeum is open only for performances, but it can be viewed from above, near the ticket booth to the Acropolis.

The **Theater of Dionysos** (☎ 01/322-4625) is open daily from 9am to 2:30pm. Admission is 500 Drs ($2.10) for adults, 400 Drs ($1.65) for seniors, and 300 Drs ($1.25) for students.

The **Center for Acropolis Studies,** on Odós Makriyáni, southeast of the Acropolis (☎ 01/923-9381), is open daily from 9am to 3pm; admission is free. Inside are plaster casts of most of the significant sculpture from the Parthenon and Erechtheum. In the main gallery upstairs is a sketch depicting the explosion that destroyed much of the Parthenon 300 years ago while it served as a Turkish munitions depot. Many vintage photos and drawings are displayed as well. Out back, archaeology students are hard at work, uncovering new layers of ancient Athens.

HOW TO SEE THEATER PERFORMANCES AT THE ACROPOLIS

Today the partially restored Theater of Herod continues to impress audiences at the **Athens Festival** with its beauty of proportion and style.

Tickets can be bought from the office of the Athens Festival at Odós Stadíou 4, just off Sýntagma Square (☎ 01/322-1459).

2 Sights Near the Acropolis

The Ancient Greek Agorá. Just north of the Acropolis. Admission (museum and archaeological site) 1,200 Drs ($5) adults, 900 Drs ($3.75) seniors, 600 Drs ($2.50) students. Museum, Tues–Sun 8:30am–3pm.

The huge, open-air excavation site called the Agorá covers the plain just north of the Acropolis. From Monastiráki, the flea market area and its metro station, you can enter the scene of archaeological work that in the past 50 years has turned up an enormous number of artifacts, along with a great deal of information about life in the Hellenistic period.

The Agorá, or marketplace, was the center of political and social life. A huge fire that roared through Athens's present-day market in 1884 helped to reveal these enormously important ruins.

If you walk down Adrianoú Street, you'll see eight elegant Corinthian columns that line the side of **Hadrian's Library,** currently being restored and not open to visitors.

At the head of Areos Street, on the right, is the Agorá and across from the entrance, on Epaminóndou Street, is an intriguing, white octagonal structure called the **Tower of the Winds** (*Aérides*), more properly known as the *Horologion* (Clock) of Andrónikos Kyrrhéstes. Dating from the 1st century B.C., this tower contained a hydraulic clock and probably a planetarium; each of its sides is decorated with a frieze depicting the wind that would blow from that specific direction. The angles of each face of the tower suggest that it could also have been used as a sundial.

At the northern entrance to the Agorá, opposite the flea market, is an excellent **site map** made of tiles and three huge statues—two Tritons and a Giant—that once held up the *propylon* (entry porch) of the Gymnasium. Bearing right to the spectacular Theseum, you'll pass a bold, headless statute of the emperor Hadrian (reigned A.D. 117–138).

The **Theseum** (*Thissíon* in Greek) is actually a temple of Hephaestus, the god of metallurgy, because in ancient times this was the quarter of the blacksmiths and other metal workers. (Its popular name derives from some of its sculptural decoration, which depicts the exploits of Theseus.) Built between 449 and 444 B.C., the Theseum is the best-preserved temple in all Greece (because of its conversion to a Christian church dedicated to St. George). The Theseum was the work of the architectural genius who created the Temple of Poseidon at Cape Soúnio (Sunium) and the Temple of Nemesis near Marathon. You can still admire the friezes under the portico on the eastern and western sides. (The frieze on the east side depicts nine of the labors of Hercules.)

The Stoa of Attalos, now the **Agorá Museum** (☎ **01/321-0185**), is a huge, red-tile-roofed building across the open Agorá from the Theseum. Constructed of marble, the stoa has 134 columns arranged in double rows of Doric, Ionic, and Aeolic capitals to form two stories; it was an upscale shopping mall during the Hellenistic era.

The Agorá Museum, created as part of the renovation, is quite interesting; the range of scientific inventions, tools, games, and machinery makes this the Smithsonian of the ancient world. Of particular interest to us is a display of artifacts from the Neolithic period to the 1st century B.C., including pottery, pottery-making tools, and bronze-casting and ceramic molds. The red-figure vessels near the center of the museum are particularly prized. There's also a collection of Roman theatrical masks, charming toys, and a pretty ivory statuette of the Apollo Lykeios, a replica of a work by Praxiteles.

If you're energetic, you can wander up the few paving stones that remain of the Panathenaic Way, which leads directly up the hill to the Acropolis, for more sightseeing. This is the shortest route to the Parthenon.

The Temple of Olypian Zeus. Vassillíssis Ólgas and Amalías aves. (entrance on Vassillíssis Ólgas). ☎ **01/922-6330.** Admission 500 Drs ($2.10) adults, 400 Drs ($1.65) senior citizens, 300 Drs ($1.25) students. Tues–Sun 8:30am–3pm.

Begun under Peisistratus in 515 B.C., this is the largest temple to the father of the gods ever built in Greece. Work on it was discontinued after the fall of Peisistratus's tyranny but recommenced under the Syrian king Antiochus IV Epiphanes. A Roman architect, Cossutius, was brought in to complete the temple according to the original plans, but he added a new Corinthian flair of his own. When Antiochus died, work was halted once more. Finally, during Hadrian's reign (about A.D. 131), the temple's 104 tall Corinthian columns were raised to the god. Only 15 of them still stand, together with the base of the colossal structure; one column, felled by an earthquake, lies in fluted segments among the wildflowers, as if to demonstrate its grandeur close up.

Beth Shalom Synagogue. Odós Melidóni 8 (off Odós Ermoú near Sýntagma Sq.). ☎ **01/325-2773.** Admission free. Daily 9am–1pm; services Mon and Thurs at 8am, Fri evening, Sat morning.

The Beth Shalom Synagogue is a living testament to the tenacity of a people and the perseverance of their faith. Prior to World War II there were more than 77,000 Jews living in Greece. After the Holocaust there were fewer than 11,000. (A fascinating account of one man's survival in the Nazi death camps is told in *Athens to Auschwitz,* published by Lycabettus Press).

Beth Shalom was built in 1939 and underwent extensive renovation in the 1970s. The white-marble facade in modern style is reason enough to make a visit, but also notice the copper pulpit *(víma)* in similar period design. Across the street, above the synagogue offices, is a reconstruction of the interior of an older synagogue.

Hadrian's Arch. Outside the archaeological site on Amalías Ave., between the Temple of Olympian Zeus and Pláka.

This squat archway overlooking the site was built to honor the emperor during his reign, perhaps in recognition for the completion of Zeus's temple. The arch symbolically separates Hellenic Athens (Theseus's city) from Roman Athens (Hadrian's city).

Panathenaic Stadium. Vassiléos Konstandínou Ave.

This is a re-creation in solid white marble of the original stadium at Olympia, now over 2,000 years old. This 60,000-seat arena was opened for the 1896 Olympic

Games, the first held since antiquity, and is still in use today. Pause and think of what an immense accomplishment the event must have been in 1896, and then imagine such an event in ancient times!

Parliament Building (*Voulí*). Sýntagma Sq.

This neoclassical building is guarded by two stiff-faced young men *(évzones)* in traditional garb. You can watch the **Changing of the Guard ceremony** at 6pm daily in front of the **Tomb of the Unknown Soldier.** Go early and buy chickpeas for 150 Drs (65¢) from any of the many vendors to feed the hordes of pigeons that know supper's coming. Then stick around for the formal marionette march as the guards' pompomed red-leather shoes clomp in unison across the marble square.

The **National Garden,** which surrounds the Parliament Building, is one of the most civilized places in Athens: several square blocks without traffic, noise, or heat. It's also the feline capital of Greece, with hundreds of stray cats all looking for love and food. (A British group is presently attempting to limit the population explosion.) It's open sunrise to sunset; entrances include those on Amalías Avenue at Sýntagma Square, on Amalías Avenue at Hadrian's Arch, and on King Constantine Avenue opposite the Panathenaic Stadium. Joggers will find the city's freshest air within its confines, with several paths of packed gravel weaving around exotic plantings. Food kiosks, birds, haggard tourists, and smiling Greeks abound. There's even a small zoo.

The **Záppion** is a large, neoclassical building used primarily for exhibitions and international conferences. It's usually closed to the public, but if you're strolling through the National Garden, take a minute to peek in and admire the fine entranceway and interior columns.

Another side of Athens rarely seen is expressed vividly in **Anafiótika,** a small quarter of island-style whitewashed homes built high up on the Acropolis hill by immigrants from Anáfi (a volcanic island in the Cyclades). Many Anáfi residents came to Athens in the 19th century to work; their low-slung stucco homes, built around large courtyards filled with caged birds, reflect the traditional Cycladic architecture of that time.

In Pláka, look for the **Monument of Lysikrates** at Epimándou and Výronos (Byron) streets, which was erected in 335 B.C. to celebrate the winning of a choral competition. It was incorporated into a Capuchin convent in the 17th century. When renovation on this square began in 1982, the site you see today was discovered, and it remains a fine example of a midcity excavation in progress. This site spans the Classical, Roman, and Byzantine eras; pottery shards, jewelry, and coins have already been found. (The Athens law requiring all contractors with building permits to submit to an archaeological review of any planned site before construction begins has indefinitely postponed many such projects.)

3 The Museums of Athens

TWO WORLD-CLASS COLLECTIONS

✪ **National Archaeological Museum.** Odós Patissíon 44. ☎ **01/821-7724.** Admission 2,000 Drs ($8.35) adults, 1,000 Drs ($4.15) students; 1-hour tours 4,000 Drs ($16.65) for 1–10 people. Mon 10:30am–5pm, Tues–Fri 8am–5pm, Sat–Sun 8:30am–3pm. Trolley: 1 or 3 from Sýntagma Sq.

This museum, a 10-minute walk north from Omónia Square, contains the best collection of Greek antiquities in the world—despite centuries of plundering by its European neighbors. The Louvre has the *Winged Victory of Samothrace* and the *Venus de Mílo,* the British Museum has the Elgin Marbles, the Arsenal of Venice is guarded by a Lion of Délos, and New York's Metropolitan Museum of Art has the largest collection of Greek ceramics; however, Athens still has treasures that outshine them.

Not until 1866 did the Greek government decide to build a central museum to house the scattered collections of archaeological societies, scholars, and wealthy patrons. Years of cataloguing and organizing were interrupted by World War II, when every artwork in the building was removed and buried underground. After 1945, Marshall Plan aid from the United States (together with other funds) enabled the Greeks to dig up the collection and renovate the museum; however, there was no comprehensive plan for the exhibition space until 1964. As other countries move rapidly into contemporary design schemes and high-technology preservation techniques, the National Archaeological Museum seems to be behind the times. Nevertheless, its collection is an unrivaled legacy; to forgo the opportunity to see some of these masterworks would be to miss a rare privilege. We believe the following exhibits are among the very best:

Room 4: The central Mycenaean Room includes gold jewelry, artifacts, and masks from the shaft graves discovered by the German amateur archaeologist Heinrich Schliemann. The famous "Mask of Agamemnon," though not actually that of the leader of the Greek forces against Troy, brings to life Homer's words from the *Iliad:* "He was the King of Men . . . distinguished among many and outstanding among heroes."

Room 6: The Cycladic Room contains marble figurines (mostly of women) from the 3rd millennium B.C.

Rooms 7–11: The Archaic Sculpture Rooms hold a collection of huge *koúri,* stylized statues of male youths, which once filled the great temples.

Room 15: The 6$\frac{1}{2}$-foot-tall bronze statue of Poseidon, the sea god, gracefully poised to throw his trident (now missing), his wet hair and beard in sensuous curls. The hand of this masterpiece was discovered off Évvia (near Artemísion) in 1926; 2 years later divers found the rest of the body.

Room 21: The *Little Jockey,* found with the Poseidon at Artemísion, still urges on his big steed. Is his anxiety fear of falling or failing?

Room 24: The eyes of the famous bronze *Ephebos* (Young Man) *of Antikythira* (c. 340 B.C.) in the middle of the room will amaze you.

Room 31: The famous (infamous to some) Hellenistic (1st century A.D.) *Aphrodite* from Délos threatens to smack Pan with her sandal for daring to get randy with her.

Room 47: The Bronze Room contains the handsome *Marathon Boy,* a bronze Hermes from the school of Praxiteles, found in 1926 off the coast of Marathon.

Room 48: The Fresco, or "Thera," Gallery, at the top of the stairs, displays the reconstructed frescoes found at Akrotíri, a Minoan city on the island of Santoríni (Thera).

Rooms 49–56: The Vase Galleries contain an incredible range of sophisticated and folk ceramics from throughout the Greek world.

✪ **Museum of Cycladic and Ancient Greek Art.** Odós Neophýtou Douká 4 (near the National Garden, off Queen Sophia Ave.). ☎ **01/722-8321.** Admission 400 Drs ($1.65) adults, 200 Drs (85¢) students. Mon and Wed–Fri 10am–4pm, Sat 10am–3pm.

In 1986 the Nicholas P. Goulandrís Foundation gave Athens a new museum, filled with the earliest sculpture, pottery, and bronzes from the Cycladic, Minoan, and Mycenaean civilizations (3000 B.C.–A.D. 300). This collection, distinguished by the early Cycladic pieces, is one of the most impressive in the world. To leave Athens without seeing it would be to miss a rare glimpse at an ancient art that speaks eloquently of the beginnings of Western civilization.

The marble figurines, their physical attributes so simply defined, so modern in their sensibility, are superbly displayed and informatively labeled. Their new white-marble home is as simply elegant as the works within. A new wing was added in 1992 to house temporary exhibits.

MORE MUSEUMS

There are many other small museums, such as the Train Museum, the Theater Museum, the Museum of the History of the Greek Costume, the Philatelic Museum, and the War Museum. You can obtain information about these museums at any office of the Greek Tourist Organization (EOT).

Benaki Museum. Leofóros Vassilíssis Sofías at Odós Koumbári 1. ☎ **01/361-1617.**

Unfortunately, the private collection of the late Anthony Benáki, a wealthy Greek from Alexandria, Egypt, was closed for restoration during our last visit, but it may reopen in 1997. This eclectic display of Hellenic, Byzantine, and medieval art objects is delightful to some and totally unappreciated by others. There's a rich collection of ecclesiastical art, including some fine icons and several rare illustrated manuscripts, as well as an interesting collection of Greek folk art, embroidery, and costumes, which appeals to many visitors interested in traditional handicrafts.

The museum shop (☎ **01/362-7367**) remains open Monday to Friday from 8:30am to 3pm.

National Gallery and Alexander Soútzos Museum. Leofóros Vassiléos Konstandínou 50. ☎ **01/723-5937.** Admission 1,000 Drs ($4.15). Mon and Wed–Sat 9am–3pm, Sun 10am–2pm.

The National Gallery and Alexander Soútzos Museum opened in 1976 with a commitment to display modern work by Greek artists. On the first floor you'll find four El Grecos and some Byzantine icons among the Renaissance through impressionist paintings of other Greek artists. The Greek artists Konstandínos Parthénis and Níkos Hatzikyriákos Ghíkas are well represented.

Byzantine Museum. Leofóros Vassilíssis Sofías 22. ☎ **01/723-1570.** Admission 500 Drs ($2.10) adults, 300 Drs ($1.25) students. Tues–Sun 8:30am–3pm.

The Byzantine Museum is housed in an 1840 mansion built by an eccentric French aristocrat, the duchess de Plaisance. The well-labeled architectural details and sculptural fragments provide an excellent introduction to Byzantine architecture, one of Greece's best-represented art forms.

To the right of the entry is a reconstruction of an early Christian basilica with sculptures (5th to 7th century A.D.) brought from many parts of Greece and reassembled here.

After walking clockwise through chronologically arranged displays, you'll arrive at an interesting reproduction of a Byzantine-domed cross-in-square Orthodox church from the 12th or 13th century lit by an exquisite carved wood iconostasis. The upper floor has a fine collection of Byzantine and post-Byzantine icons, frescoes, jewel-encrusted vestments, and other ecclesiastical memorabilia.

Museum of Greek Folk Art. Odós Kydathinéon 17, Pláka. ☎ **01/322-9031.** Admission 500 Drs ($2.10) adults, 400 Drs ($1.65) seniors, 300 Drs ($1.25) students. Tues–Sun 10am–2pm.

This museum is a real must for anyone interested in the roots of contemporary Greek culture. Elaborate embroideries from several islands, ceramics, original costumes, jewelry, silverwork, and traditional leather shadow puppets are only some of the museum's highlights. We love the plate collections from Skýros and the photo blow-ups illustrating the context in which many of these goods were used.

The nearby **Center of Folk Art and Tradition,** at Odós Angelikís Hatzimichális 6 (☎ **01/324-3987**), has a nice collection of costumes, embroidery, pottery, and musical instruments. Admission is free, and it's open Tuesday to Saturday from 9am to 1pm and 5 to 9pm.

National Historical & Ethnological Museum. Odós Stadíou 13. ☎ **01/323-7617.** Admission 500 Drs ($2.10) adults, 200 Drs (85¢) students. Tues–Sun 9am–1:30pm.

This museum is housed in the old Greek Parliament building. Its collection of Greek and Athenian historical items includes portraits of heroes from the 1821 War of Independence (for those who've often wondered whom or what many of the squares and streets are named after). A small but charming aspect of this museum is the collection of 12 watercolors by the 19th-century artist Panayiotis Zographos, depicting famous battles from the War of Independence.

Numismatic Museum. Odós Tossítsa 1. ☎ **01/821-7769.**

The Numismatic Museum houses a collection of Greek, Roman, Byzantine, medieval, and modern coins, lead seals, weights, and engraved stones. The museum was closed through 1996 so that the collection could be moved from its former home in the archaeological museum to the restored mansion of Heinrich Schliemann on Odós Panepistimíou (also known as Venizélou). We assume that the museum will reopen in 1997, but call before going.

Jewish Museum. Odós Níkis 39. ☎ **01/323-1577.** Admission free. Sun–Fri 9am–1pm.

The Jewish Museum, presently located across from the Temple of Zeus, plans to move to the address given above in 1997. This small, but expanding, collection presents a fascinating story of the region's once-flourishing Jewish culture. Few if any museums in Greece display objects with more care and understanding than does the dedicated staff here. Along with excellent changing exhibits, the museum publishes a newsletter of great interest. Although most of the Jewish community disappeared during World War II, this museum prefers to celebrate the spirit and proud history of Jews in Greece rather than create a memorial to those who died in the Holocaust. Allow enough time to visit; we stayed here for about 2 hours. The museum offers a small selection of gift items and books for sale.

Natural History Museum. Odós Levídou 13, Kifissía. ☎ **01/808-6405.** Admission 500 Drs ($2.10) adults, 100 Drs (40¢) children. Sat–Sun 9am–2pm.

This wonderful small museum was founded by Angelos and Niki Goulandris. Because of the construction of a major extension—the Gaia Center for Environmental Research and Education—the museum will be open only on weekends until 1998.

Greek Popular Musical Instruments Museum. Odós Dioyénous 1–3, Aérides Sq., Pláka. ☎ **01/325-0198.** Admission free. Tues and Thurs–Sun 10am–2pm, Wed noon–7pm.

If you're interested in Greek popular music you'll probably be delighted by this fine collection of musical instruments beautifully displayed in a handsome neoclassical mansion. You can listen on headphones to music played by the various instruments; the museum shop has an impressive library of music for sale at reasonable prices.

Hellenic Children's Museum. Odós Kydathinéon, 14, Pláka. ☎ **01/331-2995.** Admission free. Wed and Fri–Mon 10am–5pm.

Our 4-year-old became totally engrossed in excavating the new Athens metro. Equipped wth safety vests, hard hats, rubber boots, gloves, and shovels, kids can explore and "dig up" the room-size tunnel replica. There's also a small water play and bubble display, some crafts areas, a play room, a computer, and a charming

Grandparents Attic with old clothes and hats to dress up in. Most engaging for 2- to 8-year-olds, a visit to this restored Pláka mansion, opposite the Museum of Greek Folk Art, is fun for all.

Museum of Greek Children's Art. Odós Kodrod 9, Pláka. ☎ **01/331-2621.** Admission free. Tues–Sat 10am–2pm, Sun 11am–2pm.

Just around the corner from the wonderful Hellenic Children's Museum is the once-private collection of children's artwork from Mt. Pelion's Milies Museum. Paintings and a few sculptures have emerged from nationwide art competitions, revealing child-hoods steeped in Greek mythology. Remarkably, respect for natural light and a fierce national pride are evident throughout. Their catalog and reproduction postcards make excellent gifts for Grecophiles.

4 Organized Tours

If you prefer a tour, several companies offer sightseeing tours of Athens. Half-day trips, which focus on several highlights, cost about 8,000 Drs ($33.35). There are several night tours, ranging from the basic sound-and-light shows, combined with Greek folk dancing at the Dóra Strátou Folk Dance Theater, to dinner and Greek dancing afterward. Prices range from 7,000 to 12,000 Drs ($29 to $50). (Although we've never taken a night tour, we've received letters from readers who complained that the food was bland and the entertainment dull.) Day trips to Delphi, Cape Soúnio, and Corinth-Mycenae-Epidaurus are also offered, at prices ranging from 5,000 to 17,000 Drs ($20.85 to $70.85). Several companies offer day trips to the nearby islands of Aegina, Póros, and Hydra in the Saronic Gulf.

Tours can be arranged through your hotel or by calling **Viking Star Tours** at ☎ **01/898-0729.** Viking can also arrange customized individual tours, with an emphasis on historical and educational aspects of Athens, one of its specialties.

WALKING TOUR 1
Sýntagma Square & Pláka

Start: Sýntagma Square.
Finish: Pláka, at foot of the Acropolis.
Time: Allow approximately 2¹/₂ hours, not including museums or shopping stops.
Best Times: Weekdays at dusk or weekends.
Worst Times: Weekdays during rush hours or the midday heat.

Sýntagma (Constitution) Square is the heart of the city, where you'll find government offices, places of international commerce, tourist services, and elegant shops. (Metro construction will probably cause continuing inconvenience in this neighborhood for several years.) From here, a brief walk will take you to the cobblestone lanes of Pláka, a timelessly Greek neighborhood that comes as something of a surprise in this bus-tling city.

At the northern corner of the recently landscaped Sýntagma Square you'll see the venerable:

1. Grande Bretagne. Wander through the hotel lobby for a taste of old-world luxury. To the right (east), across heavily trafficked Leofóros Amalías, is the:

2. Tomb of the Unknown Soldier, and behind it is the Parliament Building, guarded by colorfully clad *évzones.*

Walk south to the corner of Óthonos and Filellínon streets (Olympic Airways is on Óthonos) and head away from the square along Óthonos Street (where it

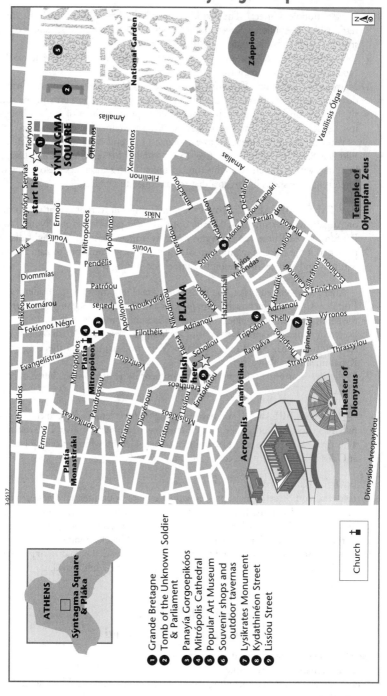

National Garden

Záppion

Vassilísis Ólgas

Temple of
Olympian Zeus

SÝNTAGMA
SQUARE

start here

Yioryíou I

Karavióryi Servías

Ermoú

Leka

Voulís

Diommías

Periktéous

Kornárou

Fokíonos Négri

Evangelístrias

Athinaídos

Ermoú

Platía
Monastiráki

Kapnikaréas

Pandróssou

Adrianoú

Dioyénous

Kírstou

Mnisikléous

Lissíou

Athinaídos

Mitropóleos

Platía
Mitropóleos

Venizélou

Pendélis

Patróou

Ipatías

Apóllonos

Thoukydídou

Filothéis

Scholiou

Fléssa

Eleftheríou

Erotokrítou

finish
here

Mitropóleos

Apóllonos

Nikis

Voulís

Nikodímou

Adrianoú

PLÁKA

Kékropos

Hatzimicháli

Áyios
Yeróndas

Afrodítis

Adrianoú

Tripódon

Shelly

Rangáva

Thespídos

Stratónos

Anafiótika

Acropolis

Theater of
Dionysus

Dionysíou Areopayítou

Othónos

Amalías

Xenofóntos

Fillelínon

Lamráchou

Nikoforou

Sotíros

Kydathinéon

Moni Asteríou Tsangári

Peta

Periándro

Plá:ou

Thálou

Lysikrátous

Ikranoú

Fríníchou

Výronos

Epimenídi

Thrassýlou

Amalías

N

3-0517

ATHENS

Sýntagma Square
& Pláka

1. Grande Bretagne
2. Tomb of the Unknown Soldier
   & Parliament
3. Panayía Gorgoepikóos
4. Mitrópolis Cathedral
5. Popular Art Museum
6. Souvenir shops and
   outdoor tavernas
7. Lysikrates Monument
8. Kydathinéon Street
9. Lissíou Street

Church

joins Mitrópoleos Street). The first left will be Níkis Street; turn here to the first right, which is Apóllonos Street, and follow Apóllonos down past six small, quiet streets till you reach the wider, brighter Adrianoú. To your left are:

3. **Panayía Gorgoepikóos,** a small Byzantine church, and towering above it, on the broad Mitrópolis Square, is the:

4. **Mitrópolis Cathedral.** The *Mitrópolis* (cathedral) is the *see* (seat) of the Ortho-dox Archbishop of Athens and the city and nation's most important church—the site of state funerals and an important gathering place in times of crisis—though its eclectic 19th-century architecture rouses little excitement in most visitors.

You can stop for something to eat at one of several cafes or make a left on Filothéis Street to Nikodímou Street to see some of Pláka's fine old neoclassical buildings with elaborate wrought-iron balconies. Each season sees the opening of interesting new shops in this area that sell antiques and collectibles.

☕ **TAKE A BREAK**   One of our favorite European tearooms is at the corner of Angelikís Hatzimichális Street, opposite the popular Hotel Neféli. **De Profundis Tea Room** serves a variety of teas, coffees, pastries, and light dishes throughout the day and night (open Monday to Friday from 5pm to 2am and on Saturday and Sunday from noon to 2am; closed in August).

After you've visited Pláka, you may want to take in a museum. Consider the:

5. **Popular Art Museum,** which is fun for kids and provides a soothing respite from the summer's heat; it's 2 blocks south of Nikodímou on Kydathinéon.

6. **Souvenir shops and outdoor tavernas** are found the length of Adrianoú, between its junction with Apóllonos at Platía Mitropóleos, and its meeting with Kydathinéon just above the:

7. **Lysikrates Monument.** Opposite the monument is the pretty little church of Ayía Ekateríni.

☕ **TAKE A BREAK**   If you have a craving for fresh lemonade, iced coffee, sin-fully rich chocolate-fudge cake, or a hearty, homemade soup, stop at **To Tristrato.** This time-worn stucco, marble, and lace cafe, cooled by whirring ceiling fans, is at Odós Dédalou 34, at the corner of Áyios Yérondas.

After dusk, stroll down:

8. **Kydathinéon Street,** which sparkles with late-night boutiques, tavernas, strolling musicians, and visitors. If you make a right, turn back down Adrianoú (now all hustle and bustle with T-shirt vendors); go past the intersection of Apóllonos Street to the first left—you'll reach Mnisikléos Street. In 2 blocks it joins:

9. **Lissíou Street,** where you'll find bouzouki tavernas crowded with drinking Greeks and dancing tourists, and some late-night action for the adult crowd.

WALKING TOUR 2
The Acropolis & Monastiráki

Start: Corner of Eólou and Adrianoú streets.
Finish: Monastiráki Flea Market.
Time: Allow 2 hours, not including the Acropolis monuments or shopping in the flea market.

The Acropolis & Monastiráki Square

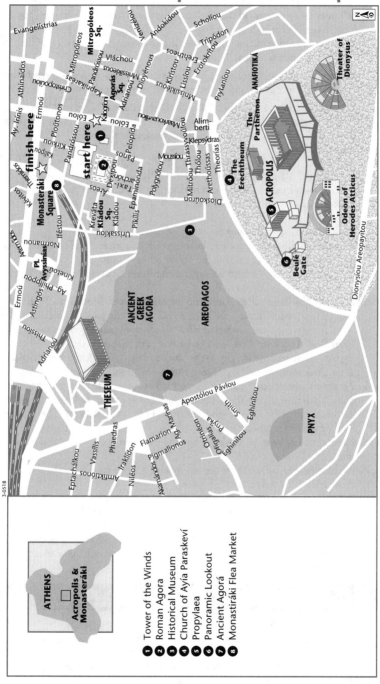

ATHENS

Acropolis & Monastiráki

1. Tower of the Winds
2. Roman Agora
3. Historical Museum
4. Church of Ayía Paraskeví
5. Propylaea
6. Panoramic Lookout
7. Ancient Agorá
8. Monastiráki Flea Market

3-0518

Best Times: Sunday, early in the day, when the flea market is in full swing but before the heat and crowds appear.

Worst Times: During the midday heat or late afternoon, because many of the Acropolis monuments close at 3pm.

A walk around Acropolis Hill to the lively Monastiráki Flea Market will satisfy those who prefer to glance at antiquities and save their energy for shopping.

From the corner of Adrianoú Street, walk south down Eólou to the:

1. **Tower of the Winds** (Aérides). Circle it clockwise. At your left is Dioyénous Street, with the remains of an old Turkish mosque at the corner.

   ☕ TAKE A BREAK If you prefer, you can begin this tour by having lunch at a favorite, old-fashioned family taverna: **Platanos,** at Odós Dioyénous 2. It serves a hearty but casual Greek spread daily (except Sunday) to passing Greeks and visitors who stray off the beaten path.

   After lunch go view the ruins of the:

2. **Roman Agorá,** which sit beside Márkou Avrilíou (Marcus Aurelius) Street, a narrow lane skirting the east side of the Tower of the Winds.

   From here, make a left on Klepsýdras and continue up the worn marble stairs at the foot of the Acropolis to the:

3. **Historical Museum** of the University of Athens (open Monday to Friday from 9am to 1pm), which has a small collection of prints and local historical materials.

   At the top of the stairs, where the hill's landscaped park begins, is the:

4. **Church of Ayía Paraskeví,** on a pedestrian path that rings the Acropolis, offering panoramic views of the city to the north and east. After 5 minutes, make a left at the cloak room sign. The path will wind uphill until you're in sight of the:

5. **Propylaea,** the majestic gateway to the Parthenon and the hilltop's other attractions. If you can't cope with such beauty (or any more uphill walking), retrace your steps to the hillside path and follow the signs to the ancient Agorá. There's a large boulder with steps leading to a:

6. **Panoramic Lookout,** from which you can look down upon your next destination, the:

7. **Ancient Agorá.** To the left is the colonnaded Stoa of Attalos and to the right is the huge, brick-red Theseum (Thissíon).

   Stroll through Athens's old Agorá, then cross the bridge over the metro (subway) tracks back to Adrianoú Street, to Athens's new agorá, the:

8. **Monastiráki Flea Market,** a collection of small shops and street vendors centered on Iféstou Street, 1 block north of Adrianoú. You can while away hours or walk across Monastiráki Square to the metro and head over to Omónia Square or out to Piraeus.

5 Spectator Sports & Active Pursuits

SPECTATOR SPORTS

The Greeks love **soccer** (football) and follow it with a passion. Games are played on Wednesday and Sunday, and you'll be lucky if you can get tickets to any game, but try it through your hotel. The **Karaý Skáki Stadium** is in Néo Fáliro (☎ 01/ 481-2902), near the metro stop on the way to Piraeus.

The **Hippodrome** is the major racetrack in Athens, located near the soccer stadium in Fáliro (☎ 01/941-7761). Horse races are held Monday, Wednesday, and Friday from 2:30 to 6pm in the winter and 6 to 10pm in the summer.

TAKING A DIP

When the thermometer tops 40°C and Athens loses its classical charm, it's time to head south to a unique swimming spot in Vouliagméni. The **Lake Spa of Vouliagméni** (☎ **01/896-2237**) is open daily from 6:30am to 7:30pm and welcomes lap swimmers as well as those suffering from a variety of ailments. This picturesque and huge natural swimming hole is part salt water, part spring-fed; its crystalline cool water is said to be therapeutic for rheumatism, neuralgia, myalgias, and gynecological troubles. Kids and adults will love its soft, sandy bottom, unique setting, and lovely poolside lounging and snacking area. Bring your own towels; they provide lockers and showers; admission is 1,000 Drs ($4.15) for adults and children over 6.

6 Shopping

AROUND SÝNTAGMA SQUARE

Surprisingly, designer shoes by such names as Charles Jourdan, Bally, and Valentino cost about half of what they do in New York! Why? Because although they're not labeled as such, many of these shoes are actually manufactured in Greece, where the cost is less. Check out the high-fashion shoe shops on **Ermoú and Mitropóleos streets,** among them **Rollini** at Ermoú 16 (☎ **01/323-4838**), **Studio Mocassino** at Ermoú 2 (☎ **01/323-4744**), and **Bournazos** at Ermoú 3 (☎ **01/322-3938**).

Marks & Spencer, the London emporium, has opened a store at Ermoú 33–35 with three floors of moderately priced apparel, as well as a sampling of its St. Michael's food products.

IN PLÁKA

Your first impression of Pláka may be that it's just an endless row of T-shirt and souvenir shops. If you stroll along **Adrianoú Street** (the center of the tourist trade), you'll get an idea of the possibilities. (The lowest prices can be found toward the west, near the flea market.)

The quality of reproductions has generally improved in recent years—though there's still a lot of shoddy kitsch—and, though the shops themselves may all look alike, a few of them are worth noting. **L'Atelier,** Adrianoú 116 (☎ **01/323-3740**), offers excellent copies of black-on-red vessels (many painted in the shop itself), as well as good Minoan frescos and marble Cycladic figures. **Amphitrion,** at Pandrossou 53 and 63 (☎ **01/321-4485**), has superior reproductions in bronze and ceramics.

If you're interested in an original work of art—not at bargain prices, but interesting browsing—look at the paintings of **Takis Moraýtis** at Adrianoú 129 (☎ **01/322-5208**); check out the enormous *pitháre* in the basement, found during excavation and left *in situ*. We particularly admire the realist paintings of Yiannis Papaioannou featured at **Topaz,** Adrianoú 67 at Mnisikléous (☎ **01/321-4320**).

Generally you'll find the more interesting and diverse shops in the eastern part around **Voulís, Iperídou, and Kydathinéon streets.** For dolls, puppets, and handmade children's toys, check out the shop of **Spiro Aravantinos** at Nikodímou 9 (☎ **01/323-6363**).

If Greek costumes are your thing, stop in at the shop of **Yoannis Iglesis,** Adrianoú and Benizélou (☎ **01/322-1262**), which makes costumes for various dance and theater companies.

On the way to Pláka from Sýntagma Square, you'll find **Aidini** at Odós Níkis 32 (☎ **01/322-6088**), selling good sculpture, jewelry, and other contemporary handcrafts by Athenian artists.

Don't miss the **Brettos Bottle Shop,** at Odós Kydathinéon 41, above the Taverna Tá Bakaliarákia; it's a wonderful shop for the finest Greek liqueurs and candies.

THE MONASTIRÁKI FLEA MARKET

The market area of Monastiráki radiates from a picturesque old square below Pláka. If you're walking, the easiest way to get there is to go down **Pandróssou Street** (which parallels Mitropóleos Street). The metro will take you right there; when you exit you'll find Pandróssou Street on the right and Iféstou Street on the left, both of them filled with knickknack displays during the Sunday flea market. On Sunday it's best to get there between 8am and 2pm, when the park behind the Theseum (Thissíon) is filled with young and old alike "walking" their canaries.

The flea market is a great place to find plates, kitchen utensils, jars, flashlights, cotton underwear (Greek sizes tend to be rather narrow), watches, new and used music cassettes and records, Chinese alarm clocks, punk clothes, Sears coveralls, leather goods, wispy cotton Isadora Duncan dresses, *kombolóia* (worry beads), and much more.

Hephaistos, at Odós Iféstou 12 (☎ 01/324-2587), is filled with old and new copper and brass products. *Remember:* It's not advisable to cook in unlined copper pots, but you can serve in them.

A few doors away at Iféstou 6, **Iakovos Antiques** (☎ 01/321-0169) offers an interesting collection of Greek and European collectibles, including porcelains, brass products, and paintings. The merchandise is high quality, with prices to match.

Next door, at Iféstou 6, you'll enjoy the handmade bouzoukis and guitars of **Vassilios Kevorkian** (☎ 01/321-0024). Theater and folk-art buffs will be intrigued by **Studio Kostas Sokaras,** at Odós Adrianoú 25 (☎ 01/321-6826). It sells a wonderful variety of puppets from the Greek shadow theater, along with folk costumes, jewelry, and textiles. For an interesting collection of art-nouveau lamps and glass shades, visit **E. & P. Sokara Antiques,** at Odós Níssou 1 (☎ 01/325-4051).

At the edge of Pláka, at Odós Pandróssou 89, is the leather shop of **Stavros Melissinos** (☎ 01/321-9247), the acclaimed poet and shoemaker to celebrities; for 3,500 to 7,000 Drs ($14.60 to $29.15), you can walk away in a pair of sandals similar to those (reputedly) once ordered by Jacqueline Onassis, the Beatles, or Rudolf Nureyev (who surely knew good shoes).

Several flight attendants informed us that Elias and Panos at **HTH Jewelry,** Pandróssou 26B (☎ 01/321-2267), have exceptionally good prices. We went to check it out and found the prices very reasonable—we also saw our flight attendants shopping there.

You may find some bulky-knit homespun wool sweaters here or in Pláka, at one of the pricier tourist-only shops. If you're off to the islands soon, you can probably find better-designed and carefully knit sweaters there; if you're off to Crete, Delphi, or other northern points, you'll probably find equally folksy sweaters at better prices.

The flea-market area functions as a regular shopping mall during the work week. The hours are primarily 8am to 2pm and 5:30 to 8pm Monday to Friday (depending on the season, Saturday is either a half day or a full day).

AROUND KOLONÁKI SQUARE

Tsakálof Street is a pedestrian mall between Iraklítou Street and Kolonáki Square, with some excellent leather and shoe shops and men's and women's fashion resort wear. Among the standouts are **Balletto** at no. 11 (☎ 01/360-0251), with a good selection of swimwear for you to take to the islands.

In case you want to see the world.

At American Express, we're here to make your journey a smooth one. So we have over 1,700 travel service locations in over 120 countries ready to help. What else would you expect from the world's largest travel agency?

do more

Travel

In case you want to be welcomed there.

We're here to see that you're always welcomed at establishments everywhere. That's why millions of people carry the American Express® Card—for peace of mind, confidence, and security, around the world or just around the corner.

do more

Cards

In case you're running low.

We're here to help with more than 118,000 Express Cash locations around the world. In order to enroll, just call American Express before you start your vacation.

do more

Express Cash

And just in case.

We're here with American Express® Travelers Cheques and Cheques *for Two*® They're the safest way to carry money on your vacation and the surest way to get a refund, practically anywhere, anytime.

Another way we help you...

do more

Travelers Cheques

East of Kolonáki Square along Odó Ypsilandou you'll find a few more interesting shops. At no. 5, **Borell's** (☎ 01/721-9772) carries an entertaining selection of gems, bijoux jewelry, and compacts from the 1940s. Across the street, at no. 8, **Miniature** (☎ 01/725-8900) has an ecletic collection of antiques, silver, glass, porcelain, and other collectibles. A celebrated shop for folk art and recent antiques, all top quality, is **Archipelagos,** Odós Iássou 6 at Moní Patráki (☎ 01/722-7308).

As Kolonáki's rents have increased, many smaller shops have opened just north around Dexamení Square, where there are many art galleries. Toward the base of Lykavittós Hill you'll find some shops tucked in the side streets. **Panayíri,** at Odós Kleoménous 25 near Ploutárchou Street (☎ 01/722-5369), is one of our favorites for gifts. It has a large selection of carved-wood items (including model ships), hand-painted stones with images of Greek villages, art books, and other contemporary artifacts.

A good budget shop for underwear, cosmetics, and a small line of clothing is the French chain store **Prisunic,** at Odós Kanári 9.

AROUND OMÓNIA SQUARE

Omónia Square is where you'll find modestly priced department stores and budget boutiques. There are three main department-like stores: **Lambropouli Bros.** is at Eólou and Lykoúrgos streets; **Athenee** is at Odós Stadíou 33; and **Minion,** the largest and most varied, is at the corner of Veranzérou and Patissíon streets (a continuation of Eólou Street).

BHS (British Home Stores), 2 blocks south of Omónia at Efpolídos and Athinás streets, has an excellent self-service restaurant (open 9am to 8:30pm), on the eighth floor, offering indoor and outdoor seating with fabulous views.

Omónia Square has several small fruit-and-nut stores, a whole-wheat macrobiotic bakery (at Stadíou and Eólou streets, next to the main post office), and many souvenir stands in narrow arcades off Stadíou Street and in the underground metro stop. Souvenirs are also sold at streetside kiosks and by mobile vendors.

A meander through the **Bazaar** (Central Market), south of Omónia along Athinás, may delight and intrigue you, even if you don't purchase anything. Although the Meat and Seafood Market may not be to your liking, you can escape it by crossing Athinás west to the Fruit and Vegetable Market. The Flower Market is around the church of Ayía Iríni on Odós Eólou, a pedestrian mall that leads south toward the Acropolis.

BEST BUYS

You get the best value for your money in Athens when you buy goods that are uniquely Greek—folk arts or internationally designed merchandise that has been manufactured in Greece. What's cheaper here than what it would cost back home? Shoes, furs, and bathing suits. What's uniquely Greek? Hand-knit woolen sweaters, flokáti rugs, cotton embroideries from the islands, ceramics, and museum reproductions.

CRAFTS

We like several stores for their still-original, handmade crafts and goods. The **Greek Women's Institution,** at Odós Kolokotróni 3 (☎ 01/323-9693), specializes in embroidery from the islands, replicas of Benáki Museum embroideries, and woven goods.

The **National Welfare Organization** (Ethnikí Pronía), at Odós Ipatías 6, off Apóllonos Street in Pláka (☎ 01/324-0017), carries woven goods, ceramics, copperware, and jewelry produced by local craftspeople. This store features a fine stock of tapestries, rugs, and small goods guaranteed to delight.

At **To Anoyi,** Odós Sotíros 1, across from the Hotel Nefeli (☎ **01/322-6487**), Kati Apostolou paints the luminous icons she sells. She also has hand-painted eggs, traditional pottery, woven goods, and ceramics from other artists on the mainland and the islands.

MUSEUM SHOPS

The **Museum of Cycladic and Ancient Greek Art,** at Odós Neophýtou Douká 4; the **Benáki Museum,** at Odós Koumbári 1; and the **National Archaeological Museum,** at Odós Patissíon 4, sell reproductions of items in their collections. The Benáki also has other goods, such as scarves, needlepoint kits, and linens whose designs were inspired by traditional Greek motifs. The National Archaeological Museum also sells castings of items exhibited at other Greek museums and copies of paintings and murals. The Museum of Cycladic Art also carries an extensive collection of books on Cycladic art and jewelry designed with Cycladic motifs.

7 Athens After Dark

Few people can match Athenians when it comes to enjoying the evening. Their midafternoon siestas (from 2 to 5pm) enable them to dine, drink, and dance till 2 or 3am (while still reporting to work at 7:30 or 8am) almost every night of the week. Sunday is the one evening when things might taper off; during the summer, though, when so many Greeks are on holiday, you probably wouldn't be able to notice any difference because the crowds will nearly always look like Saturday night prime. Put on your dancing shoes and enjoy: dining, dancing, and listening at Athens's many bouzouki clubs, international nightclubs, or discos . . . romantic nighttime vistas from mountaintop restaurants and bars . . . gambling at an elegant world-class resort . . . cultural events and concerts, the sound-and-light show at the Acropolis, the Dora Stratou Folk Dance Theater . . . movies, taverna-hopping, people-watching, and more. . . .

THE PERFORMING ARTS

The **Greek National Opera** performs at the **Olympia Theater,** 59 Akadimías St., at Mavromiháli (☎ **01/361-2461**).

The **Mégaron Mousikís Concert Hall,** 89 Vasilíssis Sofías Ave. (☎ **01/729-0391**), is an acoustically marvelous new music hall that hosts a wide range of classical music programs, including quartets, operas in concert, symphonies, and recitals. The box office is open Monday to Friday from 10am to 6pm and Saturday from 10am to 2pm. Tickets run 5,000 to 20,000 Drs ($21.30 to $85.10), depending on the performance.

The **Pallas Theater,** 1 Voukourestíou St. (☎ **01/322-8275**), hosts most major jazz and rock concerts, as well as some classical performances. It's an older, acoustically imperfect hall.

The **Hellenic American Union Auditorium,** 22 Massalías St. (between Kolonáki and Omónia; ☎ **01/362-9886**), hosts English-language theater and American-oriented music. Ticket prices vary with the performance (typically around 3,000 Drs/$12.75).

The **Athens Festival** at the **Odeum of Herodus Atticus** has famous Greek and foreign artists performing music, plays, opera, and ballet from the beginning of June through the beginning of October. The open-air setting at this ancient odeum beneath the Acropolis is beautiful. The only drawbacks are that the stone seats are hard and there are no backrests. Find out what's being presented through the English-language press or at the **Athens Festival office,** at Stadíou 4 (☎ **01/322-1459** or 01/322-3111 to 01/322-3119, ext. 137). The office is open Monday to Saturday from 8:30am to 2pm and 5 to 7pm, and on Sunday from 10am to 1pm. If available, tickets can also be purchased at the Odeum of Herodes Atticus (☎ **01/323-2771**) on the day of performance.

TRADITIONAL FOLK DANCING

Dora Stratou Folk Dance Theater. Philopáppou Hill. ☎ **01/924-4395** 8am to 2pm, 01/ 921-4650 after 5:30pm, or 01/924-4395 for the theater office at Odós Scholíou 8 in Pláka. Tickets 1,800–2,500 Drs ($7.50–$10.40)

A short walk on Philopáppou Hill from the sound-and-light show at the Acropolis, this theater provides one of the few opportunities you'll have to see genuine Greek folk dances, as opposed to the contrived bouzouki dances in the touristy tavernas. Since her company's first performance in 1953, Dora Stratou has achieved the status of grande dame of all Greek traditional dances; a night's concert will feature up to seven different styles.

Typically, a program will include dances from Macedonia, the Peloponnese, and several island groups. The choreography is accompanied by a small group of musicians, which usually include violin, drums, clarinet, *sandodri* (hammer dulcimer), and *laoúta* (lute). Each dance is performed in costumes from the appropriate region; in between dances, while the dancers change outfits, the musicians play folk music. You can see traditional Greek dances and costumes and hear music all in one place. Some may find many of the dances repetitive; but under a starlit sky, in comfortable lawn chairs in an idyllic Greek setting, most will find much to enjoy. Performances are nightly at 10:15pm, with additional matinees on Sunday and Wednesday at 8:15pm.

THE CLUB & MUSIC SCENE

Your choices range from traditional Greek music clubs—both rural *dimotiká* and urban *rebétika* (bouzouki)—to international-style discos. Athens has plenty of choices.

A warning: The police have asked us to warn readers about the scam that's most often reported to them by tourists looking for "professional companionship." It usually goes like this: A young woman will approach a man either inside or outside one of the bars, bouzouki clubs, nightclubs, or cafes frequented by tourists and will ask him to buy her a drink. The drink is usually "champagne" (actually just a carbonated beverage) that she'll consume while the man nurses his own drink. When the bill comes, it can run from 10,000 to 30,000 Drs ($40 to $125) a bottle for the "champagne"! The bartender gets his money, the girl gets her cut, and the victim gets another punch: Too embarrassed, drunk, or mad to think of it, he walks out without asking for a receipt; and when he goes to the police, he is told that an investigation cannot proceed without such proof. *Caveat emptor!*

LIVE GREEK MUSIC

It's hard to resist the lure of the bouzouki clubs, those noisy nightspots where free-flowing wine, an amplified band, and willing guests join to dance up a storm. Plate-smashing, the accepted method of showing appreciation, has been outlawed, but the tradition persists in a few clubs; check with the management before you join in, because you'll be charged by the plate! (Where allowed, they're sold before the show begins.)

Pláka is the center of the tourist-oriented music clubs, and a few key streets are wall-to-wall sound with little to differentiate the clubs. Many of the tavernas with musicians or elaborate floor shows serve a high-priced meal beforehand to get you in the mood; count on spending at least 6,000 Drs ($25) a head.

Taverna Mostroú, Odós Mnissikléous 22 (☎ 01/324-2441), is one of the oldest and best-known venues for traditional Greek music and dancing. Shows begin about 11pm and cost about 4,000 Drs ($16.65), which includes a fixed-menu supper.

Nearby, **Palia Taverna Kritikou,** Odós Mnissikléos 24 (☎ 01/322-2809), is another lively open-air taverna with music and dancing. Some of the other more reliable places for live *dimotiká* music include **Dioyenis,** Odós Séllei (Shelly) 3 (☎ 01/324-7933); **Nefeli,** Odós Pános 24 (☎ 01/321-2465); and **Stamatopoulou,** Odós Lissíou 26 (☎ 01/322-8722).

If you're interested in Greek popular music, look for **Zoom,** Odós Kydathinéon 37 (☎ 01/322-5920), where pop artists with hit albums are sometimes showered with carnations by adoring fans and the minimum is 5,000 Drs ($20.85).

For more intimate and unusual entertainment, climb Mnissikléous toward the Acropolis, turn right on Thólou, and look for **Apanemia** and **Esperides,** two smoky little *boîtes* usually filled with hip young Athenians sipping drinks (1,500 Drs/$6.25) and enjoying music that's both traditional and innovative, sometimes even humorous.

If you prefer more authentic *rebétika* music, inquire at your hotel desk or check the current issue of *Athenscope* magazine (in English and available at newsstands) to find out which clubs are featuring the best performers. Performances usually don't start until nearly midnight, and though there's usually no cover charge, drinks can cost as much as 4,000 Drs ($16.65). Most places are closed during the summer, and many are a distance from the Sýntagma/Pláka area, so budget another 2,500 to 4,000 Drs ($8.35 to $16.65) for round-trip taxi fare. Among these more distant upscale *bouzoúkia* are **Dioyenis Palace,** Syngroú 259 (☎ 01/942-4267)—a lot farther out than you might think—and **Posidonio,** Posidónos 18, Ellinikó (☎ 01/894-1033), near the airport.

One of the more central is **Stoa Athanaton,** Sofokléous 19, in the Central Meat Market (☎ 01/321-4362), which has live *rebétika* from 3 to 6pm and after midnight, and serves good food; closed Sunday; minimum 2,500 Drs ($10.40). **Taximi,** Odós Isávron 29, Exárchia (☎ 01/363-9919), is consistently popular; drinks cost 3,500 Drs ($14.60); closed Sunday as well as July and August. **Frangosyriani,** Odós Aráchovis 57, Exárchia (☎ 01/360-0693), specializes in the music of *rebétika* legend Markos Vamvakaris; closed Tuesday and Wednesday. The more downscale **Rebetiki Istoria,** Odós Ippókratous 181, Kolonáki (☎ 01/642-4937), features old-style music for a mixed crowd of cognoscenti, students, and intellectuals.

If you want some background information, buy a copy of *Greek Dances* (Lycabettus Press) by Ted Petrides, available at many bookstores for 1,000 Drs ($4.20); it has a lively, informative introduction to the country's various dances, accompanied by explicit foot diagrams, so that even a klutz can learn the *syrtáki,* one of the easiest dances.

DISCO, POP & ROCK

Athens's nightlife grows ever livelier, more various, and variable—so variable that, once again, most of our suggestions in the last edition were either gone or had changed significantly during the interval. Also, the distinctions we commonly make between various forms of popular music aren't quite so clear-cut, and clubs are rather mercurial. (*Note:* Be careful in the area just south and east of Sýntagma Square, along

Filellínon and Níkis, since there are lots of clip joints there.) Nothing beats word-of-mouth on the current best places, so ask, or at least check *Athenscope* for information, even about these suggestions.

Very few actual discos are open in central Athens during the summer; most of them are well out of town. Of these, the most popular is probably **Aerodromio,** opposite the East Terminal of the airport (☎ **01/982-0300**); admission, including one drink, is 1,200 Drs ($5) weeknights, 4,000 Drs ($16.65) on Friday and Saturday. **Boulevard,** Vouliagménis 140, Glyfáda (☎ **01/898-2557**), also attracts a young Athenian crowd. The most conveniently located disco is **Absolut,** Odós Filellínon 23, just south of Sýntagma Square. Hip students may want to head west to **Booze,** Odós Kolokotróni 57 (☎ **01/324-0944**), at the edge of Pláka. More mature readers will probably prefer to mosey north to the more glamorous **Wild Rose,** in the arcade at Odós Panepistimíou 10 (☎ **01/364-2160**). Up the street, **Mercedes Rex,** Odós Panepistimíou 48 (☎ **01/361-4591**), has even more diversity.

Exárchia remains the neighborhood favored by hip local young people seeking musical entertainment and social interaction. **Rodon,** Odós Márni 24, Platía Váthis (☎ **01/523-7418**), is still considered the best place for rock 'n' roll, with live bands—some of international stature—Friday and Saturday nights; unfortunately it's closed most of the summer. The **Green Door,** Odós Kalidromíou 52, and the **Rock Club,** Odós Emmanuíl Benáki 3, are also popular.

If you're willing to part with a little more money, you may want to hit fashionable Kolonáki to check out **The Cave,** Odós Háritos 6 (☎ **01/722-8910**), which lives up to its name; drinks begin at 1,500 Drs ($6.25) and beer at 1,000 Drs ($4.15). **Memphis,** Odós Ventíri 5 (☎ **01/722-4104**), behind the Hilton, has live music, more or less, as its name implies.

THE GAY SCENE

There's a fairly discreet gay district, including a transvestite cruising area, along Syngroú south of Hadrian's Arch, in Makriyánni. **Granazi,** Odós Lebési 20 (☎ **01/325-3979**), is a popular gay hangout, though the best-known alternative place is **E . . . Kai** ("So What?"), across Syngroú at Odós Iossíf ton Rogón 12 (☎ **01/922-1742**). In posher Kolonáki, **Alexander's,** Odós Anagnostopoúlou 44 (☎ **01/364-6660**), is considered more sophisticated and diverse.

JAZZ & PIANO BARS

If you have a more sedate taste, you may find your cup of tea in Kolonáki, near the Hilton. We suggest the **Jazz Club Diva,** Odós Andinóros 42 (☎ **01/729-0322**); **Lord Byron Bar,** at the Caravel Hotel, Leof. Vass. Alexándrou 2 (☎ **01/725-3744**); or the **Polo Bar,** at the Hilton (☎ **01/722-0201**).

True jazz aficionados will probably prefer the **Half Note,** Odós Trivianou 17, Mets (☎ **01/921-3310**), which features important international groups; performances begin after 10pm, and admission, including the first drink, is 4,000 Drs ($16.65).

Sto Gázi, in Thissío, just west of Monastiráki, is building a reputation as a sophisticated but inexpensive nightlife area. You might want to take a stroll and check it out. **Stavlos,** Odós Iráklidon 10 (☎ **01/345-2502**), several blocks south of the Thissío metro station, is an interesting spot with live jazz, art exhibits, and an occasional art film.

THE EVENING STROLL *(VÓLTA)*

Among the best and least expensive evening entertainment is the street life of Athens. To experience the joy and exuberance with which Athenians soak up the night air, simply take a turn *(vólta)* around town with them, go for a stroll along the seafront, find a sidewalk cafe table, or join them in feasting at a taverna.

The narrow, winding streets, cobblestone footpaths, and uneven stone steps of **Pláka** never fail to delight the first-time visitor. For a close-up look at the fashionable under-30 set, there's no better place than **Fokíonos Négri,** a long, broad pedestrian mall of cafes north of the National Archaeological Museum. The chic crowd strolls over to **Kolonáki Square** (a short walk from Sýntagma Square), to any of the jam-packed cafes that overlook the little planted green. Around sundown the **top of Lykavittós Hill** is particularly special. At the head of Ploutárchou Street you can catch the funicular that speeds you up or back. Our favorite spot is a little ouzerí halfway back down on the easy trail.

For those wanting a **seaside stroll,** we suggest a taxi or metro ride (to the Néo Fáliro stop) to Mikrolímano, a neighborhood built around a natural yacht harbor. Seafood restaurants line this basin, and it's a picturesque venue for a sundown stroll. (See our section on Piraeus for some dining recommendations.)

THE SOUND-&-LIGHT SHOW AT THE ACROPOLIS

Sound-and-light shows can be one of the most effective ways to bring an architectural monument to life. From the top of Philopáppou Hill (grab the seats farthest away from the public-address system), you can let yourself imagine the flawless grandeur that was. The silhouettes of the Parthenon, the Erechtheum, and particularly the Acropolis walls are enhanced by the ever-changing light. If you're disappointed by their daytime appearance when scaffolding and the effects of pollution on the temples are so obvious, you may be pleased by a distant examination of the glowing gem perched above a twinkling Athens skyline. To better endure the melodramatic delivery, you might have some ouzo or retsína before the show. You can buy a program, 500 Drs ($2.10), and read it later.

Performances are given from April to October in several languages: English is daily at 9pm. Bring a sweater and a camera (if you have high-speed film) and wear sturdy shoes. The price is 1,400 Drs ($5.85) for adults, 800 Drs ($3.35) for students. Call ☎ 01/322-4128 for information.

FILMS

The old outdoor cinemas we used to enjoy are disappearing, being pushed aside by the same modern facilities found elsewhere in Europe. We counted 70 cinemas showing "foreign" films—mostly in English, with a few French thrown in. Of these, 55 had Dolby stereo, though only the **Alexandra,** Odós Patissíon 79 (☎ 01/956-0306), and the **Apollon,** Odós Stadíou 19 (☎ 01/323-6811), were air-conditioned. What was even more amazing was the number of quality first-run and even classic American films—a couple of dozen! So if you're hungry for a movie, you won't have any trouble finding one to your liking. See *Athens News* or *Athenscope* for the current schedule.

CASINOS

Casino Mont Parnes. Párnitha. ☎ 01/246-9111.

This major casino is part of a resort complex (which includes a nightclub and a restaurant) on top of Mt. Párnitha (Parnés), about 22 miles north of Athens. There's bus service; call ☎ 142 for the schedule. If you're driving—we wouldn't want to pay the cab fare!—you can shave off the last 5 miles by taking the Parnés cable car directly to the hotel's front door. Proper dress is required. Open Monday, Tuesday, and Thursday to Sunday from 8pm to 2am.

8 The Ports: Piraeus & Rafína

PIRAEUS

Piraeus (Pireás) has been the port of Athens since antiquity. Although the Greek maritime industry isn't what it once was, the thousands of tourists who board ferries bound for the Aegean islands each day contribute to maintaining Piraeus's position as the number-one port in the Mediterranean. As a city it has the conveniences and amenities of Athens, but not the charm; as a port it has the seamier sides of a sailor's lair but also all the color and life of an active harbor.

Piraeus is one of the most seen, but least appealing places on the Greek itinerary. If you're trying to visit almost any of the islands by boat, you'll probably have to pass through Piraeus. Nighttime visitors should confine their wanderings to the port if they're waiting for a ferryboat or to Mikrolímano's expensive but scenic harborside tavernas.

ESSENTIALS

GETTING THERE & BACK FROM ATHENS   Getting to Piraeus is easy from any of Athens's centers. The fastest and easiest way, from Omónia Square or Monastiráki (a short walk from Sýntagma Square), is to take the **metro** to the last stop (75 Drs/30¢), which will leave you 1 block from the domestic port. You can also take **green bus no. 40 or 49.** No. 40 runs from the corner of Filellínon Street, on Sýntagma Square to Vassiléos Konstandínou (King Constantine) Avenue, about half a dozen blocks west of Zéa Marina or east of the international port—from which it's another 10-minute walk to the right along the water to the domestic port. Bus no. 49 runs from Omónia Square to Karaýskáki Square, the central bus terminal near the middle of the main harbor. Both buses run every 20 minutes from 5am to 1am, then hourly, but the trip can sometimes take nearly an hour. A **taxi** from Sýntagma Square will cost up to 2,000 Drs ($8.35). From the airport, bus no. 19 goes to Karaýskáki Square in Piraeus; the fare is 300 Drs ($1.25). A taxi from the airport to the port should cost about 1,500 Drs ($6.25).

There's also a **train** to Athens from the Stathmós Pireás Peloponnissíou (☎ 01/ 417-8335), 1 block north of the metro station. This station offers service to Athens, then on to Corinth, Náfplion, Pátra, Pírgos, Trípoli, and Kalamáta 8 to 16 times daily between 6am and 10pm.

Unfortunately, getting back to Athens can be more difficult. The easiest way is to take the metro to central Athens, to either Monastiráki or Omónia Square. Taxi drivers have a conspiracy to overcharge tourists disembarking from the boats. They charge 4,000 Drs ($16.65), which is two or three times the legal fare. If you stand on the dock, you'll get no mercy. Your only option is to walk to a nearby street and hail a cab.

TAKING A FERRY OR HYDROFOIL TO THE ISLANDS FROM PIRAEUS
See the section below on Rafína before you make your plans; it may be substantially cheaper to travel from Rafína to the Cyclades or the Docadenese than to depart from Pireus.

Ferry tickets can be purchased at a ticket office up to 1 hour before departure; after that they can be purchased on the boat. For booking first-class cabins or for advance-sale tickets, see one of the harborside travel agents (around Karaýskáki Square by the domestic ferries and along Aktí Miaoúli, the waterfront opposite the Crete ferries). Most open at 6am and will hold your baggage for the day (but there's no security).

The Greek Tourist Organization, EOT, publishes a list of weekly sailings, but the **tourist police** (☎ **171**) or the **Port Authority** (☎ **01/451-1311**) can provide you with schedule information.

If you need a travel agency to make reservations or to recommend a particular service, try **Explorations Unlimited,** at Odós Kapodistríou 2, just off Aktí Posidónos near the metro station (☎ **01/411-6395** or 01/411-1243), open Monday to Friday from 8am to 7pm and Saturday from 9am to 2pm.

The port spreads along the waterfront for quite a distance, so be sure you know which boat you're taking and ask for directions. Boats to most of the islands are opposite the metro station. Both regular boats to the Saronic Gulf and hydrofoils (Flying Dolphins) to Aegina are opposite and to the left of the metro station; the hydrofoils leave from the foot of Goúnari Street. Boats to the other islands are around to the right and away from the station. Boats to Italy and Turkey are a mile or so to the left. Hydrofoils to other destinations leave from Zéa Marina, a separate harbor some 3 miles southeast of the metro station.

VISITOR INFORMATION For boat schedules, transit information, and other tourist information, dial ☎ **171;** the line is open 24 hours.

The closest **EOT office** (☎ **01/453-7107**) is inconveniently located on the street above Zéa Marina (the hydrofoil port) on the second floor of a shopping arcade stocked with yacht supplies. It's open weekdays from 9am to 2:30pm, but its limited resources probably won't warrant the 20-minute walk from the ferry piers. If you're arriving and you really need information, go straight to Sýntagma Square in Athens.

FAST FACTS There are several banks in Piraeus along the waterfront. The **National Bank,** on Ethnikí Antistáseos Street, has extended hours in summer.

A portable **post office** branch opposite the Aegina ferry pier also offers currency exchange; it's open Monday to Saturday from 8am to 8pm and Sunday from 8am to 6pm. The main post office is at Ethnikís Andistáseos and Dimitríou streets.

The **phone center (OTE)** is a block northeast of the post office; there's another branch by the water, on Aktí Miaoúli at Merarchías Street, open daily from 7am to 9:30pm.

You'll find secure but expensive **luggage storage** in the metro station, at the **Central Travel Agency** (☎ **01/411-5611**); the cost is 1,000 Drs ($4.10) per piece per day.

What to See & Do

On midsummer evenings, open-air theatrical performances are given at the **Kastélla Theater,** a few blocks inland from Mikrolímano. In the wintertime performances are staged indoors, at the **Public Theater,** on the green at Vassiléos Konstandínou (King Constantine) Avenue, where you can also catch the bus to Sýntagma Square.

The **Piraeus Archaeological Museum,** at Odós Trikoúpi 31, near Zéa Marina (☎ **01/452-1598**), is open Tuesday to Sunday from 8:30am to 3pm; admission is 500 Drs ($2.10) for adults, 400 Drs ($1.65) for seniors, and 300 Drs ($1.25) for students.

The **Hellenic Maritime Museum,** at Aktí Themistokléous and Freatída Street, near the hydrofoil pier at Zéa Marina (☎ **01/451-6822**), is open Tuesday to Saturday from 9am to 1pm, closed in August; admission is 400 Drs ($1.65), free on Saturday.

The **Piraeus Flea Market** is a worthwhile Sunday excursion (8am to noon), when the enclosed, older market spills outdoors. Located off Ippodámou Street near the

Aegean Ferries ③
Bus Station ④
Crete Ferries ⑦
Cyclades Ferries ⑥
Flying Dolphins to
  Póros, Hydra, Spétses ⑨
International Ferries ⑧
Metro Station ②
Northeast Aegean Ferries ⑤
Saronic Gulf Ferries,
  Flying Dolphin to Aegina ①

metro terminus, it specializes in old ship bric-a-brac, lamps, hand-embroideries, and whatever else gets washed ashore. Nearby, **To Epineion,** Odós Godnari 1 (☎ **01/412-1735**), is a great place for a lunch of *mezédes;* after 1pm on Sunday there's live bouzouki.

WHERE TO STAY

We're not enthusiastic about an overnight stay in Piraeus, but if it makes sense in your travel plans, here are our suggestions. Be careful when walking around at night.

Hotel Mistral. Odós Vassiléos Pávlou 105, Kastélla, 185 33 Piraeus. ☎ **01/412-1425.** Fax 01/412-2096. 100 rms, all with bath; 3 suites. A/C TV TEL. 23,000 Drs ($95.85) single; 28,750 Drs ($119.80) double; 38,000–46,500 ($158.35–193.75) suite. Rates include breakfast. AE, EURO, MC, V.

The modern Hotel Mistral is only 2 blocks inland from the lively seafood dining capital of Mikrolímano, east of Zéa Marina. The spacious rooms have radios and other amenities and views of the Aegean from sunny balconies. There's a nice roof garden and plans to reopen the swimming pool.

Ideal Hotel. Odós Notará 142, 185 31 Piraeus. ☎ **01/429-4050.** Fax 01/429-3890. 31 rms, all with bath (shower). A/C TEL. 9,500 Drs ($39.60) single; 12,000 Drs ($50) double. AE.

If you want to stay close to the port, the Ideal is just 2 blocks inland from the waterfront, opposite the international ferries. It's a clean, pleasant, air-conditioned hotel that was renovated in 1995.

Lilia Hotel. Odós Zéas 131, Passalimáni, 185 34 Piraeus. ☎ **01/417-9108.** Fax 01/411-4311. 20 rms, all with bath (shower). TEL. 12,650 Drs ($52.70) single; 17,000 Drs ($70.85) double. Rates include breakfast. AE, V.

Clean, bright, comfortable rooms with ceiling fans are offered at the Lilia Hotel, a 20-minute walk from Passalimáni, the small-boat harbor fed by Zéa Marina. (A taxi to the main harbor costs 600 Drs/$2.50). The neighborhood is good for strolling, with some authentic ouzerís that are great for a sunset drink and contemplation of the pleasure boats.

WHERE TO EAT

Boat-bound travelers should get to Piraeus early enough to buy their tickets, find their ferry, and have time to walk into the market area behind Aktí Posidónos and the Aegina hydrofoils. (Snacks are expensive and dull on the boats.) There are a lot of outdoor fruit vendors, dried fruit-and-nut shops, bakeries, and knickknack traders.

Piraeus is also the most convenient destination for anyone who wants to dine by the sea. Athenians usually recommend **Mikrolímano,** but it's the single biggest source of reader complaints for us. It is, of course, very picturesque and the air (particularly in midsummer) is delightfully refreshing. Fish tavernas are piled side by side along a pretty half-moon cove hosting fishing boats and pleasure craft. Hawkers wave menus in the faces of passersby, urging them to inspect the day's catch and choose their supper. Prices are elusive, wine lists nonexistent, selected fish often disappear by sleight of hand, and rip-offs are common.

What to do? You can try one of several new cafes where drinks are served with occasional light snacks, and forget dinner; you get the ambience, the breezes, an expensive drink (rents are very high), but no miscalculated check for frozen seafood. You can try **Kanaris** (☎ 01/412-2533), the place where most bus tours stop. They have reasonably priced fish at 1,800 to 14,500 Drs ($7.80 to $63) per kilo, with calamari and octopus on the lower end of the price scale. Your meal will be good, the service is okay, and you probably won't be overcharged.

You could also head over to **Frates,** a lesser-known, less lively seafood restaurant strip near Zéa Marina and stop at whatever place catches your fancy. Or you can go to **Panorama,** where savvy Greeks go for a special meal.

For dessert or a light bite, head to **Ariston,** at Odós Bouboulínas 415, where pastries run 150 to 1,000 Drs (65¢ to $4.15). This excellent *zaharoplastío*, which lives up to its name (*áriston* means "excellent"), sells great sweets, miniature cheese pies, and rich *spanokópita* (spinach-filled pies) to take for your voyage.

Panorama Restaurant. Odós Irakliou 18–20 (above the Vearchion Music Center), Kastélla, Piraeus. ☎ **01/417-3475.** Reservations recommended in summer. Seafood 1,600–13,500 Drs ($7–$58.40) per kilo. AE, V. Daily noon–midnight. Closed August 15–30. SEAFOOD.

Ask your cab driver for Kastélla, the acropolis that once defended Piraeus harbor. In this picturesque residential quarter is a sky-high cafe with winter indoor and summer outdoor dining. The beautiful view over Mikrolímano and Piraeus harbor is now a bit marred by an apartment building rising in front of the terrace cafe, but this romantic aerie is still a lovely alternative to the hustler joints down at sea level. Our friend Vicos led us here, ordered grilled *fangrí* (sea bream), *marídes* (whitebait), *haravída* (crayfish)—and we're passing the favor on to you. This is about as close as you can get to the seaside and still expect excellently prepared, very fresh, reasonably priced seafood, with calm dignified service.

Rio-Antirio. Odós Merarchías 14. ☎ **01/451-4583.** Reservations not required. Main courses 750–1,800 Drs ($3.15–$7.50). Daily 8am–1am. GREEK.

This is a very clean, modern taverna with good salads, souvláki, pasta, and chicken, where you can peek around the display case till you're sure you understand what you're eating. Everything is tasty, freshly prepared, and inexpensive.

Tzaki Grill. Odós Godnari 7. ☎ **01/417-8932.** Reservations not required. Main courses 800–2,500 Drs ($3.35–$10.40). Daily 8am–2am. GREEK.

Look for the octopus hanging out to dry—that means you've found this clean, unpretentious grill near the Aegina hydrofoil pier and the ticket agents' offices. The specialties are inexpensive and delicious charcoal-grilled fresh fish and chicken. The octopus is also tasty.

RAFÍNA

Travelers bound for the Cyclades and the Dodecanese can save time and money by leaving from the east-coast port of Rafína. This easygoing fishing port is about 1 hour by bus east of Athens, and it's a refreshing change of pace once you reach the harborside. Everything seems much more manageable.

You'll notice many small beaches near Rafína. Villas and condos dot the coastline, and big resort hotels for Athenian weekenders crowd **Golden Beach,** the stretch south from Néa Mákri. A large joint U.S.-Greek naval base gets the prime beachfront here, leaving tourists with an incredibly diverse selection of junk-food parlors and cheap motels along the coastal highway until the more charming **Marathon Beach.**

Although Rafína doesn't have a nice beach of its own, the small harbor and sea breezes compensate by making it a refreshing change from the *néfos* (pollution) of the Greater Athens region. Life centers around the large *platía* (square), whose elevated position gives it an air of small-town dignity quite different from the dockside hustle that goes on at sea level below.

ESSENTIALS

GETTING THERE   Buses leave Athens from Áreos Park, Odós Mavromatéon 29 (☎ **01/821-0872**), every 30 minutes from 6:15am until 10:15pm, crossing the 17 miles to this Aegean port through Athens's urban sprawl and vineyards.

TAKING A BOAT OR HYDROFOIL FROM RAFÍNA TO THE ISLANDS
Boats run daily (twice a day in summer) to Ándros, Tínos, and Mýkonos (call the port police at ☎ **0294/22-300** for specific sailing times); four or five times weekly to Sýros, Páros, and Náxos (daily in summer); thrice weekly to Kos and Rhodes; and once a week to Níssiros, Tílos, Kálymnos, and Astypálea in the Dodecanese, and to Límnos and Kavála. You'll find a savings of 20% to 40% over the fares from Piraeus.

Ilio Lines (☎ **0294/22-888** in Rafína, 01/422-4772 in Piraeus) has daily hydrofoil service to Ándros, Tínos, Mýkonos, Páros, and Náxos—twice daily in July and August, several times a week in low season—continuing on to a dozen more islands that are little visited (except by wealthy Greeks with villas), as well as to Stýra, Marmári, and Kárystos on Évvia.

WHERE TO STAY & EAT

Spending a night in Rafína is a pleasant alternative to an early morning schlep to steamy Piraeus. Because many budget-tour groups use Rafína as their base for day trips, the hotel scene is dominated by a few huge Class C places. The **Hotel Avra** (☎ **0294/22-781;** fax 0294/23-320), with doubles for 21,000 Drs ($87.50), is the best. The **Hotel Akti** (☎ **0294/24-776**), with doubles for 6,000 Drs ($25), is the best value.

The immaculate **Kókkino Limanáki Campgrounds** (☎ 0294/31-603) are in nearby Kókkino Limanáki ("Little Red Port"), a beautiful red-cliff cove with a pebble beach. Rates are only 1,200 Drs ($5) per sleeping bag, with hot showers and a laundry room. If you have a long wait for the ferry, it may be worth your while to check in just for a swim.

There are two general areas where you can grab a bite in Rafína, either up around the square or down by the car-ferry pier. Colorful, awning-shaded cafes, banks, and other tourist essentials surround the spacious *platía*. On the east end of town (a 2-minute walk) a road slopes down for cars to be loaded onto ships bound for the Cyclades, Évvia, or the Dodecanese. Interspersed with the ferryboat ticket agencies are several seafood tavernas that are great fun when the ships are pulling in—far enough away to eat peacefully, yet close enough to enjoy the scene and activity. At lunchtime or suppertime watch out for the gregarious restaurateurs who'll try to rope you in for an expensive (though certainly scenic) fish fry.

9 Side Trips from Athens

It's sometimes hard to take the midsummer heat in Athens (in July and August temperatures can actually exceed 110°F!).

Our first recommendation for getting away is to head south to the beaches; all along the "Apollo Coast" between Piraeus and Cape Soúnio are resorts, beaches, tavernas, nightlife, and a relaxing change of pace. Your day could begin at the beautiful-to-behold Temple of Poseidon at Soúnio and stretch into an afternoon of beach sampling, an easy thing to do by public bus. (At the Temple of Poseidon, by the way, look for the name "Byron" carved into one of the marble columns by the English poet more than 170 years ago.)

A cool, forested retreat that's very popular with Athenians is the Kessariani Monastery, located on the verdant slopes of Mt. Imittós within a half hour drive from the center of Athens.

Architecture and archaeology buffs will enjoy an opportunity to head west to Dafní (a beautiful Byzantine monastery with an annual wine festival) and then on to Elefsína (ancient Eleusis), site of the fascinating Eleusinian Mysteries of antiquity.

The east coast of the Attic peninsula features the Plain of Marathon, site of the famous battle against the Persians. The museum and tombs uncovered here, combined with a lighthearted dip in the nearby bay, make a very interesting minijourney. North of Marathon is the Temple of Nemesis (goddess of vengeance), while south of Marathon is the Temple of Artemis (virgin goddess of the moon and hunting), at Brauron (Vravróna).

Several tour operators offer 1-day excursions to Epidaurus (see chapter 7), Delphi (see chapter 11), and the Saronic Gulf islands of Aegina, Hýdra, and Póros (covered in chapter 6). We think these sights deserve more than 1 day of your time, but if you're pressed, contact **Viking Star Tours,** Odós Artemídos 1, Glyfáda (☎ **01/ 898-0829** or 01/898-0729), for more information about the affordable packages it offers.

THE APOLLO COAST

The 40 miles of coastline curling around the Saronic Gulf between Athens and Cape Soúnio is known fondly by travel agents as the Apollo Coast.

In actuality, the first 12 miles are just an indistinguishable outgrowth of Athens. The first city south of Athens is **Glyfáda,** where the airports are located. Some readers enjoy spending the night in Glyfáda, in full view of the sea, especially on their last night in Greece. It's just 10 minutes south of Ellinikón Airport's Eastern Terminal,

Readers Recommend

Várkiza. "We stayed here the last two nights of our trip and found it the ideal place to wind down, very picturesque, with lots of activity along the waterfront and a good choice of restaurants. It's convenient to Cape Soúnio and an easy (10-mile) trip to the airport.

"We highly recommend the **Stefanakis Hotel,** at Odós Aphrodítis 17 (☎ 01/897-0528), a few blocks up from the main street, by far the best C-Class hotel we saw during our visit. The staff is very friendly, the breakfast is superior, and there's a very nice pool. A double with a real tub and shower curtain costs 12,500 Drs ($52.10)."

—Hope and Vern Boothe, Don Mills, Ontario

and there's much more of interest here than you may think from checking out the streets around the airport hotels.

EXPLORING THE AREA: THE BEACHES & BEYOND

Glyfáda is a well-to-do but hardly quiet suburb. The streets are lined with cafes, restaurants, and chic sportswear shops. Many expatriates and members of the military and diplomatic corps make Glyfáda their home, and the style and taste of the area reflect this foreign presence. The one bizarre and noisy aspect of life in this suburb is that jets from the nearby airport seem to hover over the avenues on their way in or out of Greece.

Despite the occasional rattle of windows, Glyfáda is a nice place to visit. The main drag, **King George Avenue,** is lined with cafes and restaurants, but for serious eating go around the corner from the Bank of Greece to **Konstandinópoulos Street.** There are several restaurants, sophisticated pizza parlors, steak restaurants, and bars.

If you have time to spare, explore the collection of modern Greek art found at Glyfáda's **Pierídis Gallery,** at Leofóros Vassiléos Yeoryíou 29 (☎ 01/894-8287), open Monday to Friday from 6 to 9pm and Saturday and Sunday from 10am to 1pm.

If you're looking for a beach, head south to Várkiza, about 19 miles away. The **Várkiza beach,** operated by the Greek Tourist Organization (☎ 01/897-2102), has small bungalows that rent for 6,300 Drs ($26.25), but admission is only 600 Drs ($2.50) for adults, half price for children. It's a nice public beach that will be packed on summer weekends, but at other times it makes a good day trip.

When you're there, you can walk or take the bus the 1 1/4 miles to Vári, a small town north of Várkiza known for its grilled lamb. Around the small square are several **barbecues,** serving private-label retsína and lamb on a spit. If you'll miss the Greek Easter feast, this is a way to experience every Greek's favorite meal. Several blue public buses leave Athens from Queen Olga Avenue south of the Záppion and the National Garden. Take the Soúnio coastal-route bus and get off at Vótsala/Lagoníssi.

The beaches improve in direct proportion to their distance from Athens. As you continue to Cape Soúnio, stop at **Lagoníssi** or at the small beach opposite the **Eden Beach Hotel.** Depending on crowds and season, seaside hotels may claim the right to the sand in front of their cafes and will extract 500 to 1,000 Drs ($2.10 to $4.20) from you to let you place your towel there.

SOÚNIO & THE TEMPLE OF POSEIDON

Our first-choice day trip would begin with a visit to the Temple of Poseidon at Cape Soúnio(n) (Sunium). **KTEL buses** (☎ 01/821-3203) for Soúnio leave Athens (Odós Mavromatéon 14, at Áreos Park) every hour between 6am and 6pm (it's a 2-hour ride, and the fare is 1,050 Drs/$4.40).

The 15 sun-bleached columns of the **Temple of Poseidon** stand out starkly against the Mediterranean sky, their power enhanced by the hilltop placement overlooking the sea. Their bold Doric design (no entasis, or bulging effect at the midriff, and only 16 flutings instead of 20) comes from the same master hand that designed the Theseum in the Agorá. Scholars believe that this 5th-century B.C. temple was built over the remains of an earlier Poseidon and Athena temple as part of Pericles' masterplan.

Very little remains of the *propylon* (entryway) or the *stoa* (covered arcade) that protected worshippers from the blazing sun. Yet the temple's strong columns (the square one engraved with Lord Byron's name is inside the southeast corner) and the solid base, which you can still walk on (this is one of the few temples in Greece that can be entered), convey an immediate sense of the respect felt by the architect and the worshippers for the god Poseidon. The fortress walls that once surrounded the temple defended this strategic highpoint over the Saronic Gulf and the shipping lanes to Évvia. Northeast of Poseidon's sanctuary was the Temple of Athena Sounias, but little of it remains today.

We recommend coming first thing in the morning so that you can have some time alone with this unforgettable monument. The archaeological site (☎ 0292/39-363) is open daily from 10am to 6pm. Admission is 800 Drs ($3.35) for adults, 600 Drs ($2.25) for seniors, 400 Drs ($1.65) for students.

After your first visit, walk down the hill to the tempting **Hotel Aegeon** (☎ 0292/39-200). On its beach, notice the hollowed-out storage niches in the encircling cliffs, where the Athenians dry-docked their triremes. You can picnic, eat at one of the tavernas, or have lunch and change clothes at the Aegeon's great cafe. Make sure to wander into the lobby to admire the barnacle-crusted amphorae and gemstones found in the seas below the temple.

Don't leave without returning to the Temple of Poseidon to admire it in the waning light of sunset. Looking west over the blue Aegean, your view framed by the majestic white columns nearly 2,500 years old is an experience to be relished.

MOUNT IMITTÓS & KESSARIANÍ MONASTERY

A refreshing half-day trip for travelers weary of the big city is an excursion to the **Kessarianí Monastery,** just 4¹/₂ miles east in a cool, bird-friendly forest at the foot of Mt. Imittós (Hymettus).

The healing spring waters pouring from the marble goat's head at the monastery's entrance have distinguished this as a holy site for centuries. Kessarianí, dedicated to the Presentation of the Virgin, was built over the ruins of a 5th-century Christian church, which in turn probably covered an ancient Greek temple.

The small church is constructed in the form of a Greek cross, with four marble columns supporting the dome. The lovely frescoes date from the 16th century, with the exception of those in the narthex, signed "Ioánnis Hýpatos, 1689." On the west side of the paved, flower-filled courtyard are the old kitchen and the refectory, which now houses some sculptural fragments. To the south, the old monks' cells and a bathhouse are being restored (exploration at your own risk is permitted).

The Kessarianí Monastery (☎ 01/723-6619) is open Tuesday to Sunday from 8:30am to 3pm; admission is 800 Drs ($3.35). Bus no. 224 leaves from Venizélou Street and Queen Sophia Avenue every 20 minutes; from the bus stop it's a half-hour walk up to the monastery.

Mt. Imittós offers beautiful prospects over Athens, Attica, and the Saronic Gulf—on a smogless days. At every scenic parking spot you'll find men playing backgammon, couples holding hands, and old people strolling. After sunset Imittós becomes

The Myth Behind the Mysteries of Elefsís

The names of the famous people initiated into the sacred rites performed at Elefsís would fill the rest of this chapter, yet we know almost nothing for certain about the ceremonies themselves.

We do know that they were bound up in one of the most important Greek myths: Demeter, the goddess of agriculture who had given humanity the gift of grain (our word "cereal" comes from her Roman name, "Ceres"), had a beautiful daughter, Persephone, whom Hades, god of the underworld and lord of the dead, fell in love with and abducted. Demeter could hear her daughter's cries for help coming from the cave you see immediately upon entering the site, which the ancients believed was connected to the underworld and called the Ploutonion (Pluto was the Roman name for the proprietor of Hell). Demeter was unable to find Persephone, despite her cries, and at the Kallichoron Well, to the left across the courtyard, she wept bitterly for her only child and, giving in to grief, let the earth go dry and all vegetation wither.

Eventually, she went to Mt. Olympus to plead for her daughter. Zeus declared that if the girl's grief had been equal to her mother's and she had eaten nothing, she could return. But Hades had given Persephone a pomegranate and urged her to eat it, and she had swallowed a seed. So for the 3 months of summer she was compelled to remain as queen of the Underworld, during which time Demeter grieved and let the earth lie infertile. For the remainder of the year Persephone could return to her mother, who then brought the autumn rains and let the earth flourish.

We surmise that the mysteries, celebrated in two degrees in the large central temple, the Telesterion, which was built about 600 B.C. over a Mycenaean temple, honored Demeter as the source of fertility and Persephone as the embodiment of spring. Scholars believe that these mysterious ceremonies were part purification and part drama. It's thought that priestesses promised immortality to the initiated. Cicero wrote in a letter to his friend Atticus, "Those Mysteries which, in raising us up from a brutish country life to one of culture, have gentled and ennobled us. We have learned through them not only to live in joy, but to die in greater hope."

Athens's favorite lovers' lane. The road winds around these forested slopes for nearly 11 1/2 miles, and the choice of sun, shade, cool breezes, and picnic spots is unlimited.

In antiquity, Mt. Imittós is believed to have been crowned with a statue of Zeus Hymettios, and ancient caves (including a 6th-century B.C. altar) have been found near the summit. More recently the mountain was cherished by Athenians for the honey produced by bees that fed off the mountain's fragrant flowers and herbs. Most of the bees have migrated now, although a few apiaries still exist for heather-fed bees.

THE MONASTERY OF DAFNÍ

The recently restored 11th-century monastery, one of the finest examples of Byzantine architecture in all Greece, is situated off the main Athens–Corinth highway about 6 miles west of Athens. The mosaics are among the most exquisite you'll see anywhere, and the famous *Christ Pandokrátor* ("Ruler of All") in the dome is particularly impressive. (The figures surrounding Him are the 16 Old Testament prophets who foretold His coming.)

The monastery (☎ **01/581-1558**) is open daily from 8:30am to 3pm; admission is 800 Drs ($3.35). From mid-August to mid-September an annual wine festival is usually held on the grounds; open from 8pm to midnight, entrance is 800 Drs ($3.35), and for 2,000 Drs ($8.35) you can sample many varieties of wine.

Check with the Athens Festival box office (☎ 01/322-7944) for information regarding the local **wine festival.**

Public buses no. 853, 862, and 873 leave from Elefthería (Freedom) Square, northeast of Keramikós Cemetery, every 20 minutes.

ELEFSÍS (ELEUSIS)

In the modern industrial town of Elefsís (also Elefsína in modern Greek, Eleusis in ancient Greek), farther west on the Athens–Corinth highway, you'll find the site of the most famous and revered of all the ancient mysteries, Eleusis—though it may be difficult for you to imagine the importance of the site today because of its homely setting and thorough destruction by Christians and barbarians. We probably owe our word "mystery" itself to the place.

The site and archaeological museum (☎ 01/554-6019) are open Tuesday to Sunday from 8:30am to 3pm; admission is 800 Drs ($3.35). Public buses no. 853, 862, and 873—which continue on from Dafní—leave from Elefthería (Freedom) Square, northeast of Keramikós Cemetery, every 20 minutes for the 1-hour trip to Elefsína.

On the right, after entering the site, behind the labeled **Temple of Artemis,** is the **Eschara,** a Roman-era pit where sacrificial victims were burned. To the left of the huge, sculpted marble medallion of Antonius Pius (its builder) is the **Greater Propylaea,** from the 2nd century A.D., modeled after the Propylaea of the Acropolis. Built on top of a 5th-century B.C. version, this entrance to the Sacred Way had balustrades to curb the flow of devotees to the sanctuary behind it. To the left of the Greater Propylaea can be seen one of two **triumphal arches** dedicated to the Great Goddesses and to the emperor Hadrian; this arch inspired the Arc de Triomphe, which caps the Champs-Elysées in Paris.

Nearby, the **Kallichoron Well** is where the Eleusinian women danced and chanted in praise of Demeter. Turning back, you'll see that up the marble-paved **Sacred Way** is the Ploutonion—the sacred cave through which Hades carried Persephone down into the Underworld. If you climb up beyond this you'll come to roofed-over areas where walls of several eras have not yet been fully excavated. On the right, the small carved stone steps are thought to have led to a terrace altar for worshipping the goddesses.

Behind the church is the **Telesterion,** a large square with rows of seats carved in the stone embankment. This was thought to be the Hall of Initiation (designed by Ictinus, of Parthenon fame), where devotees would gather to receive their mysterious rites.

In the small museum you can find the hacked remains of a famous **statue of Demeter** by Agorácritus, a student of Phidias, and several *kóre* (maidens). There are also various remains from the site, as well as Roman statues, including Antino's, Hadrian's favorite, in the robes of an initiate.

MARATHON

The bravery of the Athenians who defeated the invading Persian hordes at Marathon in 490 B.C. has been heralded since as one of history's greatest testimonies to the spirit of freedom and democracy.

An archaeological museum, the tomb of the Plataeans, and the tomb of the Athenians mark the spot of the battle, but the realization that this rocky plain of scrub brush and the clear blue bay beyond it were the site of such a momentous event transforms an ordinary day trip into an elevating experience.

No one tells the story of the Battle of Marathon (pronounced Ma-ra-*thón* in Greek) better than Herodotus. You may want to read about it in his *History* before you visit the site (the Penguin Classics series has a good translation).

Public (orange) buses to Marathon leave Athens from Odós Mavromatéon 29 at Áreos Park; call the **tourist police** (☎ **171**) for information and schedules. The nearby town of Marathon Beach (Paralía Marathónos) offers the closest accommodations and restaurants. Its pleasant beach, however, can get very crowded.

EXPLORING THE SITE   Near the base of Agrielíki Hill, the command post for the Athenians and their allies, a large grave site, the **Tumulus of the Plataeans,** was discovered. The tumulus was excavated in 1970 and has since been rebuilt so that you can enter and see the opened graves of the Plataean warriors. Herodotus tells us that Plataea contributed 1,000 troops to fight alongside the Athenians at Marathon. Those who fell are thought to have been buried here, about 200 yards from the archaeological museum.

Located across the highway and about 2 miles south of the archaeological museum turnoff is the **tomb of the Athenians** at Marathon, where the cremated remains of the 192 Athenian soldiers who died defending Greece from the Persians are buried. The site is marked with a simple stele (dating from 510 B.C.) carved with the likeness of Aristion, a *strategós* (general) who led the Athenians. The tomb of Miltíades has been found near the site of the present-day museum.

Marathon's **archaeological museum** (☎ **0294/55-155**) is next to the recently restored tomb of the Plataeans, 1¼ miles west of the highway turnoff marked MARATHON. The museum is certainly worth a visit. It's well organized (labels are in English as well as Greek) and features Neolithic to Byzantine-era finds from throughout the Marathon region. The small courtyard, filled with bitter orange and kumquat trees, has a large Ionic capital that's believed to be the top of a huge pedestal that supported a trophy honoring the victorious soldiers at Marathon. Archaeologists think that this column is similar in purpose to that of the Naxian Sphinx at Delphi.

The museum, the tumulus of the Plataeans, and the tomb of the Athenians are open Tuesday to Sunday from 8:30am to 3pm; admission for both museum and tomb is 500 Drs ($2.10) for adults, 400 Drs ($1.65) for seniors, and 300 Drs ($1.25) for students.

Held every October since 1972, the **Athens Open International Marathon** commemorates the run of Diomedon to announce the Athenian victory over the Persians at the Battle of Marathon (490 B.C.). The race begins outside the village of Marathon and continues along Diomedon's course for exactly 42.195 kilometers (26.2 miles) to the Panathenaic Stadium built for the first modern Olympic Games (1896) in Athens. There is no qualifying time to enter the race. Applicants should contact **SEGAS,** Leofóros Syngroú 137, 171 21 Athens (☎ **01/932-0636;** fax 01/934-2980), for information.

From Marathon, you can also make a side trip to the **Temple of Nemesis** (the goddess of vengeance) at the nearby acropolis of Rhamnous. It's accessible most easily by taxi (the fare is 10,000 Drs/$41.65) or by car from Marathon Beach. Little is left of the graceful work of the unknown architect who designed the Temple of Poseidon at Soúnio and the Theseum in the Agorá. The beautiful wildflowers that blanket the site are painful; Rhamnous means "place of spiny buckthorn."

But the Greeks have had the last laugh. The impressive three-tiered base of the goddess's temple is scarred with graffiti, particularly feet pointing in opposing directions. As an ironic touch, a smaller Temple of Themis (the goddess of eternal justice) was constructed behind that of Nemesis; its ruins are more impressive. The beautiful promontory was once lined with white-marble towers guarding the Euripus

Channel. It's now a scrub-brush slope, blocked off with fencing, but still offers a beautiful view of Marathon Bay and, beyond, the island of Évvia. The Temple of Nemesis site in Káto Soúli is open Tuesday to Sunday from 8:30am to 3pm; admission is free. Cars should follow road signs to the ferry at Ayía Marína, then bear left up the road.

THE TEMPLE OF ARTEMIS AT BRAURON

In the small village of Vravróna (also Vráona, variants of ancient Brauron) stands a Temple of Artemis that's a fabulous surprise. Not well known or frequented because the bus service is inconvenient, this lovely site is dedicated to the goddess of the moon, who was also the patroness of childbirth, unmarried girls, and chastity. Apollo's twin sister, Artemis was the protective mistress of all beasts; her role as goddess of the hunt was often chronicled in mythology.

Scholars believe that the temple was constructed in the Middle Helladic era (2000–1600 B.C.) to appease Artemis's anger over the killing of a bear. The bear was her favorite animal, and after the sanctuary was built, it was decreed that in the spring all the young girls from neighboring towns should dress like bears to honor Artemis. Every 5 years the Brauronia Festival was held, and girls between the ages of 5 and 10 would come in yellow *chitons* (full-length garments) and dance like bears on the sanctuary grounds. Many young women remained to grow up there, creating what might be called the first "feminist cell." King Agamemnon's daughter Iphigenia remained at Brauron to become a priestess when she returned from Tauris with Orestes. While Artemis was venerated in gratitude for an easy birth and the good health of the infant, Iphigenia was brought votive offerings at the death of a baby or a woman in childbirth.

The best-preserved part of the site is the **stoa,** a colonnaded way once called the Parthenon, perhaps because the young devotees of Artemis lived there during festivals. ("Parthenon" derives from the word *parthénos,* "virgin.") These ruins date primarily from the 5th century B.C. and cover earlier shrines at this site. The proportions of the temple are square; the squat Doric columns end abruptly on the limestone terrace and appear more primitive than the graceful supports of the famous Doric temples at Soúnio or on the Acropolis.

The **archaeological museum** (☎ 0294/71-020) of Vravróna is half a mile from the site, along the main road that winds through vineyards and grazing fields. Inside are 4th-century B.C. votive reliefs and friezes from the sanctuary, geometric-era ceramics from early tombs, and other finds from a prehistoric settlement discovered on a hill above the temple. The most interesting displays are those that illuminate the activities of temple inhabitants; there are terra-cotta plaques carved in relief that depict Artemis in her many incarnations, gold jewelry and ornamental objects found in the silty deposit from the sacred spring, and charming ceramic statuettes of the young girls who came to perform and worship here.

The museum and the archaeological site are open Tuesday to Sunday from 8:30am to 3pm; admission to each is 500 Drs ($2.10) for adults, 400 Drs ($1.65) for seniors, and 300 Drs ($1.25) for students. During our last visit, Vavróna, 22 miles east of Athens, could not be reached directly by public bus. We had to stay overnight in Markópoulou (not our idea of a lovely place) in order to catch the early (school) bus on to the site; the only return bus was in the afternoon. (There are a few small hotels in Vavróna, a couple of miles away through the countryside.) We hope transportation improves; call ☎ 142 for a domestic bus schedule.

The Saronic Gulf Islands

6

The calm Saronic Gulf, sheltered between Attica and the Peloponnese peninsula, has a number of attractive islands, each with a unique identity, but all so convenient to the mainland that their easy accessibility and popularity are their main drawbacks, particularly during the summer and on weekends. Our advice about visiting in the off-season is especially important here. Besides, the islands are at their most beautiful in the spring before the hordes trample the wildflowers and in the fall when the flowers seem to heave a long, luxurious sigh of relief. Unless you have reservations, go only for day trips during the summer, and then only on weekdays.

The large island of **Salamís,** visible from Piraeus, has been marred by heavy industry and construction projects, and it's no longer attractive to tourists. However, it's still famous as the birthplace of Euripides, the classical tragic poet, and as the site, in 480 B.C., of a sea battle between the Athenians and the Persians, who were roundly defeated in its narrow strait. Much-visited **Aegina** (Éyina) is also nearly a suburb of Athens, its hills covered with pines and its fertile valleys extensively cultivated, notably with numerous pistachio orchards; its graceful Doric Temple of Aphaia is one of the best preserved of all Archaic buildings, especially appealing because it's situated atop a pine-covered hill. **Póros** is an attractive if less cultivated island—very popular with the younger budget crowd and increasingly with tour groups. But it manages to keep its head above water and can be a pleasant place to enjoy good beaches and inexpensive nightlife.

Fashionable **Hýdra** (Ýdra), with its superb natural harbor, elegant stone mansions, and monasteries, is the most strikingly beautiful of the group. The whole island has been declared a national monument (vehicles have been banished), so it's a particular delight, if rather expensive. **Spétses** offers much better beaches than Hýdra, some architectural distinction, more sophisticated nightlife, and traffic (which you can escape with a little effort).

Because of good hydrofoil and ferry service, the Saronic Gulf islands can be visited on day trips from Athens, or you can find accommodations on one island and then visit the others. Hýdra is our favorite for a stay of more than 2 or 3 days, but they all offer a convenient respite from the bustle of Athens. They can also be visited on an inexpensive three-isle day cruise.

EXPLORING THE ISLANDS

One of the joys of touring the Saronic Gulf is that, with few exceptions, you can go to any island from any other island at almost any time of day. Car-ferries, excursion boats, and hydrofoils run continuously; in July and August you'll rarely have to wait more than an hour.

This efficient state of affairs is bolstered by the operation of the **Flying Dolphins,** a fleet of yellow-and-blue, Russian-built hydrofoils that fly on the surface of the water at more than twice the speed of a normal ferry. The cabin is laid out like the interior of an airplane, with bucket seats. The Ceres Company's huge new **Super Cat** hydrocatamarans are even more comfortable and faster, with food and beverage service in first class.

Generally, a hydrofoil costs about 35% more than a regular ferry. Most depart from Zéa Marina in Piraeus; the car-ferries, excursion boats, and most Aegina-bound hydrofoils leave from the main Piraeus docks. All begin operating at 6am and continue service until the late evening, stopping at Aegina, Póros, Hýdra, Spétses, Kyrapássi, Hermióne, Leonídion, Pórto, Céli, Monemvassiá, and—in the high season—Týros, Tólo, Neápolis, Náfplio, and Kýthira.

A good way to see the Saronic Gulf is by taking a three-island day cruise, which can be booked through a travel agent, such as **Viking Star Cruises** (☎ **01/898-0729** or 01/898-0829) or at your hotel desk. **Epirotiki Lines** (☎ **01/429-1000**) provides transportation to and from your hotel in Athens to Flísvos Marina, where its *Hermés* departs daily about 8:30am for Hýdra (swimming and shopping), Póros (lunch and sightseeing), and Aegina (to visit the Temple of Aphaia or swimming), returning to Athens about 7:30pm. Lunch is served on board, and there's a small pool. For about 16,500 Drs ($70) you get a good tour and an introduction to travel aboard a luxury cruise ship.

1 Aegina (Éyina)

17 nautical miles SW of Piraeus

Aegina (Éyina), the largest of the Saronic Gulf islands, is only half an hour away from Piraeus by hydrofoil, making it a convenient and pleasurable day-trip introduction to the Greek islands. Many people even treat it as an extension of the capital (in fact, Aegina *was* the capital in the early years of the modern Greek nation), commuting to and from Athens on the Flying Dolphins. An even larger group visits Aegina on weekends.

Despite the pressures of tourism and development, Aegina manages to maintain its identity. The countryside supports the usual Greek staples (olives, figs, and almonds), but there are also strangely gnarled pistachio trees. Farmers often set up temporary booths along the road to peddle these exotic nuts.

Most people come to Aegina just to escape the capital or to visit the Temple of Aphaia, one of the best-preserved sanctuaries in Greece; it ranks on a par with the Temple of Poseidon at Soúnio.

If you're interested in reading more about the island, pick up a copy of Anne Yannoulis's *Aegina* (Lycabettus Press).

ESSENTIALS

GETTING THERE & DEPARTING   **Ferry** and **excursion-boat** tickets can be purchased at the pier; call the **Piraeus Port Authority** (☎ **01/451-1311**) for schedule and departure pier information. Flying Dolphin **hydrofoil** tickets can be purchased in advance at the **Ceres Hydrofoil Joint Service** office, at Aktí

Demósthenes, one of the greatest Athenian orators and statesmen, fled to the Temple of Poseidon for refuge, but Antípater's forces pursued him, and he committed suicide by swallowing poison hidden in the nib of his pen (proving, as some wags observe, that the pen is sometimes quicker than the sword).

If you're especially interested in monasteries, you might want to visit the 18th-century **Monastery of Zoödóches Piyí** ("Life-giving Spring"), about 2^1/$_2$ miles south-east of Askéli, though monks no longer live there—you'll find only a caretaker and a couple of tavernas nearby.

There's a **beach** northwest of town at **Neório,** though it's not always very clean. There are better beaches southeast of town at **Askéli** and **Kanáli.**

Instead of touring Póros, you might want to catch the ferry across to **Galatás,** especially in the middle of June during the annual Flower Festival, when there are parades with floats and marching bands and floral displays. (Greece exports flowers, even to Holland.) From Galatás you can catch a bus the 5 miles west to **Trizína** (ancient Troezen), birthplace of Theseus and scene of the tragedy of his wife, Phaedra, and son, Hippólytus, as well as site of an ancient Temple of Asclepius. There's not a lot to see at the site, but walking through fields of carnations and along the **Devil's Causeway** (which is supposed to have the old fellow's face on one of its walls) is very pleasant and will be of even greater interest if you've read Mary Renault's *The King Must Die.*

About 2^1/$_2$ miles south of Galatás near the beach of **Alíki,** you'll find the olfactory wonder of **Limonodássos** ("Lemon Grove"), where more than 25,000 lemon trees fill the air with their fragrance. Follow the signs to the **Taverna Kardássi,** where you can enjoy freshly squeezed lemonade for about 550 Drs ($2.10) or the potent local retsína.

WHERE TO STAY

For additional accommodations, contact **Marinos Tours,** on the harbor (☎ 0298/ 23-423). Marinos handles more than 450 rooms and apartments, in addition to booking local hotels. Count on spending 6,600 to 13,200 Drs ($27.50 to $55) per night for two, depending on location and facility.

Hotel Latsi. Odós Papadopoúlou 74, 180 20 Póros, Trizínías. ☎ **0298/22-392.** 36 rms, some with bath (shower). TEL. 7,500 Drs ($31.25) double without bath, 16,500 Drs ($68.75) double with bath. No credit cards.

This blue-shuttered hotel is on the northeast side of the port, opposite the Galatás ferry pier, so it offers a scenic but somewhat quieter location. The worn but clean rooms, with balconies overlooking the Peloponnese, offer good value.

✪ **Hotel Sirene.** Askéli, 180 20 Póros, Trizínías. ☎ **0298/22-741.** Fax 0298/22-744. 120 rms, all with bath (shower). TEL. 14,500 Drs ($60.40) single; 20,500 Drs ($85.40) double. Half board optional. MC.

If you're looking for top-of-the-line accommodations, you'll like this Class B hotel situated on the road leading to the monastery, on the southern coast of Kalávria. The hotel's bright blue van meets most of the ferries, or you can take the bus or a taxi from the port; the bus fare is 165 Drs (70¢) and a taxi costs 700 Drs ($2.90). At the modern six-story building, all the spacious rooms face the sea. This exquisite view is complemented by a lovely private beach and swimming cove as well as a swimming pool near the water's edge. We enjoyed sitting on the long wrap terrace on the top floor, adjacent to the popular bar. The Sirene is usually booked with European groups, so reservations are a must.

Maria Christofa Rooms to Let. 180 20 Póros, Trizinías. ☎ **0298/22-058.** 6 rms, none with bath. 6,500 Drs ($27.10) single or double. No credit cards.

The home of Maria Christofa can be found in the narrow lanes at Póros town's highest point. Many of her simple rooms have breathtaking views of the town and harbor. We enjoyed staying in her high-ceilinged space, really the bargain of the island.

WHERE TO EAT

Caravella Restaurant. Paralía, Póros town. ☎ **0298/23-666.** Reservations not required. Main courses 1,250–4,000 Drs ($5.20–$16.65). No credit cards. Daily 10am–1am. GREEK.

This portside taverna specializes in fish entrees and other traditional dishes such as veal stifádo (veal with onions) and moussaká. We particularly liked the Caravella's octopus salad, stuffed eggplant, and roast souvláki; and we enjoyed gossiping with the owner, Takis Makris.

Lucas Restaurant. Paralía, Póros town. ☎ **0298/22-145.** Reservations not required. Main courses 1,000–4,000 Drs ($4.15–$16.65). No credit cards. Daily 7pm–1am. GREEK.

It's a pleasant quarter-mile walk southeast (right) from the central square to this casual outdoor place, opposite the private yacht mooring. A Greek dancer and his English wife, Susie, serve good fresh seafood and typical taverna fare that's reasonably priced for this upscale side of town.

Quarter Pizza. Paralía, Póros town. ☎ **0298/24-503.** Reservations not required. Pizza 1,600–2,700 Drs ($6.65–$11.25); pasta 1,250–2,000 Drs ($5.20–$8.35). No credit cards. Daily 10am–midnight. ITALIAN.

The best wood-oven–baked pizza in town is found under a grape arbor near the bridge across the canal to Kalávria. Service is friendly, and the pasta is also quite good.

PÓROS AFTER DARK

Póros is a dancer's island, and you're sure to find a club where people will be dancing to Greek music, notably the quick, energetic *hasápiko*, which will give you some idea of how many Greeks stay fit. If you're interested in something more familiar, look for the **Sirocco Disco,** at the northeast end of the harbor near the bridge to Kalávria—not to be confused with the **Sirocco Club** in the nightlife area at the opposite end of the harbor, where you'll also find **Different, Maskes,** and **Il Pirata.** In Askéli the white marble-sheathed music bar **Artemis,** an elegant nightspot, draws the yachting crowd.

3 Hýdra

35 nautical miles S of Piraeus

Hýdra (ýdra) has both natural physical beauty and superlative architectural distinction, plus the blessing of no traffic. Pedestrians are free to wander the port and the peaceful back lanes with only an occasional donkey, mule, or horse and the rare appearance of a motorized garbage truck. The whole island has been declared a monument by both the Greek government and the Council of Europe.

At first sight, the barren rocky island looks almost forbidding. Then your ship enters the perfect horseshoe harbor—surrounded by gray and white mansions, churches, and red-tiled roofs—and suddenly you see the reason for all the excitement. Hýdra was briefly an artists' colony in the 1960s; since then the artists have fled because of rising real-estate prices, leaving behind an artistic flavor that invites disdain from some, especially the more pretentious. However, if you can avoid the midday crush of cruise-ship visitors and the weekend inundation of Athenians, you'll find the island delightful and refreshing, although rather expensive. The island's one major drawback for some tourists is the lack of good beaches, though there are a few places for swimming.

The slate-gray town of Hýdra rises up like a natural amphitheater from the port; to appreciate its peacefulness, just take a short, steep walk uphill. Follow the worn cobblestone steps up to the stone wall, which surrounds a whitewashed monastery and local cemetery. At this distance, the sounds of the town and land wash over you in a flood of fresh sensations. The tinkle of goat bells, the braying of donkeys, and the chatter of children float up from below, joining the singsong chant of a monk above you.

ESSENTIALS

GETTING THERE & DEPARTING   Several car-ferries and excursion boats make the 4-hour journey from Piraeus daily; contact the **Piraeus Port Authority** (☎ **01/ 451-1311**) or the **Hýdra Port Authority** (☎ **0298/52-279**) for schedules. Several hydrofoils (both the Flying Dolphin and the super-new Flying Cat) leave Piraeus's Zéa Marina harbor for the 75-minute trip daily; contact **Ceres Hydroways** (☎ **01/ 428-0001** in Piraeus or 0298/52-019 in Hýdra) for schedules and reservations (recommended on weekends).

The **Flying Dolphin office** is on a backstreet, up the first street on the left from the ferry pier and to the right; look for the small signs. Ferry tickets are sold at **Ydraioniki** (☎ **0298/54-007**), the first small office to the left on the lane next to the National Bank.

VISITOR INFORMATION   The widely available, free publication *This Summer in Hýdra* contains a map and much useful information. **Saitis Tours,** near the ferry landing (☎ **0298/52-184**), can exchange money, provide information on rooms and villas, book excursions, and help you make long-distance calls or send faxes.

ORIENTATION   Your boat, whether ferry or hydrofoil, will dock on the left (east) side of the port. Hýdra town curls around the busy waterfront, spreads inland for several lanes, then climbs steeply uphill. Some streets have names, but signs are scarce and getting lost is part of the fun. If necessary you can always ask a local.

GETTING AROUND   Walking is the only means of transportation on the island itself, unless you come upon an available four-legged creature. Caïques provide **water-taxi** service to the island's beaches and the nearby island of Dokós, as well as to secluded restaurants in the evening; rates run about 200 to 2,000 Drs (85¢ to $8.50), depending on destination, with an extra 600-Dr ($2.55) charge if booked by phone.

FAST FACTS   The telephone **area code** for Hýdra is 0298.

The **National Bank of Greece** and the **Commercial Bank** both have offices on the harbor; they're open Monday to Thursday from 8am to 2pm, Friday from 8am to 1:30pm, and during the high season, also on Saturday from 11am to 2pm. Otherwise, the **post office,** just off the harborfront on Odós Ikonómou, the lane between the two banks, open Monday to Friday from 7:30am to 2:15pm, is your best bet for currency exchange, but several travel agents, including **Saitis Tours** on the harbor, exchange money from about 9am to 8pm.

Jasmine Laundry Service, to the right from the post office behind the central market, offers service within an hour for 2,600 Drs ($10.85) for up to 5 kilos (11 lb.).

There's a **pharmacy** (☎ **0298/52-059**) and **doctor's office** (☎ **0298/52-420**) on Odós Rafaélia, right off Odós Miaoúli above the small square a couple of blocks inland from the middle of the port. There are other doctor's offices nearby and another pharmacy off the east end of the harbor. Call the **police,** on the second floor at Odós Votsí 9 (☎ **0298/52-205**), two lanes up from near the southwest corner of the harborfront, for medical or other emergencies.

A small store near the middle of the harborfront sells English-language periodicals and a few paperbacks.

The **telephone center (OTE)** is across from the police station on Odós Votsí, open Monday to Saturday from 7:30am to 10pm and Sunday from 8am to 1pm and 5 to 10pm.

SPECIAL EVENTS If you can, come for **Greek Easter,** to share in the colorful Good Friday ceremonies. Another special time is toward the end of June for the **Miaoúlis Festival,** which celebrates a famous naval victory during the War of Independence, in which the Hydriot Admiral Andréas Vókos, known as Miaoúlis (1769–1835), defeated the superior Ottoman fleet. The battle is re-created each year, complete with the burning of a fireship, exploding cannons, and fireworks. (Be sure to reserve a room well ahead of time for both occasions.)

EXPLORING THE ISLAND

Hýdra town is the port, capital, and only town on the island, but it's chock full of enough charm and history to keep you interested for several days. The **mansions** that give the steep-sided port its special character were built in the late 18th century by Italian architects with the fortunes made by audacious Hýdriot captains, who had the skill and the courage to transport cargo wherever it was in demand regardless of embargoes and blockades; their work was especially lucrative during the Napoleonic Wars. (The map in *This Summer in Hýdra* will help you find the places we mention.) *Hýdra,* by Catherine Vanderpool (Lycabettus Press), is a good companion guide.

On the right (west) side from the ferry pier you'll find the **Tobázi mansion,** now a branch of the **School of Fine Arts**, with a hostel for students. (Call the mansion at ☎ **0298/52-291** or the Athens Polytechnic at ☎ **01/619-2119** for information about the program or exhibits.) The nearby **Ikonómou-Miriklís** (sometimes called the **Voulgaris**) **mansion** has an interesting interior. Higher up the hill is the largest and handsomest, the **Koundouriótis mansion,** built by an Albanian family that contributed generously to the cause of independence.

The closest **swimming** area is immediately below the mansion, where you can just dive off the rocks into the crystal-clear sapphire sea.

There's some interesting shopping on this side of the harbor, particularly at the **Hermes Art Shop** (☎ **0298/52-689**), which has an amazing array of jewelry, many good antique reproductions, and a few textiles, including wall hangings by the owner, Jane Stavrou, and silk paintings by her daughter.

The **shops** on the harborfront are generally overpriced, so if shopping's your game, wander the back lanes in search of diversity and better prices. On our last trip we enjoyed visiting the **Emborium,** up from the left (east) side of the harbor (☎ **0298/53-951**), where the knowledgeable owner Philippe sells his own ceramics, wooden handcrafted items from Náxos, and herbal products. Across and up the street, **Latini** (☎ **0298/53-067**) sells interesting ceramics, costume jewelry, and wooden puzzles.

On the left (east) side of the waterfront you'll find the **Spilopoúlou mansion** and the **Tsamados mansion,** now the **Merchant Marine School,** Greece's oldest college for sea captains. (You can visit if classes are not in session.) Nearby is the **Historical Archives,** which contains portraits of local heroes and celebrities, old weapons, ship decorations, and navigation paraphernalia; it's open daily from 10am to 1pm. The **Kriezis mansion** is behind the Port Authority, and the worn steps beyond lead up to the fortress that once protected the harbor.

Hýdra is famous for its many churches; there's said to be one for every day of the year, and several of them are well worth a visit. The most beautiful, the **Monastery of the Assumption of the Virgin Mary,** is conveniently situated on the central waterfront at the **Clock Tower.** The former monks' cells are now municipal offices, but the marble courtyard offers a serene retreat. (Most of the marble came from Póros's Temple of Poseidon.) There's a small chapel with precious Byzantine art, including an exquisite marble iconostasis; it's well worth the requested donation (150 Drs/65¢), for which you also get a postcard. The statues are of Lázaros Koundouriótis and Andréas Miaoúlis.

If you're interested in more religious sites, want to stretch your legs, and are wearing sturdy shoes, continue on up Odós Miaoúli, past **Kalá Pigádia** ("Good Wells," where the town still gets much of its water)—about an hour's walk—to the **Convent of Ayía Efpraxía** and the **Monastery of Profítis Ilías** (the Prophet Elijah), which offer superb views of the town and beyond. Both are still active, and the nuns sell their hand-woven fabrics. (*Note:* Men and women in shorts and tank tops will not be allowed inside.)

By continuing farther northeast you can reach the **Monastery of the Ayía Triáda** (Holy Trinity), which still has a few monks and excludes women. Walking 2 hours farther east will bring you to the **Cloister of Zourvás** and the east end of the island.

HITTING THE BEACH

The only real beach on the island is a 20-minute walk east of town at **Mandráki;** busy sand-and-shingle **Miramáre Beach,** dominated by the Miramáre Hotel, offers a **water-sports center.**

West of town you can swim off the rocks at **Kamíni,** and farther along a donkey trail you'll find **Kastéllo,** with the small fort that gives it its name and less crowded swimming on another rocky beach. Farther west (about a 45-minute walk from town), **Vlichós** offers better swimming, three tavernas, and a few rooms to let. About 2 miles farther along the trail (best reached by water taxi) is the pretty pine-lined cove of **Mólos,** favored by the jet set. The donkey path continues west to the cultivated plateau at **Episkopí,** from which a faint trail leads on west to **Bísti** and **Áyios Nikólaos** for more secluded swimming.

One fairly good beach on the south coast, **Limióniza,** can be reached with strong legs, sturdy shoes, and a good map from Ayía Triáda, though it's much easier to take a water taxi. The island of **Dokós,** northwest off the tip of Hýdra, an hour's boat ride from town, has a good beach and excellent diving conditions but few facilities, so you would need to take a picnic lunch. (It was here that Jacques Cousteau found a sunken ship with cargo still aboard—believed to be 3,000 years old.)

WHERE TO STAY

Since all the hotels are rather small, you'd be wise to book well ahead of time. In the summer and on weekends reservations are a must. All hotels are open from early April until late October unless otherwise noted. Low-season prices should be 20% to 30% less, and breakfast is often included.

DOUBLES FOR LESS THAN 10,500 DRS ($43.75)

Pension Éfi. Odós Sachíni, 180 40 Hýdra. ☎ **0298/52-371.** 15 rms, all with bath (shower). 9,250 Drs ($38.50) single or double. No credit cards.

The Éfi is a newer pension, near the police station, that offers good views of the harbor or the town's rooftops from its modern, simple rooms. You'll find the affable proprietor at a tourist shop opposite the Clock Tower. Although his English is limited, his hospitality is forthcoming.

Pension Theresia. 180 40 Hýdra. ☎ **0298/53-984.** Fax 0298/53-983. 19 rms, all with bath (shower). 8,000 Drs ($33.50) single; 10,500 Drs ($43.75) double. No credit cards. Take Tobázi St. off the southeast corner of the harbor from the ferry landing, bear right at the Amalour Club, and follow the signs to Douskos Restaurant; the pension is just off the southeast corner of the square.

One of the best budget choices in town offers comfortable rooms around a small courtyard garden with a well.

Savvas Rooms to Let. Odós Antoníou Lychnoú 13, 180 40 Hýdra. ☎ **0298/52-259.** 5 rms, none with bath. 8,500 Drs ($35.40) single; 10,500 Drs ($43.75) double. No credit cards. Closed Sept–Mar.

Up from the southwest corner of the harbor, near the Hotel Hýdra, is this gray-stone home run by the gregarious Kechayioglou brothers. Unlike most recently built rooms, the units here are spacious and handsomely furnished, if a bit worn, with two clean bathrooms outside in a plant-filled courtyard. Climbing up the steep wooden stairs with the narrow pipe handrail may remind you of maneuvering in a sailboat. The china cupboards, the sofas with flower-print cushions, and the old sloping floors leave no doubt that you're in a real home.

DOUBLES FOR LESS THAN 20,000 DRS ($83.35)

✪ **Hotel Angelika.** Odós Miaoúli 42, 180 40 Hýdra. ☎ **0298/53-202.** Fax 0298/53-698. 22 rms, all with bath (shower). 12,000 Drs ($50) single; 19,000 Drs ($79.15) double. Rates include breakfast. Air-conditioning 3,000 Drs ($12.50) extra. MC.

This friendly, good-value place—about a 10-minute walk up from the middle of the harbor—has pleasant, simple rooms overlooking a quiet arbor courtyard, where breakfast is served. Rooms 6, 8, 9, and 10 even have large rooftop terraces with panoramic views.

Hotel Greco. Odós Kouloúra, 180 40 Hýdra. ☎ **0298/53-200.** Fax 0298/53-511. 19 rms, all with bath (shower). A/C TEL. 15,000 Drs ($62.50) single; 20,000 Drs ($83.35) double. Rates include breakfast. AE, DC, MC, V.

In a quiet neighborhood away from the tourist area, this hotel, with its slick, modern interior, was created from a traditional stone fishing-net factory. All rooms are spotless and outfitted with designer-print fabrics and blue tile floors. The taverna on the large, enclosed stone patio is a pleasant spot for fresh grilled meats and Greek fare in the evening; there's also a playroom/gym with a training machine. To find the hotel, follow our directions to the Mistral Hotel; then continue up and to the left.

Hotel Hýdra. 180 40 Hýdra. ☎ **0298/52-102.** 13 rms, 8 with bath. TEL. 10,800 Drs ($45) single without bath; 15,600 Drs ($65) double without bath; 19,200 Drs ($80) double with bath. Rates include breakfast. MC, V. Closed Oct to mid-Apr. Turn left on Odós Votsí just after the Clock Tower, take the first right, then the second right, and continue up.

This is another Hydriot mansion now open to visitors, a two-story, gray-stone hotel on the western cliffs. The building was purchased from the National Tourist Organization by Dimitri Davis and has been beautifully restored. The rooms are carpeted, high-ceilinged, and simply furnished; many have balconies overlooking the town and harbor. A good value if you don't mind a hike.

Hotel Leto. 180 40 Hýdra. ☎ **0298/53-385.** Fax 01/361-2223 in Athens. 24 rms, all with bath (shower); 6 suites. A/C MINIBAR TEL. 18,900 Drs ($78.85) double; 25,650 Drs ($107) suite for three or four. Rates include breakfast. No credit cards. Take Miaoúli St. from the middle of the harbor several blocks and look for the anchor on the right.

The recently upgraded Leto has hardwood floors, bright contemporary furniture, and colorful modern-art posters on its walls. Its rooms are among the largest and most tasteful in town, and its garden is a delight. An American-style breakfast buffet is presented by the eager-to-please staff in the basement lounge. The resident Hellas Arts Club offers courses in painting, ceramics, Greek dance, yoga, and body conditioning.

Hotel Miranda. 180 40 Hýdra. ☎ **0298/52-230.** Fax 0298/53-510. 16 rms and suites all with bath (shower). TEL. 19,800 Drs ($82.50) double; 26,400 Drs ($110) double with A/C; 32,000 Drs ($133.35) suite. Rates include breakfast. V. Find the Hotel Leto and continue beyond it for a couple of blocks; the Miranda will be on the right.

Set in a sea captain's mansion from 1810, the Miranda is eclectically decorated with Oriental rugs, battered wooden chests, marble tables, contemporary paintings, and period naval engravings. Most of the renovated rooms are very spacious; some have lovely painted ceilings and antique wooden furniture. The hosts Yannis and Miranda are as gracious as one could hope for, transforming their mansion into a casual, homey abode. For families we recommend the "suites"—stylish three-bedded accommodations with Greek country antiques and oversize balconies offering harbor views.

Mistral Hotel. 180 40 Hýdra. ☎ **0298/52-509.** Fax 0298/53-411. 20 rms, all with bath (shower). TEL. 12,600 Drs ($52.50) single; 17,200 Drs ($71.65) double; 19,150 Drs ($79.75) double with A/C. Rates include breakfast. AE, V. Closed Nov–Feb. Take Tobázi St. off the southeast corner of the harbor from the ferry landing to the Ippocampos Hotel, turn right, then left, and continue up 2 blocks.

The three-story Mistral (named for those strong August winds), newly built in an old house, features a spacious stone courtyard with flowers, a bar, and comfy rattan chairs shaded by a bamboo pergola. The rooms are distinctive, suffused with the charm of the hostess Sofia. Dinner in the courtyard is available only to guests—a chance to sample the freshest seafood at bargain prices.

WHERE TO EAT

As usual, avoid the waterfront tavernas except for coffee or a quick snack. In the words of several locals: "Avoid the colored chairs. Head into the back lanes of town for a better meal and deal." In fact, two of our favorite places are at nearby beach areas west of town. Worth a special mention is the family-run **Taverna Cristina** and **Vangelis,** where simple fare, mostly fish, achieves heights of greatness.

Barba Dimas. Hýdra. ☎ **0298/53-166.** Reservations not required. Main courses 1,000–2,900 Drs ($4.15–$12.10). No credit cards. Daily 6–11:30pm. Take Tobázi St. off the southeast corner of the harbor from the ferry landing, bear right at the Amalour Club, and continue up a couple of blocks. GREEK.

One of Hýdra's few typical tavernas is this tiny (six-table) place, with a blue-and-yellow facade. The chef Yannis turns out wonderful *salingária* (snails with garlic and onion) and *souzoukákia* (lamb meatballs in tomato sauce). You won't know what's for supper until you examine his kitchen, but it's guaranteed to be fresh and cooked with loving care.

✪ Marina's Taverna. Vlichós. ☎ **0298/52-496.** Reservations not required. Main courses 1,000–3,300 Drs ($4.15–$13.75). No credit cards. Daily noon–11pm. GREEK.

For a special occasion or just for fun, take a 45-minute hike or a water taxi (2,000 Drs/$8.35) west beyond Kamíni to the best sunset view in Greece and our favorite dining experience on Hýdra. Perched high above the small pebble beach, this stunning spot, also called **Iliovasílema** (Sunset), offers a fine meal cooked by the lovely Marína. The menu is basic, handcrafted, and fresh; her *kléftiko,* an island specialty of pork pie, is superb.

Ouzeri Strofilia. Odós Miaoúli, Hýdra. No phone. Appetizers 400–3,400 Drs ($1.65–$14.15). No credit cards. Summer, daily noon–3am; winter, daily 6pm–3am. GREEK MEZÉDES.

Our favorite ouzerí for a drink and snacks—or a grazer's full meal—is 1 block up from the middle of the port. Where else can you choose from 48 *mezédes*—among them a superb mussels *saganaki, fasólia* (black-eyed peas), *kreatopitákia* (lightly fried mini meat pies), seven cheeses, and three types of olives? Strofilia also has a good, well-priced wine list.

Taverna the Garden. Hýdra. ☎ **0298/52-329.** Reservations not required. Main courses 1,400–3,600 Drs ($5.85–$15). V. Daily 7pm–1am. Follow our directions to the Mistral Hotel and turn left just before reaching it. GREEK.

One of our longtime favorites is located several blocks inland from the ferry landing, behind tall, whitewashed walls in a tree-filled garden. On a July or August evening you'll recognize this grill restaurant by the line waiting to get in. The meat is superb and the swordfish souvláki divine; don't pass up the *exochikó* (lamb wrapped in phyllo leaves).

To Steki. Odós Miaoúli, Hýdra. ☎ **0298/53-517.** Reservations not required. Main courses 1,500–1,700 Drs ($6.25–$7.10); daily specials 2,500–4,300 Drs ($10.40–$17.90). AE, EURO, MC, V. Daily 11am–midnight. Take Miaoúli St. from the middle of the harbor a couple of blocks and you'll see the restaurant on the right. GREEK.

Locals favor this small, blue-shuttered taverna for its simple fresh food and reasonable prices. The interior, where clients dine in the chilly winter months, has some colorful framed folk murals of Hydriot life. The fare is basic but very good. We don't care much for fixed-price menus, but To Steki offers four or five daily, all with salad and dessert, some menus including locally caught fish, priced according to availability.

HÝDRA AFTER DARK

The **Veranda,** up from the right (southwest corner) of the harbor near the Hotel Hýdra—look for the sign SAVVAS ROOMS TO LET—is an excellent place to sip a glass of retsína or cafe frappé and watch the sunset.

There are plenty of portside bars. The **Pirate,** near the Clock Tower (☎ 0298/52-711), is the best known, though we prefer nearby **To Roloi** for a nightcap. **Amalour,** on Miaoúli Street, off the southeast corner of the harbor a couple of blocks up from the ferry landing, features Latin American music and American blues.

There are several discos, most of them fairly low-key, usually open June to September. **Heaven** (☎ 0298/52-716), which has grand views and is favored by the younger set, is up the hill on the west side of town. **Kavos,** west above the harbor (☎ 0298/52-416), has a pleasant garden for a rest from the dancing. The louder **Scirocco** is fortunately well outside of town, on the way to Kamíni.

4 Spétses

53 nautical miles from Piraeus; 1¹/₂ nautical miles from Hermióni, Peloponnese

Of the Saronic islands, Spétses (sometimes Spétsai) is the farthest from Athens, though quite close to the Peloponnese. Boasting the best beaches in the Saronic Gulf, it's greener, more lush, and less expensive than Hýdra; its architecture is less impressive, but nevertheless distinctive. In recent years it has become increasingly popular with both Athenians and foreign visitors, especially the British, in part because of the descriptions of the island in John Fowles's masterful *The Magus;* as a consequence, there are a few too many signs advertising "English breakfast" and far too many mopeds.

Andrew Thomas's *Spétses* (Lycabettus Press) provides some good information on the island.

ESSENTIALS

GETTING THERE & DEPARTING   Several car-ferries and excursion boats make the 5-hour journey from Piraeus daily; contact the **Piraeus Port Authority** (☎ 01/451-1311) for schedules. Several hydrofoils (among them the Flying Dolphin and the super-new Flying Cat) leave Piraeus's Zéa Marina harbor for the 90-minute trip daily; contact **Ceres Hydroways** (☎ 01/428-0001 in Piraeus) or **Bardákos Tours** (☎ 0298/73-141 on Spétses) for schedules and reservations (recommended on weekends).

VISITOR INFORMATION   The local **police** and the **tourist police** (☎ 0298/73-100) are to the left off the Dápia, where the hydrofoils dock, on Odós Botássi. **Pine Island Tours,** across from the water-taxi stop (☎ 0298/72-464; fax 0298/73-255), can help you with day tours, ferry tickets, travel plans, and yacht charters; the manager, Kostas, is exceptionally well informed about the island.

ORIENTATION   Spétses is oval shaped; the ferry and hydrofoil dock at the **Dápia,** on the northeast coast. It's a 20-minute walk east to **Paleó Limáni,** the picturesque old harbor. Most visitors prefer to find accommodations near the Dápia. The lush interior is covered with Aleppo pines and fragrant herbs.

GETTING AROUND   The island's **limited public transportation** consists of two municipal buses and three or four taxis. **Mopeds** can be rented everywhere, beginning at about 3,000 Drs ($12.50) a day. **Bikes** are also widely available, and they're suitable for getting around near town; 3-speeders should cost about 1,200 Drs ($5) a day, while newer 21-speed models probably go for about 2,400 Drs ($10).

Horse-drawn carriages can take you away from the busy port into the quieter backstreets where you'll find most of the island's handsome old mansions. Take your time choosing a driver; some are friendly and informative, while others are surly and bent on getting the trip over with. A ride from the Dápia through the old residential quarter to the old harbor will cost about 2,000 Drs ($8.35). Inquire at the art shop near the post office about the possibility of private horseback riding.

The best way to get to the various beaches around the island, as well as to the one at Kósta, on the Peloponnese, is by **water taxi,** locally called a *venzína* (gasoline), little powered boats that can hold about 8 to 10 people. A tour around the island should cost about 5,000 Drs ($20.85), and shorter trips, such as from Dápia to the Old Harbor, should cost about 2,300 Drs ($9.60). Save money by joining a group; schedules are posted on the pier.

FAST FACTS   The telephone **area code** for Spétses is 0298. **Currency exchanges** are at the portside banks or at nearby travel agencies, which are open daily from 9am to 8pm in the summer. There's a **medical clinic** (☎ 0298/72-201) inland from the east (left) side of the port. The **post office** is up the street from the police station. The **telephone center (OTE),** open daily from 7:30am to 3pm, is to the right off the Dápia, behind the Hotel Soleil.

EXPLORING THE ISLAND

Unlike most island capitals, Spétses town (also called Kastélli) is quite spread out. Many of the island's neoclassical mansions are inland, screened from the busy port by all the greenery. The square where the ferries and hydrofoils arrive, the **Dápia,** is more or less the heart of the town. It was once the center of the island's defenses, but now it's the center of social life. The black-and-white pebble mosaic, called *votsalotá*—distinctive features of the island, similar to those found on Rhodes—commemorates the beginning of the Greek Revolution on Spétses, when the first flag with the motto "Freedom or Death" was raised. (You'll see other such mosaics throughout the town.) The biggest and most colorful celebration of the year falls on the weekend closest to September 8, the anniversary of the island's victory over the Turks in the Straits of Spétses in 1822.

Around the esplanade to the right (west) you'll find one of the island's most important landmarks, the grand old **Hotel Possidónion,** one of the first major tourist hotels in Greece, built in 1911 by the island's greatest benefactor, Sotíris Anáryiro, and in front of it the **statue of Bouboulína,** the island's heroine.

Laskarína Bouboulína was the daughter of a naval captain from Hýdra; legend has it that she was born in prison, which would have explained her rather piratical nature. She was already twice a widow with six grown children when the war for independence from Turkey began; she spent her fortune building the *Agamemnon,* a superb vessel on which she sailed to Náfplio and successfully blockaded the port. Both brave and shrewd, she was responsible for several naval victories, gaining the love and admiration of her compatriots, even those who claimed she could drink any man under the table and that she was so ugly the only way she could keep a lover was with a gun.

The **Laskarína Bouboulína House,** in Pefkákia, just off the port (☎ 0298/72-077), has been restored and is now open to the public Monday to Saturday from 10am to 5:30pm, with an English-speaking guide giving a half-hour tour. Admission is 800 Drs ($3.40) for adults and 400 Drs ($1.70) for children. You can see her bones, along with other artifacts, archaeological relics, and more recent folk objects, at the **Mexís Museum,** beyond the post office, behind the clinic, open daily from 8:30am to 2:30pm; admission is 500 Drs ($2.10).

Near the OTE, behind the Hotel Soleil, you'll find a very good craft shop, **Pityoússa** (no phone), which specializes in decorative folk paintings, ceramics, and interesting gift items. Across the street, **Gorgóna** has a similar collection as well as some antiques.

A little west of town, you'll find **Anáryiros College,** another gift from the great benefactor, who modeled it after an English public school. During the 1950s John Fowles taught here. Now it's closed most of the year, except for August when it hosts the **Anaryíria,** a festival of art exhibits, lectures, and theatrical performances.

East of the Dápia along the cannon-studded port you'll find the picturesque **Old Harbor** (Paleó Limáni), where the wealthy moor their yachts, and the **Cathedral of Áyios Nikólaos** (St. Nicholas), the oldest church in town, with a lovely bell tower on which the Greek flag was first raised on the island, and a nearby pebble mosaic picturing the event. (There are nearly a dozen similar mosaics in the vicinity.) Farther east is **Baltíza,** where boatyards continue to make caïques *(kaíkia)* in the traditional way. Beyond it at the tip of the peninsula is the **Fáros** (lighthouse). Walking south along the road will take you to **Ayía Marína,** the town's closest beach and most important nightlife suburb.

You can continue south and clockwise around the island to search for various isolated **beaches.** The enticing little island off the eastern shore is **Spetsopoúla,** private domain of the late billionaire shipping magnate Stavros Niarchos, whose black yacht, the largest in Greece, is still sometimes seen moored offshore.

Áyii Anáryiri, on the south side of the island opposite Spétses town, has the best beach anywhere in the Saronic Gulf, a perfect C-shaped cove lined with trees, bars, and two tavernas (the **Taverna Tássos** is considered one of the best on the island), so naturally it's very popular. You can reach it by bike, though in either direction it's a hilly trip, or by hiking across the island via Vígla—though this isn't as pleasant as it once was, because of several recent forest fires. The best way is by water taxi.

Continuing clockwise, by caïque or on foot, you'll reach **Ayía Paraskeví,** a smaller and more private beach because it's more closely bordered by pine trees. There's a cantina and a large white house, the **Villa Yasemía,** residence of the Magus himself, which can now be rented. To the west, over some rocks, is the island's official nudist beach.

The nearest good place to swim west of Spétses town is **Blueberry Hill,** though it isn't exactly a thrill and is marred by development. Farther west there's **Lambroú beach** (near **Ligonéri**) and **Vrelloú,** in a wooded valley known locally as "Paradise" (you may think of it as "Paradise Littered" because of all the plastic bottles and aluminum cans scattered around). Farther west—near the tip of the island—picturesque **Zogeriá** has a few places to eat and some pretty rocky coves for swimming. **Kósta** beach, on the Peloponnese, is a popular day trip by *venzína.*

WHERE TO STAY

Finding a good, quiet, inexpensive room in spread-out Spétses can be a bit of a hunt; we suggest that you try our recommendations or inquire at **Pine Island Tours,** across from the water-taxi stop (☎ **0298/72-464**), which can even rent you the Magus's old digs at Villa Yasemía. Avoid the main-street hotels and the group "villas," which can be noisy. Expect to pay about 7,500 to 10,000 Drs ($31.25 to $41.65) for a plain double with bath. The hotels recommended below are a little removed from the main streets and are open from late April to mid-October, unless otherwise noted.

Anna Maria Hotel. Dápia, 180 50 Spétses. ☎ **0298/73-035.** 14 rms, all with bath (shower). TEL. 11,500 Drs ($47.90) single; 14,500 Drs ($60.40) double. AE, EURO, MC, V.

This newer lodging, with a second-floor reception and breakfast lounge that make it seem more like a pension than a hotel, is above the town's post office. If it isn't overrun with British tour groups, check out the rather basic rooms. Breakfast is 900 Drs ($3.75) extra.

Hotel Faros. Platía Kentrikí, Dápia, 180 50 Spétses. ☎ **0298/72-613.** 40 rms, all with bath (shower). TEL. 9,200 Drs ($38.35) single; 11,800 Drs ($49.15) double. No credit cards.

The older Hotel Faros overlooks a busy square filled with the Taverna Faros, the Faros Pizzeria, and other restaurants whose tables and chairs curb the flow of vehicular traffic. (*Fáros* means "lighthouse," though there's none in sight.) Take the elevator to the top floor, where simple, comfortable, twin-bedded rooms offer the quietest, balconied views of the island.

Hotel Villa Christina. Dápia, 180 50 Spétses. ☎ **0298/72-218** or 0298/72-228. 15 rms, all with bath (shower); 5 studios with kitchen. 14,000 Drs ($59.35) double; 18,000 Drs ($75) triple; from 19,000 Drs ($79.15) studio. Room (but not studio) rates include breakfast. No credit cards. Closed Oct 16–Apr 14.

An old villa inside its own garden was converted into this charming hotel in a quiet neighborhood several blocks up from the ferry landing. The rooms have comfortable traditional furnishings with refrigerators and modern bathrooms, some with fine views over the garden and town to the port.

Star Hotel. Dápia, 180 50 Spétses. ☎ **0298/72-214** or 0298/72-728. Fax 0298/72-872. 37 rms, all with bath (tub and shower). TEL. 9,000 Drs ($37.50) single; 12,000 Drs ($50) double. No credit cards.

This five-story hotel—luckily situated on the *votsalotá* (pebble-mosaic) pavement that's off-limits to vehicular traffic—is the best of the older establishments. All rooms have a balcony, and the blue-shuttered front ones command a view of the harbor. The large bathrooms contain a bathtub, a Danish shower, and a bidet. Breakfast is available à la carte in the large lobby.

WORTH A SPLURGE

✪ Hotel Possidonion. Dápia, 180 50 Spétses. ☎ **0298/72-006** or 0298/72-308. Fax 0298/72-208. 55 rms, all with bath (tub). TEL. 18,400 Drs ($76.65) single with garden or sea view; 27,500 Drs ($114.60) double with garden or sea view. Rates include breakfast. AE, DC, MC, V.

The Poseidon is a grand, gracious, recently renovated hotel that dates from 1911. This belle époque classic, which boasts two grand pianos, is a landmark on the west side of the esplanade—with a handsome bronze statue of Bouboulína guarding the harbor from the plaza in front. The high-ceilinged rooms are spacious and sparsely but elegantly furnished; the old-fashioned bathrooms have large bathtubs.

WHERE TO EAT

Spétses's reputation for good living is due in part to its many fine restaurants, which can become really packed on weekend evenings. To avoid the Greek crush, try to be seated before 9pm. Spétses also has some of the best bakeries in the Saronic Gulf, and all serve an island specialty, *amigdalóta,* little almond cakes flavored with rosewater and covered with powdered sugar. Those at **Politis Cafe–Snack Bar,** on the waterfront to the right of the ferry landing (☎ **0298/72-248**), are among the best we've ever had—and they offer free coffee with breakfast.

The Bakery Restaurant. Dápia. No phone. Reservations not required. Main courses 1,100–2,800 Drs ($4.60–$11.65). MC, V. Daily 6:30pm–midnight. CONTINENTAL.

This excellent restaurant just up the street from the ferry landing (above one of Spétses's more popular bakeries) reminds us of summer dining in Berkeley, California. The food is prepared fresh, cooked with very little oil, and served piping hot by a friendly staff. The chef, who obviously understands foreign palates, prepares smoked trout salad, grilled steak, and roasted lamb with peas, as well as taverna favorites. The artichoke moussaká, baked in its own dish, is superb.

✪ Exedra Taverna. Paleó Limáni. ☎ **0298/73-497.** Reservations not required. Main courses 1,000–3,400 Drs ($4.15–$14.15). MC. Daily noon–4pm and 6pm–midnight. GREEK/SEAFOOD.

Our favorite island eatery is known to locals as both Exedra and **Siora's,** after its proprietor. The keystone of the old harbor, it's where yachts from all corners of Europe pull in and out. The specialties are fish Spetsiotá, a tasty broiled-fish-and-tomato casserole, and Argó, a shrimp-and-lobster casserole baked with lots of tangy feta cheese. Exedra's freshly cooked zucchini, eggplant, and other seasonal vegetable dishes are also excellent. If you can't find a table at supper, you could try the nearby Liyeri Taverna, also popular for its seafood.

Lazaros Taverna. Dápia. ☎ **0298/76-600.** Reservations not required. Main courses 1,000–2,600 Drs ($4.15–$10.85). No credit cards. Daily 7:30–11:30pm. GREEK.

Another favorite, where good food mixes with a normally lively local crowd, is about 400 yards up from the Dápia. It's our kind of traditional place, decorated with potted ivy and family photos; huge kegs of homemade retsína line the walls. Lazaros's small menu features daily specials (goat in lemon sauce was a tasty, unusual choice when we ate there), plus mostly grilled meat dishes. Everything's fresh and reasonably priced.

SPÉTSES AFTER DARK

There's plenty of nightlife on Spétses, with bars, discos, and bouzoúki clubs from the Dápia to the Old Harbor to Ayía Marína, and even the more remote beaches. Among the more popular bars are **Socrates,** in the heart of Dápia, and the more upscale **Anchor.** There's also the **Bracera Music Bar,** on the yachting marina; **Mourayo,** on the Old Harbor; and **Tsintsiano,** farther east. To the west of town, in Kounoupítsa, near the popular Patralis Fish Taverna, **Zorba's** and **Kalia** are nice upscale bars. For something a little more sedate try the **Halcyon,** or the **Veranda** for softer Greek music.

For discos, there's the trendy and hot **Figaro,** with a seaside patio and international music until midnight, when the music switches to Greek and the dancing follows step. The **Delfina Disco,** opposite the Dápia town beach on the road to the Old Harbor, has become increasingly popular. **Disco Fever,** with its flashing lights, draws the British crowd, and **Naos,** which looks more like a castle than a temple, features techno pop. The **Fox** is expensive but offers live Greek music and dancing; all visitors are urged to join in the fun, which gets livelier after everyone's had a few drinks. **Papagayo** also has live Greek music.

7

The Peloponnese

Though famous chiefly for its unforgettable artifacts from Greece's Classical era, the Peloponnese also boasts some of the country's most picturesque beaches and mountainous terrain. This peninsula, separated from the mainland by the Corinth Canal, is the ideal place to start your love affair with Greece. In the high season it's much less crowded here than on the island resorts, allowing residents to maintain their traditional hospitable ways.

The archaeological sites at Corinth, Mycenae, and Olympía are expressive ruins of ancient times, leaving visitors with an impression of life as it must have been lived more than 3,500 years ago. In fact, the rural Peloponnese is one of the few areas remaining today with a tangible feel of traditional Greek life.

EXPLORING THE PELOPONNESE

There are five convenient points of entry to the Peloponnese: From Athens a bus will take you into Corinth; from Italy you can ferry to Pátra; boats to and from Crete and Piraeus leave and arrive at Kalamata, Yíthio, and Monemvassía; and several port towns in the Argolid are serviced by ferry. There are also daily flights to Kalamáta from Athens.

Once you arrive in the Peloponnese, a car combined with foot power can give you the maximum in sightseeing; however, all the major areas of interest are regularly served by public bus. Even though several places, such as the Máni, have poor service, most of them can be seen in a day or less if you use another Peloponnese town as a home base. (The larger towns also have train service, which can be combined with buses for the most efficient touring.) *Note:* Pick up bus and train schedules from the Greek Tourist Organization (EOT) before you leave Athens so that you can plan ahead.

If you visited the places that we like best, it would take you about a week by car on greatly improved roads. The thought of driving 3 or 4 hours per day may not appeal to you; however, traveling by bus may require a lot of patience at some of the stops. If you want the comfort and ease of a tour, **Viking Tours,** Odós Artemídos 1, Glyfáda (☎ **01/898-0729** or 01/894-9279), books other companies' tours (principally the excellent Chat Tours). Viking offers a 4-day tour with stops at Corinth, Mycenae, Náfplio, Epidaurus, Megalópolis, Trípolis, Olympía, and Pátra, followed by Delphi; the

The Peloponnese

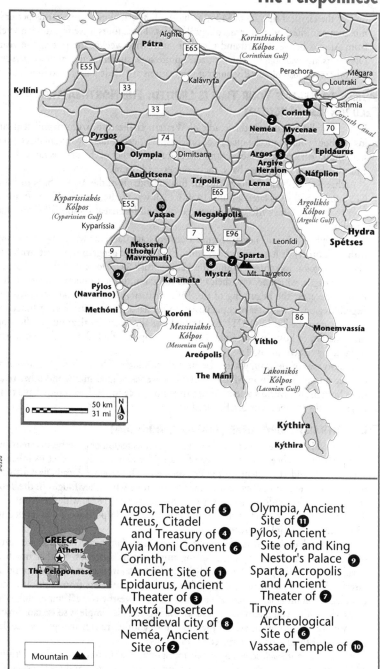

Argos, Theater of ⑤
Atreus, Citadel and Treasury of ④
Ayia Moni Convent ⑥
Corinth, Ancient Site of ①
Epidaurus, Ancient Theater of ③
Mystrá, Deserted medieval city of ⑧
Neméa, Ancient Site of ②
Olympia, Ancient Site of ⑪
Pýlos, Ancient Site of, and King Nestor's Palace ⑨
Sparta, Acropolis and Ancient Theater of ⑦
Tiryns, Archeological Site of ⑥
Vassae, Temple of ⑩

Mountain ▲▲

best of the classical sites costs $435, including first-class hotels, two meals per day, museum and site fees, and archaeological guides. These tours leave five times a week from Athens between April and October, and twice weekly the rest of the year. Discounts are available to senior citizens, professors, students, and military personnel; others can also obtain discounts if reservations are made a day or so in advance.

WHERE TO HEAD IF YOUR TIME IS LIMITED: THE NORTHEASTERN PELOPONNESE (ARGOLID)

In the Argolid (Argolída), this cradle of Western civilization, with magnificent ruins all about you, you feel a quality of timelessness. Surrounded by mountains on the west and north and by the sea on the east and south, relics of the past blend with the enduring beauty of nature's bays, rocky slopes, and plains.

Archaeological evidence now dates the first inhabitants of the Argolid back to 3000 B.C. Some 1,500 years later, around 1450 B.C., it was the heart of the Greek Empire. Every aspect of Greek life was influenced by the Mycenaeans, especially so in the Argolid.

Although this region never became a united state (factions were always warring with each other), it has always been considered a single geographical unit, with the plain of Argos as its center. Around the 12th century B.C. Dorians established themselves at Argos, which became their official capital until the Romans subjugated the Peloponnese. At the beginning of the 13th century A.D. the Franks occupied the Argolid region; it was later occupied by the Venetians. During the War of Independence against the Turks (1821), the Argolid was the major battleground; following the cessation of hostilities, Náfplio became the capital of all Greece, though it was replaced by Athens in 1834.

History was made again when a German archaeologist, Heinrich Schliemann, discovered a tomb in 1876 in Mycenae. His discoveries of gold masks and other treasures brought the world's attention to this region once more. If you only have time to sample the Peloponnese briefly, head here first.

THE CENTRAL PELOPONNESE (ARCADIA, ARKADÍA)

The central Peloponnese, an immensely mountainous region of great beauty, remains as it probably has been for thousands of years. Herodotus believed that its inhabitants were the oldest residents of the Peloponnese. The original Arcadians consisted of several different tribes that united for the first time when they fought in the Trojan War. Arcadian independence began on September 23, 1821, with the capture of Trípolis, today the capital of the central Peloponnese. Trípolis itself was leveled in 1825 and then completely rebuilt.

Several small towns surround Trípolis: Nestáni and Mantinea (Mandínia) are north of the capital, and both have interesting ruins and monasteries. Farther north is Levídi, with its Temple of Artemis Hymnia. To the southwest is Vytína, a popular Greek winter ski resort. Megalópolis lies 34 miles southwest from Trípolis, surrounded by mountains and remnants of its rich past. Nearby is the Temple of Apollo at Vassae (which you'll also see spelled as "Bassae"). This temple is so extraordinary that we urge you to see it; even if the thought of another ruin makes you wince, let the magic of this Doric masterpiece fill your senses.

All the towns are well served by public transportation, but traveling is slow. Drivers making an arc through the northern Peloponnese can cut across and see the sites between Náfplio and Olympía. The landscape changes steadily, from the low, dry hills of the Argolid to the often snow-capped peaks of the Taygetos (Taíyettos) and Parnon (Párnonas) mountains that surround Sparta.

THE SOUTHERN PELOPONNESE

Most visitors focus on the more historic north. However, for those in search of striking scenery and out-of-the-way places, the south has much to offer. Of special interest is the Byzantine village of Monemvassía, one of the most beautiful places on the Peloponnesian coast. The natural beauty of Kýthira is also worth a visit, with its flowers and groves of olives and almonds.

There are three peninsulas on the southern tip of the Peloponnese. The middle one is referred to as the **Máni,** but its history and people have also influenced the western peninsula.

THE WESTERN PELOPONNESE

The inhabitants of the Máni migrated to Elis (Ilía), the westernmost part of the Peloponnese, to pursue agriculture and livestock breeding. However, because of the heavy immigration there from other areas of Greece, feuds arose over the use of the land; eventually Maniots became known as "pirates on the sea and robbers on land." Of special interest in the western Peloponnese are the towns of Olympía (home of the original Olympic Games) and Pátra (where many visitors arrive or depart by ferry).

1 Corinth: Gateway to the Peloponnese

55 miles W of Athens

As a modern city, Corinth (Kórinthos) isn't very interesting; in its present form it has existed only since 1928, when an earthquake leveled the town for a second time. Even then the ruins of "New Corinth" were no match for those of Ancient Corinth, and today it's still primarily a stop on the way to the wonderful ruins.

On a plateau at the base of the Acrocorinth mountain stands the remains of the ancient city of Corinth (Arhéa Kórinthos)—all that's left of what once was the richest and most powerful precinct in all Greece. It occupied the land bridge between the mainland and the Peloponnese, and it took full advantage of this strategic location by charging exorbitant tolls to those who wanted to cross the isthmus in order to trade. To defend itself, Corinth became a great maritime power, able to dominate both the Corinth and Saronic gulfs because of its ability to move ships overland to the sea almost immediately.

Corinth reached its zenith in the 5th century B.C. In 44 B.C. it became a Roman colony. Archaeologists who started digging in 1896 have so far found only Roman remains. Under Roman rule the name Corinth became synonymous with luxury and excess. One of the Roman ruins is the Peirene Fountain, an enclosed-courtyard type of area with a central "pool" that appears to be about the size of an Olympic pool, now overgrown with flowers, and arched entryways flanked by pieces of columns.

ESSENTIALS

GETTING THERE & DEPARTING   By Train   Daily train service is slow but pleasant from Peloponnísou Station in Athens to Corinth. Call ☎ **01/512-4913** for schedules and information.

By Bus   Fifteen buses a day leave from the Athens terminal at Odós Kifíssou 100 for the 1½-hour trip. Call ☎ **01/512-9233** for schedules and information.

By Car   From Athens, the excellent, but ugly, seven-lane Corinth toll highway follows the winding southern coast of the mainland along the Saronic Gulf.

If you're driving from Athens to Corinth (travel time: 2 hours), you might want to stop at the monastery of Dafní; 6¹/₂ miles farther west is Elefsís, site of the ancient Eleusinian Mysteries (see chapter 5). The next 38 miles offer some sumptuous vistas of the gulf, though the superhighway may be crowded with trucks. When you reach the cluster of truck stops and souvenir stands, you'll see the bridge. Admire the **canal** as you cross it.

In ancient times Corinth was a wealthy precinct because of its location as the "middleman" between the Ionian and Aegean seas. As early as A.D. 62 Nero saw the wisdom of building a canal across Corinth to save ships from the dangerous 185-mile detour around the peninsula. He personally dug the first clod of earth with a gold shovel and carried it away on his back—more, some say, a mark of his love of theatricality than of his energy! Although 6,000 Jewish prisoners continued to dig, the canal was not finished at that time; it languished for nearly 2,000 years. Work began again in 1881, and it was completed in 1893 by a French company. The beautiful 4-mile waterway is only 30 yards wide; its smooth, flat rock sides soar 270 feet straight up.

ORIENTATION   The railway station is at Pirínis and Damaskinoú streets on the east side of town. There are two banks on King Constantine Avenue.

GETTING AROUND   Local buses going from new to Ancient Corinth (Arhéa Kórinthos) leave from Ermoú and Koliátsou streets, east of Corinth's park, every hour between 7am and 8pm, with returns on the half hour. It's a pleasant 15- to 25-minute ride. The buses that run to Náfplio, Mycenae, and Argos leave every hour from the corner of Ethnikís Andístasis and Arátou streets.

EXPLORING THE RUINS

One of the very few—but most notable—remains from the Greek period is the **Temple of Apollo,** built in the 6th century B.C. One of the oldest in Greece, it stands on a bluff overlooking the ancient marketplace, with 7 of its original 17 columns still standing. Each column was carved entirely from a single piece of stone.

Next door is the **museum** (☎ **0741/31-207**), filled with sculpture, friezes, and other relics found during the digs. The display next to the museum shows the evolution of Greek columnar architecture, culminating in the highly decorative Corinthian style. With its Roman mosaic floors, the museum is the perfect place to come in out of the sun during the summer; you can also picnic in the inner courtyard. Admission is 1,200 Drs ($5.20), free for children 17 and under. The site is open daily from 8am to 7pm (8:45am to 3pm off-season). From Corinth, the site and museum are 4¹/₂ miles south on the Argos road.

At the top of the Acrocorinth, overlooking the site, is the **Fort of Acrocorinth,** a huge fortress with foundations dating from ancient times. The rest was built and rebuilt by various other groups, including the Byzantines, Franks, and Turks. The uppermost part was originally the Temple of Aphrodite. If you haven't brought a picnic, there's the **Taverna Acrocorinth,** open daily from 8am to 10pm. It features a great view, cool drinks, and souvenirs. An ancient fountain at the first bend of the unpaved road has modern plumbing to provide you with cool running water.

To get to the Acropolis, continue past the entrance to **Ancient Corinth** and make a left at the sign (you can hire a taxi for 550 Drs/$2.30 per person, each way) and continue for 1¹/₄ miles, or hike up to the site, a 1- to 2-hour trip up an unpaved road. The reward for this sacrifice is the many gorgeous vistas you'll see at every bend in the road. The site is open daily from dawn to dusk; admission is free.

WHERE TO STAY

If you can't make it back to the new town after a day spent seeing the ruins, there are many rooms-to-let in tiny Ancient Corinth. The **Taverna Dafni** (☎ 0741/ **31-225**) was our first pick under its charming owner, Anastassios Dafni. Now that his son is in charge, you'll have to let us know how you like its 12 simple rooms. The rate is 8,000 Drs ($34.80) for two.

Bellevue Hotel. Odós Damaskinoú 41, 201 00 Corinth, Peloponnese. ☎ **0741/22-068.** 17 rms, 2 with bath (shower). 4,800 Drs ($20.90) single or double without bath, 6,000 Drs ($26.10) single or double with bath. No credit cards.

Our favorite hotel is the worn but pretty Bellevue. In 1997 the new owners may succeed in giving the old lady a new look, but we hope they don't fuss with its neoclassical detailing and remnants of charm. At press time it was still a good-value Class C pension, well-located on the main street paralleling the town marina.

Hotel Apollon. Odós Pirínis 18, 201 00 Corinth, Peloponnese. ☎ **0741/22-587.** 18 rms, all with bath (shower). 4,800 Drs ($20.90) single; 6,000 Drs ($26.10). No credit cards.

If you're weary and need a quick bed, try this hotel, which has an elevator. The first floor has been remodeled with wood paneling and all-tile bathrooms. Many rooms have small balconies. Though it's a little noisy, this is a friendly place.

WHERE TO EAT

In addition to the listings below, there are several other continental cafes on the port plaza, a few blocks west.

George Lekas Snack Bar. Ancient Corinth. ☎ **0741/31-131.** Main courses 360–2,040 Drs ($1.60–$8.90). No credit cards. Daily 8am–10pm. GREEK/CONTINENTAL.

The tour-bus crowd at the slick Taverna Ancient Korinthos forced us to try this small, friendly snack bar next door, on this village's main street. What a find! The hardworking Lekas family turn out delicious gyros, salads, spaghetti, and a garlic-rich tzadzíki. A nice respite after exploring old stones.

Kanita Pizzeria. Odós Damaskinoú 41, Corinth. No phone. Main courses 720–2,160 Drs ($3.10–$9.40). AE. Daily 8am–10pm. GREEK/CONTINENTAL.

This is next to the Bellevue, with tables under the awning across the main street. The owner George Sofikitis, who lived in Portland, Oregon, for 8 years, is one of the most helpful people in town. His international background has inspired a menu with hearty breakfasts, Greek Andístasis favorites, American and Italian courses, and a very popular "Greek-style" pizza.

2 Náfplio & Tólo

90 miles SW of Athens

Náfplio (sometimes spelled Nauplion) is a city of Venetian fortresses, an ancient harbor (much enlarged and modernized), and bustling tourism. If the city's ubiquitous church bells don't wake you in the morning, then the assorted street noises will. However, the old town's core is still so inviting that you might consider taking a breather from the usual "If this is Tuesday it must be Sparta" program that most travelers adhere to. Náfplio is the ideal base for visits to Corinth, Argos, Mycenae, Epidaurus, and the rest of the Argolid. Nearby Tólo, with its small pebble beach, is our first choice for families.

In antiquity Náfplio was a great naval power. In the 3rd century B.C. fortifications on the southern side of town were built on a clifftop rising straight up from the sea. One fort, the Palamídi, still towers over the town.

ESSENTIALS

GETTING THERE & DEPARTING   By Train   There are three trains daily from Athens to Náfplio; it takes 3 hours. In Athens, call Stathmos Peloponnisou for details (☎ 01/513-1601). To reach Tólo (4¹/₂ miles south), you'll have to take a bus or taxi.

By Bus   Buses leave hourly from Athens's Odós Kifissoú 100 terminal; call ☎ 01/513-4588 for schedule information. Buses to Tólo (a 20-minute ride farther south) leave hourly from Náfplio's station.

By Boat   In summer, two hydrofoils leave daily from Piraeus's Zéa Marina port to Náfplio and continue on to Tólo (there's only one daily off-season). Contact **Ceres Flying Dolphins** for information (☎ 01/324-2281 or 01/453-6107); it's a 3¹/₂-hour trip.

By Car   For the scenic route, drive south from Corinth, past Epidaurus, on the coast road. The quick route is the new Trípolis–Argos highway.

VISITOR INFORMATION   The local **Greek Tourist Organization (EOT)** information office (☎ 0752/24-444) is on the car road into town, at 25 Martiou no. 3, near the Public Square. It's open daily: in summer from 9am to 9pm and off-season from 10am to 5pm.

   Tolon Tours (☎ 0752/59-686; fax 0752/59-689) is the most helpful source in the beach-strip town of Tólo. It handles twice-weekly day cruises to Hýdra and Spétses, once-weekly day sails to Monemvassía, car rentals, bus tours to the major archaeological sites, tickets to Italy, and Olympic Airways flights.

   The best regional map is *Pelopónnisos,* published by F. Láppas in English, French, and German; it also includes street maps for six of the most important towns in the Peloponnese.

GETTING AROUND   Within the old town of Náfplio, you can walk everywhere. If you're staying here and using this as a base to see other nearby towns, you'll use the bus station at Syngroú Square. Local buses for Argos leave every half hour, and the bus to Mycenae and other towns departs three or four times a day. Buses going from Náfplio to Tólo and back leave every hour from 7am to 7pm daily; the 6³/₄-mile trip takes 20 minutes. You can rent a car for about $50 per day from **Safeway,** near the *paralía* (☎ 0752/22-155; fax 0752/25-738). **Kalkanakos Panagiotis Motor Technik** (☎ 0752/27-183) rents bicycles and motorcycles.

WHAT TO SEE & DO

Although Náfplio's geographical location is enough to recommend it as a base for sightseeing, the town itself is a treat. Two blocks from the waterfront is **Sýntagma (Constitution) Square,** the perfect marble-tiled, small-town square, a bit overrun with cafes, shops, a bookstore with some English-language titles, a bank, and the Hotel Athena.

   The light brick Byzantine-style building with a red-tiled dome that dominates the west corner of the square is a 19th-century **Turkish mosque,** once the palace of the Turkish governor. Today it's used for music recitals and other local events. From here, climb up any of the hand-hewn marble stairs to tour the port's older neighborhoods. This quiet, traditional neighborhood, decorated with geraniums, grape arbors, neoclassical architecture, and stray cats galore, is what you've come for.

The deluxe **Hotel Komplex Xenia Palace** (☎ 0752/28-981) is high on the hillside just below the fortress. Where the road diverges from the *paralía,* go up the several flights of stairs and follow the long entrance tunnel to elevators that ascend to a terrace built on the site of the Venetian-era fortifications. The ancient Cyclopean walls are still evident. Have a fresh lemon by the pool and soak up the views!

The **Public Square** (Kolokotróni Square and Matsíkas Street) is east, in the newer part of town; it has a park (with a children's playground), an outdoor taverna, cafes, a fountain, and fast food. It's a local hangout, with a lot of life, a lot of color. The prices at the shops and cafes are more reasonable at the east end of town than at other squares closer to the port.

The **GNTO Plage** (or **Arvanitia Beach**) is the beautifully developed town beach on the southeast side of the point, below the Hotel Komplex Xenia. There's wonderful swimming here from a smooth-stone man-made beach. With dozens of bright blue cabinas (changing rooms), showers, a few stylish cabanas (simple rest areas with sleeping platforms and linens at 3,500 Drs/$15.20 per 24 hours), rental canoes, a snack bar and ouzerí, and slate sunbathing areas, this makes for a great excursion.

Popular Arts Museum. Sofróni and Ypsilántou sts. ☎ **0752/28-379.** Admission free. Mon–Fri 4–8pm, Sat 9am–1pm.

This ethnographic/folk collection, one of the best of its kind, is just off the square. Its shady courtyard is a great place to have a drink, and the gift shop has music, tapes, posters, and replications of costumes for sale. Clothing from many regions of Greece is displayed (even the earliest animal-hide garments), and the gold embroidery is very impressive. *Note:* The Popular Arts Museum closed for a 2-year renovation in February 1997.

Archaeological Museum. Sýntagma Sq. ☎ **0752/27-502.** Admission 600 Drs ($2.60) adults, free for children 17 and under. Tues–Sun 8:30am–3pm.

On the west side of the main square is a three-story Venetian barracks with a small symbol for St. Mark, the patron saint of Venice, gracing the facade. There's an excellent collection of early and late Hellenic pottery here, finds from several Mycenaean sites, and a remarkably well-preserved 15th-century B.C. Mycenaean suit of armor.

Military Museum. Odós Amalías. ☎ **0752/25-591.** Admission free. Tues–Sun 9am–2pm.

This museum provides a look at Greece at war since its independence in the 1820s, through photographs, old prints, and weapons of various sorts.

Palamídi Castle. Náfplio. ☎ **0752/28-036.** Admission 950 Drs ($4.10) adults, free for children 17 and under, free for everyone Sun. Daily 8:30am–2:45pm.

To reach the Palamídi Castle, perched on a crag more than 700 feet high, you can walk up 857 steps; or take a car, taxi, or bus up the mile and a half. The seven forts inside the blindingly beautiful palace were built by the Venetians in the early 18th century. You'll enjoy the expansive view of the Gulf of Argolis, while the shade of the ramparts is an inviting spot for a picnic lunch.

Pasqualigo Castle. Island of Bourtzi, Náfplio Harbor. ☎ **0752/23-406.**

Below the Palamídi Castle, guarding the entrance to the harbor, is a much smaller medieval fortress on tiny Boúrtzi. The Palamídi executioners lived here because they weren't allowed to live in the town. Until recently it was only to be admired from afar. Now it's open evenings as a cafe/snack bar that's well worth a visit (see "Where to Eat," below).

WHERE TO STAY

There's a fine selection of hotels in the town, a few fancy but overpriced places on the edge of town, and a few recommended lodges on the nearby beach at Tólo.

Kyle's son really appreciated being able to play in water after a day of summer sightseeing, but Tólo is not the prettiest or cleanest beach in the Peloponnese. However, it's convenient, fun, touristy, and filled with Greek families. The EOT office keeps a list of rooms for rent, both with and without private showers; typically they cost 6,500 to 8,000 Drs ($27.10 to $33.35) for a double.

There are campgrounds about 1¹/₄ miles beyond Náfplio on the road to Argos. These are European-style "carparks" and are not recommended. However, you may like the cabanas at GNTO Plage—we think they're first rate.

If you're a hiker and want information about nearby mountain huts, call ☎ 01/323-4555.

IN NÁFPLIO

✪ **Hotel Byron.** Odós Plátonos 2, Ayíou Spyrídonos Sq., 211 00 Náfplio, Peloponnese. ☎ **0752/22-351.** Fax 0752/26-338. 13 rms, all with bath. 12,000 Drs ($52.20) single; 15,600–19,200 Drs ($67.80–$83.50) double.

This little gem lies halfway up the hill, near the historic church of St. Spyridon in the old city. Aris Papaioannou has beautifully restored an 18th-century home, appointing the small rooms with marble-topped, wrought-iron tables, Oriental rugs, and lace curtains. Four larger doubles offer air-conditioning and minibars. The Byron's idyllic terrace looks down over the rooftops and out to the harbor, perfect for sunset-view drinks. Definitely worth booking in advance.

✪ **Hotel Dioscouri.** Odós Zygomála 6, 211 00 Náfplio, Peloponnese. ☎ **0752/28-550.** Fax 0752/21-202. 49 rms, all with bath. TEL. 12,000 Drs ($43.50) single; 16,800 Drs ($73) double. Rates include breakfast. V. Walk up the same steps as for the Leto Hotel (see below), turn right, and continue for 1 more block.

Although the decor is undistinguished, this hotel has Class C prices and a Class A view, thus luring many student and academic groups. The rooms and the breakfast lounge are standard, but the views from the front and side rooms make it all worthwhile.

Hotel Epidaurus. Odós Kókkinou 2, 211 00 Náfplio, Peloponnese. ☎ **0752/27-541.** Fax 0752/27-541. 33 rms, 25 with bath (shower). 4,800 Drs ($20.90) single without bath, 8,400 Drs ($36.50) single with bath; 8,400 Drs ($36.50) double without bath, 13,200 Drs ($57.40) double with bath. No credit cards.

The original section of this hotel, at the quiet corner of Bikáki and Lambropoúlou streets, has 10 bright rooms with small terraces overlooking the town. Highlighting the classic detailing of this old house is a spiral staircase winding up to gray 8-foot double doors framed in fresh sky-blue enamel paint. A recent addition has brought more rooms, plus 20 across the street (these, handsome and comfortable, with private showers, offer the best value in town). The pension offers similarly nice accommodations, with baths across the hall.

Hotel Otto. Odós Farmakopoúlou 4, 211 00 Náfplio, Peloponnese. ☎ **0752/27-585.** 12 rms, none with bath. 9,000 Drs ($39.10) single or double. No credit cards.

We're sentimental about this place because we stayed here while researching the first edition of this book. The King Othon's classic detailing has been repainted and replastered, its walls have been whitewashed, and its wrought-iron balustrade has been polished a thousand times since then. As Náfplio has grown to include dozens of drab new places, the nice but bathless Otto, well located a block inland from the port, has begun to look better. Unfortunately, praise from such quarters as the *New York Times* makes it a bit overpriced and difficult to reserve.

Leto Hotel. Odós Zygomála 28, 211 00 Náfplio, Peloponnese. ☎ **0752/28-093.** 12 rms, 8 with bath (shower). 9,600 Drs ($41.70) single without bath; 10,560 Drs ($45.90) double without bath, 14,400 Drs ($62.60) double with bath. Breakfast 1,200 Drs ($5.20) per person. No credit cards. Follow Farmakopoúlou St. past the Otto to the end of the street and walk up the three flights of stairs; on both sides you'll see the wonderful backstreets of Náfplio.

While the Leto is not a classic, its charm lies in its quiet location. The rooms in the front offer the best view; the rest are rather nondescript. Breakfast is served on a veranda that has a view over the city's expanded harbor, mountains, and terra-cotta roof tiles.

In Tólo

Hotel Artemis. Leofóros Bouboulínas 7A, 210 56 Tólo, Náfplio, Peloponnese. ☎ **0752/59-458.** Fax 0752/59-125. 20 rms, all with bath (16 with shower, 4 with tub). 9,840 Drs ($42.80) single; 11,880 Drs ($51.70) double. V.

You'll find clean and comfortable rooms at this choice, midway along the small narrow beach overlooking the Gulf of Argos. The seaside rooms have large balconies and the street-facing rooms are all air-conditioned. The Artemis is known locally for its good Greek/continental restaurant.

Hotel Minoa. Odós Aktís 56, 210 56 Tólo, Náfplio, Peloponnese. ☎ **0752/59-207.** Fax 0752/59-707. 44 rms, all with bath (shower). TEL A/C. 8,050 Drs ($33.55) single; 9,200 Drs ($38.35) double. V.

We loved the many shades of Aegean blue at this contemporary gulfside hotel. The entrance faces a small sandy beach crowded with Europeans and well-to-do Greek families. The large, brightly accented rooms have balconies facing the town marina and Flying Dolphins' pier. It's a simple but stylish place with savvy service.

The hotel's beachside taverna serves a wide variety of continental and Greek dishes. We found the salad bar (choice of 10 Greek dips and vegetables for 1,000 Drs/$4.30) to be fresh, terrific, and the best value.

The charming Georgidakis family (all home from school and waiting on guests) also runs the stylish, hillside **King Minos Hotel** (☎ **0752/59-924**), which is pricier and away from the action but has a nice pool.

✪ **Hotel Tolo.** Leofóros Bouboulínas 15, 210 56 Tólo, Náfplio, Peloponnese. ☎ **0752/59-248.** Fax 0752/59-689. 59 rms, all with bath (tub). A/C TEL. 9,430 Drs ($39.30) single; 12,650 Drs ($52.70) double. Rates include breakfast. EURO, V.

We chose the friendly Hotel Tolo, centrally located on the main street, a 2-minute walk to the beach (the hotel's own beach is quite eroded). Spanking-clean, pastel-toned rooms face the town; the gulf-facing rooms overlooking Koronissi Islet (topped by the Church of Áyios Theodóros) offer especially beautiful views at night. At the once-a-week Greek Night, the charming Dimitris Skalidis dances up a storm! The service is excellent and the Skalidis family make all their guests feel special (they attract a lot of European groups).

Mrs. Skalidis (Yanna) runs **Tolon Tours** (☎ **0752/59-686**) and manages 14 fully equipped, air-conditioned apartments in a quiet neighborhood 250 yards off the main drag; they rent for 14,200 Drs ($61.70) for two people and 17,250 Drs ($75) for four.

Ritsa's Hotel. 210 56 Tólo, Náfplio, Peloponnese. ☎ **0752/59-418.** 30 rms, all with bath (shower). A/C TEL. 8,050 Drs ($33.55) single; 9,200 Drs ($38.35) double. No credit cards.

The Tzanis family built their small, neat hotel on the road into town, about 100 yards from the sandy public beach. Its motel-like design, wrapped around a small courtyard pool and sun deck, caught our fancy. The canopied poolside bar is nice for hanging out when the sun is highest in the summer sky. The rooms are quite simple, often attracting small family groups from Eastern Europe.

WHERE TO EAT

Be careful of the restaurants on Sýntagma Square; most are tourist traps. However, on the right-hand side of the harbor, looking out across the gentle waters of the Gulf of Argolis to the island castle of Boúrtzi, are several popular cafes where both locals and visitors can sit and admire the views. If you want to escape the more touristy restaurants, head for the ouzerís westward along the *paralía,* below the fortifications (all offer protected swimming areas open to the public). Ouzo and a tasty selection of *mezédes* (appetizers) await you at lunch or dinner. A great meal of ouzo, *saganáki* (fried cheese), octopus, and salad will cost about 2,200 Drs ($8.60) per person.

Aktaion Cafe. Aktí Miaoúli 3, Náfplio. ☎ **0752/27-425.** Snacks and desserts 540–2,160 Drs ($2.40–$9.40). No credit cards. Daily 7am–3am. SNACKS/PASTRY.

This local hotspot is next door to the Agamemnon Hotel, where the *paralía* turns. The innovative owners have refurbished it but kept its classic quality; along with the cafe's famous *ekmek* and *galaktaboúreka* dessert, it serves several excellent coffees, a luxurious tropical breakfast with fresh fruit, and beautiful ice-cream concoctions that taste almost as good as they look.

Bourtzi Cafe. Pasqualigo Castle, Boúrtzi Island, Náfplio harbor. ☎ **0752/23-406.** Snacks and drinks 600–1,920 Drs ($2.60–$8.40). Cover charge 800 Drs ($3.50) includes one drink. No credit cards. Daily 6pm–1am. SNACKS.

A former colony/prison that housed executioners from Palamídi Castle, this tiny island and pristine fort has become a government-run cafe and snack bar (it's operated by the Hotel Komplex Xenia Palace). There is no more picturesque waterside dining in all of Greece. When we last visited, none of the pizzas or sandwiches on the menu was available, the service was awful, and there was lots of shouting from the kitchen staff below. But even after that experience, and despite the cost of a water taxi and the cover charge, this cafe is a stunning treat—we recommend that you go! A colorful water taxi (500 Drs/$2.20 round-trip) departs from the central port every 20 minutes for this romantic, fabulous, and unique place.

Old Mansion Taverna (Paleó Arhontikó). Siókou and Ypsilántou sts., Náfplio. ☎ **0752/22-449.** Reservations recommended in July. Main courses 1,200–2,160 Drs ($5.20–$9.40). No credit cards. Daily 7pm–2am. GREEK.

Tassos Koliopoulos and his lovely wife, Anya, run this homey taverna, which is a block from the Epidaurus Hotel and near the Folk Museum. The delicious taverna fare comes in generous portions and the service is quite attentive (by Greek standards). The menu changes daily to take advantage of the freshest seasonal ingredients. Good local wines are available by the liter.

Readers Recommend

Kelari Taverna, Náfplio. "This restaurant is just off the main square of Náfplio and near the bank and shop that sells all the foreign newspapers and magazines. It has good inexpensive food. I can personally recommend the calamari and the marinated octopus."

—Kathryn A. Price, Woodland Hills, Calif.

Savouras Psarotaverna. Leofóros Bouboulínas 79, Náfplio. ☎ **0752/27-704.** Fish 1,320–11,400 Drs ($5.70–$49.60) per kilo. No credit cards. Daily 11:30am–11:30pm. SEAFOOD.

Several readers have recommended this seafood restaurant, located a few doors from the Customs House on the *paralía*. It's a favorite with locals for its freshly made seasonal appetizers, top-quality olive oil, and excellent preparation of the day's catch. Crisp deep-fried fish is a specialty; if they have *bakaláo* (cod) served with *skordaliá*, look no further! A kilo of fish can feed four; for $40 two can dine on *mezédes*, a medium-grade grilled fish, vegetables, and a salad.

3 Epidaurus: Where Classical Greek Theater Lives On

39 miles S of Corinth, 25 miles E of Náfplio

Epidaurus (Epídavros) is best known today for the Epidaurus Festival, superb productions of classical Greek theater held each summer in its beautifully restored amphitheater.

ESSENTIALS

GETTING THERE & DEPARTING   By Bus   Two buses leave daily from the Athens terminal at Odós Kifissoú 100 for the 2½-hour trip to Epidaurus; three local buses leave daily between the site and the port of Náfplio, where you'll find a wide range of accommodations (see section 2 of this chapter for our recommendations; Paleá Epídavros, which is about 12 miles away, has several hotels, but Náfplio is a much more interesting place to stay.) An extra late-night bus (after performances) runs on Saturday and Sunday to Náfplio or Paleá Epídavros.

By Car   Take the scenic coastal highway south from Corinth. Follow the signs to the ancient theater of Epídavros, rather than to Néa Epídavros (the dull new town) or Paleá Epídavros (the old town).

THE EPIDAURUS FESTIVAL

Only in 1900 did archaeologists (who began working at the site in 1881) uncover the magnificent amphitheater that's come to symbolize the majesty of ancient Epidaurus. Carved into the side of Mt. Kynortio, just east of the Asclepion, it once seated 14,000 healthy and recuperating spectators. Polycleitus the Younger is credited with designing this architectural masterpiece, with its scenic landscaping, excellent acoustics, orchestra (more than 22 yards in diameter), and well-arranged seating; even the poorest spectators enjoyed good sightlines and fine sound. (Strike a match above the stone podium and listen.) The theater's excellent state of preservation when found enabled the Greek government to begin presenting the modern *epidauria* (drama festivals) there in 1954. Classic works by Aeschylus, Sophocles, Euripides, Aristophanes, and others are presented in modern Greek but are staged with an eye to their original production.

Tickets to each evening's 9pm performance at the amphitheater can be purchased at the site box office after 5pm (they're usually sold out by 8pm); prices range from 2,000 to 3,800 Drs ($8.70 to $16.50), though student tickets are available for only 1,000 Drs ($4.30). Tickets can also be purchased in advance in Athens at the **Athens Festival Box Office,** Odós Stadíou 4, in the arcade off Sýntagma Square (call ☎ **01/322-1459** for information). Performances are given Saturday and Sunday nights between the end of June and September; check with the Greek Tourist Organization (EOT) for the summer's schedule. Programs sold in advance include an English translation of the entire play.

MORE TO SEE & DO

Today the name of Epidaurus is associated with its celebrated amphitheater; yet to the ancient Greeks, the place was home to the most renowned **Asclepion** (center of healing arts) in the Hellenic world. The sanctuary to the god of healing, Asclepius, was built over a 7th-century B.C. shrine to Apollo Maleatas, which had replaced that of an earlier local deity, Maleatas. Historians believe that Asclepius was a Thessalian king blessed with a talent for healing. Eventually he became deified for his abilities, and a myth developed that he was in fact a son of Apollo who was trained in the healing arts by the wise centaur Chyron. Even the Oracle of Delphi, when prompted, assured the questioners that Asclepius had come from the town of Epidaurus and that it would be important to erect a sanctuary to him there. By the 5th century B.C. the sanctuary, located near the villages of Ligoúrio and Palaiá Epídavros, drew the infirm from all parts of Greece. Within a century the Asclepion reached its peak. Most of the buildings (now in ruins) that can be seen date from this period. Belief in cult practices was diminishing at this time, so the priests were training physicians, called *asclepiadae,* who could treat patients in a more organized manner. Worshippers would come for a miracle cure, but then remain for a longer period to rest, exercise, go to the theater, take mineral baths, and diet—then depart, probably healthier.

The **archaeological museum** at Epidaurus is more than you could ask for. Tall Corinthian columns grace a facade trimmed with fragments of an ancient sculptural frieze. Inside, bright galleries are lined with statuary and sculpture found at the Asclepion sanctuary. Most of the male figures, many with snakes, represent Asclepius; most of the female figures are of Hygeia, goddess of health. Snakes symbolized regeneration connected to the underworld and the fertility of the earth.

Crude medical instruments, similar to the drill used by Hippocrates for brain surgery, are displayed in the front room. Many of the ancient cures meted out at the Asclepion were based on natural herbs and flowers, much like herbal medicine today. However, some cures were purely spiritual. A terra-cotta plaque featuring two ears was intended for patients who wanted to ask the god directly for a cure.

The architecture of the site is quite fascinating. Plans and watercolors, coupled with reconstructed facades and pediments, give a vivid picture of the scope of the sanctuary. The **tholos** was an especially noteworthy structure because of its shape, patterned floor, and interior maze design. Notice the beautiful carved lilies and acanthus flowers that bloomed from the coffered ceilings.

The archaeological site, which is still undergoing excavation, can be reached by a path behind the museum. The many stones in disarray represent the remains of the **Propylaea,** an Ionic-columned entryway; the **Abaton** (Dormitory of Incubation), where patients slept so that Asclepios could cure them in their dreams; and a temple dedicated to **Artemis,** Asclepius's aunt. Nearby was the two-story **Katagogion,** a 160-room guest house with all the amenities! The stadium to the west was the site of the Panhellenic Games, held every 4 years. The huge Temple of Asclepius (380–375 B.C.), designed by the architect Theodotos, once held a gold-and-ivory statue of the god seated with his snakes and a dog by his side, but it has never been recovered.

The **archaeological museum and site** are open Monday from noon to 7pm and Tuesday to Sunday from 8am to 7pm. Admission is 1,200 Drs ($5.21) for adults, half price for students.

WHERE TO STAY

If you decide to stay overnight in Epidaurus rather than basing yourself in Náfplio, there's a hotel at the tourist pavilion—the **Epidaurus Xenia II Hotel,** 210 52 Archéa Epídavros, Nafplias, Peloponnese (☎ **0753/22-005**). It consists of 24 units in clean, quiet bungalows of hewn stone neatly tucked behind the pines and olive trees (away from the classical setting and the hordes of day-trippers). It's a popular weekend excursion for Athenians, so book early. Rates, including breakfast, are 10,920 Drs ($47.50) single and 15,000 Drs ($65.20) double. No credit cards.

4 Mycenae (Mykínes)

71 miles SW of Athens, 31 miles S of Corinth

Mycenae may be best known as the literary setting for the tragedies of its king, Agamemnon, and his unhappy family, giving life to such characters as Orestes, Electra, and Iphigenia.

Today Mycenae is visited for its truly magnificent archaeological site. There's little happening, but archaeology buffs or those stranded by the public bus system can enjoy spending a night in the tiny commercial town.

ESSENTIALS

GETTING THERE & DEPARTING   By Bus   Fourteen buses leave Athens daily from the terminal at Odós Kifissoú 100; call ☎ **01/513-4588** for schedule information. There are four daily buses from Corinth or Náfplio to Mycenae—a pleasant 1-hour ride.

By Car   Take the Corinth–Argos highway south from Corinth for 30 miles, then follow the signs east to the site.

EXPLORING THE RUINS

In 1841 excavations were begun here, but it was not until 1874 that the German amateur archaeologist Heinrich Schliemann took an interest in Mycenae. He unearthed tombs, pieces of palaces and aqueducts, and other relics that had been mentioned by Homer, thus confirming that Homer's writings had been based on fact.

Schliemann's most famous find is the **Acropolis;** its noted **Lion Gate,** on the newer western wall, was his first discovery. The gate (from 1250 B.C.), once closed by two wooden and bronze doors, is capped by an 18-ton lintel supporting the famous lions, their front paws perched on pedestals. These cats announced to the world that within these walls was the mighty kingdom of Atreus.

On your right as you pass through the Lion Gate is the **Royal Cemetery,** the burial ground of 16th-century B.C. Mycenaean kings. These six "shaft" graves (so named because the kings were buried standing up) held many important ancient Greek artifacts; some of these exquisite gold and silver items—including the famous gold face mask that Schliemann thought was Agamemnon's—are now on display at the National Archaeological Museum in Athens.

At the top of the Acropolis are the few remnants of the **Grand Palace,** which included a throne room, a great court (its foundations still remain), and the megaron (the official reception hall), whose frescoed walls can be reconstructed—from the fragments on display in Athens—by the imaginative visitor. Behind the Acropolis is the rear gate of the fortress. This was Orestes' escape route after he had killed his mother to avenge his father Agamemnon's death by her hand. The Acropolis is 2 miles from the national Corinth–Argos road and is open daily from 8am to 7pm; admission is 1,500 Drs ($6.50) for adults, 1,100 Drs ($4.60) for seniors, and 800 Drs ($3.35) for students.

Keep your ticket from the main site and take yourself (with a flashlight) to the **Treasury of Atreus,** also known as the Tomb of Agamemnon. It's a huge, magnificent empty cone with extraordinary acoustics; it's also the coolest spot to be found during the hot Mycenaean summer. The *drómos* (corridor) approach to the tomb is nearly 100 feet long, and the interior of the *thólos* (a beehive-shaped tomb) was once decorated entirely in bronze. The cavity at the right is believed to have been used to store excess skeletons, since the main chamber was filled steadily over generations. Shepherds often used this tomb as a shelter for their flocks (notice the smoke-blackened ceiling). Several thólos have been excavated in the vicinity of the Mycenae mound; because of their scale and grandeur, names of the principal members of the House of Atreus (Agamemnon's father) have been assigned to them. All the great funerary objects discovered here come from the circular grave mounds mentioned above.

WHERE TO STAY

For campers, there are two possibilities: **Camping Atreus,** the first campground as you enter the city (☎ 0751/76-221), which charges 1,200 Drs ($5.20) per person; and **Camping Mycenae** (☎ 0751/76-247), opposite the Belle Hélène. This campground has 10 sites for pitching tents and 20 for bus groups for about the same cost.

The hotels listed below are closed from December to March, unless otherwise noted.

Dassis Rent Rooms. 212 00 Mycenae, Árgolis. ☎ **0751/76-385.** Fax 0751/76-124. 10 rms, all with bath (shower). 8,000 Drs ($34.80) single; 10,800 Drs ($47) double. AE, DC, EURO, MC, V.

Several readers have high praise for this place. Its lovely, spacious rooms are outfitted with pine furniture, big American-style bathrooms, and balconies with a countryside view. The Dassis are now offering 24-hour room service. Marion Dassis is Canadian, multilingual, friendly, and informative; her travel agency next door is a handy information source.

Hotel La Petite Planète. 212 00 Mycenae, Árgolis. ☎ **0751/76-240.** Fax 0751/76-610. 30 rms, all with bath (tub). A/C TEL. 12,000 Drs ($52.20) single; 19,200 Drs ($83.50) double. Rates include breakfast. V.

Run by an ebullient manager, this is a bright, sunny, clean, and spacious hotel high enough on a hill to catch the breeze. You'll have a wonderful view from either the front or back rooms. There's also a nice small swimming pool and a bar/restaurant under a shaded veranda. For the summer, make your reservation at least 1 month in advance.

La Belle Hélène. 212 00 Mycenae, Árgolis. ☎ **0751/76-225.** 8 rms, none with bath. 8,400 Drs ($36.50) double; 10,000 Drs ($43.50) for Room 3. Rates include breakfast. EURO, V.

La Belle Hélène has a welcome sign reading HEINRICH SCHLIEMANNS HAUS, ERBAUT 1862. Even if you're not German or an archaeology student (look at their guest book, dating from 1878, for the list of luminaries), you'll be interested in this charming inn. Take the plank-wood stairs up to Room 3, where Schliemann himself slept; its windows open out onto a view of one of his greatest accomplishments.

WHERE TO EAT

There are several places to eat, all surprisingly similar and with easy-to-understand names: the **Achilleus, Menelaos, Electra Café,** and the **Iphigenia Restaurant.** All specialize in fixed-price lunches aimed at bus-tour groups. However, tucked in near the Achilleus is the marvelous Point, a taverna-lover's taverna.

The Point. Main St. ☎ **0751/76-096.** Main courses 780–3,000 Drs ($3.40–$13). No credit cards. Daily 8pm–2am. GREEK/CONTINENTAL.

The charming Dimitris Giannikos greets visitors to his tiny taverna, while his mom turns out delicious specialties such as stuffed tomatoes and locally churned feta. His wife prepares excellent European-Greek fare, such as oven-baked pastas and filled omelets. Even if you're just passing through, stop by and sample both their traditional and more creative items.

5 Argos

8 miles S of Mycenae

According to legend, Argos is the oldest town of the Argolid, dating from prehistoric times. Around the end of the 6th century B.C. the name Argos became synonymous with fine pottery and sculpture, particularly metal and bronze work. Hageladas and Polycleitus were such excellent sculptors that their names were known throughout the Hellenic world and are still recognized today.

Today the town has about 16,000 inhabitants, a lively public market, and a yearly fair that takes place on October 1.

ESSENTIALS

GETTING THERE & DEPARTING   By Bus   Fourteen buses leave daily from the Athens terminal at Odós Kifissoú 100; call ☎ 01/513-4588 for schedule information. From Náfplion there are 25 daily buses (travel time: 30 minutes). There's also frequent local bus service from Mycenae.

By Car   Drive 36 miles southwest of Corinth on the Corinth–Argos highway.

ORIENTATION   When you arrive in Argos you'll notice the hills of **Lárissa** and **Aspída.** On top of Lárissa (the higher hill), watching over the strategic plains of the Argolid, sits a Venetian fortress on the site of an original acropolis, to which Byzantine and Turkish fortifications were later added. It remained in such good condition that its use in the 1821 War of Independence turned the tide for the Greeks (who held the Peloponnese against the Turkish onslaught). The low-to-the-ground white houses of the modern town are on the same site as the ancient city.

DISCOVERING ANCIENT ARGOS

At the southeast foot of Lárissa Hill lies the **Amphitheater of Argos.** Even larger (though now less impressive) than the one at Epidaurus, this theater has 81 tiers cut from rock and was designed to seat 20,000. It was remodeled twice, the second time, in the early 4th century B.C., in order to turn the orchestra into a water tank where nautical combat could be performed! To make it watertight, the floor was paved with blue-and-white marble. Excavations continue at the site on the lower levels. The amphitheater is located about half a mile from the main square on the road to Trípolis; it's open Tuesday to Sunday from 8:30am to 3pm; admission is free.

Next to the theater are the ruins of the **Roman baths,** with a crypt containing three sarcophagi, a frigidarium (the cold-water room), and three pools, dating from the 2nd century A.D. The tall red-brick structure in front of the theater is what remains of the **aqueduct** that serviced the city of Argos and fed the baths and swimming pool.

Just off the southwest corner of Argos's main square is the **archaeological museum** (☎ 0751/68-819). (The big St. Peter's Church there is also worth a visit.) As you enter the museum's flower-filled garden, turn left and under the covered colonnade (*stóa*) and you'll see superb Roman mosaic floors from private homes, found during various excavations. The impressive collection inside depicts the transformation from paganism to Christianity; most of the items were found by the French School of Athens. On the first floor there's a suit of bronze armor and helmet (probably from the 8th century B.C.) that the museum is rightly proud of. Downstairs you'll find a terra-cotta female figurine from about 4500 B.C.; at the top of the stairs is a gracefully strong Hercules. Don't miss the 3-foot-tall image of Dionysos and a goat, taken from the theater in Argos. The museum is open Tuesday to Sunday from 8:30am to 3pm; admission is 600 Drs ($2.60), half price for students.

WHERE TO STAY & EAT

If you decide to stay overnight, there are a few small hotels, several acceptable Greek tavernas, and a few lively cafes on Argos's main square.

Overlooking the west side of the square, the newly renovated **Hotel Telesilla,** Odos Danau 2, 212 00 Argos (☎ **0751/68-317**), has 32 rooms with telephones and air-conditioning. Bathless singles run 7,200 Drs ($31.30), or 8,400 Drs ($36.50) with bath (shower). Shiny new doubles with color TVs are 10,800 Drs ($47); with shared facilities, 8,800 Drs ($38.30).

SIDE TRIPS FROM ARGOS

TIRYNS (TÍRYNTHA)   Some 7$^{1}/_{2}$ miles from Argos, reached by a road with mountains on one side and the sea on the other, are the ruins of the Mycenaean acropolis of **Tiryns,** with its walls of Cyclopean masonry (so called because the ancients believed Cyclops himself built them to protect Proteus, the king of Tiryns). Tiryns was fortified back in the 13th century B.C., at least two generations before Mycenae. This royal vacation palace by the sea is a great treat for the modern visitor, with its upper level, or palace site, surrounded by huge, handmade walls. Although the chariot-width entrance is identical to the one at Mycenae, these ruins are in much better shape. Excavation at the lower level is slowly uncovering the foundations of several dwellings, among them the Lower Castles. These were rebuilt after a 13th-century B.C. earthquake and survived well into the Mycenaean age. The site is open daily from 8am to 7pm; admission is 600 Drs ($2.60) for adults and 400 Drs ($1.70) for students.

NEMÉA   After 22 years of excavation, the **Archaeological Site at Neméa** (☎ **0746/22-739**), known as the place where Herakles vanquished a lion as his first labor, opened to the public. You can see the ancient theater (built in 330 B.C.), the impressive stadium, and the small museum. Open daily from 9am to 3pm; admission is 600 Drs ($2.60) for adults and 400 Drs ($1.70) for seniors and students.

6 Trípolis

98 miles SW of Athens, 33 miles SE of Argos

Trípolis, the capital of Arcadia, is its chief industrial city as well as a transportation hub for the Peloponnese.

After the Turks destroyed Trípolis, it was rebuilt along more modern lines; thus its streets are unusually wide and regular, with very pretty public greens. Trípolis's altitude of 2,160 feet makes it particularly cool for the region, a pleasant respite if you're between buses.

ESSENTIALS

GETTING THERE & DEPARTING   By Train   Several trains a day leave from Peloponnísou Station in Athens. Call ☎ **01/513-1601** for information.

By Bus Thirteen buses a day leave from the Odós Kifissoú 100 terminal in Athens; call ☎ **01/513-4575** for information. Frequent local buses run from Náfplio (about 1¹/₂ hours) or Argos (2 hours).

By Car Take the Athens–Corinth highway west, then the Corinth–Argos highway south to the new Tripolis highway, about a 2-hour ride.

VISITOR INFORMATION The local **tourist police** is at Odós Spetseropoúlou 20 (☎ **071/223-030**), at the northeast corner of Áyios Vassílios Square.

WHAT TO SEE & DO

If you have time, take a stroll, visit some of the sophisticated shops, or cruise around the town. There are some beautiful public parks and gardens full of shady trees and roses, and grand cafes where you can while away a few hours.

The central *platía,* **Áyios Vassílios** (St. Basil's Square), can be reached from the bus station (located at Kolokotrónis Square) by walking west along Yioryíou Street. The exterior of **St. Basil's Church** is currently being restored, but inside it's a real beauty—cool, dark, and mysterious, with three chandeliers for soft illumination.

A right turn up Konstandínou Street will take you past the **Trípolis Theater** to the edge of the attractive city park. Or you could walk a few blocks from the bus station to the **archaeology museum** on Spiliopoúlou Street. It has a wide range of artifacts, including marbles, bronze vessels and implements, coins, even glassware, from the Neolithic period to 3rd century A.D. The displayed items are particularly well labeled in English with maps and color photographs of sites. The museum is open Tuesday to Sunday from 8:30am to 3pm; admission is 600 Drs ($2.60).

WHERE TO STAY

Arcadia Hotel. Kolokotrónis Sq., 221 00 Trípolis, Peloponnese. ☎ **071/225-551.** 45 rms, all with bath (shower). TV TEL. 9,600 Drs ($41.70) single; 15,000 Drs ($65.20) double. No credit cards.

This is a choice place in the heart of town. The rooms are freshly wallpapered, light, and cheerful, with pleasant, light furniture and carpeting. The bathrooms are large and clean, with shower curtains. There's also free parking out front if you want to take a stroll over to the city park.

Galaxy Hotel. Áyios Vassílios Sq., 221 00 Trípolis, Peloponnese. ☎ **071/225-195.** 80 rms, all with bath (tub). TV TEL. 9,000 Drs ($39.10) single; 13,000 Drs ($56.50) double. No credit cards.

The caring Angela Marinakou tends this establishment with spacious rooms, piped-in Muzak, automated wake-up calls(!), and small balconies overlooking St. Basil's Church. Even the single rooms have double beds and carpeting, making the Galaxy a better bet than you might imagine after seeing its small, spare lobby. There's a 24-hour snack bar and parking in front.

Readers Recommend

Arcadian train trip. "Rail enthusiasts might be interested in a trip through the central Peloponnese from Argos to Kalamáta. The trip takes about 4 hours. The ride through central Arcadía is spectacular, over precipices and deep gorges, with hairpin curves. The scenery is magnificent. Get a first-class ticket to ensure a seat. There are only snacks on these trains, so it would be wise to bring a loaf and a bottle."

—Helen and Stuart Landry, Endwell, N.Y.

WHERE TO EAT

Park Chalet Cafe. Áreos Sq. (at Konstandínou and Dimitrakopoúlou sts.). ☎ **071/238-491.** Snacks 480–1,080 Drs ($2.10–$4.70); main courses 960–3,200 Drs ($4.20–$13.90). Daily 8:30am–1am. CONTINENTAL.

This cafe is surrounded by the park. The indoor restaurant offers a surprising range of menu items, from pizza to fine pastas to filet mignon. The Park Chalet cake is a dessert-lover's dream, and there are five kinds of coffee to go with it.

Its outdoor affiliate, the **Kallisto Cafe** (☎ **071/237-019**), is a hip place to eat in the summer months.

7 Megalópolis

21 miles SW of Trípolis

Megalópolis today is a large, modern town that stands near the remains of the ancient town of the same name. The 4th-century B.C. ruins of Megalópolis are in such a picturesque setting that they're well worth the minor detour if you're en route from Trípolis, Sparta, or Kalamáta to Olympía.

Several local buses run there daily from Trípolis, Sparta, or Kalamáta.

An optimistic Epaminondas (famed for his leadership of Thebes) founded Megalópolis ("Large City") as a planned Utopian community between 371 B.C. and 368 B.C. Hoping to build cities (including Messene and Mantinea) to contain the aggressive Spartans, he convinced 40 smaller cities to unite into one huge capital. Villagers from all parts of Arcadia immigrated to Megalópolis. Unfortunately, dissension among the relocated inhabitants and the city's forced entry into a coalition against Sparta precipitated a very swift decline. Although the town was rebuilt several times, by the time it was visited by Pausanias in the 2nd century A.D. it lay in ruins.

The archaeological site of ancient **Megalópolis** (☎ 0791/23-275), about a mile northwest of the modern city on the Andrítsena road, is open daily from 9am to 3pm; admission is free. The **amphitheater** of Megalópolis was the largest in all of Greece, seating nearly 20,000 people. A water channel encircled the stage to allow for enhanced acoustics, thus the actors' voices could be heard in the last row. These same rows are now filled with evergreens, which make the bleachers a great spot for a picnic lunch.

Behind the stage, to the north of the site, are the column remains of the **Thersilion,** a congress hall that seated 6,000 with standing room for an additional 10,000. It was built to ensure that the Arcadian Confederacy had a meeting place; if you've ever experienced a "government by committee," you can understand why Megalópolis didn't last long. North across the river, shamefully neglected and barely accessible, are the ancient **agorá** and a **Temple of Zeus.**

WHERE TO STAY & EAT

There are two hotels, both just off the main square.

The **Achillion Hotel,** west of the square at Odós Papaioánnou 67 (☎ 0791/ 22-311), has 18 clean and comfortable rooms with phone and private shower. Every Friday a great produce market is held out front. Rates, including breakfast, are 7,200 Drs ($31.30) for a single, 10,800 Drs ($47) for a double; credit cards are accepted. The simpler, but certainly clean and acceptable, 14-room **Pan Hotel** is east of the square at Odós Papanastassíou 7 (☎ 0791/22-270). It charges about 20% less for bathless rooms.

Around the main square are several acceptable restaurants with reasonable prices. The **Deli Yiannis Christos,** at Odós Papanastassíou 10, serves moist, light, and flaky pastry and delicious *spanakópita*. Just northwest off the square is **Super Market,** a real-life American-style food shop with abundant picnic supplies.

EN ROUTE FROM MEGALÓPOLIS TO ANDRÍTSENA

On the road from Megalópolis to Andrítsena there's a fork on the right that leads to Karítena; take it. **Karítena** is a picture-perfect medieval town perched on the slopes of adjoining hills. From the town there's a wonderful view of the Alpheos (Alfíos) River as it winds through the Líkeo Valley below. The bus to Andrítsena stops in Karítena, then turns around and goes back downhill. If you've been riding too long, get off at the fork, where there's an ouzerí, and wait 15 minutes for the bus to return; then continue on to Andrítsena.

8 Andrítsena & Vassae

ANDRÍTSENA

Andrítsena is a lovely mountain village with hillside homes, foliage, and an old church, all of which make it a worthy stop on the way to Vassae. The best thing is the air; in the deep summer it's crisp and light, in winter invigorating. If you've ever been to India, this village will remind you of the imperial retreats to which the British escaped during the summer months (only it's less luxurious).

WHERE TO STAY & EAT

If you want to spend the night in Andrítsena (bus riders may have no choice), we can recommend two places, both open from April to November if the season has been busy (neither accepts credit cards).

The renovated **Hotel Pan** (☎ 0626/22-213) is at the north end of town. It has six small neat guest rooms with private shower, and a common marble staircase lined with voracious plants. The room rate is 5,300 Drs ($23) for a single or double.

The **Theoxenia Hotel** (☎ 0626/22-219; fax 0626/22-235), at the south end of town, is somewhat larger (28 rooms) and more expensive. The rooms (all with shower and private phone) are spacious and provide a great view of the mountains. The hotel's public spaces feature a weird collection of needlepoint, including Greek, European, and Walt Disney pieces! Rates, including breakfast, range from 7,200 to 9,000 Drs ($31.30 to $39.10) for a single, 9,600 to 12,000 Drs ($41.70 to $52.20) for a double.

The Theoxenia has its own restaurant with pretty good food, including some quasicontinental choices. The best cafe in Andrítsena, which doubles as the bus station, is across the street from the Hotel Pan.

Our Greek friends urged us to visit **Dimitsána** and **Vytína,** two small, charming hill towns (within 20 miles of Andrítsena) where time has stood still. If you're driving, you might want to spend a night at the **Xenonas Kazakou** (☎ 0795/31-660), a rustic traditional settlement with only five rooms, or the larger **Dimitsana Hotel** (☎ 0795/31-518). Doubles at the former start at 10,000 Drs ($43.50); at the latter, at 12,200 Drs ($53); both offer suites as well.

VASSAE

Vassae (Bassae, Vassés in modern Greek) is located 14 miles from Andrítsena, at the end of a winding, mountainous, and dusty road that offers a fine view of the village and the Alpheos Valley. At the top is one of mankind's greatest works of art, the ♦ **Temple of Vassae,** also called the Temple of Apollo Epikourios ("the Helper").

Set on a rocky plateau nestled in the highlands (and oaks) of Arcadia, this inspiring temple stands alone, aware of its own grace and majesty. This isolation well served the Phygalians, who hid in the hills around Vassae during their retreat from the Spartan army. They erected the temple to thank Apollo for saving them from a plague that erupted during the Peloponnesian War.

The Vassae temple was built by the famed architect Ictinus. Unlike his more famous Parthenon, Vassae was constructed of limestone hewn from the huge deposits in the area. It's much studied because it encompasses the three great Greek architectural traditions: Doric, Ionic, and Corinthian. Ictinus's genius lay in his ability to integrate these three differing styles into one cohesive whole; fortunately, it remains one of the best-preserved temples in Greece. Unfortunately, you must go to London to see the exquisite frieze that once adorned it, for, like its more renowned Athenian cousin, the sculptures are in the British Museum.

Because of its location the temple is not a typical tourist stop, but those who go will be well rewarded. You'll have to arrange private transportation since it's not accessible by public transportation; a taxi from Andrítsena should cost about 3,500 Drs ($15.20) per person (including 1 hour of waiting time).

9 Sparta (Spárti)

134 miles SW of Athens, 34 miles S of Trípolis

Modern Sparta (Spárti) is a prosperous town with much construction and a lively, gregarious population—quite unlike the ancient city-state that won the Peloponnesian War with its famed totalitarianism, discipline, and universal military training.

Ancient Sparta was a union of five communities within four villages built on six hills under one set of laws. This curious experiment was launched in the 9th century B.C. when a race of Dorians invaded the Laconian plain and subsequently settled there and intermarried with the locals. The four villages were united by a man who is both a historical and a legendary figure, the legislator Lykourgos, who set down the laws and principles of this new state, Sparta. He felt that three classes of residents, two kings, and one senate would ensure stability. The constitution he drafted was so strong that this new state remained intact for centuries.

After the Persian War, Sparta became increasingly jealous of Athens's influence. This led to the bloodbath known as the Peloponnesian War, which lasted nearly 30 years. Sparta emerged the victor, but never regained its dominance in Hellenic affairs. From the 6th century B.C. on, austerity was Sparta's modus operandi; since austerity prevailed in architecture and the arts as well as in daily life, even its ruins are disappointing. So ended an experiment in urban development that left its mark on history.

ESSENTIALS

GETTING THERE & DEPARTING   By Bus   Nine buses a day leave from the terminal in Athens at Odós Kifissoú 100 for the 4¹/₂-hour ride; call ☎ **01/512-4913** for schedule information.

By Car   It's a 1-hour trip along newly widened mountain roads south of Trípolis.

VISITOR INFORMATION   Tourist information (☎ **0731/24-852;** fax 0731/26-772) can be found on the second floor of the Town Hall, Lykoúrgou Street, central square. The local **tourist police** are at Odós Hilonos 8, just east of the main square (☎ **0731/20-492**).

SEEING THE SIGHTS

You can join today's less austere Spartans at the Eurocafe on Odós Paleológou, the bustling produce market in the Kleomvroutou pedestrian mall (Wednesday or Saturday mornings), or in their nightly *vólta* (stroll) around the main square. Stop to admire the gleaming contemporary decor of the high-style **Leski Saradon Cafe;** it's worthy of a peek and a glass of wine.

About 2 blocks east of the central square, on Dionysos Dafnou Street, is the **Museum of Sparta** (☎ **0731/28-575**). It houses a small but interesting collection of marbles (including the famous *Spartan Soldier* thought to be by Leonidas), friezes, mosaics, pottery, and even jewelry ranging from the 6th century B.C. to the 2nd century A.D. A new wing has opened to house items from local excavation sites which offer much insight into the character of ancient Sparta. There's also a fragrant, charming garden in the front laden with shaded benches for contemplation of the statuary that surrounds you. The museum is open Tuesday to Saturday from 8:30am to 3pm and Sunday from 8:30am to 2:30pm; admission is 600 Drs ($2.50).

At the north end of the city (about a 10-minute walk from the Hotel Apollon) is the site of **Ancient Sparta.** To visit this site, leave town by the Trípolis road until you reach Leonidas Street, and then turn left; about 300 yards farther down the road you'll see the "tomb" of Leonidas. Proceed up a dusty road and through a grove of olive trees until you come to five column bases, some old stones, the echo of a theater, and a very nice vista of the city. Beyond are the ruins of two Byzantine churches and a Roman portico. Little remains of this former great power except the legendary dedication of its men, who left their homes when they were 7 years old to live by the river, read Homer, and harden themselves to become warriors.

WHERE TO STAY

Hotel Cecil. Odós Paleológou 125, 231 00 Sparta, Laconia. ☎ **0731/24-980.** 13 rms, 8 with bath (shower). TEL. 6,240 Drs ($27.10) single without bath; 9,360 Drs ($40.70) double without bath, 9,600 Drs ($41.70) double with bath. No credit cards.

The small, old Cecil has lots of charm. Your host, Gaterina Katrani, presides over a beautifully renovated establishment, just a 5-minute walk from the central square. The front rooms can be a little noisy, but are otherwise attractive. Many have new tiled showers and tile floors, or balconies overlooking the broad avenue.

Hotel Maniatis. Odós Paleológou 72, 231 00 Sparta, Laconia. ☎ **0731/22-665.** Fax 0731/29-994. 80 rms, all with bath. A/C TEL. 11,400 Drs ($49.60) single; 14,400 Drs ($62.60) double. EURO, MC, V.

With its pastel colors and carpeting, this is quite a nice modern hotel a block from the square. Besides convenience, it offers a large, comfortable TV lounge and the slick Dias continental restaurant. The Maniatis is popular with tour groups since it has so many clean, air-conditioned rooms. Its moderate prices also help to make it a popular Class C spot for solo travelers too, but make advance reservations.

WHERE TO EAT

Dias Restaurant. Odós Paleológou 72. ☎ **0731/22-665.** Main courses 720–2,880 Drs ($3.10–$12.50). EURO, MC, V. Daily noon–4pm and 7pm–midnight. GREEK/CONTINENTAL.

Next door to the Maniatis Hotel, this smart restaurant is appealingly decorated with mirrors and pastel colors. It's air-conditioned and popular with a business crowd at lunch; the varied dishes are up-to-date, quite good, and reasonably priced.

Elysse. Odós Paleológou 113. ☎ **0731/29-896.** Main courses 840–1,680 Drs ($3.70–$7.30). No credit cards. Daily 11am–1am. CONTINENTAL.

This place looks as French as its name, but in fact the owners Stavros and Katarina spent 20 years in Canada, so they welcome diners in fluent English. The large and eclectic menu features charcoal-broiled chicken and meats, and chicken *bardouniotiko,* a Spartan specialty sautéed with onions and tomatoes, topped with feta cheese. Elysse also features daily specials made with seasonal produce.

10 Mystrá

2.7 miles W of Sparta

The Byzantine ghost town that lies in the foothills of Mt. Taygetos is populated today by birds, wildflowers, and rabbits. Mystrá was a site of great learning, a Byzantine retreat where Theophilus tried to reconcile the precepts of ancient Greek philosophy with the new religion of Christianity.

GETTING THERE

The easiest way to reach Mystrá is via Sparta; the bus leaves Sparta regularly from the corner of Leonídou and Lykoúrgou streets, 3 blocks west of the central square. From Mystrá's Xenia Restaurant bus stop there's a hearty uphill walk.

Drivers leaving Sparta should follow the signs west off Paleológou Street, along Lykoúrgou Street, and up toward the Taygetos mountains.

WHAT TO SEE & DO

If you visit Mystrá in spring you'll see the wildflower population running wild on the hills and in the cracks of the ruins. Equally colorful species of birds and insects have also made Mystrá their home. Hike up the worn stairs and crisscross the paths of this solitary spot, listening to the donkeys' bells and studying the abstract shapes of the ruined buildings as you climb. Then rest in the shade of a tree that's older than most nations and you'll be transported back to a world, ascetic and removed, where you can coexist with the spirits of those monks who inhabited this place 500 years ago.

The spirit of old Mystrá is reflected in its beautiful churches, which include **Perívleptos,** with its wall paintings; the **Evangelístria,** which boasts sculptured decor; the **Monastery of Pantánassa** and its frescoes; and the **Church of St. Dimitri** (Áyios Dimítrios), in the lower city, whose architecture, paintings, and mosaics are fine examples of Byzantine art.

At the summit is **Church of St. George** (Áyios Yióryios), which is in excellent condition and whose assorted emblems testify to the Franks' influence. The double-headed eagle marks the exact spot where the last Byzantine emperor was crowned in Mystrá's long-ago heyday. The church is open daily from 8:30am to 3pm; admission is 1,500 Drs ($6.50), half price for students, free on Sunday and holidays. Wear suitable clothing (no shorts or halter tops); if you're not appropriately dressed, cloth aprons or shawls may be available from the nuns who live in the convent.

WHERE TO STAY & EAT

The town of Mystrá itself, about 1 1/2 miles below the ancient city, exists (as do many others) primarily to service the vast hordes of tourists that pass through, but there's only one hotel. The **Byzantion,** Mystrá, 231 00 Sparti, Laconia (☎ **0731/93-309**), is a Class B hotel with 22 plain, clean rooms, all with bath; bed-and-breakfast singles cost 9,600 Drs ($41.70); doubles run 14,400 Drs ($62.60). American Express, EuroCard, and MasterCard are accepted.

There's an excellent new campground within a 15-minute walk of the monastery called **Castle View Camping** (☎ **0731/93-303**), run by a Greek-American couple. The grounds include hot showers, a snack bar, a minimarket, an information center, and a sparkling swimming pool; it's open April to October.

When you're ready for a bite, try the **Taverna To Kastro** (☎ 0731/93-526), opposite the hotel—a good choice at dinnertime. Just below the site and in a gorgeous setting is the **Restaurant Marmara,** one of the better cafes in the area for lunch. Your hostess Ann grew up in New Jersey and prepares fine Greek cuisine. Note the mineral springs behind the restaurant, which fed the marble bath where the emperor Constantine used to bathe.

11 Monemvassía

210 miles SW of Athens, 57 miles SE of Sparta

Two miles from the port town of Monemvassía, over a narrow stone causeway is the "Gibraltar of Greece," the Kástro ("Castle") of Monemvassía, one of the most beautiful spots on the Peloponnesian coast. It's a 13th-century Byzantine village, more complete than Mystrá architecturally, yet even more overrun by flowers. Tucked away on the south face of a hill, shadowed by an imposing fort, is a tiny bit of paradise.

ESSENTIALS

GETTING THERE   By Bus   Nine buses leave daily from the Athens terminal at Odós Kifissoú 100 for Sparta (travel time: $4^1/_2$ hours), then change for the bus to Monemvassía; two buses go directly to Monemvassía (travel time: 7 hours). Call ☎ 01/512-4913 for schedule information.

By Boat   The car-ferry to Kýthira from Piraeus makes calls at Monemvassía twice weekly; check with the **Port Authority** in Piraeus (☎ 01/451-1311) or in Monemvassia (☎ 0732/61-219).

By Hydrofoil   A hydrofoil leaves twice daily from Zéa Marina in Piraeus, going to Monemvassía. The **Ceres Flying Dolphin** (☎ 01/324-2281 in Athens or 0732/61-219 in Monemvassía) will save you almost 3 hours over the ferry's travel time.

VISITOR INFORMATION   Most tourist services and the local police are in the mainland village of Monemvassía, near the causeway/bridge crossing to the island rock ("Monemvassía Castle").

The most helpful and knowledgeable person on the mainland is Peter Derzotis at **Malvasia Travel** (☎ 0732/61-432; fax 0732/61/432), at the bus station; he sells ferry tickets and arranges accommodations, car, and motorbike rentals.

EXPLORING THE TOWN

When you enter the vaulted gates to this walled community, you'll be delighted by the charm and tender beauty of the vehicle-free village. Hordes of day-trippers mob the few cafes and souvenir shops nestled in grottoes of the original Byzantine dwellings, but at dusk peace returns. On top of the hillside is the 13th-century **Ayía Sofía,** similar in style to the Byzantine church at Dafní (open from dawn to dusk). The half-hour walk up through the Citadel, or "Upper City," is well worthwhile.

The crystal-clear, inviting Aegean below can be reached by the paths that corkscrew down the hill. It's beautiful to see, but difficult to reach over large, craggy rocks.

Shoppers might enjoy browsing through some of the high-priced, high-quality antiques shops. One place we loved for its contemporary artistry and moderately priced older pottery was **Hartinos Kosmos** (World of Paper; ☎ 0732/61-769). The proprietor, Thanassis, makes elegant papier-mâché gift items and hand-painted religious icons. He's open daily till after supper; from November to April he's open only weekends.

WHERE TO STAY

We say, if you can't get a room on the rock, don't even bother to come. The dozens of undistinguished mainland apartments and rooms are only good options if you're stuck. To find the best accommodations, leave your car outside the castle gate, and, wearing sturdy shoes, proceed through the carved stone tunnel to the village's only pedestrian lane. Then just ask a local.

The Castle of Monemvassía, which now encompasses three hotels, is a marvelous vacation resort, a romantic port, or an idyllic retreat for the weary traveler, especially after most tourists depart at day's end.

Hotel Byzantino. Castle of Monemvassía, 230 70 Monemvassía, Peloponnese. ☎ 0732/61-254. Fax 0732/61-331. 25 rms, all with bath (shower). 14,400–19,200 Drs ($62.60–$83.50) for rooms sleeping two to five. AE, EURO, MC, V.

We're delighted to see more restoration of Monemvassía's crumbling homes, such as the popular Cafe Byzantio's hotel complex off the main lane. Large beige-on-beige rooms have stone floors inlaid with marble, medieval carved stone fireplaces, old family armoires, and wooden storage chests. Most rooms offer air-conditioning, minifridges, and balconies with sea views; some have kitchenettes, telephones, and lofts that sleep up to five. Very grand for medieval times, though not plush and comfy. Nevertheless, a special place.

Hotel Kellia. Castle of Monemvassía, 230 70 Monemvassía, Peloponnese. ☎ 0732/61-520. 12 rms, all with bath (shower). 14,400–19,800 Drs ($62.60–$86.10) for rooms sleeping one to six. Rates include breakfast. No credit cards.

This is a government-sponsored traditional settlement project at the east end of the village beyond a pretty church. Though simple in scale, castle homes of lesser grandeur were restored in 1991. They sleep up to six people (40 beds total), and have private showers, sea views from old seafarer's windows, and a breakfast room with a sun deck.

✪ **Hotel Malvasia.** Castle of Monemvassía, 230 70 Monemvassía, Peloponnese. ☎ 0732/61-113. Fax 0732/61-722. 28 rms and suites, all with bath. 10,200 Drs ($44.40) single; 13,200–18,000 Drs ($57.40–$78.30) double; 17,250–51,570 Drs ($71.85–$215.65) suite. EURO, MC, V.

One of the greatest assets on this mesmerizing rock is the Hotel Malvasia, which occupies three separate restored locations in the old castle. Some stone quarters have handcrafted suites complete with living rooms decorated in woven flokotis, kitchenettes, solid-marble bathrooms, and beautiful bedrooms. Others offer terraces, stone balconies, built-in stucco banquettes, and sleeping alcoves. Kyle dreamed of coming here for her honeymoon, but finally made it with her family. It's expensive, but a real treat.

WHERE TO EAT

There are many pizzerias, tavernas, and snack bars in the mainland village, and several pricey snack cafes on Kástro, the island rock. Most are open only for the April-to-October tourist season, but our favorite choice is open year-round.

Restaurant Marianti. Castle of Monemvassía. No phone. Main courses 1,200–2,400 Drs ($5.20–$10.40). No credit cards. Daily 8am–midnight. GREEK.

Some exceptional women and some village cats own this pleasant taverna, a few doors down from the Hotel Malvasia. You can dine inside, where red-and-white checked tablecloths and wine casks complete the setting, or outside along the narrow village lane. Delicious *stámna* (a pork, veal, and lamb stew), *tyrokrokétes* (cheese balls), tender grilled calamari, and the fragrant house white wine just thrilled us.

I love 0-800-99-0011
in the springtime.

Every country has its own AT&T Access Number which makes calling from France and other countries really easy. Just dial the AT&T Access Number for the country you're calling from and we'll take it from there. And be sure to charge your calls on your AT&T Calling Card. It'll help you avoid outrageous phone charges on your hotel bill and save you up to 60%.* 0-800-99-0011 is a great place to visit any time of year, especially if you've got these two cards. So please take the attached wallet card of worldwide AT&T Access Numbers.

All you need for the fastest, clearest connections home.

12 Kýthira

108 nautical miles S of Piraeus

The rugged, scrub-covered island of Kýthira is isolated off the south coast of the Peloponnese. Officially it's one of the Ionian islands—and it shares their Venetian and even British background—but its whitewashed flat-roofed architecture and arid landscape make it look much more like one of the Cyclades.

It's believed that the Minoans had a trading post on Kýthira, off the Peloponnese's southernmost coast, as early as 2000 B.C. Over the centuries the island followed closely the development of the peninsula, with the Achaeans, Dorians, and Argives all in their turn taking over and settling in before being displaced by someone else. During the Peloponnesian War the island was held by Athenians and used as a base from which to raid the Laconian Plain. They settled at the ancient capital (Kýthira), on the southern hill of the island, which was topped by a fortified acropolis.

Because of Kýthira's unspoiled beauty, many Greeks have chosen to build villas there; there's also a large community of friendly Australian Greeks. Kýthira is renowned for its honey, olive and almond groves, the abundant bright-yellow semperviva, and the hospitality of its residents. It's worth a visit because of its natural beauty, traditional small villages, and general absence of tourists.

ESSENTIALS

GETTING THERE   By Plane   Olympic Airways has two daily flights from Athens; its Athens office can be reached at ☎ 01/926-7251.

By Ferry   Miras Ferries (☎ 01/412-7225 in Piraeus, 0735/33-490 in Kýthira) runs two daily ferries from Neápolis and one from Yíthio. The **F/B *Theseus*** (☎ 0752/61-219) departs twice weekly from Piraeus; three times weekly from Kastélli, Crete; and once weekly from Monemvassía.

By Hydrofoil   Ceres Flying Dolphins (☎ 01/454-7107 in Piraeus) offers service five times weekly from Zéa Marina.

VISITOR INFORMATION   Conomos Travel (☎ 0735/33-688) books accommodations and sells ferry and Olympic Airlines tickets.

GETTING AROUND   In summer one bus daily goes from Ayía Pelayía to Hóra, making local stops. Motorbike and car rentals are available.

FAST FACTS   The **police** are in Hóra (☎ 0735/31-206) and Potamós (☎ 0735/33-225); the **harbor police** are in Ayía Pelayía (☎ 0735/33-280). There's a **medical center** (☎ 0735/33-203) and a post office in Potamós. The National Bank of Greece has branches in Hóra and Potamós.

WHAT TO SEE & DO: THE BEACHES & BEYOND

Today the capital city is **Hóra,** an ingratiating village with cobblestone lanes and crooked streets that faces south toward the Cretan Sea. It has many Byzantine churches and a small **archaeological museum** (☎ 0735/31-739). Hóra's neighbor to the south is the active port of Kapsáli, site of the remains of an ancient Venetian fort perched 900 feet up on a hill.

Some 4¹/₂ miles north of Ayía Pelayía is the sandy stretch of **Platiá Ámmos,** with a taverna that's open in summer. To the south along a paved 3-mile road are three more nice beaches: Fíri Ámmos, Kalamátis, and Káko Lagádi, where there's a lake and a gorge. From **Potámos,** the central market town, you can visit **Diakófti beach** and the church of **Áyios Yíorgos,** noted for its mosaics.

Continue south to Áyios Nikólaos Bay, where there are three beaches: Asprogas, Kastráki (with the remains of a Minoan settlement nearby), and Avlémenos, where there's a campsite and Sotiros Taverna.

The west side of the island is accessible only by boat—except for **Mylopótamos,** site of a ravine and waterfall, and the **Cave of St. Sofia (Ayía Sofía),** a quarter mile west. Farther south is **Myrtidía** and the **Church of Our Lady of the Myrtle,** patron saint of the island, whose festival is held on August 15.

If you're addicted to island-hopping, there's **Antikýthira,** a smaller island just off the coast that's quite the place for explorers. Art buffs may enjoy scuba diving off its coast, where in 1900 divers found a wrecked ship full of marble and bronze sculptures, as well as fragments of superb relief work. In 1802 nearly 20 crates filled with the Parthenon's sculptural frieze (on their way to London under the aegis of the notorious Lord Elgin) "fell" off the freighter and into the deep sea—the Kýthira Triangle?—off Kýthira.

WHERE TO STAY & EAT

The comfortable **Hotel Kytheria** in Ayiá Pelayía (☎ **0735/33-321;** fax 0735/ 33-825) has 10 rooms, all with bath, for 8,000 to 10,900 Drs ($34.90 to $47.40) for a single and 9,600 to 15,600 Drs ($41.70 to $67.80) for a double. Presided over by Frieda Megalokonomos, a genial Australian Greek, the hotel is open all year, and is a stone's throw from the town beach.

There are a few tavernas and an authentic ouzerí on the "strip." Fortunately for the tourists who visit Kythira, most visitors are Greek and therefore more demanding of local chefs. Prices are reasonable everywhere.

13 Yíthio: Gateway to the Máni

186 miles SW of Athens, 27 miles S of Sparta

Yíthio (Gýthio, Gythion) is a small coastal town on the Gulf of Laconia; in ancient times it was known as Cranae, the port of Sparta. This was the first refuge of the lovers Paris and Helen when they eloped over the Taygetos mountains from her home in Sparta and set off by ship to Troy. Today Yíthio is the gateway to the Máni, the isolated southern fringe of the Peloponnese, which is named after Maina Castle, built by William de Villehardouin in the 13th century, the same gentleman who gave us the castles at Monemvassía and Mystrá.

ESSENTIALS

GETTING THERE   By Bus   Four buses leave daily from Athens's Odós Kifissoú 100 terminal; call ☎ **01/512-4913** for information.

By Boat   There's one ferry daily from Piraeus, and one car-ferry weekly to and from Kíssamos (Kastélli), Crete. Call ☎ **0733/22-207** or **Miras Ferries (☎ 0733/24-501)** for information.

By Car   From Monemvassía, follow the scenic coast road 42 miles west around the Gulf of Laconia, or head due south from Sparta on the faster highway.

Impressions

When God finished making the world all He had left was stones, and He made . . . Máni last of all.

—Old Greek man, in Kevin Andrews' *The Flight of Ikaros,* 1959

FAST FACTS   The telephone **area code** is 0733. Perivoláki ("Public Garden") Square is the heart of Yíthio; the **bus station** is across from it on the north side. As you face the square from the water, walk up the first street on your left (Vassiléos Pávlou Street) and you'll find most hotels and tavernas. The **police station** is at Vass. Pávlou 21 near the harbor (☎ **0733/22-271**). **Ferry tickets** to Kýthira, Crete, and elsewhere can be bought at the **Rozákis Agency,** Vass. Pávlou 5 (☎ **0733/22-207;** fax 0733/22-229); boat schedules are posted daily on the front door.

WHAT TO SEE & DO

Not much happens in Yíthio. Several faded tavernas, rooms to let, and tourist-worn shops line the waterfront to Perivoláki Square, all catering to those who await the twice-weekly ferries to Kýthira or Crete. The Máni museum may be here, but go to Areópolis for a tour of the authentic Máni region.

Tall old houses along the seafront look west to a lighthouse on the tiny island of Marathoníssi, now connected by a roadway to the mainland. In its midst towers the **Pyrgos Tzanetakis, "Museum of the Máni,"** in a restored 19th-century Maniot tower. On our last visit there was an impressively displayed collection of books and prints by travelers who had come to the region over the past eight centuries. It's open daily from 9am to 1pm and 5 to 9pm; admission is 500 Drs ($2.20).

Kostas Vrettos has a treasure chest of an antiques shop, **Paliazures,** next to the Pantheon Hotel, with all sorts of "old things"—pots, furniture, lamps, paintings, pottery, guns, farm implements, and coins—all legally exportable.

WHERE TO STAY & EAT

The **Hotel Kranai,** Odós Vassiléos Pávlou 17 (☎ and fax **0733/24-394**), a well-kept century-old hotel with modern amenities, offers doubles for 12,000 Drs ($52.20). The **Hotel Pantheon,** Odós Vassiléos Pávlou 31 (☎ **0733/22-289;** fax 0733/ 22-284), has plain but carpeted rooms, with balconies jutting over the boardwalk; doubles go for 16,000 Drs ($69.60); American Express, Diners Club, MasterCard, and Visa are accepted.

At the **Pension Kondoyiannis,** Odós Vassiléos Pávlou 19 (☎ **0733/22-518**), Martina Kondoyiannis makes you feel at home on the second floor above her own cozy home next to the town police station, where bathless rooms are priced at 6,000 Drs ($26.10).

We didn't think much of the portside cafes in the village, at least not for a full meal, but don't overlook the traditional ouzerís. Yíthio is the octopus capital of Greece, so most seaside cafes serve this tasty denizen of the gulf. Hidden under a brightly striped canopy at the far east corner of the port is **Ouzaki** (☎ **0733/ 22-944**). While we enjoyed an excellent salad at lunch, the owner stood by the canopy railing flipping over all the octopuses drying in the sun while his jovial family sat nearby, eating delicious-looking grilled fish.

14 Areópolis: Capital of the Máni

16 miles SW of Yíthio, 49 miles SE of Kalamáta

Areópolis was named for Ares, the god of war—and indeed the enclosed courtyards, small cobblestone lanes, and houses give the impression that the town was at one time heavily fortified. Today's Areópolis is girded by gas stations and souvenir shops catering to every kind of tourist. The fascinating older part of town is still intact and well worth a visit.

An Underground Venice: The Caves of Pýrgos Diroú

About 5 miles south of Areópolis are the famous Caves of Pýrgos Diroú. They're part of an underground river, and the approximately 5,000 yards that have been exposed are fascinating. From the entrance, skillful, whistling gondoliers steer small boats through narrow passageways, around beautiful formations of stalagmites and stalactites, their colors created by rain water penetrating the calcium carbonate in the rock. The caves served as places of worship in Paleolithic and Neolithic times, as hiding places during the Resistance movement, as cold storage for local cheesemakers, and as refuge for weary sheep.

The caves are a must-see natural marvel, although some of their beauty was destroyed when the natural passages were enlarged for boats to get through. After a half hour on water, you'll have a fascinating 5-minute walk back to the outside world (imagine you're crossing the River Styx). After the walk, a long white-rock beach, restaurant, snack bars, and a fascinating museum await.

The 39 caves are a refreshingly cool place to visit in summer (averaging 50° to 70°F), but you may have to wait up to 2 hours for an eight-person boat unless you go early. At our last visit the admission was an absolutely worthwhile 3,500 Drs ($15.20) for adults and 1,500 Drs ($6.50) for children and students. Open daily: June to September from 8am to 5:30pm, and in May and October from 8am to 2:45pm; call ☎ 0733/52-223 for more information.

The **Neolithic Museum of Diros** has excellent displays of finds from Lepotrypa, an adjoining cave that's still being excavated. Scholars believe that the original settlers (ca. 7000 B.C.) were traders carrying obsidian that was mined on Mílos. They came for the caves' fresh water (now partly salted) and flourished until 3000 B.C. when an earthquake sealed the caves' entrance, silencing this civilization. This extraordinary museum is open year-round Tuesday to Sunday from 8:30am to 3pm; admission is 500 Drs ($2.20).

ESSENTIALS

GETTING THERE   **By Bus**   Twelve buses a day leave Athens for Kalamáta from the terminal at Odós Kifissoú 21; call ☎ 01/512-4913 for schedules. From there, you can catch one of several local buses that run daily from Kalamáta. There's also local bus service from Yíthio.

By Car   The quickest route (about 2 hours) is the highway west from Sparta to Kalamáta, then the incredibly scenic coastal road from Kalamáta south to Areópolis. Keep your eyes peeled for towers dotting the hills. The seaside village of **Kardamýli,** with many rooms to let, is a fine example of the beautiful local stonework. Farther south is **Langáda,** a breathtaking, picture-perfect hilltown where strolling priests still nod at passersby and *kafeneions* (coffeehouses) are full at dusk. The striking natural beauty changes from fertile plains and terraced olive groves at Kalamáta to the arid high desert and occasional fruit trees of the Máni. Within a few miles of every village are the rocky beaches facing the Gulf of Messinía, which make this an ideal vacation spot for hikers.

VISITOR INFORMATION   You'll find the local **Greek Tourist Organization (EOT)** office (☎ 0733/51-233), the **police station** (☎ 0733/51-209), and the **bus station** all on the main square of Areópolis.

WHAT TO SEE & DO

The simplest thing to do (especially if you have a car) is to visit one of the restored Máni towers; several are described in "Where to Stay & Eat," below. The **Towers Kapetanákos,** restored by the Greek government as part of its laudable Traditional Settlements program, is within a short walk of the village square, and is well worth a visit even by those just passing through.

In addition to exploring the underground caves (see the accompanying box), you museum mavens may also want to check out the popular **Historical Museum of Máni** (☎ **0733/74-414**), located at Koutifari (Thalames). It's housed in a Máni dwelling restored by a local Mániot, Níkons Demanghelos. The collection of artifacts (unlabeled), lithographs, and costumes is sure to interest Máni-acs. The loom on display is the actual one used to produce the multicolored weavings that you'll see in all the area's shops and hotels. Open April to September, daily from 9am to 7pm; admission is 500 Drs ($2.60).

WHERE TO STAY & EAT

The traditional pensions below are scattered throughout the Máni, within a 2-hour ride from Areópolis. They're open April to October only, unless otherwise noted.

We found good, solid taverna fare at most of the hotels; the food was especially good at the **Tsitsiris Castle** (see below), open daily for lunch and dinner. Another fine choice is the **Alipas Grill,** off the main *platía* of Areópolis, convenient for those passing through. The **Diron Taverna,** at the site of the caves of Pýrgos Diroú, is also popular.

Pension Bozagregos. 230 62 Areópolis, Laconia. ☎ **0733/51-354.** 8 rms, none with bath. 8,400 Drs ($36.50) single; 9,600 Drs ($41.70) double. No credit cards.

In the middle of the old town, you can't miss the Máni home of the Bozagregos clan. Tucked behind the blond stone walls are plain, twin-bedded rooms with small garret windows. The rooms are not too distinctive, but this is a good price for a heart-of-town location.

Towers Kapetanakos. 230 62 Areópolis, Laconia. ☎ **0733/51-233.** Fax 0733/51-401. 6 rms, 1 with bath (shower). 9,350–13,200 Drs ($40.70–$57.40) room without bath, 12,000–17,400 Drs ($52.20–$75.70) room with bath. Rates include breakfast. No credit cards.

This 1820 tower, reconstructed in 1979 and surrounded by a beautiful garden, still dominates the tiny town of Areópolis. Its five tower rooms, sleeping two to six, share a common bath and excellent views over the countryside. One room, with a private bath, is situated off the ground-floor courtyard. The walls are more than 3 feet thick (you urbanites will appreciate this) and the simple furnishings are all traditional, employing old Máni motifs throughout.

Readers Recommend

Hotel Geracoulacos, Kavorastássi. "We want to rave about our new discovery of a brand-new hotel exactly on the edge of the Ionian Sea in a tiny village. The owner George Geracoulacos gives you a wonderful large double room with ocean view and breakfast for only 10,000 Drs ($43.50). It's about 5 miles away from the Pýrgos caves and a great place to tour the raw beauty of the Máni. The host and hostess George and Pitza made us feel what Greek hospitality is all about."

—Angela Van Cott, Boxford, Mass.

Traditional Tower Hotels of Vathia. EOT Paradosiakós, Ikismós, 230 71 Váthia, Laconia.
☎ **0733/55-244.** 44 rms, all with bath. 15,000–19,200 Drs ($65.20–$83.50) per room, depending on season. Rates include breakfast. No credit cards. Closed Oct–Feb.

Since the 1980s the Greek Tourist Organization (EOT) has continuously added to
its Traditional Settlement in Váthia, 23 miles south of Areópolis, near the southern
tip of the peninsula. Clusters of well-furnished rooms with up to six sleeping lofts,
all uniquely decorated in the Máni style, are arranged in 12 tall, imposing stone
towers once used to fortify this small Máni hill village. If you have a car, this is an
interesting place to spend the night.

Tsimova Tower. 230 62 Areópolis, Laconia. ☎ **0733/51-301.** 4 rms, none with bath. 9,600
Drs ($41.70) single; 12,000 Drs ($52.20) double. Rates vary with the season. No credit cards.

This is a great place for those who relish the bed-and-breakfast experience of living
with your hosts. The ebullient Versakos family keeps four simple yet ornately styled
rooms tucked into a restored Máni dwelling in the heart of Areópolis village. Visitors are welcomed with family curios, stuffed Snoopy dolls, photo albums of relatives
living in America, and lots of warmth.

✪ **Tsitsiris Castle.** Stavrí, 230 71 Yeroliménas, Laconia. ☎ **0733/56-297.** For reservations
in Athens, call ☎ **01/685-8960;** fax 01/685-8962. 20 rms, all with bath. A/C. 11,200–13,800
Drs ($48.80–$60) single; 15,500–18,500 Drs ($67.40–$80.40) double. Rates depend on season. Rates include breakfast. No credit cards.

A ritzier experience can be had at this 200-year-old guest house, lovingly restored
in harmony with the environment by a local family. It's traditionally furnished, but
with modern comfort and conveniences; the rooms have private bathrooms
equipped with tubs and shower curtains. About 14 miles south of Areópolis, it's
situated in a hiker's paradise, surrounded by the wild beauty and timeless serenity
of the Máni. (Most of the other towers in Stavrí are sparsely populated with the
elderly.) In a picturesque wine cellar, both the guests and the gracious hosts enjoy
continental cuisine.

15 Kalamáta

171 miles SW of Athens, 50 miles S of Trípolis, 36 miles W of Sparta

Kalamáta, "the southernmost city in Europe" seems almost tropical—green and abundant with bougainvillea, geraniums, and hibiscus. There's little to remind you of the
earthquake that devastated the city in 1986 except ubiquitous construction and many
new buildings.

Most readers will probably be content simply to pass through Kalamáta. If you're
stuck here, however, you may want to take a 20-minute ride southwest of the city
to the long sandy beach at **Paralía Messinía.** It's nicer than the city strip's narrow
pebble beach, and many water sports and snack cafes are available.

The region's main business, agriculture, has fully recovered from the earthquake.
Kalamáta continues to be famous for its olives, fine olive oil, and excellent figs. Shoppers may also want to look for silk *mandíli* scarves made by nuns at the local Monastery of Áyios Konstandínos.

ESSENTIALS

GETTING THERE   By Plane   Olympic Airways has one daily flight from Athens;
call ☎ **01/926-7251** in Athens or ☎ **0721/22-376** in Kalamáta for information.

By Train   There's daily train service from Athens's Stathmós Peloponnísou (train
station); call ☎ **01/513-1601** for information.

By Bus   Twelve buses leave daily from the Athens terminal at Odós Kifissoú 100 (travel time 4¹/₂ hours); call ☎ **01/513-4293** for information. Two local buses run daily from either Sparta (via Pýlos) or Areópolis.

By Boat   There are two car-ferries weekly to and from Kíssamos (Kastélli), Crete. Call **Miras Ferries** at ☎ **0721/22-059** for information.

By Car   The fastest route (about 4¹/₂ hours) is to take the highway from Athens to Corinth, then south to Trípolis and southwest to Kalamáta.

VISITOR INFORMATION   Tourist information is available at the **town hall** (no phone) on Thoukidídou Street, or at the **Office of Tourism Development,** Odós Pháron 221 (☎ **0721/22-059;** fax 0721/21-959). Additional branches are open from July to September at the riverside Makedonías Street and at the airport. The **tourist police** (☎ **0721/23-187**) are at Odós Aristoménous 46, off the central square.

One recommended travel agent is **Maniatis Travel,** at the port (☎ **0721/25-300**). It offers day trips through the Máni, to the Pýrgos Diroú caves, and it sells Crete ferry tickets.

ORIENTATION   Kalamáta is a large modern city with regular streets—except near the citadel—following the Nedón River and then opening onto a long central square. You'll find the train station to the south and the bus station to the north of the square.

WHERE TO STAY

The post-earthquake beachfront development of Kalamáta means that many hotels, busy tavernas, cafes, and nightclubs line Navarínou Street, the 3-mile-long waterfront that was named after Greece's big naval victory. This "new" beach has been touted as a "beach resort" by the local tourism industry, but it's not as appealing as more picturesque, less commercial coastal areas elsewhere.

Hotel Nevada. Odós Santarosa 9, 241 00 Kalamáta. ☎ **0721/82-429.** 12 rms, none with bath. 4,800 Drs ($20.90) single; 6,000 Drs ($26.10) double. No credit cards.

We were so pleased to find this adorable, simple four-story building just 1 block inland and 1 block east of the Crete ferry pier, off Faleron Street. Every horizontal surface in both the tidy rooms and high-ceilinged halls is covered with colorful rugs, tiles, fabrics, or flowers. Though your hostess speaks little English, she has tremendous style.

WORTH A SPLURGE

Hotel Filoxenia. Paralía Navarínou, 241 00 Kalamáta. ☎ **0721/23-166.** Fax 0721/23-343. 398 rms, all with bath. A/C TV TEL. 17,400 Drs ($75.70) single; 27,600 Drs ($114.80) double. Rates include half board. AE, DC, EURO, MC, V.

This enormous, landscaped and groomed Class B resort is another choice, on the *paralía* at the east end of the sand-and-pebble beach. Totally renovated after the earthquake, it's a bit worn at the edges from hosting so many budget European tour groups who've been promised a beach vacation. However, there's a satellite dish for their TV, and many of the modern rooms overlook a large pool. The pool plus the Hilton-like amenities may make this splurge worthwhile if you're stuck in Kalamáta for any length of time.

WHERE TO EAT

The waterfront has several cafes and tavernas where you'll find souvláki, pastries, retsína, and so on. Fresh produce, including the famous local figs, can be found in the New Market north of the main square on Aristoménous, near the bus station.

Village Tavern (To Kastráki). Berga. ☎ **0721/41-331.** Main courses 1,080–2,500 Drs ($4.70–$10.90). AE, EURO, MC, V. Daily 6pm–midnight. GREEK.

Actually, the best place for a meal isn't in Kalamáta at all. It's this pretty taverna high on the hillside east of town, 2 miles off the road to Areópolis, in the village of Berga. It certainly serves some of the best food in these parts, with a wonderful specialty of tender baby goat baked in foil.

16 Pýlos

196 miles SW of Athens, 67 miles W of Sparta

Pýlos (Pílos) is a pleasant town strategically located on Navaríno Bay and guarded by two medieval castles. "Sandy Pýlos," as Homer called it, was the home of the venerable King Nestor, whose palace has been found 10 miles north.

Pýlos's long and interesting history stems from the fact that it has one of the finest natural harbors in the world. In 425 B.C. the island of Spacteria (Sfaktiría), across the mouth of the bay, was held for months by 400 Spartans against 14,000 Athenians during a critical engagement of the Peloponnesian War. A Byzantine-era fortress there attests to Venice's former domination over the bay, which they named Navaríno. The Turks built the new castle (Neó Kástro) on a hill south of Pýlos in 1573; Ibrahim Pasha made this castle his headquarters for the Turkish forces who were trying to quash Greece's rebellion. When a fleet of English, French, and Russian vessels sailed into the bay in 1827, an unwise shot precipitated their attack, and the Turkish fleet was soundly defeated, losing 58 of 87 warships and nearly 6,000 troops. This inadvertant Battle of Navaríno won Greece its independence!

Today Pýlos is filled with tourists, but somehow it manages to carry on with its shipping trade and still seem serene.

ESSENTIALS

GETTING THERE   By Bus   Two buses leave Athens daily from the terminal at Odós Kifissoú 100; call ☎ **01/513-4293** for schedule information.

By Car   To reach Pýlos, drive for about 3 hours west of Sparta, taking the highway that goes through Kalamáta. Or it's about a 2-hour drive south of Olympía on the coast "highway."

VISITOR INFORMATION   M Travel, at Odós Filellínon 11 (☎ **0723/22-356;** fax 0723/22-676), on the main street, 2 blocks past the central square, can be extremely helpful with travel plans. The **OTE** and **post office** are just off the south side of the square.

WHAT TO SEE & DO

Fishing boats, caïques that make the 1-hour **sightseeing cruises** around the bay (1,000 Drs/$4.40) four times a day, and the occasional yacht bob up and down in the newly enlarged marina. There's a pleasant, tree-shaded central **Square of the Heroes** and a scenic harbor with some cafes.

All in all, this is a very pleasant place to while away time. In town there's the **Neó Kástro,** the Turkish fortress built in 1573. The older castle, **Paleó Káastro,** across the bay, is also well worth exploring. It belongs to the city, which in turn leases out part of it to experienced innkeepers who maintain it.

The **Pýlos Archaeological Museum** (☎ **0723/22-448**), 2 blocks from the *platía,* displays objects from the Battle of Navaríno as well as various archaeological finds from the area; it's open Tuesday to Sunday from 8:30am to 3pm; admission is 500 Drs ($2.20).

More interesting is **Nestor's Palace** (Anáktoros Néstoros), a 30-minute drive north. The excavations that unearthed the largest palace yet discovered in Greece were begun by the University of Cincinnati in 1939. (During Kyle's recent visit, its summer-school students were still there, digging up a dust storm.) Archaeologists estimate that Nestor, the wealthy king of Pýlos, founded this capital in 1300 B.C. After the fall of Troy (to which his fleet had greatly contributed) Nestor returned to settle in Pýlos. His fabulous palace has been reconstructed in prints drawn by Piet de Jong (reproduced in the local guidebook); some say that the palace itself fell prey to fire during a Dorian attack around 190 B.C.; other scholars claim that it was a 12th-century fire. The site is hard to appreciate, despite what was obviously a painstaking effort. Nonetheless, as we stood on the hilltop site surveying the unspoiled natural beauty of the Peloponnese and the Gulf of Kiparíssia (over which Nestor reigned), we were spellbound.

To reach the palace, take Kalamátas Street, which rises at the north end of the harbor, and follow the signs to Korifás (Romanou). Here the unmarked right fork will lead you (after another 6 miles) right to the site, which is open Tuesday to Sunday from 8:30am to 3pm; admission is 500 Drs ($2.20) plus any video camera fees.

The **archaeological museum** is located 2 miles north of the site, in Hóra. On display are several three-handled pithoid jars used for burying the dead, plus a good collection of artifacts uncovered at the palace site. (Many others are at the National Archaeological Museum in Athens.) Museum hours are the same as those at the site; admission is 500 Drs ($2.10).

WHERE TO STAY

Hotel Galaxy. 240 01 Pýlos, Messinía. ☎ **0723/22-780.** Fax 0723/22-208. 30 rms, all with bath (shower). TEL. 8,400 Drs ($36.50) single; 10,800 Drs ($47) double. MC, V.

Though its halls and common areas are somewhat worn, this contemporary-style hotel has neat, clean rooms with tiled showers. Most overlook Pýlos's lively Square of the Heroes. The Galaxy also has its own popular cafe with umbrella-shaded tables below.

Nilefs Hotel. Odós René Payot 4, 240 01 Pýlos, Messinía. ☎ **0723/22-518.** Fax 0723/22-575. 14 rms, 1 with bath. 10,200 Drs ($44.40) single; 14,400 Drs ($62.60) double. Rates include breakfast. No credit cards.

This former pension has become a fine small hotel and cafe, around the corner from the Pýlos Archaeological Museum. The attractive balconied rooms are quite large and modern, have new showers, and share a communal refrigerator. The slightly inland location, half a block from the west side of the port, makes it a quiet choice in the evening.

WHERE TO EAT

Athanasiou Bakery. Odós Pissistratou 2. No phone. Snacks/pastries 360–600 Drs ($1.60–$2.60). No credit cards. Mon–Sat 7am–2pm and 5–8pm. SNACKS/DESSERTS.

In earlier editions of this book we raved about Mr. Karabatsos's terrific bakery. Fortunately, the new owners of this hallowed place are also great bakers. Just walk up the central stairs on the east side of the *platía* and sample their wares. Try their fresh-made *spanokópita!* We each bought one, plus a doughnut twist, then two large, fresh-baked cookies, and devoured them all before we were halfway to Methóni.

Filip Restaurant. Pýlos–Kalamáta Rd. ☎ **0723/22-741.** Main courses 960–2,000 Drs ($4.20–$10.40). MC, V. Daily 7:30am–midnight. GREEK/CONTINENTAL.

We agree with our Pýlos buddies that this place, on a balcony above the hillside road as you begin the descent into Pýlos from Kalamáta, is the best around. It's a steep half-hour hike up from the port, but easy for drivers to find. The menu is mixed Greek and elegantly continental; the ambience is absolutely local. Litsa and her family serve a superb fish soup and super grilled swordfish or veal cutlets.

Upstairs, you'll find seven modern rooms for rent with great port views; the prices are comparable to those at the hotels listed above but, of course, with a deluxe breakfast thrown in.

17 Methóni & Koróni

248 miles SW of Athens

From Kalamáta you'll cross inland to Methóni or tour the east coast to Koróni. This part of the western Peloponnese has a wild, superlative beach along the Gulf of Messinía. Koróni and Methóni are the two principal ports for this region, known as the "Two Eyes of Venice" because of their respective Venetian fortresses (or lighthouses).

METHÓNI

Methóni is an out-of-the-way treasure that has been discovered. You're likely to run into Greeks playing on Methóni's sand beach, German tour groups in for a weekend romp, or Swedish kids in the portside playground. Like Koróni, Methóni is a medieval town, but it's much less claustrophobic than its neighbor. The Venetians fought long and hard to capture Methóni, and when they eventually succeeded they were less than delighted, since the entire town had been devastated. Starting with a fresh canvas, these Renaissance men constructed a superb **fortress and lighthouse,** both of which stand today as a testament to their skill and taste. The castle site has a marvelous moat and a series of well-preserved walls that are beautifully engineered; the wall extends out into the harbor, culminating in the medieval lighthouse that is known in these parts as one of the "eyes of Venice." The site is open Monday to Saturday from 8:30am to 7pm and Sunday from 9am to 7pm.

WHERE TO STAY

Methóni is a very comfortable seaside resort with many inexpensive rooms to rent.

Alex Hotel. 240 06 Methóni, Messinía. ☎ **0723/31-219.** Fax 0723/31-212. 20 rms, all with bath (shower). 10,800 Drs ($47) single; 13,200 Drs ($57.40) double. No credit cards.

The Paulogiannis family manages this portside inn, as well as the similar but newly constructed **Giota** across the road. It's a personable, full-service place with clean, modern rooms, a restaurant, and the town beach about 80 yards away. The Giota is smaller and a bit cozier.

Readers Recommend

Hotel Aris, Methóni (☎ 0723/31-666). "This hotel is extra-clean and comfortable. It's facing a small quiet square with lots of trees and is about 2 blocks from the beach. There's a refrigerator for guest use on the landing—very handy. The landlady is a sweetheart. Her name is Eleni Psychari."

—Kathryn A. Price, Woodland Hills, Calif.

Galini Hotel. 240 06 Methóni, Messinía. ☎ **0723/31-467.** 11 rms, all with bath (shower). 12,000 Drs ($52.20) single; 14,400 Drs ($62.60) double. No credit cards.

This is a somewhat superior hotel for its class, with a few extra touches. We liked the homey lobby lounge with a big TV. There's parking for those with their own wheels.

Hotel Castello. 240 06 Methóni, Messinía. ☎ **0723/31-300.** 14 rms, all with bath (shower). 12,000 Drs ($52.20) single; 14,400 Drs ($62.60) double. Rates include breakfast. No credit cards.

The flagstone trim and carved wood paneling in the Castello's lobby seems like something you'd find in northern Greece's hill-village hotels rather than in a beach resort. The newly built rooms are basic and clean, and the garden (where breakfast is served) is very pretty.

WHERE TO EAT

George's Cafe. Central Sq. ☎ **0723/31-640.** Snacks/desserts 480–1,560 Drs ($2.10–$6.80). No credit cards. Daily 7am–midnight. SNACKS/DESSERTS.

This is a big place for such a small town, but it's friendly and has good casual fare. The full breakfasts are particularly good, especially with one of the imported coffees. Upstairs, George rents several simple rooms with private shower. You'll find this place inland, right on Methóni's main square.

✪ **Taverna Klimatería.** Methóni town. ☎ **0723/31-544.** Main courses 1,200–1,800 Drs ($5.20–$7.80). MC, V. Daily noon–3pm and 6:30pm–midnight. GREEK.

This quiet, walled garden under a grape arbor is situated opposite the Kástro, just a few blocks south and east of central square (ask the locals). It's probably the best restaurant in the southern Peloponnese—just look at the food displayed and *try* to resist sampling all the delectables. Between mid-May and mid-October the Klimatería's owners grow all their own vegetables and even raise rabbits, which they use for a fabulous stew. Reader Kathryn Price wrote us: "My personal favorites are those light-green mild peppers; the marinated octopus; a concoction with potatoes, egg, and ham; the *keftédes;* and the *dolmadákia.* But there's lots more. Be sure to order the house wine."

EN ROUTE TO KORÓNI

Traveling directly between the west and east coastal towns can be a jarring experience—the roads are in poor condition for more than half the journey. If you're going by bus, you may have to go from Methóni, via Pýlos and Kalamáta, to Koróni; this would be just 10 miles if you went directly! Try to negotiate a shared taxi; it's faster and easier. Those who undertake the trip will be amply rewarded by some of the sights.

About 10 miles from Koróni, not far out of Methóni, is the tiny beach town of **Finikóundas,** which we once called the "soul of Greece." It has now become known for its fine windsurfing (beyond the breakwater) and sandy beach, but remains relatively quiet. The **Finicounda Hotel** (☎ 0723/71-208) has 30 cheerfully furnished rooms with private showers, phones, and views over the peaceful village. It's open year-round; doubles begin at 9,000 Drs ($39.10), and MasterCard and Visa are accepted. There are also many rooms-to-let, and the town square is a comfortable eating area, with food available.

Along the road, as you head out of town, you'll see cypress trees, vineyards, and rows of tomatoes and other vegetables growing under Long Island–style plastic canopies.

KORÓNI

This small, medieval coastal town is set on the hilly western side of the Gulf of Messinía near a 13th-century Venetian fortress: in short, it's another Greek port-and-fort town. Its compact three- and four-story buildings have wrought-iron "lace" balconies, and the stairways and streets are all narrow and worn. The entire town is built amphitheatrically—spread out at the highest hill, then angled down to the harbor below. For thousands of years foreign armies have marched in and out, obliterating what preceded them and then leaving their own brand on the town. Today Koróni has a small protected harbor that makes for a pleasant visit, but not much else.

There are many rooms-to-let above the various tavernas and restaurants on the waterfront. Mr. Costas Sipsas manages some plain, neat rooms plus **Sipsas Apartments,** 240 04 Koróni, Messinia (☎ 0725/22-312), with some tidy apartments with kitchenettes at 15,600 Drs ($67.80) per unit. The recently opened **Auberge de la Plage** (☎ 0725/22-401; fax 0725/22-508) is a large 43-room hotel on the waterfront. It's a fancier choice and charges 14,400 Drs ($62.60) for a double with bath.

18 Pýrgos

190 miles W of Athens, 13 miles W of Olympía

Pýrgos (Pírgos), the capital of Ilía, is an unattractive agricultural town with a population of about 25,000, a minor transportation hub.

Many people change trains or buses here on their way to Olympía, Athens, or elsewhere. From here you head north to Pátra for the ferry to Kefalonía or Italy, south to Kiparíssia, or east to Trípolis in order to connect with transportation to Sparta or Náfplio or . . . we'll spare you the rest.

ESSENTIALS

GETTING THERE   By Train   There are daily trains from Athens's Stathmós Peloponnísou to Pýrgos; call ☎ 01/513-1601 for schedules.

By Bus   Buses leave 10 times daily from the Athens's terminal at Odós Kifissoú 100; call ☎ 01/513-4110 for schedules and information. Local buses leave Olympía hourly for the 30-minute ride to Pýrgos.

By Car   Take the Athens–Corinth highway west to the new national highway at Pátra, then the coast highway south to Pýrgos.

VISITOR INFORMATION   The friendly **tourist police** are at Odós Karkavítsas 4 (☎ 0621/37-111), next to the Olympos Hotel. If you'd like a tour to Olympía, contact **Achtypis Tours,** Odós 28 October no. 26 (☎ 0621/26-301; fax 0621/22-200); it offers excursions there and to other regions.

GETTING AROUND   Local buses to Athens, Olympía, and Pátra leave from Manolopoúlou Street. Pýrgos **town buses** leave from Ypsilándou Street; the **train station** is at the foot of the same street.

WHERE TO STAY & EAT

If you must spend the night in Pýrgos, here are some places where you can get a good night's sleep. All town hotels cater to businesspeople and are expensive; some have restaurants.

The **Ilida Hotel,** Odós Patrón-Deliyiánni 50 (☎ 0621/28-046; fax 0621/33-834), 2 blocks from the railroad station off broad Ethnikís Andístasis Street, has modern air-conditioned doubles for 14,400 Drs ($62.60). The **Hotel Marily,** Odós Deliyánni 48 (☎ 0621/28-133; fax 0621/27-066), also off Ethnikís Andístasis near the train station, has small but clean and nicely furnished air-conditioned doubles at 16,800 Drs ($73), including breakfast; EuroCard, MasterCard, and Visa are accepted.

The newly renovated **Olympos,** Odós Karkavítsa 2 (☎ **0621/33-650**), 4 short blocks uphill from the railroad station, has comfortable, clean air-conditioned doubles (with big old-fashioned bathtubs) for 16,800 Drs ($73); EuroCard, MasterCard, and Visa are accepted.

We had a great souvláki at the **Kynigou Grill,** next to the Ilida Hotel, and some okay cheese pies at the **Zapeki Bakery,** across the street from it. When it's time to munch, you'll find lots of options just by walking around.

19 Olympía

199 miles W of Athens, 14 miles E of Pýrgos

Olympía (Olymbía) hardly needs an introduction. For more than a millennium it hosted the most important Panhellenic games, and today it's one of the most popular destinations for visitors to Greece. Olympía is at its best in the early spring before the tourist hordes descend.

The first Olympic Games were held in 776 B.C. By 576 B.C. the games had been restructured as a footrace held every 4 years for 5 days, during the summer full moon. At this time messengers would travel to announce a sacred truce in Greece's wars, and athletes from all over Greece would stop fighting in order to compete in the games.

The original Olympic event, a run down the length of the stadium (465 feet), was soon expanded to include multilap races, the pentathlon (running, wrestling, discus, jumping, and javelin), boxing, chariot races, and contests of strength. To preserve the integrity of the athletes, strict rules were imposed and stiff fines were levied against offenders. Anybody who bore arms at the sanctuary during the period of this sacred truce was fined, and bronze casts of Zeus were made and displayed from these earnings. Marble bases from these casts still exist and dot the site.

Women were not allowed to watch the competitions, possibly because the participants were nude. However, one priestess, representing Demeter, the goddess of fertility, was always present. Women did participate in the chariot races and had their own Olympics at another time—the Heraea, in honor of Zeus's wife, Hera.

As Greek civilization declined, so did the allure of the laurel wreath (with which winners were crowned); eventually corruption and vice plagued the sanctuary at Olympía. In A.D. 393 the emperor Theodosius banned the games by decree; 30 years later his son ordered all the temples at the sanctuary destroyed.

ESSENTIALS

GETTING THERE & DEPARTING   By Train   Five daily trains leave from Athens's Peloponnísou Station going to Pýrgos; call ☎ **01/513-1601** for schedules. From Pýrgos, you'll have to change to the spur line to Olympía.

By Bus   Buses leave Athens terminal at Odós Kifissoú 100 10 times daily going directly to Olympía; call ☎ **01/513-4110** for schedules and information. There are also hourly local buses between Pýrgos and Olympía.

By Car   Take the Athens–Corinth highway west to the new national highway at Pátra, then the coast highway south to Pýrgos, then turn east (inland) to Olympía.

VISITOR INFORMATION   The city of Olympía operates an excellent **tourist information office** right on the main street, Praxitélous Kondýli, near the ancient site (☎ **0624/23-100** or 0624/23-173; fax 0624/23-125), open daily from 9am to

9pm in summer and 11am to 6pm in winter. The staff can exchange traveler's checks and provide a city map and brochures, plus lists of rooms and camping and hotel facilities in the area. The **tourist police** are at Odós Ethnossinélefseos 6 (☎ 0624/22-100).

ORIENTATION Modern Olympía is a half-mile tourist strip, overflowing with very commercial cafes, shops, and hotels. The prices everywhere in town are high, but if you slip off the main drag, either 1 block up or down, you'll find that the hotels and tavernas tend to be less expensive and better.

The **telephone office (OTE),** also on Praxitélous Kondýli near the site, is open Monday to Friday from 7:30am to 2pm. Most of the town's banks, as well as the bus station, are on the main street. The **train station** is off the main street, on the north end of town. The town **bus stop** is next door to the tourist information office.

GETTING AROUND If you don't have a car, you can walk, take the **bus,** or call a **taxi** (☎ 0624/22-555) to pick you up. It's an easy 15-minute walk to the site and museum.

SEEING THE SIGHTS

The Games were revived in 1896, when the first modern Olympiad was held in Athens. The tradition of bearing a flame from the original sanctuary at Olympía to the site of the new Olympiad began in 1936. Today the flame is lit by focusing the sun's rays through a magnifying glass located at the Temple of Hera. The lit torch is then conveyed by a "priestess" through the arched entrance to the stadium and then to the field, where the first runner in the relay to the site starts the journey that the whole world watches. Olympic competitors always ran toward the Temple of Zeus; start your race at the far end. (We had fun picking olive branches and making "Olympic" wreaths after our modest marathon jog.)

The site (☎ 0624/22-529) is open Monday to Friday from 7:30am to 6pm and on Saturday and Sunday from 8:30am to 3pm; admission is 1,200 Drs ($5) for adults, 900 Drs ($3.75) for seniors, and 600 Drs ($2.50) for students. You can ride a donkey from town to the site, but bargain with the wranglers until you get the price down to about 1,200 Drs ($5.20) for the journey.

For the utmost appreciation of this site, go to the nearby ✪ **archaeological museum** (☎ 0624/22-742). Superb pediments from the Temple of Zeus have been reconstructed and are displayed in a room with the same spatial dimensions as the original setting. The statuary is remarkable for its attention to anatomical detail and the fluid facial expressions. After seeing this, you'll probably develop a respect for the word "monumental," and you'll better understand the religious aspect of the original games. The other great treasure here is the statue of Hermes by Praxiteles, which was discovered amid the ruins of the Temple of Hera; notice how the archaeologists have reconstructed the legs from the knees down, with only the right foot to work from. Finds from ongoing excavations at the site are often moved to the museum; the most interesting dig is at the monument of Pelops. This is really a one-of-a-kind museum.

You'll find signs indicating the way to the museum at the site entrance and on the road. It's open Monday from 11:30am to 6pm, Tuesday to Friday from 8:30am to 5pm, and Saturday and Sunday from 8:30am to 3pm; admission is 1,200 Drs ($5) for adults, 900 Drs ($3.75) for seniors, and 600 Drs ($2.50) for students. To take flash pictures and use video cameras, you'll need additional (pricey) permits.

The **Museum of the Olympic Games** is in town, about 3 blocks north of the bus station. The hours are Monday to Saturday from 8:30 to 3:30pm and Sunday from 9am to 4:30pm; admission is 500 Drs ($2.10).

If you're as hot as Kyle's family was when they toured Olympía, you can take advantage of the huge pool at the **Touris Club** (☎ **0624/23-001**), a 5-minute walk north from Main Street. It serves snacks and beverages after 9am daily, and diners may use the pool free. If you prefer a beach, head to **Kaïáfas** or **Zacháro,** long, broad, gold-sand beauties less than 12 miles away on the Ionian Sea.

WHERE TO STAY

Olympía is the most popular archaeological site on the Peloponnese; tour buses and individuals pass through town all summer long. If you plan to arrive between July and the middle of August, call ahead for reservations. The hotels listed below are open from late May to late September unless otherwise noted.

Hotel Achilleus. Odós Stefanopoúlou 4, 270 65 Ancient Olympía, Peloponnese. ☎ **0624/ 22-562.** 7 rms, none with bath. 4,800 Drs ($20.90) single; 6,600 Drs ($28.70) double. No credit cards.

This former pension has clean, large rooms above a snack bar, about two lanes up from the busy main street. Inquire out front about available rooms; the manager often tends the cafe downstairs. There's a shower down the hall for guests.

Hotel Phedias. Odós P. Spiliopoúlou 2, 270 65 Ancient Olympía, Peloponnese. ☎ **0624/ 22-667.** 9 rms, all with bath (tub or shower). 7,200 Drs ($31.30) single; 8,400 Drs ($36.50) double. AE, MC, V.

This Class C hotel is down the block from the prominent Hotel Hercules and opposite one of Olympía's pretty churches. The charming owner, George Bournas, has provided the nicest bathrooms in Olympía; the showers are also half-tubs. All the rooms have balconies, many overlooking his famous pastry shop.

✪ Pelops Hotel. Odós Varéla 2, 270 65 Ancient Olympía, Peloponnese. ☎ **0624/22-543.** Fax 0624/22-213. 26 ms, all with bath (20 with shower, 10 with tub). TEL. 7,800 Drs ($33.90) single; 10,000 Drs ($43.50) double. EURO, MC, V. Closed Nov–Feb.

Located at the quiet end of the village, this hotel offers the best value in this price range, with more than a few touches of distinction. Susan Spiliopoulou, the lovely owner/manager, is an Australian with travel experience. She's the perfect hostess, providing spotless rooms, good cheer, and local baby-sitters. Susan is also constantly making improvements. She and her family (together with their dog, Nora) are truly terrific; you'll leave Olympía having made good friends. Summer guests may enjoy free use of the nearby Touris Club pool.

Pension Posidon. Odós Stefanopoúlou 9, 270 65 Ancient Olympía, Peloponnese. ☎ **0624/ 22-567.** 10 rms, none with bath. 6,000 Drs ($26.10) single; 7,200 Drs ($31.30) double. No credit cards.

This pension, located two lanes up from the main street, is comparable to the nearby Achilleus. Though the rooms aren't quite as large, they're cleaner and quieter; the common showers were better during our last visit. Breakfast (1,000 Drs/$4.40) is served in the snack bar next door.

WORTH A SPLURGE

Hotel Europa. Odós Droúva 1, 270 65 Ancient Olympía, Peloponnese. ☎ **800/528-1234** in the U.S. for reservations, or 0624/22-650. Fax 0624/23-166. 42 rms, all with bath. A/C TEL. 18,900 Drs ($82.20) single; 27,350 Drs ($118.90) double. AE, DC, EURO, V.

The most luxurious hotel in town is high above it; both modern and traditional, open and spacious, it's beautifully decorated. The rooms are very comfortable, with peaceful vistas from each balcony. The public spaces are equally fine; the top-floor dining room serves Greek and continental fare indoors or on the roof terrace; the outdoor pool and tennis courts share a casual outdoor grill/snack bar. Two big surprises for Greece: 24-hour in-room beverage service and overnight laundry service. The Europa is open year-round and plans to begin offering regional day trips in 1997.

CAMPING

Camping Alphios. 270 65 Ancient Olympía, Peloponnese. ☎ **0624/22-950.** Fax 01/34-65-262. 1,800 Drs ($7.80) per person; 800 Drs ($3.50) per tent site. No credit cards.

On Droúva Hill, just below the Hotel Europa, the site has glorious views of the town and hills. There's a pool, minimarket, snack bar, and restaurant.

Camping Diana. Kalamáta Hwy., 270 65 Ancient Olympía, Peloponnese. ☎ **0624/22-314.** 1,800 Drs ($7.80) per person; 800 Drs ($3.50) per tent site. No credit cards.

This campground is near the Museum of the Olympic Games in a quiet, shady spot. It's very homey, with solar-powered showers, a swimming pool, facilities for washing clothes and dishes, and a small grocery store.

WHERE TO EAT

George Bourna's Pastry Shop. Odós P. Spiliopoúlou. ☎ **0624/22-548.** Breakfast 960 Drs ($4.20); desserts 360 Drs ($1.60). No credit cards. Daily 7am–11:30pm. SNACKS/DESSERTS.

Half a block up from the main street near the Olympic Games museum, next to the Phedias Hotel, you'll find this delightful bakery with some outdoor tables. George is charming, and a terrific cook turns out great pastry, hearty breakfasts, homemade yogurt with honey, freshly made feta, and lots of goodies at much higher quality and lower prices than you'll find at the countless fast-food shops.

Taverna Kladeos. Ancient Olympía. ☎ **0624/23-322.** Main courses 980–2,000 Drs ($4.30–$8.70). Daily 7pm–1am. GREEK.

This simple grill taverna is tucked in the woods near the railroad tracks, on a wooded rise above the river Kládeos. It was recommended to us by locals for its seasonal stuffed vegetable dishes, but we also enjoyed the roast pork and grilled chicken plates. You can dine at tables set up under the shade trees, or under the awning of a small tiled-roof house. Call ahead to make sure they're not hosting a big (read: boisterous) group the night you plan to eat there.

Taverna Praxitelis. Odós Spiliopoúlou 7. ☎ **0624/23-570.** Main courses 960–3,360 Drs ($4.20–$14.60). V. Daily 11am–3pm and 7pm–1am. GREEK.

Next door to the police station, this taverna owned by Saris Floras enjoys the best reputation among the locals for traditional Greek cuisine at moderate prices. Daily specials include fresh seafood, game such as rabbit and quail in the fall, grilled chicken, and a tasty sausage-and-pepper stew.

OLYMPÍA AFTER DARK

If you're not too tired from jogging around the Olympic Stadium, reserve seats at the **Touris Club** (☎ **0624/23-001**), on the hill north of town near the Olympic Games museum. We really enjoyed it. During the day you can lounge, sunbathe or swim in the large pool, and enjoy snacks or drinks. At 9:30pm nightly from May to October an excellent traditional Greek dance performance is given on a stage above the pool. Dinner is optional—the restaurant's typical Greek fare is quite good and reasonably priced—although there's a stiff 3,600-Dr ($15) cover charge, which includes one drink. Two dance groups made up of talented, enthusiastic locals perform at least a dozen folk dances, after which they teach spectators; then they expect you to join in. Kyle loves this and thinks everyone should at least *see* some authentic Greek folk dancing, if not actually learn the *syrtáki*. This top-quality show makes an evening in Olympía a rare cultural treat.

If live performances aren't your thing, try the **open-air cinema** behind the railroad station. Nightly shows begin at sundown (about 9:45pm) and cost 600 Drs ($2.50) per person. At our last visit, Johnny Weismuller was starring in the original *Tarzan!*

20 Kyllíni & Kástro

181 miles SW of Athens, 47 miles SW of Pátra, 23 miles NW of Pýrgos

ESSENTIALS

GETTING THERE   By Bus   Buses leave the Athens terminal (Odós Kiffísoú 100) 10 times daily going to Pýrgos; call ☎ **01/513-4110** for schedules and information. There are frequent local buses between Pátra or Pýrgos and Kyllíni or Kástro. A taxi from Lechína (outside Kyllíni) to Kástro, our favorite destination, costs 1,200 Drs ($5).

By Car   Take the Athens–Corinth highway west to the Pátra highway, then the new national highway (E55) to Lechína. Then it's local roads south to Kyllíni, Kástro, or Loutrá Kyllíni.

FAST FACTS   The telephone **area code** for the Kallíni and Kástro area is 0623. You should plan to have enough Greek currency on hand here, since the tiny port of Kyllíni has no bank or American Express office, and there are few tourist services. **Ferries** depart for the Ionian isles nine times daily to Zákynthos (1½-hour trip), four times daily to Kefalonía (2 or 3 hours, depending on the port), once daily continuing on to Ithaka (4 hours), and once daily to Corfu via Pátra (10 hours). Confirm your departure time by calling **Miras Ferries** (☎ **0623/92-100** or 0623/92-080 in Kyllíni, or 0695/41-500 in Zákynthos).

WHAT TO SEE & DO

Kyllíni is a small port with a wide stretch of dirty and busy beach on each side of the busy ferry terminal that services the Ionian islands. Plan ahead so that you have only a little time to kill and walk the side streets till the boat arrives. If you're staying overnight, we must warn you that in August the whole region is infested with mosquitoes; bring a garlic necklace and repellent for a good night's rest.

Better yet, go 3½ miles to Kástro, a charming still-Greek village in the shadow of an enormous medieval fortress. The **kástro** (castle), built in 1220 by the Frankish crusaders, is already well reconstructed and hosts popular music concerts weekly during the summer. Our tour was enlivened by a group from the **Ionian Village**, a summer camp based in nearby Vartholomío, run by the Greek Orthodox Archdiocese of North and South America. Its reputedly excellent program reacquaints Greek-American children with their parents' homeland. You can contact them at 8 E. 79th St., New York, NY 10021 (☎ **212/570-3500**), for more information.

The old-fashioned hamlet of Kástro boasts three *kafenía* (one with a billiards table), a minimarket, a telekarta payphone, and a few tavernas. It also has one of the best family beaches in the country, with clean gold sand and gentle surf, just 1¼ miles south of town.

Loutrá Kyllíni (Kyllíni Hot Springs) is home to a hydropathic spa shrouded in eucalyptus trees. There's a manicured public ✪ **beach** and sulfurous hot mineral springs, famed for curing arthritis and respiratory ailments.

WHERE TO STAY
IN KYLLÍNI

There are acceptable rooms and a hotel within sight of Kyllíni's port. Also there's a nearby campground, **Cabin Kyllíni** (☎ 0623/96-259), with four-person bungalows renting for 11,500 Drs ($50) a night; tent sites go for 2,880 Drs ($12.50). The setting makes this one of the best camping spots we know, with great beaches close at hand.

Hotel Ionian. 270 50 Loutrá Kyllíni, Ilías. ☎ **0623/92-318.** 22 rms, all with bath (shower). TEL. 9,600 Drs ($41.70) single; 12,400 Drs ($53.90) double. No credit cards.

If you don't have your own car and you happen to miss the last boat, the Hotel Ionian is just north of the port but far enough away to provide some quiet. The rooms are average and clean, and swimming is available across the road.

Xenia Hotel. 270 50 Loutrá Kyllíni, Ilías. ☎ **0623/96-277.** Fax 0623/96-474. 80 rms, all with bath (shower). TEL. 8,520 Drs ($37) single; 11,000 Drs ($47.80) double. Rates include breakfast. AE, EURO.

Arthritics will want to know about the faded, government-run Xenia Hotel. It's close to the hot springs, with undistinctive rooms but with volleyball, basketball, and tennis facilities. You can unwind by lowering yourself into a spring-water thermal bath, famous since antiquity for its curative powers.

IN KÁSTRO

Kástro has a wonderful small hotel and many rooms to let: Litsa from the **Afroditi Souvenirs Shop** (☎ 0623/95-431) on Kástro's only street has volunteered to help visitors find suitable rooms from the 100 or so that are available in local homes.

✪ **Chrissi Avgi Hotel.** Odós Loutropóleos 9, 270 50 Kástro, Ilías. ☎ **0623/95-224.** 10 rms, all with bath (9 with shower, 1 with tub). TEL. 7,500 Drs ($32.60) single; 9,800 Drs ($42.60) double. No credit cards.

This is the friendliest place to stay in the northern Peloponnese—if you can get a room. It's not architecturally noteworthy, but a cozy library and flower-filled patio, where a delicious breakfast is served (for 1,320 Drs/$5.70), enhance its appeal. Your hosts, Christos Lepidas and his lovely French wife, Catherine, make everyone feel at home. Their pleasant and quiet lodging even has some balconied rooms facing the illuminated castle. It's convenient for drivers visiting Olympía, Pátra, and the Ionians, and great for families who will appreciate Kástro's small-town charm and the excellent beaches just minutes away.

Katsenou Rooms to Let. Main St., 270 50 Kástro, Ilías. ☎ **0623/95-431.** 4 rms, all with bath (shower). 9,500 Drs ($41.30) single or double. No credit cards.

Freshly painted shades of blue accentuate the clean, quiet rooms at this small pension behind Ms. Eleni Katsenou's home. Each has its own toilet and shower, and all permit access to an adjoining kitchen and garden dining area.

WHERE TO EAT

At the ferry port of Kyllíni, up one lane from the village post office is a **bakery** with mouth-watering selections, and a half dozen ordinary cafes in the car-ferry terminal. In Kástro there are two delightful choices.

Castello Pizzaria. Main St. ☎ **0623/95-360.** Menu items 540–2,000 Drs ($2.40–$8.60). No credit cards. Daily noon–11pm. GREEK/CONTINENTAL.

Just off the lazy small-town *platía* is this elegant *mezedopolíon,* a French-inspired Greek bistro. Try the sardine or mixed vegetable pizza, aubergine salad, fresh veal roasted with garlic and olive oil, and lighter-than-air crêpes. This is the place to sit under trumpet vines or an ancient olive tree, listen to the gurgling fountain, and just let life flow by.

Restaurant Grill Toula. Kástro. No phone. Main dishes 900–1,500 Drs ($3.90–$6.50). No credit cards. Daily 11am–11:30pm. GREEK.

You can't miss this small family-run grill, where the freshest meats and locally grown vegetables are served daily to guests, then later to the other family members. The limited menu of local specialties guarantees absolutely pure flavors.

21 Pátra

128 miles NW of Athens

Pátra (Pátrai; Patras in English) is the largest town in the Pelponnese, the second most important port in Greece, and a major transportation hub—with ferry connections to Italy and the Ionian islands, bus and train connections to Athens and throughout the Peloponnese, and passage across the Gulf of Corinth to western Greece via the ferry at Río.

The modern city of Pátra stands just below the site of the ancient city where, according to legend, St. Andrew preached Christianity and was crucified for his efforts; he was later buried here. Capital of Achaea (Ahaía), the northwest part of the Peloponnese, Pátra derived its name from its founder, Patreus, the leader of the Achaeans who drove out the Ionians. This area is very mountainous, yet ruins indicate that it has been settled since the Paleolithic Age. The ancient acropolis was capped with a Byzantine castle that still dominates the city. The city's heart is Platía Vassiléos Yioryíou (King George Square).

ESSENTIALS

GETTING THERE & DEPARTING   By Train   There is frequent daily service from Athens's Peloponnísou Railroad Station (☎ 01/513-1601) or Piraeus's Peloponnísou Station (☎ 01/417-8335). Call for schedule information. The Pátra train station (☎ 061/221-311) is at the port.

By Bus   Buses leave Athens every half hour daily from the Odós Kifissoú 100 terminal; call ☎ 01/513-6135 for information.

By Car   Take the Athens–Corinth highway west to the Pátra highway, continuing west along the Gulf of Corinth.

VISITOR INFORMATION   The **National Tourist Office (EOT)** is at Odós Iróon Polytechníou 110, outside Customs at the New Port by the entrance to Gate 6 (☎ 061/653-358). It has the largest collection of free brochures in the entire country, so try to stock up. The helpful staff is here Monday to Friday from 7am to 9:30pm. The **tourist police** (☎ 061/651-833 or 061/651-893) are in the same building as the tourist office, beyond it and upstairs; they're open daily from 8am to 11pm.

GETTING AROUND   Long-distance buses leave the KTEL station (☎ 061/ 623-886) at Zaïmí and Óthonos-Amalías streets, which services hubs such as Athens, Pýrgos, Kalamáta, and Thessaloníki, as well as all parts of Greece. The bus to Athens costs 3,250 Drs ($14.10) and takes about 3 hours. Local buses stop across from the train station and follow the coastal highway as far as Río.

By Car   You can rent a car at one of several agencies; we had good luck and great prices at **AutoEurope,** Odós Kolokotróni 36, just off the port (☎ **061/524-029**).

By Ferry   Ferry tickets are sold by several travel agents along the port. For information about ferries to the Ionian islands, call **Strintzis Lines** (☎ **061/622-602**) or Joanne at the **Tsimara Shipping and Travel Office,** Odós Óthonos-Amalías 14, down the street from the National Bank (☎ **061/277-783**). There are about 15 daily **ferries to Italy**—Brindisi, Ancona, or Bari. The **Hellenic-Mediterranean Line** and **Adriatica Line** transport EurailPass holders free; call HML (☎ **061/652-521**) or Adriatica (☎ **061/422-138**) for schedule and fare information.

FAST FACTS   The telephone **area code** for Pátra is 061. The main **post office** is at Zaïmí and Mezón streets, and the **telephone center (OTE)** is at Dimitriougoúnai and Kanakári streets; both have New Port branches. If you want to book a domestic flight or just confirm one, the **Olympic Airlines** office is at Odós Ayiou Andréa 16 (near the Hotel Astir), at the corner of Arátou Street (☎ **061/222-902**). The **American Express** office is at Odós Óthonos-Amalías 48 (☎ **061/224-609**) and is open daily. The Óthonos-Amalías branch of the **National Bank of Greece** is open Monday to Friday from 8am to 2pm and 6 to 7:30pm.

SPECIAL EVENTS   For 3 weeks during February or March every year (ending the night before the begining of Orthodox Lent), the annual **Carnival**—claimed to be the world's largest noncommercial celebration of the event—features a chariot parade, traditional Greek theater, and wild Saturnalia (private and public parties with drinking, dancing, and general lack of inhibition).

The **Pátra International Festival,** in July and August, features concerts, art shows, and the usual hoopla. Young Greek directors such as Victor Arditti have presented experimental plays, and major musicians have appeared. Call ☎ **061/278-730** for schedule information. The **Pátra Summer Festival** (☎ **061/275-272**), a smaller performing arts event, takes place each year between May and September. The **Pátra Wine Festival** is held every year during the last 2 weeks of August; wine sampling and entertainment are offered nightly. Call ☎ **061/279-866** for information on the festival.

WHAT TO SEE & DO

The city's arches are the first thing many travelers see of Greece, for Pátra is where thousands of Europeans disembark from ferries arriving from Brindisi, Ancona, or Bari, Italy, or from the Ionian isles of Corfu and Kefalonía or the northern mainland at Igoumenítsa. As you might have guessed, Pátra is always crowded with visitors, backpacks, and camping caravans heading from chilly northern Europe to the sunny south of Greece. In Pátra there's actually plenty to see, including the largest cathedral—though not a great beauty—in all of Greece, Áyiou Andréas (St. Andrew's).

Pátra is also the home of the **Achaïa Clauss winery** (☎ **061/325-051**), one of the largest Greek manufacturers/exporters of (okay) wine. Call for information on tours; it's open daily from 9am to 7pm.

The **archaeology museum,** Odós Maízonos 41 (☎ **061/275-070**), exhibits fragments of sculpture, bronzes, clay vases, gold and ivory work, jewelry, and mosaics; it's open Tuesday to Sunday from 8:30am to 3pm; admission is 500 Drs ($2.20). And, needless to say, Pátra has its quota of Byzantine, Turkish, and Frankish architecture and ruins.

Some say the modern city is best viewed as you depart by boat, but if you're caught here, begin by strolling around Platía Yioryíou, 3 blocks south (right) from the train

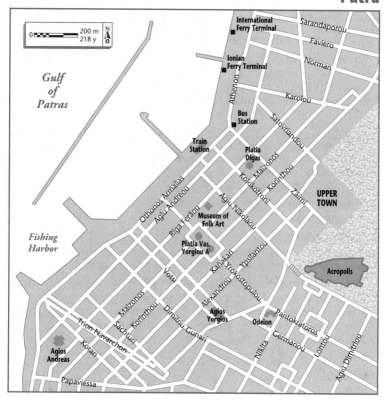

station and 3 blocks inland. You won't need any direction from us to discover the lively nightlife around the square. Continuing south up Yerokostopoúlou, you'll find several fast-food places as well as stairs leading to several bistros and all-night cafes. Keep climbing and you'll reach the **ancient odeum,** built during the Roman period and razed in the 3rd century A.D.; it's still used for concerts and theater performances. Farther up Pantokrátoros Street, you'll pass the handsome church that gives the street its name (well worth a peek inside). A left road beside the church leads to the **acropolis** and the old Turkish-built towers of the **kástro,** where you can enjoy a bird's-eye view.

WHERE TO STAY

Hotel Acropole. Odós Óthonos-Amalías 39, 262 23 Pátra, Peloponnese. ☎ **061/279-809.** Fax 061/221-533. 33 rms, all with bath (shower). TEL. 6,720 Drs ($29.20) single; 8,880 Drs ($38.60) double. EURO, MC, V.

It's centrally located, just across from the port and railway station, and 1 block from the bus station. The gracious Charmaine and Perikles Foundas are certainly one reason the Acropole welcomes so many repeat guests, but there is also the laundry service and room deliveries from their ground-floor cafe (open daily from 7:30am to 11:30pm). The hotel is well kept, but sweetly worn, with large enameled bathtubs and a groaning elevator. The front rooms, which face the port, are surprisingly quiet, because of the recently installed thermalpane windows.

Hotel Adonis. Odós Zaïmí 7 (at Kapsáli St.), 262 23 Pátra, Peloponnese. ☎ **061/224-213.** Fax 061/226-971. 56 rms, all with bath (shower). A/C TV TEL. 12,000 Drs ($52.20) single; 14,500 Drs ($62.80) double. Rates include breakfast. AE, EURO, MC, V.

A typical American-style hotel, completely refurbished in 1994, this is a pleasant, quiet place just 1 block inland from the port. The modern rooms have peach-colored wallpaper, very firm beds, piped-in classical Muzak on the radio, and even TVs. It's also close to the city center, across from the bus depot and near all ferry ticket offices.

Hotel El Greco. Odós Ayíou Andréou 145, 262 23 Pátra, Peloponnese. ☎ **061/272-931.** Fax 061/226-179. 24 rms, 8 with bath (shower). TEL. 6,000 Drs ($26.10) single or double without bath, 8,050 Drs ($35) single or double with bath. No credit cards. Head 1 block inland from the portside Gate One.

This is one of the best budget choices in town (the cheaper hotels are pretty awful). George Vlachoyianis, the friendly manager, speaks English, and the rooms are clean and comfortable.

A YOUTH HOSTEL

GYH Hostel. Odós Iróon Polytechníou 62, 264 41 Pátra, Peloponnese. ☎ **061/427-278.** 7 dorms, none with bath. 2,000 Drs ($8.70) dorm bed. No credit cards.

This hostel is located about half a mile east of the New Port on the harborfront road. It's in a handsome old villa that served as a German barracks during World War II. Within its enclosed courtyard, the hostel offers shared hot showers and laundry facilities, both very clean. It's definitely one of the best GYH facilities in Greece. (There's a possibility that the hostel will move nearer the port, so call or ask before you go.)

CAMPING

There are several campgrounds outside Pátra; the closest one is **Kavouri Camping** (☎ **061/428-066**), 1¹/₄ miles east of the port; call for current rates since they fluctuate seasonally. It should cost about 1,500 Drs ($6.50) per person, 550 Drs ($2.40) for a small tent. There are also two campsites at Río, 5 miles east: **Río Camping** (☎ **061/991-585**) and **Río Mare** (☎ **061/992-263**).

WHERE TO EAT

There are tons of hotels in Pátra, and even more restaurants. Most of them are tourist traps, and we hope you can spot them—by their telltale signs—and thus avoid them. Sweet tooths and Nesfrappé freaks might want to walk up to the shaded Platía Ólgas. **Cafe Kentri** (☎ **061/279-623**) is one of the many good places that surround this small park.

There are also a few enticing places to eat around the central Platía Yioryíou, including an excellent pâtisserie, **Tilidadis,** half a block west of the square at Odós Maízona 123 (☎ **061/338-182**), which features fresh bread, pizza, cookies, and pastries. There's a cluster of trendy new bistros on the "new" pedestrian-only stairs above Platía Yioryíou, where you'll also find **Traffic, Vengera,** and **Cafe Cinema,** with Hollywood decor.

Rocky Raccoon Bistro. Odós Yerokostopoúlou 49. ☎ **061/222-627.** Snacks 920–2,000 Drs ($4–$8.70); main courses 1,500 Drs ($6.50). No credit cards. Daily 9am–2am. INTERNATIONAL/ GREEK.

Grab a table—if you're lucky enough to get one—on the sidewalk, inside the contemporary music-filled dining rooms, or in one of the side alcoves. Beverages are the priority with most diners, but the food ranges from sandwiches and snacks to

EuroGreek and Greek favorites. Overnighters to Pátra will enjoy mingling with the local intelligentsia.

Tricoyia Brothers Restaurant. Odós Óthonos-Amalías 46 (at Ermoú). ☎ **061/279-421.** Main courses 1,300–2,900 Drs ($5.70–$12.50). AE, DC, MC, V. Daily 10am–11pm. GREEK.

Our favorite dining room is the lively Tricoyia Brothers across from the train station. There's an old-world professionalism to the place that's a relief from the nearby string of huckster- and billboard-promoted cafes. Among the many dishes that we tried, John particularly liked the beef with zucchini, carrots, and potatoes, while Kyle went for the lamb fricassee with vegetables in a creamy lemon sauce. You'll find that all the waiters are nice, too.

SIDE TRIPS TO RÍO & ANTÍRIO

Río's claim to fame is that it's the port city (5 miles north of Pátra) that connects the Peloponnese to the mainland at Antírio. The curious and museum-happy crowd may want to head over to the pier to see the ruins of **Morea Castle,** built in 1499 by the sultan Beyazid; the let's-get-on-with-it crowd may prefer to make a beeline to the souvláki trucks and the small and sometimes expensive markets.

If you have a car, the 15-minute ferry ride across this mile-wide divide will cost 1,000 Drs ($4.40); tickets are sold on board. Bus riders crossing to and from the Peloponnese will find themselves changing buses before the ferry and paying the 130-Dr (70¢) fare, the same as their noncar companions. When you reach the other side, you'll be greeted by the fortress ruins of Roumelia, built by the Turks to fortify the strait. In ancient times a Temple of Poseidon stood at each port, checking out all those who sailed through the Gulf of Corinth.

8 Crete

Every Mediterranean culture in history has coveted Crete (Kríti) because of its natural resources and artistic richness, and today's traveler will find it just as desirable.

Nature lovers will be delighted by Crete's mountainous heartland, unparalleled for its varied scenic beauty. The island is the longest link in a geological chain stretching from the mountainous Peloponnese through Kýthira to Rhodes and beyond to Asia Minor; its terrain reflects these different landscapes, particularly on the eastern and western coasts. Crete's developed northern coast is defined by a national highway linking several harbors on the azure Aegean. The once-great centers of ancient maritime powers have now become overdeveloped beach resorts and picturesque fishing ports. The untamed rugged southern coast curls lazily along the Libyan Sea, facing the coast of Africa across the Mediterranean. Crete's wealth comes from the south's thriving year-round agribusiness—tomato hothouses line the roads curved above huge canyons and rocky gorges; date palms and vineyards are interspersed with placid, sandy beach coves and dense banana plantations.

The Minoan culture that many consider the foundation of all Greek (and European) civilization originated on Crete. The variety of archaeological treasures from the Minoan civilization will delight even visitors bored with "old stones." The great palaces at Knossós, Mália, and Phestós (Phaistos) are only the first leg of a historical odyssey that leads to Hellenic, Byzantine, and Venetian sites throughout the island.

Crete has been discovered by tour groups in a big way, but it's still Greece's single most fascinating island, especially if you're willing to venture out to the less obvious destinations. Try to allow at least 1 week to sample its many pleasures.

The northern coast has been heavily developed, to the detriment of most of its once-picturesque fishing ports, especially Áyios Nikólaos. We'd recommend **Sitía** as a base for exploring the eastern part of the island and **Haniá** for exploring the central and western part.

Of the south-coast beaches, Soúyia is perhaps the quietest. Mátala is our favorite place because it has a good beach and there is only modest development. Árvi (with a poorer beach) makes a good, tranquil base for beach seekers with cars or hikers with strong legs.

Crete

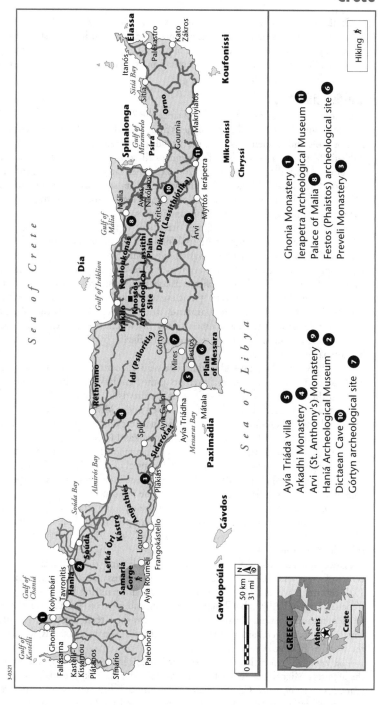

Ghonia Monastery ❶

Ierapetra Archeological Museum ⓫

Palace of Mália ❽

Festos (Phaistos) archeological site ❻

Preveli Monastery ❸

Ayía Triáda villa ❺

Arkadhi Monastery ❹

Arvi (St. Anthony's) Monastery ❾

Haniá Archeological Museum ❷

Dictaean Cave ❿

Górtyn archeological site ❼

205

On the northern coast, the tourist season extends only from April to October; after that, many accommodations and restaurants close. The southern coast advertises itself as a year-round destination because of its mild climate, but here, too, many accommodations are seasonal. If you're planning an extended winter holiday on Crete, contact a local travel agent.

A BRIEF HISTORY

We know that Crete has been inhabited since the 7th millennium B.C., but it was not until about 2600 B.C., when immigrants from Asia Minor and Africa arrived with bronze tools and implements, that the first distinct civilization was born; it was dubbed "Minoan," after the island's legendary King Minos. The most exciting archaeological finds date from 1900 to 1700 B.C., when large palaces were founded at Knossós, Phestós, and Mália. In the archaeological museum there's a collection of faïence plaques in the shape of two- and three-story local houses, indicating the relative sophistication achieved by the Minoan builders.

The archaeological evidence indicates that about 1650 B.C. a disaster, possibly a tidal wave caused by the volcanic eruption of Thíra (Santoríni), destroyed Knossós and other Minoan palaces. Knossós was rebuilt about 1600 B.C.; its population may have numbered about 50,000. Once again the palace was partly detroyed and rebuilt about 1500 B.C.—this is the magnificent palace, partly restored, that you can see today. About 1450 B.C. another cataclysmic event, possibly an earthquake or an invasion by Mycenaeans from the mainland, dealt a severe blow to the Minoan civilization. Once again there was some recovery, but within a century Crete was overrun by Dorian invaders from the Greek mainland; finally, by 1100 B.C. Minoan civilization had come to an end.

By 1000 B.C. the Dorians had established a new aristocratic government on Crete while adopting many Minoan legal precepts as the foundation for their new Spartan state on the mainland. Under the Dorians a militaristic mood predominated on Crete, and cities that had flourished while united under Minoan rule became rivals. Successful trading continued with Asia Minor and Africa, introducing Oriental styles to an island that was still largely isolated from mainland Greece.

Although not abandoned, Knossós was ruled from mainland Greece (and occasionally from Egypt) until the Romans finally took control of Crete in A.D. 67 and chose Górtyn as their capital. For 800 years under Roman rule Crete was a prosperous colony, which saw the arrival of Christianity in the 5th century.

In A.D. 826 the Saracens invaded, destroying Górtyn and establishing themselves in the newly fortified port of Candiá (Khandak)—the present-day Iráklio. Nikephóros Phokás retook Crete from marauding pirates in 961, and Venice purchased it from from the Byzantines.

Settled by Greek and Venetian nobility, Candiá became the artistic and political center of the island. Scholars speak of the Cretan Renaissance during the 16th and 17th centuries, when local poetry, architecture, and painting flowered. Iráklio's Venetian Loggia, Réthymno's Rimondi Fountain, and some of Haniá's stately homes all date from this period. However, few works from the Cretan School of Painting, which produced several artists (including Doménikos Theotokópoulous, known to the world as El Greco), remain on Crete.

The Venetians refortified the ramparts of Iráklio's fortress under the direction of the architect Michele Sammicheli, and it withstood the Turkish onslaught for 21 years. From 1669, when Candiá, the last free port, fell, little was heard from Crete until its liberation in 1898. In 1912 the island joined the Greek nation, but even today you hear people say, "Cretans first, Greeks second."

CRETE ESSENTIALS

GETTING THERE & DEPARTING   By Plane   Iráklio and Haniá airports both serve visitors flying to Crete from Athens (once a week from Thessaloníki), from Rhodes to Iráklio, or from Kássos and Kárpathos to Sitía. We recommend using the Iráklio airport because of the greater number of flights available and its proximity to the capital, where most tourist services are located.

By Ferry   There are year-round, twice-daily ferries from Piraeus to Iráklio (presently departing at nearly the same time), once daily to Haniá, and three times a week to Réthymno. A steamer from Piraeus connects Crete at least once a week with the island of Kýthira, the Peloponnesian coast at Yíthio, and the Dodecanese islands. (See the sections on Kastélli, Iráklio, Áyios Nikólaos, and Sitía for more information.) In the summer, excursion boats usually sail daily between Santoríni and Iráklio. (Hydrofoil service has been available on this route in the past, and perhaps it will resume; check with a travel agent.) Contact the Greek Tourist Organization (EOT) for information on cruises from Crete to Israel and Egypt.

GETTING AROUND THE ISLAND   A fully satisfying tour can be made over the course of a week or more by using the excellent public bus system. If you have only 3 to 5 days, it might be best to rent a car. Jeeps are particularly popular (and fun) because they expose you to the ever-changing scents and breezes while allowing free travel on unpaved roads to the more remote areas.

Getting around on this large, scenic island is part of its pleasure. There's a recently upgraded network of very passable but still treacherous roads extending to the main resort areas. After driving nearly every mile of highway and local road up and down Crete's hilly and curvaceous interior, we'd suggest that you rent a car with more horsepower than the smallest "subcompact," especially if you want to visit the western- or southern-coast beaches and the island's picturesque inland mountain villages.

By Bicycle   Bicycles, an excellent means of sightseeing on Crete, are appearing more frequently now. However, most of the visitors you see in Spandex sportswear have probably brought their own bikes. Throughout Crete you'll typically find only old one-speed bikes to rent in the major resort areas—though mountain-bike rental companies are beginning to emerge.

By Ferry   The **Sofia Company** has developed a network of caïque shuttles between nearly all of the southern-coast towns and Elafonísi island. During the summer service is generally daily; during the cooler winter months it's usually weekly.

By Bus   Public bus service is frequent, fairly inexpensive, and—except in midsummer—comfortable; most sites of tourist interest are easily reached from nearby resorts. In general, service is more frequent to the northern-coast towns than to towns on the southern, eastern, and western coasts.

By Car   Rental cars and Jeeps, which are affordable for those traveling in small groups, can greatly simplify south-coast travel. Rental-car companies such as **Avis, Budget,** and **Hertz** have offices in nearly every major tourist center; however, we found the lowest prices at locally owned outlets, such as **Caravel** and **Motor Club** in Iráklio (you'll find details later in the chapter). Be sure to either buy or carry insurance.

By Moped   Mopeds are inexpensive and easy to rent, but be sure to buy insurance and wear a helmet. Even Crete's newest paved roads can disintegrate to gravel paths after a sudden rain or harsh weather.

Impressions

The people of Crete unfortunately make more history than they can consume locally.
                                    —Saki (H. H. Munro), *The Jesting of Arlington Stringham,* 1911

Knossos is of course immensely interesting historically, but it is all on a small scale, and gives no aesthetic pleasure.
                                                            —Logan Pearsall Smith, 1926

By Taxi Metered taxis are widely available for sightseeing and for group transport to sites outside the main towns. However, if you plan to sightsee for more than a day, a rental car is cheaper and offers greater independence. Taxis are available at fixed rates at the Iráklio airport; they'll take you to nearly any of the resort towns.

AREA CODES   When calling from outside the various towns, use the following area codes: **081** for Iráklio, **0821** for Haniá, **0831** for Réthymno, **0841** for Áyios Nikólaos, and **0842** for Ierápetra. Many smaller districts with their own area codes are also noted in the text.

SPECIAL EVENTS   The island whose most famous native son is Níkos Kazantzákis's fiercely individualistic Zorba the Greek is certain to celebrate many unique holidays. Before leaving Athens you can get information on national holidays such as **Naval Week,** celebrated in mid-July at the port of Soúda near Haniá; **Greek Easter;** the **Wine Festival,** held in August in Réthymno; and the government-sponsored arts festivals, such as the **Iráklio Festival.** Don't forget to check with the local tourist office or with the police for information on Sitía's **Sultana Raisin Festival** in September; **Kritsá's Folk Festival,** where a mock wedding is performed; **Élos's Chestnut Festival;** and Ayía Galíni's **Sheep Shearing Festival.**

A SUGGESTED ITINERARY

If you treat Crete as only a stopover on a race-around-Greece tour, plan to allow at least 1 day for Iráklio (including its archaeological museum) and Knossós. If you have an additional day, consider taking an excursion to Festós and spending an afternoon on the beach at Mátala. Alternatively, you could visit Réthymno and Haniá, returning to Iráklio the following day.

If you have at least a week, we suggest renting a car—if it's within your budget—and following this course:

Day 1   Arrive in Iráklio and visit the archaeological museum and Knossós.

Day 2   Continue to Haniá, passing through Réthymno and nearby rural villages.

Day 3   Hike the Samariá Gorge and either return to Haniá or stay in one of the southern-coast beach towns (Ayía Roúmeli or Hóra Sfakiá, or take an extra day and go to Soúyia).

Day 4   If you return to Haniá, travel southeast, back through Hóra Sfakiá, and continue on to Frangokástello; otherwise, continue to the ruins at Phestós and spend the rest of the day on Mátala's beaches.

Day 5   Travel east, through Ierápetra and head north, stopping overnight in Sitía.

Day 6   If you have sufficient time, visit the palm beach at Vái or, even better, visit the Gorge of the Dead and the nearby beaches at Káto Zákros or Itanós.

Day 7   Stop in Mochlós for a quick seaside lunch and swim, and return to Iráklio.

1 Iráklio (Iráklion, Herakleion)

If you have only 1 or 2 days to see Crete, spend them in Iráklio, the largest city and principal port. We recommend a stay in this busy capital, with its cosmopolitan air and superb artistic and cultural treasures (including the world-class archaeological museum and the nearby palace of Knossós), to anyone touring Greece.

ESSENTIALS

GETTING THERE & DEPARTING   By Plane   Iráklio Airport is served by direct charter flights from all over Europe.

Olympic Airways (☎ **800/223-1226** in the U.S. or **01/966-6666** for reservations in Greece) handles most flights from within Greece. There are several flights daily from Athens, plus less frequent service from Thessaloníki and Rhodes.

Air Greece (☎ **081/241-397** in Iráklio or **01/325-5011** in Athens) has daily flights from Athens, twice weekly from Rhodes, and once weekly from Thessaloníki.

The **Iráklio Airport** is 15 minutes outside the city. City buses run frequently (every 15 or 20 minutes) between the airport and the center of town, making several stops; the fare is 230 Drs (95¢). A taxi into town should cost approximately 1,750 Drs ($7.30). There's a tourist information desk run by the Civil Aviation Authority at the Iráklio Airport and a board to make free phone calls for tourist information.

To buy airline tickets, we found the **Blavákis Travel** office at 10 Kallergón Sq. (☎ **081/282-541;** fax 081/288-176), near Venizélos Square, to be helpful and efficient. The **Olympic Airways office** in town is on Elefthería (Liberty) Square (☎ **081/229-191**).

By Bus   There are a few different **bus stations** in town.

The station for northwest-bound buses (including service to and from Haniá and Réthymno) is about 400 yards west from the ferry dock under the red canopy (☎ **081/282-637**). The stop for buses to Knossós and the airport is just south across the road, and the northeast-bound bus station, Station A (☎ **081/245-019**), is to its left.

The station for southwest-bound (including Mátala, Phestós, and Ayía Galíni) buses, Station B (☎ **081/283-073**), is just west outside the Venetian wall opposite the Haniá Gate, at Kalokerinoú and Makaríou streets.

Tickets must be purchased before boarding. There is frequent bus service to all parts of the island; a complete schedule is available from the Greek Tourist Organization (EOT) office.

By Ferry   Ferries depart daily from Piraeus for Iráklio and Haniá, and three times weekly for Áyios Nikólaos. The most convenient steamers leave at 6:30 or 7pm for the overnight 12-hour trip to Iráklio or Haniá. The steamers that service Áyios Nikólaos directly tend to be local boats, which make stops throughout the Cyclades, then at Áyios Nikólaos and Sitía, and continuing on to Kássos, Kárpathos, and the other Dodecanese islands. For schedule information, contact the **Piraeus Port Authority** (☎ **01/451-1311**).

Excursion boats and scheduled ferries ply the popular Iráklio–Santoríni route at least 5 days a week. Tickets are available from local travel agents for about 3,000 Drs ($12.50) for the 5¹/₂-hour trip. For information, contact nearly any travel agent, such as **Arabatzóglou Travel** (☎ **081/226-697**) or **Blavákis Travel** (☎ **081/282-541**) near Venizélou Square.

VISITOR INFORMATION   The **Greek Tourist Organization (EOT),** at Odós Xanthoudídou 1, off Elefthería Square (☎ **081/228-203**), is open Monday to

Friday from 8am to 3pm. The **tourist police,** at Odós Dikeosýnis (☎ **081/ 283-190**), a couple of blocks south of Venizélos Square, are open daily from 7am to 11pm. There's also a Civil Aviation Authority information office (no telephone) at the Iráklio Airport, open daily from 7:30am to 4:30pm.

One of the most helpful travel offices in Iráklio is **Arabatzóglou Travel,** at Odós 25 Avgoústou 54 (☎ **081/226-697;** fax 081/222-184).

GETTING AROUND   By Bicycle   Just off the port at Odós 25 Avgoústou 20, **Porto Club** (☎ **081/285-624**) has mountain bikes that rent for 1,700 to 4,000 Drs ($7.10 to $16.65) per week. Guided tours are also available.

By Car   Hertz (☎ **081/341-734** in Iráklio at the airport) has several offices on Crete. **Avis** (☎ **081/225-421**) and **Hellascars** (☎ **081/226-385**) also have Iráklio offices, as well as additional offices on the island. As always, it's *much* cheaper to re-serve your rental car before you come to Greece than to make arrangements after you arrive.

Some of the best rental deals can be made by the week with local companies such as **Caravel** (☎ **081/288-060;** fax 081/220-362) and **Motor Club,** 18 Anglon Sq., no. 1, Iráklio (☎ **081/222-408;** fax 081/222-862). On our last trip we drove an ex-cellent little Fiat Panda with a sun roof for about 75,000 Drs ($312.50) a week. It's often difficult to book a car from a small company during the high season (June to September); be sure to call ahead for reservations. Remember to carry insurance on any rental.

By Moped   During the high season, automatic 50cc mopeds, which can be rented everywhere, average 7,500 Drs ($31.25 per day), including insurance and taxes. **Motor Club** has its central office in Iráklio at 18 Anglon Sq., no. 1 (☎ **081/ 222-408**).

By Taxi   Taxis cruise around Iráklio and can be booked by calling ☎ **081/210-168** or 081/210-102. There's also a **taxi stand** across the street from the archaeological museum. Iráklio has the same taxi problems as Athens. Drivers may tell you that the hotel you request is booked and insist on taking you elsewhere. If you're suspicious, confront the driver or insist on getting out of the cab. At the airport look for a posted list of long-distance taxi rates to different parts of Crete. Prices are lower if you have a group of three or four people. In Iráklio there's a minimum charge of 575 Drs ($2.40) and a surcharge of 400 Drs ($1.65) for trips to the airport.

FAST FACTS   The **American Express agent** for Crete is the Adámis Travel Bu-reau, Odós 25 Avgoústou 23, Iráklio (☎ **081/246-202;** fax 081/224-717), open Monday to Saturday from 8am to 5pm and Sunday from 10am to noon and 6 to 8:30pm for emergency traveler's check services; mail is handled during these hours.

A **Bank of Greece** and an **Ionian Bank** on Odós 25 Avgoústou are open the stan-dard banking hours: Monday to Thursday from 8am to 2pm and Friday from 8am to 1:30pm. The post offices, some EOT offices, and many of the larger hotels throughout Crete will cash traveler's checks at extended hours for a nominal fee.

In case of emergency, contact the local **police** (☎ **081/283-190**) at Venizélos Square. There's usually an English-speaking officer on duty.

Venizélio Hospital is on Knossós Road, Iráklio (☎ **081/237-502**). The more modern **University Hospital** (☎ **081/269-111**) is 3 miles south of town. For gen-eral **first-aid information,** call ☎ 166 or 222-222.

Luggage can be left at the northeast-bound bus station, Station A (☎ **081/ 245-019**); each piece costs 250 Drs ($1.05) a day (compared to 800 Drs at the airport).

The main **post office** is on Daskaloyánnis Square, in Iráklio. It's open Monday to Friday from 8am to 8pm. The portable branches at El Greco Park and the port are open on Saturday from 8am to 8pm and on Sunday from 9am to 6pm.

Iráklio is a relatively safe city, and is suitable for late-night walks. Nevertheless, stay alert and be aware of your surroundings.

The **central telecommunications office (OTE)** is over and down one street from the back of El Greco Park; it's open daily from 7:30am to 11pm, with limited services after 8pm. There's a mobile OTE on Elefthería Square, open Monday to Friday from 8am to 11pm. The OTE at the airport never closes (theoretically). *Telekárte* phones are common; cards can be purchased at kiosks.

TWO SIGHTS NOT TO MISS

To get the most from a visit to Iráklio's two greatest sites, the archaeological museum and the Palace of Knossós, we recommend purchasing the excellent guidebook *Crete* (in the Greece Museums and Monuments series), by J. A. Papapostólou (it costs 2,500 Drs/$10.40), especially if you'd like to go on your own.

Otherwise, a guided tour of what remains of the fascinating Minoan culture is strongly recommended. Half-day guided bus tours to Knossós and the museum are offered daily by several travel agents, either as separate sites—at 4,500 Drs ($18.75) and 3,250 Drs ($13.50), respectively—or as a combined tour for 6,000 Drs ($25), not including entrance fees.

✪ **Archeological Museum.** Xanthoudídou St. (north of Eleftherías Sq.). ☎ **081/226-092.** Admission 1,500 Drs ($6.25) adults, 1,100 Drs ($4.60) seniors, 800 Drs ($3.35) students. Apr–Sept, Mon 12:30–5pm, Tues–Sun 8am–5pm; Oct–Mar, Mon 12:30–3pm, Tues–Sun 8am–3pm.

The archaeological museum merits at least a 2-hour visit by anyone interested in Minoan civilization. The museum includes Neolithic, Hellenic, and Roman finds from throughout Crete, but is unique for its comprehensive Minoan collection. Superb examples abound of terra-cotta icons and ceramic ware, decorated in typically Minoan black swirls and spirals. There are marble, bronze, ivory, and stone figurines worshipping, fighting with bulls, dancing, making music, and performing acrobatic feats. Precious faïence plaques depict styles of housing, clothing, sports, and worship. Several pieces of exquisite gold jewelry are displayed. There are drawings, sculptures, reliefs, and seals representing every aspect of the bull in secular and religious terms. The spirit of the Minoans—their love for natural and physical beauty, their delight in depicting the wonders of the world around them—is to be seen everywhere in this exquisite collection.

The labeled ground-floor exhibits are grouped chronologically in 15 galleries. Upstairs on the first floor is the marvelous collection of frescoes from the palaces at Knossós (copies have been installed at the site itself), Mália, and Phestós, and the smaller villas of Amnissós and Ayía Tríada. Erect, lean young men with long curls; buxom, topless maidens; graceful lilies and dolphins; bulls and ornate, multicolored decorative patterns bring the Minoan culture back to life.

✪ **Knossós.** 3 miles south of Iráklio. Admission 1,500 Drs ($6.25) adults, 1,100 Drs ($4.60) seniors, 800 Drs ($3.35) students. Daily 8am–5pm. Bus no. 2 leaves every 20 minutes from Station A, near the New Harbor; it also stops for passengers near Venizélos Sq. and at Elefthería (Freedom) Sq.; the fare is 250 Drs ($1.05).

The archaeological site at Knossós contains the Central Palace, which dominated Minoan civilization from 2000 to 1400 B.C. The remarkable excavation of ruins by the British archaeologist Sir Arthur Evans includes an elaborate re-creation of large parts of the original palace.

Try to come before 9:30am or after 11:30am, so you can avoid the cruise-ship crowds that come here on half-day tours.

Evans began his work in 1900 (after some artifacts were found in 1878 by a local scholar); as his dig progressed, he steadily bought up the land behind the growing port of Iráklio. He found that a town had existed before Minos built his palace, so he conjectured that the king (and spiritual leader of the Minoans) may have been a wealthy landowner. The huge complex (more than 4 acres in size) is thought to have had 1,400 rooms, on many levels; it's known that the east wing of the palace had five stories and the west had three.

Evans used lots of concrete and a color code to evoke images of the original structure. The round red columns were painted wood, used in building because their tensility made them earthquake resistant. The column bases and the lower portions of walls were covered in marble or alabaster, in contrast to the stuccoed top half, decorated with lively, multicolored frescoes. Wood was used in the brick walls and for door and window frames; the panes were alabaster. Remember that the fabulous frescoes have been removed from the site and can be seen at Iráklio's archaeological museum.

Eighteen storerooms were uncovered containing 150 *píthoi* (large urns) holding liquids (perhaps olive oil) used to light lamps. Evans believed that the palace was finally destroyed by a fire that roared through its wooden structure, fueled by the oil from lamps overturned in an earthquake. The little that remains of the palace is still a marvel.

Most of the lower flights of the original, expertly crafted stairs are still used, and near the queen's megaron is what's considered to be the first flush toilet! Horizontal and vertical clay pipes (evidence of the Minoans' expert sewage system) can still be seen. In the administrative wing of the palace, a wooden throne, thought to have belonged to Minos, has been re-created from a void fused in some volcanic ruins by a casting process. Outside the palace buildings are the paved stones of Europe's oldest road and the collapsed steps of Europe's first theater.

Evans also found the remains of what may have been an area (outside the palace grounds) for the celebrated bull dances, part of the mysterious religious cult surrounding this animal. If the colorful restoration of Knossós is too much for your historical sensibilities, at the knee-high ruins of Mália and Phestós you can imagine what the palaces must have looked like all by yourself.

MORE TO SEE & DO

Many of Iráklio's visitors arrive on cruise ships in the morning and depart the same evening, so many local tourist services are geared to these hit-and-run sightseers. One of the biggest tour operators is the **Creta Travel Bureau,** Odós Epiméndou 20–22 (☎ **081/227-002**).

A popular way of touring is by horse-drawn cart or on horseback. This opportunity is offered by the **Heraklion Riding Centre,** Finikia Stables (☎ **081/253-166; fax 081/316-837**). Guides lead riders through the surrounding hill villages for a look at traditional life.

A STROLL AROUND IRÁKLIO

Ferries from Piraeus usually arrive between 7 and 8am, a perfect time to explore the still-quiet city. From the new harbor, turn right and continue along the waterfront to the old **Venetian Arsenal,** an arcaded storage area awaiting development. New historical-preservation laws have been enacted in Iráklio to ensure restoration (rather than destruction) of its historic monuments.

At the tip of the old port is the **Venetian Fortress,** the "Koules" or "Rocca al Mare," a wonderfully preserved 14th-century fortress, rebuilt between 1523 and

1540. A Lion of St. Mark proudly guards the doorway. The fortress (☎ **081/ 246-211**) is open Tuesday to Sunday from 8:30am to 3pm; admission is 500 Drs ($2.10) for adults and 300 Drs ($1.25) for students.

Each morning the old harbor comes alive, with brisk trading in fish brought in by the fishing boats. If you continue west along the waterfront (Makaríou Street) and uphill, you'll soon see the austere Xenia Hotel, and across from it the small **Historical Museum of Crete** (☎ **081/283-219**). It houses a private collection of Cretan folk art, Venetian and Turkish antiquities, memorabilia of Crete's celebrated son, the author Níkos Kazantzákis, and the only El Greco painting on this island where the artist was born. The museum is open Monday to Friday from 9am to 4:30pm and Saturday from 9am to 2pm; admission is 1,000 Drs ($4.15).

If you turn left opposite the old port at Odós 25 Avgoústou, you'll be on Iráklio's travel agent / ticket office / rental-car row. Behind the first small square on your left is the **Church of Áyios Títos,** built in the 16th century and dedicated to Títos, who first brought Christianity to Crete. Just beyond is the lovely **Venetian Loggia. (El Greco Park** is a block west.) Farther up you'll find the **Basilica of San Marco** (dating from 1303, it was converted into a mosque by the Turks and is now used as an exhibition hall).

Across the street is the **Morosíni Fountain** (often referred to as the Lion Fountain), built by the Venetian general Francesco Morosini and dedicated in 1628. The lion's support, believed to have come from another 14th-century fountain, dominates **Venizélos Square,** named for Elefthérios Venizélos, a Cretan revolutionary who later became one of modern Greece's great leaders. This popular square is now usually called the Fountain Square. Stop by one of the many cafes for a breakfast of Crete's flavorful bread with local jams or honey. (To avoid any misunderstanding if there's no set menu, be sure to ask the prices in advance. As you revive, you can watch the pace of the city quicken.)

From Venizélos Square continue a few blocks south down 1866 Street to Kornáros Square to reach the **Bembo Fountain;** it's often called the "Turkish Fountain," although it was built by the Venetians—seemingly out of whatever was at hand. The ornate building next to it, presently housing a snack bar, was actually built later by the Turks.

Return to the north end of the square, turn left, and then walk northeast on Karterou Street to Platía Ekaterínis and the **Cathedral of Áyios Mínas** on the left. Inside on the right side of the transept are four icons attributed to Michael Damaskinós, a master of the Cretan School (and perhaps a teacher of El Greco). At the nearby **Church of Ayía Ekateríni** is a collection of icons by members of this same school.

If you still have energy, you may want to go a block north to Kalokerinoú Street and head west to the massive **Venetian Wall** and the **Porta Haníon** (Haniá Gate). A right turn along the wall will take you back to the sea; a left turn will take you counterclockwise around the wall past the **Katzantzakis Tomb** near the well-preserved **Martinengo Bastion,** at the southern corner of the fortifications, then back northeast to the **Public Gardens** and **Platía Eleftherías** (Freedom Square). The archaeology museum is just a block north.

SHOPPING

Iráklio has some very Greek shopping opportunities. There's a daily **meat and produce market** at the head of Odós 25 Avgoústou, along Odós 1866, a few blocks inland from the Morosíni Fountain. It's best in the early morning, but always a lot of fun. There's also an interesting outdoor market every Saturday morning on the **New Port Road.**

Several shops carrying souvenirs, cassettes of local music, photo greeting cards, and kitschy worry beads are found around **Elefthería Square,** along **Dikeosínis Street,** and, parallel to it, along the pedestrian mall of **Dedálou Street.**

Eléni Kastrinouyanni has a weaving, handcraft, jewelry, and museum-reproduction shop on Elefthería Square, across from the archaeological museum at Odós Íkarou 3 (☎ **081/226-186**).

WHERE TO STAY

Many of the Class C hotels originally built to handle Iráklio's tourist boom now find themselves in the middle of a noisy, crowded city. Some of the best of the newer lodgings are located outside the city center, but we've also included many of the older pensions, whose remnants of European charm compensate for the area's big-city drawbacks.

BY THE NEW PORT

✪ **Hotel Poseidon.** Odós Posidónos 54, Póros (New Harbor area), 713 07 Iráklio. ☎ **081/245-360** or 081/222-545. Fax 081/245-405. 26 rms, all with bath (shower). TEL. 10,000 Drs ($41.70) single; 14,000 Drs ($58.35) double. Rates include breakfast. V.

The outstanding choice here is the Hotel Poseidon, at the end of the street on the hill above the New Port, because of the hospitality, warmth, and helpfulness of its staff. And it recently got better with a redecoration that included new sound-insulating windows. The owner, John Polychronides, is sophisticated and well traveled, and keeps up-to-date on visitors' needs. He and his staff are knowledgeable about historical sites and the ever-changing resorts on Crete. All of the Poseidon's rooms (spotless, with plenty of hot water) have balconies overlooking the port or face west with a view of the Stroumboúlis mountains (ensuring a welcome breeze during Crete's hot summer). Breakfast is served in a lounge decorated with embroidery and local handicrafts. Readers who make a reservation and pay in cash can receive a 15% discount.

BY THE OLD PORT

Ilaira Hotel. Odós Ariádnis 1, 712 02 Iráklio. ☎ **081/227-103.** Fax 081/227-666. 20 rms, all with bath (shower). TEL. 10,350 Drs ($43.15) single; 15,000 ($62.50) double. Rates include breakfast. AE, EURO, MC, V.

Several blocks above, and commanding a somewhat obscured view of, the Venetian harbor is the Ilaira, which has modern, whipped-stucco-walled rooms. It's an acceptable choice, but we found it in need of some freshening up.

✪ **Kris Hotel.** Odós Bófor 2, 712 02 Iráklio. ☎ **081/223-211** or 081/223-944. 12 rms, all with bath (shower). MINIBAR. 9,000 Drs ($37.50) single; 11,000 Drs ($45.85) double. Rates include breakfast. No credit cards.

The first choice for value in this part of town is the Kris Hotel. The wonderfully friendly Maria rents single- and double-occupancy rooms with kitchenettes and balconies in this converted apartment building. The rooms have some homey touches (flowering vines, for instance) and are spacious.

Marin Hotel. Odós Bofor 10, 712 02 Iráklio. ☎ **081/220-737.** Fax 081/224-730. 48 rms, all with bath (shower). TEL. 9,200 Drs ($38.35) single; 115,000 Drs ($62.50) double. Rates include breakfast. AE, EURO, MC, V.

Several of the Marin's rooms have large balconies overlooking the harbor, and there's a bar, open evenings, on the roof garden.

Worth a Splurge

Lato Hotel. Odós Epiménidou 15, 712 02 Iráklio. ☎ **081/228-103.** Fax 081/240-350. 50 rms, all with bath (shower). A/C MINIBAR TV TEL. 17,825 Drs ($74.20) single; 23,000 Drs ($95.85) double. Rates include breakfast. AE, DC, EURO, MC, V.

Readers Joel and Nili Goldschmidt of Red Bank, New Jersey, recommended this hotel just above the old harbor. We found it modern, clean, and comfortable, with some of the bathrooms added outside on the balconies. There's a nice little cafe-bar downstairs, and room service is available from 7am to 11pm for a 20% surcharge.

DOWNTOWN

Hotel Daedalos. Odós Dedálou 15, 712 02 Iráklio. ☎ **081/244-812.** Fax 081/224-391. 60 rms, all with bath (shower). TEL. 9,200 Drs ($38.35) single; 11,000 Drs ($45.85) double. No credit cards.

Our friend Suzanna stays here on the busy pedestrian shopping lane when in town; on both our most recent visits we found it attractive enough but full—not a bad sign. Breakfast is 1,400 Drs ($5.85). Check it out.

Hotel Lena. Odós Lachaná 10 (off Výronos St.), 712 02 Iráklio. ☎ **081/242-826.** 18 rms, 9 with bath (shower). 5,300 Drs ($22.10) single without bath; 6,700 Drs ($27.90) double without bath; 9,000 Drs ($37.50) single or double with bath. V.

The bargain-priced Lena is well run by the Manganas family. It's a major step up from the more budget-oriented hostels in the area but is still quite modest.

Mirabello Hotel. Odós Theotokopoúlou 20, 712 02 Iráklio. ☎ **081/285-052.** 25 rms, 7 with bath (shower). 6,900 Drs ($28.750) single without bath, 9,000 Drs ($37.50) single with bath; 9,200 Drs ($38.35) double without bath, 10,000 Drs ($41.65) double with bath. No credit cards.

The Mirabello occupies an attractive old building, and its balconies overlook the neighborhood's quiet residential streets. The host Costas Kamaratakis, ex-captain in the Greek merchant navy, runs a tight ship here and is renovating the hotel. All bathrooms and showers have been newly tiled.

A Youth Hostel

GYH Youth Hostel. Odós Výronos 5, 712 02 Iráklio. ☎ **081/286-281** or 081/222-947. 5 rms, all with bath (shower); 100 dorm beds. 1,600 Drs ($6.65) dorm bed; 4,600 Drs ($19.15) family room. No credit cards.

The GYH Youth Hostel has about 100 beds in dorm-style rooms, 40 beds on the roof, and a limited number of double private "family" rooms. There's a spacious sitting/dining/breakfast room where the hostess Irene is reputed to make the best Greek salad on the island (460 Drs/$1.90) as well as tasty omelets.

Worth a Splurge

✪ **Galaxy Hotel.** Odós Dimokratías 67, 713 06 Iráklio. ☎ **081/238-812.** Fax 081/211-211. 140 rms, all with bath. A/C (summer only) TV TEL. 28,750 Drs ($119.80) single; 37,500 Drs ($156.25) double. Rates include breakfast. AE, DC, EURO, MC, V.

The starkly modern design of this cast-concrete hotel, considered one of Iráklio's better inns, gives a hint of its many high-end facilities, such as a sauna and cappuccino bar. The Galaxy, which was renovated in 1996, is a 15-minute walk south from the center of town. All rooms are spacious and paneled in cane matting; they have the latest amenities and, best of all, have views of the fabulous pool and sun deck below. Because of its focus on groups and business travelers, the Galaxy is busy year-round.

NEAR THE MUSEUM

Pension Vergina. Odós Hortatson 32, 712 02 Iráklio. ☎ **081/242-739.** 8 rms, none with bath. 3,700 Drs ($15.40) single; 5,800 Drs ($24.15) double. No credit cards.

The Vergina is a calm place behind the historical museum. All eight old-fashioned rooms are clean and spacious, with sinks. The lovely garden with banana trees is a real bonus, especially refreshing after a long day of sightseeing.

Rea Pension. Kalimeráki and Handákos sts., 712 02 Iráklio. ☎ **081/223-638.** Fax 081/242-189. 16 rms, 5 with bath (shower). 5,700 Drs ($23.75) single without bath, 7,000 Drs ($29.15) single with bath; 6,300 Drs ($26.25) double without bath, 7,800 Drs ($32.50) double with bath. EURO, MC, V.

The Rea Pension has spare, spotless rooms, some with balconies. Compared with others in this price range in the center of Iráklio, the guest rooms and facilities here are a tad cleaner and better maintained. A good value.

WHERE TO EAT

Iráklio boasts some excellent restaurants. Their special dishes are attributed to the variety of fresh produce (grown year-round in the south) and the Cretans' special flair with food. Crete is also known for its subtle wines—the rich, dry Minos Cava white and the Cava Lato reds.

Dedálou Street, a pedestrian mall running between Elefthería and Venizélos (Fountain) squares, is lined with restaurants that are great for people-watching.

Baritis Taverna. Póros (New Harbor area). ☎ **081/225-859.** Main courses 1,150–1,400 Drs ($4.65–$5.85); fish 6,900–9,200 Drs ($28.75–$38.35) per kilo. No credit cards. May–Oct, daily noon–4pm and 7pm–2am; Nov–Apr, Mon–Sat noon–2:30pm and 7pm–2am, Sun 7pm–2am. CRETAN/SEAFOOD.

Fish is the specialty at this lovely garden taverna run by the Baritis family, though there's much more on the menu. A canopy of grape vines shades the dining area where locals (and a scattering of visitors) sup leisurely while Greek tunes waft through the warm summer air. We sampled and enjoyed grilled octopus, calamari, salad, and crisply fried potatoes, and had a wonderful time of it in this sublimely simple setting.

Ippocampos Ouzerí. Odós Mitsotáki 3. ☎ **081/282-081.** Main courses 1,400–2,900 Drs ($5.85–$12.10); fish 9,700 Drs ($40.40) per kilo. No credit cards. Mon–Sat 1–3:30pm and 7pm–midnight. CRETAN.

Three seahorses identify the small Seahorse Ouzeri on a hill, near the foot of August 25 Street, a perfect introduction to Cretan cuisine. Sample any of its long list of *mezédes* (appetizers) with a carafe of the tasty house white wine, and watch the cruise ships pulling into the harbor. We liked the small, fried whole fish; fresh shrimp; veal meatballs; petite rice-stuffed *dolmádes;* large tender calamari with lemon; fried sliced potatoes; and smooth mashed eggplant. A good value.

✪**Kyriakos.** Leofóros Dimokratías 43. ☎ **081/224-649.** Reservations recommended. Main courses 1,500–3,200 Drs ($6.25–$13.35); fish 10,000 Drs ($41.65) per kilo. AE, DC. Thurs–Tues noon–4pm and 7pm–midnight. Closed June 15–July 15 and Sun July 16–Sept. CRETAN/GREEK.

Many residents consider Kyriakos the finest restaurant in town and definitely worth the 15-minute walk south of the archaeological museum, near the Galaxy Hotel. You'll find seating indoors and out at tables with lively pink tattersall cloths, a wine display, and a largely Greek clientele. Try the lamb fricassee or the veal with onions and the piquant *taramosaláta.* If you can't get in—it's often solidly booked—consider nearby **Tartufo** for fine pizzas.

Minos Taverna. Odós Dedálou 10. ☎ **081/246-466.** Main courses 1,000–3,200 Drs ($4.15–$13.35); fish 9,200 Drs ($38.35) per kilo. AE, EURO, MC, V (service charge added to bill). Mon–Sat 11am–3pm and 6–10pm. Closed every other Sun. CRETAN.

The Minos Taverna is favored by locals for its special Cretan veal with onions, the seasonal stuffed zucchini flowers, the house wines, and the exotic lamb-baked-in-yogurt dishes. Harris runs the show here and makes sure that the service is attentive, if sometimes too rushed in summer; don't expect to be allowed to linger after your meal. The Minos is one of the few restaurants in Iráklio open year-round. (We also recommend the **Klimataria** next door.)

IRÁKLIO AFTER DARK

If you'd like to sample Cretan wines or just need some coffee, stroll over to the Lion Fountain, where the action is, and grab the nearest empty chair.

Onar, Odós Handákos 36, west of Fountain Square (☎ **081/288-298**), is a good place to listen to Greek rock 'n' roll, sip a drink, and enjoy the scenic outdoor area.

A quieter, more intimate setting is **Pub La Palma,** at Odós Idomenéos 14, a couple of blocks inland from the Old Harbor, where you can have a drink on the comfortable patio under Bob Marley and James Dean banners, or the nearby **Dore Piano Bar.** A little farther east on Odós Bófor you'll find **Kastro** (☎ **081/226-148**), which features traditional Cretan music and bouzouki.

Opposite the old Venetian port, at the foot of Odós 25 Avgoústou (across from the Ippocampos Ouzerí), is **To Trata,** a pleasant outdoor cafe cooled by the sea breezes that swirl around the fortress. It's a very nice spot to while away the cocktail hour and watch the cruise ships.

More determined rockers should look for Bófor Street, southeast of the old harbor—follow your ears—for **Scala** and **Trapeza;** they open at 10pm, and admission (including one drink) costs 1,500 Drs ($6.25). Just around the bend, on Íkarou, are two newer discos, **Fougaro** and **Anaktoro,** where admission (including one drink) costs 1,800 Drs ($7.50).

For another kind of diversion, try the **Vincenzo Kornaros Cultural Center,** 9 Malikouti St., for cinema, theater, dance, and music; call ☎ **081/243-921** for the current schedule.

SIDE TRIPS FROM IRÁKLIO

The region south of Iráklio is similar to California's Napa Valley or France's Bordeaux region. Low, rolling hills and gently shaded valleys are resplendent with groves of trellised grapes cultivated for many of Crete's fine wines and powerful *rakí.* Sun worshippers should try the long Thombrouk Beach east of the city in Amnissós.

A WINE TOUR TO ARHÁNES (ARCHÁNES)

If you want to experience the full sensuality of this region, drive or take one of the frequent buses to Arhánes (9¹⁄₄ miles south of Iráklio) and walk to some of the nearby vineyards. You'll be saturated with the fragrance of the air as you behold the exquisite vistas. Stop by a vineyard during August or September (depending on the weather) and you can watch the harvest. Each year several visitors hire themselves out as day laborers during the harvest period. Most vineyards pay about 5,000 Drs ($22) a day, and it really is tough, back-breaking work. But there's nothing like jumping in and participating in a tradition that dates back thousands of years.

A delightful stop in Páno (Upper) Arhánes is the shaded ouzerí **Miriófito,** located at the base of the hill on which the village is built. Miriófito serves local drinks and light food, and you can watch the goings-on from under the cool of the trees.

The region has a long history of wine growing. At Vathypétro, 3 miles south (you must walk), excavations have unearthed a Minoan palace (from about 1600 B.C.) with facilities for pressing grapes. Olive presses and kilns for firing pottery have also been found. Nearby, archaeologists have uncovered what they believe are the remnants of an early, important center of worship. Traces of blood have led researchers to the conclusion that sacrifices (animal and human) took place near the palace.

Southeast of Arhánes is the town of **Thrapsánou,** where local craftsmen still make the huge ceramic urns *(píthoi)* that have been made since Minoan times. **Paradosiakí Keramikí,** seven-tenths of a mile outside Thrapsánou (☎ 0891/41-374), open Monday to Saturday, is an ideal place to watch the age-old method of pottery making. The potter's small shop has some tantalizing bargains, such as glazed espresso cups at 1,000 Drs ($4.15) for a set.

SPÍLI

Spíli is the perfect antidote to the Dionysian excesses of Crete's beach resorts. In this hillside village of grapevines, roses, and cherry trees, the old stone houses, built generations ago, are linked by winding, pebble-strewn paths only wide enough for donkeys. Immaculate courtyards are filled with geraniums and drying herbs left for the family goats to nibble on; whitewashed terraces are covered with grape-filled trellises, palms, and a variety of fragrant flowers; and the square has a fountain that spouts mountain spring water from 19 stone lions' heads.

The charmingly bucolic character of this community, its chief attraction, seems somewhat threatened as Spíli gains popularity as an excursion site and its residents, mostly farmers and their families, attune themselves to today's world. Serving the village and its steady stream of visitors, for example, are seven nearby cafes, two gas stations, a video store, two banks, a post office, a dry cleaner, a "supermarket," and a small hotel. But you can easily lose the crowds by abandoning the main street and striking out on Spíli's back lanes.

To get there, take the bus from Réthymno to Ayía Galíni and tell the driver to let you off at Spíli (in Greek: *"Thélo ná katevó stí Spíli."*).

Where to Stay & Eat
Green Hotel. 740 53 Spíli, 740 53 Réthymno. ☎ **0832/22-225.** 15 rms, all with bath. TEL. 6,900 Drs ($28.75) single; 8,600 Dr ($35.85) double. No credit cards.

We've dubbed it the "Green House" because plants have overtaken the hotel's light natural-wood interior and every room has a balcony filled with potted geraniums that overlooks flower-covered houses on the main street or the valley below. George Maravelakis, its owner, claims to speak a "Greek salad" of English, French, and German. Stay and you'll have the opportunity to try his yogurt (drenched in home-grown honey and nuts) for breakfast.

George's brother, Yannis, runs **Yannis' Restaurant,** near the fountain square (☎ **0832/22-707**), heartily recommended for its two specialties, pork gyros and lamb with vegetables. It's open daily from 7am to midnight; closed November to February.

GÓRTYN (GÓRTYNA, GÓRTYS)

Górtyn (☎ 081/226-092) is one of Crete's most important archaeological sites. Ruins from several eras have been found there in excellent condition, among them the remains of the three-aisled Basilica of Áyios Títos (St. Titus), dedicated in the 6th century A.D. to a pupil of Saint Paul who founded the first Christian community on Crete at this site in A.D. 65. It's considered Crete's finest Christian monument.

The basilica is at the foot of the ancient acropolis of Górtyn, which served as the capital of Crete during the Roman period. Surrounding the basilica are the remains of a 2nd-century Roman odeum. Across the highway, enter the olive grove past the Metropolis road to see the remains of a 2nd-century praetorium (governor's house), a nymphaeum that the Byzantines converted into a fountain, and a temple dedicated to the Egyptian gods Isis and Serapis; there's even a temple to the Pythian Apollo. Farther back are remains of a small amphitheater.

The earliest settlement dates from the post-Mycenaean period (10th century B.C.), and almost every succeeding generation has used materials from existing temples to construct edifices of its own. The best evidence of this is the Code of Górtyn, written in an ancient Doric dialect, designating the rights and property of man. It's carved in stone blocks that make up part of the much later odeum. You'll see the stone tablets in the reconstructed facade behind the theater.

Admission to the site is 800 Drs ($3.35) for adults, 600 Drs ($2.50) for seniors, and 400 Drs ($1.65) for students. It's open daily from 8am to 5pm.

PHESTÓS (FESTÓS, PHAESTÓS, PHAISTÓS)

If you've come to see the fascinating ruins of Crete's second-largest Minoan palace, we hope you've purchased the guidebook *Crete*, by J. A. Papapostólou, which has excellent drawings and maps of Minoan sites.

Excavations were begun on the palace of Phestós by the Italian archaeologist Federico Halbherr in the same period that Arthur Evans was working at Knossós, but little reconstruction was attempted, and it wasn't until 1950 that a systematic examination of the site was completed.

As you walk down the stairs to the site, you'll be in the middle of the court from the older palace (dating from about 2000 B.C.). On your right, the grand stairs mark the entrance to the newer palace built on the earthquake-shattered remains of the older one, in about 1750 B.C.—a grand Minoan palace dominating the Messará Plain, where civilization flourished until 1450 B.C.

To the 20th-century traveler the highlights of the palace are the royal apartments, which can be found under protective plastic canopies on the northern side of the site. In the first apartment, the remains of four columns make it easy to envision the arched roof they supported and the well of the light created in the courtyard. The benches and flooring that have survived in places at the western end of the room are still sheathed in alabaster slabs, mortared with red plaster. A staircase between the royal suites led up to the palace's second story.

Phestós is still an active archaeological site. We managed to visit the lower part of the site, where a team was uncovering a vast new section of the palace. (Those with a serious interest in archaeology may be able to obtain permission from the director of antiquities at the archaeological museum in Iráklio to consult with on-site scholars of the Italian Archaeological School.) Call ☎ **0892/91-315** for more information. Admission is 1,200 Drs ($5) for adults, 900 Drs ($3.75) for seniors, and 600 Drs ($2.50) for students. The site is open daily from 8am to 5pm.

Near the palace at Phestós is the villa of **Ayía Triáda** (☎ **0892/91-360**), a small Minoan palace dating from 1700 B.C. It's believed to have been the summer home of the king who resided at Phestós, and it makes a refreshing side trip at midday because of the cool breezes blowing off the Libyan Sea, just 6 miles south. The archaeological museum at Iráklio contains two carved vases, incredible sculpture with reliefs depicting boxers and harvesters, and beautiful frescoes found at this site. Admission is 500 Drs ($2.10). Open daily from 8:30am to 3pm.

THE PALACE OF MÁNIA

Crete's northern coast is heavily developed for tourism—too heavily, in our opinion—with the worst concentration of resorts east of Iráklio. The satellite cities of

Néa Kydoniá, Ayía Mariná, Arína, and Thémis Beach are full-service resorts housing budget-tour groups who've flown in on charters from Brussels, Frankfurt, or London for a "Week at the Beach" package that's cheaper than staying at home. Lager louts abound.

Hersónisos is the first major autonomous town, although the hundreds of white prefab Mediterranean-style hotels, boutiques, and scooter-rental outfits must have been cloned from the model issued at the Bureau of Greek Hotel Standards. It goes on for miles, and we suggest that you keep going, too. Farther east, you'll reach Stális, a much smaller development of the same ilk, and then Mália.

On the way through, stop to see the **palace of Mália** (☎ **0897/31-597**), an interesting Minoan site just outside this uninteresting, unappealing beach resort. Buses run from Iráklio every 30 minutes; they turn off the main highway and will leave you at the foot of the public beach in town, or you can continue to the site, which is 2 miles outside the town. (If you feel compelled to stay in Mália, you'll find several cheap accommodations just like those in Hersónisos.)

This was Crete's third most important Minoan palace (built about 2000 B.C., rebuilt between 1700 and 1550 B.C., and abandoned about 1450 B.C.). As with other Minoan palaces, it was not fortified, but unlike the rest, it occupies a plain rather than a hill. Archaeologists think the lack of frescoes and the simple style of the Mália palace indicate that it was a provincial outpost. However, evidence of considerable wealth and sophistication—such as two golden bees on a honeycomb and the exquisite leopard-head axe now in the museum in Iraklió—has been found and excavation continues.

To the right just as you enter the site are eight circular pits, which are believed to have been used to store grain. To their left are various storerooms, then the royal apartments. By skirting the circular pits to the right you can reach the south entrance of the palace and enter the central courtyard. Just off the nearest corner of the courtyard to the left is *kernós,* a round sacrificial stone with 34 holes arranged symmetrically around a larger one in the middle. (A smaller but similar table is still used today by Orthodox priests to receive offerings of food and wine.)

Admission to the palace ruins is 800 Drs ($3.35) for adults, 600 Drs ($2.50) for seniors, and 400 Drs ($1.65) for students. They're open Tuesday to Sunday from 8:30am to 3pm. We were asked to let readers know that "proper" attire is required.

LASSÍTHI PLAIN

You can visit the mountainous inland region of the Lassíthi Plain as a day trip from Iráklio. Tour guides have earmarked **Psyhró** (Psychró) as the best vantage point for clear views over the Lassíthi Plain, a sight best seen in midmorning when thousands of white sailcloth windmills are spinning wildly, pumping water to irrigate the lush wheat fields. It's breathtakingly gorgeous.

On the far side of the village you can begin the ascent to the **Dicteon Cave** (Diktéo Ándron), where, according to myth, Rhea gave birth to Zeus—in secret, to save him from the fate of his brothers and sisters who were swallowed at birth by their father, Kronos. Zeus was then left alone in the cave to be suckled by the goat Amalthea. Archaeologists have uncovered many icons and votive symbols, confirming that the cave was an important worship area during the Minoan period. You can make the steep climb to the cave in less than half an hour if you have strong legs and good shoes, or you can hire a mule or donkey for about 2,200 Drs ($9.15). Guides at the cave will ask about the same for their services. (You don't need a guide, but you will need a flashlight; be careful of the slick surfaces.) The cave is open daily from 10am to 5pm in summer, 9am to 3pm in winter; admission is 1,000 Drs ($4.15).

If you join a tour or go by public bus, you'll exit the north-coast highway just before Mália and head south through the fertile Mochas area, past the villages of Potamiá and Kéra.

A more dramatic mountain road, practical only for travelers with their own wheels, leads from the mountain town of **Neápolis.** This small settlement, on a plateau west of the Dikti range, offers its own view of windmills. The left side of the road is covered with the tall stone towers of now-idle traditional windmills, while the right, or valley, side of the drive is filled with bright aluminum ones, with spinning cloth-covered blades. It seems that most of Crete's 30 million olive trees are clinging vigorously to the hillsides here, nurtured by the continuous flow of water.

Just after Neápolis, a left turn off the highway at the flower-filled village of **Kastélli** will bring you to the more scenic, original road to **Áyios Nikólaos.** You can go left at the coast up to **Pláka,** a fishing village whose two tavernas overlook the tip of Spinalónga Island. At the dock, skillful negotiation can get you a private boat trip to the island.

Bearing right will bring you to the once equally appealing, though now very developed, port at **Eloúnda.** We recommend that you approach **Áyios Nikólaos,** the megaresort of this sparkling coastline, via the new highway with its impressive vistas, rather than via the resort hotel strip that's been developed from its northern end toward Eloúnda. As you approach Áyios Nikólaos you pass by **Ístron Bay,** a beautiful stretch of beach that has also been tremendously developed.

2 Áyios Nikólaos

The once-sleepy little port town of Áyios Nikólaos was a well-kept secret for many years, but now the local publicity hawkers have proudly dubbed it the "St-Tropez of Crete."

It took years to spoil one of Crete's most ideal vacation spots. When the summer season cranks up and tourists pour in, discos, loud tavernas, overcrowding, and moped madness make Áyios Nikólaos oppressive. We don't recommend visiting between May and September.

Áyios Nikólaos has developed around the Gulf of Mirabello, so named by Venetian conquerors for its "beautiful view." When its sheltered cove protected Cretan rebels from the Turkish navy, the port was renamed for the Church of St. Nicholas, which stood on its shore. In 1867 the governor, Kostas Adosidis Pasha, built a canal to link the village's stagnant pond with the nearby sea, creating the picturesque harbor so admired today.

ESSENTIALS

GETTING THERE & DEPARTING   By Bus   Áyios Nikólaos is well connected by bus to the main centers of Crete. From Iráklio buses make the 1¹/₂-hour run every half hour from 6:30am to 8:30pm; the fare is 1,350 Drs ($5.65).

By Taxi   Expect to pay about 14,000 Drs ($58) to have a taxi drive you from central Iráklio or the airport to Áyios Nikólaos.

By Ferry   Ferries arrive three times weekly from Sitía.

VISITOR INFORMATION   The **municipal tourist office** (☎ 0841/22-357; fax 0841/26-398) is at the bridge between the lake and the port; it's open April to November 15, daily from 8:30am to 9:30pm. The staff is fairly well informed and will change traveler's checks, provide a map, and help you find a room—if any are available.

The **tourist police,** at the intersection of Látous and Kondoyánni streets (☎ 0841/26-900), are open Monday to Friday from 8:30am to 2pm.

ORIENTATION   The town is built on a couple of low hills and centered around a small pond—referred to by the locals and all of the maps as a "lake." It's one of the most tranquil places to while away the hours at a cafe and watch the little fishing caïques pull in.

The lake meets the sea under a small bridge that divides Aktí Koundoúrou, the seaside street and focus of all development, roughly into two halves. The southeast end, Aktí I. Koundoúrou, runs below the older and quieter part of the village, where hotels and pensions have been built on a bluff high above the sea. This location puts them somewhat above the noise.

The northwestern half of the portside road is called Aktí S. Koundoúrou. Here bars and cafes look down on the town beach with steep stairs leading to the water, where concrete piers encourage sunbathing and swimming. The mopeds that eternally ply this beach route make it tough for those staying here to get a good night's sleep.

Three commercial streets run perpendicular to the port, alongside the lake, where stores provide whatever a visitor might want. (The middle street is R. Koundoúrou, yet another variation on this popular name.)

GETTING AROUND   Stathis, near the tourist office (at the bridge between the lake and the port) rents **bikes** for 1,200 Drs ($5) per day.

FAST FACTS   All town **banks** are open Monday to Thursday from 8am to 2pm and Friday from 8am to 1:30pm. The Commercial Bank is also open Saturday from 9am to 1pm. You can also **change money** at the tourist information office daily from 8:30am to 9:30pm.

Massaros Travel (☎ 0841/22-267) sells tickets for the ferries that head three times a week to Sitía, Kássos, Kárpathos, and Rhodes, and the twice-weekly ferries to Mílos and Piraeus.

The **Áyios Nikólaos General Hospital** is on Lasithíou Street (☎ 0841/25-221 or 0841/22-537).

The **post office** is on October 28 Street, open Monday to Friday from 7:30am to 8pm and Saturday and Sunday from 9am to 1pm.

The **OTE office,** open daily 6am to midnight, is south of the post office, on March 25 and Sfakináki streets.

EXPLORING THE TOWN

Our Greek friends don't think the town beach is clean enough. Instead, they head 2 miles south to **Almirós,** to a pebble beach whose chilly water is said to come from fairies bathing there at night. Two other beaches are closer, though they're both crowded: **Kitroplatía beach** is just south of the western spit of land and **Ammoúdi beach** (the most packed of all) is half a mile north on the Eloúnda road.

Just 1.3 miles from the village is a little-known Byzantine church with fine frescoes, **Áyios Nikólaos,** which gave the town its name. The church is normally closed, but you can get the keys next door from the reception desk at the Minos Palace Hotel. (You'll probably have to leave your passport or a credit card as a deposit.)

A church devoted to the Virgin, **Panayía Vrephotróphou,** dating from the early 12th century, is on Meletíou Street, near the bus station. The fine **archaeological museum,** at 17 Paleológou St. (☎ 0841/22-462), has artifacts from this district, particularly from the ancient towns (now beach resorts) of Mohlós, Mýrtos, and Kritsá; it's open Tuesday to Sunday from 8:30am to 3pm; admission is 500 Drs ($2.10) for adults, 400 Drs ($1.65) for seniors, and 300 Drs ($1.25) for students.

A small but fun **Museum of Popular Art,** next door to the tourist office, is open Sunday to Friday from 10am to 1:30pm and 5:30 to 9pm; admission is 300 Drs ($1.25).

At sunset the activity picks up, especially on the northwest side of the harbor, where bars buzz with young people trying to converse above loud music. Later in the evening the town starts to sizzle, especially on the southeast side of the harbor, where the **Lipstick Disco** is especially wild and **Jimmy's** is packed because it serves the cheapest drinks.

WHERE TO STAY

Both the southeast (village area) and the northwest (beach area) of Áyios Nikólaos have good accommodations. The trick is finding one that's kept some of the magic that made this such a popular tourist destination in the first place. And another difficulty is that most hotels are often fully booked by tour groups throughout the season.

The number-one choices above the east side of the port are the **Hotel Odysséas** and the **Pension Mýlos.** If you'd like to be closer to the swimming and nightlife, try the **Hotel Linda.** It's on the west side, sandwiched between the much larger and more expensive hotels Coral, Hermes, and Rea (see below). On the low end, Evans Street, which runs inland from the southeastern part of the harbor (just after you pass all three commercial streets), has several buildings offering rooms for rent at about 8,500 Drs ($35.40) for two.

If you plan to visit in winter, contact the **Municipal Tourist Office** (☎ 0841/22-357) to find out which facilities are open. The small **Hamburg Pension,** at Odós Látous 2 (☎ 0841/28-639), near the town hall, is one of the few.

Hotel Linda. Odós Salamínas 3A, 721 00 Áyios Nikólaos. ☎ **0841/22-130.** Fax 0841/26-433. 22 rms, all with bath (shower). TEL. 9,000 Drs ($37.50) single; 10,800 Drs ($45) double. Rates 30%–50% less off-season. No credit cards. Open year-round.

We found the Linda both clean and attractive. The decor of the rooms is what we refer to as "Hessian Greek moderne" but the bougainvillea-covered, trellised canopy over the breakfast patio is lovely. Breakfast is 1,200 Drs ($5).

Hotel Odysséas. Aktí Themistokléos 1, 721 00 Áyios Nikólaos. ☎ **0841/28-440.** 24 rms, all with bath (shower). TEL. 6,900 Drs ($28.75) single; 9,800 Drs ($40.85) double. Rates include breakfast. No credit cards.

This is where many longtime English visitors choose to stay. It has a "homely" feel (as the English like to say) but is often filled with guests who are up for a good part of the day and night. Recent improvements include the addition of an elevator and new carpets and curtains. It frequently hosts tour groups, which completely buy out the hotel.

Hotel Vasilia Inn. Odós Ariádnis 5, 721 00 Áyios Nikólaos. ☎ **0841/23-572.** 9 rms, all with bath (tub). 4,600–6,500 Drs ($19.15–$27.10) single; 5,400–9,500 Drs ($22.50–$39.60) double. No credit cards.

Near the seaside bluff, on quiet Ariádnis Street, you'll find the small Hotel Vasilia Inn. Paintings, Cretan weavings, embroidered curtains, mismatched upholstery, and a friendly staff give it a comfortable feeling. (On our last visit, however, we noticed that it could still use some improvement.)

Pension Ístron. Odós Sarolídis 4, 721 00 Áyios Nikólaos. ☎ **0841/23-763.** 9 rms, none with bath. 4,200 Drs ($17.50) single; 6,250 Drs ($26.05) double. No credit cards.

The Pension Ístron, run by the Dachis family, is a reasonably attractive choice; the rooms are enlivened by fresh-cut flowers and crisp new paint.

Pension Marilena. Erythroú Stavróu (Red Cross) 4, 721 00 Áyios Nikólaos. ☎ **0841/22-681.** Fax 0841/24-218. 14 rms, all with bath (shower). 6,200 Drs ($25.85) single; 10,500 ($43.75) double. AE, MC, V.

We met the friendly owner and her baby granddaughter on the street, just up from the Linda and Hermes hotels, when we asked for directions. First we tried the food in her small cafe, where her son cooks up traditional Cretan cuisine, then we looked at her nice, clean, comfortable rooms. We recommend them both.

Pension Mýlos. Odós Sarolídis 24, 721 00 Áyios Nikólaos. ☎ **0841/23-783.** 10 rms, 5 with bath (shower). TEL. 8,000 Drs ($33.35) single or double without bath, 9,800 Drs ($40.85) single or double with bath. No credit cards.

The Pension Mýlos is a spotless pension offering fine views of the sea. The two sisters who run it, Maria and Georgia, will greet you with their warm and generous Cretan hospitality. A stay in one of the rooms above theirs will make you feel as if you're visiting a Greek family.

WHERE TO EAT

Áyios Nikólaos has plenty of fast food and takeaway, much of it inferior. For breakfast, try tiny **Glaros Fast Food,** on Paleológou Street, where omelets start at 400 Drs ($1.65). (A Nescafé alone at one of the portside cafes would cost twice that!) The **Candiá Café,** at Odós I. Koundoúrou 12 (☎ **0841/26-355**), serves very nice cakes and Cretan desserts daily from 7:30am to 3am.

Aouas Taverna. Odós Paleológou 44. ☎ **0841/23-231.** Main courses 1,200–3,200 Drs ($5–$13.35). No credit cards. Daily 6pm–1am. TAVERNA/GRILL.

This large outdoor taverna/grill, which is popular with a local crowd, specializes in grilled food as well as the usual taverna dishes. We particularly liked the grilled lamb and chicken, but found their garden a bit crowded.

Klimataria. Odós Ethnikís Antistáseos 3. ☎ **0841/28-687.** Main courses 1,000–2,800 Drs ($4.15–$11.65). No credit cards. Daily 6pm–1am. TAVERNA/GRILL.

We're sure that the talented family behind the Klimataria will make your dining experience special. We savored a meal of veal *yuvétsi,* pork cooked in wine, and cheese balls accompanied by a sweet mountain wine from Agrilos (near Sitía). The restaurant is set in a lovely garden off the northeast corner of the lake.

DINING WITH A VIEW

A view has its price, but we liked the **Blue Lagoon Taverna** on the paved pedestrian walk on the east side of the lake, where two can dine well for about 11,000 Drs ($45.85) and up. Those who want the Riviera ambience of the busy beach coast promenade should try **Zefiros,** at Odós Aktí S. Koundoúroe 1 (☎ **0841/28-868**), open daily from 8am to 2am. You'll pay more here, but you'll get a fine meal.

A SPLURGE CHOICE IN NEARBY LÍMNES

Dionyssos. Límnes. ☎ **0841/33-401** or 0841/28-321. Fixed-price menu 8,000 Drs ($33.35). No credit cards. Thurs–Sun in high season only (call for hours). CRETAN.

At the Dionyssos, everyone joins in the fun. Four nights a week waiters will show off a variety of Greek specialties, then leap onto the dance floor to the beat of live musicians. Dionyssos is close to an authentic bouzouki club, yet serves better food and is reasonably priced.

SIDE TRIPS FROM ÁYIOS NIKÓLAOS

SPINALÓNGA ISLAND This island is one of the most popular destinations from Áyios Nikólaos; boat tours cost about 4,000 Drs ($16.65). Small boats can also be hired for much less from the ports at Eloúnda and Pláka for short visits.

Check with the **Massaros Travel Agency,** at Odós R. Koundoúrou 29 (☎ **0841/ 22-267;** fax 0841/23-077), open 7 days a week. They've got all the information on various trips, sell ferry tickets, and even list villas for rent.

Spinalónga was a peninsula until the Venetians built a powerful fortress over the ruins of the ancient city of Olonte and in 1526 made it more secure by cutting a canal through the peninsula. This insular bastion provided the Venetians with an impregnable stronghold against the Turks for 50 years, until 1715. In modern times (until 1958) Spinalónga was the site of a leper colony, earning it the poignant nickname "Island of Pain and Tears," but now it's extremely picturesque and inviting.

ELOÚNDA & PLÁKA   Just 6¹/₂ miles north of Áyios Nikólaos, along a resort-encrusted road, is the once-sleepy port of Eloúnda, a perfect example of a picturesque fishing village nestled in a sheltered cove that's been swallowed whole by tourism. Its pretty harbor can provide some respite from the midsummer crowds.

One of the overlooked highlights of Eloúnda is the underwater ancient city of **Oloús.** This Minoan town can be seen from the land only when the water is perfectly calm and clear. If you have snorkeling gear, you may be able to obtain permission from the police station in Eloúnda to explore underwater.

We suggest that you continue on through Eloúnda another 4¹/₄ miles north to quiet Pláka, where you'll find a new all-purpose place, **Taverna & Rooms Spinalonga** (☎ **0841/41-804**), where friendly Evangelia can provide you with very attractive accommodations—doubles for 7,000 Drs ($29.15) and apartments for 8,300 to 10,800 Drs ($34.60 to $45)—and serve you good Cretan food, including fresh fish caught by her husband, John, who can also take you out to Spinalónga island. There's good swimming nearby on a clean, smooth-stone beach.

KRITSÁ   The hill town of Kritsá, located 6¹/₂ miles south of the main north-coast highway, provides a welcome glimpse of the way life used to be in this part of Crete before mass tourism. The traditional weavings seen throughout the island provide much of the village's income, and the small handcraft shops on the main street offer many good buys. The town is known for its almond juice drink, *soumáda,* which is drunk cold in summer and hot in winter. Much of *Zorba the Greek* was filmed here.

Just before you reach town is the celebrated 14th-century Byzantine church of **Panayía Kerá,** with some of the finest medieval frescoes on Crete. The style of the renderings, which is comparatively primitive, is marked by decorative elements (from nature), somber colors, and the brooding expressions of saints, villagers, and kings. The church is open daily from 9am to 3pm; admission is 500 Drs ($2.10). It's a wonderful place to experience the religious devotion once expressed in this isolated village and confirms the town's past as one of the most important centers of Byzantine art during the Venetian period. There are also beautiful frescoes in several other churches, especially in Áyios Yióryios Kavousiótis.

GOURNIÁ   The superbly restored remains of the village of Gourniá (14 miles east of Áyios Nikólaos) are unique on Crete because this is the only settlement dating from the earliest Minoan period (before the cataclysm of 1450 B.C.). From the road, the rough stone walls and even the layout of Gourniá's "streets" could be mistaken for a well-organized olive grove, minus the trees. If you climb up the 3,500-year-old main street to the top of the mound, where there once stood a modest palace, you'll enjoy a wonderful view of the houses, back alleys, and agorá, as well as the Bay of Ístron beyond.

Call ☎ **081/226-092** for more information. Admission to the site is free; hours are Tuesday to Sunday from 8:30am to 3pm. The public bus from Áyios Nikólaos costs 440 Drs ($1.85).

MOHLÓS (MOCHLÓS) We don't really want to say too much about this exquisitely simple fishing port (and thus spoil one of the island's last quiet places), but we must point out that one of the most important newly excavated archaeological sites on Crete, evidence of a postvolcano Minoan settlement, is just 100 yards offshore on a rocky island. Finds from Mochlós are on display in the museums in Áyios Nikólaos and Sitía. If you decide to stay overnight, you'll find a scattering of rooms to rent, a couple of waterfront cafes, a tiny pebble beach, but not much to do at night.

3 Sitía & the Northeast

Sitía was a Venetian stronghold until the Turkish pirate Barbarossa laid siege to the fort in the late 16th century. The Kazarma (Casa di Arma) Fortress is one of the few legacies of the Venetians' stay. Once only a way station between Áyios Nikólaos and the palm-lined beach at Vái, or an embarkation port for the weekly ferries to the Dodecanese and Cyclades, Sitía has now grown into a bustling seaside town built amphitheatrically on a hill. The new Sitía overlooks a newly renovated and enlarged harbor, now lined with hotels and cafes. We recommend it mainly as a good base for sightseeing.

The bus route to Sitía follows the highway, the only road extending to the eastern tip of Crete at Vái. Beyond the clutter of development from Kaló Horió until Ístron (a secluded spot where you might consider stopping for the rest of your life) you'll see some of the most exquisite vistas of mountain and sea on the whole island. The scent of pressed olives wafts through the air, mingling with the sweet flowers in sensual confusion.

As the road climbs, cascades of yellow tumble down the hillside, where olive trees grow at an alarming 45° angle. Donkeys burdened with herbs and grape leaves are led by old farmers in their traditional baggy black pants, and you often see Crete's unique *krí-krí,* a curly-horned goat, nibbling at the road's shoulder.

About 6 miles before you reach Sitía is a turnoff for the "Minoan House of Chamaizi," a site for avid Minoanphiles. A 1,100-yard walk along the stone road leading down from the highway will take you to the ruins of this old home, safely settled among olive groves. In the nearby hamlet of Hamésio you can see local artifacts at the Cretan Home Museum.

ESSENTIALS

GETTING THERE & DEPARTING **By Plane** Olympic Airways (☎ 800/ 223-1226 in the U.S., or 01/966-6666 for reservations in Greece) has flights twice a week from Athens to Sitía and once a week from Kárpathos and Kássos to Sitía.

By Bus During the high season there are six daily buses that run from Ierápetra, six daily from Áyios Nikólaos and Iráklio, and hourly buses from the popular hamlet of Palékastro (and on to Vái).

VISITOR INFORMATION There's a portable **tourist information** trailer (☎ 0843/24-955) on the central harbor.

FAST FACTS The **bus station** is on Itanós Street, which runs perpendicular to the harbor at the east end of town. There's an **Olympic Airways** office at Odós Venizélos 56 (☎ 0843/22-270); there are infrequent flights to and from Kárpathos, Kássos, and Athens. The **airport** is quite close, about a 10-minute walk up the hill; a taxi costs about 700 Drs ($2.90). **Tzortákis Travel,** at the port (☎ 0843/28-900; fax 0843/ 22-731), sells ferryboat tickets for the weekly daytime sailings to Kássos, Kárpathos,

Halkís, and Rhodes, and for the thrice-weekly night sailings to Áyios Nikólaos, Mílos, and Piraeus.

SEEING THE SIGHTS

Sitía is pleasant but unexciting—unless you're interested in Minoan remains. If you are, plan on spending at least 1 night here. You'll want to see the remains of the **palace at Zákros** (and maybe take the hike through the Gorge of the Dead leading to Káto Zákros), or perhaps visit the archaeological site at **Palékastro** and tour the new **archaeology museum,** just south of town on the Ierápetra road. The core of this splendid small collection has been culled from the most recent excavations at the eastern end of Crete, including exciting finds that postdate the tidal wave that was thought to have ended the Minoan culture. Proof of the vitality of this "post-Minoan" work is a delicately crafted ivory sculpture that greets you as you enter the exhibition space. The museum (☎ **0843/23-917**) is open Tuesday to Sunday from 8:30am to 3pm; admission is 500 Drs ($2.10) for adults, 400 Drs ($1.65) for seniors, and 300 Drs ($1.25) for students.

Sitía also boasts an interesting **Museum of Folklore** above Arkadíou Street, open Tuesday to Saturday from 9am to 1pm and 5 to 8pm, admission free.

There's a not-too-appealing 2-mile stretch of **beach** just east of town; swimmers will find that the cleanest water is at the far east end.

The seaside has several cafes, providing tables for excellent *zaharoplastía* (pastry shops). The central square on the harbor is Platía Polytechníou, where you'll find a portable post office and a taxi stand. Venizélos Street, which runs parallel to this square, 1 block in, is home to a variety of shops and businesses.

Don't miss **Sitian Arts,** 2 blocks from the port at Odós Vitséntsou Kornárou 148 (☎ **0843/22-600**), open daily from 9am to 1pm and 2:30 to 8pm. Jane Kafetzákis, formerly of the Isle of Man, is a wonderful painter who sells watercolors, painted bags and scarves, decorated stones, jewelry, and other excellent gift items.

WHERE TO STAY

The **GYH Youth Hostel,** Odós Theríssou 4 (☎ **0843/22-693**), about a 400-yard climb up the hill from the bus stop, is a shoestring choice. The hostel offers hot showers and shared kitchen facilities for only 1,200 Drs ($5) per bed.

Arhontiko Hotel. Odós Kondilákis 16, 723 00 Sitía. ☎ **0843/28-172.** 10 rms, none with bath. 5,200 Drs ($21.65) single; 6,000 Drs ($25) double. No credit cards.

The Arhontikó ("Gentleman's House"), up the steps toward the cathedral, is redolent with atmosphere. The building itself is an early 1900s wooden house, with slightly sloped wooden floors, surrounded by orange and lemon trees; the rooms are spacious, well maintained, and clean. The hosts, Apostolis Kimalis and Brigitte Hurdalek, are as hospitable as can be. Apostolis also rents three rooms with private facilities attached to his own home; the rates are 7,000 Drs ($29.15) single or double and 9,000 Drs ($37.50) triple.

El Greco Hotel. Odós Arkadíou 13, 723 00 Sitía. ☎ **0843/23-133.** 15 rms, all with bath (shower). TEL. 9,700 Drs ($40.40) single; 11,200 Drs ($46.65) double. Rates include breakfast. No credit cards.

The El Greco Hotel, owned and operated by the professional Manuel Tzikelakis, is up the central steps from the harbor and to the left of the main church. Cretan weavings and dark-wood decor give the hotel the homey feel of a mountain lodge, and the large, balconied rooms offer fine vistas of the harbor and the Gulf of Sitía.

WHERE TO EAT

Kali Kardia Taverna. Odós Foundalídou 22. ☎ **0843/22-249.** Main courses 800–2,000 Drs ($3.35–$8.35). No credit cards. Daily 8am–1am. TAVERNA.

The Kalí Kardiá ("Good heart"), opposite the Cultural Arts Center, is a wonderfully local Greek space, where grizzled elderly men sit frozen in an "ouzoed" state. Rifles, carved walking sticks, and scythes compete for wall space with impossible beach and mountain oil paintings. Everything we sampled was superb—not fancy, mind you, but absolutely delicious. Start with an ouzo and a few *mezédes* (appetizers), then move on to a house specialty, *tiropitákia* (small cheese pies), and to any of the daily specials.

Mihos Taverna. Odós Vitséntsou Kornárou 117. ☎ **0843/22-416.** Main courses 1,000–2,200 Drs ($4.15–$9.15). EURO, MC, V. Daily noon–4pm and 7pm–midnight. TAVERNA.

The Mihos Taverna, another fine backstreet choice, presents an ascetic interior—all the flair goes into the food. Two spacious, whitewashed rooms are linked by a simple arched doorway. We dined on an excellent variety of traditional taverna cuisine: octopus, *tirópita, dolmádes,* stuffed zucchini flowers accented with cumin, and chicken and lamb prepared on the spit—all tasty and low priced.

Zorba's. Platía Kosmazótou. ☎ **0843/22-689.** Main courses 1,000–2,500 Drs ($4.15–$10.40); fish 8,000 Drs ($33.35) per kilo; lobster 10,000 Drs ($41.65) per kilo. AE, EURO, MC, V. Daily 8am–2am. GREEK/CONTINENTAL.

This large, pleasant taverna and the affiliated Zorba's II, a few cafes away, have an extraordinarily varied menu, and both are reliably good, although priced for the harbor views. The original has a better view of the harbor, but Zorba's II will appeal to those who prefer grilled meat. Our only complaint at both places is the harried, verging on rude, service during the busy summer season.

SIDE TRIPS FROM SITÍA

HITTING THE BEACH AT VÁI   Some 17 miles northeast of Sitía, Vái is a highly touted destination. Cretans and Europeans take this palm-lined, sand-beach inlet very seriously, though those familiar with Caribbean beaches will probably not be too impressed—especially since most of the palms are fenced off. This is very out of the way for a beach excursion, but a large parking lot, a cafeteria, and (best of all) private showers ensure its year-round popularity.

The hardy who scale the hill beyond the tourist restaurant will descend to a more secluded cove where nude sunbathing is acceptable. If you really want to sample the farthest-out beaches, continue straight for 1 1/2 miles past the right turnoff for Vái.

ITANÓS   At the northeastern tip of the island near Ermoúpolis is the ancient city of Itanós, unearthed by French archaeologists. The remains of the eastern acropolis indicate that this picturesque promontory was inhabited from the Geometric period. On the taller, western acropolis the remains date from the 3rd century (the height of the city's naval power). The Byzantines occupied the land between the two sites. Two isolated sandy coves, easily viewed from the height of either acropolis, provide superb swimming and sunbathing without the crowds at Vái.

PALÉKASTRO (PALAÍKASTRO)   At Roussolákos, 12 1/2 miles east of Sitía, are the remains of the Minoan port of Palékastro, which are producing some spectacular finds. However, it's the newer village of Palékastro, on the road between Sitía and the major Minoan site at Káto Zákros, that draws most visitors today. This popular town is still somewhat typical of old Crete, despite its hotels, rooms to rent, and two discos.

From Palékastro, surrounded by olive groves, it's a short commute to nearby **beaches.** Besides the swimming at Vái or Itanós, there's Agathía, a smaller, traditional village east of Palékastro that provides access to a popular beach called **Shona.**

Those drawn to peaceful Palékastro will find the 32-room **Marina Village** (☎ **0843/61-284;** fax 0843/61-285), a small resort with a pool and tennis courts outside the town, where doubles run 17,500 Drs ($72.90). The **Hellas Pension** (☎ **0843/61-240**), and several *domátia* (rooms to rent) offer lower-cost accommodations above the shops off the main square.

ZÁKROS   Some of the most magnificent Minoan artifacts have been unearthed at Káto Zákros, 23 miles from Sitía, on Crete's far east end, south from Palékastro. Though Zákros is the smallest of the four Minoan palaces found on Crete, archaeologists have determined that the location was strategic and of great commercial importance for the Minoan empire. It provided a base for trading and keeping tabs on the other major powers of antiquity: Syria, Egypt, and the whole of Asia Minor.

Zákros is the only unplundered **Minoan palace** yet found on Crete, and excavation, which began in the early 1960s and continues, has unearthed some major finds, including some remarkable carved stone vases. Several vessels are in the archeological museum in Sitía; the best, however, are among the highlights of the archeological museum in Iráklio. As with the other Minoan palaces, Zákros was built about 1700 B.C. over the remains of an earlier palace, but unlike them it was then abandoned completely, leaving behind many everyday objects from which much is being learned. Unfortunately, it's not as well preserved as Knossós and Phestós and its surroundings are often marshy, but it's certainly worth a visit for those who are fascinated by Minoan culture and history. The site is open daily from 8:30am to 3pm; admission is 500 Drs ($2.10) for adults, 400 Drs ($1.65) for seniors, and 300 Drs ($1.25) for students.

The town of Zákros (5 miles from the site) has the Class C **Hotel Zákros** (☎ **0843/93-379**), with bed and breakfast for two at 7,500 Drs ($31.25), plus rooms to rent.

There's a good **beach** at Káto Zákros; so if the heat of ancient stone gets to you, cool off in the sea. Hikers should inquire about exploring the nearby **Gorge of the Dead,** the site of an ancient necropolis.

For the truly intrepid, there's the usually deserted and totally wonderful **beach at Xerokámpos,** located south of Zákros, via a very funky, winding road.

4 The Southern Beach Resorts: Ierápetra to Ayía Galíni

With its sandy beaches and clean waters, Ierápetra is the star of the southern coast, the next willing victim of tourist inundation. Fortunately for Crete, it's already the wealthiest city (in terms of per capita income) because of its thriving agricultural industry. From here, tomatoes, eggplants, cucumbers, herbs, and raisins are exported to other parts of Greece and to northern Europe. The hothouses seen on both sides of the road as you approach from Sitía keep those ripe tomatoes coming year-round for Greek salads in Athens. Unfortunately for the hoteliers, the processing plants and business offices that service this vital industry have made Ierápetra a rather homely, bustling seaside city.

Nonetheless, Crete's southern coast along the Libyan Sea boasts the clearest waters and warmest climate in Europe, and the national highway system has made

Ierápetra one of its gateway cities. The small beach communities at Mýrtos, Árvi, and Mátala are overnight options on the way west to the resort of Ayía Galíni.

IERÁPETRA

If you want to sightsee along Crete's beautiful southern coast, Ierápetra's long harbor, pleasant cafes, and urban activities make a fairly nice base.

For advice on local sightseeing, contact the staff of the Ierápetra **Express Tourist Office,** on Platía Elefthería (☎ **0842/28-123** or 0842/22-411; fax 0842/28-330), opposite the National Bank. The multilingual guides and group representatives who share the space are available daily from 8am to 1:30pm and 4:30 to 9pm to book tours and rooms and to exchange money. Contact them for information about organized tours.

If you're interested only in the beach, backtrack east for about 17 miles to **Mávros Kolymbós** at Makriyialós, a small fishing village with a long public beach. Staying in one of the few Spartan rooms to rent above the main street will give you solo time on the beach before the day-trippers arrive.

From Ierápetra's harbor, three 60-passenger cruise boats depart daily April to October for an excursion to the tiny uninhabited **Chryssí Island,** for 6,000 Drs ($25) round-trip. Its sand beaches are considered among the finest on Crete. There's only one taverna, so bring a picnic or adequate supplies if you plan to rough-camp in this nearly African isle.

An easier (and less expensive) excursion is to the less frequented **beach at Ayía Fotía,** 12 miles east of town. The privately run KTEL buses to Sitía, which leave from the central square, will drop you there. Between Ayía Fotía and Makriyialós, you can climb down to **Galíni Beach,** near Koutsoúras, where snorkeling is popular. Recent development, however, has made all these beaches more crowded.

In Ierápetra town is a small **archaeological museum,** open Tuesday to Sunday from 8:30am to 3pm; admission is free.

For one of the most pleasant evening activities, take a sunset stroll, or *vólta.* We recommend starting at the central part of the harbor down from Elefthería Square. Turning right, you'll pass an old, official-looking iron building. A stroll past the drydocked fishing boats and worn hulls in the midst of repair will lead you to taverna row, where you can judge the local action, and then on past the town beach. At the west end of the harbor is a Venetian fortress and a mosque.

WHERE TO STAY

Heightened tourist (or should we say tour operator?) interest in Ierápetra has led to higher prices at all the official hotels, but there are many alternatives. We preferred places along the quieter east end of the harbor (where cars are turned back and pedestrians take over the flagstone promenade), although lower rates can be found at several pensions on Ioanídou Street or inland from the central square.

El Greco Hotel. Odós Michaíl Kothrí 40, 720 00 Ierápetra. ☎ **0842/28-471.** Fax 0842/26-547. 33 rms, all with bath (shower). TEL. 10,350 Drs ($43.15) single; 12,950 Drs ($53.95) double. MC, V.

The El Greco has a front door on the street and a seaside backdoor on the east end of the harbor. Its rooms are clean and pleasant, and many of them have great views from their balconies. The seaside rooms not only command a better view but also tend to be quieter. Hotel guests receive a 15% discount on meals taken at the downstairs restaurant.

Hotel Castro. Odós Stratigoú Samouíl 54, 720 00 Ierápetra. ☎ **0842/23-858.** 7 rms, 5 with bath (shower). 5,350 Drs ($22.30) single; 7,200 Drs ($30) twin. V.

At the far west end of the town beach, near the fortress, where things are a bit quieter, the Hotel Castro stands above the Cretan Arts Tourist Shop. Twin-bedded rooms in this clean pension have minifridges, but share bathing facilities. The owner, George Rainakis, also owns a 15-meter boat that holds up to 30 people and can be chartered for trips to Chrissi Island, fishing, or other excursions.

Hotel Katerina. Odós Michaíl Kothrí, 720 00 Ierápetra. ☎ **0842/28-345.** 16 rms, all with bath (shower). 8,000 Drs ($33.35) single or double. V.

Almost next door to the El Greco, on the harbor just before the eastern stretch of sand begins, this delightful hotel is run by the friendly and accommodating Katerina. Walk up to the reception desk and check out the small but clean balconied doubles with private showers.

Pension Diagoras. Odós Kyrvá 1, 720 00 Ierápetra. ☎ **0842/23-898.** 9 rms, all with bath (shower). 5,000 Drs ($20.85) single; 7,200 Drs ($30) double. No credit cards.

Behind the city hall and toward the beach end of the harbor is the Pension Diagóras, where clean doubles with Danish showers and a good view nestle above the inexpensive and old-style cafe/bar of the same name. The front-facing rooms may be quieter.

WHERE TO EAT

Since Ierápetra has a life beyond tourism, there are several good and inexpensive tavernas inland from Venizélou Street. If you've come for the view (as we did), try the beachside tavernas. The **Konaki Restaurant,** Odós Stratigoú Samouíl 32 (☎ **0842/24-422**), open daily from 8am to midnight, offers a grilled shrimp, fresh *barboúnia,* or mixed-seafood meal for about 5,000 Drs ($20.85) per person. You can order meat or vegetable specialties for about half that price.

The pedestrian promenade at the eastern end of the harbor has the best cafes for a sunset drink or after-dinner dessert and coffee.

MÝRTOS

From the road, Mýrtos looks like any of the many "hothouse" towns on Crete's attractive southern coast. Walk into town and you'll see lovely gardens in small homes and grapevines creeping up rickety trellises. If you continue walking, you'll come to Mýrtos's black-sand and pebble beach, which, unfortunately, is more likely than not to be strewn with trash (the western side of the town beach is much cleaner).

Mýrtos is a pleasant town, with a few narrow streets squeezed between the highway to Ierápetra (only 10 miles away) and a concrete promenade (really a bulkhead) that prevents the seaside tavernas from being swept away. It's quiet, picturesque, and clean (while strolling, you'll probably encounter old women in black dresses busily sweeping the sidewalk) and not yet quite overrun with tourists.

WHERE TO STAY & EAT

If you decide to stay, try the 10-room **Villa Mare Pension,** near the church on the western side of town (☎ **0842/51-274;** fax 0842/51-328). It has good sea views from its top-floor rooms and roof garden. Single or double rooms run 9,400 Drs ($39.15).

Superior but more expensive lodgings are available at the crenelated pseudotowers of the 13-room **Kastro Studios** (☎ **0842/51-444**) and at the slick eight-room **Myrtini Apartments** (☎ **0842/51-386**) on the vanguard of Mýrtos's development; doubles cost about 12,000 Drs ($50) at both places.

One of the nicest accommodations in town is **Mertiza Studios and Apartments** (☎ **0842/51-208;** fax 0842/51-036), with spacious studios from 9,400 Drs ($39.15) and apartments from 12,950 Drs ($53.95).

If the choices mentioned above are booked, another alternative is the older, but still attractive, 21-room **Hotel Mirtos,** Odós Main 140, 720 56 Mýrtos (☎ **0842/ 51-266**), where a double costs 6,000 Drs ($25). There are also clean, newer rooms to rent above the supermarket, near Mýrtos's church, and above several *kafenía.* These newer rooms usually have Danish showers in private-stall bathrooms, plus small balconies with views over the nearby tomato greenhouses and construction sites.

Unless you're here from June to September, you can probably bargain the rates down by half. Off-season is also the best time to appreciate the "Greekness" that still remains in the town.

During the day, **Katerina's Taverna** serves a respectable *horiátiki saláta* (Greek salad) and stewed-beef dish, and is popular for people-watching. Mýrtos boasts three beachfront cafes; our favorites are the **Taverna Votsal** and **Aktí.** At night, **Eros,** on the beach promenade, beckons the beer-and-wine crowd with live bouzouki.

ÁRVI

The small south-coast village of Árvi has become a favorite of those in search of less crowded beaches—and so it's no longer quite so idyllic. Its long, narrow beach, only 100 yards from banana plantations and melon fields, isn't quite the paradise some people imagine. Locals prefer the wider **beach** about a mile west of the town.

There's a spectacular **gorge** about a 15- to 20-minute hike from town, and the path—delightfully free of signs, guard rails, and tourists—leads through tilled fields of bananas, cucumbers, and grapes. You'll probably run across farmers bringing goods from town, laborers working on the water pipes, goats, and a stray dog or two. The path parallels a small stream, and at the mouth of the gorge you have to wade in knee-deep water. The sinewy curves of the rock there were formed by thousands of years of rushing water.

Árvi also has a 300-year-old **monastery** that's a more moderate walk from town. From its hillside perch you have a good view of the town's unusual layout.

If Árvi isn't to your taste and you don't mind an even bumpier road, visit the quiet fishing port of **Tsoutsoúros,** which has a wide beach, some of the best fishing on Crete, and lower priced rooms to rent.

WHERE TO STAY & EAT

The 17-room **Hotel Gorgona,** 700 04 Árvi (☎ **0895/71-353**), charges about 10,000 Drs ($41.65) for two. The 14-room **Ariadni** (☎ **0895/71-300**), right on the shore, offers doubles for 11,400 Drs ($47.50); it's a bit beach-worn but offers a discount for students, which tends to make it a great meeting place. A less expensive pension, run by the elderly Aliki Christaki, is spotless and homey.

There are also numerous rooms to rent above the shops on the main street and along the shore, where doubles with private showers run about 5,750 Drs ($23.95). The **Arvi Villa Apartments** (☎ **0895/71-324**) offer a more spacious alternative. Unfortunately, motorcycles frequently disturb the tranquillity, so choose your room carefully.

Of the half-dozen family-run tavernas in the village, we found the **Taverna Diktines** (☎ **0895/71-249**), on the eastern end, to be the most popular; it's open daily from 7am to 1am. Our favorite dining room, run by **Avios Dias** (☎ **0895/ 71-256**), is in the center of town with outdoor tables overlooking the water, open daily from 8am to 1am. We especially enjoyed the locally caught grilled fish with vegetables, served *zestó* (hot)—a rarity in these parts.

MÁTALA

One of Crete's southernmost beach communities, Mátala is known for the cave dwellings carved by early Christian refugees in the cliffs that encircle its beach. During World War II, Cretan resistance forces hid there, and young foreigners inhabited them during the 1960s and 1970s. The town boasts several of the best fine-pebble beaches on Crete, and the natural cove, formed by a horseshoe of sandstone cliffs, has perfectly clear warm water. Busloads of very young vacationers pour in every day.

Beach aficionados should climb the hill behind the pensions or take the new street to **Red Beach,** about a 20-minute walk, where some of Mátala's visitors sun in blissful seclusion; there's a drink stand there if you need to quench your thirst. If you climb over the tourists who are gaping at the once-inhabited caves—on the opposite side of the cove, fenced off but still explored by the public—you'll get to **Kómos Beach,** another 5-mile-long stretch of sand. If you feel less energetic, you can take the hourly bus or drive and then walk for about 10 minutes back through town; take the first unpaved road on the left for 2¹/₂ miles. There are a few tavernas and restaurants on the beach.

Because of the very pleasant year-round weather, several hundred Europeans have made Mátala their permanent abode. During the winter most residents of the seaside town migrate just a few miles north to the less touristed village of Pitsídia. You, too, can stay here in a private room during the busier season, usually for a lot less.

WHERE TO STAY

The quality and price of accommodations in Mátala varies according to season and location; this is truer here than in other coastal villages. Former hippies and their families tend to come in the off-season, while the "sun-and-fun" budget-tour groups arrive in July and August. Many hotels and even small pensions cater exclusively to groups and are fully booked in the high season. Mátala's few larger hotels differ by offering views over the town parking lot (toward the beach cove beyond) and balconies that face the moped-filled main street. Available housing depends on the number of presold tours; sometimes it seems easier to sleep in a cave than to find a free room.

Just up the road from Nikos are a host of perfectly acceptable guest house/pensions that we've stayed in over the years. The **Pension Fantastic** (☎ 0892/45-362) has nine neat rooms with showers and charges 8,600 Drs ($35.85) for a double. Rates are similar at the nearby guest house of **Silvia Spinthákis** (☎ 0892/45-127) and at **Antónios' Rooms** (☎ 0892/45-123). Antonios is a talented and diligent gardener with a self-proclaimed "paradise"—a small flower garden with bananas and pomegranates.

Nikos Hotel. 702 00 Mátala. ☎ **0892/45-375** or 0892/42-765. Fax 0892/45-120. 25 rms, all with bath (shower). 7,900 Drs ($32.90) single; 9,800 Drs ($40.85) double. Closed Nov–Mar 15. No credit cards.

The best choice is Nikos Kefalakis's hotel, which is near the beach on an unnamed street. Friendly and charming Nikos and his geranium-filled courtyard draw some of Mátala's nicest regulars, many of whom have been visiting since the 1970s. Call far ahead, since reservations are often tough to come by in high season.

WHERE TO EAT

Just below the portable post office on the shopping street (on the beach under a blue-striped awning) is the **Blue Restaurant** (☎ 0892/45-107), open daily from 11am to 11pm, which specializes in pizza and souvláki. Delicious pizzas with various meat, seafood, and fresh vegetable toppings run about 1,200 to 2,000 Drs ($5 to $8.25) for a single-person size.

The **Corali,** on the main square in the center (☎ **0892/45-744**), open daily from 8am to 1am, serves traditional Greek fare, with an emphasis on grilled meats. Main courses are 900 to 1,600 Drs ($3.75 to $6.65).

A good budget choice is the souvláki at **Gyros Nasos,** near the main steps leading to the beach.

KÓKKINOS PÝRGOS

The village of Kókkinos Pýrgos ("Red Tower"), less than 6 miles from Ayía Galíni on the south-coast highway, has recently developed a reputation along wandering adventurers. It has a small caïque port on the western end and a scruffy pebble beach on the eastern end.

On our last visit we were struck by the large number of new hotels, pensions, and rooms to rent, especially since the village's long beach seems so unattractive in comparison with those at other nearby beach towns. Water views from the main coastal street are also blocked by several tavernas and souvláki stands built on the rocks or bulkheading above the narrow sand-and-stone shore.

There are several *domátia* (rooms to rent) above storefronts. The small **El Greco Hotel** (☎ **0892/51-182**) is also a possibility, but we can't even imagine why anyone would want to stay in Kókkinos Pýrgos overnight!

AYÍA GALÍNI

Local legend tells of a Byzantine emperor who set sail in quest of the Holy Grail. After months of difficult travel, he met with a great storm at sea and took refuge in a quiet cove at the Bay of Messará. He prayed fervently for the storm to end, and when it did he built a small church on the nearest shore, dedicating it to Ayía Galíni, "Holy Calm."

A small, overbuilt beach community has sprung up at this once-peaceful spot. The narrow streets, packed with shops and cafes, provide a lively, informal resort atmosphere. It's a popular base for budget-charter groups (especially from Germany and Britain) that come for a week in the sun; it's not as well suited for assisting independent travelers who want to explore Crete's south coast from an inexpensive and comfortable resort. Unfortunately, the massive overbuilding of the past few years has managed to spoil Ayía Galíni's pretty port. We can't imagine coming here during the high season, when the place is a total zoo, but during the winter it more closely resembles the traditional village it once was.

ESSENTIALS

VISITOR INFORMATION   The knowledgeable staff at the **Candia Tours** office (☎ **0832/91-278,** or 081/226-168 in Iráklio; fax 0832/91-174), open daily from 8:30am to 1pm and 5 to 9pm, rents cars, exchanges money, and offers trips to all of Crete's outstanding sights. Day trips include a visit to the Samariá Gorge for a hike (10,000 Drs/$41.65), several cruises to nearby Libyan Sea beaches, a tour to the Minoan palace at Phestós, the ruins at Górtyn, and the beach at Mátala (5,000 Drs/$20.85).

ORIENTATION   The steep hill overlooking the port is tiered with hotels, and from the plusher ones there are fine views of the placid Libyan Sea. A switchback road leads steeply down through the town, and at the lowest level is **Fountain Square**—now a quiet pool—and the town **parking lot** and main **bus stop.** (Buses leave once daily at 8:30am for Iráklio, five times daily for Réthymno, and three times daily for Plakiás.) One lane above the fountain are the **post office** and **National Bank.** Pebble beaches are a short walk east around the point.

WHERE TO STAY

If you decide to stay, we recommend choosing a smaller hotel or rented room off to the side yet closer to the port; you'll still have a view, with less noise, and be a little closer to the action.

The 11-room **Hotel Selena,** 740 56 Ayía Galíni (☎ **0832/91-237**), has spotless doubles, nearly all with tubs as well as showers in the bath, and an excellent view from the common breakfast terrace; prices run 7,900 Drs ($32.90) for two, including a hearty breakfast. It's managed by the friendly Eleni Mavroyioryi (a former English teacher) and is open year-round.

Nearby, the nautical-style **Ariston Pension** (☎ **0832/91-285,** or 0832/91-122 in the Ariston Taverna), where Helen Mougarakis runs a tidy ship, has five spic-'n'-span doubles with bath for 6,700 Drs ($27.90). Helen's mother runs a budget alternative: the **Acropol** (☎ **0832/91-234**), which has doubles without bath for 4,500 Drs ($18.75); showers are 700 Drs ($2.90) extra.

The **Dedalos** (☎ **0832/91-214**) and the 12-room **Candia** (☎ **0832/91-359**) are both quiet, good-value hotels.

Camping Ayía Galíni, in an olive grove by the sea just 2 miles southeast of town (☎ **0832/91-386**), has 45 spaces, a restaurant, and a market.

WHERE TO EAT

In the cluttered pedestrian main street, the choice spot for pizzas and for good-value, tasty Greek dishes is the **Libya Sea;** try the **Thessaloníki** for good snacks. At **Bozos,** on the port, they serve a great Greek salad *(horiátiki saláta)* and many seafood dishes. The nearby **Whispers Bar** and **Jazz in Jazz Bar** are fairly priced and popular. **Sweet Bar** is the spot for Greek coffee and pastry while you pore over the *International Herald Tribune.* Among establishments open year-round are **To Steki** and the **Acropol.**

The tiny **Onar Taverna** has a narrow stairway entrance off the main street; its three-story perch above two other less distinctive cafes offers great vistas, and its small menu offers carefully prepared food.

For dancing after dinner, try the loud disco **Soroco Le Club,** on the beach, and the **Disco Juke Box,** both open nightly from 9:30pm.

5 Réthymno

The port of Réthymno, dominated by the impressive Venetian Fortezza (fortress) of 1574 on a peninsula at its western end, has retained more of a medieval flavor than Iráklio. Réthymno played a historic role as capital of the province under the Venetians and the Turks, and it carried on an active trade with the Orient. More recently it has become one of Crete's most stylish resorts.

If you're staying in Réthymno for a while, pick up the excellent book *Rethymno,* by A. Malagari and H. Stratidakis; it's sold at the comprehensive International Press bookstore, 1 block from the archaeological museum and Venizélou Street, open daily from 9am to 11pm.

ESSENTIALS

GETTING THERE & DEPARTING   Réthymno is on the northern coast 49 miles west of Iráklio, and it can be visited as a day trip from Iráklio or Haniá or it can serve as a lively and pleasant vacation base. **Buses** from Iráklio run daily every half hour from 5:30am to 8:30pm (cost 1,650 Drs/$6.90). There's also frequent bus service from Haniá (cost 1,500 Drs/$6.25).

The one-way **taxi** fare from Iráklio is 16,000 Drs ($66.65), and from Haniá, 11,000 Drs ($45.85). Every Sunday and Tuesday in high season there's an excursion ferry to Santoríni. Tickets are sold by several travel agents.

VISITOR INFORMATION   The **Greek Tourist Organization (EOT)** is on Venizélou Street along the public beach (☎ **0831/229-148;** fax 0831/56-350), open Monday to Friday from 8:30am to 8pm and Saturday and Sunday from 8:30am to 2pm.

The **tourist police** (☎ **0831/28-156**) are in the same building on Venizélou Street as the EOT, open daily from 7am to 10pm.

The excellent **Creta Travel Bureau,** Odós Venizélou 3 (☎ **0831/22-915**), offers day trips to Iráklio's archaeological museum and the palace of Knossós for 13,800 Drs ($57.50), as well as to most other sites of tourist interest on Crete. **Adamis Tours,** Odós Giaboudáki 9 (☎ **831/25-073**), offers excursions to the Samariá Gorge for 9,200 Drs ($38.35).

ORIENTATION   The **old quarter** of the city, surrounding the **Fortezza** and bordered by the rocky sea coast, consists mostly of two-story stucco houses, whose Turkish wooden balconies shade narrow, twisting lanes. Small, typical churches, *kafenía* (coffeehouses) filled with locals, flowering vines, and nesting sparrows crowd this tranquil quarter. The two small **museums** that record Réthymno's intriguing history are both in this area.

To the east is the **Customs House** on Neárchos Street, as well as the charming **Old Harbor.** From the Old Harbor, the main commercial waterfront road broadens to become **Venizélou Street,** along which the government has created a pleasant sandy beach. **Arkadíou Street** runs parallel to the waterfront, 1 block in. Most small hotels, rooms to rent, and shops are located on Arkadíou between the old port and the newly built jetty that marks the beginning of Réthymno's startlingly modern apartment and beach hotel row.

The main east-west street is **Koundouríotou,** which passes through **Platía Mártyron** (Martyr's Square) and on the north side of the **Public Garden,** where the name changes to Igoúm Gavríl.

GETTING AROUND   The **bus station,** on Perifériakos Street on the west side of town (☎ **0831/22-212**), has daily buses every half hour to Iráklio and Haniá between 5:30am and 7:30pm. The station is located 3 long blocks west of the Municipal Garden.

The **taxi station** is near the northeast corner of the Public Park; there's a stand opposite the tourist office.

FAST FACTS   The state **hospital** is on Trantallídou Street (☎ **0831/27-814**).

There's a self-service **laundry** next to the Youth Hostel on Tobázi Street, open Monday to Saturday from 8am to 8pm.

The **Olympic Airways office** is on Koumoundoúrou Street behind the city park (☎ **0831/27-353**).

There's an **OTE telecommunications** branch on Koundouríoti Street and a kiosk station on Venizélou Street. The main branch is open daily from 7:30am to midnight; the kiosk's hours are Monday to Saturday from 8am to 11:30pm and Sunday from 9am to 2pm and 5 to 10pm.

EXPLORING THE TOWN

Sightseers should start from the sheltered end of the harbor and turn left. A 4-minute walk up Paleológou Street will take you to the lovely 17th-century

Rimondi Fountain, also called Mégali Vrýssi. A block away is the **Neradzés Mosque,** with its minaret—one of the many signs of former Turkish occupation that give Réthymno so much color. There's also a fine mosque (now empty) near the Great Gate to the Fortezza. On Arkadíou Street is the early 17th-century **Venetian Loggia,** once used as a clearinghouse by local merchants. Near the Fortezza is the **archaeological museum** (☎ **0831/29-975**), open Tuesday to Sunday from 8:30am to 3pm; admission is 500 Drs ($2.10) for adults and free for students.

During the last half of July, go straight past the Neradzés Minaret to the well-groomed, flower-filled **Public Garden,** where the annual **wine festival** is held.

West of the Neradzés Mosque on Vernardou Street is the **Historical and Folk Art Museum,** a private collection of Cretan folk art that's well worth seeing. It's open Monday to Saturday from 9am to 1:30pm and 5:30 to 9pm; admission is 300 Drs ($1.25).

Now that you've had a land tour, return to the Venetian **Fortezza** for an aerial view. Its thick, low stone walls were built to deflect cannon fire. From its parapets you can see Réthymno and imagine what the Venetians saw nearly 400 years ago. Inside its 1,131 yards of wall are wells, the remains of a prison, a Greek Orthodox chapel, a mosque, and several small buildings. Open daily from 8:30am to 7pm; admission is 500 Drs ($2.10).

Shoppers will find lots of new kitsch in the touristy boutiques that line Arkadíou Street, but there are also fun handcrafts, gifts, and attractive, reasonably priced sportswear, especially up Soulíou Street. More fashionable European styles and imports can be found inland on Várda Kalleryí Street.

Hikers may want to contact the **Happy Walker,** Odós Tobázi 56 (☎ and fax **0831/52-920**), which offers daily guided hikes through various local areas. Horses are available at the **Riding Center,** Odós N. Phokás 39, Plataniás (☎ **0831/ 289-07**), southeast of town.

WHERE TO STAY

Réthymno has a wide range of accommodations in the busier new section of town by the sand beach, and just a handful in the more tranquil and picturesque old quarter by the Fortezza. Most accommodations are open only between April or May and October.

From the central taxi square in front of the Church of the Four Martyrs, go through the Porta Guora arch and take the first street on the right to reach the welcoming **Réthymnon Youth Hostel** at Odós Tobázi 4 (☎ **0831/22-848**), where you'll find 82 beds, plus 30 on the covered roof, for 1,600 Drs ($6.65); the hostel offers hot showers, three lounge areas, breakfast, and inexpensive snacks.

IN THE OLD QUARTER

The backstreets encircling the Fortezza—the city's prettiest area—hark back to the port's former days of glory under the Venetians. We'd spend our hotel money at an older lodging on the narrow twisting streets behind the Venetian port.

If you want to stay to the west of the new jetty (northeast of the Fortezza), along the rocky seaside coast road, there are many rooms to rent including the 14-room **Lefertis Pension,** Odós Plastíra 26 (☎ **0831/23-803**), where doubles run 7,500 to 8,000 Drs ($31.25 to $33.35). Another decent place is the nine-room **Kastro Hotel,** Odós Plastíra 15 (☎ **0831/24-973**), also overlooking the scruffy pebble beach, where doubles with breakfast cost 9,200 Drs ($38.35).

Pension Anna. Odós Yoryíou Kataháki 5, 741 00 Réthymno. ☎ **0831/25-586.** 7 rms, all with bath (shower). 6,900 Drs ($28.75) single or double; 8,000 Drs ($33.35) single or double with kitchen. No credit cards.

Flanking the steps leading to the Fortezza are two buff-colored, restored houses. On the right is Anna's family house and on the left is her inn, the Pension Anna. Some of the renovated rooms are equipped with small kitchenettes, while others have minifridges; all rooms are spotless.

Worth a Splurge

✪ **Fortezza Hotel.** Odós Melisínou 16, 741 00 Réthymno. ☎ **0831/55-551.** Fax 0831/54-073. 51 rms, all with bath; 3 suites. A/C TEL. 24,100 Drs ($100.40) single; 28,700 Drs ($119.60) double. Rates include breakfast. AE, DC, EURO, MC, V. Closed in winter.

The recently built Fortezza Hotel blends in admirably with its historic setting. The pink stucco, traditionally styled building has parquet marble floors, a large lounge off the lobby with a huge fireplace and TV, and a large pool surrounded by a private, tiled sun deck with snack bar. The rooms, decorated in contemporary pastel colors, are carpeted, spacious, and modern. Most have balconies overlooking the pool or Fortezza. To reserve rooms during high season, contact the hotel at least a month in advance.

IN THE HEART OF TOWN

The modern section of Réthymno is roughly the area south (inland) from the sandy beach. (The newest, most recently developed beachside strip to the east is usually booked by package tours, so we don't include it here.) Choose your hotel room carefully because the portside cafes and broad avenues of this busy city can be very noisy—day and night.

Hotel Minoa. Odós Arkadíou 62, 741 00 Réthymno. ☎ **0831/22-508.** 32 rms, all with bath (shower). MINIBAR TEL. 6,900 Drs ($28.75) single; 7,500 Drs ($31.25) double. No credit cards.

Turning your back to the fortress behind the marina, walk along Arkadíou Street; up the block you'll find one of the few older inns whose bright, creamy-colored rooms are spotlessly maintained. The family-based staff is helpful and hospitable. Twin rooms offer shared balconies.

Hotel Valari. Odós Koundouríotou 86-88, 741 00 Réthymno. ☎ **0831/22-236.** Fax 0831/29-368. 35 rms, all with bath. TEL. 11,500 Drs ($47.90) single; 16,000 Drs ($66.65) double. Rates include breakfast. No credit cards.

Our first choice here is the friendly Hotel Valari, 3 blocks inland from the tourist office. It's well maintained with fresh paint and carpeting in all rooms. Although all the rooms have balconies, we liked the back rooms, which overlook the small pool and snack bar. The Valari also has a roof garden where you can sunbathe and take in a view of the harbor.

Zania Hotel. Odós Pávlou 3, 741 00 Réthymno. ☎ **0831/28-169.** 5 rms, none with bath. TEL. 6,800 Drs ($28.35) single; 12,650 Drs ($52.70) double. No credit cards.

Near the Hotel Minoa is the captivating Zania Hotel, run by Foni Psarokalou. In excellent French, she'll describe the history of this 150-year-old house. The prices are high considering that a huge old bathroom must be shared with others, but the Zania's special qualities make it worthwhile.

Worth a Splurge

Kyma Beach Hotel. Platía Iróon, 741 00 Réthymno. ☎ **0831/55-503.** Fax 0831/27-746. 34 rms, all with bath (shower). A/C TV TEL. 19,000 Drs ($79.15) single; 23,000 Drs ($95.85) double. Rates negotiable in low season. Rates include breakfast. AE, EURO, MC, V.

If you're ready to splurge, this modern and stylish hotel is on Platía Iróon (Heroes' Square), on the beach east of the tourist office. You can't miss its contemporary Santa Fe–cum–art deco styling, or the broad white Japanese umbrellas that shade its chic, beachside Station Café. The rooms are small but very tasteful, with fridges, balconies, marble floors, and furnishings; some have loft beds and simple Greek watercolors on the walls. Room service is available, with a 10% surcharge. Reservations need to be made at least a week in advance.

WHERE TO EAT

Go through the arch of the Rimondi Fountain and turn right to find the best budget choice we know of, **Kyria Maria** (☎ 0831/29-078); here you can enjoy traditional Greek food while being serenaded by a couple of dozen songbirds; a vegetarian plate costs 900 Drs ($3.75); with meat it's 1,400 Drs ($5.85).

There are a few other notable spots in the Old Quarter. **Ovelistirion** is the name of Stelios's taverna on Theo. Arambatzoglou Street, just a block from the Fortezza's entrance. Its simple tables overlook the Orthodox Church of the Annunciation, which dominates the quiet square. Typical Greek dishes are served in the old style; fried calamari, rich moussaká, a country salad, and retsína will satisfy two for 3,500 Drs ($14.60).

Nearby at Odós Nikiphórou Foká 93 is the **Yermaniki Bakery** (☎ 0831/ 28-084), a traditional shop with brick ovens that turns out crusty loaves in the shape of chickens, baskets, geese, and rabbits, plus other prize-winning decorative baked goods. It's open daily from 8am to 3pm and 5 to 8pm.

On the sea side of the Fortezza, on the road leading to the Haniá Gate, is **Iliovasilirata,** an ouzerí popular with locals for its large variety of appetizers and the sunset view.

For desserts and snacks, there are several appealing but pricy seaside cafes and inexpensive souvláki and pizza places inland along Arkadíou Street.

Famagusta. Odós Plastíra 6. ☎ **0831/23-881.** Main courses 1,250–3,100 Drs ($5.20–$12.90). AE, DC, EURO, MC, V. Mon–Sat 9am–midnight. CRETAN/CONTINENTAL/CYPRIOT.

On the beach road between the harbor and the fortress is a perpetual favorite with a lovely view of the sea. Diners can enjoy various local specialties prepared in the Cretan style or sample Famagusta's expanding menu of continental dishes, including steaks and an assortment of pasta creations.

Restaurant Apostolis. Odós Kallirons Siganou 10. ☎ **0831/24-401.** Main courses 1,000–2,300 Drs ($4.20–$9.75). No credit cards. Daily 6am–11pm. TAVERNA.

This 60-year-old, family-run choice is the perfect spot for moussaká or beef stifádo. Just a 10- to 15-minute walk away from the tourist area in a quiet residential neighborhood, the Apostólis is completely unassuming, which is why it makes our short list of "real" places. The food is terrific, and Yóryios and Nikólaos are your friendly hosts.

RÉTHYMNO AFTER DARK

Luckily for pedestrians, traffic is barred from the harbor promenade at night, ensuring large sunset crowds for the evening *vólta*. Head east along the new port if you prefer splashier and more expensive evening entertainment or into the Old Quarter for more intimate spots, such as **Apple, Galero, Cinema,** and **Opera.** To find the best traditional Cretan music, continue along Paleológou past the Church of the Annunciation and along P. Koronéou to **Nikolaou Gounaki.** If you want to dance, look for the **Fortezza Disco,** at the old port, where the action peaks about 11:30pm; the cover charge of 1,200 Drs ($5) includes the first drink. The newer **Sound Motion,** on the newly constructed Beach Road, offers serious competition.

SIDE TRIPS FROM RÉTHYMNO

Among the most popular excursions for visitors who are in pretty good shape is the hike down the **Samariá Gorge,** the so-called "Grand Canyon of Europe." We've covered it more fully later in this chapter, but the gorge could be seen as a full-day trip from Réthymno; nearly every travel agent in town offers a trip there.

Other possible excursions from Réthymno include a visit 16 miles southeast to Crete's famous **Monastery of Arkádi**—a 16th-century Venetian work with a lovely rococo church. During the 1866 rebellion against the Turks, the monastery became a rebel stronghold and hundreds sought refuge here. When the Turks besieged the monastery and defeat was inevitable, the abbott Gabriel chose to ignite the monastery's powder magazine—killing 800 refugees and attacking soldiers—rather than surrender. Four daily buses go the monastery; the last returns to Réthymno at 4pm.

Another side trip is 19 miles south to the nearly perfect mountain village of **Spíli,** which was covered as a side trip from Iráklio in section 1 of this chapter. On the way you'll pass by the old church on the square in the village of **Arméni,** a pretty town filled with outspread fan cacti and dripping with bougainvillea.

If you're more adventurous, you may want to take a full-day trip or camping expedition to the coast due south of Réthymno. You can also stay overnight in Plakiás or the nearby mountain village of Mýrthios. Another option is to take a detour to the Préveli Monastery and Frangokástello.

PREVELI MONASTERY

This monastery has long been a stronghold of resistance against hostile armies. Its remarkable location, high on the rocks overlooking the blue Libyan Sea, is both remote and strategic. For the monks who live here it's a sanctuary of calm and beauty. For the Greek Resistance it was a base for counterattack against both the Turks and, during World War II, the Germans. Allied forces also took refuge here before they were evacuated from the coast during the Battle of Crete.

The monastery, built in 1836, contains several panels that were painted in the 1600s; a carved crest above the medieval marble fountain bears a Crusader cross. The monastery maintains a small museum that exhibits priests' vestments, religious symbols, and ornaments. It's open daily from sunrise to sunset. The sign at the gate says NO SHORTS.

The monastery also has a plaque commemorating the British, Australian, and New Zealand forces that took part in the Battle of Crete. The week of May 21 marks the anniversary of these events, and is duly noted by the people of Crete. Details of the battle are discussed in the book *Greece and Crete 1941,* by Christopher Buckley, published by the Efstathiádis Group of Athens.

To reach the monastery, take the infrequent Plakiás bus and get off at the intersection of the north-south road and the south-coast highway. It's a 2¹/₂-mile hike from there. You can also catch a caïque from Plakiás to Préveli (or "Palm" Beach) and hike up to the monastery, but be warned that this lovely beach has been sullied by campers and day-trippers and the path up to the monastery is a difficult scramble.

FRANGOKÁSTELLO

The impressive 14th-century Venetian Fortress of Frangokástello dominates a wide stretch of sandy coastline west of Plakiás. The fort is totally intact, with flowers growing inside and outside its massive walls. The worn sign of Saint Mark (the Lion of Venice) is still visible over the southern portal.

Buses run twice daily from Hóra Sfakía and once a day from Haniá to Frango-kástello, where you can get off at the castle.

Today the most compelling aspect of Frangokástello is its haunting legend, the story of Fata Morgana. In 1829, during the War of Independence, a small battalion of Greek soldiers was massacred by Turkish forces. Since that time local inhabitants swear that late at night when the sea is calm (at the end of May or September), a ghostly image of the gallant battalion appears hovering above the ocean. A coterie of young Greeks and foreigners return annually to camp out or stay at Frangokástello's pensions and await the visitation of the restless souls of the soldiers.

Tourist development elsewhere has made this once-mystical spot something of a miniresort, with a number of rooms to rent and apartment complexes along the south-coast highway. Their presence has diminished the power once radiated by this isolated, majestic fortress. Among the accommodations is **Apartments Castello,** Frangokástello, Sfakía (☎ **0825/92-068**), an 11-unit complex where tidy and taste-fully furnished apartments with kitchenettes rent for 9,000 Drs ($37.50) for two and 17,000 Drs ($70.85) for four; Diners Club and Visa are accepted. **Mr. Yannarakis** rents eight rooms attached to his taverna (☎ **0825/92-137**) on the bluff above the beach, 100 yards from the castle, where doubles cost 7,500 Drs ($31.25).

PLAKIÁS

Plakiás is a burgeoning south-coast fishing town whose attractive sand-and-pebble beach and year-round warm water have been discovered by travelers (especially charter groups). It's still a fine place for those who enjoy hiking and climbing over rocks. On the far left side of the beach is a series of caves, and on either side of the cove are many more isolated beaches.

Essentials

Getting to Plakiás is a snap during the high season and a chore during off-season. There are eight **buses** a day from Réthymno to Plakiás and two a day from Sfakía. The roadway from Réthymno (23 miles north) winds up and down hills until just a few miles outside of town, and the more scenic bus route passes through the rug-ged but beautiful Kourtaliótiko Gorge and the lovely mountain village of Mýrthios, where there are a few rooms to rent, a good youth hostel, and a couple of tavernas.

Plakiás has a **mobile post office,** open Monday to Saturday from 8:30am to 2pm and Sunday from 9am to 1pm, which also changes money. There's also a moped dealer, supermarket, several minimarkets, some souvenir and sunblock shops, and a self-service laundrette (☎ **0832/31-471**), open daily except Sunday, where you can wash and dry a load for 2,000 Drs ($8.35).

Where to Stay

Since the completion of new roads from Réthymno to the north, and from Sfakía (Hóra Sfakía) to the west, Plakiás has developed at a rapid pace but with some plan-ning. The dozens of two-story pensions that have sprung up along its beach and on a newly built back lane are supported by European tour operators who buy out their rooms from mid-June to September.

Off-season is the best time to visit, because prices are lower in the few older ho-tels, in the rooms to rent above the small row of storefronts, and in the newly built pensions.

There are lots of rooms to rent, with doubles for 6,000 to 9,000 Drs ($20.85 to $33.35), depending on the season. Our favorites are on the far northwestern end of Plakiás, beyond the main strip. We especially liked the **Aponimos Rooms** (☎ **0832/28-813**) and the next-door **Rooms on the Rocks** (no telephone), a handful of doubles above two tavernas; ask for the top-floor rooms that rent for 9,000 Drs

($37.50) and come with extra-large balconies and terrific views. Back in town is the lively 27-room Class C **Hotel Lamon** (☎ **0832/31-279;** fax 0832/31-424), next to the Candia Tours office on the waterfront; basic doubles with breakfast run 8,600 Drs ($35.85). A second choice is the 16-room **Hotel Livykon** (☎ **0832/31-216**), where clean, Spartan doubles cost 8,600 Drs ($35.85).

The new, secluded **Plakias Youth Hostel,** a 5-minute walk from the beach, is one of the best on Crete. It has 80 beds (1,125 Drs/$4.70), a very nice bathroom with handwashing facilities, mosquito screens, a snack bar, and a volleyball court.

Alianthos Beach Hotel. Áyios Vassílios, 740 60 Plakiás. ☎ **0832/31-280.** Fax 0832/31-282. 150 rms, all with bath (shower). TEL. 9,700 Drs ($40.40) single; 14,800 Drs ($61.65) double. Rates include breakfast. AE, DC, EURO, MC, V.

The fanciest choice has large, bright rooms, their balconies dripping with geraniums, overlooking the central part of the cove. Newer rooms, behind the original building, face the interior. The large pool and sun deck, small children's pool, and TV lounge make it perfect for kids who tire of frolicking on the beach across the road.

Flisvos Hotel. 740 60 Plakiás. ☎ **0832/31-421.** 11 rms, all with bath (shower). 6,500 Drs ($27.10) single; 8,600 Drs ($35.85) double. No credit cards.

When we last visited the Flisvos, this sparkling-white inn was still the cleanest place in town and the management was the friendliest. There's also a good snack bar downstairs.

Where to Eat

Petit Plakiás has a large number of restaurants, many of which are snack/toast/cafe bars, but you can still find some places that serve excellent, locally caught seafood. The best among them is the **Sofía Grill,** near the middle of the *paralía,* where tender, freshly grilled octopus, a large *horiátiki saláta* with Crete's famous tomatoes, and a glass of the local rosé will cost about 3,000 Drs ($12.50). Next door, the **Corali Restaurant,** another year-round place with similar prices, is popular with Plakiasotis.

The **Taverna Christos,** on the west side of the port at the caïque harbor, is another of our favorites. Two can eat hearty portions of moussaká, stuffed vegetables, or pastítsio, prepared with that special Cretan flair, for under 4,000 Drs ($16.65).

Plakiás has a few inexpensive choices left, which are frequented by the locals. **Platia** is an overgrown souvláki stand that's both good and cheap and thus very popular. If you're up for an evening walk, hike to Lefkóyia, the tiny village 3 miles east of Plakiás, and try the **Stelios Taverna,** where Greek specialties are delicious and affordable.

Plakiás After Dark

The cafes on the central part of the beach alternate between bars that fill up at sunset (such as **Ostrako**), and the hip late-night cafes that serve drinks, ice cream, and popular music. The high-tech gray, pink, and mirrored **Swing** is, as of our last visit, still the most popular.

Night owls should try the **Meltémi Dance Club,** on the road leading into town, or the **Hexagon,** behind the cafeteria of the same name.

6 Haniá (Chaniá) & the Southwest Coast

The city of Haniá bears the stamp of its Renaissance-era Venetian occupants more than any other city on Crete. Narrow streets with 600-year-old slender wood-and-stone houses still grace the old city, and thick stone walls fortify the small, secluded harbor. A solitary lighthouse stands watch at the point across from the narrow entrance to the port.

Today vestiges of Venetian rule can be seen around the port, its fortifying walls, and the graceful stone mansions that tower over the narrow-paved lanes of the Old Quarter. The best hotels, restaurants, and shops are found here.

Surrounding the historic Venetian center of Haniá is a modern vibrant city. As with Iráklio, many areas are of little interest to visitors (for example, busy market sections with trucks bringing produce in and out amid the endless buzzing of motorbikes and compact cars). Haniá's popularity as a group-tour destination has greatly diminished the appeal of the newer city surrounding this quarter.

We strongly recommend that you try to visit this picturesque and intriguing city off-season, the best time to find rooms in one of the lovely restored mansions of the Old Quarter and to experience the charms of a bygone era.

ESSENTIALS

GETTING THERE & DEPARTING **By Plane** Olympic Airways flies to Haniá from Athens at least three times daily in the high season. There's also a weekly flight from Thessaloníki.

Olympic Airways, Odós Tzanakáki 88 (☎ **0821/57-701**), offers bus service 90 minutes before departure time from its office to the Haniá airport; the cost is 600 Drs ($2.50).

By Ferry Ferry tickets for the nightly Piraeus boats departing from Soúda (15 minutes from the market by bus) are sold by several travel agents for 5,900 Drs ($24.60) for the 12-hour voyage. Tourist-class cabins cost 9,200 Drs ($38.35).

By Bus Buses depart from Iráklio and Réthymno for Haniá every half hour between 5:30am and 8:30pm; the fare is 3,100 Drs ($12.90) from Iráklio and 1,550 Drs ($6.45) from Réthymo.

VISITOR INFORMATION The helpful **Greek Tourist Organization (EOT)** office is just east of central Platía 1866 at Odós Kriári 40 (☎ **0821/92-943**), on the fourth floor, open Monday to Friday from 7:30am to 3pm. The **tourist police** are at Odós Kareskaïki 44 (☎ **0821/73-333**), a couple of blocks southeast of the EOT.

Stavros Paterakis and the helpful staff of **Spa Tours,** Odós Mihelidáki 10 (☎ **0821/57-444;** fax 0821/55-233), can take care of all your tour and travel needs. You can also make travel arrangements through **Interkreta,** Odós Kanevaro 9 (☎ **0821/27-221**).

ORIENTATION The **bus station** is on Kydonías Street, southwest of **Platía 1866.** From the north end of this central square, **Hálidon Street** leads north toward the **Venetian Harbor,** past the **Schiavo Bastion** on the left, the **cathedral** on the right, and the **archaeology museum** on the left, to **Platía Sindriváni** (Fountain Square), also known as Harbor Square, and the **Tzamasi Mosque.**

Turning left from the north end of the central square, Platía 1866, **Yianári Street** will take you east to the **Central Market.** Turning right at the National Bank onto **Tzanakáki Street** will take you past the post office and OTE to the **Public Garden.**

GETTING AROUND Haniá is definitely a walking town and nearly everything you'll want to explore is within a fairly small area. If you plan to visit something nearby, there are lots of taxis available.

FAST FACTS The **post office,** open Monday to Friday from 8am to 8pm, is south of the market on Tzanakáki Street. There's a **laundry** at Odós Kanevárou 38, north of the cathedral. The local **Haniá Hospital** is off Venizélou Street (☎ **0821/27-231**).

SEEING THE SIGHTS

Strolling around old Haniá should be the first activity for new arrivals, followed by some interesting shopping.

Begin by exploring the old cobbled **Venetian Harbor.** Behind the "white" **Tzamasi Mosque** (Mosque of the Janissaries) is **Kastélli,** the oldest part of the city, where you can glimpse the remains of several cultures, particularly the Venetian and Turkish. Turning right (east) along the harbor will bring you to the **Inner Harbor** and the **Venetian Arsenals** so often featured in photos of Haniá, now used as meeting and exhibition space. Across the harbor the **Lighthouse** and **San Salvatore** guard the entrance to the harbor. Farther east you'll find the remains of the eastern **Wall,** which is being reconstructed.

Turn and walk back around the harbor to the opposite rampart to visit the **Naval Museum of Crete** (☎ 0821/91-875), with interesting artifacts and displays chronicling the island's profound connection with the sea; open Tuesday to Sunday from 10am to 4pm (to 2pm November to April); admission is 400 Drs ($1.65) for adults and 250 Drs ($1.05) for students.

Make your way through the maze of charming streets back south along the still-imposing western **Wall.** The large round hill at the southwest corner of the Old City is the **Schiavou Bastion Schiavou** (Promahóna), constructed as a vantage point and damaged by recent erosion.

Eventually you'll find yourself on busy Odós Hálidon, a major commercial street, and near the harbor you'll find the **archaeological museum** (☎ 0821/90-334), with artifacts from the area. It's open Tuesday to Sunday from 8:30am to 3pm; admission is 500 Drs ($2.10) for adults, 400 Drs ($1.65) for seniors, and 300 Drs ($1.25) for students. A couple of streets behind it you'll find a ruined **synagogue,** waiting to be restored since the World War II German occupation. The **Catholic church,** with its pretty pink interior, is just south on Hálidon, and not far away across the street is the **Orthodox cathedral.**

Turn left after the cathedral on Odós Skridlóf, famous for its leather; a few blocks farther on you'll reach the large **Central Market,** built about a century ago in the shape of a Greek cross, which is well worth a visit and a good place to buy fresh produce and other food, as well as souvenirs. Going south and west from the market will take you into the modern commercial and official center. Going south and east along Odós Dimokratías will bring you to the lush **Municipal Garden,** begun in 1870, and the nearby stadium. Head north again to reach the **Venetian Rampart** or wander through the labyrinth of streets where you'll find no end to sights and delights, including several old churches and a minaret.

For **walking tours** of the area, contact Kosta Chronakis at the **Wander Team** (☎ 081/227-128; fax 081/224-392).

SHOPPING

There are dozens of souvenir and jewelry shops on the side streets off the old port, particularly on Hálidon Street up to Platía 1866, and along the pedestrian mall on Skridlóf Street. The **Haniá District Association of Traditional Handicraft,** Odós Afendoúli 14, has a cooperative store on Tobázi Street on the harbor, filled with the ceramics, paintings, and crafts of local artists. Next door are a few small souvenir shops with a collection of *máti,* those blue glass eyes thought to ward off evil.

Haniá also has an old **bronze and brass foundry** run by the metalsmith Apostolos Papadakis in a Turkish-style building at Odós Hálidon 35.

There's an incredible selection of old and antique Cretan blankets and kilims at Odós Angélou 5 (near the Naval Museum). **Kostas Liapakis** (☎ 0821/98-571) has some century-old embroideries and weavings from local dowries. Geometric patterns on rich backgrounds are quite stunning. Prices are high, but you'll certainly enjoy browsing. The shop is open daily from 9am to 8pm, and shipping is available; American Express, MasterCard, and Visa are accepted.

One of the coolest shops in Haniá is **Anatolia,** Odós Hálidon 5 (☎ 0821/41-218), run by Juliette and Patrick Fabre, a boutique specializing in Asian antique (and near-antique) jewelry, open Monday to Saturday from 10am to 9:30pm.

We particularly liked **Carmela,** next to Kostas Liapakis's rug shop (see above) at Odós Angélou 7 (☎ 0821/90-487). Carmela Iatropoulou has put together a stylish collection of contemporary (as well as a few older pieces) silver and gold jewelry and ceramics designed and made throughout Greece. She's open daily from 10am to 9:30pm; American Express, EuroCard, MasterCard, and Visa are accepted.

Across the street is the **Ornatus Jewellery Work Shop** at Odós Angélou 12 (☎ 0821/75-661), another interesting jewelry boutique, open daily from 10:30am to 11pm.

WHERE TO STAY

Haniá has a wonderful selection of hotels, many of which are converted 14th-century Venetian homes and boarding houses.

There are a couple of wonderful splurge choices reviewed below, but if you're running low on drachmas, try one of the several pensions housed in 600- to 700-year-old homes next to the Naval Museum on Angélou Street. A stay in any of these homes is enjoyable for the portside atmosphere, winding creaky stairs, and high, decorative ceilings. The one closest to the harbor is the **Meltémi** (no telephone), and it's followed by **Theresa, Ekati,** and **Stella** (☎ 0821/43-756). The **Theresa,** at no. 8 (☎ 0821/92-798), is by far the nicest (and most expensive); doubles go for about 10,800 Drs ($45), including shower and harbor views from the roof terrace. Expect to pay about 6,500 Drs ($27.10) for a double without private facilities at the other guest houses.

DOUBLES FOR LESS THAN 16,000 DRS ($67)

El Greco Hotel. Odós Theotokopoúlou 63, 731 31 Haniá. ☎ **0821/90-432.** Fax 0821/91-829. 25 rms, all with bath (shower). TEL. 8,500 Drs ($35.40) single; 11,400 Drs ($47.50) double. AE, MC, V.

Several readers have recommended this hotel on a quiet street behind the harbor next to the west Wall, and we're glad to say it's just as charming and friendly as they claimed. Some of the upper rooms even have good views.

Hotel Contessa. Odós Theofánous 15, 731 31 Haniá. ☎ **0821/98-565.** 6 rms, all with bath. TV TEL. 9,200 Drs ($38.35) single; 16,100 Drs ($67.10) double. Rates include breakfast. V.

To call the Hotel Contessa venerable would be an understatement. Housed in a 300-year-old Venetian-era home across the lane from the Amphora, with antiques decorating the lobby, it's dripping with Old-World elegance. A good value.

Maria Studios. Odós Áyios Phanouríou 189 (on the beach west of town), Kalamáki, 731 00 Haniá. ☎ **0821/31-870.** 7 rms, all with bath (shower). MINIBAR TEL. 12,000 Drs ($50) double; 13,500 Drs ($56.25) triple. No credit cards.

The friendly owners, Charlie and Maria, lived in Philadelphia for 15 years, so they speak excellent English. The place is relatively new, and each room includes a small

The Samariá Gorge: The Grand Canyon of Greece

The Samariá Gorge connects the small inland mountain hamlet of Omalós to the southern-coast beach town of Ayía Roúmeli. An 11-mile footpath leading through the narrow canyon is the only passage into or out of the area.

The rigorous hike takes about 4 to 5 hours. You don't have to be in mountaineer condition, but you should be in good shape with enough stamina to walk 11 miles. Don't imagine that "downhill all the way" means easy. Wear light hiking boots or sturdy shoes, and bring food for a picnic and a towel and swimsuit for a postdescent dip. (Reader Rochelle Schermer of Sacramento, California, writes that you really should have hiking boots and that the trek may take a whole day—6am to 8pm for her group.)

The trail begins at a well-marked entrance at Omalós—the *ksylóskalo* ("wooden stairs"). The path drops steeply for the first 2 miles with lots of switchbacks and loose stones. Good views of the gorge are available within less than a mile, so if you decide that the full trek isn't for you, you can still see the 654-yard drop to the bottom of the canyon. A multitude of wildflowers lines the path.

The trail continues to drop until it levels out at the deserted town of Samariá, 4¹/₂ miles into the gorge. The residents of Samariá were forced to leave in 1962 after the gorge was declared a national park. (No one is permitted to spend the night in the park.) They were relocated quite conveniently at the end of the trail (6¹/₂ miles away), where they now own and service the lucrative tourist concession. As at many points along the trail, there's an abundant supply of fresh mountain water.

The second segment of the journey is the real payoff. The trail finally hits the river bottom and then meanders through the rocky bed. The deep gorge becomes narrower and the water-eroded striations and patterns on the rocks and walls are exquisite. The river-cut trail passes through a chasm for about 2¹/₂ miles; then, in the more scenic part of the canyon, fast-running, turquoise-hued water suddenly emerges, enticing more than a few for a quick swim, but this is *strictly forbidden*. At

kitchenette and a shower. The Studios should be open during the off-season at prices about 30% less than in the summer.

WORTH A SPLURGE

✪ **Amphora Hotel.** Párados B. Theotokopoúlou 20, 731 31 Haniá. ☎ **0821/93-224.** Fax 0821/93-226. 20 rms, all with bath (8 with shower, 12 with tub). TEL. 16,675 Drs ($69.50) single; 23,000 Drs ($95.85) double. Rates include breakfast. EURO, MC, V.

The white-and-blue Amphora Hotel, behind the Amphora Restaurant on the east side of the Old Harbor, is a converted 600-year-old Venetian villa with unique rooms. Extremely high ceilings, French doors opening onto harbor views, simple furnishings, and modern private bathrooms grace each one. Room no. 7 is especially romantic, with its matrimonial bed, a single bed behind a curtain, and working fireplace. If you plan to come during the off-season, contact the hotel in advance.

✪ **Doma Hotel.** Odós Venizélou 124. 731 33 Haniá 73133. ☎ **0821/51-772.** Fax 0821/41-578. 28 rms, all with bath; 1 suite. A/C TEL. 17,250 Drs ($71.85) single; 25,300 Drs ($105.40) double; 52,300 Drs ($217.90) suite. Rates include breakfast. MC, V. Closed Dec–Mar.

All in all, the Doma is our favorite lodging on Crete. Housed in a stately neoclassical mansion, it's a converted family home on the edge of the Haleppa district on the

the end of the official park boundaries the gorge is only 9 feet wide and at its most dramatic. Thereafter the canyon widens, and $2^{1}/_{2}$ miles beyond leads to the great **black-pebble beach at Ayía Roúmeli** (see below). Cold drinks, restaurants (our favorite was the Taverna Tara; try the tasty dolmádes!), and the inviting water of the Libyan Sea make the end of this journey particularly pleasurable.

Although there are many conveniently packaged tours for visiting the Samariá Gorge, they all tend to be scheduled for the same time, thereby clogging the trail and forcing hikers to stay more or less in line instead of permitting everyone to experience the canyon. A better, and less costly, approach would be to stay overnight in Haniá and then take the early-morning (6:15am) public bus to Omalós. This will get you into the gorge well before the crowds descend. When we visited, there were three morning buses (at 6:15, 7:30, and 8:30am) leaving Haniá for the 1-hour trip. If you plan to stay overnight on the coast, ask for a one-way ticket. The gorge is normally open (depending on the weather) from April to October; there are many restrictions, including no camping and no singing.

If you enjoy the beach at Ayía Roúmeli after your hike through the gorge, you might want to stay overnight. There's the small **Ayia Roumeli Hotel** (☎ **0825/ 91-293**) and several Spartan and some newly constructed rooms to rent at the **Livikon, Tara, Stratos,** and **Kri-Kri guest houses.**

There's an even better **beach at Áyios Pávlos** (St. Paul), a 1-hour walk east. Simple, bathless, beach-shack doubles rent for about 4,000 Drs ($16.65), including the occasional hot shower.

The only way out of Ayía Roúmeli, short of hiking back, is the **Sofía Company** ferry to Hóra Sfakía. The ferries run six times a day between May and October, once daily in April, and cost 1,700 Drs ($7.10). The ferry makes a brief stop at Loutró, a small cove with lots of rooms, a beach, a few places to eat, and a few too many tourists for our taste. As always, check the schedule. Daily ferry service is also available to Paleohóra from April to October, costing 2,200 Drs ($9.15) each way.

east side of town. This elite 19th-century neighborhood is where the Greek statesman Elefthérios Venizélos lived and where many regal homes can still be seen. The owner and gracious proprietress, Ms. Irene ("Rena") Valyraki, has tastefully decorated the inn with family photos and heirlooms. We have yet to find such a comfortable space in any other lodging on Crete. The parlor is filled with distinctive Cretan embroideries, copper pots, and ancient marbles. The Doma's rooms are large, comfortable, and pleasant. (If you like to sleep with your windows open, choose a quieter back-facing room.) There's even laundry and room service.

A tiny elevator goes up to the homey third-floor dining room, where gourmet cuisine is served in full view of the Gulf of Haniá; be sure to take your breakfast here, since it easily ranks among the best we've had anywhere in Greece.

WHERE TO EAT

Haniá's lovely harbor has been somewhat overrun by ice-cream cafes and loud music bars, where visitors on package tours plus sailors from the nearby Greek and U.S. Navy bases congregate to have a good time. In the quieter spring and fall months it's a pleasant place to dine. We recommend the **Amphora Restaurant.**

Most of our favorites are set away from the central waterfront scene, in and around the quiet eastside residential neighborhood of Haleppa.

One of our favorite places is **Rudi's Beer House,** Odós Sífaka 24 (☎ **0821/ 50-824**)—recently discovered by the *New York Times*—where Rudi, a friendly Austrian, and his lovely Greek wife, Elpída, serve 58 kinds of beer and excellent snacks, including vegetarian dishes, at budget prices. We particularly like their tuna salad.

Nearby at Odós Sífaka 37 is **Anaplous** (☎ **0821/41-320**), the only vegetarian restaurant we know of on Crete; it also serves simple traditional food at uncommonly low prices.

Aeriko. Aktí Miaoúli and Odós Ípirou. ☎ **0821/59-307.** Reservations recommended. Main courses 1,100–2,900 Drs ($4.60–$12.10). V. Daily 6pm–1am. CRETAN/TAVERNA.

Aeriko is a well-designed waterside ouzerí/taverna that attracts a sophisticated Greek and European crowd. The owner, Stelio Blazakis, opened this attractive spot in 1990, and since then we've come to appreciate it for its fairly unusual Greek *mezédes* (appetizers), especially stuffed calamari and green peppers with cheese. Among the most popular dishes is pork with mushrooms, but we prefer the Cretan favorites such as lamb pie baked with cheese, *tirópita* with Cretan cheese.

Doma. Odós Venizélou 124. ☎ **0821/21-772.** Reservations required a day in advance. Main courses 1,800–4,400 Drs ($7.50–$18.35). MC, V. Daily 6:30–11pm. CRETAN.

The Doma is not only the city's top lodging alternative, it also has one of the most attractive dining rooms. Traditional Cretan cuisine is served home-style. Among the top dishes are an excellent Cretan-style cheese pie, marrows (zucchini) pie, lamb cooked with herbs in wine, and all the veal dishes. We also heartily recommend stopping here for an exceptional breakfast of freshly made yogurt, homemade quince jam, spices, dried fruit, and nuts.

✪**Thalasino Ayeri Fish Taverna.** Odós Viviláki 35, Haléppa. ☎ **0821/56-672.** Reservations recommended. Main courses 1,000–3,600 Drs ($4.15–$15). No credit cards. Daily 8:30pm–midnight. FISH/SEAFOOD.

Nektarios and Maria Lionaki opened "The Sea Breeze" in 1990; we made our first visit in 1991 and have enjoyed it ever since. The setting is both secluded and attractive, making it a wonderfully romantic escape from the in-center food outlets, and the fish is as fresh and as well prepared as you could hope for. There's also a limited menu for non–seafood eaters. (Take a HALÉPPA bus from the Market Square, get off at the Elefthérios Venizélou House, and ask the locals for additional directions; the taxi fare is only $2.50.)

To Karnayo. 8 Kateháki Sq. ☎ **0821/53-366.** Main courses 1,100–3,100 Drs ($4.60–$12.90); fish 9,000–10,000 Drs ($37.50–$41.65) per kilo. AE, EURO, MC, V. Daily 7am–midnight. CRETAN.

To Karnayo is a fine choice for authentic Cretan fare in a relatively tranquil environment. The grilled chicken, zucchini bourekis, and Cretan cheese pie smothered in local honey are sure to be as good. Your gregarious host Dimitris does his best to keep the food up to the highest level—using organically grown produce whenever possible—and he has succeeded on our visits.

HANIÁ AFTER DARK

Start by joining the evening *vólta* (stroll) along the harborfront. On the far east end of the Inner Harbor you'll find the area known as Dio Lux (after two old gas lamps that once stood there), where the local young people go to mingle.

Pyli, atop the Wall, is the bar with the most spectacular setting, a place to savor a drink to soft rock under trees and the stars. Across the Old Town near the Catholic church you'll find three somewhat more sophisticated places: **Ideon Andron** (after the cave where Zeus was born), Odós Hálidon 26, is probably the most inviting, but if it doesn't appeal to you, stroll around the block and check out **Anagenesis** ("Born Again") and **Babel** (no translation necessary, we hope). Midway along the harbor the **Ariadne Disco** is still holding its own against **Scala.** Jazz connoisseurs will want to visit **Fagotto,** favorite of the local artists and literati, on Odós Angélou near the Naval Museum. If a cold brew and conversation is more your speed, find **Rudi's Beer House** at Odos Sífaka 24.

The **Attikon II Cinema,** Odós Venizélou 118, plays American films in English in the open air June to September every night at 8:45 and 11pm; admission is 1,500 Drs ($6.25). In the summer the municipality sponsors **Kypos,** an open-air theater in the Public Garden.

SIDE TRIPS FROM HANIÁ

Among the most popular excursions is a full-day trek down the Samariá Gorge and back via Ayía Roúmeli. This is usually undertaken as a day trip and is covered in the box above.

Save some of that shopping money for a boat cruise around **Soúda Bay,** an evening barbecue and cruise, or a swimming excursion offered by **Domenico Tours,** Odós Kaneváro 10 (☎ 0821/53-262; fax 0821/53-262). Tours are 4,000 to 9,000 Drs ($16.65 to $37.50); check the office for more information.

Diktynna Travel, also on Kaneváro Street (☎ 0821/41-458), offers full-day Cretan craft tours for 8,000 Drs ($33.35) and walking tours of the Old Town for 3,500 Drs ($14.60).

Haniá's well-organized **taxi drivers** have published their own brochure advertising day trips to all of Crete's major sites. Call them at ☎ 0821/98-700 or 0821/98-701 for information and fares. The most popular excursion from Haniá is a hike through Europe's largest canyon to the south coast of Crete.

The prefecture of Haniá is the least developed part of Crete, because of its poor infrastructure. The snow-capped inland mountain ranges, fertile valleys, and startling palisades that tumble into the navy-blue Mediterranean make it impossible to link the isolated beaches and villages to the national highway system. To reach most of the west's idyllic beaches takes time, patience, a boat or Jeep, or an invigorating hike through the Samariá Gorge (see above).

We were tipped off about a detour to **Élos,** on the road that connects Kastélli to Paleohóra. This tiny mountain gem is little more than a bakery, taverna, and a few houses, but, oh, does it feel like a timeless place! We know that it's pretty far out of the way and that you'll likely pass it by, but if you despair about the commercialization of Crete or the insanity of its resorts and overly developed cities, take the time to visit Élos. If you're there in late September or early October, you'll probably catch the chestnut harvest.

HÓRA SFAKÍA (CHÓRA SFAKÍON)

Hóra Sfakía has become one of the most popular south-coast beach towns, both because it's the bus departure point for the popular Samariá Gorge trek and because it's linked by a paved road to the north-coast highway at the yogurt capital, Vrýssi. Do stop for a lovely plate of the village specialty (750 Drs/$3.15).

After a long hot walk, it's easy to become enchanted with Sfakía's diminutive gray pebble beach lying idly below the tour-bus parking lot.

There are still some days (though certainly not from June to September) when Hóra Sfakía can be a great place to get away from it all. But such a privileged location unfortunately subjects the tiny village to the mad crush of exhausted tourists who arrive between 3 and 7pm each evening to meet return buses—we counted more than 50 on our last visit!—after having hiked the 11 miles through the Samariá Gorge and taken a boat from Ayía Roúmeli. In addition to those who come by bus from Iráklio, many hikers passing through decide to stay, which puts a strain on the tiny town. The town tends to be jammed until about 7pm, when most visitors depart for Haniá and points north; then Sfakía returns to a semblance of calm until early the next afternoon when the parade begins anew.

If you take any of the local caïque trips to Sweetwater Beach or to the tranquil island of Gávdos, you'll find their more natural state a stark contrast to the whitewashed *domátia* that are creeping up Sfakía's steep hillside.

Essentials

There is **bus** service to and from Haniá five times daily, and twice daily to Plakiás via Frangokástello. The 2-hour bus trip to Haniá costs 1,500 Drs ($6.25). There's **boat** service to Loutró, Ayía Roúmeli, Soúyia, Paleohóra, and Elefonísi.

The **police station** is on Odós 25 Martíou, which is also the town bus parking lot. A **post office** that exchanges money is open Monday to Friday from 7:30am to 8pm, Saturday from 7:30am to 2pm, and Sunday from 9am to 1:30pm. There are some souvenir shops, a moped dealer, a bakery, and a market on the skinny lane behind the main coast street; the **OTE** is on the *platía*. Taxis are available for local transport.

We must issue a *warning about wind:* When we were there in September, a veritable gale spoiled our hope for a tranquil beach day.

Where to Stay & Eat

The 34-room **Hotel Stavris** is on a quiet lane above the port (☎ **0825/91-220;** fax 0825/911-52); clean doubles with a private shower and balcony cost 7,500 Drs ($31.25). The Perákis brothers also run a traditional *kafeníon* downstairs. Doubles at the 12-room **Xenia Hotel,** on the west side of the harbor (☎ **0825/91-238**), cost 9,200 Drs ($38.35).

Rental rooms are available above the tavernas and up the hillside along the road out of town, where you'll also be able to enjoy superb views out over the Libyan Sea; they generally run 4,000 to 7,500 Drs ($16.65 to $31.25) for a double, usually with a private bath.

For dining, we preferred **Limani,** on the west end of the port (next to the Xenia), and on the east side, **Samariá.** The grilled fish is delicious, if rather expensive, but fish fetches a premium everywhere now that many fishermen have turned their caïques into "buses" for coastal day trips. These two normally alternate staying open during the winter months.

LOUTRÓ

If Sfakía's trekker-bus scene is too busy for you, jump on one of the caïques to Loutró, a just slightly sleepier port west along the coast. It's a good destination for those who seek unsanctioned camping in the many nooks and crannies of this lovely coast.

This fast-growing fishing village is connected by a terrible winding road to Hóra Sfakía, and by the **Sofía Company**'s caïque shuttle (480 Drs/$2) that runs seven times daily in the summer between the busier ports of Ayía Roúmeli to the west and Hóra Sfakía to the east. Like its sibling ports, Loutró has a few hundred inexpensive rooms to rent and a few tavernas; expect to pay 5,000 to 8,500 Drs ($20.85 to $35.40) for a double with private facilities.

Loutró's fine, small **beach** is named Phiníkia after the nearby ancient Phoenician city, though the local Turkish-era castle is a much better preserved historic site.

7 Western Crete

On our last visit Crete's west coast, west and south of Haniá, was taking the heat of new resort development. Since the north-coast highway would collapse under the weight of any further construction to the east, small developers fueled by European tour operators have set their sights farther west.

KASTÉLLI (KÍSSAMOS)

Modern-day Kastélli is built on the site of the ancient city of Kíssamos. ("Kastélli Kissámou" was an earlier name for the town; Kíssamos is now its official name, in deference to another Kastélli southeast of Iráklio—though locals still call it Kastélli, which also refers to the area.) Today Kastélli-Kíssamos, as you'll often see it on ferry schedules, retains that lazy seaside feeling of a charmless port that receives only two big steamers per week. A rush of backpackers from the Peloponnese briefly descends on the small main square, but then most catch the first bus to other beaches or urban centers.

ESSENTIALS

Kastélli has a **post office,** where you can exchange money, a bank, and some shops on the main square where the privately run KTEL buses arrive. About 50 yards off the northeast corner of the main square toward the water is another smaller square with a fountain where you'll find a couple of travel agencies, a hotel, a restaurant, a **cafe,** a news kiosk, and a bakery. During our last visit the office of **Manólis Xirouchákis** (☎ **0822/22-655**) sold tickets for the Minoan Lines and rented bicycles, while two doors north the **Iris Travel Agency** (☎/fax **0822/23-606**) sold tickets for Anek Lines and rented cars.

If you'd like to purchase a ferry ticket to the Peloponnese—Kalamáta (three times a week), Yíthio (twice a week), Kýthira (three times a week), Antikýthira (three times a week), or Neópoli (twice a week)—go about 100 yards east (left) of the fountain square to **Horeftakis Tours** (☎ **0822/23-250**).

EXPLORING THE AREA: THE BEACHES & BEYOND

East of Kastélli, the narrow, winding, but well-paved road leads north to Kolymbári, 12 miles away. Here is a small pottery school for the preservation of traditional Cretan arts, the Orthodox Academy of Crete for religious training, and the Monastery of Goniá, a lovely 17th-century Venetian-style building.

Beach seekers should head 7 miles south of Kastélli to **Plátanos,** a village with access to the beach (some say this is Crete's best) at **Fallasárna;** locals advised us that it's best appreciated from April to June and in late September. The ruins of an ancient city are here, as well as some tavernas, a few rooms to rent, some tar washed up from passing steamers, and a long, stretch of rocks, pebbles, and fine sand. It's isolated enough so that nude swimming is tolerated. However, it does get many adventurous visitors in the summer season who frequently leave their camping litter behind.

Returning to Plátanos and continuing south, you'll find another remote beach enclave in tiny **Sfinári,** where there are a few rooms to rent. Heading south on this dizzyingly curvaceous north-south road, you pass a few inland villages and come to a fork in the road. If you bear east (left), the road connects to the slightly wider route to the very popular Paleohóra.

WHERE TO STAY & EAT

The small but very pleasant 11-room **Castell Hotel** (☎ 0822/22-141), run by the knowledgeable Michális Xirouchákis, is on the fountain square. Large, comfortable doubles with balconies and private showers cost 6,850 Drs ($28.50). There's a good unnamed restaurant next door.

The rocky but long and quiet beach is a 5-minute walk from town through cultivated fields. There you'll find several rooms to rent and more under construction.

A recommended fish taverna, **Stimadoris** (☎ 0822/22-057), named for its owner, is located just before you reach the small fishing harbor, less than a mile west of the town; it's open daily for lunch and dinner.

PALEOHÓRA (PALAIOCHÓRA)

This once-quiet fishing village was just another mystery stop on the Sofía Company's south-coast caïque shuttle, a route used primarily for traveling between Ayía Roúmeli and Hóra Sfakía. Now that Paleohóra is also connected by the picturesque but winding road to the north-coast highway, there has been new development and many big changes.

There are now enough visitors to justify the caïques for hire that make day trips to the ancient city of **Lissós,** where you can see the ruins of some houses, a theater, faded mosaics, government buildings, a partially excavated temple of healing, and an Asclepion. There's also a small, quiet, and clean **beach** that you'll enjoy if you visit when the boats aren't running—plan on a 1½-hour hike.

ESSENTIALS

GETTING THERE & DEPARTING   In the summer there are six **buses** daily between Paleohóra and Haniá, 48 miles (2 hours) to the northeast. Another bus makes a 3-hour run between Paleohóra and Haniá via Omalós (the entrance to the Samariá Gorge). The **Sofía Company** boats run daily in the summertime from Ayía Roúmeli, at a cost of 1,900 Drs ($7.90), as well as daily to Soúyia and Elafonísi.

VISITOR INFORMATION   A **Municipal Tourist Information Office** at Odós Venizélou 43, the main street (no telephone), is open May to October, daily from 9am to 2pm and 5 to 9pm.

Mrs. Vou Politopoulou at **Interkreta,** Odós Kontekaki 4 (☎ 0823/41-393; fax 0823/41-050), books rooms and hotels; sells air, boat, and bus tickets; and offers a Samariá Gorge day trip for 6,000 Drs ($25) three times a week.

FAST FACTS   The **National Bank of Greece,** at Odós Venizélou 51, is open during the usual banking hours. A **health clinic** is open Monday to Friday from 8:30am to 2:30pm and 5:30 to 9pm, and for emergencies at other times. The **post office,** beyond the school on the west side of town, open Monday to Saturday from 7:30am to 2pm and Sunday from 9am to 1:30pm, exchanges money. A **movie theater,** the Attikon, often shows films with English subtitles. **Taxis** can be reserved by calling ☎ 0823/41-140.

WHERE TO STAY & EAT

If you want to make Paleohóra your base (and a great many students and tie-dyed travelers do), plan to spend some time shopping around for your room. We found that many of the proprietors were grumpy and their places were pretty basic.

Among the best (and most expensive) hotels is the 50-room, beachfront-facing **Pal Beach Hotel,** 730 01 Paleohóra (☎ 0823/41-512); it offers simple doubles with private showers and air-conditioning for 16,400 Drs ($68.35), including breakfast.

A good midprice option is the very clean **Polydóros Hotel** (☎ **0823/41-068**), where doubles run 10,500 Drs ($43.75).

One of the best budget accommodations is the seven-room **Eleni** (no telephone; contact Interkreta at ☎ **0823/41-393**), where doubles cost a very reasonable 6,400 Drs ($26.65). If you have a sleeping bag, there's **Camping Paleohóra** (☎ **0823/41-120**), about a mile northeast of town.

The **Wave Restaurant,** a seaside restaurant run by a friendly bunch, offers a small menu but good food. The **Galaxy,** open daily from noon to 1am, is next to the post office on the sandy beach, and serves excellent fish. The **Third Eye,** near the Pal Beach Hotel, serves vegetarian food. For taverna fare, try the **Dionysos,** next to the National Bank. If you're in the mood for grilled lamb chops or souvláki, head over to **Akrogiali** by the stone beach.

OFF THE BEATEN TRACK
SOÚYIA (SOÚGIA)

A long hike or brief caïque ride will take you from Paleohóra to the port of Soúyia. A cistern, a tomb, and some house foundations provide evidence of the ancient city of Syia, which may have been a settlement of ancient visitors who were attracted by the long beaches, striated pebbles, and calm Libyan Sea.

Even at the height of summer the long pebble and smooth-black-stone beach is relatively free of crowds, and so Soúyia remains our favorite out-of-the-way beach resort on the southern coast.

The daily boat from Paleohóra costs 1,000 Drs ($4.15); there's twice-daily bus service to Haniá, taking 2¹/₂ hours and costing 1,350 Drs ($5.65).

Syia Travel, along the river (☎ **0823/41-198**), can arrange rooms, exchange money, and issue tickets; it's open Monday to Saturday from 8:30am to 12:30pm and 5 to 9pm.

The nine-room, well-kept **Pikilassos Pension** (☎ **0823/51-242**) offers doubles for 6,600 Drs ($27.50). The **Santa Irene** (☎ **0823/51-342**) has furnished apartments for 10,500 Drs ($43.75). There are several rooms to rent where you can stay for 4,000 to 6,000 Drs ($16.65 to $25) a day.

There are a couple of basic beachside tavernas—we like the **Galini Restaurant/ Bar**—where you can dine for about 2,400 Drs ($10) per person.

GÁVDOS

If Soúyia isn't remote enough, you can always catch a boat to the heavily wooded, sparsely populated island of Gávdos—the southernmost point in Europe—which is claimed to be the island where Calypso seduced Odysseus. There are rental rooms (which can be booked by Interkreta Travel), a few tavernas, a post office, a telephone center, a police officer, and even a doctor.

Gávdos can be reached year-round from Paleohóra on the post boat (Monday and Thursday, weather permitting); the 4-hour ride costs 2,800 Drs ($11.65). Between mid-April and mid-October there's service three times a week from Hóra Sfakiá and Ayía Roúmeli (both 2¹/₂ hours). Since the open Libyan Sea can get very rough, cancellations are common; check with Interkreta Travel.

CHRYSOSKALÍTISSAS

Another fabled destination is the **Monastery of Hrysoskalítissas** (Chrysoskalítissas), in the southwestern corner of the island, 3 miles north of Elafonísi (the bus to Elafonísi will stop here). The name "Golden Staircase" comes from the legend that one of the 90 steps leading up to this nunnery is made of solid gold. Dress modestly for your visit here, please.

ELAFONÍSI

Farther south on a very rough road you can wade out 100 yards through knee-deep water to Elafonísi ("Deer Island"), a once-deserted, pure-sand islet. Cretans say that here "the sun sets like on no other place on earth," and there's some buzz among Western backpackers. Unfortunately, campers and day-trippers have left a lot of trash there, and the place can get very crowded in summer. At other times it can be quite pleasant, but certainly not paradisiacal; there are some simple tavernas. Several tour operators offer weekly day trips to Elafonísi by bus from Haniá and Réthymno. About half of the 12-hour excursion is spent on a bus; if you take this trip, bring along enough food and water.

The Cyclades 9

Still spiraling around Délos, Greece's spiritual center in classical times, the Cyclades (Kykládes, "Circling Islands") are the best known and most popular of the Aegean islands. From an abstract white marble sculpture of a harpist carved nearly 4,000 years ago to the billowing sails of a windmill, snow-white village churches, brilliant blue sky, and a hammy pelican or two, the Cyclades are the quintessential Greek islands.

Mýkonos is known the world over for its extraordinary beaches, picture-postcard villages, and wild nightlife. It's a miracle that in spite of the island's continuous development so much of its original beauty and appeal survive. **Délos** is a short trip from Mýkonos. The entire island is a vast archaeological treasure; the French have been excavating the site for 100 years—and they're still at it.

Not touristy at all, **Sýros** is the administrative capital of the Cyclades, and its wealth is evidenced by the lavish neoclassical mansions that grace its port, Ermoúpolis. Another star in this chain of islands is **Páros**—a crowded destination with many of the same attractions as Mýkonos, including nightlife and excellent windsurfing. **Náxos,** the largest, most fertile and self-sufficient of the Cyclades, is directly across from Páros. Its mountains and steeply terraced villages make it one of the best islands for hiking and camping.

Íos is a party island—a popular hangout for American, British, and European students since the 1960s, with one of the best beaches in the country.

Santoríni is a super-touristy volcanic paradise complete with black-sand beaches, astonishing excavations, and donkeys that transport visitors up the switchback trail to the picturesque town of **Firá. Ía,** a restored village on the northern tip of Santoríni, offers a breathtaking view of the rest of the island and adjacent volcanos.

Each year Greeks in the tens of thousands descend on **Tínos** to visit the Church of the Panayía Evangelístria in hopes of receiving a cure or blessing. They keep Tínos quintessentially Greek.

It's hard to miss green **Ándros,** the Cyclades' second-largest island and the site of excellent archaeological and modern art museums (though little else). Even more overlooked by Americans are the western islands—**Sérifos, Sífnos, Mílos,** and **Folégandros**—which are ideal destinations for those who cherish a quieter beach and rural village life with fewer mopeds and postcard shops.

The Cyclades

Akrotíri ❼

Kamári Beach ❻

Kolymbíthres Beach ❸

Panayía
  Ekatondapyilianí ❹

Panayía
  Evangelístria ❶

Panayía Paraportianí
  Church ❷

Temple of Apollo ❺

Ferry Route ⚓ – – – – –

256

A SUGGESTED ITINERARY

If you have 1 week to see the Cyclades, here's a quick tour of the "greatest hits":

Days 1–3   Fly to Mýkonos from Athens (you can also get there from Crete or Rhodes). Sample the beaches, take a day trip to the archaeological site on the island of Délos, shop, see the museums, and enjoy the nightlife.

Day 4   Take the ferry to Páros, find accommodations in Parikía, sightsee, and spend the evening in the agorá.

Day 5   Head to Páros's north-coast beaches and dine in Náoussa.

Day 6   Take the ferry from Parikía to Santoríni; visit the site of Akrotíri and swim/dine at Kamári beach.

Day 7   Shop and sightsee in Firá, visit the coastal village of Ía, and return to Firá for sunset and an evening meal. Fly back to Athens tonight or in the morning.

1 Mýkonos

96 nautical miles E of Piraeus

Nearly everyone planning a trip to Greece dreams of visiting Mýkonos—an island of universal appeal. It's the most accessible, but also the most expensive of the Greek islands. Its special blend of simple and sophisticated pleasures attracts a wide range of visitors. Whether you've come to see or be seen, Mýkonos is a delightful introduction to the latest trends in Greek fashion, music, and lifestyles.

Even after years of popularity, the island's unique gifts remain unspoiled. The five bold-white windmills that have greeted rock stars and prime ministers for decades still dominate the harbor from their perch on Káto Mýli Hill.

ESSENTIALS

GETTNG THERE & DEPARTING   By Plane   Olympic Airways has 7 to 10 daily flights from Athens; 1 daily from Iráklio (Crete), Rhodes, and Santoríni; and 2 weekly to Híos, Lésvos, and Samós. It's often difficult to get a seat on planes that fly in and out of Mýkonos, so make your reservations early and reconfirm them with Olympic Airways in Athens (☎ 01/926-7251) or Mýkonos (☎ 0289/22-490).

By Boat   From Piraeus, the **Ventouris Lines** has at least 1 daily departure, usually at 8am; in the summer, a second, afternoon ship is added. Check schedules in Piraeus at ☎ 01/451-1311. There are daily ferryboat departures from Rafína on the **Strintzis Lines;** to check the schedule, call ☎ 0294/25-200.

Ferries leave daily from Mýkonos going to Ándros, Páros, Sýros, and Tínos; 5 to 7 times a week going to Íos, Náxos, and Santoríni; 4 times a week going to Iráklio, Crete; and twice a week to Ikaría, Sámos, Skíathos, Skýros, and Thessaloníki.

Check each travel agent's current schedule; most ferry tickets are not interchangeable among different ships. **Sea & Sky Travel** on Taxi Square (☎ 0289/22-853; fax 0289/24-753) represents the Strintzis Lines, the Flying Dolphins, Agapitos Lines, and the Sea Jet (2$^{1}/_{2}$ hours to Rafína). It also changes money at good rates, offers excursions to Délos, sells airline tickets, offers transportation to the airport, and can help you find accommodations. The **Veronis Agency,** on Taxi Square (☎ 0289/22-687; fax 0289/23-763), also offers information, safekeeping of baggage, and other services.

Hydrofoil (catamaran) service to Páros, Íos, Náxos, and Santoríni is still irregular. For schedules, call the Port Authority in Piraeus at ☎ 01/451-1311, in Rafína at ☎ 0294/23-300, or on Mýkonos at ☎ 0289/22-218.

VISITOR INFORMATION   The **Mýkonos Tourist Office** (☎ **0289/23-990**) is on the west side of the port near the excursion boats to Délos. There's also a desk at the airport during the summer. The free *Mýkonos Summertime* magazine contains lots of information.

The **tourist police** (☎ **0289/22-482**) are on the west side of the port near the excursion boats to Délos.

ORIENTATION   **Mýkonos town** (also called **Hóra**), the port, owes its special character to the whitewashed, cube-shaped houses, trimmed in every shade of blue, lining its narrow cobblestone streets. The twisting passages and alleyways of the village, constructed to thwart pirates, invariably bewilder visitors; however, on Mýkonos serendipity rewards those who are lost.

If you arrive by ferry, you'll dock at the modern, northern section of Mýkonos's small harbor. Most tourist services are located around the southern half of the port, to your right as you exit the boat. (If you arrive by Olympic Airways, its airport bus will drop you off at the bus station near its office.) Past the small, sandy town beach on your right, you'll find **Mandó Mavroyénous Square.** "Mavro" or **"Taxi Square"** is the town's taxi stand (☎ **0289/23-700** in season or 0289/22-400 in winter).

Continuing along the crescent-shaped harbor you'll see cafes and souvenir stands on your left and small fishing boats, beach shuttle caïques, and Délos excursion boats on the right. Ferryboat ticket agents and tour operators' offices are in the central section. Foreign newspapers and maps (the Mýkonos-Délos map published by Stamatis Bozinakis is especially good at 300 Drs/$1.70) can be purchased at nearby kiosks.

What Mykoniots call the "Main Street," narrow **Matoyánni** leads south off Taxi Square behind the churches. Like so many other streets in town, Matoyánni is jammed with chic bars, boutiques, cafes, and bakeries; if you pass Pierro's Bar, you'll know you're on the right road. The blue arrows labeled PLATÍS YIALÓS that run along Main Street lead to the beach bus station on Hóra's south side.

GETTING AROUND   One of Mýkonos town's greatest assets is the government decree that declared it an architectural landmark and prohibited all motorized traffic from its backstreets. There's only one way to get around the town—walking.

For the rest of the island, frequent and comfortable public transportation is by far the best value. Mýkonos has one of the best organized and most useful bus systems in the Greek islands; the buses run frequently and cost 200 to 800 Drs (85¢ to $3.35) one-way. There are two bus stations in Mýkonos town: the **north bus station,** near the middle of the harbor by the Leto Hotel, has buses leaving for Áyios Stéphanos beach, northwest-coast hotels, the inland village of Áno Méra, and the far east coast beaches at Elía, Kaló Livádi, and Kalafátis.

The **south bus station** is a 10-minute walk from the harbor—follow those helpful blue arrows on Main Street and you won't get lost—near the Olympic Airways office. From here buses leave for the airport, Áyios Ioánnis, Órnos, Psárou, and Platís Yialós. Schedules are posted, though subject to change, and buses usually leave when they're full. Ask your driver when buses will return from your destination. If you miss the last bus, you can always walk or call a taxi; cab rides cost about five times the one-way bus fare.

Caïques leave the town harbor every morning, weather permitting, for Super Paradise, Agári, and Elía beaches. You can also catch the bus to Platís Yialós, from which caïques run more frequently to Paradise, Super Paradise, Agári, and Elía. (In the high season caïque service is almost continuous, and there's service from Órnos.) Although there are posted departure times for the beach buses, they often leave as soon as they're full.

Mýkonos Town

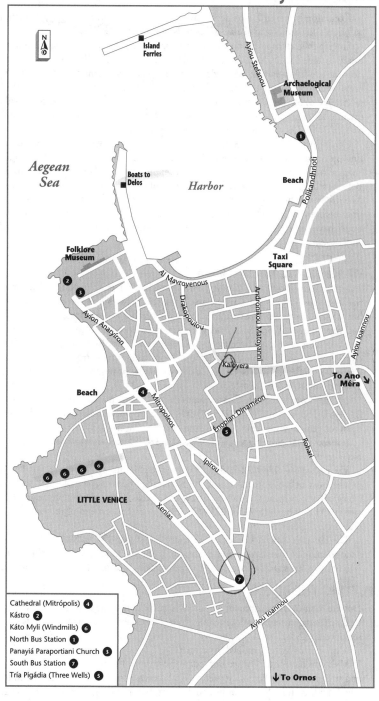

Island
Ferries

Ayíou Stefánou

Archaelogical
Museum

1

*Aegean
Sea*

Boats to
Delos

Harbor

Beach

Polikandhrióti

Folklore
Museum

Taxi
Square

2

3

Al Mavroyenous

Ayíon Anayíron

Drakopoúlou

Andronikou Matoyanní

Ayíou Ioannou

Kalpyéra

**To Ano
Méra**

Beach

4

Mitropóleos

Enóplan Dínameon

5

Rohari

Ipírou

6 **6** **6** **6**

LITTLE VENICE

Xenías

7

Ayíou Ioannou

Cathedral (Mitrópolis)	**4**
Kástro	**2**
Káto Myli (Windmills)	**6**
North Bus Station	**1**
Panayiá Paraportiani Church	**3**
South Bus Station	**7**
Tría Pigádia (Three Wells)	**5**

↓ To Ornos

Excursion boats to Délos depart from the west side of the harbor near the tourist office daily at 9am. (See a travel agent for more information.)

Since public transportation to the principal tourist sites is excellent, it's not necessary to spend your drachmas on renting a car. **Mountain bikes** are now available near the south bus station. **Mopeds** and **motorcycles** (too dangerous for the novice) are available at shops near either bus station. Expect to pay 3,700 to 6,400 Drs ($15.40 to $26.65) daily during the high season, depending on machine size. Explorers should gather in groups of four to rent a **Jeep,** available from travel agents for about 23,000 Drs ($95.85) per day, including full insurance.

Getting a **taxi** in Mýkonos town is easy; either walk to Mavro (Taxi) Square and line up or call ☎ **0289/23-700.** If you're outside town and call a taxi, you'll be charged from Mýkonos town to your pickup point, plus the fare to your destination. Before calling, try to find a taxi returning empty or flag one down along the road. The driver will be happy to make a few extra drachmas—be sure you know the set price before you take off, though. *Another budget tip:* Many of the posh out-of-town hotels have private shuttle service back to Mýkonos town. A friendly request to the concierge may get you a free ride.

FAST FACTS   The local **American Express** agent is Delia Travel, on the harbor (☎ **0289/22-322;** fax 0289/24-400).

If you need a **bank,** the Credit Bank is on Main Street. The National Bank is at the south bus station. The Credit Bank is midway between the harbor and the south bus station in the area of Limáni. All have ATMs that accept MasterCard and Visa, and they're open Monday to Friday from 8am to 2pm and 6 to 8:30pm. The National Bank is open only for currency exchange on Friday from 8am to 1pm, Saturday from 9am to 12:30pm and 5:30 to 8:30pm, and Sunday from 5:30 to 8:30pm. Traveler's checks can also be cashed at the post office, as well as at many tourist agencies and hotels, at less-than-bank rates.

The **Mýkonos Health Center** handles minor medical complaints (☎ **0289/ 23-944**). The **hospital** (☎ **0289/23-994**) offers 24-hour emergency service and is open for general visits from 9am to 1pm and 5 to 10pm.

International Newspapers (☎ **0289/23-316**) is near the church behind Sea & Sky Travel.

The **police** (☎ **0289/22-235**) are behind the grammar school above Tría Pigádia.

The **post office** is in Láka near the Mýkonos Market, open Monday to Friday from 7:30am to 2pm. You can cash traveler's checks here and get a pretty good rate.

The **OTE** phone office (☎ **0289/22-499**) is on the west end of the harbor, open daily from 7:30am to 10pm.

The **Hellenic Travel Center,** at the south bus station (☎ **0289/23-897**), offers a wide selection of special tours and excursions: a photo safari, an early-morning walking tour of town, an island bus tour, and 1-day excursions to Páros, Tínos, and Santoríni.

HITTING THE BEACH

Despite their overdevelopment and crowds, the island's gorgeous sandy beaches and fresh, clear water remain very inviting. The erratically shaped coastline offers several secluded stone-and-sand beaches; we'll review the better-known ones that are accessible on foot or by bus, moped, or caïque.

Mýkonos has learned to accommodate every type of tourist—family and solo, gay and straight, backpacker and jet-setter. Each beach attracts its own crowd with their own unwritten rules for wardrobe and conduct, but in the high season, anything goes anywhere.

NEAREST TO TOWN

Megáli Ámmos ("Big Sand") is a pleasant family beach about a 10-minute walk south of the south bus station; it's too accessible to the cruise-ship day-trippers even for consideration by those who want peace and quiet.

From the south bus station you can walk or catch a bus to **Áyios Ioánnis,** which has a small chapel and a lovely view of its bay, but the beach is small and rocky. The restaurants fill up at sunset, when romantics come for the splendid view. There are two other sand beaches accessible by poor-quality roads or on foot from Áyios Ioánnis: **Kapári,** to the north, and **Glyfádi,** on the southeast side of the peninsula, where you might find breathing room in summer.

You can also catch a bus or walk the 2 miles south to **Ornos Beach,** on calm and shallow Ornos Bay. Ornos is preferred by families and bathtub bathers who relish its still, tepid clean water. Ornos has a few fair tavernas, some overpriced rooms, and the **Lucky Divers Scuba Club** (☎ 0289/23-579), which offers lessons as well as daily dive excursions.

If you hop on a bus at the south station, you have a choice of several other beaches. From the waterfront bus stop you'll find **Psárou Beach** on your right, a popular family beach with diving, waterskiing and windsurfing facilities, and a water slide. To the left is busy **Platís Yialós,** lined with multicolored striped umbrellas, bright windsurfers, and a mixed bag of sun worshipers, including a few topless women.

Many visitors stepping off the ferry grab the nearest bus to the popular **Áyios Stéphanos,** 2 miles north of town. Unfortunately, this mediocre beach, crowded with guests from nearby hotels, isn't really worth the trip. Most water-sports facilities are available.

All these beaches are within a half-hour walk from Mýkonos town, but we wouldn't suggest that you attempt it in the midday heat of July and August. There's frequent transportation from the southside bus station. Buses to Ornos run hourly from 8am to 11pm and five or six times daily to Áyios Ióannis for 230 Drs (95¢). Buses to Platís Yalós and Psárou run every 15 minutes 8am to 8pm, then half-hourly until midnight, for 210 Drs (90¢). Buses to Áyios Stéphanos leave from the north station hourly from 8am to 10pm, for 240 Drs ($1).

AROUND THE ISLAND

From the Platís Yialós pier or, less frequently, from Ornos you can catch caïques to other beaches. Between 9:15am and 6:30pm brightly colored boats shuttle eager tourists back and forth to the pristine, fine-sand beaches of Paradise, Super Paradise, Agrári, and Elía.

As you'd expect, **Paradise** is crowded with blissful souls, mostly bared, who treasure its pure gold sand and crystal-clear water. This was the original nude beach, and today it's still where the action is and where the beautiful people look for each other, in addition to having an excellent taverna. **Super Paradise** is not quite as attainable, and so less crowded. The beach is predominantly gay and bare, and has a cafeteria-style taverna playing nonstop pop music. Clothed sunbathing by heterosexuals is tolerated, and some water sports are available. Across the little peninsula from Super Paradise is **Agrári,** a pretty cove with some green shade and a good little taverna, where all states of dress are found.

Paradise and Super Paradise are also accessible by road with private transport, though the road to Super, in particular, is of dubious quality. Paradise can be reached in a 30-minute hike from Platís Yialós. This walk is highly recommended to the lover of anonymous beaches, who will find many semiprivate niches along the way.

Apostolis Taverna, Áno Méra (☎ 71-760). "We visited Áno Méra instead of Délos because the death of the former prime minister stopped all boats. Found a wonderful eatery, with giant calamari at 1,200 Drs ($5), tomato and olive salad, better than Jersey's and only 500 Drs ($2.20), and stuffed tomatos and peppers. Ask for Apostolis."
—John Paul Basile, Philadelphia, Penn., and Cynthia Moore, Los Angeles, Calif.

Paránga is a tiny cove that's popular with nudists and usually not too crowded, with a large camping area nearby.

Caïques from Platís Yalós take about 45 minutes to get to ✪ **Elía Beach,** one of the largest and best pale-sand beaches. Bus service from the north station via Áno Méra is making it more crowded, but it remains pleasant, with two good tavernas and a new attraction, **Watermania** (☎ 0289/71-685), a huge hillside aquapark that draws funseekers from all over the island. From Mýkonos town free buses run daily from 10am to 9pm to this full-service resort, where constant disco rock, a minimarket, scuba school, bath shop, ouzerí, and more-than-adequate cafeteria entertain those taking a break from the water. There are two huge pools, great towering slides, hundreds of inflatables, boat rides, lockers, showers—you name it. Day-long admission is 3,500 Drs ($14.60) for adults, 1,750 Drs ($7.30) for children 6 to 12, and free for kids 5 and under.

If Elía becomes too busy, head back west to Agrári or scramble over the peninsula to the east to **Kaló Livádi** ("Good Pasture"), a beautiful beach with a good restaurant that has bus service from the north station in the summer.

The village of **Áno Méra** is worth a stop on the way to get a tan somewhere else. It's the transportation hub for the central, northern, and eastern parts of the island, with about 200 inhabitants and much of its original character. Once it was a community of farmers, but most now work in the booming construction trade. Besides the remains of a Venetian-era fortress, ancient ruins show that Áno Méra was once the ancient capital, with a harbor at Pánormos Bay.

Nearby is the **Tourlianí Monastery,** with a collection of baroque wood carvings, marble sculpture, and ecclesiastical vestments.

Around the Cape of Kalafáti is another long, sandy stretch. The beach that beckons sunbathers is actually near the port of the most ancient citadel of Mýkonos (about 2000 to 1600 B.C.), which crowned the peninsula between here and the Bay of Ayía Anna. **Kalafáti** is now dominated by a new citadel, the **Paradise Aphroditi Beach Hotel** (☎ 0289/71-367). A large pool, two restaurants, and 150 large rooms with balconies march down the gentle, rocky slope to the shore. May, June, and October rates are the best deal here, at 46,000 Drs ($191.65) for two, with breakfast. Buses run regularly to Kalafáti from the north bus station.

If you have more time and stamina, you might want to check out some of the lesser-known beaches around the island. Some of our recommendations require private transportation for access, and some, up to a few miles of walking from public bus stops.

West of Kalafáti is the little-known sand beach at **Ayía Anna,** reached by a terrible road off the paved road (due west of it) that leads to popular Kaló Livádi. East of Kalafáti, and reached by a direct, passable road, is **Lía Ammoudiá**—a favorite for its fine sand and small taverna.

The north-coast beaches get even smaller crowds because they're often buffeted by strong Aegean winds. If you take the bus to Áno Méra and get off at the road for the

Áyios Pandelímon Monastery, you'll be within 2 miles of **Pánormos,** a sand beach in the cove below the Áyios Sóstis church. About 2³/₄ miles east of town on the Áno Méra road is a Jeep-passable road to the north, and a half mile farther, a footpath that will put you within a 15-minute walk of **Ftelía** beach. Ftelía is excellent for wind-surfing because its recessed cove creates strong cross currents and its sandy sea bottom helps prevent accidents.

MORE TO SEE & DO

For a quick tour of ❂ **Mýkonos town,** walk up the main street, **Matoyánni.** Several "blocks" up you'll find a "major" crossroad, **Kaloyéra,** where a right turn will take you to several of the hotels we recommend. At the south end of Matoyánni, turn right on **Énoplon Dinaméon** (at the Vengera Bar), which leads through the neighborhood called **Tría Pigádia** ("Three Wells")—only 20 years ago they were the town's only water source—past the **Nautical Museum** and **Lena's House.** Turn right again on the first major street, **Mitropóleos,** and off to your right is the charming quarter known as **Little Venice.** (A left on Mitropóleos would take you to the neighborhood known as **Láka** and the south side of town.) Continue north a few blocks to the **Greek Orthodox cathedral** (Mitrópolis) and, on its right, the **Roman Catholic cathedral;** behind them are the famous windmills of **Káto Mýli,** which can be reached by a short climb.

If you continue north from the cathedral, you'll reach **Ayíon Anaryíron,** one of Mýkonos's best shopping lanes for artwork and handcrafts, and **Panayía Paraportianí** ("Our Lady of the Port"), the island's quintessential Cycladic church. Four small chapels have been joined into a whitewashed asymmetrical structure that has become a favorite of artists and photographers because of the endless variation of light and shadow playing over it. Just beyond it is the old Venetian **Kástro** and the **Folk Art Museum.** The harbor is only a few blocks back to the east.

On Mýkonos, a "What to See" section should be called "What to Do When It Rains." For those who are determined, there are a few nonhedonistic pursuits of interest. First and foremost, of course, is a day trip to the sacred island of **Délos,** a marvelous island/museum with vast archaeological ruins of great beauty and interest. This island site is so amazing and important that it's treated separately later in this chapter.

For those going to Délos, a visit to the archaeological museum may be of interest. The **Mýkonos Archaeological Museum,** northeast of the harbor across from the north bus station (☎ **0289/22-325**), has a lot of ceramic pieces (some dating from as early as 2500 B.C.), gravestones, and funerary jewelry from the island of Rhénia, and some interesting 6th-century B.C. Cycladic finds. It's open Tuesday to Sunday from 8:30am to 3pm; admission is 500 Drs ($2.10) for adults, 400 Drs ($1.65) for seniors, and 300 ($1.25) for students.

The lovely **Panayía Paraportianí** ("Our Lady of the Port") Church on the southwest side of the port is considered by architects around the world to be a superb example of the Cycladic style. The sloping, whitewashed stucco exterior is reminiscent of the sensual adobe churches of Taos, New Mexico. Hidden within its organically shaped walls are four small chapels, each of which is oriented toward a point on the compass. It's not uncommon to see artists of all ages sketching, painting, or maneuvering to photograph this Cycladic landmark. Don't leave until you've walked completely around this amazing building to see it from every angle.

Next to the church on the square is the **Folk Art Museum,** which has a fun collection of local handcrafts, furniture, silver figurines, and ship memorabilia. Outstanding in this large collection are some petrified bread samples, baked in braided shapes with red Easter eggs, and the wax life-size sailor who stands beside the huge

---

Cruising the Greek Islands

In 1995 more than 50,000 Americans cruised the Greek islands. The easiest way may be to island hop on a chartered yacht cruise; that way you don't have to worry about such things as hotel reservations and ferry connections. **Viking Star Cruises,** Odós Artemídos 1, Glyfáda, 166 74 Athens (☎ **800/341-3030** in the U.S. or 910/350-0100, or 01/898-0729 in Athens; fax 01/894-0952 in Athens or 910/791-9400 in North Carolina), can customize a tour through the Cyclades for groups, and often pair individual travelers with an organized group to reduce costs. Kyle and her family recently took the 7-day Aegean islands cruise aboard the charming but slightly funky *Viking Star.* We thought it was a great family value and relaxing holiday, with rates from $745 per person in a four-person cabin, including 2 nights in an Athens hotel, transfers, and a half-board meal plan on board. **Zeus Tours and Cruises** (☎ **800/447-5667** in the U.S. or 212/221-0006) offers cruises to the Cyclades and Dodecanese on a newly built, 18-cabin ship (starting at $1,750 per person) as well as on an older wooden ship (starting at $790 per person in a four-bunk lower cabin).

---

model of a warship from 1821. This museum is open Monday to Saturday from 5:30 to 8:30pm; admission is free.

The **Aegean Maritime Museum** (☎ **0289/22-700**) in Tría Pigádia contains a delightful and very informative collection of old maps, prints, coins, and seafarer's memorabilia. You can use the 19th-century English prints to identify the notables for whom every *platía* and *odós* is named, or study the excellent ship models to learn how the Athenian navy defeated the Persians. Make sure to get to the back garden, where you can climb up a reconstructed Armenistis lighthouse tower from 1890, with its prisms and globe still intact. It's open daily from 10:30am to 1pm and 6:30 to 9pm; admission is 500 Drs ($2.10).

Next door, **Léna's House** is an homage to Mýkonian daily life. In an original, 19th-century middle-class home, furnishings, housewares, and utensils typical of the period have been preserved. It's a wonderful contrast to the international style commonly seen today. It's open daily from 7 to 9pm and admission is free.

If you haven't climbed to **Káto Mýli,** you'll be wondering why we said there were five windmills when only three tall whitewashed ones are visible from a distance. If you go up to explore, wait until early evening, when the windmill closest to the stairs is usually open for viewing.

If you're interested in acquiring or just admiring the best local art, we recommend **The Studio** (☎ **0289/23-527**), two streets up after a left turn off Main Street at the Vengera Bar, which features Monika Derpapas's neo-Byzantine mosaics (which grace the residences of many local connoisseurs) and Richard James North's mythical, magical painted-wood objects that give new meaning to the term "flight of fantasy." There are also hand-painted T-shirts that are last word in body art fantasy—and washable! Whether or not you're interested in buying jewelry, don't miss the **Lalaounis Gallery,** just up (north) from Taxi Square.

WHERE TO STAY

Mýkonos is probably Greece's best-known island, and what qualifies as the low season here (April to June 15 and October, with most places closed all winter) would look overcrowded on most other islands. The many visitors who've been enchanted in the past return annually, while newcomers arrive daily, increasing the pressure on hotel rooms that are often booked a year in advance.

Most of the hotels and rooms listed below will accept reservations 1 to 3 months in advance only if accompanied by a deposit equal to one-third of the total amount due for your entire stay; your reservations will be accepted only after their past customers have been accommodated. If at all possible, go to Mýkonos during the low season, when sky-high prices are slightly lower and you have a good chance of finding a bed.

However, if you're determined to be in the hottest spot at the hottest time, we have a suggestion: make your reservation early and plan your trip around it. If you don't receive a reply from any of these hotels, try an outfit that's the best thing that's happened to Mýkonos in years: the **Mýkonos Accommodations Center (MAC),** off the upper end of Matoyánni Street in Tría Pigádia at Énoplon Dinaméon and Malamatenias, above the ice-cream parlor (☎ **0289/23-160** or 0289/23-408; fax 0289/ 24-137; e-mail mac@mac.myk.forthnet.gr). Their multilingual and helpful staff will correspond, talk by phone, or meet with you to determine the best accommodation for your budget (and they're not stuffy about booking cheap rooms in local houses, though of course there aren't many on Mýkonos). Mýkonos is one of Greece's most expensive islands, and MAC offers a wide range of Class C and D hotels—from 18,000 to 24,000 Drs ($75 to $100)—and some private rooms. For ensuring you an affordable bed, they charge 15% of the rental or a 6,000-Dr ($25) minimum fee, which may be worthwhile if you can visit only during the peak season. MAC will book rooms on other islands for the same fees (lower if the hotel pays a commission, too). The center is pricey, but John van Lerberghe and his staff do come through for you and can spare you disappointment.

Note: If you haven't made reservations or talked to MAC, we strongly recommend that you *don't* go to Mýkonos during the high season.

If you're reading this during the low season while sunbathing on a ferry speeding toward the island, don't despair. You may find a room in one of the in-town hotels (discussed below), all of which are within minutes of the port. If anyone offers you a private room as you disembark, grab it and be grateful if it's affordable and nice (you can always move the next day). Be prepared to accept lodging in another community outside Mýkonos town, whose old hotels sell out to regulars every year.

IN MÝKONOS TOWN

Pensions & Rooms to Let

Since the local government stopped issuing hotel building permits, the big news on Mýkonos is that many of the pensions, rooms-to-let, studios, and villas are larger and more comfortable and offer better views than the small, older hotels listed below. Most of the pensions and rooms don't serve breakfast on the premises, but they can be a very good deal; at this writing no rooms had been consigned to tour operators.

At the port there are three agencies as well as the tourist police where you can check what's available. Otherwise, the two best areas to find rooms are along Main Street, between the Hotel Matogianni and Kaloyéra Street, and along Kaloyéra Street between Ayíon Saránda and Ayíou Yerasímou streets.

If you're not carrying a lot of luggage, follow the blue arrows that direct you to Platís Yialós southwest away from the port. There are several tour operators' villas near the south bus station, and the odd rooms that remain empty are rented out by the group's booking agent, who's usually on the premises.

Maria and Mike Mitropia. Láka Sq., Hóra, 846 00 Mýkonos. ☎ **0289/23-528.** 20 rms, 13 with bath (shower). 12,000 Drs ($50) double without bath, 14,400 Drs ($60) double with bath. No credit cards.

This couple keeps very tidy and comfortable rooms above Mike's locksmith shop on Láka Square, near the town police station and opposite the Mýkonos Market. Try to reserve one of their quiet, good-value rooms.

Pension Stelios. Hóra, 846 00 Mýkonos. ☎ **0289/24-641.** Fax 0289/26-779. 20 rms, all with bath (shower). 19,200 Drs ($80) double. No credit cards.

This whitewashed, blue-shuttered addition to the hill behind the OTE office, on the northeast end of the harbor, is close to the Piraeus/Rafína ferryboat pier. It's easily reached by broad stone steps above the road, making it a quiet, scenic, and convenient place to stay. The modern, twin-bedded rooms have small balconies with good views and a common lounge.

Hotels

Hotels on Mýkonos are more expensive than those elsewhere in Greece, but here are some of the best values in town.

Hotel Apollo. Paralía, Hóra, 846 00 Mýkonos. ☎ **0289/22-223.** 20 rms, 8 with bath (shower). 15,600 Drs ($65) double with bath, 13,250 Drs ($55.20) double without bath. No credit cards.

The harborside Hotel Apollo, one of the island's oldest and best-value hotels, has a carefully maintained 19th-century facade that blends in with the central section of the port. The rooms are simply furnished, a little worse for wear, but pleasant and comfortable.

Hotel Delphines. Odós Mavroyénous, Hóra, 846 00 Mýkonos. ☎ **0289/22-292.** Fax 0289/27-307. 7 rms, all with bath (shower). 19,200 Drs ($80) single; 24,000 Drs ($100) double. Rates include breakfast. No credit cards.

Near the Hotel Manto is Capt. Kostas Zouganelis's blue-shuttered hotel. It's older and more homey than some of the other choices. The seven doubles are cozy, and the singles aren't a bad deal in this crowded port, considering that many hotels on Mýkonos charge a single person the price of a double.

Hotel Matina. Odós Fournakíon 3, Hóra, 846 00 Mýkonos. ☎ **0289/22-387** or 0289/24-501. 14 rms, all with bath (tub). 21,000 Drs ($87.50) single; 27,600 Drs ($115) double. Rates include breakfast. AE, V.

The Hotel Matina is another good choice, with small modern rooms. A real plus here: it's ideally situated inside a large garden, which insulates it from the noise of its central location.

Hotel Matogianni. Odós Matoyánni, Hóra, 846 00 Mýkonos. ☎ **0289/22-217.** Fax 0289/23-264. 22 rms, all with bath (shower). TEL. 18,000 Drs ($75) double. Rates include breakfast.

Although the Matogianni is on swinging Main Street, the modernized rooms overlooking a pretty garden are quiet.

Hotel Terra Maria. Odós Kaloyéra 18, Hóra, 846 00 Mýkonos. ☎ **0289/24-212.** Fax 0289/27-112. 25 rms, all with bath (shower). A/C TEL. 24,000 Drs ($100) double. Rates include breakfast. AE, V.

Around the corner from the Marios (see below) and much like it, the Maria offers rooms that are just as nice and modern, even a little sunnier.

Hotel Zorzis. Odós Kaloyéra, Hóra, 846 00 Mýkonos. ☎ **0289/22-167.** Fax 0289/24-169. 10 rms, all with bath (shower); 2 two-bedroom cottages. 24,000 Drs ($100) double; 60,000 Drs ($250) cottage. No credit cards.

Very centrally located, this midtown hotel has just had a complete face-lift. English pine four-poster or sleigh beds are graced with patchwork quilts. The rooms in the back face the garden and are quiet for this busy neighborhood.

Marios Hotel. Odós Kaloyéra 24, Hóra, 846 00 Mýkonos. ☎ **0289/22-704.** 12 rms, all with bath (tub). 23,000 Drs ($95.85) single or double. Rates include breakfast. No credit cards.

The quaint Class C Marios Hotel, located across from the small Zorzis, is distinguished by its dark wood-beamed ceilings. The Marios has spotless doubles with modern facilities, some with balconies overlooking a garden.

ON THE EDGE OF TOWN

Most of the new construction is along Odós Ayíou Ioánnou, the road that circles the pedestrians-only older Mýkonos town. In addition, the south beach road that begins at Xenías Street in the southwest part of town, intersects with Ayíou Ioánnou, and then runs south to the beaches at Platís Yialós has also seen much recent development. Both are good areas, with great views of old Mýkonos town and the sea, with easy access by vehicle and within a 10-minute walk of the nightlife. Many of the newer places boast a swimming pool, larger rooms, private telephones, breakfast terraces, balconies or patios, and the buzz of a larger hotel.

Pension Giovanni. Odós Giovanni 3, Hóra, 846 00 Mýkonos. ☎ **0289/22-485.** Fax 0289/22-485. 9 rms, all with bath (shower). 15,000 Drs ($75) single; 24,000 Drs ($100) double. Rates include breakfast. EURO, MC, V.

Rena Giovanni runs this whitewashed, brown-shuttered pension (located near the edge of Mýkonos town on the west side) with a personal touch. It was converted from a medical clinic, so all the rooms are quite large.

Pension Marina. Ayíou Ioánnou and Láka sts., Hóra, 846 00 Mýkonos. ☎ and fax **0289/24-960,** or 094/473-273 for a mobile phone. 15 rms, all with bath (shower). 18,000 Drs ($75) single; 21,600 Drs ($90) double. No credit cards.

Like the Pension Giovanni across from it, this small pension is very close to the edge of Mýkonos town on the west side. It's next to the church and just behind the minimall, which contains a butcher, baker, souvláki shop, car-rental agency, and travel office. The friendly owner, George Athimaritis, and his manager, Tom, maintain spic-and-span twin-bedded rooms with bureaus, chairs, and good lighting. There's also a patio for sunning or snacking.

Worth a Splurge

Edem House Hotel. Schóli Kalón Téchnon, Áyios Loukás, 846 00 Mýkonos. ☎ **0289/22-774.** Fax 0289/25-619. 24 rms, all with bath (tub or shower). TV TEL. 30,000 Drs ($125) single; 36,000 Drs ($150) double. Rates include breakfast. AE, MC, V.

This new hotel above the District Road around the town, near the south bus station, has spacious, comfortable, well-furnished rooms, all with balconies with views over the town. Some rooms have half bathtubs with shower curtains. The Edem has a nice new pool.

Hotel Ilio Maris. Despotiká, 846 00 Mýkonos. ☎ **0289/23-755.** Fax 0289/24-309. 26 rms, all with bath (tub). A/C TV TEL. 33,600 Drs ($140) single; 43,200 Drs ($180) double. Rates include American breakfast. AE, V.

Built on a slope down from the south beach road, this attractive hotel has balconied rooms with a fridge and a view of the pool and the sea beyond. The comfortable bar, lounge, and rooms are tastefully decorated with traditional Greek art—a small touch that adds style to the surroundings. Bicycle rental is available.

Hotel Poseidon. Hóra, 846 00 Mýkonos. ☎ **0289/24-441.** Fax 0289/23-812. 41 rms, all with bath (shower). A/C TV TEL. 31,200 Drs ($130) double. Rates include breakfast. AE, EURO, MC, V. Parking available.

The Hotels Poseidon A and B, near the sea on the road to Ornos, have attractive surroundings, a pool, and particularly attentive service. Poseidon B has air-conditioning.

Hotel Rochari. Odós Áyios Ioánnou, Rohári, 846 00 Mýkonos. ☎ **0289/23-107.** Fax 0289/24-307. 61 rms, all with bath (shower). A/C MINIBAR TV TEL. 15,600 Drs ($65) single; 26,400 Drs ($110) double. Closed Nov–Mar. AE, MC, V.

This hotel is on the hill above town in the quarter known as Rohári. Regular guests like the homey ambience, TV lounge, swimming pool, and comfortable rooms.

K Hotels. P.O. Box 64, 846 00 Mýkonos. ☎ **0289/23-415** or 0289/23-431. Fax 0289/23-455. 135 rms, all with bath (shower). A/C. 32,400 Drs ($135) single; 36,000 Drs ($150) double. Rates include breakfast. AE, EURO, MC, V.

The four K Hotels (Kalypso, Kohili, Korali, and Kyma) form a complex just off the south beach road. The modern air-conditioned rooms are stacked on two levels to offer views of the sea, the hills, the pool, or the tennis courts. Each building has a small bar and breakfast lounge, and there's a common restaurant.

AROUND THE ISLAND

There are hotels clustered around many popular beaches on the island, but most people prefer to stay in town and commute to the beaches. For those who need to curl their toes in the sand before breakfast, a few selections follow.

At Costa Ílios

This village, nestled atop a small cove on Ornos Bay, is one of the most beautiful spots on the island. Private homes, in the traditional style, of course, with accommodations for two to six people and with twice-weekly maid service, can be rented by the week for 230,000 to 358,000 Drs ($958 to $1,491); Diners Club and MasterCard are accepted. The village has its own beach, tennis court, swimming pool, and children's pool. For details on rentals, contact **LEMA,** Odós Makrás Stoás 1, 185 31 Piraeus (☎ **01/417-5988** or 01/417-6741; fax 01/417-9310). You can also write to Maria Koulalia, Cósta Ílios, 846 00 Mýkonos (☎ and fax **0289/24-522**), or contact LEMA by e-mail at lemacim@ibm.net or on the Web at http://www.who-is-who.gr/tour/htmlcostaoou.htm.

At Ornos Beach

This beach on calm Ornos Bay is particularly recommended to families, who will appreciate its water-sports facilities, tavernas, and shallow waters. The sleek modern **Club Mýkonos Hotel** (☎ **0289/22-600;** fax 0289/24-560) has two stories of spacious bungalow-style rooms, suites, and studios (plus time-share units). Double rooms overlooking the water, breakfast, and transportation to and from the airport cost 39,600 Drs ($165) and studios are 43,200 Drs ($180); American Express, EuroCard, MasterCard, and Visa are accepted.

The family-owned, comfortable **Hotel Asteri** (☎ **0289/22-715**), near the beach, has doubles with breakfast for 28,800 Drs ($120). No credit cards are accepted.

Splurge Choices at Platís Yialós

Some 15 minutes by bus or 30 minutes on foot south of Mýkonos town is the sandy, crescent-shaped beach of Platís Yialós, the caïque stop for shuttles running to Paradise and Super Paradise beaches. There are several excellent hotels, most very similarly named.

Hotel Petassos Bay. Platís Yialós, 846 00 Mýkonos. ☎ **0289/23-737.** Fax 0289/24-101. 21 rms, all with bath (shower). A/C MINIBAR TEL. 33,500 Drs ($139.60) single; 36,500 Drs ($152) double. Rates include breakfast. AE, V.

Large air-conditioned rooms with phones, personal Muzak, and balconies overlook the beach, which is only 33 yards away. There's a good-sized pool and sun deck, and the hotel offers free transfers to and from the airport or ferry pier.

○ **Hotel Petassos Beach.** Platís Yialós, 846 00 Mýkonos. ☎ **0289/22-437.** Fax 0289/21-101. 64 rms, all with bath (shower). A/C MINIBAR TV TEL. 29,600 Drs ($123.35) single; 31,000 Drs ($130) double. Rates include breakfast. AE, V.

Next door to the Petassos Bay and under the same capable management, this excellent choice offers rooms and facilities that are quite similar, and there's a sauna, gym, Jacuzzi, an excellent restaurant and bar, and room service. The friendly multilingual staff is one of the best on the island.

Hotel Petinos. Platís Yialós, 846 00 Mýkonos. ☎ **0289/22-913.** Fax 0289/23-680. 66 rms, all with bath (tub). TEL. 22,800 Drs ($95) single; 24,000 Drs ($100) double. Rates include breakfast. AE, EURO, MC, V.

Here you'll find nice attractive rooms with large balconies shaded by an arcaded facade.

Nissaki Hotel. Platís Yialós, 846 00 Mýkonos. ☎ **0289/22-913.** Fax 0289/23-680. 14 rms, all with bath (shower). A/C TV TEL. 25,200 Drs ($105) single; 26,400 Drs ($110) double. Rates include breakfast. AE, EURO, MC, V.

On a slope not far from the beach, this Petinos-owned hotel has good, nicely furnished rooms and patios with beach views.

At Áyios Stéphanos

About 2¹/₂ miles north of Mýkonos town is the popular resort of Áyios Stéphanos. The several hotels, pensions, tavernas, and a disco that make up this village are within reach of a pleasant, though crowded, sandy beach.

Near the coast, the best Class C choices are the **Hotel Artemis** (☎ **0289/22-345**), 30 yards from the beach, near the bus stop, with 23 rooms with bath (shower) for 20,400 Drs ($85), breakfast included; and the **Hotel Panorama** (☎ **0289/22-337**), 75 yards from the beach, with 27 rooms with bath (shower) for 26,400 Drs ($110). The small **Hotel Mina** (☎ **0289/23-024**) is uphill behind the Artemis and offers 15 double rooms with private bath for 15,000 Drs ($62.50).

CAMPING

Paradise Camping. Paradise Beach, 846 00 Mýkonos. ☎ **0289/22-58.** Fax 0289/24-350. 1,800 Drs ($7.50) per person; 1,000 Drs ($4.15) for tent; 9,000 Drs ($37.50) beach cabin with breakfast. MC, V.

The official campground on Mýkonos is at Paradise Beach. The fee includes the use of all facilities: showers, a bar, a restaurant, a minimarket, and transportation to and from the port and town. It offers rooms and bungalows as well at one of the loveliest spots on the island. How could a night in any hotel or villa compare to sleeping under the stars at the edge of Paradise?

Paranga Beach Camping. Paránga Beach, 846 00 Mýkonos. ☎ **0289/24-578.** 1,800 Drs ($7.50) per person; 1,000 Drs ($4.15) for tent. No credit cards.

This newer and even nicer facility a few miles east offers all Paradise can and more—including cooking and laundry facilities.

WHERE TO EAT

Mýkonos is famed for its restaurants, and the fashionable ones change as rapidly as the seasons. Nevertheless there are several favorites that have stood the test of time. Wait until 9:30 or 10pm to have dinner—it's the Greek way and everything's much livelier at this hour.

For breakfast or snacks, there's a classic bakery just off the harbor. (The harbor itself is lined with expensive cafes, where an early-morning or late-night coffee is the best value.) The **Andreas Pouloudis Bakery,** Odós Flórou Zuganéli 3 (☎ **0289/22-304**), off Mavro Square in the tiny lane behind the gold store, can be identified by the contented weight-watchers outside eating cheese pies. It's run by a grumpy, talented baker, who offers a variety of *"kookis," "caik,"* and "tutti frutti pies" as well as yummy cheese, spinach, and zucchini pies for 480 to 600 Drs ($2 to $2.50).

On Taxi Square, the **Alexis Snack Bar,** open at all hours, features a salad bar, as well as good, inexpensive burgers, gyros, and other snacks and refreshments.

On Kaloyéra Street near the Hotel Philippi is the more refined **Hibiscus Croissanterie,** offering a large variety of croissants plus fluffy quiche Lorraine and other authentic delights created by its French owner, Anna.

Mýkonos town's mass-market popularity has spawned mass-market eateries, and you'll find full-color photo displays of pizza, hamburgers, souvláki, club sandwiches, ice cream, and other international junk food in many back lanes.

Antonini's. Taxi Sq., Hóra. No telephone. Main courses 1,700–2,400 Drs ($7.10–$10). No credit cards. Daily 11am–3pm and 7pm–1am. GREEK.

Next to the Alexis Snack Bar, this casual, inexpensive taverna favored by Mykonians serves typical, yet satisfying Greek peasant fare.

Delphines. Odós Matoyánni, Hóra. ☎ **0289/24-269.** Main courses 1,300–3,400 Drs ($5.40–$14.15). V. Daily noon–midnight. GREEK.

Irini, the cook at this small, family-owned spot on Main Street, runs the kitchen like a grandmother feeding her only grandchild. The food is delicious and the portions are generous. Makis, the charming owner, has decorated the taverna in antiques with a maritime theme and advises you not to miss the special dessert, *prálina,* made from his mother's secret recipe. Take his advice!

El Greco/Yorgos. Tría Pigádia, Hóra. ☎ **0289/22-074.** Main courses 1,500–5,100 Drs ($6.25–$21.25). AE, DC, EURO, MC, V. Daily 7pm–1:30am. GREEK/CONTINENTAL.

El Greco, on Three Wells Square, is a traditional taverna with a large patio and a sophisticated menu, specializing in grilled meats. Start with the *kipouroú* (garden salad) and a bowl of grandma's delicious fish soup. You can splurge on chateaubriand for 5,500 Drs ($22.90) each, or have a simpler meal for half that price. Yorgos's sister, Katerina, runs the **El Greco by the Sea** at Ornos Beach.

Gatsby's. Odós Fournakíon, Hóra. ☎ **0289/23-217.** Main courses 1,140–3,000 Drs ($4.75–$12.50). AE, MC, V. Daily 7pm–2am. INTERNATIONAL.

Turn right at the south end of Main Street and on your left you'll find what locals call the "Nut Man's Shop"; turn left and you'll find Gatsby's. Our expatriate friends recommend it for well-prepared food in a lovely garden with friendly, attentive service and modest (for Mýkonos) prices. The menu is varied, with pastas, burgers, Greek dishes, and a nice range of salads. We didn't much care for the chili, but the chicken salad and hamburger were terrific.

Lotus Bar Restaurant. Odós Matoyánni, Hóra. ☎ **0289/22-881.** Main courses 2,000–4,500 Drs ($8.35–$18.75). V. Daily 9am–5am. CONTINENTAL.

One of the oldest restaurants on the island, tucked away under a profusion of greenery on Main Street, offers a health-food breakfast of bran muffins, protein shakes, and egg-white omelets. For dinner, try the the kalamari "Lotus," squid stuffed with rice and veggies in a Pernod sauce.

Niko's Taverna. Hóra. No phone. Main courses 1,450–3,000 Drs ($6.05–$12.50); fresh fish 12,500 Drs ($52) per kilo. No credit cards. Daily noon–11pm. GREEK/CONTINENTAL.

Bustling Niko's Taverna spans a narrow lane near the Paraportianí Church, and is quite popular with locals. It's one of the few good places that's also open for lunch and has a varied, inexpensive taverna menu and a very friendly staff.

WORTH A SPLURGE

Having surveyed all manner of elegant restaurants, we've come up with three that fit our criteria of more formal dining, attentive service, interesting menus with Greek specialties, and great food (not necessarily in that order).

✪ **Edem Restaurant.** Sbove Panahrándou Church, Hóra. ☎ 0289/22-855 or 0298/23-335. Reservations recommended July–Aug. Main courses 2,000–5,000 Drs ($8.35–$20.85). AE, DC, EURO, MC, V. Daily 11am–1am. GREEK/CONTINENTAL.

Superb food is the attraction of this casual garden restaurant with plenty of elbow room and a very nice pool. The Edem is famous for its meat dishes, but it has a wide range of continental and Greek specialties on its menu. Try the spaghetti with lobster. The service is second to none.

Philippi. Odós Matoyánni, Hóra. ☎ **0289/22-294.** Reservations recommended July–Aug. Main courses 4,700–6,200 Drs ($19.60–$25.85); fish 15,000–22,000 Drs ($62.50–$91.65) per kilo. AE, DC, EURO, MC, V. Daily 7pm–1am. GREEK/CONTINENTAL.

Long a favorite with locals and tourists, Philippi is set in an enchanting olive tree garden. Woven fabrics cover the tables and banquettes, which are spaced to provide intimate, romantic dining by candlelight. When you step down into the garden off busy Main Street, you'll enter a quiet European world where elegant dining prevails. The continental menu includes French classics, curry, and many elaborately prepared traditional Greek dishes. There's a sizable wine list.

Yves Klein Blue. Odós Kaloyéra, Hóra. No phone. Main courses 2,600–5,400 Drs ($10.85–$22.50). AE, DC, EURO, MC, V. Daily 7pm–2am. ITALIAN.

This elegant trattoria, just up from the Credit Bank, named after the French painter from the 1960s, who used the indigo that dominates the interior, is our favorite of the many Italian restaurants. The food is classical northern Italian, superbly prepared. When the diners thin out later in the night, it becomes a piano bar.

MÝKONOS AFTER DARK

Mýkonos really sparkles at night, so whatever your budget, plan on dressing up for the evening and walking the streets to admire everyone else admiring you.

For early drinks, try the **The Coffee Bar** at the end of Main Street—a great place to watch people—or head west to **Little Venice.** At sunset the intimate **Kastro,** behind the Paraportianí Church, and the rocking **Caprice,** down the block on Skárpa, are perfect for watching the sunset's rosy reflection on the calm Aegean. Both are enhanced by the sea splashing on the low wall.

For live piano music, try the **Montparnasse** (☎ 0289/23-719), on the same lane, a cozy bar with Toulouse-Lautrec posters. The hipper **Argo** (☎ 0289/24-674), a favorite of our Mykoniot friends, is at Three Wells, just down the street from the Maritime Museum. Look for Richard James North's Cowboy Boot on Main Street to find **Uno** (☎ 0289/22-365), a cool addition to the scene.

The longtime king of the scene in Mýkonos, **Pierro's,** on Main Street just a mob scene away from the harbor, is an elegant old bar that's seen so many fads and celebs come and go it's a wonder it's still around, but it's still the happening spot and a must-see for everyone. You may have to go into **Mantos Bar** next door to buy a beer because you can't squeeze through the flesh out front, but then you're set for the best people-watching and pickup action on the island—some would say, in all of Greece. Pierro's is in full swing after 11pm.

If it's true that blondes have more fun, the hottest spot around is the **Scandinavian Bar,** on a narrow lane behind Nikos Taverna, near the Paraportianí Church. Two indoor bars draw such a huge, mixed crowd with cheap drinks and an "anything goes" policy that you'll have to fight your way through to the nearby **Down Under,** which often has live music, where the drinks are less expensive and foreign under-20s consort with Greek under-20s.

If you're ready for some authentic Greek dancing, try **Thalami** (☎ 0289/23-291), a small underground club near the Nikos Taverna underneath the town hall on the port. You can push your way through the beaded curtains to see fine, authentic dancing by local men and visiting professionals.

The **Mýkonos Club,** opposite the Caprice Bar in Little Venice (☎ 0289/23-529), is a bouzouki nightclub that's frequented by locals and tourists in search of *rebétika* (Greek blues). The **Lucky Star,** at the juncture of the roads to Ornos and Áyios Ioánnis, features Greek popular music, both old and new; it really jumps on Saturday night when the locals head there for a good time.

If you're looking for an after-hours dance club, Dimitra LeGoff has opened the elegant and wildly popular **Bar Aristote,** on Main Street near Kaloyéra (☎ 0289/22-800). This same crowd moves on to the chic **Mercedes** or the even more sophisticated **Remezzo Disco,** near the telephone center (OTE) on the port. To party on under the stars into the morning, head for **Cavo Muses** at Áyios Stéphanos.

Newer bars include the **Anchor Club,** on Main Street near Pierro's, which is stylishly spare with just enough lighting and volume from its jazz, blues, and 1960s rock repertoire to earn a devoted mid-30s clientele; the already-mentioned Argo, which turns into a rockin' disco with great music after midnight; and the **Astra,** near the Three Wells, which is more high-tech, hard-edge rock.

Another after-1am hotspot is **MADD,** on Taxi Square, where a super DJ plays fun dance music, the drinks are good, and the view of the port is fabulous.

2 Délos (Dílos)

95 nautical miles E of Piraeus, 2 nautical miles SW of Mýkonos

This tiny island where Apollo and Artemis were born was considered by the Greeks to be the holiest of sanctuaries, the sacred center around which the Cyclades circled. The entire island of Délos, off-limits to all but day-trippers, is now an archaeological museum that's one of the best sites in Greece.

Organized excursions leave Tuesday to Sunday from Mýkonos for the 40-minute ride to the island, and cost 2,500 Drs ($10.40) round-trip for transportation alone or 8,400 Drs ($35) for a guided tour, such as that offered by **Sea & Sky Travel** (☎ 0289/22-853). Boats leave from the harbor between 9am and noon and return 3 to 5 hours later—ample time for most visitors to explore. There are daily sailings from Tínos to Délos and Mýkonos; the full-day trip costs 4,500 Drs ($19.60) with no guide.

The 3 hours on Délos scheduled by excursion boats should allow even avid archaeology buffs enough time to explore the principal sites. To the left of the new pier

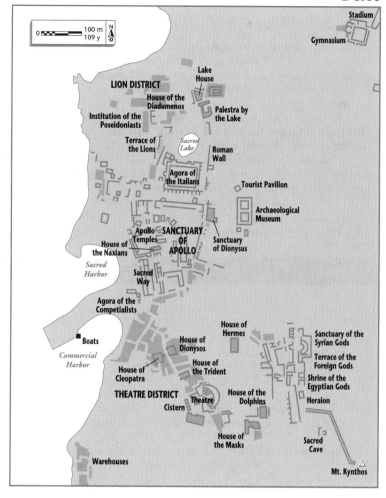

where you'll dock is the partially filled-in **Sacred Harbor,** where pilgrims and traders from throughout the ancient world landed. Site plans and picture guides are available at the ticket kiosk, and even the cheapest is adequate. Our favorite, with an excellent text, good pictures, and a foldout map in the back, was *Délos: Monuments and Museum,* by P. Zaphiropoúlou (Kreve Edition).

The site is open daily from 8:30am to 2:30pm; admission is 1,200 Drs ($5) for adults, 900 Drs ($3.75) for seniors, and 600 Drs ($2.50) for students.

Proceed up past the **Agorá,** where festivals were celebrated by the freed men and traders on the island. Bear right up the hill to explore the south side of the site dominated by **Mt. Kýnthos,** which the hardy may want to climb for its fine views over the sanctuary, and to the west the nearby islet of Ekáti, the Delian burial ground of Rhénia, and beyond them, Sýros, as well as Tínos to the north, Mýkonos to the northeast, and Náxos and Páros to the south. Along the way, a maze of ruined warehouses will be on your right. Be sure to check out the various houses, or "maisons," once inhabited by wealthy Athenians, where some exquisite mosaics have been found.

Most of the mosaics on Délos were designed and installed by artists brought in from Syria.

The large, roofed **House of Masks** contains Délos's best-known treasure, a superb colored mosaic of Dionysus on a panther, in the room at the right and some geometric patterned borders in the central room, with five elaborate masks depicting a range of theatrical expression. The bright color of these Syrian works, now over 2,000 years old, is astounding.

To the south toward Mt. Kýnthos you'll find the **Sanctuary of the Syrian Gods,** the **Temple of Serapis,** the **Shrine of the Great Gods,** and other temples. Near the top of the hill is the **Sacred Cave,** once an oracle of Apollo.

The **museum,** open the same hours as the site (admission included with entry), houses some fine sculpture, masks, and jewelry. North (left) from the **tourist pavilion** next door you'll find the filled-in **Sacred Lake,** where Leto is supposed to have given birth to Artemis and Apollo, and the famous guardian **lions** facing east over the Lake.

Northeast from the Lake is the large courtyard of the **Gymnasium** and just beyond it the long narrow **Stadium** where the athletic competitions of the Delian Games were held.

3 Sýros

78 nautical miles E of Piraeus

Only 10 years ago Ermoúpolis ("City of Hermes," patron of commerce), the administrative capital of the Cyclades, was also its shipping capital—the hub for passengers switching ferry lines to other island chains. Since Páros became the new transport hub, few people stop here anymore. The islanders' off-handed style with foreigners and the lack of tourist savvy can be rather refreshing. (No one will pay much attention to you, but you won't be neglected if you need help.) Sýros offers a rare opportunity to vacation as the Greeks do, on an island whose lack of beautiful sand beaches, archaeological wonders, and discos has spared it rampant overdevelopment.

Since antiquity Sýros's central position has made it a prosperous trading and shipping port. Excavations at Halandrianí have revealed the existence of an early Cycladic civilization from the 3rd millennium B.C. The northern tip of the island is said to have been the home of the philosopher Pherecydas, whose best pupil was Pythagoras.

After the Greek Liberation of 1821, the northern Aegean islanders who'd been driven out by the Turks sought refuge on Sýros. Throughout the 19th century Sýros flourished as a maritime center, becoming the most important port in Greece.

Today the affluent population of 20,000 doesn't rely on tourism as the mainstay of their economy. Besides the huge shipping industry, textiles and inland greenhouses are main sources of revenue. Some visitors would swear that the economy turns on *loukoúmia,* the locally produced Turkish delights that look like Jell-O cubes in powdered sugar and taste like . . . well, you'll have to try them yourself. *Halvadópita,* a locally made nougat pressed between two thin wafers, is also extremely popular.

Ermoúpolis is a busy harbor, enlarged by a huge modern breakwater that provides anchorage for many tankers and container cargo ships. Still lovely in their fading glory are the large neoclassic mansions overlooking the water, vestiges of Sýros's prosperous past.

ESSENTIALS

GETTING THERE & DEPARTING   By Plane   Olympic Airways has one to three flights daily from Athens. Call Olympic Airways at its Ermoúpolis office (☎ **0281/81-244**) or in Athens (☎ **01/926-7251**) for reservations.

By Boat   Sýros is connected daily (more frequently in summer) by ferryboat to Piraeus, Íos, Mýkonos, Náxos, Páros, Santoríni, and Tínos; four or five times weekly to Ándros; twice weekly to Folégandros and Síkinos; and once a week to Mílos, Sífnos, and Sérifos. Check the schedules with a local travel agent; **Alfa Sýros,** on the harbor (☎ **0281/81-185**), is helpful.

VISITOR INFORMATION   There's a **Greek Tourist Office (EOT)** upstairs at Odós Dodekanissíou 10, just off the port (☎ **0281/82-375**), open Monday to Friday from 7am to 2:30pm. The city of Ermoúpolis **Tourist Information Office** is on the second floor of the town hall (on the central square) (☎ **0281/87-027**), open Monday to Friday from 8am to 2:30pm. The **police** (☎ **0281/83-555**), open Monday to Friday from 7:30am to 3pm, are opposite the town hall; the **port police** (☎ **0281/82-690**) are close by.

Teamwork Holidays is on the *paralía* (harborfront) at the north end of the port (right from the ferry pier), at Odós Rálli 10 (☎ **0281/83-400;** fax 0281/83-508), and is open daily from 9am to 2pm and 6 to 9:30pm to book rooms, handle travel plans, change money, sell Olympic Airways tickets, arrange rental cars, and offer a round-the-island half-day bus tour or a full-day beach tour by motorboat.

Alfa Sýros, at the New Port (☎ **0281/81-185;** fax 0281/83-508), sells boat tickets and changes money.

ORIENTATION   Ferryboats dock at **Ermoúpolis** (our recommended base for visitors), which served as the island's major port in ancient times. At the north end of the port from the winged World War II monument, **Venizélou Street** leads inland 4 blocks to **Platía Miaoúli** (Miaoúlis Square), the city's central square.

Above the city, the taller hill on the left (west) is **Áno Sýros,** the old Catholic quarter. The hill to the east (right), topped with the blue-domed Greek Orthodox Church of the Resurrection, is **Vrondádo,** built up after the Greek immigration of 1821.

GETTING AROUND   The **bus station** is on the *paralía* near the ferry pier; schedules are posted on the board in front. Buses circle the southern half of Sýros about eight times a day (more frequently in summer) between 10am and 8pm, stopping at Possidonía/Dellagrazia, Fínikas, and Galissás. The southeast-coast beaches of Vári and Mégas Yialós are included about six times a day—restricting the possibilities of swimming and sunbathing on the southeast coast.

The **taxi stand** is on the south side of the central square. You can call ☎ **0281/ 86-222** for service.

FAST FACTS   The **telephone office (OTE)** is on the west end of the central square, open daily from 6am to 11pm. For **medical emergencies** call ☎ **0281/ 82-555.** The **post office,** open Monday to Friday from 7:30am to 3pm, is opposite the town hall.

WHAT TO SEE & DO
IN ERMOÚPOLIS

A stroll along the harbor will give an introduction to the busy and affluent port, with its numerous cafes. Two streets from the port is **Protopapadáki** or **Proíou Street,** which is open to car traffic and chock full of shops. Turn inland at the World War II monument to reach spacious marble-paved **Platía Miaoúli,** which is dominated by the buff-colored neoclassic **town hall,** designed in 1876.

Híos Street, 1 block west of Venizélou Street (off the west side of Platía Miaoúli), is the town's market street, where fresh produce, meat, fish, and other comestibles are sold.

The **Sýros Archaeological Museum** (☎ 0281/28-487) is up off the northwest corner of the central square. Its small collection includes some fine Cycladic sculptures from the 3rd millennium B.C., two beautiful miniature Hellenistic marble heads, and Roman-era sculpture from Amorgós. It's open Tuesday to Sunday from 8:30am to 3pm; admission is free.

The **Apollo Theater,** a 19th-century miniature of Milan's La Scala, is up off the east end of the main square. A major renovation funded by the European Union was nearly completed during our visit in October 1996, but the hall was still in need of seating and a sound system; it should be open soon.

Áno Sýros, the taller of the hills, on the west (left) above Ermoúpolis, is an interesting old quarter that offers a spectacular view over the harbor. It was a Christian medieval town built by the Venetians and Genoese in the 13th century on this summit for protection from pirate raids. Several Roman Catholic churches still stand, the most important of which is the **Church of San Giorgio.** The large buff-colored square building on the hilltop is the medieval **Monastery of the Capuchins.** Remnants of castle walls, stone archways, and narrow lanes still delight visitors. On foot it's a fairly demanding half-hour hike up Odós Omírou, a couple of blocks west (left) of the central square, then up the old stairs of Odós Ándréa Kárga. Most people will prefer to take a taxi or local bus up and walk down.

Vrondádo, the old Orthodox quarter, reached by going up to the right from the main square, is also well worth a visit. Turn right in front of the Apollo Theater and continue up to the handsome **Church of Áyios Nikólaos,** and from its left side you'll reach **Vapória** on the hillside above the sea, with its fine mansions, built by wealthy shipowners, merchants, and bankers, in various states of repair.

Just south of the port the huge **Neórion Boatyards** handles the construction and repair of vessels as large as 80,000 tons, and farther south the east coast is lined with piers for fishing boats.

AROUND THE ISLAND

The southern half of the island, particularly between **Áno Mána** and **Possidonía,** is neatly terraced with vineyards, wheat fields, tomato greenhouses, and fruit trees, and there are several beaches—none of them anything special, though they'll probably satisfy most people. Most bathing is off the rocky bluffs that jut from the tree-lined shore into the many bays and inlets on the south and west coasts. **Mégas Yialós,** as its name suggests, is the largest beach on the island, a sandy beach shaded by tamarisk trees and gently shelved, making it a good place for children.

Across the southwest corner of the island is **Posidónia** (often referred to as **Dellagrazia,** the Venetian name for the village dominated by the Madonna of Grace Church), an attractive village with Italianate neoclassical mansions. Its beach is small and rocky, but **Agathopés,** a 10-minute walk south, has a nice sandy beach and a little offshore islet.

North across the bay, **Fínikas** ("Phoenix," thought to be the site of an early Phoenician settlement) is another popular resort. Farther north across the headland is **Galissás,** the best sheltered beach on the island—a bit too popular in the high season when it's overrun by backpackers.

Kíni, on the west coast of sheltered Delfíni Bay—and reached on a separate bus route from Ermoúpolis—is valued for its sunsets. **Delfíni beach,** north over the headland, is a nudist hangout.

In the more mountainous north, dairies produce the popular St. Michali cheese, milk, and butter that visiting Greeks love to take home.

WHERE TO STAY
IN ERMOÚPOLIS

The small office of the **Sýros Hotelier Association,** right as you come off the ferry, can help you find a room in one of the better hotels, and there are plenty of rooms for rent in the smaller streets off the harborfront.

There are also several renovated mansions in Vapória that are above our budget. We especially like the new **Syrou Melathron,** Odós Babayiótou 5 (☎ **0281/85-963;** fax 0281/87-806), which has the most luxurious accommodations on the island, and several blocks farther along the **Arhontiko Vourli** (☎ **0281/88-440;** fax 0281/88-440) has the most faithfully restored and furnished rooms, with doubles from 23,000 Drs ($95.85).

Esperance Rooms. Aktí Papagou and Folegandrou, Ermoúpolis, 841 000 Sýros. ☎ **0281/81-671.** Fax 0281/85-707. 8 rms, all with bath (shower). A/C TV TEL. 11,500 Drs ($47.90) double. No credit cards.

This new pension is on the southwest end of the harbor, left from the ferry pier. The rooms are light and spacious, with a fridge; double-paned windows keep them quiet. Nikos Voutsinos also has eight more rooms back from the port.

✪ **Hotel Omiros.** Odós Omírou 43, Ermoúpolis, 841 00 Sýros. ☎ **0281/84-910.** Fax 0281/86-266. 13 rms, all with bath (shower). A/C. 21,000–28,000 Drs ($87.50–$116.65) double. MC, V.

Our first choice is this graciously managed, stylish yet traditional hotel on a pedestrians-only lane above the Metamórphosi Church, several blocks northwest of the main square. The rooms are pleasant, quiet, and spacious, with particularly high ceilings, and tastefully furnished with handsome antiques.

Hotel Kymata. Platía Kanári, Ermoúpolis, 841 00 Sýros. ☎ **0281/82-758.** 8 rms, all with bath (shower). 9,200 Drs ($38.35) single or double. No credit cards.

Walk to the northeast end of the harbor (right from the ferry pier) to reach this restored neoclassic home across from the Hotel Hermes. The rooms are spacious, bright, and spotless, with simple style, high ceilings, and great port views from the front—though the rooms in back are quieter. There's a pretty little smooth-pebble beach just a few yards across from its front door. Open year-round.

Ipatia Guesthouse. Odós Babayiótou 3, Ermoúpolis, 845 03 Sýros. ☎ **0281/83-575.** 8 rms, 5 with bath (tub). 8,800 Drs ($36.65) double without bath, 13,500 Drs ($56.25) double with bath. No credit cards.

This lovely restored Syriot mansion dating from 1870 is behind the Áyios Nikólaos Church, in Vapória. Walk up the east side of Platía Miaoúli and bear right. The rooms at the Ipatia have fine views, and stone steps across from it lead down to concrete bathing platforms. The Lefebvre family from Philadelphia open it to guests and friends every June to September. High-ceilinged rooms have brass beds, stone floors, and simple Syriot furnishings. Frescoed ceilings, carved wood doors, spotless rooms, and sloping stairs add enough charm to compensate for a little wear, though all is being continually updated. In the winter you can contact the Lefebvres at 1049 Anna Rd., Huntington Valley, PA 19006 (☎ **215/663-9262**).

AROUND THE ISLAND

Those drawn to the outer villages will find the most happening—still not much—at Galissás, which is a beach town 5¹/₂ miles southeast of Ermoúpolis. In Galissás, there's **Camping Yianna** (☎ **0281/42-447**), about 100 yards from the beach, with its own open-air disco—something to weigh carefully before unfurling your sleeping

---

Readers Recommend

Dendrinos' Rooms-to-Let, Galissás, Sýros. "I find the sandy-bottom bay and beach at Galíssas to be the best on the island of Sýros and one of the best in Greece. I also have found a wonderful place to stay, close to the bus stop. Nana and Takis Dendrinos are wonderfully hospitable and the rooms are spotlessly clean. In addition, there's a great taverna, Nikos' Restaurant, where the Kapellas family has delicious food and very good prices."

—Rev. Martin A. Peter, Indianapolis, Ind.

---

bag!—minimarket, snack bar, restaurant, and exchange, transportation, and informa-tion service. Rates are 1,200 Drs ($5) per person; 800 Drs ($3.35) per tent. The **Hotel Françoise** (☎ **0281/42-000**) has 34 rooms with private facilities on the road-side, about 5 minutes from the beach, with doubles from 8,500 Drs ($35.40). The **Maistrali Pension** (☎ **0821/42-059**) is another choice, with balconied rooms only 75 yards from the beach and doubles from 9,500 Drs ($39.60).

In Posidonía the attractive, 60-room Class B **Posidonion** (☎ **0281/42-100**) has the best facilities for those who want to hike the area, with doubles for 7,000 to 20,000 Drs ($29.25 to $83.35).

WHERE TO EAT

Kyle loves the numerous *zaharoplastía* (pâtisseries), which serve pastries and café frappé to idlers. The **Pantheon Cafe,** to the right of the town hall, is a fine place for breakfast, with several different kinds of coffee. A kindly Orthodox priest showed us to **Mavrákis,** just off the *paralía* behind Teamwork Holidays, that he claimed had the best *loukoúmia* on the island; gift-wrapped boxes with photos of Sýros's scenic highlights come flavored with rosewater, mint, mastic, or almond and cost about 800 Drs ($3.35) per pound (500 grams). Another excellent place for *loukoúmia* and *halvadópita* is nearby **Passari,** where you can get a glimpse of the making.

Many of the harborside restaurants serve very good food because there are too few tourists to try to get by with mediocre fare. Just look for the places favored by locals and vacationing Greeks.

Loukas Restaurant. Platía Miaoúli, Ermoúpolis. ☎ **0281/80-677.** Main courses 1,000–1,600 Drs ($4.15–$6.65). MC, V. Daily 9am–4pm and 7pm–midnight. GREEK/INTERNATIONAL.

Loukas, on the east end of the central square, has a varied taverna menu of vegetable dishes and meat casseroles. We'll vouch for the stuffed tomatoes and *papoutsákia* ("little shoes"), baked eggplant with ground meat and potatoes. The interior is air-conditioned.

✪ **Tavern Foliá.** Odós Athanasíou Diakoú, Vrondádo. ☎ **0281/83-715.** Main courses 900–2,000 Drs ($3.75–$8.35). No credit cards. Summer, daily noon–3:30pm and 5pm–2am; win-ter, daily 6pm–2am. GREEK.

George Palamaris calls his taverna Foliá ("Pigeon House") because he specializes in pigeon and rabbit dishes—though you'll find a full range of spit-cooked and grilled meats, some fish, and several vegetarian choices. We particularly recommend the de-lectable hot appetizers, such as the *bourekákia* (small meat pies), *tyropitákia* (small cheese pies), and *phyloyéres* (ham and cheese rolled in phyllo pastry). To find this spe-cial place, walk up from the northwest corner of the central square past the Apollo Theater, turn left in front of the St. Nikolas Church, climb up 6 blocks, and turn left on A. Diakoú Street.

4 Páros

91 nautical miles SE of Piraeus

Since Páros became the transportation hub of the Cyclades, thousands of travelers have passed through Parikía's caged-in piers on their way to other Cyclades islands or faraway Crete and Sámos. Inevitably, many people—those whom Mýkonos can no longer accommodate or those looking for an alternative Greek isle experience—decided to disembark. In recent years windsurfing on the excellent west-coast beaches has attracted an increasing number of visitors.

Parikía, the island's capital and major port, is most alluring in the narrow, stone-paved backstreets of the *agorá* (market) area, where the enveloping and often disorienting whitewashed walls block off all connection with the sea. The north-coast port of Náoussa, once a sleepy fishing village, has become one of the Cyclades' most stylish resorts, with excellent accommodations and gourmet restaurants.

Fortunately, the island's high season doesn't begin until school is out, so travelers searching for the island's more subtle charms have from April until late June and September through October to explore Páros at their leisure. Those arriving in July and August will probably prefer to make Náoussa their base.

PÁROS ESSENTIALS

GETTING THERE & DEPARTING   By Plane   Olympic has 10 daily flights to Páros. For schedule information and reservations, call **Olympic Airways** (☎ 01/926-7251 in Athens or **0284/21-900** in Parikía).

By Boat   The major port, Parikía, is serviced at least once daily from Piraeus (a 6-hour trip). Schedules should be confirmed with tourist information in Piraeus; call ☎ 01/451-1311. The **Ventouris Lines** leave three times a week from Piraeus via Sýros to Páros; call ☎ 0294/25-200 for schedules. The **Strintzi Line** *Ionian Sea* (☎ 01/422-5000) sails three times weekly from Piraeus via Sýros. **Ilio Lines** (☎ 01/422-4772) has hydrofoil service almost daily from Rafína.

When you're ready to move on, Parikía is linked to the other Cyclades via daily ferry service to Náxos, Íos, and Santoríni (Thíra). The F/B *Golden Veryina* has overnight service to Ikaría and Sámos four times a week. For information call the **port authority** in Parikía (☎ 0284/21-240). Tickets are sold by several agents around Mavroyénous Square. We recommend the **Vintsi Agency,** toward the north (left) end of the port (☎ 0284/21-830; fax 0284/23-666), for the best service; schedules are posted along the sidewalk. Day excursions to Mýkonos, Santoríni, Náxos, and Sífnos cost 5,600 to 11,200 Drs ($23.35 to $46.65) and are widely sold.

GETTING AROUND THE ISLAND   There are many scenic attractions within easy walking distance of both Parikía and Náoussa, but there are many options when you want to cover more territory.

By Bus   The public bus provides hourly service between Parikía (leaving on the hour from 8am to 8pm) and Náoussa (leaving on the half hour from 8:30am to 8:30pm). Other public buses from Parikía run regularly from 8am to 9pm to Poúnda (for Antíparos); to Alikí via Petaloúdes and the airport; and to Dríos inland via Léfkes and Márpissa to the southeast-coast beaches at Píso Livádi and Chryssí Aktí. Schedules are posted at the stations or call ☎ 0284/21-133.

By Bicycle   The island's rolling hills are great for exploring by bike, though the pebble-and-dirt roads require good tire pressure. A good regular bike should cost about 2,000 Drs ($8.35) a day. The **Mountain Bike Club of Páros,** left from the bus station, near the post office (☎ 0284/23-778), offers guided trips for 8,600 Drs

($35.85), as well as such essentials as a helmet, insurance, repair kits, and water bottles.

By Car & Moped   There are several moped dealers along the harbor (between the windmill and the yacht marina to the north). It's a seller's market in July and August, and most of the rental shops stand firm on their prices. Mopeds can be dangerous, so check them out carefully before deciding on a rental. Depending on size and season they'll cost about 4,000 to 6,000 Drs ($16.65 to $25) per day. Another alternative is a Jeep or dune buggy. Shop around.

We've had good luck with **Rent-A-Car Acropolis** (☎ 0284/21-830; fax 0284/23-666), run by the good-natured Boyatzis Brothers, and **Budget Rent-a-Car** (☎ 0284/22-302), along the harborfront. Groups of three or four might enjoy renting one of the Acropolis's wildly painted buggies at 16,000 Drs ($66.65) per day or a Suzuki Swift, which costs 21,000 Drs ($87.50) per day. Full insurance, which we recommend, is an additional 3,500 Drs ($14.60) per day.

By Taxi   Taxis can be booked (☎ 0284/21-500) or hailed at the windmill taxi stand. If you're coming off the ferry with lots of luggage and a hotel reservation in Náoussa, it's worth the 1,700 Drs ($7.20) to take a taxi directly there.

PARIKÍA

If you've come to Páros to party, meet fellow travelers, or luxuriate over a glass of Crevellier wine, then Parikía's the spot for you. It's a sophisticated resort with a diverse selection of restaurants and discos, comfortable hotels, and excellent shops. You can easily explore the island's sights by moped or by joining one of the many excursions offered by local travel agents. Pleasant beaches are within a half-hour walk to the south. (The beaches in town are crowded but acceptable.)

ESSENTIALS

VISITOR INFORMATION   The **Páros Tourist Information Bureau** is inside the windmill on the harbor (☎ 0284/22-079); it's open June to September, daily from 9am to 11pm. The staff speaks English and French, provides local schedules, and changes traveler's checks. For information, the helpful **tourist police** (☎ 0284/21-673) can be found in Parikía behind the windmill.

ORIENTATION   Most ferryboats land at Parikía, site of the ancient capital and the largest town on Páros. In front of the pier is Parikía's best-known landmark, a squat, whitewashed **windmill.** To the left is the open triangular **Central Square,** and if you continue along the water, you'll find the **bus station** and a very handy luggage storage (open from 8am to midnight; 300 Drs/$1.25 per piece per day), the post office, the yacht marina, and a slew of new hotels.

To the right from the windmill, the road curves out of sight and follows coastline around the telephone center (OTE) to the old **Kástro** (Venetian castle) neighborhood.

Behind the windmill to the right is the long irregular **Mavroyénous Square,** the town's commercial center. There's a scowling bust of Mandó Mavroyénous in the garden. (After her exploits during the War of Independence, she settled on Páros, where she died, impoverished and forgotten, in 1848.)

On the left side of the square are travel agents, ferryboat-ticket vendors, round-the-island excursion operators, and offices that help with accommodations. The lane that runs straight back through the square, between the two banks, leads to the enticing and picturesque **agorá** (market).

FAST FACTS   There are three **banks** on Mavroyénous Square, open Monday to Friday from 8am to 2pm, plus evenings and Saturday during the high season.

The new private **Medical Center of Páros** is left (west) off Central Square (☎ 0284/24-410), across from the post office in Parikía. The **Parikía Health Clinic** is down the road from Ekatondapylianí (☎ 0284/22-500).

If you need the **police,** call ☎ 100 or 0284/23-333.

The **post office** in Parikía is left from the windmill on the waterfront road (☎ 0284/21-236), open Monday to Friday from 7:30am to 2pm, with extended hours in July and August. It offers public fax service (☎ 0284/22-449).

The **telephone center (OTE)** in Parikía is right from the windmill on the waterfront road, open daily from 7:30am to midnight. (If the front door is closed, go around to the back; wind direction determines which door is left open.)

EXPLORING THE TOWN

Thousands of pilgrims flock to Páros each year to see its beautiful Byzantine cathedral, **Panayía Ekatondapylianí** ("Our Lady of a Hundred Doors"). To reach it, turn left from the windmill and take the street up to the right off Central Square. Notice the graceful lines of the bright-white **Áyios Nikólaos Church,** on its little traffic island. The street leads past the public gardens to Panayía Ekatondapylianí, which is considered the most superb example of Byzantine architecture in the Cyclades. (There are a number of hotels in the winding alleyways between Mavroyénous Square and Ekatondapylianí.)

According to local legend, the church was founded by St. Helen, mother of Constantine, the first Byzantine emperor, in gratitude for the shelter the port had given her during a storm—though the massive yet graceful sanctuary you see today wasn't constructed until the 6th century A.D., incorporating the 4th-century chapel on the left. (It was badly damaged by an earthquake in the 8th century and rebuilt in the 10th century.) The name means "100 Doors," but those who count will find only 99. Legend says that when the 100th door is found, Constantinople (the holiest Greek Orthodox city, known now as Istanbul) will be returned to the Greek nation. The church can be visited daily from 8am to 1pm and 5 to 8pm; admission is free.

Of special interest is the ornately carved iconostasis of luminescent Parian marble. The swing doors that lead to the altar are carved wood painted to resemble marble. The marble floors and columns add lightness and grace to the stone walls. At one time the ceiling and walls were covered with frescoes, and remnants can still be seen. Behind the main basilica on the right is the baptistry, now partly restored. On August 15, the Feast of the Assumption, great festivities are held at the site. Don't miss the beautiful installation of Byzantine icons at the **Ecclesiastical Museum,** open daily from 9am to 1pm and 5 to 9pm; suggested contribution is 500 Drs ($2.20).

The island's **archeological museum,** behind the baptistry of the Ekatondapylianí, is open Tuesday to Sunday from 8:30am to 3pm; admission is 500 Drs ($2.10) for adults, 400 Drs ($1.65) for seniors, and 300 Drs ($1.25) for students. The museum contains finds from the 3rd millennium B.C. at Saliágros to the 1st century B.C. The museum's most valued holding is a fragment of the famous Parian Chronicle (no. 26); the Ashmolean Museum at Oxford University has a larger portion. The chronicle, carved on marble tablets, was found in the 17th century and contains valuable information from which many of the events of Greek history are dated. (Interestingly, it gives us information about artists, poets, and playwrights, but doesn't bother to mention political leaders or battles.) The museum also contains a *Winged Victory* from the 5th century B.C., some objects found at the local Temple of Apollo, and part of a marble monument with a frieze of and information about the poet Archilochus, one of Páros's most famous sons, the important 7th-century B.C. lyric poet who first used iambic meter and ironic detachment. ("What breaks me, young friend, is tasteless desire, lifeless verse, boring dinners.")

Another neighborhood of great interest to those who delight in the architecture is the **Kástro,** about a 10-minute walk south of the windmill on the seaside road. The remains of the 13th-century Venetian fortifications are all the more interesting because of the marble fragments from the ancient Temples of Demeter and Apollo that were incorporated into the walls of the Venetian castle. Traditional Cycladic housing now clings to the old Venetian tower and ramparts in a fascinating melange of architectural styles that spans nearly 3,000 years.

Parikía also offers excellent **shopping,** particularly in the agorá. The wide range of galleries, handcrafts boutiques, clothing shops, and food markets make Páros one of the best spots in all of Greece for memorable souvenir and folk-art shopping. Just off Market Street, almost at its end, you'll find the **Aegean Center for the Fine Arts,** founded by the late American artist Brett Taylor, who left behind an enduring arts institution where artists, photographers, and writers come to study year-round. (For further information, write to the center at Parikía, 844 00 Páros, Cyclades; or fax 0284/23-287.)

A unique shop in the agorá directly across from the Levantis Restaurant is **The Teapot** (☎ 0284/21-177), filled with teas, spices, herbs, henna, and folk art; its assorted packaged herbs and potpourri of local Greek wildflowers make inexpensive and easy-to-carry gifts. There's also interesting shopping (particularly for "hippie" memorabilia) along the *paralía* at night, when traveling European artists and vendors display their wares for passersby.

WHERE TO STAY

The port of Parikía has three basic hotel zones: the agorá, the harbor, and the beach. Because of Páros's immense popularity most hotels now require reservations for July and August, and these should be made at least a month in advance. All written requests must be accompanied by a deposit equal to 1 night's rent. Once you arrive in Greece, a follow-up phone call is highly recommended for those who haven't received a written confirmation.

In the Agorá

The agorá is the heart of Parikía—its pulse beats 24 hours a day. This is the most intriguing place to stay, but it can get noisy. Note that accommodations are available on the outskirts of the agorá in the quiet backstreets, where the tourist presence is less pervasive.

Floga Hotel. Parikía, 844 00 Páros. ☎ **0284/22-017.** 12 rms, all with bath (tub). 8,000 Drs ($33.35) single; 10,000 Drs ($41.65) double. V.

The Floga began as rooms-to-let above the Lobster Restaurant near Livádi. Niko and his wife, Anna, turned their pleasant twin-bedded rooms into a small hotel with views over the surrounding fields. It's a block beyond Mrs. Mavro's (see below), and unless there's a lobster party below, it's very quiet.

✪ **Hotel Argonauta.** Agorá, Parikía, 844 00 Páros 84400. ☎ **0284/21-440.** Fax 0284/23-422. 15 rms, all with bath (shower). TEL. 9,800 Drs ($40.85) single; 12,500 Drs ($52.10) double. Rates include breakfast. EURO, MC, V.

The rustic stone facade and second-floor inner courtyard of this comfortable hotel fit in well with the traditional architecture found behind the Emborikí (Commercial)

Bank and above the very good taverna of that name, overlooking Mavroyénous Square. Soula and Dimitris Ghikas own and operate modern, well-equipped rooms that draw a tamer crowd than many of Parikía's hostels, so it's refreshingly quiet.

Hotel Dina. Market St., Parikía, 844 00 Páros. ☎ **0284/21-325.** 8 rms, all with bath (shower). 11,500 Drs ($47.90) double. Off-season, 30% less. No credit cards.

Our favorite small lodging in Parikía is 200 yards from the port. It would be indistinguishable from its pure-white neighbors if not for the discreet sign mounted outside. All the spotless rooms in this quiet family hotel were recently renovated, with new furniture and curtains. A beautiful garden is another plus.

Hotel Platanos. Parikía, 844 00 Páros. ☎ **0284/24-262.** 12 rms, all with bath (shower). TEL. 17,200 Drs ($71.65) double. No credit cards.

Located 350 yards south of the windmill and 1 block in from the *paralía*, the Platanos comes highly recommended by reader Garry Wabba. The neighborhood is quiet, the rooms comfortable. Ursula Antionou is a most gracious hostess.

Mrs. Zambia Mavro. Parikía, 844 00 Páros. ☎ **0284/21-628.** 4 rms, 1 with bath (shower); 1 studio. 5,200 Drs ($21.65) double without bath, 6,200 Drs ($25.85) double with bath; 9,400 Drs ($39.15) studio. No credit cards.

Mrs. Mavro's large home and two-story pension is in front of a vineyard off the road leading to the Hotel Galinos-Louiza. She speaks very little English, but she's friendly and hospitable. The buzzing, salon-style hair dryers in her living room reveal her main occupation.

Pension Vangelistra. Parikía, 844 00 Páros. ☎ **0284/21-482.** Fax 0284/22-464. 6 rms, all with bath (shower); 3 apts. 11,500 Drs ($47.90) double; 15,000 Drs ($62.50) apt. No credit cards.

This is definitely the coziest and most attractive lodging in the neighborhood down the lane across from the Hotel Louiza. You can't miss its flower-covered veranda, which brightens the whole street. Yorgos and Voula Maounis and their outgoing, English-speaking kids make every guest feel welcome. The rooms are spotless and four have balconies.

At the Harbor

The harborside near the windmill is a convenient and lively place to spend your evenings, and at sunset the views are magnificent.

Hotel Georgy. Platía Mavroyénous, Parikía, 844 00 Páros. ☎ **0284/21-667.** Fax 0284/22-544. 38 rms, all with bath (shower). 10,800 Drs ($45) single; 16,400 Drs ($68.35) double. Continental breakfast 450 Drs ($1.90) extra. No credit cards.

The Kontostavros family takes pride in providing good service to their guests. You have a choice of views over a richly planted inner courtyard or out toward lively Mavroyénous Square.

Hotel Kontes. Platía Mavroyénous, Parikía, 844 00 Páros. ☎ **0284/21-096.** 27 rms, all with bath (tub). 13,000 Drs ($54.15) single; 16,000 Drs ($66.65) double. No credit cards.

The broad arched doorway of this older inn faces Mavroyénous Square. The balconied second-floor rooms provide great views of the windmill and the sea; the first-floor rooms, with shuttered French doors, open onto a large, pleasant sun deck. This is a well-maintained, stylish building where cleanliness more than makes up for a little peeling paint.

Hotel Kýpreos. Parikía, 844 00 Páros. ☎ **0284/21-383** or 0284/22-448. 5 rms, all with bath (shower). 7,000 Drs ($29.15) single; 9,400 Drs ($39.15) double. No credit cards.

Diamanto Apartments, Parikía (☎ **0284/22-448**). "The white building was only 3 years old and had nine apartments, each with balcony or patio—clean, well maintained, and walking distance to all shops and restaurants in Parikía. In early June [1996] we paid only $25 per night. The owner took us to rent a moped as well as back to the ferry after our stay."

—G. W. and Donna Bulman, Woodinville, Wash.

Just north of the windmill, Anne, the warm and helpful hostess, offers neat, simple rooms that include double beds and balconies that shade her husband's car-rental shop below. (A night's stay at the Kýpreos might get you a discount on a car rental.)

At the Beach

The strip of hotels that line Livádi Beach, about a 10-minute walk north (left) of the windmill, offer proximity to the crowded town beach and Aegean sea views. We'll review a few of the hotels briefly, in order of their closeness to the ferryboat pier.

Hotel Argo. Parikía, 844 00 Páros. ☎ **0284/21-367** or 0284/21-207. 45 rms, all with bath (shower). TEL. 13,500 Drs ($56.25) single; 16,000 Drs ($66.65) double. Breakfast 1,000 Drs ($4.15) extra. V.

The Argo's cozy, overfurnished lobby may remind you of your grandmother's. There's is an elevator, and the spacious rooms have balconies.

Hotel Asterias. Parikía, 844 00 Páros. ☎ **0284/21-797** or 0284/22-171. Fax 0284/22-172. 36 rms, all with bath (shower). TEL. 13,900 Drs ($57.90) single; 17,500 Drs ($72.90) double. AE, EURO, MC, V.

This attractive white stucco Cycladic-style hotel is the closest to the beach, and it's one of the best hotels in the area, with a flowering garden out front. The spacious rooms have wooden-shuttered doors that open onto balconies, all with sea views.

Hotel Páros. Parikía, 844 00 Páros. ☎ **0284/21-319.** 15 rms, all with bath (shower). 12,500 Drs ($52.10) single; 14,500 Drs ($60.40) double. MC, V.

This older but well-maintained hotel offers good-value rooms with Aegean views, and Peter, the friendly owner, and his family will help make your stay pleasant.

Villa Ragousi. Parikía, 844 00 Páros. ☎ **0284/21-671.** 10 rms, all with bath (shower). 13,500 Drs ($56.25) single or double. No credit cards.

Recommended by readers, this modern three-story house up the hill from the Taverna Skouna has rather pleasant rooms, some with balconies overlooking the bay. Gavrilla Ragousi speaks English and drives a cab during the day; ask for him at the taxi stand.

Camping

Northwest of the harbor, about 900 yards from the ferry pier, is **Camping Koula** (☎ **0284/22-082**), charging 800 Drs ($3.35) per person; tents are free. It's the area's first-choice campground, but in the summer it gets so busy that most people find it unpleasant.

Parasporos Camping (☎ **0284/21-944**) is a newer facility south of Parikía on the road to Eloúnda. It has all the amenities on large, well-landscaped grounds; this ensures breathing room and quiet, even during busy July and August. The charge is 1,200 Drs ($5) per person; tent sites are free.

WHERE TO EAT

The neon-lighted souvláki/pizza/burger joints near the port seem to suffice for the college crowds, but we've looked for places where the food is tastier and more substantial. For a more elegant meal, we'd suggest that you go to Náoussa.

Aligaria Restaurant. Aligaría Sq., Parikía. ☎ **0284/22-026.** Main courses 1,700–4,000 Drs ($7.10–$16.65). EURO, MC, V. Daily 9am–midnight. GREEK.

The Kontos family runs this traditional Greek kitchen which serves a delicious assortment of simple Greek fare. We tried the lemon roasted potatoes with our grilled chicken and a salad so fresh that the cucumbers were as crunchy as potato chips.

Argonaut Restaurant. Mavroyénous Sq., Parikía. ☎ **0284/21-440.** Main courses 1,200–2,800 Drs ($5–$11.65). EURO, MC, V. Daily 8am–midnight. GREEK/INTERNATIONAL.

Breakfasts are good and reasonably priced, salads are fresh and generous, grilled meats are well prepared, and Greek standards are especially good at this dependable, unpretentious place on the upper end of Mavroyénous Square.

Dionysos Taverna. Agorá, Parikía. ☎ **0284/22-318.** Reservations recommended July–Aug. Main courses 1,100–2,400 Drs ($4.60–$10.05). AE, EURO, MC, V. Daily 6pm–midnight. GREEK/INTERNATIONAL.

This popular taverna has most of its seating outdoors in a pretty garden filled with bright-red geraniums. Inside, a flaking fresco depicts mortals frolicking around Dionysus, who oversees the sale of the Parian favorites: Lagari, a strong red wine, and Kavarnis, a dry white.

Hibiscus Cafe. Platía Valentza, Parikía. ☎ **0284/21-849.** Main courses 1,000–2,000 Drs ($4.15–$8.35). AE, MC, V. Daily noon–midnight. GREEK/PIZZA.

Next to the town hall, about 100 yards south of the port, this is one of the few casual yet stylish places. It's inexpensive, with sea-view tables, a large snack menu, and brick-oven pizza.

Levantis Restaurant. Agorá St., Parikía. ☎ **0284/23-613.** Reservations recommended July–Aug. Main courses 1,500–3,000 Drs ($6.25–$12.50). AE, DC, EURO, MC, V. Wed–Mon 7pm–2am. GREEK/EASTERN MEDITERRANEAN.

Dinner is served under grapevines that some of the older residents remember being there when they were young. Vivacious Mariana is happy to recommend her favorite of the day, and her husband, Nikolas, offers a friendly glass of wine. The fish can be disappointing but the Eastern specialties are excellent.

Poseidon Grill. Livádi Beach. ☎ **0284/22-667.** Main courses 1,000–2,000 Drs ($4.15–$8.35). No credit cards. Daily 8am–midnight. GREEK.

Across from the Stella Hotel near the beach, this fancier taverna has a wide range of vegetable entrees and excellent fish. Share a swordfish, grilled calamari, some *mezédes* (appetizers), salad, and a bottle of Nissiotissa wine.

PARIKÍA AFTER DARK

Warning: Several places on the strip offer very cheap drinks or "buy one, get one free"—usually it's locally brewed alcohol that the locals call *bómba.* It's illegal, and it makes you intoxicated quickly and very sick afterward.

Just behind the windmill is another Parikía landmark, the **Port Café,** a basic *kafenío* lit by bare incandescent bulbs. It's filled day and night with tourists waiting for the ferry, bus, taxi, or just waiting. The Port Café serves coffee, drinks, and pastry, and you can pass the time kibbitzing with a wide variety of fellow travelers.

The **Saloon d'Or,** south of the port (☎ **0284/22-176**), is the most popular place for starting the evening with fairly inexpensive drinks; on good nights the Saloon attracts the liveliest young crowd around. Continue south along the coast road, turn left at the bridge, and about 100 yards farther you should have no difficulty finding a complex with the **Dubliner** (☎ **0284/22-759**), which presents live Irish music several nights a week; **Down Under** (Australian, mate); and the **Hard Rock Café** (☎ **0284/21-113**).

If partying's not your thing, Parikía offers several elegant alternatives. The **Pebbles Bar,** on the port, plays classical music. The **Pirate Bar,** a few doors away from the Hotel Dina in the agorá, is a tastefully decorated bar whose stone interior is braced with dark wooden beams. Mellow jazz, blues, and classical music accompany the slightly more expensive drinks.

Back at the bustling *paralía,* there's a more sophisticated choice with wonderful Aegean views. The **Evinos Bar** is above the three-tiered retaining wall south of the OTE, high enough above the din so that you can appreciate the music streaming subtly from the bar speakers and take in the lovely scenery.

If you're a party type, you might enjoy the **Rendezvous,** down from Evinos, with pretty good pop music. **Black Bart's** (☎ **0284/21-802**) is midway on the *paralía*—a good spot for very loud rock music and a boisterous, big-drinker clientele.

There are two outdoor cinemas. **Ciné Rex,** right off the south-coast road (☎ **0284/21-676**), has two nightly "B" pictures, usually in English. The **Cine Páros** is in the opposite direction, up from the north end of the *paralía.*

There are enough discos tucked away in the back lanes of the agorá and at the far end of the *paralía* that it would be futile to recommend one over another.

NÁOUSSA

Náoussa is perched on Páros's north coast, between two fat peninsulas lined with rocky coves and sandy beaches. Fortunately, recent tourist development has focused on the beach areas, keeping the village relatively unspoiled. The small active port where fishermen still fish and the maze of whitewashed back lanes contribute to the town's genuine charm.

Náoussa offers a sizable selection of good restaurants and shops, most tucked into the pedestrian lanes off the town's main square. Some of the island's most exquisite beaches are within walking distance, nestled in the convoluted northern coastline. Many of the better hotels are scattered across the rolling hills and narrow, unpaved coastal paths leading to these beach coves, so Náoussa appears less developed than it actually is.

If you continue across the **main square** to an arched entryway, you'll be at the medieval gates of the **old city.** Within are the fascinating back alleys of Náoussa; they're best explored in midafternoon, when the inhabitants retire inside for siesta. Meandering quietly along the cobblestone paths and peeking into the geranium-filled gardens provides an undisturbed view of Greek life.

Beyond the National Bank is the busy **harbor** on Áyios Dimítrios Bay. It's most active at sunrise and late afternoon, when the fishers are setting out or returning home with the day's catch. From the portside cafes you can watch the nets being spread out on the dock, then carefully folded for the next day's outing. The blue, green, orange, and yellow caïques are scrubbed, rinsed, and fixed to their moorings. Across the way, the small whitewashed **Áyios Nikólaos Church,** dedicated to the patron saint of sailors, stands out strikingly in a sea of primary colors. A legacy of the 15th-century Venetian occupation of this tiny port is the old stonework of the breakwater on the eastern side. The ruined ramparts submerged in this part of the harbor are lighted at night.

ESSENTIALS

VISITOR INFORMATION   The helpful **Nissiótissa Tours** office is off the left side of main square (☎ **0284/51-480** or 0284/51-094; fax 0284/51-189), across the lane from the Náoussa Sweet Shop. Cathy and Kostas Gavalas, Greek-Americans who returned to Náoussa, know this area better than anyone else and are exceptionally well qualified to help you find a hotel, room-to-let, apartment, or villa. The Gavalas also book Olympic flights and arrange other plane, ferryboat, and excursion tickets, island tours, and rental cars (EuroCard, MasterCard, and Visa are accepted).

ORIENTATION   If you're traveling the 7 miles north from Parikía, you'll know you're approaching Náoussa by the hotels and restaurants that line the paved roadway. After crossing a street-level **bridge,** Archilochus Street and Náoussa's **main square** will be on the right. The square, shaded by tall eucalyptus trees, contains the **bus station** and **taxi stand.**

GETTING AROUND   Náoussa's sudden growth in popularity has meant expanded transportation connections to other parts of Páros and the Cyclades islands.

By Bus   Buses leave from the main square for Parikía on the half hour between 8:30am and 8:30pm (they run more often in July and August); the fare for the 15-minute trip is 300 Drs ($1.25). There's bus service to Santa Maria beach twice daily. Service to other island villages on poorly paved or narrow dirt roads is infrequent.

By Moped & Car   Because there are so many excellent beaches within 12¹/₂ miles of Náoussa village, a **moped** is a good way to sample them at your own pace. There are several moped dealers on the square and the prices are comparable to those in Parikía (you probably won't be able to bargain during the peak-demand summer season).

   Nissiótissa Tours rents **Suziki Swifts** for about 18,000 Drs ($75) daily, including third-party insurance and unlimited mileage in the high season—about half this in the low season.

By Taxi   Taxis are an expensive option for beach hopping; they're difficult to find outside the village, but for getting to and from Parikía, they're often worth the 2,000 Drs ($8.35). Luggage costs about 100 Drs (40¢) per bag extra.

By Boat   Daily **excursion boats** leave from the Náoussa harbor for Mýkonos and Délos; the 2-hour trip costs 5,800 Drs ($24.15) one-way, and the full-day round-trip excursion is 11,000 Drs ($45.85). In summer there are round-trip excursions to Náxos for 5,000 Drs ($20.85) and to Santoríni for 13,000 Drs ($54.15); one-way tickets are half price. Local caïques provide service to Kolymbíthres, Monastery, and Langéri beaches for about 800 Drs ($3.35) and to the Santa Maria beach (about 4 miles away around the eastern peninsula) for about 1,800 Drs ($7.50) round-trip.

FAST FACTS   The town **police** (☎ 0284/51-202) are on the road to Parikía, across from the **telephone office (OTE).** (You can also use metered phones at travel agencies.) The **post office** is 600 yards out on the road to Ambelas. The town **doctor** is on the main square, on the right side before the church. There's a **foreign periodicals shop** on the square.

WHERE TO STAY

In the quiet backstreets surrounding the Hotel Minoa—and in the whole area behind the Sagriótis Monument—you'll find a scattering of whitewashed buildings carrying signs for ROOMS, CHAMBRES, and ZIMMER. If you haven't made high-season reservations and can't find a hotel room, try **Nissiótissa Travel,** just off the square (☎ **0284/51-480**).

Hotel Fotilia. Náoussa, 844 01 Páros. ☎ **0284/52-581.** Fax 0284/52-583. 14 rms, all with bath (shower). TEL. 19,500 Drs ($81.25) single; 22,000 Drs ($91.65) double. Rates include breakfast. AE, V.

Climb to the top of the steps at the end of town and to the left of the church you'll see a restored windmill behind a stone archway. Here the companionable Michael Leondaris greets you with a glass of wine or a cup of coffee. The rooms are spacious and furnished in an elegant country style. Crisp blue-and-white-striped curtains open to balconies that overlook the old harbor and bay.

Kalypso Hotel. Ayíi Anáryiri Beach, 844 01 Páros. ☎ **0284/51-488.** Fax 0284/51-607. 40 rms, all with bath (shower). 14,000 Drs ($58.25) single; 21,000 Drs ($87.50) double. Rates include breakfast. AE, MC, V.

This is a very nice beachside hotel built around a cobblestone courtyard, although many of the outer, balconied rooms overlook the sea. The upper-floor rooms, quite spacious, are reached via an ornately carved wooden mezzanine that overlooks the Kalypso's bar.

Papadakis Hotel. Náoussa, 844 01 Páros. ☎ **0284/52-504.** Fax 0284/51-269. 16 rms, all with bath (shower). 16,500 Drs ($68.75) single; 19,000 Drs ($79.15) double. Rates include breakfast. No credit cards.

If you like hillside locations, the friendly Papadakis offers the best views over the village and bay. After a brisk 5-minute walk from the square, you'll arrive at its sunny breakfast lounge, where fresh carnations grace every table. The large, newly built rooms have balconies overlooking the bay and village or open out onto a common patio; those who climb the steps to the highest balconied rooms are most rewarded.

Hotel Petres. Náoussa, 844 01 Páros. ☎ **0284/52-467.** Fax 0284/52-759. 16 rms, all with bath (shower). A/C MINIBAR TEL. 13,500 Drs ($56.25) single; 19,000 Drs ($79.15) double. Rates include American buffet breakfast. DC, V.

You enter a charming reception area furnished with antiques. Claire Hatzinkolakis has decorated her rooms with loving care: handsome woven covers on the beds, hand-crocheted lace draped over the lamps, and prints from the Benaki Museum on the walls. There's a swimming pool, and a kitchen and barbecue are available to guests. Her "honeymoon suite" has her grandmother's marriage bed in it.

Apartments

There are a number of newly built apartments and studios in this area—at Áyíi Anáryiri Beach. Most function like small hotels, with a reception desk, common switchboard, lounge, and—occasionally—breakfast service.

Batistas Apartments. Náoussa, 844 01 Páros. ☎ **0284/51-058,** or 01/975-7286 in Athens. 8 apts. 17,000 Drs ($70.85) apt for two; 27,000 Drs ($112.50) apt for four. No credit cards.

Mrs. Batistas's homespun lace, crochet, and needlework give these handsome apartments an extra feeling of home.

Kapten Nikolas Apartments. Ayíi Anáryiri, 844 01 Páros. ☎ **0284/51-340.** Fax 0284/51-519. 17 apts. TEL. 17,000 Drs ($70.85) apt for two; 27,000 Drs ($112.50) apt for four. No credit cards.

These apartments near the Hotel Kalypso are handsomely furnished with marble-top tables and colorful furniture. The neighborhood is quiet and the sea views are lovely.

The larger apartments have two bathrooms. (Contact Nissiotissa Tours for reservations.)

Lily Apartments. Náoussa, 844 01 Páros. ☎ **0284/51-377,** or 01/958-9314 in Athens. Fax 0284/51-716, or 01/958-9314 in Athens. 17 apts. TEL. 17,000 Drs ($70.85) apt for two. EURO, MC, V.

Lily Ananiadou has our favorite apartments: simple, pleasantly modern, fully equipped—with kitchens, telephones, and balconies overlooking dry, scrub-brush hills.

A Splurge Choice

Hotel Contaratos Beach. Ayíi Anáryiri Beach, Náoussa, 844 01 Páros. ☎ **0284/51-693,** or 01/491-3530 in Athens. Fax 0284/51-740. 33 rms, all with bath (tub). TEL. 21,000 Drs ($87.50) single; 28,500 Drs ($118.75) double. Rates include breakfast. EURO, MC, V.

This is one of the best hotels on Páros, with rooms (most with balconies) that have large bathrooms, good reading lights, safety boxes, and views to Ayíi Anáryiri beach. There's a large swimming pool and sun deck, a tennis court, a private beach, and water sports, and the hotel offers laundry service and bicycle rental.

WHERE TO EAT

Náoussa's main square has most of the casual eating establishments in the area. Go past the church near Christo's Taverna to reach the village's **bread bakery.** The **Náoussa Pâtisserie,** on the east side of the main square, has delicious snacks of cheese pies, biscuits, espresso, and pastries. Fast-food/pizza/sandwich/ice-cream shops have proliferated in Náoussa as elsewhere, so you'll have plenty of choices for a snack or breakfast.

Barbarossa Ouzerí. On the waterfront. ☎ **0284/51-391.** Appetizers 550–1,200 Drs ($2.30–$5). No credit cards. Daily 1pm–1am. GREEK.

This authentic local *ouzerí* is right on the port. Old, windburned fishers sit for hours nursing their milky ouzo in water and miniportions of grilled octopus and olives. If you haven't partaken of this experience yet, this is the place to try it.

Kavarnis Bar. Archilochus St. ☎ **0284/51-038.** Crêpes 900–2,200 Drs ($3.75–$9.15); pasta 1,200–2,800 Drs ($5–$11.65). No credit cards. Daily 7:30pm–2am. CONTINENTAL.

This beautiful bar, just around the corner from the post office, has an interior that reminds you of another time—Paris in the 1920s or an American private club from the 1940s. The menu is crêpes, stuffed with everything from fruit to meat to ice cream. Try the famous cognac crêpe. The restaurant also serves elaborate cocktails with some modern jazz.

✪ **Lalula.** Náoussa. ☎ **0284/51-547.** Reservations recommended July–Aug. Main courses 2,000–3,600 Drs ($8.35–$15). No credit cards. Daily 7–11:45pm. GREEK/VEGETARIAN/MEDITERRANEAN.

Take a left at the post office and you'll find Lalua across from the Minoa Hotel. This is the venture of two chefs favored by past readers who loved their Tria Asteria Restaurant. A gifted German restaurateur is responsible for the delicious and distinctive food, subdued decor, and interesting but unobtrusive music. The cooking is light and refined, more health-conscious and vegetarian-oriented than one usually finds in Greece. Specials change daily to reflect what's fresh at the market; regular menu offerings include vegetable quiche, sweet-and-sour chicken with rice and ginger chutney, and fish steamed in herbs.

Minoa Restaurant. In the Minoa Hotel. ☎ **0284/51-309.** Main courses 1,000–3,500 Drs ($4.15–$14.60). No credit cards. Daily 7:30am–midnight. GREEK.

Uphill from the village square, the Minoa is one of Náoussa's best tavernas. A feast of rich, old-fashioned Greek fare steeped in olive oil and oregano, with fresh bread and wine, will cost about $25 for two.

Perivólaria. Náoussa. ☎ **0284/51-721.** Main courses 1,400–3,600 Drs ($5.85–$15). AE, V. Daily 7pm–midnight. GREEK.

About 100 yards back from the port are tables set in a lush garden of geraniums and grapes, or inside a whitewashed stucco house decorated with local ceramics. Favorite courses here include the schnitzel à la chef (veal in cream sauce with tomatoes and basil) and the tortellini Perivólaria (with pepperoni and bacon), both original, but the Greek plate with souvláki and varied appetizers is also popular.

Taverna Christo's. Archilochus St. ☎ **0284/51-442.** Reservations recommended July–Aug. Main courses 1,200–3,500 Drs ($5–$14.60). No credit cards. Daily 7:30–11:30pm. EURO-GREEK.

Taverna Christo's is known for its eclectic menu and Euro-Greek style. Dinner is served in a beautiful garden filled with red and pink geraniums. The trellised roof is dripping with grape clusters whose dark-purple color in late August is unforgettable. You can listen to classical music while dining on elegantly prepared, fresh veal, lamb, or steak dishes.

NÁOUSSA AFTER DARK

If holding hands while strolling under the stars doesn't fill up your evening, you can take in an outdoor "B" picture at the **Makis Cinema** (☎ **0284/21-676** or 0284/22-221). The show times are usually 10pm and midnight; the films are often in English, and the cost is 1,200 Drs ($5). A local friend recommends the **Sofrano Bar,** on the harbor, for relaxed conversation. If you had something a little more active in mind, try **Banana Moon,** a 10-minute walk up the hill on the main street.

EXPLORING THE REST OF THE ISLAND

If your time is limited, rent a moped or share a car for a 1-day around-the-island tour. Solo travelers may find it more economical to book a bus tour offered by several local travel agents for about 3,000 Drs ($12.50). **Páros Travel** (☎ **0284/21-582;** fax 0284/22-582) offers a variety of tours for 2,000 to 4,000 Drs ($7.20 to $14.35).

A day of sightseeing around Páros should begin in Parikía, include Petaloúdes and a visit to a beach such as Kolymbíthres on the way north, then a stop in Náoussa for a seafood lunch at the picturesque harbor. From Náoussa, the tour should continue south to one of the finest east-coast beaches, such as Ormós Mólos. On the return trip across the heartland of Páros to Parikía, be sure to stop at Léfkes, the medieval capital, and at the marble quarries of Maráthi.

PETALOÚDES   The valley of Petaloúdes ("Butterflies") is a lush oasis of pear, plum, fig, and pomegranate trees 4 miles south of Parikía. Take the beach road out of town, continue for about 2$^{1}/_{2}$ miles until you reach the left-hand turnoff for the Monastery of Christoús to Dássos ("Christ of the Forest"), which has been a nunnery since 1805. Then head a little over half a mile downhill to what Greeks call *Psychopianí* ("Soul Softener") because it lightens the heart and mind.

Kóstas Graváris opens his home daily from 8am to 8pm, closing it for siesta from 1 to 4pm. He recommends coming in the early morning or evening, when the butterflies leave the ivy leaves they cling to and fly around. The butterflies, actually tiger moths *(Panaxia quadripunctaria poda),* look like black-and-white-striped arrowheads until they fly up to reveal their bright red underwings. (They're most abundant from July 15 to August 15.) The unique combination on this arid island of a freshwater spring, dense foliage, flowering trees, and cool shade is what has lured butterflies here for at least 300 years (since the Graváris family has had this property). There's a small snack bar at the site; the butterfly keeper's fee is 800 Drs ($3.35). Donkey or mule rides from Parikía along a backroad cost about 2,000 Drs ($8.35).

LÉFKES Head south from Náoussa to Márpissa, then take the westward inland road to Parikía. It begins to ascend steep hills, and when you spot the elaborate Léfkes Village Resort, you've come to the perimeter of Léfkes. The amphitheatrical tiers of whitewashed houses with red-tiled roofs surround a central town square. It's said that Léfkes, the medieval capital of Páros, was built so that if pirates ever reached it, its sharply angled, narrow streets and confusing levels would thwart them. Even today, trying to reach the famed Ayía Triáda (Holy Trinity) Church, whose carved marble towers are easily visible from a distance, is a feat.

THE MARBLE QUARRIES AT MARÁTHI Parian marble, prized for its translucency and soft, granular texture, was used by ancient sculptors for their best works, including the *Hermes* of Praxiteles and the *Venus de Milo*. The marble quarries at Maráthi are the last stop on the return trip to Parikía; to reach them, take the winding mountain roads about 3 miles west of Léfkes, where the tiny farming community of Maráthi lives on a plateau. From the road, walk up to the left beyond the few farmhouses toward the deserted buildings that once belonged to a French mining company which in 1844 produced the marble for Napoleon's tomb. If not for the prohibitive cost, modern-day sculptors could still work with this incomparable material.

Continue 1¼ miles farther to the village of Kóstos; perched above it you'll find **Studio Yria** (☎ 0284/29-007), where local craftsmen Stelio and Monika Ghikis produce functional earthenware with indigenous designs, including an abstract octopus motif, as well as weavings and objects of cast bronze, forged iron, and Parian marble.

WEST-COAST BEACHES South from Parikía, along the west coast, which faces the island of Antíparos, are several fine beaches. Just 2 miles from the port is **Ayía Iríni,** a secluded sandy beach cove visible from the elevated main road just before the turnoff for Petaloúdes. Here you'll find a taverna, the **Ayía Iríni Campgrounds** (☎ 0284/22-340), and a handful of palm trees. Another 10 minutes south by moped is the turnoff for **Poúnda,** the largest of the "Points" on the island, a popular sandy beach, with many rental rooms, that gets crowded in July and August. Poúnda is at the narrowest stretch of the Aegean between Páros and Antíparos, and you can sit in a cafe and examine Antíparos's main port.

Alikí, a fishing village turned tourist resort, is about 12½ miles south of Parikía, beyond the airport. Many hand-built caïques are moored in the small natural harbor, and tucked around a large clean sandy beach cove are discos, cafes, and many new prefab buildings (with more to come).

Buses run hourly from Parikía—though they're sometimes unreliable—and there are many rooms near this friendly port. Our first choice would be the **Hotel Angeliki** (☎ 0284/91-235), a 13-room Class C place at the far end of the town's pier, where doubles with private bath are 7,800 Drs ($32.50) in the summer and all the balconies have beautiful views of the busy port and beach.

The **Aphrodíti,** on the road into town (☎ 0284/91-249), is another good pension. The friendly Aliprantis family has 20 modern spacious, spotless, and simply furnished rooms with balconies; doubles with bath are 8,200 Drs ($31.15).

Many shops and the **general store** (where you park your vehicle, as you have to walk through most of the town) also have rooms for rent.

NORTH-COAST BEACHES The north-coast beaches, hugging the two peninsulas that jut into Áyios Dimítrios Bay around the village of Náoussa, are the best sheltered beaches on the island. To the west of Náoussa (a caïque ride there will cost 800 Drs/$3.35, or it's about 10 minutes by moped) is the picturesque **Kolymbíthres Beach.** Small sandy coves are punctuated by smooth, giant rocks, which must be scaled or swum around to reach the next cove or the open sea. Reminiscent of the weird rocks that jut into the air above Metéora, this lunar seascape is well worth a visit even for those who can't stand sparkling azure water and golden sand.

The very attractive **Hotel Kouros** (☎ **0284/51-565;** fax 0284/51-000), with beautifully landscaped grounds and a freshwater pool, is only a 10-minute walk south. Its 55 spacious, full-amenity rooms are often booked by German tour groups, but it's well worth a try; doubles cost 19,500 Drs ($81.25) and American Express, EuroCard, MasterCard, and Visa are accepted.

When you're hungry, we recommend the **Dolphin Taverna,** about 100 yards from the Kouros, open from 7am to 2am, for traditional Greek food; dinner for two with wine will cost about 7,000 Drs ($29.15).

Camping Naoussa, about 60 yards from the beach (☎ **0284/51-595**), has hot showers, a shared kitchen, and laundry and dishwashing facilities; tent sites are free and camp guests pay 1,250 Drs ($5.20) each; tents can be rented for 800 Drs ($3.35).

North of Kolymbíthres, by the Áyios Ioánnis Church, is **Monastery Beach,** the north coast's nudist beach, and the new **Monasteri Beach Club,** a bar-restaurant with music and beach service. Most of the other beaches west of Náoussa are overcrowded because of all the hotels.

About 2¹/₂ miles north of Náoussa on a poorly paved road is the popular **Langéri Beach.** Before you reach Langéri, the road forks to the right, and bearing right will bring you to **Santa Maria Beach,** one of the most beautiful on the island because of its clear water. Shallow sand dunes (rare in Greece) line the broad banks of fine sand that curve around the irregular coastline. Although Santa Maria is only about 20 minutes from Náoussa by public bus or moped, most tourists don't make it that far.

Those who do can't miss the **Aristophanes Taverna,** a simple, shaded outdoor deck behind the dunes where you can have grilled fish (particularly good are the foot-long *barboúnia,* red mullets) or meats, and in the cooler spring and fall weather, a daily soup. A lunch feast of fresh grilled *astakós* (local lobster) with wine, cheese, and a salad will cost about 14,000 Drs ($58.35) for two of you—it's a splurge, that's for sure, but you'll never forget the experience. (The Aristophanes also offers villas for rent.)

Nearby, the **Santa Maria Surf Club** provides windsailing gear and lessons. Check here or at Ayía Iríni, Kolymbíthres, or Logáras on windsurfing lessons and equipment rental.

Southeast of Náoussa, available by public bus, is the fishing village of **Ambelás,** which has a good small beach, inexpensive taverna, rooms for rent, and several small hotels. The **Hotel Christina** (☎ **0284/51-573**) has 18 simple rooms (all with shower), with doubles for 9,500 Drs ($39.60), and a good restaurant.

EAST-COAST BEACHES The east-coast beaches can be reached by private transportation or public bus from Parikía or Náoussa; buses leave hourly in the summer from either village.

The east-coast roadway runs about a third of a mile inland from the sea, so you can't scope out the beaches from the bus window. Ask around—the local beach-bum grapevine will provide the latest update—and choose wisely; once you've disembarked, it's several miles to the next beach.

Mólos, at the tip of a small peninsula, is beautiful and convenient to the attractive inland villages of **Mámara** and **Márpissa,** where there are rooms for rent, so it's

---

Readers Recommend	

Antíparos. "I just wanted your readers to know that Antíparos is a diamond waiting to be found. The town and the Artemis Hotel are made for couples and especially families for a peaceful getaway to an enchanted island."

—Dennis Sciotto, Imperial Beach, Calif.

---

often crowded. **Píso Livádi,** about 6 miles from either Parikía or Náoussa, is a small, dirty, sandy beach cove surrounded by hotels and pizza parlors. The shallow harbor makes an unappealing swimming hole in full view of the overtouristed town. The next cove south, **Logáras,** has a good sandy beach, but it gets the overflow from busy Píso Livádi.

The next major beach, **Chryssí Aktí** ("Golden Coast"), $15^{1}/_{2}$ miles south of Náoussa, is generally considered the best beach on the island, as well as the windiest. It has half a mile of fine golden sand and has become a major windsurfing center, the site of the 1993 World Windsurfing Championship competition. There are two windsurfing clubs, the **Sunwind BIC Center** and **Force Seven,** with lessons for beginners to advanced surfers.

Chrissí Aktí has some tavernas, rooms for rent, hotels, and even a disco and bar. The community is about half a mile off the paved main road, with a parking lot at the end for beach commuters. At the parking lot, the **Golden Beach Hotel** (☎ **0284/41-194;** fax 0284/41-195) has 35 rooms with beach views, doubles with shower for 14,400 Drs ($60). Next door, the newer, 38-room **Amarilis Hotel** (☎ **0284/41-410;** fax 0284/41-600) has doubles with shower for 18,000 Drs ($63.75).

Many overnight visitors, however, head south $1^{1}/_{2}$ miles to **Dríos,** a pretty village that's fast becoming a resort town. The **Julia Hotel** (☎ **0284/41-494**) has 12 rooms with doubles for 7,600 Drs ($31.65) near the small pebble beach. The very nice **Hotel Annezina** (☎ **0284/41-037**) has 13 double rooms with shower, at 8,200 Drs ($31.15) each, and a good restaurant in the center of tiny bustling Dríos. It's wedged in next to a good supermarket, by the bus stop, and near the popular **Anchor Tavern.** Buses run to Dríos from Parikía five times daily, hourly in the summer.

A SIDE TRIP TO ANTÍPAROS (ANDÍPAROS)

A visit to Antíparos is likely to be appreciated by anyone who wants to get away from all the crowds in Parikía. This 7-mile-long island, just "anti" ("opposite") the western coast of Páros, was once connected to it by a natural causeway. For centuries its huge cave drew distinguished tourists who otherwise had little reason to go to Páros. King Otto of Greece and Lord Byron visited the cave and carved their names in the many stalagmites and stalactites.

Tourists who arrive on the excursion caïques from Parikía no longer descend the 100 yards into the cave by rope—a safer concrete staircase has been built. Nonetheless, an hour spent in the dark, echo-filled cave trying to decipher some of the inscriptions is a lot more adventuresome than—and a stark contrast to—sitting on a beach; it also makes for good storytelling long afterward.

Excursion caïques leave the port of Parikía regularly beginning at 8am for the 45-minute ride to the busy port of Antíparos. Round-trip excursions that include a visit to the caves (about a 2-hour walk from the village of Antíparos) cost about 3,000 Drs ($12.50) from Parikía and 1,600 Drs ($6.65) from Náoussa. When the boat docks, you'll have to climb the hill to the Church of St. John of the Cave. From here you'll have an excellent view south to Folégandros (farthest west), Síkinos, and Íos, with a bit of Páros to your left. There are also local shuttle boats plying the channel between Poúnda and Antíparos continuously from 9am. The fare is 300 Drs ($1.25).

Besides the several pensions and rooms-to-let, the newer **Hotel Artemis,** at the end of the *paralía* (☎ **0284/61-460;** fax 0284/61-472), has 30 comfortable rooms; a double with breakfast is 13,200 Drs ($55). The **Mantalena** (☎ **0284/61-206**) has 35 rooms, with doubles from 7,300 Drs ($30.40). There's also a **Camping Antiparoes** (☎ **0284/61-221**) with full facilities about a 10-minute walk north from the port.

5 Náxos

103 nautical miles SE of Piraeus

Náxos is the largest, most fertile, and most self-sufficient of the Cyclades. Its capital, **Hóra (Náxos town),** has the famous Portára, a portal to an ancient Temple of Apollo, and its Kástro, an impressive 13th-century Venetian castle surrounded by a pleasant maze of pedestrian lanes, plus a well-developed resort area just south of town. The interior of the island is unspoiled, with abundant charm, thriving agriculture, a number of interesting villages, and spectacular scenery, including Mt. Zas, the highest point in the Cyclades.

Náxos provides the setting for the mythical story of the Cretan princess Ariadne, daughter of King Minos, who fell in love with the Athenian hero Theseus. In exchange for his promise to marry her, she gave him a ball of thread to find his way out of the Labyrinth. After he had slain the Minotaur—the half-bull, half-man monster born of her mother Pasiphaë's union with a white bull—and escaped from the Labyrinth, she fled with him to Náxos, where he abandoned her. (An Athenian spin claims that he intended to come back for her.) But the god Dionysus happened to be in the neighborhood, having recently commandeered a ship from pirates who had seized him for ransom, and he took pity on the abandoned young woman and married her. When she died, Dionysus set the crown he had given her in the heavens to form the constellation of Corona.

ESSENTIALS

GETTING THERE & DEPARTING   **By Plane**   **Olympic Airways** has two flights daily (three in summer) between Athens and Náxos. For information and reservations call its office in Athens (☎ **01/926-7251**) or on Náxos (☎ **0285/22-095**).

By Boat   There's one ferry daily (more in the summer) from Piraeus; at present service is offered by several carriers, although it's irregular. For schedule information in Piraeus call ☎ **01/451-1311,** or call the **Náxos Port Authority** (☎ **0285/22-340**).

There is daily (several times a day in the summer) ferry service to and from Íos, Mýkonos, Páros, and Santoríni. And several times weekly there's also ferry service to/from Sýros and Tínos, less frequently to/from Folégandros, Rhodes, and Sámos, and once a week to/from Sífnos. **Ilio Lines** (☎ **01/422-4772** in Athens or 0294/22-888 in Rafína) offers hydrofoil service daily except Saturday from Rafína.

VISITOR INFORMATION   There's no official tourist information office; the commercial **Náxos Tourist Information Center** (☎ **0285/22-923** or 0285/24-525; fax 0285/25-200), across the plaza from the ferry pier (not to be confused with the small office on the pier itself, which is usually closed), is run by Despina and Kostas Kitini. Their office is the most reliable and helpful on the island; current bus and boat schedules are posted out front. They sell Olympic Airways and ferry tickets, book island excursions, make hotel and villa reservations, exchange money, store luggage, help make card and collect phone calls, and offer 2-hour laundry service!

The **tourist police** (☎ 0285/22-100) are located 2 blocks behind the Panayía Pantanássa Church, just before the Agrarian Bank—about 200 yards south from the ferry pier; there's a list of hotels and private rooms there, and they'll make reservations for you.

ORIENTATION   Boats arrive at the harbor on the northern end of Náxos in the main town, **Hóra (Náxos town).** South (right) of the pier, built on a tiny islet nestled in the harbor, is the whitewashed **Myrtidiótissa Church.** On the north side of the port, to the left as you disembark, is the **Portára,** an ancient portal that has welcomed visitors to the island for more than 2,500 years.

Above the town stands the **Kástro,** and below it is the old town of **Boúrgos.** To the left, on the northern coast of Hóra is the neighborhood called **Grotta.** Just south of town is the beachfront resort of **Áyios Yióryios,** which can be reached most directly by walking down the *paralía,* the cafe- and souvenir-lined esplanade that overlooks the harbor.

GETTING AROUND   Walking is the best way to experience Náxos because it gives you the opportunity to join the local pace and to meet the friendly residents face to face. If you plan to walk around in the interior, save your energy by catching a bus to a village that interests you, then explore it at your leisure on foot.

By Bus   You can't miss the **bus station** right in the middle of the port plaza on the north end of the harbor; ask at the nearby KTEL office, across the plaza to the left, for specific schedules. There's regular service throughout most of the island two or three times a day, more frequently to the more important destinations. In the summer there's hourly service to the nearby south-coast beaches at Áyios Prokópios and Ayía Ánna.

One of the most popular day trips is to Apóllonos, near the northern tip of the island, but the bus only makes this trip twice a day and the competition for seats is often fierce. The trip takes over 2 hours, and if you don't want to stand all that time and miss the scenery, you should be at the station well ahead of time.

In addition to the public buses there are various **excursion buses** that can be booked through travel agents.

By Bike   Bikes will suffice for getting to the beach and back, but the interior becomes too mountainous. There are good bike-rental places near the bus station and the post office.

By Moped or Motorcycle   The island's roads are fairly good and the traffic is sane. **Moto Naxos,** on Post Office Square (☎ 0285/23-410), and **Stelios Rent-A-Bike,** near the police station (☎ 0285/24-703), offer a good selection. Expect to pay about 4,000 to 9,000 Drs ($16.65 to $37.50) a day, including insurance, depending on size and season. Make sure your vehicle is in good running condition before you accept it; Náxos has some major hills that require a strong motor and good brakes.

By Car   A Jeep or small car might better suit your requirements, and most travel agents rent them. **ZAS Travel,** near the bus station (☎ 0285/23-444), rents buggies, cars, and Suzukis for about 11,000 to 20,000 Drs ($45.85 to $83.35) per day, including full insurance, free mileage and road service, a map, and good advice.

By Taxi   A half-day taxi tour around the island should cost you about 15,000 Drs ($62.50). The **taxi station** (☎ 0285/22-444) is on the port; drop by and talk it over, selecting a compatible driver who speaks English well enough to serve as a guide, bargain, and agree on a price before you depart.

FAST FACTS   The **telephone office (OTE)** is at the south end of the port; open daily in summer from 7:30am to midnight. Turn inland (left) at the OTE and take the first right to reach the **post office** on the left; it's open Monday to Friday from 8am to 2:30pm.

The town **police** (☎ **0285/23-280**) are off the north end of the port, up from the bus station, across from the elementary school.

Náxos has a good 24-hour **health center** (☎ **0285/23-333**), just outside town on the left off Odós Papavasíliou, the main street off the port just after the OTE.

The **banks** all keep the same hours—Monday to Thursday from 8am to 2pm and Friday from 8am to 1:30pm—but travel agencies can exchange money during extended hours.

English-language **newspapers and periodicals** are available at an old shop behind and to the right of the Captain's Cafe, at the entrance to the Old Market, or at Zoom, on the harborfront.

EXPLORING HÓRA

Find a good map as soon as possible, since Hóra (Náxos town) is old, large (with a permanent population of more than 3,000), and complex. The free *Summer Náxos* magazine has the best map of the city. The new Harms-Verlag *Náxos* is the best map of the island. John Freely's guide *Náxos* (Lycabettus Press) is a short, colorful account with excellent descriptions of walking tours.

The **Portára** ("Great Door") and a foundation is all that remains of an ancient **Temple of Apollo,** which stands on the islet of Palátia, a hill before the Mediterranean rose, now accessible by a causeway off the northern tip of the harbor. It was once thought to have been a Temple of Dionysus, the island's patron, but now it's believed to be Apollo's because of a brief reference to it in the Delian Hymns and because it directly faces Délos, his birthplace. On a clear day you can see that island through it. The temple was begun in 530 B.C. by the tyrant Lygdamis, but he was deposed before it was finished. Most of the marble was carted away to build the Kástro, but fortunately the massive posts and lintel were too big for the Venetians to handle.

The exquisite Venetian **Kástro,** the medieval citadel that dominates the town, is Hóra's greatest treasure, and you should allow at least several hours to explore it. Begin by turning left off the first square and entering the **old town** through the lancet (pointed) archway on the right. The lower part of the old town, **Boúrgos,** where the Greeks lived when the Venetians ruled the island, is a pleasantly confusing maze of narrow cobblestone lanes. The Kástro ("castle") itself, the domain of the Catholic aristocracy, was built by Marco Sanudo, nephew of the doge of Venice, probably on the ancient Mycenaean acropolis, in the 13th century when he declared himself the duke of Náxos. It remained the seat of Venetian power in the Cyclades for more than 300 years.

If you continue up in any direction you'll reach the outer wall of the castle, which has three entryways. Inside you'll find various buildings, some of which are being restored. Beginning at the northern gate you'll find the **Glezos Tower,** residence of the last dukes; then by turning left, **Sanudo's Palace** on the right, and across the plaza, the **Catholic cathedral.** To the right behind the cathedral is the **French School of Commerce** and the **Ursuline Convent and School.**

The French School has housed schools run by several religious orders; among its more famous students was the Cretan writer Níkos Kazantzákis, who studied here in 1896. It now houses the **archaeology museum** (☎ **0285/22-725**), which is open Tuesday to Sunday from 8:30am to 3pm; admission is 500 Drs ($2.10) for adults, 400 Drs ($1.65) for seniors, and 300 Drs ($1.25) for students. If you're interested in Cycladic culture, you may want to spend some time here. You might wish that there were fewer items and that they were better displayed and labeled; nevertheless the following treasures can be seen: Early Cycladic vessels that exemplify growing refinement, some excellent examples of white marble figurines, and many objects from the prosperous Late Mycenaean period (1400–1100 B.C.) found near Grotta, including vessels with the octopus motif that still appears in local art.

North of the Kástro and Boúrgos is the **Greek Orthodox cathedral,** built in 1789 and well worth a visit. Material from several ancient temples was used in its construction; the granite pillars are thought to be from Délos. The interior is quite ornate, and the iconostasis is particularly noteworthy. Next to the cathedral is the **ancient agorá,** which has been partly excavated. Farther north is the area called **Grotta,** below which can be seen the underwater remains of a Cycladic village.

SHOPPING

Shopping in Hóra offers both value and variety. Toward the north end of the *paralía,* near the bus station, you'll find **O Kouros** (☎ 0285/25-565), which has excellent copies of Cycladic figurines in Naxian marble, other reproductions, and interesting modern ceramics; credit/charge cards are accepted.

To the right and up from the entrance to the Old Market, you'll find **Techni** (☎ 0285/24-767), which has two shops, the first containing a nice array of silver jewelry at fair prices, and above it a more interesting one which has textiles (many hand-woven, and some crafted by local women).

Continue south along the *paralía* to the OTE, turn left on the main inland street, Odós Papavasilíou, and continue up on the left side of the street until your nose leads you to the **Tirokomiká Proïónia Náxou** (☎ 0285/22-230), a delightful old store filled with excellent local cheeses—*kephalotíri,* a superb sharp one, and milder *graviéra*—barrels of olives, spices, and other dried comestibles; it's also a good place to pick up a bottle of *kítron,* the island's famous sweet citron liqueur.

THE ISLAND'S BEST BEACHES

From Hóra, head south to reach **Court Square,** which is also called Cemetary or Post Office Square. The post office is to the north, and the **cemetery,** well worth a visit, is on the southwest corner. It's only a few blocks farther to the town's beach and resort suburb of Áyios Yióryios.

Áyios Yióryios is lined three or four blocks deep with resort hotels, restaurants, and bars, and swarming with tourists, and yet it remains remarkably civilized. It seems that everyone has come to enjoy a quiet and relaxing vacation. Many people head farther south by bike, bus, or caïque to the less crowded beaches at Áyios Prokópios and Ayía Ánna.

Áyios Prokópios is a longer, broader, cleaner fine-sand beach with a number of hotels, pensions, and tavernas built along the road back from the beach. The **Hotel Kavoúras** (☎ 0285/23-963) is a good lodging option; a double with shower is 8,500 Drs ($35.40), and studios for four are 11,500 Drs ($47.90).

Ayía Ánna, the next cove south, is much smaller, with a small port for the colorful caïques that transport beachgoers from the main port. The **Hotel Kapri** (☎ 0285/23-799; fax 0285/24-736) has 36 rooms and 12 studios; doubles with shower are 8,500 Drs ($35.40) and studios are 11,500 Drs ($47.90); minibus service to Hóra is available several times a day. The **Iria Beach Hotel** (☎ 0285/24-022; fax 0285/24-656) has a restaurant, minimarket, and 21 apartments at 10,150 Drs ($42.30) for two, 11,500 Drs ($47.90) for three. The **Taverna Gorgóna,** at the pier where the caïques dock (☎ 0285/23-799), has an excellent buffet dinner daily, with fresh grilled fish and meat, salads, vegetables, and complimentary wine.

Both beaches have windsurfing and are ideal day trips, but not for those seeking nighttime activites. **Camping Maragas** (☎ 0285/24-552) is a good facility at Ayía

Ánna. **Camping Apollon** (☎ 0285/24-117) is closer to Hóra and inland, with modern facilities and space for RVs.

Both Áyios Prokópios and Ayía Ánna are accessible over dirt roads by public bus in the summer, when school buses run vacation routes; they run almost hourly from Hóra and cost 400 Drs ($1.65). Ayía Ánna has caïque service from the small caïque jetty south of the Myrtidiótissa church islet in Hóra hourly from 9:30am to 5:30pm for about 800 Drs ($3.35) each way. From Ayía Ánna it's a 10-minute walk north to Áyios Prokópios.

South of Ayía Ánna you'll find **Pláka beach,** considered the best on the island, a 3-mile stretch of almost uninhabited shoreline where nude sunbathing is common. You can reach it by caïque from Hóra in the summer or by walking south from Ayía Ánna.

Farther south (10 miles from Hóra) is **Kastráki Beach,** with waters recently rated the cleanest in the Aegean and a 4¹/₂-mile stretch of beach. The **Summerland Complex** (☎ 0285/75-461; fax 0285/75-399) has 12 studios for 21,000 Drs ($87.50) and three apartments for 28,000 Drs ($116.65), a pool, gym, tennis court, children's playground, snack bar, and minimarket.

Farther still (13 miles from Hóra), **Pyrgáki,** the last stop on the coastal bus route, offers excellent swimming in the large protected bay, and 2¹/₂ miles farther, **Ayiássos** has the small **Hotel Neráïda** (☎ 0285/75-301), with its own restaurant.

MORE TO SEE AROUND THE ISLAND

By car, bicycle, or moped, you can make a nice round-trip tour of the interior of the island, which we'll describe briefly in a somewhat counterclockwise order. You can make a similar tour, though not so easily, by public bus; bus excursions are available to those places that pique your interest.

East from Hóra, left from the OTE along Odós Papavasilíou past the medical center (about half a mile from town) you'll reach a fork in the road; take the one to the right toward **Galanádo,** where you'll find the handsome Venetian tower, **Pýrgos Belónia,** the fortified house of the local Italian rulers. (Towers were strategically located around the island as refuges from invading pirates, and fires were lighted on the roofs to warn of an attack, both for the neighboring villagers and for adjacent towers, which could relay the alarm.) In front of the tower is the 13th-century **Church of Áyios Ioánnis** (St. John), an interesting monument to Venetian religious tolerance: the left side is a Catholic chapel and the right is Orthodox.

About 2 miles farther along on the road to Sangrí just off the right of the road is the 8th-century Byzantine **Cathedral of Áyios Mámas,** which was neglected during the Venetian occupation but has recently been partly restored. **Sangrí** is a corruption of Saint Croix, the French name for the three villages near the **Monastery of Tímiou Stavroú** ("True Cross"), which has so many remains from the past that it's sometimes referred to as "little Mistrá." At **Káto** ("Lower") **Sangrí,** the first village, is another ruined Venetian tower, and south of the pretty little village of **Áno** ("Upper") **Sangrí** is the small Byzantine chapel of **Áyios Ioánnis Yiroúlas,** built over an ancient Temple of Demeter, which is accessible by foot or by an unimproved road off the main road south from Sangrí. Farther south is the Byzantine castle of **T'Apalirоú,** the last stronghold on the island to fall to Marco Sanudo. West of Sangrí is **Kalorítsa,** with the ruins of a 13th-century monastery above a cavern containing three small churches.

From Sangrí the road descends into the lush and picturesque **Tragéa Valley** toward **Halkí,** where both the Byzantines and the Venetians built fortified towers. The lovely 11th-century white church with the red-tile roof, **Panayía Protóthronos** ("Our

Lady Before the Throne"), is sometimes open in the morning. Turn right to reach the **Frankópoulos (or Grazia) Tower;** the name says it's Frankish, but it was originally Byzantine, and a marble crest gives the date 1742, when it was renovated by the Venetians. Climb the steps for an excellent view of Filóti, one of the island's largest inland villages. Halkí's other tower is to the southeast. Northwest the **Apáno Kástro,** a Mycenaean fortress last renovated by the Venetians—possibly as a summer residence for Marco Sanudo—commands the valley.

You could go north to Moní, but we'd suggest that you continue east to **Filóti,** at the base of Mt. Zas, a pleasant place to stroll around for a look at local life. In the center of town is the **Church of Kímisis tis Theotókou** ("Assumption of the Mother of God"), with a lovely marble iconostasis and a Venetian tower. The town has several tavernas and a few rooms for rent, as well as a number of abandoned houses, which may be available for longer term rentals.

The main reason to stop in Filóti, however, is to hike up **Mt. Zas,** the high-point of the Cyclades, about a 3-hour climb beginning west of town. There's an interesting **cave** near the top, which in ancient times was sacred to Zeus and used during the Turkish occupation as a Christian chapel; on the western slope is the well-preserved Hellenistic tower, **Pýrgos Himárou,** built by Ptolemy.

The road continues along the slope of Mt. Zas to **Apíranthos,** the most beautiful of the mountain villages, which has marble streets as well as marble embellishments on the interesting architecture, which incorporates elements of both the Cycladic and Venetian. There are also two Venetian towers and a small archaeological museum near the main square with interesting Cycladic finds. It's usually open from 8:30am to 1:30pm, no admission charge; if you're interested in visiting it, ask and the curator might appear. The people, originally from Crete, have their own peculiar and colorful customs. Some local weaving and needlework is sold by the village women, and **Stiastó** (☎ 0825/61-392) offers a nice selection of popular art, including fine ceramics.

The road continues north toward Apóllonas, and you may want to turn left back toward Hóra at the crossroads—about 2¹/₂ miles north of Apíranthos. As you proceed north the road becomes extremely winding as it passes through the pretty villages of **Kóronos** and **Skádo.** There are a number of marble quarries in the area, but about 7 miles south of Apóllonas you'll see steps leading off to the left to the famous **koúros,** a colossal statue 28 feet tall begun in the 7th century and abandoned probably because of the fissures produced by the elements. Some archaeologists believe it was meant for the nearby Temple of Apollo, but the beard suggests that it's probably the island's patron deity, Dionysus.

Apóllonas itself is a small fishing village on the verge of becoming a rather depressing resort, with a sand cove and a pebbled public beach in full view. There are plenty of places to eat, rooms for rent, and a few hotels. We don't recommend a stay, but the **Hotel Kouros,** on the beach at the far end of town (☎ 0285/81-340), is hospitable and well maintained, with doubles for 9,000 Drs ($37.50). Don't be tempted to take the coastal road back to Hóra, since the road itself is poor, the scenery is not attractive, and you'd miss Moní.

Just south of **Moní,** near the middle of the island, is the important 6th-century **Monastery of Panayía Drossianí** ("Our Lady of Refreshment"), three unimpressive gray chapels huddled together that contain excellent Byzantine frescoes. Visits by those properly dressed are permitted at all hours of the day, but you may have to ring the bell to get someone to let you in. There are a couple of tavernas and some rooms to rent in Moní. If you continue back to Hóra along the more northerly route, you'll pass several more marble quarries; between the villages of Kinídaros and Míli on the left, with some help from locals or a good map, you'll find two more *koúri,* not as large but more finely detailed, also abandoned because of flaws.

WHERE TO STAY

Hóra's long, broad *paralía,* so popular for an evening *vólta* (stroll), is traffic-filled, overrun by cafes, and overpriced. We recommend hotels elsewhere, all within a 10-minute walk of the port. Grotta, the cliffside area northeast of the port, is quite developed but still offers tranquillity, wonderful views of Hóra and the sea, and a small pebble beach for swimming. The picturesque and charming Boúrgo quarter below the Kástro has a few smaller hotels nestled in its winding backstreets. Áyios Yióryios, the town's sand beach south of the port, offers many hotels and rooms for rent. Note that this area can become very crowded with day-trippers, especially in July and August, and can become quite noisy because of the night visitors to its bar and club scene.

IN GROTTA

From the bus station, take the closest major street (with traffic) off the port and continue up.

Apollon Youth Hostel. Hóra, 843 00 Náxos. ☎ **0285/22-468.** 25 rms (70 beds). 2,600 Drs ($10.85) per person. No credit cards.

Bear right after the school and police station, and continue up past the cathedral to reach the well-managed youth hostel on the left.

Hotel Grotta. Hóra, 843 00 Náxos 84300. ☎ **0285/22-215.** Fax 0285/22-000. 22 rms, all with bath (shower). TEL. 11,300 Drs ($47.10) single; 17,250 Drs ($71.90) double. Rates include breakfast. No credit cards.

This modern hotel overlooking the Bay of Grotta on the coast road is one of our favorites. The host, Mr. Lianos, is gracious to a fault, and he and his family run a sparkling inn. The spotless rooms have polished marble floors, minifridges, and large balconies. The attractive dining area has a gallery overlooking the sea and the Portára. If you call ahead, the owner will pick you up at the ferry.

IN BOÚRGO

Our Boúrgo district recommendations are most easily reached from the bus station by taking the nearest major street (with traffic) off the port, turning right through the lancet archway into the Old Market area, and following the green stenciled arrows to the Anixis Hotel. There are also many new rooms priced according to season at 7,000 to 12,000 Drs ($26.10 to $43.50), including twin beds and shower.

✪ **Chateau Zevgoli.** Hóra, 843 00 Náxos. ☎ **0285/22-993,** or 01/651-5885 in Athens. Fax 0285/24-525. 14 rms, all with bath (shower). 12,500–16,500 Drs ($54.30–$71.70) double. Rates include breakfast. V.

The stylishly restored Chateau Zevgoli is Boúrgos's most attractive hotel. In a Naxiot fashion, the cozy rooms are built around a marble-tiled courtyard smothered in potted plants. The stucco and enamel blue-trimmed rooms are simple, letting ornately carved wood furnishings, lace curtains, and modern tiled bathrooms sparkle. We think it offers the best of both worlds at worthwhile prices.

Hotel Anixis. Hóra, 843 00 Náxos. ☎ **0285/22-932.** Fax 0285/22-112. 16 rms, 12 with bath (shower). 8,600 Drs ($35.85) single or double without bath, 11,500 Drs ($47.90) single or double with bath. No credit cards.

This small hotel near the Kástro's Venetian tower offers comfortable accommodations in this quiet, desirable area. It's a contemporary-looking place with comfortable, twin-bedded rooms on two levels sharing a long balcony. The common facilities are well maintained.

Hotel Panorama. Hóra, 843 00 Náxos. ☎ **0285/24-404.** 16 rms, 10 with bath (shower). 6,250 Drs ($26.05) single without bath; 9,600 Drs ($40) double without bath, 11,000 Drs ($45.85) double with bath. No credit cards.

Just across the lane from the Anixis, this stone-and-stucco hotel is a good choice for those who want to stay in Hóra's most atmospheric neighborhood, below the Kástro amid whitewashed homes and twisting lanes. Kiki keeps a spotless place with great port views from its neat small rooms.

Hotel Pantheon. Hóra, 843 00 Náxos. ☎ **0285/24-335.** 7 rms, 5 with bath (shower). 8,400 Drs ($36.50) single or double without bath; 11,500 Drs ($50) double with bath. No credit cards.

This little-known family home tucked up on a quiet lane below the Kástro features small neat rooms and loving attention from its elderly owners. Balconied room 1, with port views and private shower, is a great value, especially during low season when prices usually drop 40%.

IN ÁYIOS YIÓRYIOS

From the edge of the port all the way down to the end of sandy Áyios Yióryios is an endless strip of hotels, bungalows, private rooms, discos, bars, and restaurants. If you can't find a room at one of the suggested places (all near the beach), be assured that there'll be other inns to welcome you.

The **Hotel Galini** (☎ 0285/22-114; fax 0285/22-677) and its sibling, the **Sofia Latina,** are both run by the wonderful Sofia (who has a great green thumb) and her amiable son George. Her quiet, spotless rooms have marble floors, phones, mini-fridges, and balconies with sea views and cooling breezes.

The **Hotel Glaros** (☎ 0285/23-101; fax 0285/24-877) has 13 comfortable, shuttered rooms with balconies overlooking a pretty rock-strewn end of the beach. The Papadopoulos family owns and operates the **Hotel Nissaki** (☎ 0285/25-710), whose pool makes it an exception to the blur of beach hotels. Many of its large, well-furnished rooms have balconies, too. The large open-air restaurant serves three meals a day at the edge of the sand, and its gift shop sells plenty of sunblock. Rates at all three run 16,500 Drs ($71.70) double, including breakfast, in high season; Visa is accepted at the Galini and the Nissaki. Transportation is provided to and from port if you have a reservation.

A SPLURGE CHOICE

Mathiassos Village Bungalows. Hóra, 843 00 Náxos. ☎ **0285/22-200,** or 01/291-8749 in Athens. Fax 0285/24-700. 110 bungalows, all with bath (tub). TV TEL. 24,000 Drs ($104.30) bungalow for two. Rates include breakfast. AE, DC, MC, V.

This resort complex provides amenities not common on Náxos. In lushly landscaped grounds are these semiattached but private bungalows, plus a large swimming pool and sun deck, tennis court, children's playground, cafeteria, taverna restaurant, and an ouzerí with gaming tables. Large bungalows come with patios, radio, and the option of TV and refrigerator; some are two-story units to accommodate families. Mathiassos Village is isolated on the ring road behind the town and doesn't have sea views, but there's a bus to the beach.

WHERE TO EAT

Although Náxos isn't the most sophisticated island in the Cyclades, the food is generally quite good. The **bakery** (☎ 0285/22-613) on the *paralía* has good baked goods at fair prices, and farther north, across from the bus station, **Bikini** is a good place for breakfast and crêpes. The **Braziliana Pâtisserie** (☎ 0285/23-777), near the post office, is a good place for a sweet treat.

Manolis Steak House. Hóra. ☎ **0285/23-619.** Main courses 1,100–1,800 Drs ($4.80–$7.80). No credit cards. Daily 11:30am–3am. GREEK/CONTINENTAL.

Continue past the post office about 40 yards, near the Galini and Sofia hotels, to reach this casual place for good Greek fast food (very tender lamb and crisp french fries) at budget prices. It's refreshingly unpretentious and traditional.

Nikos. Paralía, Hóra. ☎ **0285/23-153.** Main courses 1,200–2,750 Drs ($5.20–$12). MC, V. Daily 8am–2am. GREEK.

The most visible and popular restaurant in town is above the Commercial Bank. The dining room is enormous but has a view of the harbor on one side and the old town on the other. Don't be put off: the real star at Níkos is the seafood, which is expensive but fresh and well prepared. Try the barbecued fish—the red snapper and swordfish are perfect—lightly topped with oil and locally grown lemon. Nikos Katsaganis is himself a fisherman.

✪ **The Old Inn.** Hóra. ☎ **0285/26-093.** Main courses 1,850–2,500 Drs ($8–$10.90). No credit cards. Daily 11am–1am. INTERNATIONAL.

Whether or not you're traveling with a child (as Kyle does), this brand-new (despite the name) inn is appealing. The enormously varied menu features specialties such as camembert cheese baked with cranberries, a hearty salade niçoise, fresh grilled veal chops with local oregano, or fish fingers and chips (from the children's menu). All are interesting, well prepared, flavorful, and generously portioned. Diners relax in a tree-shaded stone courtyard, surrounded by the inn's original parlors which have been converted into a bar, a gallery of eclectic knickknacks, and an indoor dining room. Kids can await their meals in Mickey's Garden, a sandbox and play area filled with an international array of toy cars, action figures, pails, and shovels. The staff, polite and proficient, manages to please all types of patrons.

Oniro. Hóra. ☎ **0285/23-846.** Main courses 1,600–2,500 Drs ($7–$10.90). No credit cards. Daily 6pm–midnight. GREEK/CONTINENTAL.

This new taverna is tucked up under the Kástro, by the south gate of Boúrgos, with its own miniature windmill and views over the Aegean that are especially lovely at sunset. On its plant-filled roof deck you can enjoy grilled local fish, pastas and salads, and a few traditional Greek items. The local Náxos potatoes are delicious.

NÁXOS AFTER DARK

Apostolis, an ouzerí on the port near the ferry pier, is one traditional place for a superb sunset and a leisurely sip; **Apolafsis** is another, newer one.

There are many bars and cafes; the loud ones are, of course, the easiest to find. We liked **The Loft** (☎ 0285/23-339), a two-tiered cafe with a cozy bar and a wrought-iron enclosed balcony. Popular and classical Greek music accompanies the conversation.

At the south end of the port is the equally sophisticated **Vengera** cocktail bar and garden (☎ 0285/23-567), which opens at 9pm but gets livelier nearer to its 3am closing.

The **Kahlua Music Club,** on the beach at Áyios Prokópios (☎ 0285/23-287), is a barefoot and bikini type place that offers good rock, reggae, and soul from sunset to 3am.

The **Diogenes Cafe,** on the *paralía* (☎ 0285/24-084), is the best for late-night coffee and dessert, but you'll have to fight with the hundreds of locals who come to watch the evening *vólta* (stroll) and eat their special *kítron* desserts and puddings.

The long-popular **Ocean Club,** on the road to Áyios Yióryios (☎ 0285/24-323), is the best of the indoor discos. This is a nightspot where volume and youth know no bounds.

6 Íos

107 nautical miles SE of Piraeus

After 3 decades as the hippest, loudest, and most plugged-in rock in the Aegean, Íos is coming into its own. The tourist infrastructure has improved so that the multitudes of young people who arrive daily can now safely get around on public transportation. The rooms for rent are cleaner and cheaper. Drug consumption seems to have declined in favor of overimbibing colorful fruit drinks at happy hour. Discos have evolved into slam-dance clubs, and almost all the bars now feature big-screen videos each night, so patrons don't have to contemplate the stars!

Most surprising to us, and most revealing of the way Greece has matured since joining the EU, is that many of the under-20s on Íos are Greek! Miniskirted girls in platform shoes and brawny young men with earrings ferry over from Athens to celebrate the holidays here, leaving their prosperous families behind. It's a scene, and even if you don't want to participate, it sure is fun to watch.

Join Generation X on Íos—still the global village of Dionysus and all merry bands of revelers!

ESSENTIALS

GETTING THERE & DEPARTING   By Ferry   There are two daily boats from Piraeus; for specific departure times call the **Port Authority** (☎ 01/451-1311 in Piraeus or 0286/91-264 on Íos). Íos is well connected to the surrounding Cycladic islands with daily ferry service to Náxos, Páros, Mýkonos, and Santoríni; and service three times a week to Sýros; five times a week to Mílos, Sífnos, and Sérifos; and two or three times a week to Folégandros, Síkinos, and Anáfi.

By Hydrofoil   There is hydrofoil service daily in summer connecting Íos to Mýkonos, Páros, Santoríni, and Naxos. Tickets for the **Ilio Lines** are sold by travel agents, but if the seas are rough it may not run.

VISITOR INFORMATION   The most knowledgeable, helpful, and all-around useful travel agents on Íos are at **Acteon Travel** (☎ 0286/91-343 or 0286/91-318; fax 0286/91-088), the American Express agent, located on the port square in Hóra and at Milopótas Beach. Both offices usually stay open daily from 7:30am to midnight, and will assist you with information and maps, finding a room (come on in after you disembark), making phone calls, changing money, booking tickets, and storing luggage.

ORIENTATION   Like many of the Cyclades, Íos is a barren, rocky island that suffers from a lack of fresh water. Today the only foliage is in the center of the island and at the extreme north, although Homer once wrote that he'd like to be buried here, one of the most verdant of isles.

Picture a small pyramid with a port at one base, a party at the peak, and a beach paradise at the other base. That's Íos. All boats dock at **Yialós,** the port. To the left of the pier as you alight from the ferry is a beach that sometimes collects harbor debris, but is certainly acceptable, especially if you're stuck in the heat waiting for a ferry. Yialós itself has little of interest; most of the action is up the hill in **Hóra,** the pyramid's peak, where sound sleepers will probably want to stay. On the other side, downhill from Hóra, is highly regarded **Milopótas Beach**—far and away the most popular beach on the island. (There are many others, though; see below.)

GETTING AROUND   By Bus   There's excellent bus service among the port, Hóra, and Milopótas Beach—cheap, at 190 Drs (80¢) from Yialós to Hóra, and frequent (every 15 minutes between 8am and 2am). You can walk to these same points, but it can be very hot, especially up to Hóra from the beach (about a 30-minute walk). If you plan to walk after dark, bring a flashlight since the path is poorly lit. The island's only other public bus route crosses from the port to Ayía Theodóti on the east coast; it's infrequent and runs only during July and August.

Acteon Travel (☎ 0286/91-343) runs an **air-conditioned tour bus,** daily in July and August, to Manganári beach on the south coast. Other travel agents also offer a daily tour bus to Ayía Theodóti for 1,700 Drs ($7.50). Again, walking is an alternative, although it's about 2 hours away by foot.

By Moped & Motorbike   Fortunately for those living in altered states, public and private bus service is now plentiful. But if you must relive your *Easy Rider* phase, you can pick up a **moped** (about 4,500 Drs/$19.70 a day) or 50cc motorbike (about 5,750 Drs/$25) and tear across the gravel and dirt to various out-of-the-way beaches. **AutoEurope,** on the south side of the port, is the biggest outfit. Its rates include a tankful of gas, third-party insurance only (if you damage the bike, you pay), and an optional helmet. On an island where bars boast ONE DRINK FOR THE ROAD, you should drive with extreme caution.

FAST FACTS   The **police station** (☎ 0286/91-222) is conveniently located across from the bus stop in Hóra.

The **post office** (open Monday to Friday from 8am to 2pm) is a couple of blocks south of the main square; the **telephone center (OTE)** is in Hóra, behind the police station. Both have extended summer hours. If you want to make a collect call, be aware that you must book it at the OTE Monday to Friday between 7:30am and 1pm, although the office stays open until 10pm.

For **medical emergencies** call ☎ 0286/91-227. Starting in 1997 medical assistance will be available from three small hospitals under construction at the port, in Hóra, and in Milopótas.

There are two **banks**—open Monday to Friday from 8am to 2pm, with extended summer hours. Most travel agencies and many shops are also authorized to exchange money.

FUN ON & OFF THE BEACH

The nighttime party is in Hóra's backstreets. The daytime party is on ✪ **Milopótas Beach,** one of Greece's longest sandy beaches. The water is clean, and notwithstanding the usual mob scene, it's a fabulous place to spread out a towel or mat to bake under the strong Aegean sun. Perhaps 90% of those visiting Íos go no farther than Milopótas, yet Íos has beaches on almost every cove, indentation, or stretch of coastline—each with its own character. Other than Milopótas, most other beaches can be reached by private bus tours, moped, or caïque.

Manganári, on the extreme south coast, has a sandy beach, rooms to rent, a taverna, and even deluxe accommodations. You can explore the other beaches from there on foot or by moped. A 1¹/₂-hour walk northeast from Manganári is the lonely **Three Churches beach,** a haunt of those looking for undisturbed, private bathing. On the east coast are **Psáthi** (an hour away by moped-able dirt road) and **Ayía Theodóti,** both with beaches, food, and camping.

Of some historical interest are the swimming cove and caves at **Plakátos,** which archaeologists incorrectly claimed to be Homer's tomb. You'll have to hire a boat to visit.

WHERE TO STAY

Íos is a mob scene in the summer: Visitors outnumber islanders 14 to 1. Literally, we remember the days when the port police would not allow ferry passengers to disembark on the island. The hotel scene isn't totally hopeless, for on Íos, as on most of the islands during the high season (here, a particularly apt term), you can always go to a local travel agency to inquire about a private room. The other alternative is, of course, to make reservations; it may violate the free spirit of life on Íos but at least you'll know that you have a room. Most places are open only from June to mid-September, and most charge the same for single or double rooms!

The **tourist police** (☎ 0286/91-222) have a complete list of private rooms and hotels, as well as official prices for all accommodations. The friendly force is acutely aware of pricing violations, and they encourage tourists who have been overcharged to report the problem.

AT THE PORT

Now that tour groups have struck Yialós, some of the better hotels are booked early or don't even open until July when their travel agents' contracts begin. The port has one official camping spot—though people are known to camp all over when rooms are all filled—**Íos Camping Porto** (☎ 0286/91-329). It's near the small south-side beach; fully equipped, it boasts a new swimming pool. The gregarious manager and staff are friendly; they charge 1,750 Drs ($7.60) a night for a space by the water.

Acteon Hotel. Yialós, 840 01 Íos. ☎ **0286/91-343.** Fax 0286/91-088. 15 rms, all with bath (shower). 7,300 Drs ($31.80) single; 9,200 Drs ($40.10) double. AE, MC, V.

Conveniently situated above the ever-helpful Acteon Travel agency, this place saved Kyle's sanity when her delayed ferry arrived at 3:30am one moonless summer night. You'll find nice rooms at bargain rates, but those late-night ferries and nearby cafes can sometimes be noisy.

Hotel Mare-Monte. Órmos, 84 001 Íos. ☎ **0286/91-564.** 30 rms, all with bath (tub). 18,600 Drs ($80.90) single or double. Rates include breakfast. V.

One of the best conventional, contemporary hotels is on the town beach to the left (south) of the pier. Quiet double rooms offer balconies and sea views. Everything is kept clean, and the breakfast lounge is very pleasant.

IN HÓRA

In the village (which locals call "the jungle"), you can choose between a few hotels and hundreds of rooms. Visit the Acteon Travel office or police for a current "Rooms to Let" list and official prices; in 1996 they ran about 4,500 Drs ($19.70) for a single and 5,850 Drs ($25.50) for a double.

Francesco's. Hóra, 840 01 Íos. ☎ **0286/91-223.** 35 rms, 30 with bath (shower). 4,000 Drs ($17.40) single without bath, 5,550 Drs ($24.10) single with bath; 9,500 Drs ($41.30) double with bath. No credit cards.

Francesco has renovated the "last" house in town (a 300-year-old mansion) into a charming collection of rooms with a bar and several gathering places, some with splendid views. A little above the "jungle," though certainly not isolated, it made us fondly recall our first big trip to Europe.

The Hill. Hóra, 840 01 Íos. ☎ **0286/91-481.** 18 rms, all with bath (tub). 4,800 Drs ($20.90) single; 9,500 Drs ($41.30) double. No credit cards.

Some very nice, and completely sober, young Americans on their way home from Israel were pleased to show us their place across from the village, up left from the museum and police station. Simple and quiet. The family that own it didn't speak much English, but they were friendly and hospitable.

Hotel Aphroditi. Hóra, 840 01 Íos. ☎ **0286/91-546.** 12 rms, all with bath (shower). 10,080 Drs ($43.80) single; 12,600 Drs ($54.80) double. No credit cards.

This hotel, on the west side of town, has modern, pleasant rooms, and its all marble floors lend a touch of elegance. We've heard that it just opened new suites (which cost about 40% more than the doubles); let us know what you think. Unfortunately, since this expansion it's no longer Íos's only year-round hotel.

AT MILOPÓTAS BEACH

Milopótas Beach has become the most popular place to stay, with new hotels going up at an amazing rate.

A classic, and a nostalgic favorite of ours for rock-bottom prices is **Ios Camping Stars** (☎ **0286/91-302**). Petros runs this comfortable place at the bus stop corner. It's decked out with all the facilities any camper could possibly need: a restaurant, snack bar, disco, bar, a small market, showers, and lockers—all inexpensive. It's situated close to the beach, and the price is right—1,500 Drs ($6.50) per person plus a tent. It accepts American Express, MasterCard, and Visa.

The newer competition shows you exactly which way our youth are headed—straight into the lap of luxury! The amazing new **Far Out Camping** (☎ **0286/92-301;** fax 0286/92-303) has an air-conditioned restaurant and bar; a minimarket; kitchen facilities; handicapped-accessible toilets; a huge swimming pool; water-sports facilities; an athletic center with regulation tennis, volleyball, basketball, and squash courts; and free transfers from the port. All this costs only 1,750 Drs ($7.60) per person and tent—but we must warn you that it can accommodate 2,000 campers! New, comfortable bungalows (65 round stucco "huts" with a double and single bed, plus shower), scheduled for completion by late 1997, cost 4,500 Drs ($19.60) per person; American Express, MasterCard, and Visa are accepted. If you find better camping facilities anywhere in Greece, please write us.

Hotel Acropolis. Milopótas, 840 01 Íos. ☎ **0286/91-303.** 14 rms, all with bath (shower). 6,850 Drs ($29.80) single; 9,200 Drs ($40) double. No credit cards.

This place is located at the top of the donkey path above the beach. All the very simple rooms have showers, and most have balconies with great views of the beach below. This place is for the hardy hill-hiker, unless you're patient with the public bus service, which actually does run door to door.

Hotel Aegeon. Milopótas, 840 01 Íos. ☎ **0286/91-392.** Fax 0286/91-008. 16 rms, all with bath (shower). 10,000 Drs ($43.50) single or double. V.

All the rooms have balconies and patios, and all are kept spotless by Elisabet and her friendly family. The rooms are simply furnished but comfortable.

Hotel Marcos Beach. Milopótas, 840 01 Íos. ☎ **0286/91-571.** Fax 0286/91-671. 35 rms, all with bath (shower). 11,000 Drs ($47.80) single or double. MC, V.

A rooftop pool deck is one of the highlights here, though the rooms and entryway all display good taste, cleanliness, and comfort. There's handicap access to the premises, a communal TV room, two bars, and parking. Remember, though, that it's a 150-yard walk up and down to the beach.

Worth a Splurge

The following two hotels are unusually posh for Greece, maybe the kind of place young honeymooners—or the wild at heart—might contemplate. Note that both offer discounts up to 50% during the low season.

✪ **Far Out Hotel.** Milopótas, 840 01 Íos. ☎ **0286/91-446,** or 0286/91-701 in winter. Fax 0286/91-560. 45 rms, all with bath (shower). A/C TEL TV. 13,800 Drs ($60) single; 18,000 Drs ($78.30) double. Rates include breakfast. AE, MC, V.

Don't be put off by the name; it's only 5 minutes uphill from the beach cove, with comfortable, beautifully appointed rooms. Each well-kept guest room has a personal safe-deposit box and sea views; there's a swimming pool, a friendly, helpful staff, and transportation to and from the port. Quite luxurious for this island.

Íos Palace Hotel. Milopótas, 840 01 Íos. ☎ **0286/91-269,** or 01/898-3387 in Athens. Fax 0286/91-082, or 01/898-3389 in Athens. 64 rms, all with bath (shower). A/C MINIBAR TEL. 13,200 Drs ($57.40) single; 16,200 Drs ($70.40) double. Rates include breakfast. AE, MC, V.

The island's first great anomaly was this palatial hotel, once the envy of many young budget travelers. The Palace is built on terraces on the steep hillside at the north end of the beach with modern, built-in furnishings, marble tile bathrooms, excellent Aegean views from private balconies, and geraniums cascading down from hidden planters. It's well designed and very pretty. The large pool, with a flagstone sun deck and dozens of bikinis, is rimmed by a lively poolside bar. The rooms (whose rates vary according to season) get snatched up by tour groups a month in advance of busy July and August; a 1-night deposit will guarantee you a bit of well-priced luxury.

WHERE TO EAT

Food is cheap here; restaurateurs are forced to keep prices low because so many visitors shop at grocery stores and bakeries, then eat in their rooms. Most places serve pretty mediocre European fast food, but we've noted a few exceptions below.

IN HÓRA

Kalypso Restaurant. Hóra. ☎ **0286/91-120** or 0286/91-377. Main courses 1,000–2,400 Drs ($4.40–$9.10). AE, MC, V. Daily 5pm–1am. GREEK/CONTINENTAL.

Below the bend in the main road you can eat outdoors or on the more pleasant roof garden across the pedestrian lane. This is a modern taverna where good food and quiet company prevail over boisterous nearby snack bars.

Lord Byron. Hóra. ☎ **0286/92-125.** Appetizers 675–1,700 Drs ($2.90–$7.40). No credit cards. Daily 6pm–1am. GREEK.

On a tiny, quiet lane off Church Square is the grape arbor–covered Mezedopolíon Lórdos Výronos, opened in 1995 in homage to the classic Greek mezéde ouzerís of the last century. More than 40 small appetizer plates clamor to be sampled, accompanied by any of dozens of wines and liqueurs on the menu. The food is imaginative and fresh; it's a wonderful place to start off or wind down an Íos night.

The Mills Taverna. Hóra. ☎ **0286/91-284.** Main courses 1,000–2,950 Drs ($4.40–$13). AE, DC. Daily 6pm–midnight. GREEK.

Opposite the windmills on the highest point in Hóra is where you'll find classic Greek food at its best. The salad is made with *misíthra* or *xinó* cheese, a delicious alternative to feta. The goat meat and *kontosoúvli* are tender and savory. Some swear by the lamb on a spit, but our favorite is a classic moussaká. The Mills has withstood several seasons of fads and kids, but still caters to the small discerning crowd that returns to Íos each summer.

By the way, they've recently built apartments on a hill opposite Hóra to accommodate old friends; call ☎ 0286/92-027 or fax 0286/91-249 for more information.

The Nest. Hóra. No telephone. Main courses 825–2,000 Drs ($3.50–$8.70). No credit cards. Daily 12:30–3:30pm and 5pm–midnight. GREEK.

Northeast of the main square, across from the pharmacy, you'll find one of the best budget places, with big portions of well-prepared typical Greek (and a few Italian) dishes. Over time it has consistently won approval from locals and tourists, and remains open year-round.

Romantica Patisserie & Snack Bar. Hóra. ☎ 0286/91-506. Snacks 125–950 Drs (55¢–$4.20). No credit cards. Daily 8am–11pm. CONTINENTAL.

Two blocks over from the vehicle street, this is part of a heavenly aromatic bakery, and sort of romantic. Good breakfasts and snacks are served on outdoor tables.

IN YIALÓS

Enigma Cafe-Bar. Yialós. ☎ 0286/91-847. Snacks 800–1,800 Drs ($3.50–$7.80); main courses 950–2,100 Drs ($4.20–$9.10). MC, V. Daily 8am–1am. FAST FOOD.

There's plenty of fast food at the port, but the best selection and quality is on the far right of the plaza. Here the owner and chef Stelio Nicolaou prides himself on 20 varieties of pizza, Greek *mezédes,* and fine draft beers.

Stavedo. Yialós. No phone. Main courses 980–2,600 Drs ($4.30–$11.40). No credit cards. Daily 7pm–1am. SEAFOOD.

The best place on the island for fresh fish, according to locals, changed hands at our last visit. However, another sea palace wannabe has taken its place in this homely patio, left of the port, before the town beach. Check out the day's catch before you settle on a meal.

OTHER CHOICES AROUND THE ISLAND

At **Koumbára Beach,** across the little penisula east of the port overlooking the beach, you'll find the **Polydoros Restaurant** (☎ 0286/91-132), a place recommended by our Greek friends, where hearty traditional cooking is served native style, evenings only. If you overeat, you can crash in one of their new rental rooms.

At **Milopótas Beach** we recommend one or both **Drakos Tavernas**—otherwise known as the "Drakos Twins" because of these brothers' matching nearby establishments, where you'll find fresh fish and grilled meats at modest prices. They also rent rooms at their south-beach venue.

Another upstart at Milopótas is the hillside **Harmony Mexican Kitchen** (☎ 0286/91-613), not quite Acapulco but a scenic and tasty change of pace. We hadn't been to the rugged, barefoot, funky, and ultimately Greek **Christos** on Manganári for many years, and now find a phone, tablecloths, and electricity. However, the elder fisherman Christos still presides over this beach's best restaurant.

ÍOS AFTER DARK

Imagine a giant all-night street party of intoxicated teenage nomads—this is nighttime on Íos. Hóra is the epicenter.

Clubs and discos there are aplenty. A casual stroll up Hóra's twisting lanes and main street will take you past at least 10 good danceterias. You don't even have to poke your head in to hear what kind of music they play—it'll be obvious. The clubs change names and musical styles even more frequently than on Mýkonos, but below we've listed some recent favorites (with the visiting crowd, not with us). If you can't stand the volume, park yourself at a cafe across the narrow lanes and savor the people parade.

On the main street, below the stairs, is the long-standing **Disco 69,** for cheap drinks and up-to-date tunes. The **Tropicana** was an early boogie bar with rap music and contemporary top-40, still going strong. The **Slammer Bar** and the **Orange Bar** are on or near the main square, where the clash of musical styles creates a cacophony that was heretofore deemed scientifically impossible. Fringe clubs (in location, not style) include the **New Look,** especially hot after 2am, and next door to it, **Scorpion,** one of the oldest, but newly redecorated, dance clubs.

The Dubliner, where dancing on the tables is acceptable, and **Sweet Irish Dream,** both behind the big church on the east side of town, have taken to accosting passersby with offers of cheap booze and a Kool Krowd. We hate that hawking, but these places are really popular with those who like to rev up for a night's revelry and drink till dawn.

7   Santoríni

126 nautical miles SE of Piraeus, 75 nautical miles N of Crete

One of the most spectacular islands in the world, Santoríni (Thíra) is unique among the arid, whitewashed, rocky Cyclades for its dramatic volcanic landscape. Visitors arriving by boat are likely to be stunned by the sheer black cliffs that stretch around a fantastic cauldron-shaped bay, the ✪ **caldera,** which was left by an enormous volcanic eruption more than 3,600 years ago. Deep red soil and long streaks of white pumice stripe the cliffs, although these are gradually becoming obliterated by the whitewashed development dripping down from the hilltop capital of Firá. Besides the breathtaking first impression, Santoríni's black-sand beaches, plentiful cheap wine, and links to the legendary Atlantis lure American visitors by the hundreds of thousands.

The geology of Santoríni separates it visually and historically from the other Cyclades islands. In ancient times this volcanic island was called Strongylí ("Round"), because of the shape of the caldera, and Kálliste ("Most Beautiful"). The fishers who lived in traditional villages on nearby Thirasía found themselves inhabiting mountaintops that remained above water after the eruption. In fact a land bridge is submerged between the two islands. To the southwest, the tiny Asprónisi ("White Island") is another small remnant.

In the 10th century B.C. Santoríni was renamed Thíra, after a Dorian ruler from Sparta who invaded the island and settled seven villages. The ruins of Ancient Thíra, the Dorian hilltop capital, also reflect the later presence of Roman and Byzantine conquerors. The Venetian crusaders occupied the island from the 13th to the 16th century; Italian sailors called it Santoríni after its patron, St. Irene, who died in exile here in A.D. 304. (Most Greeks still call it Thíra.) In the village of Embório you can see several hillside homes built within the only Venetian fortress walls that still remain.

The volcanic eruption which occurred sometime between 1647 and 1628 B.C. (according to the most recent information) that caused the collapse of the island was so forceful that archaeologists think it produced tidal waves that totally flattened Crete and reached the shores of Africa. The fascinating city of Akrotíri, uncovered on Santoríni by Prof. Spyridon Marinatos in 1967, was apparently an ally or member of the Minoan kingdom that flourished on Crete until 1500 B.C., and may have been the legendary Atlantis. The ruins of Akrotíri, well preserved under lava and volcanic ash, have been immensely important in understanding Minoan culture. The exciting excavations continue today in the "Pompeii of the Aegean" and are an incredible sight to see.

The two islets in the center of the caldera bay are the original lava cones. The smaller one, Paleá Kaméni ("Old Burnt"), emerged after an eruption in 197 B.C. and grew, then shrank and grew again, to its present size, during 700 turbulent years. In 1707 a mild earthquake caused the larger islet, Néa Kaméni ("New Burnt"), to rise. It's been an active volcano ever since; its last eruption was in 1950. (Let us say right away that there are more interesting places to visit than the litter-strewn source of the smoke, although if you enjoy hot mud baths you may find an excursion to be worthwhile. Don't jump into the volcano, since there are sharp rocks beneath the surface.)

In 1956 an earthquake registering 7.8 on the Richter scale destroyed about two-thirds of the homes on the island. Because it struck early in the morning, when most of Santoríni's residents were working in the fields or on their boats, only 40 people were killed. Many homeless islanders, unable to secure government loans to rebuild their homes, fled to other Greek ports, the United States, or Australia to begin new lives. Now Santoríni's 11,000 residents subsist (or "get rich quick," depending on whom you talk to) principally on tourism. There's still a thriving wine industry; vines coiled in baskets over low supports (to protect grapes from the extreme heat and *meltémi* winds) grow everywhere in the rich, volcanic soil.

Most first-time visitors stay in super-touristy **Firá** (even if only for a day or two), where the majority of services are located. Its boutique-lined pedestrian lanes are filled with the hundreds who arrive daily on cruise ships. They pause briefly to admire the scenery and then gallop by on mules to buy gold, furs, and ceramics that are priced the same here as anywhere else in Greece.

ESSENTIALS

GETTING THERE & DEPARTING   By Plane   There are four direct flights from Athens daily to the "international" (it receives European charter flights) airport at Monólithos. There are three flights per week from Iráklio, Crete; four from Rhodes; and six from Mýkonos. For schedule information and reservations, check the **Olympic Airways** office in Firá (☎ 0286/22-493) or in Athens (☎ 01/926-7251).

By Ferry   Several companies offer at least two ferries a day between Piraeus and Santoríni (10 to 12 hours). There are daily ferries to other Cyclades: Sýros, Páros, Náxos, Íos, Mýkonos, Tínos, Folégandros, Síkinos, and Anáfi. Five weekly ferries ply the long route north to Skiathos and Thessaloníki. Twice-weekly ferry service from the Dodecanese calls first at Rhodes, Kárpathos, Kássos, Hálki, and Crete. To and from Crete, there are almost daily smaller excursion boats leaving Iráklio. (Beware of this open-sea route in stormy weather—6 hours of nausea may make the airfare seem cheap.) **Schedules** should be confirmed with Tourist Information in Athens (☎ 171) or in Piraeus (☎ 01/451-1311), or with the Thíra Port Authority (☎ 0286/22-239).

When you're ready to move on, most ferry tickets are handled by **Nomikos Travel** (☎ 0286/23-660), with offices in Firá, Kartarádos, and Périssa. Almost all the ferries now dock at the port at Athiniós, a one-lane town with a few snack bars, ferry ticket agents, bad shops, and rooms at the Motel A. Buses meet each ferry (fares run 450 to 900 Drs / $1.90 to $3.75) and wait to take arrivals to the central bus station in Firá, from which buses depart for various villages. To catch your ferry, check returning bus schedules or book a taxi. Standard taxi fares to or from the port are 1,800 Drs ($7.80) from Firá, 3,500 Drs ($15.20) from Ía, 2,900 Drs ($12.50) from Kamári, and 3,500 Drs ($15.20) from Périssa. The original, highly photographed port at Skála (below Firá) is too exposed for the larger steamships; often the small

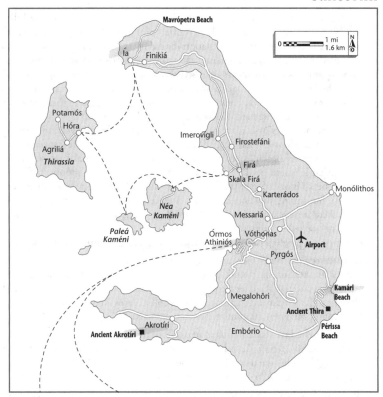

ferries that do dock there have to shuttle passengers in to shore on small caïques. If you dock at Skála, you can choose between a tough 45-minute hike uphill, where you'll encounter around 250 pushy mules; a mule ride costing 800 Drs ($3.50), including luggage (negotiate during low season); or a cable-car ride (cost 750 Drs/ $3.30) to reach Firá. We recommend taking a donkey up and a cable car down.

By Hydrofoil   Ilio Lines' high-speed hydrofoils connect Santoríni with Íos, Parós, Mýkonos, and Naxos three times weekly during the low season, and almost daily in the high season—*if the winds are not too strong.* Think twice the speed of the ferries, at least twice the fare, and contact a travel agent for schedule information.

VISITOR INFORMATION   There is no official government tourist office but we found the **Kamari Tours** office in Firá (☎ **0286/22-666;** fax 0286/22-971), 2 blocks south of the square, open daily from 8am to 11pm, particularly helpful. Kamari Tours also offers day trips to most of the island's sites, and if you have difficulty finding a room or a moped, they'll do what they can to help you. **Nomikos Travel** (☎ **0286/23-660;** fax 0286/24-942) has three offices in Firá, offering day tours, rental cars, room and villa rentals, and more.

ORIENTATION   For decades, to the tourists' delight, mules were used to make the steep ascent from the old port at **Skála** to Firá. The hardy beasts are now augmented by a Doppelmayer cable car that makes the lava rock cliff look like an Austrian ski resort, and adds 800 tourists per hour to the capital city. Unfortunately, almost all ships now dock at the colorless port of **Athiniós,** south of Skála.

After you arrive at the port at Athiniós, your first stop will be the hilltop, shopping-mad capital of **Firá** (which is often pronounced Fíra, probably a confusion with Thíra), the central bus station for around-the-island and beach bus connections. A 10-minute walk along the cliff north from Firá will lead you to **Firostepháni,** where the hotels are a better value and the view looking back to Firá is breathtaking. If you've come for more than 2 days (or at the height of the season), consider renting a room in one of the smaller villages. The pace in these villages is a little less tourist-oriented and the local beaches are less congested.

Because no rivers or lakes appeared on this island after the volcanic eruption, Santoríni's development has depended on water supplied by the few springs discovered near **Kamári Beach.** Kamári's black-sand beaches and natural water supply guaranteed that it would be the first resort to attract charter-tour groups. Off-season, Kamári Beach is one of the island's highlights (superior to the nearby scruffier **Périssa Beach**), but during July and August it's a place you'll want to stay away from. Instead, there are several small inland villages where hotels, pensions, and rooms for rent won't be booked by groups.

GETTING AROUND   By Bus   Santoríni is one of the few Cycladic islands with good bus service. Buses meet arriving ferries at Athiniós and take passengers to the island's **bus station,** just south of the central square in Firá, where they depart for other destinations. Schedules are posted on the station building, destinations are displayed on the windshields, and conductors collect fares after the bus has departed. Most routes run every 20 minutes between 7am and 11:30pm.

By Taxi   The **taxi stand** in Firá is across from the bus station or you can call for a taxi at ☎ **0286/22-555.** Taxis booked by phone base their rates from Firá. They cost 200 Drs (85¢) plus the meter for a phone-called taxi, and 500 Drs ($2.10) more if the pickup time is also reserved. Typical fares run about 2,000 Drs ($8.35).

By Moped & Car   Santoríni's young crowd seems to prefer two-wheel vehicles. Moped dealers are ubiquitous and offer single-person mopeds for 3,850 to 9,400 Drs ($16.70 to $40.90) per day, depending on the season and length of the rental. There's limited medical care on the island; wear a helmet and drive carefully!

Most travel offices can provide rental cars, or you can contact **AutoEurope** (☎ **0286/22-022**), a block south of the Firá bus stop square.

FAST FACTS   X-Ray Kilo Travel Services (☎ **0286/22-624;** fax 0286/23-600), on the main square, is the less-than-helpful American Express representative here.

The **National Bank** (open Monday to Friday from 8am to 2pm) is at the south end of the cliff path, near the post office. Many travel agents also exchange money during working hours (usually daily from 8am to 9:30pm).

Firá's small **hospital** is on 25 Martíou (☎ **0286/22-237**).

Also in Firá, the **police station** is on 25 Martíou south of the bus station (☎ **0286/22-649**). The **port police** can be reached at ☎ **0286/22-239.**

The **Firá post office,** open Monday to Friday from 8am to 1pm, is next to the bus station. The **telephone center (OTE),** up from the post office, is open daily from 7:30am to 10:30pm. **Santo Volcano Travel,** on the main square (☎ **0286/22-127;** fax 0286/22-955), will also help you send a fax or make a phone call for a nominal fee.

EXPLORING THE ISLAND

A visit to Santoríni would not be complete without a stop at the archaeological site of **Akrotíri.** The impact of this startling 1960s find has been compared to the discovery of Egypt's King Tut's tomb in the 1920s. If you don't have an archaeological background, you might want to take advantage of one of the many excellent local tours and see the site with a knowledgeable guide.

Another personal favorite is a self-guided tour of **Ancient Thíra.** The standard around-the-island day tour used to include a visit to the fascinating, highly revered Monastery of Profítis Ilías. However, during our last visit we found that it was closed because the elderly monks who'd tended it had all passed away. On island tours, the monastery has now been replaced by a winery stop. Isn't that the way of the world?

AN OUTSTANDING ARCHAEOLOGICAL SITE: AKROTÍRI

The Minoan satellite city of ✪ **Akrotíri** is an incredible monument to that culture and to the efforts of the archaeologist who discovered it far below layers of volcanic ash. From the early 1930s, Minoan expert Spyridon Marinatos devoted his life to the search for Akrotíri. The findings from Akrotíri have provided the world with some of the most beautiful Minoan stone artifacts and the most impressive frescos of the prehistoric world. The high artistic quality of the finds suggests that Akrotíri was a city of wealthy merchants and ship captains.

As you enter the covered site you'll be walking on the main street. Most of the remains on either side were stores or warehouses for Akrotíri's commercial trade. In one room 400 clay pots were found, all stacked according to size. Another room held large urns with traces of olive oil, onion, and fish inside. Continuing down the street, you'll come to a "square" in the shape of a triangle, and in front of you is the West House. This multistoried home is also called the Captain's House because of the richly decorated fresco of a Minoan and Libyan sea encounter (perhaps a battle) unearthed on the second floor.

Continuing along the main street, you'll see many more houses where remarkably preserved frescoes were discovered. Unfortunately, the best works from Akrotíri were taken away to Athens, where they can be seen at the National Archaeological Museum. It's hoped that eventually the frescoes can be housed in a museum in Firá.

Akrotíri can be reached by public bus or private bus tours. Admission is 1,250 Drs ($5.40); the site is open daily from 8:30am to 3pm, but it tends to be hot and crowded at midday. Try to arrive early in the morning, if possible, then hike over to the pebbly Red Beach for a good seafood lunch and a swim.

ANCIENT THÍRA

The acropolis of the island's ancient capital, now called Arhéa Thíra, was inhabited by Dorian colonists from the 9th century B.C. Its impressive remains are situated on the hill towering 1,200 feet above Kamári Beach. Be sure to check out the springs in the cliff. Most of the buildings on the acropolis date from the Ptolemaic period (300 to 145 B.C.).

After entering the site, follow the path on the left. Carved in the rocks at a small shrine are the eagle symbol of Zeus, the lion of Apollo (you can sit on his throne and put your foot in his imprints) to the left, the dolphin of Poseidon, and a portrait of a Dorian admiral. Just south is the open Agorá, and behind it the hewn-stone ruins of the Governor's Palace. On the southern tip is a terrace, believed to have been the center of religious practices; stone tablets found here told of naked young boys who would frolic in homage to Dionysus. From this point you have a fantastic aerial view of the ancient port at Kamári and the long black-sand streak of Périssa, and a clear idea of how valuable this acropolis was to the defense of the ancient capital. Behind this point is a partially shaded, smooth-stone sanctuary of the Egyptian gods, ideal for picnicking. Nearby is an underground sanctuary, whose Doric columns still support a stone canopy for an alternative shaded picnic spot.

Getting to Ancient Thíra requires some forethought: Wear good shoes, bring water, and by all means bring a picnic. At the nearest bus stop, you can negotiate for half-day excursions by mule up the stone path for about 4,000 Drs ($16.65). It's possible to arrange a round-trip taxi tour from Firá, which will cost about 12,000 Drs ($50), including waiting time. Ancient Thíra is open Tuesday to Saturday from 9am to 2:30pm and Sunday and holidays from 9am to 1pm.

VILLAGES

The large southern village of **Embório,** at the turnoff for Périssa Beach, still displays aspects of traditional Greek life that have long been lost at the beach resorts. Second in size to Firá, it has some unusual houses built inside the ruins of a large Venetian fortress. In the signposted TRADITIONAL AREA, stuccoed homes and closed blue-wood shutters lend an air of perpetual siesta. Our friend George Kokkinis at Kamari Tours told us that Jean-Paul Sartre spent 6 months in a castle here, writing *The Flies.* Scale the hillside to the windmills and imagine the solitude that a writer might find today.

Pýrgos is another pretty inland village, the oldest and highest on Santoríni. There are several small churches to see and the crumbling stucco and exposed stone of original Cycladic houses clinging to remnants of a Venetian-era kástro. From Pýrgos, you can stop at the **Santos** or **Canava Roussos** wineries. They're open to wine tasters, who can sample the local reds, rosés, and white wines (a Santorinian specialty) for a nominal fee. Of course, wine is packaged for sale as well. If you don't want to drink on an empty stomach, Pýrgos is the home of one of our favorite island eateries, the **Pýrgos Taverna** (☎ 0286/31-346), with its gurgling waterfalls, colored lights, circular architecture, glass-enclosed panoramic views, great steaks, baked potatoes in foil, excellent *mezédes,* Ia wine, and gracious service.

FIRÁ

To reach the famous view, just head up from the bus station and **central square,** Platía Theotokopoúlou (named after El Greco), to **Ypapantís Street,** more popularly known as **Gold Street** because of its many jewelry shops.

The **donkey station** is down to the left on little Odós Marinátou, and the lower, and much quieter street is called Ayíou Miná. By following it north you could reach **Odós M. Nomikoú** (Nomikós Street), which follows the edge of the caldera all the way to the northern tip of the island.

The main vehicle street through Firá is **25 Martíou,** which leads north past the central square to Ia.

Most people are content to stroll along Gold Street, shop, and stop at a cafe to take in the view. Generally the farther north you go the higher the prices get, the less certain the quality, and the greater the pressure. Kyle recommends the **Garanis Gallery** (☎ 0286/24-352), below in the Lagoudera Shopping Center, for the best prices and selection of handmade jewelry.

At the north end of Gold Street you'll find the **cable-car station** and up and to the right the archaeology museum. The attractive **archaeology museum** (☎ 0286/22-217) has some early Cycladic figurines, vases from Ancient Thíra, and some interesting Dionysiac figures, as well as finds from Akrotíri. It's open Tuesday to Sunday from 8:30am to 3pm; admission is 800 Drs ($3.35) for adults, 600 Drs ($2.50) for seniors, and 400 Drs ($1.65) for students. There's also an **international bookshop** nearby.

KAMÁRI BEACH

Kamári Beach is Santoríni's most popular destination because its beautiful black-pebble beach, 4¹⁄₂ miles long, was long ago discovered and exploited by tour operators. Each week about 20 planeloads of Europeans land directly at Santoríni's airport for a packaged vacation at this unique resort. If you're able to visit Kamári in the spring or fall, you can probably find a room at a price comparable to that in Firá or the less attractive Périssa Beach.

There's little to do but dance, dine, drink, and soak up the sun at Kamári Beach. The local **Kamári Tours** office (☎ **0286/31-390** or 0286/31-455) runs excursions to all of Santoríni's sites, in addition to booking most of Kamári's rooms and booking cruises to other islands. When you're ready to leave for Firá (where you can get transportation to other villages), you'll find that buses depart every half hour from 7am to midnight. If you're a spontaneous type, you can order a taxi (☎ **0286/ 31-668,** or 0286/22-555 in Firá) but the 10-minute ride will cost about 1,500 Drs ($6.25).

ÍA

The ruined **Lontza Castle,** at the west end of town, is the best place to catch the sunset. There's a small **Naval Museum of Thira** (☎ **0286/71-156**), open Wednesday to Monday from 10am to 1pm and 5 to 8pm. Loungers will find many caldera-view cafes, and hikers can tackle a vigorous walk down the cliffside to the fishing port of **Arméni.** The nearest sand beach is **Baxédes,** partially accessible by bus from the town square. A half-mile walk over the black sand will bring you to a relatively isolated, undeveloped bathing area. Ía's overnight guests often walk north and down to the rock-and-pebble beach at **Ammoúdi.** You can actually drive down, but locals have told us about rental cars parked under the cliff overhang that are soon blanketed in rockfall. *Another Ammoudi hazard:* Tourists sometimes leave their beach gear and wallets on the stone swimming platform or along the pebble beach, then find everything swept away by the enormous wake of a passing steamer. A safer beach excursion might be a walk down the west side of the island (a gently banked, cultivated area) to **Kolumbus Beach.**

If you haven't seen enough gold in Firá, check out the antique jewelry, vintage watches, and high-fashion clothes on the main street on either side of church square. **Ifanderi,** the government-sponsored shop run by the EOT, sells all-cotton rugs handwoven by the women of Santoríni.

WHERE TO STAY

Santoríni is exceptionally crowded in July and August, and visitors without sleeping bags need to make a reservation, accompanied by a deposit, at least 2 months in advance of arrival. Otherwise, head straight from the ferry to Firá's bus stop square and ask one of the travel agents to help you find a room. Unless noted, the hotels listed below are open from about April 15 to October 15.

IN FIRÁ

Most of the Firá hotels with views of the spectacular caldera charge a premium, which puts them way beyond our budget. Fortunately, there are a few good-value choices that offer quiet, comfort, and the wonderful view. Rooms-to-let (that is, unlicensed hotel construction) is such a big business that most families build impersonal multiroom additions to their charming and homey residences. Many offer modern private facilities and hotel amenities at a better price than the hotels. Between April and mid-June as well as in September and October, double rooms are available for 6,000 to 9,600 Drs ($25 to $40), while in July and August the prices soar to 10,800 to 14,400 Drs ($45 to $60). Very few hotels are open year-round.

Super-Budget Choices

International Youth Hostel Kamares. Firá, 847 00 Santoríni. ☎ **0286/24-472.** 66 beds, with 100 more on the roof. 1,800 Drs ($7.50) per person. No credit cards.

This official IYHF hostel, 200 yards north of the bus station on the left, is newer, cleaner, and better managed than some of the private ones. There are separate dorms, crowded with bunk beds, for men and women, and no curfew. There are 14 communal showers. Though less spacious in dorms and common areas, the IYH has a pretty rooftop bar.

Thira Youth Hostel. Firá, 847 00 Santoríni. ☎ **0286/22-387** or 0286/23-864. 9 rms, all with bath (shower); 80 dorm beds. 9,600 Drs ($40) double; 1,800 Drs ($7.50) dorm bed. No credit cards.

A youth hostel and nine high-ceilinged simple double rooms occupy this newly restored Thiran mansion. Though it's Spartan in amenities, its dorm bunks are painted cerulean blue, the ceilings are vaulted in the classic antiseismic design of the Cyclades, and the 20-foot-tall parlors lend an old-world dignity. This is a great value for the young-at-heart, and it's terrific for families. Elpida leads the friendly staff, there's no curfew, there are 24 communal showers, the hot water runs 24 hours, and the rooftop cafe is cheap and pretty good. The front entrance is about 300 yards north of the bus stop, right off 25 Martíou Street; the back door is opposite the Megaron Gyzi Cultural Center in the heart of town.

Moderately Priced Choices

Hotel Asimina. Firá, 847 00 Santoríni. ☎ **0286/22-989.** Fax 0286/23-958. 14 rms, all with bath (shower). 12,000 Drs ($50) single; 18,000 Drs ($75) double. AE, MC, V.

This small Class E hotel, run by Mendrinos Tours, is located in a quiet spot next door to the archaeological museum. The petite rooms all have private facilities and adequate, if simple, furnishings. We've received complaints about mosquitoes, but this remains a fair-value choice because of its central location.

If you're interested in something more plush, the same owners run the fancier **Hotel King Thiras,** about 200 yards north of here; its posted rates are about 35% higher. (You could try bargaining.)

Hotel Delfini II. Firá, 847 00 Santoríni. ☎ **0286/24-340.** Fax 0286/22-780. 4 rms, all with bath (shower); 3 apts. TEL. 18,000 Drs ($75) double; 26,400 Drs ($110) apt with kitchen. No credit cards.

The Delfini II is just below the cliff path, under the Atlantis Hotel, near the Selene Restaurant. It's a terrific blend of contemporary style and facilities with traditional Cycladic caves. The cleverly designed studios and apartments sleep two to four people; the simpler, smaller but attractive doubles are a steal. Units open out onto shared terraces or balconies, and all have minifridges and that drop-dead caldera view.

Hotel Tataki. Firá, 847 00 Santoríni. ☎ **0286/22-389.** 10 rms, all with bath (shower). 10,800 Drs ($45) single; 13,200 Drs ($55) double. No credit cards.

This small but simple hotel is built above the family home of an older couple. Though short on English, they maintain their small, plain rooms well, with many homey touches. In high season, rates vary according to view, but all rooms are situated around a geranium-filled courtyard. It's a good value for the location, just up the lane behind Pelican Travel, off the main square.

Villa Haroula. Firá, 847 00 Santoríni. ☎ **0286/23-469.** 10 rms, all with bath (shower). 12,000–18,000 Drs ($50–$75) per room, depending on season. No credit cards.

This homey, lace- and embroidery-touched pension is off a small lane at the south end of town, not far from the Selene Restaurant. Though the rooms are plain, with blond wood bedsteads and small balconies, the decorated common space adds charm. Orange bougainvillea leads up to the second-story vaulted-roof rooms, whose shared terrace is shaded by a brilliant blue arbor. These rooms provide valley views and are a better value.

Worth a Splurge

Daedalus Hotel. Firá, 847 00 Santoríni. ☎ **0286/22-834.** Fax 0286/22-818. 43 rms, all with bath (shower). A/C TV TEL. 19,200 Drs ($80) single; 24,000 Drs ($100) double. AE, DC, MC, V.

This newly built hotel stands out for its large pool and pleasant sunning area. Set off the main road in the heavily under construction south part of town, it boasts carpeted rooms with curtained showers, fridges, piped-in Muzak, and balconies. There's no view to speak of, but it's pretty plush for these parts; the sky-blue quilted leatherette headboards give it a Wild West flair.

✪ **Loucas Hotel.** Firá, 847 00 Santoríni. ☎ **0286/22-480.** Fax 0286/24-882. 25 rms, all with bath (shower). A/C TEL TV. 21,000 Drs ($87.50) single; 30,000 Drs ($125) double. Rates include breakfast. MC, V. Closed Nov–Mar 19.

Our first-choice inn underwent a total renovation in 1995, and with its priceless caldera views it remains a great value still. Opened in 1959 on the site of cliffside donkey stables, the Loucas has simple cave rooms, each with a fridge and vaulted ceilings to prevent collapse during an earthquake. The simply furnished rooms are elegantly detailed with accents of white and Aegean blue, and provide safe-deposit boxes and luxurious style. Best of all, they share a tiered stone terrace tacking down the steep cliff. The Ziras family has recently added a new bar and a full-service Greek/continental restaurant, also with a great view of the caldera.   •

✪ **Santoríni Tennis Club Apartments.** Kartarádos, P.O. Box 39, 847 00 Santoríni. ☎ **0286/22-122** or 0286/23-013. Fax 0286/23-698. 9 villas. TEL. 20,900–40,000 Drs ($78–$166.65) villa for two to five. Rates include breakfast. AE, MC, V.

The Santoríni Tennis Club is a particular favorite, a complex of restored early 19th-century Cycladic homes in the village of Kartarádos. Nine vaulted-roof dwellings and a cozy lobby bar have been created from abandoned villagers' homes nestled in the soft stone cliffs. Gorgeously simple caves sleeping two to five people are all white-washed stucco and stone inside, some duplexes, all with carved-in furniture, tiny shut-tered windows, Greek weavings and cotton rugs, and niches filled with ceramics. Fully stocked kitchenettes are for those who never want to leave; breakfast is brought daily into each home or served outside on the bluestone patio. True to its name, the Tennis Club has two porous "quick" concrete courts (nonguests are charged 1,800 Drs/$7.50 per hour), plus a garden, large swimming pool, kiddie pool, and sunbathing deck. We loved our stay and found it to be a wonderful family environment, with room for everyone to spread out.

Tzekos Villas. Firá, 847 00 Santoríni. ☎ **0286/22-755,** or 0286/22-958 in winter. Fax 0286/24-944, or 0286/22-686 in winter. 22 villas. A/C MINIBAR TV TEL. 34,800–55,200 Drs ($145–$230) villas for one to four. Rates include breakfast. AE, DC, MC, V.

These enormous deluxe, newly built "cave" dwellings have traditionally been avail-able only in Ía. Now honeymooners and other splurgers—families should inquire whether or not children would *really* be welcome here—can be next to the action, be wowed by caldera views, lounge by a lovely long lap pool, and frolic in two-story, very private and plush housing. The style is decidedly Euro-Greek, with white-on-white tiles, pastel fabrics, and a gracious but aloof staff. The Tzekos Villas are located near the old pumice quarry at the cliff's south side, close by the Selene Restaurant.

In Villages Just Outside Firá

You may not want to stay in fast-paced Firá, but most visitors will want to visit the capital city for an infusion of society. Staying in a nearby village (by this, we mean within a 20-minute walk) seems to be the best alternative.

Firostepháni

This community is just a 10-minute walk north from Firá; to our minds, it offers the loveliest view of the caldera and the active volcano at Néa Kaméni.

There are many rooms for rent in the area, but the **Hotel Galíni,** P.O. Box 9, Firostepháni, 847 00 Santoríni (☎ **0286/22-095;** fax 0286/23-097), in the center, stands out for its modern, tiered architecture, which assures that all 15 rooms with private bath have a fabulous view and the privacy of separate entrances off a common veranda. Doubles run 18,000 Drs ($75); American Express, MasterCard, and Visa are accepted.

A little north of these on the cliffside path is the **Hotel Mylos** (☎ **0286/23-884**), more of a pension above a popular snack bar. Eight small rooms with private shower, some with views, rent for 13,800 Drs ($57.50).

The **Heliovassílema (Sunset) Hotel** (☎ and fax **0286/23-486**) is just below the Mylos. It's a colorful, kitschy interpretation of traditional houses. Stucco, curving lines, and some details found in the original Ía dwellings make these 31 comfortable double rooms with telephones a good value at 15,600 Drs ($65), plus 1,800 Drs ($7.50) each for breakfast on the caldera-view terrace.

Kartarádos

This attractive, whitewashed village, 1¼ miles south of Firá, offers rooms for rent and some hotels for those who shun the singles pubs, discos, and jewelers of main-street Firá. Even if you're only passing through, take time to explore this village's still-original and very traditional core around the old cathedral just below the square.

A few minutes from Kartarádos's main square is the whitewashed **Hotel Cyclades** (☎ **0286/24-543;** fax 0286/22-948), which looks like your rich Greek aunt's private villa. The friendly Sigalas family has 26 double rooms near the moped shops for 8,400 to 18,000 Drs ($35 to $75) with breakfast, according to season, but they're open year-round.

Readers have loved their stays at the **Pension George** (☎ **0286/22-351**) because of its gregarious host, George Halaris, whose wife, Helen, is English. For a nice room with private bath, just a quick walk from the Kartarádos square, expect to pay 8,160 Drs ($34) single and 9,240 Drs ($38.50) double.

Two spiffier in-town hotels are the **Hotel Lodos** (☎ **0286/22-146;** fax 0286/25-070), which has a big pool with a fun bridge over it, a kiddie pool, a large sunning area above street level, and 21 rooms—all with bath—with singles for 10,800 Drs ($45) and doubles for 18,000 Drs ($75); and the **Villa Odyssey** (☎/fax **0286/23-681**), with 17 rooms, all with bath and minifridges for 9,000 Drs ($37.50) single and 18,000 Drs ($75) double. What a deal for singles!

Also, you can visit the helpful **Nomikos Travel** office (☎ **0286/23-660**) on the square, where George Nomikos and his generous staff will find you a room, exchange traveler's checks, and arrange ferry tickets.

In Kamári

Almost all hotels and rooms are listed with travel agents. You can contact the local **Kamári Tours** office (☎ **0286/31-390**) to get an affordable beachside room—the hotels, not the guests, pay the commission—or walk to the south end of the beach and into the little village, where you'll find other choices.

The large **Kamári Camping** (☎ 0286/32-452 or 0286/31-453) is about 800 yards from the beach. Services include a tourist information center, restaurant, cafeteria, minimarket, laundry, hot showers, and bus service. They charge 1,800 Drs ($7.50) per person including tent site.

Moderately Priced Choices

Argiris Studios. Kamári Beach, 847 00 Santoríni. ☎ **0286/33-059.** 4 apts, all with bath (shower). 18,000 Drs ($75) double. No credit cards.

Our favorite in-town taverna has been reborn as a modern complex of studio apartments. Each is bright white and simple, and contains a small kitchenette. The best deal here is that one child under age 12 may stay free with parents in a three-bedded room.

Esperides Rooms. Kamári Beach, 847 00 Santoríni. ☎ **0286/31-670.** Fax 0286/31-423. 17 rms, all with bath (shower). 14,000 Drs ($58.35) single; 15,000 Drs ($62.50) double. AE, MC, V.

The Akis Hotel manages these rooms, which are tucked in a pistachio grove, surrounded by the excavations of a Byzantine city, new housing, and several snack bars.

Hotel Glaros. Kamári Beach, 847 00 Santoríni. ☎ **0286/32-601.** Fax 0286/33-442. 16 rms, all with bath (shower). 9,600 Drs ($40) single; 13,200 Drs ($55) double. No credit cards.

The newly built Glaros is on the main street leading into the village. Though a bit less convenient, it's a cheerful spot, with a lobby full of lush ficus trees and rooms sharing a common terrace overlooking a flower-filled sidewalk snack bar.

Korali Hotel. Kamári Beach, 847 00 Santoríni. ☎ **0286/31-904** or 0286/32-990. Fax 0286/32-987. TEL. 12 rms, all with bath (shower); 1 apt. 10,800 Drs ($45) single; 18,000 Drs ($75) double; 22,500 Drs ($93.75) apt. MC, V.

This is a very handsome small hotel, with a private entrance leading to each room. It's not beachside, but it's comfortable, quiet, and a good value, especially for singles. It even rents bicycles. Both the hotel and its restaurant (Greek cuisine)—longtime locals—are open year-round.

Worth a Splurge

Akis Hotel. Kamári Beach, 847 00 Santoríni. ☎ **0286/32-309.** Fax 0286/31-423. TEL. 18 rms, all with bath (shower). 18,500 Drs ($77.10) single; 21,500 Drs ($89.60) double. Rates include breakfast. AE, MC, V.

The Akis Hotel, on the main street, is the closest—just 30 yards away—of the in-town hotels to the black beach. It has a cafeteria/cafe downstairs with good food and a local clientele. The rooms are bright and well kept.

Kamári Beach Hotel. Kamári Beach, 847 00 Santoríni. ☎ **0286/31-216** or 0286/31-243, or 01/482-8826 in Athens. Fax 0286/31-243. 92 rms, all with bath (tub). 30,000 Drs ($125) double. Rates include breakfast. AE, DC, MC, V.

This hotel has the best beachfront location, close by the little village. All the Kamári Beach's spacious, balconied rooms take advantage of the view over the Aegean and the lovely pool down below. It looks like a resort, and it's run like one. A longtime favorite.

Matina Hotel. Kamári Beach, 847 00 Santoríni. ☎ **0286/31-491.** Fax 0286/31-860. 27 rms, all with bath (shower). 23,400 Drs ($97.50) single or double with breakfast; 18,000 Drs ($75) single or double without breakfast in the pension annex. MC, V.

This thoroughly modern hotel is just a 2-minute walk from the beach. Services include room service, laundry, bike rental, and tourist information; landscaped gardens surround a nice new pool. The spacious, airy rooms are often group-booked, but try them or the nearby annex, Pension Matina. The pension is somewhat plainer, but guests can use the hotel's pool and gardens.

Venus Hotel. Kamári Beach, 847 00 Santoríni. ☎ **0286/31-183.** 60 rms, all with bath (shower). 24,000 Drs ($100) single or double. Rates include breakfast. Open year-round. MC, V.

Next to Kamári Beach, the Venus has white-on-white, marble-floored bedrooms with flashes of tasteful pastel to break up the coolness. All rooms have central heating and radios. Our favorite aspect of this popular hotel is its beachfront snack bar, which overlooks the surf, sand, and bikini action.

IN PÉRISSA

Périssa is Santoríni's other beach resort, a much smaller enclave of pensions, tour-group hotels, and cafes near a wide, long beach of black pebbles on the southeast coast. In the summer Périssa's cheaper lifestyle ensures its popularity with backpackers fleeing from high-priced Firá, Kamári, or Ía. The beach gets very noisy, crowded, and badly littered. If you can afford it, it would be better to stay elsewhere.

Buses run from Firá to Périssa every half hour from 7am to 11:30pm. On **Platía Timíou Stavroú** (Holy Cross Square) you'll find public showers and toilets, a worn miniature golf course with video games, a few markets, a moped dealer, a **mobile post office,** and the **OTE.** Both **Kamari Tours,** on the road (☎ **0286/81-127**), and **Nomikos Travel,** on the beach (☎ **0286/23-085** or 0286/81-060), can change traveler's checks, help you book rooms, and handle problems.

Périssa is a struggling wannabe resort and there are many lodgings comparable to those we've listed below. Doubles at most of these hotels (usually booked by groups) run about 14,000 Drs ($58.35) with bath.

Perissa Camping, right behind the beach (☎ **0286/81-343**), has tent sites from 1,200 Drs ($5) per person; car parking is 600 Drs ($2.50) extra. It's also the nude sunbathing center of Périssa, and provides free hot showers for guests, a minimarket, bar, snack bar, and a very active canteen with great music.

The **International Youth Hostel Périssa,** on the main road 100 yards from the beach (☎ **0286/81-639;** fax 0286/82-668), is well established and very together. The owner Yannis Drossos and the manager Loukas Gavelas send a minivan to the port to meet each ferry, offer hot showers, a music bar with live DJ and big-screen video, a communal kitchen, and coin-operated washing machines! The IYH has 82 dorm beds (in single-sex dorms) at 3,000 Drs ($12.50) per person, as well as newly built traditional-style housing with two- to eight-person private family rooms with showers for 1,450 to 1,800 Drs ($6.05 to $7.50) per person, depending upon the number of people sharing.

Vassilis Rooms (☎ **0286/81-739;** fax 0286/82-070), our best recent find, is located in a new housing cluster on the road into town, about half a mile south of the square. There are 31 rooms, many overlooking the nearby sea, all with a minifridge and tea kettles. There's an enormous sign saying THE BEST!—and we do admire the laid-stone paving, painted shutters, and attention to landscaping. This is a great deal at 9,600 Drs ($40) for two.

The **Irene Darzenda Pension,** just 60 yards from the beach (☎ **0286/81-236**)— at the bus stop on the north end of town—offers good value, with 13 simple rooms, all with bath and refrigerator (some with balconies) that cost 7,200 Drs ($30).

The modern **Meltemi Hotel** (☎ **0286/81-325;** fax 0286/81-139), which has its own pool, is one of the slickest hotels around. It has 47 fresh new rooms, all with private phones and baths. Singles are 8,700 Drs ($36.25) and doubles are 13,500 Drs

($56.25); MasterCard and Visa are accepted. It has recently added air-conditioned Class A apartments that rent for 16,500 Drs ($68.75) for two.

IN ÍA

Famous for its spectacular sunsets, Ía (spelled Oía in Greek, but pronounced as we've spell it), at the northernmost tip of the island, is the most beautiful and pleasantly unconventional village on the island.

Public buses run from Firá to Ía every half hour from 7am to 11pm; the last bus leaves Ía at 11:30pm. Taxis from Firá to Ía cost 2,200 Drs ($9.15); from Ía to Firá taxis sometimes have to be booked by phone (☎ **0286/22-555**) and so cost more.

The **EOT** information office (☎ **0286/71-234**) is near the church; Eleni Lagonikakou is there daily from 10am to 10pm to help you find rooms, suggest vendors, locate goods, and so forth.

If you're planning a long stay, it might be a good idea to touch base with Ía's goodwill ambassador, Markos Karvounis. **Karvounis Tours** (☎ **0286/71-090** or 0286/71-209; fax 0286/71-291) has a metered phone for long-distance calls and can do the following: exchange money, book wonderful villas and rooms at exceptionally low prices, find taxis, book island day trips, and sell ferry and plane tickets; it accepts American Express, MasterCard, and Visa. Karvounis Tours also offers special monthly winter rentals ($300 to $500) for those seeking peace, quiet, and real village life.

Ía is basically a two-street community: the west-facing vehicle road that leads into the bus stop and, almost parallel to it, Nikólaos Nomikós Street, the pedestrians-only, marble-paved walkway along the east-facing cliff. The Karvounis Tours office and most services are located off the cliffwalk near the village's main church.

As more traditional-style houses are restored or newly constructed to meet the growing demand, it's become possible for many more visitors to use Ía as a base to explore the island. Ía may be somewhat more expensive; only the simplest of modern hotels and hostels charge typical Greece rates.

There are a few simple rooms for rent as well, but prices run 12,000 to 18,000 Drs ($50 to $75)—about 25% more than in Firá. If you can reserve accommodations in advance, we recommend:

Hotel Anemones. Ía, 847 02 Santoríni. ☎ **0286/71-220.** 10 rms, all with bath (shower). 12,000 Drs ($50) single or double. No credit cards.

Good accommodations at a good price, with a fabulous view from the breakfast room. The modern rooms are comfortable, but without much traditional Cycladic style.

Hotel Finikia. Finikiá, 847 02 Santoríni. ☎ **0286/71-373,** or 01/654-7944 in Athens. Fax 0286/71-338. 15 rms, all with bath (shower); 3 studios. 17,000 Drs ($70.85) single or double; studios 25%–40% higher, depending upon the season. Rates include breakfast. MC, V.

This newly built sparkling-white Cycladic complex has a nice pool. Each balconied room has its own personality and a small front patio garden. Recently constructed "studios" have their own minifridges and a bit more room.

Laokasti Villas. Ía, 847 02 Santoríni. ☎ **0286/71-343.** Fax 0286/71-116. 17 villas, all with bath (shower). TEL. 28,000 Drs ($116.65) villa for two. Rates include breakfast. Extra person 5,000 Drs ($20.85). AE, MC, V.

Eight original small villas are on the west side of the vehicle road, and nine more have been added, all fashioned and fully furnished in the typical style. Kitchenettes, plus the space to accommodate three or four in some rooms, add a homey feel. Laokasti, though, has the amenities of a hotel—a swimming pool, reception room with a fireplace, cafeteria, cozy bar, and breakfast room with a panoramic view toward the beach and coast.

Lauda Rooms & Houses. Ía, 847 02 Santoríni. ☎ **0286/71-204** or 0286/71-157. 11 rms, all with bath (shower); 8 studios. 14,000–24,000 Drs ($58.35–$100) double; 40,000 Drs ($166.65) studio with kitchen. Open year-round. MC, V.

These are charming traditional rooms on Ía's cliffwalk, and we found them equally pleasant as rooms or as spacious, renovated, well-designed studios. The caldera view is priceless, making them a good value.

Youth Hostel Ía. Ía, 847 02 Santoríni. ☎ **0286/71-465.** Fax 0286/71-291. 60 beds. 3,600 Drs ($15) dorm bed. Rates include breakfast.

This privately owned "international" youth hostel is about 50 yards north of the bus stop square. The rooms are comfortable, traditional-style dormitories, and the complex includes a minimarket, bar, and restaurant, as well as telephone, postal, and travel service.

WHERE TO EAT
IN FIRÁ

There are restaurants aplenty to cater to those with a bit more money, those with sophisticated tastes who are tired of Greek food, and those young enough to live on french fries and pizza. The restaurants listed below stand out above the rest.

Warning: We've had numerous reports of exorbitant charges for seafood and wine in several of the newer restaurants.

Aris Restaurant. Odós Ayíou Miná, Firá. ☎ **0286/22-480.** Main courses 1,800–4,200 Drs ($7.50–$17.50). MC, V. Daily noon–1am. GREEK/INTERNATIONAL.

On the lowest pedestrian street, below the Loucas Hotel, you'll find Aris Ziras's fine restaurant in a converted old winery (used for interior dining in inclement weather). The chef was formerly with the Athens Hilton, service is gracious, and the dishes are mainly Greek. The *mezédes* are excellent, the moussaká is among the best we've ever had, and the napkins are white linen! Try the personalized Santorini Nykteri Aris, a fine white wine.

Kástro. Cliffside, Firá. ☎ **0286/22-503.** Breakfast, snacks, desserts 960–2,900 Drs ($4–$12.10). AE, MC, V. Daily 8am–midnight. INTERNATIONAL.

The very popular Kástro's major selling point is its site at the north end of the cliffwalk, opposite the cable car entrance. You get the caldera view as well as a sweeping vista over the cliffside's many dwellings. Simple snacks, omelets, sandwiches, and desserts are surprisingly well priced for this location, on this island. Kástro's full-service tablecoth restaurant occupies the lower levels. It's almost 50% to 100% more expensive, draws lots of day-trippers, and serves a more varied and complete menu with a large wine and drink list.

Naoussa Restaurant. In the Lagouder Shopping Center, Firá. ☎ **0286/24-869.** Main courses 900–4,200 Drs ($3.90–$18.30). V. Daily noon–1am. GREEK.

A vivid blue-and-white canopy shades this second-floor terrace taverna in the heart of town. At our lunch, the chef was boasting about her daily specials of local cuisine. She did admit that most tourists ordered beef fillet or the souvláki platter, probably more for budgetary reasons. We loved the grilled fish with lemon, which obviously cost more than meat, but is a real treat when freshly caught.

Nicholas Taverna. Erythroú Stavroú St., Firá. ☎ **0286/24-550.** Main courses 1,080–1,920 Drs ($4.50–$8). No credit cards. Mon–Sat noon–3:30pm and 6–11pm, Sun 6–11pm. GREEK.

For the closest thing to authentic taverna fare try the atmospheric Nicholas in the heart of town, on Red Cross Street. The fava-bean dip and stuffed calamari are island specialties prepared very well. This family taverna grew from a busy green market after World War II, and we find their food and untrendy decor a relief.

Nick's Café-Bar. Next to the National Bank of Greece, Firá. ☎ **0286/84-700.** Breakfast, snacks, desserts 720–2,100 Drs ($3–$8.75). No credit cards. Daily 8am–1am. INTERNATIONAL.

One of the best places for breakfast or a light lunch is near the main square, in a quiet shaded corner off the heavily trafficked street. Nick's nice waiters serve fresh-squeezed tropical juice drinks, ice-cream concoctions with lots of flags and doo-dads, and crisp tasty salads.

Sphinx Restaurant. Mitropóleos St., Firá. ☎ **0286/23-823.** Reservations recommended. Main courses 2,000–6,000 Drs ($8.35–$25). AE, MC, V. Daily noon–3pm and 7pm–2am. INTERNATIONAL.

In a restored old mansion opposite the Atlantis Hotel you'll find one of the finest restaurants on the island, appointed with antiques, sculpture, and interesting ceramics by local artists. (Competing with the smart crowd and fine art may make you want to get dressed up.) The service is friendly and attentive; every meal is fresh and superbly prepared. The seafood specials (including fresh Mediterranean lobster) and imaginative preparations of typical Greek fare are wonderful.

IN KAMÁRI

Kamári has been popular for so many years that both the tiny village and the long beach road are jammed with mediocre, moderately priced restaurants. We suggest the following:

Alexis Grill. Kamári Beach. No phone. Main courses 780–2,100 Drs ($3.25–$8.75). No credit cards. Daily 11am–midnight. GREEK/INTERNATIONAL.

No shirt, no shoes, no hassle. On the beach road, in the pine grove toward the north end of the beach—just as you'd suspect—you'll find charcoal-grilled chicken, lamb chops, moussaká, souvláki, and fish at reasonable prices.

✪ **Camille Stephani.** Kamári Beach. ☎ **0286/31-716.** Evening reservations recommended July–Sept. Main courses 1,800–4,900 Drs ($7.50–$20.40). AE, DC, MC, V. Daily 11am–midnight. INTERNATIONAL.

This pine grove–shaded restaurant has brought excellent continental cuisine and more formal dining to the north end of Kamári Beach, about 500 yards from the village bus stop. Though it's formal in service and cuisine, we had brunch here one Sunday in bathing suits and cover-ups and were treated as graciously as the Greek church crowd seated nearby. Their special is a tender beef fillet with green pepper in madeira sauce, plus a large grill menu, many fresh salads, and lower priced Greek specialties. It's a great value when compared to Firá's bastions of gourmet fare.

IN PÉRISSA

Périssa's oldest beachside eatery is **Marco's Taverna** (☎ **0286/81-205**), on the north end of the beach. **Vachos** is a newer popular choice. Both are open daily noon to midnight, serving a wide variety of food, all well prepared and costing 850 to 1,950 Drs ($3.55 to $8.15) per main course; MasterCard and Visa are accepted. **Makedonia,** on the main road, open daily from 8am to midnight, is quite popular for its inexpensive pizza.

IN ÍA

Katina Restaurant. Ammoúdi Beach. ☎ **0286/71-280.** Main courses 1,400–4,000 Drs ($5.85–$16.65). MC. Daily 9am–1am. SEAFOOD.

Locals consider Katina Koletta's the best place to eat in Ía, though it isn't in town but down at the port of Ammoúdi—best reached by donkey (a 950-Dr/$4.20 ride). Katina is better known as a fisherman's wife than a chef, so that's why the locals claim that she serves the freshest seafood! It's actually a very romantic spot on moonlit nights when the Aegean glitters at your feet.

Minim's Patisserie. Ía. ☎ **0286/71-149.** Snacks and breakfast 950–1,900 Drs ($3.95–$7.90); main courses 850–1,800 Drs ($3.55–$7.50). No credit cards. Daily 9am–11pm. CONTINENTAL.

We have friends in Firá who race to Minim's, a 2-minute walk south of the church square, on weekend mornings for delicious croissants and breakfast pastry. It's also a petite and tranquil caldera-view option for a rich breakfast, divine coffees and teas, homemade pies, pastries, cookies, cakes, various pizzas, simple pastas, classical music, and fully sated company.

Neptune Restaurant. Odós Nikólaos Nomikós, Ía. ☎ **0286/71-294.** Main courses 1,200–3,800 Drs ($5–$15.85). MC, V. Daily 6pm–midnight. GREEK.

A solid Greek establishment with a rooftop garden—with a partial sunset view—near the church square, the long-standing Neptune enjoys a reputation for moderately priced, typical Greek dishes. We suggest the vegetable specials, always made with the season's best pick.

Taverna Iliovassilema. Ía. No phone. Main courses 900–2,200 Drs ($3.75–$9.15). No credit cards. Daily 7–11pm. GREEK.

Our friend Eleni sent us to look for the lilac plastic chairs outside this tiny taverna, seen just below the old road into Ía. The "Sunset" has a perfect vantage from which to watch that superb sight. It also has great food, with specials including local cucumbers and tomatoes from nearby gardens. The taverna's caring hostess offers only a few dishes daily, such as tomato *keftiédes,* a Santorinian specialty, but always has a smooth, rich *krassí* (house wine) to go with them.

SANTORÍNI AFTER DARK

Firá's nightlife is a bubbling maelstrom that satisfies both the young looking for quick action and those who prefer to while away the night in communion with the island's natural gifts.

If you're looking for some jovial company, cruise the inner pedestrian lanes filled with boutiques and you'll find that several discreet storefronts burst to life after 9pm. The **Town Club** packs in a clean-cut rock crowd, **Just Blue** has good food and music, and **Tithora** is for the backpackers: the chummiest and most casual young drinking crowd outside of Íos. We always have fun at the parrot-crowned, outdoor **Tropical Bar,** which attracts a loud party gang, really mixed, from all over the world. You'll find everyone up on the cliff road, a bit north of the restaurant and cafe strip.

The **Kirathira Bar,** underneath the little square north of the main square, has for many years drawn jazz devotees with its great music, as well as those interested in conversation.

Discos are a tough call in Firá, where trendy spots change more rapidly than the style of beachwear. In the height of summer, when there are enough movers and shakers on the island to crowd every dancehall, the old-time **Enigma** is still most popular with those interested in good music. The **Koo Club** boasts a large, open-to-the-sky dance area, a fountain, and a tropical bar. The enormous billboards for **La Mamounia** (of Athens fame) assure us that you'll notice it easily. Whether or not you enter depends on your taste for Greek popular music, suave crooners, and the Euro-Greek scene that's arisen since Greece joined the EU. However, all these discos are fun to check out, and free—you don't pay until you start ordering the 2,500-Dr ($10.40) drinks.

Despite many distractions, Firá's unique attribute is its remarkable natural beauty. Among the many cafe-bars and tavernas below Ayía Mina on the cliff, we like the long-recommended **Franco's Bar,** whose view over the caldera is unbelievable, particularly at the magic sunset hour. You can unwind to classical music, sip local wines, and admire the stylish crowd. Franco's is expensive, but highly recommended because the charming Italian host has combined his native flair for food with a wonderful esthetic sensibility to create a delightful, elegant, and totally Cycladic cafe.

Many visitors with their own vehicle (or who take a cab) can enjoy a seaside stroll in the evening. Kamári Beach's promenade is the best suited for a moonlit *vólta*. You can stroll past the many cafes and tavernas, take in the glinting black-pebble beach, and pause for a glass of wine or even a dinner at **Camille Stephani,** one of the island's best and more formal restaurants (see above). Kamári also has an **outdoor cinema** (☎ 0286/31-974), where English-language films are shown nightly at 9:30pm; it's on the main road next to Kamári Camping and charges 1,200 Drs ($5) per seat.

Also in Kamári, **Valentino's,** a chic open-air bar on the beach near the bus stop, is still a sure bet, as is the nearby **Yellow Donkey Disco. Limbo,** above the beachside bakery, is another hotspot.

In Périssa, the party crowd might like to try **The What Club,** near the north end of town, for drinks; then on to either the **Florida Disco** or the **Lullaby Club,** both of which have music from 10pm to 3am and are located on the main vehicle street into town.

8 Tínos

87 nautical miles E of Piraeus, 66 nautical miles E of Rafína

Tínos is the most important place of religious pilgrimage in Greece, and yet it remains one of the least commercial of the Cyclades and a joy to visit for that very reason. Besides the famous Church of Panayía Evangelístria, where the miraculous icon that excites so much religious interest is enshrined, Tínos has an attractive port town, a lovely green landscape with hundreds of white Venetian dovecotes for which the island is also famous, some beautiful beaches, charming traditional villages, and friendly people who don't speak much English but make up for it with warm hospitality.

ESSENTIALS

GETTING THERE & DEPARTING   By Ferry   There are four ferries daily from Piraeus and three daily from Rafína; **schedules** should be confirmed with Tourist Information in Athens (☎ 143), the Piraeus Port Authority (☎ 01/451-1311) or the Tínos Port Authority (☎ 0283/22-348). Information and departure times from Rafína can be checked at the Rafína Port Authority (☎ 0294/25-200).

There are several sailings daily from nearby Mýkonos, Sýros, and Ándros, and several daily excursions to Mýkonos and Délos, at 4,500 Drs ($19.60).

The **Ilio Lines** hydrofoils and **SeaJet catamaran** also service Tínos daily from Rafína and Mýkonos.

There are two piers in Tínos harbor, the newer one 600 yards north of the main one; be sure you know where your ship will depart. The **port authority** can be reached at ☎ **0283/22-348.**

VISITOR INFORMATION   Tínos Mariner (☎ **0283/23-193**) can provide information and a good map of the island. The **Nicholas Information Center,** at Odós Evangelístria 24, the main market street to left and perpendicular to the port (☎ **0283/24-142;** fax 0283/24-049), is open daily from 6:30am to midnight and can supply information, sell ferry tickets, and book rooms. The **tourist police** have an office opposite the bus station (☎ **0283/22-255**).

GETTING AROUND   The **taxi stand** and **bus station** are on the harbor; check at the KTEL office there for schedules (which may be erratic) and rates. There are several shops that rent **mopeds** at 3,000 Drs ($13) a day. We recommend **Jason Rent A Car** ☎ **0283/24-283**), next to the Hotel Avra on the port, for mopeds as well as cars—a bargain at 7,200 Drs ($31.30) with insurance.

FAST FACTS   There are several banks and travel agents along the waterfront. The **telephone office (OTE),** open daily from 8am to midnight, is on the main street leading up to the Church of Panayía Evangelístria on Odós Lazárou Dóchou. The **first-aid center** can be reached at ☎ **0283/22-210.**

SEEING THE SIGHTS AROUND THE PORT

The ✪ **Church of Panayía Evangelístria** ("Our Lady of Good Tidings"), the "Lourdes of Greece," attracts thousands of pilgrims every year from all over Greece seeking the aid of a miraculous icon enshrined there. In 1822, during the War of Independence, Pelayía, a nun at the Kehrovouníou Convent, had a dream that an icon was buried on a nearby farm. She summoned her neighbors to help excavate it, and they soon discovered the foundation of a Byzantine church; a workman there found a gold icon, said to be the work of St. Luke, depicting the Annunciation of the Virgin Mary. This icon is believed to have been sent by the Virgin to cure the faithful. Work was begun immediately on the elegant neoclassical church that can be seen today.

On August 15 (Feast of the Assumption) and on March 25 (Feast of the Annunciation), the faithful—particularly the handicapped, infirm, and sick—make a pilgrimage to the holy icon of the Madonna, hang their votives, and await a miracle cure.

Almost any day of the year you can see people, particularly elderly women, with padded arms and knees, crawling from the port up the street to the church in supplication—often to ask for intercession for a loved one. If you find this a disturbing sight, try to concentrate on the colorful stalls that line Leofóros Megaloháris ("Avenue of Great Grace"), the street leading up from the left of the port, where icons, incense, candles (up to 6 feet tall), gold and silver medallions, and *támata* (tin, silver, and gold votives) are sold, or you can hurry on up to the church, which is a spectacle well worth the short climb.

The church and its galleries are open daily from noon to 6pm year-round (8am to 8pm in the summer). Men must wear long pants and sleeves, and women must wear skirts and sleeves, to enter.

Grand marble stairs lead up into the church itself, which is filled with the offerings of those who have received the miracle or blessing they sought. Hundreds of lamps overhead light a truly fantastic array of gold, silver, precious jewels, and thousands of flickering candles. The object of adoration is to the left of the central aisle, but even if you manage to make your way through all the faithful you won't be able to see the icon itself, because it's encased in gold, diamonds, and pearls. (Reproductions, however, can be seen in various shops.) Services are held regularly thoughout the day, and if you haven't yet attended an Orthodox service and experienced its resonance and mystery, you might wait for one. Notice the marble; the white is Parian, of course, and the green-veined marble is from Tínos itself and justifiably prized.

Below the church is the crypt where the icon was found, surrounded by smaller chapels; the spot in the rocks where it lay is now lined with silver, always crowded, but especially so in August, with Greek parents waiting to baptize their children with water from the font, which is filled with gold and silver offerings. The water from the spring here is believed to be both curative and beneficent.

The church is surrounded by various museums, galleries, and hostels for pilgrims. One of the galleries contains 19th-century works of religious art, including many from the Ionian school, as well as paintings said to be by Rembrandt and Rubens. Another houses Byzantine icons. One museum contains sculpture by a famous local artist, Lázarou Sóchou, and above it another contains works by other Greek sculptors, such as Vitális and Ioánnis Voúlgaros. You could spend half a day and not even begin to see half the sights.

The **archaeological museum,** about a half a block below the church, is open Tuesday to Sunday from 8:30am to 3pm; admission is 500 Drs ($2.10) for adults, 400 Drs ($1.65) for seniors, and 300 Drs ($1.25) for students. The small collection includes finds from the ancient sanctuary of Thesmophoríon, near Exóbourgo. Some red clay vases from the 8th century B.C. are particularly prized. In the museum's courtyard there are marble sculptures, including a sundial, from the 2nd century A.D. found at the Sanctuary of Poseidon and Amphitrite (his wife) at Kiónia.

The town is a pleasant place for strolling, with a **flea market** area behind the port, up the street from Ferry Boat Naias office. Besides a huge variety of candles and religious paraphernalia, you'll find local embroidery, weavings, and the delicious local nougat, as well as *loukoúmia* (Turkish delight) from Sýros. Several ceramic shops on the waterfront—**Margarita, Bernardo, Manina**—offer interesting pottery, jewelry, and copperware at moderate prices.

Harris Prassas Ostria-Tínos, Odós Evangelístrias 20 (☎ **0283/23-893;** fax 0283/24-568), is particularly recommended for his fine collection of gold and silver jewelry in contemporary, Byzantine, and classical styles, silverwork, and beautiful religious objects, including reproductions of the miraculous icon. Harris is friendly, informative, and famous for the quality of his work, and he accepts credit/charge cards.

EXPLORING THE ISLAND

The famous **Venetian dovecotes,** many dating from the 17th century, are scattered throughout the island. You can see several, as well as the **Temple of Poseidon and Amphitrite,** by taking the coastal road 1 1/2 miles west of town to **Kiónia** ("Columns"), a pleasant 30-minute hike past the Hotel Aigli. There are two dovecotes behind the tennis courts of the large luxury resort complex, the Tinos Beach Hotel, and past the hotel on the beach road you'll find the scant remains of the excavated temple.

A pleasant day trip from Tínos to **Pýrgos** will take you through many island villages to the region where the green marble is quarried and local sculptors work. Buses leave the port five times a day for the 1-hour trip beginning at 6:30am; check the schedule at the stop in Pýrgos for the return time. From Pýrgos you can go to **Pánormos,** from which the marble was once exported; there you'll find a nice beach and rooms to let. Dovecote devotees may want to include a detour along the way to **Tarambádos** and **Smardákito,** which have some of the most elaborate ones.

The scenery above Tínos town in the vicinity of the Venetian fortress of **Exóbourgo** is particularly appealing. The fortress itself was ruined by the Turks, but it still contains the remains of some houses, three churches, and a fountain, as well as a superb view. **Tripótamos** is known for its lovely architecture. **Xinára** is a Catholic village, seat of the island's bishop. **Loutró** is an especially attractive village with a 17th-century Jesuit monastery which is now an Ursuline convent and carpet-making school. You can continue on to **Krókos,** which has a couple of nice restaurants and from which it's an hour hike to one of the highest and most remote villages on the island, **Vólakas,** known for its excellent baskets. You can also continue on another 3 miles to **Kómi,** where an unimproved road leads down to the island's best beaches at **Kolymbíthres,** where there's a taverna and some rooms for rent.

There's a bus to the **Convent of Kehrovouníou,** one of the largest in Greece and still active, where Pelayía dreamed of the icon. You can visit her former cell and see her mummified head. Nearby **Dío Horiá** and **Arnádos** are both well worth a visit.

HITTING THE BEACH

You may want to head east of town. The first beach, about 1¼ miles out, is busy **Áyios Fokás,** which has the very nice little **Golden Beach Hotel** (☎ **0283/22-579**), with a lovely garden and comfortable doubles from about 11,000 Drs ($45.85).

A little farther east is **Vyrócastro,** with the walls of an ancient town and a ruined Hellenistic tower, and the nearby beach of **Livádi,** which is rather exposed. There's bus service (usually four times a day) 4½ miles east to the resort of **Pórto,** which has two beaches and several hotel complexes but little in the way of restaurants, so you may want to take a picnic. If it's crowded, walk back southwest to **Xerés,** which is less developed.

WHERE TO STAY

You'll have no problems finding a room if you avoid the Panayía festivities in March and August; hotels may also be crowded in July, when most Greeks vacation, and on summer weekends. Because it has been a popular destination for travelers of modest means for more than a century, the town has plenty of economical accommodations. People will offer you their rooms, more politely than elsewhere, at the landing.

You can find rooms to rent for 5,700 to 9,800 Drs ($23.75 to $40.85) for two on several streets behind the port. **O Yánnis,** next to the Hotel Oceanis on Odós Gízi (☎ **0283/22-515**), has large, homey, high-ceilinged rooms with clean shared facilities for about 6,700 Drs ($27.90) for two—a fair price for such a warm, friendly environment. Strátis Keladítis, at the **Nicholas Information Center,** Odós Evangelístrias 24 (☎ **0283/24-142**), has plain rooms upstairs for about 5,550 Drs ($22.90) for a double with shared facilities, as well as friendly advice, inexpensive moped rental, and so forth.

Avra Hotel. Tínos town, 842 00 Tínos. ☎ **0283/22-242.** 14 rms, all with bath (shower). 9,150 Drs ($38.15) single; 13,500 Drs ($56.25) double. No credit cards.

This century-old hotel east (right) on the waterfront has simple, spacious, high-ceilinged rooms off a tiled plant-filled courtyard. Old-fashioned and unusual.

Hotel Eleana. Platía Ierarchón, Tínos town, 842 00 Tínos. ☎ **0283/22-561.** 17 rms, all with bath (shower). 7,950 Drs ($33.15) single; 10,000 Drs ($41.65) double. No credit cards.

Tínos's best-value hotel is about 400 yards from the port, up the street to the right of the Hotel Posidonios. It doesn't have harbor views, but the rooms are large,

Readers Recommend

Boussetil Rooms, Odós Ioánnou Voúlgari 7, 842 00 Tínos (☎ **0283/22-675**). "I spent a glorious week with the Boussetil family on the island of Tínos. Their clean rooms, with private bath, are a brief walk to town, the beaches, the harbor, Panayía Evangelístria, and a grocery; everything needed is close, yet there's a sense of real privacy. The balcony room view is fantastic, overlooking Tínos town and the sea. Lower rooms open into the lush garden, where an optional breakfast is served. An exceptional place operated by exceptional people. To make a reservation, contact the English-speaking host, Manthos Boussetil."

—Sandy Clendenen, Kansas City, Mo.

comfortable, and quiet. The couple who operate it speak very little English, but they're friendly and hospitable.

✪ **Hotel Tinion.** Odós Alavánou 1, Tínos town, 842 00 Tínos. ☎ **0283/22-261.** Fax 0283/24-754. 20 rms, all with bath (10 with shower, 10 with tub). 10,500 Drs ($43.75) single; 17,500 Drs ($72.90) double. Rates include breakfast. EURO, MC, V. Closed Nov–Mar.

After a recent renovation this venerable hotel to the right from the harbor retains its old-world charm, with a marble staircase and hand-polished wood. The spotless rooms have 14-foot ceilings, balconies, marble-top tables, black-and-white prints of old Greece, lace curtains, and tilework floors.

WHERE TO EAT

Tínos has some very good restaurants, probably because most of their customers are Greeks. *Loukoumádes* (doughnuts served with cinnamon and honey) are a national treat and quite popular at this port. **Serano** is one of the few breakfast cafes offering sizzling dough, though at night several back-alley establishments also open their deep fryers.

Palea Pallada (Old Pallada). Tínos town. ☎ **0283/23-516.** Main courses 800–1,800 Drs ($3.35–$7.50). AE, MC, V. Daily noon–4pm and 6:30–11:30pm. GREEK/SEAFOOD.

Tucked under a groaning grape arbor, in a small alley 1 block west of the ferry pier, this family-run place stands out with specialties such as the sharp, hard village feta served with the smooth house wine, fresh *koliós* (a long, tasty, silver mackerel), and the grilled *loukániko*, local sausage with a hint of fennel. The Mintzas are proud to display old murals of the original "Pallada" harbor of Tínos, and treat guests with the hospitality this Greece-for-Greeks island is known for.

✪ **Peristerionas.** Odós Paksimádi Fraiskóu 12, Tínos town. ☎ **0283/23-425.** Main courses 1,000–1,750 Drs ($4.15–$7.30). No credit cards. Daily noon–3pm and 7–11:30pm. GREEK.

Our favorite meal for ambience and new flavors is usually had at Peristeriónas ("Dovecote"), which is decorated to resemble one of the Venetian towers built as dove perches that are found all over Tínos. The restaurant is on a small lane uphill and left behind the Lido Hotel, and its outdoor tables and chairs fill the walkway. The Dovecote's special courses are grilled meats and fish. Its delicious contribution to Greek cuisine is the wonderful dill, onion, and vegetable fritters called *marathotiganítes.*

Skouna Pizza Grill Restaurant. Harborfront, Tínos town. ☎ **0283/22-741.** Main courses 900–3,300 Drs ($3.75–$13.75). MC, V. Daily noon–2am. GREEK/INTERNATIONAL.

Stella is the busy overseer of the crowded tables under the yellow canopy at the west side of port square. Her Skouna is one of the few harborfront eateries we can recommend for value and service. The varied menu includes tender swordfish souvláki, pizzas, grilled meats, moussaká, seasonal stuffed vegetables, and a healthy *horiátiki saláta* (Greek salad) sprinkled with the island's fresh capers.

9 Ándros

43 nautical miles E of Rafína

Evergreen-covered Ándros, the second-largest and most northerly of the Cyclades, has long been cherished by Greek tourists for its pine-shaded beaches, old-fashioned family values, and uninflated prices. Today, however, the island is becoming more popular with foreign tourists and prices are going up.

After centuries in which the mercantile trade made Ándros one of the few islands that prospered without foreign tourism, the economic realities are slowly changing. The fabulously wealthy Goulandris family, shipping magnates and global jet-setters, have given sleepy Ándros an international cachet with enormous gifts: Hóra's stunning museum of modern art and the excellent archaeological museum next door are both courtesy of Basil and Elise Goulandrís. Their grand entry into the international art scene has done more to popularize the island than any travel agency and has assured that foreign tourism will flourish.

Ándros's earlier moment in the spotlight was in 1833 when archaeologists unearthed two statues, the *Hermes of Ándros* and the likeness of a woman from Iráklio, thought to be by Praxiteles. Later, however, scholars concluded the sculptor must have been a 1st-century B.C. artisan from a little-known Parian workshop. Both figures were on display in the National Archaeological Museum in Athens until 1981, when Elise Goulandrís persuaded the Greek government that two of its finest treasures should be returned to the new museum home that she'd created for them.

ESSENTIALS

GETTING THERE & DEPARTING   Ándros can be reached only by ferry from Rafína, but there are twice-daily connections to Tínos and Mýkonos, and a once-daily connection to Sýros. Contact **George Batis Travel** (☎ 0282/71-489) at the port of Gávrio or the **Strintzis Lines** in Gávrio (☎ 0282/71-235), or at their Rafína office (☎ 0294/25-200), for schedule information. For the Ándros Port Authority, call ☎ 0282/71-213.

VISITOR INFORMATION   There is no EOT office or tourist police on Ándros. In Gávrio there's a **tourist information office** right (south) of the ferry pier on the harborfront, but it seems to be closed most of the time. The **Achivida Tourism Office,** above the Ydroussa Bar (☎ 0282/71-556; fax 0282/71-571), exchanges money, sells ferry tickets, and arranges accommodations.

ORIENTATION   Most ferries arrive at the main port of Gávrio, but most foreign tourist activity is centered 3¹/₂ miles south in Batsí, a small village with an ordinary sand beach. The main town, Hóra (or Ándros town), is on the east coast, where strong winds make its beaches less pleasant for swimming. However, this pretty hilltop town filled with narrow steps, winding lanes, and some fine neoclassic mansions has two museums that are the island's newest attractions.

In high season the frequent ferries to and from Tínos and Mýkonos mean that you can take an extended day trip just to visit the museums. If you plan to stay overnight, we'd recommend Batsí as your base, so you can squeeze in a refreshing swim at the beach. If you're looking for a very Greek experience, make Hóra your home.

GETTING AROUND   By Bus   Most ferries to the port of Gávrio are met by a bus that runs to Hóra via Batsí, six times a day in high season. The fare is 200

Drs (85¢) to Batsí and 450 Drs ($1.90) to Hóra. (The trip to Hóra takes about an hour.)

By Taxi   The fare from Gávrio to Batsí is 2,800 Drs ($11.65), and from Batsí to Hóra is an additional 4,000 Drs ($16.65); call ☎ **0282/22-316** for information.

FAST FACTS   In Hóra (Ándros town), the capital, on the east coast, the **telephone center (OTE),** the **post office,** the **taxi station,** and a bank are on the main square, Platía Goulandrís. There are several ferry ticket offices in Batsí and Gávrio, on the west coast.

The **police** can be reached at ☎ **0282/23-300** in Hóra, **0282/41-204** in Batsí, and **0282/71-220** in Gávrio. For **medical emergencies,** call ☎ **0282/41-326.**

EXPLORING THE ISLAND

Your first stop will be the island's only active port, **Gávrio,** where the three boat lines that service Ándros from Rafína call. (You cannot come here directly from Piraeus.) Ticket offices are opposite the ferry pier at the north side of the small C-shaped fishing cove. In the center of Gávrio is the local's favorite, **Valmas Taverna.** The small pebble-and-sand beach at Gávrio's south end is reserved for the fishers, some wild ducks, a few chickens, stray cats, and odd litter.

Batsí, 3¹/₂ miles south, is built amphitheatrically around a C-shaped cove with a small caïque port at its south end. There' a portable post office, an OTE (telephone) center, and a moped-rental shop near the Hotel Scouna.

Heading south from Batsí to Hóra (Ándros town), you'll come to **Paleópolis,** site of an ancient acropolis 300 yards above sea level. Many beautiful Hellenistic sculptures, including the *Hermes of Ándros,* came from this site and can be seen in the archaeological museum. At **Stavrópeda** you turn east over Ándros's tall central mountains to **Messariá,** with its noted Byzantine-era **Church of the Taxiarchis.**

The monumental marble **Kabánis Fountain** is the centerpiece of **Platía Theophílis Kaïrí,** the central square, with a good taverna overlooking the sea and these two museums.

The **Archaeological Museum of Ándros** (☎ **0282/23-664**) features sculpture from the archaic through Roman periods (700 B.C. to A.D. 330) on the ground floor. These modern, well-lit galleries include the beautiful *Hermes,* thought to be a marble copy of a bronze by Praxiteles. There's also a gallery of marbles from many of the island's Byzantine- and Venetian-era sites. The museum is open Tuesday to Sunday from 8:30am to 3pm; admission is 500 Drs ($2.10) for adults, 400 Drs ($1.65) for seniors, and 300 Drs ($1.25) for students.

Down the steps from the archaeological museum is the ✪ **Goulandrís Museum of Modern Art** (☎ **0282/22-444**) with a separate **Museum of Sculpture** across the lane. Both contain a remarkable collection of contemporary Greek and European art. Unfortunately, they're open only May through September, Saturday to Monday from 10am to 2pm and 6 to 9pm; admission is 700 Drs ($2.90) for adults, 350 Drs ($1.45) for students, and free for seniors.

Just north of Hóra is **Steniés,** an older village known for the **Bistis Mouvelas Tower,** one of the few remaining 17th-century fortified homes left on the island. This village has been well preserved by the merchant seamen who still live here and in Hóra.

WHERE TO STAY
In Batsí

Dimitris and Thanie **Marousas** (☎ **0282/41-080**) have spacious comfortable apartments in a quiet location 150 yards from the bus stop, a 5-minute walk from the center of town; doubles are 16,300 Drs ($67.90).

If they or the central Chryssí Aktí Hotel (see below) are full, head to the **Andrina Tours** office (☎ **0282/41-064;** fax 0282/41-620), where between May and October you can find a place to stay, exchange money, and arrange car or motorbike rental or a bus tour around the island for 6,500 Drs ($27.10). (A few other hotels in Batsí consign all their rooms to travel agents and won't deal with individual tourists.) A studio with kitchenette in one of the area's many private lodgings typically costs 9,000 Drs ($37.50) for one, 12,000 Drs ($50) for two, or 14,000 Drs ($58.35) for three per night. Long-term stays, private villas, and other accommodations are negotiable. There's camping outside Gávrio at **Camping Andros** (☎ **0282/71-444**).

Chryssí Aktí Hotel. Batsí, 845 03 Ándros. ☎ **0282/41-236.** Fax 0282/41-268. 61 rms, all with bath (shower). MINIBAR TV TEL. 9,500 Drs ($39.60) single; 12,000 Drs ($50) double. No credit cards.

If the central Chryssí Aktí Hotel, across from the town beach, has rooms available, grab one. The older doubles are a bit worn, but they're acceptable and provide big balconies and private showers.

IN HÓRA (ÁNDROS TOWN)

Platía Goulandrís is the heart of Hóra, with the bus and taxi stations, post office, and an OTE (telephone) center. Goulandrís Street is the main pedestrian thoroughfare. Ándros's capital is built on a promontory with houses tumbling down both sides to sandy beaches (too rough for swimming because of the north winds). Steep stairs and narrow lanes are the only way to navigate the backstreets.

On Main Street above the Ionian Bank is the old **Egli Hotel** (☎ **0282/22-303**), with 15 doubles for 8,650 Drs ($36.05). You'll find many *zaharoplastía* (pâtisseries), most selling *karydáki* (walnuts with honey and spices), *loukoúmia* (Turkish delight), and *amygdalóta* (small almond cakes covered with powdered sugar).

WHERE TO EAT IN BATSÍ

Batsí has several good restaurants, markets, and sweet shops, where you might ask for the island's specialty—*karydáki*, walnuts with honey and spices.

The **Gallery Coffee Bar,** near Andrina Tours on the beach, is a good place to watch the sun set and enjoy a cocktail or ice-cream concoction. There are plenty of bars for later hours and two popular discos: the **Blue Sky,** on the hillside road above the Chryssí Aktí, and **Sunrise,** just off the same road. If you have your own vehicle, try the **Marabout Pizza Disco,** halfway between Batsí and Gávrio on the main road.

O Ti Kalo. Batsí. No phone. Main courses 1,000–3,400 Drs ($4.15–$14.15). No credit cards. Daily noon–3pm and 7pm–1am. SEAFOOD.

This small place one level up from the caïque port is great for fish; check out the day's catch. It also offers a popular combo platter of lobster, *barboúnia* (red mullet), and red snapper called "Georgy Porgy."

Rainbow Restaurant. Batsí. ☎ **0282/41-467.** Pasta 1,000–1,500 Drs ($4.15–$6.25); pizza 1,500–2,400 Drs ($6.25–$10). MC, V. Daily 6pm–3am. INTERNATIONAL.

A 10-minute stroll up from the beach is this delightful sparkling-white place with spacious seating in the garden or inside under flickering chandeliers with fountains splashing. The food is interesting and widely varied in style, and the staff is friendly and attentive.

Taverna Oasis. Batsí. ☎ **0282/41-590.** Main courses 1,000–1,600 Drs ($4.15–$6.65). No credit cards. Daily 7pm–1am. GREEK.

On the hillside next door to the Rainbow is this less formal taverna that serves grilled fresh meat and chicken specialties under a vine-covered pergola. There's plenty of room to dance to the Greek music.

10 The Western Cyclades: Sérifos, Sífnos, Mílos & Folégandros

None of the western Cyclades are nearly as developed for tourism as their more pub-licized cousins, though they're beginning to receive the overflow from the hugely popular Mýkonos, Páros, Íos, and Santoríni. Sérifos has a pretty hilltop Hóra, but its port, Livádi, is rather marshy and troubled by mosquitoes. Sífnos is a gorgeous is-land, with an equally attractive beach that's becoming increasingly popular. Mílos offers interesting archaeological sites and striking scenery. Folégandros, which ap-peared only recently on the tourism scene, has the loveliest Hóra in the Cyclades, with surprisingly good accommodations.

SÉRIFOS

Sérifos ("Bare One"), from its rocky landscape, is one of the least visited of the Cyclades, except during July and August when hordes of northern Europeans descend on it. Few of its residents speak English, and they're not especially hospitable to for-eigners.

ESSENTIALS

GETTING THERE & DEPARTING   Ferries depart five times weekly (daily in summer) from Piraeus on the Sérifos–Sífnos–Mílos route. Sérifos is also connected to Kýthnos, Íos, and Santoríni, although only once or twice a week. For **schedules,** check with the Port Authority in Piraeus (☎ 01/451-1311) or in Livádi (☎ 0281/51-470).

VISITOR INFORMATION   The **Sérifos Travel and Tourist Office** in Livádi behind the market will change money, provide information, and help you find a room—if it's open. Otherwise, see Mr. Bouris at the Hotel Areti.

ORIENTATION   **Livádi** ("Meadow"), the port, lies in a small relatively verdant lowland, where family farms grow apricots, figs, grapes, beans, and tomatoes in a helter-skelter fashion. Mosquitoes abound, so it might be wise to use repellent. Some hotels have screens or repellent systems. You may want to purchase an inexpensive, small electrical device that burns an odorless tablet—a good investment.

Ferries land on the south side at a modern pier, yachts and caïques moor in the middle, and a narrow, pebble-and-sand beach with rooms for rent extends to the north.

On the barren hill above Livádi is **Hóra** (or Sérifos town), a startling image of whitewashed houses and churches clinging like melted ice cream to the peak at Kástro. Hand-hewn rock steps wind their way up the steep hillside from Livádi (the car road is 3 miles) to Hóra.

GETTING AROUND   The island's two **buses** run several times daily between Livádi and Hóra from the ferry pier. (Like much of Sérifos, they're somewhat erratic; sometimes they meet the boat, sometimes they run hourly, and sometimes they're not seen for hours.) Cars and mopeds can be rented at **Blue Bird Rentals** (☎ 0282/51-511).

FAST FACTS   There are **ferry ticket agents** near the port, but no banks.

The **telephone center (OTE)** and the **post office** are up the hill in Hóra, just off the main square. The OTE is open daily from 7:30am to 12:30am. The post office, which will change money, is open Monday to Saturday from 7:30am to 2:30pm.

The **police** can be reached at ☎ **0282/51-300.** There's a **medical clinic** and a doctor can be reached at ☎ **0282/51-202.**

WHAT TO SEE & DO

Beetle-shaped Sérifos is the third-largest of the western Cyclades; most of its development is on the southeast side, facing toward Sínos. **Hóra** is a must-see for anyone visiting the island. There's a direct cobblestone donkey path much of the way. If you decide to climb it, go early in the day and wear good shoes for the 45-minute climb up the moderate slope, or take the bus up and walk down. Just as you enter the town, there's a small **Folk Art Museum** up on the right.

From the bus stop there are a few signs, some of them in white on the pavement, that will lead you to the central square and the handsome (though faded) yellow-and-red neoclassical **town hall;** in its basement (which you enter from the street on its left) is a small collection of marbles that barely qualifies as an **archaeological museum;** admission is free. Continue through the square and up to reach the Kástro.

Parts of the ancient fortress of the **Kástro** are believed to date from Roman times, but it was left in its present state of ruin after a 13th-century pirate raid. The small chapel of **St. John Theológos** is at its peak, on the site of an ancient Temple of Athena. Downhill from here, through lanes of crumbling stone houses flanked by pristine white-and-blue Cycladic restorations, are homes with Venetian medallions over their doors or ancient marble steps.

It's a brief walk to the square, where Kýklopos Street and the car route meet, site of a few coffeehouses and tavernas, where you can view old windmills. Their disabled spokes used to drive huge grinding stones to mill flour from wheat brought to Hóra by the island's farmers.

On the centuries-old path between Hóra and Livádi you'll pass donkeys carrying old women to the port, men on their way to the farms, and children rushing uphill to school. In Hóra, the village elders calmly wash oregano to fix lunch or pluck weeds from between the marble tiles outside their homes. If you look in the cracks of walls and stone you may find a rare pink carnation that's known to grow only on the island.

Just a 10-minute walk over the hill above Livádi's ferry pier on the southwest side of town is **Livadákia,** a popular family beach community. There's a very nice coarse-sand beach lined with tamarisk trees, some snack bars, pedal-boat rentals, lots of rooms for rent, and the aptly named Relax Pub. Isolated **Karávi Beach,** a 20-minute walk from Livadákia (the road is only partially passable by moped), is a favorite spot for nude sunbathing.

Northeast of Livádi, a 2-mile walk or moped ride from the town beach to the next cove, is **Psilí Ámmos,** one of Sérifos's best sand beaches. You'll find some rooms for rent here, and snack cafes on the way. A bit farther across the headland is pretty **Áyios Ioánnis** beach, where those who wish can more fully expose themselves to the elements.

About 3½ miles west is **Koutalás,** an old iron-ore–mining village whose now-devastated buildings are quite picturesque. There's a small snack bar in the village and a narrow road leading to the tree-lined, sand beach at Ganema. An unpaved road leads east to **Méga Livádi,** and in this small sheltered cove you'll find another beach.

In northern Sérifos, near Galaní, is the grand **Monastery of the Taxiarchs,** built in 1600 and dedicated to Sérifos's patron saints, Michael and Gabriel. Unfortunately, if any of these excursions interest you, you'll have to rent a moped or car to see them.

WHERE TO STAY

Most of the island's hotels and pensions are in Livádi, the main port.

Hotel Areti. Livádi, 840 05 Sérifos. ☎ **0281/51-479.** Fax 0281/51-547. 12 rms, all with bath (shower). 10,500 Drs ($43.75) single; 13,500 Drs ($56.25) double. Breakfast 900 Drs ($3.75) per person extra. No credit cards.

This excellent pension up the stairway closest to the ferry pier is the best value on the island, and you'll be close to Livadákia Beach, just over the hill. The Areti is built on a hill and offers great views, especially from its top-floor, balconied rooms.

Maistrali Hotel. Livádi, 840 05 Sérifos. ☎ **0281/51-381** or 0281/51-220. Fax 0281/51-298. 19 rms, all with bath (shower). 18,500 Drs ($77.10) single or double. Rear rooms about 20% less. No credit cards.

This attractive hotel with pleasant modern rooms is midway on the port beach (called Avlomonas). It's the closest hotel to the nearby, much nicer, sand and swimming beach at Psilí Ámmos, and it has its own restaurant.

Sérifos Beach Hotel. Livádi, 840 05 Sérifos. ☎ and fax **0281/51-209.** 40 rms, all with bath (shower). 10,500 Drs ($43.75) double. AE, DC, MC, V. Open year-round.

The older Sérifos Beach Hotel is one lane back from the beach. The tall tamarisks in front block the view, but it's a comfortable if somewhat homely choice.

WHERE TO EAT

Livádi has most of the island's restaurants, most of which front along the beach. On the first stairway up on the left as you leave the ferry pier you'll find **Ta Skalakia,** which has excellent gyros.

Taverna O Mokkas. Livádi. ☎ **0281/51-242.** Main courses 1,000–4,000 Drs ($4.15–$16.65). AE, EURO, MC, V. Daily noon–midnight. GREEK.

One of the first places on the town beach is also one of the best. Seafood is the specialty, but the standard Greek fare is well prepared and the service is prompt and friendly. We particularly liked the moussaká, *yemistá* (stuffed tomato), and french fries.

Taverna O Stamatis. Livádi. ☎ **0281/51-309.** Main courses 900–2,400 Drs ($3.75–$10); fish 7,500–10,000 Drs ($31.25–$41.65) per kilo. No credit cards. Daily 7pm–midnight. GREEK.

This typical taverna with good, inexpensive Greek fare is on the far side of the beach around Livádi's broad bay, with a red neon sign on its roof. It's a favorite of locals for fresh fish.

SÍFNOS

One of the best-kept secrets in the Cyclades, Sífnos is a favorite destination for Greeks who want to escape the hordes of tourists on the other islands. Like Sérifos, the island was famed in antiquity for its mines, but in the case of Sífnos the ore that was extracted was gold. Each year the islanders sent a solid-gold egg to Delphi as a tribute to Apollo. But one year they succumbed to their greedier impulses and substituted a gilded egg. Apollo, incensed, sank the mines deep into the Aegean. Since that time no gold has been found on the island, imparting significance to its name which means "Empty One."

ESSENTIALS

GETTING THERE & DEPARTING   There's at least one **ferry** daily from Piraeus, in addition to daily connections to the other western Cyclades—Sérifos and Mílos. There's also a ferry three times a week to Folégandros, Íos, and Santoríni, and once a week to Áyios Nikólaos on Crete. There is weekly **hydrofoil** service in summer to Rafína via Sérifos, Páros, Mýkonos, Tínos, and Ándros. Contact the **Port Authority** in Piraeus (☎ **01/451-1131**) or on Sífnos (☎ **0284/31-617**) for information.

VISITOR INFORMATION Your first stop should be the excellent **Aegean Thesaurus Travel and Tourism** office on the port (☎ **0284/31-804**), where you can book a room, buy ferry tickets, rent a car or motorbike, arrange excursions, and leave your luggage.

The main office of **Aegean Thesaurus** (☎ and fax **0284/31-145**), 20 yards north of the square up the pedestrian lane, is a one-stop help center, where you can cash traveler's checks, pick up a bus schedule and buy a good map of the island for 700 Drs ($2.90), book a flight, and avail yourself of their other services every day from 9am to midnight; all credit and charge cards are accepted.

ORIENTATION To ferry passengers, almond-shaped Sífnos appears to be a barren rock stretched lazily across the western Aegean. In fact, the island's west coast, dominated by the port at Kamáres, is much drier than the east. Most visitors arriving during the cooler weather (facilities are open from mid-April to late September) will probably want to base themselves at Apollonía, the island's inland capital. It's the most interesting village and just 3 miles northeast of the port.

During the high season things get very busy and rooms can be almost impossible to find. A room at the east-coast beach resort at Platís Yialós tends to be highly prized, but the yachting crowd and lively cafes of Kamáres also make it desirable. If you're not a dedicated sun worshipper, head to Apollonía or the picturesque village of Artemóna.

From Apollonía's **Platía Iróon** ("Heroes Square"), site of a monument to Sífnos's World War II veterans, gently sloped, winding pedestrian paths of flagstone and marble lead through this beautiful Cycladic village. Along the village's only car route are a few shops, a small market with island maps, and everyone's favorite hangout—the Lakis Kafeníon.

GETTING AROUND Getting around Sífnos is one of its pleasures; many visitors come for the wonderful hiking and mountain trails. We don't think a car or moped is necessary. Apollonía's Platía Iróon is the main **taxi stand** and the island's **central bus stop.** The bus system is fairly efficient, and can be combined with delightful walks up and down the cultivated hillsides so that they're not too tiring. Apollonía does have a few moped dealers; try **Yoni's,** on the main square (☎ **0284/31-155**), or **Easy Rider,** on the road circling the village (☎ **0284/31-001**). Cars can be rented at **FS** (☎ **0284/31-795**) and **Aegean Thesaurus** (☎ **0284/31-145**) in Apollonía or in Kamáres at **Sífnos Car** (☎ **0284/31-793**).

FAST FACTS Tourist services are centered around the main square, Platía Iróon, in Apollonía. The **post office** (☎ **0284/31-329**) is open Monday to Friday from 8am to 3pm and on Saturday and Sunday from 9am to 1:30pm in the summer. The **National Bank** (☎ **0284/31-237**) is open Monday to Thursday from 8am to 2pm and Friday from 8am to 1:30pm. The **telephone center (OTE),** just down the vehicle road, is open daily from 8am to 3pm, and also 5 to 10pm in summer. (The news kiosk on the square has a metered phone for after-hours calls.)

The **police station** (☎ **0284/31-210**) is just east of the square, and a **first-aid station** is nearby; for **medical emergencies** call ☎ **0284/31-315.**

EXPLORING THE ISLAND

In Kamáres, the town **beach** is the main attraction.

When you levitate from the sand, explore the shops filled with the island's best-known contemporary commodity: ceramics. Sifniot ceramics and everyday pottery are exported throughout Greece and are still in wide use because of their durability and charming folk designs. One of the most interesting shops is the ceramics workshop of **Antonis Kaloyirou,** on the main harborside lane (☎ **0284/31-651).** Antonis sells folk paintings of island life and the typical pottery of Sífnos, which is manufactured in his showroom from the deep gray or red clay mined in the inland hill region. Most of the pottery sold is usable and inexpensive, but there are also decorative pieces.

From the Kamáres pier you can hire a caïque to **Vathí,** a small coastal village due south, with a nice sandy beach. Vathí's twin-domed **Monastery of the Taxiarchs** watches over the skimpily clad bathers. Vathí is also the site of some old potteries, which can be explored, and it has several tavernas. **Hersónissos** is an even better beach on the north coast that's accessible by a new unpaved road or by caïque from Kamáres. In the summer season visitors gather at the caïque port and bargain with fishermen, who usually charge about 7,000 Drs ($29) each way for a boat that will seat 10.

The 3-mile drive between Kamáres and Apollonía reveals the island's agricultural heart and almost obsessive neatness. Every hillside is impeccably terraced with walls of schist and flagstone slabs. Rocky surfaces, delineated by higher walls, serve as footpaths over the hills, and carved stone and marble steps between the olive and almond trees are common. Small Cycladic farmhouses with the occasional ornamental dovecote are scattered throughout, most sporting geraniums, hibiscus, or apricot trees. Apollonía is spread over three mounds in the foothills of Mt. Profítis Ilías, site of an 8th-century Byzantine monastery.

In **Apollonía,** there's a small **Popular and Folk Art Museum** on Platía Iróon; it's open July to September 15, daily from 10am to 1pm and 6 to 10pm; admission is 300 Drs ($1.25). To its left on the pedestrian lane, **Hersonissos** (☎ **0284/32-209)** offers a choice selection of contemporary jewelry and ceramics. There are several other contemporary ceramics galleries in the winding backstreets featuring the excellent work of Greek artisans, including **Mouses** (☎ **0284/32-165),** 50 yards north of the main bus stop on the road to Artemóna.

Kástro is a beautiful east-coast village, just 2 miles south. Enter through either of the carved marble loggias; well-preserved and decaying whitewashed houses adjoin each other in irregular chains circling the sheer cliff. The Venetians took Sífnos in 1307 and built this fortress on the foundation of the ancient acropolis. Venetian coats-of-arms are still visible above the doorways of the older houses that abut the fort. The Kástro is built overlooking the sea, with a small pebble swimming beach at sea level. Within this maze are a few shops, rooms-to-let, and a small **archaeological museum** that's open daily from 10am to 2pm.

Pretty **Artemóna** fans over a hillside crowned by two blue-domed windmills and the remnants of others; it's just a 1¹/₂-mile walk from Apollonía. Some impressive neoclassic mansions belonging to the island's oldest families are on its borders near the encircling outer vehicle road.

Platís Yialós is the largest and most southern of the west-coast beaches. It's a long stretch of fine suntanned sand lining a shallow cove and a great place for beach bums, particularly in late May, June, and September when the sea is warm but calm. From here, it's a half-hour walk through the olive groves and intoxicating oregano and thyme patches over the hill to **Chryssopiyí,** another good beach.

The Apollonia-bound bus stops at **Panayía Chryssopiyí,** near the village of **Apókofto,** a remarkable monastery built on a sacred rocky promontory. The double-vaulted whitewashed church is built on a rock that was split after two women prayed to the Virgin Mary for protection against a band of pirates. The icon inside the church was said to have radiated light when it was discovered. There's good swimming immediately below the monastery and along the coast where secluded bays protect swimmers from rough water.

From this sheltered cove you can scale the point crowned by the **Harálambos Church** to the twin coves at **Fáros.** You'll pass a stone-and-metal structure below the pathway, the remains of a chute that once brought iron ore from a mine above you to the cargo ships anchored below. The path behind the south-cove beach leads to an enclave of rooms to let, a seaside taverna, and a small fishing-boat port.

WHERE TO STAY

In Apollonía

Many young Athenians vacation on Sífnos, particularly on summer weekends, and it can be rather difficult to find a room. **Aegean Thesaurus** (☎ and fax **0284/ 32-190**) can place two in a room in a private house with your own bathroom for 7,000 to 8,500 Drs ($29.15 to $35.40), in a studio with a kitchenette for 12,000 Drs ($50), or in other accommodations ranging up to a stylish villa that sleeps six for 60,000 Drs ($250) per night.

Hotel Anthoussa. Apollonía, 840 03 Sífnos. ☎ **0284/31-431.** 7 rms, all with bath (shower). 10,500 Drs ($43.75) single; 12,000 Drs ($50) double. MC, V.

This hotel is above the excellent and popular Yerontopoulos cafe-pâtisserie. Although the streetside rooms offer wonderful views over the hills, they overlook the late-night sweet-tooth crowd and in high season can only be recommended to night owls. The back rooms are quieter and overlook a beautiful bower of bougainvillea.

✪ **Hotel Sífnos.** Apollonía, 840 03 Sífnos. ☎ **0284/31-624.** 9 rms, all with bath (shower). 8,200 Drs ($34.15) single; 12,000 Drs ($50) double. AE, EURO, MC, V.

This is the best in the village, located southeast of the main square, on the pedestrians-only street to the cathedral. The hotel's manager, Helen Diareme, and her son Apostolos will do their best to make your stay comfortable. The Sífnos is open year-round and is the most traditional choice in terms of island architecture.

Hotel Sofia. Apollonía, 840 03 Sífnos. ☎ **0284/31-238.** 11 rms, all with bath (shower). 6,200 Drs ($25.85) single; 8,600 Drs ($35.85) double. No credit cards.

This newer hotel is on the road circling the town, a 2-minute walk from the square. Most of the rooms are large with private shower, many with balconies overlooking the town roofs, and a supermarket on the ground floor.

In Artemóna

Hotel Artemon. Artemóna, 840 03 Sífnos. ☎ **0284/31-303,** or 0284/31-888 in winter. Fax 0284/32-385. 23 rms, all with bath (shower). TEL. 12,650 Drs ($52.70) single; 17,250 Drs ($71.90) double. Rates include breakfast. EURO, MC, V.

This quiet, comfortable hotel is on the road just before the *platía.* Patios or balconies show off the pastoral view of wheat fields and olive groves sliding slowly to the sea. The Artemon has a large terrace restaurant shaded by grape vines, and a lobby lounge that's spacious enough for families to play in.

In Kamáres

Though Kamáres has the largest concentration of hotels and pensions on the island, make reservations by May if you plan to be there during the high season.

Hotel Boulis. Kamáres, 840 03 Sífnos. ☎ **0284/32-122,** or 0284/31-640 in winter. Fax 0284/ 32-381. 45 rms, all with bath (shower). TEL. 10,350 Drs ($43.15) single; 16,000 Drs ($66.65) double. Rates include breakfast. AE.

This newer hotel, right on the port's beach, has a spacious marble-floored reception and some amenities, including large carpeted rooms with ceiling fans and beach-view balconies.

Hotel Kamari. Kamáres, 840 03 Sífnos. ☎ **0284/32-383.** Fax 0284/31-709. 18 rms, all with bath (shower). TEL. 10,350 Drs ($43.15) single; 16,000 Drs ($66.65) double. AE, EURO, MC, V.

This is a nice, attractive lodging with balconied rooms at the quiet end of town, 300 yards from the ferry pier, where the road and beach meet. The friendly and attentive management offers safe-deposit boxes, car rental, and transfer to other villages by minibus.

Hotel Stavros. Kamáres, 840 03 Sífnos. ☎ **0284/32-383.** Fax 0284/31-709. 14 rms, 10 with bath (shower). TEL. 8,000 Drs ($33.35) single or double without bath; 11,500 Drs ($47.90) double with bath. AE, EURO, MC, V.

The same friendly management that runs the Hotel Kamari also tends this simple place about 100 yards from the ferry pier, on the *paralía* next to the church. Kyle found it quiet, and the Spartan rooms and common showers are kept very clean.

In Platís Yialós

July and August bring the stormy *meltémi* winds as well as the many Greek and European tourists who return annually to this resort's few pensions and hotels. The new **Community Camping,** just 600 yards from the beach (☎ **0284/31-786**), costs 650 Drs ($2.70) per person, with free showers for guests.

Hotel Benakis. Platís Yialós, 840 03 Sífnos. ☎ **0284/32-221.** 24 rms, all with bath (shower). 10,600 Drs ($44.15) single; 18,400 Drs ($76.65) double. Rates include breakfast. No credit cards.

This small hotel run by the friendly, helpful Benakis family is on the main road. Attractive, comfortable rooms offer lovely views of the sea or hillside.

Hotel Philoxenia. Platís Yialós, 840 03 Sífnos. ☎ **0284/32-221.** 9 rms, all with bath (shower). 13,000 Drs ($54.15) single or double. Rates include breakfast. No credit cards.

This small, simple hotel on the main street has nice large rooms, some with balconies offering sea views.

✪ **Hotel Platis Yialos.** Platís Yialós, 840 03 Sífnos. ☎ **0284/31-324,** or 0831/22-626 in winter. Fax 0284/31-325, or 0831/55-049 in winter. 26 rms, all with bath (tub). A/C TEL. 26,200 Drs ($109.15) single; 31,750 Drs ($132.25) double. Rates include breakfast. No credit cards.

It's a splurge, but the island's best hotel is ideally situated overlooking the beach from its perch on the west side of the cove. A recent renovation has added modern bathrooms with tubs and tiling throughout, large private patios to the ground-floor rooms and wonderful ceramics, painted tiles, and small paintings as a final touch. The hotel's flagstone sun deck extends from the beach to a diving platform at the end of the cove, with a bar and restaurant sharing the same Aegean views.

WHERE TO EAT

In Apollonía

Apostoli's Koutouki Taverna. Apollonía. ☎ **0284/31-186.** Main courses 1,000–2,900 Drs ($4.15–$12.10). No credit cards. Daily noon–midnight. GREEK.

There are several tavernas in Apollonía, but this is the best for Greek food, though the service is usually Greek leisurely. Any of the vegetable dishes, most made from locally grown produce, are delicious.

Readers Recommend

Themonia Restaurant, crossroads of Káto Petáli and Kástro (☎ **0284/31-866**). "We discovered a restaurant on the beautiful island of Sífnos so special we thought we'd spread the word. This family operation (Smaragda Georgouli doesn't speak much English but is a perfect hostess) uses only the freshest local ingredients. It offers a truly unbeatable combination: delicious home-cooking, generous portions, and low prices. And in case your stomach is beginning to overdose on taverna dishes drowning in oil, you'll find the fare tasty but light. What's more, it's probably the cleanest restaurant anywhere in the islands."

—Aspassia Yaga and Daniel Tai, New York, N.Y.

Sífnos Cafe-Restaurant. Apollonía. ☎ **0284/31-624.** Main courses 1,000–2,800 Drs ($4.15–$11.65). AE, EURO, MC, V. Daily 8am–midnight. GREEK.

On the main pedestrian street up to the cathedral, between the Sífnos Hotel and a quiet plaza, under a grape arbor, you'll find the best all-around place to eat in town. Breakfast includes fresh fruit juice and a dozen coffees. Choose from a variety of snacks, light meals, and desserts during the day. Have ouzo and *mezédes* for a mellow sunset. Go in and check out the refrigerator case when you're ready for a big evening meal.

In Artemónia

✪ **To Liotrívi (Manganas).** Artemóna. ☎ **0284/32-051.** Main courses 1,000–3,200 Drs ($4.15–$13.35). No credit cards. Daily noon–midnight. GREEK.

The island's favorite taverna has a handsome new building, with dining inside, down in a charming cellar, on the roof, or streetside. Taste for yourself why the Sifnians, who pride themselves on their fine distinctive cooking, consider Yannis Yorgoulis one of their finest cooks. Try his delectable *kaparosaláta* (minced caper leaves and onion salad), *povithokefiédes* (croquettes of ground chickpeas), or *ambelofásoula* (crisp local black-eyed peas in the pod). Or go for something ordinary; even the beef fillet with potatoes baked in foil is a mouth-watering delight!

In Kamáres

Captain Andreas. Kamáres. ☎ **0284/32-356.** Main courses 1,000–1,700 Drs ($4.15–$7.10); fish 3,000–17,000 Drs ($12.50–$71) per kilo. No credit cards. Daily 1–5pm and 7:30pm–12:30am. SEAFOOD.

The favorite place for seafood, with tables right on the town beach. Andreas the fisherman serves the catch of the day, usually simply cooked but terrific with chips or a seasonal vegetable dish.

Pothotas Taverna (O Simos). Kamáres. No telephone. Main courses 800–2,100 Drs ($3.35–$8.75). No credit cards. Daily 11am–midnight. GREEK.

This unobtrusive portside place has a basic Greek menu, but everything is well done. The bread brought to your table is sprinkled with sesame seeds, and the *horiátiki* salad is made with locally aged *mizíthra* cheese. The fish is fresh and not expensive; the individually baked pots of moussaká are delicious.

In Platís Yialós

Ampari Café. Platís Yialós. ☎ **0284/71-345.** Snacks 400–1,400 Drs ($1.65–$5.85). DC, MC, V. Daily 9am–1am. BREAKFAST/SNACKS.

The "Ship's Hold," on the central beach, has two decks, cozy indoor and outdoor spaces, and a beach bar, where you can enjoy breakfast, light snacks, salads, and fresh fruit. It's a popular cafe-bar on weekends, when two Sifniot musicians bring out a violin and a 200-year-old *láouto* to play indigenous folk music.

Sofia Restaurant. Platís Yialós. ☎ **0284/31-890.** Main courses 800–2,800 Drs ($3.35–$11.65). No credit cards. Daily 9pm–1am. GREEK.

At the east end of the beach is the best restaurant for Greek peasant fare, popular for its outdoor terrace and large wine list. For many in Apollonía, the casual seaside ambience warrants an evening outing.

SÍFNOS AFTER DARK

In Apollonía the **Argo Bar, Botzi,** and **Volto** on the main street are good for the latest European and American pop at very loud volumes. In summertime, the large **Dolphin Pub** becomes a lively and elegant nightspot, closing in mid-September.

Even if you're staying in Apollonía, consider taking a cab to Kamáres for a special evening. At sunset, you can seek relative tranquillity near the beach at the picturesque **Old Captain's Bar** or join the yachting set drinking Sífnos Sunrises and admiring the gang at the rival **Collage Club** above it. Later, the **Mobilize Dance Club** and the more elegant **Follie-Follie,** right on the beach, start cranking up the volume to become seaside discos.

MÍLOS

Best known for the *Venus de Milo,* the 4th-century B.C. statue of Aphrodite that was found in an island cave and spirited away by the French (it's on display in the Louvre), Mílos is the site of one of Greece's oldest civilizations. During Minoan times, Mílos became one of the richest islands in the Aegean as a result of its obsidian trade. A particularly dark moment in the island's history took place during the Peloponnesian War, when Athens, angry with the Milians for siding with Sparta, wiped out the male population.

Mílos is rich in mineral deposits, and though mining has scarred the landscape, it has made Mílos prosperous and independent of its tourist trade. Until recently there has been little inclination to exploit its natural beauty for tourism, although the recently constructed airport promises to increase the flow of tourists.

ESSENTIALS

GETTING THERE & DEPARTING   By Plane   There's one flight daily from/to Athens. Call **Olympic Airways** at its Adámas office (☎ **0287/22-380**) or in Athens (☎ **01/926-7251**) for reservations.

By Ferry   Mílos is served by daily ferries from Piraeus (three times a week during low season); the trip takes 5 to 7 hours. There are twice-weekly connections with Kímolos, Páros, Sérifos, Sífnos, and Sýros. The F/B *Ierápetra* makes the 8-hour voyage from Mílos to Áyios Nikólaos and Sitía, on Crete, twice a week. Check with the **Port Authority** in Athens (☎ **143**), in Piraeus (☎ **01/451-1311**), or on Mílos (☎ **0287/22-100**) for information.

VISITOR INFORMATION   The town-run **Mílos Tourist Information Centre** (☎ **0287/22-286** or 0287/22-287) is near the pier. The helpful and knowledgeable **Milos Travel** (☎ **0287/22-000;** fax 0287/22-688), nearby, will store your luggage and exchange currency. The staff sells ferry tickets and books a daily round-the-island boat tour that makes stops for swimming and costs 4,500 Drs ($18.75).

ORIENTATION   Mílos is the largest of the western Cyclades. Most tourist activity is concentrated around Adámas on the east side of the port, where the ferryboats dock. The island's capital, Pláka (or Mílos), just 2 miles north and inland, is well worth a visit for its authentic, decorative Cycladic architecture and its archaeological and folk-art museums. On the road between Adámas and Pláka are catacombs carved in the soft rock by early Christians.

The Mílos airport is at Alíkes, 5 miles south of Adámas on the port's coastal road. Most of the island's industrial development is in this vicinity.

The best-known beaches are on the south and east coasts and can be reached in an hour by car or moped, or by the infrequent buses. The western half of the island is more mountainous and is traversed by small, often unpaved roads.

GETTING AROUND   By Bus   In Adámas the **bus stop** is on the main road about 200 yards east of the pier; schedules are posted. There's frequent service to Pláka via Tripytí, every half hour from 7:30am to 11:30pm; six times a day to Pollónia, on the northeast corner of the island; four times a day to Paleohóri, on the southeast corner; and three times a day to Provatás, on the south coast.

By Car & Moped   Speed Rental (☎ 0287/22-440) is just east of the pier. The friendly Dimitrios Kassis, a former Houstonite, rents cars and Jeeps starting at 10,000 Drs ($41.65) per day plus 2,000 Drs ($8.35) for insurance. He also rents mopeds starting at 3,250 Drs ($13.55) a day, including liability, and has helmets available—take one.

FAST FACTS   Tourist services are found along the *paralía* (harborfront) in the port of Adámas. The **telephone center (OTE)** is open Monday to Friday from 7:30am to 3pm; the **post office** is open Monday to Friday from 7:30am to 1:30pm. The **police** can be reached at ☎ 0287/21-204. The **health center** (☎ 0287/22-700 or 0287/22-701) in Pláka can deal with medical emergencies.

Exploring the Island

Two of the most interesting sites on Mílos are within 2¹/₂ miles of Adámas. The island's capital, **Pláka** (or Mílos), is one of the best-preserved Cycladic villages in Greece. Gently sculpted, whitewashed houses lean side by side on narrow pedestrian lanes. Old marble and bluestone paving tiles, even where patched by concrete, are neatly outlined in both white and blue. Pots of geraniums and flowering succulents catch the sun on the stucco windowsills.

From the bus stop follow signs through the car-free lanes to the **Folk and Arts Museum** (☎ 0287/21-292). A small but fine collection of old photographs, ceramics, traditional Milian costumes, and embroidery is housed in an old building opposite one of the many churches of Pláka. From this square, you'll have the most striking vista of mountains, sea, and sky. The museum is open Tuesday to Saturday from 10am to 1pm and 6 to 9pm, and on Sunday from 10am to 1pm; admission is free.

After touring Pláka, head to the village of Trypytí (a 10-minute walk) where you'll find the **archaeological museum** (☎ 0287/21-620), which has a nice collection of Hellenistic-era sculpture and finds from Milian archaeological sites. In the foyer is a French-made reproduction of the Louvre's *Venus de Milo;* the original was found in a cave nearby. The museum is open Tuesday to Sunday from 8:30am to 3pm; admission is 500 Drs ($2.10) for adults, 400 Drs ($1.65) for seniors, and 300 Drs ($1.25) for students.

A short walk below is **Klíma,** a picturesque fishing village with old houses built on the water's edge. It was the capital during the Roman era, and there are fantastic **katakómbes** (catacombs) dug by Christians in the 1st century A.D.; they're open Monday, Tuesday, and Thursday to Saturday from 8:30am to 2pm; admission is free. Ancient inscriptions are etched into the walls—along with modern graffiti—and burial crypts that once held a half-dozen bodies are now fully excavated. You'll have to walk through very narrow corridors and low tunnels to see the full extent of the catacombs, so it's not for claustrophobics. There are also remains of a Roman theater and temple within a 15-minute walk of the Trypití bus stop.

Pollónia (or Apollonía), a sandy strip on the northeast coast, is the second most popular resort on Mílos—especially with windsurfers, who appreciate its strong winds. There are some pensions in this small community and more catacombs to explore nearby. You can take the same bus to Fylakopí, one of Mílos's most important archaeological sites.

The excavations at **Fylakopí**, 2^{1}/$_{2}$ miles west of Pollónia, show the influence of both the Minoans and mainland Greeks on this Middle Cycladic (2000 B.C.) settlement. Many obsidian tools were found here that actually date from pre-Minoan times.

Caïques leave from Pollónia three times daily in summer for the trip to the nearby island of **Kímolos.** The whole island is built on a foundation of chalk; absolutely everything is a dusty grayish white. There's a great beach and some interesting archaeological finds dating from Mycenaean times.

Paleohóri is the most popular of the south-coast beaches, but buses from Adámas through the village of Zefýria run only four times daily. A small village of rooms-to-let and tavernas caters to beach folk, who have unofficially divided Paleohóri's two coves into a family beach (with the tavernas) and a nude beach.

WHERE TO STAY

There are many rooms for rent above the businesses along the *paralía,* Aktí Pávlou Damouláki. Take a moment to inspect any room that may interest you before you take it—just imagine what a moped might sound like at 2am! Private rooms with attached bathrooms should cost about 10,000 Drs ($41.65) for two. **Mílos Travel** (☎ 0287/22-000) also rents apartments on the hill above Adámas for about 14,000 Drs ($58.35) for two.

Hotel Corali. Adámas, 840 01 Mílos. ☎ **0287/22-204** or 0287/22-216. 16 rms, all with bath (shower). TEL. 12,500 Drs ($52.10) single; 15,800 Drs ($65.85) double. No credit cards.

Over the hill behind the ferry pier, just beyond the church clock tower, is this comfortable place—quiet, but quite a hike if you have luggage. It has good-quality rooms, so if you're not afraid of commitment, make a reservation and the hotel minivan will pick up you and your luggage at the pier.

Hotel Delfini. Adámas, 840 01 Mílos. ☎ **0287/22-001.** 17 rms, all with bath (shower). 14,000 Drs ($58.35) double. No credit cards.

Our favorite local lodging is this small tranquil hotel run by the gregarious John Mathioudakis. The rooms have been recently freshened up, and the balconied side-facing rooms have views around the large Venus Village complex to the sea. Back rooms overlook an olive and citrus grove.

Hotel Milos. Adámas, 840 01 Mílos. ☎ **0287/22-087** or 0287/22-306. Fax 0287/22-306. 31 rms, all with bath (tub). TEL. 13,100 Drs ($54.60) single; 15,800 Drs ($65.85) double. Breakfast 1,200 Drs ($5) per person. No credit cards.

The Hotel Milos is a slightly more expensive option, and its location off the road to Pollónia isn't ideal, but the rooms are quiet and attractive.

WHERE TO EAT

O Flisvos. Portside, Adámas. ☎ **0287/22-349.** Main courses 800–2,200 Drs ($3.35–$9.15). No credit cards. Daily 11am–1am. GREEK.

The best and least expensive of the portside restaurants is known locally as Panórios. Peek into the roasting pans at fat stuffed tomatoes, crisp baked eggplant, fresh grilled souvláki, and other Greek favorites.

Trapatselis Restaurant. Pollónia Rd., Adámas. ☎ **0287/22-010.** Main courses 1,000–2,400 Drs ($4.15–$10); fish 2,000–12,000 Drs ($8.35–$50) per kilo. No credit cards. Daily 1–4pm and 7pm–midnight. GREEK/CONTINENTAL.

This very good full-fledged restaurant, about 100 yards east of the bus stop on the waterfront road, has a much more varied menu, with a large selection of appetizers and continental dishes, brighter lighting, and spiffy waiters. Locals come for the fresh grilled fish.

MÍLOS AFTER DARK

Kynigós (☎ **0287/22-349**) is a funky ouzerí on the *paralía*. Kyle thought it was a good place for her sunset ouzo and octopus ritual, but some of the locals were skeptical about foreigners hanging out with its authentic, somewhat rowdy, seamen crowd.

Adámas has a few portside cafe-bars, the best places to admire the nightly *vólta* (stroll), and the **Vipera Lebetina Bar** (☎ **0287/22-501**) on the steps uphill behind the small portside tourist information office. The **White Disco** is directly on the town beach, in front of the Venus Village complex.

FOLÉGANDROS

Most tourists who know of Folégandros have seen it only when passing its rather forbidding northern coast where precipitous cliffs rise up almost 1,000 feet. Maybe they catch a glimpse of Hóra hovering high up, white and maybe a little forlorn, and probably some imagine how lovely and pristine the little capital is, but so far relatively few have ventured up to experience its austere beauty.

Since Roman times Folégandros has been used as a place of exile, but for the last decade it has become increasingly of the self-imposed sort. Those wanting to get away from the tourist hordes have discovered it, and for now it remains unspoiled. The fewer than 1,000 residents still go about their daily lives of growing barley in terraced fields, raising livestock, and fishing, except in the summer when they welcome visitors from Athens and a growing number of foreign tourists—mostly from Scandinavia and England.

ESSENTIALS

GETTING THERE & DEPARTING   Three ferries a week (five in high season) stop at Folégandros on the Piráeus–Síkinos–Íos–Santoríni route. Two or three a week stop on the Náxos–Páros–Mílos–Sérifos–Sífnos run.

VISITOR INFORMATION   The **Maraki Travel Agency,** on the left just around from the southwest corner of the bus stop square in Hóra (☎ **0286/41-273**), can exchange money, help with travel arrangements, and sell you a map of the island for 600 Drs ($2.50).

ORIENTATION   Visitors arrive in the unimpressive port of **Karavostássi,** where there's a decent beach and a few hotels and rooms for rent. Campers may head half a mile south to **Livádi Beach.** Most people, however, tend to jump aboard the bus that's waiting to chug the 2¹/₂ miles up to **Hóra.**

GETTING AROUND   There are no taxis on the island, no cars for rent (and no reason to rent one), and as yet not even any motorcycles for hire. (Please, please let that continue to be the case!) The **bus** meets all ferries and has a regular route along the main road that runs along most of the spine of the island eight or nine times a day; the fare is 90 Drs (40¢). In summer there are daily **excursion caïques** from Karavostássi to the beaches at Angáli, Áyios Nikólaos, and Livadáki.

FAST FACTS   The **post office** and **OTE,** open Monday to Friday from 8am to 3pm, are right off the central square in Hóra. The **police** (☎ 0286/41-249) are behind nearby.

WHAT TO SEE & DO

✪ **Hóra,** one of the most beautiful capitals in the Cyclades, would be enough in itself. Above it the handsome all-white **Panayía Church** beckons you to climb the hillside for a closer look and to enjoy incredible views. Even from the bus stop square the sheer drop of the cliff offers a pretty awesome sight. On the right in the next square you'll find the picture-perfect **Kástro,** built when Marco Sanudo ruled the island in the 13th century and it's been inhabited ever since. The town itself centers on five closely connected squares, along and around which you'll find churches, restaurants, and shops.

About half a mile south of Hóra is **Áyios Eleforthérios,** the highest point on the island. Continue west on foot or by bus to reach the village of **Áno Meriá,** made up of small farms so widely dispersed that they're barely recognizable as a community. Swimmers will want to get off at the first crossroad and walk down to **Angáli,** the best fine-sand beach on the island, where there are a few tavernas and rooms to let. **Áyios Nikólaos,** another good beach, is a couple of miles farther west, and yet another $2^1/2$ miles will bring you to **Livadáki.**

If you're more adventurous, you may want to make it to the far northwest end of the island to the beach at **Áyios Yióryios,** an hour's walk beyond the last bus stop. The truly intrepid may want to hire a boat and guide to visit **Chrissospiliá,** a cave with stalactites and other curiosities, below the Panayía Church.

WHERE TO STAY

If you like the pebbled beach at Karavostássi, you may want to stay there. The **Aeolos Beach Hotel** (☎ 0286/41-205) offers comfortable doubles for about 10,000 Drs ($41.65). Campers will probably want to head south to **Livádi Camping** (☎ 0286/41-204), where the fee is 800 Drs ($3.35) per person and tents cost 500 Drs ($2.10). We suggest that you stay in Hóra, where there are also a number of nice rooms for rent.

Anemomilos Apartments. Hóra, 840 11 Folégandros. ☎ 0286/41-309. 17 apts. 20,000 Drs ($83.35) for two up, rising to 29,000 Drs ($120.85) for five. AE, V.

The best and most traditional looking of the luxury apartments are on the right up from the bus stop. They're all simply elegant, each with its own personality (one especially configured for the handicapped), most with sensational views.

✪ **Castro Hotel.** Hóra, 840 11 Folégandros. ☎ 0286/41-230, or 01/778-1658 in Athens. Fax 0286/41-230. 12 rms, all with bath (shower). 16,000 Drs ($66.65) double; 20,000 Drs ($83.35) triple. Breakfast 1,500 Drs ($6.35) extra. AE, V.

Our favorite hotel was built in 1212 and fully renovated in 1992. Of course the rooms are small and your own private bathroom may be down the hall, but they're both faithfully restored and comfortable, and there's nothing like having a window with the ocean right under it 200 yards below. The charming owner, Despo Danassi, makes you feel at home—her family has owned the building for five generations— and serves you a homemade breakfast.

Hotel Odysseus. Hóra, 840 11 Folégandros. ☎ **0286/41-239.** Fax 0286/41-366. 9 rms, all with bath (shower). 8,000 Drs ($33.35) single or double. No credit cards.

The best budget choice is on the west side of town, a few blocks beyond the OTE/ post office, then left. The rooms are simple, quiet, and comfortable, and the sunsets are splendid.

Polikandia Hotel. Hóra, 84 011 Folégandros. ☎ **0286/41-322.** Fax 0286/41-323. 31 rms, all with bath (shower). 12,000 Drs ($50) single; 15,000 Drs ($62.50) double. No credit cards.

This handsome new traditional-style hotel is on the left as you enter town. The rooms are large and comfortable with colorful furnishings, but we saw those dreaded group-tour stickers on the front door.

WHERE TO EAT

Hóra has a number of tavernas along the central squares. Locals recommend the **Pounda,** on the bus stop square (☎ 0286/41-063). A nice English couple recommended **Nikolas,** on the second square (☎ 0286/41-216), but more for the friendly, informative owner than his "turbo service" and food. We recommend **Piatsa,** on the third square (☎ 0286/41-274), a simple, family-run taverna with main courses costing 900 to 2,100 Drs ($3.75 to $8.75). **O Kritikos** (☎ 0286/42-218) is another local favorite for grilled chicken. In Áno Meriá, the **Iliovasílema** (☎ 0286/41-357) is known for its local specialties and sunsets.

HÓRA AFTER DARK

Folégandros isn't exactly buzzing with nightlife, but on the far side of town there's the large and fairly stylish **Bzut Disco,** which operates in the summer, and there are a couple of bars, including the nearby small and mellow **Kaliteremi Music Bar.**

The Dodecanese

10

The *dódeka,* or 12, islands that comprise the Dodecanese (Dodekánissos) form Greece's far eastern strategic border, within kissing distance of neighboring Turkey. From tiny Kastellórizo in the far south—just look at a map—to Pátmos at the northern end, they span a diverse landscape that makes for pleasant travel. As with most of the islands, the Dodecanese have been or are presently being subjected to the onslaught of European tour groups, just the latest horde to pass this way from the continent.

From the Asian tribes of Anatolia in antiquity to the Crusaders in the Middle Ages, the unfortunate 12 seem to be perennially in the way of this or that conquering swarm. It's hardly surprising that these particular islanders, credited with organizing the rebellion against the Turks, are among the most politically minded Greeks and have often been in the forefront of new social movements.

Of all those who overran the islands, it was the Italians (they occupied the Dodecanese between 1913 and 1943) who left the greatest mark. Many older residents here speak Italian fluently and there are Italian influences in the cuisine and culture of the region. Romans, Venetians, Genoese, and Crusaders constructed most of the islands' magnificent temples and fortresses. Under Mussolini's direction the ancient and medieval sites on Rhodes and Kos were restored in a particularly Fascist style. Though repeatedly occupied by different nations, the Dodecanese have remained essentially Greek.

Of the major islands, **Rhodes** is the largest and most developed, with a seemingly endless stretch of beach resorts on both sides of its main port and capital, Rhodes city. It's now the most popular package-tour destination in Greece, but don't let that put you off; we still love to explore the back lanes of the Old Town.

Just 1¹/₂ hours away by ferry is tiny **Sými,** once a secret and now a ballyhooed neoclassical gem that still manages to elicit "oohs" and "aaahs" from its many day-trippers and longer-term guests. Nearby and north is **Kos,** which used to be a favorite island but is now a Scandinavian colony where visitors just Ping-Pong on the beach-bar axis.

Kálymnos has made a fairly positive transition from sponge island to tourist enclave. **Léros** is also trying to attract tourists with mixed results: some love the seclusion; others find it dreary. When we vacation in Greece, we head straight to **Pátmos.** Who knows how, but it manages to resist the ravages of tourism while embracing all who visit. And far-off **Kárpathos,** site of the Dodecanese's newest international airport, has just bitten into the apple of tour groups.

The "other Dodecanese"—**Kássos, Hálki** (Chalkis), **Tílos, Nísyros, Astypálea,** and **Kastellórizo** (Meyísti)—are still relatively unscathed by foreign invaders. Many can be visited on day trips from one of the larger neighboring islands, and so we have included them in our section at the end—"Baker's Dozen."

1 Rhodes

250 nautical miles E of Piraeus

Rhodes (Ródos) is the largest island in the Dodecanese, the most cosmopolitan resort in the Aegean, and the most popular package-tour destination in Greece because of its picturesque Old Town, long stretches of sandy beaches, and lively nightlife. In the high season it swarms with British, German, Scandinavian, and Italian tourists and can be among the most challenging and expensive destinations in the country. However, the island's delightful weather—with more than 300 days of sunshine each year, according to several sources—means that you can enjoy a visit at a less hectic time without sacrificing the benefits of the high season.

Greek myth maintains that after the gods' battle against the giants, Zeus was dividing the spoils of victory, and Helios, the sun god, was gone when lots were cast for the division of earth. Upon his return, Helios appealed to Zeus, proposing that a piece of land, rising from the "foaming main," be granted as his sole possession. Zeus complied, and as Pindar wrote in the 5th century B.C., "From the waters of the sea arose an island, which is held by the Father of the piercing beams of light, the ruler of the steed whose breath is fire." The legend continues that Helios wed the nymph of the island, Rhodos, daughter of Poseidon, and was so taken with her beauty that he declared he would make the whole island an equal delight.

What we really know from history is that the three ancient Doric cities of Ialyssós, Líndos, and Kámiros banded together in 408 B.C. to create a new capital, Ródos, in order to gain greater access to the rich trading and shipping routes of the Mediterranean and Asia Minor, particularly with Egypt. Rhodes flourished and great temples were erected on the Acropolis and a wide, straight road was paved down to the harbor, where the Colossus, one of the Seven Wonders of the Ancient World, was built as a symbol of Rhodian wealth and power. A remarkably modern code of law was instituted. Proud, autocratic Rhodians were extremely independent and commercially minded; this was demonstrated in their steadfast opposition to Athens in every major conflict. During the Persian Wars, Rhodes sided with Persia, and in the prolonged Peloponnesian conflict, Rhodes helped Sparta.

However, Rhodes's authority declined as Rome, once an ally and trading partner, eventually overran and annexed the island. Julius Caesar, Pompey, Cato the Younger, Cicero, Brutus, and Mark Antony studied at Rhodes's famous School of Rhetoric. When Rhodes backed Augustus after the death of Caesar, Cassius seized or destroyed its fleet and sacked the city.

Not until the early 14th century did Rhodes once again emerge as a major force. In 1306 the Order of the Knights of St. John of Jerusalem took refuge on Rhodes and 3 years later took control of the island. For more than 2 centuries knights from Spain, France, Italy, and England came to join the order, dedicated to returning Jerusalem to the Christian fold. The Knights renovated the huge fortifications over the ancient city and built the inns and castle, the hallmarks of Rhodes. Each "Tongue," or foreign contingent with the monastery, had a headquarters, while the grand master (the life-term leader of the Knights) resided in the palace or castle.

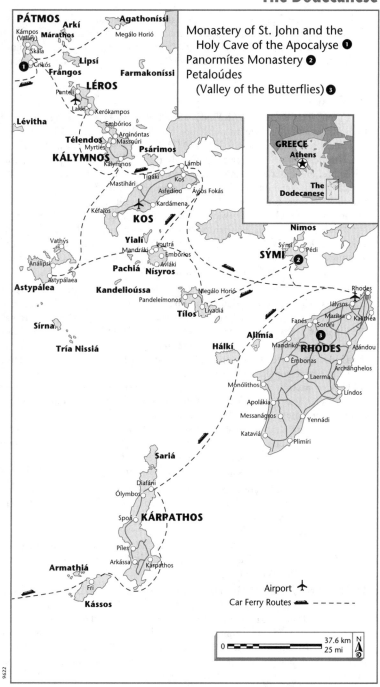

PÁTMOS Arkí **Agathoníssi**
Kámpos (Valley) **Márathos** Megálo Horió
Skála
❶ Grikós **Lipsí**
Frángos **Farmakoníssi**
Pantéli **LÉROS**
Lakkí Xerókampos
Lévitha Embórios
Arginóntas
Télendos Massoúri
Myrtiés **Psárimos**
KÁLYMNOS
Kálymnos **Lámbi**
Tigáki
Mastihári Kos
Asfendíou **Ávios Fokás**
Kéfalos Kardámena
KOS
Vathýs **Yiali**
Mandráki Koutrá
Análipsi Embórios
Astypálaea Avláki
Astypálea **Pachiá** **Nísyros**
Kandelioússa
Sírna Megálo Horió
Pandeleímonos Livadiá
Tría Nissiá **Tílos**
Nímos
Sými Pédi
SÝMI ❷
Rhodes
Iálysos
Fanés Marítsa Kalithéa
Soróni
Alímia
Hálkí Mandríko **RHODES** Afándou
Émbonas
Archánghelos
Laermá
Monólithos Líndos
Apolákia
Messanágros Yennádi
Kataviá Plimíri
Sariá
Diafáni
Ólymbos
Spoá **KÁRPATHOS**
Píles
Armathiá Arkássa Kárpathos
Fri

Monastery of St. John and the
Holy Cave of the Apocalyse ❶
Panormítes Monastery ❷
Petaloúdes
(Valley of the Butterflies) ❸

GREECE
Athens
The
Dodecanese

Airport ✈
Car Ferry Routes

0 ⊨⊨⊨⊨⊨ 37.6 km
25 mi

Kássos

9622

Turkish invaders assaulted the city through the residence of the Knights. In 1522 the Knights' numbers had dwindled to a mere 650, and Suleiman the Magnificent brought an army of 100,000 to beseige the city. After 6 months the few remaining knights surrendered and were allowed to withdraw and set up a new headquarters on Malta.

ESSENTIALS

GETTING THERE & DEPARTING   By Plane   Air Greece has one flight daily from Athens and three flights a week from Thessaloníki and Iráklio, Crete. Its office on Rhodes is at Odós Plástira 9 (☎ **0241/21-690,** or 01/325-5011 in Athens).

Olympic Airways offers five flights daily from Athens; four flights daily from Kárpathos; one flight daily from Kássos and Kastellórizo; four flights weekly from Santoríni (Thíra) and Iráklio, Crete; three flights weekly from Mýkonos and Kos; and two flights weekly from Thessaloníki. Reservations and ticket information can be obtained from the Olympic Airways Office, Odós Iérou Lóhou 9 (☎ **0241/24-571** or 0241/24-555). Flights fill quickly, so make your reservations early. Taxis cost about 1,600 to 1,900 Drs ($6.65 to $7.90) between the airport and Rhodes city. There's a duty-free shop at Rhodes International Airport to accommodate European charter travelers as well as an information desk with erratic hours.

By Ferry   Rhodes is the ferry hub of the Dodecannese, and there are usually several ferries daily via various routes from Piraeus. It can be a grim 18-hour (or even 28-hour) ride on some vessels; the F/B *Patmos* and *Rodos* are newer vessels that make the trip in 14 hours. There's one ferry weekly from Alexandroúpoli, Crete (Iráklio), Híos, Lésvos, Límnos, Náxos, Páros, Santoríni, and Sýros. Several ferries weekly ply the Dodecanese waters to Tílos, Nísyros, Hálki, and Kárpathos, while daily ferries service the more popular Sými, Kos, Léros, Kálymnos, and Pátmos. There's a once-weekly ferry to Astypálea via Kálymnos. In the summer there are three ferries a week to Limassol, Cyprus (18 hours), and then on to Haifa, Israel (30 hours). There's a daily (except Sunday) ferry to Marmaris, Turkey. Your best bet is to check the EOT office for the printed schedule of weekly departures; the staff can tell you which travel agents sell tickets for each boat. Ferryboat tickets as well as tickets to Turkey can be purchased from several agencies on Amerikís Street or from the very helpful **Triton Holidays** office near the entrance to the Old Town (see "Getting Around," below).

By Hydrofoil   The **Dodecanese Hydrofoils** and **Ilio Hydrofoils** operate from April to October, weather permitting, with daily service to Kos and Marmaris (Turkey); five times weekly to Léros and Pátmos; twice weekly to Nísyros, Sými, and Tílos; and once weekly (in July and August) to Astypálea.

There are daily **caïque** excursions between Rhodes and Sými for 3,500 Drs ($14.60) round-trip, and daily excursions from Skála Kamírou (an east-coast port 19 miles south of Rhodes city) to Hálki.

VISITOR INFORMATION   The **EOT** office, at the intersection of Makaríou and Papágou streets (☎ **0241/23-655** or 0241/21-921; fax 0241/26-955), is open Monday to Friday from 7:30am to 3pm; you can get advice there about the whole island, as well as check on the availability of accommodations. There's also a **Rhodes Municipal Tourist Office,** down the hill at Rimíni Square (☎ **0241/35-945**), near the port taxi stand, open in high season Monday to Friday from 8am to 7pm and Saturday from 8am to 6pm. The **tourist police** office, next door to the EOT office (☎ **0241/27-423**), is open daily from 7am to 9:30pm.

ORIENTATION   Rhodes city is the northernmost and by far the largest and most diverse city on the island, and makes the best base for sightseeing and beach going.

Líndos, on the southeast coast, is a scenic gem, with an ancient acropolis, traditional architecture, and a lovely beach cove. Unfortunately, it's overrun with tourists and finding a room in July and August is almost impossible. Unless you have a reservation, stay in Rhodes (advance reservations here are also highly recommended).

The best beaches lie on the east coast of the island below Líndos, from Lárdos Bay 16 miles south to Plimýri; our favorite stretch is between Yenádi and Plimýri. Compared with the rest of this woefully overbuilt island there is little development; however, a strip of burgeoning resorts catering to Scandinavian, German, and British groups makes life along this coastline extremely difficult for individual travelers. The greatest concentration of Miami Beach–style monoliths is in the north, around the perimeter of Rhodes city, covering a 9^1/$_2$-mile stretch along both east and west coasts. The interior section of Rhodes is mountainous and green, with small villages dotting its rugged terrain.

Rhodes city, the largest town and capital of the Dodecanese, is divided neatly into the Old Town, dating from the medieval period, and the New Town. The **Old Town,** which is surrounded by the massive walls (nearly 8 feet thick) built by the Knights of St. John, overlooks the harbor. The **New Town** surrounds the old on three sides and extends south to meet the resort strip. At its northern tip is the town beach in the area called 100 Palms, and nearby **Mandráki Harbor,** where private yachts and tour boats are moored.

Walking away from Mandráki on Plástira Street, you'll come to **Cyprus Square,** near which most of the New Town hotels are clustered. Veer left and continue to the park where the mighty fortress begins. Opposite the fortress is the **EOT** office; there's also a **Rhodes Municipal Tourist Office** down the hill at Rimíni Square (see "Visitor Information," above, for information on both).

GETTING AROUND   Rhodes is so big that you'll need public buses, taxis, a rental car, or a bus tour for around-the-island excursions. Within the town, walking is the best and most pleasurable way to get around; you'll need a taxi only if you're going to splurge at one of the farther-out restaurants or if you're dressed up for the Casino and don't want to walk.

The **Dodecanese Association for People with Special Needs** (☎ **0241/73-109;** fax 0241/33-278; e-mail dis12isil@compulink.gre) provides free door-to-door minibus service from the port, airport, hotel, or if you just want to go out for coffee or a swim.

By Bus   There's a good public bus system throughout the island; the EOT publishes a schedule of routes and times. Buses to Líndos and east-coast beaches leave from the East Side Bus Station, on Rimíni Square, several times daily. Buses to Ialyssós, Kámiros, and the airport leave from the nearby West Side Bus Station just down Avérof Street.

By Taxi   In Rhodes city there's a large, well-organized taxi stand (☎ **0241/64-712**) in front of Old Town, on the harborfront in Rimíni Square. There, posted for all to see and agree upon, are the set fares for sightseeing throughout the island. Since many of the cab drivers speak "sightseer English," they can chauffeur and lecture to a family or small group at a very reasonable cost. Taxis are metered, but fares should not exceed the minimum for short round-the-city jaunts. For longer trips, negotiate the cab fare directly with the driver. (For radio taxis call ☎ **0241/64-790** or 0241/64-712.)

By Car   There are several car-rental companies in each community, and a local travel agent may be able to give you the best price. We've had good luck with **AutoEurope** (☎ **0241/37-756** or 0241/22-508), which has three locations, including the airport, but delivered our car to the hotel. There are many rental offices on

Odós Oktovríou 28, where you can compare prices, but count on spending any-where from 16,000 to 24,000 Drs ($66.65 to $100) per day. *Caveat emptor:* Don't just grab the lowest price; make sure you have full insurance coverage and under-stand the terms!

By Tour/Cruise   There are several tour operators featuring nature, archaeology, shopping, and beach tours of the island. **Triton Holidays,** near Mandráki Harbor, behind the Bank of Greece, at Odós Plástira 9 (☎ **0241/21-690;** fax 0241/31-625), is one of the largest and best agencies. It also offers a wide variety of day and evening cruises, hiking tours, and excursions within the Dodecanese group and to Turkey. There are new 1-day boat trips to Líndos, which leave about 9am from the yacht harbor in Rhodes and return about 6pm, for 5,500 Drs ($22.90).

FAST FACTS   Most of this information applies to Rhodes city.

The local **American Express agent** is Rhodos Tours, at Odós Ammochóstou 23, at the New Market (☎ **0241/21-010**), open Monday to Saturday from 8:30am to 1:30pm and 5 to 8:30pm.

The **National Bank of Greece,** on Cyprus Square, keeps extended hours for ex-changing currency Monday to Thursday from 8am to 2pm and 6 to 8pm, Friday from 8am to 1:30pm and 3 to 8:30pm, Saturday from 8am to 1pm, and Sunday from 9am to noon.

For medical emergencies, call **Rhodes General Hospital** on Erythroú Stavroú Street (☎ **0241/22-222**). For other emergencies call the **tourist police** (☎ **0241/27-423**) or dial ☎ **100**.

The main branch of the **OTE (telephone office),** open daily from 6am to 11pm, is at Odós Amerikís 91 in the New Town. There's also a branch just off Sými Square, open daily from 7:30am to 11pm.

The **police** (☎ **0241/22-344**) in the Old Town are open daily 10am to midnight to handle any complaints of overcharging, theft, swindles, or other price- or goods-related problems.

The main branch of the **post office,** open daily from 8am to 2:30pm, is at Odós Amerikís 91 in the New Town.

RHODES CITY

Although the modern-day city of Rhodes has attractions dating from every era of its history, some people come to Rhodes just to shop for gold or furs and lap up the sun (they never venture out to sightsee)!

EXPLORING THE OLD TOWN

The best introduction to the old walled city is through **Eleftheria (Liberty) Gate,** where you'll come to **Sými Square,** containing ruins of the **temple of Venus,** which was identified by the votive offerings found there, which may date from the 3rd cen-tury B.C. The remains of the temple are next to a parking lot (driving is restricted in the Old Town), which rather diminishes the impact of the few stones and columns still standing. Nevertheless the ruins are a reminder that a great Hellenistic city once stood within these medieval walls.

Sými Square is also home to the **Municipal Art Gallery of Rhodes** (open Mon-day to Saturday from 8am to 2pm, plus Wednesday from 5 to 8pm), above the Ionian and Popular Bank. One block farther on is the **Museum of Decorative Arts,** which contains finely made Rhodian objects and crafts and is open Tuesday to Sunday from 8:30am to 3pm; admission is 500 Drs ($2.10) for adults, 400 Drs ($1.65) for seniors, and 300 Drs ($1.25) students. Continue through the gate until you reach the Museum Reproduction Shop (with a precious painted tile of the

Rhodes Attractions

Archeological
Museum of Rhodes **3**
Church of Our Lady
of the Castle **4**
Clock Tower **5**
Municipal Baths **7**
Palace of the Villiers
of the Isle of Adam **2**
Site where Colossus
is believed to
have stood **1**
Stadium **9**
Suleiman Mosque **6**
Theater **8**

Lighthouse
Information

Madonna above its door), then turn right on Ippotón Street toward the Palace of the Knights.

The **Street of the Knights** (you'll see the name Ippotón on maps) is one of the best-preserved and most delightful medieval relics in the world. The 600-yard-long, cobblestone street was constructed over an ancient pathway that led in a straight line from the Acropolis of Rhodes to the port. In the early 16th century it became the address for most of the inns of each nation, which housed knights who belonged to the Order of St. John. The inns were used as eating clubs and temporary residences for visiting dignitaries, and their facades reflect the various architectural details of their respective countries.

Begin at the lowest point on the hill (next to the Museum Reproduction Shop), at the Spanish house now used by a bank. Next door is the **Inn of the Order of the Tongue** (language) **of Italy,** built in 1519 (as can be seen on the shield of the order above the door). Then comes the **Palace of the Villiers of the Isle of Adam,** built in 1521, housing the Archaeological Service of the Dodecanese. The **Inn of France** now hosts the French Language Institute. Constructed in 1492, it's one of the most ornate of the inns, with the shield of three lilies (fleur-de-lis), royal crown, and that of the Magister d'Aubusson (the cardinal's hat above four crosses) off-center, over the middle door. Typical of the late Gothic period, the architectural and decorative elements are all somewhat asymmetrical, lending grace to the squat building. Opposite these inns is the side of the **Hospital of the Knights,** now the archaeological museum (see below).

The church farther on the right is **Ayía Triáda** (open daily from 9am to noon), next to the Italian consulate. Above its door are three coats-of-arms: those of France, England, and the Pope. Past the arch that spans the street, still on the right, is the **Inn of the Tongue of Provence;** it's shorter than it once was because of an explosion in 1856. Opposite it on the left is the traditionally Gothic **Inn of the Tongue of Spain,** with vertical columns elongating its facade and a lovely garden behind.

The Inn of France is open daily. The ground floor houses the Institut Français, but you can see its garden and an occasional art show held in the second-floor gallery. The other inns now serve as offices or private residences and are closed to the public.

The **Mosque of Suleiman** and the public baths are two reminders of the Turkish presence in Old Rhodes. Follow Sokrátous Street west away from the harbor, or walk a couple of blocks south from the Palace of the Grand Masters, and you can't miss the mosque with its slender, though incomplete, minaret and pink-striped Venetian exterior.

The **Municipal Baths** (what the Greeks call the "Turkish baths") are housed in a 7th-century Byzantine structure. They merit a visit by anyone interested in the vestiges of Turkish culture that still remain in the Old Town, and are a better deal than the charge for showers in most pensions. The *hamam* (most locals use the Turkish word for "bath") is located in Ariónos Square, between a large old mosque and the Folk Dance Theater. Throughout the day men and women go in via their separate entrances and disrobe in the private shuttered cubicles. A walk across the cool marble floors will lead you to the bath area—many domed, round chambers sunlit by tiny glass panes in the roof. Through the steam you'll see people seated around large marble basins, chatting while ladling bowls of water over their heads. The baths are open Tuesday to Saturday from 11am to 7pm; the baths cost 600 Drs ($2.50) on Tuesday, Thursday, and Friday, but only 360 Drs ($1.50) on Wednesday and Saturday. The ticket sellers warn that Saturday is extremely crowded with locals.

The Old Town was also home to the Jewish community, whose origins go back to the days of the ancient Greeks. Much respected as merchants, they lived in the northeast or **Jewish Quarter** of the Old Town. Little survives other than a few homes with Hebrew inscriptions, the Jewish cemetery, and the Square of the Jewish Martyrs (Platía ton Evreón Martyrón, also known as Seahorse Square because of the seahorse fountain). There's a lovely synagogue, where services are held every Friday night; a small black sign in the square shows the way. The synagogue, usually open daily from 10am to 1pm, is located on Dosiadou Street, off the square. This square is dedicated to the thousands of Jews who were rounded up here and sent to their deaths at Auschwitz. If you walk around the residential streets, you'll still see abandoned homes and burned buildings.

After touring the sites of the Old Town, you might want to walk around the walls. (The museum operates a 1-hour tour, Tuesday to Saturday at 2:30pm, beginning at the Palace of the Knights.) The fortification has a series of magnificent gates and towers, and is remarkable as an example of a fully intact medieval structure. Admission is 1,200 Drs ($5) for adults, 900 Drs ($3.75) for seniors, and 600 Drs ($2.50) for students.

Palace of the Knights. Ippotón St. ☎ **0241/23-359.** Admission 1,200 Drs ($5) adults, 900 Drs ($3.75) seniors, 600 Drs ($2.50) students. Tues–Sun 8:30am–6:30pm.

At the crest of the hill on the right, through the grand gates, is the amazing Palace of the Knights (also known as the Palace of the Grand Masters), which is believed to be the original site of the ancient Temple of Helios. It was neglected by the Turks (they turned it into a prison), and in 1856 it was accidentally blown up, along with the Church of St. John. During the Italian occupation the Fascist government undertook the enormous project of reconstructing the castle. Only the stones in the lower part of the building and walls are original; the rest is the work of 20th-century builders. The palace reflects a happy Gothic style of architecture, with large, bright windows flooding the interior with light. Inside, offsetting the dark, weighty Renaissance furniture is a collection of pastel-colored Hellenistic, Roman, and early Christian mosaics "borrowed" from Italian excavations on neighboring Kos. The intricately painted urns are Japanese and were presented as gifts from Italy's allies across the Pacific.

Church of Our Lady of the Castle. ☎ 0241/27-674. Admission 600 Drs ($2.50) adults, free for students and children. Daily 8:30am–2:30pm.

Formerly the Byzantine Museum of Rhodes, the Church of the Virgin of the Castle (also known as Our Lady of the Castle) was reopened in 1988, occupying the renovated interior of this 11th-century church. Inside is a permanent exhibition of paintings of Rhodes from the early Christian period to the 18th century, including icons, wall paintings, and miniatures.

Archaeological Museum of Rhodes. Museum Sq. **☎ 0241/27-657.** Admission 800 Drs ($3.35) adults, 600 Drs ($2.50) seniors, 400 Drs ($1.65) students. Tues–Sun 8:30am–3pm.

The medieval Knight's Hospital now houses the archaeological museum. The first floor is lined with tombstones of knights from the 15th and 16th centuries, many of which are festooned with extravagant coats-of-arms and wonderfully overblown inscriptions.

One of the masterpieces of the collection of ancient works is an elegant and expressive funeral stele dating from the 5th century B.C. showing Crito, the grieving daughter of Timarista, embracing her mother for the last time. The museum's most famous piece is the kneeling *Aphrodite of Rhodes,* on the second floor, a small 1st-century B.C. Parian marble statue of the lovely goddess fresh from her bath, holding up her long hair to dry. In the next room is the 4th-century B.C. *Aphrodite Thalássia,* the subject of Lawrence Durrell's *Reflections on a Marine Venus.* The head of Helios, patron deity of the island, was found near the site of the palace in this old city. Metallic rays, representing flashes of brilliant flames from the sun, were attached around the crown. There's also a fine collection of ancient vases and jewelry from Ialyssós and Kámiros in the Knights' Hall.

EXPLORING THE NEW TOWN

The two major attractions within the confines of the new city are **Mandráki Harbor** and Mt. Smith. The harbor is perhaps more famous for the legend of the Colossus than its present use. Two columns capped by a stag and doe, symbols of Rhodes, mark the supposed location of the Colossus. Mandráki also has a Venetian-era watchtower, three picture-postcard windmills, and boats of all varieties, from funky excursion boats that go to Sými to space-age hydrofoils, regal sailing vessels, and super-sleek jet-powered yachts.

Mt. Smith, named after a British admiral who used it for observation during the Napoleonic wars, is a modest hill north of the present city and the site of the ancient **Acropolis,** which dates from 408 B.C. Traces of its north-south main street have been found under the modern New Zealand Street. On top of Mt. Smith are remnants of temples dedicated to Athena and Zeus Polieus. Archaeologists believe that this very large temple complex was easily visible to ships in the Straits of Marmaris, and

The Colossus of Rhodes

The bronze Colossus, one of the Seven Wonders of the Ancient World, was a statue of Helios cast from 304 to 292 B.C. and estimated to have been between 90 and 110 feet tall. (The Statue of Liberty is 93 feet tall at her crown.) It tumbled down in an earthquake only 66 years after it was completed. The shattered giant lay on the ground for more than 800 years, until 653 A.D., when the Saracens sold it as scrap and it was carried away through the Syrian desert by a caravan of 900 camels. The Colossus was probably melted down to make weapons. Its exact site has never been firmly established. Myth makers and romantics have it straddling the entrance of Mandráki Harbor, where ships would pass under it between its legs. Recently a psychic led some divers to the harbor, swearing they'd find big chunks of the Colossus. Large pilings were found, but Greece's culture minister denied that they were part of the Colossus. More serious historians and archaeologists place the site farther inland, near the Temple of Helios, now the Palace of the Grand Masters.

therefore all treaties and allegiance documents between Rhodes and her warring neighbors were kept here. Below this are the three tall columns and a pediment that remain from the vast Temple of Apollo.

Below the Acropolis is a long **stadium** built into the side of Sandourli Hill. It was reconstructed by the Italians in the early 1940s, though some of the original tiers from the 2nd century B.C. can be seen. To its left is the totally reconstructed 800-seat theater once used to teach rhetoric. In the vicinity are the remains of a gymnasium, and above it, near the acropolis, a nymphaeon where caves and water channels indicate river divinities may have been worshiped.

MORE TO SEE & DO

The **Aquarium,** officially known as the Hydrobiological Institute, stands on the northern point of the city, where an amazing variety of Mediterranean marine life is on display. It's open daily from 9am to 9pm; admission is 600 Drs ($2.50) for adults, 300 Drs ($1.25) for children.

Antique-ophiles should drop into the **Ministry of Culture Museum Reproduction Shop** on Ippotón Street, open daily from 8am to 8pm, for excellent plaster and resin reproductions of favorite sculptures, friezes, tiles, and other works from throughout ancient Greece.

For a break from the run-of-the-mill tourist shops, try George Affendoulidis's **Traditional Art Shop,** Odós Ippodámou 40–42 (☎ **0241/38-431**), which features wonderful icons, unusual ceramic pieces designed and made by a local archaeologist, handmade marionettes, silver and enamel jewelry, and hand-blown glass frames and candle holders.

WHERE TO STAY

Hotels and pensions in the Old Town are cheaper and less sterile than those in modern Rhodes, and there's a special feeling along the dimly lit medieval streets. With all of the following recommendations, reservations are suggested, at least 6 weeks in advance for the high season. Note that hotels are open from late April to mid-October unless otherwise noted, and that rates may drop as much as 40% during the low season. The **Dodecanese Association for People with Special Needs** (see "Getting Around" under "Essentials," above) provides information on hotels that are equipped for those with special needs.

The true budget traveler will have a hard time in expensive Rhodes. If you can't get into one of the recommendations given below, contact the EOT for its list of rooms for rent or look for one of the small pensions off the Square of the Jewish Martyrs (Platía ton Evreón Martyrón), in the southeast quarter of the Old Town. From the several we inspected, we liked the styleless **Hotel Spot** at Odós Perikléos 21 (☎ **0241/34-737**), run by an old couple who told us that their nephew said "A spot is a good place to be." There are nine spotless rooms with common baths; rates run 8,400 Drs ($35) for two or 10,200 Drs ($42.50) for three. Across the lane at Odós Dimosthenous 21 is the **Fantasia Rooms to Let** (no phone), where for 7,200 Drs ($30), two can share a simple room with attached shower in a home overlooking a large, walled garden. The new **Rodos Youth Hostel,** in a handsome, restored 400-year-old building at Odós Eryíou (☎ **0241/30-491**), has 50 beds at 1,450 Drs ($6.05), a common-use kitchen, hot showers, a self-service laundry facility, a bar, and no curfew.

Note: Taxis are required to take passengers *with baggage* into the Old Town if so requested; the prohibition against entering this vehicle-free zone is only for those *without luggage.* Insist on getting the service you've paid for and resist drivers who want to take you to commission-paying New Town hotels.

In the Old Town

Hotel Kastro. Odós Ariónos 14, 851 00 Rhodes. ☎ **0241/20-446.** 12 rms, 3 with bath (shower). 6,000 Drs ($25) single or double without bath, 7,200 Drs ($30) single or double with bath. No credit cards.

These simple, twin-bedded rooms are a good value. The owner, Vasilis Caragiannos, sculpts benches and friezes in a medieval style, speaks fluent Italian, and has a dog called Rambo and a turtle called Papandreou. You'll see his artwork in the garden that adjoins the hotel. The taverna next door is occasionally noisy with tourists dancing to electric bouzouki, but it usually closes before midnight.

✪ Hotel La Luna. Odós Ierokléous 21, 851 00 Rhodes. ☎ **0241/25-856.** 7 rms, none with bath. 13,200 Drs ($55) single; 17,400 Drs ($72.50) double. Rates include breakfast. No credit cards.

This small, delightful hotel is 1 block from the taverna-lined Orféous Street in a quiet residential neighborhood. La Luna has a large, shaded garden with a cozy bar and breakfast tables. The real highlight is the setting of the common bathrooms: built into this old home is a genuine 300-year-old Turkish bath! Each eclectically decorated room has flower-print wallpaper, and though bathless, all are spacious and bright. The manager, Tony Kaymaktsis, maintains a fresh, lovely, and very friendly place, and will regale you with stories of Ben Kingsley's stay during the filming of the British epic *Paschali's Island.*

Maria's Rooms. Odós Menekléous 147-Z, 851 00 Rhodes. ☎ **0241/22-169.** 8 rms, 3 with bath (shower). 7,200 Drs ($30) single or double without bath; 8,400 Drs ($35) double with bath. No credit cards.

We like this pristine little pension near the Café Bazaar, which for price and quality merits the highest marks. The rooms are sparkling white and squeaky clean, and Maria is a warm and welcoming hostess.

Pension Minos. Odós Omírou 5, 851 00 Rhodes. ☎ **0241/31-813.** 17 rms, none with bath. 10,200 Drs ($42.50) single or double. No credit cards.

This contemporary pension, though in a soul-less concrete edifice, is one of the best budget choices. The hostess, Maria Lenti, is an indefatigable cleaner and the large airy rooms with private sinks, the common toilets, and the showers all gleam. We loved the balconied room no. 15 with its glorious view across the Old Town's minarets and

Readers Recommend

Hotel Marie, Odós Kos 7 (P.O. Box 214), 851 00 Rhodes. ☎ **0241/30-577;** fax 0241/22-751. "The front door is actually on a side street—to enter from Kos Street, you have to walk through a store or a quiet pub. The price was 10,000 Drs ($41.65 in August 1996) a night for a room with private bath, hair dryer, a nice balcony, and two large Scandinavian-style breakfasts. And the Marie has a pool! One caution though: You must get a room on the pool side; the street is dreadfully noisy."

—Edelgard Mahant, Toronto, Ontario

---

domes to the harbor. Go to the minimarket or bakery across the street for a take-out breakfast or snacks, then dine like royalty on the scenic rooftop terrace.

✪ **S. Nikolis Hotel.** Odós Ippodámou 61, 851 00 Rhodes. ☎ **0241/34-561.** Fax 0241/32-034. 10 rms, 6 suites, 4 apts, all with bath (shower). A/C MINIBAR TV TEL. 18,000 Drs ($75) single; 21,600 Drs ($90) double; 14,400–18,000 Drs ($60–$75) per person suite. Rates include breakfast. AE, EURO, MC, V.

This restored lodging is run by the energetic and knowledgeable Sotiris and Marianne Nikolis. It's a splurge, but it offers compact, tidy rooms with modern tiled showers. In 1990 a 10-ton marble pediment dating from the 2nd century was found beneath the medieval foundations in their backyard. After excavations were complete, the garden became the excellent Ancient Agora Bar and Restaurant. A delicious, full and very hearty breakfast is served daily on their marble rooftop terrace overlooking the Old Town. They also have attractive, nearby apartments with kitchens that are great for families (the rates are the same as for the hotel, but breakfast isn't included), a deluxe honeymoon suite with a Jacuzzi, and some simpler rooms to rent. Usually open year-round, but between November and April call ahead to be sure.

Sunlight Pension. Odós Ippodámou 32, 851 00 Rhodes. ☎ **0241/21-435.** 10 rms, all with bath (shower). 7,200 Drs ($30) single or double. No credit cards.

The small, modern rooms, each with its own refrigerator and coffeemaker, were ultra-clean when we visited and the host, Stavros Galanis, seems intent on maintaining the standard. Downstairs from the guest quarters is a secluded garden and the diminutive Stavros Bar, a place that seems to be a popular late-night meeting ground.

In the New Town

The modern hotels, even in the New Town, are more expensive in Rhodes than on other islands and mediocre breakfasts are usually exorbitant. Most of these bland establishments cater to groups and are rarely available to individual travelers.

Hotel Despo. Odós Lambráki 40, 851 00 Rhodes. ☎ and fax **0241/22-571.** 64 rms, all with bath (shower). TV TEL. 19,200 Drs ($80) double. Rates include breakfast. No credit cards.

From the usual Class C fare, this colorful hotel, in the heart of the New Town, is one of the best. It's so well managed that the 1950s-era black-and-white leather furnishings in the lobby don't show any signs of age. The bright, sunny rooms have carpeting, modern attached showers, fridges, and balconies.

International Hotel. Odós Kazoúli 12, 851 00 Rhodes. ☎ **0241/24-595.** Fax 0241/30-221. 42 rms, all with bath (shower). TEL. 10,200 Drs ($42.50) single; 14,400 Drs ($60) double. Rates include breakfast. V.

This is a clean, simple, relaxed, and friendly hotel on a quiet street a couple of blocks east of the National Theater, near the beach and tennis courts. There's a nice little bar in the open lobby with fairly inexpensive drinks, soft jazz, and modern Greek music.

Kamiros Hotel. Odós 25 Martíou 1 (P.O. Box 45), 851 00 Rhodes. ☎ **0241/22-591.** Fax 0241/22-349. 48 rms, all with bath (tub). A/C MINIBAR TV TEL. 20,400 Drs ($85) single; 27,600 Drs ($115) double. Rates include breakfast. AE, DC, MC, V.

This recently renovated hotel is a bit of a splurge, but it's a good value and a good location, in the heart of town overlooking Mandraki Harbor, just a few blocks from the Old Town. The rooms are large, the bathrooms especially are spacious, and double-paned windows make them especially quiet for the central location. The spacious lobby is attractively furnished with large contemporary blue leather sofas and chairs. The buffet breakfast is unusually substantial. (During July and August the nearby discos are supposed to close at midnight.)

Marieta Pension. Odós 28 Oktovríou, 52, 851 00 Rhodes. ☎ **0241/36-396.** 8 rms, all with bath (shower). 9,600 Drs ($40) single or double. No credit cards.

The clean, spacious Marieta Pension is a welcome alternative to the overpriced New Town hotels. The hosts, Michael and Marietta Potsos, ran the Gold Star Supermarket chain in St. Louis for many years. Now they've returned to Rhodes and run a pleasant, home-style pension in a 52-year-old traditional villa. The rooms are huge and high-ceilinged.

WHERE TO EAT

With some effort, well-prepared, tasty, and imaginative meals can be found, but prices vary widely, usually from expensive to outrageous, and restaurateurs continue to swindle tourists by overcharging, underweighing portions, or just not displaying a menu. Unless you're in one of the better restaurants, don't be shy about determining the cost of your meal before you order it. If you have any problems, keep that receipt and head for the **market police** (☎ **0241/23-849**). Most of the restaurants listed below claim to be open year-round, but experience has taught us that many close some of the time between November and April for a break, repair work, or lack of customers.

In the Old Town

The Old Town is crammed with tavernas and restaurants, all hungry for tourist dollars. Hawkers stand in front of restaurants and accost passersby—handing out business cards, ushering people in for a look at the kitchen, and finally strong-arming them into sitting down. It's all part of the game. The best way to handle a restaurant bully is to continue walking to one of the restaurants listed below. Lest you think that Old Town restaurants are strictly for visitors, many Rhodians consider this section of town to have some of the best food in the city, particularly for fish, although low-cost seafood feasts are an impossible contradiction.

Cleo's Restaurant. Odós Ayíou Fanouríou 17. ☎ **0241/28-415.** Reservations recommended in summer. Main courses 1,900–4,600 Drs ($7.90–$19.15). AE, V. Mon–Sat 7pm–midnight. ITALIAN.

This tranquil, whitewashed courtyard and two-story interior are found down a narrow lane off the noisy Sokrátous Street. Excellent Italian and nouvelle European fare is served: the pasta pomodoro mozzarella, the well-seasoned mussels, and the tender beef fillet are all excellent. Don't miss the light-as-air gourmet desserts.

Garden Restaurant Diafani. Platía Ariónos 3. ☎ **0241/26-053.** Main courses 1,400–1,800 Drs ($5.85–$7.50); fish 5,000–16,000 Drs ($20.85–$66.65) per kilo. No credit cards. Daily noon–midnight. Closed Nov–Apr. GREEK/SEAFOOD.

Don't be put off by the unassuming exterior. Head straight for the kitchen and check out the daily specials, then go back to the garden to enjoy your meal. We opted for cream *melitzanosaláta* (eggplant spread) and *dolmádes*, which were freshly made by the owner, Archondoula Propata. For the main course we had *keftália* (succulent spicy meatballs), with local wine, of course.

Manolis Dinoris Fish Taverna. 14A Museum Sq. ☎ **0241/25-824.** Fish 8,500–15,000 Drs ($34.40–$62.50) per kilo. AE, EURO, MC, V. Daily noon–3pm and 7pm–midnight. SEAFOOD.

We happened upon this special place by the Old Town's front gate while hunting for an exhibit sponsored by the municipality. What a treat! Housed in the stables of the 13th-century Knights of St. John's Inn, with vaulting arches and impossibly thick masonry, the building was restored as a restaurant. We tried a full panoply of seafood delights (including the lobster); everything was delicious and fresh. We preferred the quiet garden on the side to the front patio, but in winter there's a roaring fire going indoors at the old stone hearth that makes it very cozy.

Romeo Taverna/Grill Room. Odós Menekléous 7–9. ☎ **0241/25-186.** Main courses 1,300–2,600 Drs ($5.40–$10.85); fish 6,000–10,000 Drs ($25–$41.65) per kilo. AE, DC, EURO, MC, V. Daily 10am–12:30am. Head up from Sokrátous St., midway between Ippokrátous and the Suleiman Mosque. GREEK/GRILL/SEAFOOD.

So many of our readers raved about Romeo's that we had to go, and we weren't disappointed in this beautiful 500-year-old building with a roof garden. Our appetizers of eggplant *papoutsákia* ("little shoes") and *saganáki* cooked over charcoal were mouth-watering. For a main course we tried the *bekrí mezés* ("drunkard's appetizers"), a luscious concoction of chunks of pork cooked with pepper, onion, green peppers, and fresh tomato, which we washed down with local wine. There's the additional delight of live music on traditional instruments.

✪ **Yiánnis Taverna.** Odós Appélou 41. ☎ **0241/36-535.** Main courses 900–3,400 Drs ($3.75–$14.15). V. Daily 9am–midnight. GREEK.

For a budget homemade Greek meal, visit this small place on a quiet lane behind the popular Kavo d'Oro. Chef Yiannis spent 14 years in New York's Greek diners. Not every dish is available daily, but the excellent moussaká, stuffed vegetables, and meat dishes are well made and flavorful. Portions are hearty, it's cheap, and the friendly service is a welcome relief from nearby establishments. The breakfast omelets are a great deal, too!

In the New Town

There are some good just-for-locals restaurants in the New Town, but few with as much style as those in the Old Town. A tourist favorite is the **Mandráki Market Square,** in the agorá—1 block inland from the harbor. There are more than a dozen small outdoor grill restaurants in this circular courtyard; throughout the day lambs are rotating on spits, chickens are roasting over gas fires, and pork is being hacked from roasted torsos to make souvláki. You'll also find cafe bars, juice stands, postcard stalls, and other distractions to make this a fun (but not so cheap) lunch spot. Los Angelenos will feel nostalgic for the Farmer's Market!

Readers Recommend

Restaurant Latino, Odós Ippodámou 11. "Just down Ippodámou Street from the S. Nikolis Hotel was a restaurant that I couldn't tear myself away from! I ate there every night. It wasn't extremely pricey (for Rhodes) and the Italian food was amazing."

—Heather Howard, Beverly Hills, Calif.

Rhodes Accommodations & Dining

Accommodations
Hotel Despo **6**
International Hotel **1**
Kamiros Hotel **4**
Hotel Kastro **9**
Hotel La Luna **7**
Maria's Rooms **11**
Marieta Pension **3**
Pension Minos **17**
S. Nikolis Hotel **16**
Sunlight Pension **12**

Dining
Aris Taverna **2**
Break Delicatessen **5**
Cleo's Restaurant **14**
Garden Restaurant
  Diafani **10**
Manolis Dinoris
  Fish Taverna **8**
The Old Story **18**
Romeo Taverna/
  Grill Room **13**
Yefira Restaurant **18**
Yiannis Taverna **15**

Aris Taverna. Odós G. Leóntos 4–6. ☎ **0241/32-320.** Main courses 1,800–3,300 Drs ($7.50–$13.75). EURO, MC, V. Daily 10am–11pm. GREEK/CONTINENTAL.

This favored place around the corner from the Marietta Pension is often crowded with local businesspeople and their out-of-town guests. Kyle liked the tuna salad, butter beans, and fried peppers.

Break Delicatessen. Odós Sof. Venizélou 8. ☎ **0241/73-493.** Menu items 300–1,800 Drs ($1.25–$7.50). No credit cards. Daily 7am–3am. FAST FOOD.

Two blocks west of the EOT off G. Lambráki Street, Break is a New Age fast-food place, actually much nicer and better than you'd imagine. The counter chef huddles over a crêpe grill, turning out a dozen varieties priced as low as 400 Drs ($1.65). If you want an inexpensive salad, burger, fried chicken, croissant, spinach pie, or ice cream, it's here—and at all hours!

✪ **The Old Story (Paleá Istoría).** Odós Mitropóleos 108 (at Dendrínou). ☎ **0241/32-421.** Reservations recommended in summer. Main courses 2,500–4,200 Drs ($10.40–$17.50). EURO, V. Daily 7pm–midnight. GREEK.

This is a splurge choice, but it's one of the best restaurants in Rhodes, well worth the 10-minute cab ride (or 25-minute walk) into the New Town south of Diagora Stadium. Most of the patrons are Greek, attracted by the subtle cuisine and absence of tourists. We had unusual *mezédes* (appetizers): a finely chopped beet salad; lightly fried zucchini; a true country salad with potatoes, olives, and tomatoes; *saganáki* (fried cheese); then a fluffy greens-and-cheese soufflé, delicious meatless dolmádes, and a moist and tender roast pork with potatoes. A feast indeed!

Yefira Restaurant. In Pastida village. ☎ **0241/47-031.** Main courses 1,400–3,000 Drs ($5.85–$12.50). No credit cards. Mon–Sat 5pm–midnight, Sunday 11am–midnight. GREEK.

About 9¹/₂ miles south—about 3,000 Drs ($12.50) by taxi—inland between Rhodes and the airport is this fine grill mentioned by all our Rhodian buddies as their favorite dining spot. Go for wonderful *mezédes* (appetizers)—try the codfish with garlic and potato spread—and then anything that's fresh from the spit. We went wild for the lamb and chicken, but don't ignore the pork souvláki. This is excellent Greek food in a real Greek village.

RHODES CITY AFTER DARK

Rhodes by night is brimming with energy.

Try one of the many outdoor cafes lining the **harborside** of the New Town. There's a string of them under the lit arches outside the Agorá (New Market). You'll have a good time watching the Greek guys engage in *kamáki* (girl-chasing).

For entertainment of a strictly adult nature, try walking Ayíou Fanaríou Street in the Old Town. On and around the street you'll find bars, music, and willing company. *The* party-scene street in the New Town is Iróon Politechníou Street; if you don't want to go home alone, this is the street to stroll through, as is the surrounding neighborhood.

Local Cultural Entertainment

Sound and Light. Odós Papágou (south of Rimíni Sq.), Old Town. ☎ **0241/21-922.** Admission 1,200 Drs ($5), free for children 11 and under.

The Sound and Light (Son et Lumière) presentation dramatizes the life of a youth admitted into the monastery in 1522, the year before Rhodes's downfall to invading Turks. In contrast to Athens's Acropolis show, the dialogue here is more illuminating, though the lighting is unimaginative. Nevertheless, sitting in the lush formal gardens below the palace on a warm evening can be a pleasant and informative experience, and it's heartily recommended to those smitten by the medieval Old Town. There are twice-nightly performances (including one in English) according to season (check the posted schedule).

Traditional Folk Dance Theater. Odós Adronikou (off Arionos Sq.), Old Town. ☎ **0241/ 20-157.** Admission 3,000 Drs ($12.50) adults, 1,500 Drs ($6.25) students. May to early Oct, performances Mon, Wed, and Fri at 9:20pm.

The Greek folk dance show, presented by the Nelly Dimoglou Dance Company, is always lively, filled with color, and totally entertaining. Twenty spirited men and women perform dances from many areas of Greece in colorful, often embroidered, flouncy costumes. The five-man band plays an inspired and varied repertoire, the choreography is excellent, the dancers skillful, and even the set (an open square surrounded by two-dimensional Rhodian houses) is effective—a thoroughly recommended evening.

Discos & Nightclubs

There are at least 100 **nightclubs** on Rhodes, so you're sure to find one to your liking. We're hesitant to make any specific recommendations because the scene changes so quickly. **Amazon** (☎ **0241/37-830**) was still the hottest spot on the coastal Ialyssós Road during our last visit. **Privato Disco,** near the port, was outstandingly garish and sure to help attract a crowd to a lively quarter.

Elsewhere in the New Town, **Le Palais,** on Odós 25 Martíou (☎ **0241/34-219**), was still bringing in a lively young crowd on Friday and Saturday nights, but several hipper young locals said that they preferred the nearby **Blue Lagoon.** The action doesn't start until after 10pm, and the usual admission charge is 2,500 Drs ($10.40), which includes the first drink.

The Old Town tends to be a bit less wild and loud, so if you're not up to a serious spree, you might like the stylish new **Symposium,** off lively Sokrátous. Nearby, at Odós Omírou 70, the **Ancient Agora Bar** offers a more sedate venue for actual conversation; there's even a no-smoking section.

Rhodes sports a variety of Greek nightclubs, where bouzouki bands strum and singers croon. The **Minuit Palace** in Ixiá and the **Melody Palace** (☎ **0241/93-777**) and the **Stork** in Kremastí (near the airport) were considered the best clubs at the time of our last visit. International pop entertainers come on at 10pm, the Greek bouzouki kings at midnight. Admission is buried in the exorbitant drink charges: bottles of whisky run about 20,000 to 30,000 Drs ($83.35 to $125); anyone dining should expect to pay 12,000 to 18,000 Drs ($50 to $75) per person.

Gambling

Gambling is a popular nighttime activity in Greece. Rumor has it that there's a network of private high-stakes (and illegal) gambling dens scattered throughout the city, much as there is in Iráklio. But if you want to bet in a less subterranean atmosphere, saunter over to one of Greece's three legal casinos, the **Casino Grand Hotel,** in the Grand Hotel Astir Palace–Rhodes, off Óthonos Amalías Street on the northwest side of New Town (☎ **0241/26-254**). Open daily 8pm to 2am year-round, the casino attracts visitors from around the world. Those with visions of Las Vegas or Atlantic City will find this casino on the small side. Only those 21 years and older are admitted; they'll check your passport. Dress nicely: Closed shoes and, between November and April, jacket and tie are required.

LÍNDOS

Líndos is without question the most picturesque town on the island of Rhodes. Be warned, however, that it's often deluged with tourists; your first view of Líndos will be unforgettable for the wrong reasons. The Archeological Society controls all development in the village, and the traditional white stucco homes, shops, and restaurants form the most unified, classically Greek expression in the Dodecanese. Far too many vehicles are left by a towering, centuries-old plane tree whose roots are enclosed in a pebble-paved bench. Here, next to an ancient fountain with Arabic script, the old village women in black chatter in the shade, watching hundreds of skimpily clad tourists cross back and forth to the beach below.

Bear right into the maze before you, aim to get lost, and you'll find the reason for Líndos's aesthetic reputation. Avoid the Disneyland atmosphere of the high season and—with luck—the peasant blouses, ceramic plates, and rock-star posters (David Gilmore of Pink Floyd has a house here) hung along the shopfronts won't distract you from the village's architectural purity.

There are two entrances to the town. The first and northernmost leads down a steep hill to the bus stop and taxi stand, then veers downhill to the beach. At this square you'll find the friendly, informative **Tourist Information Kiosk** (☎ **0244/ 31-900**), open April 1 to November 1, daily from 9am to 10:30pm. (You can purchase phone cards and international newspapers here.) This is the commercial heart of the village with the Acropolis above. The rural **clinic** (☎ **0244/31-224**) and **post office** are nearby. The second road leads beyond the town and into the upper village, blessedly removed from the hordes and a better area for architecture enthusiasts.

WHAT TO SEE & DO

In Líndos, try to stay away from the village's commercial heart. Instead, stroll through the maze of narrow streets and look for ancient scripts carved in the wooden door lintels. There's the Byzantine Church of the Virgin, **Ayía Panayía,** dating from 1479. Inside there are intricate frescoes painted by Gregorios of Sými in 1779. The floor is paved with *hoklákia,* a mosaic of upright black and white pebbles, worn smooth over the centuries. Scout out a chaise longue on one of the two beaches encircling the main port to admire the luxury yachts docked at the point.

The Acropolis. ☎ **0244/31-258.** Admission 1,200 Drs ($5) adults, 900 Drs ($3.75) seniors, 600 Drs ($2.50) students. Tues–Sun 8:30am–3pm. If you don't want to walk, you can arrange for a donkey ride (1,200 Drs/$5) at the town's entrance.

Past the bus stop square and donkey stand you'll see ACROPOLIS signs. A visit to the superb remains of the Castle of the Knights on a hill above the town will help to orient you. From the east ramparts of the castle you can see the lovely beach at St. Paul's Bay below and more of Rhodes's less-developed eastern coastline.

The Acropolis contains the ruins of one of Rhodes's three Dorian towns (settled by Líndos, one of Helios's and Rhodes's three grandsons), and within its medieval walls are the impressive remains of the Sanctuary of Athena, with its large Doric portico from the 4th century B.C. St. John's Knights refortified the Acropolis with monumental turreted walls and built a small church to St. John inside—though their best deed was to preserve the ancient ruins still standing. Stones and columns are strewn everywhere, and at the base of the stairs leading to their Byzantine church is a wonderful large relief of a sailing ship, whose indented bridge once held a statue of a priest of Poseidon. From the north and east ramparts you'll have the most wonderful views of new Líndos below, where most of the homes date from the 15th century. Dug into Mt. Krana across the way are caves left by ancient tombs.

WHERE TO STAY & EAT

During the high season (ironically, when the weather is hottest!) 4,000 resident tourists are joined by up to 10,000 day-trippers from Rhodes. Since no hotel construction is permitted, almost all the old homes have been converted into pensions (called "villas" in the brochures) by English charter companies. However, during the peak season, the local **Tourist Information Kiosk** (☎ **0244/31-900**) maintains a list of the homes that rent rooms to individuals and they will help to place you; plan to pay 7,000 to 10,000 Drs ($29.15 to $41.65) for a bed in a tiny room with shared facilities.

Triton Holidays (☎ **0241/21-690**) books six-person villas with kitchen for 35,000 Drs ($145.85) a day during low season; reservations are usually made a year in advance. If Líndos is booked or not to your taste, consider the attractive beaches to the south at Péfkos, Lárdos, or Kaláthos. **Heliousa Travel** in Lárdos (☎ **0244/44-057;** fax 0244/44-041) can help you find a room as well as make other travel plans.

There are plenty of restaurants in tiny Líndos, but the best is probably **Mavrikos,** on the main square (☎ **0244/31-232**), which the Italian Restaurant Association recently rated as one of the five best restaurants on the island. It's not especially expensive by local standards. We recommend the chef's superb moussaká, delectable prawns in garlic sauce, and roasted lamb.

ELSEWHERE AROUND THE ISLAND

This island is known for scenery, and one of the greatest pleasures provided by an around-the-island tour is a chance to view some of its wonderful variations. The sights described below are not of significant historical or cultural importance, except for Ialyssós and Kámiros.

Ialyssós was the staging ground for the four major powers that have controlled the island of Rhodes. The ancient ruins and monastery reflect the presence of two of these groups. The Dorians ousted the Phoenicians from Rhodes in the 10th century B.C. and during the 3rd to 2nd centuries B.C. they constructed a **Temple to Athena** and **Zeus Polius** (similar to those on Mt. Smith), whose ruins are still visible below the monastery. Walk south of the site and you'll come to a well-preserved 4th-century B.C. fountain.

When the Knights of St. John invaded the island, they, too, started from Ialyssós, a minor town during the Byzantine era. They built a small, subterranean chapel decorated with frescoes of Jesus and heroic knights. Their little whitewashed church is built right into the hillside above the Doric temple. Over it, the Italians constructed the **Monastery of Filérimos,** which is a lovely spot to tour. Finally, Suleiman the Magnificent moved into Ialyssós in 1522 with his army of 100,000 and used it as a base for his eventual takeover of the island.

The site is open Tuesday to Sunday from 8:30am to 3pm; admission is 800 Drs ($3.35) for adults, 600 Drs ($2.50) for seniors, and 400 Drs ($1.65) for students. Proper dress is required. Ancient Ialyssós is 3 miles inland from Triánda on the island's northwest coast. There is presently no public bus service to the site, but the airport bus stops at Triánda.

The ruins at **Kámiros** are much more extensive than those at nearby Ialyssós, and many people consider it the island's best ancient site. The upper porch served as a place of religious practice and provided the height needed for the city's water supply. Climb up to the top and you'll see two swimming-pool-size aqueducts, their walls still lined with a nonporous coating. The Dorians collected water in these basins, assuring themselves of a year-round supply. The small valley contains ruins of Greek homes and streets, as well as the foundations of a large temple. The site is sufficiently well preserved for you to imagine what life was like in this ancient Doric city more than 2,000 years ago.

Consider wearing a swimsuit under your clothes; there's a nice beach and a couple of tavernas near the bus stop and, after your hike up the hill, you may want to go for a swim. The site (☎ **0244/21-954**) is open Tuesday to Sunday from 8:30am to 3pm; admission is 800 Drs ($3.35) for adults, 600 Drs ($2.50) for seniors, and 400 Drs ($1.65) for students. Kámiros (not to be confused with Skála Kamírou, its ancient port) is 21 miles southwest of Rhodes town, from which the public bus departs at 9am and 1:20pm.

Petaloúdes is a popular tourist attraction because of the millions of black-and-white-striped tiger moths that have overtaken this verdant valley. When resting quietly on flowering plants or leaves, the moths are well camouflaged. When disturbed by clappers, screamers, wailing infants, or blaring Greek disco/rock, they rise toward the sky in a flurry of red, their underbellies exposed as they try to hide from the summer crush. The setting, with its many ponds, bamboo bridges, and rock displays, is too precious for us, and there are far too many tour buses. (Real butterfly hounds would probably prefer the Petaloúdes on Páros.) Petaloúdes is 15 1/2 miles south of Rhodes and inland; it can be reached by public bus but is more easily visited with a tour.

Kalithéa is an attractive east-coast beach resort, 7 miles south of Rhodes, celebrated for its medicinal hot springs. The old-fashioned bathing facilities are now closed, but plans are being made to restore them. On the southwest tip of the island, the stretch from **Plimýri** to **Yenádi** has seen much less development and offers a contrast with most other beaches on the island. If Yenádi's dark sand-and-stone beach appeals, there are rooms to rent and tavernas. Bus service to this part of the island is, at best, infrequent. If you have a car and are making an around-the-island tour, don't miss the east-coast town of **Monólithos,** with its spectacularly set monastery; rooms are available for rent there.

2 Sými

244 nautical miles E of Piraeus, 6 nautical miles N of Rhodes

Tiny, rugged Sými is distinguished by the pastel-yellow neoclassical homes of its capital, Sými town, with the ports of Yialós and Horió, on the hillside above. The refreshing absence of modern architecture is due to an archaeological decree that severely regulates the style and methods of construction and restoration for all old and new buildings. Sými's turn-of-the-century prosperity from trading and shipbuilding is evident in the richly ornamented churches scattered over the entire island. Islanders proudly boast that there are so many churches and monasteries that one could worship at a different one every day of the year.

During the 1940s and 1950s Sými's economy was based on sponges. In the following decades sailors and fishermen used their skills to service the burgeoning commercial shipping industry. When the maritime business soured, Symians fled abroad to work, leaving their pristine home in the hands of developers. Picture-perfect traditional-style Sými is now the star of many Greek postcards. It has become a magnet for wealthy Athenians in search of long-term real estate investments, and a highly touted "off the beaten path" resort for European tour groups that are trying to avoid other tour groups.

ESSENTIALS

GETTING THERE & DEPARTING   Several excursion boats arrive daily from Rhodes; two boats are owned cooperatively (the *Sými I* and *Sými II*) and are booked locally in Rhodes through **Triton Holidays** (☎ 0241/21-690). Round-trip tickets cost 5,000 Drs ($20.85). Most boats leave at 9am daily (two or three times weekly in the off-season) from Mandráki Harbor, stop at the main port of Yialós, then continue onto the Panormítis Monastery or the beach at Pédi for sightseeing, before returning to Rhodes. There are daily car-ferries from Piraeus, two ferries a week to Crete via Kárpathos, and two local ferries weekly to Kálymnos.

VISITOR INFORMATION   Several travel agents are open Monday to Saturday from 9am to 1pm and 5 to 8pm. We found **Kalodoukas Holidays** (☎ 0241/ 71-077; fax 0241/71-491) to be the most helpful; it's at the end of the harbor past the Ionian Bank, up the steps behind the Cafe Helena. The *Sými News* is a free local paper with useful information.

ORIENTATION   Ferries and excursion boats usually dock first at hilly Yialós on the barren, rocky northern coast of the island. There's a pretty **clock tower** on the right as you enter the port; it's useful as a local landmark when defining the maze of vehicle-free lanes and stairs. Yialós is the liveliest village on the island and the goal of most overnighters. Sými's main road leads to Pédi, a developing beach resort one cove east of Yialós, and a new road rises up to Horió, the old capital.

GETTING AROUND   The island's 4,000 daily visitors usually take an excursion boat that stops at the major ports. However, there are three **public buses** a day between Yialós and Pédi, a few **motorbike** rental shops in Yialós, and a few **taxis**—the fare should be about 600 Drs ($2.50).

Kalodoukas Holidays (☎ 0241/71-077) organizes walking excursions and bus tours to the island's few sites. **Caïques** shuttle people to Emboriós beach from Yialós—for about 500 Drs ($2.10) per person each way—leaving the port when full. Most other beaches can be reached either from Yialós or Pédi by caïque: Ayía Marína, Áyios Nikólaos, and Nanú Beach usually have daily connections with the two towns; expect to pay about 1,200 Drs ($5) for a round-trip excursion.

FAST FACTS   The **OTE,** about 100 yards behind the *paralía*, up from the left side of the central square, is open weekdays 7:30am to 3pm. The **police** (☎ 0241/ 71-111), **port police** (☎ 0241/71-205), and **post office** are next to the clock tower.

EXPLORING THE ISLAND

Sými's southwestern portion is hilly and green, and the medieval **Panormítis Monastery,** near the southernmost tip, is popular with Greeks as a haven from modern life. Young Athenian businessmen speak lovingly of the monks' cells and small apartments that can be rented for R&R. Rates are about 3,500 Drs ($14.60) for a room with two beds; 8,000 Drs ($33.35) for a two-room studio with kitchenette, shower, and five beds. The whitewashed compound is appreciated both for its verdant, shaded setting and for the 16th-century gem of a church inside. The Moní Taxiárchis Mihaíl (Monastery of the Archangel Michael) boasts icons of the Archangels Michael and Gabriel adorned in silver and jewels. The town of **Panormítis Mihaílis** is most lively and interesting during its annual festival in early November, but can be explored year-round via local boats or bus tours from Yialós. The hardy can hike there—6 miles, about 3 hours—and enjoy a refreshing dip in its sheltered harbor as their reward.

In Yialós, by all means hike the gnarled, chipped stone steps of the Kalí Stráta, the wide stairway that goes up to **Horió** ("village"). This picturesque community is filled with images of a Greece that in many ways has long departed. Heavy-set, wizened old women sweep the whitewashed stone path outside their homes. Occasionally a young girl or boy or a very old man (too old to have left for America or Australia to make his fortune) can be seen retouching the bright-blue trim over the doorways and shutters. Nestled between the immaculately kept homes are the abandoned villas, their faded trim and flaking paint giving them a wistful air. While young emigrés continue to support their parents who live on Sými, renovated villas are now rented to a growing number of tourists; where tourists roam, tavernas, souvenir shops, and bouzouki bars soon follow. Commercialization has hit once-pristine Sými, but for now it's at an acceptable level.

Crowning Horió is the Byzantine and medieval **Kástro,** on the site of the ancient acropolis. Within it the **Church of Megáli Panayía** ("Great Virgin") is adorned with the most glorious frescoes on the island, which can be viewed only when services are held (weekdays from 7 to 8am and all morning on Sunday).

Sými is, unfortunately, not blessed with wide sandy beaches, though there's talk of creating a fine-sand beach at Pédi. Close to Yialós, the main town, are two **beaches:** The first is called **Nos,** with a 50-foot-long rocky "beach." **Emboriós** is a pebble beach a bit farther than Nos (a 15-minute walk west of Yialós); it's a much larger beach and has a taverna as well as the nice new **Neraïdes Apartments** (☎ 0241/ 71-784).

Two local crafts that continue to be practiced on this island are **shipbuilding** and **sponge fishing.** Walk along the water toward Nos beach and you'll probably see boats being constructed or repaired. It's a treat to watch the men fashioning planed boards into a graceful boat, an old tradition on Sými. It was a boatbuilding center in the days of the Peloponnesian War, when spirited sea battles were waged off Sými's shores.

Sponge fishing is almost a dead industry in Greece, and Sými is no exception. A generation ago 2,000 sponge divers worked the waters around the island; today only a handful undertake this dangerous work, mostly in the waters around Italy and Africa. Working at depths of 150 to 180 feet, often without gear in the old days, many divers died or were crippled by the turbulent sea and too-rapid decompression. The few sponges that are harvested—many more are imported from Asia or Florida—are sold at shops along the port. Even if they're not the real thing, they make interesting, inexpensive gifts to take home to friends.

WHERE TO STAY

Many tourists bypass hotels in favor of private apartments or houses. Between April and October, rooms for two with shower and kitchen access go for 9,500 to 15,000 Drs ($39.60 to $62.50); more luxurious two-bedroom, villa-style houses with maid service rent for 18,000 to 30,000 Drs ($75 to $125). The best way to tap into this alternative is to visit **Kalodoukas Holidays** (☎ **0241/71-077**), at the end of the harbor, up the steps behind the Cafe Helena. It also represents two newly renovated villa-hotels—the six-room **Forei Hotel** and the five-room **Hotel Marika,** both above the clock tower on the north side of the harbor, where doubles with private bath (shower) cost 10,000 Drs ($41.65).

Hotel Aliki. Yialós, 856 00 Sými. ☎ **0241/71-665.** Fax 0241/71-655. 15 rms, all with bath (shower). A/C TEL. 13,200 Drs ($55) single; 20,000 Drs ($83.35) double. Rates include breakfast. No credit cards.

The well-restored, traditional Alíki is the standard by which all Sými lodgings are judged, with elegantly styled rooms, including some with dramatic waterfront views. The level of service doesn't quite match the high standard of the interior decor. The non-sea-view rooms are a poor value when compared with the equally priced sea-view rooms. The hotel is a popular overnight getaway from bustling Rhodes, and reservations are required, often months in advance.

Hotel Dorian. Yialós, 856 00 Sými. ☎ **0241/71-181.** 9 rms, all with bath (shower). TEL. 12,500 Drs ($52.10) single; 13,500 Drs ($56.25) double. No credit cards.

This very pleasant, traditional-style hotel climbs the hill above the Hotel Aliki and offers very nice if simple rooms with minimal service. Prices are good for the sea-view rooms, many of which have balconies or terraces.

✪ **Hotel Village.** Horió, 856 00 Sými. ☎ **0241/71-800.** 17 rms, all with bath (shower). A/C TEL. 12,600 Drs ($52.50) single; 14,400 Drs ($60) double. Rates include breakfast. No credit cards.

This hotel, also known as the Horió, is in the center of the upper town, about a 15-minute walk from Pédi. The pastel gold-and-blue hotel is made up of a cluster of small buildings perched high on the shoulder of the hill that blends naturally with the village around it. The rooms are plainly furnished and spotless; some have porches and the upper rooms offer balconies.

WHERE TO EAT

Family Taverna Meraklis. Yialós. ☎ **0241/71-003.** Main courses 1,000–3,600 Drs ($4.15–$15). EURO, MC, V. Daily 8am–midnight. GREEK.

This tiny storefront taverna, hidden on a back lane behind the Ionian and Popular Bank, away from the day-trippers, is welcome more as a respite from the crowds than as a great dining experience. From a limited daily menu, some small fish, stuffed vegetables, meat, and *mezédes* (appetizers) are served, all for moderate prices. Chefs Anna and Sotiris pride themselves on their home-cooking, which is especially evident in their fresh vegetable dishes.

Taverna Neraïda. Town Sq., Yialós. ☎ **0241/71-841.** Main courses 1,300–2,400 Drs ($5.40–$10); fish 7,000–9,000 Drs ($29.15–$37.50) per kilo. MC, V. Daily 11am–3pm and 7pm–midnight. SEAFOOD.

Following our time-proven rule that fish is cheaper far from the port, this homey taverna has the best fresh fish prices on the island, as well as a wonderful range of *mezédes.* We're especially fond of the black-eyed-pea salad and *skordaliá* (garlic dip). The grilled daily fish is delicious and the very typical ambience is a treat.

3 Kos

200 nautical miles E of Piraeus

Tour groups have taken their toll on lovely Kos. In the summer, foreign visitors—mostly brought in on cheap package tours—outnumber the island's 30,000 inhabitants nearly two to one, so we recommend that you avoid the island during the high season. In the spring and fall you'll find that Kos still has more than its share of archaeological sites, unspoiled beaches, friendly people, and good food. If you're interested in an authenic Greek experience, you'll have to look hard or elsewhere.

Many first-time visitors prefer to stay in the northern port town of Kos, then explore the rich variety of archaeological and historical sights and sample the capital's lively nightlife. After exploring the beaches on bicycle excursions, long-term visitors often move out and look for accommodations closer to the golden sand. Our recommendation for beach-goers is to head to the southwestern end of the island near Kéfalos, particularly Áyios Stéfanos.

Since ancient times Kos has been associated with the healing arts and the practice of medicine. Prior to the Dorian settlement of Kos in the 11th-century B.C., a cult dedicated to the worship of Asclepios, the god of healing and medicine, had already been established. Asclepios was either a son of Apollo (from whom he acquired his knowledge) or a mortal (perhaps the physician of the Argonauts) who was deified because of his great healing power. An Asclepion, a sanctuary dedicated to the god, was built so the sick could make offerings in order to receive a cure. Throughout the centuries Kos produced many notable doctors, but none more renowned than Hippocrates (born 460 B.C.), the "Father of Medicine." He established the first medical school and a canon of medical ethics which is, to this day, the code of doctors throughout the world.

ESSENTIALS

GETTING THERE & DEPARTING   By Plane   Olympic Airways has two flights daily from Athens. The airport is inland 16 miles southwest of Kos town, but Olympic provides bus service to and from its office at Odós Vas. Pávlou 12 (☎ **0242/28-330**); buses leave 2 hours before the flight and cost 1,200 Drs ($5).

By Ferry   One or two car-ferries run daily from Piraeus via Pátmos, Léros, and Kálymnos. There's a daily car-ferry and excursion ship from Rhodes and connections with the other Dódecanese by local excursion ships; connections three to five times weekly with Kálymnos, Kastellórizo, Pátmos, Nísyros, Sými, and Tílos, and once weekly to Astipálea. There's one ferry a week to Sámos, Ikaría, Híos, Lésvos, Límnos, and Alexandroúpoli; one a week to Páros, Náxos, and Sýros; and one a week to Thessaloníki. In summer, several caïques depart daily from the beach of Mastihári for nearby Kálymnos.

By Hydrofoil In the summer there's daily hydrofoil service to Pátmos, Rhodes, and Sámos; five times a week to Léros; twice a week to Kálymnos, Nísyros, and Tílos; and once a week to Sými. Tickets are sold at the various travel agencies near the port. Check schedules with the **Piraeus Port Authority** (☎ **01/451-1311**).

VISITOR INFORMATION Your first stop should be the very helpful **Municipal Tourism Office,** located at Odós Vas. Yióryiou 1, near the east-side hydrofoil pier (☎ **0242/24-460**), open in summer Monday to Friday from 8am to 9pm and Saturday and Sunday from 8am to 3pm; off-season, Monday to Friday from 9am to 3pm. **Pulia Tours,** at Odós Vas. Pávlou 3, on the south end of the harbor near the Credit Bank (☎ **0242/26-388**), changes money and sells ferry, hydrofoil, and excursion tickets. The **tourist police,** at the police station on Aktí Miaoúli (☎ **0242/22-444**), are open 24 hours a day; you can ask them about available rooms to rent.

GETTING AROUND Residents of Kos town can easily walk to most sights, and in fact a stroll along the harbor or the busy backstreets of the Agorá is one of the greatest pleasures offered by the island.

By Bus Public bus service is inexpensive but infrequent; the fare to far-off Kéfalos is 1,000 Drs ($4.15). Buses serve all the beach areas, but this is not the place to get stranded after sunset; a return taxi will be very costly. The **KTEL bus station** is on Kleopátras Street. Local city buses leave frequently from the **town bus stop,** on the south side of the harbor, and pass by such local sights as the Asclepion.

By Bicycle A bicycle is the best means of transportation for nearby tanning. You can rent them anywhere for 800 to 1,200 Drs ($3.35 to $5) per day, but remember that the best bikes go early, so get there before 9am.

By Moped/Car Mopeds are great for longer excursions (or lazier people) and can be rented all over town for 3,500 to 6,000 Drs ($14.60 to $25). Several companies rent cars and Jeeps—including **Avis** (☎ **0242/24-272**) and **AutoEurope** (☎ **0242/27-691**)—but this can be expensive unless you do some heavy-duty touring. Expect to pay 14,000 Drs ($58.35) for a subcompact or 18,500 Drs ($77.10) for a Jeep, per day, including insurance.

By Taxi Taxis actually use meters on Kos, and most trips in Kos town will not exceed the 350-Dr ($1.45) minimum fare. However, a ride to the airport is 6,000 Drs ($25) and to the beaches even more. There's a taxi stand near the southeast corner of the harbor; call ☎ **0242/23-333** to book a cab.

FAST FACTS For medical assistance contact the **Hippocrates Hospital,** Odós Ippokrátou 32 (☎ **0242/22-300**). The **OTE** is on Výronos Street, and the **post office** is on Venizélou Street, both about 2 blocks beyond the Ancient Agorá. The **International News Stand Patmios** is at Vas. Pávlou 2.

THE PORT OF KOS

From the time of the Roman Empire until the Allied victory over the Germans in World War II, Kos was occupied and ruled by foreign forces. Nowhere is the legacy of foreign domination more apparent than in the area of the port and capital city, Kos (also called Hóra). The town has a network of Greek and Roman excavations, as well as Byzantine remains, Venetian buildings, a medieval castle, and a Turkish mosque, all within a 1-square-mile area. Only 3 miles northwest of Hóra is the Asclepion, the most important archaeological site on the island. From July to September, you can catch the many art exhibitions, theater, and dance performances funded by the Kos Hippokratia Festival.

WHAT TO SEE & DO

Kos's many archaeological sites can be seen in 1 day. Consider touring the outdoor sites such as the Odeum, western excavations, agorá, and plane tree after seeing the Asclepion, Roman villa, castle, and museum.

The best way to reach all these sites is by bicycle; if you're in good shape for bicycling about 7¹/₂ miles, you can visit everything in a day. Starting from town, take the main road to the intersection of Koritsas, Alexandrou, and Grigoriou streets and follow the signs for the Asclepion. You'll pass through the hamlet of **Platáni** (also called "Turkish Town," where the residents still speak Turkish). It's a great place to stop for an inexpensive snack; you might want to return for dinner during the quieter evening hours. The **Clarisse Ceramic Factory,** on the left, is a good place to buy souvenirs. You'll know you're nearing the Asclepion when you enter an exquisite cyprus-lined roadway.

Asclepion. ☎ 0242/28-763. Admission 800 Drs ($3.35) adults, 600 Drs ($2.50) seniors, 400 Drs ($1.65) students. Tues–Sun 8:30am–3pm (to 6:30pm in summer).

The Asclepion was excavated in the early part of this century, first by the German archaeologist Herzog in 1902, then by a team of Italians. The Italians unearthed the lowest of four levels of the terraced site. The second level is the Propylaea, thought to be where the treatment of the sick actually took place (sulfur springs and a Roman-era bath, on the left, were central to the ancients' idea of exorcising disease). This level of the Asclepion (the largest) was bordered by a Doric portico on three sides, and contained many rooms to house visitors and patients. A number of niches and pedestals were found here, as well as statues and other votive offerings. Don't miss the refreshingly cool drinking fountain next to the stairway; it is Pan who, from his shaded enclave, leaps out at the parched visitor. Continue climbing the magnificent stairway to the two upper terraces, both containing temples from the Greek and Roman eras.

In the center of the third level is the **Altar of the Asclepion** and two temples, the left one dedicated to Apollo and the right the original Temple of Asclepios. Pilgrims placed their votive offerings (sometimes of enormous value) in the cella of these temples prior to therapy. The Ionic temple on the left, with the restored columns, dates from the 1st century B.C., while the Temple of Asclepius dates from the beginning of the 3rd century B.C.

As you ascend the stairs to the highest level, look back toward Turkey and you'll see the 7th-century B.C. ally of Kos, Halikarnassos (present-day Bodrum), which was part of the Doric Hexapolis uniting Kos, Halikarnassos, and Knidos with the Rhodian cities of Líndos, Ialyssós, and Kámiros. The fourth story contains the once-monumental 2nd-century B.C. Temple of Asclepius. This huge sanctuary, built in the Doric style of contrasting black and white marble, must have been an awe-inspiring sight, visible for miles around.

Castle of the Knights. Admission 800 Drs ($3.35) adults, 600 Drs ($2.50) seniors, 400 Drs ($1.65) students. Tues–Sun 8:30am–2:30pm.

Walk across the bridge and you'll be at the Castle of the Knights of Rhodes. When entering this impressive fortress, built in the late 14th century and restored by the Grand Masters d'Aubusson and d'Amboise in the 16th, you'll see fragments of statues, columns, pedestals, and doorways from ancient times. It illustrates a ubiquitous phenomenon in Greece: succeeding generations pulled down existing structures to build new edifices.

The design of the castle was considered innovative because of its system of inner and outer walls and the numerous subterranean tunnels and rooms that facilitated covert movement within them; the entire fortress was surrounded by a moat. The views of the harbor and beach from the top of the far wall are unsurpassed.

Archaeological Museum. ☎ 0242/28-326. Admission 800 Drs ($3.35) adults, 600 Drs ($2.50) seniors, 400 Drs ($1.65) students. Tues–Sun 8:30am–2:30pm.

The central room contains finely executed 2nd-century A.D. mosaics and sculptures found at the House of Europa. The mosaic (completely intact and in color) depicts the two most famous figures in the Koan pantheon, Asclepios and Hippocrates. The "must see" in this museum's excellent collection of Hellenistic and Roman sculptures is the figure of a man assumed to be Hippocrates. Whatever his identity, the statue is a deeply expressive work, showing the pathos of a man who has taken on the suffering of the world.

The Western Excavation

Returning to Kos, turn right on Grigoriou Street and proceed until you reach the site of the Western Excavation, on your left; through the tall trees the Odeum is on your right. The Western Excavation, also known as the ancient Greek and Roman city, connects the site by two 3rd-century B.C. perpendicular roadways. Follow the road leading away from the Odeum until you come to the large reconstructed building on the right; it was originally thought to be a **nymphaeum** (a place where virgins were readied for the fulfillment of their destiny); however, later research led archaeologists to conclude that it was a public toilet! Nevertheless it's a great toilet, with a superb mosaic floor; you'll have to climb up on the right side of the building to peer inside. Across from the toilet is the **Xystro,** a restored colonnade from a gymnasium dating from the Hellenistic era. If you continue walking along the road, you'll come to a covered area that houses a lovely 2nd-century A.D. mosaic showing the Judgment of Paris and various Roman deities. The buildings in the center of the site are, like the Xystro, from the 3rd century B.C.; if you climb up you'll see the fine marble parquet floor and remarkable mosaics (many of which are covered by a thin layer of sand for protection).

Walk back through the site along the road and make a left to reach the second part of the site. The remains here date from the Roman and early Christian eras. The highlight is the splendid mosaic in the **House of Europa** (the first on your left) depicting a lovely, terrified-looking Europa being carted away to Crete by Zeus in the guise of a bull.

Roman Sites

Cross the modern road and proceed to the **Odeum,** excavated during the Italian occupation of the island in 1929. Many of the sites on the island have exceptional carved marble and the Roman-era Odeum is no exception. The famous sculpture of Hippocrates (among others) was found in the covered archways at the base of the Odeum.

Continue down the modern road to the restored Roman villa known as the **Casa Romana,** adjacent to a Roman bath and a Greek temple of Dionysius. Reconstruction of the Roman villa was the work of the Italians who, one can only surmise, were going around the Mediterranean world fixing up ancient edifices to demonstrate the connection between the great Roman Empire and the newly established Fascist state. It's a fascinating archaeological achievement, and presents a unique opportunity to tour a complete Roman villa. Open Tuesday to Sunday from 8:30am to 2:30pm; admission is 800 Drs ($3.35) for adults, 600 Drs ($2.50) for seniors, and 400 Drs ($1.65) for students.

Hippocrates' Tree

Follow the Odeum road for 3 blocks and turn left to see the recently relandscaped ruins of the **Temple of Dionysus.** Continue down Pávlou Street, and to the right of the nursery on Elefthería Square you'll find the **Ancient Agorá,** a 2nd-century B.C. market. Walking along the northern edge of the Agorá toward the harbor, you'll come to a well-preserved mosque and the **plane tree of Hippocrates,** under which he was supposed to have taught his students. (It's extremely unlikely that this tree was alive during his time, but who knows? Anyway, you can't help feeling for the aged trunk that supports still-virile branches propped up with old columns and pedestals.)

WHERE TO STAY

Try to arrive in Kos during the morning, or you might find yourself sleeping in the park or on the beach. If you don't have a reservation, your first stop should be the tourist police. There are basically three areas for hotels in Kos town: Lámbi Beach to the west, the central area behind the harbor, and the beach on the east side.

Kos Camping (☎ **0242/23-910**) is 1¹/₂ miles out of town toward the east, opposite a rocky beach in Psalídi. The sleeping-bag charge is 1,400 Drs ($5.85) per night, with tents going for an additional 800 Drs ($3.35).

Hotel Affendoulis. Odós Evripílou 1, 853 00 Kos. ☎ **0242/25-321.** Fax 0242/25-797. 17 rms, all with bath (shower). TEL. 8,500 Drs ($35.40) single; 12,000 Drs ($50) double. Rates include breakfast. No credit cards.

Our first choice is this fine modern hotel on a quiet side street a mere 200 yards from the eastern beach. First of all, this spotless hotel, with its polished marble floors and ultra-white walls, is the domain of the Zikas family, as helpful and gregarious a clan as we've found in Kos. We enjoyed sitting (and writing) in the open lobby decorated with more Greek style than is usually found. There's a shaded outdoor breakfast area and a much-used honor-system kitchen for drinks and snacks. The bright, balconied rooms have firm mattresses on the beds and are comfortably furnished, with decorative touches. A good value.

Hotel Galini. Platía 3 Septemvríou, 853 00 Kos. ☎ **0242/23-368.** Fax 0242/23-747. 31 rms, all with bath (shower). TEL. 8,600 Drs ($35.85) single; 11,000 Drs ($45.85) double. Rates include breakfast. No credit cards.

This Class C inn is pleasant, but it's beginning to show the wear and tear of German, Finnish, and Italian tour groups. It's a good choice because of its quiet location in a newly developed quarter of town. The rooms are quite plain but clean.

Hotel Maritina. Odós Výronos 19, 853 00 Kos. ☎ **0242/23-511.** Fax 0242/26-124. 80 rms, all with bath (shower). A/C MINIBAR TV TEL. 11,500 Drs ($47.90) single; 18,400 Drs ($76.65) double. Rates include breakfast. AE, DC, EURO, MC, V.

This is a fine Class C hotel where last-minute arrivals may find a room, though it's pricey compared to the competition. The rooms overlook a quiet side street and were recently renovated with colorful new decor. The hotel has wheelchair access to the lobby and in several rooms.

Hotel Theodorou. Odós G. Papandréou, 853 00 Kos. ☎ **0242/23-363.** Fax 0242/23-526. 60 rms, all with bath (shower). TEL. 8,400 Drs ($35) single; 13,800 Drs ($57.50) double. Rates include breakfast. V.

This lively place is a three-story hotel filled with northern Europeans who seem to be perpetually ready for a party. The location is ideal for those who want to be close to the beach and close to the town's nightlife. The rates are on the high side for the pleasant but totally standard Class C accommodations; you're paying for the ever-popular Psalídi Beach. Breakfast usually consists of ham, cheese, and seasonal fruit. The hotel has a bar on the beach and rents bicycles and mopeds.

Pension Alexis. Odós Irodotóu 9 (at Omírou St.), 853 00 Kos. ☎ **0242/28-798.** 12 rms, none with bath. 6,150 Drs ($25.65) single; 7,500 Drs ($31.25) double. Rates include breakfast. No credit cards.

If you're on a tight budget, we recommend this inexpensive place. All rooms share common facilities, including a homey kitchen and breakfast area. We particularly liked the spacious upstairs rooms with their parquet floors, balconies, and fine views of the harbor. Since the pension is in the Zikas family home, you have the feeling of living in a Greek house.

Pension Anna. Odós Venizélou 69, 853 00 Kos. ☎ **0242/23-030.** Fax 0242/23-886. 18 rms, all with bath (shower). TEL. 6,300 Drs ($26.25) single; 13,200 Drs ($54.15) double. Rates include breakfast. AE, EURO, V.

If all else fails and you need a room, try the Pension Anna, a simple, family-run place. (Anna lived for many years in New York.) The balconied rooms are plain but comfortable, and the location is fairly quiet and convenient. There's a well-stocked lobby bar.

Pension Kalamaki Nitsa. Odós G. Avérof 47, Lámbi Beach, 853 00 Kos. ☎ **0242/25-810.** 12 rms, all with bath (shower). 8,000 Drs ($33.35) single or double. No credit cards.

Across the road from the popular Lámbi Beach is a simple pension above a liquor store. The rooms are basic but adequate. Although it's only a short walk to the beach, the sand and water are cleaner a bit farther away from town.

Where to Eat

Don't forget to try some of the local Kos wines: the dry white Lafkos, the red Appelis, or the light subtle Theokritos retsína.

Arap (Platanio) Taverna. In Platáni. ☎ **0242/28-442.** Main courses 1,100–2,000 Drs ($4.60–$8.35). No credit cards. Daily noon–midnight. TURKISH/GREEK.

Because of Kos's proximity to Turkey, a number of tavernas serve both Turkish and Greek cuisine. The best is in the village of Platáni (Kermete, in Turkish), on the road to the Asclepion, about 1¼ miles south of town. Among the many fine dishes are *souzoukákia, imam biyaldi* (Turkish stuffed eggplant), and delectable cheese pies.

Restaurant Olimpiada. Odó Kleopátras 2. ☎ **0242/23-031.** Main courses 1,000–1,500 Drs ($4.15–$6.25). EURO, MC, V. Daily 11am–11pm. GREEK.

The best value for simple Greek fare is the Olimpiada, around the corner from the Olympic Airways office on Pávlou Street. The food is mostly fresh, flavorful (if not original), and inexpensive, and the staff is remarkably courteous and friendly. The okra in tomato sauce and the several vegetable dishes are the best. The Olimpiada is open all year.

✪ **Taverna Mavromatis.** At Psalídi Beach. ☎ **0242/22-433.** Main courses 1,400–2,600 Drs ($5.85–$10.85). DC, EURO, MC, V. Daily 9am–midnight. Closed mid-Oct to Apr. GREEK.

For some of the best food on the island, take a 20-minute walk southeast of the ferry port to the vine- and geranium-covered taverna run by the Mavromati brothers. Their Greek food is what you came to Greece for: melt-in-your-mouth *saganáki*, mint- and garlic-spiced *souzoukákia*, tender grilled lamb chops, moist beef souvláki. Prices are reasonable (even for fresh fish) and the gentle music, waves lapping at your feet, and shaded back patio are delightful.

KOS AFTER DARK

To our minds, the portside cafes opposite the daily excursion boat to Kálymnos are best in the early morning. **Opera,** on Odós Arseníou 2 blocks inland from Vas. Yióryiou, is a popular music bar that plays mostly jazz and blues. If you prefer something considerably more raucous, look for **Odós Nafklíroú** on the northeast side of the Ancient Agora. There are of course many nightspots along the port and a few up Odós Bouboulinas. The lively **Playboy Disco,** Odós Kanári 2 (☎ **0242/22-592**), has an impressive light show.

If you like bouzouki music and Greek dancing, friends recommend **Imam's** at Mármari Beach. We suggest that you pick up a copy of *Kos: Where and How* (for 400 Drs/$1.70) and let your fingers do the walking.

THE BEST BEACHES AROUND THE ISLAND

Although there are many fascinating archaeological sites, the reason that most people come to Kos is for its wonderful **beaches.** The two best are between Tigáki and Mármari on the north coast and between Kéfalos and Kardámena on the south. Both can be reached by bus. From Kos town the closer northwest-coast beaches are an hour away by bicycle and considerably more convenient, though rather crowded.

If you want to stay on the northwest side of the island, a good choice is to go farther south to **Mastihári,** a quieter village with its own fine beach and many rooms to rent. From Mastihári, small excursion boats make the 30-minute crossing to Kálymnos several times daily.

Tigáki is typical of the beach towns that deal almost exclusively with groups, but it's convenient for day trips and pleasant enough. From here there's also regular caïque service to **Psérimos,** a small island with a nice sandy beach, a few tavernas, and some rooms to rent—though it also gets quite crowded during the high season. **Mármari,** about 3 miles southwest, is a little quieter, but it, too, has become increasingly popular because of its windsurfing potential.

Not to be overlooked are the beaches to the west of the port town, Kos. **Lámbi Beach,** a 10-minute walk from town, is usually packed, but you can take advantage of the many tavernas that line the shore for a nice lunch. On the other side of the harbor to the east are beaches extending all the way to the cape of **Áyios Fokás.** These also become crowded, and are lined with a large number of beachfront hotels. The well-groomed pebble-and-sand **Psalídi Beach** is just 2 miles east of the main port, but it may soon fall victim to the construction of a new yacht marina.

ASFENDÍOU (RUSTIC VILLAGES) AROUND THE ISLAND

The inland villages of **Ziá, Evangelístria, Asómatos,** and **Lagoúdi** are all part of the Asfendíou region, a 30-minute drive from downtown Kos. These hamlets are situated halfway up the craggy peaks that form the island's geological backbone, in forests of eucalyptus, pine, fig, and olive trees. In spring the ground is littered with wildflowers of every hue, and the soft aromas of camomile, oregano, mint, and sage perfume the air. Locals hike to these villages during the summer for the cooling breezes that blow across the mountain. There's a wonderful mix of stately churches, crumbling houses, active farms, and new construction, and the people everywhere are among the friendliest on the island. We loved the quintessentially Greek ambience of this area.

The most efficient way to visit this area is by car, but we prefer taking the public bus, infrequent but cheap, and walking from town to town. In the village of Asómatos, we happened upon an English artist's studio that's worth a visit.

Alexandrous Alwyn is known for his bronze sculpture, though many of his highly eclectic sketches and paintings are also on display. His work is somewhat like Henry Moore's, only warmer and more expressive, and is set in a lovely courtyard outside his studio; it's open daily. Ask any local or call ☎ **0242/68-239** for directions.

It's almost worth taking the trip to enjoy the superbly simple dining at the **Sunset Balcony** (☎ **0242/69-120**), just west of the church in Ziá. We had Heineken beer and a large plate of more than a dozen *mezédes,* all of which were distinctive and delicious; then we finished our meal with near-perfect souvláki—all for less than $20 each. To view the sun setting over the Kos plains and several nearby islands dotting the sea is nearly as remarkable as it is on Santoríni.

SOUTHERN KOS & KÉFALOS

Kardámena is an overdeveloped concrete-and-sand lot with many, many places to stay; however, we prefer to head south toward the almost-connected villages of Áyios Stéfanos and Kéfalos. In between these developed areas (and just to the north, as well) is an enormous stretch of sand and stone visited by a mere fraction of the tourists who inhabit the town beaches. The names of these beaches running north to south are **Magic** (one of the best), **Paradise** (with water sports), Camel, Lagáda, and **Sunny.** All are served by frequent bus service from Kos town. The town of **Kéfalos,** overlooking the sea, used to be a wealthy place that relied more on income brought in by its many sailors and ship captains than by tourism. The seaside is now being rapidly developed, and the village has the largest number of consumer conveniences on the southern part of Kos, including a bank, post office, OTE, tavernas, and shops. It's our beach of choice for those driven out of Kos town by mopeds and music bars.

This 2½-mile-long stretch of gray sand and stone lines a gently arced cove running south from Áyios Stéfanos, site of the island's **Club Med resort** (☎ **0242/71-311**), to the blossoming resort of Kéfalos. On the mid-stretch of beach, the superorganized **Surfpool Windsurfing School** caters weekly programs to German tour groups, but also rents K2 equipment for beginners or semipros by the day. Rates, including wetsuits, are 5,500 Drs ($22.90) per hour, or 20,000 Drs ($83.35) for 5 hours, which can be used up over several days. In high season, brisk offshore breezes provide swift sailing but few waves, an ideal combination for racing back and forth parallel to the seashore. The colorful presence of so many windsurfers and sailboats (rented at Club Med) make up much of Kéfalos's scenic appeal.

WHERE TO STAY & EAT

Newly developed Kéfalos has many rooms-to-let complexes with little personality, and a few good-value hotels. Most of the beachside ones have small restaurants, but we found two casual places on the sand that really appealed. The **Restaurant Corner,** in the middle of the beach (☎ **0242/71-223**), serves only those specials that take advantage of the day's fish catch, 12,000 Drs ($50) per kilo, a bargain for such ambience. The octopus, lightly battered, fried, and served with oregano and lemon is great. **Captain John,** at the south end of the beach (☎ **0242/71-152**), has an international menu and attracts the biggest morning crowd with its 8:30am opening and large variety of breakfast eats. Both places serve lunch and dinner daily, have inexpensive food and local wines, and don't accept credit cards.

Hotel Kokalakis. Kéfalos, 853 01 Kos. ☎ **0242/71-466.** 42 rms, all with bath (shower). 8,800 Drs ($36.65) single or double. Rates include breakfast. No credit cards.

This was one of the first hotels here, and claims a prime location just off the quiet main street on the beach. The balconied rooms, most overlooking the small pool and the sea, are simple and whitewashed. There's a rattan bar next to the pool for snacks and drinks, and a lobby lounge and breakfast area. The pool is open to the public for 500 Drs ($2.10). The front desk also rents Jeeps at a good price of 18,000 Drs ($75) per day.

Hotel Kordistos. Kéfalos, 853 01 Kos. ☎ **0242/71-251.** 21 rms, all with bath (shower). TEL. 7,500 Drs ($31.25) single; 9,500 Drs ($39.60) double. Rates include breakfast. EURO, MC, V.

This is another good choice, though the quiet sea-facing back rooms overlook some unfinished (illegal), permanently halted construction. The well-kept simple twin-bedded rooms have small balconies.

Sacallis Inn. Kéfalos, 853 01 Kos. ☎ **0242/71-010.** 25 rms, all with bath (shower). TEL. 7,800 Drs ($32.50) single; 9,800 Drs ($40.85) double. Rates include breakfast. V.

Tony and Maria Sacallis's inn is well designed and very appealing. Large rooms are spic 'n' span, with fresh carpeting, modern facilities, and tiled balconies, most over-looking the picturesque Kastri islet and the azure sea. There's a large beachside pa-tio with a bar and a nice lawn. There's a Greek/continental sea-view taverna, and additional rooms are on the way.

SIDE TRIPS TO TURKEY

Many visitors to Kos find themselves staring longingly at the Turkish coastline, imag-ining an excursion into exotic Asia Minor. Boats to Bodrum, Turkey, now leave twice daily from the main harbor; ask the tourist police for ships' agents and schedules. (Tuesday and Friday are bazaar days in Bodrum.) The round-trip fare (including "taxes" and "harbor fees") is 11,500 Drs ($47.90). You can usually buy tickets on the boat, though some agents may require submission of your passport and fee 1 day in advance of your trip. Contact the tourist police regarding any necessary papers, since politically motivated visa regulations and rules change frequently.

4 Kálymnos

183 nautical miles E of Piraeus

Kálymnos is best known for natural sponges, but the island also offers some out-of-the-way beaches, a few resort developments, and—if you can get off the beaten track—peace and quiet rarely found on its better-known neighbors, Rhodes and Kos.

The thriving sponge-fishing industry (10% of Greece's total output) used to make Kálymnos refreshingly autonomous. Now the industry has fallen on hard times, and to compensate for this loss the island has amassed the largest fishing fleet in Greece, more than 1,000 registered ships.

Tourism is also being actively courted. Unfortunately, like its better-known Dodecanese neighbors, Kálymnos has been hit by the scourge of tour groups. Some of the best hotels in areas that are now overbuilt—such as the beach communities of Massoúri and Myrtiés—are rented by Scandinavian tourist companies for the en-tire season, making it difficult for the independent traveler. If it's a Greek retreat that you seek in July or August, head farther out to Emboriós or to inland villages.

ESSENTIALS

GETTING THERE & DEPARTING **By Plane** There's a new airport on Kálymnos, but no regular air service was offered at press time.

By Boat One car-ferry leaves Piraeus for Kálymnos daily, via Léros and Pátmos; schedules should be confirmed in Athens at **Tourist Information** (☎ **143**) or at the **Piraeus Port Authority** (☎ **01/451-1311**). There is irregular service (about five times a week) between Kálymnos and the other Dódecanese islands; in high season there's twice-daily service to Kos and Pátmos. There are once-weekly connections to the Cyclades, Pythagório on Sámos, and Iráklio, Crete. Schedules need to be checked at the port of departure. In high season (June to September) Kálymnos has daily **hydrofoil** connections with Léros, Pátmos, Kos, and Rhodes, and weekly connections with Astypálea, Lipsí, Nísyros, and Tílos—but you should check with a travel agent since this service changes frequently. There's a daily **excursion boat** between Myrtiés and Léros, and in the summer there's service between Mastihári on Kos and Pothiá, sometimes stopping at Psérimos.

VISITOR INFORMATION   The **tourist information office** (☎ **0243/29-310** or 0243/23-138) is just off the northwest corner of the harbor near the excursion boat docks, open daily from 8:30am to 1pm and 2 to 7pm. The **tourist police** (☎ **0243/22-100**) are on the on the east side of the waterfront square Platía Elefthería (just west of the cathedral), where you'll also find several **travel agents,** among them the helpful **Kalymnos Tours** (☎ **0243/28-329;** fax 0243/29-656).

ORIENTATION   Most visitors to Kálymnos arrive at the busy port of Pothiá (Kálymnos town), a rather homely town with a population of 11,000. Orient yourself by the silver-domed **Áyios Nikólaos Cathedral,** near the center of the harbor. The main inland road, **Odós Venizélou,** is on its right. Follow Venizélou several blocks north to the central square, **Platía Kyprou.** Left of the cathedral is **Platía Elefthería,** the harborfront square where most tourist services are found. To the left on the barren hillside above the town is a 30-foot-tall concrete **cross** and nearby the **Christ Our Savior Church,** whose rotund pink basilica is paired with a tall, slim clock tower.

GETTING AROUND   It's easy to walk around Pothiá, but the island itself is large. There is **bus** service between Pothiá and Massoúri via Myrtiés about every 2 hours between 7am and 9pm, more frequently in the summer. Service to Vathý and Emboriós is far less frequent—only 3 days a week when we were there. The **bus station** is just to the right of the cathedral on the waterfront.

Shared **taxis** cost about twice as much as buses on Kálymnos; rates are posted at the taxi stand on Platía Kyprou. Expect to pay about 400 Drs ($1.65) for a shared ride to the beach at Myrtiés. A private cab to Emboriós should cost about 2,800 Drs ($11.65).

There are **moped**-rental shops aplenty. **Hatzilaou-Mamakas Auto Moto Rent** (☎ **0243/28-990;** fax 0243/29-814), with offices in Pothiá, Massoúri, and Myrtiés, has the best selection of vehicles for hire at good prices; a Piaggio Vespa with insurance will cost about 2,800 Drs ($11.65); a Fiat Panda, 15,000 Drs ($62.50).

FAST FACTS   The **taxi stand** in Pothiá is on Platía Kyprou, a few blocks inland on Venizélou Street from the harbor behind the cathedral, and the **police** (☎ **0243/29-301**) are just beyond it to the left. The **OTE** and **post office** are to the right above the taxi square. Several **banks** are located on the east side of Platía Elefthería (just west of the cathedral).

POTHIÁ

In the middle of the pier is a modern bronze sculpture of a nude sponge diver, arms raised above his head; perhaps he should be viewed upside-down for maximum effect. This is the work of the local sculptor Michael Kokkinos, whose many other sculptures pop up in the oddest, most pleasant places.

Cream-colored **Áyios Nikólaos Cathedral** is a treasure trove of icons and frescoes. Indeed, this is one of the most elaborate churches in the Dodecanese, since it was the object of tribute by the well-to-do sponge fishermen and their families.

You can't leave Kálymnos without learning something about the islanders' nearly extinct occupation—**sponge diving.** The industry dates back to 1700 when divers, weighted by a stone belt, would dive 30 to 50 feet down (holding their breath), and collect up to 10 sponges per dive. The sponges, animals living in plantlike colonies on rocks at the bottom of the sea, were then cleaned and treated. In 1885 the Skafandre (a primitive diving suit) made it possible for the divers to remain underwater at depths of 50 to 125 feet for nearly an hour! In heavy, rubberized canvas suits, with an air tube attached to a fishbowl helmet, men would walk the sea bottom, cutting sponges with their knives and gathering them with racquet-style baskets. On board, other workers would trample the sponges to squeeze out the dark membrane and milky juices. Each year on May 10 the ships would depart from Kálymnos for the annual harvest, after much celebration, prayer, and a blessing from the high priest of Ághios Nikólaos. On October 30 another festival was held to thank God for those who returned home safely.

The riskiness of this occupation, in which many died or were crippled by the "bends," reduced the number of divers from several thousand to about 80. Today the fleets sail north to nearby Sámos and Ikaría, or south of Crete to the Libyan Sea, and the men wear modern scuba gear. The export of sponges has declined because of competition from plastic sponges, from the poorer quality natural sponges processed in the Philippines and Malaysia, and from pollution in the Mediterranean. Nonetheless, on a reduced scale this industry still thrives. Incidentally, many Kalymniots immigrated to Florida after the World War II, settling in Tampa and Tarpon Springs to continue their trade off the coasts of The Bahamas.

To get to the **Astor Workshop of Sea Sponges** (☎ **0243/29-815**), take the stairs at the left of the pier, past the tavernas up into town. About halfway up, a concrete path on your right leads to the workshop, where you can see each stage of preparation: the sponges' blackish original color, their softening after being beaten with sticks to loosen pebbles and fibers, and the subsequent whitening after a bath in sulfuric acid. Then workers trim them into a round shape with gardening shears. Sponges are for sale, priced according to size and grade.

WHERE TO STAY

If you want to make quiet Kálymnos your headquarters in the Dodecanese, you might stay in noisy Pothiá for a night until you find your own retreat (probably near Myrtiés/Massoúri). Since tourism has only recently arrived, many of the newest and brightest accommodations are to be found in private rooms. Pothiá's **Tourist Information Office** (☎ **0243/29-130**) can point you in the right direction; expect to pay about 6,000 Drs ($25) for a double with private shower in Pothiá and a little less in the villages. Accommodations are available from mid-April to mid-October unless otherwise noted.

Hotel Panorama. Ammoudára, Pothiá, 852 00 Kálymnos. ☎ **0243/23-138.** 13 rms, all with bath (shower). 6,000 Drs ($25) single; 9,000 Drs ($37.50) double. No credit cards.

This sparkling three-tiered hotel is on the hill off the northwest corner of the harbor, above the sponge-factory lane. Themelis and Desiree Koutouzi opened their marble and stucco inn in 1989. The lower-level rooms have large patios, while all enjoy a wonderful breeze and fine views over the harbor. It's a good idea to call in advance to arrange for someone to meet you at the boat; the walk uphill is fairly strenuous if you're carrying a large bag.

Hotel Pátmos. Áyíou Nikólao, Pothiá, 852 00 Kálymnos. ☎ **0243/22-750.** 15 rms, all with bath (shower). 2,800 ($11.65) single; 5,000 Drs ($20.85) double. No credit cards.

Directly behind the tourist information hut is this small, aging pension that's open year-round. Its compact, well-tended rooms in the heart of the harbor are managed by the jovial, Greek-only-speaking Christos Maragous, who allows guests to keep their rooms until 5pm if they're catching the late boat.

Olympic Hotel. Áyíou Nikólao, Pothiá, 852 00 Kálymnos. ☎ **0243/28-801.** Fax 0243/ 29-314. 41 rms, all with bath (shower). TEL. 8,400 Drs ($35) single; 13,400 Drs ($55.85) double. Rates include breakfast. AE, MC, V.

This large, modern, all-white hotel, with four stories and an elevator, dominates the northwest corner of the harbor. The large rooms have tiny bathrooms but good-sized balconies overlooking the harbor and potentially noisy *paralía*. Breakfast is served in the large, sunny lobby and there's a rooftop terrace for snacks and sunning.

WHERE TO EAT

There are several feed-the-day-tripper pizza and moussaká cafes on the central port opposite the excursion ferries, but if you take a short walk to the left side of the harbor you'll be rewarded by some fine, authentic Greek food.

Afrismeno Kyma Ouzerí / Taverna Kosari. On the port. ☎ **0243/23-427.** Main courses 1,000–3,000 Drs ($4.25–$12.50). No credit cards. Daily 11am–2am. GREEK.

This friendly taverna / ouzerí plays it both ways with grilled meat and fish, simple *mezédes,* and traditional stews. It's casual but delightful for a seaside lunch with octopi hanging out to dry. Try some cooked in the typical Kalymniot way.

Kálymnos Yacht Club (NOK). ☎ **0243/29-239.** Main courses 750–2,000 Drs ($3.15–$8.35). No credit cards. Daily 8am–3pm and 6:30–11pm. GREEK.

One of Pothiá's better eateries and a delightful place to watch the yachts at night is the Naftikós Ómilos, an old seafarers' club draped in fishnets with a huge mural of a sponge fisherman (what else?) floating above a background of the city. You can eat a hearty Greek meal of simple, inexpensive fish or meat dishes, surrounded by crusty old Greek sailors and local youngsters. It's the past and future of the island's seafarers, and it's open year-round.

Taverna Ksefteris. Christos St. ☎ **0243/28-642.** Main courses 800–1,600 Drs ($3.35–$6.65). No credit cards. Daily 11:30am–11pm. GREEK.

When you get really hungry, head up Venizélou (to the right of the cathedral) off the harbor, take the first right, and find this local favorite on the left. The same family has operated this come-into-our-kitchen taverna for nearly a century, and their quiet back garden is a treat. Try the plump *souzoukákia* or huge, freshly made *dolmádes.* Open year-round.

POTHIÁ AFTER DARK

One of Pothiá's better late-night drink-and-snack spots is **Mike's Piano Bar** (☎ 0243/29-221), otherwise known as the **Do-Re-Mi.** This popular rusticated stone lodge seems to attract a cross section of tourists, yachters, and Kalymniots until very late (if you stay late enough, you can sample the breakfast menu). You'll find the Do-Re-Mi next to the tourist information office, behind the portside Poseidon statue. Nearby is another good social spot called the **Scirocco Café-Bar** (no phone), an open-air nightspot particularly popular with ferry watchers because of its fine view of the Piraeus car-ferry pier.

EXPLORING AROUND THE ISLAND

You might like to share a cab (that will seat four) for a **round-the-island tour;** the cost is about 10,000 Drs ($41.65) for 4 hours or 18,000 Drs ($75) for 8 hours.

Kálymnos Tours (☎ 0243/28-329) offers an English-language bus tour around the island twice a week for about 4,000 Drs ($16.65), as well as round-the-island swim and barbecue cruises and daily boat trips.

Many of the island's most important sites are along the east-west road that bisects the island; though they're often scenic, they're not top-rated in significance. Just outside Pothiá is the small **Kástro Hryssoherías** ("Golden Hand"), a castle of the Knights of St. John which offers a splendid view of the west coast. At **Péra Kástro,** above the old capital of **Horió,** you can see small white chapels clinging like barnacles to the rocky hillside around the remains of a 10th-century Byzantine fortress. Beyond Horió, at Pigádia, is the island's most revered shrine, the **Church of Jesus of Jerusalem,** with the ruins of a domed basilica and some columns that were built over what is now thought to be the ancient Sanctuary of Apollo.

Kandoúni is the first sandy part of the Platís Yiálos western coast. Ticky-tacky hotels and rooms line this beach and **Linária,** the next cove. The narrow, soiled beach is crowded, with strong, direct winds that make it rough for swimming. We suggest continuing north along the oleander-lined road to **Myrtiés,** a gray sand-and-pebble beach resort below a commercial stretch of road, or better yet, to **Massoúri,** a more stylish resort.

MYRTIÉS

Just half a mile away from Myrtiés across the shimmering crystal-blue water is the small island of **Télendos,** with its several houses looking square at this village. Local boats will take you across for 150 Drs (65¢) if you're not up to swimming to it.

Where to Stay

Atlantis Hotel. Myrtiés, 852 00 Kálymnos. ☎ **0243/47-497.** 17 rms, all with bath (shower). TEL. 6,600 Drs ($27.50) single or double. MC, V.

This old-fashioned hotel and restaurant offers the friendliest, homiest service in town. The large terrazzo-floored lobby is decorated with local ceramics and weavings. The bright, large rooms have big bathrooms and new simple furnishings, most of them with a small kitchen and refrigerator; we preferred the second-floor rooms with balconies and fine sea views. The popular taverna serves seafood and grilled meats in the evenings.

Hotel Myrsina. Myrtiés, 852 00 Kálymnos. ☎ **0243/47-997.** 40 rms, all with bath (shower). TEL. 8,000 Drs ($33.35) single; 9,300 Drs ($38.75) double. EURO, MC, V.

One of the nicest hotels in this area—newly built, with a large pool and grand sea views. Spacious balconies look over the road to the bay, making the pleasant but ordinary rooms something special. The bad news is the group hammerlock, so that only the odd rooms are available to individuals in the high season.

Themis Hotel. Myrtiés, 852 00 Kálymnos. ☎ **0243/47-230** or 0243/47-893. 9 rms, all with bath (shower). 6,600 Drs ($27.50) single; 8,000 Drs ($33.35) double. No credit cards.

If you like the sound of water lapping beneath your window, you should try this little hotel on the harbor down from the church. The hardworking family that runs it and its busy restaurant spent many years in Montréal. If they're full, try the handsome new Zephyros Hotel across the street.

Where to Eat

Restaurant Argo. Main street, Myrtiés. ☎ **0243/47-825.** Main courses 1,000–2,100 Drs ($4.15–$8.75). No credit cards. Daily 11am–2am. GREEK.

This simple grill offers a good variety of meat and some fish dishes. (Ask what's fresh before you commit yourself to a meal there.) The best thing about it is the terrace dining area with stunning bay views.

MASSOÚRI

Massoúri, the best-developed resort on the island, is the next beach north of Myrtiés. Small hotels, private houses, restaurants, and tourist shops crowd the coastal road above a long picturesque rock-and-sand beach. On our last visit we found it among the most pleasant we visited anywhere. The people are friendly, the accommodations are excellent, and there's plenty of good food and even a little nightlife. Groups do have a lock on most of the rooms in the high season, but in the spring and fall there'll be plenty of rooms available. We suggest that you save time and even money by contacting **Advance Travel** (☎ 0243/48-148) on the main street. **Massouri Holidays** (☎ 0243/47-626) also books some local apartments, as well as exchanging money, selling maps, renting safe-deposit boxes, and offering telephone service.

Where to Stay

Advance Travel and Massouri Holidays book some of Massoúri's 100-odd rooms to rent; local apartments in a quiet area rent for 9,200 Drs ($38.35) a night with kitchenette, shower, and twin beds. Other choices are **Niki's Pension** (☎ 0243/47-201) and **Lina's Studios** (☎ 0243/47-017), both nearby above the road, commanding fine vistas of the sea and nearby islands; expect to pay about 7,500 Drs ($31.25) for a double.

✪ **Fatolitis Apartments.** Massoúri, 852 00 Kálymnos. ☎ **0243/47-615.** 11 studios, all with bath (shower). 7,000 Drs ($29.15) studio for two; 9,200 Drs ($38.35) studio for three. No credit cards.

This multitiered cluster of small studios tumbles down from the main road below the cheerful wicker and flower-print decor of the Fatolitis Snack Bar. The family owners run a clean, stylish place with potted plants, large sea-view verandas for lounging, and simple, natural-wood furnishings. The two- and three-bed studios have a fridge and kitchenette. A great deal if you can book one!

Hotel Massouri Beach. Massoúri, 852 00 Kálymnos. ☎ **0243/47-555.** Fax 0243/47-177. 32 rms, all with bath (shower). TEL. 8,250 Drs ($34.40) single; 10,500 Drs ($43.75) double. Rates include breakfast. EURO, MC, V.

This beachside hotel has modern rooms, complete with heating and breakfast—a pretty good deal. The hotel has a wonderful sea-view terrace and a small bar; be sure to ask for a sea-view room to take advantage of the beachfront location.

Hotel Plaza. Massoúri, 852 00 Kálymnos. ☎ **0243/47-134.** 60 rms, all with bath (shower). TEL. 10,500 Drs ($43.75) single; 13,200 Drs ($55) double. Rates include breakfast. No credit cards.

We liked the sea-facing doubles and the big pool with its own bar at this large, group-oriented hotel. It's quite spacious, with breakfast and dining geared to lots of patrons, but it's a quality Class B inn with Class C prices.

Where to Eat

Aegean Tavern. Main street, Massoúri. No phone. Main courses 800–2,100 Drs ($3.35–$8.75). No credit cards. Daily noon–midnight. GREEK.

George Pizanias returned home after many years of operating a Greek restaurant outside Atlanta to open this charming new place. It's above the street, so you miss the passing vehicles and catch the evening breeze. The service is friendly and the food is fresh and somewhat updated, with less oil than usual and attractively presented; we tried standards like a country salad, moussaká and *saganáki*—all superb.

Matheos Restaurant. Main street. Massoúri. ☎ **0243/47-184.** Main courses 900–2,400 Drs ($3.75–$10). EURO, MC. Daily noon–midnight. GREEK.

Irene and George Matheos, who were the cooks at the Aegean Fare Restaurant in Boston for 20 years, own and operate this pleasant taverna above the road on the north side of town. From their freshly made fare, we liked the *skordaliá,* stuffed tomatoes, and various lamb dishes. Friendly service, too.

EMBORIÓS

Everyone will tell you that the best beaches accessible by car are along the northwest coast above Massoúri between **Aryinóndas** (where the frequent public bus ends) and **Emboriós.** If you've missed the twice-weekly bus from Pothiá or the daily excursion boat from Myrtiés (which costs 1,800 Drs/$7.50 round-trip), you can take a moped or an older cab from Aryinóndas. We spent a magical day in Emboriós and the surrounding hills. After dining in a nearly empty taverna on the beach, swimming in clean water, and walking in the craggy hills where few tourists tread, we were convinced that this is the place for long-term visitors to Kálymnos.

There's a scattering of rooms to rent, mostly attached to (or upstairs from) a taverna. During our visit, **Harry's Apartments and Restaurant** (☎ **0243/47-434**) was the most sophisticated choice. Both the fine pension and taverna lie close to the bay, around a shaded garden. Each of six apartments has a small kitchen; two should plan to pay 9,800 Drs ($40.85) a night. Call ahead for reservations before you make the trip north. Eight very simple double rooms are 6,300 Drs ($26.25) a night at the **Pension Pizanias** (☎ **0243/47-277**), attached to the tasty **Restaurant Themis.**

ELSEWHERE AROUND THE ISLAND

Southwest of Pothiá is the village of **Vothiní** and below it the sandy beach of **Vliháda** on its own quiet little bay, which is much less crowded than the west-coast beaches.

Another good area to explore is east of Pothiá, where a winding mountain road takes you to **Vathý,** at the head of a fjord; thousands of mandarin trees fill the verdant valley along the 3-mile road to **Stimeniá.**

5 Léros

171 nautical miles E of Piraeus

For years isolated Léros, renowned in mythology as the island of Diana, was best known for its mental health hospitals. Despite this reputation and Greece's strong military presence here, Léros is now trying to lure tourists to its rocky shores and tranquil bays. The calming, hilly landscape and unaffected lifestyle offer a haven for some; others find the place too tame. We suggest that if this island appeals to you, it might be best if you could visit on a day excursion or make a stopover on the way to or from Pátmos; if you change your mind, you can always move on to your next destination. If you love the island, so much the better. Just be aware that Léros is nearly deserted in May, June, and September but absolutely packed in July and August—make your hotel plans accordingly.

ESSENTIALS

GETTING THERE & DEPARTING **By Plane** **Olympic Airways** offers one flight daily between Athens and Léros. Call its office in Athens (☎ **01/926-7251**) or in Plátanos, Léros (☎ **0247/22-844**), for information.

By Boat One car-ferry leaves daily from Piraeus (an 11-hour trip) in high season, three times weekly the rest of the year. There are **excursion boats** every day between the main port of Lakkí and Pátmos, and daily excursions between Kálymnos and Léros, with less frequent caïques from Ayía Marína to Lipsí, Nísyros, and Astipálea.

In summer there's daily **hydrofoil** service from the small port of Ayía Marína to Pátmos, Kos, and Rhodes, and weekly to Astypálea, Lipsí, Nísyros, and Tílos—be sure to check with a travel agent since the schedules change frequently. **DRM Travel,** in Ayía Marína (☎ **0247/24-303**), is the hydrofoil agent on Léros.

VISITOR INFORMATION   **DRM Travel and Tourism,** in Ayía Marína (☎ **0247/24-303;** fax 0247/24-303) or Alínda (☎ **0247/23-502**), is an excellent resource for independent travelers. Chris Christine Kokkonis can help with hotel, pension, and villa bookings, and recommend the best local restaurants and island tours. She also arranges tours and/or accommodations on Lipsí, Nísyros, Astipálea, and Tílos, as well as on Pátmos, Sými, and Ikaría.

ORIENTATION   Most boats call at **Lakkí,** a dull and rather oppressive port on the southwestern side of the island. The most visually arresting sights here are the distinctively Fascist buildings lining the harbor. The massive proportions and stream-lined shapes recall the presence of Italian troops during the first half of this century. (Lakkí's excellent natural harbor was the main port for the Italian navy in the eastern Mediterranean.) Most of the better hotels, beaches, restaurants, and other tourist services can be found only a few miles due north, beginning in **Pandéli** (our favorite village) and ending in the gray-gravel beach town of **Alínda** (the most developed base for visitors). Midway is **Plátanos,** the capital, a picturesque market town with stately 19th-century homes built on tiers below an impressive Venetian fortress. Boxy, whitewashed, flat-roofed houses cluster around the bustling main square.

A few excursion boats and an occasional hydrofoil dock at **Ayía Marína,** in between Alínda and Plátanos. The airport is to the far north, near Parthéni, close to some of the island's best beaches. At the far south of the island is **Kserókambos** (Xirócampos), the island's only sanctioned campground; this is also where you can catch the daily excursion boat to Kálymnos.

GETTING AROUND   Léros covers only 20 square miles and is easy to get around on foot or by bike. There are **bicycles** and **mopeds** for rent in all the main tourist centers; expect to pay 500 Drs ($2.10) a day for a bike and at least five times that for a motorized two-wheeler.

Buses run from Plátanos six times a day south to Kserókambos (Xirócampos) via Lakkí, and four times a day north to Parthéni via Alínda.

FAST FACTS   Lakkí and Plátanos both have banks, telephone exchanges, and post offices. The island's main **bus station** and **taxi stand** are on the main road near the central square in Plátanos. The **police station** (☎ **0247/22-222**) is in Ayía Marína.

EXPLORING THE ISLAND

If you want to explore but don't have much time, consider a 2- to 3-hour taxi tour of the island with an English-speaking guide/driver for approximately 8,000 Drs ($33.35). Among its pleasures is a visit to a local beekeeper who sells honey straight from the comb.

If it's a beach you crave, head north to **Blefoúti** where there's also a simple taverna. In the next cove south of Pandéli is the less-congested beach at **Vromólithos,** where you'll find a taverna that's open only in the summer. On the west coast is a delightful little church, **Áyios Isidóros,** built on an outcrop in Gourná Bay; you can reach the well-tended church by way of a causeway.

WHERE TO STAY

We'd suggest staying in Pandéli and using it as your base for touring the island. The small beach resorts at Ayía Marína and Alínda are nearly connected and offer a wider and better choice of accommodations and dining, though they lack charm. Avoid the main port of Lakkí; take a taxi into Pandéli or Alínda for more hospitable housing. As mentioned above, there's camping at Kserókambos (Xirócampos); **Camping Leros** (☎ **0247/23-372**) offers hot showers, a dining area with a snack bar, and a laundry room for 900 Drs ($3.75) a night.

In central **Plátanos,** there's the quiet family-run **Eleftheria Hotel** (☎ **0247/23-550**), with nice, comfortable doubles for 5,700 Drs ($23.75).

IN PANDÉLI

There are many rooms for rent above the tavernas at Pandéli's waterfront; most of these places, such as the **Alex, Rena, Kavos,** and **Pandéli,** which charge about 6,300 Drs ($26.25) for a double room with private shower, can be booked through **DRM Travel** (☎ **0247/24-303**).

Pension Afroditi. Pandéli, 854 00 Léros. ☎ **0247/23-477.** 10 rms, 8 with bath (shower). 5,300 Drs ($22.10) single; 6,600 Drs ($27.50) double. No credit cards.

A simple pension with reasonably adequate facilities and a nice garden set back from the harbor.

IN ALÍNDA

The town beach is fairly attractive and sheltered, but it's also busy and kids on motorbikes do their best to destroy the peace. We suggest that you investigate the many good accommodations away from the motorbike madness. Our suggestions are: the **Ara Hotel** (☎ **0247/24-140;** fax 0247/24-194), at the top of the hill behind the Alinda Hotel, with a swimming pool, 10 studios at 10,000 Drs ($41.65) for two, and 8 apartments at 12,000 Drs ($50) for three; the **Chrissoula Apartments** (☎ **0247/22-451**), 500 yards off the north end of the beach, with a very nice new swimming pool, 16 studios from 6,600 Drs ($27.50), and 9 apartments from 10,600 Drs ($44.15), and EuroCard, MasterCard, and Visa accepted; and our favorite even without a pool, **Effie's Apartments** (☎ **0247/24-459;** fax 0247/23-507), 50 yards off the middle of the beach (ask at the Finikas Taverna), with 8 apartments from 10,500 Drs ($43.75), and EuroCard and MasterCard accepted.

Alínda Hotel. Alínda, 854 00 Léros. ☎ **0247/23-266.** 18 rms, 13 with bath (tub). 5,300 Drs ($22.10) single or double without bath, 8,000 Drs ($33.35) single or double with bath. Rates include breakfast. EURO, MC, V.

The Alínda is situated on the *paralía,* but far enough off it for a semblance of quiet. The back rooms face an attractive garden and orchard. The management is friendly and helpful, and there's a good restaurant.

WHERE TO EAT
IN PANDÉLI

Maria's Taverna. Paralía, Alínda. No phone. Menu items 300–950 Drs ($1.25–$3.95); fish from 12,000 Drs ($50) per kilo. No credit cards. Daily 5–11pm. GREEK.

Perhaps best of all in Pandéli, this old and informal taverna offers traditional fare and fish at prices that are positively low.

Savana Bar. On Pandéli beach. ☎ **0247/23-969.** Snacks/desserts 350–1,000 Drs ($1.45–$4.15). No credit cards. Daily 8:30am–2am. CONTINENTAL.

This very popular beachside bar serves partygoers a late breakfast of fresh juices, varied coffees, croissants, pancakes, and omelets. As the sun wanes, they turn their attention to grilled sandwiches, mixed tropical drinks, and ice-cream concoctions.

IN ALÍNDA

Finikas Taverna. Paralía, Alínda. ☎ **0247/22-695.** Main courses 1,000–1,900 Drs ($4.15–$7.90). EURO, MC, V. Daily 9am–11:30pm. GREEK.

This casual place has checkered tablecloths draping wooden tables at the water's edge. You can dine under the shade-providing tamarisks or in the back garden and sample stuffed vegetables, good lamb dishes, and a flavorful *horiátiki.*

Theofilos Cafe/Pizza Restaurant. Paralía, Alínda. ☎ **0247/22-497.** Main courses 900–2,600 Drs ($3.75–$10.85). No credit cards. Daily noon–11pm. GREEK/CONTINENTAL.

We had a sumptuous little meal at this white-canopied, outdoor diner overlooking the beach. The menu features delicately prepared moussaká and a large selection of great pizza, all at modest prices. Be sure to go inside for a peek at the Theophilos-like painting.

6 Pátmos

163 nautical miles E of Piraeus

Pátmos has an unusually long tourist season, thanks to the moderating sea breezes that sweep across the island year-round. Thousands of Christians make a pilgrimage to the religious shrines of Pátmos annually, but the majority of visitors arrive on Mediterranean cruise ships and depart the same day. Any traveler seeking peace and quiet, good-hearted, gentle Greek people, and a disarmingly sophisticated social scene should stick around. Pátmos surprises all who stay long enough for a second look.

From a distance, Pátmos is all gray stone: barren rocks, no beaches, ascetic, just a rough-hewn pedestal for the huge walled fortress of the Monastery of St. John. As you round Point Hesmeris, you'll see the hidden port of Skála, cluttered with bars, tavernas, and hotels.

Since antiquity the isolated, arid island has been considered the "Siberia" of the Mediterranean world. The Romans immortalized the island by sending John the Theologian (the Younger) into exile there in A.D. 96 during the emperor Domitian's widescale persecution of all Christians in the empire. Saint John (Book of Revelation) makes this reference to his sojourn: "I dwelled in an island which is called Patmos, as to preach the word of God and have faith in the martyrdom suffered by Jesus Christ."

For centuries after Saint John's historic visit, Patmians continued to trade with the mainland port of Miletus, their link to Asia Minor, and to adhere to the Artemis cult worship practiced in Ephesus. In 313 the emperor Constantine officially recognized Christianity. Pátmos fell into relative obscurity, endured devastating raids through the Islamic period, and was eventually retaken by the Byzantine Empire.

In 1088 a devout monk, Christodoulos, went to Alexius I Comnenus to ask permission to found a monastery dedicated to Saint John on the island. Alexius realized the political favor such a bequest could earn him with the already-powerful Christian church. The 1088 Chrysobull (Alexius's imperial decree that is still proudly displayed in the monastery) granted to the monks of Christodoulos "the right to be absolute rulers to all eternity." This Chrysobull (it also exempted Pátmos from government taxation or judicial interference and granted the monastery the right to own ships tax-free) shaped the future development of the island.

Pátmos's autonomous religious community flourished. The centuries of Turkish domination that withered Greek culture elsewhere left Pátmos almost untouched. The Monastery of St. John became the finest cultural and theological school in the country, even prospering under the Italian occupation. After World War II Pátmos was reunited with the Greek nation.

Today Pátmos is one of the few Greek islands that has benefited from tourism without having to sell its soul. The monastery's real estate monopoly ensured slow, careful development of the land. The monks have never condoned nude or topless sunbathing, which has kept away the more risqué summer tourists. No military construction was permitted, so there's no commercial airport on the island (many foreign residents use Olympic's private helicopter landing pad in Skála). The revenue produced by Holy Land day-trip visitors is enough to keep Skála thriving; the less commercial sections of the island are supported by the elite foreign population. The fortuitous combination of historical and social factors has made Pátmos a unique, unspoiled island "sacred" to many.

ESSENTIALS

GETTING THERE & DEPARTING   By Ferry   There's one ferry departure daily (except Sunday) from Piraeus; it's a long, sometimes-arduous trip. Check with the **Piraeus Port Authority** (☎ **01/451-1311**) for schedules. There are daily car-ferries to Léros, Kálymnos, Kos, and Rhodes. There are three ferries a week going to Sámos and once a week going to Ikaría—both in the Northeast Aegean group. Once a week the Sámos ferry continues on to Híos, Lésbos, Límnos, and Kavála. In high season there are daily **excursion boats** to the nearby islands of Arkí and Lipsí, and from Pythagório, Sámos.

By Hydrofoil   This is the fastest but most expensive method of transport; **hydrofoils** connect Pátmos four times weekly (daily in summer) with Rhodes (4 hours) and Kos ($1^1/_2$ hours), and three times a week (twice daily in summer) with Sámos (1 hour). Contact Astoria Shipping Agency (☎ **0247/31-205**) at the port of Skála for schedules.

VISITOR INFORMATION   The **Municipal Tourist Information Office** in Skála is located in the large white building near the middle of the main pier (☎ **0247/31-666**); the tourist office entrance is at the rear. The staff can help you find a room, hotel, or house to rent. It's open daily: April to October from 8am to 9pm and in winter from 9am to 3pm. Ask about a helpful free publication—*Pátmos Summertime.*

The **Astoria Shipping Agency,** on the *paralía* near the south end of the main pier (☎ **0247/31-205;** fax 0247/31-975), changes money, sells ferry and hydrofoil tickets, and books hotels and rooms daily from 8am to 9pm.

GETTING AROUND   The port of Skála is compact enough to walk around with pleasure. We actually enjoy the 30-minute uphill trek on a rough-stone chariot road to visit the Monastery of St. John, and we certainly recommend it for coming down—before dark or with a flashlight. Outside Skála, goat paths lead up and over the many untouristed hillsides to wild, unexpected natural vistas. Hiking around the island will also bring you into contact with the lovely Patmian people, whose deep religious beliefs make them even more hospitable than the average welcoming Greek citizen.

By Bus   The island's **bus stop** is near the south end of the main pier; a schedule is posted. Buses run from Skála to Hóra eight times daily for 140 Drs (60¢), to the beach at Gríkou six times daily for 210 Drs (90¢), and to the beach at Kámbos four times daily for 180 Drs (75¢).

By Boat   During the summer season, local fishermen turn their caïques into beach shuttles and offer daily excursions to many of the island's private coves. You can walk along the harbor and read the chalkboard destination signs hanging off the stern of the boats. These small boats charge 700 Drs ($2.90) each way to Psilí Ámmos or Lámbi, and 400 Drs ($1.45) each way to Kámbos.

By Taxi The **taxi stand** in Skála is on the main pier next to the post office (☎ 0247/31-225). However, taxis are usually grabbed up by repeat visitors or commuting residents who rush off the ferry. If you want to have dinner or spend the evening in Hóra, book a taxi ahead of time; the fare is 1,000 Drs ($4.15), depending on the time of day and season, plus a 100-Dr (40¢) charge for radio calls. A taxi ride to Lámbi is 1,300 Drs ($5.40); to Grígou, 1,700 Drs ($7.10).

By Bicycle Mountain bikes are available at **Theo & Georgio's,** just behind Astoria Shipping, for 1,200 Drs ($5) per day.

By Moped Mopeds afford the greatest freedom of movement. Most roads are paved, so it's not as risky as elsewhere, but be cautious on the gravel-filled, winding, hilly roads. There are moped-rental shops aplenty in Skála; expect to pay 2,000 to 3,000 Drs ($8.35 to $12.50) per day for a single-seater.

By Car Rent A Car Pátmos, at the port near the post office (☎ 0247/32-203), has subcompacts starting at 17,000 Drs ($70.85) per day.

FAST FACTS In Skála the **post office** is located on the right of the large white building near the middle of the main pier, open Monday to Friday from 7:30am to 2pm; and the **police** entrance is in front of the building (☎ 0247/31-303). The **bus station** is to the left (south) toward the end of the pier.

The **hospital** is on the Skála–Hóra road (☎ 0247/31-211). The **OTE** is 300 yards from the port up from the post office, open Monday to Saturday from 9am to 2pm and 5 to 8pm (to 10pm in summer).

SPECIAL EVENTS If you're lucky enough to be in Greece for the Orthodox Easter (late April or early May), you can witness the **Niptíras,** a reenactment of the Last Supper that's performed only on Pátmos (in the square outside the Monastery of St. John) and in Jerusalem. The festivities and holy days extend from the Monday before Easter to the following Tuesday, when there's great feasting and dancing in Xanthos Square.

SKÁLA, HÓRA & ENVIRONS

Most visitors stay at the east-coast port of **Skála** at the island's narrow midriff, where the majority of the island's hotels and rooms are located. To the south, the hilltop **Monastery of St. John** dominates the port in much the same way that the city of Oz dominated the consciousness of those who lived beneath it. Skála is still small enough so that most commercial activity is along the waterfront, with more recent development on the low hill behind the *paralía,* on unpaved back lanes two or three deep.

The jumble of whitewashed homes that cling to the fortresslike walls of this medieval monastery comprise **Hóra** (or "City"). Hóra has been the island's main town since the 11th century, and it's an architectural delight on the order of Líndos, Rhodes. Anyone visiting the island must explore this hilltop village and its monastery, even if only for an hour or two.

The narrow, twisting lanes that encircle the monastery are lined with 6-foot-tall white stucco walls surrounding the private residences of Hóra's international elite. Even during siesta the ornately carved brown wood doors rarely open to reveal the elegant, stylish homes within. The town is a minimecca for the wealthy who scorn the splashier resort islands: actors, writers, publishers, diplomats, tycoons, and their friends. However, Hóra's exclusivity rarely affects the day visitor. The town's streets seem refreshingly deserted, even during the high season.

The wealthy who couldn't get into Hóra have built villas "down below," near the beaches. Their presence and their anonymity add to the mystique that makes Pátmos such a special island.

SEEING THE SIGHTS

The island's two great Christian monuments, the Monastery of St. John and the Holy Cave of the Apocalypse, are of such historical and artistic significance that they should be seen by everyone visiting Pátmos.

Beyond that, if you stay on Pátmos long enough, you'll begin to hear about the hundreds of "must see" sites cherished by the locals. We'll discuss only the sites that you're likely to encounter. Patmophiles may want to read Tom Stone's *Pátmos,* published by Lycabettus Press, and may want to attend the English-language Catholic mass at St. Francis House every Saturday night.

If you walk from the ferry north to the well-marked Astoria Hotel, you'll pass the busy heart of town, **Emmanuel Xanthos Square.** In the maddeningly irregular, whitewashed lanes behind the square are a scattering of hotels and shops. From the square north along the waterfront are several small tavernas, hotels, and bars. Behind is the little "neighborhood" of **Nethia,** where some fine hotel rooms are located. Ten minutes past Nethia on the path curving up to the right and over the hill is the local beach, **Órmos Méloï.**

A little way out in the harbor, opposite the Patmion Hotel, is a large red buoy that marks **"Devil's Rock."** This submerged plateau is marked not only as a warning to sailors, but to keep sinners on their toes! It's said that here, nearly 2,000 years ago, the Devil used to preach to local residents by communing with the spirits of their ancestors. An alternative telling of this folktale suggests that the Devil was Kynops, a local magician sent by priests from the Temple of Apollo to challenge Saint John's influence. In either case, one day the Devil/Kynops offered to enlighten St. John himself, but when he dove underwater to display his powers, Saint John crossed himself and the Devil was halted there, frozen in stone. Though this is a convenient fishing perch, local fishermen avoid it because "the fish caught off this rock smell funny."

Another local landmark you might be curious about is the wrought-iron fencing that encloses a nondescript flat rock, toward the north end of the waterfront. Devoted Patmians have enclosed the stone slab where Saint John is said to have baptized more than 14,000 converts from among the local population.

You might also enjoy a hike up to the site of the ancient city, **Kastélli,** about 20 minutes northwest of Skála, where you can see the remains of a Hellenistic wall, the little church of Áyios Konstandínos, and a spectacular sunset.

The **Simantiri House** (☎ 0247/31-360) belonged to the family of the same name for eight generations, beginning in 1625. Today this superbly restored Venetian-style Patmian mansion is open to the public, daily from 9am to 3pm and 5 to 8pm, for tours. (The best way to find the Simantiri House is to ask for the Zoödóhos Piyí Monastery; it's just down the street.) Admission is 350 Drs ($1.45). The **Zoödóhos Piyí Monastery** (☎ 0247/31-256) is itself a treat to behold; it's open to the public daily from 9am to noon and 3 to 6pm; admission is free.

The Monastery of St. John. ☎ **0247/31-234.** Admission to the museum 500 Drs ($2.10). Open hours change seasonally, but try to arrive between 9 and 10am—call the tourist information office (☎ **0247/31-666**) for current schedule.

The Monastery of St. John was founded in 1088 by the monk Christodoulos. Tall gray stone walls were constructed to protect the hilltop retreat from pirate raids; thus it looks like a solid medieval fortress.

Upon crossing the monastery's main threshold, the visitor is transported by the stillness and ethereal calm into a private world. Supported by heavy gray brick columns, the large covered cistern containing holy water in the center of the courtyard (an ideal bench for contemplation) held wine in the days when 200 monks inhabited Hóra. Except on major Greek Orthodox holidays, the monastery's religious activities are not as impressive as its museum-quality collection of manuscripts, religious icons, Byzantine art, and frescoes.

The **Outer Narthex,** to the left of the entrances, is richly painted with 17th-century frescoes depicting traditional tales from the life of St. John (a flashlight is needed for a thorough examination of the dark chapel). Tour guides meet the day-cruise visitors; their anecdotes of monastic life and vivid descriptions of the many parts of the monastery that are now off-limits make their tours worthwhile.

For centuries the remarkable collection of more than 13,000 documents in the monastery **library** has drawn scholars to Pátmos. The earliest text is a 6th-century fragment from the Gospel of Saint Mark; on Pátmos there are 33 leaves of this priceless work, which has been divided among museums in Leningrad, Athens, Britain, the Vatican, and Vienna. The 1088 Chrysobull issued by Alexius I Comnenus granting the monastery sovereignty over Pátmos is displayed, as well as an 8th-century text of Job and Codex 33, the 10th-century illustrated manuscript of the discourses of Saint Gregory the Theologian. In the **Treasury** are jewels and icons donated by Catherine II and Peter the Great of Russia, and other dignitaries, and the 4th-century B.C. marble tablet describing Orestes' visit to Pátmos.

After 200 years of tourist abuse (many valuable texts were taken back to Europe by visiting scholars), the library and original Treasury have been closed to view. One may visit the well-secured **Treasury-Library-Museum,** where a sampling of the rich vestments, icons, and religious artifacts belonging to the monastery are displayed.

The monastery requests visitors to "Respect the Holy Places, our traditions and our morals by your dignified attire, serious appearance, and your general behavior."

Holy Cave of the Apocalypse. ☎ 0247/31-234. Open hours change seasonally, but try to arrive between 9 and 10am—call the tourist information office (☎ 0247/31-666) for current schedule.

The Monastery of the Apocalypse was built at the site of the grotto where Saint John received his revelation from God. Located just a 5-minute walk down from the hilltop monastery, you can easily visit it on your descent to Skála.

"Dear visitor, the place which you have just entered is sacred," begins the brochure written by Archimandrite Koutsanellos, Superior of the Cave, and handed out to all visitors. The rousing brochure provides an excellent description of the religious significance of each niche in the rocks and the many icons in the cave. The little white-washed monastery that surrounds the cave was the 18th-century home of the Patmias School, an institute of higher learning unparalleled during the Turkish occupation. A large modern structure built after World War II to accommodate the school and a theological seminary dominates the barren hillside above Skála.

Appropriate attire is required: no slacks for women, no shorts for anyone. This dress code applies to everyone visiting any of the island's religious sites, including the other monasteries and nunneries, which have fine frescoes and religious icons. If you're interested in the significance of Pátmos in Christian history, you may want to read Otto Meinardus's *St. John of Pátmos* and the *Seven Churches of the Apocalypse,* published by Lycabettus Press.

WHERE TO STAY

Since there are not many hotels in Skála, the best ones require reservations 2 to 3 months in advance (if you plan to visit Pátmos at Easter, or in July or August). Most hotels are open from April to late October, according to demand.

Last-minute planners should have no trouble finding a room for rent in the surrounding hillsides; if you want to rent a kitchenette apartment or villa on a long-term lease, contact the **Astoria Shipping Agency** (☎ **0247/31-205;** fax 0247/31-975) for more information. At the nearby Méloï Beach is the well-situated, popular **Stefanos Camping** (☎ **0247/31-821**), also known as **Patmos's Flowers Camping.** This convenient campground (a mile from the port) becomes rather crowded during high season; it charges 1,500 Drs ($6.25) for tents and 3,000 Drs ($12.50) for site rental for two people.

Blue Bay Hotel. Skála, 855 00 Pátmos. ☎ **0247/31-165.** Fax 0247/32-303. 22 rms, all with bath (shower). TEL. 12,500 Drs ($52.10) single; 18,500 Drs ($77.10) double. EURO, MC, V.

Reader Robert H. Smith of El Cerrito, California, wrote to insist that we consider this handsome new hotel about 200 yards left from the port. We found it every bit as quiet, immaculate, attractive, and comfortable, and the Karantani family as hospitable, gracious, and helpful as he said. In fact, we found Mr. Smith there again, with his wife and friends—high praise indeed, we think.

Castelli Hotel. Skála, 855 00 Pátmos. ☎ **0247/31-361.** Fax 0247/31-656. 45 rms, all with bath (shower). TEL. 10,000 Drs ($41.65) single; 13,500 Drs ($56.25) double. Rates include breakfast. No credit cards.

Guests are accommodated here in two white stucco blocks framed with brown shutters. From the wood-trimmed balconies, the striking vista can be enjoyed from your own cushioned wrought-iron chairs. The spotless rooms are large with beige tile floors; the common lounge and lobby areas are filled with photographs, flower-print sofas, seashells, fresh-cut flowers from the surrounding gardens, and other knick-knacks of seaside life. Such good care and charm make this a good value.

Hotel Adonis. Skála, 855 00 Pátmos. ☎ **0247/31-103,** or 01/512-1035 in Athens. Fax 0247/32-225. 23 rms, all with bath (shower). TEL. 11,500 Drs ($47.90) single; 16,100 Drs ($67.10) double. Rates include breakfast. EURO, MC, V.

The Patmian-style, white-stucco-and-stone facade, and small rooftop neon sign distinguishes this hotel from the many residences sprouting on the hillside. Fresh, wood-trimmed rooms, with harbor-view balconies (ask for the top floor!) provide quiet and convenient lodging. The new tiled bathrooms even have shower curtains. Breakfast is served on the shaded front porch, within scent of the jasmine-covered arbor.

✪ Hotel Australis. Skála, 855 00 Pátmos. ☎ **0247/31-576.** 19 rms, all with bath (shower). TEL. 10,300 Drs ($42.90) single; 13,500 Drs ($56.25) double. No credit cards.

The welcoming Fokas and Chris Michalis, who spent many years in Australia, run this small, friendly hotel in a blooming hillside oasis that makes it feel like a high-priced villa. The grounds are covered with bright bougainvillea, geraniums, carnations, fuchsias, dahlias, and roses; they've been featured in *Garden Design* magazine. The pleasant communal porch, where breakfast is served, looks out on the harbor. (Their son, Michael, has three handsome new studios over his house on the old road to Hóra.)

Hotel Effie. Skála, 855 00 Pátmos. ☎ **0247/31-298.** Fax 0247/32-700. 35 rms, all with bath (shower). TEL. 10,000 Drs ($41.65) single; 13,500 Drs ($56.25) double. Rates include breakfast. No credit cards.

Turn left before the Old Harbor Restaurant to reach this recently built hotel on the quiet hillside. The rooms are large, light, spare, and spotless, with wood-trimmed balconies with somewhat limited views. The owners, Effie and Nick, make all their guests feel at home and are constantly busy improving the place, with a new garden on its way.

Hotel Ellinis. Skála, 855 00 Pátmos. ☎ **0247/31-275.** Fax 0247/31-846. 40 rms, all with bath (shower). TEL. 10,000 Drs ($41.65) single; 13,500 Drs ($56.25) double.

Located around the port, next to the Fina station at the Méloï end of Skála, is this Class C lodging, with a fountain in front and a wonderful evening view across the harbor to the illuminated village and sky-high monastery. It's run by Christodoulous Grillis and family, giving the otherwise plain accommodations some familial warmth. The family also maintains 14 rental rooms nearby (6,900 Drs/$28.75 for two).

Romeos Hotel. Skála, 855 00 Pátmos. ☎ **0247/31-962.** Fax 0247/31-070. 50 rms, all with bath (shower); 2 suites. TEL. 16,000 Drs ($66.65) single; 23,500 Drs ($97.90) double; 24,000 Drs ($100) suite. Rates include breakfast. EURO, MC, V.

Of all of Skála's newer lodgings, this one on the backstreets behind the OTE is especially commodious, with the biggest pool on the island and a quiet garden. It's a bit of a splurge, but it's a good buy for what you get. Run by a Greek-American family, the Romeos has spotless rooms, with woven-cotton upholstering, simple decor, and countryside-view balconies bringing sea breezes. The rooms are built like semiattached bungalows on a series of tiers on Mt. Kastélli. Another option would be one of the larger honeymoon suites, with matrimonial beds, full baths (with tubs), and a small lounge.

✪ Skála Hotel. Skála, 855 00 Pátmos. ☎ **0247/31-343.** Fax 0247/31-747. 78 rms, all with bath (tub). TEL. 14,000 Drs ($58.35) single; 20,500 Drs ($85.40) double. Rates include breakfast. DC, EURO, MC, V. Closed Nov–Mar.

The Skála, located well off the street behind a lush garden overflowing with arresting pink bougainvillea, has aged like a fine wine to become our favorite lodging in this busy town. Annual improvements include the expanding garden, a large pool with an inviting sun deck and bar, a large breakfast buffet, fridges and adjustable heat in all guest rooms, additional conference and meeting facilities, and even better and more personalized service. The host captain Gríllis and his staff offer guests the kind of hospitality you expect on such a sophisticated island. Some rooms have harbor views, but you'll have to request one well in advance since they're often booked by return guests.

Villa Knossos. Skála, 855 00 Pátmos. ☎ **0247/32-189.** 10 rms, all with bath (tub). 10,000 Drs ($41.65) single or double. No credit cards.

We're always pleased to find good budget choices on these expensive islands, and this small white villa just off the port is a find! Nicos and Despina Mourtzaki have done an impressive landscaping job, enhancing the simple twin-bedded rooms with purple and pink bougainvillea, potted geraniums, and multicolored hibiscus.

WHERE TO EAT

Because of the many foreign residents and long-term tourists, most restaurants and tavernas cater daily to repeat customers, and we found the food usually moderately priced, well prepared, and graciously served. Those restaurants listed below are open from May to September unless otherwise noted.

If you have a sweet tooth, you'll be pleased at the offerings of many local bakeries. The **Edelweiss Pâtisserie** (no phone), one lane behind the *paralía*, stays open late to serve ice cream and pastries to passersby. The traditional **Pratirio Arto** is on the second square behind the main one; it's open Monday to Saturday from 8am to 2pm to sell fresh bread, delicious *tirópitta*, and a variety of dunk-'em biscuits.

The modern, mirrored **Koumanis Bakery** is Skála's premier sweets palace, with three branches serving fine European and Greek delicacies; it's open daily from 8am to 2pm and 4:30 to 10pm to serve the special Patmian *tirópitta*, a cheese pie baked in a crust like a tart, and many of the island's special cookies. We inquired about one specialty, the half-moon *poungí*, which begins with a fragile *kourambiés* dough and then is filled with a mixture of vermicelli, nuts, and honey. They're a sinfully delicious bargain at 240 Drs ($1) each.

✪ **Arion Cafebar.** Paralía, Skála. ☎ **0247/31-595.** Snacks/desserts 500–1,400 Drs ($2.10–$5.85). No credit cards. Daily 8:30am–3am. CONTINENTAL.

Just as day cafe crowds favor the main square, sunset idlers seem to favor the harbor. The elegant old Arion on the port has high ceilings and exposed stone walls. Large old fans stir up a breeze above the long, broad, polished-wood bar. Ornate iron medieval-style wall sconces produce the intimate lighting. Late breakfasts, drinks, snacks, delicious ice-cream concoctions, and coffee are served inside and out.

The Balcony (Jimmy's). Hóra. ☎ **0247/32-115.** Main courses 1,200–2,500 Drs ($5–$10.40). No credit cards. Daily 11am–4pm and 7–11pm. GREEK/INTERNATIONAL.

Near the entrance to the monastery you'll find this simple place with good food, reasonable prices, friendly management, and a great view. Even though we weren't hungry, we thought we ought to try such a convenient place, so we had a fresh village salad with a distinctive cheese, an excellent omelet, and a couple of beers, sat drinking in the scenery, and came away completely satisfied.

Fish Taverna To Pyrofani. Central paralía, Skála. ☎ **0247/31-539.** Main courses 1,000–1,500 Drs ($4.15–$6.25); fish 8,500 Drs ($35.40) per kilo. No credit cards. Daily noon–3pm and 6–11pm. SEAFOOD.

This is our favorite for seafood, next door to the Skála Hotel. Begin with the special *tzatzíki*, have grilled *melanoúri* or *barboúnia*, wine and salad, and it's a Patmian feast! To Pyrofáni, supplied daily by local fishermen, is a casual, portside place for a Saturday-night fish fry or grilled lobster.

Grigoris Grill. Opposite the Skála car-ferry pier. ☎ **0247/31-515.** Main courses 1,400–2,900 Drs ($5.85–$12.10). No credit cards. Daily 6pm–midnight. GREEK.

This is one of Skála's better-known restaurants, formerly the center of Patmian chic. We recommend any of its grilled fish or meat dishes, particularly during the low season, when more care and attention are given to the preparation. Well-cooked veal cutlets, large, tender lamb chops, and the swordfish souvláki are favorites. Gregory's also offers several vegetarian specials.

Olympia Taverna. Theofakosta Sq., Hóra. ☎ **0247/31-543.** Main courses 1,000–1,700 Drs ($4.15–$7.10). No credit cards. Mon–Sat noon–2pm and 6:30–10pm. GREEK.

This taverna, less frequented by tourists because of its low-key presence, is one of our favorites for traditional Greek home-style cooking. On our last supper we dined on octopus *youvétsi*, stuffed aubergine, *hórta* and beet salad, and a sublime slab of cake, all delicious and inexpensive. During the summer they open the roof garden (great views) for open-air dining.

Pandelis Restaurant. One lane back from the Skála port. ☎ **0247/31-230.** Main courses 1,000–2,500 Drs ($4.15–$10.40); fish 8,000 Drs ($33.35) per kilo. No credit cards. Daily 11am–11pm. GREEK.

One of Skála's older establishments prepares delicious food at low prices in a comfortable, homey environment. The Pandelis, located right behind the Astoria Hotel, serves delicious lightly fried calamari and swordfish kebab, as well as a complement of vegetarian entrees. It's a favorite with locals, and open year-round.

✪ **The Patmian House.** Hóra. ☎ **0247/31-180.** Reservations recommended. Main courses 1,800–6,500 Drs ($7.50–$27.10) plus 23% tax and service. No credit cards. Daily 7pm–midnight. Closed Oct–May. GREEK/CONTINENTAL.

It shouldn't surprise you that sophisticated Hóra features one of the best and most interesting Greek restaurants in the entire country, one set in a restored 17th-century dwelling on the back lanes behind Xanthos Square, and glowingly reviewed in *Vogue, The Athenian, European Travel & Life,* and several German and Australian periodicals. Victor Gouras, a Patmian gourmand who worked at several top New York restaurants, and his talented wife, Irene, have created the perfect place for that splurge evening. Nick and Alex Gouras take summers off from their jobs at New York's Periyiali and the chic Aureole to help out in the family business. From several superb hors d'oeuvres we recommend Irene's special *taramosaláta,* her *yigántes* (giant beans) in garlic sauce, *spanakópita,* or the tasty zucchini fritters. The varied selection includes a superb rabbit *stifádo* flavored with juniper berries, a tender, moist lemon chicken, a melt-in-your-mouth veal parmigiana, and a Patmian vegetarian specialty *melitzánes mé revíthia* (an eggplant-and-chickpea casserole). Ask the Gouras family about any fish, steak, or meat specialties of the day, and don't miss the *diplés,* a honey-dipped roll.

Plaza Kaffeterion. On the main Square, Skála. ☎ **0247/31-266.** Snacks/desserts 500–1,100 Drs ($2.10–$4.60). No credit cards. Daily 7am–midnight. CONTINENTAL.

Start your day in the lively square across from the post office. This place is the most local in feel; favorite dishes include continental breakfast or a hearty English or American breakfast. The Plaza is also popular for early-evening drinks.

EXPLORING ELSEWHERE AROUND THE ISLAND: THE BEACHES & BEYOND

Other than the towns of Skála and Hóra, most of Pátmos's limited development has centered around the beach areas. Short-term visitors should allow a day to visit Hóra and the Monastery of St. John; after that, the island's exquisite beaches can be explored on foot (as we prefer) or by caïque excursions from Skála.

The town beach, a sand-and-pebble patch just 500 yards from the ferryboat pier, offers no privacy; it's usually filled with Greek families who don't mind sunbathing in full view of the clothed tourists who stroll along the waterfront promenade.

The nearby **Méloï Beach,** just a 15-minute walk northeast of Skála, is a little more secluded though not the island's best. Virile young Greek men who've come with their tourist girlfriends are likely to be playing cassette tapes of the latest European hits. NUDITY IS FORBIDDEN signs are prominently posted, and the locals complain when this rule is ignored. The beachside **Méloï Restaurant** (☎ **0247/31-888**) is a good taverna and a very pleasant place to while away the evening.

It takes a moped, taxi (600 Drs/$2.50), excursion boat (same price as taxi), or sturdy legs (a 10-minute walk from the nearest bus stop) to reach **Agriolivádo Beach,** about 2 miles north of Skála. Along this unspoiled, tranquil sandy cove you'll find one taverna and some efficiency apartments.

Readers Recommend

Kima Restaurant. "To reach this really great restaurant, go past the Hotel Australis and turn right as though going to Méloï Beach. A sign on the right just before the beach indicates the short road leading to the restaurant. This is the location for a romantic dinner, with the tabled terrace right on the level of the water. Small boats, some of them off yachts, moor right outside the restaurant. The food is really good and different, with special sauces and plenty of garlic."

—Diane D. Jumet, New York, N.Y.

KÁMPOS

The next beach cove north of Agriolivádo is **Órmos Kámbos,** a sheltered cove popular with families. Its pale sand-and-rock beach is shaded by a few pine trees and the water is calm and shallow enough to make it ideal for children. Kámbos village, on the hill above, has about 400 residents and is quite lively in high season.

There are very few rooms-to-let because most overnighters rent homes long term, although a local travel agent may be able to find a room if any of the villas become vacant.

Akroyialo (☎ 0247/32-590) is a popular restaurant on the beach that's not expensive. The casual Greek food and service are equally good, and the proprietors Vasilis, Panormitis, and their dog and cat are fun to visit.

There are also some small tavernas up the hill on Kámbos Square. **Ta Kavourakia,** open from early morning to late, but known for its seafood, has Greek bouzouki music every Saturday night.

Four buses ply the Kámbos–Skála road daily, but most residents hop the frequent, inexpensive beach shuttles for the 20-minute ride; taxis cost 1,200 Drs ($5).

GRÍKOU

Some 2¹/₂ miles south of Skála is the resort village of Gríkou, where many foreigners have built villas for their summer holidays. As you descend from the coast road toward the shores of Gríkou Bay, you'll see the islet of Tragonísi, its hills framing the large boulder that sits in the middle of the bay. This is called Kalikatsou ("cormorant") by the Greeks, because of its appearance at the tip of a narrow, curved spit of land. The natural caves within this rock formation have been enhanced by human hands, leading the author Tom Stone to speculate that monks might have inhabited these caves from the 4th to the 7th centuries, much as they did in Turkey's Cappadocia region.

Gríkou is a long-established resort with a rather limited, pleasantly low-key hotel and restaurant scene. There's an okay, family-oriented, pebble-and-sand beach right in town, with pedalos, windsurfers, Sunfish, and canoes for rent. The more private beach is in the cove just south at Pétras.

Where to Stay

Hotel Artemis. Gríkou, 855 00 Pátmos. ☎ **0247/31-555.** 24 rms, all with bath (shower). A/C TEL. 12,500 Drs ($52.10) single; 19,000 Drs ($79.15) double. Rates include breakfast. No credit cards.

This is a very nice alternative in the lodging scene, built in traditional style. It's furnished simply with local handcrafts, which lends an air of enchantment to the place. All rooms have balconies facing the water, and there's a TV room and a small bar downstairs adjoining a lush garden, where breakfast is served.

Hotel Gricos Apartments. Gríkou, 855 00 Pátmos. ☎ **0247/31-167.** Fax 0247/31-294. 21 rms, all with bath (shower). 9,200 Drs ($38.35) single or double with refrigerator, 13,800 Drs ($57.50) single or double with refrigerator and sink. No credit cards.

We put this in the "pretty good" and "quite unusual" category, a place where tuneful birds serenade newly arriving tourists in an atrium-style lobby. Since it's one lane inland from the beach, the sea and village views are pretty limited, but you'll get a decent twin-bedded room with some kitchen facilities, at a very good price.

Patmian House Apartments. Gríkou, 855 00 Pátmos. ☎ **0247/31-180** or 0247/31-589. 8 villas, all with bath (shower). 15,000 Drs ($62.50) two-bed villa. No credit cards.

The owners of Hóra's chic Patmian House Restaurant maintain eight attached villas and a flowering garden, just a few lanes inland from the beach. Each efficiency apartment, called a "villa," has its own cooking facilities and is furnished in a Spartan, easy-to-maintain beachhouse manner.

✪ **Petra Apartments.** Gríkou, 855 00 Pátmos. ☎ **0247/31-035,** or 01/806-2697 in Athens. Fax 0247/32-335. 25 apts, all with bath (shower). TEL. 25,000 Drs ($104.15) apt for two; 38,000 Drs ($158.35) apt for four. No credit cards. Closed Sept 11–May.

The charming Stergiou family takes loving care of our favorite lodging in Gríkou. It's a splurge, but we think it's worth it. If the folks aren't home, Christos and his sheepdog, Lumpi, will happily show you around these stylish apartments, made into one- or two-bedroom units with small kitchenettes, compact bathrooms, and verandas with wonderful views over Gríkou Bay. Each is simply but carefully decorated, with the necessities of home plus some local color. It's a perfect family place, within a 5-minute walk of the beach, but with an elegant outdoor bar for the adults. Because it's popular with Europeans in August, advance reservations are advised.

Xenia Hotel. Gríkou, 855 00 Pátmos. ☎ **0247/31-219.** Fax 0247/32-372. 35 rms, all with bath (shower). TEL. 11,500 Drs ($47.90) single; 18,000 Drs ($75) double. Rates include breakfast. AE, DC.

The older but well-located Xenia is at the north end of the cove. A couple we met from Amsterdam described it as "the perfect location for a quiet, idyllic, seaside holiday." Many of the spacious but worn doubles overlook the bay and beachside snack bar. A good choice if you want hotel amenities in a beach setting.

Where to Eat

Stamatis Restaurant. Gríkou Beach. ☎ **0247/31-302.** Main courses 1,100–2,300 Drs ($4.60–$9.60). No credit cards. Daily 10am–11pm. GREEK.

Eleni is the talented chef at the reliable restaurant located adjacent to the pier. The covered terrace is where diners consume prodigious amounts of fresh mullet, traditional Greek entrees (we had fine *pastítsio* and fresh green beans), and drinks overlooking the windsurfers.

LÁMBI & PSILÍ ÁMMOS

To the north of Skála is **Órmos Lámbis,** famous for wonderful striped and patterned smooth stones. The deep earth tones of cream, gray, lilac, and coral are particularly striking when wet, and a small bottle filled with Patmian seawater and Lámbi stones makes an unforgettable souvenir of your stay. Daily excursion caïques which round Cape Yeranós take about 1 hour from Skála, and the round-trip fare is 1,400 Drs ($5.85); one-way taxi fare is 1,300 Drs ($5.40). The last stop on the Kámbos bus line leaves you about a 15-minute walk away. There are rooms for rent by the beach at Lámbi and a few tavernas (the **Dolphin** and the **Lambi Beach** are both good) for light snacks.

On the other side of the island's southern point is what's universally acclaimed as Pátmos's best beach—the half-mile stretch of **Psilí Ámmos** ("Fine Sand"). This protected cove, dotted with shade-giving tamarisk trees and tucked on the craggy south coast, provides a special bathing experience. The water is shallow and calm until the afternoon, when breezes can bring waves, a rarity in the Aegean! Because it's so isolated, accessible only by caïque—day trips from Skála cost 1,400 Drs ($5.85)—or by a moped-worthy road plus a hike, nude bathing is as condoned as it will ever be on this Orthodox island. There's even a small taverna that opens for great home-cooking in the summer.

There are a few less known beaches that are best reached by caïque. Among these are the twin pebble-and-sand coves beyond Kámbos called **Vayiá** and **Livádi Déla Póthitou.** On the southern end of the island, on the opposite coast from Psilí Ámmos at a narrow crossover point between two bays, are two fine, rarely visited beaches near Gríkou—**Órmos Pétras** and **Órmos Diakoftoú.**

7 Kárpathos

242 nautical miles SE of Piraeus

The second-largest of the Dodecanese group is a stark contrast to the sophisticated international resort of Rhodes. Because of its relative isolation—midway between Crete and Rhodes, but southwest of the island chain paralleling Turkey—Kárpathos for years remained distinctly its own place. Sadly, the development of an international airport from a former airstrip has brought tour groups to this wild and rugged outpost. Most of the residents here have lived in the United States and so English is widely spoken, but transportation is a problem.

ESSENTIALS

GETTING THERE & DEPARTING   By Plane   There are four flights weekly from Athens, four flights daily from Rhodes, four flights weekly from Kássos, and one flight weekly from Sitía, Crete. Tickets can be purchased at the **Olympic Airways** office, 25 Martíou and Apodímon Karpathíon streets, on the main square, in Pigádia (☎ **0245/22-150**).

By Boat   Kárpathos is serviced by steamers from Piraeus via Náxos, Páros, Santoríni, and Crete two to four times weekly, depending on season. Car-ferries connect the island to nearby Kássos and far-off Rhodes one to three times weekly.

VISITOR INFORMATION   Karpathos Travel is on Dimokratías Street between the taxi stand and bus station (☎ **0245/22-148**). The **tourist police** (☎ **0245/22-218**) are a block south of Platía 5 Oktovríou, which is just off the southwest corner of the harbor.

ORIENTATION   Kárpathos is a long, narrow island with a rugged, mountainous north and a more gentle and fertile south with a number of good beaches. A road runs most of the length of the island, but in the north much of it is still unsurfaced. Most ferries stop at the southeastern port and transportation hub of **Pigádia.** The main street, **Apodímon Karpathíon,** runs east-west just south of and parallel to the harbor, and the **taxi stand** is midway along that street, at the corner of Dimokratías Street. The **bus station** is 2 blocks inland from the taxi stand.

Some ferries also stop at the northeast port of **Diafáni,** from which there's no public transportation. The **airport** is at the southern tip of the island.

GETTING AROUND   By Bus   Public transportation is quite limited, with buses serving only the southern half of the island. There are four buses a day south to

Amopí and west to Pylés via Apéri; two a day southwest to Finíki via Menetés and Arkássa; and only two a week to the west-coast resort of Lefkós. Check the schedule at the station in Pigádia.

By Taxi　Rates to various destinations are listed at the taxi stand (☎ 0245/22-705). Try to share a taxi from the airport since the fare is 2,200 Drs ($9.15).

By Moped or Car　Your choices are limited; most rental agencies are near Platía 5 Oktovríou. Ask the tourist police about road conditions and the location of filling stations (they're rather rare).

FAST FACTS　Most tourist services are found in the port of Pigádia. The local **police** (☎ 0245/22-226) and **post office** are a block south of Platía 5 Oktovríou, which is just off the southwest corner of the harbor. The **OTE** is a block farther southwest. The **National Bank** is on Apodímon Karpathíon midway on the harbor. The small **hospital** is 2 blocks west of Platía 5 Oktovríou (☎ 0245/ 22-228).

EXPLORING THE ISLAND

Lawrence Durrell called Kárpathos "an ideal hideaway." Tourists who moor at the southern port, Kárpathos town, or Pigádia, will find a sparkling village of chiseled stone houses, whose red terra-cotta-tiled roofs peek above the treetops. Pastel-colored facades are broken by bas reliefs of Doric columns; many of their ornate wrought-iron balconies depict the double-eagle symbol of the Byzantine Empire. Although 95% of the islanders have studied or worked in America for some years of their life, when they're at home on Kárpathos they shed the title "Greek-Americans" and become simply "Karpathians."

The southern half of the island—large verdant plains, fruit trees, and trellised vineyards—contrasts with the barren, mountainous reaches of the windblown north. **Apéri,** a small village 6 miles north of Pigádia and once the capital of the island, features the island's most important monastery and traditional stone homes built on both sides of a flowing stream. **Arkássa,** on the opposite coast, shows signs of the ancient Arkaseia on the bluffs above fruit orchards.

A newly built highway crossing the once-impassable Mt. Kalolímni (3,675 feet) unites Pigádia with the northern port of **Diafáni,** though there's still no bus service there. Five miles away, perched on the side of Mt. Profítis Ílías, is the famous village of **Ólýmbos.** Ethnologists have studied the oldest settlement on the island to learn more about the roots of contemporary Greek folk tradition. The 600 villagers are said to live 300 years behind the times, and it's a treat to visit this intimate community, although its rarity is already being exploited by locals and visitors. A local dialect (peppered with ancient Doric words) is still spoken, and even other Karpathians don't understand it.

Olymbian women wear full cotton skirts and lace-trimmed blouses, covered by a flower-print or black apron. Even the faces of the young, swathed in black cotton head scarves, seem timelessly Greek. The old men in their baggy black pants and stiff cotton overshirts continue to farm or herd as always; now many of the young men have gone to Athens or abroad. Ólýmbos is more authentic during one of its many festivals. The post-Easter festivities are very colorful and elaborate, involving all the villagers, who wear traditional holiday costumes. Karpathian music is much faster-paced than the bouzouki played elsewhere, and the lively dances are thought to be unique to the island.

Homespun fabrics, lace, and local handcrafts are good-value gifts from the island.

WHERE TO STAY

Outside Pigádia, most of the island's villages offer accommodations in rented rooms, an ideal way to share village life.

Kárpathos Hotel. Odós Dimokratías 25, Pigádia, 857 00 Kárpathos. ☎ **0245/22-347.** 16 rms, 11 with bath (shower). 6,800 Drs ($28.35) double without bath, 7,500 Drs ($31.25) double with bath. No credit cards.

The older Kárpathos, 2 blocks from the waterfront, has nice rooms with plenty of light. Even the bathless rooms and common toilet and shower facilities are clean, because the place is well run by the Margaritis family.

Porfyris Hotel. Pigádia, 857 00 Kárpathos. ☎ **0245/22-294.** 22 rms, all with bath (shower). 10,000 Drs ($41.65) single or double. No credit cards.

The Porfyris is one of the island's oldest and best choices with a great view toward the port. Its comfortable restaurant serves moderately priced Greek and some continental food. (We prefer the local portside tavernas at lunch or dinner.)

8 Baker's Dozen

Dodekánisos ("Twelve Islands") represents the dozen most important islands in the group. There are hundreds of other small islands tucked in and around the seven better-known ones that we've already discussed. Most are occupied by only a few fishing families, many have no electricity or indoor plumbing, and few are of interest to the average visitor. This section concludes with the six islands that round out one "baker's dozen": Kássos, Hálki, Tílos, Nísyros, Astipálea, and Kastelórizo.

Hálki, Tílos, and Astipálea do have something in common with Kárpathos—they're all included in a clever English company's brochures for "Greece: The Unspoilt Islands." **Laskarina Holidays,** at St. Mary's Gate, Wirksworth, Derbyshire DE4 4DQ, U.K. (☎ **0629/822-203** or 0629/824-881; fax 0629/822-205), offers a number of vacation packages including round-trip airfare from Britain, and hotels, rooms to rent, houses, or villas on several little-developed islands. If this is the Greece you're after, we can't think of a better resource. Its agents on each island may be able to help last-minute arrivals with temporary lodgings.

Getting to these islands can be quite difficult, and in the meltémi-blown seas of summer, often unreliable. We'd recommend contacting the **Pireaus Port Authority** (☎ **01/451-1311**) or **Athens Tourist Information** (☎ **143**) first about ferry schedules. Then you should call **Triton Holidays** on Rhodes (☎ **0241/21-690**), **Pulia Tours** on Kos (☎ **0242/26-388**), **Kalymnos Tours** on Kálymnos (☎ **0243/28-329**), or **Astypalea Tours** on Astypálea (☎ **0243/61-328**) for specific information on connections by local boats and privately run excursions.

KÁSSOS

Kássos, 3 nautical miles southwest of Kárpathos, is separated from her larger neighbor by the treacherous waters of the Karpathian Straits. Forbidding vertical cliffs, which form most of the coastline, have caused development on Kássos to be confined to settlements in the northwest.

Few inhabitants remain on Kássos since the first tide emigrated to Egypt to build the Suez Canal; many Kassiots return now only for the holidays. Ironically, every July 7, Kássos commemorates the massacre of its people by the Egyptian troops of Ibrahim Pasha, who overran the tiny island in the Ottoman offensive of 1824.

ESSENTIALS

GETTING THERE & DEPARTING **By Plane** Olympic Airways offers a daily connection with Rhodes, four times a week with Kápathos, and once a week with Athens and Sitía, Crete. The **Olympic Airways** office is on Kríti Street in Phrý (☎ 0245/41-444). The **airport** is about half a mile west of Phrý.

By Boat Kássos is serviced by steamers from Piraeus via Náxos, Páros, Santoríni, Crete, and Kárpathos two to four times weekly, depending on season. Car-ferries connect the island to nearby Kárpathos and far-off Rhodes one to three times weekly. There's an excursion boat between Kárpathos and Kássos on Sunday in the summer.

VISITOR INFORMATION/FAST FACTS **Kassos Maritime & Travel Agency** (☎ 0245/41-323) can give you information and help you with travel-related problems. The **post office,** the **police** (☎ 0245/41-222), **National Bank**, and **bus station** are on the main street, Krítis. You can find the **OTE** by its satellite dish.

GETTING AROUND The island's only **bus** makes the circuit of villages for 150 Drs (65¢); a schedule is posted at the station.

EXPLORING THE ISLAND

The charming little capital and principal town of **Phrý** (Fri) is about half a mile inland from the port. Peek into any of the fine stone houses of Phrý and you'll see interiors that have been lavishly decorated with artwork brought home by generations of seafarers.

There are only five other villages of any consequence, all in the north-central part of the island and all connected by a 3-mile circuit of road. **Emborió,** a fishing hamlet, is just east; **Panayía,** with about 50 inhabitants and a few neglected shipowners' mansions, is about half a mile south; **Póli,** the ancient capital, with the remains of a Byzantine castle and church on its acropolis, is 2 miles southeast of Phrý; **Arvanitohóri,** farther west, is a garden spot with figs, pomegranates, and brilliant bougainvillea; **Ayía Marína,** about half a mile west of Phrý, near the airport, has an acceptable beach at Ammoúa.

The most popular site on Kássos is the **Sellai Cave** (also called Hellenokamára), near Ayía Marína, which is known for its beautifully colored stalactites. The Pelasgian walls (masonry consisting of large, hand-hewn stones) that surround the grotto once provided the islanders with a haven from pirates.

Plan to spend a few days since transportation opportunities are scant. Luckily, Phrý boasts a good hotel just 50 yards from the water's edge. The **Anagennisis Hotel,** Phrý, 858 00 Kássos (☎ 0245/41-495; fax 0245/41-036), has 10 rooms with balconies and private facilities.

HÁLKI

Hálki (Chalkis), one of the smallest of the Dódecanese, is most often visited as a day excursion from her larger, glitzier neighbor, Rhodes, just 1 1/2 hours west by ferry from the main port or 2 hours from Skála Kámiros. If you're tired of discos, beach umbrellas, casinos, and honking horns, it may be the place for you—relax and share the life led by the 300 villagers who've remained on the island. Hálki is on the steamer route from Piraeus through the Cyclades to Rhodes, with service one to three times a week. There's an **excursion boat** connection with Skála Kámiros on Rhodes daily except Sunday.

There are no buses, cars, or taxis on Hálki. There are **excursion caïques** to a few beaches and the nearby uninhabited island of Alimniá.

Caïques pull into the small port of **Emborió,** where you'll find a few outdoor ouzerís and tavernas serving inexpensive, fresh seafood. This bustling village of sponge divers turned fishermen is built around a stately clock tower, the neoclassic town hall, and the beautiful Church of Ághios Nikólaos. Overnighters can find a room for rent in many of the traditional pastel stone houses overlooking the water; long-term guests should contact Laskarina Holidays (see above).

A few miles' hike above the port is **Hóra,** the island's capital during the 18th and 19th centuries, built around a 15th-century fortress (constructed by the Knights of St. John) to protect villagers from sea-level attack by Turkish pirates. It's a wonderful hike up here, rewarded by vistas looking toward Rhodes or Kárpathos. Hálki offers some antiquities (including a black mosaic-paved stone path nearly half a mile long and the remains of several temples to Apollo), two Byzantine monasteries, and uncrowded, sandy beaches. **Póndamos,** a 10-minute walk west of Emborió, is a pretty sand-and-shingle cove with a popular taverna.

TÍLOS

Tílos, equidistant (about 4 hours by ferry) from the much more diversified islands of Kos and Rhodes, gets few foreign visitors and is the least developed for tourism of these outer Dodecanese.

There are one or two car-ferries to Tílos from Piraeus or Rhodes weekly, with more frequent **ferry** connections to Kálymnos, Kos, Nísyros, and Sými. In the summer there's **hydrofoil** service twice a week to Rhodes, Kos, and Nísyros, and once a week to Kálymnos and Astypálea.

The only means of public transportation is an orange **minibus** that runs from the main square of Livádia to Megálo Horió, Áyios Antónis, and Éristos. There are a couple of places that rent mopeds in Livádia.

Ferries call at the southern port of **Livádia,** the island's most interesting village. Here you'll find a few tavernas, *kafenía,* the sleepy harbor, and most of the 200 resident Tiliots. Nearby are small, sandy beaches and several freshwater streams. It's possible to rent a room in one of the attractive arcaded houses that face east to the Turkish coast, but long-term guests should contact Laskarina Holidays (see above).

Megálo Horió, 5 miles north of Livádia, is the site of the ancient capital, a white-washed village with the remains of a *kástro,* a pretty church, and a small museum. There's very little activity here, but it's a good base from which to hike among the remnants of seven inland Crusader castles. Crossing the island's spine of pumice cliffs created by the long-ago volcanic eruption of Nísyros, you'll come to the **Monastery of Áyios Pandelímon,** a Byzantine beauty.

NÍSYROS

Nísyros (Níssyros), a volcanic island south of Kos, is frequently visited by day-trippers from Kos, though few stay overnight. Although the pentagonal island has no surface water, it's the most verdant of the Dodecanese.

ESSENTIALS

GETTING THERE & DEPARTING   Nísyros has ferry service twice a week on the Piraeus–Rhodes route and daily in the summer from Kéfalos and Kos. An **inter-island ferry** links it with Kos, Rhodes, Sými, and Tílos twice a week. In the summer there are daily **excursion boats** from Kos.

VISITOR INFORMATION/FAST FACTS   **Polyvotis Tours** (☎ 0242/31-201) has an information board and kiosk at the pier. The **police** (☎ 0242/31-222), **port**

police, and **post office** are in the same building across from the pier. The **OTE** and **National Bank** are on the main street.

GETTING AROUND   There is fairly dependable **bus** service five times daily from Mandráki to Páli, twice daily to the volcano, and twice daily on weekdays to Nikiá and Emborió. The station is on the pier; a schedule is posted outside Polyvotis Tours.

There are a couple of **taxi** companies (☎ **0242/31-474** or 0242/31-360). Rates are standard: 2,800 Drs ($11.65) to the volcano and Emborió, 1,400 Drs ($5.85) to Páli, 3,500 Drs ($14.60) to Nikiá.

There are several moped dealers on the main street.

EXPLORING THE ISLAND

Boats dock at the port and capital, **Mandráki.** To reach the center of town, continue straight ahead from the pier and bear right at the fork, cross the large square, follow the **main street** past the **town hall,** and turn left to reach the **central square,** Platía Ilikioménis.

Mandráki is an attractive town with two-story houses, many with colorful wooden balconies, and it's especially charming in the maze that surrounds its central square. (While you're exploring, watch out for the motorbikes and pickups that manage to negotiate with ease and speed.)

Signs direct visitors to the town's major attractions. The most popular is the **Castle of the Knights of St. John** with the 15th-century **Monastery of Panayía Spilianí** ("Our Lady of the Cave") within; it's open daily from 10:30am to 3pm and admission is free. (On the way there, you might want to stop in at the **Historical and Popular Museum,** if it's open.) Follow the KASTRO signs to **Paleókastro** ("Old Castle"), the impressive remains of a Doric fortress with Cyclopean walls atop the ancient Acropolis.

Most visitors come to see the **volcano** with its 2¹/₂-mile-wide caldera rimmed by gray stone hills that fall squarely to the sea. The plain of Lákki within was formed by a violent eruption in 1552. (The last minor eruption was in 1933.) There are seven extinct craters and four geothermal wells within the caldera. Plans to harness the energy with an electrical generation plant have been put on hold, at least in part because of local concern about pollution. (Our sincere thanks to Richard A. Bulloch for setting us straight on this and other matters.)

WHERE TO STAY & EAT

The **Hotel Porfyris** (☎ **0242/31-376**) has a swimming pool and 38 comfortable rooms, all with bath (shower); doubles cost 9,000 Drs ($37.50). Another good option is the **Three Brothers Hotel** (☎ **0242/31-244**), which has doubles with bath (shower) for 6,500 Drs ($27.10) and a good restaurant. (Turn left at the fork above the pier to reach both.) The most frequently recommended place to eat is the **Taverna Irini**, on the central square.

ASTYPÁLEA

Butterfly-shaped Astipálea, the westernmost of the Dodecanese, is 90 nautical miles from Rhodes. The landscape recalls both Rhodes and neighboring Amorgós, but the architecture has been influenced most by the sensual, whitewashed homes of the Cyclades islands.

ESSENTIALS

GETTING THERE & DEPARTING   By Plane   Olympic Airways has three flights a week from Athens. The **Olympic Airways** agent on Astypálea is **Astypálea**

Tours (☎ 0243/61-588). The **airport** is near the narrow middle of the island, just beyond **Maltezána**, 4¹/₂ miles northeast of Skála.

By Boat   Isolated Astypálea can be reached by the once-weekly (in summer three times weekly) car-ferry from Piraeus, which calls first at Páros and Amorgós, and takes 16 hours. There's a twice-weekly ferry from Kálymnos (a 5-hour trip) or a once-weekly excursion boat (a 3-hour trip). In summer there's **hydrofoil** service once a week to Rhodes via Tílos, Nísyros, Kálymnos, and Kos.

VISITOR INFORMATION / FAST FACTS   There's a small **municipal tourist office** on the pier (☎ 0243/61-217). The **police** (☎ 0243/61-207) and **port police** (☎ 0243/61-208) are in the same white building on the pier. The **OTE** is nearby beneath the Hotel Paradissos. The **National Bank** has a small branch at the Hotel Aegeon, just up the road. The **post office** is near the top of the road.

GETTING AROUND   There is **bus** service (more frequent and regular in summer) between Skála and Hóra, as well as to Livádia and to Maltezána via Mármara. There are a few **taxis** available at reasonable rates, though they're difficult to find. (Ask at the tourist office or at your hotel.) In the summer there are **excursion caïques** from Skála to the various inaccessible beaches and the islet of Ayía Kyriakí, as well as from the west-coast port of Áyios Andréas; check with **Gournas Tours** (☎ 0243/61-334).

EXPLORING THE ISLAND

Boats dock at **Skála** (Yialós). From the pier the main road leads off to the right behind the white police building and climbs steeply up to **Hóra** (Kástro). The best (and most crowded) little beach on the island is at **Livádia,** about 1¹/₄ miles southwest of Hóra. **Mármari,** another small sand-and-shingle beach, is 1¹/₄ miles northeast of Skála.

The main village, **Astypálea** (sometimes called Periyialós), incorporates the port of Skála (or Yialós) and the old town of Hóra (Kástro), with nine ruined windmills on a hill above it. The hike uphill to visit them is well worthwhile for the beautiful vista over Maltezána Bay, its many rocky islets, and the sand-and-shingle beach cove of Livádia.

Astipálea is crowned by a 15th-century Venetian kástro and may remind some of Pátmos's Hóra. Within the castle is a well-preserved icon of the Madonna, and above its door is the Quirini family's coat-of-arms. These noble Venetians ruled "Castello," the capital of "Stampalia," from 1207 to 1522.

Today the island is becoming a summer retreat for wealthy Athenians, who have built coastal villas or occupy many of the port's small cubist homes, now renovated as studios or rooms for rent.

The beaches also fill up with Greek families during July and August camping holidays, but there are a few inexpensive hotels to accommodate tourists, all charging about 6,500 Drs ($27.10) for a double. Near the port are the **Hotel Australia** (☎ 0243/61-338), with a friendly English-speaking owner; the okay **Aegeon** (☎ 0243/61-236); the recently renovated **Astynea** (☎ 0243/61-209), the only one that's open year-round; and across the road, the old but well-maintained **Paradissos** (☎ 0243/61-224). If you'd like to stay elsewhere on the island or for a longer period, contact Louise Edeleanu, a British expatriate, at **Gournas Tours** (☎ 0243/ 61-334).

KASTELLÓRIZO

Kastellórizo (Méyisti), made famous by the hit film *Mediterraneo*, remains more important as a symbol of Greek independence than as a tourist attraction. This tiny droplet of stone is 65 miles southeast of Rhodes and less than 2 miles from the Turkish port of Kas. (There's a lively black market tourist-and-goods trade between the two.) The 250 residents (it's said that they remain only to keep the population above the 200 mark, below which the island would revert to Turkey) are totally dependent on supplies brought in from far-off Rhodes.

The name "Kastellórizo" originated from the period of Venetian occupation of the island, when it was renamed after the red-stone fortress (Castello Rosso) built by the eighth grand master of the Knights of St. John. The Greeks call it Méyisti (the "Biggest"). Some will tell you it's because Kastellórizo is the largest among a cluster of tiny islands; others claim that the islanders deserve this title for their bravery in overcoming past misfortunes.

The island has been occupied by at least seven nations, including Egypt, Italy, Turkey, and Venice. Even the grand fortress built by St. John's Knights was used as a prison for wayward members of the order. In 1913 local residents revolted and quickly came under French control. After World War I Italy regained the island; during World War II it forced the remaining islanders to evacuate. Kastellórizo was occupied by Allied troops, which led to German bomb attacks; most of the town was burned and pillaged. The few citizens who returned after the war (the island was returned to Greece in 1948) had nothing to come home to.

ESSENTIALS

GETTING THERE & DEPARTING   By Plane   Olympic Airways offers daily flights from Rhodes in July and August; three times a week the rest of the year. The Olympic agent on Kastelórizo is **DiZi Tours** (☎ **0241/49-240**).

By Boat   Ferries run one to three times a week from Piraeus or Rhodes to Kastellórizo. When relations are positive between Greece and Turkey, there is legal **caïque service** from the Turkish port of Kas for day-trippers only (cost: about 4,500 Drs/$18.75).

VISITOR INFORMATION/FAST FACTS   DiZi Tours (☎ **0241/49-240**), the only travel agent on the island, can cash traveler's checks and give you cash advances on American Express, MasterCard, and Visa cards. The **post office** and **police** (☎ **0241/49-333**) are on the west side of the bay.

GETTING AROUND   There is only one **bus** on the island, and it's used only for transportation to and from the airport (fare: 500 Drs/$2.10).

EXPLORING THE ISLAND

Kastelórizo, the island's only town, is on a well-sheltered bay on the northeast corner of the island. Ferries dock on the east side of the bay. The **central square** is about midway along the bay. The port town, now partially rebuilt, is tiered amphitheatrically to the water's edge. The pastel-colored, red-tile-roofed houses will remind some of Sými, but here the ornate wooden balconies (vestiges of Turkish influence) overhang the oblong harbor. The sea bottom can easily be seen through the crystal-clear waters. As Kastellorizots occupy themselves only with fishing, the few portside tavernas serve some of the most superb seafood in the Dodecanese.

If sitting over a plate of shrimp or lobster and admiring the Turkish coast loses its appeal, stroll over to the harborside mosque. It's been turned into a **museum** of local folklore and handcrafts; there are displays of fascinating photographs of the island in her heyday. Otherwise, organize a group and charter a caïque for an hour's trip to the east-coast **Blue Grotto** (Galázio Spílio) or Perásta. This fantastic cave, filled with stalactites and stalagmites, reflects every hue of blue light from its deep waters and has been compared to the one at Capri. Plan a morning trip with your boat captain so you can be in and out of the grotto during low tide, when the overhanging entrance is passable. If you become stuck there, you may see why the cave is also called "Fokiali," after the seals that reportedly live inside.

In addition to the 17-room **Hotel Meyisti** (☎ **0241/29-072**), which has doubles with bath (shower) for 16,500 Drs ($68.75), there are several pensions, including the **Sydney Pension** (☎ **0241/49-302**), above the Sydney Restaurant, where bathless doubles cost 7,500 Drs ($31.25) and doubles with bath (shower) go for 10,500 Drs ($43.75); and the **Pension Kastelo** (no phone, inquire at the Taverna Mavros), behind Platía Australías, with doubles for 7,500 Drs ($31.25) and apartments for 12,500 Drs ($52.10). There are also rooms for rent above the shops and tavernas of the *paralía*.

11

Central Greece (Stereá Elládos)

Just reading the list of headings in this chapter should give you the classical tingle—Thebes, Delphi, Mt. Parnassus, Thermopylae, and Mt. Olympus. Imagine also Metéora, where James Bond, in *For Your Eyes Only,* dangled off the edge of one of its precariously perched, sky-high monasteries. All these sights and more are described in this chapter.

Fortunately, central Greece is blessed with a practical and functional transportation infrastructure. To reach most major sights you'll have a choice of train or bus, or occasionally plane. Renting a car is still the most efficient way to cram everything in, but the lack of wheels won't prevent you from enjoying the area's natural and man-made beauties.

There are no weather limitations here either, but we prefer spring or fall, when the tourist crush is not too great. In late April and May there's often snow on the slopes of Parnassus and Olympus, while a bevy of wildflowers illuminate the Thessalian Plain. In the dry, hot summer you'll probably be tempted to forget classical sightseeing and head directly to the islands. By mid-September the summer bustle has simmered down, Greek children are back in school, and central Greece has returned to its usual relaxed state—one of its main attractions.

1 Boeotia

45 miles NW of Athens, 28 miles SW of Livadiá

Boeotia (pronounced "Bee-*oh*-sha")—Viotía in Greek, though it's rarely used today—is a region of ancient Greece that we still refer to for convenience. It extends from the Aegean coast to the Pindus range and includes such legendary sights as Mt. Parnassus, haunt of the Muses; the Pass of Thermopylae, where the Spartan general Leonidas and his men fell; Aulis, the port used by warships setting sail for Troy; its capital, City of Seven Gates, the legendary Thebes; and most important, nestled at the foot of Mt. Parnassus, the site of the oracle of Delphi. If you do nothing else during your visit to Greece, try to pay a call at Delphi, one of the most remarkable places on earth.

You have several transportation options in the region. From Athens's Stathmós Laríssis, 10 **trains** depart daily for Thebes or Livadiá. Call ☎ 01/362-4402 for information. There are also **buses**

Central Greece

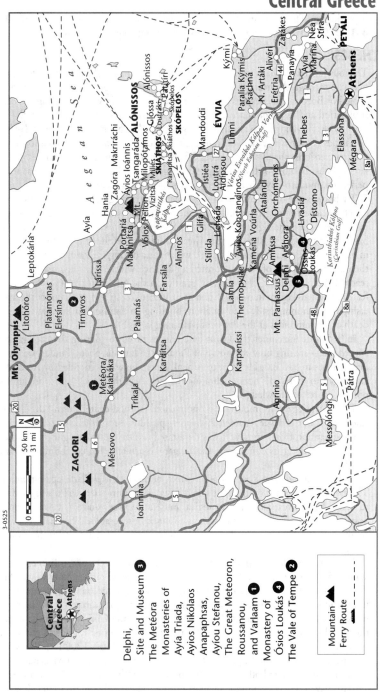

Delphi,
Site and Museum ❸
The Metéora
Monasteries of
Ayia Triada,
Ayios Nikólaos
Anapaphsas,
Ayíou Stefanou,
Roussanou,
and Varlaam ❶
Monastery of
Ósios Loukás ❹
The Vale of Tempe ❷

▲ Mountain
- - - - Ferry Route

3-0525

departing for Thebes hourly from Athens's terminal at Odós Liossíon 260 (☎ 01/ 831-7179). If you're driving, take the Athens–Lamía highway north to Thebes.

THEBES

The journey from Athens to Delphi on the Athens–Lamía high-speed motorway will take you through the heart of Thebes (Thíva or, less commonly, Thívai), the ancient capital of Boeotia. Thebes was one of the greatest of the city-states during the classical period and its prominence in modern consciousness has been assured by the literary works surviving from antiquity. Tragedies by Aeschylus *(Seven Against Thebes),* Sophocles *(Oedipus Rex* and *Antigone),* and Seneca *(Oedipus),* not to mention more modern versions, are all set in Thebes. Thebes endured much in those times and in later epochs: Because of the onslaughts, pillages, and wholesale ravaging that it experienced, modern-day Thebes offers the visitor little of its former glory.

Thebes was one of Athens's most important rivals during the classical period, principally because the oligarchy that ruled there was distrustful of democracy. Though it had developed the fighting formation called the *phalanx,* the close-knit line of battle, later adopted by Alexander the Great, it did not join the other Greek city-states in resisting the Persian invasion. It sided with Sparta during the Peloponnesian Wars, then after the defeat of Athens formed an alliance with Athens against Sparta. It reached the pinnacle of its power and prestige in the 4th century B.C., when it defeated Sparta at Tegyra in 374 B.C. and again at Leuktra in 371 B.C., under the leadership of Epaminondas. It then set about building an empire, but faltered with the death of Epiminondas at the Battle of Mantinea in 362 B.C.

In 335 B.C. Alexander the Great had Thebes razed for daring to rebel against Macedonia—sparing only the house of Pindar, the famous poet. (Pindar was born near Thebes in 518 B.C. He went to Athens, where he was befriended by Aeschylus and began to write. His odes celebrating the victors in the Greek games are an important source of knowledge.)

Thebes was again an important economic and cultural center during the Byzantine period, but it never regained its former splendor. From the time of Alexander to the liberation from Turkey, it was devastated or razed at least eight more times, numbering among its conquerors the Bulgars, Normans, Franks, Lombards, and Turks.

The **bus station** is on Epaminóndou Street, near the central Platía Epaminóndou. The **railroad station** is on the west side of town, and train riders will probably want to take a **taxi** to reach the archaeological museum. Once you're at Epaminóndou Square, though, you'll be within walking distance of several local tavernas, the museum, and the Palace of Cadmus (now only a rock-filled lot at Pindárou and Antigónis streets).

The town's **archaeological museum,** on Pindárou Street (☎ 0262/23-559), about a 5-minute walk from Epaminóndou Square, is small but certainly worthwhile if you're in town. Outside, in a garden of stelae, is an "antique" table made up of columns and sculptural fragments, shaded by a grape arbor, that makes a pleasant picnic spot. Large mosaics mounted outside include an early Christian floor depicting the months of the year as young men bearing gifts. In the first room straight ahead is a collection of Mycenaean *lárnakes* (clay coffins) from 1400–1200 B.C. Excavated at a site near Thebes, this important find revealed a great deal about Mycenaean funeral customs, through both the primitive paintings on the coffins and their contents. This display at Thebes is unique in all of Europe. There's also an unusual collection of 40 lapis lazuli cylindrical seals from far-off Mesopotamia, recovered near Thebes.

The sculpture room houses votive offerings from the Sanctuary of Apollo Ptoios, one of the most famous sanctuaries in ancient Greece. Admission is 500 Drs ($2.10) for adults, 400 Drs ($1.65) for seniors and students. The museum is open Tuesday to Sunday from 8:30am to 3pm.

LIVADIÁ

Livadiá's one important sight can be combined with a cafe or picnic break in your tour of classical Greece. This special site is the **Oracle of Trophónios,** a well-marked spot just half a mile west off the Athens–Delphi highway. Here, in the scenic **Trophónios Park,** you'll find the **Xenía,** a picturesque and expensive cafe overlooking a stream. In ancient times the stream was called the Spring of Mnémosyne (Memory), where those who came to consult the oracle could refresh themselves.

While waiting for your order, you can contemplate the reaction of the Roman traveler Pausanius, author of the original *Hellas on 50 Drachmas a Day,* who said that the place gave him the heebiejeebies—or, to be exact, "so seized by terror that I barely recognized myself or anything around me." Trophónios was an ancient god of the Underworld whose advice was much sought-after in the 6th century B.C. As you admire the Spring of Memory, glance to the left at the large square niche in the cliff. This was the sanctuary of the gods Daimon (Demon) and Fortune, where pilgrims were fed the flesh of sacrificial victims after a drink of the waters of Lethe, the Spring of Forgetfulness, which flows beneath it. Having forgotten the past—or more likely, what was about to happen to him—the pilgrim would be primed at the Spring of Memory. Late in the evening he was anointed with oil and led up to the oracle, thought to be in a gorge of what is now called Mt. Áyios Ilías—behind you—and with honeycakes in each hand, was slid into a coffinlike pit in the floor of the cave and left buried for several days. After his long communion with the oracle, he was hoisted out feet first and questioned by a priest, who would record his impressions.

When you can tear yourself away, head northwest. After 23 miles of winding, uphill roads the scenery will grow richer, as rocks and olive trees alternate with prospects over the Gulf of Corinth and an occasional glimpse of Mt. Parnassus. The less picturesque newer highway will bring you right into a charming village of Aráhova.

ARÁHOVA (ARÁCHOVA)

Just 6 miles north of Delphi, the lovely mountain town of Aráhova is perched on the slopes of Mt. Parnassus at 3,100 feet above sea level. Although the main street suffers from the invasion of tour buses and souvenir vendors, a descent or ascent by hand-hewn rock stairs leading from it will take you into another world.

ESSENTIALS

GETTING THERE & DEPARTING   At the height of the tourist season, many people may prefer to stay overnight in Aráhova when visiting the overcrowded village of Delphi. There are six local **buses** running back and forth between Delphi and Aráhova that stop in front of the Celena Cafeteria across from the main square, where **taxis** can be found.

VISITOR INFORMATION / FAST FACTS   The **tourist office,** the **OTE,** and the **post office** are on Xenía Square, a block west of the main square. The **police station** (☎ 0267/32-004) is just off the south side of the square, and there's a ski-rental shop nearby.

SPECIAL EVENTS   The **Feast of St. George** (Áyios Yióryios), the patron saint of shepherds and the village, is celebrated on April 23—unless this falls before

Orthodox Easter, when it's moved to the Monday after Easter—is celebrated with a traditional bacchanalia on the plaza outside the church. (The peculiar Dionysiac quality of the celebration here probably owes something to ancient rites dedicated to the shepherd-deity Pan and to Dionysos, who ruled Parnassus and Delphi during the winter.) The festivities extend over several days and encompass all those who are fortunate enough to be in town.

EXPLORING THE AREA

Greeks from the cities love to weekend here in winter and ski nearby. Many small tempting stores that line the main street feature the village's most celebrated products: strong, fragrant red wine *(krassí);* mild white sheep cheese called *formélla;* Parnassus honey; shaggy sheepskin *flokáti;* and, most apparent, elegant, finely patterned carpets *(haliá).*

Several markets display local products in their windows—and some of it is authentic. If the weavings interest you, go straight to the shop of **Katína Panagákou,** Odós Delphón 15 (☎ 0267/31-743), on the south side of main street about 200 yards from the tower. Katína is a superb weaver and her shop features the work of many local artisans. You can purchase new or antique rugs *(haliá)* or weavings. Her prices are reasonable for the high quality.

Mt. Parnassus (Parnassós)

The Greek Tourist Organization (EOT) has established a full-service ski resort based in Fteroláka at an altitude of 7,375 feet—a 16³/₄-mile or 50-minute drive from Aráhova. There are 12 ski runs; beginners get the chair lifts while more experienced skiers have to make do with the two upper-level T-bars. There's a ski-rental shop, snack bar, cafeteria, and clothes and accessories boutique at the **Fteroláka Center.** The ski center is open from December to April; contact its office for more information (☎ 0234/22-689) or for reservations (☎ 0267/22-693). Daily lift tickets can be purchased for about 3,000 Drs ($12.50). The center gives lessons, and you can rent gear.

In nice weather, hikers may want to try the nearly 4-hour ascent to the top of Parnassus. The Fteroláka Center (above) also has facilities higher up at Kelariá, at nearly 6,550 feet. Contact the center or the EOT in Delphi. In Athens, contact the **Hellenic Federation of Mountaineering** (☎ 01/323-4555) for information.

WHERE TO STAY

Unlike most destinations in Greece, room prices in Aráhova are higher in winter, because of its popularity as a weekend retreat and ski resort. If you're planning to be in town for the St. George's Day festivities, arrive early or telephone ahead for reservations. One alternative is to stay in a private home, although you'll have a problem making reservations. The town has formed a housing co-op and has set prices for a double at 7,500 Drs ($31.25).

Hotel Apollon. Odós Delphón 20, 320 04 Aráhova. ☎ **0267/31-427** or 0267/31-057. 10 rms, none with bath. 5,000 Drs ($20.85) single; 7,250 Drs ($30.20) double. Rates include breakfast. EURO, MC, V.

Andreas Louskou and his family keep a spotless, homey lodging on the main street with wonderful views from most of its rooms, which are attractively furnished, with common lavatories. Some have balconies.

Hotel Parnassos. Odós Delphón 18, 320 04 Aráhova. ☎ **0267/31-307** or 0267/31-189. 10 rms, none with bath. 5,000 Drs ($20.85) single; 7,250 Drs ($30.20) double. Rates include breakfast. EURO, MC, V.

One of the town's best choices is run by the Louskous, cousins of the good people at the Apollon. It shares the same fine view and has a denlike lobby with a fireplace and a cozy breakfast room.

Xenía Hotel. Xenía Sq., 320 04 Aráhova. ☎ **0267/31-230.** 45 rms, all with bath (shower). TEL. 10,500 Drs ($43.75) single; 15,800 Drs ($65.85) double. Rates include breakfast. MC, V.

Recently refurbished, the Xenía, far enough off the highway for you to enjoy the fine view, has a spacious lobby and big comfortable rooms with large balconies.

WHERE TO EAT

O Karmalis. Odós Delphón 51. No phone. Main courses 900–2,600 Drs ($3.75–$10.85). No credit cards. Daily 5pm–midnight. GREEK.

An excellent, inexpensive taverna on the south side of the main street, O Karmalis serves hearty fare on a sunny outdoor patio or inside, where the no-nonsense decor lets you concentrate on the food itself.

Taverna Karathanassi. Odós Delphón 56. ☎ **0267/31-360.** Main courses 800–2,600 Drs ($3.35–$10.85). No credit cards. Daily noon–midnight. GREEK.

Across from the small square where Aráhovan men sit sipping coffee is the family-run Taverna Karathanassi, where a recent renovation added spiffy hardwood floors, wooden tables, chairs, and walls with old Greek paintings, and even a new roof garden. The friendly chef is eager for guests to enjoy her grilled lamb, veal, or chicken. The moist bread is baked fresh daily and the *horiátiki saláta* (Greek salad) with local *formélla* cheese is a meal in itself.

2 Delphi (Delfí)

110 miles NW of Athens

If you can only see one archaeological site in Greece, make it the oracle of Delphi. Nowhere will you find more interesting remains, a more beautiful setting, or a better collection of art gathered in the same place. If any of our readers write to tell us that they didn't hear the oracle, we can only assume that they weren't listening. Delphi is the most mystical and magical site in the entire country.

According to Plutarch, there were two precepts inscribed upon the Delphic oracle: KNOW THYSELF *(Gnóthi seaftón)* and NOTHING IN EXCESS *(Medén ágan),* "and upon these all other precepts depend."

ESSENTIALS

GETTING THERE & DEPARTING   From Athens's terminal at Odós Liossíon 260 (☎ 01/831-7096), six buses leave daily for Delphi. If you're driving yourself, take National Road 1 to Thebes, exit, and continue west.

VISITOR INFORMATION   The helpful Delphi **tourist office,** at Odós Frideríkis 44 (☎ 0265/82-900), is open daily from 8am to 3pm—plus 6 to 8pm in July and August—with useful information always posted in the window. The **tourist police** are at Odós Frideríkis 27 (☎ 0265/89-920).

GETTING AROUND   Delphi is a mountain village built above and below its two main streets, the upper Apóllonos and the lower Frideríkis. You can easily walk anywhere in the small town, including all the sites. The Delphi **bus stop** is next to the Taverna Castri on the west end of the main street. The local bus to Aráhova leaves throughout the day; the fare is 180 Drs (75¢). To get to Óssios Loukás, take a bus to Dístomo (or exit the Athens bus at the highway intersection), then walk 2 miles to catch the bus directly to the monastery. (*Be warned:* This is not an easy trip; check the tourist office for current schedules.) From Delphi, you can share a **taxi** with up to four people for about 10,000 Drs ($41.65), a bargain for the 45-minute scenic drive to Óssios Loukás. (Negotiate the fare before you leave and have the driver wait for you.)

FAST FACTS Most tourist services are on Odós Frideríkis, including the **post office,** which is open Monday to Friday from 7:30am to 7:30pm, Saturday from 8am to 2:30pm, and Sunday from 9am to 1pm. The **OTE** is at Odós Frideríkis 10, open Monday to Saturday from 7:30am to 3:10pm and Sunday from 9am to 2pm. The two **banks** on Odós Frideríkis are open the usual hours as well as 5 to 7pm in summer; there are cash machines on the street. The post office and kiosk at the museum also exchange money.

EXPLORING THE MUSEUM & THE SITES

Some visitors to Delphi may wonder what they should visit first, the archaeological site or the museum. Kyle and many near-experts suggest that it's best to tour the museum first, arguing that a visit to the museum will orient or enhance your walk through the remains at the site. However, John thinks it's best to buy a detailed map or guidebook at the museum and then head straight for the site. Later, when you go to the museum, you'll be much happier and more interested in trying to translate those little signs in French that describe the museum artifacts.

We recommend that you go to the Delphi Museum and archaeological sites either early or late in the day (so you'll be there either before or after the tour groups).

✪ **Delphi Museum.** Delphi. ☎ **0265/82-312.** Fax 0265/82-966. Admission 1,200 Drs ($5) adults, 900 Drs ($3.75) seniors, 600 Drs ($2.50) students. Mon 11am–5:30pm, Tues–Fri 7:30am–6:30pm, Sat–Sun and holidays 8:30am–3pm.

One of the first things you'll see upon entering the museum is a Roman copy of the **Omphalós** (Naval Stone), a marble cone sculpted to appear as if covered with braided wool. In antiquity Delphi was held to be the center (naval) of the world. On the right-hand wall in the next room is a **frieze** from the treasury of the Sifnians (525 B.C.), depicting the war between the Greeks and Trojans, the gods at Mt. Olympus, and the war between the gods and the giants. In the same room you'll find the famous **winged sphynx of the Naxians.** The sphynx—part bird and lion and part woman—stood atop a tall pedestal at the base of the Temple of Apollo.

Enter the room with the two still and imposing archaic *koúri* (600 B.C.); to the right are the remains of sacred offerings found in a secret passage under the Temple of Apollo, one of the most exciting exhibits in the museum. The 6th-century B.C. **offerings,** thought to be from one of the Ionian cities because of their style, are made of gold and ivory; because of their value, they were moved, after a 5th-century A.D. fire, from storage in the treasury of the Corinthians to an underground vault. In 1939, French archaeologists found at least three life-size figures (of Apollo, Artemis, and possibly Leto) and a huge bull. The bull is made of wood, covered with hammered and cast silver and decorated with gold and ivory. The human figures, now charred, are made of solid ivory. Don't miss the beautiful censer in the corner, which dates from 450 B.C.

As you return to the main hall, continue through the rooms that display **metopes from the Athenian treasury;** admire the forceful imagery of the "Labors of Heracles." The exhibit of remnants and restored sections of the *thólos* from the Sanctuary of Athena Pronaea is of particular interest if you've already viewed the extraordinarily beautiful circular building standing below the main site of Delphi.

Delphi Site Plan

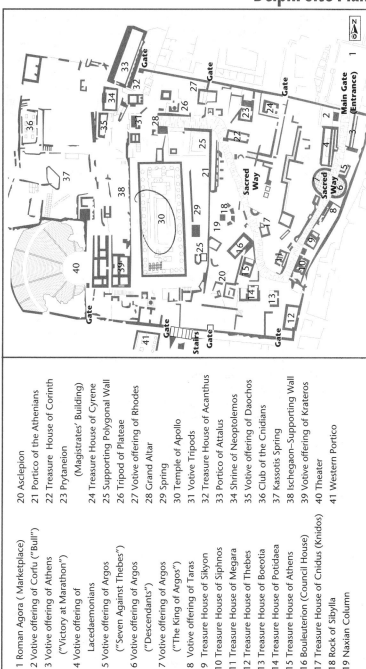

3-0526

1 Roman Agora (Marketplace)
2 Votive offering of Corfu ("Bull")
3 Votive offering of Athens
   ("Victory at Marathon")
4 Votive offering of
   Lacedaemonians
5 Votive offering of Argos
   ("Seven Against Thebes")
6 Votive offering of Argos
   ("Descendants")
7 Votive offering of Argos
   ("The King of Argos")
8 Votive offering of Taras
9 Treasure House of Sikyon
10 Treasure House of Siphnos
11 Treasure House of Megara
12 Treasure House of Thebes
13 Treasure House of Boeotia
14 Treasure House of Potidaea
15 Treasure House of Athens
16 Bouleuterion (Council House)
17 Treasure House of Cnidus (Knidos)
18 Rock of Sibylla
19 Naxian Column

20 Asclepion
21 Portico of the Athenians
22 Treasure House of Corinth
23 Prytaneion
   (Magistrates' Building)
24 Treasure House of Cyrene
25 Supporting Polygonal Wall
26 Tripod of Plataea
27 Votive offering of Rhodes
28 Grand Altar
29 Spring
30 Temple of Apollo
31 Votive Tripods
32 Treasure House of Acanthus
33 Portico of Attalus
34 Shrine of Neoptolemos
35 Votive offering of Daochos
36 Club of the Cnidians
37 Kassotis Spring
38 Ischegaon–Supporting Wall
39 Votive offering of Krateros
40 Theater
41 Western Portico

413

In the remaining rooms are three highlights that you should search out. The first is a figure of **Ayias,** a star athlete of the 5th century B.C. The best preserved of a group of six related figures, it is believed to be a copy of a bronze executed by Lysippus. The second sculpture of note is the contemplative **Antinoös,** the Greek youth loved and deified by the Roman emperor Hadrian. (He's believed to have drowned himself in the Nile at the age of 18 because an oracle demanded that a friend make a sacrifice in order for Hadrian to continue living.) The final sculpture is the highlight of Delphi: the **bronze charioteer,** offered by King Polyzalos in 474 B.C. This lithe young man was part of a larger sculpture that included a chariot; the whole commemorated the victory of the charioteer in the Pythian Games. The eyes of the victor still sparkle.

Before you rush off to the site, examine the marble **Acanthus column** (330 B.C.). Three elegant women in dancing positions pose atop the column, once used as part of a votive tripod.

Sanctuary of Apollo. Admission 1,200 Drs ($5) adults, 900 Drs ($3.75) seniors, 600 Drs ($2.50) students. Mon–Fri 7:30am–6:30pm, Sat–Sun and holidays 8:30am–3pm.

Along the hillside that hugs the road to Aráhova is the Sanctuary of Apollo. If you don't have a site guide, wait a few minutes and tag along with a guided tour in the language of your choice. (There are usually tours in English, French, German, Italian, and Greek.)

Up the stairs from the ticket booth is the **Sacred Way,** which was once lined with bronze statues offered to Apollo by Sparta, Arcadia, and several other city-states. On both sides of the walk are the **treasuries,** which used to house many of the offerings now preserved in the museum.

After the beautiful treasury of the Athenians, on the left you'll see the **Rock of the Sybil,** the legendary predecessor of the priestesses, and nearby blocks of stone that mark the shrine of Gaia, the earth goddess who was worshiped here long before Apollo. (Gaia, Gaea, or Ge gives us our modern "geo-," as in geography.) Behind this is the long "polygonal wall," covered with inscriptions on each of its beveled faces.

The vast foundations of the **Temple of Apollo** and the few Doric columns that remain invoke images of his beautiful temple at Bassae (Vásses) in the Peloponnese. The *ádyton* (inner sanctum), was on the west (left) side, partly underground; it contained the sacred *Omphalós,* a golden statue of Apollo, the sacred laurel tree, a shrine to Dionysos (who ruled here during the winter while Apollo was on Delos), and the Oracle itself.

Climbing higher to the theater will give you a wonderful view of the temple and the Temple of Athena Pronaea in the valley below. This view of the serene and magnificent landscape clearly illustrates why the ancients chose this as the "navel" of the world. The compact **amphitheater** at this level held 5,000 spectators for dramatic presentations, music, and poetry readings.

At the very top of the site is the long **stadium** (which now hosts theatrical events), one of the best preserved in Greece. The stadium is remembered as the site of chariot races during the quadrennial Pythian Games (begun in 582 B.C.; these athletic competitions did for Apollo what the Olympic Games did for Zeus).

Castalia Fountain. Admission free. Daily 24 hours.

At the curve of the road between the Temple of Apollo and the Temple Athena Pronaea, under the huge maple trees, pilgrims to Delphi would purify themselves with water from sacred Mt. Parnassus—usually by washing their hair. The fountain

The Secrets of the Oracle

The Pythia, a priestess of Apollo (at least 50 years old), made her prophecies from within the *ádyton,* separated from those seeking advice by a curtain. (Her name, by the way, is derived from the Python, the serpent son of the Earth that Apollo slew here, and she remained as a representative of the Earth Mother, whom Apollo displaced.) Here she would sit on her tripod—suspended between heaven and earth—chewing laurel leaves (sacred to Apollo) and breathing the vapors rising from a chasm so that she might go into a trance and deliver ecstatic utterings that were interpreted by the priests, who rendered them as ambiguous aphorisms in couplets. Thus for centuries the priests virtually dictated the social and political affairs of the Greek world.

house carved into the rock where the Cave of the Python was supposed to have been is now fenced off, but you can see it and the niches carved in the rock, which contained offerings brought to the nymph Castalia and Mother Earth.

The Castalia fountain is a lovely shaded spot, away from the hordes of international shutterbugs. You can still taste the deliciously pure water yourself—a free initiation into the cult of Apollo.

Temple of Athena Pronaea. Admission free. Daily 7:30am–sunset.

From the roadway, walk 5 minutes past the Castalia Fountain to the tourist cafe. Below it are the remains of the **gymnasium,** which had racetracks, boxing and wrestling rings, and baths for training local athletes. Keep walking along the roadway, past the laurels, till you see three white Doric columns, topped with one of the few in situ pediments in Greece. The 4th-century B.C. limestone Temple of Athena Pronaea ("Before the Temple") was visited by pilgrims before they entered the Sacred Precinct. Beyond it is one of Delphi's most beautiful monuments, the mysterious, circular **thólos,** which perhaps enclosed the pit where the very earliest sacrifices were made.

Thought to be the work of the master architect Theodoros (ca. 380 B.C.), the marble thólos was originally composed of 20 outer columns that surrounded 10 Corinthian semicolumns, in two tiers. This is the spot from which to admire all the ruins of Delphi, contemplate the oracle's role in the ancient world, and listen to the prophecy of the birds.

WHERE TO STAY

Hotels and pensions are cheek to cheek with bookshops, souvenir stands, and expensive tavernas, especially along Frideríkis Street, and there are some excellent places to stay at that make Delphi an ideal base camp for touring this region.

There are a few budget accommodations on upper Apóllonos Street, close to the bus stop. **Loúla Sotiríou** (☎ **0265/82-349**) rents four doubles with access to a common bathroom for 5,200 Drs ($21.65) per night. Her pleasant home is on the west end of town, at Odós Apóllonos 84, the last house on the right before the Amalia Hotel.

Apollon Camping (☎ **0265/82-762**) is basic but is the best-situated campground in the vicinity of Delphi. It's located off the main highway, 1¼ miles south of the village, and offers a swimming pool, a minimarket, a taverna, a cafe, and tent sites that overlook the mountains, the valley, and the Gulf of Corinth beyond. Rates are 1,100 Drs ($4.60) per person, plus 450 Drs ($1.90) per tent.

Hotel Aeolos. Odós Frideríkis 23, 330 54 Delphi. ☎ **0265/82-632.** 29 rms, all with bath (shower). 8,800 Drs ($36.65) single; 11,800 Drs ($49.15) double. Rates include breakfast.

The lobby of this good-value hotel has a lot of old-world charm and big, comfortable chairs. The rooms are quiet, light, and cheerful. They offer excellent views down to the valley carpeted with olive trees and out to the port of Iteá on the Gulf of Corinth.

Hotel Athina. Odós Frideríkis 55, 330 54 Delphi. ☎ **0265/82-239.** 12 rms, 8 with bath (shower). 6,250–7,500 Drs ($26–$31.35) single; 8,000–9,500 Drs ($33.35–$39.60) double. Rooms with bath 20% more. Breakfast 650 Drs ($2.70) extra. V.

This small hotel has attractive rooms with superb views from the balconies. Breakfast is served in a spot with a great view. The manager, Nicholas Zinelis, speaks English and is very helpful.

Hotel Hermes. Odós Frideríkis 27, 330 54 Delphi. ☎ **0265/82-318.** Fax 82-639. 30 rms, all with bath (shower). A/C TEL. 9,500 Drs ($39.60) single; 11,000 Drs ($50) double. Rates include breakfast. MC, V.

One of our favorite hotels was recently given such a thorough renovation that we hardly recognized the handsome wood paneling, tasteful furnishings, and gleaming fixtures during our last visit. This charming hotel is built into the hillside on a quiet part of the main street, and the top-floor rooms offer the same superb view you can enjoy in the pleasant breakfast room. Many years ago the owners, Tony and Nick Droseros, happily told us, "Your boss, Arthur Frommer, slept here!" So would we!

✪ Hotel Olympic. Odós Frideríkis 57, 330 54 Delphi. ☎ **0265/82-163.** Fax 0265/82-639. 25 rms, all with bath (shower or tub). A/C TEL. 13,500 Drs ($56.25) single; 17,000 Drs ($70.85) double. Rates include breakfast. MC, V.

If this hotel weren't so immaculate, you might assume that it was from a grander, more gracious period. It's easily the most beautiful hotel in town, with quality and distinction everywhere: handsome wood, black wrought iron, and sleek dark furnishings contrasting with cool white plaster walls. All this, and a splendid view.

Hotel Pan. Odós Frideríkis 53, 330 54 Delphi. ☎ **0265/82-294.** 17 rms, all with bath (shower). TEL. 7,000 Drs ($29.15) single; 10,000 Drs ($41.65) double. Rates include breakfast. AE, MC, V.

Check in the gift shop near the peaceful south end of the main street for Yannis and Andreas Lefas, hosts at this modern hotel; both speak English well. The lobby is spare, making the most of beautiful maroon marble floors. All rooms share a terrace with a wonderful valley view; the breakfast room is especially charming.

Hotel Panorama. Odós Ossíou Louká 47, 330 54 Delphi. ☎ **0265/82-061** or 0265/82-437. Fax 0265/82-081. 20 rms, all with bath (tub). TV TEL. 13,200 Drs ($55) single; 15,800 Drs ($65.85) double. Rates include breakfast. MC, V.

This comfortable inn high on the hill above town offers simple village style with modern amenities—central heat, direct-dial telephones, music—together with warm hospitality. The view is as its name suggests, and there's a nightclub featuring live entertainment.

Hotel Sibylla. Odós Frideríkis 19, 330 54 Delphi. ☎ **0265/82-335.** Fax 0265/83-024. 10 rms, all with bath (shower). TEL. 5,500 Drs ($22.90) single; 7,500 Drs ($31.25) double.

The lobby is small and very European. The rooms, comfortable but plain, share the same scenic views as the Aiolos and Athina. There's an in-house travel and exchange desk.

Pension Delphi. Odós Apóllonos 31, 330 54 Delphi. ☎ **0265/82-286.** 100 dorm beds; 3 rms, none with bath. 4,000 Drs ($16.65) dorm bed; 8,000 Drs ($33.35) double. No credit cards.

The former Delphi Youth Hostel was well known on the budget traveler's circuit for its gracious, helpful, and friendly staff and its better-than-average accommodations—and we have no reason to believe that the new name means much else has changed. You can call or write ahead for reservations. There are three doubles, but the 100 beds are what's really in demand. In high season new arrivals should sign up for a bed between 7:30 and 10am, before sightseeing. The hostel will also put overflow crowds out on the roof for 1,000 Drs ($4.15).

Pension Odysseus. Odós Isaía 1, 330 54 Delphi. ☎ **0265/82-235.** 8 rms, none with bath. 4,500 Drs ($18.75) single; 5,000 Drs ($20.85) double. Showers 385 Drs ($1.60) extra. AE, DC, MC, V.

Located on a small pedestrian street lined with red planters is an ideal pension: inexpensive and quiet, with fantastic views, nice rooms, and a spacious terrace. The effusive hostess, Toula, encourages her guests to buy food at the local markets and bring it back to enjoy at one of her terrace tables.

WHERE TO EAT

Castalia Spring Cafe. Near the Oracle. ☎ **0265/82-210.** Snacks 700–1,200 Drs ($2.10–$4.15); main courses 950–2,600 Drs ($3.95–$10.85). No credit cards. Daily 8am–11pm (to 1am in summer). CONTINENTAL.

This very pleasant cafe close to the archaeological site, near the entrance to the Temple of Athena Pronaiea, offers fresh-squeezed orange juice, sweets, and ice cream while you enjoy the view of the ancient gymnasium and valley below.

Isaía Cafeteria Delfi. Odós Isaía 10. ☎ **0265/82-863.** Snacks/desserts 250–1,900 Drs ($1.05–$7.90). No credit cards. Daily 8am–midnight. SNACKS/DESSERTS.

Light meals, snacks, and breakfast are offered at reasonable prices at this little bar on the pedestrian lane a few yards down from Apóllonos Street. It's a good rest stop before or after the museum.

Taverna Aráhova. Odós Frideríkis 50. ☎ **0265/82-452.** Main courses 1,000–2,700 Drs ($4.15–$11.25). Daily 6:30pm–midnight. GREEK.

This small traditional taverna specializes in fresh veal, beef, lamb, and chicken—much of it raised on Yiorgos Panagakos's own farm—roasted over charcoal. Don't miss the chips or roast potatoes.

Taverna Vakchos. Odós Apóllonos 31. ☎ **0265/82-448.** Main courses 800–2,100 Drs ($3.35–$8.75); fixed-price daily meals 2,000–3,000 Drs ($8.35–$12.50). V. Daily 7am–11pm. GREEK.

You'll find our favorite budget place up to the left from the bus stop. The Vakchos (Bacchus) is bright, spacious, and no-frills, with gorgeous views and typical taverna fare well prepared and amiably served. Locals still recommend it enthusiastically.

DELPHI AFTER DARK

Delphi has bars and discothèques on Frideríkis Street. If you're in the mood for stargazing, try **Delphi by Night.** If a Greek dance show is more your style, climb the steps to **Katói,** in a pretty garden behind the wall at Odós Apóllonos 36, where free lessons are given from 9:30 to 11:30 nightly in nice weather; in winter, classes move indoors to a more intimate and rustic setting with an old-fashioned fireplace. The nightclub at the **Panorama Hotel** also provides live entertainment for 1,200 to 1,800 Drs ($5 to $7.50).

SIDE TRIPS FROM DELPHI

With Delphi as a base, you can visit Aráhova or Mt. Parnassus (already covered in this chapter), areas of great scenic beauty. Southwest of Delphi is the 11th-century Byzantine monastery of **Óssios Loukás;** an exquisite chapel in this lovely compound boasts gold-backed mosaics that rival those at Dafní for the affections of Byzantophiles.

If you're contemplating breaking up your archaeological tour with a refreshing splash in the sea, it's most easily done along the Gulf of Corinth coast. The beaches are not very good, though nearby **Itéa** is certainly acceptable. **Galaxídi,** 10½ miles southwest, is a charming little port with several nice hotels and restaurants. The best beaches are all the way west to **Náfpaktos**—which you may more readily recognize as Lepanto, where the fleet of the Holy League defeated the Turkish fleet in the last and greatest naval engagement of oar-driven ships, in 1571—near the Antírio cross-over point for entry into the Peloponnese.

If you plan to proceed up the eastern coast of Greece to Mt. Pelio, Vólos, or the Sporades, or due north to Metéora and on to Thessaloníki, we'll take you up Boeotia on the Lamía highway.

If you're traveling (as many of the tours from Athens do) from Delphi to the monastery of Óssios Loukás, you'll pass a spot of great importance in Greek literature. Where the road continues straight to Livadiá and splits right (south) to Dístomo and Óssios Loukás is thought to be the **triple way,** the crossroads where Oedipus killed his father, King Laius. Oedipus was walking from Delphi to Thebes, having received a warning from the oracle that he would kill his father and marry his mother, from whom he had been separated since birth. At this very fork in the road Oedipus met an older man riding in a royal chariot who refused to let him pass. The man whipped Oedipus and, in defense, Oedipus killed him, fulfilling the first part of the oracle's terrible prophecy.

Monastery of Óssios Loukás. Admission 800 Drs ($3.35) adults, 600 Drs ($2.50) seniors, 400 Drs ($1.65) students. May–Sept, daily 8am–5:30pm.

The church of Óssios Loukás is one of the most ornately decorated and well-designed Byzantine sanctuaries in Greece. Its brilliant gold-backed mosaics and innovative octagonal structure make Óssios Loukás a must for those interested in Byzantine architecture. Set on the slopes of Mt. Helikon, the church is dedicated to the hermit Holy Loukás—*not* Saint Luke the Apostle—and is part of a larger monastery that's run by four bearded monks.

Óssios Loukás Stiriótis established a kind of medieval oracle, a church known for prophecies and the ascetic life, in A.D. 942. He lived there until his death in 953. The original church was replaced during the 11th century by Romanós the First, and the new church is a local variation of Haghía Sophía in Constantinople. Loukás's relics, formerly kept in the Vatican, were moved to the church in 1987, converting the status of the site from a museum to a holy place. Monks screen visitors to ensure that they are wearing the proper attire (no shorts or halter tops); those not dressed appropriately will be provided with a bright-orange pajamalike covering.

As you enter the narthex, where tickets and postcards are sold, look up and you'll see some of the best and the brightest of the sparkling mosaics. Proceed into the church and turn left at the second niche. When you step up, Loukás will be above you, sporting a helmet and beard, his intense eyes watching over tourists, arms up in resignation. Many of the mosaics, including the one decorating the main dome, were severely damaged or destroyed by an earthquake in 1659. Paintings and frescoes, which in turn were damaged by Turkish troops in the 19th century, replaced the lost mosaics. Notice the lacelike carved marble pillars in front of the altar and the patterns and columns of the marble floors.

We mistakenly entered the monastery from the back and walked down a narrow path (where we were blessed by a monk who was chopping wood) that led to the church and the crypt where old Loukás was originally buried. The crypt contains some interesting and colorful frescoes festooned with graffiti from throughout the ages.

On the grounds of the monastery is the flagstone "village" of Óssios Loukás, complete with taverna. Don't miss the view of the valley below from the patio. There isn't a sign of modern life—except the road—so the panorama is strictly medieval.

HEADING NORTH

To continue north, return to the main highway at **Amfíssa.** Surrounded by mountains and situated on the same plain as Iteá, it serves mostly as a major marketplace for all the local hillside villages. Amfíssa's abundant supply of water, hot temperatures, and flat terrain make it an ideal area for growing olives. One local resident claimed that the area is planted with more than 5 million olive trees! The town is like an oven in summer and remarkably cold in winter, so unless you want to watch the olives grow, we suggest that you continue on to the high point of your northward journey.

The Pass of Thermopylae

The mountains (west) will be to your left, the sea (east) to your right, and straight ahead the national highway system goes directly through one of the most famous places of antiquity. Watch for the **statue of Leonidas,** the celebrated Spartan leader, who stands erect, shield and spear in hand, marveling at the amount of vehicular traffic that flows through this strategic pass.

In 480 B.C., when Xerxes and the Persians reached Thermopylae, they realized that to conquer Greece they would have to fight their way through this pass. Leonidas, the commander of the Spartan forces and general of all the Greek troops, had 7,300 men stationed in the middle. Weeks of standoff went by, until an Thessalian soldier, Ephialtes, angry at the confederation, turned traitor and showed the Persians a back route over the mountains. Leonidas realized at once what had happened and ordered most of the Greek troops to retreat south. He kept with him 300 Spartans, 700 Thespians, and 300 Theban hostages as a rear guard.

Leonidas and his brave Spartans died to the last man, and their bravery is celebrated in the famous epigram of the poet Simonides engraved in the memorial: "Stranger, tell the Spartans that here we lie, obedient to their word."

Thermopylae means "Hot Gates" in Greek, and the pass was named for the hot springs that flowed through it in antiquity and are now routed to several spas on the east coast. If you've had enough driving for the day, the **Camping Leonidas** grounds are just off the highway, and to the east (about 18¹/₂ miles from the pass), on the coast, the pretty beach resort of **Kaména Voúrla.** The narrow strip of beach is matched across the highway by a row of new white two-story hotels, the architecture of a pleasant middle-class resort overlooking the island of Évvia.

3 Évvia

50 miles N of Athens

Évvia (still often confusingly written Euboea, a letter-for-letter approximation) is the second-largest Greek island, after Crete—though, because it's so close to the mainland and joined to it by a bridge at Halkída, it has little of the feel of an island. Évvia has abundant beauty and a number of good beaches, but it's not at all popular with foreign visitors—perhaps because it's so popular with the Greeks themselves.

Older Greeks will swear that the island of Évvia was actually part of the mainland until Poseidon (angry at some mortal who'd flirted with a mermaid) took his trident and sliced the Évvia piece off. Since that time long ago the Greeks have done everything possible to reconnect it, while enjoying the benefit of two additional coastlines.

Évvia is Athens's equivalent of New York's Long Island. Its proximity and sand beaches make it the place for weekend homes and minivacations. This section is for readers who need a quick break from the Athenian heat. If you're interested in the lesser-known pleasures of Skýros, turn to the section on Kými, the port city closest to this Sporades island.

ESSENTIALS

GETTING THERE & DEPARTING By Train Several trains run daily to Halkída from Athens's **Stathmós Laríssis.** Call ☎ **01/362-4402** for information.

By Bus There are 16 buses daily to Halkída from Athens's terminal at Odós Liossíon 260 (☎ **01/831-7153**).

By Boat Frequent car-ferries connect Rafína and Marmári in the south, Ayía Marína and Néa Stýra, Skála Oropoú and Erétria south of Halkída, and Árkítsa and Loutrá Edipsoú in the north. Call ☎ **0294/63-491** for schedules.

By Car Drive north on National Road 1 to Schimatari, exit, and follow the signs to Halkída. The only land bridge, which connects Áyios Minás to Halkída, extends a mere 210 feet.

HALKÍDA

Évvia's capital is Halkída (Chalkída or sometimes Chalkís, from the Greek word for "bronze," *halkós*); in antiquity this thriving port was well known for the metalwork it contributed to the sanctuaries at Delphi and Olympia and for the weapons produced during continuous wars. Over the centuries Évvia, in whole or in part, fell under the rule of the Athenians, Spartans, Thebans, Macedonians, Franks, Venetians, and Turks. Meanwhile, its sailors were opening new trade routes for the Hellenic world and founding colonies in northern Greece (Halkidikí), in Italy, and in Asia Minor.

The **Évripos Channel** is the most interesting thing about present-day Halkída because of its irregular currents, which change direction 7 to 14 times a day—or sometimes don't change at all—depending on the moon and the season. The rapid shift and brief lulls in between make it dangerous for boats to pass through, and it's said that Aristotle drowned himself here in frustration at not being able to explain the currents—though this is probably not true. Today scientists only guess that the Évripos acts as a sluice between two water levels of the Évvian (Euboean) Channel.

If you arrive by public transportation, you'll find the Halkída **bus station** on Venizélou Street (☎ **0221/22-640** or 0221/22-436), and the **train station** (☎ **0221/26-250**) nearby.

The **archaeological museum** is at Odós Venizélou 13, where you can see a small collection of artifacts, particularly from Erétria. There's also an attractive Turkish mosque near the Évripos Channel bridge. Expensive hotels and cafes line the promenade of Halkídas's harbor, with the restaurants on one side of the street and their cafe tables overlooking the water on the other side.

NORTHERN ÉVVIA

This area, signposted as BOREIOS EVVIA (Vórios Évvia, "Northern Évvia"), is best known for the medicinal hot-springs spa at **Loutrá Edípsou,** famous since antiquity. Many hotels with mineral water bubbling right into the rooms have been built for arthritis and rheumatism sufferers. If this interests you, the Greek Tourist Organization (EOT) in Athens can provide you with more information about it and other Grecian spas. **Límni,** 53 miles north of Halkída, was such a picturesque port that Zeus and Hera got married there, but times have changed: As with all good nearby places, hotels and speedboats have followed in the wake of suntanned Athenian weekenders, and idyllic Límni is no more.

SOUTHERN ÉVVIA

Heading from Halkída toward southern Évvia ("Nótios Évvia" in Greek—so don't mistake the "N" in the road sign N. EVVIA for "Northern"!) you'll notice occasional evidence of resort life. Eretria Beach, Holidays in Evvia, and the Golden Beach are all huge, full-service resorts packed with locals on summer weekends. Some 2¹/₂ miles south of town is **Evvia Camping (☎ 0221/61-081).** Erétria's narrow pebble beach makes it a nice day trip or a convenient weekend away from the Athenian *néfos* (pollution) and noise.

Néa Stýra is the most efficient ferry crossing (time- and moneywise) if you're driving up to Kými for the ferry to Skýros. If for some reason you're stuck here overnight, there's the **Hotel Plaza (☎ 0224/41-492)**—*no* relation to New York's—with a 24-hour snack bar.

KÝMI

Kými, 58 miles northeast of Halkída, is the only place on Évvia worthy of a 1-night stand. It's a charming mountaintop fishing village, and the explanation for this apparent contradiction is that the plateau it's on is more spacious and hospitable than the narrow coast. Tall, narrow stone houses are stacked in among the pine and fir forests, but everyone finds his way into the main square.

Here you'll find the **Hotel Krineion (☎ 0222/22-287)**, a charming, woodtrimmed 50-year-old lodging that's seen a lot of visitors. Large doubles go for 7,000 Drs ($29.15), and the front rooms offer great views. A more modern alternative is the **Hotel Kými (☎ 0222/22-408)**, up the hill by the post office; doubles here are 5,000 Drs ($20.85).

The best of Kými's cuisine can be sampled at any of the tavernas off the main square. For breakfast there's a bakery below the square, where you can also buy picnic supplies for the boat; or try the small *zaharoplastío* (cafe/pâtisserie) on the square that features Kými's unique all-almond baklavá.

In the surrounding region are several Byzantine churches; the remains of an ancient *kástro* (fort) are 2¹/₂ miles north of the village. The most delightful site is the charming **Folklore Museum of Kými (☎ 0222/22-011)**, located in a traditional house below the square and filled with sailors' memorabilia, embroidery, costumes, and brought-home treasures. It's open daily from 10am to 1pm and 5 to 7:30pm in summer. Call for more information.

PARALÍA KÝMIS

Kými's port is below the town, an attractive little strip with a few hotels, cafes, tavernas, and one big pier. The two or three boats that go to Skýros in the summer don't leave till the afternoon; buses stop right in front of the **ferry to Skýros,** and tickets can be purchased across from the dock on the day of departure; call ☎ 0222/ 22-020 for schedule information. There are also three sailings weekly to Alónissos, Skópelos, and Skiáthos; however, weather and demand play havoc with sailing schedules from this little port.

4 Thessaly

Thessaly (Thessalía), the home of Mt. Olympus and other famous peaks in Greek mythology, was regarded as a special place by the ancient Greeks. Olympus, of course, was the abode of the gods; Mt. Pelion was inhabited by frolicking centaurs and wood fairies; and Mt. Ossa was used as a "stepping stone" by the giant Aloadae to reach heaven and try to dethrone the gods. As you drive from Athens, entering Thessaly through the provincial town of Lamía, you'll notice the change in landscape—the stark contrast between the lowlands and the lofty, scenic heights. In the western part of the Thessalian Plain are the startling *metéora* ("rocks in air"), just outside the provincial capital of Kalabáka. When you see these incredible monoliths towering majestically over the flat plains, you can understand why the ancients—and, later, the Christians—invested this region with religious significance.

When you pass through Lamía, notice the medieval castle of the Duchy of Catalan (built between 1319 and 1393) towering on the heights above you to the northeast. From this prospect it could guard the narrow waterway curling around Évvia into the mainland ports. Scholars have found that its walls were largely built over the remains of classical ones, proving once again that once a fortress, always a fortress.

An old local through road that wends its way around tavernas, beaches, kids on bicycles, and erratic coastline is a slower, more difficult route compared with the modern toll road, but it's certainly more fun.

VÓLOS & MT. PELION

Vólos is a bustling industrial city and the third most important port in Greece, after Piraeus and Thessaloníki, the gateway to the Sporades. The verdant Mt. Pelion area to the east and south is one of the most traditional, charming, and colorful areas of Greece.

Vólos figures in one of the most famous of Greek myths. Some years before the Trojan War, King Pelias, usurper of the throne of Iolkos, agreed to return it to Jason, his nephew and rightful heir, if he could bring him the magical Golden Fleece (thought to be a symbol of the rising sun). Jason set sail on the famous quest aboard the *Argo* from Vólos (ancient Iolkós) with 50 oarsmen and such luminaries as Theseus, Orpheus, Herakles (Hercules), Asclepius, Castor, and Pollux. Jason returned from Kolchís, on the Black Sea, with the Golden Fleece and the woman who'd helped procure it, the enchantress Medea. Later he cast Medea aside in order to marry Glauce (Creusa), daughter of the king of Corinth, and Medea revenged herself famously by killing Glauce and her father, then the two sons of Glauce and Jason—the subject of eloquent tragedies by Euripides and Seneca. Jason then wandered aimlessly until his death.

Stories from mythology may constitute the only appeal that the modern-day city of Vólos will have for many. Because of the devastation of two earthquakes in 1955, today's rows of concrete housing, functional commercial buildings, and an active but unattractive port are what confront the visitor. However, it's the gateway to the Sporades islands of Skíathos, Skópelos, and Alónissos. (Skýros is more easily reached from Kými, Évvia.) Once touched by Pelion's wooded, fairyland beauty, you may decide to sample these equally blessed, verdant islands and leave the sun-bleached, arid Cyclades to others.

If you continue on a long walk (25 minutes) east along the water, past Platía Yiórgiou (a pleasant park) and past the Church of Áyios Konstandínos, you'll come to the **archaeological museum,** on Athanasáki Street, famous for its permanent exhibit of prehistoric finds from throughout Thessaly, as well as painted funerary stelae from the Hellenistic village of Dimítrias. It's open Tuesday to Sunday from 8:30am to 3pm; admission is 500 Drs ($2.10) for adults, 400 Drs ($1.65) for seniors, and 300 Drs ($1.25) for students.

ESSENTIALS

GETTING THERE & DEPARTING   **By Train**   There are four regular trains leaving daily from Athens's **Stathmós Laríssis** (☎ 01/362-4402), plus three express trains, which cut the trip by half an hour. In Vólos, call ☎ 0421/24-056 for information. There are six trains daily from Vólos to Thessaloníki, 15 to Lárissa—where connections with both Athens and Thessaloníki are frequent—and four to Kalabáka (for Metéora) via Tríkala.

By Bus   There are nine buses daily from Athens's Odós Liossíon, 12 from Lárissa, four from Thessaloníki, and two from Kalabáka and Lamía. (Service is more frequent in summer; call ☎ 01/831-7186 in Athens or ☎ 0421/25-527 in Vólos for information.)

By Boat   There's a ferry connection twice daily with Skíathos, once daily with Skópelos, once daily with Tríkeri (at the southern tip of Pelion), daily except Monday with Alónissos, every Tuesday and Friday via Kými to Skýros (12 hours!). Ferry tickets to the Sporades can be purchased from the **Sporades Travel Agency,** Odós Argonáfton 32 (☎ 0421/23-400), or from **George Skouris,** Odós Venizélou 14–26 (☎ 0421/27-204; fax 0421/30-668). In the summer there is **hydrofoil** service four to six times daily to Skiáthos, Skópelos, and Alónissos, with additional service to Tríkeri, Évvia, and Áyios Konstandínos. Hydrofoil tickets and information are available at **Falcon Tours,** Argonáfton 34 (☎ 0421/21-626).

By Car   From National Road 1, follow Highway 6 (E-87) or 30 east.

VISITOR INFORMATION   The **Thessaly region EOT (Greek Tourist Organization)** is on the north side of the main square, Platía Ríga Feréou, open Monday to Friday from 7am to 2:30pm (☎ 0421/23-500 or 0421/36-233). When it's closed, there's much useful information posted outside on the bulletin board. The **tourist police** (☎ 0421/27-094), open daily from 8am to 2:30pm, are on the second floor of the police station, at Odós 28 Oktovríou 179, 4 blocks inland from near the east end of the harbor.

ORIENTATION   The main square, **Platía Ríga Feréou,** is just off the northwest corner of the harbor. The **train station** is just west, and the **bus station** is a 10-minute walk southwest, at the corner of Grigoríou Lambráki and Lahaná streets. **Argonáfton Street** runs along the waterfront southeast from the main square, parallel to the main streets, **Iásonos** and **Dimitriádos** and **Ermoú;** the **ferry and hydrofoil dock** is about midway along Argonáfton Street.

GETTING AROUND   **By Bus**   There is bus service from Vólos to many of the most important villages of the Pelion peninsula: 10 daily southeast to Kalá Nerá, most continuing on to Áfissos; seven daily to the Vyzítsa via Miliés; 10 daily northeast to Makrynítsa via Portariá; six daily south to Milína via Argalastí and Hórto, three continuing on to Platan   á; three daily to Zagorá via Hánia; and three daily to Áyios Ioánnis via Tsangaráda. There's service also to many smaller viilages, but, as you see, the schedule is complicated; check the posted schedule at the station.

By Car Renting a car is probably the most convenient way for a group to sightsee in the Mt. Pelion region. We recommend **European Rent a Car,** at Odós Iásonos 79 (☎ **0421/36-238** or 0421/24-381; fax 0421/24-192); daily rates are about 16,000 Drs ($66.65) for a compact, including tax and mileage.

FAST FACTS There are several **banks** around Argonáfton, Iásonos, and Dimitriádos streets, but none keeps extended hours; travel offices will cash traveler's checks. The **post office** is at Odós Pávlou Melá 67 (about 4 blocks inland from the middle of the port); the **OTE** (telephone center) is nearby, on Venizélou Street, open 24 hours. Emergency **medical assistance** can be obtained at the Vólos Hospital (☎ **0421/27-531**), near the archaeological museum on the southeast side of town.

WHERE TO STAY & EAT

The best places to stay in centaur land are in the hills of Mt. Pelion. Of course, some people will prefer to stay closer to the ferryboat, train, or bus, so here are some suggestions.

When it's time to eat, you may fare best by picnicking. Try the markets along Iásonos (Jason) Street, 1 block in from the water. The only retaurant we can enthusiastically recommend is the **Tzafoliás Grill,** at Odós Argonáfton 40 (☎ **0421/ 29-626**). A dining suggestion in the unremarkable cuisine culture of Vólos: Try Dímitra retsína—it's locally made and widely acknowledged to be the best in Greece.

Hotel Iason. Odós Pávlou Melá 1, 380 01 Vólos. ☎ **0421/26-075.** 32 rms, 12 with bath (shower). TEL. 6,500 Drs ($27.10) single; 9,200 Drs ($38.35) double. Rates include breakfast. No credit cards.

The best deal around the port is the older Hotel Iáson (Jason). The friendly manager keeps a tidy place, whose spacious rooms have tidy bathrooms and balconies with port views.

Hotel Kipseli. Odós Ayíou Nikoláou 1, 380 01 Vólos. ☎ **0421/24-420** or 0421/26-020. 54 rms, 34 with bath (shower). TEL. 9,500 Drs ($39.60) single; 10,000 Drs ($41.65) double without bath, 11,600 Drs ($48.35) double with bath. Rates include breakfast. No credit cards.

The Hotel Kipséli is situated in the upscale section of the Vólos waterfront (to your right as you leave the ferry), where the rooms—some with harbor views—are fine. The people at the front desk are friendly and accommodating. Their cafeteria is also quite good.

Hotel Philippos. Odós Sólonos 9 (at Odós Dimitriádos), 380 01 Vólos. ☎ **0421/37-607.** Fax 0421/395-50. 39 rms, all with bath (shower). TV TEL. 9,600 Drs ($40) single; 13,500 Drs ($56.25) double. Breakfast 1,200 Drs ($5) extra. No credit cards.

This newer hotel, 2 blocks from the port back near Ríga Feréos Square, has quiet, comfortable rooms and a friendly manager who speaks English. The breakfast room is particularly attractive.

EXPLORING THE PELION HILLS

The area around Mt. Pelion is popular with Greeks, who rush up for long winter weekends or for the traditional Easter ceremonies. After you leave Vólos, the air is immediately cooler and fresher, and within minutes the scent of pines and basil eradicates the industrial fumes. You'll find that the farther you climb, especially when you reach the other side of the 5,305-foot massif, the more beautiful and timeless the scenery becomes.

You'll have no difficulty imagining this lush, green country as the home of the centaurs (creatures with the body of a horse and the torso and head of a man) of ancient mythology. Here they frolicked with pretty river nymphs and wood fairies who inhabited the verdant highlands and wreaked havoc with intruders. (Their hijinks are said to have kept the area from ever becoming overpopulated—and everyone who tours one of the most beautiful, scenic regions in Greece will have much to thank them for.) The cave of Chiron (Cheiron), the wise and benevolent centaur, is somewhere high on the mountainside. According to Homer, the heroes Achilles, Herakles, Asclepius, Jason, Aeneas, and Peleus all learned at his hooves. Most centaurs were known for their bawdy behavior and drunkenness, but Chiron was an expert at music, shooting, and the medicinal use of herbs and plants for which Mt. Pelion is still justly famous. (It was he who cut the *pílios* [spear] from one of the pine trees on Mt. Pelion, thereby saving the life of Achilles.)

KATIHÓRI

If you drive northeast from Vólos you'll pass through the pretty village of Anakassía on the way to Katihóri. Tucked up off the main road are a few traditional, "Pelion-style" houses lining narrow cobblestone streets. Local residents stroll through their village, skinned lambs ready for roasting tossed over their shoulders, oblivious of the occasional tourist.

Right on the side of the road is one of those special places worth coming to for a quiet and peaceful stay in the old Greek style, the **Guest House Matsangou** (☎ **0421/99-380;** fax 0421/35-030). Lily Matsangou's nine rooms are, like the exterior of the mansion, renovated in the traditional Pelion style. Her high-ceilinged, stucco-walled rooms have wood and flagstone floors, antique handcrafted furnishings, woven rugs, and tall, plush-mattressed beds. Grapevines grow over the trellis-roofed patio that overlooks the Pelion range and pine forests decending into the sea, a view undisturbed by modern life. The Matsangou is open year-round, but Lily requires a minimum booking to open in winter. Doubles with common bath are 11,400 Drs ($47.50).

PORTARIÁ

Some 2 miles from Katihóri is Portariá (altitude 1,965 feet), where a 13th-century **Chapel of the Virgin** stands next to the mid–18th-century church of **Áyios Nikólaos**. A modern Xenía Hotel intrudes on the mansions, whose roofs have been restored to their original gray slate. (Villagers usually opt for the cheaper, red terracotta tiles.) Around the picturesque square of this "commercial" center are a small bank, a post office, and some rooms for rent. A fountain, dated "1927," at the bend in the road, under the aging plane tree, offers delicious spring water. Portariá is far enough into the mysterious Pelion world to provide endless hikes and walks leading pleasantly to nowhere.

And there's an attractive hotel right here. The stone walls of the **Hotel Pelias** (☎ **0421/99-290,** 0421/99-291, or 0421/99-175) blend well with the quiet village square; inside, contemporary paintings and a handsome fireplace grace the inviting lobby. Doubles with bath, balcony, and breakfast run 12,500 Drs ($52.10) in summer (Visa accepted).

MAKRYNÍTSA

Some 10¹/₂ miles from Vólos is Makrynítsa, the star village of Pelion. It's the most traditional; centered around the charming Iríni (Peace) Square are three-story mansions, fountains, and spectacular old plane trees—one so large you can walk into it! The stone facade of the tiny Church of Áyios Ioánnis is decorated with ornate marble plaques. Next to it is a marble fountain where fresh cold water rushes from the mouths of bronze chimeras.

Right on the square, facing the church and fountain on one side and the breathtaking valley view on the other, is the **Pantheon Café** (☎ 0421/99-143), which has good food but rather indifferent service.

Whether or not you've come to spend the night, Makrynítsa is the perfect place to sample the laudable restoration work being done by the Greek government. Three mansions have already been restored and are now being used as hotels. The **Arhondiko Sisilianou** (☎ 0421/99-556) is located up the cobblestone steps behind the Church of Áyios Ioánnis. This mansion has a simple white stucco interior that's enlivened by traditional, dark earth-tone woven fabrics and gray slatted-wood doors and window shutters. Bed-and-breakfast doubles at all three restored *arhondiká* cost 15,500 Drs ($64.60).

Farther west from Iríni Square is the **Arhondiko Mousli** (☎ 0421/99-228), whose best feature is the immaculate slate-paved patio shaded by plum and plane trees. The tall stone mansion is capped with a second-story facade broken up by old wooden shutters and beautiful stained-glass windowpanes. The **Arhondiko Xiradaki** (☎ 0421/99-250) is below the road on the left before you reach the square.

Our first choice for less expensive accommodations is the **Hotel Diomídis** (☎ 0421/99-430 or 0421/99-090; fax 0421/99-114), where singles cost 9,700 Drs ($40.40) and doubles are 11,000 Drs ($45.85). Just follow the signs to the Sisilianoú Mansion and you'll walk first into the Diomídis's courtyard. The Roútsos have decorated the house cheerfully in traditional Pelion style, and each floor has a floor-length, late-night sitting lounge. Room no. 10 is the double to ask for; it has a balcony overlooking Vólos and the sea, in the direction of the Sporades.

The souvenir to buy from this region is honey, but nuts and homemade fruit preserves are also widely available and delicious. Makrynítsa is also famous for its fresh herbs (some 2,000 kinds!) gathered on Mt. Pelion, which are offered for sale.

Continuing 5¹/₂ mils from Portariá through chestnut trees, evergreens, and hairpin turns will bring you to **Hánia** (altitude 3,925 feet), the ski center of the region. You can contact the **Ski Center** in nearby Agrioléfkes (☎ 0421/96-417) for ski information, or the **Mountaineering Club Lodge** (☎ 0421/25-696 in Vólos), which sponsors area hikes and climbs. There's a **youth hostel** operating in Hánia sporadically throughout the year; call ☎ 0421/96-416 for information.

MILIÉS

In Pelion, the largest plane tree, the public fountain that sustains its neighbors, the central church, and a few tavernas usually mark the heart of a village. However, now there's a news kiosk, a mailbox, sometimes a pay phone, and occasionally a taxi stand or bus stop to complement the facilities.

Miliés, 19 miles southeast of Vólos, is no exception, with an outstanding **library** facing the village square. Two stories of historical volumes reflect the high degree of literacy and learning that has always existed in Pelion. (In the library's bookshop you can purchase a wonderful book of photographs of the region's traditional architecture.) The library is open Tuesday to Saturday from 8am to 1:30pm and 5 to 7pm and on Sunday from 10am to 1pm. Next door is the small **town hall,** and around the corner, a well-designed **folk museum.** The director, Fay Stamatis, has documented the family workshops that craft natural dyes, woven materials, tin work, and saddleries that still function in Miliés. Its open hours vary but they're posted on the front door; 20-minute cassette tours in English are available.

If you're ready to tackle some short local **hikes,** head down the hill through the village to the ramshackle mill house and abandoned train station. The railway tracks formerly served Miliés, Vyzítsa, and other villages all the way back to Vólos, and it's hoped that service will be restored. Until then, a stroll along the tracks through these green woods, roaring waterfalls, and gently sloped hills is quite rewarding.

Miliés is a wonderful place to while away time during Greece's dog days of summer. Residents can guide you down the village's stone steps to a well-kept traditional tower with a low wooden door. Knock and your hosts will lead you upstairs to several bedrooms and sitting rooms with polished wooden floors, woven drapes, hooked rugs, lead windows, and finely carved moldings. Many of the eight rooms have fireplaces, all have fresh flowers, and all overlook fields of goats, strolling farmers, rustling pines, and a valley frozen in time. A high-season double costs 15,800 Drs ($65.85).

Or you can drive (slowly) down the small, partially paved road right off the hairpin turn as you leave the town to **O Palios Stathmos** (Old Station) **Guesthouse** (☎ **0423/86-425**), a modern, three-story hotel just opposite the local landmark from which it takes its name; a double with bath costs 12,000 Drs ($50).

O Stathmos is also a popular local taverna. It serves the freshest, creamiest *tzatzíki* we've ever had and the Italian chef makes a tender beef in lemon sauce with herbed peas and crisp potatoes. With the house wine and a fresh salad, this is a real treat for two at about 3,000 Drs ($12.50). There's another taverna on the main square, next to the playground, with live music after 10pm nightly.

VYZÍTSA

Vyzítsa, northwest of Miliés, is an even more fulfilling destination, with its own square lined with plane trees, a central fountain, churches, and tavernas.

An additional feature here is the well-organized presence of the National Tourist Organization (EOT), which has opened eight restored mansions and guest houses for rent. Most are located on the right up from the main road, where signs point to the **Reception Guesthouse** (☎ **0423/86-373**). This reception also serves as the local folk-art museum, so those passing through should stop in to see the collection of snowshoes, clothing, utensils, and tools. A total of 60 beds is available; doubles with bath go for 15,500 Drs ($64.60), including breakfast. The main guest house serves breakfast for all in a common dining room; it also serves scrumptious baklavá and such spirits as *tsípouro* (strong, locally brewed ouzo).

Among the few inhabited homes are several decrepit mansions with caved-in roofs (a continual problem with slate), broken windows, and eroded stone siding; they contrast vividly with the lovely, restored mansions used as hotels. If you go to Vyzítsa, don't drink the water gushing down the main stone street to the bus stop. Instead, let the old Vyzítsians, sitting at the cafe/bar in the square above, usher you to another spring. On the way, you can sample the tunes on its aging Greek jukebox.

THE PELION BEACHES

After several miles of hairpin turns down from Makrynítsa, a left fork will take you through apple orchards to **Zagóra,** the largest town of Pelion, where traditional and more recent houses are scattered on the hillsides that slope down to the tilled fields in the valley below—and where John bought the best apples he's ever had, fresh off the trees. Taking the right fork leads to the cutoff for **Áyios Ioánnis,** 4¼ miles away. Every hotel, taverna, and campground in this small, easygoing community is a stone's throw from the water's edge without spoiling its natural beauty. Fresh fish, a lively nightlife, and a sandy beach keep travelers happy, and since it's off the beaten track it may remain this peaceful for a few more years.

The **Captain George Hotel and Bar** (☎ **0426/31-297**) is well known because of its colorful manager, Freddie Kourkouvellos, who spent many years in Boston.

Double rooms with bath and American-style breakfast cost 12,800 Drs ($53.35). Media freaks will appreciate the phone in every room and the availability of TV and VCR with almost-current films. Among Captain George and his crew, Chinese, Portuguese, English, and Greek are spoken.

Many less expensive rooms to rent are advertised in the village and are widely available for about 7,500 Drs ($31.25).

If you follow the road south, you'll go through Makriráhi to Tsangaráda, midway along the Pelion coast and 38½ miles from Vólos. Trucks of hay often snarl traffic—only one can pass at a time—and donkeys carrying bundles of wood plus old women out picking herbs also vie for a portion of roadway. **Mylopótamos,** 5 miles from Tsangaráda as the road forks east, is considered one of the prettiest, unspoiled beach areas of Pelion. It's a broad sandy stretch interrupted at intervals by surf crashing over the rocks.

On the hillside, about 1¼ miles from the beach road, is a unique guest house, clinging to the cliffs. The **Milopotamos Guesthouse** (☎ 0421/49-203) has more than a dozen double rooms whose balconies face the sea; rates are 8,800 Drs ($36.65) for two.

Local residents sent us to their favorite gourmet restaurant—a cookout! We bought fresh fish near the beach, grabbed a loaf of fresh bread, and headed to the grill to cook it, all the while sipping a fine local retsína and chomping pungent fresh tomatoes and cantaloupe.

EN ROUTE FROM VÓLOS TO KALABÁKA

The 37 miles between Vólos and Lárissa on the toll highway pass quickly. Lots of watermelon, heat, and unpaved roads make Lárissa feel like a midwestern cow town on a summer's day—in other words, a place to breeze through. It's a well-connected transportation hub, and there are several recently built hotels, but we think you'd do better to continue on.

TRÍKALA

From Lárissa, head due west to Tríkala. Here's another 37-mile drive one could do without; however, any route that shortens the way to Kalabáka and the marvelous monasteries of Metéora is okay with us. Tríkala, a friendly town of some interest, is believed to be the birthplace of Asclepius, the god of medicine. In the southwest part of town, Hellenistic-era walls and Roman baths mark the site of the oldest Asclepion in Greece. The ancient Doris became the Homeric city of Tríkki; it rose near the acropolis built above the Lítheos River. A rather picturesque Venetian fortress sits on St. Nicholas Heights, south of the city, and an old Muslim mosque can be found near the bus station.

If you're coming straight from Athens, **buses** run from Athens to Tríkala seven times daily, departing from the terminal at Odós Liossíon 260 (☎ 01/831-1434); between Tríkala and Lárissa there's a bus every half hour. Bus service to Vólos runs four times daily, to Kalabáka every 20 minutes all day, to Ioánnina twice daily, and to Metéora directly three times daily. Five daily **trains** pass through Kardítsa, departing from Athens's Stathmós Laríssis (☎ 01/821-3882, or 041/236-259 in Lárissa).

The **Hotel Lithaeon,** Odós Óthonos 6 (☎ 0431/20-690; fax 0431/37-390), conveniently located at Tríkala's bus station, is surprisingly pleasant; doubles with breakfast are 9,800 Drs ($40.85). A budget alternative is the small, older **Hotel Palladion,** Odós Výronos 4 (☎ 0431/28-091), a couple of blocks toward the river, where simple, but nice doubles with shared toilet facilities cost 6,800 Drs ($28.35).

If you're staying overnight in Tríkala, you'll want to find King George Square (Platía Vassiléos Yioryíou), on the banks of the river, for some nightlife, tavernas, and local color. From the bus station, follow the curving riverbed away from the abandoned mosque. The **Panorama Café,** atop the tallest building in town, is a good place for a drink. Our friends recommend the **Taverna Psatha,** on Kitrilákis Square, for the best traditional taverna fare.

KALABÁKA

Kalabáka (frequently written as Kalambáka) is a pleasant provincial town that was almost completely destroyed by the Germans during World War II. Most of what you see today is modern, but the people are friendly, and there are plenty of facilities for tourists because of the town's proximity to the astonishing monasteries of Metéora.

In this part of Thessaly the two great mountain ranges of Pindus (Píndos) and Ossa split apart to let the Pínios River flow into the Vale of Tempi, and from there to the sea. Kalabáka, at the foot of the Pindus massif, sits at the point where the Pínios reaches the level valley floor; it's believed that the unique rock formations of Metéora were formed by the heavily eroded riverbed of the Pínios at a time when it was a much more active and deeper river. It's said that the monks from Metéora believe that during the time of Noah's ark all of Thessaly was under water, which disappeared as the result of an earthquake. In much the same way that the ark landed on the peak of Mt. Ararat when the waters receded, the persecuted monks of the Convent of Stagón built their churches atop inaccessible pinnacles of time-worn stone. In the 12th century these small religious cells began to attract the devout from all over the Byzantine world, and by the 14th century Metéora was a community of such religious learning, art, and wealth that its only rival was Mt. Áthos. At this point the monks of the Monastery of Metéoron (Great Metéoron, the largest) had gained independence from the rule of the abbot of the Convent of Stagón and tried to take control of other, less influential, monasteries in the area. Such in-fighting led to a reduction in the number of monasteries.

The Turkish occupation of Greece had a favorable effect on Metéora, because Suleiman the Magnificent put strong bishops in charge of Thessaly's ecclesiastical matters. The Monasteries of Varlaám and Roussánou benefited most from the influx of funds and new recruits; their libraries were enriched with new manuscripts, their churches decorated with brilliant frescoes, and their chapels enlarged and refurbished. Over the next few centuries the fortunes of the Metéora monasteries again declined, and now only four still function (the former total had been 24).

ESSENTIALS

GETTING THERE & DEPARTING   By Train   There are seven trains daily from Athens's **Lárissa Station** (☎ **01/821-3882**)—three are express trains, which cut the 6-hour trip by 2 hours. There are also four trains daily to and from Thessaloníki, and three trains daily to and from Vólos. Kalabáka is at the western end of the narrow-gauge line to Vólos. Trains connect 10 times daily with the Athens–Thessaloníki line at Paleofarsálos (which locals usually call Stávros); check the schedule carefully in order to avoid a long wait there. Tickets can be bought at the **Kalabáka station** (☎ **0432/22-451**).

By Bus   Seven buses from Athens to Tríkala depart daily from the Athens terminal at Odós Liossíon 260 (☎ **01/831-1434**). Between Tríkala and Kalabáka there's a bus every 20 minutes all day, and to Metéora directly there's one three times daily. Call ☎ **0432/22-432** in Kalabáka for schedule information.

By Car   From Athens, take the Athens–Thessaloníki highway north to Lamia; from there, take the highway northwest to Kalabáka. From Delphi, take the

Lamia–Karditsa–Tríkala–Kalabáka highway north. Allow at least 6 hours for the Athens–Kalabáka trip.

ORIENTATION   Most of the town's main traffic arteries converge at the **central square,** from which the road veers right up through the village of **Kastráki** to Metéora. From the central square the main road, **Odós Trikálon,** leads southeast to another larger roundabout square, **Platía Ríga Feréou.** The **bus station** is a few blocks south of the main square, at the corner of Plátanos and Ikonómou streets. The **train station** is several blocks south of Platía Ríga Feréou, on the Tríkala–Ioánnina highway. There are tavernas on both squares, some hotels near the railroad station, and several hotels on the small streets around the central square and on the road to Metéora.

GETTING AROUND   By Bus   Local buses run five times daily from Kalabáka's central square to Metamórphosis (Great Metéoron) via Kastráki and the Áyios Nikólaos Monastery; the fare is 250 Drs ($1.05). You can walk from the bus stop in front of Metamorphosis to the Óssios Varlaám monastery, only 150 yards away. To reach the Ayía Triás and Áyios Stéphanos monasteries entails a 3-mile walk along the paved roadway. (Check with your hotel reception desk for bus schedules.)

By Taxi   If you don't have a car, we recommend taking a taxi to visit the monasteries. Kalabáka's **taxi stand** (☎ **0432/22-310**) is on the main street; for about 8,000 Drs ($33.35) you can book a cab for the $11^3/_4$-mile circuit to the six monasteries that are open to visitors, including a half-hour wait at each one; the drivers are generally quite knowledgeable.

FAST FACTS   The **police** can be found near the bus station on Hatzipétrou Street (☎ **0432/22-109**). The **post office** is 1 block above the central square. The **OTE** (telephone center) is at Odós Kastrakíou 27, on the right side of the road to Metéora. The **National Bank** is on Platía Ríga Feréou. For **medical emergencies** call ☎ **0432/22-222.**

THE MONASTERIES OF METÉORA

If you were to drive the $11^3/_4$-mile circular path through the valley of monasteries, you'd approach them in this order: Áyios Nikólaos, Roussánou, Metamórphosis (Great Metéoron), Óssios Varlaám, Ayía Triás, and Áyios Stéphanos. Below, however, we list the monasteries in the order of importance (according to our criteria). The following information will help you plan your tour:

Men in shorts and women in trousers or sleeveless dresses are not allowed to enter. This sign is posted in front of each monastery and convent, and the monks are quite serious. Women must wear skirts below their knees, men must wear long pants, and your arms must be covered.

For **disabled travelers,** the exquisite configuration of Metéora and its monasteries is best appreciated at a distance, but if you want to go inside a monastery, Áyios Stéphanos is the most easily accessible; it's just 20 yards across a footbridge (which will support a wheelchair) from the paved road. The easiest climb up is the 3-minute hike to Óssios Varlaám, which has lovely examples of frescoes and religious objects. If you have the stamina for just one solid 10-minute hike, then you *must* visit the area's largest creation—the Metamorphosis (Great Metéoron).

For more information, pick up a copy of the beautifully illustrated book *Meteora* by D. Z. Sofianos, or perhaps *Meteora, the Sacred Rocks and Their History,* which has a small foldout map; both are widely available at kiosks and souvenir shops in the area.

Metamorphosis (Great Metéoron, Megálou Meteórou). 422 00 Kalabáka. ☎ **0432/22-278.** Admission 600 Drs ($2.50). Wed–Mon 9am–1pm and 3:20–6pm.

The first monastery of Metéora was founded by St. Athanássios, a monk from Mt. Áthos, between 1356 and 1372. The church was built atop Platýs Líthos (Broad Stone), one of the largest flat-topped rock formations. Metéoron achieved its autonomy and religious authority after the king of Serbia's son became a monk there. The new monk, Joasaf, ensured royal donations to the monastery's coffers, making Metéoron the wealthiest and most powerful of the existing units. The sanctuary was enlarged in the middle of the 16th century to the size of the present-day church. It's decorated with colorful frescoes, elaborately carved wood, and an inlaid ivory pedestal for the bishop. In the narthex, notice the particularly gruesome images of the saints being tortured.

The museum is housed in the old dining room, part of the 16th-century addition to the original monastery. The museum contains a collection of rare manuscripts; most are modest illuminations of the Gospel and the Book of St. John, dating from between the 9th and 16th centuries. Next to the museum is the old kitchen that once served meals for the guests of the Meteoron Hostel. As you leave the museum and church, turn left at the base of the stairs. A small wooden door with a hole large enough for your head contains a bizarre array of the skulls of monks who served the monastery long ago.

Óssios Varlaám. 422 00 Kalabáka. ☎ **0432/22-277.** Admission 400 Drs ($1.65). Sat–Thurs 9am–1pm and 3:20–6pm.

The monastery of Óssios Varlaám, about 150 yards from Grand Metéoron, is an easier walk up, and well worth a visit. The stone corridors are filled with admonitory signs: DO NOT MAKE NOISE, NO SMOKING, PRIVATE ENTRY; but the lovely flowering garden softens the austerity of the place. The frescoes in the chapel (on the right) were done by Franco Catellano in 1565, 48 years after the monastery's founding by two wealthy brothers from Ioánnina. These frescoes were restored in 1870.

Áyios Nikólaos. 422 00 Kalabáka. ☎ **0432/22-375.** Admission 400 Drs ($1.65). Daily 9am–6pm.

The first monastery you'll come to on the road north from Kalabáka (and the first bus stop) is Áyios Nikólaos, perched on a lone rock towering above the road. You'll have to climb up there to see it—notice the pulley-and-basket system the monks once used—but the stairs can easily be climbed in 10 minutes. There are stairs to the left and a ramp to the right. (On our last trip, there were two donkey meisters offering to take visitors up for a small fee.)

Áyios Nikólaos is no longer inhabited and thus receives few visitors, making it the most intimate and serene of the monasteries. This monastery was built in 1388 and later expanded. Its small chapel is filled with excellent frescoes by the Cretan School painter Theophánes the Monk (done in 1527), which are low enough for close study. The chapel's ornately painted and carved-wood ceiling is in surprisingly good condition. We heartily recommend Áyios Nikólaos to sightseers with energy to spare after Metéoron.

Roussánou. 422 00 Kalabáka. No phone. Admission 400 Drs ($1.65). Daily 9am–1pm and 3–6pm.

This precariously perched nunnery, also known as Moní Ayías Varváras, was until a few years ago accessible only by a series of ladders. Now there's a path, staircase, and bridge to Roussánou and its smiling nuns. The monastery is thought to have been built in the late 13th century as a hermitage, and it has now been rebuilt and restored. It became a monastery by decree in 1545. The highlight here is the 16th-century Cretan frescoes depicting gory scenes of martyred saints (highly recommended).

Áyios Stéphanos. 422 00 Kalabáka. ☎ **0432/22-279.** Admission 400 Drs ($1.65). Tues–Sun 9am–1pm and 3:20–6pm (3–5pm in winter).

Áyios Stéphanos, the most distant of the monasteries open to the public, is also the richest and most accessible. It was founded as a hermitage in 1312 by Jeremias and built during the 1330s by the emperor Andrónicus III Paleológos. In 1961 it was converted into a nunnery, which includes doctors and scholars who are actively involved in social work as well as preserving and teaching Byzantine art and music. The older of the two churches, Áyios Stéphanos, dates from 1350 and its impressive frescos have recently been cleaned and restored. Murals are now being painted in the newer church, Áyios Harálambos (which dates from 1798). The small museum inside displays liturgical vestments, post-Byzantine icons, carved wooden crosses, and rare manuscripts. The view over Kalabáka and the plain of Thessaly is superb.

Ayía Triáda. 422 00 Kalabáka. ☎ **0432/22-220.** Admission 400 Drs ($1.65). Daily 8am–1pm and 3–6:30pm.

The Convent of Ayía Triáda (Holy Trinity), also called Ayía Triás, founded by the monk Dométios in 1438, is perhaps the most amazing sight of Metéora. Its solitary placement, approached by 139 steep steps, gives it the most remote and primitive feel and makes it one of the least visited sites. After you've caught your breath and are ready to enter, you can see in the first room the platform, attached to guide wires, that swings out to the nearby plateau to bring back materials and people. Inside, the small chapel is filled with frescoes, which are, sadly, blackened by the smoke from votive candles and the modern heater.

Ayía Triáda, on its lone, seemingly inaccessible peak, was the star location of *For Your Eyes Only,* a James Bond movie. The monastery is a superb construction that's best admired from afar; most of its interior is just not worth the climb.

Byzantine Church of the Assumption. On Kímisis Theotókou, Kalabáka. No phone. Admission free.

The cathedral *(mitrópolis)* of Kalabáka itself is well worth a visit. It's located on the highest street in the village, Kímisis Theotókou. The church, built in the 7th century and restored in 1326, is the only three-aisled basilica of its type other than Haghía Sophía in Istanbul. Its most prized object is the marble pulpit in the center in front of the doors of the sanctuary. The worn frescoes depicting the *Crucifixion* and *Ascension of Elijah* are the work of the Cretan monk Neóphytos, son of the artist Theophánes who painted the fine frescoes in the Áyios Nikólaos monastery. At the back of the altar is an ancient sun throne, and beneath it is a large crypt where local Christians once found refuge. In a corner of the apse, closed to the public, are mosaic fragments of a peacock image dating from the 11th century. A brief history of the church, in several languages, is available at the door. When we visited, a local religious holiday was being celebrated and all the women in their traditional black cotton, apron-covered dresses insisted on giving us cookies and servings of a delicious wheat, walnut, and cinnamon cereal called *kóliva.* It was one of those unexpected moments that make Greece so delightful.

WHERE TO STAY

We've heard a number of complaints about rooms that are offered by people who meet arriving buses and trains; be cautious about accepting such a room. Most of the hotels we recommend here are conveniently situated.

Hotel Aeolic Star. Odós Diákou 4, 422 00 Kalabáka. ☎☎ **0432/22-325.** Fax 0432/23-031. 18 rms, 9 with bath (shower). TEL. 4,950 Drs ($20.65) single without bath, 6,500 Drs ($27.10) single with bath; 6,600 Drs ($27.50) double without bath, 9,600 Drs ($40) double with bath. Rates include breakfast. V.

Above the central square, the friendly Papadelli family will make you feel right at home. John stayed here during his last visit and found the family getting ready to enlarge and renovate the breakfast room. The rooms are comfortable and pleasant, all with balconies, some with views of Metéora.

✪ **Hotel Antoniades.** Odós Trikkálon 148, 422 00 Kalambáka. ☎ **0432/24-387.** Fax 0432/24-319. 24 rms, all with bath (shower). TEL. 10,500 Drs ($43.75) single; 13,500 Drs ($56.25) double. Rates include breakfast. V.

Although it doesn't provide views of Metéora, the Antoniádes is the best all-around hotel value in town, with superior accommodations, a friendly staff, congenial atmosphere, and excellent food in its restaurant—which is recommended even for those not staying here. They've just added a new swimming pool and sun deck on the roof.

Hotel Astoria. Odós Kondíli 93, 422 00 Kalabáka. ☎ **0432/22-213.** 10 rms, 6 with bath (shower). 4,500 Drs ($18.75) single without bath, 8,000 Drs ($33.35) single with bath; 6,600 Drs ($27.50) double without bath, 9,900 Drs ($41.25) double with bath. No credit cards.

The Astoria is a smaller and older hotel, just half a block up from the train station. Its rooms are large, pleasant, and comfortable—especially good for a family. The friendly owner, who speaks good English, informed us that the hotel was named after New York's Waldorf Astoria, where his father used to work.

Hotel Helvetia. Odós Kastrakíou 45, 422 00 Kalabáka. ☎ **0432/23-041.** 18 rms, all with bath (shower). TEL. 11,300 Drs ($47.10) single; 14,500 Drs ($60.40) double; 18,000 Drs ($75) triple. Rates include breakfast. No credit cards.

The pleasant Hotel Helvetia is situated up from the main square on the road to Metéora. Its upper-floor rooms have windows facing across the street to the pock-marked "cave" rocks where many hermits had hidden homes. The hosts, Christos and Vassiliki Gasos, encourage camaraderie among guests in their cafe/bar. Their son, who often works at the reception desk, speaks English.

Hotel Rex. Odós Kastrakíou 11, 422 00 Kalabáka. ☎ **0432/22-042.** Fax 0432/22-372. 34 rms, all with bath (shower). TEL. 5,750 Drs ($23.95) single; 8,000 Drs ($33.35) double. Rates include breakfast. V.

One of the town's best values is just up from the main square on the road to Metéora. It's quiet for its central location and well maintained, with large rooms, attractive furniture, and some of the most comfortable beds in town.

Hotel Xenos. 422 00 Kalabáka. ☎ **0432/24-445** and 0432/24-991. Fax 0432/23-031. 61 rms, all with bath (shower). 12,000 ($50) single; 14,500 Drs ($60.40) double. V.

Those with their own transportation will enjoy the quiet isolation of this new hotel on the hillside off to the right of the highway just as you enter town from Tríkala. The rooms are large, tastefully furnished in modern style, with comfortable beds and pleasant views.

WHERE TO EAT

✪ **O Kipos Taverna.** Odós Trikálon. ☎ **0432/23-218.** Main courses 1,000–1,800 Drs ($4.15–$7.50). V. Daily 11am–3:30pm and 7:30pm–2am. Closed Mon in winter. GREEK.

This traditional taverna, "The Garden," at the east edge of town on the road to Tríkala, is picture perfect. Its food is all prepared to order, and it plays authentic Greek music you're welcome to dance to. Its charcoal-broiled chicken is among the best we've ever tasted.

Santa Lucia Pizza. Odós Trikálon 85. ☎ **0432/23-024.** Pizza 1,250–2,000 Drs ($5.20–$8.35). No credit cards. Daily 11am–3pm and 5pm–midnight. ITALIAN/GREEK.

If you're hungry for something Italian-American, Santa Lucia has 15 kinds of pizza, five kinds of spaghetti, and 10 kinds of salad, as well as Greek dishes—and they deliver.

THE MT. OLYMPUS REGION

From Kalabáka you can return east through Tríkala to Lárissa, then follow the National Highway north to the Mt. Olympus region. About 1¼ miles north of the Ambelákia turn-off, you'll enter the **Vale of Tempe** (Témbi), which runs for nearly 6 miles along the Piniós River between the Olympus and Ossa mountain ranges—one of the few approaches to Greece from the north, which was taken by Xerxes and Alexander. There's an active scenic attraction road stop at **Ayía Paraskeví,** where you'll see hundreds of cars parked and Greek men pulling their wives and children by the hand across the busy highway to the shaded rocks and gushing waterfall at the **Spring of Daphne,** where, according to myth, Apollo chased and caught the beautiful nymph, who changed herself into a laurel tree *(dáphni),* which then became sacred to Apollo. A narrow footbridge crosses the river: to one side is a modern chapel; to the other, a pleasant cafe and souvenir shops selling tokens of Paradise.

Continuing north through the vale, you'll see the ruins of the **Castle of the Beautiful Maiden** (Kástro tis Oreás), a Frankish outpost. At the north end of the vale you'll see another impressive **castle** crowning the hill above **Platamónas,** from which it guarded the Gulf of Thermae. It was built between 1204 and 1222 by the Crusaders, and was spared by the Turks only because they used it to guard against pirates from the east. Here you'll be entering Macedonia.

About 43 miles north of Lárissa is the tiny village of **Litóhoro,** at the base of Greece's legendary **Mt. Olympus** (Óros Ólymbos); at 9,550 feet, it's the highest mountain in Greece. Litóhoro is the starting point for climbing the mountain.

Mount Olympus, the equivalent of Heaven (or the Top of the Sky) for the ancients, was, of course, the home of the gods. Apollodorus and Homer tell of the Gigantomachy, the War between the Olympians and the Giants, sons of Uranus (Sky) and Gaia (Earth), creators of our cosmos, the ordered world created from chaos. Their many sons, the Titans, included the one-eyed monster Cyclops. His brother Cronus eventually led an uprising of Titans to take over leadership of the cosmos.

Uranus predicted that some day Cronus, too, would lose his throne to one of his sons. Each time his wife, Rhea (the Earth Mother), bore him a child, Cronus swallowed it whole to forestall the outcome of Uranus's prediction. Finally, when her sixth child was born, Rhea dressed a large stone in baby clothes and fed it to Cronus. Her hidden son, Zeus, was given to the goat Amalthea, to be raised in Crete. When Zeus reached manhood, his mother helped him to feed a special potion to Cronus, which made him throw up the other five children, all gods, who were ready to do battle. Zeus (with the help of his siblings) took over Cronus's kingdom and established his home on Greece's highest peak, Olympus.

Homer describes the attempt made by the Giants to return the attack: "Ossa they strove to set upon Olympus, and upon Ossa leafy Pelion, so that the heavens might be scaled." Zeus had cunningly enlisted the aid of the Cyclops, uncle of Cronus, who forged for him the powerful thunderbolt that became his symbol. Ovid wrote about the battle's outcome: "Then the omnipotent Father with his thunder made Olympus tremble, and from Ossa hurled Pelion." Thus was Mt. Olympus secured for the gods, and it was not until 1913 that a mortal dared to scale this highest peak.

Mount Olympus is by no means an easy climb, but in summer fit and fairly experienced trekkers with good boots, warm clothes, water, and provisions will be able to make it in 2 or 3 days. The climb requires preparation, however; the Greek Tourist Organization (EOT), the Federation of Mountaineering and Skiing (EOS), or the Association of Greek Climbers (SEO) can help you plan the trip. There are some English-speaking guides available in Litóhoro, as well as lodgings, tavernas, minimarkets, and provision stores along 28 Oktovríou, which is up from the central square.

The most popular trail up Mt. Olympus starts at the village of Priónia, 11 miles southwest of Litohóro. There's no bus service from Litóhoro to Priónia; if you don't have a car, you could hitch a ride or take a **taxi**. Alternatively, you could rent a **motorbike** for about 6,000 Drs ($25) or a **bike** for about 1,800 Drs ($7.50) from the YHA Hostel (☎ **0352/82-176**). Another option (for the energetic) is to hike along a marked trail following the Enipeas River.

ESSENTIALS

GETTING THERE & DEPARTING   By Train   There are 10 trains daily to Litóhoro, continuing on to Thessaloníki; they depart from Athens's **Stathmós Laríssis** (☎ **01/821-3882**). (The station is near the coast, 5¹/₂ miles from Litóhoro; you must walk 150 yards to the highway and catch a bus on to Litóhoro.)

By Bus   There are three daily buses to Kateríni from Athens's terminal at Odós Liossíon 260 (☎ **01/831-7059**); get off at Litóhoro. There are seven buses a day from Athens to Lárissa (☎ **01/831-7109**), where there is frequent local bus service to Litóhoro. There are eight buses daily from Thessaloníki to Litóhoro. There is hourly bus service from 6am to midnight between Kateríni and Litóhoro.

By Car   Take National Road 1 for 43 miles north of Lárissa; Litóhoro is 6 miles east of the highway.

VISITOR INFORMATION   There's a small **Greek Tourist Organization (EOT)** office on the main street just before the road to Priónia. The **Federation of Mountaineering and Skiing (EOS)** has a regional office (☎ **0352/81-944,** or 01/323-4555 in Athens) in Litóhoro—turn left off the main street opposite the Myrto Hotel and follow the signs—open Monday to Friday from 9am to 1pm and 6 to 8pm and on Saturday from 9am to 1pm; the staff speaks English and can give you advice, as well as a free pamphlet with details on most trails. The federation maintains three shelters on Olympus: one at Spílios Agapitós (altitude 6,875 feet, 13¹/₂ miles from Litóhoro); on the eastern face of Olympus at Vryssopoúles (altitude 6,225 feet); a 15-bed shelter at King Paul (altitude 8,840 feet, 1¹/₂ hours away from Spílios Agapitós). The shelter at Stavrós (altitude 3,275 feet, 1¹/₂ hours from Litóhoro) is maintained by the **Thessaloníki Alpine Club** (☎ **031/224-710**).

ORIENTATION   The **main street** of Litóhoro is Ayíou Nikoláou, the road from Kateríni, which leads to the **central square** *(kentrikí platía)*. The **road to Priónia,** where the trail up the mountain begins, is off to the right just before the square. **Odós 28 Oktovríou** leads up off to the left from the central square.

FAST FACTS   The **OTE** and **police station** (☎ **0352/81-100**) are near the Greek Tourist Organization (EOT). The **post office** and **National Bank** are on the central square.

12 The Sporades

Greeks have been vacationing in the Sporades (Sporádes, "Strewn") islands for years, attracted by fragrant pine trees growing down to the edge of golden-sand beaches. Few foreign tourists had ventured to any of the Sporades, preferring the oft-sailed passages leading to the Cyclades. With so few foreign visitors, prices stayed low and hotels and restaurants remained relatively empty.

But it was only a matter of time before this idyllic state of affairs would come to an end. Groups began to visit Skiáthos, and later Skópelos. An airport was built on Skiáthos with flights to and from Athens several times a day and, in the summer, up to 80 charter flights a week from Europe. Now there's hydrofoil service linking the islands as well as connecting them to several mainland ports.

The islands are lush with plum, fig, olive, grape, and almond orchards planted in the midst of pine and plane forests. The long crescent-shaped beaches—some sandy, others of polished snow-white stones—are superior to nearly any in the Aegean islands.

The downside is that overdevelopment and package-tour groups have marred beautiful **Skiáthos,** and it has now become one of the most expensive Greek islands. We don't recommend it in summer—unless, of course, you're looking for an active social scene on the crowded beaches and in the many nightclubs.

Skópelos has one of the most beautiful ports in the country, and it's faring somewhat better—though it, too, is getting expensive and crowded in the summer. More distant **Alónissos** is less attractive at first sight, and package-tour groups are making inroads, but it still has a lot of low-key charm and is less expensive, and its people are considerably friendlier than on its more popular neighbors. More remote **Skýros** remains one of Greece's most interesting island destinations, with its own distinctive culture, Cycladic-like whitewashed cube architecture, an arid landscape, and some very nice beaches. Some people find it a bit odd, even pretentiously New Age, but we still recommend it for those who want to get away from the crowd.

There are good ferry, hydrofoil, and excursion-boat connections between the mainland at Vólos and Áyios Konstandínos and the three northern Sporades (Skiáthos, Skópelos, and Alónissos); in summer you'll rarely have to wait more than an hour from early morning to mid-evening. If you're departing from Athens, you might want to contact **Alkyon Travel,** Odós Akademías 97, near Omónia Square (☎ **01/384-3220** or 01/384-3221); it can arrange bus transportation to Áyios Konstandínos and hydrofoil or ferry tickets. Boats to Skýros run much less often; it's best to take a boat from Kými on Évvia.

1 Skiáthos

41 nautical miles from Vólos

Skiáthos (sometimes Skíathos) offers natural beauty and sophistication. Most people come for the exquisite fine-sand beaches and sparkling blue water. Others are attracted to the lively nightlife, excellent restaurants, elegant shops, and handsome villas. Most Greeks continue on the ferry to Skópelos or Alónissos, both of which are less inundated by foreign visitors during the high season.

If there's any possibility for you to visit Skiáthos before July 20 or after September 20 (during this period the tourist crush is at its worst), try to do so. If not, the overwhelming demand for accommodations may force you to visit Skiáthos as a day trip. But make the effort in any case; if you don't like Skiáthos or can't find a room, you can always take a hydrofoil to another, less crowded destination.

ESSENTIALS

GETTING THERE & DEPARTING   By Plane   Olympic Airways offers daily flights from Athens (twice daily in April and May, five time daily June through September); contact **Olympic Airways** information in Athens (☎ **01/926-7251**) for reservations. The Olympic Airways office on Skiáthos (☎ **0427/22-200**) is on the right side of the main street inland from the port. There is presently no bus service from the airport to town; expect to pay about 1,500 Drs ($6.25) by taxi.

By Boat   Skiáthos can be reached by ferry (3 hours) or hydrofoil (75 minutes) from Vólos or Áyios Konstandínos. There's also ferry service once or twice a week from Kými, on Évvia (5 hours). During the high season there are four hydrofoils daily from Vólos, three from Áyios Konstandínos, and almost daily from Thessaloníki (3 hours). If you're in Athens, depart from Áyios Konstandínos; **Alkyon Travel,** Odós Akademías 97, near Omónia Square (☎ **01/384-3220** or 01/384-3221), can arrange bus transportation to Áyios Konstandínos and hydrofoil or ferry tickets. From the north, Vólos is closer, enabling you to make a quick side trip to the Mt. Pelion region. If you're going to Skiáthos, it makes little sense to leave from Kými unless you're coming from Skýros. For hydrofoil information, contact the **Ceres Hydrofoil Joint Service** in Piraeus (☎ **01/453-7107** or 01/453-6107), **Skiáthos Holidays** on Skiáthos (☎ **0427/22-018**), in Áyios Konstandínos (☎ **0235/31-614**), in Thessaloníki (☎ **031/223-811**), or in Vólos (☎ **0421/39-786**) for schedules and details. For ferry schedules contact the **port police** on Skiáthos (☎ **0427/22-017**). Ferry tickets can be purchased through several local travel agents (Skiáthos information is ☎ **0427/22-216** or 0427/22-209). Plan your itinerary carefully in order to make good connections between buses and ferries (or hydrofoils).

ORIENTATION   Hydrofoils and ferries dock at the port town of **Skiáthos,** also called Hóra, on the island's southern coast toward the east end of the island. It lies on the main roadway that links the 7^1/$_2$ miles of southern resort developments together. Skiáthos's north coast is much more rugged and scenically pure: steep cliffs, pine forests, and rocky hills predominate.

Skiáthos is a relatively modern town, built in 1830 on two low-lying hills, then reconstructed after heavy German bombardment during World War II. The handsome **Boúrtzi fortress** jutting out into the middle of the harbor is an islet connected by a broad causeway. Ferries and hydrofoils stop at the port on the right (east) of the fortress and fishing boats and excursion caïques dock on the left (west). The **Church of Áyios Nikólaos** dominates the the hill on the east side and the larger **Church of Tríon Ierarchón** ("Three Archbishops") balances it lower on the west side.

The busy **main street,** Odós Papadiamándis, with car traffic, leads off the harbor and up through town; most services are found here. On the west flank of the harbor (the left side as you disembark the ferry) are several cheerful outdoor cafes; a few traditionally built small hotels; the excursion caïques for the north-coast beaches, adjacent islands, and around-the-island tours; and in the corner, the broad steps leading up to the town's next level.

Climbing the stairs above the Oasis Cafe will bring you to **Platía Tríon Ierarchón,** a stone-paved mall around the town's most important church, with many boutiques, bars, and ornate villas around it. The eastern flank is home to many tourist services as well as a few recommended hotels; beyond it the harborfront road branches right along the yacht harbor, an important nightlife area in the summer, and left toward the **airport.**

VISITOR INFORMATION   The nearest **Greek Tourist Organization** office is in Vólos (☎ **0421/23-500**), a 1-hour ride away from the mainland; the staff is very knowledgeable about the Sporades, Metéora, and the Mt. Pelion region. There's information and a good map of the island and town in the free magazine *Summer Skiáthos.*

The **Mare Nostrum Holidays Office,** at Odós Papadiamándis 21 (☎ **0427/ 21-463** or 0427/21-464; fax 0427/21-793), is open daily from 8am to 10pm; it books villas, hotels, and rooms; sells tickets to many of the around-the-island, hydrofoil, and beach caïque trips; books Olympic flights; exchanges currency; and cashes all traveler's checks without commission. Katerina Michail-Craig, the charming managing director, speaks excellent English, is helpful and exceedingly well informed, and has lots of tips on everything from beaches to restaurants. **Skiáthos Holidays,** the grumpy Flying Dophin agent, is right on the *paralía.* (☎ **0427/22-018** or 0427/ 22-033); call for up-to-date departure schedules. Tickets may be bought at most travel agencies. **Nomikos Lines,** at the base of Papadiamándis Street and the *paralía* (☎ **0427/22-209** or 0427/22-276), operates the ferryboats to the other islands.

GETTING AROUND   By Bus   Skiáthos has public bus service along the south coast of the island from the **bus station** on the harbor to Koukounariés, with stops at the various beaches in between. The conductor will ask where you're going and determine the fare after the bus is under way; the maximum fare is 350 Drs ($1.45). In April and November buses run six times daily; in May and October every hour from 9am to 9pm; in June and September every half hour from 8:30am to 10pm; and in July and August every 20 minutes from 8:30am to 2:30pm and 3:30pm to midnight.

By Taxi   Taxis can be found on the harborfront. They are unmetered and much in demand, so you'll have to negotiate the fare.

By Car & Moped   Two reliable car-rental agencies are **Creator,** at Papadiamándis 8 (☎ **0427/22-385**), and the local **Avis** licensee, on the *paralía* (☎ **0427/21-458;** fax 0427/23-289), run by the friendly Yannis Theofanidis. Expect to pay 18,000 to 24,000 Drs ($75 to $100) per day in the high season, somewhat less at other times. Mopeds are available from **K. Dioletta Rent a Car,** on Papadiamándis Street, starting at 3,500 Drs ($14.60) per day.

By Water Taxi   The north-coast beaches, adjacent islands, and the historic Kástro are most easily reached by caïque. These smaller vessels sail frequently from the fishing harbor west of the Boúrtzi fortress; their beach and island tour schedules are posted on signs over the stern. An around-the-island tour that includes stops at Lálaria Beach and Kástro will cost about 4,000 Drs ($16.65).

FAST FACTS The local **American Express** agent is Mare Nostrum Holidays, at Odós Papadiamándis 21 (☎ **0427/21-463**), open daily from 8am to 10pm.

There are many **banks** in the town, such as the National Bank of Greece on Papadiamándis Street, open Monday to Friday from 8am to 2pm and 7 to 9pm and on Sunday from 9am to noon (closed Saturday).

For medical emergencies contact the **Skiáthos Hospital** (☎ **0427/22-040**). The **police station** is about 400 yards from the harbor on Papadiamándis Street (☎ **0427/21-111**), on the left.

The **post office** is on Papadiamándis Street (☎ **0427/22-011**), inland from the harbor about 300 yards on the right, open Monday to Friday from 7:30am to 2pm; it also exchanges money.

The **OTE (telephone office)** is on Papadiamándis Street, inland from the harbor about 300 yards on the right, open Monday to Friday from 7:30am to 10pm and on Saturday and Sunday from 9am to 2pm and 5 to 10pm.

SPECIAL EVENTS The **Aegean Festival** presents nightly performances of ancient Greek tragedies and comedies, traditional music and dance, modern dance and theater, and visiting international troups in the outdoor theater at the **Boúrtzi Cultural Center,** on the islet in the harbor, from mid-June until the beginning of October. Performances begin at 9:30pm and cost 4,000 Drs ($16.65), half price for students; call ☎ **0427/23-717** for information.

EXPLORING THE ISLAND

Skiáthos town itself, with its two-story whitewashed villas, is a pleasant place for strolling.

The main street is named after Alexándros Papadiamándis, the island's best-known son, an author who made his fame writing about island life and Greek customs in an idiosyncratic style and vernacular language that defies good translation into other languages. The **Papadiamándis House,** off the main street on the right a couple of blocks inland from the port, has been turned into a museum filled with his works and memorabilia; it's open Tuesday to Sunday from 9:30am to 1pm and 5:30 to 7:30pm.

The handsome little **Boúrtzi** is also well worth a visit. Its **Cultural Center,** open daily from 10am to 2pm and 5:30 to 10pm, hosts art exhibits during the summer.

The natural beauty of the island makes it a special place for those who love the outdoors. From the port to the northern tip, **Kástro** (see below for details) is an enjoyable 2-hour hike over scrubby brush, rolling green hills, and fields of wildflowers.

If you take the first paved road to the left off the airport road and follow the signs, you can visit the island's most beautiful architectural site, the **Evangelístria Monastery,** and beyond it on the mule path is the abandoned **Áyios Harálambos Monastery.** Hikers may want to pick their way down to Lálaria or continue west to Kástro. Mule trips are offered by the various travel agencies.

THE BEACHES

Skiáthos is most famous for its beaches, and we'll cover the most important ones briefly, clockwise from the port. Through the years, Europeans and Greeks alike have voted with their sandals and umbrellas for Koukanaries, although we prefer the more remote Lálaria. Either way, our point is, head straight for the sands!

The most popular beaches are west of town along the 7¹/₂ miles of coastal highway. You can rent an umbrella and two chairs at most beaches for about 1,750 Drs ($7.45) per day.

The first, **Megáli Ámmos,** the sandy strip below the popular tour-group community of Ftélia, is so close to town and in such company that it's hardly worth mentioning. **Vassílias** is usually also dismissed with a shrug. **Achládias** is said to have been very nice before it became overwhelmed by resorts. **Tzanérias** is thought to be a slight improvement; then farther out on the Kalamáki peninsula, south of the highway, **Kanapítsa** begins to excite some interest, especially among those interested in water sports; the **Kanapítsa Wat-Sport** [*sic*] **Center** (☎ **0427/21-298**) offers water and jet skis, windsurfing, air chairs, sailing, and speed boats for rent. Scuba divers may want to stop by the **Dolphin Diving Center** (☎ **0427/22-520**) at the big Nostos Hotel.

Across the peninsula, **Vromólimnos** ("Dirty Lake") is fairly attractive and usually relatively uncrowded, perhaps because of its unsavory name and the cloudy (but not polluted) water from which that name comes, and it offers waterskiing and windsurfing. **Ayía Paraskeví** is also highly regarded. **Platánias,** the next major beach, is usually uncrowded, perhaps because the big resort hotels there have their own pools and sun decks. Past the next headland, **Troúlos** is one of the prettiest beaches because of its relative isolation, its crescent shape, and the islets that guard the small bay. The major road north from the coastal highway here leads to the **Kounístria Monastery,** a pretty 17th-century structure that contains some beautiful icons, in a lovely spot with a nice taverna. Horseback riders should note that the **Pinewood Horse Riding Club** is located on this road.

The last bus stop is at the much ballyhooed **Koukounariés.** The bus, usually so packed with barefoot, bikini-clad visitors that it's a wonder it doesn't tip over, chugs uphill past the Pallas Hotel luxury resort. As the bus descends, it winds around the inland waterway, Lake Strofílias, and then stops at the edge of a fragrant pine forest. *Koukounariés* means "pine cones" in Greek, and behind this grove of trees is a half-mile-long stretch of fine gold sand in a half-moon-shaped cove. Tucked into the evergreen fold are some changing rooms, a small snack bar, and the concessionaire for windsurfers. The beach is extremely crowded with an easy mix of topless sunbathers, families, and singles, all out to polish their suntans. On the far west side of the cove is the island's Spartan Xenia Hotel, presently unoccupied. (There are many lodgings in the area, but because of the mosquito population and ticky-tacky construction, we prefer to stay back in town or in a villa.)

Ayía Eléni, located a short but scenic walk from the Koukounariés bus stop (the end of the line) west across the tip of the island, is a broad cove popular for windsurfing because it's a bit rougher than the south-coast beaches but not nearly as gusty as those on the north. Across the peninsula behind the deserted Xenia Hotel, a 20-minute steep-grade walk from the Koukounariés bus stop, is **Banana** (still sometimes called Krássa), which is the island's most fashionable nude beach. It's slightly less crowded than Koukounariés, but with the same sand, pine trees, chairs, umbrellas, and windsurfer/jet-ski rentals and a snack bar or two. **Little Banana** is presently the gay beach.

Limonáki Xerxes (also called **Mandráki**), north across the tip of the island, a 20-minute walk up the path opposite the Lake Strofílias bus stop, is a cove where Xerxes brought in 10 triremes to conquer the Hellenic fleet moored at Skiáthos during the Persian Wars. It's a pristine and relatively secluded beach for those who crave a quiet spot. **Elía,** east across the little peninsula, is also quite nice. Both beaches have small refreshment kiosks.

Mégas Asélinos, east along the north coast, is a windy beach where free camping has taken root; it's linked to the coastal highway via the road that leads to the Kounístria Monastery (continue north when the road forks off to the right toward the monastery). There's also an official campsite and a fairly good taverna. **Mikrós Asélinos,** farther east, is smaller and quieter, and you can reach it via a road that leads off to the left just before the monastery. Most of the other north-coast beaches are only accessible by boat.

✪ **Lálaria,** on the island's northern tip, near Kástro, is (in our estimation) one of the loveliest beaches in Greece. One of its unique qualities is the Trípia Pétra, perforated rock cliffs, that jut out into the sea on both sides of the cove. These have been worn through over time by the wind and the waves to form perfect archways. From the shore these "portholes" frame a sparkling seascape. You can lie on the gleaming white pebbles—while gulls squawk in the distance—and admire the bright-blue Aegean and cloudless sky through their rounded openings. The water at Lálaria beach is an especially vivid shade of aquamarine because of the highly reflective white pebbles and marble and limestone slabs on the sea bottom. The swimming here is excellent, though the undertow can sometimes be quite strong. If you swim through the arches against the brisk *meltémi* winds, you can play with the echo created inside them. Out in the water you can admire the glowing silver-white pebble beach and jagged white cliffs above it. There are many naturally carved caves in the cliff wall that lines the beach, providing privacy or shade for those who've had too much exposure. Lálaria can be reached only by an excursion caïque from the port; the fare is 4,000 Drs ($17) for an around-the-island trip, which usually includes stops at one or more of the other sights along the north coast.

There are also two acceptable beaches on the east end of the island, gray-sand **Mégas Yialós** and **Órmos Xánemos,** which can be reached by car, both windy, unprotected coves that also suffer from proximity to the airport. Excursion caïques can also take you to the small island of **Tsougriá,** opposite Skiáthos town, where there's a small taverna and more isolated swimming.

KÁSTRO

Kástro, the old fortress capital, was built in the 16th century when the island was overrun by the Turks; its remote and spectacular site offered protection from pirate raids, but it was abandoned shortly after the War of Independence when such measures were no longer necessary. Once joined to firm ground by a drawbridge, the fortress can now be reached by concrete stairs. (If you visit, carry up a load of building materials for use in the current reconstruction.) The remains of more than 300 houses and 22 churches have largely fallen into the sea, but three of the churches, with porcelain plates imbedded in their worn stucco facades, still stand, and the original frescoes of one are still visible. From this citadel prospect there are excellent views to the Kastronísia islet below and the sparkling Aegean.

Kástro can be reached on foot, a 2-hour hike from the port. Starting out on the uphill path just west of the harbor will take you by the Monasteries of Áyios Fanoúrias, Áyios Dionísios, and Áyios Athanássios to Panayía Kardási, where the road officially ends. You can also reach Kástro by excursion caïque, by mule or donkey tour (available through most travel agencies), or by moped via the latest road that runs to the north coast from just south of Ftélia.

SHOPPING

Skiáthos offers excellent shopping. The merchandise is by no means cheap, but the quality is high and there is considerable variety. The highlight for Greek crafts and folk art is ✪ **Archipelago** (☎ **0427/22-163**), adjacent to the Papadiamándis House. This brilliantly designed space is the work of Marcos and Andrea Botsaris, who are among the premier collectors of folk art in the country. The exquisite objects of art and folklore, both old and new, generally come from outside the Sporades, specifically from Epirus, Macedonia, Thrace, Lésvos, and the Peloponnese, and include costumes, jewelry, sculpture, painting, and all manner of objects.

A good place for clothing is **Aris,** Odós Agliánous 4 (☎ **0427/22-415**), where Maria Drakou sells bright, unusual dresses, T-shirts, and short, flirty, washable shirts hand-painted with lively floral and abstract patterns.

Gallery Castello, off Papadiamándis Street (☎ **0427/23-100**), is run by Maria Veyena, a woman with an eye for the eclectic: Greek jewelry, ceramics, rugs, weavings, and an assortment of objects varying from artistic to the everyday, old and new, make up the ever-changing inventory. We especially like Maria's taste in antique silver jewelry as well as weaving from Pelion, Epirus, and Crete. Open daily from 9:30am to 2pm and 6 to 11pm.

Galerie Varsakis, on Tríon Ierarchón Square, above the fishing port (☎ **0427/ 22-255**), has another excellent collection of folk antiques, enbroidered bags and linens, rugs from around the world, and other collectibles. We found reasonably priced gifts, admired the superb antiques, and discovered that Harris, the proprietor, speaks English and is quite an original himself.

Island, on upper Papadiamándis across from the OTE (☎ **0427/23-377**), is a pleasant surprise in the world of look-alike T-shirt shops; it stocks all-cotton shirts, designed and made in Greece, as well as other casual wear both attractively styled and priced, and is open daily from 9:30am to 1:30pm and 5:30 to 10:30pm.

WHERE TO STAY

If you enjoy the restaurant/shopping/nightlife scene, or you've arrived with reservations at one of the resort communities, we'd recommend setting up a base for exploration in the port town. From here, you can try caïque excursions to the island's magnificent beaches or take public buses to various villages. Many families prefer to rent two- to four-bedroom villas outside the town or overlooking a beach, with only an occasional foray into town.

Between July 20 and September 20 it can be literally impossible to find a room on Skiáthos. If you're traveling at this time of year, try phoning ahead from Athens to book a room, or better still, book your accommodations well before you leave home. Many hotels will accept reservations when a deposit equal to one-third of the anticipated total amount is wired to them through an Athens bank or, if you book through an agency, is secured by check or by credit or charge card. (If you make plans in advance, most of these hotels ask that you reserve by mail 2 or 3 months before the summer season.) However, if you get off the ferry between 8am and 10pm without a reservation, head to **Mare Nostrum Holidays,** on Papadiamándis Street (☎ **0427/21-463**). They'll try to help you secure a place when all else fails.

Most of the "luxury" hotels were hastily built some years ago and have since been managed and maintained poorly, so even if you prefer to stay at a beach resort, we recommend that you check into one of the hotels in town and then investigate other possibilities before you commit yourself to one of the smaller properties offered by various agencies. If you plan to book lodgings through an agency, expect to pay at least 10,000 Drs ($41.65) a night for a first-class room, 40,000 Drs ($166.65) for a studio, or 80,000 Drs ($340) on up for a fully equipped three-bedroom villa on the beach. Most of these will be located on or near one of the island's popular beach resorts. Lower-cost housing is available in the town—which is where we usually stay.

All over the hillside above the eastern harbor are several unlicensed "hotels," which are actually recently constructed rooms to rent. When you're hotel hunting, talk to passersby and they can tell you which buildings are lodgings (you may be surprised).

One of the most pleasant parts of town is the quiet neighborhood on the hill above the bay at the western end of the port. Numerous private rooms-to-let can be found on and above the winding stair/street. Take a walk and look for the signs, or ask passersby or neighborhood shopkeepers.

Hotel Akti. Skiáthos, 370 02 Skiáthos. ☎ **0427/22-024.** 14 rms, all with bath (shower). TEL. 15,000 Drs ($62.50) single; 21,000 Drs ($87.50) double. AE, EURO, MC, V.

This thoroughly redone hotel has tastefully furnished rooms. However, it's on a fairly noisy, harborfront street and thus is not recommended for light sleepers.

Hotel Athos. Ring Rd., Skiáthos, 370 02 Skiáthos. ☎ and fax **0427/22-477.** 15 rms, all with bath (shower). TEL. 15,000 Drs ($62.50) single; 21,000 Drs ($87.50) double. AE, EURO, MC, V.

A relative newcomer (it opened in 1991), the Hotel Athos is on the bypass road that skirts above the town. It should be especially attractive to those who want easy access to the town without the bustle. The rooms, many facing the sea, are spotlessly clean and an especially good value in the low season.

Hotel Australia. Párodos Evangelístrias, Skiáthos, 370 02 Skiáthos. ☎ **0427/22-488.** 16 rms and studios, all with bath (shower). 8,000 Drs ($33.35) single; 15,000 ($62.50) double; 17,500 Drs ($72.90) studio with kitchen. No credit cards.

Turn right off Papadiamándis Street before the post office, then take the first left to find this plain, quiet hotel run by a couple who lived in Australia and speak English quite well. The rooms are sparsely furnished but comfortable, with small balconies; guests can share the refrigerator.

Boúrtzi Hotel. Odós Moraitou 8, Skiáthos, 370 02 Skiáthos. ☎ **0427/21-304.** Fax 0427/23-243. 23 rms, all with bath (shower). MINIBAR TEL. 13,600 Drs ($56.65) single; 14,200 Drs ($59.15) double. No credit cards.

The Boúrtzi caters largely to groups, but a few rooms are available to individuals; it's an attractive hotel in the middle of town. The back, garden-facing rooms are sure to be quieter. The owners also run the nearby 22-room Pothos Hotel (same telephone number), which has similar rooms and facilities.

Hotel Morfo. Odós Ananiniou 23, Skiáthos, 370 02 Skiáthos. ☎ **0427/21-737.** Fax 0427/23-222. 17 rms, all with bath (shower). TEL. 14,000 Drs ($58.30) single; 17,600 Drs ($73.30) double. Rates include breakfast. EURO, MC, V.

Turn right off the main street at the National Bank, then left at the big plane (sycamore) tree to reach this attractive hotel on your left on a quiet backstreet in the center of town. You enter through a small, well-kept garden into a festively decorated lobby. The guest rooms are comfortable and tastefully decorated.

WORTH A SPLURGE

Hotel Meltémi. Skiáthos, 370 02 Skiáthos. ☎ **0427/22-493.** Fax 0427/21-294. 18 rms, all with bath (shower). TEL. 14,500 Drs ($60.40) single; 22,000 Drs ($91.65) double. Rates include breakfast. EURO, MC, V.

On the east side of the harbor, opposite the many moored yachts, is the modern and comfortable Hotel Meltémi. Its spacious rooms may be booked by April, but give it a try; it's best to reserve at least 3 weeks in advance. The hosts, Yorgo and Giuliana Rigas, run a very friendly bar out on the waterside. The front rooms, which have balconies facing the harbor, are noisy.

Hotel Orsa. P.O. Box 3, Skiáthos, 370 02 Skiáthos. ☎ **0427/22-430.** Fax 0427/21-952. 17 rms, all with bath (shower). TEL. 22,000 Drs ($91.65) double. No credit cards.

One of the most charming small hotels in town is on the western promontory beyond the fishing harbor. To get there, walk down the port west past the fish stalls and Jimmy's Bar, go up two flights of steps, and look for a recessed courtyard on the left, with handsome wrought-iron details. Most of the rooms have windows or balconies overlooking the harbor and the islands beyond. A lovely garden terrace is a perfect place for a tranquil breakfast. Contact **Heliotropio Travel** on the east end of the harbor for booking.

✪ **Troulos Bay Hotel.** Troúlos, 370 02 Skiáthos. ☎ **0427/49-3909** or 0427/21-223. Fax 0427/21-791. 43 rms and studios, all with bath (tub). TEL. 23,500 Drs ($97.90) double; 27,500 Drs ($114.60) triple; 31,500 Drs ($131.25) studio. Rates include breakfast. AE, EURO, MC, V.

Though it's not exactly luxurious, this is our first choice of beach hotels, set on handsomely landscaped and well-kept grounds on the south coast's prettiest little beach. Like most of Skiáthos's hotels, the Troulos Bay is booked mostly by groups, but it performs well for them—it has won Thompson's "small and friendly award" 3 years in a row. The restaurant serves good food at reasonable prices, and the staff is refreshingly attentive and truly helpful. The rooms are large, attractive, and comfortably furnished, most with a balcony overlooking the gorgeous beach with lovely wooded islets beyond.

WHERE TO EAT

The harbor and the lanes around Papadiamándis Street are lined with mediocre, overpriced tavernas and cafes. As with most overdeveloped tourist resorts, there's a plethora of ice-cream parlors, fast-food stands, and minimarkets, but there are also lots of good (even excellent) eateries.

Kypséli, near the west end of the harbor, serves a good English breakfast with eggs and bacon, fresh orange juice, toast, cake, and coffee for 1,600 Drs ($6.65), but an extra cup of coffee will cost you 600 Drs ($2.50)!

There are a number of attractive, well-regarded places above the west end of the harbor beyond Tríon Ierarchón Church. Climb the steps to the left of the church under the awning at To Steki and you'll find **Stamátis Taverna,** recommended for traditional fare, and then on the left, **Le Bistro** (which we review below); **Ánemos,** most often mentioned by locals for seafood; **La Casa,** with Greek/Italian food; and up on the right, **Chez Julien,** with French cuisine.

✪ **Asprolithos.** Mavroyiáli and Koraï sts. ☎ **0427/23-110.** Reservations recommended. Main courses 1,600–6,000 Drs ($6.65–$25). AE, EURO, V. Daily 7pm–1am. GREEK/INTERNATIONAL.

Walk up Papadiamándis Street, a block past the high school, and turn right for a simply superb meal of light, updated taverna fare. You can order a classic moussaká here if you want to play it safe, or try such specialties as artichokes and prawns smothered in cheese. We devoured their snapper baked in wine with wild greens, served with thick french fries that had obviously never seen a freezer. The main dining room is dominated by a handsome stone fireplace, and there are also tables outside where you can catch the breeze. An elegant ambience and friendly, attentive service.

Carnayio Taverna. Paralía. ☎ **0427/22-868.** Main courses 1,800–4,500 Drs ($7.50–$18.75). Daily 8pm–1am. TAVERNA/SEAFOOD.

One of the better waterfront tavernas is across the road from the Alkyon Hotel. It disappointed us during our most recent visit, but it still enjoys a good reputation locally. Among our favorites over the years are *exóhiko,* fish soup, lamb *youvétsi,* and, of course, grilled fish. The garden setting is still special, and if you're there into the wee hours, you might be lucky enough to see a real round of dancing waiters and diners.

Kampoureli Ouzerí. Paralía. ☎ **0427/21-112.** Menu items 450–3,500 Drs ($1.90–$14.60). Daily noon–1am. GREEK.

This ouzerí, facing toward the ferries on the waterfront, is one of the most authentic eateries in town, though it caters to a largely nonlocal crowd. You can have the authentic ouzo-and-octopus combo at 600 Drs ($2.50) or sample the rich supply of cheese pies, fried feta, olives, and other piquant *mezédes* (hors d'oeuvres).

Le Bistro. Martínou St. ☎ **0427/21-627.** Reservations recommended. Main courses 2,000–5,000 Drs ($8.35–$20.85). EURO, MC, V. Daily 7pm–1am. CONTINENTAL.

This intimate, continental restaurant is easily spotted by its twin, across the street, which functions as a bar, overlooking the water. Both the bar and the dining room are lovely spaces. The full-course meals are beautifully prepared from their own stocks and sauces. Swordfish, roast pork, and steamed vegetables should be savored slowly, so there'll be room for the delicious desserts.

Taverna Limanákia. Paralía. ☎ **0427/22-835.** Main courses 1,500–5,200 Drs ($6.25–$21.65). MC. Daily 7pm–midnight. TAVERNA/SEAFOOD.

Very much in the style of its next-door neighbor the Carnáyio, the Limanákia serves some of the best taverna and seafood dishes in town. We vacillate about which of the two we prefer, but we've always come away feeling satisfied after a meal in this reliable eatery.

Taverna Mesoyia. Grigóriou (off Dimitriádou St.). ☎ **0427/21-440.** Main courses 1,100–2,400 Drs ($4.60–$10). No credit cards. Daily 7pm–midnight. TAVERNA.

You'll have a hard time finding the best authentic traditional food in town, since this little taverna is in the midst of the town's most labyrinthine neighborhood, above the Tríon Ierarchón Church, but when you find the very attractive Taverna Alexandros, which also has good food, you'll be just a turn or two away. Try the *melitsána papoutsáki* (eggplant shoes), the special chicken, or fresh fish in season. The management is refreshingly straightforward in admitting when something is frozen—as some fish must be at certain times of the year when it's illegal to fish.

Stavros Gyros & Souvlaki. Trión Ierarchón Sq. No phone. Main courses 700–1,500 Drs ($2.90–$6.25). No credit cards. Daily 7pm–1am. GRILL.

To the left of the Varsakis Gallery, this unassuming souvláki stand with a green awning is one of our favorites in the Sporades. Outside you'll see picnic-style pine tables and a chalkboard menu offering souvláki and lamb chops. Complement this with a peasant salad with cheese, and chase it down with soda, beer, wine, or ouzo; or order the peasant salad with feta, and you'll be ready to tackle more sightseeing. Everything is delicious and offers great value.

Readers Recommend

Taverna Ilias, Skiáthos. ☎ **0427/22-664.** (Turn right off the main street before the post office and take the third street to the left.) "My wife and I have traveled extensively in Greece, and the best restaurant we've eaten at anywhere is the Taverna Ilias in Skiáthos. My wife recommends the chicken curry, and I recommend the moussaká, the aroma of which comes right through the crust. The food is great and the service is impeccable."

—Bruce Bassof, Boulder, Colo.

⭐ **The Windmill Restaurant.** Above Áyios Nikólaos Church. ☎ **0427/21-105.** Reservations recommended. Main courses 2,000–3,600 Drs ($8.35–$15). EURO, V. Daily 7–11pm. INTERNATIONAL.

The town's most special dining experience is found at the top of the eastern hill beyond the white church with the clock. You couldn't ask for a better place to enjoy the sunset, and the menu has such distinctive dishes as smoked salmon and prawn filo parcels, spareribs with barbecue sauce, and demi-spatchcock of chicken with bourbon glaze and chili sauce. Even the deserts are unusual, including lemon and orange terrine with butterscotch sauce and poached pears with red-wine/toffee glaze. There are nearly two dozen wines from which to choose, including the best Greek wines.

SKIÁTHOS AFTER DARK

Skiáthos town offers lively nightlife, more concentrated on each end of the port—and you might begin your evening with a *vólta* along the harbor—around and above Platía Tríon Ierarchón, and in the heart of town, especially along Odós Polytechníou, parallel to the main street and 1 block to the left (west).

The **Borzoi** (not to be confused with the Boúrtzi), left off the main street, is the oldest club on the island and one of the most easily found; you may want to check it out several times during the evening, which generally gets livelier toward midnight.

Continue past the Borzoi to reach the **Banana Bar** (☎ **0427/21-232**), for "surprising dance music" on the right, then the **Admiral Benbow Club,** for something more soulful—across from flashy **Spartacus** and next door to the **Kazbar** (which claims to be the Aussie Consul-General of Skiáthos)—and to rock until 3am. At the next intersection south you'll find **Kyrki,** which plays jazz and blues, and the **Totem Musik Bar,** recommended by the local young people. **Vengera,** also on Polytechníou (☎ **0427/21-935**), plays "real Greek music." **Down Town** (☎ **0427/23-102**) plays jazz, rock, folk, and pop and features live music from 10pm to midnight on Wednesday and Friday.

Back across Papadiamándis Street, just before the post office along Párados Evangelístrias, you can find **Adagio** (☎ **0427/23-102**), which is discreetly gay and plays classical music and Greek ballads that allow conversation. Wander back down the main street to reach the **Kentavros Bar,** on the left beyond the Papadiamándis House, which plays heavier rock 'n' roll.

On the east end of the harbor you'll find Fresh, Cavos, and **Kalua.** The **BBC Disco,** on the airport road just off the harbor, is said to be a good place for all-night dancing. The **Apothiki Music Hall** reportedly has some of the best live Greek music.

On the west end of the harbor, **Jimmy's** (☎ **0427/22-816**) promises the "get-away feeling." If you enjoy watching videos while drinking, try the **Oasis Cafe,** where the draft beer is only 450 Drs ($1.90) a stein; if any kind of game is being played, it'll be on the tube. Farther along the old harbor, just up the steps on the far side, you'll find the **Jailhouse Cafe,** which plays rock music and has a fun young menu with such items as Cajun-style chicken and ribs with barbecue sauce; you can also have breakfast there. **Remezzo,** on the water near the old shipyard, gets rather wild downstairs but offers a quieter upstairs if the scene becomes too much for you.

2 Skópelos

58 nautical miles from Vólos

It was inevitable that handsomely rugged Skópelos would follow Skiáthos in its development, but it has done so more wisely and at a slower pace. Its beaches are not nearly so numerous or as pretty, but Skópelos town is one of the most beautiful ports in Greece, and the island is richer in vegetation, with wind-swept pines growing down to secluded coves, wide beaches, and terraced cliffs of angled rock slabs.

Skópelos is one of Greece's most architecturally pristine islands—on a par with Hydra and Sými. The main town, also called Skópelos (or Hóra), scales the low hills around the harbor and has the same winding, narrow paths that characterize the more famous Cycladic islands to the south. The interior is densely planted with fruit and nut orchards. Skópelos's plums and almonds, which are justly famous, are liberally used in the island's unique cuisine. The coastline, like that of Skiáthos, is punctuated by impressive grottos and bays; you'll surely get some lovely photographs here.

If you've never been to Skópelos, it's best to find a room in Skópelos town and begin your exploration there; you'll find all the necessary tourist services, the starting point for many bus and boat excursions, as well as a large number of hotels. After you've acquainted yourself with the rest of the island, you can move to one of the villages or beaches. However, if you're looking for a quieter, purer Greek village, we recommend Glóssa. Its name means "tongue," because the hill on which the town is built looks like a tongue when viewed from the sea.

ESSENTIALS

GETTING THERE & DEPARTING   By Plane   To reach Skópelos by air, you'll have to fly to nearby Skiáthos and take a hydrofoil or ferry.

By Boat   From Athens, it's best to depart from Áyios Konstandínos; **Alkyon Travel,** Odós Akademías 97, near Omónia Square (☎ 01/384-3220 or 01/384-3221), can arrange bus transportation to Áyios Konstandínos and hydrofoil or ferry tickets. From the north, Vólos is closer and would enable you to make a quick side trip to the Mt. Pelion region. The ferry to Skópelos from Skiáthos takes 45 minutes to Glóssa/Loutráki, 90 minutes to Skópelos town. The price for a ticket is the same, about 1,000 Drs ($4.15). The Ceres **hydrofoil** takes 15 minutes to Glóssa/Loutráki (four times daily; 1,750 Drs/$7.30), 35 minutes to Skópelos town (eight times daily, 2,050 Drs/$8.55). In Skópelos, hydrofoil tickets can be purchased at the port from the Flying Dolphin agent, **Madro Travel,** opposite the dock (☎ 0424/22-300 or 0424/22-145). There are infrequent connections to Kými, on Évvia. Check with the **Port Authority** (☎ 0424/22-180) for current schedules since they change frequently.

VISITOR INFORMATION   The **Municipal Tourist Office** of Skópelos (☎ 0424/23-231) is on the waterfront, to the left of the pier as you disembark; it's open daily from 9:30am to 10pm during the high season. It provides information as well as exchanges money and reserves rooms. A well-written guide to the island (with photos and a fold-out map) is *Discover Skópelos,* by Joanne Bramhall and Aneta Prosser.

The English-speaking staff at **Skopelorama** run an excellent travel agency, next door to the Hotel Eleni on the left (east) end of the port (☎ 0424/22-917 or 0424/23-250; fax 0424/23-243), open daily from 9am to 1pm and 5 to 10pm. They can help you find a room or exchange money, they offer excursions and provide information, and they know the island inside out and are really friendly folk.

ORIENTATION   Ferries from Alónissos, Skýros, and Kými and most hydrofoils and other boats from Skiáthos dock at both Glóssa/Loutráki and Skópelos. Most boats stop first at **Loutráki,** a homely little port near the northern end of the west coast, with the more attractive town of **Glóssa** high above it. We suggest you stay on board for the trip around the northern tip of the island and along the east coast, getting a better sense of why the island's name means "cliff" in Greek, to the island's main harbor, especially if this is your first visit to the island. You'll know why as the boat pulls around the last headland into that huge and nearly perfect C-shaped harbor and you get your first glimpse of **Skópelos town** rising like a steep amphitheater around the port.

To the right, as you leave the boat, are a few of Skópelos's 123 churches (which must be an ecclesiastical record for such a small village). The *paralía* (waterfront) is lined with banks, cafes, travel agencies, and the like, interspersed with a few huge trees. Many of the hotels are on the far left (as you leave the dock) end of the *paralía*. The bus station / taxi stand is under a giant plane tree about 200 yards to the left of the dock. Most of the shops and the OTE are up the main street leading off the *paralía*. The backstreets are amazingly convoluted; the best plan is to stroll around and get to know a few familiar landmarks. There are beaches on both sides of the harbor; Gliphóneri (or Áyios Konstandínos) beach, on the north end, is a 15-minute walk away, and there's a mediocre beach stretching south from town.

A good paved road runs south from Skópelos to **Stáfilos,** then west to **Agnóndas,** and up the beach-filled west coast to the northern villages of **Klíma, Glóssa,** and **Loutráki.**

If you're island-hopping, you might want to take advantage of Skópelos's two ports. The northern port at Loutráki is just a short jaunt from Skiáthos, while Skópelos town is closer to Alónissos. Depending on where you've been and where you're going, consider starting at one end of the island, crossing to the other, and moving on to the next island.

GETTING AROUND   By Bus   Skópelos is reasonably well served by public buses; the **bus stop** in Skópelos town is on the east end of the port. Since there are four routes, it's important to know your destination before boarding; check the schedule posted at the bus stop or ask the driver. Buses run the main route every half hour during the high season; they begin in Skópelos and make stops at Stáfilos, Agnóndas, Pánormos, the Adrina Beach Hotel, Miliá, Élios, Klíma, Glóssa, and Loutráki. The fare from Skópelos to Glóssa is 600 Drs ($2.55).

By Taxi   The taxi stand is in the middle of the waterfront; taxis will take you to almost anyplace on the island. Since taxis aren't metered, you'll need to negotiate your fare beforehand; the typical fare from Skópelos town to Glóssa is about 5,500 Drs ($22.90).

By Moped & Car   The most convenient way to see the island is to rent a moped at one of the many shops on the port. The cost should be about 2,800 Drs ($11.90) per day. A Jeep at **Motor Tours** (☎ 0424/22-986), for example, will run around 24,000 Drs ($100), including third-party insurance; expect to pay a few thousand drachmas less for a Fiat Panda.

By Boat   To visit the more isolated beaches, take one of the large excursion boats that go to the more secluded beaches in a day and provide a barbecue lunch. These excursions, which should cost about 14,000 Drs ($58.35), need to be booked a day in advance during the summer. Caïques operate during the peak season to Glistéri, Gliphóneri, and Sáres beaches, for about 1,500 Drs ($6.25). From the port of Agnóndas, there are fishing boats traveling to Limnonári, one of the island's better beaches.

FAST FACTS   The only **telephone center (OTE)** on the island is in the middle of the waterfront in Skópelos town, and there are also phone booths along the harbor; these phones require cards that can be purchased at the OTE or kiosks (press "i" for information in English). In Glóssa, Klíma, Moní Evangelístrias, Moní

Prodromoú, Agnónda, and Pánormos, you can try a kiosk, travel agent, or hotel for telephone service. The **post office** is on the east side of the port, on the road behind the Bar Alegari, open Monday to Friday from 8am to 2:30pm.

The **National Bank of Greece** and the **Commercial Bank** are on the *paralía;* both are open Monday to Friday from 8am to 3pm (until 1:30pm on Friday) and 6:30 to 8:30pm, and on Saturday from 10:30am to 2pm. The **police station** (☎ **0424/ 22-235**) is up the steps to the right of the National Bank, on the left; they can help you find a room as well as handle emergencies. There's a self-service **laundry** just down the street from the Adonis Hotel (☎ **0424/22-602**); it's open Monday to Saturday.

EXPLORING THE ISLAND

Most of the island's sights and activities are outdoors. The whole of Skópelos's 35 square miles is prime for hiking, biking, climbing, horseback riding, sailing (ask at the Skópelos travel agencies), and most of all, sunning and swimming. Skopelorama (see "Visitor Information" under "Essentials," above) operates a fine series of excursions such as monasteries by coach, traditional Skópelos, a walking tour of the town, several cruises, and a day trip to Alónissos.

A walk through the backstreets and alleyways of Skópelos town will delight almost anyone, and you can't stay lost for long. Some of the older buildings are rather Italianate, the similarity enhanced by the red-tile roofs that replaced the old slate roofs destroyed by an earthquake in 1965 (they were too expensive and impractical to rebuild). Other houses are of the more stolid Mt. Pelion design, and some are more Macedonian, with colorful wooden balconies. Even the newer buildings have been built in traditional style, so there's a pervasive sense of harmony.

Flowering plants fill pots, small plots, the precariously overhanging wooden balconies, and even crevices all along the steep meandering streets. Here and there you'll find an intensively cultivated garden with intricate trellises, and a number of the whitewashed houses have meticulously reconstructed green and gray slate roofs. Old women sit outdoors in front of their homes in groups of three or four, knitting and embroidering—the speed of their needles nearly keeping up with their rapid conversation, though they're likely to smile and speak to you if you greet them.

Even the town's Venetian **Kástro,** which overlooks the community, has been whitewashed, so that it looks too new to have been built over an archaic Temple of Athena (another indication of Athens dominence) and too serene to have been singled out for attack by the Turks during the War of Independence.

Once you have a better sense of the town's architecture, you may prefer to focus on interiors; in this case, you might want to visit the **Folk Art Museum,** near the OTE. (It was being renovated during our most recent visit, but it is normally open Tuesday to Sunday from 10:30am to 1pm and 6 to 11pm.) This is an old house furnished in the traditional style, and it has displays of traditional dress, pottery, old photographs, and local crafts. There's also the new **International Center for Photographic Exhibition,** which will surely interest shutterbugs.

Skópelos has a variety of galleries that exhibit local photography, ceramics, and jewelry. The Skópelos branch of **Archipelagos** (☎ **0424/23-127**) is one of the best of these; it faces the waterfront near the bus stop. **To Sinnefo** (no telephone) is located on a backstreet off Velizaríou Street (one of the few named streets), and specializes in handmade puppets, mobiles, and marionettes. **Nick Rodies,** whose gallery is located next door to Skopelorama (☎ **0424/22-779**), is from a Skópelos family that have produced ceramics for three generations. His elegant black vessels, at once both classical and modern, are among the finest we've found in Greece. The studio is open daily from 9am to 1pm and 5 to 11pm; credit cards are accepted.

There are five monasteries south of town, all strung along a pleasant path that continues south from the beach hotels. The first, **Evangelístra,** was founded by monks from Mt. Athos, but it now serves as a nunnery, and the weavings of its present occupants can be bought at a small shop there; it's open daily from 8am to 1pm and 4 to 7pm. The fortified Monastery of **Ayía Bárbara,** now abandoned, contains 15th-century frescoes. **Metamórphosis,** almost abandoned, is very much alive on August 6, when the feast of the Metamorphosis is celebrated there. **Prodromoú** is a 30-minute hike farther, but it's the handsomest and contains a particularly beautiful iconostasis. **Taxiárchon,** abandoned and overgrown, is at the summit of Mt. Poloúki, to the southeast; this hike is recommended only to the hardiest and most dedicated.

The first spur off the highway south from Skópelos town leads off to the left to **Stáfilos,** a popular family beach recommended by locals for a good seafood dinner—which you must order in the morning; also this is where the tomb of the Minoan prince Stáfilos, containing the sword now on display at the National Archaeological Museum, was found. About a quarter mile across the headland is **Velanió,** where nude bathing is common.

The next settlement west is **Agnóndas,** named for a local athlete who brought home the gold during the 569 B.C. Olympics; this small fishing village became a tourist resort despite the absence of a beach. **Limnonári,** a 15-minute walk farther west and accessible by caïque in the summer, has a nice fine-sand beach in a rather homely and shadeless setting.

The road then turns inland again, through a pine forest, to **Pánormos,** with a sheltered pebble beach, which has become the island's best resort; there are a number of tavernas, restaurants, hotels, and rooms to rent, as well as water-sports facilities. The road then climbs again toward **Miliá,** which is considered the island's best beach. You'll have to walk down about a quarter of a mile from the bus stop, but you'll find a lovely curving light-gray sand-and-pebble beach opposite the island of Dassía, and water-sports facilities at the **Beach Boys Club** (☎ 0424/33-496). There are also isolated beaches between the two.

The next stop, **Élios,** is a town that was built to house those who were displaced by the 1965 earthquake; it has become home to many of the people who operate resort facilities on the west coast, as well as something of a resort itself. At **Káto Klíma** ("Lower Ladder") the road begins to climb to **Áno Klíma** ("Upper Ladder") on its way to Glóssa.

Glóssa is a lovely hilltop town constructed during the Turkish occupation; it was mostly spared during the earthquake and remains one of the most Greek and charming towns in the Sporades. It has a number of rooms to rent, a nice hotel, and a very good taverna for those who are tempted to stay.

Most of the coastline is craggy, with just a few hard-to-reach beaches. Among the best places to catch some sunshine and do a bit of swimming is on the small beach below the picturesque Monastery of **Áyios Ioánnis,** east of town, which reminds many of Metéora. (Be sure to take food and water with you.) It's a winding 2 miles down to **Loutráki,** which has some rooms to rent and places to eat, but we don't recommend staying there.

Continuing in our clockwise course around the island you'd come to **Glistéri,** which is best reached by caïque from Skópelos town. It's a small pebbled beach with a nearby olive grove offering some respite from the sun, and a good bet when the other beaches are overrun in the summer.

You can also go by caïque to the grotto at **Tripití** for the island's best fishing; the little island of **Áyios Yióryios,** which has an abandoned monastery; **Gliphóneri** (or Áyios Konstandínos), the best beach just north of Skópelos town; and **Sáres,** the best beach just south.

WHERE TO STAY

Skópelos is nearly as popular as Skiáthos; because of its increase in tourism, several new hotels have cropped up, especially in Skópelos town and at Pánormos.

If you need advice about one of the in-town hotels or pensions or accommodations farther out, talk to the people at **Skopelorama,** the police, or the town hall officials. Be sure to look at a room and agree on a price before accepting anything or you may be unpleasantly surprised. To make matters more confusing, there are no real street names in the main, older section of town, so you'll probably have to ask for directions several times before you find your lodging.

New camping facilities have been constructed 4¹/₄ miles from Skópelos town on the road above Agnóndas Beach. For budget prices, they offer dormitory accommodations with showers (there's still no phone!).

There are about 100 rooms to rent in Glóssa; expect to pay 9,500 Drs ($39.60) for single or double occupancy. The best way to find a room is to visit one of the tavernas or shops and inquire about a vacancy; it's a small town with an informal reservation system. If you can't find a room in Glóssa, you can always head down the hill to Loutráki and check into a pension by the water.

Hotel Atlantes. Glóssa, 370 03 Skópelos. ☎ **0424/33-223,** 0424/33-756, or 0424/33-767. 10 rms, all with bath (shower). TEL. 7,250 Drs ($30.20) single; 9,250 Drs ($38.55) double. No credit cards.

The owner and host, Lee Chokalas, born in Mississippi but raised here, has returned to his native island after a 30-year absence to build this comfortable hotel, across from the bus stop. All rooms have balconies that overlook the flower-filled garden or out to sea. If Lee has no room in the inn, ask him or George Antoniou at the Pýthari souvenir shop (☎ **0424/33-077**) in town for advice on a room for rent.

Hotel Denise. Skópelos, 370 03 Skópelos. ☎ **0424/22-678.** Fax 0424/22-769. 25 rms, all with bath (shower). A/C MINIBAR TEL. 13,200 Drs ($55) single; 19,200 Drs ($80) double. Rates include breakfast. EURO, MC, V.

One of the best hotels in Skópelos because of its prime location, nice facilities, and swimming pool, the Hotel Denise stands atop the village and commands spectacular views of the harbor and the Aegean. It was upgraded several years ago, but it still fits in well with Skópelos's architectural style. Each of its four stories is ringed by a wide balcony, and the rooms have hardwood floors and furniture. Since the Denise is quite popular, call for a pickup and check on room availability before you hike up the steep road. Better yet, reserve in advance.

Hotel Drosia. Skópelos, 370 03 Skópelos. ☎ **0424/22-490.** 10 rms, all with bath (shower). TEL. 8,600 Drs ($35.85) single; 9,800 Drs ($40.85) double.

This small, older hotel is next to the Denise, atop a hill overlooking the village, with exceptional views. The rooms are well maintained, clean, and simply furnished. All in all, it's a very good value.

Hotel Eleni. Skópelos, 370 03 Skópelos. ☎ **0424/22-393.** 37 rms, all with bath (shower). TEL. 9,500 Drs ($39.58) single; 13,000 Drs ($54.15) double. EURO, MC.

The Hotel Eleni is a gracious modern hotel, 100 yards from the waterfront, and all rooms have balconies. The owner, Charlie Hatyidrosis, returned from the Bronx and built this establishment after he and his brother had managed several pizzerias in New York City.

Hotel Rania. Skópelos, 370 03 Skópelos. ☎ **0424/22-486.** 11 rms, all with bath (shower). TEL. 10,000 Drs ($41.65) single or double. No credit cards.

The Rania is down by the waterside, just beyond and to the left of the larger Amalia. Its very simply furnished rooms provide bath, balcony, and phone, and are reasonably well maintained. The Rania is one of the few hotels that remain open all year.

Pension Andromahi. Velizaríou St., Skópelos, 370 03 Skópelos. ☎ **0424/22-941.** 7 rms, all with bath (shower). 8,050 Drs ($33.50) single; 11,000 Drs ($45.83) double. MC, V.

The Andromahi feels like an old-fashioned bed-and-breakfast with many homey touches and painted furniture. Our only objection—and it's fairly serious—is that the Andromahi tends to be pretty noisy in the late evening. Otherwise, this is a gem—and it's open year-round.

Pension Katarina. Skópelos, 370 03 Skópelos. ☎ **0424/23-307.** 7 rms, all with bath (shower). 13,750 Drs ($57.30) single or double. No credit cards.

Built in 1991, the attractive Katarina commands a wonderful view of the town from its south-side waterfront perch. We much admired the well-kept rose garden as well as the attractively built lobby and guest quarters. The only down side here is that the Katarina is situated just a couple of doors from two popular bars. Request a top-floor, water-facing room.

WORTH A SPLURGE

✪ **Hotel Prince Stafilos.** Skópelos, 370 03 Skópelos. ☎ **0424/22-775** or 0424/23-011. Fax 0424/22-825. 70 rms, all with bath (shower). TEL. 21,500 Drs ($89.60) single; 39,500 Drs ($164.60) double. Rates include breakfast. AE, EURO, MC, V.

The handsomest and most traditional hotel on the island is about half a mile south of town. (They'll give you a ride from the ferry dock.) The friendly owner, Pelopidas Tsitsirigos, is also the architect responsible for the hotel's special charm. The lobby is spacious and very attractively decorated with local artifacts. There's a pool, restaurant, and bars. A large buffet breakfast is served.

Skópelos Village. Skópelos, 370 03 Skópelos. ☎ **0424/22-517.** Fax 0424/22-958. 36 studios and apts, all with bath (tub). MINIBAR TEL. 30,000 Drs ($125) studio; 35,000 Drs ($145.85) apt.

These buildings are tastefully constructed as "traditional island houses." Each studio or apartment is equipped with kitchen, private bath, and one or two bedrooms. The units share a common swimming pool, barbecue, and snack bar where breakfast is served. Each villa can comfortably sleep from two to six people.

WHERE TO EAT

✪ **Anatoli Ouzerí.** Skópelos. No phone. Main courses 1,400–2,600 Drs ($5.85–$10.85). 9pm–1am. GREEK.

You'll have quite a climb to reach this diminutive ouzerí high above town, but we found the food superb, more than justifying the effort. Our meal featured several delicious *mezédes* (appetizers), including lightly fried green peppers, black-eyed peas with fresh spices, and an exceptional octopus salad. Luckily the Anatoli is largely unknown except by residents or long-term guests. If you're in luck, Yórgos Xindáris, the rail-thin proprietor/chef, will play his bouzoúki and sing classic rebétika songs, sometimes with accompanists. If you come early or late in the season, bring a sweater.

Crêperie Greca. Skópelos. ☎ **0424/23-310.** Menu items 600–1,600 Drs ($2.50–$6.65). Daily noon–3pm and 7pm–2am. CRÊPES.

If you like crêpes, don't miss Crêperie Greca, across from the Adonis Hotel on the sloping street up from the waterfront bus stop. Zucchini and cheese, or chicken and mushroom, are the most filling, but for drama try the flaming fruit and cream crêpes, all prepared by the French owner on a tiny burner.

Finikas Taverna & Ouzeri. Skópelos. ☎ **0424/23-247.** Main courses 1,700–2,100 Drs ($7.10–$8.75). Daily 7:30pm–2am. GREEK.

Tucked away on the upper backstreets of Skópelos is a picturesque garden taverna/ ouzerí dominated by a broad-leaf palm. The Finikas may offer Skópelos's most romantic setting, perhaps by dint of its isolated location as well as its lovely garden dining area. Among the many fine dishes are an excellent ratatouille and pork cooked with prunes and apples, a traditional island specialty.

Molos Taverna & Ouzerí. Skópelos. ☎ **0424/22-551.** Main courses 1,400–3,000 Drs ($5.85–$12.50). Daily noon–2:30pm and 6pm–1am. GREEK.

This local favorite right near the ferry on the *paralía* is open year-round. Molos features many specialties, including stuffed pork with cheese, garlic, and vegetables; *abeloúrgos* (stuffed chicken with ham, wrapped in grape leaves); and *koukiar,* a slice of thinly cut veal with eggplant, covered with a béchamel sauce.

Platanos Jazz Bar. Skópelos. No phone. Menu items 600–1,800 Drs ($2.50–$7.50). 5am–3am. BAR.

For everything from breakfast to a late-night drink, try the Platanos, the jazz pub, beneath the enormous plane tree just to the left off the ferry dock. Breakfast in the summer starts as early as 5 or 6am for ferry passengers, who can serve themselves German drip-style coffee, fruit salad with nuts and yogurt, and fresh-squeezed orange juice, all for 2,200 Drs ($9.15). Platanos is equally pleasant for evening and late-night drinks (expect to pay about 1,200 Drs/$5), to be enjoyed while listening to their phenomenal collection of jazz records.

Spiro's Taverna. Skópelos. ☎ **0424/23-146.** Menu items 600–3,000 Drs ($2.50–$12.50). Daily noon–midnight. GREEK.

Spiro's Taverna, to the left as you leave the ferry dock, is often packed with a crowd eager for its spit-roasted chicken. This simple outdoor cafe is popular with locals, expatriates, and travelers alike, and it's open year-round.

Taverna Koutoúki. Skópelos. ☎ **0424/22-380.** Main courses 1,000–2,400 Drs ($4.15–$10). No credit cards. Daily 5:30pm–1am. GREEK.

You'll find this unpretentious, excellent-value taverna in a small grapevine-draped garden on the main backroad behind the Amalia Hotel near the Health Center. The decor is basic, the music is traditional, the service is friendly, and the food is excellent—fresh and hot, with a few specialties such as beef in a delicious sweet tomato sauce with garlic, meatballs, and pork stuffed with garlic.

Taverna T'Agnanti. Glóssa. ☎ **0424/33-606** or 0424/33-076. Main courses 1,000–3,400 Drs ($4.15–$14.15). Daily 7am–midnight. GREEK.

A seasonal resident sent us to this modest taverna, and since then we've received several letters from happy readers about the inexpensive food, friendly staff, and spectacular view. The menu is standard taverna style, but we enjoyed everything we sampled. The Stamataki and Antoniou families run this and the nearby Pýthari souvenir shop, and if requested, will even help you find a room in town. This is the place to meet, greet, and eat in Glóssa—about 180 yards up from the bus stop.

SKÓPELOS AFTER DARK

The night scene isn't nearly as active on Skópelos as on neighboring Skiáthos, but there are still plenty of bars, late-night cafes, and discos. Most of the coolest bars are on the far (east) side of town; follow the plentiful signs above the Hotel Amalia to reach the indoor **Kyrki Disco,** or continue on along the beachfront to the outdoor **Karyatis;** on the way you'll pass **Akti Panorama** (☎ **0424/23-132**), a beachside taverna that often features live Greek music. The best place for bouzouki music is **Meidani,** in a handsomely converted olive-oil factory approximately in the middle of town; it doesn't open until 11pm or so, but there's a nice little bar close by where you could wait. Or you could wander around town checking out the night scene around Plátanos Square, beyond and along the *paralía*. Don't forget the **Platanos Jazz Bar** and the possibility of live music at the **Anatoli Ouzerí,** above the town.

3 Alónissos

62 nautical miles from Vólos

Since Alónissos has been buffered from mass tourism by its more popular neighbors, Skiáthos and Skópelos, it remains largely undeveloped and unpretentious. Most of the island is mountainous and green, covered largely with olive trees and pines. The coast, especially along the inhabited southeastern part, is quite rugged and irregular, and there aren't a lot of beaches—though there are several very nice ones, all refreshingly free of motorboats, jet skis, and crowds—except in August when the island becomes an Italian possession. There's enough sophistication for some nice restaurants, and there are a number of good hotels, but the residents remain remarkably easygoing, open, and friendly.

If recent history is a guide, then Alónissos, the least known and one of the most naturally attractive of the major Sporades, would have to be considered a star-crossed island. For many centuries when Alónissos was a major producer of wine, vineyards covered over one-fourth of the island. Then, in 1950, phylloxera devastated the vines and contaminated the soil. The island still cannot produce wine, but olive groves cover the hills.

Another trying year for Alónissos was 1965: A minor earthquake hit the island, damaging the hilltop Byzantine capital. Roofs caved in and many walls cracked, but ironically the greatest damage was caused by a military commission sent in to study the situation. Instead of recommending rebuilding the old town, they suggested moving the entire population of the capital to a minor port, Patitíri ("Winepress"). The homely, substandard housing of their "model community" created yet another blight on the island. (A Canadian film group even came to Alónissos a few years ago to make a documentary on how *not* to build a town.) However, purple bougainvillea now hides many architectural flaws and the islanders' spirit has rebounded, so that today the port is no longer ugly, and it has the familiar and pleasant blend of tavernas, hotels, and tourist services.

The total population of Alónissos is about 3,000; most people live between Patitíri and the old capital, so you can imagine how little development has taken place on the rest of the island.

ESSENTIALS

GETTING THERE & DEPARTING   By Plane   The fastest way to get there is to fly to Skiáthos and connect with a hydrofoil. You could come from Skýros, but there are far fewer boats and it's a much longer trip.

By Boat Alónissos connects with Skiáthos and Skópelos by ferry, so during the busy summer months there is frequent daily service. Seven hydrofoils arrive and depart daily. Excursion boats from Alónissos's neighbors also operate daily throughout the summer. There's at least one boat a day from either Vólos or Áyios Konstandínos, and one weekly from Kými. In the spring and fall service to the island drops off considerably; check with the local **Port Authority** (☎ **0424/65-595**) for the schedule.

VISITOR INFORMATION If you're just arriving, a good place to begin is the **Ikos Travel Office,** right on the *paralía* (☎ **0424/65-320;** fax 0424/65-321). Pákis Athanassíou runs the agency and knows the island as well as anyone you're likely to meet; he and his staff are the very best source of information and advice. They sell hydrofoil and ferry tickets, can book Olympic Airways flights, and offer a number of interesting excursions. They also have the best **map** of the island, prepared by Hans Jörg Rothenberger, a must if you plan to walk or hike—and you should.

ORIENTATION Excursion boats, hydrofoils, and the Nomikos ferry call at the port of **Patitíri,** on the southern tip of the island. The old capital, **Old Alónissos,** is above it to the northwest. Most of the island's beaches are north and east of Patitíri, and are best reached by excursion boats.

Patitíri has a small but well-sheltered harbor; most shops are located either along the waterfront or up one of the two main streets that lead off it—the left toward Old Alónissos and the right toward Vótsi and points north. The steep hill on the right (north) as you leave the ferry has most of the town's hotels and private rooms to rent, many overlooking the harbor. There's another cluster of hotels on the southern side of the port beyond the small rocky (but acceptable) town beach. The waterfront has the usual mix of cafes, hotels, fish tavernas, and shops.

GETTING AROUND **By Bus** There is irregular bus service from the port in Patitíri to Old Alónissos four times a day—more often in high season, less often off-season; the fare is 250 Drs ($1.05) one-way. Tickets may be purchased on board or at Ikos Travel.

By Moped & Car Mopeds and motorcycles are available in Patitíri for 4,000 Drs ($16.65) and up per day, depending on the size. A Jeep/truck can be rented for about 30,000 Drs ($125) per day, including insurance. Be very careful on the twisting mountain roads in the remote, northern parts of the island.

By Taxi The taxi stand (☎ **0424/65-573** or 0424/65-425) is on the right side of the port; although the island has only three or four taxis, you'll have to be a firm negotiator to get a fair price. A taxi from Patitíri to Old Alónissos should cost about 1,000 Drs ($4.25) each way.

By Boat Most of the excursion boats to the nearby beaches leave the port sometime between 9 to 11am and cost about 1,000 Drs ($4.15) round-trip. Ask at Ikos Travel about chartering a boat, or at least convincing a fisher to go to some of the nearby Lesser Sporades. Rental boats are available; one with a 9-hp motor will cost about 20,000 Drs ($83.35) per day.

On Foot This is our favorite means of getting around on Alónissos. Old Alónissos is an hour's walk up a winding trail through olive groves. The new island map (see "Visitor Information," above) will show you the route, which begins near the post office. Ask and the way will be shown. Some visitors may prefer to take a bus or taxi up and then return on foot. The road from Patitíri to Old Alónissos is one of the few paved roads, though there's a large network of dirt and unimproved roads that crisscross the island.

FAST FACTS   The **police** have an office in Patitíri (☎ **0424/65-205**). There's a newsstand up the left-hand road on the left with English-language newspapers, magazines, and a few paperbacks. The **post office** is on the road to Hóra, the left-hand road off the harbor, open Monday to Friday from 8am to 2pm. The **telephone office (OTE)** is on the waterfront, but it's open only in the summer, daily from 7:30am to 9pm. There's a **doctor** who can handle most emergencies (☎ **0424/65-208**). The local **pharmacy** is on the right-hand road, just off the harbor.

EXPLORING THE ISLAND

The southeastern tip of the island, **Marpoúnda,** while not exactly off-limits, is dominated by the big Marpoúnda Village Club, which caters to fun-loving Italians; you may not feel welcome there. Continue past the complex until you reach a path that leads off to the left through the pines and follow it down to **Vithísma,** a nicer beach which you'll have to share with windsurfers in the summer. A little farther along the upper trail you'll find **Megálo Mourtiá,** a pebble beach with a couple of tavernas and a path leading up to Old Alónissos.

Most visitors will probably want to make their first destination **Old Alónissos** (Paleá Alónissos, sometimes called Hóra, though most locals say Horió), the old Byzantine capital, with its spectacular views, especially at sunset. Many of the houses are still in ruins, while others were bought at bargain prices, mostly by English and German visitors, who have restored them. A few locals have also returned; although the ongoing restoration is largely faithful to the original architecture, the town has a rather sophisticated international feel.

Most of the foreigners come only for the summer, and until recently most residents went without electricity and rejected modern comforts and conveniences, hoping thereby to achieve a greater psychic connection to the past. Some residents use electricity only in the bars, tavernas, and shops, but not at home. Tavernas, bars, minimarkets, a few rooms to rent, and a growing number of arts and crafts shops have opened in the last few years, and it looks as if the capital may once again regain some of its lost dignity, as local resentment of the foreign invasion abates.

Even at the busiest time of year, there is much tranquillity; even the derelict houses are interesting in what they reveal about the past (including the Venetians, who rebuilt the fortifications). It's a rather steep climb up a path that begins near the post office and will require about an hour's time plus sturdy shoes; you might want to take a bus or taxi up. We recommend that you walk down, either along the more direct footpath during the day or along the vehicle road at night (unless you have a flashlight).

If you're fortunate enough to find a room, you can go swimming below the town at **Vrisítsa** by taking a 20-minute walk north. When you come down from Old Alónissos on the vehicle road, you'll see Vrisítsa below on the left. The windmill there is being restored, and the town holds promise as a charming retreat.

BEACHES & ACTIVE PURSUITS

The closest beach to the north of Patitíri is **Roussoúm Yialós,** which may suit the less ambitious. Beyond it is **Vótsi,** the island's second-largest settlement, with another well-protected harbor, a fishing village that's becoming a resort. If you go to Vótsi by the vehicle road you'll pass the new **International Academy of Classical Homeopathy** on the left (Ikos Travel can give you information about it). There's a beach beyond Vótsi, **Spartínes,** but while you're moving you might as well continue on to **Miliá Yialós,** where pines grow down to the beach and the water is clearer, good for snorkeling. The next beach, **Chrissí Miliá,** has a more gradual slope, which makes it better for children, and it has a good taverna.

Kokkinókastro, over the hill, is believed to be the site of ancient Íkos, and, as its name suggests, the pebbles on this beach are red. The remains of an even older settlement, one of the oldest in the Aegean, dating back to the Middle Paleolithic era, have recently been discovered there. It's a very pretty place, but you'll have to take a picnic and water if you want to spend the day there.

Beyond it, **Tzórtzi** is another pretty beach, with especially beautiful water that's ideal for snorkeling. (Since you'll probably not want to walk this far, you may want to catch a caïque from the port.)

Stení Vála, the last village of any size, with a fjordlike harbor, has a few tavernas, a market, a campsite, and enough rooms so that it might be a possibility for an overnight stay. It's the gateway to the National Marine Park, which you cannot enter without special permission unless you're with a guided tour.

Kalamákia, farther north on the coast, also has a couple of tavernas and a few rooms. There's still plenty of territory to explore both along the coast and inland farther north, but be aware that the roads are quite poor, the population sparse, and facilities meager if they exist at all.

The coast also has a number of grottos of exceptional beauty, and Ikos Travel runs several excursions that take you along the coast. A short walk outside Vótsi—in **Platsoúka**—will bring you to a cave that's particularly picturesque. (It's most accessible on calm days.) Alónissos offers opportunities for spearfishing, skin diving, and underwater exploration of the ruins off **Psathoúra,** site of a huge modern lighthouse.

There are a number of other minor **islands** off Alónissos, some of which can be visited by excursion boat during the high season. **Peristéra,** to the east, the largest and one of the closest, can be visited by excursion boat, and there are fine beaches within a 30-minute walk from the place where the boat docks at Vassilikó. On summer evenings boats carry parties out for special barbecues. **Kyrá Panayía** (Pelagós), which belongs to the Orthodox church, has two abandoned monasteries and a cave that's often identified as the one belonging to the Cyclops Polyphemus, who was blinded by Odysseus. Beyond it, **Yioúra** has a rare breed of wild goats and another large cave that makes the same claim to fame. **Pipéri,** to their east, is a wildlife sanctuary, home to a small colony of monk seals and Elenora falcons.

Increasingly, visitors are coming to Alónissos to **hike,** both with and without backpacks, and to observe sea mammals such as dolphins and seals in the **National Marine Park.** We've never had the time to do this, but if you have, write and share your experiences with us. Was it worth it? Did you see any Mediterranean seals?

WHERE TO STAY

Quite a few private homes rent rooms; if you want to save money, they're usually comparable to most of the Class D and some of the Class C hotels and pensions. Expect to pay 6,000 to 8,000 Drs ($25 to $33.35) per person for a room. Most of the rooms are on the north side of the port, such as **Pension Lucy** (☎ **0424/ 65-016**), run by one of the most gracious hostesses in town; a double runs 7,500 Drs ($31.25). By the time you arrive on Alónissos there may be accommodations available in the old capital. The folks at Ikos Travel can arrange to rent houses that will sleep three to four people for 16,000 to 18,000 Drs ($66.65 to $75).

Hotel Gorgona. Rousoúm Yialós, 370 05 Alónissos. ☎ **0424/65-317.** Fax 0424/65-629. 17 rms, all with bath (shower). TEL. 13,500 Drs ($56.25) single or double. No credit cards.

Take the right-hand road up from the harbor, continue east past the school, and look for a mural of a mermaid (*gorgóna*) flanking the front door of a hotel up on the right. It's one of the cleanest and quietest places in town, and all the beds have firm, orthopedic mattresses. Ask for a sea-facing room; for the price, this is one of the best values in town.

Hotel Liadromia. Patitíri, 370 05 Alónissos. ☎ **0424/65-521.** Fax 0424/65-096. 20 rms, all with bath (shower). TEL. 14,500 Drs ($60.40) single or double. Rates include breakfast. EURO, MC, V.

This is a very nice hotel on the right above the harbor. Many of its rooms provide great views, and a roof garden is an extra treat. The hostess, Maria Thansiou, an Alónissos original, has brought considerable style to this attractive inn. Lace curtains, wall hangings, murals, and wrought-iron fixtures distinguish this hotel from the average lodging. There are also six studios with a kitchenette for the same price, but without breakfast.

✪ **Paradise Hotel.** Patitíri, 370 05 Alónissos. ☎ **0424/65-213** or 0424/65-160. Fax 0424/65-161. 31 rms, all with bath (shower). TEL. 16,000 Drs ($66.65) single; 21,500 Drs ($89.60) double. Rates include breakfast. MC, V.

The Paradise Hotel, run by the gracious and gregarious Kostas, is also on the right above the harbor. You'll enjoy the new pool and relaxation area, late-afternoon drinks on the hotel's pine-shaded terrace overlooking the water-worn rocks, or a swim in the clean, clear sea below. There's a smaller pool for kids. The staff will arrange transportation from the dock.

Pension Vótsi. Vótsi, 370 05 Alónissos. ☎ **0424/65-510** or 0424/65-066. Fax 0424/65-449. 15 rms, all with bath (shower). TEL. 10,000 Drs ($41.65) double. Rates include breakfast. No credit cards.

This handsome new pension is pleasant and quiet, with Pelion-style slate floors, ceiling fans, and fridges in every room, and such homey touches as hand-embroidered curtains. The friendly, relaxed family that operates the pension makes it feel even more like home.

Theodorou Hotel. Stení Vála, 370 05 Alónissos. ☎ **0424/65-158** or 0424/65-558. Fax 0424/65-321. 12 rms, all with bath (shower), 2 with kitchenette. MINIBAR TEL. 9,750 Drs ($40.65) single or double; 12,500 Drs ($52.10) double with kitchenette. MC.

If you really want to get away from it all, there's the Theodorou Hotel, a basic inn located about halfway up the east coast of the island in Stení Vála. The rooms are simply furnished and transportation to the hotel is provided by Land Rover or boat. The village has two restaurants, a minimarket, and a pub.

WHERE TO EAT
IN PATITÍRI

Argo. Patitíri. ☎ **0424/65-141.** Main courses 1,400–12,000 Drs ($5.85–$50); fish priced per kilo. EURO, V. Daily 10am–2am. TAVERNA.

This attractive outdoor taverna is on the cliffside around from the right (north) side of the harbor, offering a view down the rocky eastern shore of the island. Late breakfasts are quite good. Fresh seafood is the specialty, and you can have the local lobster *(astakós)* for 9,000 Drs ($37.50) or crayfish *(karavída)* for 12,000 Drs ($50) per kilo.

✪ **Kamaki Ouzerí.** Patitíri. ☎ **0424/65-245.** Main courses 900–4,000 Drs ($3.75–$16.65). Daily 6pm–1am. GREEK.

The gregarious Spiros is in charge of the grill at this ultra-popular ouzerí, about 100 yards up the left-hand road off the harbor on the left. A wide selection of super *mezédes* (appetizers in larger portions) and fresh fish distinguish this fine, but very basic eatery from the more touristed establishments. This restaurant probably has the best food in town, especially the grilled seafood and fish.

Ouzerí Leftéris. Patitíri. No phone. Main courses 900–3,000 Drs ($3.75–$12.50). Daily 10am–4pm and 6pm–1am. GREEK.

We come here for the best bargain in town: an ouzo and hot-plate combo, a bargain at 310 Drs ($1.70), including an assortment of *mezédes* (appetizers). The Leftéris also offers many salads, freshly grilled fish, and their delicious house specialty, saganáki shrimp with onions, tomatoes, pepper, mustard, and feta.

IN OLD ALÓNISSOS

Astrofengiá Restaurant & Bar. Old Alónissos. ☎ **0424/65-182.** Reservations recommended. Main courses 1,400–2,200 Drs ($5.85–$9.15). Daily 6pm–midnight. Closed Oct–May. GREEK/INTERNATIONAL.

Good food, some of the island's best nightlife, and stunning 360° views are all to be found at Astrofengiá ("Starlight"), on the top level of Old Alónissos. The menu includes traditional Greek cuisine and some surprisingly sophisticated dishes, including artichoke hearts with cream-dill dressing and grilled swordfish with capers, all reasonably priced. Iannis Toundas and his sister, Mina Xenaki, try to use organic vegetables as much as possible.

Paraport Taverna. Old Alónissos. No phone. Main courses 950–2,800 Drs ($3.95–$11.65). Daily 9am–2pm and 6pm–1am. GREEK.

At the top of old Alónissos village, the head chef Ilias and family serve good standard Greek taverna fare. There's live music about once a week.

IN STENÍ VÁLA

I Stení Vála. Stení Vála. ☎ **0424/65-545.** Main courses 900–3,400 Drs ($3.75–$14.15). Daily 7am–midnight. GREEK/SEAFOOD.

Locals consider this handsome taverna the best on the island, especially for seafood. There's a large interior dining room and a spacious veranda with a nice view of the harbor and fjordlike cove. The cook's *tirópita* (cheese pie) is among the very best, a large spiral filled with excellent feta and fried crisp in olive oil.

ALÓNISSOS AFTER DARK

The cafes, bars, and ouzerí near the port get fairly lively at night, and you don't have to walk far to see which one suits your fancy. **La Vie, Neféli,** and **Nine Muses** are generally considered superior, and are above the harbor on the right. **On the Rocks** is a good place for late-night dancing. **4 X 4 Disco,** up to the left off the road to Old Alónissos, plays American and European rock, and a little farther up the road, **Rebétika** plays the best Greek music on the island. You might want to go on up to the **Astrofengiá Bar** in Old Alónissos to get a little closer to the stars. The **Elias Pub,** in Vótsi, is considered the island's best pub.

4 Skýros

25 nautical miles from Kými, 118 nautical miles from Piraeus

Skýros is an island of wide, fine-sand beaches, attractive whitewashed sugar-cube architecture, picturesque surroundings, fairly low prices, and relatively few tourists. Why? First, it's difficult to get to Skýros. The ferry leaves from either the isolated port of Paralía Kými, on the east coast of Évvia (with a 2-hour boat ride to Skýros), or from Vólos (or the other Sporades), which is the starting point for a 4-hour hydrofoil ride to the island. Second, Greek tourists prefer the other, more thickly forested Sporades. We think that Skýros's scruffy vegetation and stark contrast between sea, sky, and rugged terrain make it all the more interesting.

Also, many Skyrians themselves have been ambivalent, at best, about developing this very traditional island for tourism. Until recently there were only a handful of hotels on the whole island. Since 1990, however, Skýros has seen a miniboom in the accommodations-building business; with the completion of a giant marina, it's setting itself up to become yet another tourist mecca. Direct charter flights from Europe, always a harbinger of accelerated change, now land at the island's airport. None of this should deter you, however; be assured that, at least for now, Skýros remains an ideal place for an extended stay.

ESSENTIALS

GETTING THERE & DEPARTING   By Plane   Olympic Airways has two flights a week (daily in the summer) between Athens and Skýros; in Athens call ☎ 01/926-7251 for information and reservations. The planes are small, so reserve well in advance. (You can also fly to Skiáthos and then connect by hydrofoil, but this isn't such a good idea unless you want to visit the other Sporades first.) The local Olympic representative is **Skýros Travel** (☎ 0222/91-123 or 0222/91-600). A taxi from the airport costs about 3,000 Drs ($12.50).

By Boat   There's only one ferry company serving Skýros, the **Lykomides Co.,** and it's owned by a company whose stockholders are all residents of Skýros. The old company provided great service during the busy summer months but lousy service off-season. So the Skyrians bought their own boat, the *Lykomídes,* and allow it to dock only at Skýros. During the summer it runs twice daily from Kými to Skýros (at 11am and 5pm) and twice daily from Skyros to Kými (at 8am and 2pm); the trip takes about 2 1/2 hours. Off-season there's one ferry each way, leaving Skyros at 8am and Kými at 5pm. The fare is 1,800 Drs ($7.50). For schedules, call ☎ 0222/22-020 in Kými or ☎ 0222/91-790 or 0222/91-789 in Skýros. The Lykomides offices in Skýros and Kými sell connecting bus tickets to Athens; the fare for the 3 1/2-hour ride is 2,850 Drs ($12.15).

The Ceres Flying Dolphin **hydrofoils** now go from Skiáthos, Skópelos, and Alónissos to Skýros five times a week, starting in mid-May (daily in July and August). This is easily the most convenient way to go, though pricey compared to the ferry. One-way tickets cost 10,500 Drs ($44.70) for the 4-hour plus Vólos–Skýros trip.

The tricky part of getting to Skýros by ferry is the connection with the ferry from the other Sporades islands. The off-season ferry from Skiáthos, Skópelos, Alónissos, and Vólos is scheduled to arrive at Kými at 5pm, but is frequently late. It's not uncommon to see the Skýros ferry disappearing on the horizon as your ferry pulls into Kými. You might have to make the best of the 24-hour layover and get a room in Kými or Paralía Kými.

Buses from Athens to Kými leave Terminal B at Odós Liossíon 260 six times a day, though you should leave no later than 1:30pm; the fare for the 3 1/2-hour trip is 2,850 Drs ($12.15). From Kými you must take a local bus to Paralía Kými. If you're not sure about the connection, ask the bus driver.

VISITOR INFORMATION   The largest tourist office is **Skýros Travel & Tourism,** next to Skýros Pizza Restaurant on the main street (☎ 0222/91-123 or 0222/91-600; fax 0222/92-123); it's open daily from 8am to 2:30pm and 6:30 to 11:30pm. The English-speaking Lefteris Trakos is very helpful on many counts, including accommodations, changing money at bank rates, Olympic Airways flights (he's the local Olympic and charter flight agent), long-distance calls, some interesting bus and boat tours, and car rental, as well as Flying Dolphin and bus tickets.

ORIENTATION　　Ferries and hydrofoils dock at **Linariá,** a plain mostly modern fishing village on the west coast, pleasant enough but not recommended for a stay. Catch the bus waiting at the dock to take you across the narrow middle of the island to the west-coast capital **Skýros town,** which is built on a rocky bluff overlooking the sea. The island is divided almost evenly by its narrow waist; the northern half is fertile and covered with pine forest, while the southern half is barren and quite rugged. The **airport** is near the northern tip of the island. As you exit the bus at the **bus stop square** in Skýros town, head north up the **main street** toward the center of town and the main tourist services.

GETTING AROUND　　**By Bus**　　The only scheduled bus run is the Skýros–Linariá shuttle that operates four to five times daily; the cost is 220 Drs (95¢). Skýros Travel offers a twice-daily beach-excursion bus in high season.

By Moped & Car　　Mopeds and motorcycles are available in Skýros, near the police or taxi station, for about 4,000 to 5,000 Drs ($16.65 to $20.85) per day. A Seat Marbella can be rented from **Pegasus Rent a Car** (☎ **0222/91-600**) at Skýros Travel for about 15,500 Drs ($64.60) per day, including third-party insurance. The island has a relatively well-developed network of roads.

By Taxi　　Taxi service between Linariá and Skýros is available but relatively expensive, about 3,000 Drs ($12.50). Rates to other, farther destinations are similarly high.

FAST FACTS　　The **post office** is near the bus stop square, open Monday to Friday from 8am to 2pm. There's only one **bank** (with no extended hours), also located near the bus square; the best idea is to bring lots of drachmas. The **telephone office (OTE),** open Monday to Friday from 7:30am to 3pm, is just above the main square across from the **police station** (☎ **0222/91-274**).

EXPLORING THE ISLAND

Skýros (which is called Horió and, of course, sometimes Hóra) looks much like a typical Cycladic hill town, with whitewashed cube-shaped houses built on top of each other. The main street, Agorás ("Market"), leads up to the **central square,** Platía Iróon ("Heroes Square"), which is actually just a widening of the street. The winding streets and paths that are called streets are too narrow for cars and mopeds, so most of the traffic is by foot and hoof.

Signs point up to the town's **Kastro.** It's a 15-minute climb, but worth it for the view; on the way you'll pass the **Church of Ayía Triáda,** which has some interesting frescoes, and the **Monastery of Áyios Yióryios,** which was founded in 962 and contains a famous black-faced icon of St. George that was brought back from Constantinople during the Iconoclasm. A lion of St. Mark over the gate of the citadel identifies the structure as Venetian, but actually it's mostly Byzantine built atop a classical foundation. (According to myth, King Lykomídes pushed Theseus to his death from here.) From one side the view overlooks the rooftops of the town, and from the other the cliff drops precipitously to the sea.

The terrace at the far end of town is **Rupert Brooke Square,** where the English poet, who is buried on the southern tip of the island, is honored by a nude statue of *Immortal Poetry,* which is reported to have greatly offended the local people when it was installed. You'll probably be amused when you see how pranksters have chosen to deface the hapless bronze figure.

The Carnival of Skýros

The 21-day Karnaváli is highlighted by a 4-day period leading up to Lent, the most important of which is Katharí Deftéra (Clean Monday). On this day Skyrians don traditional costumes and perform dances, including the famous "goat dance," on the *platía*. Unleavened bread *(lagána)* is served with *taramasaláta* and other meatless specialties. (Traditionally, vegetarian food is eaten for 40 days leading up to Páska, Orthodox Easter.)

Prior to this, and culminating on Sunday in the midafternoon, are a series of ritual dances and events performed by a group of weirdly costumed men. Some dress as old shepherds in dark animal skins, with a mask made of goatskin and a belt with numerous sheep bells. Others dress as young women and flirt outrageously. (Skýros has a long history of transvestism; it was here that Achilles successfully dodged the draft during the Trojan War by dressing as a woman, until shrewd Odysseus tricked him into revealing his true gender.) Other celebrants caricature Europeans, and all behave outlandishly and rather aggressively, reciting ribald poetry and poking fun at any and all bystanders. This ritual, generally believed to be pagan in origin, causes some people to reflect on the antics of ancient Greek comedy and even tragedy ("goat song"), with men playing all the roles and catharsis the goal.

The **archaeology museum** (☎ 0222/91-327) is just below on the steps leading down to Magaziá Beach. It has a small collection of Mycenaean and late Helladic funerary objects, proto-geometric vessels, and artifacts from the Roman period, as well as a reconstruction of a typical 19th-century house. It's open Tuesday to Sunday from 8:30am to 3pm; admission is 500 Drs ($2.10) for adults, 400 Drs ($1.65) for seniors, and 300 Drs ($1.25) for students.

Nearby, the **Faltaïts Museum** (☎ 0222/91-232) houses the private collection of Manos Faltaïts. It's one of the best island folk-art museums in Greece and contains a large and varied collection of plates, embroidery, weaving, woodworking, and clothing, as well as photographs, including some of local men in traditional Carnival costumes. There's a workshop attached to the museum where young artisans make lovely objects using traditional patterns and materials. Proceeds from the sale of workshop items go to the upkeep of the museum. It's open daily in the summer from 10am to 1pm and 5:30 to 8:30pm; off-season just ring the bell and someone will open the door for you; admission is free. The museum also has another shop in the town called **Argo,** on the main street (☎ 0222/92-158); it's open daily from 10am to 1pm and 6:30pm to midnight.

Local customs and dress are being better preserved on Skýros than on any island we know of. Older men can still be seen in baggy blue pants, black caps, and leather sandals constructed with numerous straps, and older women still wear their long head scarves. The embroidery you'll often see women busily working at as they gossip is famous for its vibrant colors and interesting patterns, such as people dancing hand-in-hand with flowers twined around their limbs. Peek into the doorway of any Skyrian home and you're likely to see what looks like a room from a dollhouse with miniature tables and chairs, and colorful plates—loads of plates hanging on the wall.

Skýros is also the home of a unique breed of **wild pygmy ponies,** often compared to the horses depicted on the Parthenon frieze and thought to be related to Shetland ponies. The Meraklídes, local Skyrians who care for these rare animals, have moved most of the diminishing breed to the nearby island of Skyropoúla, though tame ones can still be seen grazing near town. Ask around and you might be able to find a Meraklíde who'll let a child ride one.

THE BEACHES

To reach **Magaziá,** continue down from Rupert Brooke Square. (If you're carrying a heavy load, take a taxi.) From Magaziá, once the site of the town's storehouses (magazines), it's nearly half a mile to **Mólos,** a fishing village, though the two villages are quickly becoming indistinguishable because of development. There's windsurfing along this more developed beach, and there are some fairly isolated beaches beyond Mólos, with some nudist bathers.

There's a very nice beach just below the Kástro, though getting to it is somewhat of a problem. (We're sorry, but we just can't provide any easy directions; you'll have to ask—probably more than once.)

South of town the beaches are less attractive until you reach **Aspoús,** which has a few rooms to rent and a couple of tavernas. **Ahíli,** a bit farther south, is where you'll find the big new **marina,** so it's no longer much of a place for swimming. Farther south the coast becomes increasingly rugged and there's no roadway.

We recommend that you head back across the narrow waist of the island to **Kalamítsa,** the old safe harbor, 2 miles south of Linariá, which has a good clean beach and bus service in the summer.

Both halves of the island offer attractions, though the most scenic area is probably to the south toward **Tris Boukés,** where Rupert Brooke is buried. The better beaches, however, are to the north.

North of Linariá, **Aheroúnes** is a rather pretty beach, and beyond it, **Péfkos,** where marble was once quarried, is better sheltered and has a taverna that's open in the summer. The next beach north, **Áyios Fokás,** is probably the best on the island, with a lovely white-pebble beach and a taverna in the summer. Locals call it paradise, and as is true for all such places, it's very difficult to reach. Most Skyrians will suggest walking, but it's a long hilly hike. To get there, take the bus back to Linariá, tell the driver where you're going, get off at the intersection with Péfkos, and begin your hike west from there.

Atsítsa is another beach with pines growing there, but it's a bit too rocky; it can be reached by the road going across the Óros Olýmbos mountains in the center of the island. It has a few rooms to rent and a holistic health and fitness holiday community. A 15-minute walk farther north at **Kyrá Panayía** will bring you to a sandy beach that's a bit better.

A MEMORABLE HIKE

The northwest of the island is covered in dense pine forests, speading down to the rocky shore and opening into gentle bays and coves. This area provides wonderful hiking for sturdy walkers. Take a taxi (4,000 Drs/$17) to **Atsítsa.** If you're cautious, arrange for the taxi to return in 5 or 6 hours. Explore the ruins of the ancient mining operation at Atsítsa, then head south for about $4^1/2$ miles to Áyios Fokás, a small bay with a tiny taverna perched right on the water. Kali Orfanou, a gracious hostess, will provide you with the meal of your trip: fresh fish caught that morning in the waters before you, vegetables plucked from the garden for your salad, and her own homemade feta cheese and wine. Stay, swim in the bay, and hike back to your taxi. The ambitious will continue south for 7 or 8 miles to the main road and catch the bus or hail a taxi. This part is mainly uphill, so beware. In case you tire or can't pry yourself away from this secluded paradise, Kali offers two extremely primitive rooms with the view of your dreams, but without electricity or modern toilets.

SHOPPING

Skýros is also a good place for shopping, especially for local ceramics. For the very best handmade museum copies, go to the **Pottery Studio Kallio,** up the main street on the left; the proprietor, George Nittis, speaks English and is extremely knowledgeable. **Ergastiri,** also on the main street, sells interesting ceramics, Greek shadow puppets, and a great selection of postcards. For simpler, more naïve Skyrian plates, try the small shop at **no. 307,** across from Fragoules hardware, or **Skyriana Keramika,** across from Skýros Travel. You'll find Stamatis Ftoulis's **Skyriana Keramika Workshop** (☎ 0222/91-559) near the Stephanos Restaurant in Magaziá, not far from the Xenia Hotel. Nice hand-carved wooden chests and chairs made from beech—in the old days it used to be blackberry wood—can be purchased from **Lefteris Avgoklouris,** a former student of the recently departed master, Baboussis, in Skýros town; his studio (☎ 0222/91-106) is on Konthili Road, around the corner from the post office. Another fine carver is **Manolios,** who can be found in the main market.

WHERE TO STAY

The whole island has only a few hotels, so most visitors to Skýros stay in private rooms. Facilities on Skýros are somewhat more primitive than on the other islands, so before you accept any accommodation, check it over to make sure it's what you want. The best rooms are in the upper part of the town, north from the bus stop. Walk beyond the *platía,* up the main street. Women will offer you rooms here, so look them over and make your choice. A more efficient procedure is to stop in at the Skýros Travel Center. Rates for in-town or beach rooms during the high season are about 6,000 Drs ($25); so-called Class A rooms run 7,000 Drs ($29.15).

IN SKÝROS

✪ **Hotel Nefeli.** Skýros, 340 07 Skýros. ☎ **0222/91-964.** Fax 0222/92-061. 12 rms, all with bath (shower). TV TEL. 13,500 Drs ($56.25) single; 19,500 Drs ($81.25) double. Rates include breakfast. AE, MC, V.

One of the best in-town options is the excellent Hotel Nefeli, built in the modern Skyrian style. All rooms have fridges, many offer fine views, and the large, downstairs lobby is a welcoming space, always filled at breakfast time. The hotel also has some very handsome traditonal-style studios with fireplaces for 30,000 Drs ($125). Since the Nefeli is one of the more popular hotels, you'd do well to reserve in advance.

ON MAGAZIÁ BEACH/MÓLOS

Hotel Angela. Mólos, 340 07 Skýros. ☎ **0222/91-764.** Fax 0222/92-030. 14 rms, all with bath (shower). TEL. 15,000 Drs ($62.50) single or double. No credit cards.

Among the most attractive and best-kept beach abodes is the Hotel Angela, adjacent to the sprawling Paradise Hotel complex. All pleasant and tidy rooms have balconies, but because the hotel is set back about 100 yards from the beach, there are only partial sea views. Nevertheless, the facilities and hospitality of the young couple who run the Angela make it one of the best bets for your money.

Pension Galeni. Mólos, 340 07 Skýros. ☎ **0222/91-379.** Fax 0222/91-379. 13 rms, all with bath (shower). 13,500 Drs ($56.25) single or double. AE, MC, V.

The small but delightful Pension Galeni has recently upgraded its rooms, so that all of them now have private facilities. We like the front (sea-facing) rooms on the top floor for their (currently) unobstructed views. The Galeni overlooks one of the cleanest parts of the beach—at least it was clean when we visited. They also have studios with kitchenettes for 17,000 Drs ($70.85).

Xenia Hotel. Magaziá Beach, 340 07 Skýros. ☎ **0222/91-209.** Fax 0222/92-062. 24 rms, all with bath (tub). TEL. 14,000 Drs ($58.35) single; 19,000 Drs ($79.15) double. Rates include buffet breakfast. AE, DC, V.

The recently upgraded Xenia occupies, arguably, the best location on Magaziá. In 1989 it added a controversial (and ugly) concrete breakwater that's supposed to protect the beach from erosion. The rooms have handsome 1950s-style furniture and big bathrooms with tubs, as well as wonderful balconies and sea views.

In LINARIÁ OR AHEROÚNES BEACH

Linaria Bay Hotel. Linariá, 340 07 Skýros. ☎ **0222/96-274** or 0222/96-275. 9 rms, all with bath (shower); 2 apts. A/C TV TEL. 9,000 Drs ($37.50) single; 11,500 Drs ($47.90) double; 19,500 Drs ($81.25) apt. No credit cards.

For those who want to spend the night near the port, we recommend this pleasant white hotel with blue shutters up to the right, below the church. All rooms have a fridge.

Pegasus Apartments. Aheroúnes Beach, 340 07 Skýros. ☎ **0222/91-552.** 7 studios, 1 apt, all with bath (shower). MINIBAR. 10,150 Drs ($42.25) studio; 20,250 Drs ($84.50) apt. EURO, MC, V.

The resourceful Lefteris Trakos built these fully equipped studios which can accommodate two or three people (the apartment can sleep up to six). New additions include a taverna, minimarket, and pretty garden. Another plus is the chance to see (and ride, if you're under 15) Katerina, a Skyriot pony.

WHERE TO EAT

The food in Skýros town is generally pretty good and reasonably priced. **Anemos,** up from the square on the main drag (☎ **0222/92-155**), is a good place for breakfast, with filtered coffee, omelets, and freshly squeezed juice. The **Skyros Pizza Restaurant** (☎ **0222/91-684**) serves tasty pies as well as other Greek specialities in generous portions. **I Trýpa** ("The Hole"), near the square, is a good place for a light snack, croissant, *tirópita,* or ice cream. For gyros *(souvláki me píta)* and french fries try **K. Hioti,** just below the square.

The best **bakery** in town is hidden away up in the hills on the edge of Skyros. Walk up along the stairs to the statue of *Immortal Poetry,* bear right up the whitewashed stone path, and ask a local. It's tucked away, but your nose can be your guide. (It also sells its bread in the market.)

In Linariá, look for **Kyría Maria** (over the headland near the power station), which is especially good for fish—if you ask her not to overcook it—or **Michaeli's Psistariá,** which specializes in grilled meats.

Glaros Restaurant. Skýros. No phone. Main courses 800–2,600 Drs ($3.35–$10.85). Daily 7pm–1am. GREEK.

This venerable establishment, favored by locals during the busy summer season as a reward for staying open all year, serves from a very small list of traditional taverna fare. We've been regulars at this basic place on nearly every trip to the island over the past 10 years and can report that the moussaká is still as good as ever.

Kristina's Restaurant. Skýros. ☎ **0222/91-778.** Main courses 1,200–3,800 Drs ($5–$15.85). No credit cards. Mon–Sat 7pm–midnight. GREEK/INTERNATIONAL.

Those searching for something a little different should try this newer restaurant down from the bus stop square, about 100 yards south from the Nefeli Hotel, off to the right from the Supermarket. Kristina, the Australian chef, brings a lighter touch to everything she cooks. Chicken fricassee is the house special, and patrons keep coming back for it. Other favorites are the hot herb bread, vegetarian mixed plates, and cheesecake.

Marietes Grill. Skýros. ☎ **0222/91-311.** Main courses 1,000–2,000 Drs ($4.15–$8.35). Daily 1–3pm and 6am–midnight. GREEK.

One of the oldest places in town is a second generation–run grill that's popular with locals and visitors. The dining room is as simple as simple gets, but the food is extremely fresh and very good. We recommend the grilled chicken and meats. There's a small sampling of salads.

✪ **Pegasus Restaurant.** Skýros. ☎ **0222/92-580.** Main courses 1,600–2,200 Drs ($6.65–$9.15). No credit cards. Daily noon–3pm and 7pm–midnight. GREEK/INTERNATIONAL.

The town's prettiest and most romantic restaurant is down the side street above Skýros Travel. We had a delicious salad with *kasséri* (Skyrian cheese), excellent bread, and superb lobster with spaghetti.

Restaurant Kabanero. Skýros. ☎ **0222/91-240.** Main courses 1,000–1,700 Drs ($4.15–$7.10). Daily 6am–midnight. GREEK.

The perpetually busy Kabanero serves the usual Greek menu: moussaká, stuffed peppers and tomatoes, various stewed vegetables, and selected meats. We found the preparation up to snuff and prices about 20% less than at most other restaurants in town. The Kabanero is a treat and one of the best dining values in town.

SKÝROS AFTER DARK

If you've gotta dance, try the **Kastro Club** in Linariá, the **Skyropoúla Disco** located between Skýros beach and the nudist beach, or the **Skyros Club** in the Skyros Palace Hotel. Aside from these, there are few evening diversions other than bar-hopping on the main street. **Apocalypsis** attracts a younger crowd. **On the Rocks** rocks. **Renaissance** is loud and lively. **Rodon** is the best for actually listening to music.

Western Greece   13

The Ionian coast offers some of the most varied and impressive landscapes in Greece. In the south the flat marshes around Messolóngi give way to a coastline that's handsomely austere and especially appealing because of its striking contrast with the deep emerald green of the Ionian Sea. About midway up the coast, the landlocked Ambracian Gulf (Kólpos Amvrakikós) interrupts, its hospitable waters offering refuge to millions of waterfowl in the winter. From Vónitsa you can head west across a causeway to the island of Lefkáda, east around the gulf to Árta, or cross the narrow mouth of the gulf by ferry to Préveza.

North of the Ambracian Gulf the coastline becomes more irregular, with some particularly exquisite scenery, including postcard-beautiful Párga, en route to Igoumenítsa, the most important port of the region. From Igoumenítsa you can catch a ferry to most of the Ionian islands, Pátra, or Italy—or you can head east through the mountains toward the picturesque capital of Ioánnina. (Albania is less than 15¹/₂ miles north, but you can reach it more easily from Corfu.)

Epirus (Ípiros) is the green mountainous northwest region that stretches inland to the plains of Thessaly on the east. Plentiful rainfall and a more temperate climate make it an interesting contrast to the Aegean region that most people equate with Greece. Deep-set rivers, evergreen slopes, lush valleys, and picturesque villages of timbered houses with slate and tile roofs give it an alpine quality. Wildlife is more plentiful here than anywhere else in southern Europe, and it's a splendid area for hiking. Tourism is not yet an important source of income, and the mountain people are remarkably independent, retaining many of their traditional customs, clothing, and building styles. Little English is spoken, except at hotels, restaurants, and other businesses that offer services to visitors—so it remains indeed a fine place to get away from it all.

Most people visit western Greece in conjunction with a beach break on the nearby Ionian Islands, or as part of a tour of northern Greece. (See the map of western Greece and the Ionian Islands in chapter 14.) If you have some extra time, we'd recommend driving up the scenic west coast (from the Peloponnese or Athens) and spending a night at the miniresort of Párga. Then continue east to Ioánnina, where you might visit the Oracle of Dodóni and spend a few nights absorbing the town's charming ambience. From there, it's a pleasant drive to Métsovo, where hikers especially will enjoy having a few days to explore.

1   The Ionian Coast

There are no government tourist offices in this region, so local travel agents are the best source of information.

GETTING THERE

By Bus   The 9-hour bus trip to and from Athens operates three times daily on the privately run **KTEL** lines; call ☎ **01/512-5954** in Athens for information on schedules and fares. Most other destinations are served by local buses from Igoumenítsa, Ioánnina, and Préveza.

By Boat   If you follow our advice, you won't jump your steamer from Italy when it calls at Corfu just to cross over to Igoumenítsa. But if you do, the informative Baláskas Brothers at **Milano Travel,** at Odós Ayíon Apostólon 9, opposite the ferry pier (☎ **0665/23-565**), can answer all your questions; they're open daily from 8am to 10:30pm in summer. **John Kantas,** at Odós Ayíon Apostólon 13, is also very helpful. From Igoumenítsa to Corfu, the passenger fare is 850 Drs ($3.55) per person; for a car and driver the cost is 7,500 Drs ($31.25). Ferries depart almost hourly from 5am to 10pm.

Generally speaking, from Igoumenítsa there are at least half a dozen **ferries** daily in summer to Brindisi; the voyage takes 11 hours and costs about 10,000 Drs ($41.65) in high season (and about half that amount in spring and fall). In summer there are two or three ferries daily to Ancona, taking 24 hours, at a cost of 18,500 Drs ($77.10); two to four a day to Bari, 14 hours, 10,000 Drs ($41.65); three a week to Ortona, 24 hours, 18,000 Drs ($75); and two a week to Otranto, 9 hours, 10,000 Drs ($41.65). There's **hydrofoil** service in summer every other day to Brindisi via Corfu, 4 hours, 12,000 Drs ($50); and twice a week to Trieste, 18 hours, 19,000 Drs ($79.15). Schedules and even companies are subject to change, but all the ticket offices are on the waterfront Ethnikís Andistásis, across from the landing. For general information, contact the **Port Authority** (☎ **0665/22-240**). Reservations are recommended in summer.

For tickets to Ancona, contact **Strintzis/Minoan** (☎ **0665/22-952**); to Brindisi, **Hellenic-Mediterranean Lines** (☎ **0665/22-180**); to Bari, **Ventoúris** (☎ **0665/24-237**); to other destinations, the **Chris Travel Agency** (☎ **0665/25-351**).

By Car   From the Peloponnese, drive west on the coastal highway, then cross the Gulf of Corinth from Río, near Pátra, and drive northwest along the coast. From Athens, the inland highway north through Livadiá, Tríkala, and Ioánnina is the quickest route to Igoumenítsa.

MESSOLÓNGI

This town was founded 400 years ago after the Evinos River began to silt up, uniting three islets. The shallow lagoons surrounding the town provide excellent fishing and breeding grounds for eel and *avgotáraho* (a local fish roe). Messolóngi does not have charming seaside tavernas serving these local delicacies; rather, it features incomplete tract housing overlooking dirty marshland to the sea and bountiful mosquitoes. From the local army base, hundreds of uniformed soldiers spill out to roam the streets or crowd the ouzerís.

This town played a pivotal role in the fight for independence from the Turks. The brave inhabitants of Messolóngi held out for 4 years against the Turkish assault.

Finally, when it was captured in 1826, its population was massacred and the town was razed by fire. These events proved decisive in prompting the Great Powers (Great Britain, France, and Russia) to send a fleet in an attempt to prevent further atrocities—which resulted in the serendipitous victory at Navarino that eventually led to Greek independence. For those who've come this far to see **Byron's grave,** it's in the Garden of Heroes, which is signposted just before you enter the town.

North of Messolóngi, the road curves inland through green fields where you'll see olive groves, cypress trees, and plastic tents for drying tobacco.

ASTAKÓS

About 30 miles north of Messolóngi is the lovely port of Astakós, with ferry service to Ithaka, Kefalonía, and Pátra. Handsome 19th-century villas line the broad streets, and newer houses spill up the gentle slope of forested hills that surround this cove. A simple pier juts out into the placid water, and the waterfront is lined with taverna tables.

From Astakós, there are daily **sailings** in summer to Ayía Efimía on Kefalonía or Ithaca; call ☎ **0674/61-487** for schedule information.

If you decide to spend the night, there are rooms for rent above the storefronts around the town square, or try the **Stratos Hotel** (☎ **0646/41-096**), a relaxed, modern place where comfortable doubles with half-tubs with showers and large balconies overlooking the harbor cost 18,000 Drs ($75); the cafeteria downstairs serves midday and sunset beverages to the parade of port watchers.

Astakós has a few tavernas; we like **Spíros,** on the port, for its fresh fish, stewed vegetable dishes, and baked eggplant.

MÍTIKAS

Mítikas is another charming port on the Ionian coast, 50 miles north of Messolóngi. This quiet village has several hotels and a few tavernas, built during the boom times when ferries docked here on their way to and from Ithaca and Kefalonía. Now there's only the daily caïque to the nearby island of **Kálamos.** Occasionally boats from Lefkáda circle the nearby Pringiponíssi (four private islands) so that tourists can ogle Skorpiós, the island owned by the late Aristotle Onassis, and then stop at Mítikas for lunch.

The friendly residents seem little touched by their brush with tourist fame. They proudly tell Americans of the days when the young John Kennedy Jr. and Onassis used to water-ski off their shores. The calm waters are broken now by fishing boats that bring back their mullet and eels to local tavernas. The most satisfying thing to do in Mítikas is watch life go by. Older women, dressed in black, sweep their patios along the waterfront. Crisply dressed young girls promenade along the main street, holding hands. Old men in dusty blue and gray sit at the cafe/bars and watch you as you look at them. Robust young men clean the eels on the long thin stretch of pebble beach, swapping stories about Australia, where they return each winter to earn money for their families.

On our last trip we stayed at **Gláros Rooms,** across from the church on the main street (☎ **0646/81-240**), owned and operated by the friendliest people in town; the son, Miltiádes, speaks English and his wife, Mary, who comes from Toronto, teaches English at the local school. Doubles with common bath, and some with balconies overlooking the peaceful harbor, cost 5,600 Drs ($23.35). The **Hotel Kymata,** a little farther down the street (☎ **0646/81-258**), offers comfortable doubles with bath for 10,400 Drs ($43.35).

The **Gláros Restaurant,** across from the church, has the best food in town. Much of it is grown on the owners' farm.

En Route to Préveza

The Ionian coast banks sharply here, leaving drivers at a 30° angle to admire the fairy-land greenery and small stone fragments that appear to have been tossed randomly into the sea. Near the crossover to Lefkás at the water's edge are more ramparts from the well-preserved Venetian fortress at **Santa Maura** (Mávra), built by Giovanni Orsini in 1300.

Near **Vónitsa** is a well-preserved Byzantine castle that was so impregnable it was able to hold out against the Turks until 1479. At **Áktio** (Actium), site of the famous naval battle where the forces of Octavina (later Emperor Augustus) defeated those of Mark Antony and Cleopatra, there's another break in the road—the Ambracian Gulf. Here a small car-ferry shuttles back and forth across the quarter-mile waterway from the parking lot to the busy, crowded Préveza harbor. The Áktio–Préveza shuttle runs every half hour; the charge is 800 Drs ($3.35) for a car; people pay 100 Drs (40¢) each.

PRÉVEZA

Préveza is a pleasant town that has recently experienced considerable renovation; it's a good place to stop for a meal or even an overnight. There are a number of tourist services and good cafes along its busy, well-protected harbor. Préveza's harbor is in full view of the steady crawl of vehicles waiting for the next shuttle and the nightly *vólta.* The stone paved shopping lane *(lithóstrotos),* 1 block up from the port, is a good place to stock up on picnic supplies.

Essentials

For information or travel arrangements, we suggest that you contact Lucia at **Leopoulos Travel** (☎ 0682/24-473; fax 0682/25-671), just north of the Áktio shuttle landing, on the left. The **municipal tourist office** (☎ 0682/28-120), **post office,** and **National Bank** are farther north on the harborfront. The **bus station** is several blocks inland on Leofóros Irínis, the main commercial street; from the harborfront turn left just before the Castle. The **police station** is a couple of blocks north of the bus station, on the left. **Olympic Airways** (☎ 0682/28-343) has daily flights to and from Athens. In the summer there's **hydrofoil** service to Corfu via Páxi daily except Tuesday and Thursday at 3pm; the 2¹/₂-hour trip costs 6,800 Drs ($28.35).

What to See & Do

For archaeology buffs, there's the large, intriguing site of Nikópolis nearby, and veering east, the transportation hub of Árta.

Nikópolis is 5 miles north of Préveza, a Roman town built in A.D. 31 by the emperor Augustus to commemorate his victory at Actium (Áktio). It's a nice place to visit on a sticky summer day since it's shaded by olive trees and carpeted with grass. Several walls have survived with triple gates, and you can climb around to see the remains of the Temples of Mars (Ares) and Poseidon, part of an aqueduct, and some baths. In the Byzantine period Nikópolis prospered, and the remains of five basilicas can be examined at the site. Unfortunately, their fine mosaic floors are covered with gravel. The foundation wall of the outer city wall is 1 mile long and can be found (by the diligent) above the village of **Smyrtoúla.** The upper part of the Roman theater is visible on the Nikópolis slope; the rest is still beneath it. The

museum at the site (☎ 0682/41-336) has more burial monuments; its guard will also open one of the basilicas for you (for a tip). The site and museum are open daily from 8:30am to 3pm; admission is 500 Drs ($2.10) for adults, 400 Drs ($1.65) for seniors, and 300 Drs ($1.25) for students. Visitors without vehicles can catch the local bus from Prevéza to Igoumenítsa or Árta and get off at the site.

If you're an archaeology buff, watch for the signs to **Kassópi** on the road north from Prévéza to Árta (the local bus passes by). Kassópi is a well-preserved ancient town designed by Hippodamus according to ideas set forth in Aristotle's *Politics.* Cobblestone streets, many with a gutter down the center, were sloped to carry off rainwater; about 20 blocks have been laid out in a geometric pattern. Between visitors the guard passes his time by tending the sheep that inhabit Kassópi; they give it such a lived-in feel. The site is open daily from 9am to 3pm; admission is 500 Drs ($2.10) for adults, 400 Drs ($1.65) for seniors, and 300 Drs ($1.25) for students. The view is quite impressive from here, but don't pass by the next site, nearby Zalónga.

The men of **Zalónga** were massacred by the troops of Ali Pasha almost 200 years ago. It was on this cliff at Zalónga that, in 1822, 62 Souliote women, with children in their arms, danced to the edge and stepped off, one by one. A monument celebrates these women, who preferred death to rape or submission to Turkish rule. The monument can be seen high up on the mountain from miles away; a 15-minute walk plus a climb up some steps will take you there. Just below it is the small chapel of **Áyios Dimítrios,** whose frescoed interior tells the sad story of the women of Soúli.

Árta is the second-largest town in Epirus after Ioánnina and is known for its bridge, the oldest stone bridge in Greece, which spans the Árakthos River. The Church of Panayía Parigorítissa ("Our Lady of Consolation"), an interesting 13th-century work in the center of town, has been converted into a museum for local artifacts from Roman and Byzantine times. The major attractions here are the church, the ruins of a temple along Pýrrou Street, the nearby remains of the ancient theater, and a crumbling fortress above the town. In Áyios Vassílios and Ayía Theodóra, rare icons and fine frescoes, gifts of the Komnines and Angeli imperial families, are exhibited.

WHERE TO STAY & EAT

The best place to stay in Prévéza is the recently renovated **Dioni** (☎ 0682/27-381; fax 0682/27-384), on Papayioryíou Square—follow the signs up from near the Port Authority on the harbor—where air-conditioned doubles cost 17,500 Drs ($72.90), with American Express, MasterCard, and Visa accepted. Just south of it you'll find the **Hotel Mínos** (☎ 0682/28-424), where comfortable doubles with bath cost 13,250 Drs ($55.20).

For an excellent dinner, look for the **Taverna Psatha,** Odós Dardanellía 4 (☎ 0682/28-424), open daily from 7pm to 1am, where main courses cost 900 to 2,000 Drs ($3.75 to $8.35) for such dishes as lamb with potatoes, meatballs, and stuffed cabbage with lemon sauce. From the harborfront, turn inland after the small square with the octagonal fountain, left in front of the church with the clock tower on the shopping street *(lithóstrotos),* then take the second right up at their sign.

EN ROUTE TO PÁRGA

As you continue north from Prévéza to Igoumenítsa, you'll notice that the irregular coast still offers some of the best scenery in Greece. The changing light, especially as the day wears on, creates subtle images, and the emerald depths of the Ionian Sea are particularly luminous.

PÁRGA

Beach lovers may want to continue for 35 miles to Párga, a picture-perfect resort for great R&R—in the off-season. You'll find it very built-up to accommodate Corfu's overflow traffic and it's booked solidly by tour groups in the high season, but the two long beach coves that fan out like outstretched wings from its long central pier provide enough room for everyone to enjoy the clean, calm waters.

The town beach is a scenic stretch of white sand (with a few scattered rocks) facing the gorgeous bay. The water is emerald and turquoise, with perfectly positioned little rocky islands, and a handsome *kástro* crowns the town. Unfortunately, the word is out on all this beauty, so it's nearly impossible to find rooms here in the summer— though you'll find them being eagerly offered in the spring and fall.

ESSENTIALS

The **West Travel Tourist Office,** upstairs at Odós Alexándrou Vága 1 (☎ **0684/ 31-223;** fax 0684/31-948), sells ferry and excursion tickets to the local caïques, and can rent cars, book rooms or apartments, and help you with other travel-related needs.

The **police station, post office,** and **bus station** are all in the same building at Odós Alexándrou Vága 18, near the big church. Turn left from in front of the bus station and you'll find yourself on the main pedestrian lane that winds through the market and uphill to the *kástro.* The **OTE** (telephone center) is on the right at the first cross street, open Monday to Friday from 7:30am to 3:10pm, with longer hours in summer. Continue past the OTE to reach the **National Bank** on the tiny market square, Platía Vasilá. There are also several **souvenir shops** that act as banker's agents on this square.

WHAT TO SEE & DO

The transparent water makes this a fine place for snorkeling—and several souvenir shops sell snorkels, masks, and fins. Small paddleboats are ideal for touring Párga's other nearby coves. Caïques advertise their **excursion trips** on small signs on the pier; our favorite sign advertises a DAY TRIP TO HADES, which departs at 9am. (Does it ever return?) There are several boats running to **Paxí** for 1,650 Drs ($6.90) and to the **Nekromantío Cave,** on the Aherón River, for 1,350 Drs ($5.65).

If you walk up the lane that runs behind the harbor, the "tost," burger, and disco joints disappear. You can explore the walls of the Venetian **kástro** that straddles Párga's two coves, or cross over and reward yourself with a swim at long, sandy **Váltos beach** (the best local beach).

The **Nekromantío of Ephýra** (Sanctuary of Persephone and Hades) is the most popular day trip from Párga—15$^1/_2$ miles south at the village of **Messopótamos.** At the ancient grounds of the "Necromantic Oracle" is the estuary of the Aherón River—the mythical River Styx—where the souls of the dead used to board the ferry to Hades. Today you can explore the dry subterranean lake of **Aherúsia** (where the ancients believed Hermes led the souls of the dead who paid Charon to row them across to Hades) and visit the famous **oracle** that was recommended by Circe to Odysseus for its wise counsel. Excavations have revealed a dark, twisting corridor leading into the main sanctuary, a labyrinth created to remind petitioners of the tortured wanderings of restless souls in Erebos, the last stop before Hades.

WHERE TO STAY & EAT

New hotels are still being constructed and there are rooms for rent all over town and beyond Váltos beach. Don't come without reservations during the high season, but before July 1 or after September 15 you can shop around and bargain.

Our favorite place is the older **Hotel Paradissos,** Odós Livadá 33, in the center of town (☎ **0684/31-229;** fax 0684/31-226), which has been renovated while still preserving its charm, attentive service, and friendly atmosphere; doubles with bath cost 9,980 Drs ($41.60), and American Express, EuroCard, MasterCard, and Visa are accepted. The **Ayios Nektários,** at Odós Ayías Mánnas 36, up the street from the bus station (☎ **0684/31-150**), is also quite acceptable; doubles with shower are 9,700 Drs ($40.40). During John's last visit he stayed at the lovely new **Hotel Maistrali,** 4 Kryonéri Place (☎ **0684/31-275**), just 50 yards from the town beach—they're booked many months in advance for the summer season—where spacious doubles with bath and balcony cost 10,900 Drs ($45.40).

Walk up to the center of "town" and you'll find **To Kantouni** (no phone) in a niche off Vasilá Street, under a canvas canopy. Wander into the dark, cool interior of this little storefront and the cook will show you her dinner entrees. Everyone says that she has the best moussaká in town, and the prices are hard to beat. The best fresh seafood can be found at **Tzimas** (or **Four Brothers**) **Restaurant,** Odós Anexartisías 63 (☎ **0684/31-251**), the last place on the right at the harbor. Climb the pedestrian street to the fortress and continue on past to **O Flisvos** (☎ **0684/31-694**), one of the most beautiful outdoor restaurants you'll ever see, with a glorious view and good food at surprisingly reasonable prices. If you come to watch the sunset, you won't need reservations.

IGOUMENÍTSA

This west-coast city is the jumping-off point for maritime excursions to Corfu and Italy. Fortunately, there is frequent service to these points because there's not much to do here but wait for your ship to come in. The restaurants are generally awful, and if you should be unlucky enough to have to spend the night, you'll find the hotels vastly overpriced. There are no archaeological sites nearby, and there are few beaches. (The water in this heavily trafficked channel isn't so great either.)

If you're coming from Italy with a Eurailpass, resist any urge to jump ship unless you're going to northern Greece first. Since trains don't go to Igoumenítsa, you'd have to pay for a bus. Our suggestion is that you continue by ship to Pátra, where you can get a train to Athens or elsewhere.

To find the bus station and escape the portside gougers, turn left (north) from the ferry pier. The **bus station** is about 400 yards north; turn right at the little park with the bearded bust, go 2 blocks inland, and turn left.

If you get stuck here, make your way a quarter mile north of the ferry pier toward Ioánnina to the gracious **Hotel El Greco,** Odós Ethnikís Andístasis 86 (☎ **0665/ 22-245;** fax 0665/25-073), where attractive doubles with bath cost 16,500 Drs ($68.75)—a lot less than you'd pay closer to the ferry—and credit cards are accepted. The **Hotel Epirus,** on Odós Párgas, about 100 yards above the port on the road to Párga (☎ **0665/22-504**), is the only other place we find acceptable; a nice, fairly quiet double with bath costs 13,500 Drs ($56.25).

2 Epirus

The capital of Epirus (Ípiros), **Ioánnina** (Yánnina), is a city of nearly 120,000 inhabitants. It's a bustling metropolis with lots of light industry and traffic—not the ideal place for relaxation, but well worth a visit. Its archaeological museum has some surprisingly interesting finds, including objects related to the nearby Oracle of Zeus at Dodóni (Dodona). The Aslán Tzamí (mosque), in the city's special walled-in Old Town on the lake, houses an intriguing collection of folk art and political memorabilia.

And don't leave without visiting **Nissí,** the islet in Lake Pamvótis (now often called Lake Ioánnina) where a small community of homes and monasteries has been built; it's one of northern Greece's most colorful and pleasant excursions. Even more important, don't leave the region without visiting **Dodóni,** site of an oracle much revered in antiquity that still speaks to the modern pilgrim who goes with open ears.

From Ioánnina you can work your way through dramatic mountain countryside over the Athamanon range to the traditional hill village of **Métsovo,** where weavers and other craftsmen thrive in a foundation-funded, creative environment that seeks to preserve the best of the past.

The best way to explore and experience this dramatic region is to rent a car (or take a bus) through the area referred to as **Zagóri** or the **44 Villages.** These mountain hamlets are simple, traditional places, with low-built houses overlooking fertile valleys and rushing waterways. For hikers, there's a 7$\frac{1}{2}$-mile walk through the **Víkos Gorge,** in Víkos-Aóös National Park. **Robinson Expeditions** in Ioánnina (☎ 0651/29-402) offers outdoor excursions in the Epirus area.

GETTING THERE & GETTING AROUND

By Plane　Olympic Airways (☎ 0651/26-218) has two flights a day to and from Athens, as well as five flights a week to and from Thessaloníki. Its office is on the central square near the EOT. Bus no. 7 runs every 20 minutes between the airport and the main bus station; the fare is 200 Drs (85¢).

By Bus　Buses leave from the **main bus station,** on Zozimádou Street, 1 block above the intersection of Venizélou and Avérof streets (☎ 0651/26-286), for Igoumenítsa nine times a day (2$\frac{1}{2}$ hours, 1,600 Drs/$6.65); for Athens nine times a day (8 hours, 6,800 Drs/$28.35); for Thessaloníki five times a day (7 hours, 5,500 Drs/$22.90); for Métsovo four times a day (1$\frac{1}{2}$ hours, 1,000 Drs/$4.15); and for Párga once a day (3 hours, 1,800 Drs/$7.50). There is also infrequent bus service to Zagóri from this station; check with the EOT for the latest schedules. From the **secondary bus station,** on Bizaníou Street south of the central square (☎ 0651/25-014), there are two buses a day to Pátra (4$\frac{1}{2}$ hours, 4,000 Drs/$16.65), as well as buses to Dodóni, Párga, and Préveza.

By Car　The route along the coast we've described is more scenic and diverse; Highway 5 (E-19) is more direct. The new direct route from Igoumenítsa to Thessaloníki is reportedly near completion.

IOÁNNINA

270 miles NW of Athens, 62 miles E of Igoumenítsa

The city has a rich and colorful history, a thriving traditional culture, a highly regarded university, a picturesque setting on ancient Lake Pamvótis, and several colorful sights associated with its most infamous resident, Ali Pasha.

ESSENTIALS

VISITOR INFORMATION　The helpful **Greek Tourist Organization (EOT)** office, at Odós Zérvas 2, off the southwest corner of the central square (Platía Pýrrou) (☎ 0651/25-086), is open Monday to Friday from 7:30am to 2:30pm, with extended hours in the summer. The **tourist police** are on the first floor (Room 10) of the main police station, at 28 Oktovríou 11, north of the central square (☎ 0651/25-673), open daily from 7am to 2pm.

Robinson Expeditions, Odós 8 Merarhías 10, on the north side of town (☎ 0651/29-402; fax 0651/25-071), offers a program of outdoor adventures

including trekking in the Pindus mountains, gorge hiking, hang-gliding, rafting, kayaking, and flora and fauna walks in the Epirus area.

ORIENTATION   Ioánnina spreads out along the western bank of **Lake Pamvótis.** The walled **Old Town** juts out into the lake and the new city rises above it. The center of town is dominated by what seems like one large irregular **central square,** which is actually several squares—Platía Pýrrou (on the southwest), Platía Dimokratías, and Platía 25 Martíou.

Five main traffic arteries intersect near the middle of the central squares: **28 Oktovríou,** leading northwest; **Bótsari,** leading north; **Avérof,** leading northeast down to the Old Town and the lake; **Bizaníou,** leading south; and **Dodónis** (also still called King George), leading southeast—as you might expect—to Dodóni and Athens.

Most tourist services, hotels, and restaurants can be found near the central square. It's a 5-minute walk down Avérof (you'll pass the **Old Bazaar** on your left) to the walled Old Town, then another 5 minutes around its perimeter or through an opposite gate out to the shore of the lake. The tall, brown brick **Litharítsia Prison** is on a rise in the green park surrounding the old clock tower; this can be used to orient yourself to nearby Pyrrus Square.

GETTING AROUND   By Bus   Ioánnina has a fair public bus system. Tickets, which cost 90 Drs (38¢) must be purchased before boarding. There's a kiosk on the west side of Platía Dimokratías (Central Square).

By Car   A rental car is one of the most efficient ways of getting around, especially for a small group. There's a **Budget Rent A Car** office on Leofóros Dodónis (☎ **0651/43-901;** fax 0651/45-382) with a branch at the airport (☎ **0651/25-102**).

By Taxi   Local taxis don't have meters, so you must negotiate a price before you get in. Each hour's drive should cost about 4,000 Drs ($16.65), plus about 1,200 Drs ($5) per hour for waiting. To get the most for your money, take the time to find a driver who speaks some English.

FAST FACTS   The **post office** is at 28 Oktovríou 3; the **telephone center (OTE)** is next door at Odós 28 Oktovríou 4, open daily from 7am to midnight. For a wide selection of foreign-language **periodicals,** try Athanasios Daktylithos, at Odós Pirsinela 14 (☎ **0651/28-005**).

SPECIAL EVENTS   During the summer in the **Ioánnina Theater,** performances are often given of *Ipirótika,* a festival of indigenous songs and dances (with older singers specializing in the popular *dimotiká,* traditional ballads and folk songs), as well as other cultural events. Contact the EOT for more information, including the date of the 1-day-only performance of classical theater at Dodóni.

What to See & Do

There's lots of interesting **shopping** for folk art, silver jewelry, icons, carpets, and hammered copper, brass, and tin dishware. Ioánnina is most famous for its silver work, especially filagree, and you'll find the largest concentration of shops and widest selection along Avérof. (There's not much chance to bargain here, but the prices are often half what you might pay on the more touristic islands.) **George Minas Moschos,** with shops at Avérof 56 and 65 (☎ **0651/20-542**), has an excellent assortment of more traditional designs and a few interesting antiques. **Stathis Detsikas Silver,** Avérof 72 (☎ **0651/32-313**), offers more contemporary designs. **Asimika Lagou,** Karamanlí 35, near the bottom of the hill (☎ **0651/34-163**), is more fashionable.

If the repoussé copper and brass interest you, wander off Avérof to the left into the Old Bazaar area, and follow your ears to the tink-tink of the craftsmen. Some of this work is also engraved and sometimes given a light wash of silver. You'll also find some cloisonné and even some wood carvings in this area.

Archaeological Museum. March 25 Sq. (northwest side of City Park). ☎ **0651/24-490.** Admission 500 Drs ($2.10). Mon noon–6pm, Tues–Fri 8am–6pm, Sat–Sun 8:30am–3pm.

A special surprise in town is this lovely, well-lit, modern museum with many artifacts from Dodóni and other archaeological sites in the Epirus region. Pieces include pottery, jewelry, and coins, primarily from the 5th to 3rd centuries B.C., when Dodóni (Dodona) was one of the most important oracles in Greece. Don't miss the collection of lead tablets inscribed with questions for the oracle. A highlight of the museum is the small bronze statue from Dodóni (it shows intricate and amazing details on a boy holding a dove), and a paleolithic hand axe from Kokkinopolis, Préveza. Outdoor alcoves adjoining the galleries display pieces of the marble capitals and grave stelle from various neighboring archaeological sites.

Municipal Popular Art Museum in Aslán Tzamí (Mosque). Alexander Noustou St. ☎ **0651/26-356.** Admission 600 Drs ($2.50) adults, 300 Drs ($1.25) students. Mon–Fri 8am–3pm, Sat–Sun 9am–3pm.

The museum is located on the lake side of the Old Town, up some cobblestone-paved lanes. Displayed haphazardly in the various prayer areas are some fine local costumes, weapons, old documents, and photos of military men, plus memorabilia from the War of Independence and World War II. The eclectic collection includes some

Judaica: three *katubahs* (marriage contracts in Hebrew from 1762) and a gold-embroidered velvet curtain from an old Jewish synagogue in Ioánnina.

Synagogue. 18-B Joseph Eliyiá, Old Town. Admission free. Wed and Sat by appointment (call Avram Negreen at ☎ **0651/28-043** or Maurisis Eliazaf at ☎ 0651/25-195 or 0651/29-429).

The Synagogue of Ioánnina is a handsome building located just inside the walls of the Old Town on Ioustinianoú (Justinian) Street. You'll find it by walking down Avérof Street and making a quick left after entering the main gate. Continue for about 2 blocks and the synagogue will be on your right. As with others in northern Greece, this religious building is no longer in normal use because most of the local Jewish population was murdered during the German occupation. (There's a Holocaust Memorial nearby, outside the walls, at Karamanlí and Soútsou streets.) Although the gate will almost certainly be locked, you can gain entrance by contacting one of the gentlemen listed above. (Mr. Negreen runs a small shop at Odós Anexartisías 8 and is usually available to open the synagogue on Wednesday and Saturday afternoons.)

An Island in the Lake

A boat leaves the lakeside just left of the old fortress every half hour for the island. The 10-minute trip costs 175 Drs (75¢). The water is too murky with green algae to see much, but you get the impression of plenty of life there.

Nissí (which simply means "island") was settled in the 17th century by refugees from the Máni in the Peloponnese. Its most colorful inhabitant was the dissident Turkish ruler Ali Pasha, who arrived in 1820 and took refuge here for 2 years. After much cajoling, he received a royal pardon from Constantinople (Istanbul), which was just a trick on the Ottoman sultan's part: troops had been dispatched to Ioánnina to end his command. When they arrived, he hid on the second floor of the guest house of the Monastery of Áyios Pandelímon, but soldiers killed him by firing through the floor. He was beheaded and his head was paraded about the province before being taken to Constantinople.

The **Ali Pasha House** is straight up the blessedly car-free pathway of souvenir shops. The "museum" was actually the pre-1820 home of Ali's wife, Vassilikí, who betrayed his presence in the monastery next door. The 17th-century Monastery of Áyios Pandelímon is closed to visitors, but just behind the Ali Museum is the **Prodrómou Monastery** (dedicated to St. John the Baptist, the "Forerunner" of Christ), built in 1506–07 and filled with frescoes.

Continue back up Souvenir Street; where the other side of the island comes into view is the **Moní Philanthropínon,** built in 1292. If you walk through the richly decorated, frescoed church, you'll come to the wing used as a "secret school" during the Turkish occupation. It's obvious that the frescoes have been grossly defaced (because of the Muslim taboo against worshiping human images), but are still worth seeing. Next door, the **Moní Stratigopoúlou** (11th century) was dedicated to St. Nicholas, whose portrait is inside the first entry. The frescoes are much darker and eroded here. If the door is closed, an old woman in black will open it up for you; give her a small contribution. Farther along this path is the 16th-century **Eleoúsis Monastery,** which is also closed to the public. Even if you have only a few hours between buses in Ioánnina, it would be worth your while to visit the island briefly and stop for lunch.

Nearby Attractions

Oracle of Dodóni. ☎ **0651/82-287.** Admission 500 Drs ($2.10) adults, 400 Drs ($1.65) seniors, 300 Drs ($1.25) students. Summer, Mon–Fri 8am–7pm, Sat–Sun 8:30am–3pm; off-season, Mon–Sat 10am–3pm. From the Vyzaníou St. station in Ioánnina, there are two buses a day to Dodóni; taxis from Ioánnina charge about 5,000–6,000 Drs ($20.85–$25) round-trip, including waiting time.

Set in a valley amid tall, rugged, gray-blue mountains 13 miles south of Ioánnina, Dodóni (Dodona) was the most famous oracle of Zeus, possibly the oldest in Greece. It's now believed that the site was used for religious purposes as early as 2000 B.C.— at first sacred to an earth goddess, Naea, who was supplanted by Zeus in his aspect as god of the sky and weather by about 1200 B.C., although she was still honored as Dione. A large oak near an earlier sacred oak (which was chopped down in the late 4th century A.D.) marks the site of the oracle and Temple of Zeus. The priests, who, as Homer tells us through Achilles's prayer, slept on the ground and never washed their feet, listened to the god's voice in the rustling of the leaves. For centuries kings and commanders would consult the oracles at both Dodoni and Delphi, hoping that at least one would respond to their questions with an answer they liked.

At the site today you'll see a mass of temples with eroded columns, tumbled upon each other. The theater, one of the largest in Greece, is still impressive in its bulk. During the Roman era the first five rows were removed and replaced with a retaining wall for use during gladiator events. A theatrical performance is given in the theater once a year, in August, in honor of the Dodona Festivals of antiquity.

Pérama Caves. Admission 1,000 Drs ($4.15) adults, 500 Drs ($2.10) students. Summer, daily 8am–8pm; winter, daily 8am–4pm. Bus: 8 from the west side of the central square (Plátia Dimokratías) to Pérama; then walk 10 minutes from the bus stop.

These spectacular caves, 3 miles north of Ioánnina (near the village of Pérama), were discovered during World War II by guerrillas hiding from the Germans and are believed to be the most extensive caves in Greece. They're filled with galleries of stalactites and stalagmites that are well lit and fun to explore.

Vrellis Museum. Bizáni, Epirus. ☎ **0651/55-055.** Admission free. Daily 8:30am–7pm.

We aren't sure what to say about this wax museum. Locals speak about it reverentially, describing it as a moving tribute to the courage of Epirus's religious and political patriots from the time of the Ottoman occupation until the modern era. It has recently moved into new, larger, and better lighted quarters in Bizáni, about 7 miles south of town on the highway to Athens.

WHERE TO STAY

Ioánnina has a number of budget hotels near the bus station, an area off the noisier thoroughfares but convenient to the lake and shopping. Many hotels no longer accept credit cards because ATMs can be found nearby.

Hotel Egnatia. Odós Aravántinou 20 (at Daglí St.), 454 45 Ioánnina. ☎ **0651/25-667.** Fax 0651/75-060. 52 rms, all with bath (shower). TEL. 9,600 Drs ($40) single; 13,200 Drs ($55) double. No credit cards.

The Egnatia is on the small, quiet part of Skobourdi Square, near the main bus station. The comfortable lobby is modern with a few rustic touches. The guest rooms are plain but acceptable, with good firm beds and curtains for all showers.

Hotel El Greco. Odós Tsirigóti 8, 454 45 Ioánnina. ☎ **0651/30-726.** Fax 0651/30-728. 36 rms, all with bath (shower). TEL. 10,400 Drs ($43.35) single; 14,300 Drs ($59.60) double. Rates include breakfast. No credit cards.

Turn left from in front of the main bus station, take the second street to the left, and you'll reach this charming hotel on the right. It's a quiet family hotel, with the friendliest atmosphere in town. There's a cheery breakfast room and parking in back.

Hotel Galaxy. Platía Pýrrou, 452 21 Ioánnina. ☎ **0651/25-056.** Fax 0651/30-724. 38 rms, all with bath (shower). TEL. 12,000 Drs ($50) single; 18,000 Drs ($75) double. Rates include breakfast. No credit cards.

This older hotel just off the southeast corner of the central square recently underwent a thorough renovation, and it's now the handsomest traditional-style hotel in town—with double-paned windows for extra quiet. Ask for a room with a lake view.

Hotel King Pyrros. Odós Goúnari 3, 45 444 Ioánnina. ☎ **0651/27-652.** Fax 0651/29-980. 23 rms, all with bath (shower). TV TEL. 9,200 Drs ($38.35) single; 13,800 Drs ($57.50) double. EURO, MC, V.

This attractive hotel is right off the central square, opposite the clock tower, and the windows facing the main street are double-paned. The rooms are small but comfortable, neat, and pleasant.

✪ **Hotel Olympic.** Odós Melanídi 2, 45 332 Ioánnina. ☎ **0651/22-233.** Fax 0651/22-041. 54 rms, all with bath (tub or shower). A/C TV TEL. 14,400 Drs ($60) single; 19,200 Drs ($80) double; 27,600 Drs ($115) deluxe double. Rates include breakfast. No credit cards.

This tip-top lodging is in the center of town off Dodónis Street near 28 Oktovríou. It's one of the more popular hotels and professionally managed, so a reservation is recommended. The guest rooms have double beds and well-lit bathrooms; all have fridges and some include minibars. The new top-floor rooms are the most comfortable and luxurious in town.

Hotel Paris. Odós Tsirigóti 6, 454 44 Ioánnina. ☎ **0651/20-541.** 55 rms, 20 with bath (tub or shower). 5,200 Drs ($21.65) single without bath; 7,500 Drs ($31.25) double without bath, 9,200 Drs ($38.35) double with bath. No credit cards.

This budget hotel is down the street from the bus station, near the Hotel El Greco. It's no great shakes, but it's convenient, well kept, and has decent shared bathrooms. Some of the rooms with private baths boast tubs—a real bargain.

WHERE TO EAT

The huge **Oasi,** on the north end of the central square (☎ **0651/33-942**), is open 24 hours a day, and has a good local reputation—good enough for a big wedding dinner during our last visit. For the most delectable desserts, cross the street to **Diethnes** (☎ **0651/26-690**).

Litharitsia Cafeteria. Ayías Marínas and Yervassíou sts. ☎ **0651/20-043.** Snacks 450–1,200 Drs ($1.90–$5); main courses 1,100–2,900 Drs ($4.60–$12.10). No credit cards. Daily 11am–1am, depending on season. INTERNATIONAL.

Walk east toward the lake from the clock tower and up the stairs to the plaza to reach this unique complex made from the Turkish-era prison where Greek insurgents were jailed. The prices for snacks and beverages tend to match the elevation, but the view from the rooftop terrace is splendid and well removed from traffic. Downstairs is a large, handsome dining room with arched windows and rich wood decor, as well as several smaller facilities.

Taverna Gastra. Igoumenítsa Rd. No phone. Main courses 1,200–4,000 Drs ($5–$16.65). No credit cards. Daily dusk–midnight. GREEK.

The highly popular Taverna Gástra ("Flower Pot") is 1 1/4 miles west of the airport, on the right side just before the road branches. A wide variety of well-prepared dishes are served, and dancing is encouraged.

Taverna O Kipos. Odós Karaïskáki 20. ☎ **0651/78-287.** Main courses 1,100–3,800 Drs ($4.60–$15.85). No credit cards. Daily dusk–midnight. GREEK.

Walk down 28 Oktovríou and turn right after Zalóngou Park to reach this excellent garden taverna (*kipós* means "garden") with traditional decor and music but contemporary cuisine—fresh beef, pork, lamb, veal, and chicken grilled to your taste—it won first place again during our last visit. The menu is in Greek, but ask for Vangelis, the chef/owner, who picked up some English while working for many years in a New York restaurant.

Taverna O Fomas. Nissí, Lake Ioánnina. ☎ **0651/81-819.** Main courses 700–1,400 Drs ($2.90–$5.85); fish from 3,500 Drs ($14.60) per kilo. Daily from when the first customer arrives until the last one leaves. GREEK/SEAFOOD.

Several attractive restaurants greet you as you get off the boat. They're all good—and you can wangle a better price by comparison shopping—but we found this homely, tree-shaded place, about 250 yards along the path to the Ali Pasha Museum, to be the most inviting since we saw several Greek families enjoying their meal. The trout was tasty, tender, and succulent. For a special treat in season, try the local delicacy, *karavída,* a shellfish that's something between crayfish and lobster.

MÉTSOVO

This delightful alpine village, perched at nearly 3,300 feet above sea level, holds on to its traditions while managing some sophistication. Its unique flavor comes in part from the ethnic heritage of its inhabitants, who are Vlachs (originally from Walachia, in Romania). These former shepherds, who have settled all over the Balkans and beyond, pride themselves on their peaceable communities, traditional garb, exquisite weaving, and special cuisine—all of which may be found in Métsovo. The village acquired both its relative wealth and independence by guarding the nearby Katára Pass for the Ottoman Empire. A school was established here in 1659, which became a center of commerce based on sheep farming. It suffered some damage from Turkish troops in 1854, but by this time the village's most famous son, George Avérof (1815–99) had already made his fortune; he restored the town and later bequeathed a considerable sum to help preserve its special legacy.

Greeks are lured to Métsovo year-round: in the summer for its cool, fresh air, and in the winter for its abundant Swiss-village charm. We've never found it anything short of exhilarating!

ESSENTIALS

GETTING THERE   Drive 36 miles west on Highway 6 (E-87) from Ioánnina or 57$\frac{1}{2}$ miles west from Tríkala in Thessaly. There are two daily buses from Kalabáka, five from Ioánnina (but only two on weekends), and one from Thessaloníki, so you shouldn't find it difficult to get here. The only problem is leaving.

VISITOR INFORMATION   The **bus stop** is on Platía Avérof, the central square. Your hotel should be able to provide you with the most information about the local area. The **police station,** opposite the bus stop (☎ **0656/41-233**), is friendly and fairly helpful. The **post office** is on the main street above the square, open Monday to Friday from 7:30am to 2:30pm. There are two **banks** on the square, open Monday to Friday from 8am to 2pm, but several shops accept traveler's checks and credit cards. If you need **medical assistance,** call ☎ **0656/41-111.** Contact the **Métsovo Alpine Club** (☎ **0656/41-249**) for information on trails and the nearby ski center.

SPECIAL EVENTS   If you're here on July 26 for the local religious festival, you'll be treated to dancing in the square, as well as traditional costumes (a more elaborately embroidered version of the daily wear) and roasted lamb on publicly shared skewers.

WHAT TO SEE & DO

The handsome new traditional-style **Averof Gallery,** on the south side of the central square, houses an impressive collection of more than 250 paintings, drawings, and sculptures of the most important 19th- and 20th-century Greek artists. It's open Tuesday to Sunday from 9am to 1:30pm and 5 to 7:30pm; admission is 500 Drs ($2.10).

The Tosítsa family's mansion has been restored and modernized as a **folk-art museum.** Its heavy wood, stucco, and roomy interior is quite typical of the *arhondiká* that can be seen in the hill country of Mt. Pelion, Kastoriá, and parts of Crete. The simple rooms are filled with decorative woven fabrics or warmth-giving rugs, tapestries, and carpets. The displays are a little too "stagey" for Kyle's tastes, but overall it's an excellent introduction to the best of northern Greek folk craft. The museum is open Wednesday to Friday from 8:30am to 1pm and 4 to 6pm. Admission is 300 Drs ($1.25).

Métsovo's main street provides wonderful **shopping** for embroidered wool capes, scarves, sweaters, carpets, pillow covers, and other souvenirs, but you should stick to items from the northern region. (We've seen inferior copies from Albania, embroidered silk blouses from China, synthetic linen tablecloths from Asian factories, and other overpriced junk.)

Having warned you about foreign-made products, we want to rave about the Pratírio Laïkís Téchnis, the **Métsovo Folk Art Cooperative** supported by the Tosítsa Foundation, which runs the folk-art museum. The cooperative store, which is located on a cobblestone path about 50 yards above the Egnatía Hotel, has a large variety of weavings, embroidery, and charming sculpted wooden dolls. The Laïkís Téchnis's gifted women will also tailor some great-looking clothes to order; if you don't want to look like an extra from the Dora Stratou folk-dance troupe in Athens, they'll whip up a cape, shawl, or suit in heavy hand-carded wool that'll knock 'em out on Fifth Avenue.

Another special shop is that of **Ares Talares,** next door to the Egnatía Hotel (☎ **0656/41-901**), where Mr. Talares carries on the family tradition of silversmithing; you'll find superb articles in the local style and exquisite free-form jewelry, at about half of what you'd pay in Athens. (His gold is also an exceptional value.)

You can hike, explore, or spend days roaming the hills around here, but don't forget that other Métsovo specialty—cheese. **Tiropolío** (literally "Cheese Store"), on the main square, is one of many such shops, but it gives out free samples! Smoked cheese is a regional specialty. Try *metsovoné* (which can be stored a long time—good for travelers), *vlachotíri* (made from sheep's milk), or *metsovélla* (another, lighter sheep's-milk cheese). The **Tirokomío** is the local cheese factory, on the right as you enter Métsovo from the west. Go visit it and sample away, but don't forget to search out a bottle of **Kastoyi,** the region's legendary, aged red wine. (We found a bottle at Stani on the square.)

The **Cathedral of Ayía Paraskeví,** just above the main square, is worth a visit to see its carved wood screen, silver chandeliers, and copies of the Ravenna mosaics. (On Sunday the local women can be seen going to church wearing their embroidered traditional dresses.) The **Church of Áyios Yióryios,** on the small road leading off to the left just as you enter the village, is also well worth searching for, and there's a **park** next door where children can play. The **Monastery of Áyios Nikólaos,** in a gorge below the village, has some interesting frescoes and a handsome hand-carved wood iconostasis. To reach it, turn left just after the Hotel Athinae and follow the signs; it takes about half an hour to walk down and an hour to walk back up.

Have we convinced you to spend the night in this special village?

WHERE TO STAY

✪ **Egnatia Hotel.** 10 Tosítsa Rd., 442 00 Métsovo. ☎ **0656/41-263.** Fax 0656/41-485. 36 rms, all with bath (shower). TEL. 12,800 Drs ($53.35) single; 17,500 Drs ($72.90) double. Rates include breakfast. AE, DC, EURO, MC, V.

A canary singing in the foyer is just the start of the award-winning hospitality of this excellent hotel on the quiet main street. The sitting and dining areas are charmingly decorated with local weavings and artifacts. The rooms are pleasant and comfortable, with flower-trimmed balconies and splendid views of the hills.

Hotel Athinae. 442 00 Métsovo. ☎ **0656/41-332.** 8 rms, 5 with bath (shower). 4,800 Drs ($20) single without bath; 7,200 Drs ($30) double with bath. Rates include breakfast. No credit cards.

Métsovo's only real budget choice is located above a tavern around the corner from the main square. It's quiet and the rooms are small, but the place is so charming that you may soon find this to be one of its attractive qualities. The owner's daughter and son, who speak English, will gladly show you the 16 new family-run rooms with bath and great views just beyond the square; they rent for 6,000 to 11,000 Drs ($25 to $45.85).

Hotel Bitounis. 25 Tosítsa Rd., 442 00 Métsovo. ☎ **0656/41-217.** Fax 0656/41-545. 30 rms, all with bath (shower). TEL. 12,000 Drs ($50) single; 14,400 Drs ($60) double. V. Free parking.

The large, comfortable carpeted rooms, most with balconies, overlook the spectacular valley below. The owner's son, Yannis, speaks English.

Hotel Flokas. 442 00 Métsovo. ☎ **0656/41-309.** Fax 0656/44-200. 10 rms, all with bath (shower). TEL. 9,250 Drs ($38.55) single; 11,250 Drs ($46.90) double. Rates include breakfast. V.

This inn, well above the square on the road leading off to the right before the bank, has rooms that overlook some red-tile rooftops and the valley below. You're greeted by a dripping fountain and a skylight above the stairs. The rooms have warm, natural-wood floors and simple furnishings with traditional decor.

Hotel Galaxias. 420 00 Métsovo. ☎ **0656/41-202.** Fax 0656/41-124. 10 rms, all with bath (shower). TEL. 18,000 Drs ($75) double. Rates include breakfast. AE, MC, V.

Attached to the excellent Galaxias Restaurant (see "Where to Eat," below) is this equally fine hotel. The decor is standard Métsovo, but there's a quiet, homey feel about the place because of the Barbayanni family's gracious management. The breakfast room is cozy, but our favorite space here is the garden/cafe. Not the fanciest lodging in town, but a good value.

Hotel Kassaros. 442 00 Métsovo. ☎ **0656/41-800.** Fax 0656/41-262. 31 rms, all with bath (shower). TV TEL. 11,400 Drs ($47.50) single; 16,800 Drs ($70) double. Rates include breakfast. AE, DC, EURO, MC, V.

The Hotel Kassaros is another fine lodging in the traditional style, on the road leading up just before the square. The rooms are spacious, comfortable, and attractive; all have balconies, most with splendid views.

Worth a Splurge

Hotel Victoria. 442 00 Métsovo. ☎ **0656/41-771** and 0656/41-898. 37 rms, all with bath (shower). TEL. 20,400 Drs ($85) single; 22,200 Drs ($92.50) double. Rates include buffet breakfast. MC, V.

The newest and largest hotel is on the small road leading off to the left just as you enter the village. The gray-stone first story is topped with a typically whitewashed stucco-and-plaster second story, covered with a red-tile roof. Inside, the gray-slate–paved lobby has big picture windows that reveal exquisite views. Natural-wood beams, balconies, beds, tables, and chairs provide a warm, homey feeling that's enhanced in winter when the tall stone fireplaces are ablaze. The dining room and bar are trimmed with locally produced weavings and rugs.

WHERE TO EAT

Athinae Restaurant. Near the central square. ☎ **0656/41-332.** Main courses 600–1,550 Drs ($2.50–$6.45). No credit cards. Daily 7am–11pm, depending on season. GREEK.

Maria Papapostolou offers down-home cooking Métsovo style, in keeping with her rustic inn and low prices. She offers vegetarian dishes as well as grilled meats, but her specialties include a delicious *píta* (mild leeks baked with a cornbread-like crust), *práso keftédes* (meatballs with leeks), and *spetzofái* (sausage with peppers).

Galaxias Restaurant. Just before the central square. ☎ **0656/41-202.** Main courses 750–2,000 Drs ($3.15–$8.35). EURO, MC, V. Daily 7:30am–midnight. GREEK.

With its soaring ceiling and decorations of local antiques, this is easily the handsomest restaurant in town, with the best food. Try the delicious bean soup and the roast goat, as well as the *kokorétsi,* a Métsovo favorite.

ZAGÓRI (ZAGÓRIA)

No visit to Epirus would be complete without a trip to the dramatic mountainous region of **Zagóri.** Also known collectively as the **Zagorohória,** or the **44 Villages** (though many of them are sadly depopulated), the area is part of the vast Víkos-Aóös National Park system, which means that development is strictly controlled: All buildings must be constructed of the traditional stone and slate of the Pindus mountains—there's not a red-tile roof in sight! As a result, the traditional mountain hamlets seem to have sprouted magically from their surroundings.

The Zagóri villages combine a surprising architectural sophistication with their setting of natural beauty. Square, handsome 18th- and 19th-century gray-stone houses overlook rushing waterways, flinty slopes, lush valleys, and stunning Víkos Gorge, a rocky 10-mile fissure in the earth that has sometimes been compared to the Grand Canyon. These are the wilds of Epirus: wild bear, boar, and wolves are said to inhabit the thickly forested hills, though all we've ever seen are flocks of sheep and a stray cow or two wandering through cobblestone streets and tranquil squares.

As with any unspoiled place in the modern world, development is a big political issue here. We've heard several Zagorians bless the sparse bus service that makes their villages less accessible to the masses. The tourists who make it up the mountain tend to be a sophisticated lot, often European or Greek, and they're willing to pay for the quaintness. You could spend about the same for a week in Zagóri as you would spend in the islands, but it's every bit as magical and considerably more serene.

ESSENTIALS

GETTING THERE & GETTING AROUND   By Bus   Bus service in Zagóri is rather inadequate: from the main bus station in Ioánnina there's service to Pápingo on Monday, Wednesday, and Friday at 5:30am and 2:30pm, with a return at 6:30am and 4:15pm; and to Skamnélli via Vítsa, Monodéndrini, Kípi, and Tsepélovo on Monday, Wednesday, and Friday at 6am and 4:15pm, with a return at 7:45am and 5pm.

By Car The roads are good, although winding, and you can see much of Zagóri in a day by car. You can rent a car in Ioánnina (see "Getting Around" in the Ioánnina section, above). Take the airport road north out of Ioánnina and you'll see clearly marked signs from there. The **EOT** in Ioánnina (☎ 0653/25-086) has free maps.

On Foot The Víkos Gorge, from Monodéndri to Pápingo, is a challenging 8-hour trek. We've been advised that although it's perfectly safe for hikers in pairs, one should not go alone, not only because of possible injury but because there have been a few unpleasant encounters with groups of Albanian immigrants who wander around down there. The friendly, helpful **EOT** in Ioánnina (☎ 0653/25-086) provides excellent maps and information about Víkos as does the local **mountain club** in Megálo Pápingo (☎ 0653/41-138 or 0653/41-230), but you can also go with a tour.

By Organized Tour Try the old veterans at **Robinson Expeditions** (☎ 0651/29-402) in Ioánnina, or the resourceful and well-organized **Ares Talares** of the Hotel Egnatia in Métsovo (☎ 0656/41-263).

KÍPI

On your way to Tsepélovo, be sure to detour to Kípi to see its famous 16th-century Turkish-style **bridges,** especially the graceful triple-arched one known as Plakídas.

TSEPÉLOVO

Tsepélovo is 30 miles from Ioánnina, built on a slope with charmingly crooked paths, and the few tumbledown houses show up the beautifully preserved ones. As one of the more populated Zagóri towns, it's an inexpensive base for exploring the area and consequently attracts budget travelers.

If you want to spend the night here, try one of the tasteful, rustic rooms, about 7,500 Drs ($31.25) with private bath, in the homey guest house run by **Alexis Gouris** (☎ 0653/81-214 or 0653/81-288). You'll have to lock the gate so that a stray sheep doesn't get Mr. Gouris's prize roses. Mr. Gouris is a spry, cultured gentleman who learned English while working as a translator for NATO; he's a wonderful host and a veritable font of information about the area. He recommends one long (about 5¹/₂-hour) local hike, which will take you to Drakólimni (Dragon Lake) and Mt. Astráka (see "The Pápingos," below).

MONODÉNDRI

Monodéndri is where the classic trek through the gorge begins. The town is much celebrated by guidebooks, and it certainly has ravishing views of Víkos, particularly from the lovely 15th-century **Monastery of Ayía Paraskeví** on the lower *platía,* which should not be missed. If you're not planning to hike, we suggest stopping here for lunch and pushing on to the Pápingos, only about a 1¹/₂-hour drive away.

The town is organized around two squares, connected by a steep cobblestone path: the upper tier is where the bus stops and where you'll find the **Monodendri Pension & Restaurant** (☎ 0653/61-233), which is justly famous for its cheese pies and other delicacies. It's a handsome, modern building interpreting traditional Zagóri style, where doubles with private bath cost 9,800 Drs ($40.85). It's best to book ahead.

On the lower *platía,* near the monastery, is the well-run **Vikos Pension** (☎ 0653/61-323), which is built around a garden courtyard. The rooms are large with slate floors, furnished in tasteful traditional style, though unfortunately none of them offers good views; doubles with private facilities cost 10,200 Drs ($42.50).

On your way out of Monodéndri, be sure to make the 2¹/₂-mile detour northwest of Monodéndri to the Víkos Balcony, following the signs to Osia, for even more spectacular vistas of the gorge and mountains!

THE PÁPINGOS

Megálo (Big) Pápingo and Mikró (Little) Pápingo combine the classic fairy-tale Zagóri architecture with the area's friendliest ambience and most varied scenery. This is the point at which trekkers emerge from Víkos. You can see both the 2,000-foot drop of the gorge and the twin mesa-shaped peaks of Mt. Gamíla, which tower more than 8,000 feet overhead.

Megálo Pápingo is a relaxed, sprawling community whose unofficial center is between Koulis's cafe-bar and **Yiorgos's restaurant** (☎ 0653/41-124), where we had a wonderful meal of fresh, savory broiled chicken, yogurt as thick as ice cream, and a flaky cheese pie for about 2,200 Drs ($9.15). There's a 1¹/₄-mile road that snakes up to tiny Micró Pápingo, with more breathtaking views along the way.

The Greeks love these towns, so it's wise to book ahead, especially for Christmas, Easter, or the dog days of August. There are many options:

A few years ago the EOT's four traditional *arhondiká* guest houses in Megálo Pápingo were sold to private owners, and the **Guesthouse Astraka** (☎ 0653/ 41-693) is now the only one that still accepts visitors. The furniture and decorations are no longer authentically Zagóri, but the 130-year-old mansion is still gorgeous, with its carved wooden ceilings and other details. A double with private bath should cost about 12,500 Drs ($52.10); EuroCard and MasterCard are accepted.

It's a little like staying at your grandmother's, but we liked the few *domátia* (rooms) available next door to Astraka at the house of **Eleni Economides,** with its garden courtyard; contact Mrs. Economides through Nikos at the Hotel Koulis (see below). The best deal is the small tower with two brass four-poster beds, private bath, and a spectacular mountain view, for 12,500 Drs ($52.10), but the other two rooms have such details as painted ceilings, family icons, and antique furniture.

The **Hotel Koulis** (☎ 0653/41-138 or 0653/41-115) is a simple, traditional family house where whitewashed doubles with hand-decorated curtains and private baths go for 11,400 Drs ($41.25), no credit cards accepted. The friendly young Nikos speaks excellent English and knows the local trails like the back of his hand. This is also the home of a popular bar-restaurant.

There are many enjoyable hikes of varying difficulty in the immediate vicinity, and you don't have to go far for a great view. The most famous—and strenuous—hike will take you up Mt. Astráka to the **Gamíla Refuge,** where you can stay overnight. (To obtain maps and the key, call the local mountain club in Megálo Pápingo at ☎ 0653/41-138 or 0653/41-230.) It's only 1¹/₂ hours from Gamíla to Drakólimni (Dragon Lake) and 4 hours beyond that to Tsepélovo (see above). Other pleasant expeditions include a local swimming hole on the road between the Pápingos. Ask any of the locals to show you the way.

14 The Ionian Islands

Of all the Greek islands, the Ionians are the most fortunate recipients of nature's bounty. All have plentiful rainfall, fertile land, temperate climate, and lush, semitropical scenery. Their strategic position put them in the way of every conqueror set on annexing the mainland of Greece. As a result, the Ionians reflect aspects of many cultures, and they're the most European part of the country—and thus in many ways the least Greek.

Corfu (Kérkyra), one of the great tourist meccas, has always been the gem of the Ionians, its culture and architecture reflecting the elegant styles of the Italian, French, and English occupiers. Tiny **Páxos** (Paxí) and **Antipáxos** (Andípaxi) are small verdant links in the Ionian chain, miniretreats that offer a change of pace from the frenzy of the others. **Lefkáda** (also Lefkás) is a large, slowly developing island just a stone's throw away from the mainland, known for its Arts and Letters Festival and embroidery exports. **Ithaca** (Itháki) is the island immortalized by Homer, the kingdom of Odysseus and the object of his long, adventure-filled *Odyssey*. **Kefaloniá** is the largest, most self-sustaining of the Ionians; successful sea trade and agriculture have enabled many residents to ignore the recent influx of foreign tourists flocking to see its natural beauties and historic sights. **Zákynthos** (Zante) is the southernmost island, its proximity to the Peloponnese, pebble beaches, and moderate climate have made it one of the most popular destinations for Greek tourists.

1 Corfu

132 nautical miles from Pátra, 18 nautical miles from Igoumenítsa

Corfu (Kérkyra) is the first glimpse of Greece for many travelers, but its beauty and culture are not typically Greek. The Italians have strongly influenced the island's cuisine, art, and language; the French affected its architecture and education; and the British helped form its laws and lifestyle. The traditional blue trim of Greece is more apt to be the green of the Venetians. Some Greeks say the Corfiots are too refined, too European, too cosmopolitan to be Greek, yet ever since Homer immortalized the island of the hospitable Phaeacians, the Greek people have held Corfu in high regard.

The verdant beauty of the island, so unlike the stark, arid islands of the Aegean, has drawn visitors for centuries. European royalty frequently summered there, bringing their native artists and

Western Greece & the Ionian Islands

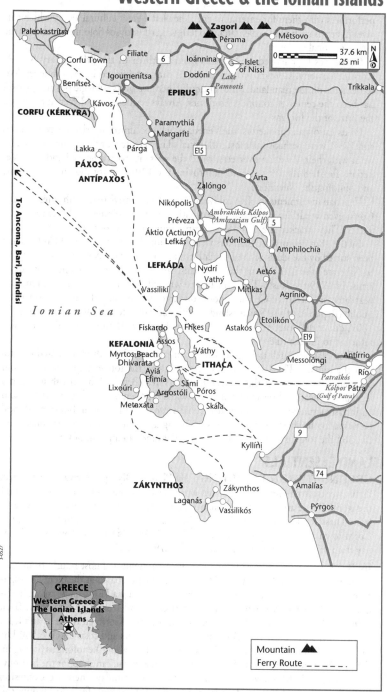

Paleokastrítsa

Corfu Town
Filiate
6
Ioánnina
Dodóni
Islet of Nissi
Pérama
Zagori
Métsovo

0   37.6 km
25 mi
N

Igoumenítsa
Benítses
CORFU (KÉRKYRA)
Kávos
EPIRUS
5
Lake Pamvotis
Tríkkala

Paramythiá
Margaríti
Lakka
PÁXOS
Párga
ANTÍPAXOS
E15
Zalóngo
Árta

Nikópolis
Préveza
Áktio (Actium)
Lefkás
LEFKÁDA
Nydrí
Vathý
Ambrakikós Kólpos (Ambracian Gulf)
Vónitsa
5
Amphilochía
Aetós
Mítikas
Agrínio

To Ancoma, Bari, Brindisi

Vassilikí
Ionian Sea
Etolikón
Astakós
Fiskardo
Flíkes
KEFALONIÀ
Assos
Myrtos Beach
Dhivarata
Ayiá
Efimía
Lixoúri
Sámi
Argostóli
Póros
Metaxáta
Skála
Váthy
ITHACA
Messolóngi
Patraïkós
Kólpos Pátra (Gulf of Patra)
E19
Antírrio
Río

Kyllíni
9

ZÁKYNTHOS
Zákynthos
Laganás
Vassilikós
Amalías
74
Pýrgos

3-0527

GREECE
Western Greece & The Ionian Islands
Athens

Mountain
Ferry Route

performers with them for entertainment. They left a great cultural legacy which survives in artists such as the celebrated modern writer Dionysos Solomos, author of the Greek national anthem.

Corfu was first settled by Dorians from Corinth in the 8th century B.C. As Corinth's colony, Corcyra prospered and in time established its own independent settlements on the mainland. Since antiquity, because of its strategic position, Corfu has been the center of countless hostilities. Always resilient after defeat, it remained the prize of the Ionians.

Of its European conquerors, the Venetians, who occupied the island between 1386 and 1797, were perhaps the most influential. They created a titled gentry of Greeks, who, with their Venetian overseers, ruled the peasants with a heavy hand. The Venetians fortified the entire island, improving the 12th-century Byzantine Old Fort and building the New Fort.

Venetian investments in olive cultivation and the extensive trade with Europe made Corfu even wealthier, attracting the attention of many pirates, and eventually the Turks. They attacked the island several times but failed to conquer it.

By the 18th century the islanders were ready for change. Intellectual Corfiots had been stirred by the ideals of the French Revolution, and when Napoleon sent his fleet to "liberate" the island from the Venetians, the French were welcomed with open arms. In 1799 the Russo-Turkish Alliance wrested Corfu away from the French. A year later the Treaty of Constantinople declared the creation of the Septinsular Republic (Republic of the Seven Islands), with allegiance to the Ottoman Empire. In 1807, under the Peace of Tilsit between Napoleon and Alexander I of Russia, it was returned to French rule.

When Napoleon fell from power both Austria and Great Britain wanted control over the Ionians. The 1815 Treaty of Paris created the Ionian Republic, a free and independent state under the protectorship of Great Britain. The British installed a legal and educational system (Italian was widely spoken on Corfu until 1851), and an infrastructure and network of roads that served the island well, but quelled local participation in liberation movements springing up throughout the Greek mainland. In 1864 the Ionians became part of the newly founded kingdom of Greece.

ISLAND ESSENTIALS

GETTING THERE & DEPARTING   By Plane   Olympic Airways offers direct flights weekly from Geneva, Milan, and Rome, as well as flights from 35 cities around the world. There are three or four flights daily from Athens and two or three weekly from Thessaloníki. For reservations and information, contact the Olympic office in Corfu town at Odós Kapodistríou 20 (☎ **0661/38-694**), open Monday to Saturday from 9am to 4:45pm, or in Athens (☎ **01/926-7251**).

By Boat   Car-ferries run daily to and from Igoumenítsa almost hourly from 5am to 10pm (1¹/₂ hours, 800 Drs/$3.35); tickets can be purchased at the pier. The high-speed catamaran *Neárchos* runs from Préveza to Corfu via Páxos daily except Tuesday and Thursday. Most international ferries to and from Italy (Ancona, Bari, Brindisi, Ortona, Otranto, Trieste, and Venice) stop at Corfu en route to and from Pátra and Igoumenítsa. The trip to Pátra takes 10 hours and costs about 6,500 Drs ($27.10). Most of the international ticket agencies are along Xenofóndos Stratigoú, the waterfront road leading up from the New Port, and you can shop for the best buy. Four times daily Monday to Saturday, and once on Sunday, there are **excursion boats** from the Old Port to the isles of Páxos and Antipáxos; for information, call ☎ **0661/32-655**. There's also service to Albania; limited service to the minor islands of Eríkousa, Mathráki, and Othoní; and from Corfu's second port of Lefkými to

Igoumenítsa. A complete schedule is posted at the **port police** kiosk (☎ 0661/ 32-655). The tourist information office (EOT) also has a schedule in its office.

ORIENTATION   The sickle-shaped island of Corfu is approximately 230 square miles in area; within this are more than 300 large and small villages. Our first-choice base is **Corfu town,** a wonderfully picturesque European city.

If you can afford it, try to rent a car to explore the rest of the island, which is justly famed for its scenic beauties. The eastern coastline, facing Albania and the northern Greek mainland, has been developed à la Miami Beach. Though it has undergone tremendous development in the recent past, the acknowledged beauty queen of the island is **Paleokastrítsa,** on the west coast.

Most ferries arrive at the **New Port,** just west of Corfu town, from where you can see the **Néo Froúrio** (New Fort) up to your left (east). Many tourist services, including ferryboat tickets, travel agencies, and car-rental companies, are in the immediate area of the New Port.

GETTING AROUND   Corfu town and most of the island's major resorts are small enough to walk around in, once you're there. The island itself is too large and too heavily trafficked for walking around; public buses are cheap, fairly efficient, and safer than mopeds. However, we'd encourage hikers to plan a walking trip between the many picturesque hill villages in the island's north.

By Bus   Around-the-island buses leave from two terminals. Green and cream-colored buses to the distant towns and beaches of Paleokastrítsa, Áyios Gordis, Glyfáda, Kassiópi, Kávos, and other villages leave from the long-distance bus station on Odós Avramíou, beneath the Néo Froúrio 3 blocks up from the east end of the New Port, behind the Ionian Hotel. Most run several times daily, with fares ranging from 300 to 700 Drs ($1.25 to $2.90).

Dark-blue buses going to the suburbs, nearby villages, and the major sights such as the Achilleion, Áyios Ioánnis, and the resorts of Benítses, Kontokáli, and Dassía, leave from the central San Rocco Square (also called Platía Theotóki), at Avramíou and Theotóki streets. The no. 2 bus to Kanóni leaves from the east side of the Esplanade every half hour from 7:30am to 10pm. Be sure to ask when the last bus returns, as some service ends as early as 8pm. The blue local buses cost 125 Drs (50¢); tickets can be bought at the station on San Rocco Square or on board.

By Taxi   Taxis usually meet all the ferries, outside the Customs House at the New Port or by the small park at the Old Port.

The taxi problem, serious in Athens and other highly touristed destinations in Greece, is particularly acute on Corfu. Finding a driver willing to use a meter (and on a legal basis) is as tough as finding inexpensive fresh fish. Below are the posted legal rates (expect a 20% increase during the lifetime of this edition).

Legal Taxi Rates

Type	Amount
Minimum	400 Drs ($1.65)
Luggage supplement	250 Drs ($1.05)
Port or airport supplement	250 Drs ($1.05)
Single mileage tariff (in town)	100 Drs (40¢)
Double mileage tariff (out of town)	150 Drs (65¢)
One-way and from 1am to 5am	150 Drs (65¢)
If taxi waits	1,000 Drs ($4.15) per hour
Radio-call surcharge	250 Drs ($1.05)

Although this table is a good guideline, rates can vary by a factor of 10! Of those drivers who use their meter, some actually doctor it to charge double for a legitimate single-tariff ride. The best advice is to ask a local, non–taxi driver for the approximate fare. Armed with that, and insisting that the driver use the meter, you might get there for close to the official rate. For out-of-town trips, we've found it easiest to bargain for a flat rate. We've also heard that the radio taxis (☎ **0661/33-811** or 0661/33-812) are generally more trustworthy.

Sample Taxi Fares

From Corfu Town	Rate
To the airport	1,400 Drs ($5.85)
To the international port	1,200 Drs ($5)
To Paleokastrítsa	4,200 Drs ($17.50)
To Sidári	5,500 Drs ($22.90)

Note: If you think you've been overcharged, get the driver's identification number and report it immediately to the **traffic police** (☎ **0661/39-294**) at the central police station, just off the north side of San Rocco Square.

By Car   There are lots of car-rental companies around the island. We recommend **AutoEurope** on Ethnikís Andistáseos, across from the New Port (☎ **0661/41-700**). High-season travelers should reserve a car before leaving home; **Avis** is at Ethnikís Andistáseos 42 (☎ **0661/24-404**). If you have the time you should shop around; expect to pay $90 to $150 per day, including unlimited mileage and a stiff 18% tax. We've had good service from Kostas Ginis at the small **Sunrise Rent A Car,** Odós Arseníou 1 (☎ **0661/44-325** or 0661/33-519), as well as from **International Rent Cars,** Odós Kapodistríou 20A (☎ **0661/37-710**).

Tip: Check your hotel reception desk first to see if they can get you a good rate on a rental car.

By Moped   Most of the more interesting parts of the Old Town are pedestrian only, but mopeds are a fun way to get around the nearby parts of the island. We find them too small to be comfortable for the 2- or 3-hour ride each way required to explore the north or south coasts from Corfu town. Rates vary from 6,000 Drs ($25) for a one-seater Vespa to 10,000 Drs ($41.65) for a Suzuki 125cc cross-country model. *Warning:* Collision or damage insurance is limited—you will be liable for most accidents.

CORFU TOWN

We've found no better place to stay if your interest is in things antique, historical, luxurious, romantic, swinging, fashionable, or gastronomic. The airport is only 10 minutes south of town, and the best sightseeing is an arm's length from elegant boutiques, gourmet restaurants, excellent museums, and sophisticated nightlife.

The most picturesque part of the city is east of the Néo Froúrio (New Fort), around the **Spianáda** (Esplanade), the big park where Corfiots play and stroll, and the **Paleó Froúrio** (Old Fort), on a peninsula just east. A 15-minute walk up east along the waterfront will take you there. On the way you'll pass the New Fort on your right, then the **Old Port** on your left, with an attractive park/square in front of Zavitsianoú Street.

From here you can bear right and wend your way uphill through the cobblestone maze of the **Old Venetian Quarter,** or you can follow the roadway to the left to Arseníou Street, which skirts the cliff rising above the sea and leads to an irregular plaza with the **Palace of St. Michael and St. George** above it and the picturesque **Mandráki Harbor** off to the left. The Esplanade is just beyond the palace.

ESSENTIALS

VISITOR INFORMATION   From May to October the **Greek Tourist Organization (EOT),** Odós Rizópaston Vouleftón (☎ **0661/37-638** or 0661/37-639; fax 0661/30-298), is open Monday to Friday from 9am to 8pm and on Saturday from 9am to 2pm. In the winter it's open Monday to Friday from 9am to 2:30pm. To get there, take Alexándras south off San Rocco Square; turn left (east) on the second street and it's in the peach-colored building on the left. The **Municipal Tourist Office** (☎ **0661/42-602**) has branches at the New Port, inside the Customs House, open Monday to Saturday from 7am to 1pm; and on the Esplanade, open Monday to Saturday from 9am to 8:30pm and on Sunday from 9am to 3pm. It offers information and a free brochure with a good map of the town, as well as a map of the island for 350 Drs ($1.45).

The **tourist police** (☎ **0661/30-265**) are at the central police station, just off the north side of San Rocco Square; the office is open daily from 7am to 2:30pm for simple complaints about hotels, taxis, and so on.

The travel agency **Greek Skies,** Odós Kapodistríou 20A, on the southwest side of the Esplanade (☎ **0661/39-160;** fax 0661/36-161), open Monday to Saturday, is generally helpful and will book rental cars, confirm flights, and assist with hotel reservations. **Charitos Travel,** upstairs at Odós Arseníou 35, on the north side of town above the Old Port (☎ **0661/44-611;** fax 0661/36-825), has long been helpful to Frommer's readers for arranging island tours (including mountain-bike tours), renting private villas, arranging wedding logistics, and booking top-quality hotel rooms at a discount. Charitos runs several bus and boat excursions; for example, a full-day coastal tour that stops at two beaches, with a barbecue and wine, costs about 1,200 Drs ($50).

FAST FACTS   Corfu's **American Express agent** (for lost or stolen cards, emergency check cashing, lost traveler's check replacements, and mail) is **Greek Skies,** Odós Kapodistríou 20A (☎ **0661/39-160**), on the southwest side of the Esplanade. If it's closed, report stolen checks to the U.K. office (☎ **00-44-27/367-5975**).

Most **banks** are open Monday to Thursday from 8am to 2pm and on Friday from 8am to 1:30pm, though several have extended hours in summer. The National Bank branch at the Customs House is open to meet ferryboats; the Ionian and Commercial banks on San Rocco Square have evening hours (Monday to Friday from 5 to 7pm) and are open weekends from 8am to 2pm.

The **British consulate** is at Odós Menekrátous 1 in Corfu town (☎ **0661/30-055**).

For medical emergencies, contact the **Corfu General Hospital,** Odós Polihróni Konstánda, west of San Marco Square (☎ **0661/45-811**). For general **emergencies,** dial ☎ **100**; for **ambulance** service dial ☎ **166.**

There's **luggage storage** opposite the New Port, next door to the Commercial Bank, at Odós Avramíou 130 (☎ **0661/37-673**).

The *Corfu News,* an advertiser-supported yet discriminating judge of Corfu, is free and available in many hotels and at the EOT office. The politically conscious *Corfiot* is sold by subscription at 250 Drs ($1.05) per issue. The daily *Athens News* is widely sold and contains local performance schedules.

Thefts should be reported to the **security police,** Leofóros Alexándras 17, across from the post office (☎ **0661/22-340**).

The central **post office** is on Alexándras Avenue, 2 blocks southeast from San Rocco Square (☎ **0661/25-544**), open Monday to Friday from 7:30am to 8pm, Saturday from 7:30am to 2pm, and Sunday from 9am to 1:30pm.

The main **telephone office (OTE)** is at Odós Mantzárou 9, 2 blocks east of San Rocco Square, open daily from 6am to midnight. There's a convenient branch (with international phone directories) at Odós Kapodistríou 34 on the Esplanade, open daily from 7:30am to 11pm.

SPECIAL EVENTS   Corfu's favorite holidays are celebrated in honor of its patron saint, **St. Spyrídon,** four times a year—on Palm Sunday, Orthodox Easter Sunday, August 11 (to commemorate the Corfiots' resistance against the Turks during the siege of 1716), and on the first Sunday in November. St. Spyrídon is credited with saving the medieval town from the plague in 1630, from the Turks on several occasions, and again during World War II when a bomb dropped through the roof of his cathedral but didn't explode.

Easter, as it is everywhere in Greece, is a major holiday on Corfu. The biggest night is Holy Saturday, when a processional leads to the Esplanade where the bishop will announce at midnight "*Christós anésti!*" (Christ is risen). After his proclamation, the hymns, fireworks, bands, bells, and dancing begin as the lights are turned on everywhere. On Easter Sunday the feast of roast lamb and wine continues until the afternoon, when everyone goes out again to dance.

The **Corfu Festival** has been one of the highlights of the September season for the past few years, presenting internationally acclaimed ballet, opera, dance, and music performances. Check with the EOT upon arrival to confirm the season's schedule of events.

SEEING THE SIGHTS

This island may be hedonistic, but it offers plenty besides sunning and touring. Museum aficionados will find plenty to hold their interest. Shoppers will find souvenirs, jewelry, ceramics, and high-fashion boutiques, especially in the charming Old Quarters. Sports enthusiasts have a wide range of options, including tennis, golf, yachting, and windsurfing. Party animals can find numerous bars, clubs, and discos.

The superb collection at the **Museum of Asiatic Art** is apparently being moved from its former quarters in the Palace of St. Michael and St. George, but it's well worth finding. There are excellent examples of Japanese netsuke and wood-block prints, porcelain, sculpture, and watercolors, as well as a large collection of Chinese art, so well labeled that it provides novices with a comprehensive introduction to art, culture, and religion from the Shang Dynasty (1500 B.C.) to the Ching (19th century).

The **Palace of St. Michael and St. George,** on the north end of the Esplanade, was built in 1819–24 as the residence of the British lord high commissioner of the Ionian Islands, and it's a fine example of the English neoclassical style seen along the Esplanade and throughout the Old Town.

Like many towns in northern Greece, Corfu once had a substantial Jewish population; only 70 people survived the Holocaust out of a population of over 3,000. Today the only visible sign of the community is a reasonably well-preserved **synagogue** built approximately 300 years ago, on the 4th Parádos (lane) off Velissaríou Street, about 2 blocks up from the New Fort. The synagogue is still in use (every Saturday morning beginning at 9am) and has much of its original ornamentation. Members of the community claim that their ancestors, from Puglia, Italy, brought locally made treasures with them. The display of Torah crowns is the most interesting

Ayios Spyrídon Church ⑤	Long-distance Bus Station ④	Palace of St. Michael & St. George ⑥
Bus Stop for Kanóni ⑩	Mandráki Harbor ⑦	San Rocco Square (Local Bus Station) ⑨
Byzantine Museum ③	New Port ①	Town Hall ⑧
EOT (Greek Tourist Office) ⑪	Old Port ②	

aspect of the Sephardic-style interior. To gain access to the synagogue during the week, call the Jewish Community Center (☎ **0661/38-802**).

The beautifully planted **British Cemetery**, several long blocks south of San Rocco Square, is dedicated to the British soldiers and civilians who lost their lives in the Ionians during its term as a British protectorate. The cemetery entrance is on Kolokotróni Street.

Archaeological Museum. Odós Vraíla 1. ☎ **0661/30-680.** Admission 800 Drs ($3.35) adults, 600 Drs ($2.50) seniors, 400 Drs ($1.65) students. Tues–Sun 8:30am–3pm.

The collection is diverse, interesting, and well labeled—and it has outgrown the museum, so that recent finds, such as bronze statuettes from the late archaic to Roman periods, including a Hercules, two soldiers, and a shepherd, are now exhibited in the lobby. Upstairs, the first gallery contains ceramics and a large archaic lion of the late 7th century B.C., found near Menekrates' tomb. To the left is an impressive coin collection.

The back room houses the museum's highlight, the **Gorgo Pediment** from the Doric Temple of Artemis in Kanóni, the oldest stone pediment yet found, and one of the largest. These sculptures (from about 585 B.C.) have been installed in a re-creation of their original setting. The grinning Gorgon Medusa is shown running, one knee on the ground, with her offspring, the winged horses Pegasus and Chrysaor on either side. (Myth says that they were born of her blood when Perseus cut off her head, but she looks far from dead.) This is considered the finest extant work of the archaic period, and it represents a major advancement for the Corinthian artists who sculpted it. Pegasus was the symbol of Corinth. The two "leopanthers" (half lion, half panther) on each side suggest to some that this is actually Artemis in one of her more terrible aspects.

The next room contains objects found at Monday Repos, including large clay figurines of Artemis. The last room features a marble torso, a copy of the *Apollo Parnopios* of Pheidias, as well as two Roman statues of Aphrodite, and portrait busts of the historian Thucidides and the comic poet Menander.

Achilleion Museum. Gastouríou, Corfu. ☎ **0661/56-210.** Admission 700 Drs ($2.90) adults, 450 Drs ($1.90) seniors, 300 Drs ($1.25) students. Daily 9am–4:30pm. Bus: 10 from San Rocco Square to the Achilleion (six times daily between 7am and 8pm, returning four times daily between 7:20am and 8:20pm); visit early or late during the summer to avoid the crush of tour groups.

In 1890 the empress Elizabeth of Austria decided to build herself a retreat away from the intrigues of the Hapsburg court. The Achilleion was named after her hero Achilles, who she identified with her son Rudolph, and many sculptures of him adorn its outdoor garden. She thought of herself as his mother, the dolphin Thetis—hence the many dolphin images throughout the well-maintained grounds and extraordinary interior. Shelf tops, commodes, and mantelpieces are filled with family memorabilia, portraits, and war mementos. The ground floor has bright murals, frescoes, and a painted ceiling. Wrought-iron handrails sweep up the marble staircase supported by 12 gods and goddesses; garish architectural trim, lots of gilt, and a saddle-seated throne of Kaiser Wilhelm II of Germany (who bought the estate for himself after Elizabeth was assassinated by an Italian anarchist) fill the parlor rooms. At night the Achilleion becomes a casino.

Byzantine Museum. Off Arseníou St. ☎ **0661/38-313.** Admission 500 Drs ($2.10) adults, 400 Drs ($1.65) seniors, 300 Drs ($1.25) students. Tues–Sat 8:45am–3pm, Sun 9:30am–2:30pm.

This small museum is in the beautifully restored 16th-century Church of Andivouniótissa, which overlooks the sea on the north side of the Old Town. It contains a fine collection of icons, frescoes, and religious paintings by well-known Greek artists. Artifacts date to the 11th century; a Russian altar cloth donated by Nikifórou Theotóki is of particular interest.

The Old Fort (Paleó Froúrio). ☎ **0661/48-319.** Admission 800 Drs ($3.35) adults, 600 Drs ($2.50) seniors. Tues–Sun 8:30am–3pm.

The promontory was connected until the Venetians dug the *contrafossa* (moat) in the 16th century to improve their fortifications built over the 12th century Byzantine structure. It was able to resist several sieges by the Turks. Each of the two peaks that gave the island its name—*kórfos* means bosom—is topped by a castle, offering fine views east to Albania and west over the town and island. The Doric-style Church of St. George was built by the British in 1830.

A Stroll Around Corfu Town

Anyone on Corfu for at least a day should seize the opportunity to walk around its Old Quarter. If you're coming from the New Port, begin by walking up **Xenofóndos Stratigoú** (General Xenophon) past the New Fort and the Old Port and along **Arseníou Street,** the road that leads uphill around the point. This walk provides wonderful views of Vídos Island (home of the Kérkyra Bird and Wildlife Sanctuary), Epirus (on the Greek mainland beyond it), and the Albanian coast up to the north. You'll pass many elegant neoclassical buildings from the various European occupations; notice the French consulate on the corner of Arseníou and Kapodistríou.

From this corner you can gauge the layout of the **Old Fort,** on its own rocky point with the yacht-filled **Mandráki Harbor** beneath it. Up ahead is the neoclassical Palace of St. Michael and St. George, and beyond it is the spacious **Spianáda** (Esplanade). If you continue south along Kapodistríou, the arcaded structure on your left is the **Listón,** built during the brief French occupation in the early 19th century. It may remind you of the rue de Rivoli in Paris; the same architect designed both. This is a popular, if rather expensive place, to stop for a coffee or ouzo and watch a cricket match and children playing.

Across the Esplanade, near the entrance to the Old Fort, is the **statue of Schulenberg,** an Austrian mercenary who assisted in the defense of the island against the Turks in the great seige of 1716. On the right above the Old Fort is the tiny **Church of St. George.** The building beyond the bandstand at the south end of the Esplanade is the **Maitland Rotunda,** which commemorates the first British lord high commissioner.

The street running west from the entrance to the Old Fort through the center of the Esplanade is **Dousmáni.** By following it to the right (west) you'll reenter the maze of the Old Town along Voulgáreos and will soon encounter the **Town Hall.** The most interesting streets are to the right (north) in the Old Venetian Quarter known as **Campiello.** Shoppers will be particularly interested in the streets running parallel to Voulgáreos—Windmann, Ayíon Pándon, and Sevastianoú—which are full of boutiques, jewelers, souvenir stands, and Greek handcraft stores. The deeper you walk into this old quarter, the more enchanted you'll be. Many little streets never intersect; many alleys are dead-ends, and often a gate or fence will lead nowhere. The magic of Old Corfu is in the buildings left from its colonial days, when so many cultures left their mark to create this teeming cosmopolitan town.

About 6 or 7 blocks north of the Town Hall, at the corner of Filellínon and Áyios Spyrídon streets, you'll find the **Cathedral of Áyios Spyrídon,** dedicated to the island's patron saint. Inside you'll see gold and silver icons and the embalmed body of the saint himself. (It's said that the embalmed body of Spyrídon, a 4th-century bishop of Cyprus, was smuggled from Istanbul.)

When you've tired of the Old Town, turn east toward the Esplanade and approach the Old Fort, the site of the nightly *son-et-lumière* (sound-and-light) show. Just below it to the south is Corfu's closest swimming spot, the Yacht Club, and to the north, the old Mandraki Harbor and its glamourous yachts.

At the end of the Esplanade past the Maitland Rotunda you'll pass the Corfu Palace Hotel. At the next corner, Vraíla Street, are the archaeological museum and the town tennis courts. Keep strolling south on **Dimokratías Avenue** (also still known as King Constantine Street) as it parallels the water. In less than 1 1/4 miles you'll reach **Plage Mon Repos.** The beautifully landscaped grounds were part of the overall concept of Sir Frederick Adam, a British lord high commissioner who built this as his summer residence. Begun in 1831, it soon became known as "Sir Frederick's Folly." After Greece became independent, Mon Repos (My Repose) was used as the summer palace of the Greek royal family, but since the abolition of the monarchy it's been closed to the public. Today it's a pleasant pebble-and-sand swimming beach.

Joggers and walkers will enjoy the 6-mile jaunt south to the suburb of **Kanóni,** a picturesque peninisula named for the cannon once fixed on the bluff there; others can catch the no. 2 bus from the east side of the Esplanade, across from the statue of Schulenberg. From this scenic, if overly popular, area you can see the picturesque inlet with its two little islands. You can reach the first one, **Vlahérna,** with its oftenphotographed little monastery, via a little causeway. **Pondikoníssi** (Mouse Island), with its 12th-century Church of Áyios Pnévmatos, can be reached only by boat—usually available.

Allow about 2 hours to explore the town, another hour if you visit Kanóni, and another few hours if you enter the museums or go for a swim.

FAMILY FUN

The **Shell Museum,** said to be the best private collection in Europe, can be found on Platía Néou Frouríou, on the east side of the New Fort. It's open daily from 10am to 7pm; admission is 500 Drs ($2.10).

The glass-bottomed *Kalypso Star* (☎ 0661/46-525) departs for an underwater odyssey from the Old Port in Corfu. Adult fare is 3,500 Drs ($14.60); children are charged 1,750 Drs ($7.30).

The **Danilia Village** is the Colonial Williamsburg of Corfu. Within its confines are a reconstructed traditional village, fields for goatherds and shepherds, pottery makers, perfume cells, weavers, wine and olive presses, an Orthodox church, an agricultural museum displaying traditional Greek objects, fields being tilled—in short, everything needed to re-create a day in the life of a 200-year-old Greek village. In the evening the Greek taverna opens, offering a filling meal of local specialties, much free retsina, and loud bouzouki; a troupe of *syrtáki* and *zeibékiko* dancers and musicians will entertain you, and ask you to join in with them. The results can be great fun. Remember to bring your camera.

Several tour companies offer excursions to the village, located 5 miles northeast of Corfu town, off the Paleokastrítsa road. The average cost is 12,000 Drs ($50), which includes a tour of the grounds, dinner, wine (as much as you want), entertainment, and transportation to and from your hotel. Independents can make reservations directly with Danilia Village—call its in-town office at Odós Kapodistríou 38 (☎ 0661/36-833)—and take the no. 7 bus to Goúvia, then walk 1 1/4 miles to the site. It's open Monday to Saturday from 10am to 1pm and 6pm till the action stops (dinner starts at 8:30pm).

WHERE TO STAY

Hotels on Corfu (as with Rhodes and Mýkonos) tend to be much more expensive than on other, less touristed islands. Happily, some of the older lodgings in and around the Old Town (the most convenient location) have been maintained and provide clean, if Spartan, living for moderate prices. There are also some budget hotels around the New Port, and some good choices in the nearby suburbs with reasonable rates. Most hoteliers urge that reservations be made 1 to 2 months in advance (particularly at the budget hotels).

Note: Most hotels are open from April 1 to October 31 unless otherwise noted.

The tourist police are responsible for rooms-to-rent that are government licensed, and will give you the names and phone numbers of those that are available. Contacting a travel agent is probably your best bet for last-minute, high-season accommodations.

In & Around the Old Town

Hotel Arcadion. Odós Kapodistríou 44, Corfu, 491 00 Corfu. ☎ 0661/37-671. Fax 0661/45-087. 55 rms, all with bath (shower). TEL. 12,000 Drs ($50) single; 18,000 Drs ($75) double. Rates include breakfast. AE, V.

This neoclassical hotel is an aging but good-value choice along the Esplanade. It offers a central location and simple twin-bedded rooms with balconies overlooking the ancient citadel and Mandráki Harbor. The compact single rooms with showers are good value, though the facilities are somewhat worn and the cafe crowd below can make it noisy in the summer.

Bella Venezia. Odós Zambéli 4 (P.O. Box 32), Corfu, 491 00 Corfu. ☎ **0661/44-290.** Fax 0661/20-708. 32 rms, all with bath (tub or shower). A/C TV TEL. 19,200 Drs ($80) single; 25,200 Drs ($105) double. DC, EURO, MC, V.

This wonderfully restored neoclassical mansion on the fringe of Old Town houses a newly renovated hotel. The large, high-ceilinged rooms, fitted with heaters for year-round guests, have a simple old-world charm that will please traditionalists. Though it's plainer than the Cavalieri, the well-decorated common spaces, attentive service, attractive breakfast patio, and snack kiosk outside make this an excellent value, though it's a bit of a splurge for us.

Around Corfu Town & the Suburbs

✪ **Arhondikó Hotel.** Odós Athanasíou 61, Garítsa, 491 00 Corfu. ☎ **0661/36-850.** Fax 0661/38-294. 10 rms, 10 suites, all with bath (shower). MINIBAR TV TEL. 15,500 Drs ($65.60) single; 20,000 Drs ($83.35) double. No credit cards.

This retrofitted *arhondikó* (mansion) built in 1903, on the seafront road south of town overlooking Garítsa Bay, still retains some of its original grandeur. Although the floors have been cut up to accommodate a larger number of rooms, many suites are large enough for three to six beds. The first two floors have frescoed cathedral ceilings. The rooms are large and simply decorated, with spotlessly clean modern bathrooms, and the common spaces are accented with flowers and ancient urns. Breakfast and snacks are served outside under a vine-covered arbor. Although it's a bit out of the way, the waterside walk is pleasant and the neighborhood is quiet.

Hotel Atlantis. Odós Xenofóndos Stratigoú 48, New Port, Corfu, 491 00 Corfu. ☎ **0661/ 35-560.** Fax 0661/46-480. 61 rms, all with bath (shower). TV TEL. 15,500 Drs ($64.60) single; 18,000 Drs ($75) double. AE, DC, EURO, MC, V.

This comfortable, well-kept business hotel is across from the Customs House at the New Port, a 10-minute walk from the Old Town. The rooms are spacious, clean, comfortable, and remarkably quiet for the busy location. The staff is friendly and helpful, and the cafe serves a good breakfast at a fair price.

Hotel Europa. Odós Yitsiáni 10, Mandoúki, Corfu, 491 00 Corfu. ☎ **0661/39-304.** 34 rms, 20 with bath (shower). 4,800 Drs ($20) single without bath; 5,750 Drs ($23.95) double without bath, 7,200 Drs ($30) double with bath. No credit cards.

The cute, homey Hotel Europa is a bit difficult to find, but its isolation from the portside traffic is well worth the minor inconvenience. (From Customs at the New Port, take Venizélou south and look for the sign; it's 2 blocks behind the AutoEurope office.) It's aging but clean, with acceptable common toilets and hot-water showers. The bright twin-bedded rooms are a good value for this almost "in town" location.

Hotel Marina. Anemómilos, Corfu, 491 00 Corfu. ☎ **0661/32-783.** 110 rms, all with bath (tub). TEL. 20,650 Drs ($86.05) single or double. Rates include breakfast. EURO, MC, V.

This newer hotel has bright, comfortable, and quiet rooms directly across the street from Plage Mon Repos, the small but popular sand beach a 15-minute walk south of Old Town. Each has a balcony with sea or town views, fresh white stucco walls, marble floors, and tiled bathrooms with a full-size tub and shower curtain. Breakfast is served outdoors in an adjoining garden, and there's a large TV lounge off the lobby. Though a little less convenient than some hotels, the Marina offers good value among the larger, full-amenity hotels.

Hotel Royal. Odós Figaréto 110, Kanóni, 491 00 Corfu. ☎ **0661/37-512.** Fax 0661/38-786. 121 rms, all with bath (tub or shower). TEL. 12,000 Drs ($50) single; 15,600 Drs ($65) double. Rates include breakfast. No credit cards.

The rooms of the Royal (Vassilikón in Greek) tower over a marble veranda and three swimming pools, terraced on a verdant hillside so that each one spills into the one below. The abundant, glittery decor might be described as wildly ornate or simply modern rococo. The only drawback is that it overlooks the international airport. A reader wrote us a rave review of her honeymoon stay at the Royal: "It's next to the Olympic runways, but flights stopped in the evening and during the day we were touring the island, so the noise didn't bother us. When we were at the hotel, it was actually interesting to watch the planes take off." Although flights now run into the wee hours, the Royal is still quite a popular place.

WHERE TO EAT

Corfu, perhaps because of its Italian heritage, has some excellent restaurants serving Greek and Italian cuisine. There are many pricey, touristy cafes (open from mid-April to the end of October) scattered throughout the Old Town. However, several locally known tavernas around the New Port or south of Old Town in Garítsa will show you a traditional Greek meal at its best.

In & Around the Old Town

Chambor. Odós Guildford 71, Town Hall Sq., Old Town. ☎ **0661/39-031.** Main courses 1,800–5,800 Drs ($7.50–$24.15). DC, MC, V. Mon–Sat 9am–2am, Sun 5pm–2am. INTERNATIONAL.

Chambor has a fine setting across from Corfu's illuminated and imposing Town Hall, an interesting decor, and an exotic and imaginative menu. We began with a mixed appetizer plate of both spinach and eggplant croquettes, saganaki, sausage, tart *tzatzíki,* and potent taramasaláta; followed it with a rich, creamy pasta carbonara and a casserole of bream baked with vegetables; and finished with a heavenly chocolate mousse. An excellent choice if you need a break from the roughshod presentation and simplicity of most taverna fare and don't mind service that's just a bit pretentious.

Grill Room Chrissomalis. Odós N. Theotóki 6, Old Town. ☎ **0661/30-342.** Main courses 1,200–2,600 Drs ($5–$10.85). No credit cards. Daily noon–midnight. GREEK.

Standard Greek dishes are served in very generous portions by a friendly staff at this old-fashioned *zythopsistopolíon* in the Old Quarter, a block west of the Listón. One good indication of the quality of the food and the fair prices is that most of the clientele is Greek, many regulars. Even the french fries are freshly prepared—not the frozen ones that have become very nearly ubiquitous.

Pizza Pete. Odós Arseníou 19, Old Town. ☎ **0661/22-301.** Main courses 1,200–3,400 Drs ($5–$14.15). MC, V. Summer, daily 9am–3am; off-season, daily 9am–10pm. ITALIAN/GREEK.

For casual Italian and Greek fare in a scenic, waterside setting, try this outdoor pizzeria on the north side of the Old Town, overlooking Vídos Island. The new owners, Takis and Yiannis, still serve "Pizza Pete's" menu as well as their own Greek dishes. You can have a full English breakfast for 1,500 Drs ($6.25), plus snacks, juices, ice cream, milkshakes, and Greek dishes, as well as the crisp-crust pizza. It's a good place to watch the sunset over drinks. The vegetarian pizza is topped with fresh peppers, tomatoes, onions, olives, and mushrooms, and the homemade, oven-baked moussaká is quite good.

Restaurant Aegli. Odós Kapodistríou 23, Old Town. ☎ **0661/31-949.** Main courses 1,650–3,200 Drs ($6.90–$13.35). AE, DC, EURO, MC, V. Daily 10:30am–midnight. GREEK/CONTINENTAL.

This is our favorite among the higher-priced cafes in the Listón overlooking the Esplanade. It's very pleasant to sit on the comfy, leather-cushioned chairs and watch life drift by, especially if you're waiting for one of the Aegli's Corfiot specialties. It features *sofríto* (veal in garlic sauce), swordfish, spicy salami, a selection of pastas, and *pastitsáda* (baked veal in tomato-and-cheese sauce). The new cafeteria offers 40 kinds of ice cream, croissants, cakes, and draft beer.

Yoryias Taverna. Odós Guildford 16, Old Town. ☎ **0661/37-147.** Main courses 900–2,200 Drs ($3.75–$9.15). No credit cards. Daily noon–midnight. GREEK.

It's becoming increasingly difficult to find a genuine taverna in the Old Town, but this is a typical grill on a humble scale, located 1 block inland from the Esplanade behind the Olympic Airways office. You can choose from oregano-scented, fresh grilled lamb, souvláki, moist barbecued chicken, and numerous other meat specialties for a modest sum. Everything tastes fresh and is obviously cooked with great care. And it's open all year.

Around Corfu Town & the Suburbs

Bekios Grill. Odós Ethnikís Andistáseos, Mandoúki, Corfu town. ☎ **0661/25-946.** Main courses 1,200–2,350 Drs ($5–$9.80). No credit cards. Daily 8:30pm–1am. GREEK.

This grill restaurant about 500 yards west of the New Port, opposite the Port Police, is a favorite of Mandoúki residents and Corfu town workers. Most of the fresh meat is sold by the kilo, with roast lamb, grilled pork chops, and roast chicken being the top choices. The large *horiátiki* salad and crispy fries go well with everything. We think the modest prices justify the 20-minute waterfront evening stroll from the Old Town. Open year-round.

Ciao. Odós Vlachernón 46, Garítsa. ☎ **0661/26-462.** Main courses 1,350–2,350 Drs ($5.65–$9.80). DC, EURO, MC, V. Daily 7pm–2am. Closed Mon off-season. ITALIAN.

This contemporary bistro behind the Ethnikí Stadium (a 20-minute walk south of the Esplanade) is favored by our Corfiot friends for the city's best Italian fare. From the varied selection (18 pastas and 19 varied pizzas), we found the spaghetti carbonara and the ecological pizza (a vegetarian delight) to be particularly good, and appropriately light for an August evening on the outdoor terrace. Our friends rave about the chicken cacciatore and veal marsala.

✪ **Iannis Taverna.** Iássonos (at Sosípatros St.), Anemómilos. ☎ **0116/33-061.** Main courses 1,100–2,350 Drs ($4.60–$9.80). No credit cards. Mon–Sat 8pm–1am. GREEK.

At this taverna south of town near Mon Repos, you enter that most public of Greek enclaves, the kitchen, where the amiable staff will take you on a tour of about 20 courses simmering in pans. The variety, especially in the early evening, is outstanding and each dish is a paradigm of *haute grecque.* The list of offerings changes nightly, so just point and enjoy. On our last visit we sampled a flavorful veal *stifádo* with sweet pearl onions, picante potato, and *koukí* (broad bean), and an octopus-and-potato stew—all delicious. Vegetarians will find at least three dishes nightly. Don't ignore the tasty house *krassí,* a local vintage. Iannis is open all year and is always packed with the loyal and adoring.

Sossi Fish Taverna. Mandoúki, Corfu town. No phone. Main courses 1,250–2,300 Drs ($5.20–$9.60). No credit cards. Daily 8:30pm–midnight. GREEK.

Mr. Sossi's tiny *psarotavérna* (fish taverna) is a block inland from the waterfront, about 500 yards west of the New Port at the end of the Mantouki bus line. A haven for fish lovers who remember when fishing was Corfu's main enterprise, it serves up fried sardines, bream, and small snapper cooked in affordable stews, soups, and casseroles. Hearty bread, thick *tzatzíki,* or a very garlicky *skordaliá* sustain diners until the nightly special is ready. It's the place to join cabbies, dock workers, and neighborhood folk in a wholesome, tasty, traditional meal—year-round.

Viceroy Indian Restaurant. Nafsiká (Nausicaa) St., Kanóni. ☎ **0661/44-656.** Reservations recommended in summer. Main courses 2,250–3,300 Drs ($9.40–$13.75). Daily 7–11:30pm. INDIAN.

If you're staying in the area or are looking for a change of taste, this new, highly re-garded North Indian restaurant with a Sri Lankan chef and British management is a piquant choice. Specialties include the lamb korma and chicken chili masala, both well—but not *too* hotly—spiced, fragrant with coriander and curry. The Viceroy Biryani, a rice pilaf with pieces of moist chicken, lamb, and prawns, graced with saf-fron and egg, is a good dish in combination with one of the vegetable curries.

CORFU TOWN AFTER DARK

Recent community laws have established an 11pm noise curfew in Corfu town, and a more liberal 3am (4am on Saturday) curfew outside the town limits. Therefore, most of the noisy, swinging nightlife is found in the resort complexes, though the town has its share of glamour and glitz.

The **Acteon Bar** is one of the best choices for an affordable drink and *mezédes* (appetizers) at sunset. This casual cafe, about 100 yards south of the Old Fort gate on the waterside, has a first-rate view over Corfu's serene waterway. Later, after you've had dinner and the mandatory walk along the Esplanade, you can stop for a drink or dessert at **Biston Serano,** one of the nicer outdoor cafes, at no. 8 on the Esplanade.

There are several other choices within a 10-minute walk south. **The Lobby,** at Odós Kapodistríou 39, is decorated in trompe-l'oeil antiquities to contrast with its contemporary pop-music track. The bartenders are elegant and fun and the latest American releases play through the night.

Nearby, occupying the ground floor of a fading Venetian mansion at Odós Kapodistríou 10, is **Tequila.** Its outdoor terrace is filled with palm trees and cafe tables shaded by thatch umbrellas, while the dimly lit interior is shrouded in minimalist style and loud New Wave music.

An older, more sophisticated foreign crowd gathers after 5pm in winter at the **Cavalieri Hotel bar,** an English-style wood-paneled and red-leather pub off the charming lobby. In summer, most regulars go directly up to the hotel's colonnaded rooftop bar, particularly stunning at sunset.

Another option is the elegant piano bar at **Quattro Stagioni,** an attractive, very European bistro on N. Theotóki Street in the Old Town; from 7pm to 2am nightly a pricey menu of light Italian fare is served at the bar or to those enjoying the out-door cafe.

If action is your aim, head a mile northwest of the New Port to "Disco Mile," a strip of waterside dancing clubs. We saw Greeks, Scandinavians, Germans, Britons, and Australians drinking outside the doors, waiting for clubs to empty so they could take their turn stomping the night away to European and American hits. Most clubs impose a 3,500-Dr ($14.60) cover charge, which includes one drink, and are open nightly after 10pm (often only Thursday to Saturday off-season).

A disco we particularly liked on the waterside Ethnikís Andistáseos was **Apocalipsis** (☎ **0661/40-345**), whose wild limestone "Fall of the Roman Empire" facade really caught our eye. You'll know it by the Olympic Flame burning on its roof. Nearby at Ethnikís Andistáseos 52 is **Hippodrome** (☎ **0661/43-150**), marked by freestand-ing classical columns draped in gold lamé, with a pool and huge video screen and a reputation as a *kamákia* hangout. Talk to the locals to get their advice on nightclubs and discos so you don't drop your drachmas at last year's hot spot.

Between Alíkes and Goúvia on the coast road are three of the most popular night-clubs, those super-energized plugged-in bouzoúki joints where plate smashing and

Greek crooners dominate the scene. **Esperides** (☎ **0661/38-121**), **Ekati,** and **Corfu By Night** (☎ **0661/38-123**), expensive supper or late-drinks clubs, will provide some of the most unforgettable experiences of your stay. The air-conditioned **Adonis** (☎ **0661/91-381**) and **Reflections** (☎ **0661/91-735**), another disco with a British DJ, are both up in Goúvia.

PALEOKASTRÍTSA

Just 16 miles due west of Corfu town is the small community of Paleokastrítsa, set high on the rocks above a lovely bay. If you approach this community from the heavily wooded road from Corfu town around the sunset hour, its beauty is still breathtaking. The clear waters, black rocks that break the still surface of the bay, and the misty glow of the evergreens in the dying light are an unforgettable picture. (Paleokastrítsa also lays claim to having been the home of King Alcinoos, and the boulder in its harbor is said to be the Phaeacian ship petrified by Poseidon for daring to help Odysseus.) Tourist development has lessened the appeal of Paleokastrítsa and it's overcrowded in the summer, but in the spring and fall it remains an attractive resort.

Several rounded coves forming rock-and-pebble beaches and the pure transparent water draw divers and fishermen. Bathers seeking less crowded areas should walk down to the Ayía Triáda beach—a path descends from the clifftop roadway just past Paleokastrítsa Rent a Car—or try some of the less visible pebbly coves around the marina. Of all the other resorts on the island that we cover—Áyios Yióryios, Sidári, Glyfáda, and Kassiópi—we find Paleokastrítsa to have the most dramatic scenery, which, combined with restaurants and nightlife, makes it the top alternative to Corfu town.

WHAT TO SEE & DO

The area's scenic beauty is best taken in on leisurely walks. Especially spectacular views of the coast can be had along the path through cypress and pines on the way to the village of **Lákones,** an hour's walk uphill behind the Hotel Odysseus (about 3 miles). The village's Bella Vista Cafe boasts "the most beautiful view in Europe." You can continue on to the **Kríni** and up to its hilltop acropolis, **Angelókastro,** a 13th-century Byzantine bastion perched atop a precipice nearly 1,000 feet high.

Another spectacular walk can be made up to the **Monastery of Panayías Paleokastrítsas** (also called Theotóki or Zoodóhos Piyí), on a promontory above Paleokastrítsa. The path looks steep, but don't let it scare you; it's only about 15 minutes to the top. This hike is best made at sunset when the light is constantly changing over beautiful little bays and inlets interrupted by lush greenery. The monastery is still in use and a walk around the top provides the visitor with peaceful gardens and lots of grape arbors to rest under. There's a small museum with some 17th-century icons; it's open daily from 7am to 1pm and 3 to 8pm and admission is free, but a donation should be made. A monk at the door usually offers long black skirts for the underclothed.

Shoppers will find several points of interest on the road between Corfu town and Paleokastrítsa. China collectors should definitely stop at the **Ceraco Fine Bone China Factory** (☎ **0663/22-650**), which sells discontinued patterns and fine-quality seconds. Because the cost of labor is significantly lower here than in other European countries, the prices are unbelievably low for such superior quality goods. They're open Tuesday to Saturday from 9am to 5:30pm and accept American Express and Visa.

There's also the **Mavromatis Company** (☎ **0663/22-174**), manufacturers of *koum kouat* (kumquat) liqueurs. You can sample many of the clear amber fruit liqueurs and brandies, and purchase these special gifts there. Those interested in objects, including bowls, made of handsome and durable olive wood should stop at the **Wood's Nest** olive wood workshop.

WHERE TO STAY

Other than the few super-plush hotels on the cliffs, most housing is in group-booked villas or rooms to rent. Unfortunately, the proliferation of groups has made it extremely difficult to find high-season rooms, so call ahead or check with the Corfu Sun Club in Corfu town before you venture out here with your luggage. Some readers may prefer a room farther away from the bay in the height of mosquito season, August.

We rented a wonderful room from **George Bakiras** and his wife, Eleni (☎ **0663/ 41-311** or 0663/41-328); write to him at: Michalas/Bakiras, Lákones, Paleokastrítsa, 490 83 Corfu. Look for their sign on the left of the road, 100 yards past the Odyssey Hotel: ROOMS FOR RENT/ GREEN HOUSE/ 30 M. FROM BEACH/ G. BAKIRAS. The Bakiras family's modest bungalow in a wooded setting has eight large doubles; four have kitchenettes and all have private facilities. Their front porch overlooks the marina. Rooms are 9,300 Drs ($38.75) per night, and their hospitality can't be beat. They also now rent nine rooms with kitchenette above the Paleokastrítsa main street, with "superb sea view."

On this embankment below the Odyssey Hotel is the **Villa Georgina;** contact the villa ℅ Spiros Loulis, Lákones, Paleokastrítsa, 490 83 Corfu (no phone). The kindly Mr. Loulis rents eight modernized rooms with private shower and bidet; rates are 9,000 Drs ($37.50) per night. The common balcony offers a sea view barely visible through dense evergreen trees. You'll also find other rooms for rent tucked up on the wooded hillside above the village's main street.

Camping Paleokastritsa (☎ **0663/41-104**) is set in a densely wooded area about a 10-minute walk east of the Ayía Triáda beach.

Hotel Apollon-Ermis. Paleokastrítsa, 490 83 Corfu. ☎ and fax **0663/41-211.** 43 rms, all with bath (tub or shower). TEL. 10,800 Drs ($45) single or double; 14,400 Drs ($60) triple. Rates include breakfast. No credit cards.

This small hotel owned by the Ionian Yacht Club has green-shuttered rooms with small balconies overlooking the roadway and town beach. The ground-floor cafe is very popular with beachgoers (see "Where to Eat," below).

Hotel Zefiros. Box 2, Paleokastrítsa, 490 83 Corfu. ☎ **0663/41-244.** 15 rms, all with bath (shower). 4,800 Drs ($20) single; 6,000 Drs ($25) double with toilet outside, 9,600 Drs ($40) double with bath. Rates include breakfast. No credit cards.

The dark-pink hotel next door to the Apollon-Ermis is a decent choice. All the well-kept rooms have showers inside, but some have shared toilets outside in the hall. The front-facing rooms have balconies facing the small harbor and town beach.

Oceanis Hotel. Paleokastrítsa, 490 83 Corfu. ☎ **0663/41-229.** Fax 0663/22-368. 71 rms, all with bath (tub or shower). TEL. 9,600 Drs ($40) single; 18,000 Drs ($75) double; 21,500 Drs ($89.60) triple. Rates include breakfast. AE, V.

This handsome resort well off the road usually has some rooms left over for individual travelers. The lobby is spacious and airy, and the staff is friendly and helpful. The spacious modern rooms offer spectacular views throughout the region; many overlook the good-sized swimming pool and panoramic sun deck. The Oceanis also organizes theme nights, Greek night buffets, and poolside barbecues.

WHERE TO EAT

The **Belvedere Restaurant** (☎ 0663/41-583), next door to the Green House, has a great view of Belvedere Cove and good food at reasonable prices; American Express, MasterCard, and Visa are accepted.

Apollon Restaurant. Opposite the village beach. ☎ **0663/41-211.** Main courses 1,300–3,000 Drs ($5.40–$12.50); fish 1,200–4,000 Drs ($5–$16.65) per portion. No credit cards. Daily 11am–3pm and 7–11pm. CONTINENTAL.

The Apollon, on the ground floor of the Apollon-Ermis Hotel, is the friendliest, best-value eatery around the beach area. At lunch you'll find families, barefoot and damp, having thick, extra-cheesey pizzas with myriad toppings. At sunset, the low-volume Greek folk music serenades young couples enjoying cheese pies and a beer. About 9:30pm, everyone turns out for the good-value daily specials—a four-course meal for 2,500 to 4,000 Drs ($10.40 to $16.65)—or hearty portions of Greek and continental fare.

AROUND THE ISLAND

Pagí, a petite mountaintop village northwest of Paleokastrítsa, is the turning point for buses snaking down the cliff north to the beach at Afiónis, or south to the beach at Áyios Yióryios. The hour ride from Corfu town spent twisting in and out of the shaded, wooded, cool forests and valleys will remind you what all the hoopla was about this island.

ÁYIOS YIÓRYIOS

Órmos Áyios Yióryios (not to be confused with the St. George's Beach resort area on the southwestern coast) is a spectacular 1 1/4-mile stretch of pale gold sand curving gently around a broad bay of the same name. Though undergoing rapid small-scale development, for now it remains a haven from the white concrete hotel strip lining Corfu's better-known beaches.

The far north end of this cove (not connected by road to the mid-beach stretch) is a little-devcloped area for beach lovers called **Afiónis.** There's a charming set of rooms at the Taverna Afiónis, run by George Bardis, formerly of Brighton Beach, New York; a double with twin beds and a private bath just a stone's throw from the water costs 7,500 Drs ($31.25). The Taverna Vrahos next door also rents simple rooms. (There were still no phones during our last visit.) To reach Afiónis, jump on the "Arilás" bus, which runs twice daily from Corfu town.

At the small but much bigger central beach of Áyios Yióryios, most development is due to **Thompson Holidays** and **Nur Travel,** those enterprising European budget travel companies that stake out new resort turf with their modest "villas." Limited traveler amenities include **Costas Cars and Bikes** (☎ 0663/96-298) for moped and car rental, and several minimarkets and souvenir shops that double as money changers. Three buses a day make the 1-hour trip from the long-distance bus station near the New Port.

Where to Stay & Eat

Several of the small hotels and rooms-for-rent complexes claimed that they would accept individual travelers from April to June and mid-September to late October, when their contracts with ▮▮▮ operators expired. You can also check for vacancies during the high season.

The **Hotel Belle Hélène,** Áyios Yióryios Armenadon, 490 81 Corfu (☎ 0663/96-201), is the best of the new beachside lodgings. Good basic rooms, most with sea views, are complemented by a comfortable lounge with a terrace and outdoor pool. The attached continental and Greek restaurant has a Teutonic bias, reflecting Nur Tour's clientele. The 54 rooms cost 15,600 Drs ($65) single or double with breakfast or 24,000 Drs ($100) with a half-board plan; American Express and Visa are accepted.

The **Kostas Golden Beach Hotel,** Áyios Yióryios Pagí, 490 81 Corfu (☎ **0663/96-207**), is another mid-beach choice, with 40 modern balconied rooms and a small beachside pool. When Thompson Holidays hasn't packed it with Brits, the Golden Beach is another good choice in the same price range. The **Hotel Corfu Star,** Áyios Yióryios Pagí, 490 81 Corfu (☎ **0663/96-210**), is uphill from these and another, cheaper option.

In the central part of the beach there are several rooms for rent above a few undistinguished tavernas and near the Arista Market. Prices will average 7,500 Drs ($31.25) for a double with private toilet and shower. The very pleasant **San George Camping** (☎ **0663/51-194;** fax 0663/51-759) is farther uphill on the cliffside; a tent for two costs 3,600 Drs ($15).

Dining highlights include the beachside **Taverna Nafsika,** which has Greek dancing on Friday nights when there are enough people gathered in this tiny outpost, and the **Moonlight Grill Room,** another simple taverna about 500 yards inland on the road back to Pagí.

NORTHWESTERN VILLAGES

Hikers (or drivers with Jeeps) can ascend the steep cliff road for 2 miles to **Makrádes,** then continue another, more level 2½ miles to **Alimatádes,** both small villages of stone homes. The dusty lanes are filled with load-bearing donkeys and women carrying bundles of grape leaves on their heads. At periodic roadside stands, couples sell packets of hand-picked oregano, thyme, rosemary, and bay leaves, and bottles of home-brewed red and white wine.

From **Pagí,** there's also a better road through the north country. Follow the enchanting fern-filled stretch of road that crosses a stone bridge to the traditional hill village of **Vatónies.** Old women with white cloths shading their heads from the sun and black dresses with colorful aprons carry twigs, herbs, and hay for chickens. Drivers coming from Paleokastrítsa can take the turnoff for Doukádes, a tiny, unspoiled mountain village whose square is still filled with goatherds, women in traditional clothes, and aging farmers playing cards. There's one **taverna** in town, a good place to stop and refuel.

The larger road from Kastellani Yírou leads 7½ miles north to **Sidári,** past ancient gnarled olive trees, with chartreuse ferns and furry moss patches in the crannies and valleys. Sidári is popular with families because of its small fine-sand beach and calm, shallow water—which isn't overly clean. We found better swimming just around the rocky point to the west, an area known to locals as **"Canal d'Amour."** It's said that all who sail through the eroded half cave at this point will be able to marry whoever is on their minds at the time. The "Canal d'Amour" is more picturesque than the bustling, wildly commercialized village. Buses run from Corfu town to Sidári five times daily between 9am and 7:30pm.

The best-priced hotels and pensions are monopolized by the travel agencies in the village, but a few said that they would do business with individual travelers if they had any extra rooms. Your best bet is to contact the **Kostas Kantarelis Travel Office** (☎ **0663/95-314**), which, like most of Sidári, is open only from April 15 to October 30; expect to pay 11,500 Drs ($47.90) for a double with private bath, 16,000 Drs ($66.65) for a studio with a kitchenette. It also rents cars, mopeds, and bicycles at good prices. Most Sidári hotels have their own restaurants, and there are several undistinguished fast-food parlors on the main street.

THE NORTHERN COAST

East of the village of Sidári, the north-coast roadway disintegrates into a picturesque, backwoods country lane with lots of cabbage and tomato patches. If you detour to **Kanaloúri** you'll be treated to a lovely little village where inhabitants wear traditional homespun cotton clothes. Drivers must watch out for the donkeys, who like to swing their bottoms out into the road when they hear a car approach!

The nondescript roadstop of Róda is being developed as the next resort, with construction raging along its narrow pebble beach. At the coastal boomtown of **Aharávi,** there's a good, sandy beach, but it gets jammed with day-trippers from Sidári (out to find an isolated beach) as well as the local sybarites.

The beach at Ayía Ekateríni, known as **Kalamáki Beach,** is a gray sand-and-pebble stretch, as is Áyios Spyrídon, named after Corfu's patron saint. Both have developed with clusters of rooms for rent and tavernas, but not until you get to the harbor of **Kassiópi** do you find the next full-blown resort.

The once-sleepy fishing village of Kassiópi is one long strip of billboards, pizza parlors, discos, souvenir stands, and rooms-to-let, leading to a relatively peaceful, attractive port lined with several tavernas. The nearby beaches have narrow rocky banks, though while bathing you get a distant view of Albania. Kassiópi is serviced eight times daily from the long-distance bus station near the New Port.

If the charter business from England and Holland is off, there may be rooms available at the ubiquitous "villas" in town, where doubles with bath run 7,500 Drs ($31.25) a night. *Note:* Kassiópi is plagued with strong mistral winds in August and has a short tourist season; most businesses open only from mid-May to the end of October. The **Salco Holidays Tourist Bureau,** off the main square by the harbor (☎ **0663/81-317** or 0663/81-437), will help you find a room, rent a car, organize a day trip, or rent a motorboat for water sports. It's well organized to entertain tourists locked into 14-day Kassiópi packages, even offering day trips to Albania.

THE EASTERN COAST

Between Kassiópi and Corfu town is 22¹/₂ miles of cove and beach-lined coastline. The pretty little tree-lined port of **Áyios Stéfanos** is a new destination for day-trippers, who enjoy lounging at the two tavernas overlooking a cove filled with colorful fishing boats.

Most of the housing along the more upscale east coast is in private villas, the best of which are booked by the **CV (Corfu Villas) Travel Office,** Odós Donzelótou 7, Corfu, 491 00 Corfu (☎ **0661/24-009**); or 43 Cadogan St., Chelsea, London SW3 2PR, England (☎ **0171/581-0851**).

Kouloúra, Kalámi, and **Kéntroma** are small boating ports farther south with pebbly bathing areas. All are densely packed with tourists who've descended from the brush-covered slopes of villa land to partake of the water. Many of these communities have been written of in Lawrence Durrell's *Prospero's Cell.*

About 12¹/₂ miles north of Corfu town, the coast road runs high above the water through forests of olive and cypress. The pretty hillside beach community of **Nissáki** has one huge Class A resort, several tavernas, and wooded slopes coated with newly built whitewashed villas. The long, crowded white-sand stretch of **Barbáti,** where many water sports are offered, runs south to Pýryi. **Ýpsos** is a very commercialized resort area; across the roadway from myriad hotels and rooms is a narrow pebble shore and very placid water. The town float is packed with kids and sunbathers. Looking out to sea, the views of evergreens growing along the waterfront reminded us of New Hampshire.

There are several campsites in this vicinity, until we come to **Dassía,** home of Corfu's own Club Med. At **Komménos** the coast breaks out into a lush spit of land occupied by one of our favorite luxury resort developments, the **Daphnila Bay** (☎ **0661/91-520**).

The coast south from Goúvia has undergone great upheaval and construction to become an undistinguished, budget-group-tour destination. **Pérama** is the first community south of the inlet below Corfu town. Many villas-to-let and hotels crowd the coast road, but some hardy olive trees manage to poke their heads through. Just above Gastoúri is **Achillío,** the inland retreat of the wealthy where many of the European royal villas (including the Achilleion of the empress Elizabeth of Austria) can be seen. As in so many wealthy enclaves, the lush overgrowth obscures the sightseers' view of many of the finest homes.

Benítses (7³/₄ miles or 15 minutes by bus south of Corfu town), once a scenic fishing village along this coast, has become the island's most jam-packed beach town. For 1¹/₄ miles of coast road there are lots of bars (including *karaoke* clubs), fast-food joints, seafood restaurants, laser and video discos, boutiques, and travel agents. At night it's chaos, but during daylight there's a lazy summer feel.

There are a great number of resort hotels all the way down the coast to the once-sleepy beach of **Kávos,** now inunudated by the many boat excursions emanating from Corfu in search of a quiet beach. (There are even day trips to Páxos, easily seen from the point at Asprókavos.) Along this road (about 12¹/₂ miles south of Corfu town) are the sibling resorts of **Moraítika** and **Messóngi,** separated by the narrow Messóngi River, both with narrow sand and shingle beaches leading to calm, shallow seas.

THE WESTERN COAST

From Vrakaniótika village and its fortress, near the site of the island's largest enclosed lagoon, one major road leads down into the narrow tip of Corfu's "tail." Some 4¹/₂ miles south, at the village of Aryirádes, a narrower road veers west to the other Áyios Yióryios, a small beach and sand-lined swimming cove that's favored for weekend outings with the kids. Heading north to the island's midpoint is **Áyios Górdis,** a very popular beach and swimming area, about 40 minutes by public bus from Corfu town.

Most visitors based in Corfu town head for **Glyfáda** as a day beach trip, for good reason. Glyfáda is conveniently reached and is one of Corfu's best beaches: it's long, large, with room for everybody, and the sand is kept remarkably clean. Unfortunately, the recently built Grand Hotel Glyfáda monolith and several new condos dominate the once-rural skyline. The bus from Corfu's long-distance bus station near the New Port runs nine times daily between 7am and 7:30pm to this sandy, active cove.

The hilltop village of Pélekas (above Glyfáda beach) is touted as the place from which to watch the sunset; only on Corfu could this attribute create a full-fledged resort! It's terribly overcrowded and overbuilt, and filled with well-dressed families and coeds; there are as many moped dealers as rooms for rent. Yet the half-hour ascent to the top of **Pélekas Hill** to watch the sunset makes your visit here worthwhile. Before the sun goes all the way down, circle the parking area on the hilltop for magnificent views over the entire island and the Ionian Sea.

North of Glyfáda there's a one-lane roadway that continues along the coast to the **Myrtiotíssas Monastery;** after a visit, you can walk down behind it and arrive at a lovely sand beach. Inland from the newly built seaside resort at Ermónes is the 18-hole golf course at **Livádi Toú Rópa** (Ropa's Meadow), nestled in a valley near **Vátos** on Ermónes Bay.

This agricultural heartland of Corfu is quite remarkable. In the cooler hours of the early evening, the fields fill up with farmers and you begin to see the true islanders emerge. Old, wind-burnt women in black cotton head scarves just sit out on their stoops, head in hand, contemplating the sky. Wiry old men and young boys and girls comb the countryside, removing olives from the glistening black nets where they've landed. At **Gardeládes** you must choose either the left-hand turn to the beautiful Paleokastrítsa Bay or the right-hand turn for Corfu town.

2 Páxos

31 nautical miles SE of Corfu, 21 nautical miles W of Igoumenítsa

Páxos (Paxí) is a pretty island covered with more than 200,000 olive trees, with a population of less than 3,000. British package-tour companies are exploiting it as a destination for discerning travelers; it's popular with vacationing Greeks and Italians in July and August; and numerous day-trippers come from Corfu and Párga. During the high season tourists outnumber residents. At other times tranquillity returns and it can be a most pleasant place to visit, especially for those who want to explore its unspoiled interior and discover its resident fishermen, tiny villages, traditionally dressed women, and lively tavernas. Its beaches are not at all special, but there is frequent caïque service to **Antipáxos,** a small neighboring island just 3 miles south, which is well endowed with stretches of pale-sand beach.

ESSENTIALS

GETTING THERE & DEPARTING   By Boat   There's at least one ferry daily from Corfu's Old Port (2¹/₂ hours, 1,700 Drs/$7.10). In high season there are two high-speed boats daily from Corfu's Old Port (1¹/₂ hours, 6,600 Drs/$27.50 round-trip—return coupons can be used after the date of purchase). The high-speed catamaran *Neárchos* runs from Préveza to Corfu via Páxos daily except Tuesday and Thursday. The minicruisers *Petrakis* and *Sotirakis* (☎ 0661/38-690) sail to Páxos and Antipáxos from the beach resorts of Kassiópi (near the northeast tip of Corfu) and Kávos (near the southern tip of Corfu) on regular day trips. From the mainland the *Rena S II Love Boat* (☎ 0661/25-317) provides daily service between Páxos and Párga, and other boats provide irregular service from Igoumenítsa and Moltos. Call the **Gáïos Port Authority** (☎ 0662/31-259) for more information.

VISITOR INFORMATION   There is no tourist information office on Páxos, but the regular **police,** just off the port in Gáïos (☎ 0662/31-222), will handle complaints and emergencies. There are a handful of **travel agencies** on the island, on the waterfront in Gáïos and in the village of Lákka; all sell boat tickets. The friendly office of **Paxos Sun Holidays,** 1 block in from the waterfront in Gáïos (☎ 0662/ 31-201; fax 0662/32-036), is an Olympic Airways agent.

ORIENTATION   Páxos is only 6 miles long and less than 2¹/₂ miles wide, with low hills on its east coast and more precipitous cliffs on the west. **Gáïos,** the main port and town, is on the east coast toward the southern end of the island, with the wooded islets of **Panayía** and **Áyios Nikólaos** (Kástro) crowding its harbor. Smaller boats still use the Old Port, but ferries dock at the New Port, about 500 yards to the northeast.

From Gáïos a paved road leads northwest through the interior of the island to **Lákka,** a resort on a small horseshoe-shaped bay at the tip of the island. About halfway along this road a branch leads off to the right to **Longós,** a small fishing village. **Oxías,** a couple of miles south of Gáïos, is known for its mineral springs. The island's best beach is on the island of **Mongoníssi,** joined to the south end of the island by a causeway, a 45-minute walk southeast from Gáïos.

GETTING AROUND   Walking is our favorite mode of transport, but there is an island **bus,** which runs four or five times a day from Gáïos to Lákka, making a stop in Longós. If you want to contribute to the noise pollution, small **mopeds** and **motorbikes** of all sizes are available for rent at agencies on the waterfront in Gáïos. There's an informal **taxi** stand on the main square in Gáïos.

FAST FACTS   There is a **medical clinic** (☎ 0662/31-466) in Gáïos. The **post office** and **telephone office (OTE)** are near the main square in Gáïos. Several travel agents and two general stores will exchange traveler's checks; during the low season they're open Monday to Friday from 8am to 1:30pm, with evening and weekend hours in high season.

SPECIAL EVENTS   Festivities spill over from the local monastery into the town on its holy day, the **Feast of the Assumption (August 15).** Páxos's other cultural highlight is the annual **Music Festival;** every September a number of internationally known classical musicians perform in the villages of Lákka and Longós.

EXPLORING THE ISLAND

Páxos is still so unspoiled that the affable locals wish you a passing "*Yássou!*" or "*Kaliméra!*" along the road. The whole island has a kind of anachronistic quality, and its modest whitewashed stucco houses, except for their green shutters, are more like those found in the Cyclades than the neoclassical Ionian-style mansions found on neighboring islands. And unlike the other Ionians, the deep silence of Páxos or Antipáxos is more often broken by the crowing of a rooster than by the mechanical buzz of a moped.

The streets of **Gáïos** are too narrow for cars, and the town has both a 15th-century **Venetian fortress** on the islet of Áyios Nikólaos (Kástro) and a **monastery** on the islet of Panayía.

North of Gáïos are several villages and beachside communities—most notably **Lákka** and **Longós.** Opinion differs on which is the more charming—and both are dominated by British tour groups—but we recommend Lákka as your base if Gáïos proves too busy. The large, enclosed Lákka Bay is favored by sailors and windsurfers for its calm, if not pure, water and steady breezes. Longós, 2½ miles south of Lákka, has rooms for rent, with most activity centered around the bus stop or small marina. There's a quiet pebble beach nearby. In both communities, **Planos Holidays** (☎ 0662/31-744; fax 0662/31-010) can arrange for rooms, excursions, and other travel needs.

If you've come this far for a deserted beach, head farther south to the island of **Antipáxos** (Andípaxi). Well-traveled locals call it the "Barbados of Greece" because of its clean white beach. Boats to Antipáxos run many times daily in high season. Captains normally wait for a full boatload of sun worshipers before setting sail for the brief commute; a round-trip ticket is 1,000 Drs ($4). Once on Antipáxos, you can walk everywhere. Most of these boats stop at the superb soft-sand beach at **Vríka** and the even better **Voutoúmi** before docking at **Órmos Agripídias.** The picturesque port opens out to a broad cove that's almost blocked by a verdant islet that seems to have drifted in too close. The hilltop village is surrounded by stone walls, taking advantage of the island's most plentiful building material.

Antipáxos, about one-fourth the size of Páxos, has a population of less than 200, and it's known for its good white and red wines. There are a few foreign-owned deluxe villas, wired with personal generators and radio phones, sprinkled around;

between are the fine, golden-sand beaches the island is noted for. There are tavernas at the beaches but no accommodations, though Vríka has a small unofficial campsite. (If you plan to camp overnight, bring provisions.)

WHERE TO STAY

Gáïos has most of the island's accommodations, including two small Class E hotels, the **Ilios** (☎ **0662/31-808**) and the **Lefkothea** (☎ **0662/31-807**). The **Adamantia** (☎ **0662/31-121**) has traditional furnished apartments for 15,000 to 25,000 Drs ($62.50 to $104), depending on the season. The **Paxos Club,** half a mile from the port (☎ **0662/32-450;** fax 0662/32-097), has a large swimming pool and furnished apartments for 25,000 to 65,000 Drs ($104 to $271).

There are plenty of rooms for rent around the island, primarily in Gáïos, Longós, and Lákka. Although there may be a few rooms on Antipáxos, it's impossible to know what might be available unless you're based in Gáïos and go over in person to check it out. Most visitors still prefer private rooms, and it's estimated there are at least 5,000 private beds, three-quarters of which are in Gáïos. In high season, category A private rooms, with bath, run approximately 7,300 Drs ($30.40) single, and 8,300 Drs ($34.60) double. Before and after the impossible-to-find-a-room high season, there is some softening in the market and you have increased negotiating power, though most places are open only from mid-April to October.

If at all possible, contact the **Planos Holidays** office in Lákka, 490 82 Páxos (☎ **0662/31-744** or 0662/31-821; fax 0662/31-010), before you arrive. This office in the central part of Lákka's waterfront provides travel information, currency exchange, and most important, villa and apartment rental information. It's the agent for two British firms—the Greek Islands Club and Villa Centre Holidays—and really keeps a finger on the pulse of available housing in Gáïos, Longós, and Lákka.

As you step off the boat, there may be townspeople at the pier offering rooms. Ask to look at the accommodations before you make a commitment—unless you're traveling in August. In that case, grab any available room!

Páxos Beach Hotel. Gáïos, 490 82 Páxos. ☎ **0662/32-211.** Fax 0662/32-166. 42 rms, all with bath (shower). A/C TEL. 22,000 Drs ($91.65) single; 32,500 Drs ($135.40) double. Rates include half board. No credit cards.

This attractive, rustic hewn-stone resort, set in olive groves above a pretty pebble beach, has a good restaurant, bar, TV lounge, and table tennis room. The simply furnished, twin-bedded bungalow rooms have sea-view verandas.

WHERE TO EAT

At the time of our last visit, the favorite tavernas in Lákka were the **Kapodistrias** and the **Souris,** both inexpensive and centrally located. The locals singled out **Nassos, Vassilis,** and **Iannis** as the finest taverna proprietors in Longós, where everyone specializes in fish.

Restaurant Rex. Gáïos. No phone. Main courses 1,200–2,500 Drs ($5–$10.40). No credit cards. Daily noon–10pm. SEAFOOD/GREEK.

Residents who want to eat fish head for the Restaurant Rex, just off the main square. The restaurant usually offers several fixed-price meals, most prepared with locally caught fish. If it's too jammed with day-trippers, try the Blue Grotto, on the waterfront opposite the Páxos Sun Holidays office.

Taka-Taka. Gáïos. ☎ **0662/31-323.** Main courses 1,200–1,800 Drs ($5–$7.50). No credit cards. Daily 11:30am–10pm. GREEK.

From its quiet setting 2 blocks behind the main square, this grill offers a nice selection of traditional Greek cuisine. The specialty is grilled meat and fish, but the stuffed tomatoes, shish kebab, and fish courses are also delicious. One of Taka-Taka's main attractions, other than its friendly proprietor, the food, and its super-clean kitchen (a rarity), is the vine-covered garden dining area.

3 Lefkáda

87 nautical miles NW of Pátra, 31 miles S of Igoumenítsa

Lefkáda (also called Lefkás) is the fourth largest of the Ionians, a fertile island with plenty of rainfall, yet it remains relatively poor and undeveloped. It was connected to the mainland by a narrow isthmus until the Corinthians dug a canal through it in the 8th century B.C., but the gap has once again been closed by a floating bridge.

The lyric poetess Sappho is most often associated with her native island of Lésvos (and her love for women), but the legend of her love for a man links her with Lefkáda. It's said that she fell in love with a handsome boatman, Phaon, a favorite of Aphrodite. Phaon soon tired of her, but she followed him to Lefkáda, where for centuries the priests of Apollo had made a devotional dive from the white cliffs on the southwest coast that give the island its name (*lefkós* means white). In despair or following the example of Aphrodite, who is supposed to have made such a lover's leap after the death of Adonis, she is said to have thrown herself from Kávos tís Kyrás (236 feet) to her death at the foot of the white cliffs of Cape Lefkátas.

Today the floating bridge that conveniently connects the island to the mainland seems to diminish Lefkáda's appeal to many foreign tourists. However, long sand-and-pebble beaches on the island's west coast (including the stunning Pórto Katsíki, voted one of the Mediterranean's best beaches by *Condé Nast Traveler* magazine) and the windsurfing potential of Vassilikí Bay (considered the eastern Mediterranean's best) are now being developed—and both are strong attractions for those looking for someplace off the beaten track.

ESSENTIALS

GETTING THERE & DEPARTING   By Plane   Olympic Airways has daily flights to and from Préveza, a mainland city 25 minutes by bus from Lefkás. Tickets and information can be obtained from Olympic's office in Lefkás (☎ 0645/22-430), in Préveza at Spiliádou and Bálkou streets (☎ 0682/28-674), or in Athens (☎ 01/926-7251).

By Bus   There are four buses daily from Athens's Terminal A, Odós Kifissoú 100; the 6-hour trip costs 6,950 Drs ($28.95) each way. There are two express buses daily from Igoumenítsa to Préveza, for those coming from Corfu. Call the terminal in Athens (☎ 01/513-3583) or the one in Lefkás (☎ 0645/22-364) for information; reservations are recommended a day in advance.

By Boat   The F/B *Meganissi* connects the port of Nydrí, Lefkáda, with Fríkes, Ithaca, and Fiskárdo, Kefaloniá. The F/B *Captain Aristides* connects Vassilikí, Lefkáda, with Píso Aetós, Ithaca, and Fiskárdo or Sámi on Kefaloniá. **Four Islands Ferries** now coordinates the ferry service among Lefkáda, Ithaca, Kefaloniá, and Meganíssi; call its office in Nydrí (☎ 0645/92-427), Fríkes (☎ 0674/33-120), Fiskárdo (☎ 0671/51-478), or Sámi (☎ 0671/22-000) for schedules and information. In summer there's additional service among Lefkáda, Ithaca, and Kefaloniá; for current information, contact the **Lefkáda Port Authority** (☎ 0645/22-322).

VISITOR INFORMATION   There is no tourist information office on the island, but the **tourist police** are at Odós Politehníou 30 in Lefkás town (☎ 0645/26-450).

Travel agents can exchange currency daily from 9am to 9pm throughout the high season. **Post offices** can exchange money Monday to Friday from 8:30am to 1pm.

   Lefkas Travel, Odós Dörpfeld 18 (☎ **0645/22-430;** fax 0645/23-566), open daily from 9am to 1pm, has a metered phone and fax service, can book accommodations, and sells air and ferry tickets.

ORIENTATION   The island's main town, capital, and port, **Lefkás** (also called Lefká and Lefkáda), is at the northeastern tip of the island directly across the canal, joined to the mainland through the marshland by a ribbon of paved roadway. Although visitors will find accommodations most easily in the main town of Lefkás, as well as the east-coast resort of Nydrí (which is overly tourist oriented), we suggest the newly developed south-coast village of Vassilikí as a more attractive base camp.

   Since 1988, when the local government began building roads west down the dramatic cliffs of Cape Lefkátas, several stunning beaches have been revealed. The finest is **Pórto Katsíki,** which some say was the late Aristotle Onassis's favorite beach. (He arranged for boatloads of its sand to be brought to Skorpiós to make his own beach.) We're voting for this as one of "Greece's 10 Best Beaches"!

GETTING AROUND   By Bus   The **bus station** in Lefkás is on the southeast side of town near the New Port. Island buses run frequently to Nydrí, four times a day to Vassilikí, and twice a day to Póros, on the southeast coast.

By Taxi   The main **taxi stand** is also near the New Port. Fares are high; the trip from Lefkás to Vassilikí, about 21 miles, costs about 5,400 Drs ($22.50). You'll have to ask your hotel to call a taxi for you if you're staying outside the main town. If you want to explore beaches, **caïques** depart daily from Lefkás, Nydrí, and Vassilikí for beach cruises and round-the-island jaunts; check out the signboards posted on their sterns or ask a travel agent.

By Jeep   Jeeps are widely available from any local travel agent. Rates start at 15,000 Drs ($62.50) per day plus mileage.

By Moped   Mopeds are available everywhere from about 3,500 Drs ($14.60) per day, but the best west-coast beaches can be reached only by rough roads—too challenging for our moped abilities!

FAST FACTS   The **Lefkáda Hospital** is at Odós A. Valaóritis 24 in Lefkás town (☎ **0645/25-371**); there's a **health clinic** in Vassilikí (☎ **0645/31-065**). The regular **police** are at Odós Mela 55 in Lefkás town (☎ **0645/22-346**), with offices in Nydrí (☎ **0645/95-207**) and Vassilikí (☎ **0645/31-012**). In case of **emergency,** call ☎ **0645/22-100.** The **telephone office (OTE),** near the city hall in Lefkás, is open 24 hours; in Vassilikí the OTE is on the main street, open Monday to Saturday from 2:30 to 11pm, with a portable branch at the harbor in high season, also open Sunday from 9am to 2pm.

SPECIAL EVENTS   Lefkáda attracts many tourists each August to its popular **Festival of Arts and Literature** and **International Festival of Folklore,** 2 weeks of lectures, folk dances, theater pieces, and exhibitions. If you're here for either festival, August 11 is **St. Spýrídon's Day,** when colorful folk dancing, dining, and singing take place in the inland village of Kariá, 8³/₄ miles south of Lefkás town. A traditional wedding ceremony is performed in the central square, and locals don festive costumes.

LEFKÁS

The port of Lefkás is definitely the busiest town on the island. Its interior is more appealing than the developed coast with its prospects over the marshy lagoon, and the shore facing the mainland is lined with hotels, tourist offices, parking lots, and a wide roadway. The main street running southwest through the middle of town can be found by wandering north from the New Port or west from the Public Gardens; it's officially called **Dörpfeld,** after a German archaeologist who proposed that Lefkáda was actually Homer's Ithaca—though many locals don't recognize the name—and after a few blocks it widens to become the **main square,** after which it becomes **Stratigoú Méla.**

In Lefkás, you can shop in the *agorá* (**market**) for the intricate lacework and embroidery for which local women are known. There are no bargains among the handmade products, but since they are exported to Europe and America, they're certainly cheaper here than what you'd pay at home.

From the port of Lefkás, Nydrí, or Vassilikí, you can join a fun **day cruise,** our favorite way to explore the islets of the Ionians. The dense green foliage and stark black rocks that protrude unexpectedly from the calm waters are all scenic hallmarks of a region best appreciated from the water. Bring your binoculars!

The east coast faces directly on the mainland and thus offers sheltered coves and inlets ideal for boating and, in less crowded areas, recreational swimming. At **Nikianá,** about 5 miles south of Lefkás town, there's a mild surf.

WHERE TO STAY

Lefkas Travel (see "Visitor Information" under "Essentials," above) can assist you in finding a room to rent. Doubles with private bath (shower) run about 10,500 Drs ($43.75) in town, about 20% less in the villages.

Byzantio Hotel. Odós Dörpfeld 4, Lefkás, 311 00 Lefkáda. ☎ **0645/22-629.** Fax 0645/24-055. 15 rms, none with bath. TEL. 5,250 Drs ($21.90) single; 9,200 Drs ($38.35) double. No credit cards.

An old but good value choice near the waterfront, the Byzantio is comfortable and homey, with old photos and prints in the hallways. The public areas, communal baths, and toilets are well kept. Both the older and the new wing have high-ceilinged, well-lit rooms that share a long terrace overlooking the harbor. There's also a small bar and TV lounge.

Hotel Santa Maura. Odós Sp. Vlánti 2, Lefkás, 311 00 Lefkáda. ☎ **0645/22-342.** Fax 0645/26-253. 19 rms, all with bath (tub or shower). A/C TEL. 8,500 Drs ($35.40) single; 11,350 Drs ($47.30) double. Rates include breakfast. No credit cards.

Continue past the Byzantio on Dörpfeld to reach this converted 1850s mansion off to the left. There's a lot of variation in the rooms, and eight of them have private but unattached bathrooms, but they're all pleasant, comfortable, and quiet. The friendly family that owns it speaks English and knows the island. The hotel is open all year.

WHERE TO EAT

Kostas Taverna. On the main street. No phone. Main courses 1,150–2,650 Drs ($4.80–$11.05). No credit cards. Daily noon–10pm. GREEK.

Kostas Logothetis runs another good taverna near the main square. For a quick, inexpensive meal, try the delicious souvláki or lamb kebabs with garlic-filled *tzatzíki.* The moussaká and grilled squid are also very good.

Regantos Taverna. Odós Dimárhou Verióti 17. No phone. Main courses 1,000–2,600 Drs ($4.15–$10.85). No credit cards. Daily 7–11pm. GREEK.

This old taverna just north off the main square is still a local favorite, loved for its home-style cooking and robust Greek fare, including local salamis and beef dishes that are the island's specialty.

VASSILIKÍ

The south-coast port of Vassilikí, 21 miles from Lefkás town, is our pick for an overnight stay. Though newly built, its small size, bustling harbor, and the pebble Pónti beach are very appealing. There's a ferry connection with Fiskárdo, Kefaloniá, and Fríkes, Ithaca, but the big attraction is windsurfing—considered the best in the eastern Mediterranean because the deep cove surrounding the bay provides a natural windbreak, which guarantees steady west winds yet smooth water. Several European tour operators fill the hotels and rooms for rent with clients on week-long windsurfing packages, who lend a continuity and athletes' seriousness of purpose not usually found at other resorts.

Friendly **Samba Tours,** on the main street (☎ 0645/31-520; fax 0645/31-522), open daily from 8:30am to 9pm, can change money, sell ferry tickets, and arrange accommodations, car, windsurfing, and yacht rentals.

Vassilikí Travel (☎ 0645/31-509; fax 0645/31-081), open May to October, daily from 9am to 1pm and 6 to 10pm, can help you find a room, rent a car or moped, or make long-distance calls. It also offers day cruises with a picnic to Porto Katsíki, the island's best beach, just around Cape Lefkátas, for about 2,000 Drs ($8.35), or to Sívota Bay, Skórpios, and Meganíssi for about 4,000 Drs ($16.65). A few miles (a 45-minute walk) south of town is the pretty beach at **Áyiofýli,** also served by regular caïques from Vassilikí's port.

Windsurfers may want to contact **Club Vassiliki,** on Vassilikí Beach (☎ 0645/31-588); its week-long board program costs about 45,000 Drs ($187.50) and can be booked in advance as a tour package with Club Vass, 30 Brackenbury Rd., London W6 0BA, U.K. (☎ 0181/741-4471 or 0181/741-4686). Day rentals can be arranged locally for 18,000 Drs ($75), or 2,800 Drs ($11.65) per hour. **Wildwind Sailing Holidays** (☎ 0645/31-588) has sailing programs from Póndi Beach; its local instructors will rent you a catamaran for 7,000 Drs ($29.15) per hour when they're off duty from the package-tour students.

WHERE TO STAY

There are a few hotels and hundreds of rooms for rent in Vassilikí, but many are booked for the short season (typically May 15 to October 10) by European tour operators. For assistance and advance reservations (25% deposit requested), contact **Samba Tours** (☎ 0645/31-520; fax 0645/31-522) or **Vassiliki Travel** (☎ 0645/31-081; fax 0645/31-081); double rooms with private bath (shower) start at 9,000 Drs ($37.50), two-person studios with kitchenette at 10,500 Drs ($43.75), and two-bedroom apartments at 14,500 Drs ($60.40). **Vassiliki Beach Camping** (☎ 0645/31-308) is inland from the waterfront behind Póndi Beach.

✪ **Hotel Apollo.** Vassilikí, 310 82 Lefkáda. ☎ **0645/31-122.** Fax 0645/31-142. 34 rms, all with bath (shower). TEL. 11,500 Drs ($47.90) single; 19,500 Drs ($81.25) double. Rates include breakfast. AE, MC, V.

These simple but spacious, full-amenity (including a fridge) rooms overlook the marina and Póndi Beach, where windsurfers provide plenty of color. The hotel has a good garden restaurant—which we recommend to those staying elsewhere—and a pleasant roof terrace for evening drinks. The friendly, helpful staff also offers travel services, such as daily cruises and coach trips. If you call ahead, the Apollo's mini-bus will pick you up at the airport.

Hotel Paradise. Vassilikí, 310 82 Lefkáda. ☎ **0645/31-256.** 15 rms, 10 with bath (tub). TEL. 7,250 Drs ($30.20) single or double without bath, 10,000 Drs ($41.65) single or double with bath. No credit cards.

This old hotel dates from Vassilikí's pre-boom days. The rooms are bright and very well kept, and the common bathrooms are scrubbed clean. The Paradise's central location and pretty garden make it a good value; the hotel is open year-round.

WHERE TO EAT

Livanakis Kafeníon. On the port. No phone. Snacks 400–1,200 Drs ($1.65–$5). No credit cards. Daily 8am–9pm. SNACKS/COFFEE.

This very old-fashioned portside cafe has postage stamp–size outdoor tables overlooking the day-excursion boats and fishing caïques. We liked their early breakfast of fresh bread, honey, cheese, and strong Greek coffee (600 Drs/$2.50) so we could watch the locals primping their boats in anticipation of the 10am onslaught of day-trippers. Livanakis serves coffee to old-timers playing *távoli* (backgammon) throughout the day, then gets into ouzo mode at dusk when it serves the cheapest drinks in town.

Restaurant Miramare. Paralía, near the ferry dock. ☎ **0645/31-138.** Main courses 1,100–2,500 Drs ($4.60–$10.40). No credit cards. Daily 8:30am–2am. GREEK.

The Miramare has a very welcoming feeling to it, with vine-laden walls and a great view of the sea. The service is friendly and the food delicious. After a very filling meal of chicken, garden-fresh *maroúli* (lettuce) salad, and potatoes, fresh fruit was brought "from the house."

Taverna No Problem. Sívota Bay. ☎ **0645/31-182.** Fish 5,000–11,000 Drs ($20.85–$45.85) per kilo. No credit cards. Daily noon–11pm. SEAFOOD.

This is the best of the row of tavernas lining the yacht marina at beautiful Sívota Bay, just 3³/₄ miles east of Vassilikí. Day or night, it's worth an excursion to sample the simply prepared, excellent, freshly caught seafood. The fried calamari is tender and light, the *horiátiki saláta* (village salad) has ripe red tomatoes and lots of olives, the chips are made fresh, and the local fish, particularly the fleshy white *lythríni* (sea bream), are wonderfully grilled.

VASSILIKÍ AFTER DARK

In the evening the small harbor comes alive with strollers and some good bars. The **Byzantio** is an old stone building on the south side of the port with a post-hippy crowd; the nearby **Zeus** has a slicker, younger crowd of foreigners enjoying its loud rock sound track. **Sam's Place,** just off Póndi Beach, serves a walloping English breakfast called "The Works" for 1,500 Drs ($6.25) from 10am to 1pm; then it closes until 10pm when it becomes a rocking music bar, with a jam session on Monday and "Paddy's Night" (Irish music) on Friday. On our last visit a group of young Brits, celebrating their graduation from an advanced windsurfing course, recommended **Tunnel** and the **Remezzo Club** for partying and **Yellow Taffy** for breakfast and sweets.

NYDRÍ

The eastern coast port of Nydrí, 10 miles south of Lefkás town, was the island's first resort area because of its picturesque location facing the mainland. The port's popularity with sailors and tourists has made these calm waters too polluted and crowded for swimming. Across the placid blue Ionian, you'll see the islet of **Madoúri** with the cream-colored 18th-century mansion of the poet Aristotelis Valaoritis—presently off-limits. Behind it is tiny green uninhabited **Spartí.** To the south are **Skorpídi** and **Skórpios,** famed home of the Onassis family. (It's usually possible to take a boat tour around Skórpios from Lefkás, Nydrí, or Vassilikí, and even to swim off its beach— if Athina Onassis, Tina's daughter and Ari's only surviving descendant, isn't vacationing there.)

Some 4 nautical miles out from Nydri is **Meganíssi,** a much larger island with some beaches and villages for stranded day-trippers. Although Nydrí's waterfront was extended and dozens of gelaterias, cafes, discos, and pizza bars have opened, old women still sit beside the sailing yachts, grilling ears of corn and selling oregano to passersby.

If the hustle-bustle of Nydrí and its countless tour groups sound appealing, you'll want to contact **Nydri Travel,** located in the middle of the town's long main street (☎ **0645/92-514;** fax 0645/92-256) and open daily from 7am to 11pm. Since there are few hotels, the travel bureau can help you find a suitable room to rent in the village. Many rooms are actually in "villas" that European budget-tour operators have constructed to house clients; rates start at 9,000 Drs ($37.50) for a double with private bath (shower). The bureau is a good source of information on local goings-on, attractions, day tours, and water sports.

A SCENIC DRIVE TO THE ISLAND'S BEST BEACHES

South of Nydrí is a very scenic drive along the curving peninsula that forms Vlihó Bay. **Sívota** is on the island's southeast tip, facing the larger islet of Meganíssi. This peaceful port offers three tavernas (see "Where to Eat" in Vassilikí) at the harbor for a relaxing lunch.

The road winds west to **Vassilikí** (see above). From here, only the fit and daring should hike out to the white cliffs of Cape Lefkátas.

An inland road north from Póndi will take you to **Komíli** (8³/₄ miles), a small village on the newly built coast road down the length of Cape Lefkátas.

About 6³/₄ miles south is our favorite beach, ✪ **Pórto Katsíki (Goat Port),** with two small coffee and snack *kantínas* perched up on the cliffs. It's a stiff but glorious walk down to the heavenly gold-sand beach cove, certainly one of the best in Greece. Even closer to the Komíli turnoff are the 3-mile-long **Yialós,** a deserted sand-and-pebble beach, and **Grammí,** another fine-sand beach accessible only by caïque. These areas are destined for the next wave of development.

Kalamítsi is set high on a hill above the west coast; its traditional housing and sea views are well worth a detour if you're on your way to the pretty little resort of Áyios Nikítas. You'll first pass **Káthisma,** a long sand beach where, to our disappointment, car traffic is permitted on the sand. It's the best and most easily reached by public bus from Lefkás town, only 7¹/₂ miles north.

At **Áyios Nikítas** there's a clean beach and rough cold water that experienced sportsmen say is better than at Vassilikí for windsurfing. Information central in this tiny group resort (everything is within 100 yards of the seaside) is **Vantage Travel** (☎ **0645/97-415**). Vantage will book rooms, exchange currency, place long-distance calls, arrange a rental car, and generally introduce you to the bustle of clubs, cafes, and shops that have just opened.

Áyios Nikítas's best place to stay is the **Odyssey Hotel,** Áyios Nikítas, 310 80 Lefkáda (☎ **0645/97-351;** fax 0645/97-421), where 31 bright new rooms, all with bath (shower) and phone, some with double beds, open onto sea-view balconies. They have a popular bar and breakfast lounge. Singles run about 11,500 Drs ($47.90) and doubles are 19,500 Drs ($81.25); Diners Club, EuroCard, MasterCard, and Visa are accepted.

4 Ithaca

53 nautical miles NW of Pátra, 82 nautical miles S of Igoumenítsa

Ithaca (Itháki) is best known as the home of Odysseus. This is the island to which he yearned to return throughout his journey of 10 long and lonely years. From its rugged, stony, uninviting west coast, the modern visitor might rightly wonder why anyone would be anxious to return there; the island offers little in the way of beaches. Inland, however, Ithaca boasts wildly beautiful rocky hills and verdant pine-covered valleys.

A sign on the Lazaretto reads EVERY TRAVELER IS A CITIZEN OF ITHACA, but, for all its fame, few go there. We hope that that continues to be the case, since the island is a refreshing respite from its more popular neighbors. Bars, discos, resort hotels, and boutiques are probably still a few years away—Ithaca is still most attractive to those who have been enchanted by Homer's *Odyssey*. There are a number of interesting archaeological sites on the island, and the landscape is lovely. The locals are not yet jaded by tourism; they may not be as open and hospitable as southern Greeks usually are, but they're not unfriendly. The few beaches are mostly of white pebbles, which contrast exquisitely with the pure turquoise and sapphire water.

Better days returned to Ithaca in the 19th century, when the nearby cove of Loútsa was the headquarters of a large shipbuilding operation. Today marine service shops cater to passing yachts. The former fishing village of Fríkes, on the east coast, is a hub for intra-Ionian ferries. It, and nearby Kióni, are both picturesque villages where group-booked tourists occupy traditional housing, enjoy small-town life, and hike to nearby pebble beaches. Both may have more appeal than Vathý for long-term visitors.

ESSENTIALS

GETTING THERE & DEPARTING   By Boat   The F/B *Meganissi* connects the port of Fríkes, Ithaca, with Nydrí, Lefkáda, and Fiskárdo, Kefaloniá. The F/B *Captan Aristides* connects Píso Aëtós, Ithaca, with Vassilikí, Lefkáda, and Fiskárdo or Sámi on Kefaloniá. **Four Islands Ferries** now coordinates the ferry service between Ithaca, Lefkáda, Kefaloniá, and Meganíssi; call its office in Fríkes (☎ 0674/33-120), Nydrí (☎ 0645/92-427), Fiskárdo (☎ 0671/51-478), or Sámi (☎ 0671/22-000) for schedules and information. In summer there's service twice daily between Vathý and Sámi, Kefaloniá, and daily service between Fríkes, Ithaca, and Fiskárdo, Kefaloniá. Vathý is served by a daily car-ferry from Pátra via Sámi, Kefaloniá, on **Strintizis/Minoan Lines** (☎ 0674/33-120); it's a 5-hour ride. The F/B *Thiaki* runs from Astakós on the mainland to Vathý and Ayía Evfimía, Kefaloniá. For more information, contact the **port police** (☎ 0674/32-909).

ORIENTATION   Ithaca is shaped like an irregular bow tie, and most ferries call at its capital and most important port, **Vathý** ("Deep," also called Itháki), an impressively protected and picturesque harbor on the east coast, south of the island's waist. As you approach the harbor, the small islet of **Lazaretto** is on the right. From the ferry landing on the west side of the harbor, turn left and follow the waterfront to the **main square,** Platía Drakoúli, on the southwest corner of the harbor.

The island's one main road leads northwest from Vathý along the Bay of Dexiá, with a spur off to the left (west) to the new port at **Píso Aëtós,** then turns north along the west coast, passing below the **Monastery of Katharón** en route to the island's second town, **Stavrós.** The small resort of **Fríkes** is northeast across the island, and the road continues southeast along the coast to the picturesque little port of **Kióni.**

GETTING AROUND   The main **bus stop** is on the main square in Vathý. The island's only bus runs once daily (three times daily in high season) to Kióni via Stavrós and Fríkes. (The bus doesn't run to Píso Aëtós, which has little but a good new pier; the taxi fare is about 2,000 Drs/$8.35.) Travel agencies on the *paralía* (harborfront) in Vathý and in Fríkes and Kióni rent **mountain bikes** suitable for the hilly terrain for about 2,000 Drs ($8.35) per day, **mopeds** from 6,500 Drs ($27.10), and **cars** starting at 16,500 Drs ($68.75) per day; most accept MasterCard and Visa.

If you've only got a day on Ithaca, we'd recommend a 4-hour round-the-island tour by **taxi** with an English-speaking driver. Those stationed at the main square in Vathý charge about 15,000 Drs ($62.50). Several travel agents sell intra-Ionian ferry tickets, and caïque captains in Fríkes and Kióni also organize around-the-island boat excursions.

FAST FACTS   The **National Bank** has a branch southwest of the main square, and several nearby travel agents change traveler's checks during extended hours. The **hospital** in Vathý (☎ **0674/32-222**) is 200 yards south from the harbor, on the road to Arethoúsa. The town **police** (☎ **0674/32-205**) are on the same road, about 500 yards from the port. The **post office** is midway along the port, open Monday to Friday from 7:30am to 2:30pm. The **telephone center (OTE)** is a handsome, two-story building on the south side of the harbor, open Monday to Saturday from 7:30am to 10pm.

SPECIAL EVENTS   Each year from mid-August to mid-September, there's a **Festival of Greek Music** in Vathý to celebrate national culture.

EXPLORING THE ISLAND

The port of **Vathý** has most of the island's tourist services, good white-stone beaches south of town, and caïque service to other beaches, such as Gidáki. There's also a small **archaeological museum** (☎ **0674/32-200**) behind the portside OTE, open Tuesday to Sunday from 10am to 3pm; admission is free.

The **"Cave of the Nymphs"** (Marmarospiliá) is a signposted hike southwest above Vathý; here, according to some, Odysseus hid the gifts bestowed upon him by the hospitable Phaeacians. The **"Fountain of Arethoúsa,"** where Odysseus is supposed to have met his faithful swineherd Eumaeus, is a 2-hour hike south of Vathý. It, too, is signposted from town, but keep your eyes open for the turnoff down to the left about halfway there. Take water and a snack.

Having a car makes a day tour around the island practical and enjoyable. South of Vathý two prongs of roadway pierce the mountainous southern half of the island. Some 1¼ miles above the port is the larger village of **Perahóri,** a very scenic spot at sunset. If you have a four-wheel-drive vehicle, you might continue southwest to the **Monastery of Taxiarchón,** founded in 1693 and known for its El Greco icon.

Hilly routes climb up and down through rapidly changing countryside, and at the narrow waist the deep blue of the sea is ever present. **Aëtós** is the village at the island's narrowest point. Above it are the ruins of ancient Alakomenae, believed by Schliemann and others to be the site of Odysseus's palace; most archaeologists, however, place it at Pilikáta, north of Stavrós, a more strategic setting. (New excavations are certain to inspire new theories and dash old ones.) The beach at **Órmos Aëtós**— not to be confused with Píso Aëtós (Behind Aëtós) on the west coast—about a 15-minute drive north of Vathý, is one of the island's prettiest rocky beach coves.

On Mt. Níritos north of Aëtós is the **Monastery of Katharón,** whose belfry provides views over the Bay of Pátra and the Greek mainland to the east. **Stavrós** (10½ miles north of Vathý) is the hub city of the north, and Pólis Bay below it is thought by many to have been the port of Odysseus's capital. (The Cave of Lízos, just south—no longer accessible—was an ancient sanctuary, thought by some to have been Homer's Cave of the Nymphs.) Stavrós also has a small but interesting archaeological museum, open Tuesday to Sunday from 10am to 3pm; admission is free.

Northeast of Stavrós is the small port of **Fríkes,** where day-trip boats arrive from Fiskárdo, and just 3 miles south (a very scenic 45-minute walk) is the picturesque port of **Kióni,** home to many of the island's seafaring families. Kióni ("Columns") over-looks three abandoned windmills topping the hills that enclose the harbor. Not much happens here, so the favorite activity (other than swimming, fishing, sailing, or sleeping) is to sit at an outdoor cafe and soak up the ambience. The locals support themselves by tourism, boat repair, sailing (mostly in the merchant navy), and rudi-mentary agriculture, and everyday life has a very informal air. Both harbors are quiet and clean; the water is so inviting that people swim off the rocks only a few hundred yards from the boats. In addition, there are even better rock-and-pebble beaches within a 10-minute walk of either port.

Fríkes is less developed, but just a bit busier than Kióni because of the excursion boats connecting Lefkáda with Kefaloniá that stop here. The more architecturally authentic Kióni—building styles are now governed by local preservation laws—has fewer services but more charm.

WHERE TO STAY
IN VATHÝ

Vathý has only two hotels, so most people rent private rooms, which are offered by owners to those arriving by ferry or, except during the height of summer, easily booked through one of the town's many travel agents. **Polyctor Tours,** on the main square (☎ **0674/33-120;** fax 0674/33-130), can help you find a room or house to rent. Rates run about 8,000 Drs ($33.35) for two with shared toilet facilities to about 14,000 Drs ($58.35) with private shower and fridge; American Express, EuroCard, and MasterCard are accepted. Most places are open from late April to mid-October; up until July 1 and after August 31 the rates are usually 40% less.

Hotel Mentor. Vathý, 38 300 Ithaca. ☎ **0674/32-433.** Fax 0674/32-293. 36 rms and suites, all with bath (shower). TEL. 9,200 Drs ($38.35) single; 12,650 Drs ($52.70) double; 19,350 Drs ($80.65) four-bed suite. No credit cards.

The Mentor, on the southeast corner of the harbor, is the better and quieter of the two hotels. It has pleasant, comfortable rooms and a large roof garden, which pro-vides sunset views. There's a small gift shop off the lobby, and a port-view taverna, run by the Livanis family. They also rent apartments above the east side of the port, starting at 14,000 Drs ($58.35) for two, with a kitchenette.

Hotel Odysseus. Vathý, 28 300 Ithaca. ☎ **0674/32-381.** Fax 0674/32-381. 9 rms, all with bath (shower). TEL. 13,500 Drs ($56.25) single or double. No credit cards.

The Odysseus is on the quiet residential side of the harbor, a 10-minute walk north-west (right) from the ferry pier. The high-ceilinged rooms with French doors open-ing out onto harbor-view balconies are our first choice, because there's little traffic at night to disturb your sleep. There's also a large terrace cafeteria and restaurant for moderately priced Greek fare.

IN FRÍKES

Polyctor Tours (☎ **0674/31-771**) or **Kiki Travel** (☎ **0674/31-728** or 0674/31-387) overlook the waterfront at Fríkes. Both agencies change money, book rooms, and rent apartments, and Polyctor sells ferry tickets. In July and August, finding a room can be a problem; contact these agencies well in advance of your trip or plan to stay in Fríkes's only hotel. Two-person apartments with kitchenettes and shower rent for 9,000 to 16,000 Drs ($37.50 to $65.65); four-person two-bedroom houses with verandas start at 27,000 Drs ($112.50).

Hotel Nostos. Fríkes, 28 300 Ithaca. ☎ **0674/31-644.** Fax 0674/31-716. 32 rms, all with bath (shower). TEL. 10,800 Drs ($45) single; 16,500 Drs ($68.75) double. Rates include breakfast. No credit cards.

This friendly, top-quality hotel was brought to our attention by readers Patricia and William E. McCulloh of Gambier, Ohio. The hosts, Niki and Andreas Anagnostatos, are friendly and helpful, and speak English.

IN KIÓNI

There are plenty of rental rooms, but all are booked by travel agents or handled by the Greek Islands Club (an English touring company). **Kióni Vacations** (☎ 0674/ **31-668** June to October, or off-season 01/523-1462 in Athens) can help you find a room for about 14,500 Drs ($60.40), find a two- or three-person studio with kitchenette, rent a moped, or change traveler's checks at its portside office. Ask if the Greek Islands Club has a vacancy in the **Hotel Kióni;** expect to pay around 16,000 Drs ($66.65) for a double.

WHERE TO EAT

Vegetable dishes are particularly flavorful because of the locally pressed olive oil used for cooking. The island's special desert *ravaní,* sponge cake soaked in honey, can be found in Vathý's harborside *zaharoplastía* (pâtisseries), and occasionally in the village tavernas. Note that most places are open only from May to October.

In **Fríkes,** you'll find the **Votoalo** and **Penelope** tavernas, some snack cafes, and a market (great for picnics). The **Hostel Nostos** (see "Where to Stay," above) is also known for its fine Greek food.

In **Kióni,** the **Sunrise Café** and **Koutsouvelis Taverna** are both on the central harbor, with tables spread over a waterfront terrace. Fried snapper and typical Greek fare are available at each; expect to pay about 3,500 Drs ($14.60) per person for a meal with wine.

✪ **Gregory's Taverna.** Paleó Karábo. ☎ **0674/32-573.** Main courses 1,000–2,200 Drs ($4.15–$9.15). No credit cards. Daily 9am–4pm and 6:30pm–1am. GREEK.

Across from Vathý, on the northeast side of the harbor (about a 1¼-mile walk), is the outstanding country-style taverna of Gregory Vlismas. Many diners come by boat from other parts of the island, though we thoroughly enjoyed the 25-minute stroll from town and found it well worthwhile for the fresh fish, fine Ithacan barrel wine, and homemade Greek specialties.

O Batis Cafe Pizzeria. Vathý. ☎ **0674/33-048.** Main courses 1,200–3,400 Drs ($5–$14.15). No credit cards. Daily 6pm–midnight. GREEK/ITALIAN.

For a change of taste, try something Italian at this pleasant little waterfront cafe north of the main square. There are 16 varieties of wood-oven–baked pizza and a dozen pastas; we recommend the arabiatta sauce, which is nicely spiced but not too hot. Fresh fish is available, too.

Trehadiri Taverna. Vathý. ☎ **0674/33-066.** Main courses 950–1,600 Drs ($3.95–$6.65) No credit cards. Daily 6pm–midnight. GREEK.

Turn right off the waterfront at the post office, then left on the next block to find Gerrys Dorizas and his wife, Maria, whipping up fresh vegetable and meat dishes, including a fragrant eggplant imam, baked with spices, and a tasty moussaká. The grilled leg of lamb, if available, and the tender roast veal are delicious.

5 Kefaloniá

71 nautical miles NW of Pátra, 44 nautical miles W of Kyllíni

Kefaloniá (Kefalónia, Kefallínia, Cefalónia, or Cephallonia, among other variations) is one of Greece's best-kept secrets: a large, unspoiled island with spectacular scenery, beautiful beaches, traditional housing, and excellent wine. Since antiquity it's been an island of prosperous sailors and traders.

Each summer this large island attracts thousands of visitors, particularly British and Italian, who settle into apartments or "villas" with their families and rent cars for sightseeing and day trips to the beach. In addition, so many Kefalonians return in the summer that there are often not enough facilities for foreigners. In line with the island's flush economy, hotel and restaurant prices are higher than on most comparable islands, and foreign visitors will have little luck bargaining.

ESSENTIALS

GETTING THERE & DEPARTING   **By Plane**   **Olympic Airways** has daily flights (twice daily in summer) from Athens. Its office in Argostóli is at Odós R. Vergóti 1 (☎ **0671/28-808**), toward the harbor from the archaeological museum. The airport is 5¹/₂ miles south of Argostóli; there is shuttle-bus service between it and the Olympic office in Argostóli.

By Boat   One car-ferry leaves daily from Pátra going to Sámi; for information call ☎ **061/277-622** in Pátra or ☎ **01/823-6012** in Athens. Two car-ferries run weekly from Piraeus to Sámi on the **Strintzi/Minoan Lines,** and continue on to Corfu; for information call ☎ **01/751-2356** in Piraeus. From Kyllíni, on the west coast of the Peloponnese, two or three car-ferries run daily to Argostóli; for information call ☎ **0623/92-211,** or **01/822-8198** in Athens. The **Hellenic Mediterranean Lines** (☎ **061/42-95-20** in Pátra) has daily departures in summer from Pátra to Kefaloniá, then on to Brindisi, Italy.

The F/B *Meganissi* connects Fiskárdo, Kefaloniá, with Fríkes, Ithaca, and with Nydrí, Lefkáda. The F/B *Captan Aristides* connects Fiskárdo and Sámi, Kefaloniá, with Píso Aëtós, Ithaca, and Vassilikí, Lefkáda. **Four Islands Ferries** now coordinates the ferry service between Kefaloniá, Ithaca, Lefkáda, and Meganíssi; call its office in Fiskárdo (☎ **0671/51-478**), Sámi (☎ **0671/22-000**), Fríkes (☎ **0674/33-120**), or Nydrí (☎ **0645/92-427**) for schedules and information. In the summer there's service twice daily between Sámi and Vathý, Ithaca, and daily service between Fiskárdo and Fríkes, Ithaca. The F/B *Thiaki* runs from Astakós on the mainland to Vathý and Ayía Evfimía, Kefaloniá. For the latest information call ☎ **0671/51-478** in Argostóli, ☎ **0674/51-496** in Fiskárdo, or the **Argostóli Port Authority** (☎ **0671/22-224**).

By Bus   There is one bus daily from Athens's Terminal A, Odós Kifissioú 100, via ferry to the port of Póros (8 hours, 6,500 Drs/$27.10).

ORIENTATION   The odd-shaped island of Kefaloniá, the largest of the Ionians, looks rather like a high-heeled shoe with a high tongue reaching up to parallel the shores of Ithaca. Under the instep is the capital and main town, **Argostóli;** directly opposite it on the inside of the heel is the coastal resort town of **Lixoúri.** Behind the heel and up the inside of the tongue (the west coast of the island) are the best beaches, usually at the foot of spectacular, steep chalk-white cliffs. On the instep of the shoe is the island's main port, **Sámi,** a village where most Piraeus and Pátra ferries stop, to avoid having to round the "sole" of the island to Argostóli. The northern port of **Fiskárdo** is to our minds Kefaloniá's most charming town. We recommend jumping on the first bus from Sámi to Argostóli, spending a few nights there, then heading north to Fiskárdo.

GETTING AROUND   **By Bus**   The privately run **KTEL buses** (☎ **0674/ 22-276** or 0674/23-364) serve most of island; however, it's so big and hilly that service is slow and not nearly frequent enough. From Sámi, where most ferries arrive, there are four buses daily (only two on Sunday) to the island's central bus station on the south end of Argostóli.

From Argostóli there are two buses daily (once daily on Sunday and off-season) north to Fiskárdo, but its route provides the most exquisite scenery. There are three buses daily to the southeast port of Póros. In the summer there are buses every half hour from 9:30am to 6:45pm to the nearby beaches at Lássi, Makrís Yialós, and Platís Yialós. There's only one bus daily between Sámi and Fiskárdo.

By Taxi The island's main taxi station is off Valiánou, the central square in the heart of Argostóli. A four-passenger Mercedes taxi will cost about 27,000 Drs ($112.50) for an around-the-island 8-hour tour. On the way the driver may choose to pick up anyone who flags him down, and then charge them whatever fare seems equitable. (This in no way reduces *your* fare!) Use of the meter is legally compulsory, though rarely practised. Flat rates are agreed upon by most drivers; for example, from the airport to Argostóli, 1,600 Drs ($6.65); Argostóli to Sámi, 4,500 Drs ($18.75); Argostóli to Fiskárdo, 9,000 Drs ($37.50), or 12,500 Drs ($52.10) round-trip, including 1-hour waiting time.

By Car **AutoEurope** has an office in Lassí, near the airport (☎ **0671/24-078**), and **Pefanis Rent-a-Car** has an office off the main square at Valiánou 4 (☎ **0671/22-338**). Their rates are approximately 18,000 Drs ($75) per day for a compact car. There are 20 rental-car companies in town, so shop around and book one early, as most rental cars are taken by visiting ex-islanders.

By Moped Mopeds are too slow to cover much ground, but if you're based in a village and want to explore locally, they can be a lot of fun because the roads on wealthy Kefaloniá are very good. In high-priced Argostóli, 3-day moped rentals are 12,000 to 18,000 Drs ($50 to $75) for a two-seater Vespa; about 50% less by the day.

By Ferry The car-ferry to Lixoúri—a fun, 30-minute voyage between two points of land jutting into the Argostolion Gulf—leaves from the northern ferry dock of Argostóli, in front of the Cephallonia Star Hotel. This car-ferry runs 22 times daily (a schedule is posted near the pier); the fare is 220 Drs (90¢). Landlubbers can take a round-about roadway by car or public bus.

AREA CODE The telephone area code for Argostóli, Lixoúri, and Skála is **0671;** for Sámi and Fiskárdo it's **0674**.

ARGOSTÓLI

The island's capital is an amusing, lively, modern town totally rebuilt after the devastation of the earthquakes of 1953. The village proper is on its own spit of land tied to the mainland by the **Trapanós Bridge.** This broad causeway was originally built in 1910 by the British C. P. de Bosset in 15 days; 2 years later it was replaced by masonry. The center portion of the bridge was adorned with an obelisk dedicated by Kefalonian residents in gratitude to the "Glory of the British Nation." Greater Argostóli spreads to the main part of the island and connects to the north-south highway.

ESSENTIALS

ORIENTATION The **Trapanós Bridge** is at the south end of town, off **Metaxá Street,** the harborside road. The bustling **agorá** (market) is in this area, running two and three streets in from the water. During the day it's a beehive of activity as trucks unload produce and fishermen bring their catch in. This is the best place to get a behind-the-scenes look at Greek life, as well as the best place to get Gentilini or

Calliga wines (the island's best-known export and a perfect gift to bring home) and groceries for campers and picnickers. The handsome new **bus station** is to the south, about half a mile south of the main square.

Walking north along the harbor will bring you to the **Port Authority** building; the main square, **Valiánou Square,** is 2 blocks inland from the water, lined with hotels, tavernas, cafes, and shops. The **Lithóstroto,** a cobblestone pedestrians-only shopping lane (also still known as Diádahos Konstandínou "Crown Prince Constantine"), leads south from the main square parallel to the waterfront. Most travel services and related businesses are found in the narrow lanes to the south and east of the main square; the museums and library are to the south and west, and above them are houses banked on a steep hillside. If you climb over this hill and descend the other side—a paved roadway winds down—you'll arrive at the excellent but crowded town beaches of **Makrí Yialós** (Long Beach) and **Platís Yialós** (Wide Beach).

VISITOR INFORMATION The very helpful **Greek Tourist Organization (EOT)** office is next to the Port Authority building on the harbor (☎ 0671/22-248; fax 0671/24-466), open daily from 8am to 10pm (off-season, Monday to Friday from 8am to 3pm). Dennis Messaris and his multilingual assistant, Vassiliki, are enthusiastic experts about the island. The **tourist police** (☎ 0671/22-200) are at the police station, across from the Port Authority on the harbor.

Ferry tickets can be purchased from Argostóli travel agents or at the port in Sámi. Maria at the **Bartholomos Agency** (☎ 0671/28-853; fax 0671/22-809), just east of Valiánou Square, is especially helpful. **Filóxenos Travel,** Odós G. Vergóti 2, on the southwest corner of Valiánou Square (☎ 0671/23-055, or 01/571-2820 in Athens; fax 0671/28-114), rents rooms, books air and ferry tickets, and runs many island excursions. The owner, Paul El-Zerey, is very helpful; he offers a 1-day round-the-island tour for 5,500 Drs ($22.90), and day trips to Lefkáda and Ithaca.

FAST FACTS There are several **banks** around Valiánou Square open regular hours, plus several commercial **currency exchanges** open daily from 9am to 6pm, as well as a growing number of **ATMs.** The **post office** is on the Lithóstroto, 9 blocks south of Valiánou Square, open Monday to Friday from 7:30am to 2pm (later in August). The **telephone office (OTE)** is 3 blocks south off the southwest corner of Valiánou Square, behind the archaeology museum, open daily from 7:30am to 11pm. The **Argostóli Hospital** is on Souidías Street (☎ 0671/24-641), 6 or 7 blocks inland from the causeway and 1 block to the left.

EXPLORING THE TOWN

Take a stroll along the Lithóstrotos to get an idea of the island's wealth and sophistication. Keep an eye out for Kefalonía's rich "Golden" brand honey, tart quince preserves, and almond pralines in the various shops.

For the best selection of Greek handicrafts, find **Alexander's Shop,** on the east end of the museum square opposite the Olympic Airways office (☎ 0671/23-057), where Thalia Marangaki has interesting jewelry (some her own work), embroidery, crochet, handmade glass and ceramics (including traditional dolls of the island), excellent icons, and clothing; she's open daily from 9am to 2pm and 6 to 9pm; MasterCard and Visa are accepted.

Koryialenios Historical and Cultural Museum. ☎ 0671/28-221. Admission 500 Drs ($2.10), free on Fri. Mon–Sat 9am–2pm. Walk south from Valiánou Sq. to the small square with the archaeology museum and Kéfalos Theater; turn left in front of the theater and take the first right up.

This incredible museum is a must for anyone interested in the island's history and culture. It's housed on the ground floor of the stately Koryialenios Library and includes a large, superb collection of artisans' tools, costumes, European antiquities, old photographs (including many from 1904 depicting Argostóli as it was before the earthquakes), maps, and 19th-century articles used throughout the island. Excellent lace pieces are for sale in the lobby. An hour spent in this museum is a better introduction to modern Kefalonian history than you're likely to find in any book.

Archaeological Museum. One block south of Valiánou Sq. ☎ **0671/28-300.** Admission 500 Drs ($2.10) adults, 400 Drs ($1.65) seniors, 300 Drs ($1.25) students. Tues–Sun 8:30am–3pm.

Its small but interesting collection includes Mycenaean finds (pottery, jewelry, and bronze tools), classical pottery, Roman sculpture and mosaics, and an impressive array of coins—well displayed but not well labeled.

LOCAL WINERIES

The **Calliga Vineyards** is open for tours; contact the EOT for the current schedule. When present shopping, buy the fine white Robola in a burlap sack with Greek writing and the Calligata wax seal that sells for about 1,800 Drs ($7.50); Calliga Cava is a popular aged red wine for the same price.

Tucked away in a remote spot in nearby Miniés, north of the airport, is the **Gentilini Vineyard** (☎ **0671/41-618**). The superb quality of this modestly scaled winery is testament to one man's determination to produce a Greek export wine. Spiros and Anna Cosmetatos are the very capable vintners, and gracious and informative hosts. Although they don't run organized tours or wine tastings, if you call ahead, and if it's convenient for them, the Cosmetatoses will conduct an informal tour of their vineyard. Oenophiles should note that Kefalonía's Gentilini, which sells for about 3,500 Drs ($14.60), is considered one of the very best wines in all of Greece.

WHERE TO STAY

Most accommodations are open from mid-April to late October.

Filóxenos Travel (☎ **0671/23-055;** fax 0671/28-114) is a good source for available rooms to rent around the island. In Argostóli, these discreetly marked complexes (geared to Kefaloniots returning home) are usually of better value than hotels. We've stayed in the modern, sky-blue stucco apartment complex of Chicago expatriates **Jerry and Lákis Zérvos** at Odós Metaxá 3 (☎ **0671/28-919**), 1 block east of Valiánou Square. Eight spacious doubles with private bath (many with balconies) cost about 9,000 Drs ($37.50).

Camping Argostóli Beach (☎ **0671/23-487**), the closest facility, is north of town in Fanári, on the beach.

Castello Hotel. 11 Valiánou Sq., Argostóli, 281 00 Kefaloniá. ☎ **0671/23-250.** Fax 0671/ 23-252. 20 rms, all with bath (shower). TEL. 8,575 Drs ($35.75) single; 13,700 Drs ($57.10) double. Rates include breakfast. AE, EURO, MC, V.

The recently redecorated interior of this hotel at the northwest corner of the main square is part pastel chiffon, part go-go moderne: large beige glass globes hang like Christmas-tree balls from the lobby ceiling. The renovated doubles are bright and cheery, though the rooms overlooking the square can be noisy.

Cephallonia Star. Odós Metaxá 50, Argostóli, 281 00 Kefaloniá. ☎ **0671/23-181.** Fax 0671/ 23-180. 42 rms, all with bath (27 with shower, 15 with tub). A/C TV TEL. 11,500 Drs ($47.90) single; 18,500 Drs ($77.10) double. Rates include breakfast. MC, V.

This older hotel on the waterfront opposite the Lixoúri ferry pier is very well kept. The rooms are pleasant and comfortable, all with fridges and many with balconies with fine views over the water. In August we found a mobile amusement park set up across the street. It's a good value and becomes an even better one for those who stay longer.

Hotel Aenos. 11 Valiánou Sq., Argostóli, 281 00 Kefaloniá. ☎ **0671/28-013.** Fax 0671/22-740. 40 rms, all with bath (shower). A/C TEL. 11,500 Drs ($47.90) single; 16,000 Drs ($66.65) double. Rates include breakfast. AE, DC, EURO, MC, V.

This refurbished hotel at the northeast corner of the main square has cottage cheese–textured ceilings, dark natural-wood furnishings, a picturesque and usable roof garden, and an active outdoor cafe. The Aenos seems to attract returning Greeks, who are really the soul of its lively, active social life.

Hotel Allegro. Odós Andréas Hoïdá 2, Argostóli, 281 00 Kefaloniá. ☎ **0671/22-268.** 16 rms, 10 with bath (shower). TEL. 6,900 Drs ($28.75) double without bath, 11,500 Drs ($47.90) double with bath. No credit cards.

This small older hotel offers convenient but Spartan lodgings half a block off the waterfront about halfway between the causeway and the Port Authority, near the post office. The rooms are small but comfortable; many have balconies and all have sinks. Singles go for 10% less.

✪ **Hotel Ionian Plaza.** Valliánou Sq., Argostóli, 281 00 Kefaloniá. ☎ **0671/25-581.** Fax 0671/25-585. 43 rms, all with bath (shower). A/C TV TEL. 12,300 Drs ($51.25) single; 19,500 Drs ($81.25) double. MC, V.

Vassilis Vassilatos returned to Argostóli after 15 years in New York and Australia to build this impressive hotel on the north side of the main square and the adjoining **Restaurant Palazzino** in the neoclassical Kefalonian style. It's lovely and elegant, with an excellent staff. The rooms are spacious, attractive, and more than comfortable, well worth the extra drachmas.

WHERE TO EAT

There are several good tavernas near the center of town and a number of pastry shops on Valiánou Square, our favorite spot for people-watching; we especially like the **Paloma Pâtisserie,** on the east side, for its variety of desserts, both European and Greek. **Quick's,** on the north side, is not only that, but also inexpensive; you can get burgers, fries, souvláki, moussaká, and ice cream in a bright Formica and fluorescent establishment. For fresh fruit, visit the market area on the waterfront near the causeway; on Saturday local farmers and gardeners bring in their own fresh produce. There's also a seafood market here before 10am daily.

Don't miss the local specialty, *kreatópita,* a Kefalonian meat pie—pork and beef or lamb with rice and a touch of spinach in filo pastry; we found it delicious.

The Cottage (I Kalýva). Off the southwest corner of Valiánou Sq. ☎ **0671/24-849.** Main courses 900–2,500 Drs ($3.75–$10.40). No credit cards. Daily noon–4:30pm and 7:30pm–midnight. GREEK.

Just off the main square you can dine in the intimate taverna-style dining room or next door in the more open area behind a wall of ivy, under a rattan ceiling, with rustic touches of copper pots and wagon wheels. Service is friendly and the food is well prepared. The grilled chicken is tender and juicy, and the *horiátiki* salad is excellent, with a generous portion of local *féta.* Those of vegetarian inclination should try the *briám,* zucchini and potato "in oven."

⭕ **Patsoura's.** Odós Metaxá 32. ☎ **0671/22-779.** Main courses 1,000–2,800 Drs ($4.15–$11.65). No credit cards. Daily noon–4:30pm and 7pm–midnight. GREEK.

Our favorite cook, Christianthou Patsoura, should be in his new place on the waterfront north of the Cephallonia Star Hotel by your visit. One of his best dishes is an island specialy, *krasáto,* pork cooked in wine. His aubergine pie is also exceptionally tasty.

ARGOSTÓLI AFTER DARK

Some people will be content with the lively activity on the main square, Valiánou; try the popular cafe/bar in the **Aenos Hotel** on the northeast corner, or the **Mythos Bar,** on the south side. There's a small nightlife area a block off the southeast corner of the square, where you'll find the **Old House Pub,** one of the few places to survive the earthquake and a favorite watering hole of the cognoscenti, where the music rocks until 2am, and **Cassis Music.** Just south on St. Metaxá (a block in from the waterfront) are the **Romeo Music Bar** and **Paradise Pub.** The **Phoenix Dancing Bar** is off the southwest corner of the square. If you want to join the fashionable young Greek set, saunter up Leofóros Rizópaston, still also called Vassiléos Yioryíou (King George) and check out **Da Cappo** and **Koúklos.** The seaside **Limanaki,** farther north, is a popular disco.

FISKÁRDO

Fiskárdo, 28^{1}/$_{2}$ miles north of Argostóli, survived the earthquake of 1953 almost totally unharmed. When you come down the hill and turn the corner into its tiny square, you see a tranquil harbor with the hills of Ithaca rising beyond it. The charming village spreads mainly to the right around the C-shaped cove; a lighthouse dots the left side. Flotillas of yachts moor around the bay. It's no wonder people come to dote on this tiny village; it's an architectural gem unlike most left in Greece. And they do come—the winter population of fewer than 100 swells tenfold with Brits and Italians in July and August.

Although there's increasing tourist congestion—particularly during midday, when the day-trip cruises from Lefkáda and Ithaca arrive—a quiet pace prevails among the fig, cherry, peach, and apricot trees. A Doric-columned schoolhouse sits proudly amid stucco villas with colonnaded porticos and overgrown grape arbors. The port is made for idlers, whether you choose to sit in a taverna with ouzo and schmooze with the locals—almost everyone speaks English—or sample the exceptionally clear water. The ambience is so fetching that we were content to loll on the flat rocks at the far end of the cove.

Fiskardo Travel (☎ **0674/41-315;** fax 0674/41-352), near the steps up to the church, open daily from 9am to 10pm, changes money, sells excursion and ferry tickets, arranges yacht and car rentals, and books accommodations. **Fiskardo Rent a Car and Moto** (☎ **0674/41-401**), toward the north (left) end of the harbor, is the largest car-rental agency; a Suzuki compact will cost you about 15,000 Drs ($62.50), 20% less off-season. The friendly folks at the **Maestro Cafe,** south (right) on the harbor, will hold your luggage for you—and they serve good food at modest prices.

WHERE TO STAY

Try to stay in Fiskárdo overnight to sample the essence of Greek life before it disappears, preferably in one of the classic villas or the former Traditional Settlements (government-renovated 150-year-old villas). Each house has been divided into simply furnished twin- or triple-bedded rooms with attached showers. Only two of the government-renovated homes, recently returned to their original owners, are still used for private rental. Contact these family owners directly: **Mrs. Athanasia Dendrinou** (☎ 0674/41-326) or **Mrs. Vasso Palikisianou** (☎ 0674/41-303) by phone, or by writing them at Fiskárdo, 290 84 Kefaloniá, Greece, for information on availability and prices. Most of the restored rooms (with shared baths) go for about 12,000 Drs ($50), regardless of season (not open in winter). The **Dendrinos family** (☎ 0674/41-205; fax 0674/41-247) also offers a variety of other accommodations, including doubles with bath for 8,000 to 14,000 Drs ($33.35 to $58.35) and apartments with beautifully landscaped gardens for 17,000 to 26,000 Drs ($70.85 to $108.35).

The EOT, the Greek Tourist Organization, estimates that there are at least 250 private rooms available for about 9,500 Drs ($39.60) for a bathless double, or 11,800 Drs ($49.15) for a double with bath. We liked the seven simple rooms rented by **Stella Barzouka** (☎ 0674/41-310) in a newly built, old-style house in the village. There are common showers, a large kitchen, and a landscaped garden for guests to share. **Makis Market** also represents several four- to six-person apartments with kitchenettes that rent for about 30,000 Drs ($125) per night (25% less between November 30 and April 1).

Erisos Pension. Fiskárdo, 280 84 Kefaloniá. ☎ 01/934-2992 in Athens. 6 rms, all with bath (shower). 13,900 Drs ($57.90) single or double. No credit cards.

Spyridoula Manousardiou has transformed her traditional home just off the port by adding private bathrooms with showers to each tidy, tile-floored room. Aegean-blue shutters enclose these bright, high-ceilinged spaces. The flowering bougainvillea shrouding the stone exterior makes this one of the village's prettiest homes.

✪ **Fiskardona.** Fiskárdo, 280 84 Kefaloniá. ☎ 0674/41-316. 7 rms, all with bath (shower). 15,700 Drs ($65.40) single or double; 17,900 Drs ($74.60) triple. No credit cards.

This yellow-shuttered stone-and-stucco house sits right behind the port on a tiny square. The gracious Mr. Tzamarelos and his family have rebuilt and modernized this mid–19th century villa, while maintaining many original architectural details. The front-facing rooms have small balconies overlooking the town (potentially noisy in high season), and there's a common kitchen, dining area, and TV lounge on the ground floor.

Fiscardo Philoxenia. Fiskárdo, 280 84 Kefaloniá. ☎ 0674/41-319, or 01/561-2037 in Athens. 6 rms, all with bath (shower). 16,400 Drs ($68.35) double or triple. No credit cards.

Makis Kavadias's restored villa is in the heart of the village to the left from the stairs. Inside the bright-green wooden gate are several large, modernized rooms that share a fully equipped common kitchen. Ask for an upstairs room with a porch overlooking the harbor.

WHERE TO EAT

Choosing a restaurant in Fiskárdo won't be hard. Most are on or near the waterfront, and you'll quickly get a feel for the style of each.

Maestro serves a good breakfast and pizza. For ice cream (19 flavors), sweets, or yogurt try **Grace's**, on the *paralía*. Although every establishment fills up with tourists for a drink, ouzo, or coffee at night, **Le Barbare** is the slickest nightspot; it's just off the port in the tiny town square. **Harry's Bar,** no relation to the famed Venetian haunt, and **The Captain's Cabin,** a good pizza, sandwich, and pastry spot, are both popular choices on the port.

Restaurant Faros. Paralía. ☎ 0674/41-277. Main courses 1,400–2,100 Drs ($5.85–$8.75). V. Daily 11am–11pm. GREEK.

This is a friendly portside place with less of a crush than at other tavernas, but with similarly rushed service at supper. Go for a leisurely lunch; we loved their *kreatópita,* Kefalonian meat pie, with a salad. Fresh fish is well priced and excellently prepared.

Tassia Restaurant. Paralía. ☎ **0674/41-205.** Main courses 900–2,600 Drs ($3.75–$10.85). V. Daily 11am–midnight. GREEK.

This is the fanciest and priciest of the local choices, befitting its location overlooking the yacht harbor, near the north (left) end of the port. We found it packed again during our recent visit, but the service was very efficient and the food was quite good. The Greek standards and fresh fish are very well prepared.

Next door, the **Gaïta,** a traditional grill, is owned by the same capable family.

ELSEWHERE AROUND THE ISLAND

If Argostóli is under the "arch" of the high heel–shaped island, then **Livathó** is the region around the "sole." This prosperous area of fertile rolling hills, heavily striped with narrow, scenic, winding roads, is the home of some of the island's wealthier merchants and sea captains. **Metaxáta** (where Lord Byron stayed for 4 months in 1823) is one village with several modern luxury villas.

Kourkoumeláda, to the south, is the product of one man's faith and generosity. After the earthquake of 1953, George Vergotis, a wealthy entrepreneur, rebuilt the entire village and all its former homes by himself. **Ormos Lourdáta** is one of the island's longest, loveliest, and most crowded beaches. A nature trail leads off the town's main square, offering a 2- to 3-hour walk through olive and orange groves, scrubby hillsides, and pine and oak forests; it's at its best in the spring when the wildflowers are blooming.

Markópoulos, near the southern end of the island, claims to have been founded by ancestors of Marco Polo. During the week before the Feast of the Assumption (August 15) its residents are said to catch harmless snakes with black crosses on their heads, which then disappear until the following year.

At the island's "toe" is the village of **Skála,** called Néa Skála by those who saw it after the earthquake. It's now a budding resort of rooms for rent favored by the British.

The east coast's principal port, **Sámi,** is a calm, sheltered harbor in a niche of the white cliffs that score the east coast's verdant palisades. The ruins of a Roman bath (with its mosaic floor intact) led archaeologists to conclude that this was indeed the port of ancient Sámi. It has little to offer today, but if you're stuck overnight you can find a nice room at the **Castle of Sámi** (☎ 0674/22-656).

There's a good road north from Sámi along the east coast. About 1 1/2 miles (a half-hour walk) north of town you'll find the **Melissáni Grotto** (☎ 0674/ 22-997), a large purple (as its name says) and blue cave that encloses a huge underground lake, where you can take a boat ride for 800 Drs ($3.35). For many years it appeared that water flowed backward into the land at Katavóthres, near Argostóli. Now scientists say that in fact this water is flowing due east, through an underwater tunnel into the underground lake at Melissáni.

Another interesting cave, **Drogaráti,** with yellow and orange stalactites and stalagmites, can be found about 2 1/2 miles southwest inland from Sámi, to the right just off the road to Argostóli. It's open all day during the summer; admission is 800 Drs ($3.35). One of its large chambers has such good acoustics that concerts are sometimes held there in the summer. Maria Callas once sang there.

The village of **Áyía Evfimía,** 6 miles north of Sámi, is the port of call for the daily ferry from Astakós on the mainland via Fríkes, Ithaca. From here north, the coast rises to tall rocky heights and the roadway moves inland to some charming, small villages and finally to Fiskárdo.

The west coast of Kefaloniá has the best beaches on the island and some of its most breathtaking scenery. The main road south from Fiskárdo winds down through sweet little villages to **Ássos** (about 8 miles south), where the tongue of Kefalonía's shoe butts out into another small peninsula. Topping it is a Venetian castle from 1595; the buff-colored stones ramble across this acropolis, once used to safeguard Kefaloniá's western flank. Within its protective arc is the picturesque port of Ássos, one of the loveliest in Greece, with an abundance of figs, peaches, flowering oleander, and geraniums. Boxy, pastel-colored houses unified by red-tile roofs are the summer cottages of Greeks and Italians who stroll through the portside in bikinis and diaphanous dresses. The village square is called Platía Parison, dedicated to the city of Paris for its "generous contribution to the reconstruction of Ássos after the earthquakes of 1953."

The drive between Assos and **Ormós Mýrtos** (about 6 miles) is one of the prettiest on the island. For your efforts, you're rewarded with a long, wide stretch of fine pearl-colored pebbles and the most Paul Newman–blue waters, with only a scattering of fellow sun worshipers. We voted for ✪ **Mýrtos Beach** as one of Greece's top 10 beaches.

South of this, on the green, rugged coast is the **Monastery of Kipouréon,** built in 1744. It's still inhabited by the original sect of monks, who zealously guard its fine collection of antique icons. Rounding the cape to Lixoúri you'll find many more good beaches, best reached by boat. The newly built resort at **Lixoúri** is easily reached by ferry from the Argostóli pier (see "Getting Around" under "Essentials," above). It's a pleasant half-hour minicruise for a day trip to this area's fine, dark-sand beaches. Day-trippers may want to rent a scooter from one of the numerous shops along the *paralía* in Lixoúri, particularly if you consider heading northwest to the peninsula's best beach at **Petáni,** on Ortholithías Bay, or south to **Mégas Lákos** and **Kounópetra,** both with good, small-pebble beaches.

6 Zákynthos

53 nautical miles NW of Patras, 18 nautical miles W of Kyllíni

Zákynthos (also known as Zánte) is the southernmost of the islands in the Ionian Sea, and the closest to the Peloponnese. The Venetians called it Fior' di Levante ("Flower of the Orient"); it's an island of remarkable natural beauty, with a number of excellent beaches. Its southern location in the warm Ionian Sea provides an especially pleasant climate in the winter; the many sheltered coves on the north end of the island provide cooler water and temperate breezes in the summer.

The island is not as heavily developed as Corfu and doesn't yet cater solely to tour groups; however, Italian, British, and Scandinavian holiday makers are in full force, so reservations are necessary in the summer. Prices have climbed dramatically, reaching parity with the other Ionian resorts. There are several thousand available beds in private homes around the island, and we've found that staying with a local is the best way to vacation inexpensively on this first-class, Greece-for-Greeks resort. The lively port of **Zákynthos (Zánte)** is our recommended base for first-time visitors.

The island, first noted in history by Homer as Yliessa, was settled by Zákynthos, son of Dardanos, king of Troy. In Hellenic times this tiny democracy was wooed by both Athens and Sparta because of its fertile soil and strategic location. In 1204 Zákynthos fell to the Byzantine conquerors and was ruled by a succession of Frankish princes; during this time the *kástro,* whose ruins reflect the extent of the entire city at that time, was built. In 1484 the Venetians took Zákynthos and ruled it for over 300 years. They began what became one of the nicest legacies of this fertile island: the lucrative cultivation of grapes, made into wine and, of course, Zante currants. In 1500 the Venetians expanded the city of Zákynthos outside the fortress walls.

The narrow streets, open squares, and arcades that form weatherproof promenades along the harbor were designed by the Italians, but date only from the 1950s. That's because 1953 brought catastrophe—more than 90% of the island's buildings were leveled by a tremendous earthquake that damaged parts of many of the Ionian islands, but which started in Zákynthos.

ESSENTIALS

GETTING THERE & DEPARTING   By Plane   There is one flight daily (two daily in summer) on **Olympic Airways** from Athens. For information, contact its office at Odós Alexándrou Róma 16 on Ayíou Márkou Square (☎ **0695/28-611**), or in Athens (☎ **01/926-7251**). The airport is 3³/₄ miles southwest of Zákynthos town. There's no shuttle bus; a taxi will cost you about 1,200 Drs ($5).

By Boat   Several **car-ferries** make the 1¹/₂-hour trip daily from Kyllíni, on the Peloponnese mainland. Call the **port authority** of Kyllíni (☎ **0623/92-211**) or Zákynthos (☎ **0695/22-417**) for schedule information.

By Bus   There is bus service four times daily to and from Athens's Terminal A, Odós Kifissoú 100, via Pátra (7 hours, 4,125 Drs/$17.20).

VISITOR INFORMATION   There is no municipal or government tourist office and we have never found the local tourist police very helpful, but you could ask for help at the **Tuo Travel Agency,** Odós Filíta 42 (☎ **0695/22-255**), 1 block west of the harbor opposite the bus station; or at **Potamitis Tours,** 3 San Marcos Sq. (☎ **0695/23-118**).

Several travel agents (most are open daily from 9am to 9pm in summer) will cash traveler's checks outside banking hours. The **tourist police** (☎ **0695/22-550**), on the *paralía* 2 blocks from the second gas station toward Platía Solomoú, are open Monday to Friday from 8am to 2:30pm.

GETTING AROUND   The **bus station** is 5 blocks south of the central square and 1 block in from the water. There's frequent service north to Tsilívi and Alykés, south to Argási, and west to Laganás, but only once or twice daily to other villages and beaches on the island. **Mopeds** are an adequate means of transport and can be rented at several places. **Stamatis,** Odós Filíta 9 (☎ **0695/23-673**), is one friendly place, and **Moto Sakis,** Leofóros Dimokrátias 3 (☎ **0695/23-928**), is another. Both rent mopeds for about 2,750 Drs ($11.45) per day. You can rent **bicycles,** too, but the many hills require pretty strong calf muscles! The faster mopeds allow you to fully enjoy the cool pine forests and scent of roses that line every roadway. If you've got a few days to explore, buy one of the widely available maps for 600 Drs ($2.50), and you can jog, hike, or wander along the roadways to appreciate the island's beauty.

FAST FACTS   The **hospital** (☎ **0695/22-514**) is west of the port. The **police station** is off Lombárdou at Odós Tzoul, áti 5. The **post office** is at Odós Tertséti 27 at Gouskos, west of the Government House, open Monday to Friday from 7:30am to 2pm; it will cash traveler's checks outside the usual banking hours. The **telephone center (OTE),** just east of Platía Solomoú, beyond the museum, is open daily from 7am to midnight.

EXPLORING THE ISLAND
ZÁKYNTHOS TOWN

Zákynthos town is the capital, sporting excellent restaurants, elegant (and expensive!) boutiques, and rousing nightlife; the beach is within a few miles' walk. There are several small, reasonably priced Greek-style pensions tucked into the backstreets, away from the harbor and among the bakeries, markets, and service businesses that the locals use. Several churches crop up in the small alleys and many tree-lined squares, so that a walk through Zákynthos alternates between the screech of mopeds, cars, and hustle-bustle activity and the quiet, shaded relief of monumental churches and plazas.

Note: Zákynthos has undergone some changes in street names, which may be confusing.

The harborside lane, **Lombárdou,** runs between the two spindly arms of the man-made breakwater that form the docking area. You'll disembark facing **Platía Solomoú,** the main square, where the statue of Solomós dominates the busy port patrol.

The fourth right turn off **Venizélou,** the main street running inland from Solomoú Square, is **Vassiléos Konstantínou** (King Constantine) Street (also signposted as May 21), the town's main drag for shops, restaurants, cafe-bars, and markets. This street leads into the 16th-century **Platía Áyíou Márkou** (St. Mark's Square), a rare exception to the postquake rebuilding. Here you'll find some "fast-food cafes" (the most chic) and on the west side, the Solomós Museum.

Farther up the museum street are several **banks;** opposite them is the island's **taxi stand.**

If it's a rainy day in Zákynthos town, head for the **Solomós Museum,** at Odós Vassiléos Konstandínou 6, next to the Áyios Márkos Cathedral, open daily from 9am to 2pm, for a look at the author's lifelong collection of literary memorabilia.

The **Byzantine Museum,** a small, well-presented collection (labeled in Greek and French) of Byzantine-era through 19th-century church paintings from the Ionian School of Art, is open Tuesday to Sunday from 8:30am to 2:30pm.

The **Cathedral of Áyios Dionýssios** (St. Denis), across from the harbor on the south end of town, is one of the island's finest because of the wrought-silver casket in which relics of Zákynthos's patron saint repose. Twice a year, on August 24 and December 17, there are processions throughout the town for St. Dionýssios, who must pass over streets strewn with myrtle branches.

There are many pricey boutiques at the port, but there's also a **handcrafts cooperative** at Odós Lombárdou 42, on the *paralía* (harborfront), where locally made items are sold. We admired tablecloths, place mats, and curtains, as well as hand-knit sweaters and woven rugs.

ELSEWHERE AROUND THE ISLAND

Readers with a SCUBA license might enjoy a dive into the Ionian. **Zante Diving / Driftwood Club,** on Laganás Beach (☎ 0695/51-196), offers a range of cruises and dive trips off the west coast, where they claim there are more than a thousand underwater caves to explore.

The **Tuo Travel Agency** (☎ 0695/22-255) offers round-the-island day trips, plus tours to Kefaloniá, Olympia, Delphi, Mycenae, and Athens. Vasilis, the man to see on Zákynthos, also books diving and horseback-riding trips.

While on Zákynthos, you just may find a beach resort that can lure you away from the port town. We thought that **Alykés** was truly the prettiest white-sand beach on the island. Alykés is 6 miles north of Zákynthos town, along an inland road that winds up around the verdant hills through vineyards and olive groves.

There are a few hotels on the beach. The Tsoukalas brothers—guess where they've lived abroad?—run the **Montreal Hotel,** Alykés, 290 90 Zákynthos (☎ 0695/ 83-241). All 31 bright, cheerful rooms, angled to face the sea, overlook the *léfka* (poplars) that shade the hotel's seaside cafe, where you can rent a canoe for under $4 an hour. Bed-and-breakfast singles cost 11,250 Drs ($46.90); doubles run 14,500 Drs ($60.40).

Tsilívi Beach is another beach area that developed just $2^1/_2$ miles north of the port, near the village of Plános. In August the most preferred location on the island is undoubtedly **Kalamáki Beach,** where the Crystal Beach Hotel offers a bird's-eye view of the famous **loggerhead turtles,** which come late each evening during the month to lay their eggs on the shore. The **Crystal Beach** (☎ 0695/22-774), with 58 doubles with bath (shower) for 16,500 Drs ($68.75), is one of two hotels that managed to get a license during the years when everyone thought turtle footprints were just tractor marks. The World Wildlife Fund has established a "biogenic reserve" at Kalamáki to protect the turtles, which were only discovered 9 years ago by locals. Besides attracting curious tourists, the turtles actually serve a secondary purpose: they eat jellyfish, making the waters safer for swimming.

South of Zákynthos town the island becomes heavily wooded with pine and olive forests. At **Cape Yérakas** there are few buildings except a few older hotels and some tavernas. There are turtledoves and hidden coves filled with crafty fishermen. Going back toward the city, there are many ROOM TO LET signs among the olive groves decked out with laundry lines and fields filled with grazing cows. There are also several all-amenity, Class C hotels in the resort areas of **Vassilikós** and **Argássi.** In Argássi, the traditionally styled and furnished 60-room **Hotel Levante** (☎ 0695/ 22-833) is the most attractive; doubles with private facilities cost 15,500 Drs ($64.60).

WHERE TO STAY

European tour groups have recently established a strong presence here, booking up many hotels for years in advance, so it may be difficult for the individual budget traveler to find a room. Listed below are several hotels (open May to October unless otherwise noted) where you may be able to get a room in high season; if everything is booked, ask the tourist police for assistance. They might be able to find you accommodations in a private home. Expect to pay about 6,000 Drs ($25) for a double room with private bath, 4,500 Drs ($18.75) for shared facilities.

The following recommendations are all in Zákynthos town; for suggestions at the various beaches around the island, see "Exploring the Island," above.

Apollon. Odós Tertséti 30, Zákynthos, 275 75 Zákynthos. ☎ 0695/42-838. 15 rms, all with bath (shower). TEL. 10,000 Drs ($41.65) single; 12,500 Drs ($52.10) double. Rates include breakfast. EURO, MC, V.

The Apollon is conveniently located a few blocks up from the harbor near the post office. Though central, it's blessedly quiet, with clean, undistinguished rooms and a pleasant breakfast lounge.

Hotel Bitzaro. Odós Dionysíou Roma 46, Zákynthos, 275 75 Zákynthos. ☎ 0695/23-644. Fax 0695/23-493. 40 rms, all with bath (shower). TEL. 12,200 Drs ($50.85) single; 17,200 Drs ($71.65) double. Rates include breakfast. No credit cards.

This attractive family-run hotel is just a few blocks south of Platía Solomoú, far enough away from the port and town traffic. The rooms are comfortable, ultra-clean, and extremely well maintained (try to avoid those closer to the bar, which can get noisy). The family has recently opened a new hotel at Kalamáki Beach (☎ 0695/ 25-773).

Hotel Phoenix. Platía Solomoú, Zákynthos, 275 75 Zákynthos. ☎ 0695/42-719. Fax 0695/ 45-083. 34 rms, all with bath (shower). TEL. 8,700 Drs ($36.25) single; 12,300 Drs ($51.25) double. No credit cards.

This older hotel on the main square has merged with the neighboring Hotel Astoria. The facilities are clean, spacious, and well furnished, and some rooms have balconies overlooking the square.

Omonia Hotel. Odós Xanthopoúlou 3, Zákynthos, 275 75 Zákynthos. ☎ 0695/22-113. 12 rms, all with bath (shower). TEL. 11,200 Drs ($46.65) double. No credit cards.

The Omonia is a small, homey place in a peaceful residential neighborhood a few blocks inland from the *paralía*. The rooms are small and dark, but kept clean. It's open year-round.

Palatino Hotel. Odós Kolokotróni 10 (at Kolýva St.), Zákynthos, 291 00 Zákynthos. ☎ 0695/ 45-400. Fax 0695/45-400. 30 rms, all with bath (tub and shower). A/C TEL. 16,500 Drs ($68.75) single; 19,800 Drs ($82.50) double. AE, DC, EURO, MC, V.

One of the newest and most comfortable hotels in town is a block in from the town beach. It's spacious, quietly elegant, cheerful, and relaxed. All bathrooms have full bathtubs with shower and shower curtains. The rooms with balconies are the best deal, because the hotel is far enough away from traffic so you can enjoy them.

WHERE TO EAT

Café Olympia. Odós Alexándrou Roma 3. ☎ 0695/28-747. Main courses 350–700 Drs ($1.45–$2.90). No credit cards. Daily 7am–10pm. SNACKS/DESSERTS.

For breakfast, try the Café Olympia, opposite Platía Solomoú and the Government House. Cheese pies, yogurt, Greek coffee, butter biscuits, and other treats are good and inexpensive.

The Clock. Odós Vassiléos Konstandínou 11. ☎ 0695/23-587. Main courses 1,200–2,000 Drs ($5–$8.35). No credit cards. Mon–Sat 9am–2pm and 6:30–11:30pm, Sun 6:30–11:30pm. INTERNATIONAL.

A good, inexpensive "restaurant, steak house, cafe bar, pizza"—that's how The Clock (Tó Rolói) describes itself, and this family-run place lives up to its claim. Some Englishmen weary of "breakfest complet" extolled the virtues of the Clock's bacon and eggs, but we like it for lunch and dinner. The large and varied menu will satisfy meat lovers and vegetarians alike, at moderate prices. The chefs deserve praise for serving hot (not tepid) food.

Orea Hellas. Odós Ioánnou Logothétou 11. ☎ 0695/28-622. Reservations recommended on weekends in summer. Main courses 1,200–2,500 Drs ($5–$10.40). Daily 7am–1am. GREEK.

Oréa Héllas ("Fair Greece") is a sentimental favorite with Zantiotes, set in the heart of what was the restaurant district before the earthquake of 1953. The host, Takis Kefalinos, is a friendly and excellent chef. The small indoor restaurant (open all year) is decorated with turn-of-the-century prints of Zante; across the street is an outdoor lot, lit with Christmas-tree lights, that opens at dinner for food and live music. One of Oréa Hellas's best dishes is *sáltsa*, an island specialty that's something like a beef goulash. The lamb, with big, rice-flake-like noodles, is very tasty, and the loin of pork is one of the best-sellers.

Tres Jolie. Odós Dennis Stefánou 15. ☎ **0695/24-621.** Snacks 400–800 Drs ($1.65–$3.35). No credit cards. Daily 9am–9pm. SNACKS/DESSERTS.

You'll find this new little place by walking south from the government building on Alexándrou Róma and turning left toward the harbor. It's pretty, as its name suggests, with delicious sandwiches, pastries, confections, and ice creams made on the spot. Everything's fresh daily, as they sell out by midafternoon.

Zohios. Odós Psarón 9. No phone. Main courses 1,000–1,400 Drs ($4.15–$5.85). No credit cards. Daily 8pm–1am. GREEK.

This is a traditional taverna favored by locals, just off El. Venizélou and Dessila behind the little green square. A typical moussaká, sautéed vegetables, stuffed tomatoes and eggplant, some pasta dishes, and fried seafood are particularly good and inexpensive.

ZÁKYNTHOS AFTER DARK

Zákynthos really comes alive at night. The harborside promenade fills with Greeks out for their nightly *vólta,* taking a slow turn around the port to relish the cool evening breezes. Especially popular with the younger set is the **Ship Inn,** on the *paralía* near the tourist police office. Inside at the bar and clustered out front you'll find adolescent and early-twenty-something Greek mopeders downing beer.

The two most popular discos near the town are on the road to Argássi. **Video Disco** is the newer, therefore superior by local standards; **Argassi** is just a bit farther on and ranks a close second.

15 Northern Greece

The capital of Macedonia (Makedonía), Thessaloníki is Greece's second-largest city and third-largest port—but it was also the second most important city of the Byzantine Empire, so it has its own proud history. Macedonia also includes the Halkidikí peninsula, one of Greece's most scenic resorts, with Mt. Áthos, a totally independent religious community over 1,000 years old, at its easternmost tip.

There are great Hellenic-era antiquities at Pélla, Veryína, and Véria; Roman ruins at Philippi and Amphípolis; and one of the world's great museums in Thessaloníki. Macedonia was one of the wealthiest members of the Hellenic Federation more than 2,000 years ago, and still prospers in agriculture, industry, and trade today. The fur industry of Kastoriá, the tobacco of Kavála, the shipping of Thessaloníki are the kind of growth industries that will keep Greece alive forever. Unlike so many of the islands or the southern cities which survive on tourism generated by historic events, much of Macedonia (and Thrace, too) can live on its own. Visiting them can become an exploration into the heart and soul of modern Greece. Thrace, because of its high Muslim population, bridges the cultural gap that might exist at the border of two countries with such a volatile past; it also provides a good introduction to Turkey.

Macedonia, for many, will always be known as the land of Alexander the Great. It is the land that nourished his ambitious dreams until, a young man in his 20s, he took up the reins of his assassinated father, Philip II, and set out to subdue all of Greece. However coarse and provincial, it was Macedonia, rather than cosmopolitan Athens, that inspired this conqueror, who created, as Constantine Cavafy says in his poem "In the Year 200 B.C.," "the great new Hellenic world . . . with our far-flung supremacy and our common Greek language, which we carried as far as . . . India."

If you only have 3 or 4 days to spare, spend your time based in Thessaloníki, one of our favorite Greek cities. We'd recommend a half-day jaunt to Pélla (23$^{1}/_{2}$ miles northwest, the birthplace of Alexander the Great and a fascinating site and museum), followed by an afternoon at the archaeological museum. After this we suggest a full-day walking tour of the city itself, its Byzantine and Roman sights, cafes, shops, and waterfront.

The next day you can take a guided bus tour across Halkidikí, then cruise around the holy peninsula of Mt. Áthos to admire the monasteries. History buffs will want to take another expertly guided day trip to the archaeological sites that illuminate Macedonia's past. If by this time you crave a beach, head east to Kavála to catch the ferries for the Northeast Aegean island of Thássos.

1 Thessaloníki

335 miles N of Athens

Thessaloníki (often called Salonica), with about 750,000 inhabitants, is not even a close second to Athens in population, but it's even more sophisticated and cosmopolitan. Its downtown area was destroyed by a fire in 1917, so with the rebuilding, it's now rather modern. Thessaloníki doesn't have the classical remains of the capital, but it has a few Roman ruins, a number of superb Byzantine churches, and two excellent museums. It has been designated the 1997 Cultural Capital of Europe.

We dreaded going to Thessaloníki after everything we'd heard about it, but were delighted with the city when we arrived. Yes, there's some air pollution, but the winds often carry it away. The harbor isn't pristine—what busy port is?—and it's a little smelly, but you soon get used to it. And the traffic whizzes past, but at least it's moving. Give it a chance and you'll find it one of the most cosmopolitan cities in Europe, full of vital, friendly people enjoying good shops, sights aplenty, excellent food, and a vibrant, varied nightlife. In recent years many Albanian and Serbian immigrants have arrived, contributing their culture and energy to life in this city.

One of Thessaloníki's many charms is that it isn't touristed-out. People won't eye you with contempt or as the next mark for a pitch, and there are no rows of tacky souvenir stalls.

Thessaloníki is the capital of Alexander's country, a city founded as recently as 316 B.C. by the Macedonian general Kassandros. Just two decades earlier King Philip had won a decisive victory for his Thessalian allies at the Plain of Crocus; the daughter (Alexander's half-sister) born to him that year was named Thessaloníki ("Victory in Thessaly") to commemorate it. When she was wed to General Kassandros, he renamed the city given to them as a home after her.

During the Roman occupation Via Egnatia was paved as a through road between Rome, on the Adriatic coast, and Constantinople, capital of the Byzantine Empire. (Egnatía Street is still one of Thessaloníki's major arteries, paralleling the sea.) Under the Romans Thessaloníki became the most powerful city of northern Greece. Cicero had been exiled here; Antony and Octavius were welcomed in 42 B.C. after the Battle at Philippi, where Brutus and Cassius, conspirators against Julius Caesar, met their deaths and all hope of maintaining a republic in Rome was lost. In gratitude, they made Thessaloníki a free city. Politarchs (magistrates) were elected from the people to govern this Roman city, now independent like Athens.

Saint Paul arrived here about A.D. 49. From the Acts of the Apostles, we're told: "They came to Thessaloníka, where there was a synagogue of the Jews. . . . And Paul went in, as was his custom, and for three weeks he argued with them from the scriptures . . . and some of them were persuaded, and joined Paul and Silas; as did a great many of the devout Greeks and not a few of the leading women." After he was forced to leave the city, he wrote his "Letter to the Thessalonians" to the newly converted Christians of Thessaloníki. (The Jewish population at that time, called the Romaniote, spoke Greek and traced their lineage to the days of Alexander's mission to Jerusalem in 333 B.C.)

The emperor of the eastern Roman empire, Galerius, made Thessaloníki his capital. In A.D. 306 he had Saint Dimitrios, the city's patron, put to death, but he also left the city his triumphal arch, the remains of his palace, and his mausoleum, which

Thessaloníki

was later converted into the Church of St. George. By the 7th century Thessaloníki was one of the greatest Byzantine cities and enjoyed a rare prosperity. In 1430 the Turkish forces of Murad II laid siege to the city; the Turks continued their rule here until 1912.

The expulsion of the Jews from Spain during the reign of Ferdinand V and Isabella (late 15th to early 16th centuries) led nearly 20,000 of them to settle in Thessaloníki. By the time the Germans invaded Greece, the Jewish population exceeded 60,000 and there were more than 35 synagogues. (The few Jews who survived World War II still speak Ladino, the old Sephardic tongue from their Basque homeland.)

Most of the architectural and artistic legacy of the Turkish occupation was eradicated by the Greeks, although two minarets and some *hamams* (Turkish baths) still stand. In this century alone, Thessaloníki has suffered terrible fires and severe bombings, yet something from each era has survived to sustain the patchwork whole we see today. From the Roman era there is the Arch of Galerius; then the great Byzantine chapels, mosaics, and frescoes; the White Tower on the harbor, a 16th-century

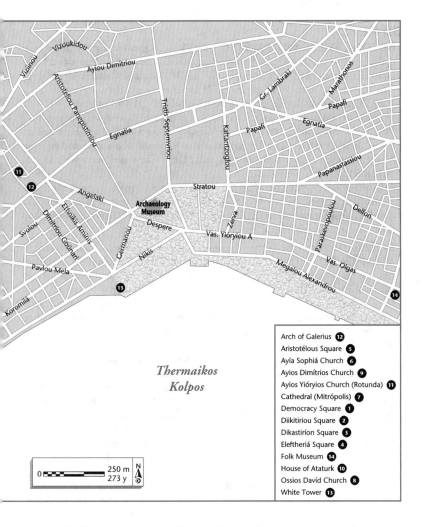

Arch of Galerius 12
Aristotélous Square 5
Ayía Sophiá Church 6
Ayios Dimítrios Church 9
Ayios Yióryios Church (Rotunda) 11
Cathedral (Mitrópolis) 7
Democracy Square 1
Diikitiriou Square 2
Dikastiríon Square 3
Eleftheriá Square 4
Folk Museum 14
House of Ataturk 10
Ossios Davíd Church 8
White Tower 13

Ottoman fortification; a stone on the waterfront marking the spot where the Greek king George I was assassinated; some exquisite neoclassical office buildings and art deco apartments; the parklike exhibition grounds of the International Trade Fair begun in 1926 (which now attracts more than a million traders in mid-September); the tiered communications tower that dominates the field opposite the archaeological museum. Thessaloníki's Aristotle University complex was built after the war over the old Jewish Cemetery.

Today it's best known as a Byzantine city because of the wealth of art and architecture that remained from the centuries when Thessaloníki was second only to Constantinople. A major earthquake in 1978 damaged most of the Byzantine churches, and most are still being restored. Recent archaeological excavations at Dervéni and Veryína (site of King Philip's tomb) have turned up such remarkable artifacts from the Macedonian period that we consider Thessaloníki notable for its archaeological museum and nearby sites.

ESSENTIALS

GETTING THERE & DEPARTING   By Plane   Olympic Airways has several daily flights to and from most European capitals and major American cities. Contact the Olympic office in Thessaloníki, at Odós Koundouriótou 3 (☎ 031/230-240), or in Athens (☎ 01/926-7251) for schedule and fare information.

Lufthansa Airlines has daily service from Frankfurt.

There are at least seven daily flights to and from Athens; one daily to and from Ioánnina, Límnos, and Lésvos; five a week to Corfu; four a week to and from Iráklio, Crete; three a week to and from Mýkonos and Santoríni; two a week to and from Alexandroúpolis, Híos, Rhodes, Sámos, and Haniá, Crete; and one a week to and from Kavála.

City bus no. 78 runs between the train station and the airport, stopping at Aristotélous Square; the fare is 125 Drs (50¢). There is a tourist police station, a **Greek Tourist Organization (EOT)** office (☎ 031/471-170), and a duty-free shop at the airport for international travelers.

By Train   Trains arrive at the Thessaloníki station on Monastiríou Street; call ☎ 031/276-382 or 031/517-517 for information. The Information Booth is open daily for the arrival of all trains; if it's out of maps, study the mural map of the city outside the station. There are two banks, a post office, and a telephone center (OTE), all open daily, located to the right as you exit. The luggage-storage bureau (the only official one in the entire city) is open 24 hours and charges 220 Drs (90¢) per piece until midnight each day. Train tickets can be bought at the station or at the OSE office at the northeast corner of Aristotélous Square.

There are four regular trains daily (one with sleeper) to and from Athens: trip time is 7¹/₂ hours; the fare is 5,200 Drs ($21.65) in first class, 3,500 Drs ($14.60) in second class. In addition, there are five express trains to and from Athens: trip time, 6 hours; fare, 9,000 Drs ($37.50) in first class, 7,200 Drs ($30) in second class. On the express train, the only real difference we noticed between first and second class was that most first-class seats face forward and most second-class seats face toward the rear. There are four trains a day to and from Kozáni (with a connection to Flórina), three regular and two express trains to and from Alexandroúpolis, and three daily to and from Vólos.

At present international service is limited to two trains daily from Belgrade; one daily from Budapest (via Belgrade), with connections to other European cities; one daily to and from Sophia; and one daily to and from Istanbul.

By Bus   There are eight buses daily from Athens's Terminal A, Odós Kifissoú 100; the 8-hour trip costs 5,500 Drs ($22.90) each way; call ☎ 01/514-8856 for reservations.

A consolidated **bus station** was still not completed when we last visited Thessaloníki, but most bus stations are near the train station. Buses to Athens leave from Monastiríou 65, opposite the train station; those to Pélla, Édessa, Vólos, and Kastoriá leave from Anayeniséos 22; those to Flórina, from Anayeniséos 42; for Véria, from 26 Oktovríou 10; and for Halkidikí, from Karakássi 68, farther east. Check with the EOT for additional details.

The Greek Railway (OSE) runs three buses a day to Sophia and one daily (except Wednesday) to Istanbul, leaving at 3am; the 14-hour trip costs 11,500 Drs ($47.90). OSE buses leave from in front of the train station, and tickets can be purchased inside; call ☎ 031/538-416 for more information.

By Ferry   There are three car-ferries per week between Thessaloníki and Skiáthos or Skópelos, and one a week to Alónissos; call ☎ 01/417-8084 for schedules and information. There's also weekly service on Saturday to Límnos, Lésvos, and Híos. In the summer there's ferry service twice a week to Iráklio, Crete, via Páros and Santoríni.

By Hydrofoil   The **Ceres Hydrofoil Company** (☎ **01/453-7107** in Athens or 031/534-376 in Thessaloníki) offers daily service in summer between Thessaloníki and Skiáthos (3¹/₂ hours, 11,350 Drs/$47.30); Skópelos (4¹/₂ hours, 12,700 Drs/ $52.95); and Alónissos (5¹/₂ hours, 13,335 Drs/$55.55).

VISITOR INFORMATION   The **Greek Tourist Organization (EOT),** on the east side of Aristotélous Square (☎ **031/271-888**), open Monday to Friday from 8am to 8pm and on Saturday from 8am to 3pm, is probably the best, friendliest, and most helpful in Greece.

The **tourist police** are at Egnatía 10, though the entrance is around the corner on Tandalidou (☎ **031/271-888**). The office is open daily: 24 hours in the summer, 7:30am to 11pm October to March.

ORIENTATION   Don't be surprised if you find that this city of three-quarters of a million seems to be as large and bewildering as Athens. Those arriving by train or bus will be at the west end of the city, near Monastiríou Street, which then becomes **Egnatía Street.** You'll probably do most of your sightseeing within a rectangular area (about a 20-minute walk east) bordered by Egnatía Street on the north; Venizélou and Dragoúmi streets, which end at Eleftherías Square, to the west; **Níkis Avenue** (still also known as Leofóros Vassiléos Konstandínou), the harborside avenue, on the south; and the park, archaeological museum, and exhibition grounds to the east. **Platía Aristitélous** is a central meeting area on the waterfront at Níkis Street.

While you're here, walk over to the waterfront: to the left you'll see Thessaloníki's famous landmark, the **White Tower,** recently converted into a museum of local archaeological finds and Byzantine treasures. From there, a 5-minute walk northeast on N. Yermanou Street will bring you to the **archaeological museum** and the exhibition grounds behind it. To the right (west) of Platía Aristotélous is **Eleftheria Square** and the large pier for commercial vessels as well as the sporadic North Aegean islands ferry. Between the port and the train and bus stations, there are several budget hotels.

Ladádika, the area to the west of Elefthería Square, in from the waterfront, was once the red-light district, but recent gentrification has filled it with chic tavernas, bars, and restaurants.

If you walk straight up (north) through the square to Aristotélous Street, the second intersection is **Ermoú Street.** There are several hotels to the left, and to the right is the 8th-century **Church of Ayía Sophía.** The next major intersection north is Egnatía Street, for more than 2,000 years a major thoroughfare. However, Egnatía Street has become so noisy that we can no longer recommend the older hotels along it.

To the right, at the intersection of Aristotélous and Egnatía streets, you can look east to the 3rd-century **Arch of Galerius.** Straight ahead, across Egnatía, is **Dikastiríon Square.** On the southwest corner of the square is the 11th-century **Panayía Halkéon Cathedral,** and behind it the remains of the **Roman agora,** which is being excavated and restored. The northwest corner of the square serves as the **local bus terminal** for most of Thessaloníki's bus lines. The **Bazaar** is south of Dikastiríon Square.

GETTING AROUND   Thessaloníki is the major transportation hub for all vehicular, air, train, and water traffic in Macedonia and Thrace. Thousands of Europeans pour through Greece's northern borders with the former Yugoslavia and Bulgaria every July and August, though recent unrest in these countries has significantly lessened the traffic.

By Car If you've driven into Thessaloníki, good luck finding a parking space downtown. Many of the new hotels have parking lots and charge 800 to 1,500 Drs ($3.35 to $6.25) a day; there's a free municipal parking lot near the White Tower and archaeological museum. To explore Thessaloníki, park your car and walk, or try the public buses.

Driving is the easiest way to reach **Panorama,** just 7¹/₂ miles northeast of the city center, a quieter and prettier suburb, with classy hotels, restaurants, cafes, and street life.

Renting a car when you're ready to move on and explore Alexander the Great country is the most convenient way to go. There's **AutoEurope** at Odós Komninón and Níkis (☎ 031/242-121); **Avis** at Odós Níkis 3 and the airport (☎ 031/227-126); **Hertz** at Odós Venizélou 4 (☎ 031/277-787) and the airport (☎ 031/473-952); **Europcar** at Odós G. Papandréou 5 (☎ 031/826-333; fax 031/826-205) and the airport (☎ 031/473-508); as well as smaller local rental companies. A compact car will cost about 22,500 Drs ($93.75), including insurance, per day. (Remember, it's cheaper to make a reservation in North America before you leave home.)

By Bus Orange double buses with an accordion connection run regularly along the major streets; the fare is 75 Drs (30¢), and you pay the conductor as you board. Blue buses and orange single buses serve the surburbs as well as the city; the fare is 100 Drs (40¢) in town and 115 Drs (50¢) to more distant destinations, and tickets are usually sold by exact-change-only machines—or you can drop your fare into the box next to the driver. A 12-ticket card can be purchased at city bus kiosks for 850 Drs ($3.55). Call ☎ 031/513-734 or visit the **EOT** office for more information.

By Taxi Taxis are blue and white with meters, and the drivers here are generally more cooperative than they are in Athens, though you must compete for taxis by standing at the curb and shouting your destination. You can call for a radio taxi at ☎ 031/217-218.

FAST FACTS At the **American Express bank,** Odós Tsimiskí 19 (☎ 031/272-791), open Monday to Friday from 8am to 1:30pm, you can cash or replace traveler's checks and pick up mail.

The **National Bank of Greece,** Odós Tsimiskí 11, has extended hours Monday to Friday from 8am to 1pm and 6 to 8pm, on Saturday from 8am to 2pm, and on Sunday and holidays from 8am to noon. **Kapa Bureau d'Echange,** Odós Egnatía 49–51 (☎ 031/280-145), with slightly less favorable rates of exchange, is open every day from 8:30am to 8:30pm. **ATMs** are common in the center of town.

Foreign-language periodicals are available at several kiosks near the port or Aristotélous Square, but the best selection is at **Malliaris Kaisia,** Odós Aristotélous 9, open daily from 9am to 9pm. **Molhos,** Tsimiskí 10 (at Dragoúmi), has a similar selection, including books about Mt. Áthos.

The **American consulate** is at Odós Níkis 59 (☎ 031/266-121), open Tuesday to Thursday from 9am to noon; the **British vice consulate** is at Odós Venizélou 8 (☎ 031/278-006).

In an **emergency,** dial ☎ 100 for the English-speaking 24-hour help line. Call ☎ 166 for medical emergencies; the **Thessaloníki Red Cross** is at Koundouriótou 10, near the port (☎ 031/530-530).

The **Ministry of Northern Greece,** Dikitríou Square (☎ 031/270-092), is the place to apply for and pick up permits to visit the holy site of Mt. Áthos.

The central **post office,** open daily from 7:30am to 8pm, where you can also change money, is at Odós Tsimiskí 28, off Aristotélous Street. The **telephone office (OTE),** open 24 hours a day, is at Karólou and Ermoú streets.

SEEING THE SIGHTS

✪ **Archaeological Museum.** Platía Hánthi (YMCA Sq.; at the intersection of Angeláki and Tsimiskí sts.). ☎ **031/830-538.** Admission 1,500 Drs ($6.25) adults, 1,100 Drs ($4.60) seniors, 800 Drs ($3.35) students; video, 400 Drs ($1.65) extra. Apr–Oct 15, Mon 12:30–7pm, Tues–Fri 8:30am–7pm, Sat–Sun 8:30am–3pm; Oct 16–Mar, Mon 10:30am–5pm, Tues–Fri 8:30am–5pm, Sat–Sun 8:30am–3pm.

This museum, situated 2 blocks northeast of the White Tower, is organized in two circles: the inner galleries are dedicated to recent finds from Sindos; the outer circle is most of the older portion of the museum. A new wing houses the magnificent artifacts from Dervéni and Veryína.

The Sindos wing, opened in 1982, displays 6th- to 5th-century B.C. examples of gold hair ornaments, jewelry, filigree pendants, dollhouse-size tables and chairs, and some delicate miniature glass amphoras. Most of these were found in tombs that were underwater, so all metal other than gold has been badly damaged. The buried warrior's golden face mask and helmet, which date from 520 B.C., are particularly impressive.

In the next galleries there are grave steles from Véria and fine marble statues from the ancient Agorá of Thessaloníki, from around the 1st to 2nd centuries A.D. In the central gallery you'll find a fascinating display devoted to 2,300 years of Thessaloníki daily life, including a striking 3rd-century mosaic from a local house. In the fourth gallery there's a bold, strong sculpture of the Roman emperor Augustus.

At Dervéni, gold and bronze from the last half of the 4th century B.C., as well as ornate silverwork burial gifts, were found. In the beginning of the gallery are finds from a royal tomb at Kateríni and from Thérmi and Stavroúpolis. But the real prizes are from Veryína, the first great capital of Macedonia, birthplace of Philip II. Excavations in the late 1970s unearthed one of the most important archaeological finds since the Tut tombs, the royal tomb of Philip himself, untouched in 2,100 years. The riches of the find are astonishing, especially the exquisite crown of the great king. The solid-gold funerary box is another example of the fine level of craftsmanship of the Macedonians; even the bones of Philip are displayed, providing an eerie experience for the viewer. Imagine the man that was Philip—a great leader, warrior, king—now a set of surprisingly small bones overshadowed by the splendor of the objects found with him. This gallery is not to be missed! Professor Andronicos's museum guide (1,200 Drs/$5) is excellent, with especially fine reproductions.

The White Tower (Historical and Art Museum of Thessaloníki). Níkis and Pávlou Méla sts. (on the waterfront, 2 blocks west of the archaeological museum). ☎ **031/267-832.** Admission 800 Drs ($3.35) adults, 600 Drs ($2.50) seniors, 400 Drs ($1.65) students. Mon 12:30–5pm, Tues–Fri 8am–5pm, Sat–Sun 8:30am–3pm.

The interior of the city's best-known landmark has recently been renovated and turned into a superb museum housing local archaeological finds and Byzantine treasures. The White Tower (Lefkós Pýrgos), also called the "Bloody Tower" because it was the site of a Turkish massacre of Janissaries in 1826, was built as a prison in the early 16th century after designs by the renowned Ottoman architect Sinan. Take time to visit the display downstairs before you climb the broad stone stairs that spiral up and around inside the cool cylinder and lead to five small display floors. Marble architectural ornaments, column fragments, mosaics, 4th- to 5th-century tombs with wall paintings, and Byzantine jewelry, coins, and icons are wonderfully displayed in vaulted, low-ceilinged galleries. Don't miss the small side rooms (you have to stoop to enter); also be sure to see the two enameled, carved gold Byzantine bracelets on the third floor. There's a small cafe at the top, and you can usually step outside for a grand view of the city.

Macedonian Folk and Ethnographic Museum. Odós Vassilísis Ólgas 68. ☎ **031/830-591.** Admission 200 Drs (85¢) adults, 150 Drs (65¢) students. Fri–Wed 9:30am–2pm. Walk 1 block inland from the harbor; it's 2 long blocks south from the archaeological museum.

This museum exhibits items connected with the preindustrial era of northern Greece. There are myriad ornaments, weapons, and household items. We particularly liked the costumes and folk-arts displays. (The museum may be closed for renovation during your visit.)

A STROLL THROUGH THESSALONÍKI

Our walking tour begins at Thessaloníki's most attractive square, **Platía Aristotélous,** on Níkis Street, the waterfront drive along the city's busy port. Make a left on the portside avenue and continue east until you come to the **White Tower,** the city's most famous landmark, now a fine museum (see above).

If you want to include the **archaeological museum** in your tour, continue east 2 blocks and turn left. Otherwise, turn left and continue north 7 or 8 blocks until you reach busy Egnatía Street, on which you'll find the massive **Arch of Galerius,** now shrouded in scaffolding. The arch was constructed in A.D. 303 to commemorate the Roman emperor's victories over the Persians in 297. The reliefs, which portray the battle with the Persians, have been badly eroded, though the arch is still impressive. Walk through it and continue north to the domed **Rotunda,** now the **Church of Áyios Yióryios** (St. George). It was built only a few years after the arch, as an imperial mausoleum, and was later converted to a Christian sanctuary and decorated with masterful mosaics. In 1590 it was converted into a mosque and remained in use under the Ottomans until 1912; the minaret is still there. The church has remained closed for restoration since the earthquake of 1978 and is open only occasionally for concerts and exhibitions, though it's hoped that it will reopen soon.

If you're interested in Turkish history, continue north from the Rotunda until you reach the next main avenue, Ayíou Dimitríou. Turn left until you reach the Turkish consulate on the right at no. 151, at the corner of Apostólou Pávlou Street, and next door, the **House of Ataturk,** the founder and first president of the modern state of Turkey, who was born here in 1881 as Mustafa Kemal. The house, usually open daily from 9am to 1pm and 2 to 6pm, contains historical photos, Turkish-style furniture, and other paraphernalia. Admission is free, but in order to enter you must surrender your passport (temporarily) to the Turkish consulate. (Security is tight because relations between Greece and Turkey remain strained.)

Return to Egnatía, and just west of the Arch, at the intersection with Iassonídou, you'll find the 14th-century **Church of Áyios Pandelímon,** and across the street, the subterranean **Church of the Metamórphosi** (Transfiguration). These aren't on the normal tour route, but we especially like the latter for its sunken, listing foundation and the perfectly preserved Byzantine brick-and-tile exterior. (If you've stopped at the Church of the Metamórphosi and are looking for a bite to eat, try the **Koubarakia Restaurant,** which overlooks this tiny sanctuary.)

Two blocks southeast, on diagonally running Patriárhou Ioákim, is one of Thessaloníki's most important Byzantine churches, the 8th-century **Ayía Sophía,** a copy of the more famous Ayía Sophía (Hagia Sofia) in Istanbul, which marks an important turning point in Western architecture by incorporating the Oriental cupola and a cruciform style over the older basilica form. When the Ottomans ruled Thessaloníki, the church was converted to a mosque. The interior mosaics, including an Ascension of Christ enthroned on a rainbow and surrounded by the Apostles and olive trees, date from the 11th century.

Return north past Egnatía on Ayía Sophía Street to reach the **Panayía Ahiropíitos,** the oldest surviving church in Thessaloníki. The name means "Our Lady Not Done [that is, painted] by [human] Hands," referring to the icon that's said to have miraculously appeared in the 5th century. The mosaics on the upper walls and finely filtered light from the arched windows are reason enough to take a quick look inside, though the opening hours are erratic.

Continue west on Egnatía, turn right at the bus station, and follow the road 2 blocks to the **Roman Agora** and **theater.** The large square that was once the center of Roman business life was discovered in 1962 when the foundation for a new court-house was being dug. Excavation and restoration have proceded slowly but seemed to be nearing completion when we last visited. The small amphitheater is already being used for concerts. Above the northern perimeter of the market is a small, shaded park that's ideal for a rest, picnic, or cool drink.

If you have the time and energy, you may want to continue north a couple of blocks to **Áyios Dimítrios,** the city's largest church, built during the 5th century to honor the city's patron saint. It burned down during the great fire of 1917 and was rebuilt over the next three decades. A few small mosaics from the 7th century remain in the huge interior. During the reconstruction, a crypt, thought to be the remains of the Roman bath in which Dimítrios was martyred, was discovered below the apse. The church and crypt are open to the public Tuesday to Sunday from 8:30am to 3pm. On Sundays there are baptismal ceremonies all morning long and it's quite an experience!

If you're up to seeing another Byzantine church, with perhaps the finest mosaics in the city, wend your way north to **Óssios Davíd,** a 5th-century church in the old Turkish quarter known as Epiménidou or Kástra. (This is a charming place for a stroll, but if you want to get there directly, continue east of the Church of Áyios Dimítrios on Ayíou Dimitríou Street 3 blocks to Ayía Sophía Street, turn left/north, and continue up half a dozen long blocks.) The second-oldest church in the city was considered otherwise unremarkable until Independence Day in 1921 when an Orthodox monk from Egypt, who had been told in a dream to go and pray there, came and was rewarded with an earthquake that revealed a superb mosaic in the apse depicting a beardless Christ seen in a vision of Ezekiel. The monk died on the spot.

Return to Platía Dikastiríon on Egnatía and the small, charming **Panayía Halkéon** ("Our Lady of the Copper Workers"), which according to an inscription was built in 1028, with its soft Byzantine curves and domes and highly articulated doorways. Alternating brick, mortar, and stone add a subtle pattern to the church's classical design. (There are still a few copperware shops across the street.)

South across Egnatía and east is the lively **Bazaar,** the main shopping streets, where shoes and clothes are often a bargain.

WHERE TO STAY

In Thessaloníki there are plenty of older budget hotels, though most of them have become intolerably noisy in recent years. So, although you'll have to walk an extra few blocks to sightsee if you choose one of our recommendations, at least you'll be getting enough sleep to enjoy it.

The surge of visitors in late August and September for the International Trade Fair makes rooms very difficult to find, and many hotels raise their prices by 15% to 20% or make continental breakfast compulsory. Demand remains high through the Dimitría in October, when the city celebrates its patron saint with a month of festivities and cultural events.

The most popular of the nearby campgrounds on a beach—the water is polluted at the commercial port—is **Ayía Triáda,** where the EOT has organized campgrounds (☎ 0392/51-360).

AROUND DIIKITIRÍOU SQUARE

This area, northwest of central Dikastiríon Square, was once a quiet enclave of professional people, fashionable shops, and government offices; it remains pleasant enough, and some good-value hotels can still be found here. Locals complain about Albanian immigrants in a nearby park, though it looked peaceful enough to us.

Hotel Bill. Odós Amvrossíou 16, 562 30 Thessaloníki. ☎ **031/537-666.** 23 rms, 14 with bath (shower or tub). TEL. 4,000 single without bath, 6,350 Drs ($26.45) single with bath; 7,500 Drs ($31.25) double without bath, 9,775 Drs ($40.75) double with bath. No credit cards.

An excellent value, with balconies and baths in some of the large double rooms that compete with much pricier establishments. Kyle slept well here!

Hotel Esperia. Odós Olýmbou 58, 546 31 Thessaloníki. ☎ **031/269-321.** Fax 031/269-457. 70 rms, all with bath (shower or tub). A/C TV TEL. 20,500 Drs ($85.40) single; 23,000 Drs ($95.85) double. Breakfast 1,900 Drs ($7.90) extra. No credit cards.

The rooms are carpeted, each has a large tiled bathroom, and the front balconies overlook the classical Ministry of Northern Greece building. Newly refurbished, it offers very high quality and a friendly staff.

Park Hotel. Odós Dragoumi 81, 546 30 Thessaloníki. ☎ **031/524-121.** Fax 031/524-193. 56 rms, all with bath (tub). A/C TEL. 20,750 Drs ($86.45) single; 25,300 Drs ($105.40) double. Rates include breakfast. V.

This hotel was renovated in 1994 and has a large modern lobby and bar that come as close to a Hilton as you'll find in this price range. The spacious rooms have air-conditioning and music; many have refrigerators and televisions.

NEAR THE PORT

The port in Thessaloníki is one of the best areas for budget hotels.

Hotel Continental. Odós Komnínon 5, 546 24 Thessaloníki. ☎ **031/277-553.** 39 rms, 15 with bath and A/C. TEL. 6,900 Drs ($28.75) single without bath; 13,800 Drs ($57.50) double with bath. No credit cards.

A block off the water between Elefthería and Aristotélous squares, it's "continental" on the outside only. Inside it's ordinary, but nice and quiet, with a little lobby and an exposed elevator.

Hotel Luxemburg. Odós Komnínon 6, 546 24 Thessaloníki. ☎ **031/278-449.** 29 rms, 6 with bath (tub). 8,000 Drs ($33.35) single without bath; 13,350 Drs ($55.65) double with bath. No credit cards.

The rooms (except for the ceilings) don't live up to the the spiffy beaux arts exterior, but they're pleasant, quiet, and comfortable.

Hotel Tourist. Odós Mitropoléos 21, 546 24 Thessaloníki. ☎ **031/276-335.** Fax 031/229-796. 37 rms, all with bath (shower or tub). TEL. 10,550 Drs ($43.95) single; 18,650 Drs ($77.70) double; 20,500 Drs ($85.40) triple. No credit cards.

The exterior of this old-fashioned hotel on a fairly quiet street has been recently renovated, and the lobby is spare with an attractive glass-doored cage elevator. The older gentleman at the front desk doesn't speak much English, but his son does and can usually be reached by phone. The halls are spacious with high molded ceilings, as are most of the rooms, and all are well kept. There's a good place for a light breakfast across the street at the opposite end of the block.

Near the Railway & Bus Stations

Though not our favorite neighborhood, the area just east of the railway station may be convenient for late-night bus or train arrivals—though our other hotel recommendations are all within a 5-minute 1,000-Dr ($4.15) cab ride or 20-minute walk from the railroad station.

Hotel Rex. Odós Monastiríou 39, 546 27 Thessaloníki. ☎ **031/517-051.** 59 rms, 22 with bath (tub). TEL. 9,200 Drs ($38.35) single without bath; 12,650 Drs ($52.70) double without bath, 16,675 Drs ($69.50) double with bath. No credit cards.

At the Rex, across the street and 1 long block to the left (east) of the station, the sixth-floor sun roof has an urban sort of charm. The rooms are plain but nice, and the rear ones are quieter. The new manager, whom we met during our last visit, was friendly and helpful.

Hotel Veryina. Odós Monastiríou 19, 546 27 Thessaloníki. ☎ **031/516-021.** Fax 031/529-308. 133 rms, all with bath (tub). A/C. 19,500 Drs ($81.25) single; 23,700 Drs ($98.75) double. Rates include breakfast. AE, MC, V.

Up the road a bit east from the station, this well-managed eight-story, white concrete edifice has pleasant, spacious rooms with balconies—most with telephones, televisions, and ceiling fans.

Near Egnatía Street

The hotels along busy Egnatía Street are convenient, but are not for light sleepers.

Hotel Acropol. Odós Tandalidou 4, 546 26 Thessaloníki. ☎ **031/536-170.** 30 rms, none with bath. TEL. 5,200 Drs ($21.65) single; 5,950 Drs ($24.80) double. No credit cards.

This modest budget hotel is around the corner from Egnatía—and a bit removed from the noise—with an attractive vine hanging over the entranceway. The large rooms with their own sinks are drab but clean, and the shared bathrooms are immaculate, with real bathtubs. The Acropol is no beauty, but the owners, the Hatjitheodorou family, speak English and are outstandingly helpful and friendly.

Hotel Amalia. Odós Ermoú 33, 546 24 Thessaloníki. ☎ **031/268-321.** Fax 031/233-356. 66 rms, all with bath (shower or tub). TEL. 12,250 Drs ($51.05) single; 15,700 Drs ($65.40) double.

This modern hotel was recommended to us by locals, and it's not a bad value. The blue-and-white rooms are large and bright, many with balconies. Although it's right on Ermoú, the thick glass windows seem to provide some insulation against noise.

Hotel Ariston. Odós Karaóli-Dimitríou (Diikitiríou) 5, 546 23 Thessaloníki. ☎ **031/519-630.** 35 rms, 11 with bath (tub). TEL. 7,600 Drs ($31.65) single without bath; 12,800 Drs ($53.35) double with bath. No credit cards.

This older hotel is about 50 yards northeast of the point where four other streets intersect at Platía Dimokratías (Democracy Square). (The street signs read Karaóli and Dimitríou, and some maps label it Churchill, but everyone still calls it Diikitiríou.) Some of the bathless rooms have amusing "Murphy"-style pull-out shower stalls; others are American style, with the toilet outside in the hall. It's an adventure staying at the Ariston, so if you don't like what you're shown, ask for something else—they're very accommodating.

Hotel Augustus. Odós Svorónou 4, 546 23 Thessaloníki. ☎ **031/522-550.** 24 rms, none with bath. 5,100 Drs ($21.25) single; 5,700 Drs ($23.75) double. No credit cards.

You'll recognize the beaux arts–style "Avgoústos" near Platía Dimokratías by its handsome flatiron shape. The interior doesn't live up to its ornate facade, but the plain rooms are pleasant and recently renovated, and come with their own sinks. The shared bathrooms are well maintained. It's a block north of Egnatía, so it's relatively quiet.

Hotel Averof. Odós Leóndos Sofoú 24, 546 25 Thessaloníki. ☎ **031/538-840.** Fax 031/543-194. 33 rms, 10 with bath (shower). TEL. 5,200 Drs ($21.65) single without bath; 9,200 Drs ($38.35) double without bath, 11,500 Drs ($47.90) double with bath. No credit cards.

This pleasant hotel with a friendly manager is just far enough off busy Egnatía to be acceptably quiet. The rooms are pleasant and comfortable, with nice pine furniture.

YHA Hostel. Odós Svólou 44, 546 21 Thessaloníki. ☎ **031/225-946.** Fax 031/262-208. 2,200 Drs ($9.15) bed in double or triple dorm. No credit cards. Bus: 10 from the railway station to the Kamana stop.

The manager of this co-ed hostel near the archaeological museum is helpful when he's there (8:30am to noon and 7pm to midnight), but there's no linen or cooking facilities. Hot water for showers is available only in the evenings, and the bedrooms are closed from 11am to 7pm for cleaning—not sleeping! There's an 11pm curfew, which may be ignored if you enter quietly, and an IYHF card is usually required.

WHERE TO EAT

There's a joie de vivre among the Salonicans that makes dining out in this cosmopolitan city an unexpected pleasure. There are many tried-and-true restaurants that the International Trade Fair has kept alive, as well as many inexpensive, simple tavernas and grills, and Westernized fast-food chains that a traveler in any budget range can afford.

NEAR THE PORT

You'll find most of the older and better restaurants, as well as some glitzy new ones, near the harbor and Aristotélous Square. One block up from Aristotélous Square on the right you'll find the **Terkenlis Bakery and Confectionary,** at Odós Tsimiskí 30, with the best pastries and sweets in town, probably in Macedonia, and possibly in all Greece.

Clochard. Odós Koromilá 4. ☎ **031/239-805.** Reservations recommended. Main courses 1,500–4,800 Drs ($6.25–$20). DC. Sun–Fri 8pm–2am, Sat noon–3pm and 8pm–2am. INTERNATIONAL.

As you'd expect from the name, the accent is on the French in this *très chic* piano bar on a small street 1 block off the harbor in the center of town, which serves only the very best meats and fresh fish in season grilled to perfection in its international kitchen. You'll want to dress up for this very sophisticated restaurant.

Olympos-Naoussa. Odós Níkis 5. ☎ **031/275-715.** Reservations recommended. Main courses 700–1,650 Drs ($2.90–$6.90). No credit cards. Mon–Fri noon–4pm. CONTINENTAL.

Just down the street from the port, traditional continental cuisine is served in this elegant, older restaurant that caters to the suit, tie, and grandmother lunch crowd. We recommend the *mýdia tiganitá,* a local specialty of fried mussels. The service is good, even when the place is busy, and there's also less formal outdoor seating in summer.

Roğotis Restaurant Grill. Odós Venizélou 8. ☎ **031/277-694.** Main courses 1,100–3,500 Drs ($4.60–$14.60). AE, DC, MC, V. Mon, Wed, and Sat 10:30am–5:30pm; Tues and Thurs–Fri 10:30am–11:30pm. GREEK/CONTINENTAL.

This old-fashioned dark-wood taverna is just off Eleftherías Square. Known by its former street address but actually named Vairlis Souzoukákia, and famous for its *souzoukákia* (ground veal patties), it has a large and interesting menu with varied *mezédes* (appetizers), meat dishes, and grilled and skewered fish.

Stratis. Odós Níkis 19. ☎ **031/279-353.** Reservations recommended. Main courses 1,100–3,500 Drs ($4.60–$14.60). AE, V. Daily noon–midnight. GREEK.

This very attractive, low-key restaurant across from the harbor has a varied, traditional Greek menu: lots of meats, excellent imported wines, seafood specialties, and a range of skillfully prepared and displayed *mezédes* (the traditional array of appetizer-size portions of piquant foods, best had with ouzo or wine). The regionally produced Corona white wine is particularly good.

✪ Ta Nicía. Odós Koromilá 13. ☎ **031/285-991.** Reservations recommended. Main courses 1,600–4,200 Drs ($6.65–$17.50). V. Daily noon–5pm and 8pm–1am. SEAFOOD.

"The Islands," a block off the harbor, is a charming little place with fresh white walls, a wood-beam ceiling, lively blue trim, and interesting ceramics. It serves the best seafood in town prepared in a *nouvelle* Greek manner all its own. You won't often find mussels, crab, and cuttlefish cooked so originally or served with such simple elegance. Grilled meats are also available, and you might find walnut pie or quince baked in white wine for dessert.

Ta Spata. Odós Aristotélous 29. ☎ **031/277-412.** Main courses 400–1,500 Drs ($1.65–$6.25). No credit cards. Daily 10am–midnight. GREEK.

One of the best budget bets is north of Aristotélous Square on the right. This *psistariá/estiatório* is a basic Greek eatery where you walk inside and pick out what looks good and it will be served to you by a friendly waiter. Some choices include beef with chips, pork with cabbage or "cooked in rich sauce," pasta, and a dozen vegetables. For desert try the *halvá*, which isn't cloyingly sweet.

Zythos. Odós Katoúni 5, ☎ **031/540-284.** Reservations not required. Main courses 900–2,800 Drs ($3.75–$11.65). No credit cards. Daily 7am–1am. GREEK.

This very popular restaurant was one of the first to open in Ladádika, the newly hip area west of Eleftherías Square. There are four other fine-dining choices right on Odós Katoúni, but this is the busiest. Zythos has airy wooden tables and canvas chairs on the street outside; an elegant interior of high ceilings, little wooden cafe tables, and tiled floors; and especially pleasant, efficient service. But the inventive, delicious food is the real drawing point. We loved the deep-fried mushroom fritters and cheese-stuffed squid, and devoured a chicken souvláki plate of tender skewers wrapped in smoky bacon.

NEAR THE ARCHAEOLOGICAL MUSEUM

Impero Pizza. Odós Smýrnis 12. ☎ **031/239-103.** Main courses 500–2,200 Drs ($2.10–$9.15). No credit cards. Daily 9am–4pm and 6pm–3am. PIZZA.

Just up the street from the U.S. consulate (at Odós Nikis 59) you'll find this little cafe that serves delicious pizza. Resident Yanks claim that it's the best in town—and who knows more about pizza? Besides which, they speak English, thanks to the American music they play.

Ta Koubarakia. Odós Egnatía 140. ☎ **031/271-905** or 031/268-442. Main courses 1,200–2,600 Drs ($5–$10.85). AE, V. Daily noon–5pm and 7pm–1am. GREEK.

This cafe, centrally located for day-tour walkers across from Egnatía and west from the Arch of Galerius, behind the sunken Byzantine Church of the Metamórphosi, is always filled with Greeks enjoying excellent grilled calamari and broiled whole fish.

If you can't read the menu, politely venture inside this very clean little place and choose from the fresh, attractive selection.

Tiffany's. Odós Iktínou 3. ☎ **031/274-022.** Main courses 1,100–4,500 Drs ($4.60–$18.75). No credit cards. Daily noon–midnight. GREEK.

No breakfast, but lunch and dinner are exceptional at this attractive outdoor and indoor taverna on a quiet, shaded pedestrian mall in the shopping district, just a 5-minute walk east from the archaeological museum. We suggest the tangy *magarítsa* (lamb liver with egg-and-lemon soup), *ambelophýlla* (the chef's delicious variation of stuffed vine leaves), and *kolokythákia yemistá* (zucchini stuffed with minced meat in egg-and-lemon sauce).

THESSALONÍKI AFTER DARK

The liveliest and most varied nightlife in Thessaloníki can be found late at night along and off the harbor, in what the locals call the center of town, especially along and around Proxénou Koromilá Street. If you're looking for something a little wilder, meander east toward the White Tower; you might enjoy just watching others enjoy themselves. The **Divus Dancing Hall,** Proxénou Koromilá 51 (☎ **031/286-067**), pretty much lives up to its name after 10pm. **Entasis,** Proxénou Koromilá 29, is a gay and lesbian bar.

The younger crowd gathers a little farther east along and in from Níkis Street; you can't miss them. During our last visit the coolest spot was the **Club Privé,** at Odós Pávlou Méla 40, a music bar with chic decor.

The bar scene changes seasonally, so this year's picks may be next year's duds. In summer the disco crowd moves outdoors and out of town, on the road just past the airport; last summer's favorites were said to be **Amnesia,** which, if we remember correctly, has held on for a few years now, and **Swing.** But don't take our word for it—ask around. Most are open June to September and charge about 2,000 Drs ($8.35) for cover and one drink. It's about a $7\frac{1}{2}$-mile cab ride out (1,500 Drs/$6.25), but don't bother going before 11pm because the crowds are still at the bars.

From September to June the liveliest disco is said to be **Traffic,** on Trítis Septemvríou, a couple of blocks south of Egnatía. **L'Apogée,** at Ethnikís Andistásis 16, on the east side of town, is also said to be hot. For live Greek music, look for **Avantaz,** opposite the Turkish consulate at Ayíou Dimitríou 156. Again, expect to pay about 2,000 Drs ($8.35) for cover and a drink, but don't expect much to be happening until around midnight.

A popular nightlife center is **Mýlos,** Odós Yioryíou 56 (☎ **031/525-968**), an old mill and satellite building transformed into a very attractive entertainment complex with an art gallery, theater, several excellent restaurants, bars, and live music clubs ranging from classical to heavy metal. It's southwest of the port in a rather creepy part of town, best reached by taxi; the fare should be about 1,200 Drs ($5) one-way.

If you're up for a nighttime *vólta,* that leisurely Greek saunter, there's no better place for it than **along the harbor in front of Aristotélous Square.** Beyond the White Tower you can escape the traffic and be romanced by the moon and the waves, or at least entertained by others enjoying romance and various other quiet amusements. If you wander west to the waterfront around the commercial and ferryboat pier, and particularly up to the region of Polytéchniou and 26 Oktovríou streets, you'll find some colorful ladies of the night, along with clubs, bars, and neon signs.

To escape reality, sample the cinemas near the White Tower. The **Aristotelion,** at Ethnikís Amínis Plaza 2 (☎ **031/232-557**), is a grand old 1,000-seat palace that plays recent American films in full Dolby stereo. Farther east at Odós Níkis 73 is the **Cinema Pallaso** (☎ **031/278-515**), for recent European fare and schlock

American B-movies. Both the **White Tower** on N. Yérmanou Street and the **Dimotiko Teatro Kipou** have outdoor performances (check with the EOT for schedules).

2 Halkidikí & Mt. Áthos

Halkidikí (Chalkidiki, Chalcidice), the three-fingered peninsula settled centuries ago by sailors from Halkís in Évvia, is beloved by the Greeks for its lush pine forests and gold-sand beaches. Now, however, most of the forests have been cut back to make way for condos, and the narrow beach strips are so overcrowded that sometimes it's hard to differentiate the sand from the flesh.

Kassándra, the westernmost finger of the peninsula, was the first to be developed. The roads throughout are packed with condominiums and vacation villas for Thessalonikans, and there are hotels or megaresort complexes for European tour groups around each sandy strip.

Sithonía, the middle finger, has a more densely forested interior and a very rugged and beautiful coastline, whose few sand beaches have been much less developed. Campers will find ample opportunities along the west coast, especially at **Nikitas, Tripótamos,** and **Pórto Koufó.** Along the east coast there are campsites at the beaches of **Sárti, Áyios Sikiás,** and **Kalamítsi,** and—as always—rooms for rent along the coast road and in the larger inland villages such as Sikiá. Sithonia's biggest resort complex is at Néos Marmarás, now renamed **Pórto Carrás** after its developer—the oil tycoon John Carras. He planted a million grape vines, almond trees, orange and grapefruit groves, and flowering bushes after filling in a mosquito-breeding lake at this picturesque site. Besides its three hotels—the Meliton, the Sithonia Beach, and the slightly more modest Village Inn—there's a casino, a marina, several swimming pools, tennis courts, a riding stable, and an 18-hole golf course.

The eastern (or right) finger of Halkidikí is **Mt. Áthos** (Áyiou Óros, the Holy Mountain), an independent Greek Orthodox state revered by the Greeks. The 20 monasteries of this most scenically beautiful of the fingers are not open to women visitors; only 10 men are allowed ashore each day to visit. (See the Mt. Áthos section below for information regarding permits.) You can visit **Ouranópoli** (the closest "open" city) by bus, but this small village is often overrun with day-trippers who join the Round-Áthos Cruises; it does not provide the spiritual experience that women readers might seek. Instead, you'd do well to join a Mt. Áthos day trip or quietly explore **Ierissós** (the ancient Acanthos), **Gomati,** or **Megáli Panayía** on your own. Also of interest in the eastern sector is **Arnéa,** a mountain town whose women are known for their colorful hand-woven rugs and fabrics. Aristotle, the great philosopher, was born in nearby Stáyira.

EXPLORING THE REGION

You can take a public bus to **Políyiros,** the capital of Halkidikí. It's 43 miles from Thessaloníki, and is served by regular buses from the Thessaloníki station at Odós 26 Oktovríou 100 (☎ **031/513-734**), but unfortunately the route does not go through any of the peninsula's beautiful scenery. Your best bet is to rent a car in Thessaloníki (see "Getting Around" under "Essentials" in section 1 of this chapter for details) and explore on your own.

Políyiros has become a fair-sized modern town of little interest to most tourists, except for the **archaeological museum** near its north end. Museum and archaeology fans are likely to find the collection of primitive clay figurines from the 5th century B.C., and the Picasso-esque style of painting on the black figure vases, particularly pleasing. For the cognoscenti, there are fragments from the Sanctuary of Zeus

Ammon near Kallithéa on the Kassándra finger and artifacts from the ancient city of Acanthos (Ierissós), where Aristotle taught. The museum is open Tuesday to Sunday from 8:30am to 3pm; admission is 500 Drs ($2.10) for adults, 400 Drs ($1.65) for seniors, and free for students.

If this is as far as you'll go in Halkidikí, and you still have energy, you might enjoy hiking up **Profítis Ilías hill** for a wonderful view.

West of Políyiros is the village of **Petrálona,** famous for its natural cave where a skull and some remains were found, indicating habitation by an early man more than 700,000 years ago (the first tourist?). The cave is filled with colorful stalagmites and stalactites and the paleontological museum at the site is quite interesting; it's open daily from 9am to 6pm. Petrálona can be reached twice daily by bus via Néa Kalikrátia and it's also the destination for many local day tours.

If you have only a day, we'd recommend one of the **Mt. Athos cruise** excursions that originate in Thessaloníki. **Doucas Tours,** Odós Venizélou 8 on Platía Eleftherías (☎ 031/224-100), offers a coach tour across Halkidikí to Órmos Panayía on the central finger of Sithonía, then a cruise along the west coast of Áthos to Ouranópolis; the cost is 11,500 Drs ($47.90). (Go to the second floor and ask for Panayótis.)

If you'll have an opportunity to visit other resorts in Greece, we suggest that you avoid the crowded Halkidikí resorts.

MT. ÁTHOS

The monastic community consisting of 20 monasteries and 700 related houses perched on the Holy Mountain has remained largely untouched by time since St. Anathasios founded the Lávra Monastery in A.D. 963. At its peak, Áthos had 40,000 monks (the Crusaders sold 39,000 of them into slavery). Today Mt. Áthos is an independent religious state that's not even part of Greece: The monks follow their own Orthodox calendar—their year begins 17 days after ours—and their time zone is 4 hours later than at Ouranópolis, the nearest lay community. A recent census found that Áthos had 1,500 residents; only 20 to 25 monks still live at each of the open monasteries.

Many of the customs practiced at Mt. Áthos are unique, but the basic precepts of the Orthodox religion are the same as those studied at Tínos, Pátmos, and Metéora (Greece's other religious enclaves). The Orthodox service you'll hear on Áthos is the same one you'd hear in Moscow, Bucharest, or Sofia. Visitors with some knowledge of the Orthodox faith can learn a lot from their conversations with the monks, all of whom are well educated and speak several languages. The Bibles, icons, frescoes, and religious art displayed in the monasteries comprise one of the best collections of its kind in the world.

Laymen (but not women) can get permission to stay for up to 4 days on the Holy Mountain. Days are spent hiking among the monasteries and exploring the lush, forested, and flowering countryside. You must reach the monastery where you'll spend the night by sunset because the doors are locked then. The monks farm (they grow their own food), study, and pray in the early morning, and then sleep in the afternoon. Nights are spent dining and talking with the few guests they receive. Meals consist of locally grown eggplant, onions, olives, and bread, with the occasional tomato, cucumber, or fresh fish. The monks will offer wine and their homemade ouzo to soften the austerity.

Of the 20 monasteries that are open, **Lávra,** the oldest and one of the few that hasn't been rebuilt, is the most architecturally pure. Fortress walls surround this stone, wood-trimmed Byzantine compound. The **Monastery of Símonos Pétras** is perched on top of a 6,700-foot-high cliff, where Simon built it in the mid–14th century. It was rebuilt by the Serbians, and after a 1581 fire, was restored by funds from the Orthodox faithful of Bucharest. Between 1821 and 1891 it was closed by the Turks—Mt. Áthos as a whole remained fairly autonomous under the Turkish occupation—and in 1891 suffered another fire that destroyed the library. As with many monasteries, Símonos Pétras boasts such treasures as the left hand of Saint Magdalene and the hand of Saint Dionysios of Zákynthos.

The 13th-century **Monastery of St. Gregory** was deserted in 1500, rebuilt by the governor of Moldovlahia, and burned down in 1761. It was restored and its church dedicated to St. Nicholas. At St. Gregory are the two legs and right palm of St. Anastasia Romaia, as well as beautiful icons and frescoes in the church. The **Monastery of Zográphou** is famous for its library, which contains early ecclesiastical codes and 66 codes on parchment of 16th- to 19th-century Byzantine music. Fortunately, a 1976 fire that destroyed one wing left the library unharmed.

The 12th-century **Monastery of Pandelímon** has been called the Russian monastery since the 14th century, when it was rebuilt (after a fire) with Serbian and Byzantine funds. After Greek monks abandoned it for another monastery near the coast, a Russian abbot was elected, and for 100 years the main mass has been given in Russian and Greek. The 19th-century influx of Russian Orthodoxy has left its mark visually on all the monasteries that have been partially rebuilt or restored since that time. (Recently the patriarch of Moscow has expressed some interest, which is reported to be of concern to the Greek government.) In 1963 the Holy Mountain celebrated its first millennium of religious occupation, an event that brought the unique Mt. Áthos to the attention of the world.

Only 10 foreign male visitors are permitted to remain overnight on Mt. Áthos each night. If you're interested, apply 3 to 4 months in advance; a dated **entry permit** will then be issued. To obtain the permit, you must send a letter that includes: details from your passport (or send a photocopy); personal or professional information, including why you want to visit Mt. Áthos; a declaration of your "intention to be a pilgrim"; and a letter of recommendation from your consulate. Address your letter to the Ministry of Northern Greece, Diikitiríou Square, 546 23 Thessaloníki. They will preapply for you, requesting your dates. Applicants in Athens may contact the EOT or the Ministry of Foreign Affairs, which will then forward your request to the Thessaloníki office. If you're a religious professional, you should apply by writing to the Ecumenical Patriarchate, Istanbul, Turkey, and noting your religious background.

Once you've been notified in writing that your request has been granted and your date has been specified, you'll have to pick up your permit personally from the Ministry of Northern Greece on Áyíou Dimitríou Street in Thessaloníki, which is open Monday to Friday from 11am to 1:45pm.

To reach Mt. Áthos, take a bus from Odós Karakássi 68 in Thessaloníki, to Ouranópolis on Halkidikí. There's one boat a day to Dafní (2 hours), the harbor of Mt. Áthos. You must show your letter of permission to board the boat. From Dafní, you can take the bus 7½ miles uphill to Karyés, the administrative capital of Áthos. There, you'll present your letter for a *diamonitírion*, a pass enabling you to visit other monasteries. There's no charge for room or board at any of the monasteries, but the boat trip and pass will cost about $60.

Note: Women should not even try to win this battle; **Doucas Tours** (☎ **031/ 224-100** or 031/269-984 in Thessaloníki) and others have organized well-guided day cruises around the Holy Mountain for about 12,000 Drs ($50).

3　Alexander the Great Country

From Thessaloníki: 38 miles W to Veryína, 42 miles W to Véria, 21 miles NW to Pélla, 48 miles S to Dión

Hesiod traces the settlement of Macedonia to the descendants of Makednos and Magnes, sons of Zeus who populated the region after about 2000 B.C. These Makednian tribes spread southward to the Pieria Mountains in the Pindus range, eventually moving over the next thousand years into the Peloponnese as Dorian peoples. Herodotus called the Makednia a "wide-wandering" Greek race, accurately foreshadowing the goals and eventual triumph of Macedonia's most celebrated son, Alexander.

Historians believe that King Perdikkas first founded the Macedonian capital at Veryína in the 7th century B.C. It was known as Aigaes in antiquity.

The region is linked in history and in the popular imagination with Alexander the Great, who lived from 356 to 323 B.C. He was only 18 at the time of his father's death, but he had already served as a general at the Battle of Herónia, and he had been tutored by Aristotle, who had surely broadened his mind and deepened his appreciation of Greek culture.

In 334 he set out to conquer Persia, to avenge its invasion of Greece and to finance future expeditions. He took Miletus, Tyre, Phoenicia, Palestine, and Egypt on the way, founding Alexandria, the great city that still bears his name. After he had met and defeated the forces of the Persian king, Darius, at Gaugemela, he pushed farther east to Babylon, Sousa, and Persepolis, where he burned the palace of Xerxes in revenge for Thermopylae.

He pushed farther east into the mountains of what is now Afghanistan, planning to invade India. His troops were weary and homesick, but he managed to cross the Indus River, in what is now Pakistan. But the monsoon rains had come, and his soldiers refused to cross the Hyphasis River; after much pleading, Alexander agreed to turn back.

The return trip was extremely difficult, with natural disasters and shortages of food and water, and it took him nearly a year to reach Sousa. There he married a Bactrian princess and presided over the marriage of 10,000 of his men to Asian women. He prosposed retiring thousands of his loyal Macedonian soldiers and replacing them with Persians, but their anger and resentment dissuaded him.

He announced that his next objective was Arabia, but in June of 323 he fell ill with a fever in Babylon and died. He had conquered most of the known world and introduced Greek culture, which continued to exert an extraordinary influence throughout the ancient world.

After his death the Macedonians only held on to their own kingdom until 168 B.C., when the Romans defeated them at the Battle of Pidna, but Alexander's legacy will never be forgotten.

East of the present-day city of Veryína, on both sides of the national highway, are small mounds that have contributed a great deal of information about the dress, burial customs, and weaponry and tools manufactured by these families. Archaeologists found that some mounds had been opened and reused later during the Hellenistic era by Macedonian settlers. The Frenchman Leon Heuzey began excavating at Veryína in 1861, thinking that it was probably the small Macedonian village of Balla. Over the years archaeologists uncovered a Macedonian tomb (in 1937) and a royal palace, both thought to date from the early 3rd century B.C. In 1959 Professors Bakalakis and Andronicos joined the team of Greek archaeologists and historians at the site. In 1977 Professor Andronicos made the most envied find of the century, a royal tomb that had never been plundered!

EXPLORING THE REGION

Although each of the sites can be reached by **public bus** from Thessaloníki's west-side KTEL stations, we found the schedules too limited to permit viewing more than one or two sites on any given day. Bus fares to the many connecting points between Pélla, Véria, Veryína, and Dión are $6 to $9 each and add up quickly.

Two or more travelers can see more in less time by **renting a car** from one of the many companies in Thessaloníki. See "Getting Around" under "Essentials" in section 1 of this chapter for details.

Many travelers prefer the convenience and expert narration that comes with a guided bus tour. The **Greek Tourist Organization (EOT)** in Thessaloníki maintains a list of tour agents in the area who offer such excursions. One of them is **Doucas Tours,** Odós Venizélou 8 (☎ **031/269-984;** fax 031/286-610), which is among the largest operators in this area.

VÉRYINA

The magnificent hoard of gold funerary objects, now on display at the archaeology museum in Thessaloníki, were assumed to belong to Philip II, largely because of a misshapen greave that fit the historical description of Alexander's father's lame leg—but there was still some dissention. Finally, in 1982, Professor Andronicos found the first row of seats of an ancient theater, which established a direct link with King Philip and his death and confirmed this as his capital. As Professor Andronicos said, "We know that King Philip II was killed by one of his seven bodyguards while attending the wedding of daughter Cleopatra in the theater of Aigaes."

The **royal tomb** that has yielded such wealth is in the midst of excavation and study, and may not be opened to the general public for several years. One can visit the Macedonian tomb and royal palace near the modern-day village of Véryina, and see from above the early stages of excavation at the theater.

The **Macedonian tomb** has been partially cleared from under the mound of soil that was piled over it in antiquity to thwart vandals. Unfortunately, it didn't work. When the huge white marble doors were pushed aside, the tomb was empty. The facade is almost perfectly intact; four Ionic semicolumns in relief grace the entry. Through the grated, modern iron protective gate you can see the halves of the marble sealing doors, carved in relief to resemble wood joined by metal studs. If you bring a flashlight, you can see to the right the damaged remains of the marble throne.

The **royal palace,** which archaeologists presume was the summer residence of the royal family, is thought to have been built for King Antigonas Gonatas, who preceded Philip by almost half a century. Although the knee-high remains are difficult to appreciate, the dimensions of the palace—475 by 310 feet—are impressive. The central courtyard, whose walls of buff-colored Poros stone can be discerned, once had 60 Doric columns. Archaeologists have found traces of several badly damaged mosaics, and have come to the conclusion that early Christian squatters at the site may have been offended by the nudity or religious frolicking portrayed in some; the only intact mosaics are of floral patterns and geometric designs. Along with the obviously high level of artistry, scholars have determined that there was great architectural and engineering sophistication in Macedonia at the time. Even in the largest palace rooms, no trace of internal support columns has been found, indi-cating a technical expertise capable of designing walls to hold the weight of the heavy, tiled roofs.

The partially uncovered **theater** can be viewed in the plains below the hillside palace. The site of the tombs and royal palace is open Tuesday to Sunday from 8:30am to 3pm.

VÉRIA

Nine miles northwest of Véryina, and the largest nearby town to make bus connections to the site, Véria is better known for its Byzantine-era churches than for remains of the Roman era. Some are housed in its **museum** (open daily from 9am to 5pm), with exquisite painted stelae, pottery, and figurines from Véryina and exceptionally high-quality finds from the Macedonian tomb at Lefkádia. Véria was later one of two Macedonian capitals during the reform period of the emperor Diocletian (3rd century A.D.). The **Cathedral of St. John Theológos** and the **Church of Christ** display some fine frescoes from the later Byzantine period.

Before we head east to the second Macedonian capital, Pélla, we'll note some other sites south of Thessaloníki. There is very little of interest at Pýdna, but recent finds at the site of Dión may one day prove to be as exciting as those at Veryína.

DIÓN

About 50 miles south of Thessaloníki, at the foot of the magnificent Mt. Olympus, is the village of Dión. Recent excavations have revealed that this was an important religious center for worshiping the gods of the sacred mount. Philip II celebrated his victories here, and his son, Alexander the Great, came to sacrifice to Zeus to bless his famous expedition. The choice of this site for such important worship is no mystery, for the landscape is very blessed. Springs pour out of the hills and run down to the nearby sea. The thunderstorms that were thought to be the god's battles roll off the mountain and across the oak groves of Dión, lending credence to the legends that grew around it.

Much progress has been made in the **excavations** in recent years, filling the new museum with some very fine works. As you reach the town of Dión, turn down a small road toward the sea to the east and you'll pass a small, badly preserved theater on the right. About a quarter mile farther is the main part of the site, to the left. There are ancient paved roads running by stores, workshops, an odeon, and the well-preserved foundations of public baths. The short, standing pillars supported the floor under which heated air would flow. Across the modern road is the Temple of Demeter, where finds date back to 500 B.C. Farther down the public road on your right is the most interesting part of the area. Under 6 feet of water, archaeologists found an intact Sanctuary of Isis, the Egyptian goddess. Water and mud heaved into place by an earthquake had protected it from vandals for centuries. Rich finds of sculpture were uncovered still standing in place, including the wonderful cult statue of Aphrodite that stands in the museum. A copy sits in the reeds and water that have partially reclaimed the temple, although the foundations are still clearly visible.

The archaeological site (☎ 0351/53-206) is open daily from 8am to 5pm (to 3pm in winter); admission is 800 Drs ($3.35) for adults, 600 Drs ($2.50) for seniors, and 400 Drs ($1.65) for students.

The **Dión Museum** is on the same road as the archaeological site, but back in the quiet village. The brand-new building (with scholarly teams cataloging recent finds out back) contains tasteful displays of very exciting finds from the site. The sculptural works, votive offerings from throughout the ancient world, are especially impressive, particularly the cult statue of Aphrodite found underwater in the Temple of Isis. Upstairs is a collection of household items, including surgical tools, dentist's instruments, and rusted iron nails used in house construction.

The museum is open on Monday from 12:30 to 5pm, Tuesday to Friday from 8am to 5pm, and on Saturday and Sunday from 8:30am to 3pm; admission is 800 Drs ($3.35) for adults, 600 Drs ($2.50) for seniors, and 400 Drs ($1.65) for students.

PÉLLA

At the end of the 5th century B.C. the Macedonian capital had moved from Veryína (Aigaes) to Pélla. It was traditional in the Macedonian culture to bury royalty in the ancient capital—a tradition that Alexander, who died in Babylon and was buried in Alexandria, was not to fulfill. Philip II ruled his kingdom from Pella, and from here launched more successful military missions than the Greek world had ever seen. He was an early exponent of Panhellenism, a concept of Greek unity for mutual protection and prosperity. After defeating the combined southern Greek forces at the Battle of Herónia (Chaironeia) in 338 B.C., he called for peace and unity against the common Persian foe and was on the verge of realizing this goal. On the eve of his death (2 short years later) Philip was proclaimed head of the Hellenic Federation. Pélla became the first *de facto* capital of a united Greece, and the stage was set for Alexander.

The small **archaeological site** (☎ 0382/31-160) and its few remains have led scholars to speculate on the great wealth and high standard of living achieved by its inhabitants. Graceful fluted Ionic columns still stand, and there are superb pebble mosaic floors—most now in the museum. The site is only part of the Macedonian capital that Alexander had enlarged according to a master urban plan. The museum has a small display of statuary, pottery, and jewelry excavated at the site, as well as the carefully reconstructed late 4th-century mosaics, which are especially graceful and lively. Admission to the site and museum is 500 Drs ($2.10) for adults, 400 Drs ($1.65) for seniors, and 300 Drs ($1.25) for students. The site is open Monday to Friday from 8am to 3pm and on Saturday and Sunday from 8:30am to 3pm; the museum's hours are Monday from 12:30 to 3pm, Tuesday to Friday from 8am to 3pm, and Saturday and Sunday from 8:30am to 3pm.

In the modern town of Pélla there are several moderately priced tavernas and shops. The 51-room **Hotel Avra** (☎ 0384/91-300), in nearby Aridea, is a modern, comfortable lodging favored by tour groups for its proximity to the site.

ELSEWHERE AROUND THE REGION

Many tourists working their way west to Epirus prefer to move onward through the picturesque metropolis of **Édessa,** known for its cascading waterfalls and its Byzantine-era bridge that was one link in the Romans' Egnatía Way.

The two archaeological sites that have offered us the richest artifacts displayed in the Thessaloníki Museum are **Sindos** and **Dervéni.** There is little to see at **Dervéni** (6 miles east of Thessaloníki on the Kavála highway) or at **Sindos** (14 miles west), where a treasure-filled cemetery spanning centuries was found when excavating a site for a new factory in the industrial zone. In both areas, archaeological work continues.

4 Other Macedonia Highlights

THE KASTORIÁ REGION

Kastoriá, considered by many Greeks their most beautiful town, is set on a tree-lined peninsula on a mountain lake. It's a prosperous center of fur trade and assembly, with many Byzantine and medieval churches.

ESSENTIALS

GETTING THERE & DEPARTING   By Plane   From May to October, **Olympic Airways** has four flights a week to and from Athens; its office is at Leofóros Megálou Alexándrou 15 (☎ 0467/22-275). The airport is 6 miles south of town.

By Train   The nearest major railroad station is in Flórina; there are two trains daily from Athens; call ☎ 01/821-3882 for information.

By Bus   Two buses depart daily from Athens's Terminal A, Odós Kifissoú 100; the 11-hour trip costs 8,400 Drs ($35); for schedule information, phone ☎ 01/512-9308 in Athens or ☎ 0467/83-455 in Kastoriá. Five buses a day leave from the Thessaloníki station at Anayeniséos 22; the trip takes 4 hours and costs 3,200 Drs ($13.35).

VISITOR INFORMATION / FAST FACTS   The helpful **Greek Tourist Organization (EOT)** office is in the town hall, a block northeast of Platía Daváki (☎ 0467/24-484). The **telephone center (OTE)** is on Odós Ayíou Athanassíou northwest of the central Platía Dexaménis; the **area code** is **0467.** The **post office** is near the lake a couple of blocks south of Platía Daváki. The local **police** are at Odós Grámmou 25, near the bus station (☎ 0467/83-333).

EXPLORING THE AREA

If you're continuing west (hopefully not in the bitter cold winter), you'll first reach the prefecture of Flórina, then that of Kastoriá. **Flórina,** once home to rebel Greek forces, edges up to the Albanian and Yugoslav borders, giving it a somewhat more ethnic feel than you'll find in the hill country farther south. It's a verdant region dotted by small cold-water lakes; ice skating is a popular winter activity.

In the northwest area, tranquil **Lake Préspa,** noted for its excellent **bird-watching,** is actually the larger Megáli Préspa and tiny Mikrí Préspa, two bodies of water separated by a very narrow land bridge at the village of Lemos. Both are part Greek and part Albanian; Megáli Préspa also has the (possibly unique) distinction of being part Yugoslavian as well. In any case, this region of shallow, marshy wetlands has for centuries been an active breeding ground for wildlife and birds. Since 1977 the region around Mikrí Préspa has been a national wildlife preserve, most noted for its over 185 different species of birds. Mikrí Préspa numbers among its happy inhabitants two types of endangered pelicans and some of Europe's rare cormorants.

The city of **Kastoriá,** center of Greece's fur-producing region, is set on a promontory jutting into the still, gray-blue (polluted) waters of Lake Kastoriá (or Orestiada). Because of its influential role as a successful trading center, Kastoriá is graced with many Byzantine churches—more than 70 churches from the Byzantine and later eras are tucked in between typical Macedonian *arhondiká* (mansions). Many of these mansions have large, open fireplaces and their own exceptional frescoes.

The excellent **Kastoria Folklore Museum,** housed in the Aïvazís mansion, a traditional-style *arhondikó* on Kapetán Lázou Street, has interesting displays of locally produced embroideries and, of course, a history of the fur trade. It's open daily from 10am to noon and 3 to 5pm; admission is 220 Drs (90¢).

Kastoriá also has a **Byzantine museum** with a collection of ikons drawn from its many *arhondiká,* on the central Platía Dexaménis, near the Xenia Hotel, open Tuesday to Sunday from 8:30am to 3pm; free admission.

Kastoriá's fur trade is based on its skilled craftspeople ("trimmers"), who can take small pieces of fur, or ends, and stitch them together to form a whole cloth, from which lower-priced coats are made. In several factories you can watch as leftovers imported from European and Scandinavian furriers are melded together to form blankets and carpets. "Stop and shop" is our recommendation for Kastoriá; furs are cheaper here than anywhere else.

Kastoriá is also a lovely place to stroll. On the west side of the lake, near the Hotel Kastoriá, is a weeping willow–lined lane that attracts walkers, cyclists, and fishermen. If you climb up the heights of the town, you'll be rewarded with a fine view that reminded us of a northern Italian lake town. Kastoriá has spawned a unique, squared-off paddle boat for making your way around the lake; these funny-looking vessels are available for rent by the hour for a few drachmas.

WHERE TO STAY

Europa Hotel. Odós Áyíou Athanasíou 8, 521 00 Kastoriá. ☎ **0467/23-826.** Fax 0467/ 25-154. 36 rms, all with bath (tub). TEL. 9,700 Drs ($40.40) single; 11,900 Drs ($49.60) double. EURO, MC, V.

These well-kept rooms have partial views of the lake and are a good choice if everything else is booked.

Hotel Orestion. Platía Daváki 1, 521 00 Kastoriá. ☎ **0467/22-257.** 20 rms, all with bath (tub). TEL. 10,450 Drs ($43.55) single; 12,750 Drs ($53.15) double. V.

This comfortable hostel is located above Platía Daváki, near the bus station. The standard double rooms are well kept by the friendly proprietors. A bar and breakfast room are open year-round.

Hotel Tsamis. Odós Koromilá 3, 521 00 Dispilio, Kastoriá. ☎ **0467/85-334.** Fax 0467/ 85-777. 75 rms, 3 suites, all with bath (tub). MINIBAR TV TEL. 13,750 Drs ($57.30) single; 19,800 Drs ($82.50) double. Rates include breakfast. AE, DC, V.

This newly renovated lodging on the national road 2 miles south of town is a modern three-story inn with carefully tended grounds, willows leading down to its own dock, and spectacular views of the lake and town. The stone lobby has a fireplace that in the colder months is particularly welcoming, and there's even a gymnasium (at an extra charge). The nicely decorated guest rooms have lake-view balconies; prices are on the high side but an excellent value.

WHERE TO EAT

Choose a place to eat by walking along the lakefront and stopping in the various cafes.

Rendezvous Café/Bar. On Lake Kastoriá. ☎ **0467/24-793.** Menu items 400–1,350 Drs ($1.65–$5.65). No credit cards. Daily 11am–12:30am. SNACKS/DESSERTS.

Pizza, snacks, and pink tablecloths, pink neon, pink curtains. They serve great coffee drinks and ice cream.

Taverna Michalis. On the Flórina highway. No phone. Main courses 1,000–2,500 Drs ($4.15–$10.40). No credit cards. Daily 6:30pm–midnight. GREEK.

Everyone's favorite country taverna is on the road leading north to Flórina. It's open year-round, so items change according to season. The roast meats and stuffed vegetables are especially good.

TRAVELING EAST THROUGH MACEDONIA

Let's turn eastward from Thessaloníki and look at the Macedonia that becomes more Oriental the farther east you go. The scenic route to Dráma is along the Kavála highway which hugs northern Halkidikí; as you pass **Lake Korónia** and **Lake Vólvi** you'll see how easily an island could have been made of Halkidikí if the two lakes had been joined! North of Lake Korónia is the famous village of **Langádas,** where every year on May 21 the Festival of the Anastenarídes is held. Local firewalkers will come out and dance on blazing embers in honor of Saints Konstandínos and Eléni. (There's not much here on other days of the year.) On the north side of Lake Vólvi is the hamlet of **Philadelphia,** one of many Greek cities called "Brotherly Love."

Amphípolis, a new village on the site of an ancient, prosperous mineral-mining town, is noted for its Byzantine church and for the remarkable marble Lion Statue found in the riverbed of the flowing Strýmon River. The Strýmon, which contributed to the rich mineral deposits sought after by Thracian, Roman, and Athenian alike, also preserved for us the remnants of a large wooden bridge from the 5th century, which has recently been brought up from its bottom.

The roads leading to **Dráma,** called the "Plain of Gold" for its late-afternoon amber light, are often lined with shade-giving poplar and elm trees. The plain was the battleground for a 5th-century B.C. defeat of Athens by the more powerful Macedonian forces, yet very little of interest remains from antiquity. Consider a lunch break in one of Dráma's pretty public gardens. If you're not prepared to picnic, there's a small taverna, on its own little island in the middle of the healthy Ayía Várvara springs that bubble up in downtown Dráma.

PHILIPPI

Philippi (Phílippi), also spelled Filippi, is best known for the Battle of Philippi and as the place where Saint Paul preached his first sermon. In 42 B.C. the armies of Mark Antony and Octavius met those of Julius Caesar's assassins on the Plain of Philippi and defeated them soundly. Brutus and Cassius committed suicide and the Roman republic died with them; representative government gave way to the dictatorship of the Caesars. After their victory, Mark Antony and Octavius committed great sums of money to renewing Philippi, and most of its fascinating archaeological sites date from this period of largesse. They granted Philippi the status of a Roman colony, and a garrison guarding Via Egnatia and its language, laws, and coinage followed the Roman model.

In the Acts of the Apostles, we read about Saint Paul's visit to Philippi, probably about A.D. 49: "We went to Philippi, which is the leading city of the district of Macedonia, and a Roman colony. . . . On the sabbath day we went outside the gate to the riverside, where we supposed there was a place of prayer; and we sat down and spoke to the women who had come together." Paul and Silas set up a church in the house of Lydia, one of the women laundering who'd accepted Paul's words and been baptized. Their troubles were caused by a young prophetess who was trying to discredit the preacher. Impatiently, Paul exorcised the spirit that enabled her to prophecy, and her supporters and "agents" demanded that Paul be jailed for interfering with their livelihood. A small crypt in the Roman forum is supposed to be the cell where Paul and Silas were imprisoned.

As you enter Philippi, the **archaeological site** and museum are on the left of the main road. The **Propylon** has been restored and welcomes visitors. The largest part of the site is the **forum** or agorá (on the south side), where there are remains of the arcade that once spanned three sides. There are remnants of a Roman bath, but a much more impressive plumbing feat are the 50 marble seats still in place in the **public toilets** at the southeastern end of the agorá. At the north end, finely preserved stairs lead up to a terrace and portico. A bold, hewn-brick arch on top of rectangular columns is the striking remains of a 6th-century basilica. The tawny-colored stone and acanthus leaf–trimmed columns were made up from the Roman-era palaestra and forum, destroyed in clearing the land for the chapel. The smaller basilica A, as it's called, is near the ruins of the theater.

The **theater** dates from the 4th century B.C. and was actively used in Philip's time for the presentation of dramatic works. In the 3rd century A.D. it was converted to a gladiator's arena; wild animal exits and entrances and a guard rail for the spectator seating were added at that time. The theater has been somewhat restored, and during the summer a Historic Drama Festival is held there (check with the EOT for schedule information).

The small **archaeological museum** (☎ 051/516-251) at the site exhibits finds from the Neolithic period (Dikili-Tach and Sitagri regions) and from the Hellenic and Roman eras, when Philippi was at its prime.

The site and museum are open Tuesday to Sunday from 8:30am to 3pm; admission is 500 Drs ($2.10). To reach Philippi from Kavála, take the Dráma bus from the KTEL station, which leaves every 20 minutes, and ask the driver to let you off at Arhéa Phílipi; the half-hour ride costs 350 Drs ($1.45).

5 Kavála

107 miles E of Thessaloníki, 106 miles W of Alexandroúpolis, 285 miles W of Istanbul

Kavála is one of Greece's most attractive cities, the second largest in Macedonia and an important port—its large harbor nestled on the lower slopes of Mt. Symbólon. It rests on the remains of the ancient Neapolis, the port of Philippi, and has been occupied for at least 3,000 years. The Apostle Paul first set foot on European soil here, on his way to Philippi.

Besides its successful fishing and shipping industry, Kavála is the central market town for the area and Thrace's large tobacco industry. Tobacco has been farmed by Anatolian peoples in the Kavála area for centuries, and their integration into the community is one of the more intriguing aspects of this cross-over region.

ESSENTIALS

GETTING THERE & DEPARTING   **By Plane**   **Olympic Airways** has at least one flight daily to and from Athens; its office in Kavála is at Odós Ethnikís Andistásis 8 (☎ 051/836-639). The airport is 18 miles southeast of town; at present there is no shuttle bus, but a public bus leaves from the bus station at 6:15pm daily.

By Train   The nearest train station is 18 miles away in Dráma; it's serviced several times daily from Athens and from Thessaloníki. Contact the OSE in Dráma (☎ 051/32-444), in Athens (☎ 01/522-2491), or Thessaloníki (☎ 031/276-382 or 031/517-517) for information.

By Bus   Two buses depart daily from Athens's Terminal A, Odós Kifissoú 100 (☎ 01/512-9363) for Dráma or Kávala (11 hours). KTEL buses run along Via Egnatia (built in the mid–2nd century from Rome to Constantinople) from Thessaloníki every hour; the 2-hour trip costs 2,600 Drs ($10.85). The **KTEL bus station** is at the corner of Mitropolítou and Filikís Eterías, a block northwest from the harbor.

Buses to Alexandroúpolis stop in front of the Dore Cafe at Odós Erythroú Stavroú 34, where departure times are posted and tickets can be purchased.

The **OSE bus** to Istanbul stops in Kavála at 5:30pm daily; contact **Alkyon Travel,** Odós Venizélou 24 (☎ 051/231-096), for information and tickets.

By Ferry   There are hourly ferries to Skála Prínou on Thássos (1¼ hours, 650 Drs/ $2.70 or 4,000 Drs/$16.65 for a car and driver). There are two to five ferries weekly to Límnos and Lésvos, with additional service in summer to Híos, Sámos, and the Dodecanese. In summer there's a ferry twice a week to Samothráki. Call the EOT at ☎ 051/222-425 for further details.

By Hydrofoil   In summer there are seven hydrofoils daily to Liménas (30 minutes, 1,500 Drs/$6.25) and five to Skála Prínou (40 minutes, 1,900 Drs/$7.90)

on Thássos; tickets can be purchased at the pier. In the summer there are hydrofoil connections twice a week with Límnos, Mytilíni, and Plomári on Lésvos, and Híos; contact **Miliades Shipping,** Platía Karaóli-Dimitríou 36, off the east corner of the harbor (☎ **051/226-147;** fax 051/838-767), for information and tickets.

VISITOR INFORMATION The **Greek Tourist Organization (EOT)** office, Odós Filellínon 5, at the west end of Elefthería Square (☎ **051/222-425**), is open Monday to Friday from 7am to 2:30pm (plus 5 to 8pm in summer) and on Saturday from 8am to 1pm. You can buy tickets there to the annual summer-long Drama Festivals held on the island of Thássos and in the ancient theater at Philippi; check with them for schedules and show times.

The **tourist police** are in the police station at Odós Omonías 119, left from the northeast end of Platía Elefthería and half a dozen blocks up on the left (☎ **051/ 222-905**).

ORIENTATION Kavála is the midway point between Thessaloníki and Istanbul (there's a huge CONSTANTINOPLE 460 KM sign at the harbor). At the center of town is a main square, **Platía Elefthería,** located a block off the middle of the **harbor.** The main streets run east-west: **Venizélou,** west from the south end of Platía Elethería; **Erythroú Stavroú** (Red Cross), 1 block south from the northwest corner of the harbor; and **Ethnikís Andistásis,** 2 blocks farther south, along the waterfront. The **bus station** is 1 block south of Erythroú Stavroú, a block west of the harbor. **Ferries** to Thássos leave from the west side of the harbor, long-distance ferries from the east side. **Panayía,** the colorful old Turkish quarter, is southeast of the main square above the east side of the harbor.

Contemporary concrete-block housing descends from the west and fascinating wood-and-stucco traditional Turkish-blend villas descend from the east; the new meets a modern pier for the Thássos ferries and the old meets the original crescent-shaped port and breakwater installed for the long-range ferries. From the impressive hilltop remains of the **Byzantine fortress,** one can appreciate the amphitheatrical design of the city. The 16th-century **Kamares Aqueduct** commissioned by Suleiman the Magnificent still dominates the central part of town. If you confine your stay in Kavála to the old Panayía quarter and the scenic port lined with cafes and shops, you'll have the best possible time in this otherwise busy commercial city.

FAST FACTS The **post office,** open Monday to Friday from 7:30am to 8pm, is at Erythroú Stavroú and Mitropolítou, north of the bus station. The **telephone center (OTE)** is nearby on the west side of the harbor, at Avérof and Ethnikís Andistásis, open daily from 6am to midnight (to 11pm in winter). For English-language periodicals, try **Papadoyianis Books,** Odós Omonías 46, across the square from the EOT.

SEEING THE SIGHTS

The town's most interesting sights are found in the labyrinth of narrow cobblestone lanes in **Panayía,** the old Turkish quarter above the east side of the harbor. The view from the **Byzantine kástro** is splendid.

The **House of Muhammed Ali** (the ancient one), near the southern tip of the peninsula at the end of Poulídou Street, is now open to the public; ring the bell and the caretaker will give you a brief tour. This traditional-style Turkish house was where Ali, founder of the Egyptian dynasty that ended with King Farouk, was born in 1769. It's maintained courtesy of the Egyptian government, which also owns and is partially restoring the **Imaret** down the hill, also built by Muhammed Ali. This was a priests' school combined with a poorhouse, which at times housed and fed up to 300 people.

It's a wonderful, sprawling piece of Islamic architecture, and inside you'll find the highly popular **Refreshments Imaret** (☎ 051/836-286), open daily from 11am to 3am, down under cool white arches around a lush garden, where you can sip something cool, listen to exotic music, and drift away for a while. It's beautiful and soothing anytime, but at its most enchanting at dusk.

The handsome modern **archaeological museum,** on the west side of the waterfront (☎ 051/222-335), attractively displays a full spectrum of artifacts including some particularly beautiful jewelry, fine vases, and excellently crafted terra-cotta figurines from Amphípolis (a prosperous mining town near Thessaloníki), Avdira, Neápolis (the ancient Kavála), and Philippi. It's open Tuesday to Sunday from 8:30am to 3pm; admission is 600 Drs ($2.50) for adults, 400 Drs ($1.65) for seniors, and 300 Drs ($1.25) for students.

An extensive **bazaar** is held on Saturday mornings near the archaeological museum with an amazing array of merchandise.

There's also a small **folk-art museum,** at Odós Philippoú 4, 3 blocks northeast (☎ 051/227-820), open Monday to Friday from 8am to 2pm and on Saturday from 9am to 1pm; admission is free.

WHERE TO STAY

The higher-priced hotels are on Erythroú Stavroú and Venizélou Street, west of Elefthería Square; budget accommodations are nearer the square and east of it.

The EOT-run **Batis Camping,** at Batis Beach, 2 miles west of Kavála (☎ 051/243-051), is a luxurious resort-style camping area complete with water sports. **Irini Camping** (☎ 051/229-785) is 1¹/₄ miles east of town.

George Alvanos Rooms to Let. Odós Athemíou 35, Panayía, 654 03 Kavála 65403. ☎ 051/288-412 or 051/221-781. 5 rms, none with bath. 3,250 Drs ($13.55) single; 4,400 Drs ($18.35) double. No credit cards.

These are currently the only rooms for rent in the Panayía, Kavála's old Turkish quarter, and by far the best budget value in town: immaculate, airy, and cheerful, with a clothesline available. The two bathrooms are also very clean and pleasant. Yiórgos Alvanos or a member of his family gives you a key to the house and disappears upstairs for the rest of your visit, though they are perfectly willing to make recommendations or suggestions if you give them a shout. These rooms go quickly, so call in advance. Ask for a double with the sea view.

Hotel Galaxy. Odós Venizélou 27, 653 02 Kavála. ☎ **051/224-521.** Fax 051/226-754. 149 rms, all with bath (shower or tub). A/C TEL. 14,800 Drs ($61.65) single; 21,500 Drs ($89.60) double. Rates include breakfast. AE, DC, EURO, MC, V.

This superior hotel has balconies that face directly over the harbor with its brightly painted caïques south to the hills of Thássos, with the castle up on the left. There's a roof garden (great view!), restaurant, bar, and air-conditioned rooms, some with big bathtubs and minibars. It's popular with the "Saint Paul in Greece" tour groups, but it's so big you can almost always find a room.

Hotel Nefeli. Odós Erythroú Stavroú 50, 654 03 Kavála. ☎ **051/227-441.** Fax 051/227-440. 94 rms, all with bath (shower or tub). TEL. 13,200 Drs ($55) single; 15,200 Drs ($63.35) double. EURO, MC, V.

We stayed here across from the park near the archaeological museum during our last visit and found it quite satisfactory. Outside the street gets rather lively in the evenings, but inside all remains quiet. The rooms are simple and spacious, and the Acropolis-view roof garden competes favorably with pricier neighbors.

Panorama Hotel. Odós Venizélou 26C, 654 03 Kavála. ☎ **051/224-205** or 051/229-711. 52 rms, 16 with bath (shower). TEL. 8,850 Drs ($36.90) single; 10,750 Drs ($44.80) double. Rooms with bath 20% more. Rates include breakfast.

This hotel is just down and across the street from the Galaxy but the prices here are much more reasonable. It's nothing special to look at, but the location is convenient and the management is friendly and helpful.

Parthenon Hotel. Odós Spetsón 14, 654 02 Kavála. ☎ **051/223-205.** 12 rms, none with bath. 4,000 Drs ($16.65) single; 5,750 Drs ($23.95) double.

The only budget hotel we can suggest has flowered coverlets, wallpaper, and couches that create a strange, almost-Oriental decor in this balconied, high-ceilinged, creaky-floored abode. The shared baths are big, old but clean, and we enjoyed our stay.

WHERE TO EAT

There are plenty of decent places to eat, and you'll find good seafood in Kavála, though most of the harborside establishments are a bit overpriced. You'll find better prices away from the water and on Polídou Street up in Panayía.

Kiriakos Taverna. Odós Perigáli 14. ☎ **051/222-494.** Main courses 1,800–3,800 Drs ($7.50–$15.85). No credit cards. Daily 10am–5pm and 8pm–2am. GREEK/INTERNATIONAL/SEAFOOD.

Near the stadium, on the right about half a mile from the center of town on the road to Alexandroúpolis, overlooking the beach is a fine place for *ksifiás* (swordfish) and fried *mýdia* (mussels).

Panos Zafira. Platía Karaóli-Dimitríou 20. ☎ **051/227-978.** Main courses 500–2,600 Drs ($2.10–$10.85); fish 9,000–15,000 Drs ($37.50–$62.50) per kilo. V. Daily noon–midnight. SEAFOOD.

On the east side of the harbor along with several others you'll find this popular place known for grilled calamari and small local fish—*marídes* (whitebait), *kotsomoúres* (dark), and *gávros* (fresh anchovies)—which are cheaper than most other seafood.

Pavlidi Bakery. Odós Poulídou 5. ☎ **051/223-589.** Menu items 50–400 Drs (20¢–$1.65). No credit cards. Daily 8am–8pm. BAKERY.

Since 1923 this *artopolío* (bakery), on the left just as you start the climb to the castle and Panayía, has been baking *spanakópita, tirópita, milópita* (apple turnovers, which go fast), whole-wheat and sesame breads, and a number of delicious sweets. They have fruit juice and soft drinks if you want to make a meal.

Taverna O Faros. Odós Poulídou 25. ☎ **051/838-987.** Main courses 900–2,600 Drs ($3.75–$10.85). No credit cards. Daily noon–12:30am. GREEK/SEAFOOD.

Have the day's catch fried or broiled and served with a wedge of lime or savor exceptionally well-prepared Greek fare over some of the hearty, regional Límnos white wine at "The Lighthouse." At this special taverna high on the main street of Panayía across from the Imaret, you can watch the neighbors stroll as you enjoy warm hospitality and special ambience as well as superb food.

6　Alexandroúpolis

213 miles E of Thessaloníki, 179 miles W of Istanbul

Alexandroúpolis, the major population center of Thrace, is a sprawling modern town laid out by Russian engineers during the Russo-Turkish War of 1878. It became Greek in 1920, when it was given its present name by King Alexander.

Nearly one-fourth of Thrace's population is Muslim, in a country where more than 90% of the population shares the Orthodox faith. This story goes back to the years after World War I when the Greeks pushed their *megáli idéa* (great idea) of uniting all the areas with an Orthodox population once again under the Greek flag, perhaps reestablishing a great capital at Constantinople. They invaded the weakened Ottoman Empire and got nearly as far as Ankara before they were repulsed by Turkish forces rallied by Ataturk. Many ethnic Greeks were slaughtered, others fled, and still others were displaced during the exchange of population supervised under the Treaty of Lausanne of 1923. (More than 1,300,000 Christians were expelled from Turkey, and 400,000 Muslims were expelled from Greece.) The treaty also gave Greece the western part of Thrace. In the last decade the government has made a big push to industrialize this region. The borders shared with Bulgaria and Turkey ensure that it will always be heavily fortified as a strategic military outpost. Villages such as Xánthi and Komotiní are of the past; Alexandroúpolis is of the future.

ESSENTIALS

GETTING THERE & DEPARTING   By Plane   Olympic Airways has at least one flight daily between Athens and Alexandroúpolis; its office in Alexandroúpolis is at Odós Ellis 6, at the corner of Koletti Street (☎ 0551/26-207). The airport is 4¼ miles east of town.

By Train   There are five trains daily between Alexandroúpolis and Thessaloníki, one continuing on to Athens. For information in Alexandroúpolis, call ☎ 0551/26-212. From Alexandroúpolis, one train leaves nightly for Istanbul; the 10-hour ride costs 5,500 Drs ($22.90). The **railway station** (☎ 0551/26-395) is on the waterfront on the east side of town.

By Bus   Two buses a day leave from Athens's Terminal A, Odós Kifissoú 100; call ☎ 01/513-2084 for information. There are five buses daily to and from Thessaloníki via Kavála (6 hours, 4,800 Drs/$20). The Alexandroúpolis KTEL bus station is at Odós Venizélou 36, a block north of the main street. There is one **OSE bus** daily to Istanbul, leaving from the railway station at 9:30am; purchase your ticket there as far in advance as possible; the trip takes 7 hours and costs 6,150 Drs ($25.65).

By Ferry   There is ferry service to Samothráki at least once a day (several times a day in July and August). Tickets can be purchased from **Vatitsis Shipping** at Kyproú 5, across from the port (☎ 0551/26-721). Contact the **port authority** (☎ 0551/26-468) for more information.

By Hydrofoil   In summer there's hydrofoil service to and from Límnos, Híos, and Lésvos; contact **Kikon Travel,** Odós Venizélou 68 (☎ 0551/32-398; fax 0551/34-755), for tickets and information.

VISITOR INFORMATION / FAST FACTS   The **Municipal Tourist Office** is in the town hall, 3 blocks behind the lighthouse, at Leofóros Dimokratías 306 (☎ 0551/24-998); it's open Monday to Friday from 8am to 2pm. The **tourist police** are at Odós Karaïskáki 6 (☎ 0551/37-411), 2 blocks off the *paralía* near the lighthouse. The **post office** is on the *paralía* 2 blocks west of the lighthouse. The **telephone center (OTE)** is at Mitropolíto Kavíri and Venizelou streets, east of the bus station, open daily from 6am to midnight.

SPECIAL EVENTS   Every August there's a Wine Festival; in February a Hunter's Week (the thing to do in this rugged region) is celebrated near the city.

EXPLORING THE TOWN & BEYOND

There isn't much to see in Alexandroúpolis, though it's pleasant enough along the harbor, which comes alive at dusk when everyone comes out for the evening *vólta*.

The nearby **cave at Makri** is pushed by tour operators as the famed cave where Odysseus met the Cyclops and defeated him.

Local buses go to several nearby **beaches,** making for an easy day excursion. Another day trip goes through the **Évros Delta,** one of Europe's most important wetlands, home to nearly 300 species of birds. In **Didymótiho,** the double row of walls, 10 towers, 3 gates, a reservoir, and food storage cells of an imposing Byzantine castle can still be seen. It was one of the most important Byzantine cities, home to both the emperor Iannis Paleologos and the sultan Beyazit.

Elsewhere in the region, the coastal road swings inland as you cross the Néstos River and heads north to the fascinating village of **Xánthi,** 39 miles from Kavála. This is a tobacco town, and the odor is everywhere. Many of the villagers are dressed traditionally in Turkish peasant clothes—baggy black trousers, full skirts, and headdresses. The women who wear white bandanas are Pomaki, descendants of the Bulgarian hill people who were converted to Islam from Christianity.

Some 43^1/$_2$ miles farther east, in **Komotiní,** the locals are dressed in traditional garb too, but here the head-clothes are black and the faces are pure Turkish. The Komotinis are Musulmani—Muslims of direct Turkish descent. In Komotiní worship services are held five times daily in the 450-year-old **New Mosque.**

WHERE TO STAY

If you're waiting for the Samothráki ferry and need a place to stay, the best budget choice is the **EOT Campground** (☎ 0551/26-225), on the beach 1^1/$_4$ miles west of town. It can accommodate up to 900 people, but call ahead to find out how crowded it will be.

If you want to stay in town, look along Dimokratías Avenue.

Hotel Alex. Leofóros Dimokratías 294, 681 00 Alexandroúpolis. ☎ **0551/26-302** or 0551/ 28-400. 32 rms, all with bath (shower or tub). TV TEL. 6,050 Drs ($25.20) single; 8,725 Drs ($36.35) double. No credit cards.

The rooms are small and modestly furnished but carpeted and comfortable. Though it's on the main street downtown the front rooms are quiet because they have new double-paned windows—part of recent remodeling that's also added a bar/cafeteria.

Park Hotel. Leofóros Dimokratías 458, 681 00 Alexandroúpolis. ☎ **0551/28-607.** 24 rms, all with bath (tub). TEL. 9,650 Drs ($40.20) single; 13,325 Drs ($55.50) double. Rates include breakfast. No credit cards.

On the west side of town across from a very nice park, with a few trees and shrubs of its own, this little suburban hotel suits its name quite well. The lobby is especially homelike, with a big fireplace, comfy furnishings, and white curtains trimmed with local tatting that looks especially made for it. The rooms are attractive and comfortable, all with balconies that can be enjoyed.

WHERE TO EAT

When in Alexandroúpolis, try *lagós* (hare) and the locally produced telemes cheese.

Klimatariá. Odós Kyproú 14. ☎ **0551/26-288.** Main courses 900–1,600 Drs ($3.75–$6.65). No credit cards. Daily 7am–1am. GREEK/TURKISH/SEAFOOD.

At this popular taverna, on a small square a block off the *paralía,* near the train station, you can sample a spicier-than-usual moussaká with a delicious hunk of Greek bread. The Turkish influence can be tasted in the cuisine here. The lamb and beef dishes are also flavorful; try the *katsikáki* (baked goat).

The Northeastern Aegean Islands

16

The islands in the northeast Aegean are among the least visited of the major Greek islands, in part because they're fairly inaccessible, but also because they're simply not well known.

These islands can be divided into the the eastern islands of Sámos, Híos, and Lésvos (Mytilíni) and the northern islands, including Límnos, Samothráki, and Thássos. The better-known eastern islands are more autonomous, and they all share a cultural (and transportation) connection with Turkey. In July and August the smaller northern islands, though less visited by foreigners, become extensions or weekend resorts of Thessaloníki and the larger mainland cities.

These islands are spread out and rather difficult to hop between; therefore, we suggest that you focus on a limited area if you have only a week to travel.

1 Sámos

174 nautical miles NE of Piraeus

Sámos is an attractive and pleasant island, mountainous and green. Its peaks are the highest in the Aegean islands, and sections of the scenic interior are as thickly forested as any in the region.

Sámos has a long and honorable history with abundant evidence to prove it. During the 6th century B.C., in the glory days of the Ionian civilization, Sámos led the field in its contributions to art, architecture, and science. The island's favorite son, Pythagoras, is the most notable in a long list of native luminaries that includes the philosopher Epicurus, Aesop of *Fables* fame, and the mathematician Aristárchos. Herodotus devoted a large portion of his *History* to the island.

Because Sámos is one of the closest Greek islands to Turkey, it's a particularly convenient departure point for those who want to visit **Ephesus**—one of the most important archaeological sites in Asia Minor.

ESSENTIALS

GETTING THERE & DEPARTING   By Plane   Olympic Airways runs three flights daily (five in summer) between Athens and Sámos; its office in Sámos town is at the corner of Kanári and Smýrnis streets (☎ 0273/27-237), and in Pythagório it's at Odós Lykoúrgos 90 (☎ 0273/61-213). The airport is 2¹/₂ miles west of

Pythagório; you can take a taxi to Sámos town for about 3,000 Drs ($12.50) or to Pythagório for 1,500 Drs ($6.25).

By Boat   There are daily **ferries** (sometimes two) in high season from Piraeus via Náxos, Páros, and Ikaría to Karlóvassi and Sámos town. (Don't make the mistake of getting off at Karlóvassi, the first stop on the island, unless that's your destination.) Sámos town has ferry connections daily with Ikaría, four times a week with Híos, and once a week with Lésvos, Límnos, and Rhodes. In summer there's **hydrofoil** service from Sámos town to Híos and Lésvos, and from Pythagório to Pátmos and Kos. Smaller excursion boats leave Pythagório four times a week for Pátmos—this can be a rough trip!—and the larger, smoother-sailing steamers go three times a week. There's a once-a-week connection to Kavála and Thessaloníki on the mainland; call the **port authority** in Piraeus (☎ 01/451-1311), Sámos town (☎ 0273/27-318), or Pythagório (☎ 0273/61-225) for schedule information.

ORIENTATION   Large, almond-shaped Sámos has three ports. The ferries from Piraeus and the Cyclades normally stop first at Karlóvassi, on the northwest coast, then continue on to Sámos town, on the northeast coast. **Sámos town** (also called Vathý), the capital and main town, is an old port that has undergone extensive development but remains an essentially Greek town with lots of commerce and color.

Karlóvassi is the most Greek in feeling of Sámos's major towns, with a friendly harbor, nearby beaches, and a scattering of hotels. **Pythagório,** the third port, is a picturesque village on the southeast coast that was the ancient capital of the island. Nearby are the Efpalínion Tunnel, the remains of the ancient Heréon, and the airport. However, because it's the best base for sightseeing, it's excessively crowded with tour groups (it's believed that they occupy more than 80% of the resort's rooms!).

For years **Kokkári,** 6 miles northwest of Sámos town, was the island's least spoiled resort, but now it's overrun with tourists who prefer less touristy villages. All along the north coast, the pebble beaches, though plagued by strong winds, are also undergoing intensive development. Midway on the north-coast road between Kokkári and Karlóvassi is the **Platanákia region** of villages set on steeply terraced hills and valleys.

GETTING AROUND   By Bicycle or Moped   You can rent a bicycle or moped in Sámos town from several shops near the central square. In Pythagório, **Nikos Rent a Motor Bike,** on Odós Lykoúrgou Logothéti (☎ 0273/61-094), rents both; rates include helmets: bicycles rent for 1,400 Drs ($5.95), Vespas for 3,000 Drs ($12.75), and two-person mopeds from about 5,000 Drs ($21.75) a day.

By Bus   There's good public bus service on Sámos; the Sámos town **bus terminal** is inland from the south end of the port on Odós Ioánnou Lekáti at Kanári (☎ 0273/27-262). The bus makes the 20-minute trip between Sámos town and Pythagório frequently. Buses go to Kokkári and the inland village of Mytiliní seven times a day. There are four buses daily from Pythagório to Iréo (near the Heréon), and there's also service to Pýrgos, Marathókambos, and Votsalákia beach.

By Boat   Excursion boats from the Pythagório harbor go to Psilí Ámmos beach (on the east end of the island) daily, and to the island of Ikaría three times weekly. There's a popular day cruise to the sandy beach on Samiopoúla, a small island where there's a taverna and rooms for rent.

By Car   For the best prices and selection, we recommend **Aramis Rent a Motorbike-Car** (☎ 0273/23-253; fax 0273/23-620), 200 yards left from the harbor in Sámos town, and near the bus station in Pythagório (☎ 0273/62-267). Expect to pay about $80 per day. There are plenty of other agencies, so shop around. You'll probably find them cheaper in Sámos town than elsewhere.

The Northeastern Aegean Islands

BULGARIA

TURKEY

0 — 45 km
— 28 mi

N

Kavála

Alexandroúpolis

Liménas (Thássos)
Makryámmos
Limenária — Panayía

THÁSSOS

SAMOTHRÁKI
Kamariótissa — Hóra
Mt. Fengári

Gallípoli

Sea of Marmara

Canakkale

*A e g e a n
S e a*

Gökçeada

TURKEY

Kórnos
Mýrina
Skandáli

LÍMNOS

Ayvalik

Pergamon

Mólyvos
(Míthymna)
Mandamádos

LÉSVOS (Mytilíni)
Eressós — Pétra
Skála Eressós — Ayiássos — Mytilíni
Plomári

Skýros

Psará HÍOS
Kardámila Inóusses
Híos Town
Pasalimáni Çesme
Mestá Piryí

Izmir

Ephesus
Kuşadasi
Kokkári
Karlóvassi Sámos
SÁMOS Mytilíni
Pythagório
Psilí Ámmos

IKARÍA

GREECE

Athens

The Northeastern
Aegean Islands

3-0530

567

By Taxi   The most common taxi fare, from Sámos to Pythagório, is 2,200 Drs ($9.15). The taxi stand in Sámos town is off the northwest cornver of the main square.

SÁMOS TOWN
ESSENTIALS

VISITOR INFORMATION   The **municipal tourist office** is half a block in from the port, off the northwest (left) side of the main square, Platía Pythagóra (☎ **0273/28-530** or 0273/28-582). Open daily from 8am to 2:30pm (in high season from 7:30am to 10pm), it's manned by local people who are very helpful and informative; they cannot make room reservations over the phone, but they will help you find accommodations when you go to their office.

The travel agency nearest the ferry landing in Sámos town is **I.T.S.A.** (☎ **0273/23-605;** fax 0273/27-955); one of the best and friendliest, it can help you make all travel arrangements, find accommodations, change money at good rates, and store your luggage free. **Samina Travel,** farther along the harborfront at Odós Sofoúli 67 (☎ **0273/28-841;** fax 0273/23-616), can also change money and help you arrange day trips and plane tickets. **Pythagoras Tours,** on the harborfront (☎ **0273/27-240**), also sells ferry tickets.

FAST FACTS   The local **police** can be reached at ☎ **0273/22-100,** 24 hours a day. The police station (☎ **0273/27-333**) is near the Credit Bank at the south end of the harbor. The **Sámos General Hospital** (☎ **0273/27-407** or 0273/27-426) is on the north side of Sámos town on the waterfront north (left) of the ferry landing.

Sámos has a branch of the **National Bank of Greece** on the port, open Monday to Thursday from 8am to 2pm and on Friday from 8am to 1:30pm. Several travel agents change money at a less favorable rate, but they're open daily from 8am to 10pm.

There's a **British consulate** on Sofoúli Street (☎ **0273/27-314**).

The **post office** is on Odós Smýrnis, 3 blocks south of the Municipal Gardens and 4 blocks in from the harbor. The **telephone office (OTE)** is on Platía Iróon, southeast of the Municipal Gardens, open daily 24 hours.

SEEING THE SIGHTS IN TOWN & NEARBY

The local **archaeology museum** (☎ **0273/27-469**) has a fine collection housed in two buildings. Particularly impressive is the large and varied collection of votives, mostly bronze, found at the Heréon, illustrating its prestige in the ancient world by their value and area covered—all of Greece, the Near East, Egypt, Cyprus, even Spain. The newer building houses sculpture, including the largest (18 feet high) standing *koúros* and a group of six archaic statues found at the Heréon. Sámos was the sculpture center of Greece; being much in demand, many of the island's best sculptors (especially adept in casting) traveled all over the Hellenistic world to create their art. Admission to the museum is 800 Drs ($3.35) for adults, 600 Drs ($2.50) for seniors, and 400 Drs ($1.65) for students. Hours are Tuesday to Sunday from 8:30am to 3pm.

Áno Vathí, the upper town, is a charming quarter with narrow winding streets and neoclassical houses, a quiet residential area where there are few cars, motorcycles, tourist buses, or hotels. Because it retains much of its original villagelike character, the area is a very pleasant place for strolling.

The so-so town beach, **Plaz Gagoú,** is a short walk northwest of (left from) the ferry landing in the pleasant suburb of **Kalámi.**

A few miles east of town you can climb a path to the **Monastery of Zoödóhou Piyís** for a good look at Turkey (on the southeastern tip of the island, at **Possidonió,** you'll be even closer and can find a very good taverna for seafood). West along the coast is **Psilí Ámmos,** the better of the island's two beaches.

WHERE TO STAY

Sámos town is usually mostly booked by European tour groups during July and August. Ask the EOT for its help with finding one of the many private rooms (approximately 8,000 Drs/$33.35 for a double room with private bath), or inquire at **Samina Travel** (☎ 0273/28-841). Most hotels are open April 15 to October 31 unless otherwise noted.

✪ **Emily Hotel.** Odós Grámmou and Odós 11 Noemvríou, Sámos, 831 00 Sámos. ☎ **0273/ 24-691.** Fax 0273/24-692. 18 rms, all with bath (tub). A/C TEL. 12,300 Drs ($51.25) single; 16,600 Drs ($69.15) double. AE, V.

You'll find this charming new hotel on the right several blocks up from the port on the small street between the Samos Hotel and the Catholic church. The rooms are spacious, attractively furnished, and especially quiet, most with their own balcony. Breakfast is available for 1,000 Drs ($4.15) or 1,500 Drs ($6.25) for an American version.

Hotel Helen. Odós Grámmou 2, Sámos, 831 00 Sámos. ☎ **0273/28-215.** 18 rms, all with bath (tub). 6,900 Drs ($28.75) single; 8,600 Drs ($38.85) double. No credit cards.

Just down the street from the more elegant Emily, the Helen, well looked after by the Tsaklofas family, offers modestly furnished but spotless rooms with balconies. Most of the rooms face the back and are quieter. The small lobby bar is a good place for a drink.

Hotel La Piscine. Odós Kephalopoúlou, Kalámi, 831 00 Sámos. ☎ **0273/24-560.** Fax 0273/ 24-564. 65 rms, all with bath (tub). TEL. 11,700 Drs ($48.75) single; 13,800 Drs ($57.50) double.

This buff-colored hotel sits atop the hill on the waterfront road left from the pier, on the way to the town beach. The rooms are spacious and all have balconies; those in front face the sea, the mountains, and the pool, which is the largest on the island. Air-conditioning is available in July and August. The sophisticated Mina Vasilou has decorated the spacious lobby and corridors with prints of her favorite contemporary artists, including Miteras and Morelis.

Hotel Samos. Odós Sofoúli 11, Sámos, 831 00 Sámos. ☎ **0273/28-378.** Fax 0273/23-771. 105 rms, all with bath (tub). TEL. 11,000 Drs ($45.85) single; 15,600 Drs ($65) double. Rates include breakfast. AE, EURO, MC, V.

This comfortable lodge, the closest to the ferry, has a popular cafe-bar out front and a swimming pool. The facade has been restored to resemble that of a classic Samian-style mansion, with such interior amenities as an elevator and wall-to-wall carpeting. The spacious, simple rooms are super-clean with first-rate service. We recommend the rooms in the back of the hotel, which are quieter and have larger balconies. All in all, a good bargain.

Pythagoras Hotel. Kalistrátou Kalámi 2, Kalámi, 831 00 Sámos. ☎ **0273/28-422.** Fax 0273/ 28-893. 17 rms, all with bath (tub). 5,000 Drs ($20.85) single; 7,000 Drs ($29.15) double. MC, V.

We tried this older family hotel about 500 yards left from the port on the way to the town beach. It was plain but comfortable, and from our seaside room all we could hear was the surf and birds singing in the trees. The neighborhood cafe downstairs serves a good, inexpensive breakfast. Students are given a discount, except in July and August.

Sibylla Hotel. Platía Ayíou Nikoláou, Sámos, 831 00 Sámos. ☎ **0273/22-396.** 20 rms, all with bath (tub). 5,750 Drs ($23.95) single; 9,700 Drs ($40.40) double. No credit cards.

This pretty hotel a couple of blocks in from the middle of the port, off the northwest corner of St. Nicholas Square, is popular with tour groups but a good choice if you can get a room. All are sparkling clean, designed in the old villa style of the local mansions. (The building originally served as a tobacco factory.)

WHERE TO EAT

The real specialty on Sámos is not the food (generally, it's tourist quality, mediocre, and expensive) but the wine! As Lord Byron exclaimed, "Fill high the bowl with Samian wine!" The Samian wine preferred by those who are accustomed to California and French wines is a dry white (with a hint of green) called Saména. There's also a delicious relatively dry rosé called Fokianos. By contrast, Greeks tend to go wild over the sweet wines with names like Nectar, Dux, and Anthemis. Almost any restaurant on the island will serve one or all of these wines, and you really ought to try a bottle.

Christos Taverna. Platía Ayíou Nikoláou. ☎ **0273/24-792.** Main courses 1,100–1,600 Drs ($4.60–$6.65). No credit cards. Daily 9am–midnight. GREEK.

Bear to the left off the northwest corner of the main square to reach St. Nicholas Square and this simple little taverna under a covered alleyway decorated with odd antiques. On our first visit we played it safe and ordered a Greek salad and stuffed eggplant—excellent and each a meal in itself. An English family told us that their meal was the best they'd had on the island. We've been back several times since! It's open all year.

Gregoris Grill. Odós Smyrnis. ☎ **0273/22-718.** Main courses 800–2,400 Drs ($3.35–$10). No credit cards. Daily 7–11:30pm. GREEK.

We recently returned to this grill, 3 blocks south of the Municipal Gardens across from the post office, and can report that it's still a fine place for a good inexpensive meal. It isn't much to look at, but the lamb chops were luscious and everything was cooked just right. Although the owners don't speak English, the service is ultra-friendly and the prices are low. Highly recommended, for a great-value, typical taverna dinner.

Restaurant Ouzaría Souda. Paralía (at Odós Grámmou). No phone. Main courses 1,250–2,900 Drs ($5.20–$12.10). AE, EURO, MC, V. Daily 7–11:30pm. GREEK.

On the waterfront near the Catholic church, the Koufandakis family presides over this lively spot—a great place to catch the action along the port while you're eating. The wood-oven–baked "special pizza" came loaded with veggies and the crust was perfect. There's a nice selection of vegetarian dishes.

Taverna Stelios. Odós Kephalopoúlou. ☎ **0273/23-639.** Main courses 1,300–2,000 Drs ($5.40–$8.35). No credit cards. Daily 11am–midnight. Closed Nov–Mar. GREEK.

Northwest of the ferry landing, a few yards to the left of and around the corner from the Coast Guard building, this taverna sits back from the road amid a profusion of greenery. The menu offers a wide range of traditional fare from old Samian recipes. At the suggestion of the manager, Irene Karathanasis, we tried the *stifádo* (veal cooked with tomatoes, pearl onions, and wine) and the *soutsoukákia* (a generous portion of beef patty in spicy tomato sauce). When we thought we couldn't eat another morsel, we were persuaded to try the fresh yogurt with sour-cherry sauce—and we were certainly glad we didn't miss it!

SÁMOS AFTER DARK

The *in* place in Sámos town during our last visit was the **In Music Bar,** near the central square. Several other bars of various types can be found on the lanes just off the port. **Number Nine,** at Kephalopoúlou 9, beyond the ferry landing on the road to the town beach, on the right, is one of the oldest and best-known clubs. The hottest disco in Sámos town is **Metropolis,** behind the Paradise Hotel on the south side of town. **Totem Disco,** 2 miles from town on the main road to Pythagório, is a big place that can become rather lively in the summer. If you like bouzouki, try **Zorba's,** out of town on the road to Mytiliní.

PYTHAGÓRIO

Pythagório, south across the island from Sámos town, is a charming but overcrowded modern resort built on the site of an ancient village and harbor; it was called Tigáni until 1955, when it was renamed after the most famous Samian, Pythagoras, the great mathematician and philosopher. Under the autocrat Polykrates, what Herodotus called "three of the greatest building achievements of the world" were accomplished: the foundation for the harbor was laid (where the jetty is today), the Efpalínion Tunnel was completed, and the Heréon was enlarged, making it the biggest of all ancient Greek temples.

ESSENTIALS

VISITOR INFORMATION   The **Pythagorio Municipal Tourist Office** is on the main street, Odós Lykoúrgou Logothéti (☎ 0273/61-022), 1 block up from the harbor, and is open daily from 8am to 10pm for assistance with rooms, changing money, and making long-distance calls.

FAST FACTS   The local **police** (☎ 0273/61-333) are also on the main street to handle problems or emergencies. **Samina Travel** has an office on the port (☎ 0273/61-583); see the friendly Pavlo for advice. The **post office** is 4 blocks up from the harbor on the main street; the **OTE** is on the *paralía* near the pier. There's a **launderette** off the main street on the church street; it's open daily from 9am to 9pm (to 11pm in summer). The **bus station** (actually just a couple of benches under a tree) is like nearly everything else, on the busy main street, on the left, up from the post office.

SEEING THE SIGHTS

The **Efpalínion Tunnel** (Efpalíneo Órygma), one of the most impressive engineering accomplishments of the ancient world, is a 3,450-foot-long waterway through the mountain above Pythagório, and is located about 1 1/4 miles northwest of Pythagório. It was excavated to transport water from mountain streams to ancient Sámos.

Efpalinos directed two teams of workers digging from each side, and after nearly 15 years they met remarkably close to each other. The tunnel caved in during the 17th century when Sámos was devastated by a series of earthquakes. A few years ago a German engineering team completed 8 years of work to clear the tunnel of debris and rock and reveal this astonishing achievement.

You can walk up to the tunnel, a moderate 45-minute climb, by following the signs up from the west end of town, or you can take a taxi from Pythagório for about 600 Drs ($2.55). Some of the spaces are tight and slippery, but presently you can walk about a third of the way into the tunnel. Though it's lighted, you should bring a flashlight. It's open Tuesday to Sunday from 9am to 2pm, according to official sources, but the hours are in fact erratic so you should call ahead to determine if it's open, as they often close the tunnel for repairs. Admission is 500 Drs ($2.10) for adults, 400 Drs ($1.65) for seniors, and 300 Drs ($1.25) for students. Call ☎ 0273/61-400 for information.

The **Heréon,** or Sanctuary of Hera (wife of Zeus and queen of the gods), is 5 miles southwest of Pythagório at Iréo, a rather lackluster resort. All that survives of the greatest of all Greek temples is its massive foundation, a lone reconstructed column, and copies of the statuary seen in the archaeological museum. The temple was originally surrounded by a forest of columns, one of its most distinctive and original features. In fact, rival Ionian cities were so impressed that they rebuilt many of their ancient temples in similar style. (The Temple of Artemis in nearby Ephesus is a direct imitation of the great Samian structure.) The Heréon was rebuilt and greatly expanded under Polykrates; it was damaged during numerous invasions and finally destroyed by a series of earthquakes.

A good way to visit is by bicycle, as the road from Pythagório is flat, or you can walk for about an hour or so. The few buses a day usually leave Sámos or Pythagório in the afternoon. The site is open Tuesday to Sunday from 8:30am to 3pm. Admission is 500 Drs ($2.10) for adults, 400 Drs($1.65) for seniors, and 300 Drs ($1.25) for students. Call ☎ 0273/27-469 for details.

Columns from the city's fortifications and an unexcavated theater are visible on the left side north of the port. There are also remains of **Roman baths** about half a mile west of town, open Tuesday to Saturday from 11am to 2pm.

There's a small **archaeology collection** in the town hall on Platía Irínis (☎ 0273/61-400), 2 blocks north (right) from the main street and a block in from the waterfront, with finds from the Heréon. It's open Tuesday to Thursday and Sunday from 9am to 2pm, and on Friday and Saturday from noon to 2pm; admission is free.

WHERE TO STAY

Pythagório is almost completely at the service of European tour groups. If you arrive there without a reservation, catch the bus to Sámos town and head for its **tourist office,** 1 block off the *paralía* on the main street, for help in finding one of the many private rooms, which usually cost about 7,250 Drs ($30.20) for a double room with private bath; otherwise, inquire at **Rhenia Tours** (☎ 0273/62-224) or **Samina Travel** (☎ 0273/61-583). Most hotels operate between April 15 and October 31 unless otherwise noted.

Captain Fragoulis. Pythagório, 831 03 Sámos. ☎ **0273/61-473.** 2 rms, 6 studios, all with bath (tub). 8,000 Drs ($33.35) single or double; 12,650 Drs ($52.70) studio for two; 14,900 Drs ($62.10) studio for three. No credit cards.

This personal little pension has a facade that's mostly rustic stone; it offers a wonderful view of Pythagório from its location on the road to Sámos. The good captain's son-in-law—an artist—has lent his touch to the decor of this well-maintained hostelry.

Hotel Evripili. Pythagório, 831 03 Sámos. ☎ **0273/61-407.** 10 rms, all with bath (tub). 7,475 Drs ($31.15) single; 9,315 Drs ($38.80) double. Rates include breakfast. No credit cards.

This 400-year-old stone mansion, across the lane from the new Hotel Labito, has been converted into compact, comfortable guest rooms, most with balconies. Although Austrian tour groups often fill the place in July and August, before or after that period you can go downstairs to the cozy basement breakfast lounge to inquire about room availability.

Hotel Hera II. Pythagório, 831 03 Sámos. ☎ **0273/61-319.** Fax 0273/61-196. 7 rms, all with bath (tub). A/C TEL. 16,700 Drs ($69.60) single; 18,700 Drs ($77.90) double. Rates include breakfast. No credit cards.

The Hotel Hera II, situated on the hillside on the road to Sámos, is one of the most deluxe hotels on the island. Behind the white marble is a small, luxurious neobaroque villa with utterly fantastic views over the harbor below. The rooms, with piped-in music, are elegantly simple and the service (except during July and August, when tour groups take over) is first-rate.

✪ **Hotel Labito.** Pythagório, 831 03 Sámos. ☎ **0273/61-086.** Fax 0273/61-085. 69 rms, all with bath (tub). A/C TEL. 10,900 Drs ($45.40) single; 12,200 Drs ($50.85) double. No credit cards.

This wonderful new hotel, designed to resemble rows of two-story Samian mansions painted in classic lemon-yellow with green-and-white trim, is a welcome addition to the heart of the village. Set just two lanes behind the port, it's in an ideally quiet and convenient location. The marble lobby, simply decorated indoor and terrace breakfast and bar areas, and the matched pastel pink or blue room furnishings add a touch of luxury rarely seen in a Class C hotel. Our top-value choice in town.

Hotel Olympiada. Pythagório, 831 03 Sámos. ☎ **0273/61-490.** 10 rms, all with bath (tub). TEL. 8,000 Drs ($33.35) single; 12,600 Drs ($52.50) double. Rates include breakfast. No credit cards.

This attractive, newly built hotel has pleasant plantings and a nice view from its perch next to the pricey Hotel Hera II. Although it's about a 15-minute walk from the *paralía*—a steep uphill climb if you have luggage—the well-kept rooms provide good value.

Hotel Sandalis. Pythagório, 831 03 Sámos. ☎ **0273/61-691.** 14 rms, all with bath (tub). 7,500 Drs ($31.25) single; 11,000 Drs ($45.85) double. Rates include breakfast. No credit cards.

Also above the town, this homey establishment has very tastefully decorated rooms, balconies with French doors (rear rooms face the quiet hills), and a lovely flower garden. A reader who spent Greek Easter here assures us that this special inn had the cleanest rooms he had found on his tour. The friendly Sandalises, who have spent many years in Chicago, are the gracious hosts.

WHERE TO EAT

We can recommend several places here, although the prices at this resort are higher than in Sámos town.

After dinner, you'll find that nightlife in Pythagório is much more subdued than in Sámos town. The **San Lorenzo,** above the port on the Sámos road, and **Labito,** on the village's back lanes, are two of the island's best discos.

Esperides Restaurant. Pythagório. ☎ **0273/61-767.** Reservations recommended in summer. Main courses 1,150–4,000 Drs ($4.80–$16.65). No credit cards. Summer, daily 6pm–midnight; off-season, daily noon–midnight. INTERNATIONAL.

This pleasant, walled garden is a few blocks inland from the port and west of the main street. There are uniformed waiters and a dressier crowd. The variety of continental and Greek dishes is well presented and should appeal to a wide variety of palates. We resented the frozen french fries served with the tasty baked chicken; otherwise, all meat and vegetables were fresh.

The Family House. Pythagório. No phone. Main courses 1,400–3,200 Drs ($5.85–$13.35). No credit cards. Daily 6pm–midnight. GREEK/CONTINENTAL.

A more casual garden, enlivened by Christmas-tree lights strung through some whitewashed citrus trees, can be found a block east of the main street below the main church. The Greek food is tasty and not overcooked, and there's a respectable selection of pasta and seafood dishes for those who shun moussaká.

✪ **I Varka.** Paralía. ☎ **0273/61-636.** Main courses 1,500–3,500 Drs ($6.25–$14.60). EURO, MC, V. Daily noon–midnight. Closed Nov–Apr. SEAFOOD.

The community of Pythagório has funded "The Boat" ouzerí/taverna in a garden of salt pines at the south end of the port. Delicious fresh fish and grilled meats, plus a surprising variety of *mezédes* (appetizers), are prepared in the small kitchen built in this dry-docked fishing boat. The grilled octopus, strung up on a line to dry, and the pink *barboúnia* (red mullet) or clear gray mullet, all cooked to perfection over a charcoal grill, are the standouts.

EXPLORING ELSEWHERE AROUND THE ISLAND

In **Mytiliní,** an attractive little town northwest of Pythagório and southwest of Sámos town, you'll find the best-known paleontological remains in Greece, mostly from the nearby Stephanidis Valley, on display in the **paleontological museum** (☎ **0273/51-205**). It's open Monday to Saturday from 8:30am to 2pm and 6 to 7:30pm; admission is 500 Drs ($2.10). There's bus service to Mytiliní three times a day from Sámos or Pythagório.

From south of Mytiliní the road continues west through the fertile interior of the island through **Pýrgos,** the honey capital of the island. Due west, but accessible by a more circuitous route, is the most rapidly developing part of the coastline, on Marathókambos Bay along the southwestern shore. A long but narrow rock-and-pebble beach, several tavernas, and a mushrooming number of hotels, pensions, and windsurfers fill the once-tiny village of **Órmos Marathókambos** and, a couple of miles farther west, **Votsalákia,** a somewhat nicer beach.

The road continues north from Marathókambos to **Karlóvassi,** the least touristed of the three major ports, which has a scattering of hotels. There's an excellent beach at **Potámi,** west of town.

Midway on the north-coast road between Karlóvassi and Kokkári is the **Platanákia region** of villages set on steeply terraced hills, where Samos's famous muscadine grapes are used to make muscat wine. Samians call Platanákia "paradise." Narrow roads lead south from the costal highway through cool, densely wooded valleys with rushing streams and up through terraced hills to mountain hamlets. To visit this area from Sámos town, drive west past Kokkári, and about 11 miles out there's a left turn to Aïdónia and Manolátes.

You might stop at the **Paradisos Restaurant** (☎ **0273/94-208**), which is a large garden cafe located just at the Manolátes turnoff from the coast highway. Mr. Folas, the owner, worked in vineyards for many years and makes his own wine from the excellent Samian grapes. Mrs. Folas's *tirópita* (fresh baked after 7pm) is made from local goat cheese and butter and wrapped in a flaky pastry. Paradisos is open daily for lunch and dinner, and also has a few rooms for rent.

About 15 minutes up the winding country road to Manolátes, two more "country" tavernas have found a spot under the evergreens beside the soothing stream. Near **Aïdónia** ("Nightingale") there's a clear mountain spring that attracts scores of songbirds and is a delightful watering and washing spot.

Manolátes is farther up and now accessible by car, but it's a peaceful, half-hour hike uphill if you have the stamina. You'll be rewarded by a marvelous view of the steeply tiered vineyards strung along the foothills of Mt. Ámbelos (3,735 feet high) and down to the deep-blue sea. The small and picturesque hamlet is a typical Samian village, with stucco homes and red-tile roofs. The narrow cobblestone streets are so steep that you may find yourself bending forward to avoid falling backward. Manolátes has a simple taverna, plus a small snack bar deeper in the pedestrian lanes with panoramic views.

The **beaches** that extend westward from Avlákia to Kokkári are made of large gray sand and pebbles and they're fairly wide and attractive, but be forewarned that the winds on this side of the island are notorious, and you may have to move on to sunbathe comfortably.

KOKKÁRI

Up until a decade ago **Kokkári,** about 6 miles west of Sámos town on the north-coast highway, was a traditional Greek fishing village with small cobblestone backstreets, a few tavernas, and off in the distance, green brush-covered hills. Today it's filled with small hotels, pensions, and rooms-to-let in many of the town's older homes, and with many waterside cafes, chic boutiques, pedestrian bridges, and walkways, it can still be very charming in the spring and fall. Its small-scale commercialism, though dense, is very appealing and draws hordes competing for its few rooms and hotels in the summer months.

WHERE TO STAY IN KOKKÁRI

The **Tourist Office** (☎ 0273/92-333) staff will do their best to find you a place to stay; expect to pay 6,500 Drs ($27.10) for a room with bath, 5,250 Drs ($21.90) for one without bath. Most hotels willing to subrent a tour group–booked room to individuals will charge at least 10,000 Drs ($41.65) for two. The large deluxe **Hotel Arion** (☎ 0273/92-020), on the edge of town, with doubles for 19,750 Drs ($82.30), will surely satisfy anyone who feels like splurging.

From the many rooms-to-let we looked at, we can recommend the simple twin-bedded rooms, with private toilet and shower (some with balconies), handled by the **Café Manos** (☎ 0273/92-217) on the west end of the waterfront. They manage a small, brown-shuttered building as well as the nearby **Pension Christos,** both of which are inland just off the east end of the waterfront. The newer **Sophia Rooms-to-Let** (☎ 0273/92-431) is above the west waterfront, so the rear-facing water-view rooms would be the quietest. Both places charge about 5,500 Drs ($22.90) for a single or double room.

Hotel Olympia Beach. Kokkári, 831 00 Sámos. ☎ **0273/92-353.** Fax 0273/92-457. 12 rms, all with bath (tub). TEL. 13,200 Drs ($55) single; 15,400 Drs ($64.15) double. Rates include breakfast. No credit cards.

This bright place, which is often booked by European tour groups, overlooks the beach. If you plan to stay here, try to get a sea-facing room or you might be disturbed by noise from the road.

WHERE TO EAT IN KOKKÁRI

✪ **Taverna Avgo Tou Kokora.** Kokkári. ☎ **0273/92-113.** Main courses 1,400–3,200 Drs ($5.85–$13.35). No credit cards. Daily noon–1am. GREEK.

Locals rave about this chic seaside cafe with a refreshingly diverse menu and a postcard-perfect setting. (Its fanciful name means "Cock's Egg.") You'll find the island's largest assortment of *mezédes* (appetizers) as well as a variety of grilled meats and fish, and of course, several dishes derived from the name of the establishment.

SIDE TRIPS TO TURKEY

During the high season there are usually two boats a day going between Sámos and **Kúadasi,** Turkey—a popular, well-developed resort 20 minutes from the magnificent archaeological site at **Ephesus.** A one-way trip to Kúadasi costs about 13,500 Drs ($56.25), which includes the 4,000-Dr ($16.65) Greek port tax and the 3,000-Dr ($12.50) Turkish port tax. A round-trip ticket (including a guided tour of Ephesus and a same-day return) costs about 21,000 Drs ($87.50). If you decide to get a round-trip ticket but want to stay in Turkey for more than a day, you'll have to pay an additional port tax. Many travel agencies sell tickets to Turkey, with boats departing from both Sámos town and Pythagório. Although you must submit your passport to the travel agency that books your trip, it will be returned to you by the port police on the pier when you depart for Turkey.

2 Híos (Chíos)

153 nautical miles NE of Piraeus

"Craggy Híos" Homer dubbed it—and he should have known, since it was probably his home. It remains unspoiled by mass tourism; the wealthy shipowners who control the island simply haven't wanted tourists, and the local economy (at least until recently) has been able to get by without them.

The black-pebble beaches on the southeast coast of the island are famous (the beach at Emborió, on the southern tip of the island, is particularly beautiful), but the west coast has white-sand beaches that look as if they're visited by only a few hundred people in an entire year. (Beaches like this in the Cyclades would be packed instantly.)

There's a monastery in the middle of the island, Néa Moní, that's almost unsurpassed for the grandeur of its location and the beauty of its Byzantine mosaics. There are unique medieval villages in the south, and the major crop—mastic—grows nowhere else in the world. The northern part of the island offers excellent hiking opportunities, and the clear waters are superb for swimming, diving, and fishing.

The island residents are known for their good humor, and they still enjoy sharing their space with visitors. Enjoy it while you still can. For now Híos remains an ideal destination for those who want to escape the hordes and it's one of the most exotic places from which to cross over to Turkey.

Híos offers the adventurous visitor remote sandy coves, intact medieval villages (where you can rent a room in a 700-year-old house!), excellent fishing, a diverse landscape, and friendly people. Many of the elite families that control Greece's private shipping empires have villas here or on the smaller nearby islands.

Híos town is a thriving, refreshingly Greek port filled with Greeks, though it doesn't look typically Greek and isn't particularly attractive at first sight. Most of the city was built after a destructive earthquake in 1881 and the square modern architecture is dull and impressive. Late 19th-century mansions (and some dating as far back as the 14th century), in various states of repair, line the coast road on the outskirts of town.

The most interesting villages, dating from medieval times, are Pyryí and Mestá. Both are in the mastic region, in the southern half of Híos; they were so named because of the gum trees that still grow in the countryside (mastic in the Phoenician language was *hio,* which may account for the island's name). Pyryí is known throughout Greece for the distinctive gray-and-white geometric designs that decorate the facades of most of the village buildings. Mestá and many of the hamlets surrounding it, including Olýmbi and Véssa, are architectural gems—villages of two-story stone-and-mortar houses linked by narrow vaulted streets and quiet squares.

ESSENTIALS

GETTING THERE & DEPARTING   By Plane   Olympic Airways has about four flights a week from Athens and twice a week from Lésvos (Mytilíni) and Thessaloníki; its office in Híos town is on Leofóros Egéou, midway along the harborfront (☎ **0271/24-515**). The **airport** (☎ **0271-24-546**) is 2½ miles south of Híos town; a taxi into town will cost about 650 Drs ($2.70).

By Boat   One car-ferry leaves daily for Piraeus via Sámos, continuing on to Lésvos, and there is once-a-week service to Thessaloníki, Kavála, and the Dodecanese. Excursion boats arrive at Híos from Pythagório, Sámos, four times a week. Gianmar Lines offers **hydrofoil** service to and from Lésvos and Vathý, Sámos, in the summer. Check with the **Híos Port Authority** (☎ **0271/44-432**) for current schedules.

VISITOR INFORMATION   The **Tourist Information Office,** at Odós Kanári 18 (☎ **0271/44-389**), the second street from the north end of the harbor, can help you find a room; the office is open in summer, Monday to Friday from 7am to 2:30pm and 6:30 to 9pm, on Saturday from 10am to 1:30pm, and on Sunday from 10am to noon. The **tourist police** are headquartered at Odós Neoríon 35 (☎ **0271/ 44-427**), at the north end of the harbor.

Another good source of information is **Híos Tours,** on the harbor at Leofóros Egéou 84 (☎ **0271/29-444;** fax 0271/21-333), open Monday to Saturday from 8:30am to 1:30pm and 5:30 to 8:30pm and on Sunday from 6 to 8pm; the staff can help you find a room. Híos Tours or the tourist office can exchange currency after the portside banks' normal hours.

The free **Híos Summertime** magazine contains a lot of useful information, as well as maps of the city.

ORIENTATION   Boats dock at **Híos town,** the capital and largest town on the island, midway along the east coast. Most tourist services are located along the waterfront; **Odós Neoríon** is on the north end and **Leofóros Egéou** is on the west and south. The heart of the city, **Platía Vounakíou** (or **Plastíra**), the central square, is a couple of blocks in from the northwest corner of the harbor. Behind it is the city's **Central Park,** and to its south is the **Bazaar,** a maze of market lanes, where you can find an astonishing range of merchandise.

GETTING AROUND   By Bus   All buses leave from Híos town. The blue buses, which leave from the **blue bus station,** on the north side of the Central Park, serve local destinations. The green long-distance buses leave from the **green bus station,** a block south of the Central Park. There are four buses a day to Mestá, eight daily to Pyryí, five daily to Kardámila, but only two buses a week to Anávatos (via Néa Moní and Volissós) on the northwest coast.

By Taxi   Taxis are readily available at the port, though the **taxi station** is beyond the OTE, at the northeast corner of the central square; fares run about 1,800 Drs ($7.50) to Néa Moní, 4,000 Drs ($16.15) to Pyryí, and 5,000 Drs ($20.85) to Mestá.

By Car   Híos is a large island and fun to explore, so car pooling really pays off. Try **Vassilakis Brothers Rent-A-Car,** Odós Evgenías Hándri 3, off the south end of the harbor (☎ **0271/23-205;** fax 0271/25-659); it also has offices at the airport (☎ **0271/27-582**) and in Karfás (☎ **0271/32-284**). Compact cars rent for about 15,000 Drs ($62.50) per day, but ask about the specific terms of the insurance.

By Moped   Mopeds are a great way to get around scenic Híos—the roads are good and there's not much traffic. There are several moped-rental shops at the port. A fully insured Honda 50, suitable for two, costs about 4,600 Drs ($19.15) per day; expect to pay a few hundred drachmas less for a moped.

FAST FACTS   The **telephone center (OTE)** is across the street from the tourist office. The **post office** is on Odós Omírou, the second street from the south end of the harbor.

EXPLORING THE ISLAND

Greeks come to Híos for weeks at a time to take advantage of its many secluded beaches, scenic countryside and villages, and interesting cultural sites.

In Híos town, the former mosque situated east from the central square is now the island's **Byzantine Museum.** Open Tuesday to Sunday from 10am to 1pm, with free admission, it houses many objects including a number of marble gravestones.

The town's **Kástro** is north of the central square behind the **town hall.** It was built by the Genoese, and all but the inland walls were detroyed by the earthquake. You can enter through the **Porta Maggiora** and explore what remains of the old Jewish and Turkish quarter. The small tower to the right as you enter is the **Justiniani Museum,** which houses a collection of icons and mosaics, but was closed during our last visit.

If you enjoy museums, head south to Odós Korái, the next-to-the-last street off the west side of the harbor (after the post office), and you'll find the **Argenti Museum** near the **cathedral.** Located on the top floor of the **Korái Library,** it's open Monday to Friday from 8am to 2pm and on Saturday from 8am to 12:30pm, with free admission; it houses portraits of the local aristocracy and copies of Eugene Delacroix's *Massacre of Híos,* a masterpiece depicting the Turkish massacre of the local population in 1822, which helped galvanize European opinion against the Turks. (Actually the Samians were to blame for starting an insurrection, but it was Híos that suffered: 30,000 Greeks wree slaughtered, another 45,000 were enslaved, and the island's vineyards were uprooted.)

There's also a small **archaeology museum,** at Odós Michálon 5, south off the southwest corner of the harbor (☎ **0271/44-239**), though it, too, was closed for repairs during our last visit. It's a typical island archaeology museum with miscellaneous local finds, plus a letter from Alexander the Great to the local people.

South of town, **Kámbos** (or Campo, in Italian) is a fertile plain that was staked out by Genoese aristocrats. Most of the late 19th-century mansions (and some dating as far back as the 14th century) that line the coast road leading south toward the airport are distinctly Italian in design, golden ochre in color, with strong horizontal lines. This is an interesting area in which to stroll the narrow lanes for glimpses into the gardens and courtyards behind the high walls. Unfortunately the area is being developed, and Scandinavian, Dutch, and German tour groups are already coming in.

The beach closest to town is **Bella Vista,** but it's often crowded; a better one is **Karfás,** a fine-sand beach farther south, which can be reached by the local (blue) bus. The best beaches are near the southern end of the island, beginning at **Kómi,** which has a white-sand beach.

A couple of miles farther south, ✪ **Emborió** is considered the island's best beach. Emborió is a small fishing village built around a volcanically formed cove. The water appears black from the dark smooth stones on the ocean floor. Men wade knee-deep to catch squid and pry off crustaceans while snorkelers explore the colorful seabed. If you walk past the small man-made black-pebble beach that's overflowing with families, just over the rocks to your right is a beach that will knock your socks off—**Mávra Vólia.** Here, walking on the smooth black rocks feels and sounds as if you were walking through a room filled with marbles—the sound reverberates against the rough volcanic cliff behind. The panorama of the beach, slightly curving coastline, and distant sea is an incredible experience. There's regular bus service here from Híos town or from Pyryí (5 miles away) to Emborió.

Híos offers the adventurous visitor many more remote sandy coves on the west coast, and along the way (in the southern half of Híos) there are intact medieval villages in the mastic region. If your tour around the island takes you to the interior—and it should—you'll probably encounter huge swaths of landscape that were burned during a series of calamitous fires that spread thoughout the island in 1988.

The most interesting excursion is to the **mastic villages,** beginning with Armólia, and including Pyryí, Olýmbi, Mestá, and Vessá, continuing back along the western coast to the ghost town of Anávatos and finally to Néa Moní, the 11th-century monastery in the center of the island. (Or you could make the tour in the opposite direction, going west from Híos town.)

✪ **Pyryí** is the only village in Greece decorated with distinctive white-and-gray graffiti (we use the word in its original meaning of "designs scratched into a surface," rather than the modern sense of defacement). The walls are stuccoed with a mixture of cement and black volcanic sand, then painted over with white lime, part of which is scraped away to create the designs. From the main *platía,* what you see is like some strange neo geo or op art dream. On the main square is the 12th-century Byzantine chapel of Áyii Apóstoli, built in the style of the earlier Néa Moní, a tiny jewel, with 17th-century frescoes still in good condition.

✪ **Mestá** is quite different from Pyryí. This remarkable 14th-century "fortress" village was built inside a system of walls, with corner towers and iron gates to fend off invaders. The yard-thick attached walls of the houses create a labyrinth of streets that will charm, delight, and disorient you. Although many young people have moved away, life is thriving in Mestá thanks to many renovation projects. The arch-roofed houses that have withstood centuries of earthquakes reveal interiors of remarkable grace. Life is slow and quiet here—a perfect place for a quite retreat.

There are two beautiful churches; the newer one (only 120 years old) is the fourthlargest and one of the wealthiest in Greece. Its ornate frescoes, massive chandeliers, and lovely icons make it worth a stop on your trip through the main square. The older church, Paleós Taxiárchis, is buried deep in the village; the gatekeeper lives across the street. Its Byzantine frescoes have finally been exposed to view (they had been covered with plaster during the years the building was used as a Turkish mosque). Both churches are dedicated to the patron saints of the village, Michael and Gabriel.

Several monks lead a quiet life at ✪ **Néa Moní,** a medieval church built in 1042 by craftsmen sent from Constantinople by the emperor Constantine VIII to replace an earlier monastery—and ever since it has been called the "New Monastery." It's one of Greece's prettiest monasteries, with an octagonal chapel highlighted by exquisite mosaics of marble white, azure blue, and ruby red on a field of gold tiles. The dreamy expressions on the faces of the figures give them an artistic elevation that's unsurpassed in Greece; technically they cannot match those at Óssios Loukás and Dafní, but they outshine them in the subtlety of expression.

Be sure to wander to the back of the monastery for the view below, and look into the cistern (bring a flashlight), a cavernous vaulted room with columns, to your right as you come through the main gate. The small chapel at the monastery entrance is dedicated to those who were massacred in 1822 by the Turks, who also damaged the monastery itself. The skulls and bones are from the actual victims. Only a few buses each week go to Néa Moní, but travel agents offer excursions; alternatively, you could take a moped, car, or taxi. It's open daily from 8am to 1pm and 4 to 8pm; admission is free.

On the west coast of Híos, directly across from the main town, are a series of coves and beaches between Órmos Elinátas and Órmos Trachiloú. About half a mile northwest of the town of **Lithí** are a few tavernas, a few rooms for rent, and a shallow cove with moorings for colorful fishing boats. The most enticing accommodation is **Agistri** (☎ 0271/73-469), above the far end of the beach, which offers six rooms at about 6,000 Drs ($25). A bit farther north there's a long stretch of fine white pebbles and stones where nude bathing is common. If you plan to go to the west coast, consider renting a car or moped for the long, winding road, because the bus service to Lithí is infrequent.

The northern part of the island is craggier and the fishing and diving from rocks is superior. The road north from Híos is more picturesque, and there are several small resorts, such as **Vrondádos** and **Langáda,** in the rocky coves, many with good tavernas. Although no one knows exactly where Homer was born, most historians believe that he came from Híos. The "Stone of Homer," where the blind poet was supposed to have sat when he composed his legendary works, is outside Vrondádos in a grove of olive trees, at the ancient site of the Temple of Cybele and Rhea.

The most attractive town on the island is **Kardámila,** on the northeast corner—an enclave of shipowners and affluent ship officers and crew. There's only one hotel here and few tourist services—that's why it's so refreshing.

Nagós, northwest across the headland, is another pleasant seaside village that offers some great black-sand beaches. Most people go to the beach close to town, but it can sometimes become crowded. The secret is to hike to the two small beaches a little to the east (take the small road behind the white house near the windmill and you'll get there). To reach Nagós you'll have to take the Kardámila bus and hope that it will continue the 3 miles to the beach. If not, you can usually get a ride by waving down a private car. (There aren't enough hitchhikers on the island yet to make anyone wary.)

WHERE TO STAY
IN HÍOS TOWN

If you're just arriving on Híos, it might be best for you to find an accommodation in town before you set off for one of the island's many special villages, which are prettier and cheaper, though you'll need your own vehicle for sightseeing. Híos town has a large number of private rooms; it will probably cost about 6,500 Drs ($27.10) for two. Contact the tourist office for availabilities.

✪ **Hotel Kýma.** Odós Evyeniás Handrí 1, Híos, 821 00 Híos. ☎ 0271/44-500. Fax 0271/44-600. 59 rms, all with bath (shower or tub). A/C TEL. 13,250 Drs ($55.20) single; 17,350 Drs ($72.30) double. Rates include breakfast. No credit cards.

Our favorite in-town lodging was built in 1917 as a private villa. Though the hotel is of historic interest—the treaty with Turkey was signed in the Kýma in 1922—most of the architectural details, other than in the lobby area and breakfast room, are gone. All rooms have been renovated in a modern style; many have views of the sea, and a few have big whirlpool baths. The management, under the smart direction of the venerable Mr. Spordílis, is friendly, capable, and helpful. They also serve an excellent breakfast, complete with fresh tangerine juice, thick yogurt, tea and coffee of all varieties, and fresh fruit.

Pension Yiannis. Odós Mihaíl Livanoú 48–50, Híos, 821 00 Híos. ☎ **0271/27-433.** 13 rms, 10 with bath (shower). 7,000 Drs ($29.15) single or double without bath, 10,000 Drs ($41.65) single or double with bath. No credit cards.

This pleasant pension is one street off the south end of the harbor. The friendly hostess, Irene, grew up in New Jersey and New York, and allows you to share her refrigerator. It's a good value, the rooms are bright and pleasant, and the garden out behind is a treat.

Rooms Alex. Odós Mihaíl Livanoú 29, Híos, 821 00 Híos. ☎ **0271/26-054.** 6 rms, 2 with bath (tub). 6,000 Drs ($25) single or double without bath, 7,000 Drs ($29.15) single or double with bath. No credit cards.

Another good-value place south of the harbor, with nice rooms and a roof garden with a sea view. Alex, who speaks English very well, will meet you at the harbor or airport if you call.

ELSEWHERE AROUND THE ISLAND

Kardámila, on the northeast coast, is our first choice of the resort towns because it's prosperous, self-sufficient, and very untouristy.

Karfás, 4¹⁄₂ miles south of Híos town around Cape Ayía Eléni, is an exploding tourist resort. Its fine-sand beach is lined with expensive Greek all-inclusive holiday hotels. There are also a great many rooms and apartments for rent in the **Vrondádos** beach area north of Híos town. Contact the Tourist Information Office or Híos Tours (☎ **0271/29-444**) for specific recommendations.

In **Pasalimáni,** around the corner from the petite harbor, there's a wonderfully rustic inn called the **Mikro Castello** (☎ **0271/28-743**), which is a handmade four-room treasure trove of carved wood sculpture. Each room has a platform bed, fireplace, and rudimentary kitchen gear. We've visited twice and are always taken with it. A double with breakfast costs 10,000 Drs ($41.65); no credit cards.

Travelers attracted to even more remote destinations might visit **Psará,** a small island 18 nautical miles off the west coast of Híos, where the **EOT Guesthouse** offers rooms in a restored 17th-century parliament building; doubles without bath are 6,000 Drs ($25) and doubles with bath are 7,000 Drs ($29.15). Call them at ☎ **0274/61-293** (or 0251/27-908 on Lésvos) for information and reservations. There are also rooms-to-let on the island. There's ferry service from Híos town to Psará three times a week.

Golden Sand Hotel. P.O. Box 32, Karfás, 821 00 Híos. ☎ **0271/32-080.** Fax 0271/31-700. 108 rms, all with bath (tub). A/C MINIBAR TEL. 21,000 Drs ($87.50) single; 27,200 Drs ($113.35) double. AE, DC, EURO, MC, V.

It's a bit of a splurge, but the Golden Sand was one of the first Karfás beach resorts, an attractive, group-oriented, two-story lodge with a large roof deck and marble floors throughout. It also has a large pool, its own private beach, satellite TV and radio in the large guest rooms, and a spacious, airy breakfast area. There's even a beauty salon and kids' playground. Between mid-June and mid-September a compulsory half-board plan is in effect, adding 3,500 Drs ($14.60) per person per day to the high-season rates above.

Hotel Kardámyla. Kardámila, 823 00 Híos. ☎ **0272/23-353.** Fax 0271/23-354. 32 rms, all with bath (tub). A/C TEL. 14,200 Drs ($59.15) single; 18,000 Drs ($75) double. Rates include breakfast. No credit cards.

This modern resort hotel was built for the guests and business associates of the town's shipowners and officers, and it has its own small beach. The rooms are large and plain, with modern bathrooms and balconies overlooking the beach. The excellent Theo Spordílis has taken over its management, so you can be sure the service will be good.

Staying in Traditional Villages

There are a few centuries-old villages in Greece that seem timeless, where life seems to have changed as little as the buildings themselves. Many are outdoor architectural museums, studied and appreciated for their unique styles of construction, but unfortunately abandoned by the younger members of the community.

Mestá, 22¹/₂ miles southwest of Híos town, is just such a village, and fortunately, the Greek government acquired 33 old abandoned homes to protect them from further deterioration. Four of these homes, originally built more than 500 years ago, have been restored and opened by the EOT as part of its Traditional Settlements Program. The admirable Dimitri Pipidis (☎ **0271/76-319**) manages the four houses (a total of eight rooms), and each comes equipped with a kitchen, bathroom, and enough sleeping space for two to six people. The price is determined by the number of beds: 9,000 Drs ($37.50) for one bed, 10,500 Drs ($43.75) for two beds, and 12,000 Drs ($50) for three beds.

If there's no answer at the Mestá number, just drive to the village; Dimitri's office is on the central square. If the houses are booked, he can help you find an available private room in Mestá. A typical room costs 7,500 Drs ($31.90), depending on the house and season. During the high season it's important to make your reservations early.

There are also private rooms for rent in **Pyryí,** though it's so busy with day-trippers that we find Mestá much more relaxing. Several businesses near the main square rent rooms; **Astra Rooms** (☎ **0271/71-149**) offers rather simple, bathless rooms for 3,000 Drs ($12.50) per bed per night.

The **Women's Agricultural-Tourist Co-operative of Híos,** near the central square in Pyryí, 821 02 Híos (☎ **0271/72-496**), can find you a room in a private home for about 5,000 to 7,500 Drs ($20.50 to $31.25), depending on the season. Their members also offer bathless rooms in the towns of Mestá, Pyryí, Armoliá, and Olýmbi, as well as on local farms, for about 4,400 Drs ($18.35) for one and 6,000 Drs ($25) for two, plus an additional 750 Drs ($3.15) for breakfast. If you like, you can help cook or work in the fields with your host. In any of the villages, except Mestá, we think this is the best choice. For reservations, write or call the co-operative; the office is open year-round.

WHERE TO EAT

More sophisticated locals prefer to take a short drive south or north for fine cuisine. **Giamos,** on Karfás beach, is known as a good outlet for meat dishes. If you're in Emborió or Pasalimáni, be sure to try the fish and squid; both villages are known for their seafood, and you can watch the fishers bring in their catch right in front of your table. The same is true just north of Vrondádos at the **Ormos Lo Restaurant** near the public beach.

Apolaisi. In Ayía Ermióni Village. ☎ **0271/31-359.** Menu items 650–1,600 Drs ($2.70–$6.65); fish from 12,000 Drs ($50) per kilo. No credit cards. Daily 5pm–midnight. SEAFOOD.

This delightful fish taverna with a candlelit terrace run by Yorgo Karanikola is about 5 or 6 miles south of Híos town. Dine on fried calamari, grilled fish, and an assortment of salads while fishers below take their boats out for their night's work. You'll need to take a taxi to get to Apolaisi; plan on a 10- to 15-minute ride.

Híos Marine Club. Odós Nenitoúsi 1, Híos. ☎ **0271/23-184.** Main courses 700–3,400 Drs ($2.90–$14.15). EURO, MC, V. Daily noon–2am. GREEK.

This good taverna right in town serves the usual Greek dishes, pasta, and grilled meats and fish. Try the *galéos* (a local fish) grilled, or the *bámies,* an okra dish.

Iviskos. On the central square, Híos. No phone. Snacks/desserts 350–2,200 Drs ($1.45–$9.15). No credit cards. Daily 7am–2am. CONTINENTAL.

Iviskos serves excellent bread with its breakfast, and a dynamite Black Forest cake until 2am. This is the place for light eats and people watching.

Theodosiou Ouzerí. Paralía, Híos. No phone. Menu items 400–3,600 Drs ($1.65–$15). No credit cards. Daily 5pm–midnight. GREEK.

In the evening, many residents enjoy pulling up a streetside chair at a cafe along the water to sip an ouzo or slurp a chocolate sundae. Of the many cafes on the *paralía,* we like Theodosiou Ouzerí, located on the far right side of the port, both for the scene and its menu.

Paradise (Yiorgo Passa's). Langáda. ☎ **0271/74-218.** Menu items 600–2,800 Drs ($2.50–$11.65); fish from 10,000 Drs ($41.65) per kilo. No credit cards. Daily 11am–2am. SEAFOOD.

Langáda, a fishing village with a strip of five or six outdoor fish tavernas lining the harbor, about 12 miles north of Híos, is an excellent dining venue. Of those that we sampled, we prefer the food prepared by Yiorgo Passa at his Paradise snack bar. His place is the first on the left as you walk down to the waterfront. The prices are low, the portions generous, and the ambience is warm and friendly. *Note:* There are evening dinner cruises to Langáda from Híos; check with Híos Tours about the schedule and prices.

Zervas. Odós Neoríon 1, Híos. ☎ **0271/44-709.** Main courses 1,000–2,500 Drs ($4.15–$10.40). EURO, MC. Daily noon–2am. INTERNATIONAL.

This new restaurant on the north end of the harbor is easily the most attractive of the waterfront establishments, and the food is as good as the handsome decor promises. Try the house specialty, grilled chicken—a hit with local diners.

HÍOS AFTER DARK

Most people in Híos entertain themselves along the harborfront and around the central square, but there are a few more sophisticated bars, including **Kavos** and **Remezzo.** There are two discos: **Neraïda,** at Leofóros Enósseos 3 (☎ **0271/20-149**); and **Karnayio,** on the road to the airport.

The **Omírio** (Homeric) **Center,** off the southwest corner of the main square (☎ **0271/24-217**), sometimes hosts visiting musicians.

SIDE TRIPS TO TURKEY

During the summer there are daily departures to Çesme, Turkey, from the port of Híos. The round-trip price is about 18,000 Drs ($75), including a bus tour of the city of Izmir, or a 2-hour bus ride and tour of Ephesus, plus all taxes. The rest of the year, boats run less often; check with the portside travel agents such as Híos Tours. Çesme is a 45-minute bus ride from Izmir on the Aegean coast, where buses run frequently to Istanbul and all the coastal cities including Ephesus. *Note:* You must submit your passport (at least temporarily) to the travel agency the day before your departure.

3 Lésvos (Mytilíni)

188 nautical miles NE of Piraeus

Lésvos, frequently called Mytilíni, after its capital, is the third-largest island in Greece, with a population of nearly 120,000. Its capital and main port, Mytilíni, on the southeast coast, is a small bustling city and one of the busiest ports in Greece.

It's impossible to think about Lésvos without the island's two most obvious, and related, associations: the love of women for women and the great classical poet Sappho. Legends abound about the origin of the former, some suggesting that it developed as a cult or college devoted to Aphrodite (possibly founded by Sappho), others theorizing that the island became "lesbian" when the Athenians wreaked vengeance on its inhabitants, after a failed rebellion, by murdering all its men.

For all her fame, little is known for certain about the great lyric poet whom Plato called "the Tenth Muse." Sappho was born on Lésvos about 620 B.C. and lived most of her life in Eressós, though apparently she spent some time in exile in Sicily, probably because of the political activities of her husband or brothers. Her husband was a wealthy man from Ándros, and they had at least one daughter. ("I have a beautiful daughter, golden like a flower, my beloved Kleis, and for her I would not accept the whole of Lydia. . . .") Little remains of her poetry but such fragments, and most of that would have been lost to us if later admirers hadn't quoted her.

Most scholars now agree that she was a member of a religious association devoted to a female deity, probably Aphrodite, and the mistress of a school that prepared aristocratic young women from all over Ionia for marriage. Her poetry is called *melic,* from which we get our word "melody," because it was meant to be sung to the accompaniment of a lyre. Much of her surviving poetry, such as the exquisite "To a Bride," is addressed to young women, and there can be no doubt that she celebrates her passion for them. Probably they were sung at a gathering, perhaps something like our modern bridal shower, attended exclusively by women. There is no evidence that her contemporaries found the least offense in them. She was greatly admired and respected, even among men; the poet Alcaeus called her "holy." Few poets have expressed love with such eloquence, tenderness, and power. ("Love's unbound my limbs and set me shaking/ A demon bittersweet and my unmaking.") No one who has read the precious little that remains of her work can doubt they are among the greatest love lyrics ever composed.

That Lésvos was an artistic center is without dispute—there is still a festival each May called "The Week of Prose and Arts"—but it was most famous in ancient times for its academies and symposia. Theophrastus, director of the Athens Academy, came from Lésvos, and both Plato and Aristotle went to Lésvos to teach and study. The maxims "Know thyself" and "Nothing in excess," inscribed on the Temple at Delphi, were taken from the writings of Pitticus, one of the Seven Sages of Greece and a tyrant of Lésvos. The philosopher Epicurus came to Lésvos from Sámos to study.

Today the island's face is changing, especially the northern town of Mólyvos—one of the loveliest parts of the island—because of the growing number of British tour groups.

ESSENTIALS

GETTING THERE & DEPARTING **By Plane** **Olympic Airways** has three flights daily between Lésvos (called "Mytilíni" on schedules and boarding infor-mation) and Athens, 10 flights daily to and from Thessaloníki, a daily flight to Límnos, and two flights a week to Híos. The Olympic office in Mytilíni is at Odós Kavétsou 44, about 200 yards south of Ayía Irínis park, south from the harbor (☎ **0251/28-660**). The airport is 5 miles south of Mytilíni; a bus meets Olympic flights (cost: 400 Drs/$1.65). A taxi from the airport costs about 1,200 Drs ($5).

By Boat   In the summer there is ferry service at least once daily between Lésvos and Piraeus via Híos (12 hours, 5,500 Drs/$22.90). There's a connection two or three times a week with Kavála via Límnos, and once or twice a week with Thessaloníki via Límnos. In summer Ilios Lines and Gianmar offer **hydrofoil** service between Lésvos and Alexandroúpolis, Híos, Kávala, Límnos, Pythagório (Sámos), Pátmos, and Sámos town. Call the **Maritime Company of Lésvos** (☎ **0251/23-720**), the **port authority** (☎ **0251/28-888**), or the **port police** (☎ **0251/28-647**) for current schedules.

Always double-check schedules on Lésvos, since the harbor is extremely busy in the summer and service is often inexplicably irregular. Many of the ferries to Mytilíni are scheduled to arrive at midnight, but may be as late as 2:30am. The late boats are not necessarily met by people with rooms for rent, so be sure to call ahead for accommodations. If you're stuck, you can always wake up the night clerk at the **Blue Sea Hotel,** across from the ferry pier at Koundouriótou 91 (☎ **0251/23-994**), where doubles go for 18,800 Drs ($78.35); or at the **Hotel Sappho,** midway down the harborfront at Koundouriótou 31 (☎ **0251/22-888**), where doubles cost 12,000 Drs ($50).

VISITOR INFORMATION   The **EOT** is at Odós Aristárhou 6 (☎ **0251/42-511;** fax 0251/42-512), behind the customs office to the left (east) from the ferry pier in Mytilíni. It's open daily from 8am to 2pm, with extended hours during the high season. The staff maintain a complete listing of hotels, pensions, and rooms throughout the island, and are willing to make calls for you for accommodations in Mytilíni. The **tourist police** (☎ **0251/22-776**) are near the EOT, left (east) from the ferry pier.

ORIENTATION   Lésvos is shaped something like a rounded triangle with two huge tear-shaped inland bays (gulfs) cutting into the west and south coasts of the island. There are important concentrations of tourism on the north coast at beautiful **Mólyvos** (which is still frequently called by its ancient name, Míthymna) and south at **Plomári.**

Sappho's hometown, **Eressós,** is near the northwest coast of the island. Within the island's irregular triangle there is amazing diversity: parts of the island are industrialized, parts are fertile (with about 12 million olive trees), parts are mountainous with chestnut and pine trees, parts are desertlike plain, and there are even a few marshy areas to round out the picture. What you experience will depend a great deal on what you choose to see.

Mytilíni, the capital, main port, and airport, are on the southeastern corner of the triangle, just across from Ayvalik, on the Turkish coast. Most of the city's activity centers around the big **main harbor** along the waterfront or along **Pávlou Koundouriótou Street,** especially west of the harbor, which is the most important area of the city for tourists since it has nearly all the services and shops. Most ferries dock near the southeast corner of the main harbor. Northeast of the main harbor is a promontory dominated by a large Genoese fortress, and the main commercial thoroughfare, **Ermoú,** crosses the promontory to the the the **old north harbor.**

GETTING AROUND   By Bus   Lésvos has an expensive, infrequent, and metered bus system providing daily service in summer to Kaloní or Mólyvos (four times), to Mandamádos (once), Plomári (four times), and to Eressós and Sigrí (once). The

round-the-island KTEL bus station is at the south end of the port behind the Argo Hotel. The **local bus station** is near the north end of the harbor, near the Popular Arts Museum.

By Car   There are many car-rental offices on the port in Mytilíni, and you can bargain except during the summer. **Europcar** has offices in Mytilíni (☎ **0251/43-311**) and a desk at the airport (☎ **0251/61-200**). Expect to pay 17,000 Drs ($70.85) a day without gas for a Fiat Panda.

By Boat   **Aeolic Cruises** (☎ **0251/23-960;** fax 0251/43-694) offers daily boat excursions around the island during the high season from its portside office.

By Motorbike   There are lots of motorbike-rental agencies along the harbor in Mytilíni, as well as a few in Mólyvos, Plomári, and Skála Eressoú, but the island is so large that they're not suitable for exploring all of it.

By Taxi   The **taxi stand** in Mytilíni is near the local bus station (close to the north end of the port and the Popular Arts Museum). The one-way taxi fare to Mólyvos is 10,000 Drs ($42.55); to Eressós or Sígri it's 12,500 Drs ($53.20).

FAST FACTS   The **Vostáni Hospital,** on Odós P. Vostáni, just southeast of town (☎ **0251/43-777**), can take care of emergencies. The **post office** and the **telephone center (OTE)** are on Odós Vournázon, a long block inland behind the town hall. The telephone **area code** for Mytilíni is **0251,** for Mólyvos (Míthymna) and Eressós it's **0253,** and for Plomári it's **0252.**

EXPLORING THE ISLAND

Most people arrive on Lésvos at the big and busy harbor of **Mytilíni** and immediately rush away. It's more like a mainland city than an island capital; it has a big-city ambience that more nearly resembles Thessaloníki than any other Aegean backwater. Unlike most of Greece, Lesviots know that they're Europeans, and they feel they share a rich cultural legacy with the continent. Mytilíni is not to everyone's taste, especially at first glance, but we suggest that you take another look. Stroll around town and look at the amazing array of architecture.

Even if you're dying for white cubes over a dazzling sea, we suggest sticking around town long enough to enjoy the best sights, especially the excellent Theophilos Museum in nearby Variá, the port, and the ornate, peaked-dome **Church of St. Therápon.** There are many grand old garden villas scattered around town, especially near the archaeological museum, west of the port. To the north, toward the fortress, Mytilíni's crumbling ochre backstreets are filled with a mix of traditional coffeehouses, artisans, and food vendors, along with stylish new jewelry, antiques, and clothing stores.

The new **Archaeological Museum of Mytilini,** at Odós Eftalíou 7 (☎ **0251/28-032**), east of the harbor, has a fine sculpture collection. It contains finds from the Bronze Age up to the Hellenistic era from Therme and Mólyvos, including the latest excavations, and a rich selection of mosaics, sculpture, and tablets. It's open Tuesday to Sunday from 8:30am to 3pm; admission is 500 Drs ($2.10).

The **Popular Arts Museum** is in a small white house in the center of the port near the local bus station on Koundouriótou Street (☎ **0251/41-844**). Its current curator and guide, Ioánna, will give you an excellent tour of its fine embroideries, eccentric pottery (much of which came from Cannakale, Turkey), costumes, and historical documents. It's open Monday to Saturday from 8:30am to 2pm; admission is 250 Drs ($1.05).

The **Theóphilos Museum,** the former house of the folk artist Hatzimichális Theóphilos (1868–1934), who emigrated from the Mt. Pelion region to paint on Lésvos, is about 2 miles south of town in Variá. His watercolors of ordinary people, daily life, and local landscapes are widely celebrated, and they're also exhibited at the Museum of Folk Art in Pláka, in Athens. The museum is hung floor to ceiling with Theóphilos's extraordinary canvases. The museum is open Tuesday to Sunday from 9am to 1pm and 3 to 5pm; admission is 500 Drs ($2.10).

The mildly compelling **Tériade Library and Museum of Modern Art** is next door to the Theóphilos Museum, in the home of the noted art critic Stratís Eleftheriáde, better known by the name he assumed in France, Tériade. Copies of his published works, including the *Minotaure* and *Verve* magazines, as well as his personal collection of works by Matisse, Picasso, Miró, Chagall, Roualt, Giacometti, and other modern artists, are displayed. It's open Tuesday to Sunday from 9am to 2pm and 5 to 8pm; admission is 500 Drs ($2.10).

The **Kástro** to the north of the city was founded by Justinian in the 6th century and restored and enlarged by the Genoese in 1737, incorporating columns from a 7th-century B.C. Temple of Apollo. In the summer it's used as a performing arts center, often with popular Greek singers. There's also an **ancient theater** to the east above the town and a well-preserved **Roman aqueduct,** thought to have been built in the 2nd century, near Mória, a short distance north from Mytilíni.

The **east-coast road,** leading up to Mandamádos, is the most scenic on the island; olive and fruit trees grow down to the water's edge and thermal springs form warm pools that attract bathers. (If you want to disappear into Lésvos's seductive landscape, head to the west, where fewer visitors tread.) The long coast road, which sometimes veers inland, has a series of less-than-inviting pebble-and-stone beaches; however, if you feel like stopping for a fish lunch, we can recommend the harbors at Panayoúda, Pyryí Thérmis, and Skála Mistegnon.

Mandamádos is a large village of gray stone houses known for the manufacture of *koumária,* porous ceramic vases that keep water cool even in scorching heat.

Mólyvos (Míthymna), at the northern tip of the triangle, reached by the inland route, is a castle-crowned village with stone and pink-pastel stucco mansions capped by red-tile roofs. The town overlooks the sea, its modest harbor, and flanking pebble beaches overflowing with sunbathers and swimmers.

Although now there are altogether too many souvenir shops selling geniune plastic neon-green backscratchers and the like, the village is still a wonderful place to soak up a lot of Greek atmosphere: the men who live in cafes, studying their ouzo; the bright, colorful geraniums and roses that decorate balconies and sills; the unfathomable layout of streets, alleyways, and passages; and the women, always working, who have a special place on Lésvos. In Mólyvos you can wander up to the Genoese fortress, stroll along the port, or swim at the local pebble beaches.

About 4¹/₂ miles south of Mólyvos is the enterprising village of **Pétra,** a fishing hamlet with an enormous rock in its center, where the **Committee for the Equal Rights of the Two Sexes** started a program to place visitors in local homes, where they can help in the fields, in the kitchen, or in the handicraft cooperative. The **Women's Agricultural-Tourist Co-operative** (☎ **0253/41-238;** fax 0253/41-309) has a reception area in the village and a popular taverna on the main square.

East of Mólyvos—best reached by the coastal highway north from Mytilíni—is **Skála Sykaminiás,** the prettiest little fishing village on the island, and the setting for Stratis Myrivilis's novel *The Mermaid Madonna.* Closer to Mólyvos is **Eftálou,** with its famous hot thermal baths called **Loutrá Eftaloú.** Both villages are appealing, have modest architecture, and exemplify the unhurried pace of Greek peasant life.

The paved road to Mólyvos meets the west-bound road at **Kalloní,** a sardine center, 2¹/₂ miles north of Lésvos's largest inland body of water, the Gulf of Kalloní. The western half of the island is the least visited; **sandy beaches** run the length of the coast from Sígri to Skála Eressoú. The villages on this part of Lésvos are the island's most serene.

Eressós is an attractive village overlooking a lush green plain. Its port, **Skála Eressoú,** 2¹/₂ miles south, has the best beach on Lésvos, a wide, dark-sand stretch over a mile long lined with tamarisks; it has become a full-blown resort popular with Greek families as well as with gay women. (A few remains of ancient Eressós still stand just east of Skála Eressoú.) A long stretch of sandy beaches and coves extends north from there to Sígri. Skála Eressoú has an **archaeology museum** (☎ 0253/53-332), near the 5th-century Basilica of Áyios Andréas (St. Andrew), with local finds from the archaic, classical, and Roman periods. It's open Tuesday to Sunday from 7:30am to 3:30pm; admission is free.

Although some visitors prefer the village of Eressós, most stay at the beach. In Mytilíni, the **Cooperative Tourism & Travel Agency** (☎ 0251/21-329) maintains a list of available rooms. If you want to stay at the beach, there are some rooms for rent.

Plomári, 25 miles southwest of Mytilíni, is a town very much like Mólyvos, though not as pretty. It's Lésvos's second city and the port for one of Greece's major ouzo centers, as well as a growing resort. If you're there when the potent drink is being distilled, your nose will catch the licorice scent of fennel wafting in the breeze. Plomári town has been able to accept tourist development without completely selling its soul; it still retains something of its fishing-village character. Local houses have the traditional wooden galleries, called *sachnissínia,* so the town has a different architectural quality from Mólyvos, but also offers winding streets, mysterious passageways, outdoor cafes, a scenic harbor, and a relaxed pace. There's an Ouzo Festival every July, and the town is known for its fresh shrimp, hot red peppers, and locally produced mushrooms. Unfortunately, all this has attracted tour groups, and so hotel rooms are hard to find.

Plomári's in-town beaches are fine for swimming, but travel a few miles east to **Áyios Isodóros** for better water, a long pebble beach, and a growing number of pensions and condos. Due west on Lésvos's south coast is the popular sand beach at **Vaterá** (5 miles long, 30 yards wide), which is often jammed.

A really enjoyable day trip is to the rural hamlet of **Ayiássos,** 14¹/₄ miles west of Mytilíni, where local craftsmen still turn out their ceramic ware by hand. The town, built up on the foothills of Mt. Ólýmbos, has traditional gray stone houses, some painted in fantastic pastels, with wooden "Turkish" (Ottoman) balconies covered with flowering vines, and modest churches on steep, narrow cobblestone lanes. During our last visit Maestro Yannis Sousamlis was playing haunting music on his *sandoúri* (hammer dulcimer). You can take an excursion bus from Mytilíni or share a taxi (cost: about 7,000 Drs/$29.15 for the 1-hour, 15¹/₂-mile ride).

WHERE TO STAY

The **Cooperative Tourism and Travel Agency,** at Odos Konstantinoupóleos 5, next to the bus station in Mytilíni (☎ 0251/21-329; fax 0251/41-268), can help you find rooms in the island's rural areas.

IN MYTILÍNI

Mytilíni has a number of older hotels at the port, most of them hardly worth mentioning. The EOT office can provide information on available private rooms.

Hotel Blue Sea. Odós Koundouriótou 91, Mytilíni, 810 00 Lésvos. ☎ **0251/23-995.** Fax 0251/29-656. 61 rms, all with bath (tub). TEL. 12,000 Drs ($50) single; 18,800 Drs ($78.30) double. EURO, MC, V.

This older hotel on the southeast corner of the port near the ferry pier was recently remodeled and outfitted with double-paned windows, so now it's not only convenient but quiet enough for a good night's sleep.

Hotel Erato. Odós P. Vostáni 2, Mytilíni, 811 00 Lésvos. ☎ **0251/41-160.** 22 rms, all with bath (tub). TEL. 7,250 Drs ($30.20) single; 11,800 Drs ($49.15) double. EURO, MC, V.

This four-story lodging was converted from a medical clinic. The rooms are bright with scrubbed-clean baths and balconies, and the staff is friendly and helpful. However, many of the rooms suffer from the noise of cycles ripping by, so check your room before you make a commitment. It's open all year.

Salina's Garden. Odós Fokéas 7–9, Mytilíni, 811 00 Lésvos. ☎ **0251/42-073.** 6 rms, 1 with bath (tub). 5,500 Drs ($22.90) single; 7,250 Drs ($30.20) double. No credit cards.

These pleasant, rustic rooms, grouped around a lovely garden, are up Ermoú Street going north from the main harbor, off to the right—not far from the Kástro. There's no Salina here, just a friendly, English-speaking Greek family who create a relaxed, mellow atmosphere that's very popular with budget travelers. They also rent motorbikes for a reasonable price, and guests can use their kitchen to prepare breakfast. This place fills up fast, so call ahead.

IN MÓLYVOS (MÍTHYMNA)

In Mólyvos the **Tourist Information Office** (☎ 0253/71-347) maintains a list of private rooms to rent, many of which are up on the hill near the ochre-colored castle. A Class A room in Mólyvos typically starts at 7,500 Drs ($31.25).

Hotel-Bungalows Delfinia. Mólyvos, 811 08 Lésvos. ☎ **0253/71-315.** Fax 0253/71-524. 65 rms, 57 bungalows, all with bath (tub). TEL. 16,800 Drs ($70) single; 23,250 Drs ($98.90) double; 33,200 Drs ($138.35) bungalow. Room rates include breakfast; bungalow rates include half board. AE, DC, V.

This contemporary white stucco and gray stone resort, in a panoramic setting above the port and beach, is a splurge, but it's a good value as far as full-service hotels go. Piped-in music, minibars (in the bungalows), room service, and one-day laundry can go a long way toward making a vacation special. Though the rooms are simple, the complex is situated on spacious, well-kept grounds with a saltwater swimming pool, table tennis, snack bar, basketball, volleyball, and tennis facilities. It's open year-round.

✪ **Hotel Olive Press.** Mólyvos, 811 08 Lésvos. ☎ **0253/71-205.** Fax 0253/71-246. 41 rms, 9 studios, all with bath (tub). TEL. 14,750 Drs ($61.45) single; 19,800 Drs ($82.50) double; 30,000 Drs ($125) studio. Room (but not studio) rates include breakfast. AE, DC, V.

The most charming hotel in town is newly built in a traditional style down near the town beach. The rooms are on the small side, but they're quiet and very comfortable, with terrazzo floors, handsome furnishings, and bathtubs with shower curtains. The windows of some of the rooms open onto great sea views, with waves lapping just below. There's a nice inner courtyard with several gardens. The staff is gracious and friendly.

Nicholas Prokopiou Rooms to Let. Odós Eftaliótou 22, Mólyvos, 811 08 Lésvos. ☎ **0253/71-403.** 4 rms, none with bath. 6,600 Drs ($27.50) double; 7,900 Drs ($32.90) triple. No credit cards.

We found a lovely unnamed stone house in the old part of town that offered rooms. For a modest sum, you get a pleasant double-bedded room, kitchen facilities, and the pleasure of dining in a secluded, verdant garden.

Sea Horse Pension. Mólyvos, 811 08 Lésvos. ☎ **0253/71-320.** Fax 0253/71-374. 14 rms, all with bath (tub). 8,300 Drs ($34.60) single; 9,400 Drs ($39.15) double. Rates include breakfast. No credit cards.

There's a cluster of recently built group hotels below the old town, near the beach. Among them is this smaller, homier pension, Thalássio Álogo in Greek, where the friendly manager Stergios keeps tidy rooms with good views. There's also a restaurant and an in-house travel agency.

In Plomári

In Plomári, we like the **Pension Lida** (☎ **0251/44-320**), located in two handsome old villas right in town, where doubles with sea view and private bath are 8,650 Drs ($36.05), including breakfast in a little garden balcony.

WHERE TO EAT
In Mytilíni

Mytilíni, with its youthful, somewhat avant-garde population, has even more portside cafes and tavernas than your average bustling harbor town. At the southern end of the port (opposite the new docks) are several small ouzerís, specializing in grilled octopus, squid, shrimp, and local fish. Small portions of *tzatzíki, patátes,* and olives accompany wine or one of the many types of ouzo from Plomári. The cluster of chairs around the small lighthouse at the point is the most scenic, and windiest, of these places. For *après* ouzo there are several cafes, but on soccer night it's almost impossible to get a seat.

Averof 1841 Grill. Odós P. Koundouriótou. No phone. Main courses 600–3,400 Drs ($2.50–$14.15). No credit cards. Daily 11:30am–11:30pm. GREEK.

This taverna, midway on the west side of the port near the Sappho Hotel, is one of the better grills around, with particularly good beef dishes. Try any of the tender souvláki, or the lamb with potatoes.

In Mólyvos (Míthymna)

Mólyvos presents quite a few good choices, including the **Olive Press,** down by the harbor, which serves a nice breakfast.

Captain's Table. Mólyvos. ☎ **0253/71-241.** Main courses 1,000–2,100 Drs ($4.15–$8.75). MC, V. Daily 11am–1am. Closed Dec–Mar. INTERNATIONAL/SEAFOOD.

One of our favorite cooks, Melinda, has moved her establishment down to the harbor. Now, in addition to the scrumptious vegetarian fare, you can have seafood and grilled meats, such as a beefburger and mixed grill, several kinds of pasta, and such exotic dishes as Kashmiri curried chicken and spareribs with sweet-and-sour sauce. Lobster is 9,000 Drs ($37.50) a kilo, and two can share the Captain's plate (fish, shrimp, octopus, *kalamári,* and mussels) for 6,000 Drs ($25).

Tropicana. Mólyvos. ☎ **0253/71-869.** Snacks/desserts 400–2,800 Drs ($1.65–$11.65). No credit cards. Daily 8am–1am. INTERNATIONAL.

After lunch or dinner, stroll up into the old town to sip a cappuccino or have a tuna salad or a dish of ice cream. This outdoor cafe under a plane tree provides soothing classical music and a most relaxing ambience. The owner, Hari Prokoplou, learned the secrets of making ice cream in Los Angeles.

ELSEWHERE AROUND THE ISLAND

In **Eressós** we enjoyed dining along the water, and found one good place to the far left as you face the sea. The **Arion Restaurant** (otherwise known as "The Boy on the Dolphin"; ☎ 0253/53-384) serves a delicious moussaká and Greek specialties with a vaguely English touch; it's open for lunch and dinner.

For a great fish meal, take the first right turn past Áyios Isodóros and go about 2 miles to the town of **Ayía Várvara.** Fresh swordfish steaks are 2,000 Drs ($8.35) per person at **Blue Sea** (☎ 0252/32-834), where you sit under the stars, right beside the unspoiled rocky coastline. There are also a few rooms available here.

LÉSVOS AFTER DARK

Mytilíni has lots of nightlife on either end of the harbor. The north end tends to be younger, cheaper, and more informal. The more sophisticated stuff is off the south end of the harbor; you'll have no trouble finding it. There's also the outdoor **Pallas Cinema** nearby. Don't forget that there might be entertainment at the Kástro.

Nighttime in Mólyvos revolves around bars, of which there are plenty. When we last visited, one of the hottest spots was **Perlita. Koukos** is supposed to attract a largely gay crowd, while a local favorite, the **Castro Bar,** has been known to host an active pick-up scene.

You may have noticed a really strange structure to the right on the outskirts of Mólyvos as you entered town—a cantilevered deck with a mast and a sign saying BOAT-SPIRIT-MUSIC. That was **Gatelouzi,** which often gets rather lively at night.

Vangelis Bouzouki (no phone) is west from Mólyvos on the road to Eftálou—past the Sappho Tours office. About a 10-minute walk outside town there's a sign that points to an olive grove; follow it about 500 yards through the grove until you reach a clearing with gnarly olive trees and a few stray sheep—you've arrived at Mólyvos's top acoustic bouzouki club. A circular concrete dance floor is surrounded by clumps of cafe tables. Forget the food, but order some ouzo and late-night *mezédes* (appetizers) and sit back to enjoy the show.

SIDE TRIPS TO TURKEY

Few people heading to Lésvos realize that there's a direct connection to Turkey via the port of Ayvalik; only about 3,000 tourists make the crossing annually. In high season, ships to Turkey sail Monday to Saturday. Tickets for the Turkish boats are sold by **Aeolic Cruises Travel Agency** (☎ 0271/23-960) at the port in Mytilíni (round-trip cost: about 17,500 Drs/$72.90). You must submit your passport the day before your departure (it will be returned). Ayvalik, a densely wooded fishing village, makes a refreshing base camp from which to tour Pergamum or ancient Troy. An all-inclusive tour to Pergamum with lunch, bus, and round-trip boat fare costs about $85.

4 Límnos

186 nautical miles NE of Piraeus

Límnos (also spelled Lemnos) is pretty much all alone out in the middle of the northeast Aegean, guarding one of history's most strategic waterways, the Dardenelles (also called the Hellespont)—the strait between Europe and Asia that connects the Aegean with the Sea of Marmara, the Mediterranean with the Black Sea.

It's a rugged volcanic island, nearly treeless because of overgrazing and recent fires rather than the volcano eruptions of antiquity that made it the home of Hephaistos (Vulcan to the Romans), god of fire and metalwork. In the spring it's green with low-growing scrub and abundant wildflowers (worthy of close inspection), but by fall it has been scorched brown, the color of cinnamon. It's the home of some very important military installations and one of Greece's best-known resorts, the Akti Mirina.

ESSENTIALS

GETTING THERE & DEPARTING **By Plane** **Olympic Airways** has two or three flights daily between Límnos and Athens and one flight a day between Thessaloníki and Lésvos; its office is on Odós Garoufalídou, in Mýrina (☎ 0254/22-478). The airport bus departs 90 minutes before flight time and meets all flights; it costs 1,000 Drs ($4.15).

By Boat Límnos has **ferry** service to and from Kavála (5 hours) four or five times weekly, Piraeus (14 hours) three or four times a week via Lésvos and Híos, Rafína (10 hours) three or four times a week, and Alexandroúpolis, Ikaría, Kálymnos, Kos, Rhodes, Sámos, and Thessaloníki once a week. In summer there is **hydrofoil** service to Híos, Lésvos, Sámos, and Pátmos. The schedule changes often, so contact the **Límnos Port Authority** (☎ 0254/22-225) or the port authority or travel agency nearest you.

VISITOR INFORMATION/ORIENTATION **El Travel** (☎ 0254/24-988; fax 0254/22-697), on the far east side of the public square on the harbor, and **Petridou Travel** (☎ 0254/22-309; fax 0254/22-129), just around the corner to the right of the public square, are both helpful travel agencies. The **tourist police** can be reached at ☎ 0254/22-201.

GETTING AROUND **By Bus** The central **bus station** (☎ 0254/22-464) is 3 blocks up from the taxi square; turn right and you'll find it on the left. A schedule is posted, but you're not likely to find much on it. Except for Moúdros and Kondiás, most places on the island have bus service only once a day, usually in the afternoon.

By Bicycle Bicycles, which can be rented in town, are an inexpensive means of transportation.

By Boat Caïques on the north side of the harbor offer service to the various beaches and the grottos at Skála; the price is negotiable, and they leave when they're ready.

By Car You can rent a small Jeep from almost any of the travel agents in town for about $70 a day.

On Foot You can easily walk around Mýrina, to the Kástro, and to the beaches on either side of town. In spring the island invites you to hike almost everywhere.

FAST FACTS From the port of Mýrina, continue up to your right past the **city hall** and the Aktaeon Hotel and turn left to reach the **main street,** Odós P. Kída. Most services are found within a few blocks along this street. The **taxi station** marks what might conveniently be called a **central square.** From the central square, the **telephone center (OTE)** is to your right, as are two **banks.** The **post office** is to your right and then around to the left. The **police station** is on Odós Garoufalídou (☎ 0254/22-200). Continue a block past the police station and turn left to reach the **hospital** (☎ 0254/22-222).

EXPLORING THE ISLAND

The first thing you'll notice as your boat arrives in **Mýrina,** the capital and port, is the Kástro that dominates it—solid evidence of the island's military history.

We suggest that you explore the town itself first, a pleasant, easy-going place once you get past the crush at the ferry pier. You'll probably have to look closely to recognize much distinction in the architecture, but there's more than a trace of both Turkish and Thracian influence there. Up along the main street you'll find pleasant **shopping** for antiques, preserves made from the local black plums, Limnian honey (a favorite of the gods), the famous Limnian wines—red and rosé, "Kalavaki" (Aristotle's favorite, a dry white), and the sweet "Moschato"—and local pottery.

It won't be long until you notice a military presence, if the soldiers didn't in fact escort you ashore. Young soldiers mill through the town smiling and joking, enjoying themselves casually, and their good humor is infectious.

You may want to wander back to the right through the maze of narrow streets to the *paralía*, Navaroú Koundouriótou, and stroll along the **beach,** past some nice hotels and cafes. The first beach is called **Romeïkos Yialós** ("Roman Beach"—the Greeks have called themselves Romans since the early Byzantine period) and the second is **Ríha Nerá;** the famous Akti Marina Resort is off above the far end.

The island's **cathedral** and **archaeology museum** (☎ 0254/22-990) are along the *paralía.* The museum just had an overhaul and was named one of the best three small museums in Europe. It contains artifacts from three of the island's important ancient sites—Polióchni, the Ifestía (Sanctuary of Hephaestus), and the Sanctuary of the Kavíri. (These sites, by the way, are rather ancient and obscure; they will probably interest only relatively few people.) The objects may not appear too impressive, but if you take the time to look closely, you'll probably be impressed. It's open Tuesday to Sunday from 9am to 3pm; admission is 500 Drs ($2.10) for adults, 400 Drs ($1.65) for seniors, and 300 Drs ($1.25) for students.

Next you may want to tackle the **Kástro,** which also contains much more than is apparent. In the classical era this was a Temple of Artemis, then it became a Roman site, then Byzantine, then Venetian, then Genoese, then Turkish.

Another important military site is across the island, muddy **Moúdros Bay,** the Allied naval base during World War I (at the time of the disastrous Galipoli campaign), as well as the rather depressing town of **Moúdros** and a British Commonwealth cemetery with 800 graves.

The island's volcanic past is everywhere apparent; it's little wonder that Hephaestus was worshiped here—or that his myth emerged in association with this island, which was home to some of the earliest metallurgy on record. It's probably not mere coincidence that the ancients valued their metalworkers so much that they sometimes cut their Achilles tendons so that they could not escape, and that the smithy god should be lame.

Born ugly, Hephaestus was rejected by his father, Zeus; according to Milton, he was "Dropt from the zenith like a falling star, on Lemnos, the Aegean isle." Here he fashioned shields and spears for the Olympians and created a race of cast-gold robotic maidens who stoked the fiery furnace that caused the volcanic disturbances.

Another local myth holds that Aphrodite once made the island's women smell repulsive to their husbands since the men had favored Hephaestus over her during the couple's tempestuous marriage. The women grew angry with their men's rejection and poisoned their wine, slit their throats, and threw them into the sea from the cliffs above Akti Mirina. For a time Límnos was inhabited only by women, until the *Argo* and its crew pulled into the island's snug harbor to repopulate the island.

WHERE TO STAY

Private rooms are available, but you'll have to bargain since Limnians often double the "expected" rate for the few tourists they meet.

Aktaeon Hotel. Odós Arvanitáki, Mýrina, 814 00 Límnos. ☎ **0254/22-258.** 14 rms, 12 with bath (shower). 4,600 Drs ($19.15) single without bath; 10,400 Drs ($43.35) double without bath, 13,250 Drs ($55.20) double with bath. No credit cards.

This older hotel at the harborfront could be better maintained, but it still has some charm and is convenient. Also, it's open year-round.

Hotel Lemnos. Odós Arvanitáki, Mýrina, 814 00 Límnos. ☎ **0254/22-153.** Fax 0254/23-494. 26 rms, all with bath (shower). 10,400 Drs ($43.35) single; 13,800 Drs ($57.50) double; 16,200 Drs ($67.50) triple. MC, V.

This new hotel on the harborfront is attractive, pleasant, comfortable, and quiet. The owners, Harry Geanopoulos and Bill Stamboulis, spent many years in New Jersey, so they speak English and know what Americans want: a good night's sleep at a fair price.

Hotel Sevdalis. Odós Garoufalídou 6, Mýrina, 814 00 Límnos. ☎ **0254/22-303.** Fax 0254/ 22-382. 36 rms, all with bath (shower). A/C TEL. 12,650 Drs ($52.70) single; 16,300 Drs ($67.90) double. No credit cards.

This well-maintained hotel is above the taxi square, near the Olympic Airways office, about 300 yards off the port and 700 yards from the beach. There's a lounge with TV and a bar for guests.

WHERE TO EAT

The **Avra,** next to the Port Authority near the port, is a good basic place with fair prices. It doesn't have a menu—you go inside and choose from the steam table. The best places for seafood are behind the sheltered fishing boat mooring beyond the turn up the main street; locals rate **Taverna Glaros** the best, but it's also the most expensive. **O Platanos,** up the main street on the left—look for a small square and the giant plane (sycamore) tree from which it takes its name—is a pleasant place that serves good traditional food.

LÍMNOS AFTER DARK

Mýrina has lots of evening activities along the *paralia* north of the Kástro and in the middle of town, if you don't mind sharing it with a number of remarkably well-behaved young soldiers. The **Disco Avlonas Club** (☎ **0254/23-885**) is 1¼ miles out of town on the road to Thános. The **Gitonia Ton Angelon,** on Áyios Dimítrios (☎ **0254/23-345**), promises "a new proposition for your night's entertainment."

5 Samothráki

30 nautical miles S of Alexandroúpolis

Lonely Samothráki (Samothrace) is one of the most remote and dramatic of the Greek islands, rising precipitously from the sea, with the peak of Mt. Fengári, the tallest in the Aegean, reaching a height of 5,250 feet. According to myth, Poseidon sat atop Mt. Fengári to watch the battle at Troy. Its coast is so forbidding that docking a boat can still be difficult today; on your arrival, you may be taken ashore on a smaller caïque. In ancient times its Sanctuary of the Great Gods was an important place of pilgrimage from throughout the eastern Mediterranean, and it's still the most important reason to visit today.

Except for religious pilgrimages to the ultra-secretive Mysteries, few people have been attracted to the windy, rocky, unprosperous Samothráki; thus it has not experienced the invasions and disasters that befell other Aegean islands. The situation remains much the same today; Samothráki, with a population of only 3,000, has not attracted large numbers of tourists.

Like Mílos, the island is closely associated with a particular piece of sculpture, the dynamic *Winged Victory (Nike) of Samothrace,* which is on display in the Louvre. The

4th-century B.C. statue was commissioned by Demetrius Polyocretes—the patron of the Colossus of Rhodes—for his victory over Ptolemy in Egypt. It was found 2,100 years later, in the mid–19th century, by the French consul of Adrianople (now Edirne, Turkey), who spirited the masterpiece off the island and back to Paris. Excavations at the site of the Mysteries, the Temple of the Great Gods near Paleópolis ("Old City"), began in 1938 when an archaeological team from the United States uncovered the foundations of a complex of temples and initiation sanctuaries. The **Arisinoë Rotunda** (dedicated by one of the Ptolemies' wives) is a circular building on the order of the tholos at Delphi and the largest structure of its kind in Greece.

The Mysteries, which predate the Greek settlement of the islands, originated in Thracian religious ceremonies devoted to the Great Mother (or Great Goddess, Cybele), her virile young consort, Kadmilos, and the demonic Kavíri twins. Herodotus claimed that the Kavíri were a race of dwarfs who protected the fields, but modern scholars believe they were fertility deities. These deities were assimilated into the Greek pantheon: the Great Mother as Demeter, Aphrodite, and Hecate (who personified her underworld qualities); Kadmilos as Hermes; and the Kavíri as the Dioskoúri, the twins Castor and Pollux. The mysterious Kavíri, however, eluded complete assimilation, and remained the object of superstitious awe. Initiation into the Mysteries of the Kavíri was open to everyone, but fear of these powerful deities prevented anyone from communicating the nature of the rites. From archaeological evidence scholars have deduced that they were somewhat like the Mysteries of Eleusis and consisted of two rites, held at night, the first to invoke spiritual rebirth in the initiate and the second requiring confession for the absolution of sins. Such notables as Philip of Macedonia and his wife-to-be, Olympias, journeyed to Samothráki to take part in the rites.

ESSENTIALS

GETTING THERE & DEPARTING   By Plane   There are no direct flights to Samothráki. However, **Olympic Airways** offers daily flights between Athens and Alexandroúpolis or Kavála (both on the mainland), a handy way to save ferry time.

By Boat   Samothráki has **ferry** connections with Alexandroúpolis approximately twice a day in the summer, with Kavála approximately six times a week, and with Límnos twice a week. (Call ☎ **0551/26-721** for up-to-date information; the schedule changes from year to year and there is very little service off-season.) From May to October, there is **hydrofoil** service between Samothráki and Alexandroúpolis, Kavála, Límnos, and Thássos. Contact the **port police** in Kamariótissa (☎ **0551/41-305**) for current information.

ORIENTATION   Kamariótissa, the port town, is near the northwest tip of the island; **Hóra** (also called Samothráki), the capital and main town, is 3 miles east. When you get off the ferry in Kamariótissa, to the left you'll find the **bus station,** a branch of the **National Bank,** the **port police** (☎ **0551/41-305**), **Niki Tours** (☎ **0551/41-465;** fax 0551/41-304), and **Saos Travel** (☎ **0551/41-505**). The island's few other services are on the main street up in Hóra: the **post office, telephone center (OTE), Agricultural Bank,** and **police** (☎ **0551/41-203**). Hóra's nameless narrow and winding **main street** leads off the **main square,** where the bus turns around; follow the signs to the **Kástro.**

GETTING AROUND   Buses travel from the port up to Hóra and along the north coast to Thérma (Loutrá) via Paleópolis approximately every 2 hours in summer, much less often in winter. **Motorbikes** and **cars** can be rented at the port; a Jeep from Niki Tours costs about 15,000 Drs ($62.50) per day.

SEEING THE SIGHTS

Most visitors simply visit the **Sanctuary of the Great Gods** (☎ 0551/41-474), just south of Paleópolis (3 3/4 miles northeast of the port or an hour's hike north from Hóra), with sensational views of **Mt. Fengári** (the Mountain of the Moon). You might want to visit the attractive museum first in order to get a better idea of the site; it houses reconstructions (including a plaster cast of the *Winged Victory*), figurines, pottery, and jewelry, all well labeled in English, and sells a splendid guide written by the American excavator Karl Lehman. The site and museum are open Tuesday to Sunday from 8:30am to 3pm; admission is 500 Drs ($2.10) for adults and 300 Drs ($1.25) for students.

Thérma (Loutrá), 3 3/4 miles east of Paleópolis, is the liveliest place on the island, with the hot sulfurous springs from which it takes its name, lots of plane and chestnut trees, and what passes as a growing little resort on this simple island: a couple of hotels, a restaurant, a cafe-pub, and a port under construction which may accommodate hydrofoils in the near future.

It's possible to climb **Mt. Fengári,** but consult the local police about the conditions on the slopes; the mountain is covered with snow for much of the year.

WHERE TO STAY

In Kamariótissa there's the homely little **Kyma** (☎ 0551/41-263), with doubles and shared baths for 5,500 Drs ($22.90); the much better **Niki Beach** (☎ 0551/41-561), with 38 double rooms with private baths at 13,500 Drs ($56.25); and above it the island's most luxurious hotel, the **Aeolos** (☎ 0551/41-555; fax 0551/41-810), with a swimming pool and doubles (including breakfast) for 15,750 Drs ($65.65). There are a few rooms for rent in Hóra and Paleópolis, not to mention the old **Xenia Hotel** (☎ 0551/41-230), which offers doubles with private bath for 8,200 Drs ($34.15). The island's newest hotel, the **Kástro** (☎ 0551/41-001; fax 0551/41-000), is just west of Paleópolis, where plain but nice doubles with bath and breakfast cost 15,750 Drs ($65.65).

WHERE TO EAT

The food on Samothráki is geared to local tastes, which do not appear to be very discriminating. Kamariótissa has a couple of satisfactory restaurants, the **Horizon** and the **Klimatariá.** The **Taverna Kástro,** on the main square in Hóra, is okay. There's no place to eat in Paleópolis except at the hotels, though there are a couple of places that look promising on the road to Thérma.

6 Thássos

14 nautical miles S of Kavála

Thássos, only 7 1/2 miles off the mainland, is a pretty, almost circular island with hilly coastal plains, a mountainous interior, plenty of good sandy beaches, a number of archaeological remains, and gentle slopes covered with pine, plane, oak, olive, walnut, and chestnut trees—though some of its forests have been ravaged by fires, especially in 1985. It's a well-watered island and less troubled by the strong *meltémi* winds that buffet most of the Greek islands; as a consequence of these conditions, it has a serious mosquito problem. Thássos has long been a popular resort for Greeks, especially from Thessaloníki and elsewhere in the north, but in recent years it has become increasingly popular with foreign tourists, including budget groups. Although it can get rather crowded during the summer, there still seem to be enough beds even on the busiest summer weekends.

Thássos has always had a wealth of natural resources. Marble was quarried by the Parians when they ruled Thássos; together with other minerals, it's still being dug. Herodotus claimed that there were active gold mines on the island when he visited in the 5th century B.C. There are none today, but oil was recently discovered off the coast, proving once again that the rich get richer. Besides abundant olive, fruit, and nut crops, the island produces a lot of honey, and you'll probably see beehives along the roadside.

ESSENTIALS

GETTING THERE & DEPARTING   By Plane   If you're pressed for time, consider the twice-daily **Olympic Airways** flights between Kavála and Athens; Olympic has an office in the port of Liménas (☎ **0593/22-546**).

By Boat   There is **ferry** service hourly between Kavála and Skála Prínou (1¹/₂ hours, 420 Drs/$1.75) and once daily to Liménas. There's also ferry service from Keramotí, 28¹/₂ miles southeast of Kavála, to Liménas every 45 minutes (half an hour, 300 Drs/$1.25), continuing on to Skála Prínou. In the summer there's **hydrofoil** service from Kavála to Liménas six times daily (half an hour, 1,500 Drs/$6.25).

VISITOR INFORMATION   The **tourist police** (☎ **0593/22-500**) are open daily during the summer months. Check with the portside **Katha Travel** (☎ **0593/22-546**), open daily, for general information, and with **Prinos Travel** in Skála Prínos (☎ **0593/71-152**) about Kavála, Límnos, and Samothráki (where it has branch offices). Both the police and Katha maintain lists of available private rooms as well as current bus and ferry schedules.

ORIENTATION   The island's capital, **Liménas** (also called Thássos town and Limín—not to be confused with Limenária) is on the northeast coast. A good asphalt road circles the entire island. The second port, **Skála Prínou** (also called Órmos Prínou), is on the northwest coast. The second town, **Limenária,** is on the southwest coast.

Liménas is a modern town that was built over its ancient counterpart and is conveniently laid out. The ferry and hydrofoil **landing** is in the middle of the harbor, the **central square** is 2 blocks inland from it, and the **museum, old harbor, ancient agorá,** and **ancient theater** are to the left (east).

GETTING AROUND   Thássos has a good **bus** system, with Liménas as its hub; in summer there is hourly service to Limenária via Skála Prínou and the west-coast beaches. There are two or three buses daily that make a clockwise circuit of the island for 6,500 Drs ($27.10). **Bikes** are available for rent, and they're fine for local sightseeing; **motorbikes,** also widely available, are a better means of getting around. **Cars** can be rented from travel or rental agencies, including **Thassos Rent A Car** (☎ **0593/22-535**) in Liménas. **Avis** has offices in Liménas (☎ **0593/22-535**) and Skála Prínou (☎ **0593/71-202**).

FAST FACTS   The **local police, bus station,** and **National Bank** are all at the port in Liménas (Thássos town); the **telephone office (OTE)** is a block behind the police station, and the **post office** is 2 blocks behind it.

EXPLORING THE ISLAND

Liménas has the island's most important archaeological site, the remains of **Ancient Thássos,** most of which are near the left (east) end of the waterfront near the old harbor. The **ancient agorá,** the marketplace through the Roman era, has a massive marble altar and the foundations of stoas and porticos.

The nearby **archaeology museum** (☎ **0593/22-180**) has a nice collection of terra-cotta figurines and pottery, a remarkably well preserved and effeminate head of Dionysos, Aphrodite riding a dolphin, and a young man carrying a lamb on his shoulders. The museum was closed for renovation, but it may have reopened by the time of your visit.

Beyond the ancient agorá, steps lead up to the **ancient theater;** it has been outfitted with wooden seats since it hosts performances of classical drama during the summer. A path leads on up to the **acropolis** of the ancient city with the substantial ruins of a **medieval fortress** that was largely constructed with stone from more ancient temples and last occupied by the Genoese. From here you can follow the **wall** to the foundations of a **Temple of Apollo** and beyond it a small **Sanctuary of Pan.**

South of Liménas is the charming mountain village of **Panayía,** with whitewashed, slate-roofed houses decorated with wood carvings; below it is the attractive town beach, **Chryssí Ammoudiá,** with its fair share of tavernas. Farther south, **Potamiá** has a small **folk-art museum** and the **Polygnotos Vagis Museum,** featuring the work of a sculptor born in the village; from here there's a path that you could take to climb to the top of **Mt. Ipsárion,** or you could continue to **Skála Potomiás,** which has the island's best beach, **Chryssí Aktí** ("Golden Beach"). **Kínira,** farther south, also has a fair beach, and nearby **Paradise Beach** features pale sand and some nudist activity. There are prettier and more secluded coves farther south.

The west coast of the island is more agricultural and less picturesque. **Limenária,** the island's second town, has somewhat more charm than the capital, but it can become rather crowded in the summer. There are less populous beaches farther south at **Pefkári** and **Potós.** From Potós there's a road that goes inland 6 miles to **Theológos**—the medieval and Turkish capital, and possibly the most beautiful village on the island; accessible by public bus, it has a taverna and a few rooms for rent.

WHERE TO STAY

Unless you arrive on a summer weekend, you'll have little trouble finding a room. People with rooms to rent usually meet the ferries. Across from the bus station is a listing of the town's hotels, and there are eight campsites around the island.

The upgraded, eight-room **Astir** (☎ 0593/22-160) offers harbor-view doubles for 5,950 Drs ($24.80) per night, while the **Angelika** (☎ 0593/22-387) has doubles with private bath for 10,450 Drs ($43.55). Both are on the *paralía* and are open year-round.

Quieter and better choices can be found southwest of the central square on the road to Skála Prínos: the modern **Hotel Myroni** (☎ 0593/23-256; fax 0593/ 22-132) offers spacious doubles with bath for 12,500 Drs ($52.10), and next door, the traditional **Hotel Victoria** (with the same telephone and fax numbers) has doubles with bath for 11,000 Drs ($45.85).

Skála Prínos provides an alternative, with significantly less commercial development. The quarter-mile-long town is lined with beaches, both to the east and the west. The **Elektra Hotel** (☎ 0593/71-374), on the west (to the right as you get off the ferry), is the biggest and best-looking hotel in town; doubles with bath and breakfast here cost 11,350 Drs ($47.30). The welcoming **Hotel Prinos** (☎ 0593/71-327), on the beach (to the left as you get off the ferry), has spotless, balconied doubles with modern showers for 6,350 Drs ($26.50).

Appendix

A Basic Greek Vocabulary

Greek is relatively easy to pronounce. Every syllable in a word is spoken as written, and words of more than one syllable almost always have a stress accent—except when letters are capitalized. The pronunciation guide on the next page is intended to aid you as you go over the basic words and phrases listed in this appendix. While your pronunciation may not be perfect, you'll find that people in Greece will quickly warm to you if you try to speak to them in their own language.

The transliteration of Greek into English presents a special problem, because there is no recognized standard system to go by. Thus, for example, the island of Αιγινα is variously spelled Aegina, Aiyina, Egina, and Éyina, while the name Γεωργιοσ shows up in English as Yoryos, Yeoryios, Georgios, and Gheorghios, to cite only some of the variants. So don't be surprised if you see a street or town spelled differently on your map or on a signpost. (There are many similarities between the Greek and our Roman alphabets—we get the word from its first two letters—and it really isn't as exotic as it may at first appear.)

GREEK ALPHABET

Letter	Name	Transliteration	Pronunciation
Α, α	álpha	a	f*a*ther
Β, β	víta	v	*v*et
Γ, γ	gámma	g *or* gh *before* a, o, u	g*e*t
		y *before* e, i, *and* y	*y*et
Δ, δ	délta	d *or* dh	*th*en
Ε, ε	épsilon	e	*e*gg
Ζ, ζ	zíta	z	*z*one
Η, η	íta	i	mach*i*ne
Θ, θ	thíta	th	*th*in
Ι, ι	ióta	i	mach*i*ne
		y (before *a* and *o*)	*y*oke
Κ, κ	káppa	k	*k*ey
Λ, λ	lámbda	l	*l*amb
Μ, μ	mí	m	*m*other
Ν, ν	ní	n	*n*et
Ξ, ξ	xí	x *or* ks	a*x*e
Ο, ο	ómikron	o	*o*ver
Π, π	pí	p	*p*et
Ρ, ρ	ró	r	*r*ed (with slight trill)
Σ, σ, ς*	sígma	s	*s*ee
Τ, τ	táf	t	*t*op
Υ, υ	ípsilon	y *or* i	p*y*ramid
Φ, φ	phí	f *or* ph	*ph*ilosophy
Χ, χ	chí	h *or* ch	*h*ope or Scottish lo*ch*
Ψ, ψ	psí	ps	la*ps*e
Ω, ω	oméga	o	*o*ver (but slightly longer)

*The letter ς occurs only at the end of a word; σ occurs elsewhere in a word. For example: σεισμός "earthquake."

Diphthongs	Transliteration	Pronunciation
ΑΙ, αι	e, ai, *or* ae	like *e* above (*e*gg)
ΕΙ, ει	i	like *i* above (mach*i*ne)
ΟΙ, οι	i	like *i* above (mach*i*ne)
ΟΥ, ου	ou	Lou*v*re
ΑΥ, αυ	av before vowels and most consonants	a*v*ert
	af before voiceless consonants	a*f*firm
ΕΥ, ευ	ev before vowels and most consonants	e*v* er
	ef before voiceless consonants	e*f*fort

Double Consonants	Transliteration	Pronunciation
ΓΓ, γγ	ng (nasalised)	a*ng*le
ΓΚ, γκ	g at the beginning of a word	*g*as
	ng in the middle of a word	a*ng*le
ΜΠ, μπ	b	*b*ar
ΝΤ, ντ	d at the beginning of a word	*d*andy
	nd in the middle of a word	da*nd*y
ΤΣ, τσ	ts	hi*ts*

WORDS & PHRASES

Airport	**Aerodrómio**
Automobile	**Aftokínito**
Avenue	**Leofóros**
Bad	**Kakós,-kí,-kó***
Bank	**Trápeza**
Beautiful	**Oréos, -a, -o***
The bill, please.	**To logariazmó, parakaló.**
Breakfast	**Proinó**
Bus	**Leoforío**
Can you tell me?	**Boríte ná moú píte?**
Car (coach)	**Amáxi**
Cheap	**Ftinó**
Church	**Ekklissía**
Closed	**Klistós, -stí, -stó***
Coast	**Aktí**
Coffeehouse	**Kafenío**
Cold	**Kríos, -a, -o***
Dinner	**Vradinó**
Do you speak English?	**Miláte angliká?**
Does anyone speak English?	**Milál kanís angliká?**
Excuse me.	**Signómi.**
Expensive	**Akrivós, -í, -ó***
Farewell!	**Stó ka-ló!** (to person leaving)
Glad to meet you.	**Héro polí.**
Good	**Kalós, -lí, -ló***
Good-bye	**Adío** or **hérete**
Good evening	**Kalispéra**
Good health (cheers)!	**Stín yá sas** or **Yá-mas!**
Good morning	**Kaliméra**
Good night	**Kaliníkta**
Hello!	**Yássas!** (polite) or **Yássou!** (familiar)
Here	**Edó**
Hot	**Zestós, -stí, -stó***
Hotel	**Ksenodohío**
How are you?	**Tí kánete?** or **Pós íste?**
How far?	**Pósso makriá?**
How long?	**Póssi óra?** or **Pósso keró?**
How much is it?	**Pósso káni?**
I am from New York.	**Íme apó tín Néa Iórki.**
I am lost.	**Ého hathí.**
I'm sorry.	**Lipoúme.**
I don't speak Greek (well).	**Dén miláo elliniká (kalá).**
I don't understand.	**Dén katalavéno.**
I want to go to the airport.	**Thélo ná páo stó aerodrómio.**
I want a glass of beer.	**Thélo éna potíri bíra.**
It's (not) all right.	**(Dén) íne endáxi.**

*Masculine ending -os, feminine ending -a or -i, neuter ending -o.

Left (direction)	**Aristerá**
Ladies' room	**Yinekón**
Lunch	**Messimerianó**
Map	**Hártis**
Market (place)	**Agorá**
Men's room	**Andrón**
Mr.	**Kýrios**
Mrs.	**Kyría**
Miss	**Despinís**
My name is . . .	**Onomázome . . .** or **Me léne . . .**
New	**Kenoúryos, -ya, -yo***
No	**Óhi**
Okay	**Endáxi**
Old	**Paleós, -leá, -leó***
Open	**Aniktós, -ktí, -któ***
Passport	**Diavatírio**
Pâtisserie	**Zaharoplastío**
Pharmacy	**Farmakío**
Please	**Parakaló**
Please call a taxi.	**Parakaló, fonáxte éna taxi.**
Post office	**Tahidromío**
Restaurant	**Estiatório**
Rest room	**Toualétta**
Right (direction)	**Dexiá**
Saint	**Áyios** (masc.), **ayía** (fem.), **áyïi** (plural)
Seashore	**Paralía**
Speak more slowly, please.	**Miláte argá, parakaló.**
Square	**Platía**
Street	**Odós**
Show me on the map.	**Díxte mou stó hárti.**
Station (bus, train)	**Stathmós (leoforíou, trénou)**
Stop (bus)	**Stási (leoforíou)**
Suitcase	**Valítsa**
Telephone	**Tiléfono**
Temple (of Athena, Zeus)	**Naós (Athinás, Diós)**
Thank you (very much).	**Efharistó (polí).**
Today	**Símera**
Tomorrow	**Ávrio**
Very nice	**Polí oréos, -a, -o***
Very good	**Polí kalá**
What?	**Tí?**
What is this?	**Tí íne aftós?**
What time is it?	**Tí óra íne?**
What's your name?	**Pós leneté?**
Where is . . . ?	**Poú íne . . . ?**
Why?	**Yatí?**
Write it, please.	**Grápste to, parakaló.**
Yes	**Ne** or **málista** (of course)

*Masculine ending -os, feminine ending -a or -i, neuter ending -o.

NUMBERS

0	**Midén**	17	**Dekaeftá**	151	**Ekatón penínda éna**	
1	**Éna** or **mía** (feminine)	18	**Dekaoktó**	152	**Ekatón penínda dío**	
		19	**Dekaenyá**			
2	**Dío**	20	**Íkossi**	200	**Diakóssya**	
3	**Tría** or **trís**	21	**Íkossi éna**	300	**Triakóssya**	
4	**Téssera**	22	**Íkossi dío**	400	**Tetrakóssya**	
5	**Pénde**	30	**Triánda**	500	**Pendakóssya**	
6	**Éxi**	40	**Saránda**	600	**Exakóssya**	
7	**Eftá**	50	**Penínda**	700	**Eftakóssya**	
8	**Októ**	60	**Exínda**	800	**Oktakóssya**	
9	**Ennéa** or **enyá**	70	**Evdomínda**	900	**Enyakóssya**	
10	**Déka**	80	**Ogdónda**	1,000	**Hílya**	
11	**Éndeka**	90	**Enenínda**	2,000	**Dío hilyádes**	
12	**Dódeka**	100	**Ekató(n)**	3,000	**Trís hilyádes**	
13	**Dekatría**	101	**Ekatón éna**	4,000	**Tésseris hilyádes**	
14	**Dekatéssera**	102	**Ekatón dío**			
15	**Dekapénde**	150	**Ekatón penínda**	5,000	**Pénde hilyádes**	
16	**Dekaéxi**					

CALENDAR

Monday	**Deftéra**	Friday	**Paraskeví**	
Tuesday	**Tríti**	Saturday	**Sávvato**	
Wednesday	**Tetárti**	Sunday	**Kiriakí**	
Thursday	**Pémpti**			

January	**Ianouários**	July	**Ioúlios**	
February	**Fevrouários**	August	**Ávgoustos**	
March	**Mártios**	September	**Septémvrios**	
April	**Aprílios**	October	**Októvrios**	
May	**Máios**	November	**Noémvrios**	
June	**Ioúnios**	December	**Dekémvrios**	

B Greek Menu Terms

HORS D'OEUVRES (Orektiká)

Domátes yemistés mé rízi	Tomatoes stuffed with rice
Horiátiki saláta	"Village" salad ("Greek" salad to us)
Hórta	Dandelion salad
Melitzanosaláta	Eggplant salad
Piperiés yemistés	Stuffed green peppers
Saganáki	Grilled cheese
Spanokópita	Spinach pie
Taramosaláta	Fish roe with mayonnaise
Tirópita	Cheese pie
Tzatzíki	Yogurt-cucumber-garlic dip

FISH (Psári)

Astakós (ladolémono)	Lobster (with oil-and-lemon sauce)
Bakaliáro (skordaliá)	Cod (with garlic)
Barboúnia (skáras)	Red mullet (grilled)
Garídes	Shrimp
Glóssa (tiganití)	Sole (fried)
Kalamarákia (tiganitá)	Squid (fried)
Kalamarákia (yemistá)	Squid (stuffed)
Karavídes	Crayfish
Oktapódi	Octopus
Soupiés yemistés	Cuttlefish (stuffed)
Tsípoura	Dorado

MEATS (Kréas)

Arní avgolémono	Lamb with lemon sauce
Arní soúvlas	Spit-roasted lamb
Arní yiouvétsi	Baked lamb with orzo
Brizóla hiriní	Pork steak or chop
Brizóla moscharísia	Beef or veal steak
Dolmadákia	Stuffed vine leaves
Keftedes	Fried meatballs
Kotópoulo soúvlas	Spit-roasted chicken
Kotópoulo yemistó	Stuffed chicken
Loukánika	Spiced sausages
Moussaká	Meat and eggplant
Païdákia	Lamb chops
Piláfi rízi	Rice pilaf
Souvláki	Lamb (sometimes veal) on the skewer
Youvarlákia	Boiled meatballs with rice

Index

FLY WITH

TRAVEL NETWORK ®

AND SAVE

UP TO $400 OFF

Save Up To $400 on Airfare Valid for Flights on Most Major Airlines.

(up to $100 each for 4 airline tickets)

$25 OFF
per roundtrip ticket
of $189

$50 OFF
per roundtrip ticket
of $289

$75 OFF
per roundtrip ticket
of $389

$100 OFF
per roundtrip ticket
of $489

Coupon is good toward the purchase of four
roundtrip tickets.
Good for travel through 6/30/98.
See Reverse Side for Instructions, Terms, & Conditions

TRAVEL NETWORK®

INSTRUCTIONS FOR REDEMPTION

1. To expedite service, please have your travel dates and times ready for the reservation agent. We suggest you call an airline prior to calling Travel Network so you are aware of current published air fares.

2. Call Travel Network toll free at 1-888-940-5000 in the U.S or 1-905-707-7222 in Canada and advise agent you hold a TRAVEL NETWORK FROMMER GUIDE AIR COUPON.

3. All tickets must be purchased by credit card or cashier's check within 24 hours of receiving air fare. quote.

4. Your Travel Network agent will give you the address to mail the coupon.

TERMS AND CONDITIONS

1. This offer is valid for discounts on published round-trip fares on most airlines. Reservation and ticket purchases must be made through Travel Network. Air Discount coupons are valid for flights originating within the 48 contiguous United States to destinations in the contiguous 48 United States and select cities in Alaska, Hawaii, Europe, Mexico and Caribbean.

2. Travel Network reserves the right to select the airline carrier and to make reservations based on Travel Network's availability outside the stated blackout dates. Reservations require a 14 to 21 day advance purchase and a Saturday night stay to receive a discount. Some airlines may not allow discounts on flights originating from their respective hub cities. The maximum discount allowed is $100.00 per ticket. The maximum discount to Hawaii, Mexico and the Caribbean is $75.00

3. The minimum purchase amount for an airline ticket is $189.00 for discounts to apply. The minimum purchase applies to round-trip ticket, (coach class only) and may not be combined with any other coupon, certificate or voucher, student's fare, child's fare, group fare, senior discount program, frequent flyer award program or airline industry discount program.

4. Discounts are applied to fares before application of any taxes, passenger facility charges, governmental fees, and security charges, if applicable. Once redeemed, your Air Discount coupon cannot be reused and will not be replaced if stolen or lost. This offer is void if coupon is duplicated in any way.

5. Use of Sky Values coupon is not valid where prohibited by law.

6. All tickets issued are non-refundable, non-transferable and subject to change fees.

7. Blackout Dates: 1997: May 23,26; July 2-7; Aug. 29; Sept. 1,2; Nov. 25-30; Dec. 1, 15-31. / 1998: Jan 1-5; Feb. 12-19; Apr. 9-13; May 22-26. Reservations for travel in 1998 cannot be accepted before October 15, 1997. Some discounts may be available during stated blackout dates on some airlines while other unstated blackouts may be in effect during certain holiday periods on some airlines.

8. Travel Network is the final authority on interpretation of these Terms and Conditions.

Call Toll Free in the U.S
1-888-940-5000
and in Canada
1-905-707-7222

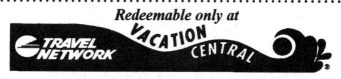

WHEREVER YOU TRAVEL, *H*ELP IS NEVER FAR AWAY.

From planning your trip to providing travel assistance along the way, American Express® Travel Service Offices are always there to help you do more.

Greece

American Express Travel Service
2 Hermou Street
Syntagma Square
Athens
1/3244976

Greek Skies Travel (R)
20A Capodistria Street
Corfu
661/33410

Adamis Tours (R)
23, 25th August Street
Heraklion
Crete
81/246202

X-Ray Kilo (R)
Main Square
Fira-Santorini
286/24301

Acteon Travel Agency (R)
Port Square
Ios
286/91343

Delia Travel Ltd. (R)
At The Quay
Mykonos
289/22322

Albatros Travel (R)
48 Othonos Amalias Street
Patras
61/220127

Rhodos Tours Ltd. (R)
23 Ammochostou St.
Rhodes
241/21010

do more
Travel

http://www.americanexpress.com/travel

American Express Travel Service Offices are found in central locations throughout Greece.